Marketing

Management

Marketing Management

Providing, Communicating and Delivering Value

Frank Bradley

University College, Dublin

Prentice Hall

London New York Toronto Sydney Tokyo Singapore
Madrid Mexico City Munich

First published 1995 by
Prentice Hall Europe
Campus 400, Maylands Avenue
Hemel Hempstead
Hertfordshire, HP2 7EZ
A division of
Simon & Schuster International Group

Typeset in 10½/12 pt Baskerville
by Goodfellow & Egan Limited, Cambridge

Printed and bound in Great Britain by TJ Press (Padstow) Ltd

Library of Congress Cataloging-in-Publication Data

Bradley, Frank, 1942–
    Marketing management: providing, communicating and delivering value /
Frank Bradley.
        p.   cm.
    Includes bibliographical references and index.
    ISBN 0-13-065343-8
    1. Marketing—Management.   I. Title.
HF5415. 13.B674   1995   94-44927
658.8—dc20   CIP

British Library Cataloguing in Publication Data

A catalogue record for this book is available from
the British Library

ISBN 0-13-065343-8

2 3 4 5 99 98 97 96

*This book is dedicated to
my wife and best friend,
Breda with love*

Contents

Contents

Part B   Select the value for markets, customers and competitors

Chapter 6   Understanding consumer markets   245

Chapter 7   Understanding organizational markets   287

Contents

Part C   Provide the value for customers

Contents

Chapter 13 Pricing decisions and methods 561

Part D   Communicate the value to customers

Contents

Part E   Deliver the value to customers

Contents

Chapter 19   Sales promotion   829

Case studies   867

Contents

Foreword

Marketing *au fin du siècle*

The antecedents of modern marketing practices go back to the time of Columbus (Fullerton, 1988). Notwithstanding this long history, marketing has matured during the twentieth century; in particular this applies to the accumulation of knowledge known as 'marketing science'.

At the end of the twentieth century marketing practice and marketing science can be characterized by a number of recent developments: the growing emphasis on building long-term relationships with customers; an increasing focus on the international aspects of marketing management; the growing diffusion of marketing theories and practices in areas in which marketing management was not known and/or was not applied; the growing emphasis on competition; the explosion of data which can be used as a basis for decision-making in marketing; and the increase in analytical frameworks, tools, methods and techniques.

Long-term relationships: Modern marketing is concerned with exchange processes. The exchange of values between marketer and customer groups is the central focus of all modern theory on marketing. The marketing function initiates, negotiates and manages acceptable exchange relationships with key interest groups in the pursuit of sustainable competitive advantages within specific markets on the basis of long-run consumer channel franchises (Day and Wensley, 1983). The focus in modern marketing theory is, and has always been, on the customer and on solving problems faced by the customer (Bradley, 1995). Seeking value from the customer's perspective means building long-term mutually profitable relationships with customers. This idea has important consequences for marketing management – consumers should be approached on a regular, more direct and individual basis, which is dealt with in the emerging area of direct marketing. It also implies that the 'personality' of products and services with which customers have a relationship should be improved. This has led to an increasing focus on branding. Brands have become the centre of attention because of the value they represent in the long-term relationship between marketer and customer. This 'value' has been translated into financial value in the brand equity debate.

Modern marketing is also concerned with relationships other than those between marketer and customer. The opening sentences of the Preface of this book indicate that marketing is a concern for all people in a company; it is an organization-wide philosophy. Modern management approaches suggest that all functions in an organization exist to serve customers, implying a diffusion of marketing theories and practices over all functional areas in an organization.

Finally, long-term relationships play an increasingly prominent role in the relation between an organization and other organizations. These relationships are studied on organizational markets and more specifically in networks between firms.

Internationalization: The development of economic blocs has played an important role in world affairs particularly since the Second World War. The phenomenon of nations agreeing on the abolition of various types of barriers between their economies is generally referred to as economic integration. Market integration in Europe (EU), South-East Asia (ASEAN) and North America (NAFTA) demonstrate the commitment of countries to put aside political and other differences in favour of selling in larger markets. In recent decades four superpowers – EU, NAFTA, ASEAN and Japan – have replaced one superpower, the USA (Bradley, 1995). This has important consequences for marketing practices (Leeflang and de Mortanges, 1994). We now face multi-country markets with multi-cultural consumers which are approached by international manufacturers, international brands and international wholesalers and retailers.

Diffusion of marketing theory: Marketing theory, methods and practices are not only used in markets with fast moving non-durable consumer goods, but also have been diffused to markets for services, ideas and people. More specifically a body of knowledge has been developed around areas such as the marketing of services and the quality of services.

Growing emphasis on competition: Prior to the economic decline in the West, companies could ignore their competitors because most markets were growing. In the 'flat eighties' companies realized that sales gains would largely occur by wresting share away from competitors. This explains the growing attention paid to competition. Today's companies are starting to pay as much attention to tracking their competitors as to understanding their consumers. This is reflected in today's marketing concept, the stages in the marketing planning process and the growing number of analyses developed to diagnose competition.

Data explosion: The introduction of scanner data has led to a data explosion in marketing. By scanning we mean methods that enable people to record electronically purchases made at home or in a store. The latter, using check-out records, are used to set up scanning-based store audits. The development of scanner data based models offers enormous possibilities to test and develop theories in marketing science. However, the data have to be transformed into information for the decision-maker in marketing management, thus explaining the growth in the development of marketing information systems.

Analytical frameworks, tools, methods, techniques: More and more individualized relationships, with different consumer groups not only require more and better data, but also better and more useful tools and analytical techniques. These tools, methods and techniques are developed in marketing science. In this area econometric marketing models, cluster analyses, multidimensional scaling methods, conjoint analyses, latent class-analyses, and so on, have been developed and applied. Furthermore, many kinds of frameworks have been developed to structure theories about markets and how to approach them.

Frank Bradley's text gives a thorough treatment to the developments briefly discussed above. In the introduction (Chapter 1), the importance of long-term relationships in modern marketing is emphasized. The relationships to other business functions in modern marketing is emphasized. The relationships to other business functions (Chapter 2) and other organizations (Chapter 9) are also discussed extensively. Topics such as brand management (Chapter 12) and direct marketing (Chapter 15) have an entire chapter devoted to them.

Marketing Management is very international in flavour, containing theory, practice and examples from Europe, the USA, the Far East, Australia and New Zealand. It considers the economic impact of the superpowers, it demonstrates the implications of the internal European Market and analyses markets in developing countries, the Far East and Eastern Europe.

The diffusion of marketing theory is demonstrated by many examples and by the explicit attention to markets of ideas and people (Chapter 5) and the management of services in marketing (Chapter 10). The growing emphasis on competition is reflected in a chapter on understanding and analysing competitors (Chapter 8). Ample attention is given to marketing data and marketing information systems in Chapter 9. The book contains a well thought out analytical framework for marketing decisions. The value orientation emphasized in this text views marketing as a series of six delivery processes whereby the business system is designed in such a way that value is delivered by the company to the customer through a number of discrete stages (Chapter 1).

Frank Bradley's *Marketing Management* is a modern book on the subject which marks the theory and practice of marketing at the end of this century. It is international, broad, deep and analytical, just like marketing *au fin du siècle.*

Peter S.H. Leeflang,
Professor of Marketing, University of Groningen, The Netherlands

References

Bradley, F. (1995) *Marketing Management,* Hemel Hempstead: Prentice Hall.

Day, G.S. and R. Wensley (1983) 'Marketing theory with a strategic orientation', *Journal of Marketing,* **47**, 4, 79–89.

Fullerton, R.A. (1988) 'How modern is modern marketing? Marketing's evolution and the myth of the production era', *Journal of Marketing,* **52**, 1, 108–25.

Leeflang, P.S.H. and Charles P. de Mortanges (1994) 'The internal European market and strategic marketing planning: implications and expectations', *Journal of International Consumer Marketing,* **6**, 2, 7–23.

Preface

Marketing is a concern for all people and organizations at all times. Successful marketing is based on an organization-wide philosophy which identifies, selects, provides, communicates and delivers value to chosen customer groups. It is not a separate departmental function in the organization. Marketing is concerned with defining customer groups and identifying and providing values which satisfy the needs of these groups more effectively than competitors while producing a profit or benefit for the company. We live by understanding our own needs and the needs of others, and by providing and exchanging something of complementary value to improve the welfare and satisfaction of all. Marketing is the study of needs and wants in society: how they arise; how they are recognized and cultivated; and how they are satisfied. People and organizations provide something of value for someone else, a good, a service or an idea. Marketing is also concerned with exchange processes: how transactions are initiated, motivated, facilitated and completed. It is, therefore, concerned with the convergence of the selling and buying processes in society. The focus is on customer creation and not just sales. Successful organizations create markets by being customer focused rather than production oriented or cost driven.

Providing, communicating and delivering value

Marketing as a management subject consists of a set of concepts and principles for choosing target markets, evaluating customer needs, developing products and services which satisfy wants, and delivering value to customers and profit or benefit to the company or organization. Customer needs are seen as business opportunities which occur in the context of a complex marketing environment consisting of the organization itself, its customers and competitors both of which are constantly changing.

Marketing management is concerned with providing, communicating and delivering value to customers. In doing so, the company must deal with strategic and operational issues in developing and implementing a competitive posture in the market. Marketing begins long before products and services reach the market and continues long after they have been delivered. In providing, communicating and delivering value, the company first identifies and selects society and customer values to be developed in the context of customer needs while recognizing the strengths and weaknesses of competing products and services. Marketing management is a six-stage process in which the organization attempts to identify society and customer values, select the appropriate values for markets and customers in the context of existing and potential competitors, provide the value for customers, communicate the value, deliver it, and implement the marketing plan which encompasses the previous stages.

Organization of the book

This book examines the above issues in detail and attempts to integrate strategic and operational marketing based on a blend of conceptual and applied material relevant to products, services and ideas in consumer and industrial markets. Marketing management is concerned with the application of marketing thinking in all areas of the business irrespective of its nature. The conceptual material reflects the most up-to-date perspectives on academic and company research. The applied material seeks to demonstrate the universality of marketing management by drawing upon illustrations, company experience and case studies from a wide range of geographic and industry settings including comparative, multicountry and multicultural industrial and consumer buying situations.

The material in the text reflects marketing management theory and practice in the USA, Europe, the Far East, Australia and New Zealand. The text is illustrated with examples of 'best practices' from each of these areas. The text does not, however, focus on any one area exclusively. It is a mainstream marketing management textbook based on the premise that marketing is a universal management function with strong strategic elements which are operationalized in different ways in different parts of the world.

The issues outlined above are addressed in 21 chapters, which are divided into six parts, on the basis of a review and integration of recent thinking in marketing management, the copious use of illustrations drawn from business practice and a series of short case studies which serve to integrate the material in the text. The emphasis throughout the text is on identifying best practice in the area of marketing management. The first part, Part A, consists of four chapters which identify society and customer values. Part B addresses the question of selecting the appropriate values for markets and customers in the context of competing products and services. Part C examines the ways in which the organization provides the values for customers. The emphasis is on the provision of value and not just its manufacture. Hence, the book applies to many different types of organization, not just manufacturing companies. Part D deals with the need to communicate the value to customers, while Part E is concerned with delivering the value to customers. The last section, Part F, examines the issue of marketing planning and implementation, and integrates the six stages as a continuous process within the organization.

Acknowledgements

This textbook has been influenced by many people. My colleagues at the Graduate School of Business at University College Dublin have had a very important role in its preparation: Teresa Brannick, Nora Costello, Derek Creevey, Brenda Cullen, A. C. Cunningham, Sean De Burca, Liam Glynn, Benoît Heilbrunn, Dympna Hughes, David Kennedy, Mary Lambkin, Caolan Mannion, Jacqui McWilliams, Tony Meenaghan and Elizabeth Reynolds. I was helped greatly by the excellent secretarial service provided by Marie Byrne, Rachel Collins and Anne Woods, and by Bernard Condon who also prepared the diagrams used. I wish to thank the Dean of the Faculty of Commerce and my long-time friend Aidan Kelly, who has provided continuous support. I also wish to thank R & A Bailey and Company for supporting my chair at University College Dublin.

I am indebted to colleagues at other universities who supplied research and teaching materials, particularly case materials, which have been used in this book: Loretta Ho, Department of Business Studies, Hong Kong Polytechnic; Svend Hollensen, Copenhagen Business School, Copenhagen; Lynn Kahle, Copenhagen College of Engineering, Copenhagen; Thomas Kim-ping Leung, Department of Business Studies, Hong Kong Polytechnic; Alkis S. Magdalinos, La Verne College, Athens; Peter Leeflang, Department of Marketing, University of Gröningen, Gröningen; Jenny Ling, Department of Business Studies, Hong Kong Polytechnic; Marcus J. Schmidt, Copenhagen Business School, Copenhagen and Miguel Otero, University of Santiago de Compostella.

My editor, Julia Helmsley, was a constant source of advice, direction and help throughout the preparation of the manuscript. Her patience and support are much appreciated. Her colleague John Yates provided much-needed research and advice on the format and structure of the text. I am most grateful to the many marketing scholars, listed separately below, who contributed by providing suggestions and constructive criticisms at the development stage of the text. I would also like to express my appreciation to the numerous reviewers who provided excellent assistance at various stages in the process.

Acknowledgements

Lastly, I wish to thank my wife, Breda, for her unstinting support and understanding throughout the past two years. This book belongs to all of us.

Frank Bradley
University College Dublin
Ireland
31 May 1994

Dennis Adcock, Coventry University; P. K. Ahmed, University of Huddersfield; Susan Auty, Lancaster University; Russell Aylott, University of Sunderland; T. Barry, South Kent College; Elanor Bennett, Basingstoke College of Technology; J. C. Bergsma, Noordelijke Hogeschool; K. N. Bernard, University of Strathclyde; C. Berry, London Guildhall University; Grete Birtwistle, Glasgow Caledonian University; Chris Blackburn, Oxford Brookes University; Per Blenker, Handelshojskole Syd; J. M. M. Bloemer, Rijksuniversiteit Limburg; A. M. A. N. Bolten, Haarlem Business School; Humphrey Bourne, City University; Margaret Bourne, South Nottingham College of Further Education; Jane Bower, Heriot-Watt University; H. C. Boxman, Hogeschool Windesheim; Michael Braithwaite, University of Luton; D. R. Brennan, Middlesex University; H. J. Brinkmann, Norges Handelshoyskole; Anne Broderick, University of Glasgow; Paul Brown, Coventry University; Patrick Butler, University of Ulster; H. D. H. A. Cabooter, Hogeschool Venlo; Ian Chaston, University of Plymouth; D. B. Cherry, Thames Valley University; Marylyn Collins, University of Birmingham; P. Copley, University of Northumbria at Newcastle; Chris Cunningham, Henley Management College; Paul Custance, Harper Adams Agricultural College; Linda Daniells, University of Northumbria at Newcastle; Barbara Davison, Salisbury College; I. M. de Blauwe, Hogeschool Eindhoven; Daan de Boer, Noordelijke Hogeschool; Leslie de Chernatony, The Open University; C. F. de Vita, University of Luton; John Desmond, University of Glasgow; F. Drent, Hotel Management School; Robert Duke, University of Leeds; William Duncan, Nene College; K. Edward, Dundee Institute of Technology; Jaafar El-Murad, University of Westminster; D. Elliott, De Montfort University; W. B. Elschot, Haagse Hogeschool; Robert Elslander, Hogeschool Eindhoven; Christine Ennew, University of Nottingham; Aka Erkkila, Stockholms Universitet; Jenny Evans, University of Hertfordshire; Nigel Evans, University of Northumbria at Newcastle; Andreas Falkenberg, Norges Handelshoyskole; Maureen FitzGerald, University of Warwick; Mike Fletcher, Staffordshire University; Edel Foley, College of Commerce; G. R. Forbes, University of Huddersfield; Holger J. Formgren, IHM Management Centre AB; Peter Frason, University of Hertfordshire; Susan Gagen, North East Surrey College of Technology; P. A. Garton, De Montfort University; P. T. Gibbs, Bournemouth University; Paul H. Gilliam, Oxford Brookes University; Sue Gilpin, Manchester Metropolitan University; Ilya Girson, University of Westminster; W. Goosens, Goosens Consultants; Jens Graff, Niels Brock School of International Business; Kjell Grønhaug, Norwegian School of Economics and Business Adminstration; Evert Gummesson, Stockholms Universitet; Stuart M. Haddock, University of Central Lancashire; Robert Hadland, Luton College of Further Education; R. Hamilton, Lancaster University; Helge Hammerich, Aalborg Universitets Centre; Graham Hankinson, Thames Valley University; Anton Hartman-Olesen, Herning Handelskole; Karoline Hauger, Oppland Regional College; Helen Haywood, Bournemouth University; Thomas Helgesson, Halmstad University College; S. J. Henderson, De Montfort University; E. T. M. Hendrilis, Hogeschool Holland; Nick Hill, South Bank University; Jeanne Hill, University of Central Lancashire; D. M. Hillyard, Nene College; Maurice Hinde, Ried Kerr College; Janny C. Hoekstra, Rijksuniversiteit Groningen; Graham Hooley, Aston University; Steven Hornshaw, Thurrock Management Centre; Andrew Inglis, London Guildhall University; Vijay P. Jain, Danish School for International Marketing and Export; Ove Daniel Jakobsen, Bodo Graduate School of Business; Stig G. Johanssen, Stockholms Universitet; Axel Johne, City University; Brian Jones,

Wirral Metropolitan College; Hapenga Monty Kabeta, Copperbelt University; Martha Lynn Kahle, Copenhagen College of Engineering; Constantine S. Katsikeas, University of Wales; Ellen Kaye, Institute for International Business Studies; F. A. Kense, Hogeschool Middem Brabant; P. J. Kitchen, Keele University; E. J. Knight, University of Derby; H. Kofstra, Noordelijke Hogeschool; Maarten Kool, Agricultural University; G. Th. Kranenburg, Haagsche Hogeschool; Peter Kristensen, Aalborg Handelskole; Tore Kristensen, IOA – Copenhagen Business School, Jornn Ladegaard, Herning School of Business Science; Marie Pascale Lapalus, Robert Gordon University; Wendy Lomax, Kingston University; Gary Love, North East Wales Institute of Higher Education; Mark A. Low, University of Salford; A. W. Macfarlane, University of Humberside; C. Mackell, University of Aberdeen; S. Maddock, University of Birmingham; Alkis S. Magdalinos, University of La Verne; R. Mann, Berufsakademie Villingen-Schwenningen; J. Marcussen-Offereins, HEAO – Utrecht; Robert L. Marshall, North Cheshire College; Rita Martenson, Vid Göteborgs Universitet; Derek Martin, Oxford Brookes University; Kenneth McClement, Dundee College of Further Education; Geraldine McKay, Staffordshire University; Steen Mejrup, Handelshojskole Syd; M. T. G. Meulenberg, Agricultural University; Blain Meyrick, Coventry University; Brian Middleton, North East Wales Institute of Higher Education; R. S. Minhas, University of Sheffield; R. E. Morgan, University of Wales; Vibeke Toft Muller, Vestsjaellands Handelshogskole Centre; Jannie Munch, Aalborg Handelskole; Laurence Murphy, Regional Technical College; Leo Murphy, Omagh College of Further Education; Peter Naudé, University of Manchester; E. Karin Newman, Middlesex University; Ed J. Nijssen, Erasmus Universiteit; Sveno Noehr, Aalborg Handelskole; Bengt Norden, University of Gothenburg; Lars Nyengaard, Handelshojskole Syd; J. J. H. Orval, International Agrarische Hogeschool; Per Ostergaard, Odense University; Stephen J. Page, Massey University; D. Palihawadana, Leeds Metropolitan University; Gordon D. Pearson, Keele University; Neils Kristian Pedersen, Aabenraa Business College; Ed Peelen, Universiteit van Amsterdam; J. M. Penn, University of Portsmouth; Helen Perks, University of Salford; Morten jul Petersen, Sonderborg Handelsskile; Chris Pierce, Leeds Metropolitan University; Carole Pimblett, Bolton Institute of Higher Education; Alison Price, Liverpool John Moores University; Andrea Prothero, University of Wales; J. R. Rance, Hanzehogeschool; Jan Randsdorp, Haarlem Business School; Erling Rasmussen, Roskilde Universitetscenter; Ruth Rettie, Kingston University; F. Patrick Roche, Cork Regional Technical College; Theo J. Roebers, Technische Universiteit Delft; H. C. A. Roest, Katholieke Universiteit Brabant; H. J. Roseboom, H. E. S. Rotterdam; Denis Scanlan, University of Hull; M. J. Schildkamp, Hogeschl S'Hertogenbosch; Janette Sheerman, University of Bradford; Brian Sheffield, University of Northumbria at Newcastle; R. C. M. T. Smit, Hogeschool West Brabant; T. M. Smith, Bolton Institute of Higher Education; Robert Smith, North East Surrey College of Technology; J. Southan, University of Salford; Barry Southern, Wigan College of Technology; F. M. Spijkerman-van Zon, Hogeschl S'Hertogenbosch; Douglas Stoddart, University of Buckingham; Marilyn A. Stone, Heriot-Watt University; L. W. Stops, Bournemouth University; Steve Storey, University of Sunderland; Jack Sumner; Blackpool and Fylde College of Further and Higher Education; David Sutcliffe, University of Central Lancashire; Stephen Swailes, Nene College; Gilbert Swinnen, Limburgs Universitair Cenbrum; Y. J. Taylor, St Helens College; Jonathan Taylor, University of North London; M. H. M. Thissew, Hogeschool Amsterdam; K. Tomlinson, Canterbury Christ Church College of Higher Education; David G. Tonks, Lancaster University; M. E. Townsend, University of Portsmouth; Peter Trim, University of Kent at Canterbury; Paris M. Tsikalakis, The American College of Greece; M. van den Bosch, HEAO – Arnhem; A. J. van der Lely, Hogeschool voor Economics and Management; G. van Ginkel, H. E. S. Rotterdam; G. F. M. van Lier, Hogeschool West Brabant; B. A. van Schelt, Hogeschl S'Hertogenbosch; T. H. Verhallen, Katholieke Universiteit Brabant; J. H. M. Verheiden, Hogeschool Eindhoven; Jens Vestergaard, Handelshojskole Syd; J. B. Vollering, Erasmus Universiteit, E. Waarts, Erasmus Universiteit; Michael Walsh, Cork Regional Technical College; Michael Ward, University College, Salford; Gary Warnaby, Manchester Metropolitan University; J. Watkinson, Tresham Institute; Gerald Watts, Lancaster University; W. A. Westgate, Henley

Acknowledgements

Management College; Hellen Westlund, Gothenburg School of Economics; Nigel Wichglo, Leeds Metropolitan University; Monika Wiklund, Hogskolan I Vaxjo; Hugh Wilkins, Oxford Brookes University; Roger Willetts, Nene College; G. Williams, The College of North East London; Alan Wilson, University of Strathclyde; Deborah K. Wilson, European University; S. H. Wilson, Manchester Metropolitan University; Laurie Wood, University of Salford; Helen R. Woodruffe, University of Salford; R. G. Woolrich, University of North London; Sheila Wright, De Montfort University.

PART A

Identify society and customer values

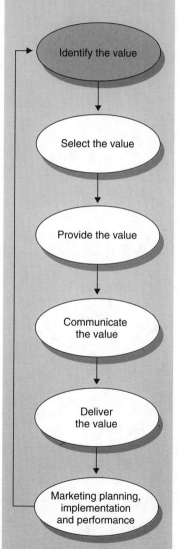

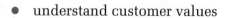

- understand customer values
- choose customer segments
- define customer benefits

Chapters

Marketing in society

1

Meaning of marketing for the company
Nature of marketing activities
Social responsibility in marketing
Theory in marketing

Introduction

This chapter introduces and explains:

- origins of and need for marketing in society;
- modern marketing thought;
- the marketing concept;
- performance of marketing activities;
- trust and ethical issues in marketing;
- cause marketing;
- consumerism and the environmental influences on marketing;
- theories to understand marketing processes; and
- an analytical framework for marketing management.

A broad description of the marketing management task in modern society is presented. Marketing is a discipline in its own right which is related to many others in the social sciences. It is a business discipline which has direct relevance to the way organizations and individuals behave in the marketplace. It relates to the wider world in which we live through its impact on society and through the impact of social norms and practices on it. Marketing is a business philosophy concerned with the way business is done and with many of the operational tasks encountered in providing products and service benefits to customers in the context of a competitive environment.

Having studied this chapter, you should be able to define the phrases listed above in your own words, and you should be able to do the following:

1. Describe the meaning of marketing in society and for an organization.

2. Understand the implications of the marketing concept.

3. Identify and describe marketing activities.

4. Recognize marketing's social responsibility.

5. Design an appropriate framework for the study of marketing management.

Meaning of marketing for the company

Marketing is a relatively new discipline which has evolved during the past hundred years or so into a formal business discipline. Although people and companies have always engaged in marketing practices, the formal study of marketing is of recent vintage. To appreciate the need for marketing management in the organization it is necessary to understand its origins, the role of marketing in society and recent developments in marketing thought and how it applies to marketing management.

Origins of marketing

In earlier times marketing did not have the managerial focus it has today. Marketing was seen to be concerned with the way in which commodities such as food, timber and other raw materials were moved from the point of production to the point of consumption. Marketing was treated as a branch of applied economics devoted to the study of distribution channels. Second, marketing was concerned with the marketing institutions through which the commodities were delivered to the market, e.g. processors, wholesalers and retailers. Third, marketing was concerned with the functions provided by these institutions. These three approaches to an understanding of marketing were very descriptive in nature and had little normative content.

Concern for the functions of marketing was the most analytical of these approaches and led directly to the development of a conceptual framework for marketing as a management discipline. Marketing was seen, therefore, as a series of social and economic processes rather than as a managerial activity. The institutional and functional emphasis began to change in 1948 when the

American Marketing Association defined marketing as the 'performance of business activities directed toward, and incident to, the flow of goods and services from producer to consumer or user', a definition modified slightly in 1960 (Webster, 1992: 2).

The managerial approach to the study of marketing appeared in the 1950s and 1960s. Early writers defined marketing management as a decision-making or problem-solving process and relied on analytical frameworks drawn from the behavioural sciences, economics, mathematics and statistics. By drawing on the behavioural and quantitative sciences, early writers derived legitimacy for marketing as a separate academic discipline.

In the early stages of the development of marketing as an academic discipline, concern rested with sellers and buyers and products and services which had utilitarian value only. The objective was an exchange between manufacturers who provided products or services, and buyers who desired the products and services and possessed money to acquire them. In these early days the market transaction was confined to the transfer of ownership of an economic good or service from one party to another in exchange for payment. Market transactions were seen to involve direct payment of some kind.

Later, by recognizing that non-market transactions also involve a transfer of assets but no exchange of payment, the domain of marketing was extended. In this view, whether it involves giving gifts, receiving public services, helping charities or paying taxes, marketing is seen as relevant to all organizations providing products and services for a customer group, whether or not payment arises. A product or service is then defined as something which has value to someone.

These various approaches to the study of marketing have led scholars to conclude that marketing is both a managerial orientation or philosophy and a business function. It is necessary, however, to distinguish between them.

Marketing as a social process

To understand the nature of marketing in the organization it is necessary to consider the types of marketing decision faced by the company. Marketing decisions are complex because markets are dynamic and the marketing environment facing the company is complex. The factors which contribute to complexity in marketing are:

- the need to consider a large number of changing variables;

- the external and uncontrollable nature of these variables;

- the unpredictable behaviour of marketing variables;

- instability in the marketing environment; and

5

- the scarcity of information

The importance of these factors in influencing marketing decisions will become more apparent later. At this stage, note that the marketing manager faces a situation where often there are no clearly defined sources of information, and where the sources of data are inadequate and may be relevant only for a short period.

Marketing as a social science

Marketing as an academic discipline is embedded in the social sciences. It is related to four groups of social science disciplines. The first are those linked directly to marketing: economics, political science and organizational studies. The second group are those concerned with human behaviour: anthropology, sociology, psychology and communications. The third group are those which deal with the broader aspects of life such as philosophy, social work and ecology. The final set of social sciences includes those concerned with tools, techniques and methods of measurement: mathematics, statistics, econometrics and computer science.

From political economy the study of marketing draws on the concept of a rational, calculating individual who attempts to maximize individual satisfaction largely isolated from the influence of others. From politics the study of marketing draws on the concept of power and the influence of pressure groups, regulations and a macro framework for ethics in business. The impact of government regulations, the value of propaganda and the extent to which advertising is regulated in different countries may also be understood in a political context.

The sociological perspective treats a person's behaviour as a product of culture, the social environment and association with others. Issues of group behaviour, individual behaviour and the role of the family are understood within a sociological perspective. The family cycle, which views people at different stages of life depending on their financial position, family commitments and purchasing behaviour, is drawn from sociology.

From communications studies it is possible to identify influences which are applicable in advertising, sales promotion, personal selling and negotiations. Communication studies enables us to determine the effectiveness of mass media, e.g. television, by measuring the extent of brand awareness in the market, the belief in the claims made for the brand, the evaluation made of the brand and the extent to which there is a desire to buy the brand.

From psychology the marketing discipline derives the impact of reference groups' influence on product and service purchasing. The role of opinion leaders, celebrities and authority figures in marketing communications may be understood with reference to psychological models.

Ecological concerns are becoming very important. No firm can ignore the effect of its activities on the environment. Damage to the environment is a social cost which must be borne by all. It is important that marketing takes due care not to do anything which would adversely affect the environment in which we live. The effect of humans on the environment may be studied within a framework based on a study of ecology and demography. Concepts of population, its size, growth and mobility are important considerations in the study of marketing. The movement of people from rural communities to urban areas affects the marketing task and must be considered by the marketing manager. For example, shopping centre location, the provision of retailing outlets, and the distribution of products and services all relate to population.

Marketing is a social process by which individuals, families, groups and other organizations obtain what they need and want by identifying value, providing it and exchanging it with others. The core concepts of marketing are needs, wants and demands, markets, products and services, values and satisfaction, exchange and communications (Figure 1.1). Needs are the internal influences which prompt behaviour. Biological needs refer to a person's requirements for food, air and shelter, while social needs refer to issues such as security, personal gratification and prestige. Wants are culture bound and refer to the way in which needs are satisfied. Wants may be satisfied using a number of technologies. A teenager may listen to music on a rock radio station or on tapes in a personal stereo system. Demand refers to the ability and willingness of a customer to buy a particular product or service which satisfies

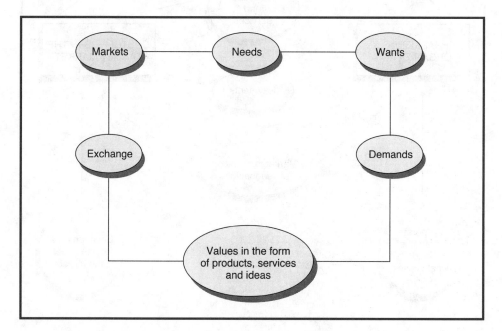

Figure 1.1   The core concepts of marketing

the want and the more latent need. A student may want a BMW but afford only a bicycle.

Products and services are values provided to satisfy needs or wants. The importance of products and services stems from their ability to satisfy these needs and wants. It is important, therefore, to think in terms of values or benefits, not products and services. For customers, value is reflected in the ability of a product or service to satisfy expectations. Consumers intuitively or explicitly attempt to determine the capacity of a product or service to satisfy a particular set of goods. Usually the consumer faces a choice of product alternatives, each of which can satisfy the particular need. Values are then exchanged, which means obtaining a desired product or service from somebody in return for something else of value, usually money but also including other factors.

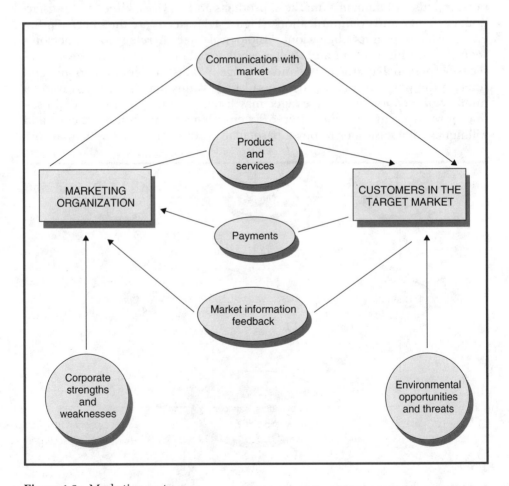

Figure 1.2 Marketing system

Marketing, markets and exchange

Marketing is considered, therefore, to be one of the social sciences. It is necessary to adopt a multidisciplinary approach to its study as it reflects many aspects of the social and human sciences. Marketing as a social science is concerned with markets and exchange, the participants in the exchange and the subject of the exchange. Markets include consumers, industrial users, the government, and intermediaries located in the domestic market and abroad. The other parties to the exchange include companies, individuals and groups. Usually marketing is performed by companies, but increasingly interest centres on the marketing functions of non-profit organizations like hospitals, political parties, universities and associations. The subject matter of the exchange is usually a product or service, but it is necessary to include ideas, people, places and other items of value which can be exchanged. Marketing depends on the exchange process to:

- provide a high material standard of living in society;

- encourage the consumption of products and services;

- increase consumer satisfaction through quality and variety; and

- develop a system of companies and organizations capable of fulfilling these functions profitably.

Marketing may be thought of as an independent system of items, people and ideas which interact on a regular basis to provide benefits to society. At its simplest, the company or organization is linked to the market through four major flows (Figure 1.2). The company communicates with the market in some way and provides products and services and other things of value for customers in that market. In return the market provides information on its needs and wants, and also provides payments. The marketing organization may be a profit-seeking company or other enterprise providing value to society. As such it has certain strengths and weaknesses, and the market served is influenced by a set of environmental opportunities and threats emanating from the broader environment in which the organization operates. The analysis of strengths and weaknesses, threats and opportunities is the subject of later chapters.

Individual and social group values

Individual and family decisions are affected by individual and social values. Values are centrally held enduring beliefs which guide actions and judgements in specific situations and in more general circumstances as people orientate themselves in their environment (Rokeach, 1973: 160). There are many types of value which must be distinguished. People possess moral values, express political values and satisfy utility values which are often mixed together, making it difficult if not impossible to be accurate in defining the concept of

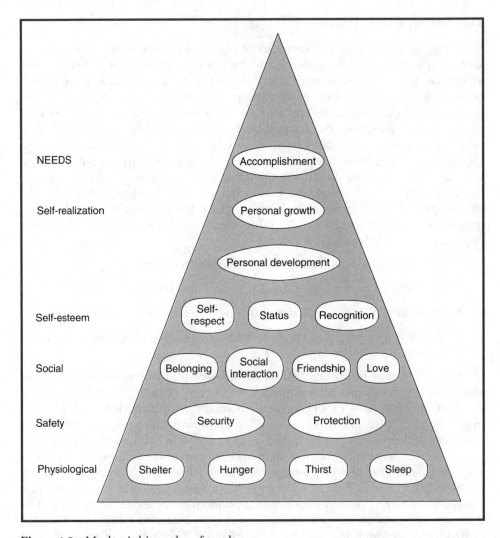

Figure 1.3 Maslow's hierarchy of needs
(Source: Based on Maslow, 1954. Reprinted by permission of HarperCollins Publishers Inc.)

values. The significance of values is determined by their function in understanding how the individual, family and groups in society adapt and behave. Values are self-centred and socially centred, since they represent an interaction between the individual and society (Grunert and Juhl, 1991: 2).

Values in society are beliefs about desirable behaviours that transcend specific situations, and are ranked by their relative importance (Schwartz and Bilsky, 1987). Values are also drawn into use when interaction between the individual and the group arises. These are the formal characteristics of values, and their meaningful content may be defined as the cognitive representation

of universal human requirements (Grunert and Juhl, 1991). These requirements refer to biological needs and wants such as food and shelter, personal
interactions such as occur in the family, and social or institutional requirements such as the welfare and survival of the group (Maslow, 1970; Rokeach,
1973). Maslow (1970) has suggested that society's needs are myriad and are
expressed in a hierarchical fashion (Figure 1.3).

The implication of this hierarchy for marketing is that the level achieved
by people and society helps to determine the kind of goods and services which
will be in demand. At the very basic level, people attempt to satisfy the physiological needs of shelter, hunger, thirst and sleep. Until these needs are satisfied, safety needs, which occur at the next level in the hierarchy, are less
important. At the third stage, social needs make a claim on society's attention,
and society expresses its need for belonging, social interaction, friendship and
love. When these needs are satisfied, issues of self-esteem become important as
people seek self-respect, status and recognition in the society in which they
live. At the highest level, people seek personal growth and development, and
accomplishment through self-realization. It is important to identify the level
that society has reached when deciding an appropriate role for marketing. For
most people in developing or poor countries, only the lower levels have yet
been reached, while some people in developed or rich countries have reached
a much more advanced level. Indeed, it is important to note that wide diver-
gences also exist within a given society. Applying the hierarchical framework
may therefore be difficult, but it does indicate the wide divergence of needs to
be satisfied which exist in society.

Need for marketing in society

Marketing is concerned with the exchange of values and the entire business
process, which consists of a tightly integrated effort to identify, develop and
satisfy customer needs. Addressing marketing issues facing the railroads, for
example, would have avoided the trap of ignoring competition from cars,
trucks and aeroplanes. To survive it is necessary to adopt a customer orientation and recognize the needs of the market.

> But mere survival is a so-so aspiration. The trick is to survive gallantly ... to
> have the visceral feel of entrepreneurial greatness. No organisation can achieve
> greatness without a vigorous leader who ... can produce eager followers in vast
> numbers. In business, the followers are the customers. (Levitt, 1960: 56)

To develop these customers it is necessary for the company to be imbued
with a customer-creating and customer-satisfying philosophy. The successful
firm must provide 'customer-creating value satisfactions', according to Levitt,
and it must push such ideas into every part of the company. The company

11

must think of itself not as producing goods and services, but as buying customers: as doing things that will make people want to do business with it (Levitt, 1960: 56).

Importance of marketing to society

From the 1950s to the 1980s, the way in which mass production industries were organized drove them to produce as much as they could. In the early part of the period, the market for such goods was only partly satisfied. In the later part, financial and economic pressures of globalization forced efficient manufacturing companies to seek markets abroad. Declining unit costs and the prospect of profits created an inordinate focus on production efficiency.

Such a mass production mentality brought with it an equally strong pressure to move output down the distribution channel to where it could be consumed, with a concomitant pressure on selling what had been produced. Selling was emphasized, not marketing. 'Marketing, being a more sophisticated and complex process, gets ignored. Selling focuses on the needs of the seller, marketing on the needs of the buyer' (Levitt, 1960: 50).

Marketing in periods of growth

The fundamental requirements of competing successfully in growth markets which may be fashion driven are:

- rapid product innovation;

- intense differentiation of products and services;

- the pursuit of fashion and diversity not uniformity; and

- flexible manufacturing systems to produce small batches of specialized products.

Car manufacturers are among the most extreme exponents of this approach in growth markets, producing limited editions and myriad variations on aspects of the vehicle such as seat adjustments, different steering wheel configurations and positions, and other more obvious options such as stereo equipment and shaded window glass.

Marketing during recessions

When growth declines and recessions affect consumers, they become frugal again. The difficulty for manufacturers and providers of products and services is to observe the change (Kotler, 1972b). Manufacturers are frequently left with diversified product ranges, sophisticated and flexible plant and equipment, and engineering teams dedicated to short product cycles.

As customers have realized that many products are at parity with each other, and as discounting has made heavily branded items available more cheaply, customers have expressed a desire for products and services which perform to an expected standard and which are promoted by informative rather than merely persuasive advertising. Customers in the 1990s are beginning to seek intrinsic value in the products they buy. Emphasizing the price aspect of value in a product is a valuable sales promotion technique in weaker economic situations.

An emphasis on value in marketing means giving the customer:

- improved products with added features;
- with better service; and
- at a lower price.

Companies have to demonstrate that their brands have value in order to justify premium pricing. Marketing in this sense means delivering value to the customer through products that are guaranteed to perform. Better products and services and lower prices mean that the advantage will go to strong competitors with a cost advantage. L'Eggs women's hosiery is sold at very competitive prices due to heavy investment in the most efficient manufacturing technology. The company maintained margins with almost no price increase throughout the 1980s. The combination of low price and a strong brand has given L'Eggs a 54 per cent share of the US market (*Business Week*, 11 November 1991: 57).

Modern marketing thought

Modern marketing thought means identifying values desired by customers, providing them in some way, communicating these values to customer groups and delivering the value. Values mean benefits focused on solving customer problems and not merely on the products and services which serve as the vehicle of the solution. The focus is on the customer and on solving problems faced by the customer.

Seeking value from the customer's perspective means building a long-term, mutually profitable relationship with customers instead of trying to maximize the profit on each transaction. An emphasis on relationships rather than individual transactions focuses on the customer, not the product, as the profit centre. It also means that attracting new customers is an intermediate objective in the process of maintaining and cultivating an existing customer base (Lambin, 1993). This approach views marketing as a continuous relationship with customers in contrast to the more traditional view which is short term and focused on immediate sales response (Dwyer *et al.*, 1987).

The first sale to a customer is often very difficult, costs a lot and results in little or no profit. With a strong continuing relationship, however, the customer becomes more profitable. Such long-term relationships are established through the exchange of information, products, services and social contacts. In this way the company–customer relationship is commercialized.

It should also be recognized that in several situations, particularly in industrial markets, there are several parties involved in the relationship. Buyers and sellers operate in a network of suppliers, customers, financial institutions and governments. The whole network becomes part of the relationship (Håkansson, 1982).

Definitions of marketing

Definitions in marketing, as in any other business discipline, are important for a number of reasons. The definition of an area of business:

- contributes to its professional image among consumers and business organizations;

- delineates the area for research and teaching purposes, including diagnostic applied research within organizations; and

- identifies and communicates a sense of purpose among practitioners and professionals in the field of marketing.

Any conceptual definition of a business discipline is an abstraction of techniques and practices that contains limitations related to the use of the definition. It is likely that no one definition describes marketing comprehensively as different definitions may be used for different purposes. A conceptual definition should distinguish the concept from other similar concepts and clearly define what is meant by the term 'marketing'. Furthermore, the definition should be clear, precise and complete.

Various definitions of marketing have been offered at different times. Early definitions, reflecting the environment in which firms operated, equated marketing with selling. A popular definition for many years stated that marketing is the managerial process of providing the right product, in the right place, at the right time and at the right price. This definition reflects the business activities required to ensure that the product or service moves from the point of production to the point of consumption. According to this view, marketing seeks to maximize customer satisfaction and profits by designing an optimal marketing mix.

As with the other management disciplines, interest also centres on how marketing is practised in the community. As a practice, marketing draws on many sciences although it is not a science itself. Marketing is a discipline with its own assumptions, objectives, methods and measurement techniques. Several definitions of marketing may be found in the literature:

- the performance of business activities that direct the flow of goods and services from producer to consumer or user;

- getting the right goods and services to the right people at the right place at the right time, at the right price with the right communications and promotion;

- the human activity directed at satisfying needs and wants through exchange processes.

Marketing has been defined by the Institute of Marketing in the United Kingdom as the management function responsible for identifying, anticipating and satisfying customer requirements profitably. Marketing is, therefore, both a concept and a set of techniques which address such matters as research, product design and development, pricing, packaging, sales and sales promotion, advertising, public relations, distribution and after-sales service. These activities define the broad scope of marketing and their balanced integration within a marketing plan is known as the marketing programme or marketing mix.

Marketing has also been defined as a 'social and managerial process by which individuals and groups obtain what they need and want through creating, offering, and exchanging products of value with others' (Kotler, 1994: 6). It is defined by Dibb *et al.* (1991: 5) as 'individual and organizational activities that facilitate and expedite satisfying exchange relationships in a dynamic environment through the creation, distribution, promotion, and pricing of goods, services, and ideas'. According to Carman (1973: 1), marketing is 'the process by which the demand structure for products and services is anticipated or enlarged and satisfied through the conception, promotion, distribution and exchange of such goods'. The emphasis in this definition is on the process involved. As Carman notes, the study of this marketing process has been organized to the point where it qualifies as a discipline but probably not as a science.

The core concept of marketing is the exchange of values between two parties where the values need not be limited to goods, services and money, but may include other resources such as time, energy and feelings (Kotler, 1972a: 48). For example, a transaction occurs when a person decides to attend a football match: time is exchanged for entertainment. This generic concept of marketing is, according to Kotler, specifically concerned with how transactions are created, stimulated, facilitated and valued (1972a: 49).

Marketing has been defined by the American Marketing Association (1985) as 'the process of planning and executing the conception, pricing, promotion and distribution of ideas, goods and services to create exchange and satisfy individual and organisational objectives'. This definition states that marketing is a process managed by the marketing function in the organization, which is a rather narrow definition. It is a production-oriented definition which identifies a list of activities to be performed by the firm, but ignores what customers expect marketing to be (Grönroos, 1987: 4). A Nordic definition of marketing, which attempts to involve the customer's view of the nature of marketing, based on the interactions and networks approach, is: 'Marketing is to establish, develop and commercialize long-term customer relationships, so that the objectives of the parties involved are met. This is done by a mutual exchange and keeping of promises' (Grönroos, 1987: 9).

Thus, the marketing function permeates the entire organization and includes all the activities which affect current and future buyer behaviour of customers. Other writers emphasize that, while marketing may be a function within the company, it is also a corporate philosophy underlying the entire approach to business (Baker, 1976). The confusion apparently arises from the shift in marketing orientation of companies over time.

Markets and marketing

Marketing is concerned with problem solving and customer benefits reflecting customer needs and wants. As we have seen, however, needs and wants are not the same thing. Needs are universal, but the means of satisfying them are local. Wants reflect the customer's education, culture, personality and financial circumstances. The housekeeper may need the carpets cleaned but may or may not want an Electrolux, or Nilfisk or Miéle to do the job! The firm must identify the problem that its customers use its products and services to solve. It is also necessary to identify the benefits that customers seek from using a product or service available in the market.

A market consists of all the potential customers who share a particular need or want, and who might be willing and able to engage in exchange to satisfy that need or want. Markets are also used to describe various groups of buyers:

- need markets, e.g. markets seeking package holidays;

- product markets, e.g. the beer market;

- demographic markets, e.g. the teenage market.

For these and other reasons, the focus is on selected customers in a target market. A construction equipment manufacturer might have a number of civil engineering customers who seek high-quality durable machines, a fair price for the value provided, on-time delivery, good credit and finance terms, and rapid and efficient after-sales service. In return, the equipment manufacturer would expect a good price, on-time payment and good word-of-mouth promotion and endorsement to other possible buyers (Figure 1.4).

A marketing orientation helps to define the firm's business. For marketing success, it is important that the company has answers to the following questions:

- What is the problem that customers are trying to solve?

- What benefits do customers seek?

- How well does the company's product solve this problem and provide these benefits?

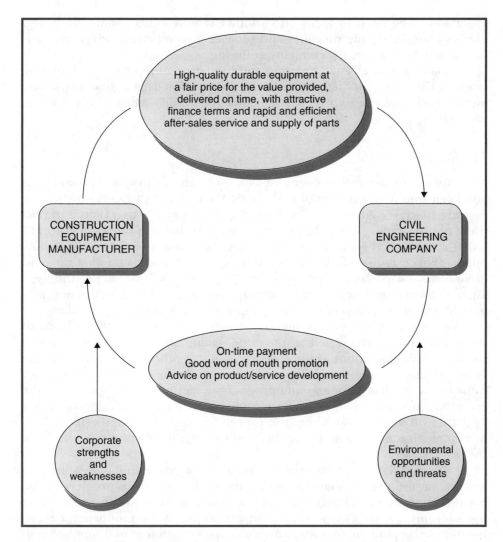

High-quality durable equipment at a fair price for the value provided, delivered on time, with attractive finance terms and rapid and efficient after-sales service and supply of parts

CONSTRUCTION EQUIPMENT MANUFACTURER

CIVIL ENGINEERING COMPANY

On-time payment
Good word of mouth promotion
Advice on product/service development

Corporate strengths and weaknesses

Environmental opportunities and threats

Figure 1.4 Hypothetical example of exchange of values in marketing

A statement that the company is in the film-making business is not very useful because it says nothing about customer needs. Some film companies merely assumed that they were in the film business when the entertainment business left them behind. In this connection it is worth quoting the statement often attributed to Charles Revson of Revlon: 'In the factory we make cosmetics but in the drugstore we sell hope.' Another version of the same idea, attributed to salesman Elmer Wheeler is, 'Don't sell the steak – sell the sizzle.' A similar point from industrial marketing is made by Levitt: 'Purchasing agents don't buy quarter inch drills, they buy quarter inch holes' (quoted in Kotler,

1988: 446). The need to focus on customer requirements competitively also implies considering the products and services of competitors which are perceived as substitutes for the company's offering.

Marketing is an all-encompassing and fundamental function of all organisations. This view conflicts with the more traditional view that marketing means marketing research or is a staff function (unlike sales, which is a line function).

Marketing concept

Marketing has long been recognized as a social and economic activity. It has also been considered as a set of tools to aid trade and exchange. However, the formal explicit recognition of the marketing concept in its own right is of relatively recent origin. 'The enigma of marketing is that it is one of the world's oldest activities and yet it is regarded as the most recent of the business disciplines' (Baker, 1976). Marketing as a discipline borrows from a wide range of theoretical and practical knowledge, and it has evolved over time. Different aspects of marketing have been emphasized at different times. In this way, promotion and pricing became important aspects of the strategy of marketing.

Depending on the environmental pressures on business, the balance of the marketing mix has varied: at one time, selling and the salesperson dominated marketing activities within the firm, while at others, advertising was the most prominent element in the marketing mix. Consequently, companies came to accept that the marketing programme had to be appropriate for the environment at any one time, while accounting for the firm's business position in that environment. Sometimes the pressure is to produce and sell, while at other times it is to be more thoughtful and strategic in responding to needs in the marketplace.

It therefore became necessary for the marketing discipline to develop into more than just a set of tools for addressing some immediate problem in the business environment. It was realized that marketing was not the preserve of the sales force, to be used to dispose of the output of the production department while keeping the finance and accounting department well supplied with sales revenues.

There has been much debate and argument in the literature about the nature of the marketing concept (Houston, 1986). This debate continues and is healthy for the development of the discipline. For present purposes, the marketing concept is a philosophy which encourages the company to ensure that the needs and wants of customers in selected target markets are reflected in all its actions and activities, while recognizing constraints imposed by society. According to the marketing concept, organizations which follow this precept should be successful and profitable.

The marketing concept first received formal recognition in 1952 by one of its leading exponents. The 1952 Annual Report of the General Electric

Company in the USA pioneered the new notion with the declaration that the marketing concept

> introduces the marketing man at the beginning rather than at the end of the production cycle and integrates marketing into each phase of business ... [M]arketing establishes ... for the engineer, the design and manufacturing man, what the customer wants in a given product, what price he is willing to pay and where and when it will be wanted. Marketing will have authority in product planning, production scheduling and inventory control, as well as in sales distribution or servicing of the product. (General Electric Company, 1952: 21)

Three aspects of this summary statement are interesting: the customer orientation, the profit orientation and the emphasis on integrated company effort. These three aspects are fundamental to the adoption of the marketing concept.

Marketing means, therefore, being oriented to the needs of customers rather than emphasizing what is convenient to produce. Effective marketing requires that the company analyzes the needs that its products are supposed to satisfy. For instance, customers do not usually buy coffee; rather they buy a warm stimulating drink. Likewise customers do not buy sisal; they buy a material to make baling rope to tie things together, or fiber to serve as backing for a floor covering. Customers do not buy handicrafts; they buy something that will look attractive in their homes or offices, or which will be acceptable as a gift. In such cases, customers are attempting to impress friends, business associates or acquaintances.

In all of the above instances, the organization should realize that many alternative products may satisfy the needs identified. In other words, there are usually many substitutes for the firm's products. For coffee include tea, cocoa, alcohol or soft drinks. For sisal include polypropylene fiber or polythene sheeting. For handicraft items include furniture or any decorative alternative.

The real lesson of the marketing concept is that better-performing firms recognize the basic and enduring nature of the customer needs they are attempting to satisfy; it is the technology of want satisfaction which is transitory (Anderson, 1982: 23). The products and services used to satisfy customer needs and wants change constantly.

The adoption of the marketing concept confers specific authority and responsibility within the company. Marketing is concerned with all parts of the organization. It is therefore more than a set of tools; it is an orientation which pervades the thinking of the organization as a whole.

Company response to the marketing concept

The responses of companies to opportunities offered by adopting the marketing concept are varied. Companies may be categorized in different ways depending on whether they place the emphasis on a functional approach to marketing, which involves sales and promotional support primarily, a customer orientation based on identifying and satisfying customer needs, a departmental or bureaucratic approach based on the activities normally found in the marketing department of a company, or a marketing philosophy approach which serves as a guide to the entire organization (Figure 1.5).

These approaches to marketing are based on different orientations of the organization. Marketing may be seen purely as one of the internal business functions which supplies the organization with the expertise associated with markets and marketing. This includes sales and advertising support, market research, analysis and marketing planning, and would be provided in conjunction with other functional support.

At the opposite extreme, the organization is seen to have a customer orientation indicating a focus on customer needs and emphasizing ways of satisfying customer wants. The marketing department orientation views marketing in a compartmentalized way with an emphasis on the procedures for providing sales and advertising support, market research, analysis and planning. The emphasis here is on a bureaucratic organization of marketing. Lastly, the marketing

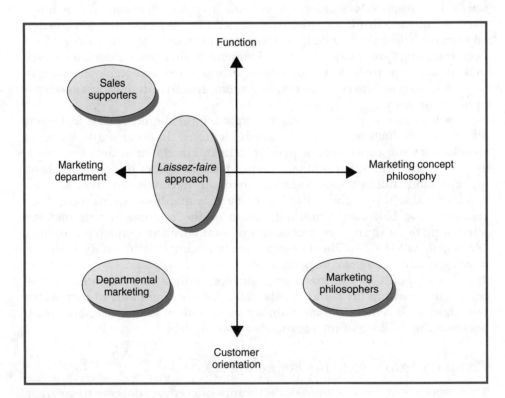

Figure 1.5   Approaches to marketing in the organization
(Source: Hooley *et al.*, 1990)

concept philosophy produces an orientation which imbues the organization with the marketing approach, focusing simultaneously on customers, competitors and the organization itself. It is strategic in that longer-term factors are considered. It is also tactical in that short-term decisions must also be made.

Based on this framework, four distinct approaches to marketing have been identified, three of which suggest a natural progression of marketing development within the company from sales support, through departmental marketing to the adoption of marketing as a guiding philosophy for the entire organization (Hooley *et al.*, 1990). The fourth approach, being a mixture of sales support and departmental marketing, suggested to these writers a *laissez-faire* approach to marketing rather than a conscious orientation (Figure 1.5). By combining the four approaches, these authors classify companies as 'sales supporters', 'departmental marketing', 'marketing philosophers' or '*laissez-faire*' organizations. The 'marketing philosophers' approach gives rise to the marketing concept and its role in organizations active in the marketplace.

Constraints on applying the marketing concept

There are certain circumstances where the marketing concept itself is limited and must be modified or adapted. The marketing concept has tended to be applied in profit-motivated businesses where transactions involve money for products. As will be seen, its application is much wider. As often applied, however, the concept may not distinguish between the short-term wants of customers and their own long-term welfare. A case in point is the manufacture and sale of large cars, which more rapidly deplete the limited reserves of a scarce resource such as oil or even oxygen.

Marketing must also distinguish between the individual consumer's needs and wants, and the welfare of society. Large cars greatly contribute to the pollution and traffic congestion of cities. Similarly, tobacco causes problems for smokers and for those who inhale the smoke. It is necessary, therefore, to integrate profitability requirements with ecological and environmental constraints.

A number of writers on marketing have agreed that a blind application of the marketing concept is undesirable as it can lead firms to depart from major product development and innovation and instead emphasize low-risk product modifications (Hayes and Abernathy, 1980). This occurs partly because consumers, when asked in marketing research studies to articulate their wants, refer to the familiar and hence suggest only minor product modifications. Applying the marketing concept in this way may discourage innovation. But consumer surveys are not the only way that the marketing-oriented firm can identify the customer's needs and wants. Furthermore, the adoption of the marketing concept implies an assessment of the competition, since the company's aim is to satisfy customers within a segment better than competitors.

The two major assumptions behind the marketing concept are that consumers know what they want and are informed and highly rational in satisfying their wants; and that consumer sovereignty prevails (Dickinson *et al.*, 1986: 9). These authors argue that, if the marketing concept were right in assuming that customers know what they want, then the key issue would be to create the product, create awareness of it and make it available at an acceptable price. The fact is that both goals and corresponding wants can be unstable, with wants being only vaguely articulated and consumers remaining open to persuasion as to what might better serve their interests (1986: 20).

The marketing concept also assumes that the consumer is sovereign: that is, companies follow the dictates of the market in regard to exactly what should be provided. But consumers do not always know exactly what they want and they may be unsure of their trade-offs among product or service attributes. Many companies see no inconsistency in referring to the marketing concept as the basis for marketing management while at the same time accepting that consumer perceptions are important and can be influenced.

Nature of marketing activities

There is a growing consensus among managers and academics that the marketing function 'initiates, negotiates, and manages acceptable exchange relationships with key interest groups, or constituencies in the pursuit of sustainable competitive advantage within specific markets on the basis of long run consumer and channel franchises' (Day and Wensley, 1983: 83). This consensus recognizes that there may not always be a large overlap between the firm's actual or potential resource base and its ability to serve the needs and wants of customers in a market. For some companies the correspondence between the two is very close, while for others the overlap is marginal.

It is the marketing orientation which is important. Marketing attempts to free the firm from the shackles of competition by identifying and developing a competitive advantage for the company. Competitive advantage derives from the company's orientation to its environment. A marketing orientation means starting with customer needs and focusing the firm's resources on these needs to produce profit. It also means matching the company's resources to the needs of the market. High-performance marketing organizations successfully identify and manage the area of overlap between resources and needs (Figure 1.6). Many organizations never succeed in matching their resources to customer requirements, while some firms succeed only partially. Very few firms achieve a perfect fit whereby the organization satisfies market and customer needs perfectly.

It is the task of the marketing function to identify and manage the area of overlap between resources and needs to ensure that the customer receives the benefits of the product and service desired, when and where wanted, at an acceptable price, while producing a profit for the firm. Marketing starts with needs and integrates and co-ordinates the organization's activities to serve

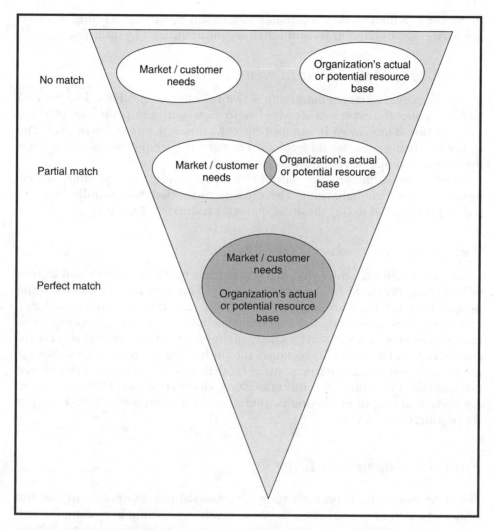

Figure 1.6 Matching the organization's resources with market needs

these needs for some reward. For companies, this reward is profit: profit, not sales, is the objective of the enterprise.

Performance of marketing activities

As will be seen throughout this text, marketing performance in companies means identifying customer value; innovating to provide high-quality products and services to meet that customer value; and communicating and delivering that value in a high-quality, acceptable way. In this context, marketing activities are performed by companies and other organizations and by individuals.

Performance of marketing in organizations

Some companies perform marketing activities better than others. The general public frequently expresses its view as to how well companies meet these expectations. They do so by sponsoring companies in various ways, primarily by buying their products and services. They are also frequently asked for their opinions on companies regarding various matters.

The general public and customers form opinions regarding various aspects of company behaviour. These opinions are believed to influence the public's disposition to buy these companies' products and services.

Performance of marketing by individuals

Some individuals recognize that marketing has a role to play in regard to how well they are accepted by the general public. This is more obvious for some people than others. For example, politicians, entertainers and, to a lesser extent, sports people recognize that the principles of marketing apply to them as well as to products and services. Very often only the promotional aspects are considered. But if the ability to satisfy the underlying needs of voters, theatre-goers, rock concert fans, participants at football games or television viewers are not satisfied, the politician, entertainer or sports person quickly loses appeal. An understanding of marketing is, therefore, important for people as well as for products and services.

Functions of marketing

For many years, writers on marketing have been at pains to point out that the principal function of marketing 'is not so much to be skilful in making the customer do what suits the interests of the business as to be skilled in conceiving and then making the business do what suits the interests of the customers' (McKittrick, 1957: 78). In a present-day context, to be skilful in conceiving the real interests of customers, the organization must balance environmental considerations against profitability requirements; society's welfare against individual needs; and the long-term welfare of customers against their short-term wants. For these reasons, therefore, we must broaden the marketing concept to include wider dimensions.

It is necessary to generalize the concept of products and services by focusing more on the exchange function than on the traditional market transaction itself. It is noteworthy in this respect that marketing is important for numerous groups in society. Industrial buyers are concerned that they are seen as good customers by their suppliers. In industrial marketing, buyers and sellers are primarily interested in establishing long-term, mutually beneficial relationships.

The role of marketing also applies to employees. The needs of employees extend beyond money incomes. It is necessary to provide employees with assurances regarding real income, job security and satisfaction, personal development and participation in decisions affecting their lives. By meeting the human development needs of employees rather than merely seeing people as a supply of labour, productivity in the organization may be improved and absenteeism reduced.

From society at large, business obtains numerous benefits, and in turn it has responsibilities to society. Benefits to business relate to such public goods as roads, subsidies and industry and trade protection. Business must recognize, for example, the social cost of physically distributing its products, which is borne by society. Close attention to such matters by business improves its standing in society and reduces costs.

Scope of marketing in the profit sector

Marketing in the profit sector may be examined either at the level of the organization, which emphasizes application, or from the point of view of marketing as a science. Furthermore, each of these views may be analyzed from a positive or a normative perspective. The scope of marketing in the profit sector divides, therefore, into four areas of concern (Hunt, 1976).

The scope of marketing at the applied level in the company or organization has both positive and normative aspects (Figure 1.7). The positive aspects of marketing at this level are concerned with buyer behaviour:

- how buyers identify their needs and wants;

- how they become aware of products and services which satisfy these needs and wants;

- how they select them; and

- where they locate and purchase them.

It is concerned, therefore, with the entire buying process.

The normative aspects at the applied level refer to the management of marketing within the firm. Concern rests with all marketing decisions regarding:

- the marketing programme;

- the marketing organization; and

- planning and implementation.

Here the issues examined include the way in which firms should determine their prices, how they should design and develop their products and services, and how they should promote and distribute them.

25

Focus / Emphasis	POSITIVE	NORMATIVE
APPLIED	Buyer behaviour	Marketing management
SCIENTIFIC	Approaches to study of marketing	Efficiency, responsibility and sovereignity in marketing

Figure 1.7   Scope of marketing in the profit sector

At the scientific level, positive aspects of marketing deal with approaches to the study of marketing as a discipline. Here concern rests with the varying degrees of emphasis placed on marketing institutions and on functional, commodity and environmental approaches to the study of marketing. Concern also rests with the legal aspects of marketing, comparative marketing systems and the efficiency of various systems of marketing.

At the normative level, while still dealing with scientific considerations, concern rests with efficiency, responsibility and sovereignty in marketing. Questions such as how can marketing systems be made more efficient, does distribution cost too much, is advertising desirable, and does marketing have a social responsibility are addressed. Broader issues such as the role of marketing in human development are also questioned. The question of the desirability or otherwise of consumer sovereignty is raised. A broader aspect of this would be the issue of cultural dominance in international markets through the spread of fast-food outlets, for example, and the effect they have on local customs and culture. A question frequently asked by marketing scholars in this context is: how desirable is it to stimulate this type of demand?

Scope of marketing in the non-profit sector

The scope of marketing at the applied level for the non-profit sector recognizes its role in forecasting demand for public goods like roads, public transport and public health care (Figure 1.8). Questions such as how do consumers buy public goods are addressed. Concern rests with developing case illustrations of the marketing of public goods.

Focus / Emphasis	POSITIVE	NORMATIVE
APPLIED	Demand forecasting for non-profit-sector goods and services	Social marketing
SCIENTIFIC	Influence and efficiency in non-profit-sector marketing	Desirability of non-profit-sector marketing

Figure 1.8   Scope of marketing in the non-profit sector

At the scientific level, concern rests with assessing the desirability and efficiency of services such as television advertising, consumer products, packaging and distribution. These aspects refer to a positive analysis. Questions such as the influence of television advertising on elections, the influence of public service advertising on behaviour (e.g. influence of drink-driving advertising campaigns), the efficiency of distribution for public goods, and the recognition of recycling as a distribution problem in reverse are all addressed in this situation. The role of television advertising to children is a very contentious issue in many countries and its desirability is frequently questioned (Exhibit 1.1).

For a normative analysis, marketing is concerned at the applied level with its role in social marketing. For example, concern rests with determining how non-profit organizations such as hospitals and charities should manage elements of the marketing mix. Similarly, concern would also rest with determining how the demand for such public goods can be predicted.

At the scientific level, normative issues such as society's view on whether politicians or causes should be promoted like products are examined. In this case, society would also be concerned with establishing the desirability of the low information content which typifies the advertisements of some political parties. As another example, marketing has a role in determining the desirability of government health warnings on cigarette packets while at the same time collecting tobacco tax. An interesting question related to this is: should the demand for public goods be promoted?

EXHIBIT 1.1   Not in front of the children!

As you settle down to a feast of television commercials bringing you red-nosed reindeer carrying power drills, aftershave and dry sherry, spare a thought for this Christmas's less privileged – the Euro-tots who are barred from experiencing some advertising ploys, and the companies who want to sell them. Across Europe advertising to children is either hamstrung, as advertisers see it, or regulated, as the governments concerned view it.

In Finland, Santa's homeland, child actors may not speak or sing the name of a product in commercials. When it comes to advertising sweets, they must not appear on the screen at all; children munching sweeties are also out of order in the Netherlands. In neighbouring Sweden no child may be depicted playing with 'war toys', and advertisements may not show the price of toys. On Swedish TV, all ads aimed at 'gaining the attention' – rather a difficult concept to quantify perhaps – of children under the age of 12 are banned.

In Turkey, children can only watch TV commercials in the presence of an adult. Continuing the 'we know what is best for you' theme is Denmark, where no-one under the age of 30 is permitted to appear in toy advertisements, slightly later than the age both of reason and enfranchisement.

Scandinavia is obviously a touchy area. In Norway, skateboards must include the following labelling: 'Do not use skateboards in areas with traffic. Skateboards are not suitable for children under the age of 12.'

In France, anyone under 16 is banned from enunicating a product name in an advertisement; they cannot wear the colours, logo, brand name or initials of any product; and they can only introduce a product in a commercial when 'there exists a direct link between the product and child usage and when shown together with adults'.

In Greece, advertising of all toys was banned from 1987 until earlier this year; that ban continues on television for all toy ads before 11 p.m. In Italy, commercial breaks are prohibited in cartoon programmes 'aimed' at children. If you think that all that is tight regulation, consider the British market. One of many regulations states that 'no product or service may be advertised, and no method of advertising may be used which might result in harm to children (anyone aged 15 or under) physically, mentally or morally, and no method of advertising may be employed which takes advantage of the natural credulity and sense of loyalty of children'.

Some of my best friends' children are already looking forward to watching a wall-to-wall diet of old Marx Brothers movies on Christmas TV, but no-one thinks to protect them from that. Merry Christmas.

Source: *Financial Times*, 19 December 1991.

Marketing costs, values and satisfaction

The successful company understands that there are certain fundamental benefits desired and for which the customer is prepared to pay a higher price. Such companies deliver superior value as perceived by the customer. Successful companies sometimes spend a great amount of resources in engineering products, sparing no cost in their design, with the objective of arriving at superior reliability at marginally higher prices. These organizations sometimes emphasize the production of value. There are many other organizations which are not interested in leading-edge technology, greater flexibility or superior power. They were interested, rather, in providing a service to customers and in communicating value to them.

Increasingly, successful companies do not manufacture but assemble, communicate and deliver the value to customers. The provision of value and its communication and delivery to customers are the key to successful marketing. This philosophy and the associated set of tasks underlies the approach of this book.

In choosing among products or services, customers base their decision on two important criteria, price and benefits, and the trade-off between the two. A positive trade-off, i.e. benefits minus price, indicates value. Products and services are demanded that customers perceive have a superior value compared to competitors, while others are not.

Social responsibility in marketing

Social responsibility in marketing means accounting for the relationship between marketing and the environment in which it operates. Social responsibility refers to the obligation of the company, beyond the requirements of the law, to take into practical consideration in its decision making the social consequences of its decisions and actions, as well as profits (Gidengil, 1977: 72). This view of social responsibility implies constraints on the company more rigorous than would arise if the company attempted to fulfil its economic and legal requirements only. The reasons for a greater interest in social responsibility stem from the greater involvement of business with government and the influence of myriad stakeholders in the company: shareholders, institutional investors, employees and other regulatory and environmental bodies. The more important dimensions of the environment which relate to an appropriate application of marketing are the social and moral environment, the business environment and the physical environment.

Ethical and trust issues in marketing

Many people believe that business is mostly profit focused and that, given the opportunity, companies would harm the environment, endanger public health, sell unsafe products and risk the health of workers and the general public. There have been many court cases supporting such claims. A survey in the USA in 1989 reported that respondents believe that companies would follow various unethical business practices to increase their profits (Table 1.1).

In recent years, ethical issues have become very important in marketing (Dubinsky *et al.*, 1985, 1992). Ethics refers to the social and moral standards which are acceptable in a society. Trust is a related issue which is an essential ingredient in building long-term relationships between organizations and their customers. Trust is well placed where ethical standards are upheld. It is misplaced where ethical standards are ignored or flaunted. The departure of José Ignacio López from General Motors to Volkswagen raised a number of ethical questions which have long-term repercussions for these companies and for business in general (Exhibit 1.2). Both trust and ethics are highly dependent on culture and vary according to the culture and background of customers. Organizations operating in many cultures, as in the case of international marketing, have greater difficulty in coping with a heterogeneous set of customers drawing on disparate cultures for their ethical standards.

The task facing the company intent on developing a workable ethical framework for marketing is easier to understand if ethical issues about marketing are divided into questions:

- directed towards the fundamental functions of marketing; and

- about the specific actions of individual companies.

TABLE 1.1   Attitudes toward business

To obtain greater profits business would …	*Respondents who agreed (%)*
Deliberately charge inflated prices	62
Harm the environment	47
Knowingly sell inferior products	44
Risk workers' health and safety	42
Endanger public health	38
Sell unsafe products	37
All of the above	25
None of the above	8
Not sure	4

Note: Based on a survey of 1247 adults in the USA conducted by Louis Harris & Associates.

Source: *Business Week*, 29 May 1989: 25.

EXHIBIT 1.2   There's another side to the López saga

The López affair just won't die. Detroit and Germany alike seem transfixed by General Motors Corp.'s increasingly credible allegations that its former purchasing guru, José López de Arriortua, and his aides stole and shredded sensitive GM documents when he defected to Volkswagen in March.

What the headlines obscure is López' legacy, far less publicized at GM. GM, now pushing prosecutors in the US and Germany to nail López for industrial espionage, apparently tolerated many questionable strategies when López turned them on its own suppliers. GM Chief Financial Officer, G. Richard Wagoner Jr, who assumed López' duties in April, admitted as much in a speech to suppliers in Traverse City, Mich., on 6 August.

GM is now in a sticky ethical situation. As Carnegie Mellon University Management Professor Gerald C. Meyers, who once headed American Motors Corp., puts it: 'When it's used for GM, it's a boon. When it's used against them, it's a terrible thing.' Even the largest and most powerful of General Motors' suppliers are unwilling to detail López' purported tactics on the record, for fear of angering their largest customers. However, dozens have privately outlined their experiencs to *Business Week*.

López, they say, often tore up long-term contracts. Suppliers also allege that López exaggerated rivals' bids to compel them to bid lower still. Foreshadowing GM's current changes, what riled suppliers more than anything was López' allegedly cavalier handling of proprietary information. Some suppliers say they were shocked to learn that López had circulated to their competitors blue-prints of their top-secret technology, in hopes of eliciting lower bids. That made it easy for competitors to underbid, since they didn't have to recoup research and development costs. 'If there's anything that sends a supplier through the ceiling, it's taking our information, our [blue]prints, to our competitors,' says Timothy D. Leuliette, head of ITT Automotive.

Volkswagen says López has started to work his magic in Europe: his measures, CEO Ferdinand Piech says, will save over $410 million this year. Pretty dramatic, but VW might do well to reflect on the potential fallout now facing GM. Some key suppliers are reluctant to take their new technology to GM and are shifting their brightest engineers to work for Ford and Chrysler Corp. The risk: future GM products will fall short in innovation and quality. To avert that catastrophe, GM must quickly rebuild supplier trust. Wagoner's willingness to discuss General Motors' missteps is a good start.

Source: *Business Week*, 23 August 1993: 22.

The first group of questions are referred to as macro-ethical marketing questions, while the latter are referred to as micro-ethical questions (Robin and Reidenbach, 1993: 104). According to these authors, basic marketing functions are seen to be ethical or unethical if measured within an understanding of their history, the times in which they are applied, their context, the expectations of society, the requirements of capitalism and an understanding of human behaviour. Thus, according to Robin and Reidenbach, it would not be appropriate to claim that marketing is unethical because it is profit oriented or because it distributes utility according to merit rather than some other form of distributive justice.

In a similar vein, the marketing function of persuasion cannot be defined as ethical or unethical until the context of its application is considered. In this regard, persuasion might be judged 'ethical' in an industrialized country but 'unethical' in a developing country, where most people would not have received sufficient formal education to be in a position to adopt a critical view of the material used to persuade.

Marketing means establishing a continuing relationship between individuals and organizations. The effectiveness of interactions within these relationships is affected by trust (Pruitt, 1981) and ethical perceptions (Tsalikis and Fritzsche, 1989). Trust is an emotional and cognitive state in which an individual relies upon information received from another person (Swan and Jones, 1988). It is an important factor in interpersonal relationships and arises due to expertise, respect and reliability (Dwyer *et al.*, 1987; Anderson and Weitz, 1989). A fundamental issue in any social exchange is proven trustworthiness. Generally speaking, product and service providers gain trust by being consistent in matching actual outcomes with those desired by the customer. Developing trust between the parties to an exchange reduces uncertainty, leads to constructive dialogue and co-operation in problem solving, and serves as a basis for carrying out agreements. Trust encourages longer-term social transactions, while its absence may terminate a relationship.

Ethical perceptions are defined as the degree to which an individual is perceived as practising moral and community standards in interpersonal relationships (Pruden, 1971). In this case the marketing manager would be influenced by an individual ethic, reflected in the moral component of the definition of ethics, which is highly culture bound, and by a company or professional ethic, which is reflected in the community component of the definition, which may be culture bound but is more likely to reflect broader management philosophies. If one party to an exchange lacks an ethical orientation, it may lead to a suspension of existing or future business between the two parties.

Cause marketing

Social responsibility in marketing has promoted the development of cause marketing, by which individuals and organizations adopt social causes or use them in their marketing endeavours. Some very well-known companies have followed this approach and found an important market segment. The Body Shop Inc. launched a campaign designed to increase awareness of HIV and AIDS among women, its major customer group. Featuring the theme 'Protect and Respect', the company distributed free educational literature on the disease as well as on safe sex.

EXHIBIT 1.3   What makes Ryka run?

Sheri Poe isn't afraid to talk about the day 21 years ago when she was raped in a car near the campus of Southern Illinois University. In fact she considers it therapeutic. The assault led to years of psychological trauma, punctuated by bulimia and financial collapse. By slowly coming to terms with what happened, Poe eventually recovered. She began a recovery process that included walking, and later aerobics. The exercise 'helped me get in touch with my body,' she says.

It also helped her come up with an idea. Having suffered back pains from workouts, Poe observed that most aerobics shoes on the market weren't designed with the narrow heel or high arch typical of women's feet. Why not design a workout shoe specifically for women? In 1987, she founded a sneaker company called Ryka Inc. to produce aerobic shoes designed especially for women.

Lately, the 40-year-old Poe has been telling her story to all who will listen. She has woven it into a potent marketing message that helped boost Ryka's sales by 53 percent last year, to $12 million. The cynics, of course, will say that Poe has attached her intimate history to Ryka's marketing message in an exploitative effort to sell more sneakers. Poe responds that selling more shoes is merely a means to an end. She has pledged seven percent of the company's profits to a fund called the Ryka ROSE (Regaining One's Self-Esteem) Foundation, which channels money to groups helping women who have been victims of violent crime. 'There's no hidden agenda for me, except helping the women who are touched by violence in overwhelming numbers,' she says.

From the start, she trumpeted the fact that the company is the only producer of women's shoes actually run by women (70 percent of the employees are female). She also kept some influential aerobics instructors decked out in Ryka products. In 1991, Poe sent Oprah Winfrey a pair of Rykas and wound up as a guest on a show featuring women entrepreneurs.

Poe didn't start telling her own story publicly until last year, when she saw Oprah testify about child abuse before a Senate committee. It shook her. 'It's not enough to make a great shoe and support women physically,' she says now. 'What about their emotions? Not only am I a survivor of violence, but our customers are touched by this.' Sensitive advertising, coupled with the ROSE Foundation, she thought, would be an effective way to give women help.

So far, Poe says, 'the response has been overwhelming'. Not only are sales growing but the company is flooded with phone calls from women victims looking for resources. 'It's a smart position to take in the 90s,' says Jane McDonnell, publisher of *Women's Sport & Fitness* magazine. 'Women tend to respond very positively to cause marketing.' Especially, it seems, when the marketer makes it clear she knows what she's talking about.

Source: *Business Week*, 14 June 1993: 60 and 62.

In 1987 Sheri Poe founded a sneaker company to produce aerobic shoes designed especially for women and at the same time adopted the cause of violent crime against women to promote its products. While the Body Shop Inc. and similar companies have led a growing number of organizations to embrace 'cause marketing' as the selling trend of the 1990s, Sheri Poe's highly personal campaign has stretched the concept past all previous boundaries. Her tactics have created a convincing niche in the market. Jennifer Black Groves, an athletic apparel analyst in the USA, referring to the growth of the company stated: 'Sure, Ryka's got a good, unique line of shoes. But what's making Ryka work is Sheri Poe and her story' (Exhibit 1.3). Issues such as violence cannot be portrayed lightly. It is necessary to communicate the statistics and the need to address the problem, while at the same time showing that recovery and successful results are possible. In this case Sheri Poe herself, by going public with her story, provides the essential elements to make such a campaign work.

Several other well-known companies have adopted cause marketing as a way of addressing difficult social problems, while recognizing that issues of importance to women can be a powerful way of reaching the market. Liz Claiborne Inc. New York launched its Women's Work Programme in 1991, which consisted of community-based, public arts projects designed to heighten awareness and foster change on issues of particular interest to women and their families. In 1993 the company extended its programme against domestic violence by using powerful images on billboards in Boston and Miami (Miller, 1993: 1). One of the billboards shows two clocks, with the headline 'Every 12 seconds a woman is beaten in the US'. All of the billboards carried the message 'Don't die for love/Stop domestic violence' and included a local telephone number to call for help.

An issue of particular importance to women, breast cancer, has been a central cause in the marketing programmes of Estée Lauder, providing funds for research into its causes and treatment, and of Avon, providing more women, especially those in low income groups, with access to early detection services.

Consumerism and marketing

Marketing has been viewed as the mechanism and philosophy by which customers can be satisfied. In the past it has not been clear whether short-run customer needs or their longer-term interests were being served. Business more often than not achieved the former, frequently at the expense of the latter (Abratt and Sacks, 1989: 26). Nowadays tobacco and alcohol are considered to provide immediate satisfaction, but may be detrimental to public health in the longer term.

Some writers argue that what is in society's long-term interests is also good for business (Dawson, 1969; Kotler, 1972b). The societal view of marketing requires companies to act in the public interest, which according to these writers safeguards future freedom of action and even the survival of business in an increasingly hostile social environment (Feldman, 1971; Abratt and Sacks, 1989: 27). The societal concept of marketing does not deny that the basic goal of business is to ensure its long-term survival and profitability.

Marketing and the environment

In the past twenty years or so, it has become very apparent that society's resources are finite and that the environment is something to be protected. The oil crisis of the 1970s and the more recent debate on the value of the rain forests are examples. As a result, some marketing scholars have been critical of the traditional emphasis in marketing on material consumption, while not taking into account the longer-term effects on society (Feldman, 1971; Kotler and Levy, 1971).

The view that marketing has a special responsibility when discussing the natural environment is now well developed. By promoting product manufacture and usage, the company may be encouraging resource depletion, pollution or other environmental deterioration. Most companies believe that it is not sufficient to make profits and generate employment while ignoring an obligation to society regarding the preservation of the natural environment, even if their behaviour is within the law. Some firms, however, continue to ignore this implied obligation, arguing that their behaviour is not illegal when they dump chemicals in watercourses, overpackage products, or damage the atmosphere. Such firms often maintain that they should not be expected to take action to protect the environment if their competitive position would be jeopardized in the process. In a general way, social responsibility is an investment in future profits which should be made even at the expense of short-term profits.

One company which has successfully linked itself with improving the environment and hence the standard of living of people is ABB (Asea Brown Boveri), the Swedish–Swiss conglomerate energy organization. In a series of magazine advertisements, ABB has linked environmental protection with an improved standard of living. In these advertisements, appearing in magazines such as *Business Week*, ABB claims to be a leader in electrical engineering, committed to the development of new and better ways of generating power, getting it to where it is needed, and using it efficiently. In its advertising, ABB demonstrates its role in improving living standards and the conditions under which people live, whether in developed or developing countries. According to the company, its role is fundamentally the same, linking improvements in the physical environment to better living standards (Exhibit 1.4).

Theory in marketing

As an applied and professional discipline, marketing is quite different from the natural sciences: it has a much wider range of options for the selection of

EXHIBIT 1.4   Bill Coleman believes in the environment and Joe Matsau brings electricity to the Kingdom in the Sky!

The following is the text of the advertising copy used by Asea Brown Boveri (ABB) in various well-known magazines to accompany pictures of Bill Coleman taking photographs of a river and of Joe Matsau among a group of villagers in the uplands of Lesotho:

Bill Coleman believes the environment is a sound investment

Bill Coleman is not an ecologist, he's a banker. He looks at the world's growing preoccupation with environmental issues from a different perspective, which has begun to influence the advice he gives investment clients at James Capel & Co. in London. 'There can be no doubt about the scale of opportunity for companies which can help bridge the gap between the demand for energy and the realities of protecting our environment', says Coleman.

'We are seeing the emergence of a new business sector spanning a range of energy and environmentally-related technologies that is going to rank alongside such things as microelectronics, telecommunications and bio-medicine in importance. Nature's energy resources are undervalued assets in more senses than one.'

Electrical engineering will be a key technology in the twenty-first century. The facts are simple. By the year 2000, the world's energy demands will have increased by 30 per cent. There will be one billion new consumers whose needs must be met whilst the effects on our environment must be minimised.

Joes Matsau is bringing electricity to the Kingdom in the Sky

The de-forestation of some parts of Africa has been a matter of survival, not profit. In the mountainous kingdom of Lesotho, generations of villagers have had to live off landscape for fuel to cook and heat their homes.

Joe Matsau of Lesotho Electrical Company has a promising alternative. He is directing a long-term rural electrification programme which will make his country energy self sufficient. Hydro-electric power is the key with transmission lines reaching up to over 2,000 metres into the 'Kingdom of the Sky' as it is known locally.

Village by village, Lesotho is switching dependency from the earth's fragile resources to the fruits of man's ingenuity. 'We still have a long way to go,' says Mr Matsau, 'but the programme would never have seen the light of day without ABB's help – not just their technology but the skill in identifying crucial aid and loan sources for us. The world is changing fast. ABB us helping us change even faster to catch up.'

its subject matter than any of the natural sciences, but at the same time it is desirable that it be purposeful in some way. Marketing is, therefore, a professional discipline with a theoretical and an applied dimension whereby marketing scientists and practitioners work alongside each other (Mueller-Heumann, 1986: 306). As with other applied and professional disciplines, marketing requires a positive and a normative orientation. The marketing concept must have a professional dimension to create a common sense of purpose among practitioners.

The environment in which modern business has to operate is characterized by two main factors: complexity and dynamism. For the individual organization, these are most commonly manifested in 'change'. From the point of view of marketing theory, the complexity and dynamism described mean that the body of theory being applied must be constantly expanded and revised, and that the area of its scope must be extended if it is to cope realistically with the fluctuating manifestations of the environment.

Marketing strategy and business theories

Marketing is related to corporate strategy where the latter is viewed as a statement of purpose and the broad means of achieving it. The basic objectives of corporate strategy are to:

- match company strengths with market opportunities;
- avoid threats posed by environmental change and competitors; and
- remedy weaknesses in the company and its operations.

Marketing strategy is an intrinsic part of corporate strategy, but not synonymous with it. Marketing's role in strategic planning for the firm means identifying the optimal long-term positions that will assure customer satisfaction and support. These optimal positions are determined largely by fundamental changes in demographic, economic, social and political factors (Anderson, 1982: 24). Thus, strategic positioning is more likely to be guided by long-term demographic and socioeconomic research than by surveys of consumer attitudes, the hallmark of the traditional market-driven firm.

Customer needs change dramatically from one period to another depending on the circumstances in the economy, changes in the environment and changes in outlook. A new trend appearing in the 1990s is the focus on customer value. Value in marketing is a combination of product or service quality, reasonable or acceptable prices and responsive service. It is noteworthy that marketing value combines high quality with acceptable prices. Value in marketing means delivering on a whole range of promises to the customer. The emphasis on value now appearing is a reaction against the perceived excesses of the 1970s and 1980s and is also a reflection of a more difficult economic situation and changing demographics.

Social exchange theory in marketing

Social exchange frameworks are based on the observation that organizations and people interact to maximize benefits and minimize the cost of exchange. The rewards from an exchange may range from the possession of some physical object like a new sweater, to the psychological benefits of being associated with a particular brand of car, to the social gains of belonging to a particular club or group. The cost of an exchange may be financial, involving the payment of money, psychological, such as the loss of an association with a particular brand, or social, such as being excluded from a group.

Underlying social exchange theories is the idea that participants in the exchange use persuasion or social influence to derive the desired response. At the same time, the exchange is conditioned by social norms and the availability of alternatives. An exchange system may be defined as 'a set of social actors, their relationships to each other, and the endogenous and exogenous variables affecting the behaviour of the social actors in those social relationships' (Bagozzi, 1974: 78). Social actors may consist of sales people, retailers, consumers, advertisers and other marketing groups, while relationships are defined as the roles and connections between the actors. The variables include social, psychological and physical phenomena. Bagozzi (1974) uses the customer–sales person dyad to illustrate the exchange system, which may be interpreted as a social influence process in which both participants to the exchange mediate a number of positive as well as negative influences on the other (Figure 1.9).

The underlying variables serve as causal determinants of the way participants respond. The product is exchanged for money depending on the relative differences between the salesperson's and the customer's subjective expected utility. These utilities usually include factors such as attraction, prestige, esteem, role position in society or within the group, the size of the benefit, its cost and value. These variables mediate the exchange decisions by influencing the subjective probabilities and utilities of the social interaction.

In this respect, the product offered by the company may satisfy the subjective expected utility of the customer, but the availability of a more attractive substitute may prevent the exchange occurring. The minimum acceptable level that both company and customer will accept is determined by some variable outside the system. For the company, these include company policies and objectives. For the customer, they involve budgets and family concerns. Social norms, legal restrictions and ethical factors also influence exchanges.

Exchange relationships in marketing

Most marketing exchanges are characterized by a transaction involving a product or service being sold for money, where the latent reasons for the transaction are economic, social and psychological in nature. Based on this latent structure, marketing exchanges may be economic, symbolic or some combi-

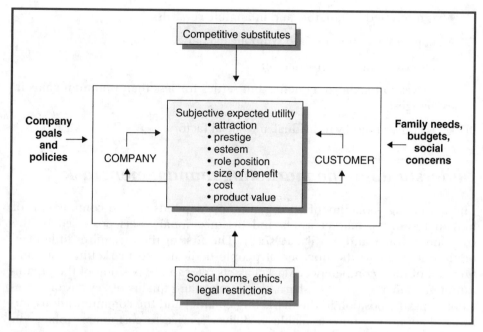

Figure 1.9 Influences in the customer–company interaction
(Source: Adapted from Bagozzi (1974: 79 and 81). With the permission of the American Marketing Association)

nation of the two. Marketing exchange as economic is built on the concept of 'economic man', which assumes that:

- people are rational in behaviour;

- they attempt to maximize satisfaction through exchange;

- they possess complete information on alternatives available to them; and

- exchanges are reasonably free from outside influences.

Symbolic exchange, in contrast, refers to the mutual transfer of psychological, social or other intangible benefits associated with products and services. 'People buy things not only for what they can do, but also for what they mean' (Levy, 1959: 118).

But experience demonstrates that marketing exchanges involve economic and symbolic dimensions which are quite often difficult to separate. Successful transactions depend on deriving an appropriate mix of the two. Customers seek economic and symbolic rewards in their purchases and dealings with companies, which leads to the suggestion of the existence of a 'marketing person' (Bagozzi, 1975: 37) who:

- is sometimes rational, sometimes irrational;

39

- is motivated by tangible and intangible rewards;

- engages in economic and symbolic exchanges;

- faces incomplete information;

- strives to maximize benefits, but settles for less than optimum gains in exchanges; and

- is constrained by individual and social factors.

Understanding the marketing management task

The marketing capability of an organization depends on the combination of human resources, market assets and organizational assets possessed by the company (Möller and Anttila, 1987: 3). The first of these requires little elaboration; it refers to the number of people dedicated to marketing tasks and the level of their competence. Market assets refer to the position of the organization in its market: market share, the number and quality of key customer relationships, the position in the marketing channel and the communications and physical support systems available to deliver service to customers (Johansson and Mattsson, 1985).

By organizational assets is meant the degree to which the company or organization is effectively and efficiently configured to produce the desired results. Included are the mechanisms used to cope with the environment, analyzing customers and competitors, developing policies and plans, and implementing and controlling marketing activities. In periods of change in the market, it is especially important that the company devotes detailed managerial attention to marketing issues. Very often organizations realize that they need to refocus their marketing efforts when the marketing environment changes (Exhibit 1.5).

The marketing capability of the organization depends on its ability to cope with a number of external environments and its ability to manage its own internal environment. In managing its own internal environment, the organization is concerned (Möller and Anttila, 1987) with how:

- the organization defines its business and develops strategies to achieve corporate goals;

- management integrates the major functions of the organization (marketing, sales operations, finance and R & D) to implement strategy;

- the marketing function is managed; and

- the operational and planning system of the firm acknowledges the role of marketing.

EXHIBIT 1.5   Taking aim! Marketing in Japan

Marketing in Japan has been shaped by two kinds of abundance: many shops and many products. Japan has 13 retailers for every 1,000 inhabitants, compared with six per 1,000 in America and Europe. Many of those small, weak shops have fallen under the control of Japan's big firms. Shiseido, a maker of cosmetics, has some 25,000 outlets selling only its products. Matsushita boasts 19,000 shops that sell mainly or only its electrical appliances. To maintain such networks, Japanese firms put their energy into frequent visits to their shops, rather than into building brands or analysing data on consumer habits.

Product proliferation also distracted Japan's firms from thinking hard about consumers. During the 1980s Japanese firms churned out new designs too fast for elaborate consumer surveys to be possible. Plentiful shops, plentiful products: both these distinguishing marks are fading. Today Matsushita makes 60 per cent of its domestic sales through small shops, down from 70 per cent in 1985. That trend is set to accelerate.

Japan's economic woes are undoing the second sort of abundance: product proliferation. With their profits collapsing, firms as diverse as car manufacturers and biscuits makers are cutting costs by launching fewer models. Ajinomoto, a big food company, launched an average of 31 new kinds of frozen food each year in the late 1980s; last year it launched 19. Rather than showering shops with new ideas, Ajinomoto says it now tries to boost the appeal of existing products. The same applies to other sectors. In 1988 Matsushita had 5,000 audio products on the market; now it has 1,000. In 1989 it sold 72 kinds of rice cooker; it now sells 38.

Market research, brand building, test marketing; the disciplines traditionally associated with western firms seem suddenly right for the Japanese market. Kao, a company which makes everything from face-packs to floppy disks, seems the perfect illustration of Japan Inc's new zeal for targeting customers precisely. Kao has for some time printed its phone number on its products; operators who field consumer's calls log the pattern of responses into the marketing department's computers. All this has led Kao to abandon its old scatter-shot approach to selling: it launched 20 new products last year, down from 70 in 1988. At the same time the firm has been keen to boost its core brands. Kao's advertising budget grew by 8.1 per cent over the period.

Source: *The Economist*, 24 April 1993: 73.

In contrast, the external environment consists of those organizations, groups or individuals which directly influence the operations of the company, such as customers, competitors, and distributors and other intermediaries.

Customer and competitor knowledge is a prerequisite for developing competitive advantage and marketing strategy. The four key dimensions of customer-related marketing capability according to Möller and Anttila (1987) are the company's ability to:

- make a profound analysis and understand the product and service needs of customers and the related value chain;

- assess the purchasing strategies of customers;

- evaluate the interdependence of key customer relations; and

- develop successful customer strategies based on the previous analysis, assessment and evaluation.

The marketing capability issues associated with competitor analysis may be summarized (Porter, 1980; Möller and Anttila, 1987) as management's ability to:

- assess the position and strategies of key competitors, i.e. products and services and primary competitive advantage;

- perform a comparative strengths and weaknesses analysis of the competitive advantages of the firm;

- analyze competitor marketing and customer strategies; and

- analyze competitor, supplier and distributor relationships.

Managerial model of marketing management

As was seen above, marketing is a descriptive discipline involving the study of how transactions are created, stimulated, facilitated and valued. In contrast, marketing management is normative, involving the efficient creation of values to stimulate desired transactions. Marketing management is essentially a disciplined view of the task of achieving specific responses from others through the creation and provision of values (Kotler, 1972a: 52).

The successful application of marketing as a management discipline presumes the possession of certain analytical and planning skills. Market analysis is required, whereby the market is identified, its needs, wants and values are specified, its size is measured and its location is determined. Associated with market analysis is the skill of product and service analysis, by which the company determines the products and services currently available and their evaluation by customer groups.

A number of planning skills are also required. Product planning requires the organization to know where to seek new ideas, how to choose and refine the core product concept, how to package the product and how to test it. The second is pricing or valuing the product or service, whereby a set of terms of exchange are developed. The third task is promotion, whereby the company develops the symbolic values and communicates the value of the product or service to stimulate market interest among customers. The fourth planning task is distribution, or how to deliver the product or service to make it accessible to customers.

Analytical framework for marketing

Traditionally, marketing in the business system was viewed as a way of producing products and services and then selling them to myriad interested customers. Managers focused on the product or service within the business system. The elements of the business system consisted of three major functions: developing the product or service in demand by customers; manufacturing the product or service; and selling it to a grateful public (Figure 1.10).

Associated with each major function were a series of subfunctions. Developing the product or service implied an emphasis on product or service design and process design. At the manufacturing stage, the emphasis shifted to seeking the best way of procuring supplies, manufacturing products and providing before- and after-sales service. In this traditional view of marketing, all the elements of marketing were associated with the selling function. Marketing research, distribution, pricing and promotion existed to serve the sales function.

The modern value orientation emphasized in this text views marketing as a series of six delivery processes, whereby the business system is designed in such a way that value is delivered by the company to the customer through a number of discrete stages (Lanning and Michaels, 1988). In this view of marketing,

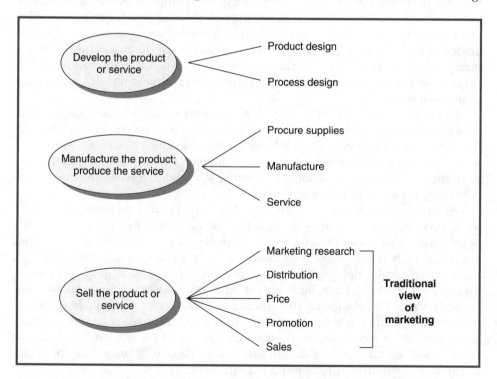

Figure 1.10   Traditional product orientation of the business system

it is first necessary to identify society and customer values to be promoted by the company. This means understanding customer values, needs and wants along the lines of the discussion above. It also means deciding the customer segments to be served and defining precise benefits for each segment identified (Figure 1.11). In the second stage, the company selects the value most appropriate for the market of interest, taking into account the special needs of customers and the activities of competitors.

In the third stage, the company attempts to provide the value identified. It does this in a number of ways. First it is necessary to design the product and process to be used. Then it is necessary to procure supplies. Manufacturing may be a part of the process, but the option is available for the firm to assemble or even to buy in, depending on the circumstances. Retailers provide a lot of value without much manufacture. The emphasis is on the provision of value not its manufacture. This is the key to an understanding of marketing. Production in the sense of manufacturing is not necessarily involved, whereas the provision of value is. In the final part of this stage, it is necessary to price the product or service, which is a major ingredient in value.

The fourth stage in the process is to communicate the value to customers and potential customers through advertising, public relations, direct marketing and personal selling. In the next stage, the company attempts to deliver the value to customers, which is done through distribution, logistics, and sales promotion. Lastly, it is necessary to plan, implement and evaluate the performance of the company's marketing strategies as part of the marketing management task. The remainder of this text is devoted to an elaboration of this process of identifying, selecting, providing, communicating and delivering value to customers.

In many companies, more attention is given to some of these stages than to others. For example, technical companies often give too much attention to the earlier stages: identifying, selecting and providing value. In industries where product innovation is quickly imitated or surpassed, competitive strength may be more sustainable by seeking advantage in communicating and delivering the value to customers.

At present, many service companies attempt to provide customized personal services which are quickly imitated. Banks and other financial institutions have used new technology to provide better branch services and improved cash delivery systems. However, by providing integrated financial information and sophisticated management of personal and corporate finance, some banks have built longer-term relationships which create imitation barriers, thereby giving the innovating firm a more sustainable competitive advantage than is available from the use of technology alone, such as automated teller machines. In these cases, success stems not from selecting a value position, but from the innovative and thorough attention to detail involved in the delivery of the value to customers.

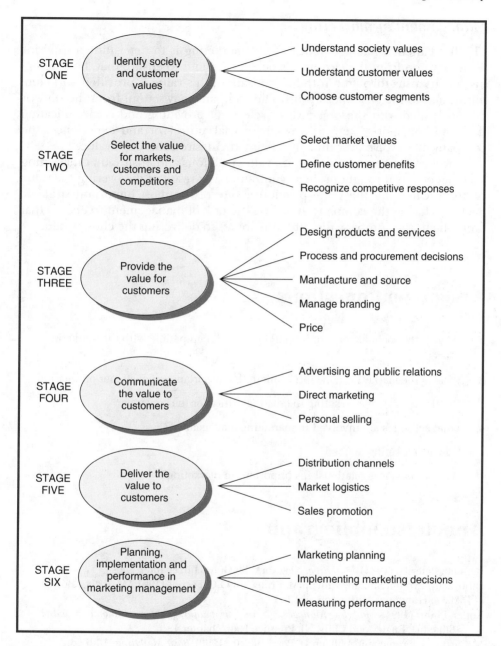

Figure 1.11 Value orientation in marketing management

Management of marketing

The fundamental management issue in marketing is to determine a superior value position from the customer's perspective and to ensure that, by developing a consensus throughout the organization, this value is provided and communicated to the customer group. The company may set out from the start or be established with the objective of selecting, providing and communicating the value; or, more likely, as a result of trial and error and experience, the company may evolve over time into being the desired source of value.

Successful companies recognize value positions and ensure that marketing learning occurs throughout the organization as a result of discovering the value position. Choosing the value position is one of the most important strategic decisions facing the company. It is then the task of management to ensure that everyone in the company directly contributes to delivering the chosen value.

Assignment questions

1 What is the societal concept in marketing? Is it compatible with the marketing concept?

2 What is the marketing concept? Explain the importance of customer orientation.

3 Discuss the role of marketing in creating utility for the consumer.

4 What activities are involved in marketing management?

5 How is marketing defined?

6 Why are business relationships important in marketing?

Annotated bibliography

Bennett, Peter D. (1988) *Marketing*, New York: McGraw-Hill, chapter 1.

Dibb, Sally, Lyndon Simkin, William M. Pride and O.C. Ferrell (1991) *Marketing*, Boston, Mass.: Houghton Mifflin, pp. 4–12.

Kotler, Philip (1994) *Marketing Management: Analysis, planning, implementation and control* (8th edn), Englewood Cliffs, NJ, Prentice Hall, chapter 1.

McCarthy, E. Jerome, and William D. Perreault, Jr (1990) *Basic Marketing* (10th edn), Homewood, Ill.: Richard D. Irwin.

Stanton, William J., Michael J. Etzel and Bruce J. Walker (1991) *Fundamentals of Marketing*, International Edition, New York: McGraw-Hill, chapter 1.

References

Abratt, Russel, and Diane Sacks (1989) 'Perceptions of the societal marketing concept', *European Journal of Marketing*, **23**, 6, 25–33.

American Marketing Association (1985) 'AMA Board approves new marketing definition', *Marketing News*, **5**, 1 March.

Anderson, Erin and Barton Weitz (1989) 'Determinants of continuity in conventional industrial channel dyads', *Marketing Science*, **8**, 4, 310–23.

Anderson, Paul F. (1982) 'Marketing, strategic planning and the theory of the firm', *Journal of Marketing*, **46**, 2, 15–26.

Bagozzi, Richard P. (1974) 'Marketing as an organised behaviour system of exchange', *Journal of Marketing*, **38**, 4, 77–81.

Bagozzi, Richard (1975) 'Marketing as exchange', *Journal of Marketing*, **39**, 4, 32–9.

Baker, Michael J. (1976) *Marketing: Theory and practice*, London: Macmillan.

Carman, James M. (1973): 'On the universality of marketing', *Journal of Contemporary Business*, **2**, 4, 1–16.

Dawson, M. (1969) 'The human concept: new philosophy for business', *Business Horizons*, **12**, 29–38.

Day, George S., and Robin Wensley (1983) 'Marketing theory with a strategic orientation', *Journal of Marketing*, **47**, 4, 79–89.

Dibb, Sally, Lyndon Simkin, William M. Pride and O.C. Ferrell (1991) *Marketing*, Boston, Mass.: Houghton Mifflin.

Dickinson, Roger, Anthony Herbst and John O'Shaughnessy (1986) 'Marketing concept and customer orientation', *European Journal of Marketing*, **20**, 10, 18–23.

Dubinsky, Alan J., Thomas N. Ingram and William Rudelius (1985) 'Ethics in industrial selling: how product and service salespeople compare', *Journal of the Academy of Marketing Science*, **13**, Winter, 160–7.

Dubinsky, Alan J., Marvin A. Jolson, Ronald E. Michaels, Masaaki Kotabe and Chae Lim (1992) 'Ethical perceptions of field personnel: an empirical assessment', *Journal of Personal Selling and Sales Management*, **12**, 4, 9–22.

Dwyer, Robert F. and Sejo Oh (1987) 'Output sector munificence effects on the internal polical economy of marketing channels', *Journal of Marketing Research*, **24**, November 347–58.

Feldman, P. (1971) 'Societal adaptation: a new challenge for marketing', *Journal of Marketing*, **35**, 3, 54–60.

General Electric Company (1952) *Annual Report*, New York: General Electric Company.

Gidengil, B.Z. (1977) 'The social responsibilities of business: what marketing executives think', *European Journal of Marketing*, **11**, 1, 72–85.

Grönroos, Christian (1987) 'Defining marketing: a market oriented approach', Working Paper 170, Swedish School of Economics, Helsinki, December.

Grunert, Suzanne C., and Hans Jørn Juhl (1991) 'Values, environmental attitudes and buying behaviour of organic foods: their relationships in a sample of Danish teachers', ISSN 0905-1392, H No. 60, October, Institut for Informationsbehandling, University of Aarhus, Aarhus, Denmark.

Håkansson, Håkan (1982) *International Marketing and Purchasing of Industrial Goods: An interaction approach*, New York: John Wiley.

Hayes, Robert H., and William J. Abernathy (1980) 'Managing our way to economic decline', *Harvard Business Review*, **58**, 4, 67–77.

Hooley, Graham J., James E. Lynch and Jenny Shepherd (1990) 'The marketing concept: putting theory into practice', *European Journal of Marketing*, **24**, 9, 7–23.

Houston, Franklin S. (1986) 'The marketing concept: what it is and what it is not', *Journal of Marketing*, **50**, 2, 81–7.

Hunt, S.D. (1976) 'The nature and scope of marketing', *Journal of Marketing*, **40**, 3, 17–28.

Johannson, Jan, and Lars-Gunnar Mattsson (1985) 'Marketing investments and market investment in industrial networks', *International Journal of Research in Marketing*, **2**, 3, 185–95.

Kotler, Philip (1972a) 'A generic concept of marketing', *Journal of Marketing*, **36**, 2, 46–54.

Kotler, Philip (1972b) 'What consumerism means for marketers', *Harvard Business Review*, **50**, 3, 48–57.

Kotler, Philip (1988) *Marketing Management* (6th edn), Englewood Cliffs, NJ: Prentice Hall.

Kotler, Philip (1994) *Marketing Management: Analysis, planning, implementation and control* (8th edn), Englewood Cliffs, NJ: Prentice Hall.

Kotler, Philip, and Sidney J. Levy (1971) 'Demarketing, yes, demarketing', *Harvard Business Review*, **49**, 6, 74–80.

Lambin, Jean-Jacques (1993) 'Priorities in marketing management practice: implications for research and for teaching', paper presented at 22nd Annual Conference of the European Marketing Academy (EMAC), ESADE, Barcelona, 25 May.

Lanning, Michael J., and Edward G. Michaels (1988) 'A business is a value delivery system', *McKinsey Staff Paper*, 41, June.

Levitt, Theodore (1960) 'Marketing myopia', *Harvard Business Review*, **38**, 4, 24–47.

Levitt, Theodore (1976) 'The industrialization of service', *Harvard Business Review*, **54**, 5, 63–74.

Levy, Sidney J. (1959) 'Symbols for sale', *Harvard Business Review*, **37**, 4, 117–24.

Maslow, Abraham H. (ed.) (1970) *Motivation and Personality* (2nd edn), New York: Harper and Row.

McKittrick, J.B. (1957) 'What is the marketing management concept?', in Frank M. Bass (ed.), *The Frontiers of Marketing Thought and Science*, Chicago: American Marketing Association.

Möller, K.E. Kristian, and Mai Anttila (1987) 'Marketing capability in small manufacturing firms: a key success factor?', paper in *Contemporary Research in Marketing*, the 16th Annual Conference of the European Marketing Academy, York University, Toronto.

Miller, Cyndee (1993) 'Tapping into women's issues is potent way to reach market', *Marketing News*, **27**, 25, 6 December.

Mueller-Heumann, Guenther (1986) 'Toward a professional concept of marketing', *Journal of Marketing Management*, **1**, 3, 303–13.

Porter, Michael E. (1980) *Competitive Strategy*, New York: The Free Press.

Pruden, Henry O. (1971) 'The interorganizational link', *California Management Review*, **14**, 1, 39–45.

Pruitt, D.G. (1981) *Negotiation Behaviour*, New York: Academic Press.

Robin, Donald P., and R. Eric Reidenbach (1993) 'Searching for a place to stand: towards a workable ethical philosophy of marketing', *Journal of Public Policy and Marketing*, **12**, 1, 97–105.

Rokeach, M.J. (1973) *The Nature of Human Values*, New York: The Free Press.

Schwartz, Shalom H., and Wolfgang Bilsky (1987) 'Toward a universal psychological structure of human values', *Journal of Personality and Social Psychology*, **53**, 3, 550–62.

Swan, John E. and J.H. Jones (1988) 'Measuring dimensions of purchase trust of industrial sales people', *Journal of Personal Selling and Sales Management*, **8**, 1, 1–9.

Tsalikis, J., and D.J. Fritzsche (1989) 'Business ethics: a literature review with a focus on marketing ethics', *Journal of Business Ethics*, **8**, 9, 695–743.

Webster, Frederick E., Jr (1992) 'The changing role of marketing in the corporation', *Journal of Marketing*, **56**, 4, 1–17.

Scope of marketing management

2

Introduction

This chapter introduces and explains:

- the difference between strategic and operational marketing;

- the components of the marketing function;

- the role of marketing as a business philosophy and the relationship with other areas of the business;

- the different orientations in companies: production and sales, customers and competitors, and the marketing orientation with a longer-term view;

- the role of mission statements, goals and strategic statements, and the importance of marketing objectives;

- the difference between corporate and marketing strategy;

- the concept of the marketing mix;

- how companies manage and plan the marketing mix; and

- the meaning of applied strategic marketing.

The chapter discusses the scope of marketing management in the company. Marketing management deals with strategic and operational issues. In both it relates to the other areas of business which influence the company's orientation

51

to the market. A marketing orientation permits the company to focus on customers and competitors while taking a longer-term view of the welfare of the company. Strategic issues involve considering the company's corporate and marketing strategies and how they affect product and market portfolios. Operational issues refer to the implementation of strategy and relate to ways of designing and controlling the marketing mix. The elements of the marketing mix are outlined and the way the company attempts to integrate them in the context of its marketing objectives is examined.

Having studied this chapter, you should be able to do the following:

1. Determine the marketing orientation of companies.

2. Specify the relevant scope of marketing management.

3. State the function of mission statements, goals and objectives.

4. Define the meaning and significance of strategic and operational aspects of marketing management.

5. Recognize the importance of marketing objectives.

6. Outline how companies identify and implement the marketing mix in the context of an applied strategic marketing plan.

Scope of marketing

In Chapter 1 the role of marketing in society was described. Much social and economic activity is influenced in one way or another by marketing. The scope of marketing is quite wide, therefore, as it applies to people, places and things. Most attention is given to things – products and services – but the scope is wider. Marketing also deals with customers and competitors and how they respond to changes in the environment, how tastes and preferences are influenced, and how innovation spreads throughout the community. The role of marketing in society is welcomed by some, but often seen as an intrusion by others. Companies welcome marketing when they see that its principles can be applied to consolidate fragmented markets (Exhibit 2.1). Marketing is also concerned with strategic issues in the company: matters that concern longer-term developments. It is concerned too with tactical issues which have their effect or influence in the shorter term.

Strategic and operational marketing

Marketing in any organization is usually conceived of at two levels. It is first thought of as a set of tools or techniques which enable the firm to achieve its

---

EXHIBIT 2.1   Upsetting the cider-apple cart

For a few days in the middle of May, London's trendiest pubs could be awash with such liquid delights as Pig Squeal and Dead Dick. The national cider festival is coming to town. Cider is undergoing a change of image.

'Rough' or 'real' cider (commonly known as scrumpy) is unfiltered, untreated and unlikely to do much for your celebral dexterity. Its oldest attraction, its sheer potency, is not much trumpeted by brewers anxious to turn it into an up-market tipple. Nor are its traditional consumers – a rough mix of yokels, tramps, and penny-pinched students – the stuff that marketing dreams are made of.

After seeing what the ad men did to promote lager, the three big cider producers – HP Bulmer, Taunton, and Showerings, which between them control 90 per cent of the market – are trying to do the same for cider. Slick adverts have been selling 'premium' ciders with sharp-edged names like Red Rock and Diamond White. Their efforts are starting to pay off. Cider sales are picking up; 77 million gallons were sold in Britain last year, up 14 per cent on 1989.

Predictably, there is little space in this commercial future for the scrumpy fraternity. The big brewers argue that the rough drink's appeal is too limited, accounting for only five per cent of the pub-cider trade. Down in the West Country heartland, the scrumpies are fighting a rearguard action against what they see as an intrusion by the big brewers into their local 'cider houses'. Attempts to introduce new ciders in Bristol pubs have had the customers up in arms.

The protesters are backed by the Campaign for Real Ale (CAMRA), a pressure group committed to traditional brewing methods. But, although real ale is flourishing, CAMRA's efforts to spread the good news about real cider have been less successful. The group, which is organising next month's London festival, concedes that the drink has a serious image problem. 'It's a drink that's connected with trouble', says a CAMRA official bluntly. With names like Pig Squeal and Dead Dick, who'd have thought it?

Source: *The Economist*, 25 April 1992: 41.

---

operational objectives, such as a sales target, within a given period. Alternatively, marketing is thought of as a concept which should imbue all long-term strategic thinking in the organisation. In such circumstances, concern rests with the long-term welfare of the organization and its customers. The second view reflects the marketing concept and means adopting a philosophical position which drives the organization to think strategically about its products and services, its customers and markets, and its competitors. It is important to note that both views of marketing are legitimate, but they should not be confused.

Many organizations introduce sophisticated management systems which incorporate sets of marketing tools and techniques. Aiming these at achieving short-term objectives, they nevertheless think they are being strategic. Strategic thinking in an organization depends on the corporate culture of the organization. Strategic marketing questions whether the firm is providing the right products and services to serve the right markets and customers, while competing with the right competitors. Operational marketing questions whether the firm is doing these things in the right way or performing them efficiently given the resources at its disposal.

The confusion between these two views of the scope of marketing in the organization arises because all functional areas in the firm experience the same difficulty. Short-term concern for the efficiency of operations focuses on operational matters, especially as marketing operations influence the other functional areas of the company and in turn are influenced by them.

Marketing relates to production by expressing market needs and design specifications, while production attempts to limit the cost of providing the product or service (Figure 2.1). At the same time, marketing relates to finance through information on budgets, sales data and pricing information. Personnel and marketing are related in areas dealing with the remuneration, performance and recruitment of staff. Lastly, marketing is related to the research and development function in the organization by providing information and guidance on changing market needs. These simple relationships

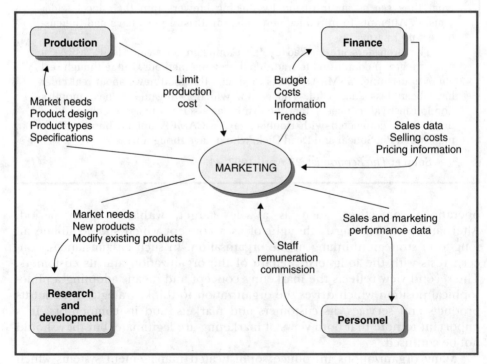

Figure 2.1 The marketing function in the organization

serve to demonstrate that no functional area of business is independent. Concern for immediate responses and efficiencies within the organization creates pressure for a short-term orientation to the detriment of the longer-term view, and this causes the confusion between strategic marketing and operational marketing discussed above.

Components of the marketing function

The marketing function is organized in many different ways to suit the needs of the organization, and consists of a number of components: customer and competitor analysis through market and marketing research, product development, promotion, distribution and selling. The company frequently depends on other organizations for assistance regarding research, advertising, public relations and consultancy support. Whichever way it is organized, it is possible to identify a number of functions which are common to all situations.

Marketing is also concerned with the sales function, by which its products and services are sold to customers and after-sales service is provided. Marketing is concerned with how its products and services are advertised and promoted to reach the right audience with the right message at the right time. It is a major function of marketing to deliver the product or service to customers where and when desired. Distribution is important under these circumstances, especially where markets are distant, requiring the physical movement of containers and packages and the service of independent market intermediaries. Market research and information collection is an important function to ensure that the organization is providing the products and services of superior value to customers (Figure 2.2).

It is unusual for most companies to be in a position to perform all the functions mentioned above from their own resources. Most organizations retain the services of independent companies from time to time, to assist the company in various ways. Market research companies are retained to collect and analyze market trends and competitor information. Advertising agencies may be asked to assist in the design of appropriate advertising material and in its placement in suitable media, such as television, newspapers or magazines. Public relations companies may be retained to ensure that the general corporate image of the company is maintained, or they may be hired to help cope with a short-term problem in the market which, if ignored, might damage relationships between the company and its customers.

Each step in the process is important and has its place in the company's approach to the market. The nature of the product or service is immaterial: the steps are the same, as may be judged from the approach followed by EMI Records in launching one of the albums of the singer Sinéad O'Connor's (Exhibit 2.2).

Occasionally companies retain the services of market and product development consultants, who provide assistance in new product development and

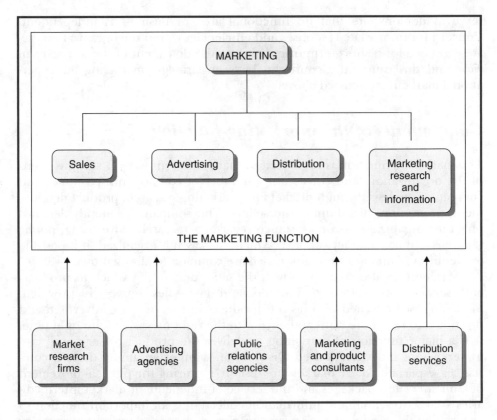

Figure 2.2 Components of the marketing function

design, or in the modernizing of the company's existing line of products and services. Lastly, companies may maintain their own distribution facilities, equipment and transport. In general, however, most companies rely on independent organizations to provide such assistance.

In most markets, the direct contact between the provider of the product or service and the customer has been severed, so it is necessary to employ independent distributors as intermediaries in the channel of distribution to reach customers. Many intermediaries exist which provide valuable service in ensuring that products and services are delivered to customers. The role of wholesalers and retailers in modern marketing illustrates the point.

Relationship to other business disciplines

Much of the difference between marketing decisions and the decisions faced by other functional areas of business arises because marketing management

---

EXHIBIT 2.2   Marketing means money

For Sinéad O'Connor's last album, 'I Do Not Want What I Haven't Got', EMI Records were very happy to get their sums completely wrong. Optimistically, they thought it might sell 15,000 copies in Ireland; in fact, final sales were over three times that figure. But the marketing machines of major record labels are well oiled operations, and there's usually little left to chance when a new album is released. The market is thoroughly analysed to tell the company how popular the record will be, and large amounts of money are then spent on promotion to encourage you and me to buy it.

The marketing and distribution campaign begins well before the record is actually brought out, and continues long after the initial hype has died down. A tour is usually planned six months in advance, to coincide with the album's release; the main aim of the tour is to promote the new record, not to make money.

Normally, a first single is released a month or two before the album comes out. The number of copies of the album that are manufactured depends on the sales of the artist's last album and the performance of the single. 'Nothing Compares 2 U' sold almost 10,000 copies in Ireland for Sinéad O'Connor, and reached Number 1 on both sides of the Atlantic. The single succeeded way beyond the wildest dreams of anyone in EMI and virtually guaranteed the success of the album when it was released. Most albums need the release of two or three singles in order to build up sales, but Sinéad was off to a flying start.

The machinery of pop promotion really moves into action once an album has been brought out. In-store displays are put up, the artist interviewed in the media and newspaper, radio and perhaps TV advertising is paid for. Retailers can phone in additional orders at any time, and these orders are processed on a weekly basis by the record distributors. Further single releases keep the momentum going behind a promotional campaign. Advertising is particularly heavy at Christmas, when huge numbers of records are sold. Record companies are frequently accused of ripping off their customers (and even their bands) and of hyping their product. With some justification, the companies defend themselves by saying that records are no different from any other products, and are promoted in the same way, using advertising, public relations, merchandising and other marketing techniques.

Source: *Irish Times*, 3 December 1991.

has the dual responsibility of holding down costs while also generating revenues for the company. The accounting and production functions, for example, are usually concerned only with reducing costs at each level of output.

Marketing is much more at the interface between the external environment in which the company operates and the internal structure of the company itself. Marketing decisions are expected to influence the environment in some way, while at the same time influencing the behaviour and circumstances of the organization itself. Successful companies understand the changes that take place in the environment, interpret them correctly and respond to them in a strategic manner, while also giving satisfaction to the customer.

The major functional areas of the company are responsible for the provision of the resources required for the firm's survival and growth. The primary objective of each of these functional areas is to ensure an uninterrupted flow of resources from the appropriate external group (Anderson, 1982: 22). In this view, the major responsibility of marketing is to satisfy the long-term needs of its customers. In seeking to achieve the objective of satisfying customers, marketing people must work within the confines of legal, technical, financial and human resource considerations. A desire to promote the marketing concept within a firm may run the risk of being thwarted by others who see the bargaining power thus obtained as detrimental to their own position within the company.

Marketing as a business philosophy

There are various ways of conceiving the appropriate role for marketing within the organization (Kotler and Armstrong, 1994). Marketing is sometimes considered as one of the functional areas of business and receives equal treatment with the other functional areas (Figure 2.3). Alternatively, in some firms marketing is seen to dominate all other functions. In some sense production, finance and personnel are considered as subservient to marketing.

A more modern approach suggests that the customer is the centre of attention and that the various functions in business exist to serve the customer. The appeal of this approach and the need to consider internal functions in the company led to the view that marketing is the interface between the customer and the company, and that marketing serves to control and integrate the business functions to meet the needs of the market.

Manufacturing and operations

Years ago the principal link between the manufacturing function in the firm and the customer in the market was through the sales force. Sales people placed their orders directly with factory managers and engineers. The link between the two was supervised by a general manager who resolved major issues of conflict or dispute. This is still the situation facing many smaller companies. But as organizations have grown and become more complex, this simple structure has been shown to be inadequate in integrating the objectives of manufacturing and sales.

Many firms responded by departmentalizing the market function, which has grown to become the principal contact between sales and manufacturing.

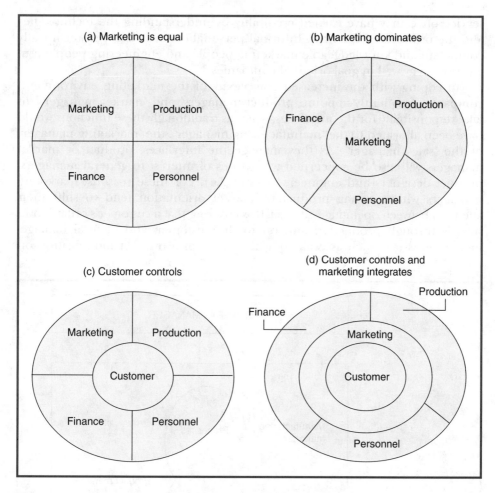

Figure 2.3 Alternative views of marketing in the organization
(Source: Adapted from Kotler and Armstrong, 1994)

Whichever way it is manifested in the company, as a philosophy imbuing every-body in the organization, or organized separately as a department, the market-ing function has become responsible for defining the firm's product strategy, selecting products and positioning them in the company's product line. Marketing often obtains market and sales information for transfer to manufac-turing. As a consequence, the marketing function is an integrative one, linking the various stages of activity within the firm and outside to customers.

At the same time, one of the key roles of marketing especially in technology-driven companies is to calibrate technology-driven ideas by screening them: determining the size and profitability of the market for them before the company commits to their production. Marketing people can provide this service once they have earned credibility by understanding the technologies and the products of the firm. Informal personal contacts between technically competent and knowledgeable marketing people and engineering people usually work very well in goal-oriented companies.

In coping with the increased complexity of the marketing environment, companies frequently appoint 'product managers' and 'market managers' to take responsibility for the interfaces, whereas traditionally these functions would have been allocated to the 'manufacturing manager', the 'marketing manager' or the 'sales manager'. As they manage the interfaces, product or market managers will also be concerned with issues of interest to general managers, product designers and engineers (Figure 2.4). For these reasons, marketing managers with a strong product or market orientation tend to shift their attention between operating issues, such as ensuring that a customer's order moves smartly through production and on to the customer, and general management-level issues, such as evaluating the effect of a product modification on

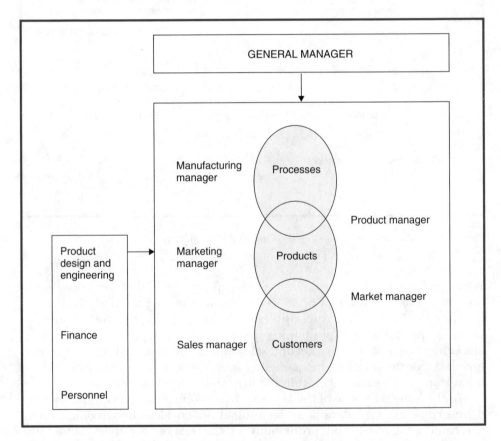

Figure 2.4   Links between marketing and manufacturing

the sales of other products in the line. To be successful in developing a sustainable competitive advantage, general managers outside manufacturing need to have a broad understanding of the company's process technology, its product line and its customers.

There are many opportunities for conflict to arise between marketing and manufacturing. Eight potential major points of conflict have been identified by Shapiro (1977). The problem areas and the typical comments made by both sides have an immediate intuitive appeal for anyone who has worked in industry (Table 2.1). Engineering people might be accused of thinking in logical, factual terms and wanting marketing people to provide market information in engineering terms. Manufacturing-oriented managers also believe that they cannot use marketing research information because 'customers don't

TABLE 2.1   Levels of interaction between marketing and manufacturing

Typical marketing comment	Problem area	Typical manufacturing comment
Why don't we have enough capacity?	Capacity planning and long-range sales forecasting	Why didn't we have an accurate sales forecast?
We need faster response. Our lead times are ridiculous.	Production scheduling and short-range sales forecasting	We need realistic customer commitments and sales forecasts that don't change like wind direction.
Why don't we ever have the right merchandise in inventory?	Delivery and physical distribution	We can't keep everything in inventory.
Why can't we have reasonable quality at reasonable cost?	Quality assurance	Why must we always offer options that are too hard to manufacture and that offer little customer utility?
Our customers demand variety.	Breadth of product line	The product line is too broad: all we get are short uneconomical runs.
Our costs are so high that we are not competitive in the marketplace.	Cost control	We can't provide fast delivery, broad variety, rapid response to change, and high quality at low cost.
New products are our life blood.	New product introduction	Unnecessary design changes are prohibitively expensive.
Field service costs are too high.	Adjunct services such as spare parts inventory support, installation and repair	Products are being used in ways for which they weren't designed.

Source: Adapted from Shapiro (1977). Reprinted by permission of Harvard Business School Press from Shapiro, Benson P. (1977) 'Can marketing and manufacturing coexist?', *Harvard Business Review*, **55**, 5, 104–14. Copyright © 1977 by the President and Fellows of Harvard College.

know what they want' or because 'they just extrapolate from current product concepts'. Manufacturing and engineering people also complain about the lack of technical knowledge among marketing people. Because marketing people spend most of their time working with existing products and services, they inevitably know less about new or advanced technologies than do engineers or technical people. It is important to note, however, that customers are not generally interested in how technology works; they are interested in obtaining benefits from its application to their problems.

Marketing high-technology products

In new product development, especially in rapidly changing technologies, the focus is on customer benefits and problem solving, not on the product itself. In rapidly changing technologies this may mean that success in new product development can depend on how well the company anticipates future requirements that customers may not be able to articulate in the present. The case of the Sony Walkman may be cited to support this point. Before its introduction it is unlikely that conventional consumer research studies would have indicated a need or want for such a product. In such circumstances, some companies draw on the advice of technology 'opinion leader-users' who have an economic incentive to explore advancement on current products and services. For such innovations it is necessary to study that segment of the market which is likely to give the information required, not just the average consumer.

Conditions resembling supply-side marketing dominate the early stages of the marketing of high-technology products. In high technology Say's Law (the supply of a product can create its own demand) appears appropriate (Shanklin and Ryans, 1984: 165). High-technology products and services appear to create a demand where none previously existed. According to these authors, 'the infancy of every high technology market has been characterized by supply side conditions in which the marketer's job is to stimulate primary or basic demand for the product, process or service at hand' (1984: 165).

Manufacturing and engineering people, however, frequently miss the broader context of markets by concentrating on individual users. Marketing people must decide if there are others who are similar, and if the segment to which they belong is sufficiently large and profitable. Marketing managers must also determine relative priorities for product and service attributes in the context of the entire market, to complement the technical perspective of manufacturing and engineering.

Finance and management accounting

It may be observed that, for the past two decades at least, companies have increasingly been dominated by financially oriented management. In a financially oriented environment, the pressures on management are usually to produce quick and predictable returns. An operational philosophy with such objectives is not compatible with the risk and uncertainty associated with marketing innovations designed to compete in the longer term.

This excessive emphasis on short-term financial controls leads companies to depend too much on the results of market research. The dependence of firms on the results of consumer surveys and the exigencies of return on investment measures encourages a low-risk, short-run investment philosophy. This argument suggests that market research can identify the current desires of consumers, but is often incapable of determining future needs and wants. The results of the short-term perspective can be dire according to some authors. 'By their preference for servicing existing markets rather than creating new ones and by their devotion to short term returns and management by numbers many [managers] have effectively foresworn long term technological superiority as a competitive weapon. In consequence they have abdicated their strategic responsibilities' (Hayes and Abernathy, 1980: 70).

Human resources and other disciplines

In organizing for marketing, it is necessary to determine the kind and number of people required. Successful marketing management depends to a large extent on developing a human resources policy appropriate for the organization. This is a human resource management issue which relates directly to marketing management. After determining the market strategy for the organization and the operational implications of that strategy in terms of marketing people, brand managers, sales and sales support staff, the human resource requirements become apparent. Most organizations carry out periodic and regular personnel audits to determine the number and kind of people required in a changing environment.

Determining the kind of marketing people required in a company is undertaken using a job analysis, which defines the specific activities to be performed and determines the personalities and qualifications suited for the jobs concerned. In completing this task, the marketing manager and staff are in regular contact with the human resources manager in preparing job descriptions, which are written statements of the nature, requirements and responsibilities of the marketing positions in the organization.

Another area where human resource management interacts with marketing management is in staff training. Many organizations carry out in-house training programmes on a regular basis or send their people on outside training programmes. The need to update management skills is an important function for most organizations and one that must be kept constantly under review by the human resources people.

Orientation of the company

It is possible to classify firms or organizations depending on whether they are production oriented, sales oriented, customer oriented, competitor oriented or marketing oriented.

Production and sales orientations

Many organizations emphasize how well they perform some function which they believe customers require. Other organizations produce some product or service and through strong selling methods attempt to convince potential customers that their offering should be purchased. Both approaches may have some value in limited circumstances, such as in periods of scarcity or little choice, but in general they have little appeal in modern markets.

Production-oriented companies

Production-oriented organizations are sometimes superior to their competitors regarding technological issues. Arising out of this dominance is an attitude which is reflected in the belief that the company produces a product which is better than others, and hence the expectation is that everybody will want to purchase it. Unfortunately for such companies, it does not work that way. While the company's product may be technically the best, competitor products or services may meet customer needs in a simpler or cheaper way. The best product or service for the customer is the one which satisfies the expressed need in the easiest possible way. Some companies easily fall into the trap of believing in their own superiority while competitors develop more attractive value-laden products and services.

In this respect, note the efforts of traditional dairy products companies in the 1970s and early 1980s, attempting to be more efficient in producing greater quantities of rectangular blocks of butter and hard cheese, while competitors were busily developing spreadable butter and cream cheeses to meet the needs of the market. In recent years, the dairy industry throughout Europe has revolutionized its approach to product development and has slowly begun to recognize the need to adapt to customer needs.

Firms operating under the production orientation assume that consumers will buy products which are available and affordable, and that they prefer products which offer the best quality at a particular price. With such an orientation the task of management is to seek more efficient production and distribution, and to improve quality. In Table 2.2 the production emphasis is contrasted with the marketing emphasis for a few well-known product categories.

TABLE 2.2   Production and marketing emphasis contested for selected product categories

Production emphasis	Marketing emphasis
● Cars	Transportation
	Convenience
● Mechanical/electrical drills	Holes
● Soft ice-cream	Refreshment
● Medical techniques	Health

Sales-oriented companies

Some companies emphasize sales in the belief that greater sales produce greater profits. These companies rarely support their customers with a good after-sales service. There is no great concern for product quality or customer needs. Eventually, it becomes more and more difficult to sell the product. Sales-oriented companies frequently have to deal with dissatisfied customers whose expectations have been misunderstood or ignored.

The sales concept assumes that the customer is passive and will not buy unless the firm makes a sustained effort to stimulate and maintain interest. A sales-oriented company believes in short-run sales volume and customers as individuals in the selling process, whereas marketing-oriented companies believe in strategic marketing planning, opportunities and threats, customers and segments, and differences among them.

Customer and competitor orientations in companies

Companies may focus their activities on customers or competitors. A customer orientation means focusing exclusively on customers as the way to achieve long-run profits, while a competitor orientation means focusing on the activities of competitors to counteract them in some way with the same overriding objective of achieving long-run profits (Figure 2.5). A narrow focus on customers or competitors is generally myopic as the two approaches are complementary.

Customer orientation

A customer orientation means directly appealing to customers by offering a better match of products or services to customer needs. A customer orientation views the firm as identifying the needs and wants of potential customers and then designing, providing and communication values to match customer requirements (Figure 2.5). As a result, the firm serves satisfied customers who produce high levels of sales and long-term profits. It is assumed that customers carry out intensive searches to find the product or service which meets their

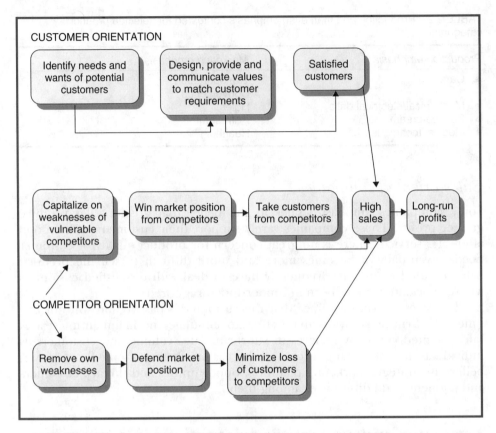

Figure 2.5 Customer and competitor orientation in the organization

(Source: Adapted with permission from McGraw-Hill from: Oxenfeldt, Alfred R., and William L. Moore (1983) 'Customer or competitor: which guideline for marketing?' in Stewart Henderson Britt, Harper W. Boyd, Robert T. Davis and Jean Claude Larreche (eds), *Marketing Management and Administrative Action*, New York: McGraw-Hill)

needs and that, once found, loyal patronage follows. A successful customer orientation states that the company must:

- identify customer needs and wants with great accuracy;

- determine how much customers value the different things they want;

- design and provide products and services to meet customer requirements and communicate these values to customers.

It has been argued, however, that a customer orientation is based on four questionable assumptions: that customers know what they want, that marketing research can ascertain what potential customers want, that satisfied customers will reward the company with repeat purchases and loyalty, and that competitive offers are significant enough to be important to customers (Oxenfeldt and Moore, 1983: 44).

These authors cite a number of situations where the above assumptions may not hold. If customers do not know or cannot articulate what they want, the company may be forced to guess. If customers cannot identify significant differences among products and the purchase is not very important, brand choice will be based not on a search of all brands in the category, but on a brand that satisfied in the past, on recall of advertising or on a sales promotion. When such product parity occurs, firms sometimes attempt to introduce significant product or service improvements, or to emphasize small differences through advertising, allowing greater retail margins so that they will promote the company's brand. None of these approaches need be in the customer's best longer-term interests.

Too great a focus on customers can lead to rapid product innovation and differentiation, short product life cycles, and an emphasis on small batch production of specialized products and services. This is especially true in affluent markets when incomes are rising. In such circumstances, it is also necessary to take account of trends in the environment and the activities of competitors.

Competitor orientation

A competitor orientation views customers as the ultimate prize to be won at the expense of rivals. Sources of competitive advantage on which this premise is based are well-developed distribution systems, preferential treatment by suppliers and lower costs. A competitor orientation implies that the firm attempts to capitalize on the weaknesses of vulnerable competitors to win market position and customers from them, which produces a high level of sales and long-run profits (Figure 2.5). At the same time, the firm attempts to remove its own weaknesses to defend market position and minimize the loss of customers to competitors.

A competitor orientation based on pursuing competitive advantage means accepting five propositions (Hunt *et al.*, 1981: 268):

- competition consists of a constant struggle of organizations to develop, maintain or increase their differential advantage over other companies;

- competition for differential advantage is the principal source of marketing innovation;

- foundations for differential advantage are market segmentation, selection of product and service appeals, product improvement, process improvement and product innovation;

- over time competitors will attempt to neutralize the differential advantage of any new entrant to the market;

- the existence of a differentiated advantage gives the firm a position in the market known as an 'ecological niche'.

Marketing-oriented companies

A marketing-oriented company examines customer needs, selects a target market, designs and packages a product to meet market requirements, and ensures customer satisfaction by consulting with its customers regarding product dimensions which require improvement. Some companies spend a significant proportion of their marketing budget to keep in touch with their customers. This research can range from formal evaluation of customer views carried out by a professional marketing research agency, to a more informal approach as would be found in a restaurant typified in the simple question, 'Did you enjoy your meal?' It may also cover many different situations. Evaluations of courses and lecturers is another example of keeping in touch with the customer. Whatever form it takes, it is important that action follows, if necessary.

Marketing and sales orientations contrasted

A sales emphasis is very different from a marketing emphasis in the organization. A marketing orientation produces very different behaviour in terms of identifying, providing, communicating and delivering value than is found in a production and sales orientation (Table 2.3). Four important areas where they differ separate the two approaches: company objectives, company orientation, attitudes to segmentation and the perceived task facing marketing in the company (Kotler, 1977). A sales emphasis results in objectives which are aimed at increasing current sales to meet quotas and to derive commissions and bonuses. Little discrimination is made between products or customers in terms of profits unless these differences are written into the incentives. In contrast, objectives with a marketing emphasis take account of profits. Marketing objectives refer to product mixes, customer groups and different marketing approaches to achieve profitable sales volume and market shares at acceptable levels of risk.

In an analysis of the performance of the 100 most profitable and the 100 most unprofitable companies in the manufacturing sector in Greece, Avlonitis *et al.* (1992: 91) concluded that the more profitable companies stressed long-term marketing planning, current marketing research and new product development, whereas the less profitable firms emphasized personal selling, reflecting a production and sales orientation.

The selling and marketing orientations produce very different emphases in the organization. A selling orientation predominantly reflects a production approach, whereby something is produced and the task is to sell it, thereby increasing consumption (Figure 2.6). A focus on sales means a focus on individual customers rather than market segments or market classes. Such companies are very knowledgeable about individual accounts and the variables which influence specific sales transactions, but they are less interested in developing an approach to an entire segment of similar needs and wants in the market.

A marketing approach attempts to determine ways of offering superior

TABLE 2.3   Marketing, production and sales orientations in an organization

Attitudes and activities	Production and sales orientation	Marketing orientation
Identifying customer value		
Attitudes toward customers	They should be delighted that we exist. If they only knew how difficult it is to produce these goods.	We are delighted that they exist – customer needs drive us.
Marketing research	Used occasionally to obtain customer reaction.	Used to identify needs and how well they are satisfied.
Providing the value		
Products and services	We sell what we can make.	We provide what we can profitably sell.
Innovation	Focus on technology and ways of reducing costs.	Emphasis on new opportunities and cost saving.
Packaging	Product protection.	Customer convenience and promotional support.
Communicating the value		
Company advertising	Aspects of manufacturing, quality, product features.	Customer benefits.
Sales force	Obtain the sale, forget the rest.	Ensure product or service satisfies the customer, co-ordinate with rest of organization.
Delivering the value		
Transportation	Extension of production, minimize cost.	Part of customer service.
Inventory	Facilitates production patterns.	Customer and cost emphasis.
Customer credit	A necessary evil.	Enhances customer value.
Profit	A residual, cover costs first.	A critical objective.

Sources: Adapted from McCarthy and Perrault (1990); Gross and Peterson (1987); Vizza *et al.* (1967).

value to the more profitable segments without damaging individual customer relationships. It reflects an integrated approach based on research and feedback. Customer needs are first evaluated, and then an integrated marketing effort is developed to satisfy customers so that the organization achieves its goals. Feedback occurs at various points, particularly between goal achievement and marketing effort, and between customer satisfaction and needs analysis and effort (Figure 2.7).

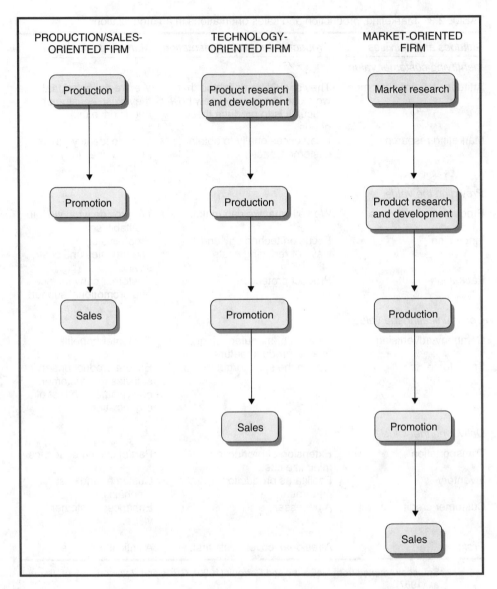

Figure 2.6   Alternative business orientations of the firm

Longer-term view of marketing management

Much management literature refers to different time frames. The short term, the medium term and the long term are common phrases found in the literature. By the short term is usually meant a period in which existing assets are used as efficiently as possible, attempts are made to cut costs, and where

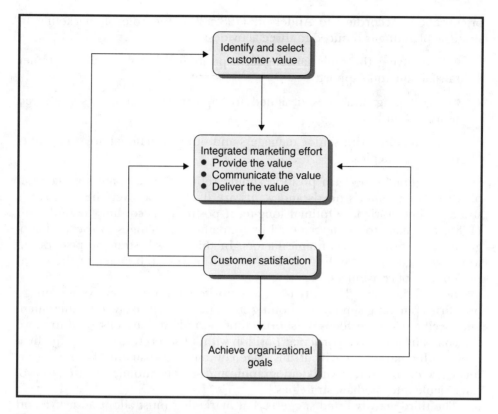

Figure 2.7   Integrated marketing orientation

necessary government assistance is sought for temporary relief when structural difficulties arise in the market. Managers operating with a short-term view are required to be tough, have strong determination and be prepared to pay close attention to detail.

By the medium term is meant a period in which labour and other scarce resources can be replaced with equipment. Medium-term management decisions require the availability of capital and a willingness to take significant financial risks. In the long term, in contrast, the company can develop new products and processes, which introduces the possibility of entering new markets or restructuring old ones. Success in the long term demands imagination and a considerable amount of innovation.

Firms which respond to short-term pressures only 'simply delude themselves into believing that consumer surveys, techniques and product portfolio procedures automatically confer a marketing orientation on their adopters' (Anderson, 1982: 23). The fundamental insight of the marketing concept has little to do with the use of particular analytical techniques. Marketing is, therefore, a management concern and not just an operational function within the organization. According to Anderson (1982: 24), the role of marketing in strategic planning is reduced to three activities:

- identifying the optional long-term position that will ensure customer satisfaction and support;

- developing strategies designed to capture the company's preferred positions; and

- negotiating with senior managers and other functional areas to implement its strategies.

The optimal long-term position should reflect the company's perception of what its customer's needs and wants are likely to be over the company's strategic time horizon. Optimal long-term positions, according to Anderson (1982) are likely to be determined by fundamental changes in social, demographic, political and economic factors. In this regard, strategic positioning will be guided by research in these areas and by research aimed at the latent preferences of consumers.

Behind the second activity is an attempt to gain a competitive advantage over firms pursuing similar positioning strategies. This is likely to be incremental. Specific strategies focus on shorter time periods and are designed to move the company towards a particular position without severely disrupting the firm itself or the market. Activity at this stage combines assessment of current performance of consumers with demographic and socioeconomic research to produce viable intermediate strategies.

The third activity listed suggests that marketing must adopt an active and assertive role in promoting its strategic view. It can do so by demonstrating the weak survival value of a short-term consumer orientation to the other functional areas and to senior management.

Implementation of marketing in the company

The implementation of the marketing concept is the responsibility of the entire company or organization, and not merely of any functional department. Strategic marketing issues must be considered at the level of senior management, whereas the operational aspects of marketing are considered at the level of a department or area within the firm. Phrases such as 'market-driven management' express this strategic view of the marketing concept.

Market-driven management addresses a much wider field than that examined in the traditional domain of marketing management, since it includes the culture of the organization, financial factors and manufacturing considerations.

This text argues that, while marketing management has a key role to play in any organization, it is important to distinguish between strategic and operational issues in implementing marketing. Frequently, marketing managers implicitly assume that theirs is the dominant function in the organization. The reality is, however, that success comes from recognizing that a broader view of the role of marketing, in which no one functional area in an organization is likely to dominate all activity, may be more appropriate. In the modern company, each functional area is beginning to recognize a broader view of its role. This means that the activities, values and power of marketing management should vary depending on circumstances.

It depends on whether strategic or operational marketing issues are being considered. In terms of strategy, it is important that strategic marketing factors are fully considered. Regarding operational marketing factors, it depends on how critical marketing is to the company's overall corporate mission. Accepting this view means that accountants are likely to have supremacy in accounting firms, engineers are likely to dominate in electronic and computer firms, financial people are likely to hold the power in financial institutions and banks, academics in universities, and marketing people in consumer packaged goods companies. In successful companies, marketing managers recognize how they fit in with the company's corporate mission, something which changes as the marketing environment changes.

Internal marketing

In addition to equipping the company to cope with the outside world of customers and competitors, it is also necessary to train and motivate all staff within the company to provide the appropriate level of service to customers. In attempting to serve the business philosophy role within the organization, marketing people must attempt to be missionaries, encouraging everybody else to practise the marketing concept (Berry, 1986). Internal marketing is very closely related to human resource management and the way in which the organization develops its own distinctive corporate culture. It is the task of successfully hiring, training and motivating able employees who want to serve the customers well (Kotler, 1994: 22). It is obvious that it is necessary to determine the organization's internal culture before venturing forth to serve customers in the external world. This internal market must be motivated to react in a certain desired way which is best described as marketing-like (Grönroos, 1984: 3). Internal marketing is, therefore, a management philosophy and a set of marketing activities designed to attain the company's overall objective.

Since satisfying customers is central to the task of marketing management, it is essential that everybody in the organization who deals with customers is imbued with a sense of marketing, which means internal marketing for some and external marketing for others. Customers exist, therefore, both within the organization and outside it. By focusing on customers in this way, a different perspective of the organization is obtained. In traditional organizations, the chief executive and senior manager appear at the top of the chart with sales and other front-office people at the bottom. In many such charts, customers are not represented at all.

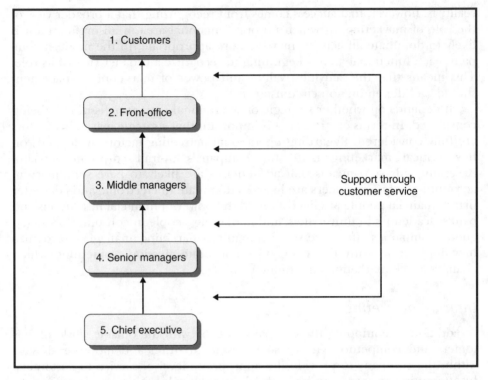

Figure 2.8   Internal marketing and a customer orientation for the marketing task

A contrary view, driven by a strong sense of marketing and especially internal marketing, places the customer on top, the front-office people next, middle managers below them, and finally senior managers (Figure 2.8). As the front-office people meet and serve customers, they must receive a lot of attention within the organization. Senior managers exist, in this view of the world, to support the layer of middle managers. It is important to note that everybody is somebody else's customer. That is why the customer is placed on top and is so important to the survival and growth of the organization.

Strategic issues in marketing management

Marketing strategy refers to the way the marketing mix is blended together to achieve the company's marketing objectives. It also refers to the process by which these objectives are attained. The process of strategic marketing means working in the context of a corporate strategic plan, a mission statement, a set of objectives and target market segments, positioning in the market and establishing policies for the other elements of the marketing mix. In formulating marketing strategy and deciding the appropriate process, companies should recognize that markets are dynamic: needs and wants change and product-markets evolve. Companies should also recognize that it may be necessary to obtain new resources.

Formulating marketing strategy

The key components in formulating marketing strategy include an analysis of the company, the market and the competition to understand better how the market functions within the competitive environment. A good marketing strategy cannot be formulated without an appropriate support and incentive system, which allows the company to think strategically rather than constantly making tactical responses. Strategic marketing thinking requires the development of a multitude of creative, entrepreneurial insights into the company, the industry and the market.

Environmental change is one feature of marketing which companies must consider on a constant basis. To make legitimate assumptions about changes in the marketing environment, the company must analyze the macro environment to discover the impact on business of changes in politics, economics, technology and society in general. At the micro level, industry and customer trends including market size, buyer behaviour, existing and emerging market segments, and developments in distribution channels are of interest.

The company must make a set of assumptions regarding resources, based on an evaluation of the company and its competitiveness, which means its ability to conceive values in demand by customers, to design products and services to match those values, to launch them in the market, to finance the operation and to manage the entire process. The company makes competitive assumptions based on an analysis of competitors, existing and potential, available substitute products and the degree of integration existing between suppliers and customers.

Defining marketing strategy

Strategy is a statement of purpose and a specification of the broad means of achieving that purpose. The future is uncertain and the more distant the future, the more uncertain it becomes. The notion of marketing strategy was devised to provide a structured approach to strategic marketing planning for the business as a whole.

Marketing strategy is defined as an integrated set of marketing-related actions taking account of the firm's resources, aimed at increasing the long-term well-being of the company, by securing a sustainable competitive advantage with respect to the competition in serving customer needs. The key words in this definition are: integrated, actions, sustainable and competition.

Mission statements, goals and strategies

Most companies and organizations can identify an explicit or implicit corporate mission, corporate goals and strategies, and a series of functional strategies. Corporate mission statements provide direction and continuity for an organization by objectively stating the broad parameters within which the organization operates and seeks to develop and grow. Such a statement attempts to establish an ethos or corporate culture for the organization, a series of ambitions within the context of the organization's perceived competences. Some companies develop mission statements which contain a very wide set of objectives and strategies. Corporate objectives and strategies for CIBA-GEIGY AG, Basle, Switzerland, in 1985 were:

> to develop a world-wide leading position in speciality chemicals through excellence in research and development, production and marketing, while satisfying a wide range of stakeholders and obtaining at least 7 per cent return on capital invested. (Albert Bodmer, then Chairman of the Executive Committee)

Marketing-oriented mission statements

Organizations sometimes emphasize different aspects of their environment in preparing their mission statement: customers, products and services, markets served, and technology. Examples of mission statements drawn from recent company annual reports (David, 1989; Lambin, 1993) and news reports illustrate the differences in emphasis.

Customer focus

> We believe our first responsibility is to the doctors, nurses and patients, to mothers and all others who use our products and services. (Johnson and Johnson)

> The purpose of Motorola is to honourably serve the needs of the community by providing products and services of superior quality at a fair price to our customers. (Motorola, Inc.)

Product and service focus

> AMAX's principal products are molybdenum, coal, iron ore, copper, lead, zinc, petroleum and natural gas, potash, phosphate, nickel, tungsten, silver, gold and magnesium. (AMAX)

> We provide our customers with retail banking, real estate finance and corporate banking products which will meet their credit, investment, security and liquidity needs. (Carteret Savings and Loans Association)

Focus on market served

> We are dedicated to the total success of Corning Glass Works as a world-wide competitor. (Corning Glass Works)

> To be a leading consumer marketing company in the US and internationally. (Sara Lee Corporation)

> BA firmly intends to take its place as the core and motivating force of one of the first and most successful of the 10–12 truly global carriers which will ultimately come about. (British Airways in the *Observer*, 19 July 1992)

Technology focus

> Control Data is in the business of applying microelectronics and computer technology in two general areas: computer-related hardware and computer enhancing services, which include computation, information, education and finance. (Control Data)

> Dupont is a diversified chemical, energy and speciality products company with a strong tradition of discovery. Our global businesses are constantly evolving and continually searching for new and better ways to use our human, technological and financial resources to improve the quality of life of people around the world. (DuPont Chemical Corporation)

Focus on problem solving

> We are selling computerised managerial solutions... (IBM)

> We are selling guaranteed waterproof solutions to roofing problems in partnership with exclusive distributors and highly qualified roofing applicators. (Derbit, a company operating in the roofing market in Europe and manufacturing membranes made of APP-modified bitumen)

> ... the air and temperature control business including air ventilation and air conditioning systems. (Sedal, a small company manufacturing ventilation metallic grids)

Linking goals and strategies

Corporate goals refer to the specific targets set by the organization which are to be achieved over a clearly defined period, while corporate strategy refers to the sequence of actions by which the corporate goals will be achieved within the specified period. Functional strategies consist of the sequence of actions at the functional level within the organization which collectively represent corporate strategy, such as marketing, finance, operations, and personnel. For success it is necessary that marketing strategy synchronizes with the other elements of strategy and with the organization's overall strategy.

Corporate and marketing strategy

The basic objectives of corporate strategy are to match corporate strengths with market opportunities, to avoid threats posed in the environment by competitors and environmental change, and to remedy weaknesses in the corporate organization and operations (Baker, 1978). Most writers on the subject of corporate strategy agree that a company's strategy is essentially a process of continuous searching and adapting to the changing environment. It is concerned with how a firm uses its resources over time. Corporate strategy attempts to help the firm decide the appropriate business in which to allocate its resources.

A major element which permeates all aspects of corporate strategy is marketing. Indeed, many authors view marketing strategy and corporate strategy as synonymous. Marketing strategy is designed to achieve some, though not all, of the organization's objectives, but rarely is it the sole element of overall corporate strategy (Baker, 1978). Marketing strategy deals with how the firm allocates resources to products and markets, and is defined in terms of the firm's portfolio of product-market positions.

The interaction between marketing activities and other operations in the firm and the basic steps in profit achievement have been identified for technological products by Hill (1973), who also shows how the marketing information system in the organization is the bridge relating marketing operations to senior management in the company (Figure 2.9).

The link between the board and senior management of the company and the marketing function demonstrates the myriad ways in which marketing imbues all levels of the organization. The board and chief executive of the company, reflecting a marketing orientation, decide corporate strategy, which involves a statement regarding the desired level of profit and the required return on assets employed in the company (Figure 2.9). The marketing function is concerned with profits and cash flow and develops a strategic position in the market, plans marketing activities and implements them in the marketplace.

Generic marketing strategies

Many writers have attempted to identify generic marketing strategies followed by companies in the market. Companies have been classified as defenders, prospectors, analyzers and reactors, depending on the degree of adaptive capability in product-market development (Miles and Snow, 1978). In this classification system, reactors manifest little adaptive capability, while prospectors are characterized by being highly capable of adapting to a changing marketing environment. In more recent years, another four-group classification scheme has become very popular among researchers and in the literature. Companies have been divided into industry cost leaders, differentiators, focused cost leaders and focused differentiators (Porter, 1980, 1985).

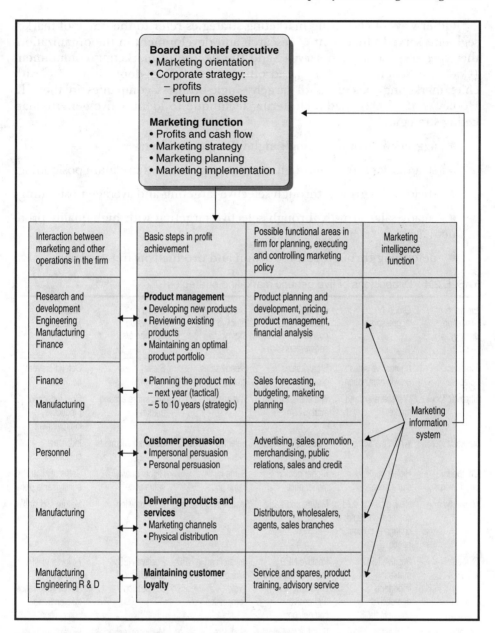

Figure 2.9   Marketing activities in a company
(Source: Adapted from Hill, 1973)

Other ways of classifying marketing strategies refer to the range of market segments served, the extent of research and development in the organization, the types of product and service, and the degree of marketing commitment (Cool and Schendel, 1987). Based on a series of 25 in-depth interviews with chief marketing executives of largely single-business companies in the UK, Hooley *et al.* (1992) used a clustering technique to identify five generic marketing strategies:

- aggressive growth through high-value positioning;
- steady sales growth through selective targeting and premium positioning;
- steady sales growth through selective targeting and average positioning;
- steady sales growth through selective targeting with high-quality products; and
- defending through cost reduction and productivity improvements.

TABLE 2.4   Dimensions of five generic marketing strategies

Elements of marketing strategy	Group 1 Aggressors	Group 2 Premium position segmenters	Group 3 Stuck-in-the-middle	Group 4 High-value segmenters	Group 5 Defenders
Strategic objective	Aggressive sales growth/domination	Steady sales growth	Steady sales growth	Steady sales growth	Defend/prevent/decline
Strategic focus	Win share/expand market	Win share/expand market	Win share	Win share/expand market	Cost reduction/productivity improvement
Market target	Whole market	Selected segments	Selected segments	Selected segments	Individual customers
Competitive positioning	Higher quality/same price	Higher quality/higher price	Same quality/same price	Higher quality/same price	Same or higher quality/same price
Market type	New, growing; fluid competition: rapid change in customer needs	Mature and stable	Mature and stable	New, growing	Mature and stable
Corporate attitudes	Positive NPD; marketing important; aggressive competitors	Positive NPD; marketing important; aggressive competitors	Imitate/lead in NPD; take on/avoid competition	Positive NPD; take on/avoid competition	Follower in NPD; marketing of limited importance; take on/avoid competition
Performance	Best across financial and marketing-based criteria	Good across most criteria	Mediocre	Mediocre, especially on profits	Worst performance overall

Note: *NPD = new product development.*

Source: Hooley *et al.* (1992: 87).

A summary of the nature of these generic strategies demonstrates the relative emphasis given to marketing objectives, focus, targeting, quality and price (Table 2.4). Certain similarities with the Miles/Snow and Porter classifications are apparent: prospector, defender, differentiator, focus and stuck-in-the-middle.

The aggressive growth strategy of group 1 is associated with expanding markets, a positive stance in new product development and a high degree of emphasis on marketing (Hooley *et al.*, 1992: 87). At the other extreme, efficiency, strong financial controls and little new product development are the characteristics most in evidence. In between these extremes are other common generic strategies found among different businesses.

Corporate branding and marketing

Corporate image is another area of marketing concern for the organization. The corporate brand affects the organization's reputation, which in turn affects the organization's ability to attain its objectives and, if quoted on a stock exchange, its share price. Share price is a vital indictor of corporate brand value.

The Economist newspaper commissioned a survey to discover which British companies are most admired by their peers. Assessment by and of rivals is thought to be the key factor in determining a manager's self-esteem, and is immune to tastes among those doing the evaluation. Those polled were asked to rank firms in their sector under nine different headings: quality of management; financial soundness; quality of products and services; ability to attract, develop and retain top talent; value as a long-term investment; capacity to innovate; quality of marketing; community and environmental responsibility; and the use of corporate assets. The results of this survey for three factors which represent the marketing dimension and the overall score for the top five companies featured in the survey are shown in Table 2.5.

Generally, the better an organization is known, the more it is appreciated.

TABLE 2.5   Britain's most admired companies, 1991

Capacity to innovate	Quality of products and services	Quality of marketing	All factors
Rankings			
1. Glaxo	1. Glaxo	1. Unilever	1. Glaxo
2. Body Shop	2. Unilever	2. Rentokil	2. Unilever
3 = Rentokil	3. Marks and Spencer	3. Glaxo	3. Rentokil
3 = Reuters	4. Guinness	4. Smith Kline Beecham	4. Guinness
5. East Midlands Electric	5. Dunhill	5. Guinness	5. Reuters

Note: = denotes same rank.

Source: *The Economist*, 17 October 1992: 79–80. Copyright, *The Economist*, London 1994.

Investors and other opinion leaders respond to images and advertising just like consumers. For industrial products and services generally, the corporate brand name is also the principal brand of the company. This is especially true in financial services and retailing.

Corporate advertising is a very effective way of communicating with customers, shareholders, opinion leaders and other interested parties. In recent years, the Benetton Company has received a great deal of publicity, and also criticism, as a result of its controversial approach to using sensitive social issues in its billboard and magazine advertising. Its focus on AIDS has been criticized severely in the media (Exhibit 2.3). The advertising may be controversial, but the corporate branding is strong.

Product-market portfolios

As a general principle, companies attempt to design and develop a portfolio of products and services which they offer to customers in various markets. Companies may also be seen to have an existing portfolio of products and services which they offer to customers in existing markets. The kinds of marketing management problem facing such companies are very different from companies attempting to extend their product portfolios to include new products and services and new markets (Figure 2.10). A company may consider entering new markets with the same products and services or with new ones. Usually it is recommended that the company proceed in the direction of new products and services, or in the direction of a new market, but not both simultaneously. Ultimately, it is the company's objective to reach the top right-hand cell in Figure 2.10. To reach this position directly by producing new products and services for new markets is considered very difficult.

Operational issues in marketing management

Operational marketing issues refer to how well the company communicates and implements its marketing strategy. The company attempts to do an effective job given the marketing resources at its disposal. An operational marketing matter of considerable importance in a rapidly changing environment is the degree to which the company reacts quickly, flexibly and effectively to sudden changes affecting its circumstances. Operational issues in marketing management are often clarified by analysis, setting attainable objectives, and identifying periodic market opportunities.

EXHIBIT 2.3   More controversy, please, we're Italian

First it was a black woman breastfeeding a white baby; then an array of multi-coloured condoms; then a nun and a priest kissing; then a new-born baby – blood-smeared, dangling from an umbilical cord. Now Benetton, an Italian clothing firm which in the past two years has used these images in its worldwide advertising campaigns, is about to release an even more inflammatory advertisement: a picture of a dying AIDS victim. Has the company gone too far?

Britain's media think so. Magazine publishers such as IPC and EMAP, and Britain's Advertising Standards Authority, are calling the advert 'obscene', 'disgusting' and 'a despicable exploitation of a tragic situation'. Together with billboard companies, many publishers have refused to run the photo, though newspapers have published it with news stories describing the outrage of the advertising industry. A similar outcry last year forced Benetton to withdraw its baby ads in Britain. Undaunted, perhaps even encouraged, Benetton plans to unveil the AIDS ad in New York on 13 February.

American magazines may react in similar ways. So far none has said it will reject the AIDS ad, which uses an award winning photograph of a man on his death-bed. But 'puritanism', as Benetton's in-house adman, Oliviero Toscani, calls it, is hardly unknown in America. Last year American editions of *Elle* and *Cosmopolitan* refused the baby advert; the kissing clerics met with even more resistance. Indeed, the Pope himself declared his disapproval.

Such noises are nothing new to Benetton. In fact the headlines they produce are precisely the point. The company has turned courting controversy into a spectacularly successful marketing strategy. The 'United Colours of Benetton' campaigns of the mid-1980s which played on themes of racial harmony, helped turn the firm into a powerful global brand. But sales really rocketed when the ads took on other 'social issues' (i.e. became intentionally incendiary). In 1990 sales rose by 25 per cent to two trillion lire ($1.7 billion); in 1991 they are thought to have increased by another 15 per cent.

There is more to this than the truism that all publicity is good publicity. Mr Toscani claims the campaigns are not designed to offend, but rather to 'raise consciousness'. A more plausible interpretation is that Benetton is trying to sell sweaters to the young and hip – and those who like to think of themselves in that way. What better means to appeal to them than by offending their elders?

The AIDS ad may, however, be seen not as tweaking society's squares but as trying to profit from people's pain. One British AIDS charity has said so. But some American gay activists disagree, saying the advert gives the issue a higher public profile. The parents of the dying man may feel the same since, according to Benetton, they approved the company's use of the photo. Either way, expect no repentance, or tamer ads, from Benetton unless its sales start to drop.

Source: *The Economist*, 1 February 1992: 74.

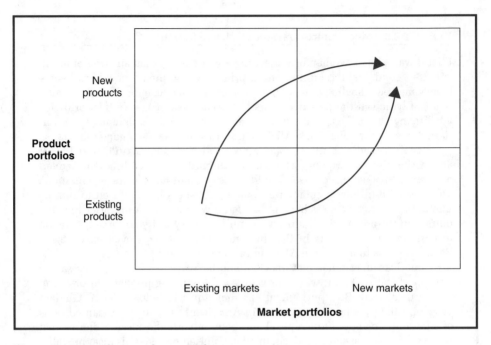

Figure 2.10   Product-market portfolios

Analysis for marketing decisions

All marketing decisions are based on somebody's judgement. Usually managers inform their judgement first. This is done through an analysis of the market. In most new ventures, for example, the company attempts to analyze the market, competition, growth rates and the possibility of failure. As the risk and costs of marketing rise, so too does the level of analysis normally carried out.

An analysis for marketing decisions helps the company understand marketing problems, diagnose them and identify possible solutions. A detailed analysis of the market provides a precise and objective understanding of the market. Analysis also implies diagnosis. A detailed diagnostic approach involves the testing and evaluation of alternative approaches. Lastly, analysis also implies possible solutions. By evaluating marketing strategies, the company may be in a position to decide upon and implement creative solutions to the problems identified.

Importance of marketing objectives

It is necessary to specify marketing objectives in the context of the company's overall business objectives. The objectives of a firm are the specific goals to be achieved within stated time periods relating to sales, profits, products, markets and assets. Policies are guidelines established to assist in operating the business to achieve the objectives e.g. how to spend capital, how to allocate an advertising budget, how to set prices, how to recruit sales staff and how to deliver value to customers. Clearly, therefore, before the company can develop a policy for marketing it is necessary to decide on marketing objectives.

Operational marketing objectives

Objectives must be operational: that is, they should provide clear guidelines. An example of a non-operational objective will make the point clearer: 'we price to make a profit'. Because such an objective does not state or imply the kind of action the firm should take in order to achieve the stated objective, it is non-operational.

There are four distinguishing characteristics of an operational objective:

- specific tasks are set for the company or product;

- it should be possible to discover whether the tasks have been performed;

- it should also be possible to state the evaluative criteria;

- a time limit for the attainment of the objective must be established.

It is because they are precise that operational objectives are operational.

Short-term and long-term objectives

Short-term marketing objectives are usually specified in annual budgets and are included with other objectives such as ones relating to profits, sales volume and market share. They are measurable and provide forecasts and targets for different activities within the firm. The most important short-term objectives in regard to marketing tend to refer to profits, sales volumes or market shares. Short-term operational marketing objectives assist the company with its management control function.

Setting strategic marketing objectives means devoting time to determining long-term levels for the various marketing variables at the company's disposal. It implies deciding the pricing, distribution and promotional strategies for the various stages of the product life cycle. In this instance, marketing variables are not conceived of as merely a tactical variable to be used to gain short-term advantage in the market. The myopia of ignoring the longer-term marketing objectives may be seen in the case of a company installing a new plant and failing accurately to forecast demand for the product. Failure to consider long-term strategic marketing issues influences all aspects of the business: financial performance (e.g. a combination of a known pattern of high fixed costs with an undesirable pattern of product prices), products and even viability.

ortunities in target markets

It is usually essential that the company identifies and serves target customer groups as attempts to satisfy all customer groups can easily result in failure. Companies which treat every customer the same use a mass market approach on the assumption that all customers have similar needs and wants, and can be satisfied with a standard product or service available at the same price through the same distribution channels and promoted in the same way throughout the market. The mass market approach is appropriate when:

- there is little variation in the needs of customers for a specific product or service; and

- the company must develop and support an approach to the market which satisfies everyone.

It is extremely rare to find the first condition in practice, since people express wide-ranging preferences for the things they buy. Regarding the second condition, if the number of customers is large, the company is involved in a heavy commitment of resources which it may not have at its disposal. By seeking opportunities in target markets, the company is better able to provide products and services appropriate to the needs and wants of these particular groups.

Most companies recognize that no two customers ever have exactly the same requirements. Different individuals and companies have varying needs and wants. The extensive range of product and service options available in retail outlets or in individual product catalogues attests to the validity of this claim.

Concept of the marketing mix

The concept of the marketing mix forms the central aspect of marketing theory and practice, and refers to the elements which comprise the marketing programme. The concept evolved from an examination of how companies approached the market for consumer products in the United States particularly after World War II, and is, therefore, conditioned by special circumstances. The originator of the concept refers to twelve elements: product planning, channels of distribution, physical handling, pricing, advertising, display, servicing, promotions, personal selling, packaging, fact finding and analysis (Borden, 1964). Borden did not attempt a definition of the marketing mix, being satisfied to provide a list of the more important elements.

Borden's twelve elements were regrouped into the popular four Ps: product, price, promotion and place (McCarthy, 1964). Each of these categories consisted of a mix of elements which resulted in a product mix, a promotion mix, a distribution mix and a pricing mix. Advertising, personal selling, sales promotion and publicity have been included as part of the promotion mix (Kotler and Armstrong, 1994). The elements of the marketing mix as Borden conceived them have been categorized under the four headings of the modern approach to marketing used in this text (Figure 2.11).

Marketing mix defined

The marketing mix has been defined as those marketing management elements which the organization is able to co-ordinate and control in adopting a position in selected markets. A definition of the marketing mix incorporating this view is now widely accepted in the literature: 'the set of controllable tactical marketing tools that the firm blends to produce the response it wants in the target market' (Kotler and Armstrong, 1994: 46). The marketing mix is, therefore, a set of controllable factors at the disposal of marketing managers.

Too great an emphasis on tactics, as in this definition, may be misplaced. A definition which also accommodates a more strategic perspective states that the 'marketing mix is the set of marketing tools that the firm uses to pursue its marketing objectives in the target market' (Kotler, 1994: 98). An alternative view specifies four controllable elements: product, distribution, promotion and price, referred to as the marketing mix decision variables because the company decides what type of each component to use and in what amounts (Dibb *et al.*, 1991: 20). These have been labelled the four Ps by McCarthy (1964), with 'place' instead of the now more common 'distribution'.

Other approaches to categorizing the marketing mix have had some popularity. Frey (1961) advocated that the marketing mix should be viewed as consisting of two parts: the offering (i.e. the product, packaging, price, service and the brand) and the methods used in marketing (i.e. the channels of distribution, personal selling, sales promotion and publicity). A simple three-way

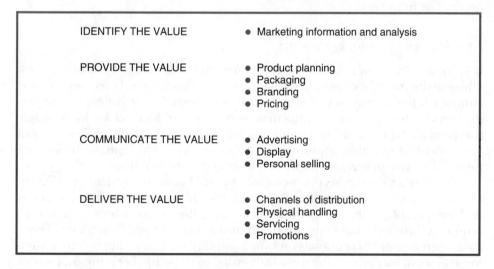

Figure 2.11 Elements of the marketing mix

classification into the goods and services mix, the distribution mix and the communications mix was suggested by Lazer and Kelly (1962).

Criticism of the four Ps framework

While the four Ps framework is very popular, it has been criticized because of its simplistic and misleading treatment of a number of issues (Kent, 1986). Much of the criticism has centred on the need to include additional elements such as packaging, public relations (Mindak and Fine, 1981), and power and public relations (Kotler, 1986). The thrust of this criticism has the effect of extending the list to resemble that originally proposed by Borden (1964).

More substantive criticism levelled at the four Ps approach relates to an inadequate treatment of industrial products and services in marketing. Because industrial products are complex and the buying process is complicated, there is a considerable degree of interdependence between buyer and seller. This buyer–seller relationship binds the two together in pursuit of their objectives (Webster, 1984: 52; 1992).

Furthermore, there is a convergence of adopted positions achieved through negotiation as much as by persuasion which underlies much of the marketing mix. Such negotiation leads to relationships based on personal contacts, something which, if not ignored in the traditional treatment of the marketing mix, is not emphasized. In the marketing of industrial products, the building of relationships is fundamental (Gummesson, 1987). Long-term relationships are more important than obtaining immediate sales as the expectation is that a network of personal relationships can be longer lasting than product or brand loyalties.

Services in the marketing mix

It is frequently argued that most companies today are collections of services. Observe the number of people in manufacturing operations in a company and compare it to those in service arenas such as engineering, logistics and marketing. Service activities such as information systems and logistics are increasingly the primary basis for adding value in the organization. Note that successful banks depend more on sophisticated computer networks than on traditional financial service operations organized in large secure buildings.

There is a growing acceptance that the marketing of services is different because of their nature. Because they are intangible, perishable, heterogeneous and inseparable from the provider and user, the arrangement is that they require a different marketing approach and a different marketing mix. There have been numerous proposals on how to modify the marketing mix to accommodate services. Perhaps the most influential of these has been the framework proposed by Booms and Bitner (1981), who suggest a modification and an

PRODUCT	PRICE	PLACE	PROMOTION
Quality	Level	Location	Advertising
Brand name	Discounts and allowances	Accessibility	Personal selling
Service line	Payment terms	Distribution channels	Sales promotion
Warranty	Customers' own perceived	Distribution coverage	Publicity
Capabilities	value		Personnel
Facilitating goods	Quality/price interaction		Physical environment
Tangible clues	Differentiation		Facilitating goods
Price			Tangible clues
Personnel			Process of service
Physical environment			delivery
Process of service			
delivery			

PARTICIPANTS	PHYSICAL EVIDENCE	PROCESS
Personnel:	Environment:	Policies
Training	Furnishings	Procedures
Discretion	Colour	Mechanization
Commitment	Layout	Employee discretion
Incentives	Noise level	Customer involvement
Appearance	Facilitating goods	Customer direction
Interpersonal behaviour	Tangible clues	Flow of activities
Attitudes		
Other customers:		
Behaviour		
Degree of involvement		
Customer/customer contact		

Figure 2.12 The marketing mix: modified and expanded for services

(Source: Booms and Bitner, 1981. With the permission of the American Marketing Association)

extension of the original framework to include participants, physical evidence and process (Figure 2.12).

In this framework, the participants are the people involved in providing and receiving the service. In services, the firm's staff occupy key positions in influencing customer perceptions of product quality, hence their training and motivation is very important. Furthermore, because customers are participants, it is also important to manage the interaction among customers themselves and the effect it can have on the perception of product quality. In this regard, note that the number, type and behaviour of people on a packaged holiday coach tour will partly determine the enjoyment of such a holiday.

Marketing of intangibles

Because services are intangible, customers use physical evidence as a tangible clue to assess the quality of service provided. The more intangible a service is, the greater is the need to provide physical evidence of its quality. The physical environment (i.e. buildings, furniture layout) is often influential in customer assessment of the quality and level of service. Restaurants, hotels and offices are frequently judged by such criteria. This physical environment becomes part of the product itself.

Services are also believed to be different due to the way they are processed. The firm must ensure that customers understand the process of acquiring a service. In most service situations, it is necessary to queue and the service delivery itself is likely to take time, but it is necessary to determine acceptable queuing and delivery times from the customer's perspective.

Supporters of the four Ps approach argue that the above are mere extensions which can be incorporated in the traditional framework. Having a separate marketing mix for services is difficult to maintain when it is noted that 'everybody sells intangibles in the marketplace no matter what is produced in the factory' (Levitt, 1981: 94). Furthermore, note that 'there is no such thing as service industries. There are only industries whose service components are greater or lesser than those of other industries. Everybody is in service' (Levitt, 1972: 41). This perspective is similar to the view that products and services form part of a continuum with products being tangible dominant and services being intangible dominant (Shostack, 1977). There are very few pure products or pure services, but rather a set of benefits which are a mixture of the two. If this position is accepted then no distinction should be made between the marketing mix for products and services. Up to 80 per cent of the output of some companies is a service element rather than a product, traditionally defined.

Managing and planning the marketing mix

There are many aspects to marketing management which involve planning. Marketing planning means designing a marketing programme around the elements of the marketing mix. Organizations provide products and services, price them, promote them and then distribute them to customers. Several chapters are devoted to discussing the elements of the marketing mix. For now a brief description will suffice.

Product in the marketing mix

Product planning means selecting what to provide and sell, and how to match products and services with the needs of the market. By concentrating on the product alone, it is not easy to gain a sustainable competitive advantage in the market, since most products can be imitated relatively easily. After a while consumers have difficulty in telling the difference between products made by different manufacturers. Consequently, other elements of the marketing mix matter.

Pricing in the marketing mix

Pricing is one of the most difficult areas in marketing, since both strategic and tactical aspects must be considered. Customers may relate price and quality: the higher the price, the higher the perceived quality. In such circumstances, if the product design is better than the average available, raising price may increase sales. Alternatively, if the market is price sensitive, any increase in price may lead to a fall in sales.

Pricing is concerned with deciding how much customers should pay for the product or service to ensure that costs are covered and a contribution is made to company profit. Here it is essential to note that customers seek value. While price may be an overrated element in the marketing mix, it is necessary to consider this element of the mix very carefully. Many companies that have not differentiated their products or services experience price pressure. In these circumstances, customers may be price sensitive. In other circumstances, however, price sensitivity may not be an issue, especially where customers perceive that the company's products and services are highly differentiated.

Promotion in the marketing mix

Promotion is a collection of methods by which the organization may inform its customers of what is offered. A second important aspect of promotion is to persuade the customers to buy the organization's products or services. There are several aspects of promotion: personal selling, advertising, merchandising and sales promotion. A decision regarding which media to use illustrates the point. Should the firm use magazines, the television or radio? Within each, the firm usually has a number of choices: newspapers, business magazines, women's magazines; various radio stations and various television channels. The decision is based on matching the medium with the audience: young people listen to certain radio stations; business people read certain magazines and technical journals. In television advertising, timing may be the critical factor.

Distribution in the marketing mix

The manufacturer of a new health product may distribute it through supermarkets or health food shops. Distribution through supermarkets means negotiating adequate shelf space in supermarkets for very large annual sales, and perhaps dealing with one or at most two supermarket buyers. The company must decide if it can cope with such a regime. A small manufacturer may be exposed to price competition or replacement by other similar products. Alternatively, the company may decide to distribute through speciality health food shops, where price would be higher, annual sales lower and the health aspect emphasized in promotion. In this case, the manufacturer might deal with as many as 150–200 small retailers. These are some of the distribution alternatives and the provider of goods and services or manufacturer must decide which is appropriate for the product and the market.

Distribution decisions are concerned with the system of marketing intermediaries which exists to channel products and services from the original producer to the final consumer.

Popularity of the marketing mix framework

The marketing mix framework is widely considered the general marketing model in most of the western world. But it is easy to forget that the model was developed in North America using empirical data drawn mainly from consumer durables and packaged goods markets conditioned by a peculiar environment, media structure and highly competitive distribution system (Grönroos, 1984: 2). It is likely that the debate as to the appropriateness of the marketing mix framework and what constitutes its elements will continue for some time. The marked advantage of the framework is that it provides a very useful analytical framework for marketing management decisions, and it appeals to managers.

Applied strategic marketing

Successful companies are increasingly focusing their attention beyond the sale or simple transaction. They attempt to build long-term relationships with customers, especially those who represent the greatest potential. To provide long-term customer satisfaction, companies must understand current and future customer expectations and requirements. To do this it is also necessary to have a structured approach to the collection of pertinent information.

The task of the organization is to maintain itself or grow by negotiating for resources in the environment. As organizations grow, they enhance the efficiency and effectiveness of their negotiations through functional specialization. In this way, finance specializes in negotiations with financial institutions, owners and other stakeholders, while marketing specializes in negotiating with customers to ensure the required level of cash flow to the organization. From this perspective, the major responsibility of the marketing function is to satisfy the long-term needs of its customers, which means implementing the marketing concept, which 'is essentially a state of mind or world view that recognises that firms survive to the extent that they meet the real needs of customers' (Anderson, 1982: 23). According to Anderson, the real lesson of the marketing concept is that successful companies recognize the fundamental and enduring nature of the customer needs they are attempting to satisfy, while at the same time acknowledging that the technology available to satisfy customer needs and wants is transitory. In these circumstances, successful companies constantly monitor and adapt to the changing technological and marketing environment.

According to Kotler (1994: 94), the marketing management process is a five-step procedure:

- analyzing marketing opportunities;

- researching and selecting target markets;

- designing marketing strategies;

- planning marketing programmes; and

- organizing, implementing and controlling the marketing effort.

For a marketing strategy to be successful it is essential that the firm recognizes that marketing and markets are dynamic, events change, products, services and markets evolve, and, even though resources may be scarce, they can be made available to the firm under certain circumstances.

Planning, implementation and co-ordination

A most important ingredient in any business plan is the company's marketing plan. A marketing plan is the foundation for company policy regarding the allocation, direction and control of marketing resources to achieve strategic and tactical objectives. It is important to distinguish between these two aspects of marketing planning. Strategic marketing planning is concerned with broad marketing objectives and relates closely to overall corporate strategy. Tactical planning considers the specific marketing decisions regarding distribution and delivery, advertising and promotion, merchandising, and pricing and service. Tactical marketing plans usually cover relatively short periods up to a year. Strategic marketing issues refer to decisions which affect the company in the longer term, usually taken to mean three to five years depending on the volatility of the marketing environment.

Components of the marketing mix

Marketing may be implemented at three different levels. As a concept, marketing represents a strategic focus on the environment to produce company and stakeholder benefits. It is a way of thinking about the company which produces profitable exchanges. As a process, marketing is concerned with the managerial direction of resources to realize environmental opportunities, while recognizing that customers have needs and wants that cannot normally be completely satisfied. Third, marketing is concerned with management decisions taken in the context of a marketing programme to ensure focused attention on customers in the market.

Assignment questions

1 What is a business mission and why is it important? How is the planning of marketing strategy affected by the business mission?

2 Describe the different stages of the development of marketing thought.

3 What are environmental opportunities or threats? Why are they so important to the firm?

4 Discuss the importance of analyzing organizational strengths and weaknesses in marketing.

5 What is market opportunity analysis? Why is it important to the firm?

6 What is a target market? What considerations must be made in selecting target markets?

7 What is a marketing programme? Why must it be co-ordinated?

8 What kinds of plan must be developed by the marketing organization? What do they involve? What are the benefits of marketing planning?

9 What bases can be used to organize a marketing department? When are different bases most appropriate?

Annotated bibliography

Bennett, Peter D. (1988) *Marketing*, New York: McGraw-Hill, chapter 1, 13–19.
Dibb, Sally, Lyndon Simkin, William M. Pride and O.C. Ferrell (1991) *Marketing*, Boston, Mass.: Houghton Mifflin, chapter 1, 13–23.
Kotler, Philip (1994) *Marketing Management: Analysis, planning, implementation and control* (8th edn), Englewood Cliffs, NJ: Prentice Hall, chapter 1, 13–30.
McCarthy, E. Jerome, and William D. Perreault, Jr (1990) *Basic Marketing* (10th edn), Homewood, Ill.,: Richard D. Irwin, chapter 2.
Stanton, William J., Michael J. Etzel and Bruce J. Walker (1991) *Fundamentals of Marketing*, International Edition, New York: McGraw-Hill, chapter 1.

References

Anderson, Paul F. (1982) 'Marketing, strategic planning and the theory of the firm', *Journal of Marketing*, **46**, 2, 15–26.
Avlonitis, George J., Athanasios Kouremenos and Spiros P. Gounaris (1992) 'Company performance: does marketing orientation matter?', paper in *Marketing for Europe –*

Marketing for the Future, 21st Annual Conference of the European Marketing Academy (EMAC), Aarhus University, Aarhus, Denmark.

Baker, Michael J. (1978) 'Limited options for marketing strategies', *Irish Marketing Journal*, **5**, 8/9, 21–3.

Berry, Leonard (1986) 'Big ideas in services marketing', *Journal of Consumer Marketing*, **3**, Spring, 47–51.

Booms, B.H., and M.J. Bitner (1981) 'Marketing strategies and organization structures for service firms', in J. Donnelly and J.R. George (eds.), *Marketing of Services*, Chicago: American Marketing Association.

Borden, Neil H. (1964) 'The concept of the marketing mix', *Journal of Advertising Research* **4**, 3, 2–7.

Cool, K.O., and D. Schendel (1987) 'Strategic group formation and performance: the case of the US pharmaceutical industry', *Management Science*, **33**, 9, 1102–24.

David, Fred R. (1989) 'How companies define their mission', *Long Range Planning*, **22**, 1, 90–7.

Dibb, Sally, Lyndon Simkin, William M. Pride and O.C. Ferrell (1991) *Marketing*, Boston, Mass.: Houghton Mifflin.

Frey, Albert W. (1961) *Advertising* (3rd edn), New York: The Ronald Press.

Grönroos, Christian (1984) 'Internal marketing – theory and practice', paper presented at the American Marketing Association 3rd Conference on Services Marketing, *Services Marketing in a Changing Environment*, Chicago, Ill., 23–6 September.

Gross, Charles W., and Robin T. Peterson (1987) *Marketing: Concepts and decision making*, St Paul, Minn.: West Publishing Co.

Gummesson, E. (1987) 'The new marketing – developing long term interactive relationships', *Long Range Planning*, **20/4**, 104, 10–20.

Hayes, Robert H., and William J. Abernathy (1980) 'Managing our way to economic decline', *Harvard Business Review*, **58**, 4, 67–77.

Hill, Roy W. (1973) *Marketing Technological Products to Industry*, Oxford: Pergamon Press.

Hooley, Graham J., James E. Lynch and David Jobber (1992) 'Generic marketing strategies', *International Journal of Research in Marketing*, **9**, 1, 75–89.

Hunt, Shelby D., James A. Muncy and Nina M. Ray (1981) 'Anderson's general theory of marketing: a formalization', in Ben M. Enis and Kenneth J. Roering (eds.), *Review of Marketing 1981*, Chicago: American Marketing Association.

Kent, R.A. (1986) 'Faith in the four Ps: an alternative', *Journal of Marketing Management*, **2**, 2, 145–54.

Kotler, Philip (1977) 'From sales obsession to marketing effectiveness', *Harvard Business Review*, **55**, 6, 67–75.

Kotler, Philip (1986) 'Megamarketing', *Harvard Business Review*, **64**, 2, 117–24.

Kotler, Philip (1994) *Marketing Management: Analysis, planning, implementation and control* (8th edn), Englewood Cliffs, NJ: Prentice Hall.

Kotler, Philip, and Gary Armstrong (1994) *Principles of Marketing* (6th edn), Englewood Cliffs, NJ: Prentice Hall.

Lambin, Jean-Jacques (1993) 'Priorities in marketing management practice: implications for research and teaching', paper presented at 22nd Conference of the European Marketing Academy, ESADE, Barcelona, 25–28 May.

Lazer, William, and E.K. Kelly (1962) *Managerial Marketing: Perspectives and viewpoints*, Homewood, Ill.: Richard D. Irwin.

Levitt, Theodore (1960) 'Marketing Myopia', *Harvard Business Review*, 38, 24–47.

Levitt, Theodore (1972) 'Production line approach to services', *Harvard Business Review*, **50**, 5, 41–53.

Levitt, Theodore (1981) 'Marketing manageable products and product intangibles', *Harvard Business Review*, May–June, 94–102.

McCarthy, E. Jerome (1964) *Basic Marketing*, Homewood, Ill.: Richard D. Irwin.

McCarthy, E. Jerome, and William D. Perrault, Jr (1990) *Basic Marketing* (10th edn), Homewood, Ill.: Richard D. Irwin.

Miles, R., and Charles C. Snow (1978) *Organisational Strategy, Structure and Process*, New York: McGraw-Hill.

Mindak, W.A., and S. Fine (1981) 'A fifth "P": public relations', in J. Donnelly and J.R. George (eds), *Marketing of Services*, Chicago: American Marketing Association.

Oxenfeldt, Alfred R., and William L. Moore (1983) 'Customer or competitor: which guideline for marketing?', in Stewart Henderson Britt, Harper W. Boyd, Robert T. Davis and Jean Claude Larreche (eds.), *Marketing Management and Administrative Action*, New York: McGraw-Hill.

Porter, Michael E. (1980) *Competitive Strategy*, New York: The Free Press.

Porter, Michael E. (1985) *Competitive Advantage*, New York: The Free Press.

Shanklin, William L., and John K. Ryans, Jr (1984) 'Organizing for high-tech marketing', *Harvard Business Review*, **62**, 6, 64–71.

Shapiro, Benson P. (1977) 'Can marketing and manufacturing coexist?', *Harvard Business Review*, **55**, 5, 104–14.

Shostack, G. Lynn (1977) 'Breaking free from product marketing', Journal of Marketing, **41**, 2, 73–80.

Vizza, R.F., T.E. Chambers and E.J. Cook (1967) *Adaptation of the Marketing Concept: Fact or fiction*, New York: Sales Executive Club of New York, Inc.

Webster, Frederick E. Jr (1984) *Industrial Marketing Strategy* (2nd edn), New York: John Wiley.

Webster, Frederick E. Jr (1992) 'The changing role of marketing in the corporation', *Journal of Marketing*, **56**, 4, 1–17.

Analytical methods in marketing

3

Introduction

This chapter introduces and explains:

- the nature and significance of the more popular portfolio models used by companies;

- the use of portfolio models in classifying product markets;

- how to assess alternative business options facing the company;

- the significance of product and market portfolio analysis;

- the application of the product life cycle framework in the company;

- the stages in the product life cycle;

- the management implications of the product life cycle;

- the theory and experience of market segmentation;

- market segmentation in practice;

- the implications of segmentation for the marketing mix;

- using market segmentation to select markets;

- segmenting consumer and industrial markets; and

- applications of analytical methods in market positioning.

The chapter presents a broad overview of portfolio and life cycle models which are frequently encountered in the analysis of business problems, and which can be applied to marketing management problems. Analysis of the company and the market at this general level then allows a more detailed analysis of the company's products and services as they move through their life cycles. The varying marketing strategies required at each stage in the cycle are identified and related to other areas of the business. This is followed by a discussion of market segmentation and how various segmentation techniques can be applied to select target markets. The process of market segmentation is related to the way that the company positions itself relative to customer needs and competitve offers.

Having studied this chapter, you should be able to do the following:

1. Apply portfolio business models to an analysis of markets and competitors.

2. Specify the implications of the product life cycle for elements of the marketing mix.

3. Identify the appropriate marketing response for each stage of the life cycle.

4. Determine the value of market segmentation for different circumstances.

5. Design an approach to segmenting consumer and industrial markets.

6. Link market portfolio analysis with product life cycle analysis and market segmentation to provide guidelines for market positioning.

Need for analytical methods in marketing

Marketing management is concerned with positioning the company and its products and services in the market and in the minds of customers, in such a way that they will form an awareness of the value provided by the company or interest in it, and a preference for it over competitive offers. This means that the company must approach the market in an analytical fashion. To achieve the appropriate position in the market, the company must analyze and understand the customers it wishes to serve, its own internal resources and capabilities, and the strengths and weaknesses of competitors (Figure 3.1). An understanding of competitors, customers and itself allows the company to select an appropriate position in the market. The market positioning decision has implications for the company's marketing strategy.

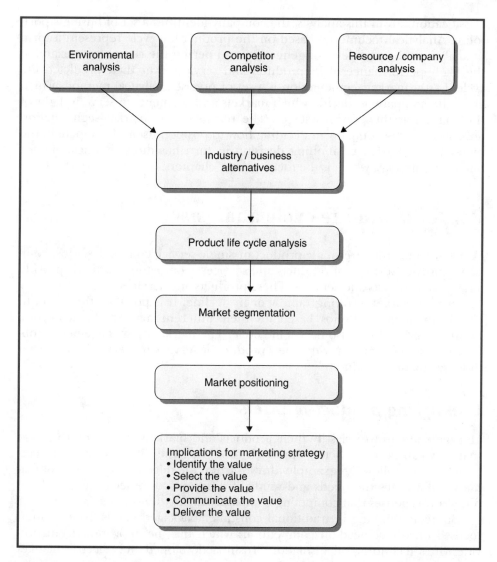

Figure 3.1 Deciding how to compete: the need for analytical methods in marketing

There are many analytical methods which assist the company in the process of understanding and serving customers. From the point of view of marketing management, it is useful to consider these methods as forming a hierarchy which includes methods that allow a very general form of analysis and very specific techniques that are applied at customer level.

Three groups of analytical techniques are discussed in this chapter. The first, analysis of industry and business alternatives, is an approach which allows the company to classify market opportunities and threats in a broad general

99

classification. From this analysis, the company identifies a set of business port-folios. Analytical techniques based on the product life cycle represent a form of analysis at the next level of generality, and permit the company to examine the likely performance of its products and services over their predicted life cycle. Lastly, market segmentation is a set of precise analytical methods which allow the company to decide which markets and segments to serve in light of the analysis at the previous stages. The results of the market segmentation analysis assist the company in deciding how to position itself to compete in the market. The market positioning decision in turn has direct implications for marketing strategy, which is the focus of later chapters.

Portfolio and life cycle analysis

Very few companies are single-product or single-service companies. Most com-panies provide a range of products and services. Competitors similarly provide a range of products and services. These products and services may be relatively new in the market, growing rapidly or in decline. It is possible, therefore, to classify them in portfolios based on their inherent market characteristics. Products and services also have a life cycle. The marketing management prob-lems facing the company with a new product or service are very different from those for mature products.

Classifying product-markets

Managers attempt to classify their products and markets in different ways so that they can design a better approach to serving the different needs of cus-tomers. The following example drawn from the electric blanket product-market illustrates the needs and wants of different customer groups and the different responses that competing companies make to those needs.

Strategic thinking in traditional consumer packaged goods firms is often focused on direct head-on competition, which may be appropriate but pro-vides little technological insulation. Toshiba developed the 'electric blanket underneath' concept to beat the 'blanket on top' products. In the late 1980s Sunbeam challenged this form of the product. Sunbeam claimed, 'You know how it feels – your feet are freezing but the rest of you is fine, then in summer you are simply too hot.'

The 'Body Responsive System' from Sunbeam recognized variations in temperature along the body and produced more heat where and when needed! Sunbeam also had a number of added features: different warmth levels, dual controls for double beds, freedom to leave the blanket on all night, safety in washing, use as a lighweight summer duvet, and ability to fit into a normal duvet cover.

100

In the above example, it is clear that very different product-markets are involved. Adding the piece of information that the price of the second product would be about fifteen or twenty times the price of the first product clearly illustrates the need to classify product-markets into managerially meaningful groups.

Using portfolio models

During the past twenty years, portfolio planning models have been very popular as support for strategic planning. They have been used as diagnostic aids and also as prescriptive guides in selecting strategic options for companies (Kotler, 1994). In general, portfolio models attempt to classify products on two dimensions: the attractiveness of markets, measured as market growth rate; and the ability of the product to compete within that market, measured as the company's relative market share.

Industry portfolio analysis

Portfolio analysis is one of the better-known techniques which companies use to analyze some of the issues outlined above. The first step in the analysis is to construct a portfolio of the company's businesses which graphically portrays the positions of the different businesses on factors such as growth rates, relative competitive position, competitive ability, stage of product-market evolution and overall attractiveness of the industry. It is also possible to analyze product-markets for any one business on the same principle. The two most common portfolio frameworks in current use are the Boston Consulting Group (BCG) growth–market share matrix (Boyd and Larreche, 1978) and the General Electric nine-cell business portfolio matrix.

Assessing business development alternatives

Because products have life cycles, they have a differential impact on company performance depending on whether they are new or growing or mature or coming to the end of their life. Using the product life cycle and portfolio frameworks ensures that the short-and long-term contributions of diverse products and businesses are balanced to achieve corporate goals. The strategies emerging from a product portfolio analysis emphasize a balance between cash flows, ensuring that there are products in the mature stage to supply cash to sustain the growth of needy products in earlier stages of the life cycle (Day, 1977). In this way, too, the firm is in a better position to allocate resources to the various products.

Portfolio frameworks also provide a uniform measurement system by which all the firm's product lines can be evaluated. It is possible to identify key issues and needs for individual products and for the firm as a whole. The product portfolio is a classification system which helps to estimate cash flows, decide investment opportunities and specify marketing strategies.

BCG growth–share matrix

In the Boston Consulting Group framework, products and markets are classified into four groups with products in each group shown as circles. The area of the circle represents the proportion of total company sales derived from a particular product. This gives a visual image of the company's existing product portfolio (Figure 3.2). The products in each cell of the matrix require different levels of investment, vary in regard to cash flows, have different growth potential and, hence, must be treated differently when preparing a marketing strategy. The four cells in the BCG growth–share matrix are referred to as cash cows, stars, question marks and dogs, depending on their position.

Cash cows are businesses or products with a relatively high market share in a low-growth market, which yield cash in excess of reinvestment needs to develop the product or business. These products or businesses generate the cash required for profits or a contribution to overheads or dividends. Cash cows support acquisitions and the necessary cash flow to invest in more recent product introductions, stars or question marks. In other words, companies use cash cow products to preserve market position while generating sufficient revenue to support newer ventures. The dilemma facing the firm is to know how much cash

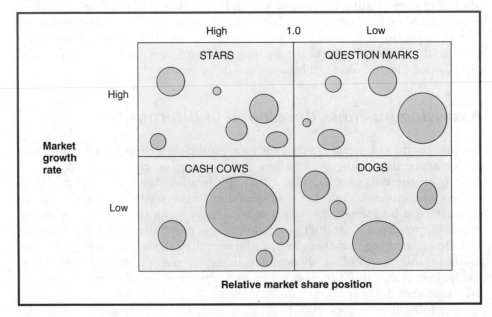

Figure 3.2   The BCG growth–share business portfolio matrix

102

to take from the cash cow to support other products, and how much to reinvest in the cash cows themselves to ensure their continued health. Many companies fail in this regard by bleeding cash cows to support questionable ventures.

Products with high shares of high-growth markets tend to be approximately self-sufficient in terms of cash flow. These products are referred to as stars and represent the best opportunities for future growth; they are attractive candidates for marketing investment. The usual marketing strategy for stars is to invest in them to maintain or build market share, so that as the market matures they become cash cows.

Cash cows were once stars: products in high-growth markets commanding high market shares. Star products offer the possibility of profit and growth. Because of their rapid growth and dominant share position, star products require large cash injections to expand manufacturing facilities and provide working capital. Stars approaching maturity generate large amounts of cash due to volume sales in high-growth markets. They are generally believed to generate as much cash as they require, and so are considered to be cash neutral. Star products still growing rapidly usually require substantial investment capital in addition to what they can produce themselves, in order to preserve their high growth and high market share.

Products with low shares in high-growth markets usually require more cash than they generate. Because of this negative cash flow, they are referred to as question marks. The usual marketing strategy for these products is to build market share by large investments of cash to ensure that they become stars and avoid falling behind the rest of the portfolio, or even becoming casualties.

Products classified as question marks experience rapid market growth, but their low share raises doubts as to whether they will ever be profitable. They require large amounts of cash to support their growth and development, but their ability to generate cash themselves is low due to their low market share and low scale economies.

It is agreed that the options for question mark products are to promote aggressive growth to obtain the benefits of a high-growth market, or divest if the costs of aggressive growth are greater than the potential returns.

Products with low shares in low-growth markets, referred to as dogs, have a bleak future. The cash flow associated with such products may be positive or negative depending on circumstances. The usual marketing strategy for dogs is to harvest them in a managed way if the cash flow is positive or to delete them rapidly if the cash flow is negative. A final decision would require detailed analysis of each situation.

The portfolio matrix recognizes that successful products follow a life cycle usually starting as question marks, becoming stars, then cash cows and finally dogs as they approach the end of their life cycle, each with different needs and opportunities (Figure 3.3). The life cycle of products is a dynamic concept that requires account to be taken of the various positions the product may hold at different stages in its life.

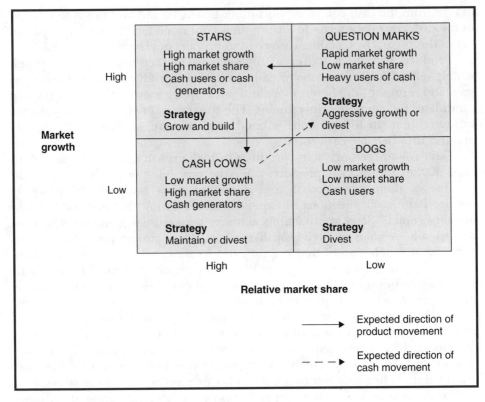

Figure 3.3 The BCG growth-share business portfolio

Evaluation of the BCG growth–share matrix

Assumptions underlying the BCG matrix have been challenged. Armstrong and Brodie (1994: 83) were unable to find a single empirical study that demonstrated that the BCG matrix was valuable as a decision aid. Indeed, they conclude that the BCG matrix interferes with profit maximizing. Wensley (1981) argues that there is little empirical evidence to support a causal relationship between market growth and profits, while Morrisson and Wensley (1991) provide a comprehensive review of previously published evaluative studies of the BCG matrix. Others have argued in its favour (Haspelagh, 1982) on the ground that the BCG matrix may lead managers to make decisions which are less irrational than those they would make without the structure provided by the BCG matrix. At a minimum, therefore, the BCG matrix provides a structure around which managers can analyze their businesses and product-markets to determine the most appropriate marketing strategy, but it must be used with care.

General Electric business portfolio matrix

The GE nine-cell business portfolio matrix has great managerial appeal and is based on assessing the company's competitive position in the market and matching it with the attractiveness of markets in the longer term. This requires a detailed analysis of the company, its products and the circumstances in the market served.

Competitive business position

A portfolio analysis of the company's products involves classifying them on two dimensions, one internal, the company's competitive position, and the other external, the attractiveness of markets. The competitive position of each business may be measured by determining the company's ability to match competitors on:

- cost;
- product quality;
- ability to compete on price;
- knowledge of customers and markets;
- technological capability;
- ability and skills of people; and
- the fit of these factors with requirements for success.

Internal factors relate to the capability of the firm or its overall competitive business position in regard to its products. The company's competitive position is influenced by its position in the market, its economic and technological position, and its resource capability. Market position is usually gauged by reference to the share of the market held by the product in question, the degree of product differentiation, the product mix, and the image the company and its products have in the market. The company's economic and technological position depends on its cost structure, the capacity in the company, and patents, trademarks and other secrets. Resource capability refers to management and marketing strengths, the company's power in the channel of distribution, and the company's relationship with workers and trade unions, government and other public bodies.

Attractiveness of markets

Many of the factors which influence the company's competitive position also influence the attractiveness of markets. Long-term product-market attractiveness is measured on the vertical axis and reflects:

- market size and growth;

- industry profitability;
- market structure and competitive intensity;
- scale economies;
- technology and capital requirements;
- cyclical and seasonal factors; and
- regulatory, environmental and social influences.

Market attractiveness derives from market, economic and technological, competitive and environmental factors. By market factors is meant the size, growth and customer bargaining power existing in the market. Economic and technological factors refer to the nature and intensity of investment in the industry, the technology used and the industry entry or exit barriers which may exist. Competitive factors include the structure of competition, the number and range of substitutes available, and the perceived product differentiation present. Environmental factors refer to a range of matters collectively subsumed under culture, social norms, and government and international regulations. Market attractiveness may be measured by obtaining a measure of the total size of the market, growth of sales volumes, and profitability. It is also necessary to obtain measures of long-term trends in the market and of any opportunity to segment the market.

Market investment opportunities

By classifying market investment opportunities in this way, the firm derives a three-way classification of opportunities (Figure 3.4). Those market opportunities which are highly attractive refer to circumstances where the market is very attractive and the firm's competitive position is strong. Those opportunities classified as unattractive refer to the situation where the market is unattractive and the firm's competitive position is weak. Companies are likely to prefer the former to the latter and invest accordingly.

Investment opportunities which are indifferent lie between the other two, being strong on one set of factors and weak on the other. In circumstances like these, advice to the firm would be to invest with care, since the risk is greater. Such investment should be treated opportunistically. If the market opportunities are good and the company does not have a competitive advantage in the product-market under consideration, it may be possible to obtain the required resources at relatively short notice to capitalize on the opportunities presented. Other circumstances, such as longer-term expectations, might shift such investment opportunities in one or other direction.

Most managers report that it is difficult if not impossible to develop and maintain a perfectly balanced portfolio. It is important to note, however, that some portfolios are viable while others are not. The portfolio of products

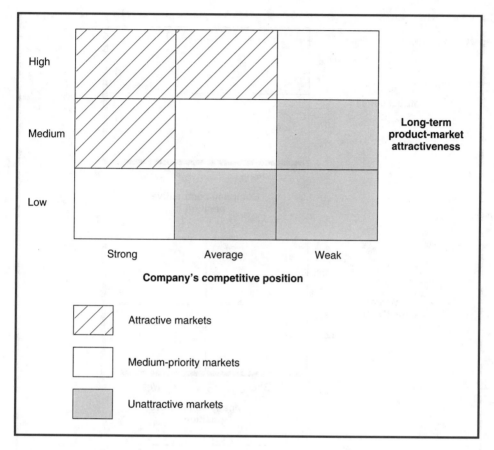

Figure 3.4 The GE business portfolio matrix

shown in Figure 3.5(a) is attractive provided that product A in the mature market continues to produce cash to support the doubtful products D, E and F. Rapidly changing and shorter life cycles, especially in high-technology businesses, could make the portfolio difficult to manage successfully. In contrast, lack of internal company resources would make it very difficult for any company to support the portfolio illustrated in Figure 3.5(b), while the portfolio shown in Figure 3.5(c) suggests an early exit from the market and the possible demise of the company or its acquisition by another.

Product and market portfolios

Rarely do businesses rely on one product or service. Generally, the company is concerned with managing a number of products or services. The problem for marketing managers is one of managing a portfolio. The portfolio concept is

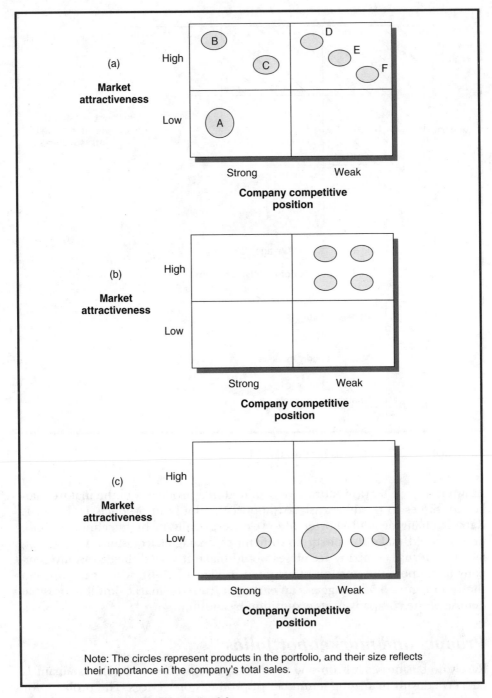

Note: The circles represent products in the portfolio, and their size reflects their importance in the company's total sales.

Figure 3.5   Viability of product portfolios

valuable, since it classifies products or services according to where they are on a life cycle and relative to competing products. In the product portfolio of most firms it is usually possible to find those products in which the firm should invest for the future, those in which it should maintain existing investment levels, and those in which investment should be limited or even withdrawn. By classifying the portfolio of products in this way, it is also easier to identify gaps in the firm's product line so that new ones might be developed and introduced.

The product portfolio for large diversified international companies can be very extensive, requiring considerable resources for its management. Product portfolios may contain a range of consumer and industrial branded and unbranded products sold through various types of channel in many markets. Such a portfolio would require a highly differentiated marketing strategy and a sophisticated approach to planning. CPC International, for example, is a very successful food company which operates over 110 plants in 40 countries with more than 60 per cent of its sales outside the USA, the home of its parent. European brands managed by CPC International include Knorr, Mazola and Hellman's. Profit performance in CPC International is dependent upon decentralized management, strong local brand identification and the use of indigenous ingredients to meet local tastes. Strategic marketing planning in an organization like CPC International is necessary for continued profitable growth.

Product life cycle

Discussions of the product life cycle are usually illustrated with an S-shaped or logistic curve, portraying the typical sales pattern for any product. The life cycle is usually divided into four convenient stages called introduction, or pioneering, growth, maturity and decline (Figure 3.6). The familiar product life cycle is based on the assumption that products have a finite life, which can be divided into sequential stages depending on changing market growth rates and changing competitive conditions.

Usually, the different stages are indicated where changes in the rates of sales growth or decline become pronounced. Even though specifying where each stage begins and ends is arbitrary, the product life cycle concept has attained a strong position in the marketing literature and in the conceptualization of marketing management problems. There have been many efforts to determine the validity of the theory. The sales behaviour of a variety of products has been analyzed and, while the evidence is not conclusive, the research that has been reported generally supports the life cycle concept and suggests that a bell-shaped curve is a reasonable model of the sale record for many types of product (Barksdale and Harris, 1982: 75). Time is the variable on the horizontal axis, but time is not the determinant of product sales. Time is a proxy variable for changes in product characteristics, competition, marketing

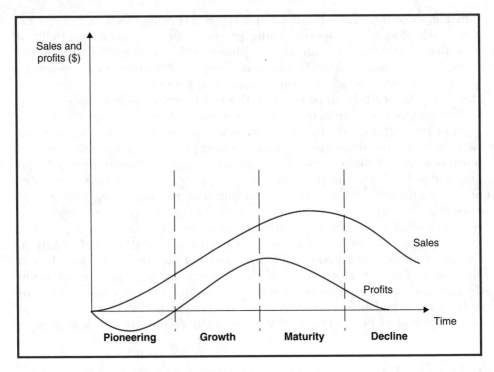

Figure 3.6   Product sales and profit life cycles
(Source: Adapted from Goulding, 1983)

strategies, environmental variables and market-related variables which occur over time (Meenaghan and O'Sullivan, 1986).

Definition of the product life cycle

The product life cycle reflects changing customer needs in a competitive marketing environment. It simultaneously recognizes the demand side and the supply side. The demand side is expressed through changing customer needs and preferences, while the supply side is represented by the activities of the company itself and its competitors. Companies recognize a latent need, and design and develop a product or service to respond to that expressed need. Initially, the innovator may be the exclusive supplier to a relatively small group of customers. With time, active marketing and competitive endeavour, the market expands and company sales increase. Then product sales begin to slow down and eventually enter a period of decline.

Like their biological counterparts, products and services are expected to move through a life cycle, which marks distinct stages in the sales history of the product or service. Each stage provides the company with opportunities and management tasks to perform. The life cycle, if not managed, becomes a self-fulfilling prophecy. Successful marketing companies attempt to move rapidly up the early part of the life cycle with the intention of staying in the maturity stage for as long as desired. These companies enter the decline stage only by design and not by default.

Stages in the product life cycle

Analysts of the product life cycle generally divide it into four distinct stages – the pioneering or introductory stage, the growth stage, the maturity stage and the decline stage – each with different characteristics. Sales of recorded music albums appear to follow a life cycle and the amounts at stake are considerable (Exhibit 3.1).

Pioneering stage of life cycle

New products, product versions or brands in the pioneering stage of the life cycle are unique and face a competitive situation which is quite different from that faced by them later in the life cycle. During this stage, new product forms or new product classes are introduced and developed. As such products are new to the world and usually do not have any direct competition when they first appear, following Barksdale and Harris (1982), this stage of the life cycle is referred to here as the pioneering stage rather than the introduction stage, which is the term used in most introductory marketing textbooks.

During the pioneering stage, the company expects sales to grow slowly, profits to be very low or non-existent, and cash flow to be negative. This is a high-cost period in the development of the product-market, since investment is needed to develop the market. The company concentrates on relatively

---

EXHIBIT 3.1   Life cycles of recorded music

Old fashioned vinyl records are playing their last waltz. Last year a total of 86 million long-playing records (LPs) were sold in Europe, America and Japan, down from 769 million in 1980. By 1995, according to a forecast by BIS Strategic Decisions, a firm of consultants, a mere 13.5 million will be sold, worth $171 million. Compact discs (CDs) have stolen the LP's song. After a shaky launch in 1983, CD sales soared to a new high of 900 million units last year. In 1995, BIS reckons, 1.3 billion CDs will be sold in Europe, America and Japan – a staggering $18.6 billion-worth of recorded music. Pre-recorded cassette-tape sales are also starting to reel in the wake of the CD. Between 1991 and 1995 annual sales of cassettes look set to fall by more than half, to 293 million units.

Source: *The Economist*, 26 September 1992: 119.

111

high-priced, undifferentiated products sold through few outlets with a marketing communications mix that concentrates on creating awareness. Customers and intermediaries must be informed of the product's existence and of any unique features it possesses.

Several causes of slow growth during the pioneering stage have been identified: delays in achieving adequate distribution, the novelty and risk associated with the new product, and customer reluctance to change existing buying patterns. The rate of growth during the pioneering stage depends on market conditions, company marketing strategy and the resources allocated to the endeavour.

If customers dislike or reject the product in the pioneering stage, word-of-mouth communication is negative and repeat sales are unlikely to develop. Achieving product trial is a central objective at this stage. Early sales success often depends on how well the company develops innovative ways to facilitate trial at low financial and psychological risk to customers.

During the pioneering stage, net cash outflows are normal, but the financial requirement for adequate working capital may be substantial. Market investment funds are required to attract distributors and other intermediaries to build up inventory. Promotional expenditures are usually at their highest ratio to sales because of the need for a high level of effort to inform potential customers of the new but unknown product, to encourage trial and to secure adequate distribution to reach customers.

At the pioneering stage there are only a few competitors who produce basic versions of the product, since the market is not yet ready for refinements or extensions to the product. Usually companies focus on innovative segments of the market, those who are most likely to make an immediate purchase and who are less price sensitive. Prices tend to be relatively high in real terms because unit costs are high. Furthermore, manufacturing problems may not have been fully resolved and high margins are required to support the heavy promotional expenditures required to achieve growth.

Growth stage of life cycle

It is difficult to state exactly when a product moves from the pioneering stage to the growth stage. Generally speaking, the company knows when it has entered the growth stage. The most telling phenomenon is the rapid growth in sales. Purchase patterns and distribution channels tend to change rapidly, and market share can be increased relatively quickly and at low cost by focusing on incremental sales, especially among new users instead of existing users. During this stage, the new product begins to experience competition for the first time as other firms move into the market.

For consumer products, repeat orders begin and the less innovative consuming majority begin to show interest in the product. Strong market growth attracts new competitors into the market. These competitors are product imitators who are attracted by the opportunities for large-scale production and profit. Their objective is to participate in the market growth with cheaper or differentiated versions of the innovator's product. They also introduce new product features.

The marketing activity of imitators and the new product features they include give credibility to the innovator's product and further expand the market. The competitive pressure may not be an issue at this stage because growth is so strong and customers seek the relatively new products. As the market expands there may be temporary room for many competitors, each producing a product version customized to particular market segments. The increased number of competitors leads to an increase in the number of distribution outlets, and industry sales increase rapidly to fill distributor channels.

Real prices tend to fall in the growth stage. Companies tend to hold nominal prices fixed and seek the benefit of falling unit costs which arise with increased production and sales. In some product-markets, the lower real price is combined with an improved product in intensive distribution to create brand preference. Brand preference established by an innovator in the growth stage is difficult to dislodge. Promotional expenditures tend to remain the same or increase as companies continue to educate the market and meet new competition. Sales increase much faster, however, causing a rapid decline in the promotion to sales ratio. Profits also tend to increase in the growth stage as promotion costs are spread over a much greater volume, and as unit manufacturing costs fall faster than prices.

During the growth stage, companies usually continue to improve the product and to innovate in order to remain ahead of imitators. Without continued investment, imitators may reach the stage of product parity among customers, leaving the innovator with no competitive advantage. Inadequate attention to continued product and market development in the growth stage may shorten the life cycle and dissipate any leadership position obtained.

With a slowdown in growth, the battle for market share and survival tends to precipitate a shake-out among competitors, leaving only the stronger to share a relatively large and stable market. A shake-out in the growth stage of the life cycle indicates the failure or disappearance of a significant number of marginal competitors as a result of the intense competition that seems to occur when sales growth slows as the market approaches maturity (Lambkin, 1993: 1). Smaller companies are the most likely victims of shake-out, since they are the ones most likely to resort to self-destructive price competition.

Maturity stage of life cycle

There comes a point when the rate of sales growth slows down to the equivalent of the general rate of growth in economic activity in the market. At this point, it is said that the product has entered the stage of maturity. The mature stage of the life cycle is of very great importance to the company. Most companies have more of their products in this stage than in other stages.

The mature stage of a market normally lasts longer than the previous stages, but it still poses formidable challenges to the company. The ideal product life cycle shows a short initial period of development, involving losses, followed by a short period of rapid introduction and growth, leading to a relatively long tranquil period of positive cash flow, sales and profits (Figure 3.7). Ideally, the company wishes to have its product in a leadership or strong competitive position in the chosen market segments by this stage. Marketing strategies in the maturity stage revolve around deepening the company's position in the market and extending the maturity stage for as long as possible.

During maturity, purchasing patterns and distribution channels stabilize, as a result of which a substantial increase in share by one company at the expense of another will be strongly resisted. Share gains during the mature stage of the life cycle are time consuming and expensive. Sales growth declines and profits begin to wane, though cash flow is at its strongest. Unit marketing costs are at their lowest. The marketing objective is to manage low-priced, differentiated products in intensive distribution for long-term brand loyalty.

Companies prolong the maturity stage by improving the product in various ways, by adapting it to new segments or uses, by developing line extensions to cater for new segments and changing customer needs, and sometimes by price decreases to attract the more price-sensitive segments of the market. In effect, the company may reposition its product to defend its market. The maturity stage of the life cycle is normally associated with strong cash flows which provide funds for further new products and profits.

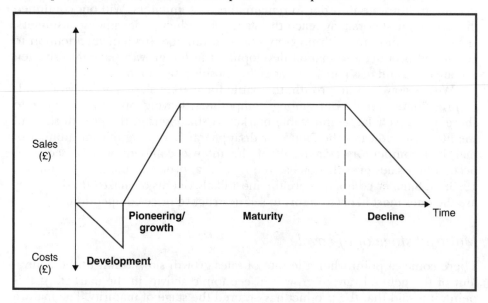

Figure 3.7 The ideal product life cycle
(Source: Adapted from Goldman and Muller, 1982; cited in Kotler, 1994: 353)

114

Decline stage of life cycle

Like living organisms, products reach the stage where they can no longer be maintained. The market loses interest in them, the company fails to up-grade and support them, or they are actually phased out deliberately in favour of new products at the pioneering stage. Whatever the reason, most products reach the decline stage and disappear from the market.

Sales decline for many reasons, most of which may be outside the manufacturer's control. Technological advances, shifts in consumer tastes and competitive activities are the principal reasons why companies discover they have too much capacity, suffer from increased price cutting and see their profits erode. For example, technological advances and competitive pressures, combined with a change in consumer behaviour, appear to have been responsible for the revolution in the recorded music business in the early 1990s (Exhibit 3.2). As sales and profits decline, some companies withdraw from the market.

EXHIBIT 3.2   Product innovation in the recorded music business

When the record companies introduced CDs in 1983, they did so in the nick of time. In most big markets, sales per head of full-length recordings had already been in decline for several years. Sales in America and West Germany had peaked in 1987 and in Britain in 1975. (By 1979 singles were also falling in all three countries; they never recovered.) It is not true that CDs killed vinyl records. They were dying anyway, and cassettes were not making up the losses.

Compact disks were typically more than twice as expensive as vinyl or cassette albums in the early 1980s, but they caught on fast. In the first five years nearly one billion were sold. And by 1988, five years after the CD's introduction, people in rich countries were buying more music than ever before.

Such salvation through technology, is nothing new. Every time a successful new format offers better or more convenient reproduction, people have flocked to buy some of their favourite music all over again. In 1992 the music business may come to regret its premature slogan for CDs, 'perfect music forever'. It will be trying to convince people that they ought to have two other new toys as well – Sony's Minidisc and Philip's digital compact cassette (DCC). One day the CD, too, will decline, as cassettes are already starting to do. The record companies expect this to start around 1995. What then? Rather a lot. In the past, the record business has merely switched from selling one sort of physical package to selling a new one. There is more of this to come: DCC, which is due to be launched next spring, will almost certainly eat into the markets for both conventional cassettes and CDs. And poorer countries still have plenty of catching up to do with the old formats.

Source: 'The Music Business', a supplement in *The Economist*, 21 December 1991: 4.

Mismanagement of the decline stage, especially if it involves too much investment in the product to retain it artificially beyond its profitable life, can result in a serious financial trap for the business and change the company's reputation among customers.

The sales decline may be slow, rapid or lingering. Careful management of the process in the decline stage usually involves the reduction of product models, the reduction of product variations and options, and the maintenance of reasonable margins. Companies may also withdraw from smaller market segments and weaker channels. In the decline stage, companies stress low costs and production and marketing efficiency. Prices may even be raised for restricted product versions in selective distribution. Reinforcement advertising is stressed. Such a combination usually produces adequate cash flows for the company to invest in new products. Since 1980 it may be said that the sales of long-playing records have reached the decline stage of the life cycle, while cassettes have more recently shown symptoms of decline (Figure 3.8). In contrast, compact disc sales have been growing and are expected to continue growing.

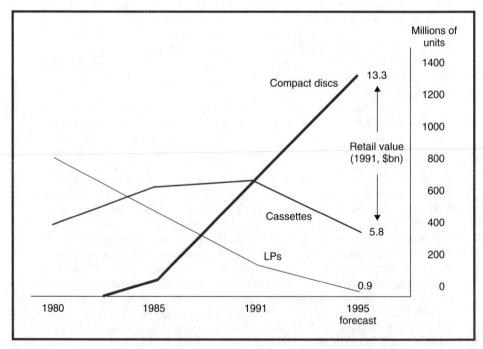

Figure 3.8 Sales of recorded music albums in Europe, USA and Japan

(Source: *The Economist*, 26 September 1992: 119. Copyright, *The Economist*, London 1994)

Management implications of product life cycle

The implications of the product life cycle are that products have a limited life expectancy, profits follow an unpredictable path, and life cycles differ for different products. The product life cycle for a product class, like confectionery, is different from that for a product form, like chocolate confectionery, and each is different for confectionery brands. Hence, the company must develop different marketing strategies which are appopriate for different stages of the life cycle, and it must also take account of the extent of brand development involved.

Normally it is good management practice to prevent the life cycle taking its full course in the manner predicted. Companies usually attempt to reach the maturity stage very quickly and remain there for a long time. The K-Swiss Inc. athletic shoe company in California is a good example of a company which was successful in remaining for a long time in the maturity stage based on a very simple product attribute (Exhibit 3.3).

Product life cycle and marketing planning

While there is much debate about whether the product life cycle is a general theory or applies only in special circumstances, it does provide the company with an insightful framework for considering the growth and development of a new product, the company itself or an entire industry. The product life cycle is used primarily in planning the company's marketing strategy, but it also affects other areas of the business, including manufacturing, finance and human resources, because of the differential demands it places on them. For example, different patterns of life cycle have a different effect on manufacturing requirements in terms of volume, variety and the dominant form of competition. Decisions regarding product customization, sales of each version and time to replacement are affected.

The stage of the life cycle affects product design, the combination of product attributes used, and the commonality of components. In the early stages, greater emphasis is placed on uniqueness and differentiation. The maturation of a market tends to lead to fewer competitors and greater price competition among survivors. In this context, it is important to ensure that marketing effort is of the correct form for each stage of the cycle. During the pioneering stage, advertising themes are likely to emphasize educational aspects which would be wasteful in the mature stage.

The life cycle concept assists the company in making financial forecasts for different stages. In the mature stage, for example, sales revenue is unlikely to increase unless price is increased. Many writers have analyzed the various predictions and suggestions for marketing strategy which emanate from a study of the life cycle. These have been elegantly classified by Porter (1980) and are summarized here (Table 3.1).

EXHIBIT 3.3   The shoe as hero

When it comes to staking a claim in the volatile $4.8 billion athletic footwear market, K-Swiss Inc. is doing a little counterprogramming: no glitz, no glamour. No big-time razzle-dazzle psychedelic designs. Instead, Pacoima, Californian-based K-Swiss' basic product line is a plain, white leather athletic shoe. K-Swiss' target buyers are boys and men who wear button-down shirts and girls and women who wear classic-looking Ralph Lauren-style sportswear.

In a fad-driven market where K-Swiss' far bigger competitors – Nike, Reebok and LA Gear – are trying to outdo each other in creating trendy envy, the no-frills approach seems to be working. Between 1988 and 1989 revenues increased 72 per cent, from $40 million to $69 million. Meanwhile, profits rose from $2.7 million to $4.7 million. K-Swiss stock, recently $26 a share, or 28 times 1989 earnings, has gained 48 per cent since it went public in June at $17.50.

Compared with its big three rivals – which together account for 59 per cent of the athletic footwear market – K-Swiss' share is a tiny 1.6 per cent. But that's up a very respectable 60 per cent in the last year, while Nike, Reebok and LA Gear together gained 5 per cent. It hasn't been easy. In 1988 retailers snickered at K-Swiss' claim that its new Gstaad court shoe would have a product life-cycle of about five years, compared with the industry average of six months to a year. But many sceptics have been won over by results at the cash register and the fact that K-Swiss is fanatical about quality control: its one per cent return rate is among the lowest in the industry. The design of its Classic, a white leather tennis shoe with five subtle stripes, pretty much hasn't changed in 24 years and is the basis for the entire product line, over 20 items.

K-Swiss was founded in 1966 by Art and Ernest Brunner, former Swiss skiers and athletic equipment importers. For 20 years their primary product was the Classic, a design they discovered in Switzerland and perfected, using high-quality rubber and leather. They set up shop in low-rent Pacoima, about 25 miles north of Los Angeles. Sales grew steadily, to about $21 million by 1986. All this without marketing or advertising. The shoe basically sold itself.

In 1985 Stride Rite briefly considered buying K-Swiss. In 1986 when Jake Nichols, MD at Stride Rite, couldn't persuade his superiors to take the plunge, he resigned to buy K-Swiss himself – a deal he completed in January 1987. Almost immediately, he pushed the one-product company into new areas such as basketball, court, boating and alpine hiking shoes. Most styles are available in men's, women's, children's and infant lines.

Nichols sees great growth potential overseas, a joint venture in Japan already accounts for 16 per cent of K-Swiss sales. K-Swiss also markets its shoes in Taiwan, Hong Kong, Singapore, New Zealand, and Central and South America. 'There are few universally accepted things,' says Nichols 'One of those is Swiss quality.' Maybe, just maybe, your LA Gears and British Knights can keep riding the roller coasters of fashion. For sheer staying power, however, we'd be inclined to bet on K-Swiss.

Source: *Forbes*, 20 August 1990: 76–7.

TABLE 3.1 Predictions of product life cycle theories: strategy, competition and performance

Strategy, competition and performance	Stage of product life cycle			
	Pioneering	Growth	Maturity	Decline
Buyers and buyer behaviour	High incomes Buyer inertia Need persuasion	Wider group of buyers Accept uneven quality	Market saturation Repeat purchases Many brands	Sophisticated buyers
Products and product change	Basic designs Low quality Key role for product development	Product differentiation improved quality Reliability in complex products	Less differentiation High quality Less frequent product changes Standardization	Little product differentiation Indifferent quality
Distribution	Specialized channels	Competition for distribution access Mass channels	Distribution channels reduce lines High market logistic costs Mass channels	Speciality channels
Other marketing mix elements	Very high advertising/sales ratios Price skimming High marketing costs	Lower advertising/ sales ratio Key role for advertising and distribution in non-technical products	Market segmentation Product extensions Heavy advertising Lower advertising/ sales ratios	Low advertising/ sales ratio Low marketing effort
Competition	Few companies	Many companies Mergers and shake-outs	Price competition Private label brands	Market exists Fewer competitors
Risk	High risk	Sales growth compensates for risk	Risk is cyclical	
Margins and profits	High prices and margins Low profits	Highest profits Lower real prices	Falling prices Lower margins and profits Stability of market shares	Low prices and margins Price increase in late decline
Overall strategy	Seek market share Key functions are R & D and engineering	Possible changes in price/quality images Marketing is key function	Difficult to increase market share Cost competition is key Wrong time to change image	Cost control is key function

Source: Adapted from Porter (1980: 159–61). Reprinted by permission of The Free Press, a Division of Simon and Schuster

In summary, the product life cycle provides an analytical framework for thinking about how the product evolves through its life cycle, while identifying the kinds of market segment that are likely to materialize at different points in time. It also provides a guide to the most appropriate marketing strategies to implement for each situation.

Market segmentation

Market theory provides a number of guidelines which can help the company in its approach to segmenting markets. In addition, there is a wide range of practical experience that the company can draw upon when evaluating whether or how to segment markets. This assistance comes in the form of guidelines in identifying, defining and choosing market segments. Assistance is also available in regard to the process of market segmentation.

Market segmentation: theory and experience

Successful market segmentation comes from a combination of theory and experience. Usually, market segments are easily identified by managers who know the industry well. From the theoretical point of view there are a number of methods of market segmentation which traditionally have been accepted, but recently have been questioned.

Identifying market segments

To the experienced manager, market segments are easily identified using criteria common in the industry. Ways of identifying market segments tend to be based on buyer demographics and socioeconomics, the size of the purchase, the motivation for the purchase and the manner of the purchase. This last is particularly relevant in industrial markets, where tendering and other forms of doing business different from buying at list price are common. Some of these approaches may not be relevant to the circumstances facing the company. Indeed, a number of them may not be practical. The company must judge which approach is the most appropriate for its purpose.

Many companies question the relevance of the approaches just described and are prepared to challenge the traditional wisdom thereby expressed. Other ways of segmenting markets reflecting life cycles, family cycles and innovation cycles may be more appropriate. However, the problem with these is that, while they may be relevant, they are difficult to use because it is difficult to measure them. Companies seek approaches to segmentation which have a strong management orientation and are thus focused on management problems.

Customer and company benefits of segmentation

A market segment is a customer group whose expected reactions will be similar when faced with a given marketing mix. A segment seeks a unique set of benefits from the product or service purchased. In this sense, a person who orders a beer usually seeks a different set of product benefits from a person who orders a gin and tonic; however, both are in the market for beverages. An industrial buyer among original equipment manufacturers in the car industry seeks performance standards, delivery and price terms different from a buyer who serves the replacement market. Both may be in the car industry, but they seek different product benefits. Market segmentation means dividing the market into customer groups which might merit separate marketing mixes, reflecting different product benefits. Market segmentation is based on identifying buyer characteristics which are correlated with the probable purchase of the firm's products, services or ideas.

There are identifiable benefits for the firm in segmenting the market. These fall under four headings: evaluate, focus, identify and calibrate (Figure 3.9). The company, through market segmentation, may be able to evaluate opportunities in the market and determine competitor positions in order to develop customized strategies for identified segments. In consumer markets, segmentation carried to the extreme would mean preparing a separate marketing mix for every customer. This does not mean that the firm loses sight of the individual customer when segmenting a market. As Jan Carlson of SAS has pointed out, 'We should treat every customer as an individual.' Having developed appropriate strategies to reach the segments identified, the firm can also position itself in the market against its competitors to serve identified customer groups.

Market segmentation may also be used to identify and allocate resources. By dividing the market into segments, it is easier to identify the resources needed to serve the segments appropriately and to allocate these resources to each segment according to some management criteria.

From time to time the firm needs to make tactical changes to calibrate its marketing programmes. By working with segments, it is easier to fine tune the marketing mix to produce a tactical response in a particular segment or series of segments. Like most areas of management, such calibration of activities is a normal process in the running of a company.

During the 1980s the VF (Vanity Fair) Corporation in the USA, despite owning some well-known brands such as Wrangler, Lee jeans, Jantzen sports wear and Vanity Fair lingerie, at first failed to observe shifts occurring in consumer markets. The company responded to the situation by paying much more attention to fashion changes obtained from detailed market research, and by establishing better relations with retailers to give a more focused, consumer-driven emphasis to the company. Instead of selling its brands to all kinds of retailers, the VF Corporatioan began to target different brand names

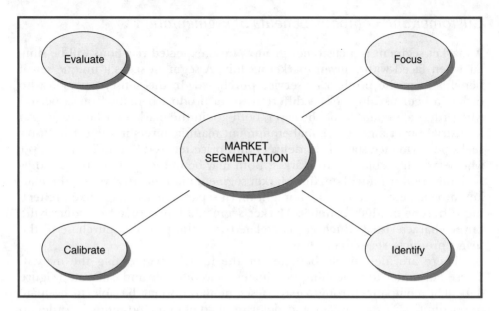

Figure 3.9   Objectives of market segmentation

precisely at specific retailers, in an endeavour to respond to the segmentation appearing in the market at retail level. Its jeans consumers could buy the more sophisticated Girbaud line in higher-priced department stores, while they entered mass marketing outlets to buy Lee jeans, Wrangler and Rustler. VF's lowest-priced jeans are now sold through discount stores. In lingerie VF's Eileen West line is aimed at more expensive department stores, while Vanity Fair is sold to mid-range shops and the Vassarette brand to discount stores.

Definition of market segmentation

Market segmentation means dividing the market into customer groups which might merit separate marketing mixes, reflecting different product benefits. Segmentation is based on identifying buyer characteristics which are related in some deterministic fashion to the likelihood that the company's products, services or ideas will be purchased. A market segment has been defined as 'a group of customers with some common characteristic relevant in explaining their response to a supplier's marketing stimuli' (Wind and Cardozo, 1974: 154). The company recognizes the role of segmentation when it begins to focus on customer needs and interests rather than on the physical dimensions of the product.

Marketing segmentation has been defined as: 'the act of identifying and profiling distinct groups of buyers who might require separate products and/ or marketing mixes' (Kotler, 1994: 265). This definition stresses the mechanics of segmentation and reflects a market research emphasis. An alternative definition treats market segmentation as the strategic marketing process of 'dividing a potential market into distinct sub-sets of consumers and selecting one or more segments as a market target to be reached with a distinct marketing mix' (Schiffman and Kanuk, 1994). A market segment is, therefore, a customer group, the expected reactions of which are similar to a given marketing mix. Buyers in a market segment seek a unique set of product benefits. As examples of market segments, note that purchasers of milk and purchasers of soft drinks are both in the market for beverages, but they seek different product benefits for different reasons.

Market segmentation in practice

Successful companies usually attempt to segment markets according to values desired by customers. Having done so, the company then evaluates opportunities in each segment to deliver a superior value to customers in the selected segments. These two steps allow the company to choose the value position in the market.

Identifying the benefits and the dimensions of price which are important to customers can be a difficult exercise and one which companies often neglect or address superficially, insisting that their customers seek quality, value for money, durability or service, whereas the values sought are much more latent, subtle and complicated. Vague general statements about benefits sought provide little support in deciding appropriate marketing strategies. Sometimes it is a question of attempting to decide what customers will want in the future.

Regarding price, it is important to distinguish between purchase price and the lifetime cost of the product or service to the customer. Different customer groups respond differently to price changes, so it is important to determine price sensitivities.

'The Holy Grail of Marketing' is how Josh McQueen, research director at Leo Burnett Advertising in Chicago, described the link between what advertisers already know about consumers – their age, sex and income – and what they so desperately want to know, namely their buying habits (*The Economist*, 26 September 1992: 76). According to research at Leo Burnett, consumers fall into four different behavioural groups:

- long loyals;
- rotators;
- deal sensitives; and
- price sensitives.

'Long loyals' are committed to one brand regardless of competitive prices. 'Rotators' switch regularly among a small number of favourite brands and are not very price sensitive but seek variety. The third group are similar, but are referred to as 'deal sensitive' because they switch among a small set of brands, almost always buying the brand which is on special offer. The final group are the 'price sensitives', who purchase whatever product is cheapest irrespective of brand.

A company whose brand already appeals to a large proportion of long loyals and rotators in a market will be cutting its own throat if it slashes prices low enough to appeal to price sensitives. Conversely, a brand bought mainly by deal and price sensitives might be wise to stop advertising on television and to shift spending into price-cutting promotions. (*The Economist*, 26 September 1992: 79).

Generic market segmentation

Three generic market segmentation strategies have been identified: an undifferentiated strategy; a differentiated strategy; and a concentrated strategy. Companies sometimes make no effort to segment the market. The company does not recognize that the market is capable of being segmented. A firm following an undifferentiated strategy gives no recognition to market segments, but rather focuses on what is common to all customers in the market. Products and services in such firms are designed and developed to suit the broadest possible customer appeals. The advantages of such a strategy are that it minimizes certain costs and helps to concentrate the attention of the competition in one or two areas of the market. This last point assumes that competitors will not attack across a broad front, but will select points where they are strong and the company is vulnerable.

In certain circumstances, it is inappropriate to attempt to segment the market (Young *et al.*, 1978). These authors identify three sets of circumstances when market segmentation is unlikely to provide any benefits:

- the market is so small that marketing to a portion of it is not profitable;

- heavy users constitute such a large proportion of sales volume that they are the only relevant target; and

- the brand is the dominant brand in the market.

In relation to the market size, in some product categories the frequency of usage is so low that the market can only sustain one of the brands. Because such a brand must appeal to all segments, decisions on product positioning, advertising, distribution and pricing must be based on an analysis of the entire market. When heavy users dominate the market for a product, conventional market segmentation is meaningless because most of the marketing effort will be directed at that group. If the heavy user group itself is large, however, other segmentation criteria may be applied. Lastly, when the brand is dominant, it draws its customers from all segments. In such circumstances, targeting a selection of segments may reduce instead of increasing sales.

An undifferentiated mass market strategy means addressing the entire market with the same marketing approach. Success depends on there being large numbers of customers with more or less common needs and a product with sufficient features and benefits to provide all of the required product benefits: for example, Coca-Cola produces nearly the same product for each market and promotes it in the same way.

When the company has decided the industry in which it plans to operate, it must decide the market segment to be served. It is usually recognized that few companies are able to serve all segments of the market. If companies ignore segmentation, customers tend to be too numerous, too widely scattered and too heterogeneous in their requirements to be treated as an integral whole. It is generally necessary, therefore, to segment most markets.

A differentiated strategy means operating in two or more segments using separate marketing strategies in each segment. A differentiated approach has the effect of enlarging the size of the total market, but costs are also increased. For example, Guinness sells several brands aimed at the beer market: Guinness Stout, Harp Lager, Smithwicks Ale and Guinness Kaliber, the non-alcoholic beer.

By following a concentrated (or niche) strategy, the company selects a single segment in the market which represents the best opportunity for the company to serve customers well, and builds a defensible competitive position against new entrants. An example of a company pursuing a concentrated strategy is Waterford Crystal. Companies following such a strategy often attempt to seek dominance through specialization. The key advantage of a concentrated strategy is that the company may be able to obtain specialization economies. The risks associated with such a strategy are usually greater.

Five important factors influence a company's segmentation strategy:

- company resources;
- type of product;
- stage in the life cycle;
- degree of homogeneity among buyers; and
- strategies followed by competitors.

Niche marketing

Niche marketing has become very popular in recent years. The business press frequently features articles referring to market niches. 'Niche marketing is all the rage these days, giving us everything from gourmet pet foods to organic bathroom tissue' (*Forbes*, 2 September 1991: 135). While market segments refer to large identifiable groups in the market, such as deodorant buyers seeking personal freshness, a niche is a more narrowly defined group seeking a special combination of benefits, such as a deodorant which provides hygiene and self-esteem benefits for young teenagers. Niche markets are typified by specialist needs among small groups of customers served by few competitors.

Evian table water has discovered a small but growing niche for its non-carbonated spring water from the French Alps: people who desire purity and no additives in what they consume, and who want to be different by carrying it in their work-out or gym bags. Evian, part of the BSN Groupe in France, offers very practical attributes to its customers in this market niche: unbreakable plastic bottles, screw-on tops that can be resealed without leaking, and easy-to-handle sizes.

To be successful in a market niche, the company must understand the needs of its customers thoroughly. In such an event, customers are usually willing to be extremely loyal and pay a premium for the attention they receive. Many companies have recognized the value of niche marketing and have attempted to build up lasting relationships with customers in selected niches.

An example of a services company which has segmented its market very effectively, and targeted a niche in it, is 1st Business Bank in Los Angeles (*Forbes*, 1 April 1991: 70). This bank focuses on serving mid-size companies with annual sales between $3 million and $100 million. The larger banks frequently relegate such customers to junior loan officers with little decision-making authority, even though they have relatively high borrowing requirements at any one time.

Criteria for effective segmentation

The value of segmented markets increases if a number of conditions are present:

- the company possesses information on the relevant buyer characteristic;
- marketing efforts can be focused on the chosen segment; and
- segments are large, profitable and stable.

Many criteria for segmentation are useless, since they are not susceptible to measurement. For example, it is very difficult to measure the number of buyers of hand-held electric drills who are motivated primarily by considerations of economy or quality or hobby.

Second, for a segment to be useful, it is also necessary that marketing efforts can be effectively focused on the chosen segments. For example, it is important to reach innovators in the pioneering stage of the life cycle, but the available communications media may not be sufficiently discriminatory to be able to access such buyers successfully.

Third, marketing segmentation also implies that the segments chosen are large and profitable, and that these circumstances are not likely to change for a considerable period. To be effective, segments must be sufficiently stable and substantial for it to be worth while developing separate marketing mixes. Within limits, market segments are treated as separate markets and so similar evaluative criteria must be applied.

Market segmentation involves a trade-off: applying the various segmentation criteria which are available could result in too great a number of segments to manage. In such circumstances, the company attempts to aggregate customer dimensions into useful categories for the purpose of segmentation. Various analytical and quantitative techniques are available to assist the company in determining the optimum number of segments to derive a trade-off between comprehensiveness and practicality.

Market segmentation strategies

Deciding the appropriate segmentation strategy means considering the impact that dividing the market into segments will have on the marketing mix, and determining how the company can respond to the needs of the various segments while accounting for competition. It is necessary to develop a set of criteria to evaluate the segments identified, enabling the company to make the most appropriate choice of segmentation strategy.

Segmentation and the marketing mix

Segmentation is related to other aspects of marketing through the customer function served by a particular product and the technology involved. Different combinations of product technology can serve different market segments and different customer functions. For example, a bicycle can be produced in many forms based on different technologies, e.g. lighweight, aluminium-framed racing machines or heavy-duty, steel-framed conventional cycles. It can serve different customer functions, e.g. transportation or recreation and sport. The bicycle can be produced to serve many different customer segments, e.g. the high-income segment (A) or the student market (B). While there are many conceivable combinations on these three dimensions, the restricted set described here serves to demonstrate that some combinations are more likely to be successful than others (Figure 3.10).

Segmenting a market means grouping buyers who share characteristics of marketing significance so that the company attains a degree of homogeneity in the strategy it develops to serve the unique needs of each segment. The essential ingredient is that the company is in a position to develop different types of marketing programme to serve chosen market segments. Market segmentation is an analytical process which precedes the setting of objectives and

127

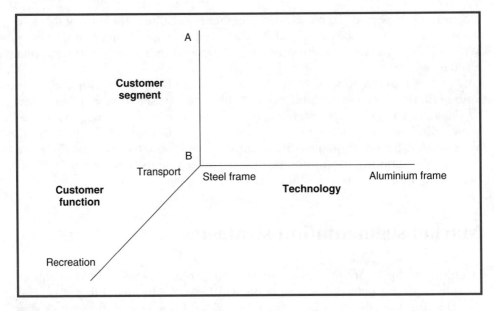

Figure 3.10 Relationship among segmentation, customer function and product technology in the market for bicycles

the formulation of strategy. By segmenting markets, the company can identify segments it can profitably serve and avoid segments for which its products and services are not suited.

A market segment is a group of customers whose needs and consumption patterns are very similar to each other, while being different in some significant way from other groups in the same general market.

Segmentation and the selection of markets

Very few firms have the resources or products to compete in all markets simultaneously, although many try to compete in too many markets. Customers are usually too numerous, too widely scattered geographically and too heterogeneous in their requirements for a single product to serve all demands.

Segmentation of markets is used by companies to achieve a better competitive positioning for existing brands. It may also be used to separate two or more brands of the same company to minimize cannibalization. Segmentation is sometimes used to identify gaps in the market which could provide new opportunities for the company, and it can serve to identify potential new buyers for existing products.

Process of market segmentation

There are many techniques which may be used in segmenting markets. Most depend on understanding underlying needs and wants, and quantifying the responses of different customer groups regarding the way in which desired benefits are related to price sensitivity.

Market segmentation variables

Identifying market segments is a two-stage process. First, it is necessary to decide who in the market might be interested in buying the company's product or services. For this the company will rely on macro segmentation variables. In consumer markets, such variables fall into the geographic and demographic categories. In industrial markets, product and organization variables serve this purpose (Figure 3.11).

In the second stage, it is necessary to determine the reasons why customers purchase. For this the company will rely on micro segmentation variables. In consumer markets, such variables fall into the psychographic and behavioural categories. In industrial markets, decision-making unit variables serve this purpose (Figure 3.11).

Segmentation on the basis of usage

Selection of the important segments may be discovered by studying several product dimensions:

- usage of the category;
- frequency of use – heavy, moderate and light users;
- brand use and brand share; and
- product attitudes.

Segmentation of markets on the basis of usage is very popular. Many markets can be segmented into non-users, previous users, potential users, first-time users and regular users of a product or service. Companies with high market share attempt to convert potential users into actual users, while smaller firms try to encourage users of competing brands to switch to their brand. Potential users and regular users require different marketing approaches.

Cultural and geographic market segmentation

One of the simpler management approaches to market segmentation is to treat different cultural and geographic regions or countries as different

MACRO SEGMENTATION VARIABLES	
Consumer Markets	**Industrial markets**
• *Geography:* country, region, administrative area, city, density, climate • *Demography:* age, family, sex, income, education, occupation, religion, nationality, language	• *Product:* industry, location, technology, user status, customer capability • *Organization:* company size, purchasing function, purchase policies, purchasing criteria, power relationships
MICRO SEGMENTATION VARIABLES	
Consumer Markets	**Industrial markets**
• *Psychographic:* social class, lifestyle, personality • *Behavioural:* occasions, benefits, user status, usage rate, loyalty, attitude to product	• *Decision-making unit:* specific application, size of order, urgency, buyer-seller convergence, attitude to risk, loyalty

Figure 3.11   Market segmentation variables
(Source: Adapted from Kotler, 1994; and Bonoma and Shapiro, 1983)

market segments. This approach is very common in large market areas like the USA or Europe. At a very general level, European markets may be treated as similar based on language, geographic proximity and level of development. This preliminary approach to segmentation has been suggested by Vandermerwe and L'Hullier (1989) who identify six market clusters for developed markets in Europe (Figure 3.12).

The value of this approach depends on the existence of regional disparities in tastes or usage, or some other important criterion. Usually there is a market variation in consumption patterns, but this is not always the case. In some markets, especially markets like the USA, mass media, transportation and multiple production locations have substantially eroded many of the differences based on geographic factors. Many differences still remain, however, and the emergence of local differences based on ethnic and cultural factors has again presented the possibility of successful geographic segmentation. In Europe, many geographic differences continue to exist in major markets. Differences in consumption behaviour among European markets present segmentation possibilities (Table 3.2).

130

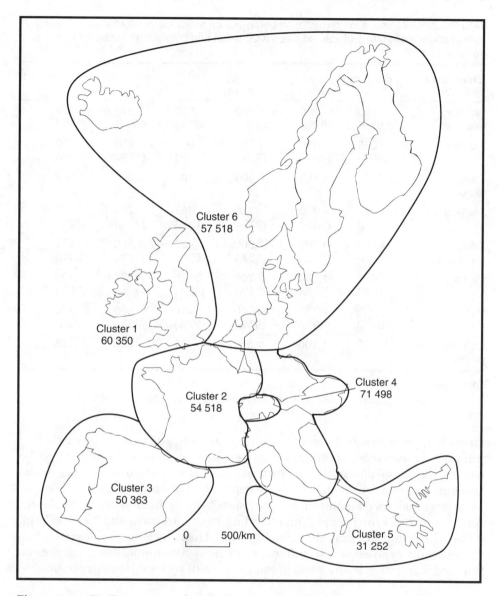

Figure 3.12 Six European market clusters (000 people, 1990)
(Source: Vandermerwe and L'Hullier, 1989. Copyright 1989 by the Foundation for the School of Business at Indiana University. Used with permission)

In esoteric societies, the existence of many social characteristics indigenous to each cultural group allows the group to function as a closed system (Tamilia, 1980: 224). In some developing countries, small island economies and regions within Europe, restricted personal and social mobility and iso-

131

TABLE 3.2   Differences in consumption behaviour on major expenditures in six Common Market countries in terms of volume sales (000 units) and percentage household ownership, 1989

Expenditure item	Belgium	France	Fed. Rep. Germany	UK	Italy	Netherlands
Washing machine	290 (86%)[1]	1,900 (87%)	1,720 (91%)*	1,910 (85%)	1,510 (95%)*	424 (93%)
Freezer	225 (61%)	1,450 (40%)	1,735 (62%)	900 (40%)	800 (51%)	360 (50%)
Colour television	370	4,100	4,400	4,100	2,600	642
Dishwasher	65 (30%)	750 (29%)	700 (37%)	487 (12%)	290 (25%)	97 (12%)
Food processor	1,050 (91%)	4,300 (83%)	2,500 (93%)	1,430 (80%)	1,580 (50%)	670 (84%)
Microwave	217 (12%)	1,600 (20%)	2,700 (24%)	2,360 (38%)	237 (3%)	190 (26%)
Vacuum cleaner	700 (91%)	2,750 (89%)	3,500 (97%)	3,410 (97%)	950 (43%)	400 (98%)
Compact disc player	60	1,100	1,570	475	385	125

[1] 1988 figures.

Source: *Consumer Europe* (Euromonitor Publications, GB), 1991.

lation help to maintain a closed cultural system. In such societies, marketing innovations and mass communications emanating from without tend to be treated with suspicion and fear. In traditional closed cultural systems, social sanctions operate for deviation from accepted behavioural norms.

In more advanced industrial societies, such as found in most of Europe, North America, parts of the Pacific Rim, including Japan, Australia and New Zealand, it is unusual to find isolated cultural groups. These societies reflect open cultural systems exposed to the influences of mass communications, transportation and marketing, leading to a greater degree of cultural homogenization.

Demographic, socioeconomic and family characteristics in segmentation

Demographic features are also used to segment markets. For some products, consumption is positively related to age. Clothing, holiday centres and confectionery snack products are examples; older customers tend to buy more than younger people. Product consumption can similarly be related to a person's sex. Men and women buy different products and have different needs. The family life cycle may also be relevant to the purchase of consumer durables. Family size can yield different consumption patterns, as may the level of education. Single men and women have very different purchasing patterns from older married people with young children. Families with older children spend more on education, food and clothing than families with no children or young children. Families with grown-up children and older people have still different needs and expenditure patterns.

Companies also segment markets by age groups, income, ethnic origin and lifestyle. Older people may be divided into age groups such as 50–64 years; 65–75; 75–84; and 85 and older. Many people in the 50–64 age group suddenly find themselves with surplus cash while still at the peak of their earning power. This group may no longer face heavy mortgage, education and other payments. People in the two middle groups have lower budgets, tend to travel extensively and favour grandchildren with attention and gifts. The oldest group spend a high proportion of their income on health care and similar products.

Socioeconomic variables are frequently used in market segmentation. Occupational and income factors are mostly used to determine a person's social class. Social class and income have been used extensively as segmentation variables as they are thought to influence consumer behaviour. Other factors, such as age, family composition, market information and advertising, may compound the direct relationship which may exist between purchasing behaviour and social class. A number of research studies have shown that social class is an important factor to consider. Using social class as a segmentation variable means classifying consumers into groups which manifest different buying behaviour (Figure 3.13).

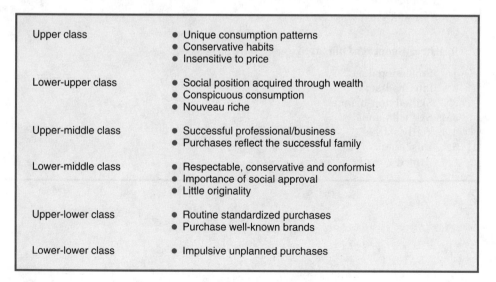

Figure 3.13 Classifying consumers into social classes

EXHIBIT 3.4   The multilayered British class system

The usual opening gambit at a New York dinner party is 'What do you do?' In Paris, it is 'What films have you seen lately?' And in London? There is no standard formula. What people want to know is where you live, what job you do, what school and university you went to – everything needed to place you in the class system. They try to tease out the answers without appearing to ask. After all, these things don't matter, do they?

John Major wants to turn Britain into a 'classless society'. He is up against a tradition bred in the bone of the British. They have an intuitive sense of class. Nuances of accent, dress and taste all serve as sorting mechanisms. Britain's unwritten class codes fascinate and bewilder foreigners. Until recently they rarely bewildered Britains. But more of those dinner-party questions are now needed to do the class placing.

The problem is that several hierarchies overlap. Feudal stratification lives on. The class of the past remains stronger in Britain than in most other countries, thanks to the monarchy, to the endurance of the landed gentry and to the private-school system which perpetuated upper-class apartheid.

Rival ways of dividing the British into class categories abound. These are some of the main ones:

Goldthorpe's Five

> Salariat (professional and managerial)
> Routine non-manual (office and sales)
> Petty bourgeois (self employed including farmers)
> Manual foremen and supervisors
> Working class

Registrar-General's Official Six

1.   Professional, etc.
2.   Intermediate
3N. Skilled non-manual
3M. Skilled manual
4.   Partly skilled
5.   Unskilled
6.   Armed Forces

Market Research Six

A.   Professional/senior managerial
B.   Middle managers/executives
C1. Junior managers/non-manual
C2. Skilled manual
D.   Semiskilled/unskilled manual
E.   Unemployed/state dependents

Lord Runciman's Seven

Upper class
Upper middle class
Middle middle class
Lower middle class
Skilled working class
Unskilled working class
Underclass

Erik Wright's Marxist 12

Bourgeoisie
Small employers
Petit bourgeoisie
Expert managers
Expert supervisors
Expert non-managers
Semi-credentialled managers
Semi-credentialled supervisors
Semi-credentialled workers
Uncredentialled managers
Uncredentialled supervisors
Proletarians

Source: *The Economist*, 5 September 1992: 34.

Classification has traditionally been determined by the world of work, but classifications based on occupation are beginning to lose their appeal because of the increasing complexity of occupations and the unrealistic assumption of such classifications that the head of household is a married male. Such assumptions give a great deal of offence to an increasing number of women, many of whom refuse to participate in studies based on these classifications. Moreover, although they are still used, it is difficult to decide which segmentation scheme based on class structure is the most appropriate (Exhibit 3.4).

Behavioural and psychographic segmentation

A person's interst in various products and services is influenced by lifestyle factors, and in many cases the products people use reflect their individual lifestyles. There is an increasing tendency among product and brand manufacturers to segment their markets based on consumer lifestyle or psychographic considerations.

Lifestyle segmentation methods classify people in different groups characterized by their opinions, activities and interests. It begins with people, their lifestyles and motivations, and then determines how various marketing factors fit into their living (Plummer, 1974: 37).

When the segments have been selected, it is necessary to describe the target customer in greater depth, with the focus on how best to reach customers and communicate more accurately with them. Understanding customer lifestyles allows the company more accurately to position, advertise and deliver its products and services.

Lifestyle has been used as the basis for segmentation in a number of studies. One such approach identifies three groups which are presumed to be homogeneous across different European markets (Martin, 1988: 57; Kossof, 1988: 43–4):

- Group 1: young people with homogeneous tastes in music, sport and culture

- Group 2: socialites and trend setters who value independence, are wealthy and well educated, and value exclusivity and reject stereotyping.

- Group 3: business people who travel abroad regularly, have a taste for luxury, and are rich and almost entirely male.

Psychographic segmentation is performed by dividing the market into sections according to lifestyles or personality factors. One way of doing this would be to survey respondents with statements like those used by Ziff (1971): 'If there is a 'flu going I'm sure to catch it' and 'Once you get a cold there is little you can do about it.' By analyzing respondents' identification with such statements, Ziff was able to distinguish four different market segments for cold remedies:

- realists;

- authority seekers;

- sceptics; and

- hypochondriacs.

The realists were not excessively concerned with protection, but neither were they fatalists. They viewed remedies positively and wanted a convenient solution which was non-prescription. The authority seekers were neither fatalists nor stoics regarding health matters, but had a strong preference for the stamp of authority on remedies. The approval of a doctor and a prescription was important for these people. The sceptics had a low health concern, were the least likely to resort to medication and did not believe in cold remedies. The hypochondriacs were very concerned with health matters and regarded themselves as prone to all germs and diseases. These people tended to take medication at the onset of the first symptom of a cold. For this group a mild authority assurance was required.

Benefit segmentation

People buy products for their perceived benefits, and different product attributes provide different customer benefits. The benefits demanded by customers vary by market segment. Companies attempt to provide differentiated products and services for different market segments, each with its own distinctive or unique customer benefit (Figure 3.14).

To illustrate the above points, assume that the Dental Equipment Company Limited, an imaginary company, has identified three major segments in the market for dental drills: public health dental practices, private paediatrician practices and private adult practices. Assume that the customers for dental drills, the dentists, seek four benefits: economy, compatibility with existing equipment, variable speed functions and accuracy. While other benefits will be sought, these are considered the more important (Table 3.3).

So far the market segments and customer benefits have been identified, but the importance of each benefit to each segment has yet to be determined. Assume that public health practices are more interested in economy and accuracy than compatibility and variable speed. Similarly, assume that in both the other segments economy is not so important, but compatibility is relatively more important as the drills must be combined with other expensive equipment. Assume that dentists pay greater attention to accuracy for adults in private practice and insist on high performance regarding variable speed in paediatric practices. It is clear from the table that model B closely corresponds to the customer benefit sought in the market segment served, whereas model A is deficient on price and model C is deficient on compatibility.

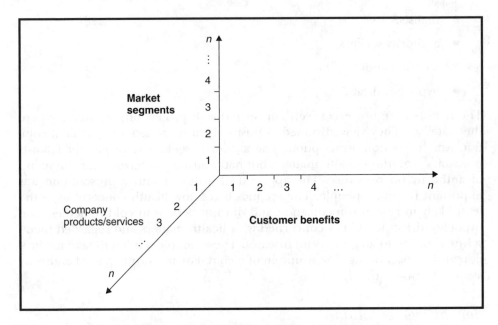

Figure 3.14 Benefit segmentation and product differentiation

By analyzing customer needs and wants in each market segment, and by determining the organization's capacity to serve these needs and wants, the manager is in a better position to decide which market segments should be selected for separate marketing mixes. This process is referred to as targeting markets to be served.

Benefit segmentation focuses on the benefits sought by customers and divides the segments accordingly. In a study of the US toothpaste market, Haley (1968) identified four benefit segments: the sensory segment, the sociables, the worriers and the independent segment (Table 3.4). In applying the

TABLE 3.3   Using customer benefits to segment the market

Customer benefits	Market segments		
	Public health clinics	Private paediatric practices	Private adult practices
Accuracy	4	5	3
Speed	4	5	4
Compatibility	3	4	2
Economy	1	4	3
	Model A	Model B	Model C
		Product range	

Note: 1–5 = degree of perceived fit between product and customer benefit sought: 5 = perfect fit; 1 = very poor fit.

138

research to this market, Haley was also able to identify various product-market characteristics of each of these segments and the brands favoured by each group.

Demographic and perhaps attitudinal descriptions of these groups could lead to distinctive advertising appeals, using different media in each case. The choice of medium would depend on determining the media exposure profiles for each segment: that is, the typical reading, listening and television viewing habits of the group. If the four groups used different publications for their reading, for example, an opportunity might exist for market segmentation.

The objectives of market segmentation may also be to compete with substitute products available in the market. Segmenting the market for competitive substitutability is a strategy frequently used by large companies with the resources to develop numerous brands aimed at different market segments. Bacardi launched five specific brands of rum, each aimed at a different segment of the market for alcoholic spirits:

- 'Silver Rum' to compete with vodka and gin;

- 'Amber Rum' to compete with American whiskey;

- 'Gold Reserve' to compete with brandies;

- '983' to compete with Scotch whiskey; and

- '151 Proof Rum' to compete in the mixed drinks and cooking segments.

TABLE 3.4   Benefit segmentation applied to the US toothpaste market

Product-market characteristics	Market segments			
	Sensory segment	*Sociables*	*Worriers*	*Independent segment*
Principal benefit sought	Flavour, product appearance	Brightness of teeth	Decay prevention	Price
Demographic strengths	Children	Teens, young people	Large families	Men
Special behaviour characteristics	Users of spearmint-flavoured toothpaste	Smokers	Heavy users	Heavy users
Personality characteristics	High self-involvement	High sociability	High hypochondriasis	High autonomy
Lifestyle characteristics	Hedonistic	Active	Conservative	Value oriented
Brands disproportionately flavoured	Colgate, Stripe	Macleans, Plus White, Ultra Brite	Crest	Brands on sale

Source: Haley (1968: 33). With the permission of the American Marketing Association

Using attitudes to segment the market

Attitudes towards a brand or towards the act of buying itself can also provide the basis for segmentation. Different attitudes among groups of customers may themselves be used as a means of discriminating among them. Regarding attitudes to the brand, it may be that different groups respond differently to many of the products' attributes. The attitude of department store buyers to various brands of women's tights available in the Dublin area appears to reflect the exclusivity of distribution and the perceived fashion and quality content of the brands (Figure 3.15).

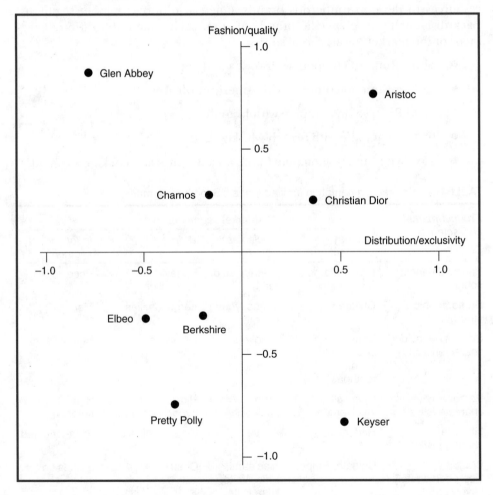

Figure 3.15   Market segments based on attitudes in the fashion industry
(Source: Bradley and Mealy, 1984)

In a study of the relation of cancer fear appeals and smoking, Quinn *et al.* (1992) discovered that a significantly higher level of fear was induced among younger people, women, and non-smokers, leading these authors to conclude that 'exposure to the health consequences of smoking may be an effective deterrent to smoking commencement ... especially when the message strategy and content are targeted according to the identified market segments' (1992: 365–6).

Segmenting industrial markets

Some writers have argued that segmentation approaches used in consumer markets can equally be applied in industrial markets (Wind, 1978: 318), while others state that the complexity found in industrial markets demands a different approach (Webster, 1978: 78). 'The choice of segmentation as a marketing strategy for industrial goods and services is predicated on the same assumptions and criteria as segmentation for consumer goods. The only differences, therefore, between consumer and industrial market segmentation involve the specific bases used for segmentation' (Wind and Cardozo, 1974: 154). In industrial markets, the benefits sought are derived from the benefits of the product in use. Industrial buyers need different products for different purposes. Product benefits are therefore relevant in segmenting industrial markets.

Product use and buying characteristics

Buyers in industrial markets usually refer to a set of purchasing criteria when evaluating competitive offers. These criteria are usually related to the product use and buying characteristics of buyers. It may be possible to use these criteria as a basis for segmenting the market. Criteria used in industrial buying include guaranteed product quality, preferred supply status, immediate and reliable delivery, technical support and price. Buyers might be classified into two segments:

- premium price, immediate delivery and high quality; and

- low price, slow delivery and acceptable quality.

Market segmentation is appropriate in industrial markets under three sets of circumstances (Johnson and Flodhammer, 1980: 203), when:

- products and services are heterogeneous;

- products are used in a variety of industries; and

- heterogeneous customers have different profitability requirements, buying structures and supplier requirements.

141

Identify society and customer values

In regard to the first point, some products and services are technologically complex and require highly technical sales, research and other support staff. Other products are less complex and less expensive, and can be sold on a more conventional basis, as might be found in consumer markets.

When industrial products are used in a variety of industries, it may be possible to segment the market to a greater extent than if only a few applications exist. Frequently, in industrial marketing, the same product or a slightly modified one has different uses which indicate the value of dividing the market into segments. For example, the same or slightly modified compressor can be used in road engineering works and on building sites, two very different market segments.

In regard to the third point, end users have different needs and expectations, which give rise to opportunities to segment the market.

Account size and importance of purchase

Account size may or may not be a useful way of segmenting industrial markets. Different buyers may use the product in different ways. Buyer perceptions of the product depend on the role and importance of the product in the company's overall purchases. The purchase of the same piece of equipment by a large organization and a small company will have a different impact. Consequently, account size and the importance of the purchase to the buyer may form the basis of an approach to segmenting industrial markets.

Structure of decision-making unit and segmentation

Many buying decisions in industrial markets are committee decisions taken by a decision-making unit within the buying organization. In other circumstances, the buying decisions are taken by one individual without the influence of others. The structure of the decision-making unit may provide a means of dividing the industrial market into segments, by identifying the patterns of influence in the purchasing process of particular decision influencers.

In some situations very few technical people are involved in the purchase, while in others most senior managers are involved. There are circumstances, too, when outside influencers such as consultants, advisers, government agencies and bankers influence the decision. Segmenting the market on the basis of the structure of the decision-making unit would seem, therefore, to be a fruitful approach to market segmentation in industrial markets.

Process of market positioning

Market positioning means understanding customer buying criteria and recognizing the performance of each competitor on each of the evaluative criteria identified. There are two aspects to positioning. The first deals with the customer and the second deals with competitors.

In positioning a product relative to customer needs and wants, concern rests with introducing products and services to fill identified gaps in the market, altering product and service positions already in the market, and altering buyer perceptions of the benefits sought. This means focusing on changing the importance that customers accord to the benefits, and identifying or emphasizing benefits previously not recognized.

To illustrate positioning strategy, assume that the beer market can be represented in two dimensions: sweet-bitter and strong-weak. The three aspects of positioning for customers are shown in Figure 3.16. In Figure 3.16(a) the firm introduces a new product X to fill an identified gap in the market. In Figure 3.16(b) the firm alters the product's position from being weak and sweet to being strong and sweet. Figure 3.16(c) illustrates the situation where the company attempts to change the evaluative criteria used by customers, from strong-weak to good value-poor value and from sweet-bitter to thirst quenching-nutritious.

Positioning strategy must also account for what competitors are doing. It is essential that the company knows who its current competitors are and who new entrants to the market might be. In Figure 3.16(a) the firm has identified a considerable number of competitors: A–P. The next step is to identify their position in the market, the benefits offered and the strategies followed. From the figure it is noted that the greatest number of competitors produce strong, sweet beer, five produce strong, bitter beer and only three produce weak beer which is also sweet. From this analysis the firm notes the principal competitive advantage and weakness of each competitor in each position. This helps to determine how each competing product is positioned relative to each other and relative to customer needs. Note from Figure 3.16(b) that the company intends moving from an area populated by two small segments to a relatively large market segment which seeks strong, sweet beer.

The process of positioning therefore involves two interrelated sets of activities (Figure 3.17). First, it requires the firm to analyze the market, to segment it and to select segments to serve. Second, it requires the firm to perform an analysis of competitors, to differentiate its products and services, and to select a package of customer benefits to promote. These two sets of activities converge to position the company's products, and this has implications for marketing strategy, including the marketing mix. In selecting the target markets to serve and the package of customer benefits to promote, the firm refers to an internal corporate resource analysis.

One of the components of James Maxmin's strategy in the early 1990s for Laura Ashley after he became its chief executive was to mix the company's floral patterns with trendy designs, a market positioning strategy aimed at younger customers and career women. But Laura Ashley had no interest in appealing to a vastly expanded customer base. According to Maxmin, 'Ninety

143

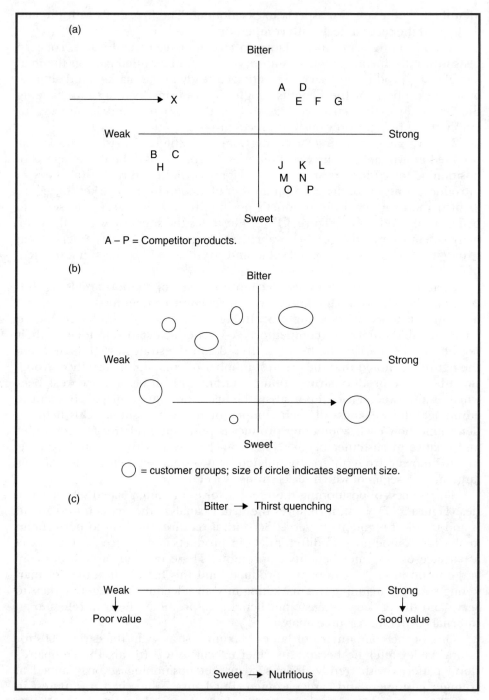

Figure 3.16 Product positioning customer preferences: hypothetical beer product

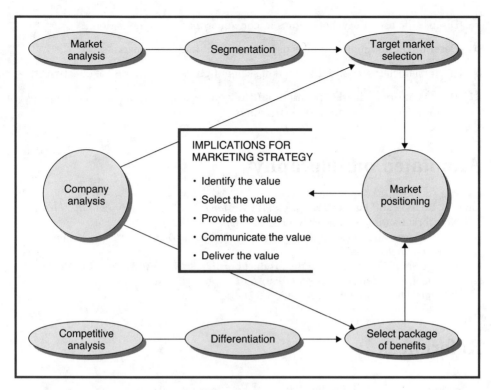

Figure 3.17 The process of positioning

per cent of shoppers are never going to like us – and that's our strength'
(*Business Week*, 23 December 1991: 67).

Assignment questions

1   Evaluate the use of portfolio models in marketing management.

2   Describe the characteristics of the product life cycle and discuss the implications of each stage for marketing.

3   How may the product life cycle be used as an aid in marketing planning?

4   Discuss the advantages that market segmentation has over mass or undifferentiated marketing.

5   Why do some firms segment their markets on a geographical basis? Give examples of product markets that you know are segmented in this way.

6   Describe the most common methods of demographic segmentation and give examples of products which are segmented in this way.

7 Discuss the use of psychographics in consumer market segmentation.

8 Describe the common variables used to segment industrial markets.

9 What characteristics should a market segment possess in order to be effective?

10 What is meant by market positioning? How does segmentation analysis and competitive analysis support positioning?

Annotated bibliography

Ames, B. Charles, and James D. Hlavacek (1984) *Managerial Marketing for Industrial Firms*, New York: Random House, chapter 5, 90–109.

Bonoma, Thomas, and Benson P. Shapiro (1983) *Segmenting Industrial Markets*, Lexington, Mass.: Lexington Books.

Day, George S. (1977) 'Diagnosing the product portfolio', *Journal of Marketing*, **41**, 2, 29–38.

Hutt, Michael, and Thomas W. Speh (1989) *Business Marketing Management* (3rd edn), Chicago: The Dryden Press, chapter 6, 171–94.

References

Armstrong, D. S., and R. J. Brodie (1994) 'Effects of portfolio planning methods on decision-making: experimental results', *International Journal of Research in Marketing*, **11**, 1, 73–84.

Barksdale, Hiram C., and Clyde E. Harris, Jr (1982) 'Portfolio analysis and the product life cycle', *Long Range Planning*, **15**, 6, 74–83.

Bonoma, Thomas K., and Benson P. Shapiro (1983) *Segmenting Industrial Markets*, Lexington, Mass.: Lexington Books.

Boyd, Harper W., and Jean-Claude Larreche (1978) 'The foundations of marketing strategy', in Gerald Zaltman and Tom Bonoma (eds.) *Review of Marketing*, Chicago: American Marketing Association.

Bradley, M. F., and J. A. Mealy (1984) 'Brand positioning in a consumer products market', *Journal of Irish Business and Administrative Research*, **6**, 1, 12–20.

Day, George S. (1977) 'Diagnosing the product portfolio', *Journal of Marketing*, **41**, April, 29–38.

Goldman, Arieh, and Muller, Eitan (1982) 'Measuring shape patterns of product life cycles: implications for marketing strategy', paper presented at the Jerusalem School of Business Administration, Hebrew University of Jerusalem, August, cited in Philip Kotler (1994) *Marketing Management: Analysis, planning, implementation and control* (8th edn), Englewood Cliffs, NJ: Prentice Hall.

Goulding, Ian (1983) 'New product development: a literature review', *European Journal of Marketing*, **17**, 3, 3–30.

Haley, Russell I. (1968) 'Benefit segmentation: a decision-oriented research tool', *Journal of Marketing*, **32**, 3, 30–5.

Haspelagh, P. (1982) 'Portfolio planning: uses and limits', *Harvard Business Review*, **60**, 1, 58–73.

Johnson, Hal G., and Åke Flodhammer (1980) 'Some factors in industrial market segmentation', *Industrial Marketing Management*, **9** July, 201–5.

Kossof, J. (1988) 'Europe: up for sale', *New Statesmen and Society*, **1**, 8, 43–44.

Kotler, Philip (1994) *Marketing Management: Analysis planning and control* (8th edn), Englewood Cliffs, NJ: Prentice Hall.

Lambkin, Mary (1993) 'Market shake-outs: a framework for research', Department of Marketing, University College Dublin.

Martin, J. (1988) 'Beyond 1992: lifestyle in key', *Advertising Age*, 11 July, 57.

Meenaghan, John A., and P.J.P. O'Sullivan (1986) 'The shape and length of the product life cycle', *Irish Marketing Review*, **1**, Spring 83–102

Morrisson, A., and R. Wensley (1991) 'Boxed up or boxed in? A short history of the Boston Consulting Group share/growth matrix', *Journal of Marketing Management*, **7**, 2, 105–29.

Plummer, Joseph T. (1974) 'The concept and application of lifestyle segmentation', *Journal of Marketing*, **38** 1, 33–7.

Porter, Michael E. (1980) *Competitive Strategy*, New York: The Free Press.

Quinn, Valerie, Tony Meenaghan and Teresa Brannick (1992) 'Fear appeals: segmentation is the way to go', *International Journal of Advertising*, **11**, 356–66.

Schiffman, Leon G., and Leslie Lazar Kanuk (1994) *Consumer Behaviour* (5th edn), Englewood Cliffs, NJ: Prentice Hall.

Tamilia, Robert D. (1980) 'Cultural market segmentation in a bilingual and bicultural setting', *European Journal of Marketing*, **14**, 4, 223–31.

Vandermerwe, Sandra, and M. L'Hullier (1989) 'Euro consumers in 1992', *Business Horizons*, January/February, 34–40.

Webster, Frederick E. Jr. (1978) 'Management science in industrial marketing', *Journal of Marketing*, **42** 1, 21–6.

Wensley, R. (1981) 'Strategic marketing: betas, boxes, or basics?', *Journal of Marketing*, **45**, 3, 173–82.

Wind, Yoram (1978) 'Issues and advances in segmentation research', *Journal of Marketing Research*, **15**, August, 317–37.

Wind, Yoram, and Richard Cardozo (1974) 'Industrial market segmentation', *Industrial Marketing Management*, **3**, 153–66.

Young, Shirley, Leland Ott and Barbara Feigin (1978) 'Some practical considerations in market segmentation', *Journal of Marketing Research*, **15**, August, 405–12.

Ziff, Ruth (1971) 'Psychographics for market segmentation', *Journal of Advertising Research*, **11**, 2, 3–9.

Understanding the marketing environment

4

Introduction

This chapter introduces and explains:

- the meaning of environmental uncertainty in marketing;

- the impact of the various elements of the macroeconomic environment on marketing;

- the economic impact of the European Union;

- the special position of new emerging markets;

- how companies cope with the marketing environment; and

- the response of companies to environmental change and market uncertainty.

It is important for companies to recognize the different levels of uncertainty in the marketing environment and how they can respond to them. This means understanding the environment and its various components. Each element has a direct impact on the welfare of the company. Demographic trends affect the size of the market, its location and the kind of goods and services required. The cultural environment also affects the kind of goods demanded and influences the elements of the marketing mix which can be employed. The political and legal environments affect business particularly in regard to

149

the participation of companies in foreign markets and in respect of the conditions under which marketing takes place. Changes in the economic environment affect marketing in regard to economic growth, interest rates and exchange rate movements. In particular, the deregulation of many markets opens possibilities to companies. Innovation and technological development introduce standards for competition and opportunities for wealth creation in the marketing of products and services. Concern for the physical environment creates many opportunities for marketing, while also raising the cost of producing and marketing goods and services. It is necessary for the company to audit the macro environment to ensure an appropriate response at the micro level. Environmental analysis allows the company to respond to change and to cope with marketing uncertainty.

Having studied this chapter, you should be able to do the following:

1. Define risk and uncertainty in marketing.

2. Determine the impact of change, complexity and diversity on marketing.

3. Relate the components of the macro environment to the behaviour of the company and consumers.

4. Recognize the impact of the new emerging markets in Europe and in the developing world.

5. Understand the stimulus to marketing provided by the deregulation of industries.

6. Specify how the company and consumer respond to environmental change and cope with market uncertainty.

Levels of uncertainty in the marketing environment

Companies make decisions regarding marketing and markets most days. It is easier to make decisions when managers know with certainty what the outcome of their decisions will be. Unfortunately, companies face considerable uncertainty when making decisions. Much of that uncertainty stems from the turbulent environment in which marketing occurs. This environment may be divided into the broad macro marketing environment at the level of governments, regional trade groups and transnational institutions, and the micro marketing environment which is closer to the company and of more immediate concern.

The marketing capability of the organization depends on its ability to cope with a number of external environments and its ability to manage its own internal environment (Möller and Anttila, 1987: 4). The external environment includes the macro environment, the industry environment and the task environment. The firm's macro environment consists of the general economic, social, legal, technological and cultural factors, and their influence on business and industry. The industry environment refers to demand and competition in an industry, the system of distributors and suppliers, and the network of relationships involving companies in several industries (Porter, 1980; Johanson and Mattson, 1985). Monitoring, analyzing and understanding the macro and industry environment is a key part of the firm's marketing capability, and according to Möller and Anttila (1987) includes an ability to understand:

- the complex influences affecting industry;

- how demand arises in an industry, the role of primary customers, derived demand and the value of marketing channels;

- the competitive dynamics of an industry, e.g. the role of strategic industry groups, price formation and changes, capacity and changing products and technology; and

- the importance of supplier markets, e.g. how the development of supplier markets influences competition.

Various approaches to environmental analysis may be found in practice. Each recognizes that the marketing environment consists of a constellation of demands and constraints to which the company must adjust in order to survive and grow.

Environmental uncertainty in marketing

The company must cope with uncertainty both at the micro level and at the macro level. Macro-level uncertainty means the uncertainty that arises among national and international institutions and political processes which are established in society to integrate the business system as a whole. At the micro level, change is usually incremental, and problems and conflicts are resolved by direct competitive and collaborative interaction among companies themselves. The firm can gain substantial competitive advantage by being able to identify issues early enough, realize their strategic significance and take specific actions to seize opportunities (Camillus and Datta, 1991).

When the environment becomes turbulent, however, interest centres on how best to stabilize it again. Uncertainty and turbulence in the competitive environment are a consequence of failure in the macro-level processes (Metcalfe, 1974). These processes would include unforeseen political events which shape a new economic context for an industry.

Meaning of environmental uncertainty

The marketing environment consists of the constellation of demands and constraints to which the company or organization must adjust in order to survive and grow (Figure 4.1). These demands and constraints are imposed directly and indirectly by customers and competitors. Suppliers and intermediaries like distributors and retailers, and agencies like banks and advertising agents, impose a different type of demand and constraint. A more pervasive long-term pressure arises from the wider environment, including the technological and scientific environment, the government, culture, ecology, legal and ethical factors, and the economy.

Most marketing textbooks define the marketing environment as consisting of external forces which directly or indirectly influence the company's acquisition of resources and the production of a range of outputs. Resources include

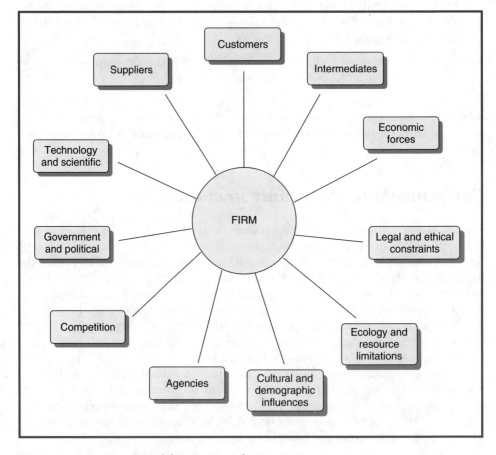

Figure 4.1 Components of the micro marketing environment

financial resources, raw materials, skills, people and information. The outputs include products, services and ideas packaged and advertised in some way.

Risk and uncertainty in marketing

Uncertainty relates to the company's confidence in expectations, while risk relates to the possible outcomes of action: that is, the loss which might arise if a given action is taken, such as entering a particular foreign market. Risk includes the probability of loss and the significance of what might be lost. As we are concerned with the effect of uncertainty on the behaviour of a company, we are dealing here with subjective or perceived uncertainty: that is, the manager's subjective estimates of the risk of loss in a particular venture. Uncertainty due to lack of information results in less confidence in judgements regarding the market.

One of the best ways of reducing perceived uncertainty about markets is to understand them and to obtain more information about the factors which are thought to affect them. A key task for the firm in an uncertain world is to obtain as much information as possible about likely outcomes. At the same time, there is no amount of information which can completely eliminate uncertainty.

The methods of dealing with risks and unavoidable uncertainty are usually part of the corporate culture of the firm, and reflect the psychological make-up of senior managers. The quality of management has a pronounced effect on the expansion of the firm. Quality of management includes a willingness to take risks; it also includes a willingness to search for ways of avoiding risk and still expand.

Companies are known to change their objectives as the economic environment changes. For many years, Japanese companies followed sales growth as their principal objective. When the environment changed to one where competition was rampant in many markets world-wide, Japanese companies began to produce new products in greater quantities than before. Sales continued to grow and so did profits. In more recent years, when growth has slowed, the environment again has forced Japanese companies to change. Sales growth in recession is difficult and, if it occurs, margins tend to be so small that profits are also very small.

The environment works in other ways too. Dominance by Japanese companies of any sector of the UK market is likely to bring with it a political backlash. The pressure on Japanese companies to ease off competitively is strong in these circumstances. Such pressure forced Toyota to drop its 'Global 10' promotional campaign among US car dealers. The objective of this campaign was to gain 10 per cent of the world car market (*Business Week*, 2 March 1992: 16).

Uncertainty and market information

Uncertainty about the environment is defined as the manager's perceived inability to predict accurately something about the company's external environment. The manager experiences uncertainty due to a lack to sufficient information on environmental factors relevant to the decision, ignorance about the consequences of the decision, and the decision maker's own lack of confidence about the forecasted consequences (Duncan, 1972). For Lawrence and Lorsch (1967) uncertainty arises due to a lack of clear information, the long wait for definitive feedback from the market, and a general uncertainty about causal relationships. Uncertainty also arises when the manager is unable to discriminate between relevant and irrelevant data (Gifford *et al.*, 1979).

Most writers on the subject accept that environmental uncertainty is a perceptual phenomenon, but there is much less unanimity regarding its nature. Uncertainty arises when there is difficulty in assigning probabilities regarding the likelihood of future events (Pfeffer and Salancik, 1978), or when there is a lack of information about cause-and-effect relationships or an inability to predict accurately what the results of a decision might be (Downey and Slocum, 1975).

Macro marketing environment

In the macro marketing environment, concern rests with uncontrollable change which occurs outside the company. This change affects the broad macroeconomic environment, including interest and exchange rates, growth in incomes, and levels of unemployment in the economy. Three dimensions of the macro marketing environment dominate the manager's concerns at this level: the rate of change in the environment, the complexity of the product technology in use and the extent of market diversity (Figure 4.2).

Change in the macro environment may be rapid or slow. The company is also concerned with the kind of product technology being used and changes occurring in it. Product technology in a particular industry may be relatively simple, as is the case in many basic and traditional industries, or it may be complex, as in electronics, fine chemicals and pharmaceuticals. The third dimension refers to the degree of homogeneity which exists in the market itself. In some markets, tastes and preferences are relatively homogeneous, while in others they are highly differentiated and diverse.

Market change, complexity and diversity

Macro marketing environments which are not complex have the advantage of fewer critical information requirements for decision making (Jurkovich, 1974: 382). The result is that in a homogeneous environment undifferentiated marketing strategies may succeed, whereas in a differentiated environment they are likely to fail.

The degree to which the components of the environment are interrelated is also of interest to the company. Industrial markets, especially those for large items of capital equipment, are more interrelated than typical consumer

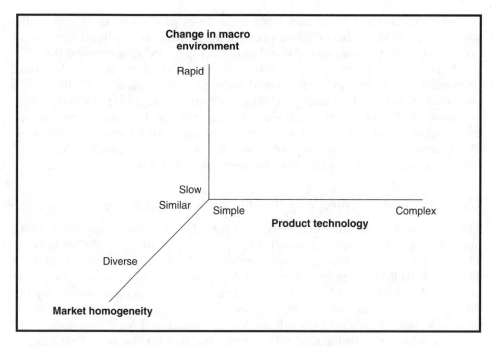

Figure 4.2 Dimensions of perceived environmental uncertainty

markets. With the integration of markets in Europe, however, the environment is becoming more interrelated even for consumer markets as a result of regulations on products, advertising, packaging and financial services. In such an interrelated environment, the company responds by integrating activities within the company through the use product and market managers.

The second dimension refers to product technology. The company may produce simple products using simple knowledge, or it may produce extremely advanced, complex products based on knowledge drawn from myriad scientific fields. Uncertainty regarding product technology means not knowing whether the company's products can meet customer needs once these needs have been identified.

The third dimension is concerned with market homogeneity. International markets may be similar in most respects to domestic markets. This may also be true for market segments within a country market. Differences in markets arise from a wide range of customers, extensive ranges of products and services, and numerous geographical locations. Uncertainty regarding the market arises when the company is unsure whether its products and services are able to satisfy customer needs. The greater the differences, the greater is the uncertainty, and hence the greater is the company's need to obtain information on many aspects of its markets. To cope with diversity, companies frequently segment the market into distinct parts.

155

When the firm is active in a large number of product-markets, especially when these markets reflect different economic, political and cultural structures, orderly and effective management within the company becomes more difficult.

As the environment becomes more complex and differentiated, the company must match the environment and become more complex and differentiated itself if it is to be effective (Weitz and Anderson, 1981). In effect, the company needs to decentralize the marketing effort and create internal structures that match the critical components in the markets: for example, divisions or departments for individual product-markets would have the effect of allowing the manager to deal with a now relatively homogeneous environment.

Uncontrollable elements of the marketing environment

The major task of the marketing manager is to design and control the marketing programme: that is, the product itself, promotion, pricing and distribution. This must be done within an environment much of which is uncontrollable. The uncontrollable elements are: the extent and rate of economic development in the market (e.g. selling dishwashers in a developing country may be difficult); social and cultural influences which prohibit or restrict product sales (e.g. selling alcohol in Saudi Arabia); political and legal decisions (e.g. the proportion of lean meat in pork pies or the ban on the sale of children's aspirin); business practices; and competitive policy (e.g. restrictions on price wars or below-cost selling).

When a firm begins to do business in foreign markets, an additional set of uncontrollables come into play. The new set of differences arise under the following headings:

- political and legal systems;

- economic trends and levels of development;

- physical features, geography and topography;

- distribution systems; and

- government-sponsored competition.

Elements of the macro marketing environment

The macro marketing environment consists of eight important dimensions, each of which affects the development of marketing and the growth of the company (Figure 4.3). Many of these components have recently taken on great significance in society. In the 1990s, for example, there has been a greater interest in the physical environment than before. Also there is a great amount of activity in the area of regulation and law, which impacts on the company. In recent years, economic factors such as exchange rates and interest rates have also been very significant influences on the behaviour of companies.

Regional market integration in Europe (European Union, EU), in South-East Asia (Association of South-East Asian Nations, ASEAN), and more recently in North America (North American Free Trade Association, NAFTA) demonstrate the commitment of countries to put aside political and other differences in favour of the competitive and economic advantages of manufacturing and selling in larger markets. Four economic superpowers, the EU, NAFTA, ASEAN and Japan, have replaced the old world economic order dominated by one superpower, the USA. These groupings are highly interdependent economically, and it is likely that dependence and co-operation will continue to be a feature of the macro marketing environment for years to come.

Economic growth in society

Within the broad economic framework in society, governments form or agree to industrial and trade policies which mean close collaboration between government and business. This collaboration to achieve society's economic objectives usually involves subsidies, tax incentives, regulations, trade protection, focused credit and certain forms of administrative guidance.

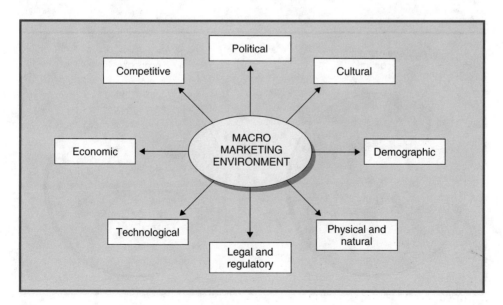

Figure 4.3   Elements of the macro marketing environment

Role of industrial policy

In many countries, the government actively seeks to promote an industrial policy which should provide an effective macroeconomic climate for society and business. In other countries, any such interference in the economic system is shunned. Directly or indirectly, through macroeconomic policies governments attempt to modernize their economies. In recent years, this has also meant liberalizing economies and opening them up to competition. It is recognized that it is necessary to equip people with new education and skills to compete in the future.

Some countries are in a better position to compete than others. Developing economies and less developed countries generally depend for their income on commodities and raw materials. Traditional industries, such as textiles, clothing and simple metal industries, are also quite important to these countries. High-technology industries are not so prevalent in developing countries (Figure 4.4).

In industrial market economies, commodities and traditional industries are less important. In these countries, high-technology industries assume a much greater importance. As countries industrialize, they attempt to move towards knowledge-based industries and products the demand for which is income elastic. Industrial policies are aimed at shifting the industrial base from low-knowledge income-inelastic commodity-markets to high-knowledge, income-elastic product-markets, such as sophisticated consumer electronics and branded personal products and services.

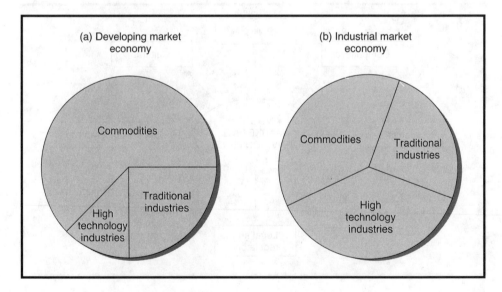

Figure 4.4   Importance of industrial base

Long-term economic competitiveness

In examining the ability of the company to compete in the longer term, it is necessary to understand the nature of the various influences on the company and the level of the influence. Competitiveness is defined as 'the immediate and future ability of, and opportunities for, entrepreneurs to design, produce and market goods within their respective environments whose price and non-price qualities form a more attractive package than those of competitors abroad or in domestic markets' (European Management Forum, 1984: 6).

Industrial policy and other influences may impact on the company and the economy generally at the macro or micro levels (Figure 4.5). The nature of the influence at the macro level may occur as 'hardware' or 'software' according to Abernathy *et al.* (1983). Hardware macro influences include government policies and EU directives aimed at improving roads, bridges, telecommunications, transport and other similar infrastructural supports required in the modern economy. At EU level, an example of such support in the 1990s is the very large financial package made available to member countries under the 'Structural Funds' policy.

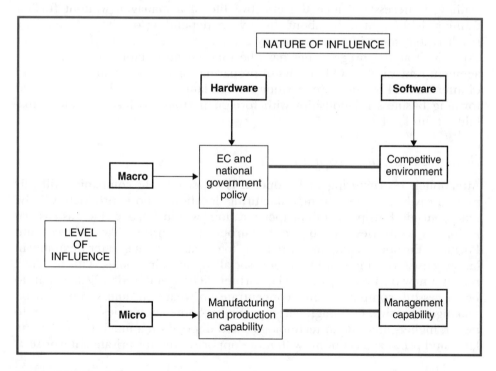

Figure 4.5 Key influences on competitiveness
(Source: Derived from Abernathy *et al.*, 1983)

Macro influences may also take the form of 'software' support to improve the competitive environment in the country. The competitive environment is improved by fostering a culture of enterprise, risk taking and innovation. Education policy regarding the teaching of foreign languages, enterprise skills and self-reliance, rather than a dependence on bureaucratic structures and central government support, is one way of fostering a competitive environment in a country.

At the micro level, hardware support for industry takes the form of financial and other assistance to establish and increase manufacturing and production capability in the country. The restructuring of the former East Germany is a good example of massive hardware support at the micro level. Any such support, whether it takes the form of building factories, supporting new technologies or providing grants or other financial incentives to industry, may be classified as hardware support for competitiveness at the micro level.

The last area to be examined, where it is thought the greatest impact on competitiveness can be made, is management. Management capability is always in need of upgrading and renewal. As the competitive environment changes, so do the pressures on management. There is, therefore, a requirement that managers are educated and trained for the tasks they face. Constant training is necessary, since the effective life of a manager, without further training, is thought to be about three years depending on the industry. The result is that short internal company training courses combined with longer executive training programmes have become an important part of the management renewal diet. Other ways of preparing for the new competitive world of international business are learning foreign languages, travelling abroad and forming business relationships with foreign partners to foster greater capability at this level.

Restructuring of European industry

After much restructuring in Europe, it is expected that companies will rely more heavily on cheaper manufacturing locations; more products will be made outside Europe or in cheaper locations within Europe, such as eastern European countries or southern European countries like Greece and Portugal. European companies are likely to demand much greater flexibility in labour costs, working conditions and social supports in homes. This in effect means a new pact among the social partners. The trend also indicates that, to be successful, companies must concentrate on what consumers want, not on making expensive, over-engineered products. Some companies may shift into newer, higher-value-added technologies and depend on a much more deregulated and privatized economy with more opportunities for private enterprise.

Value added and labour productivity

Labour productivity is the most accurate measure of economic performance in an economy. Growth in labour productivity means higher living standards. The faster the rate of productivity growth, the faster the economy can grow without inflation. In recent years, labour productivity has increased in the USA but has declined in Japan and Germany. For the whole US economy, labour productivity increased from 0.2 per cent in the period 1971–81 to 0.9 per cent in the period 1981–92 (Table 4.1). The same pattern, though more pronounced, also occurred in manufacturing. Even though the growth rates in Japan and Germany are still substantial, the trend is towards lower rates in those countries and higher rates in the USA.

The impact of the growth of labour productivity can be traced to its effect on value added in industry. In 1992 the value added for each hour worked in all businesses in Japan was 58 per cent of the value added in the USA. In Germany it was 82 per cent and in France 85 per cent (Figure 4.6). In manufacturing industry, German and Japanese value added was 80 per cent of the US figure while in the UK it was 60 per cent.

Labour productivity in services is a special case. Productivity in services tends to lag behind that in manufacturing due in the main to inadequate measurement, lower penetration of technology and lack of competition. Until recently, services have been protected from international competition. In recent years, the amount of technology in services has increased dramatically with a consequent shake-out in service industries. Shake-outs have also occurred in telecommunications, airlines and utilities due to government deregulation policies.

It has been argued, however, that many of the productivity differences in services are due more to open competition and improved labour practices than to investment in high technology (Lewis *et al.*, 1992). These authors studied a number of service businesses like telecommunications, retail merchandising and restaurants, and concluded that demand factors were the most important influences in telecommunications and general merchandising (Table 4.2). Most service businesses benefited from deregulation and changes in labour contracts. Changes in management behaviour, especially as it applies to decisions on the product mix and organization of labour, are important

TABLE 4.1 Growth in labour productivity

Country	Whole economy		Manufacturing	
	1971–81	*1981–92*	*1971–81*	*1981–92*
	(% per year)		(% per year)	
Japan	3.5	2.6	5.9	3.0
Germany	2.3	1.8	3.8	2.5
USA	0.2	0.9	1.7	3.0

Source: *The Economist*, 13 February 1993: 67. Copyright, *The Economist*, London 1994

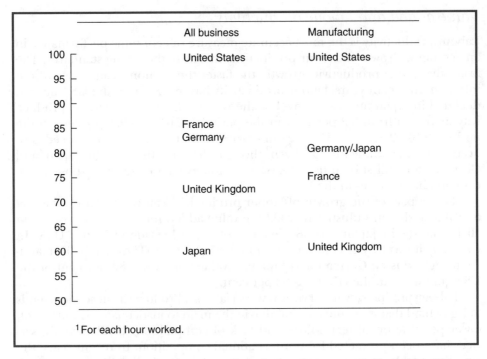

	All business	Manufacturing
100	United States	United States
95		
90		
85	France	
	Germany	
80		Germany/Japan
75		France
	United Kingdom	
70		
65		
60	Japan	United Kingdom
55		
50		

[1] For each hour worked.

Figure 4.6   Value added in selected countries,[1] 1992 (USA = 100). Copyright, *The Economist*, London 1994

determinants of labour productivity differences in most sectors. Restaurants are much less affected than the other sectors studied.

Growth in services in the economy

Sectors of the modern economy may be divided into manufacturing, services and the knowledge sector. The last includes those subsectors which produce, store, retrieve and distribute information useful to decision makers.

The modern economy needs a balance of all three sectors. The manufacturing and service sectors are interdependent and need each other for survival and growth. The computer industry needs software writers and cars need petrol stations. Many workers in manufacturing industry work in services. For example, in many industries it is possible to find people working in design, distribution, after-sales support, and financial planning and investment. These people are working in the service economy.

In industrial countries, services account for as much as 60 per cent of gross domestic product, although it is difficult to be accurate because services are difficult to define and measure, and they tend to be ignored in official statistics.

In many ways, the service economy is just as important and may be even more important than the traditional manufacturing economy. The marketing

TABLE 4.2   Causes of labour productivity differences

	Airlines	Telecom	Retail banking	General merchandising	Restaurants
External factors					
Market conditions:					
• Demand factors	□	☆[1]	△	☆	□
• Relative input prices/ factor availability	□	△	□	□	□
Policy and regulation:	☆	☆	☆	☆	□
• Competition and concentration rules	☆	☆	□	□	□
• Government ownership	△	△	□	□	△
• Labour rules and unionism	☆	☆	☆	☆	△
↓					
Management behaviour					
↓					
Production process					
• Output mix, variety, quality	△	□	△	☆	△
• Economies of scale	△	□	△	△	△
• Capital (intensity and vintage)	□	△	☆	△	□
• Skill of labour	□	□	□	□	□
• Organization of labour	☆	☆	☆	□	□
↓					
Labour productivity					

☆ = Important   △ = Secondary   □ = Undifferentiating

[1]Affects only capital productivity and total factor productivity.

Source: Lewis *et al.* (1992: 77). By permission of McKinsey and Co.

of services is also just as important as the marketing of products. In the modern industrial economy, there is now a pronounced interest in services due primarily to a recognition that services were always an important feature of the economy and that it is increasingly possible to define, measure and recognize their importance.

Macroeconomic considerations

Long-term economic growth

Trends in long-term economic growth in a country indicate the changes in the world economic environment which have occurred. Taking the USA as the standard, GDP per person in each of a number of countries for the period 1870 to 1989 shows some remarkable shifts over time (Figure 4.7). In 1870 Britain was the richest country in the world, having nearly twice the purchasing power per person of Germany. In the early part of the 1900s, the USA by-passed Britain and more recently still other countries, such as Japan, have also passed it. Japan was only slightly better off than India in 1870, but its recent performance dominates that of most other countries. Since 1950 a number of countries have shown strong economic improvement, especially those in the Far East.

Importance of discretionary income

The amount of income left after taxes is an important determinant of household expenditure. The taxes on income, for central and local government, paid by families on average manufacturing wages with two children for a number of EC countries are shown in Figure 4.8. In 1991, families in France, Iceland, Luxembourg and Portugal paid 1 per cent or less, while families in Denmark paid 36 per cent of their earnings in income tax. When non-standard tax reliefs are included, such as mortgage interest relief and pensions,

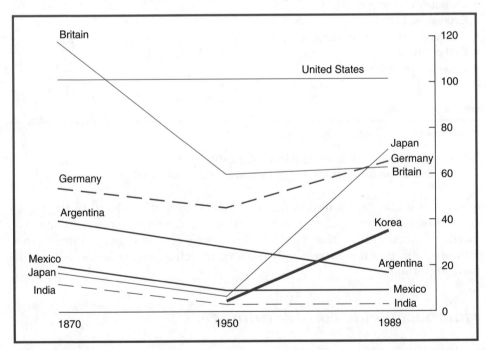

Figure 4.7 Historical trends in GDP per person, 1870–1989 (USA = 100; 1980 dollars, using PPP exchange rates)

(Source: *The Economist*, 20 June 1992: 123). Copyright, *The Economist*, London 1994

the actual burden is smaller. When employees' social security contributions and family allowances are added, workers in Denmark are left with 68 per cent of their income compared to net incomes of 117 per cent of gross incomes for Icelanders, accounted for by large family allowances.

Impact of poverty in society

Poverty challenges all parts of society, since it means social and economic exclusion and disadvantage for people who lack not only money, but also access to a range of services and opportunities. Definitions of poverty are the subject of frequent disagreement. One measure is based on the number of people receiving less than half the average income in the country where they

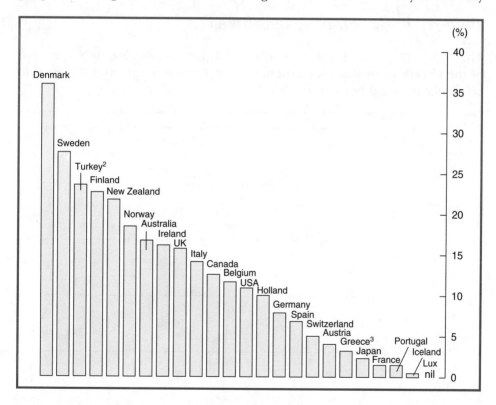

Figure 4.8 Income tax as a proportion of gross earnings in selected countries, 1991[1]
(Sources: *The Economist*, **6**, 21 November 1992: 135; OECD). Copyright, *The Economist*, London 1994.

Notes:
1. Married person on average manufacturing wage with two children, excluding the effect of non-standard tax reliefs.
2. 1990.
3. 1989.

live. By this definition there are currently about 50 million people or 15 per cent of the total population living in poverty in the European Union. And, in spite of economic growth and aid to less developed regions, the proportion of poor people in Europe is growing. Wim Van Velzem, President of the Social Affairs Committee in the European Parliament, claims that on the basis used above there were 50 million people in poverty in 1992 compared to 30 million in 1978 (*Financial Times*, 22 April 1992: 2).

The nature of poverty has changed. Poverty in the 1990s arises mainly from the consequences of industrial restructuring and long-term unemployment. While poverty used to be associated only with the sick and the elderly, it is now more likely to affect younger, unemployed families and single parents.

Poverty in developing countries

The richest 20 per cent of the world's population received nearly 83 per cent of the world's gross domestic product in 1989, while the poorest 20 per cent received a mere 1.4 per cent (Figure 4.9).

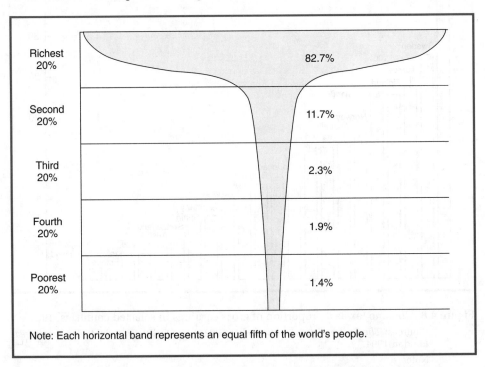

Note: Each horizontal band represents an equal fifth of the world's people.

Figure 4.9 The poverty trap: distribution of world GDP, 1989 (% of total, quintiles of population ranked by income)

(Source: *The Economist*, 25 April 1992: 56. Copyright, *The Economist*, London 1994)

Within some countries similar disparities exist. In many developing countries, the richest 20 per cent of people receive as much as 30 times more annual income than the poorest 20 per cent. Such contrasts within countries can result in strife and violent political dissent. The poor also have other ways of threatening the rich. They can despoil the environment by burning down rain forests, foster diseases such as AIDS in Africa, and destabilize regional politics as in Haiti. As producers or consumers, they engage in a mere 1 per cent of formal world trade (*The Economist,* 25 April 1992: 56).

Relevance of marketing in developing countries

The relevance of basic marketing principles to developing countries is in dispute. Environmental factors may prevent the straight transfer of marketing principles and concepts. Conditions of a strong market, increasing competition based on innovative products and services, better education and consumerism, all of which led to the acceptance of the marketing concept in the advanced world, are usually missing in developing countries. In addition, centralized planning frequently means that supply and demand are centrally controlled, which interferes with free market forces. It is often suggested that cultural factors also prevent the application of the marketing concept. In view of the growing number of developing countries that are adopting structural adjustment and trade liberalization policies, however, this traditional marketing perspective may be in decline.

The application of comparative advantage through the marketing system is an attractive proposition, since effective communications are rapidly shrinking the world market. In such circumstances, a local community can better decide which activities to develop in relation to local conditions, market structures and resources. A social system such as this exists by adapting to environmental change in a rapidly changing world.

Marketing may also be useful in countering non-economic obstacles such as value systems, attitudes and work practices which do not alter in the face of economic opportunity, but instead prevent the pace of development being maintained. Social marketing or the design, implementation and control of social ideas offers a powerful mechanism to overcome such obstacles.

Marketing can, therefore, both derive the best method of human development and reduce the obstacles to it, given the resources and cultural conditions of a country. As well as a developmental role, marketing also has a societal role to play in human development. Since there is no universal agreement about what aspects of a social and economic transformation are desirable, marketing can ensure that the values of the society are considered. It is precisely because marketing operates as a social system that it is able to identify opportunities and promote development which correspond with the values of a society. Marketing is able to achieve such objectives because its principles are versatile enough to cope with the heterogeneity of politics, natural resources, culture, population and development among and within developing countries.

167

Demographic environment

The population of the world is estimated to have been about 2.5 billion people in 1950 and 5.3 billion in 1990. By 2150 this figure is expected to grow to 11.5 billion (Table 4.3). Of greater significance are the shifts in population which are expected. Growth and shifts in population have a very direct influence on the demand for products and services. In 1950 Europe was home to 15.6 per cent of the world's population, but by 1990 this had fallen to 9.4 per cent and by 2150 it is expected to decline to 3.7 per cent. Other areas expected to decline are North America, the former Soviet Union and the People's Republic of China. Population is expected to increase in Latin America, Asia and Oceania, and especially in Africa.

Impact of demographic changes

Generation X, the generation which followed the 'Boomers', is beginning to enter the mainstream of adult life. In the mid-1990s they are at university, in their first jobs or job hunting. They set tastes and popular culture and are often referred to as 'latch-key kids', since householders are likely to be supporting two careers and some are separated or divorced. This generation has been entering the workforce as economies have run into recession, so they are economically alienated since it is difficult to progress economically and socially in such an environment. Because of over-exposure to television, they have also become cynical and selective consumers.

People are also marrying later. In the EU, the mean age of marriage for women in the late 1970s was 23; in 1992 it was 25. But to an extent the decline in marriage has been accompanied by an increase in cohabitation. Cohabitation is practised more in some countries than in others. In northern

TABLE 4.3   World population trends

Regions	1950 (%)	1990 (%)	2150 (%)
Europe	15.6	9.4	3.7
North America	6.6	5.2	2.7
Latin America	6.6	8.5	9.7
Soviet Union (former)	7.2	5.4	3.6
Africa	8.8	12.1	26.8
China	22.1	21.5	12.0
Other/Asia/Oceania	18.9	21.8	24.6
India	14.2	16.1	16.9
Total	100.0	100.0	100.0
Population (number)	2.5 billion	5.3 billion	11.5 billion

Source: *The Economist*, 11 April 1992: 119.

Europe, people tend to live together for long periods and then separate. The time to separation is shorter in the USA, while in southern Europe cohabitation is not a common practice.

Since the 1950s, the proportion of women in paid employment has risen dramatically in every industrial country. Women now go out to work even when children are very young. Almost two-thirds of all women in the OECD are in paid employment, while in Scandinavia nearly as many women as men are in the paid labour force.

Because of population changes, there are new market segments emerging which must be served. In 1985 people living alone in the USA accounted for 24 per cent of all households. In 1960 it was 13 per cent. Single parents were heads of nearly nine million households in 1985 compared with nearly four million in 1970. In 1960 there were 23 million women in paid employment; by 1985 this had increased to more than 52 million. In the late 1980s, the proportion of the population of two-income families in the USA was nearly a half compared to a quarter in the early 1960s. The impact of these demographic changes may be seen in the polarization of retailing into luxury and discount segments as growth of both low-income and high-income households is higher than that of middle-income households.

Demographic changes affect consumer expenditures as well. Because of a static population growth in Europe, manufacturers and retailers are engaged in a battle for a decreasing level of expenditure on their products. This is especially true for food, where trends have a very direct impact, since the proportion of income spent on food is expected to decline rapidly. The food industry will also have to change to provide a diet for an ageing population. The habits of older people are becoming more important than the demands of children.

TABLE 4.4   Population in eastern Europe, 1990

	Total population (millions)	Urban population (%)
Soviet Union (CIS)	287.9	68
Poland	38.4	63
Romania	23.3	51
Czech Republic	10.4	77
Hungary	10.3	60
Slovakia	5.3	74
Bulgaria	8.5	70
Albania	3.3	55
Comecon	401.1	66
EU	325.9	79

Sources: 'Survey of Eastern Europe', *The Economist*, 13 March 1993: 18; Seitz (1992: 4–5). Copyright, *The Economist*, London 1994.

Demography of central Europe

As a market there has been considerable interest in countries in central Europe in recent years. The total population of Comecon countries was 401.4 million people in 1990 compared with 325.9 million in the EU. It is a much larger market in terms of total population. Some countries have very large populations, such as the CIS and Poland, while others have very small populations, such as Slovakia, Bulgaria and Albania (Table 4.4).

From the point of view of effective demand, a number of these countries have already demonstrated a potential which will be much sought after by western companies. Urban population, a crude measure of demand for consumer products and services, approaches the EU average in the Czech Republic, Slovakia and Bulgaria. Romania is still largely a rurally based country. The level of effective demand in these countries is tempered by the need for reconstruction and basic development in many industries.

Demography of the Far East

Until recently, western companies saw business activity in the Far East in production terms only. Countries there were seen as providing a threat or an opportunity depending on the nature of the business. Textile industries and consumer electronic companies in the West saw the East as a threat. Importers of high-quality consumer products, department stores and consumers, on the other hand, saw the opportunities offered by trading with countries in the Far East.

The above situation prevails into the 1990s, but many of these countries have become richer; their peoples are now demanding a higher standard of

TABLE 4.5   Population of selected countries in the Far East, 1991

Country	Population (millions)
China (PRC)	1149.5
Hong Kong	5.8
Taiwan	20.6
North Korea	21.9
South Korea	43.3
Japan	123.3
Malaysia	18.2
Singapore	2.8
Philippines	62.9
Indonesia	181.3
India	866.5
Sri Lanka	17.2
Bangladesh	110.6
Pakistan	115.8
Thailand	57.2
Vietnam	67.8

Source: 'Survey of Asia', *The Economist*, 30 October 1993: 6.

living and can afford it due to their increased wealth. Many of the countries have themselves developed into very valuable markets in their own right. Economic growth rates and the demand for consumer and industrial products in the Far East have far outstripped economic activity in the West.

Some of the consumer markets in the Far East appear to have very great potential. In terms of population size, a number of markets stand out: China, India, Indonesia and Japan (Table 4.5). There are many other substantial markets also. While the population may be large, however, effective demand may not be correspondingly large. Another trend is the shift to the cities in those countries: Jakarta in Indonesia, Bombay in India and Karachi in Pakistan are all expected to see their populations increase very significantly in the next few years.

Cultural environment for marketing

The cultural environment influences marketing because of its direct impact on marketing practices, the kinds of product and service demanded, and the behaviour of consumers and other buyers.

Influence of culture in marketing

Culture has many dimensions. Among the more important are: language, which influences communications; education, which influences purchasing; and attitudes to various factors that can have a dominant effect in the disposition to purchase a particular product or service.

Language is the primary means of communication and is the most important cultural input in our complex communications process. Despite the fact that English is being called the 'European business language' many nations, such as Germany, France and Finland, have clung on and indeed even revised the use of their native tongue. Direct translation from one language to another often loses the proper meaning in the process. There are many examples of poor translations; some of these have become overworn jokes, yet they serve to indicate the cultural and language traps which surround the unwary as they enter new international markets.

Religion is especially relevant in some countries as it may influence purchasing patterns: for example, of certain foods and alcohol. Purchasing and consumption patterns strongly influenced by religion become an integral part of culture and change only slowly.

Education levels and educational systems also affect a group's disposition to purchasing. Among the more important factors are:

- literacy levels;
- attitudes to foreigners and foreign products; and
- consumer sophistication.

171

The role of women in society is often used as a crude measure of cultural openness and advancement in that society. One of the better ways of observing the role of women in society is to examine the changing roles of women in advertising, e.g. for cars, clothes, household appliances and cleaning liquids. It is a relatively easy matter to see the impact of culture and stereotyping used in our daily lives.

Sociocultural and business distance

Sociocultural distance is a method of accounting for the physical, economic and cultural distance between countries. The importance of sociocultural distance may be judged from the fact that companies tend to have more information and be more knowledgeable about countries which are culturally near to them than those culturally distant. Companies tend to avoid culturally divergent countries in favour of culturally similar markets. The same argument holds for the movement of products and people. Cultural distance is an impediment and restricting force which predisposes the company to closer markets.

Political economy of marketing

The development of markets is greatly influenced by politics and economics. The efficiency of markets and marketing depends on an active political and economic system where institutions grow and respond to the needs of the community. In many cases, the appropriate response will require the establishment of new institutions and frameworks for economic and political integration.

Multinational market development requires that countries co-operate at least on economic matters and on political issues as the relationship develops. Normally, a number of countries see an opportunity for regional co-operation where governments sponsor strategic industries. Internal tariff barriers are maintained, but for selected industries a common external barrier is agreed (Figure 4.10). The next level of market development occurs when countries establish a free trade area among themselves. As the relationship and co-operation develop, a full customs zone may be established, followed by a common market.

Twelve countries in Europe had until recently operated versions of a common market. In theory, a common market implies free mobility of goods, services, capital and labour, economic and monetary unity and fiscal unity. In practice, there were and continue to be many difficulties in implementing the common market as envisaged. But progress continues to be made, directives with legal standing are being promulgated, and new institutions are being established. A feature of the European common market is the application of European Free Trade Area (EFTA) countries to join: Sweden, Norway, Finland and Austria. Central European countries such as the Czech Republic, Slovakia and Hungary have also applied for membership.

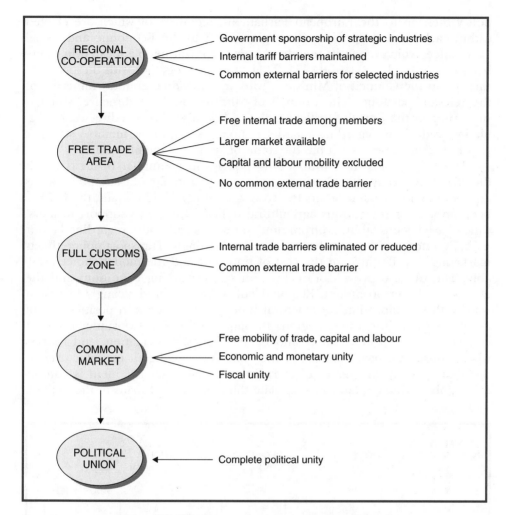

Figure 4.10 Multinational market development

The final stage of multinational market development is the formulation of full political union among members of a common market. With the signing of the Maastricht Treaty in 1993 the twelve member countries of the European Community (EC) effectively became members of the European Union (EU). Complete political union brings with it the possibility of full integration of markets and related institutions.

Internal market of the European Union

The European Commission initiates and implements decisions in the European Union. Its proposals to change something or to introduce a new policy then go to the European Parliament, members of which are elected within each country to represent regions, and to the Economic and Social Committee, which draws its members from technical people located in member states of the EU (Figure 4.11). Their opinions together with the proposal then go to the Council of Ministers, who are individual country ministers of the relevant portfolio. The Council of Ministers issues a directive which is supervised by the Court of Justice. At the end of this process, a directive or regulation or decision regarding a matter of policy is sent to the member states or to private companies, and it has the status of law in the member states.

The EU is concerned with setting policies in a number of areas which directly or indirectly affect business and marketing. Some of these policy areas are very well known and others less so (Figure 4.12). Traditionally, the EU has been known for the various agricultural policies, mostly to support farmers, which have been established from time to time. Social policy regarding labour mobility, safety and equality has also featured strongly. Transport policy affects marketing directly through the cost of transport and the modal choice available. The EU also provides directives on safety, working conditions and the effects on the environment. Regional policy has featured strongly in recent years with the allocation of structural funds, and is seen as a positive way of developing and integrating regions throughout the EU. Consumer policy is concerned with product safety and liability issues, information, and redress where consumers have suffered at the hands of a negligent manufacturer or distributor. Lastly, of greater concern in the present environment is competition policy, which attempts to regulate the behaviour of firms in the market.

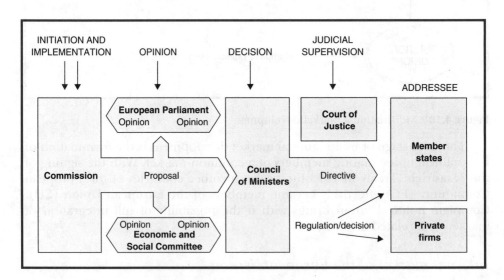

Figure 4.11 How a decision is taken in the EU
(Source: *Irish Times*, 14 December 1990)

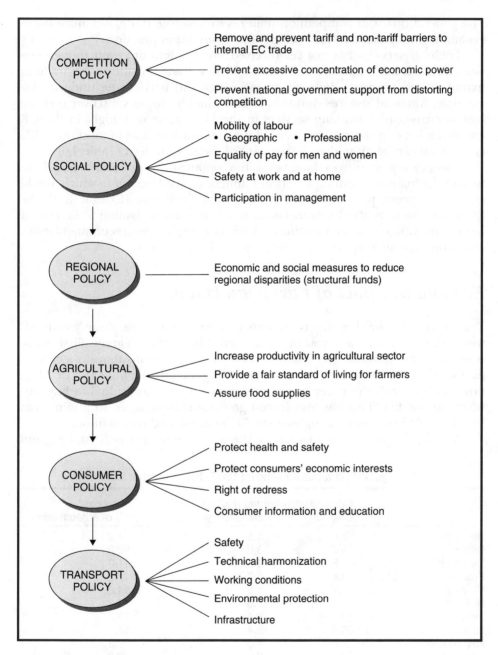

Figure 4.12 EC policy measures

The general thrust of competition policy is to promote trade, eliminate barriers and protect customers and competitors from unfair practices.

Trade in services has not yet received much attention, even though services are such an important component of total trade. Furthermore, trade in manufactured products depends on efficiency and barrier-free trade in, for example, financial services. Individuals and small businesses discover that the cost of cross-border banking services in the EU can be very high. In the UK and Spain it can be over 20 per cent of the amount lent, and in most other EU countries it can be more than 10 per cent of the amount lent (Table 4.6).

European post offices have seen the opportunity presented and have formed Eurogiro, a payments network aimed at small accounts which would guarantee speedy payments for a relatively low fixed cost (Exhibit 4.1). The EU Commission is also likely to take a direct interest by issuing a directive if banks and other financial institutions do not implement recommendations regarding customer information on cross-border payments.

Economic impact of European Union

The internal EU market affects business in a number of ways. Four 'freedoms' were promised which are now being delivered in varying degrees. First, there is the freedom to move goods across borders, which means that no technical excuse will exist to prevent the sales of most goods throughout the EU. It is now possible, with the exception of motor cars, for an individual to buy anywhere in the EU. This has also forced governments to agree to a minimum VAT rate of 15 per cent throughout the EU to avoid 'tax' competition.

As regards the mobility of services, the second freedom, only banking and

TABLE 4.6   Average bank charges for sending 130 ECUs to another EU country

| | Commission charged (ECUs) | | Total cost |
	Originator	Beneficiary	(% of amount sent)[1]
Belgium	7.6	1.5	7.2
Britain	19.2	3.0	20.3
Denmark	11.8	2.3	11.0
France	16.8	5.9	17.5
Germany	16.8	1.9	14.8
Holland	11.0	1.6	12.3
Ireland	12.9	6.4	15.8
Italy	20.6	3.4	18.7
Luxembourg	7.5	4.0	9.2
Portugal	19.4	5.0	18.3
Spain	20.0	5.9	22.7

[1] Including exchange costs.

Source: *The Economist*, 7 November 1992: 96. Copyright, *The Economist*, London 1994.

EXHIBIT 4.1　Tangled transfers of European payment systems

Every year individuals and small businesses make about 200 million cross-border payments within the European Community. Many are fleeced by their banks while doing so according to a report from BEUC, the European Consumers' Organisation ('Cost Transparency in Cross-border Financial Transfers', 4 November 1992).

The consumer group's study is based on a sample of 176 transfers, each equivalent to 130 ecus ($162), made through 22 banks in the EC members in February and March of this year. Some of the payments were telegraphic transfers and others went by mail. Customers instructed their banks to split the costs of some payments between sender and recipient; on others the sender asked to pay all the charges.

The EC does not allow any member government to control the movement of such small amounts of capital. The one Greek bank that was asked to make transfers refused to do so, and the Greek banks receiving payments would not give information about their charges. Three of the transfers – from Belgium to Portugal, Portugal to Spain and Portugal to Italy – have not yet arrived. None of the banks involved has accepted responsibility; none has offered either a refund or compensation.

In February 1990 the Commission recommended (a touch unrealistically) that a cross-border transfer be no more expensive than a domestic one, which rarely costs a typical EC customer more than half an ecu. Yet BEUC found the average cost (various commissions plus the exchange-rate spread) of its sample to be 20 ecus. Some banks charged over 20 per cent of the value of the (admittedly small) payment; it cost 51 ecus to send 130 ecus from Denmark to Britain, for example. But Sir Leon Brittan, the commissioner for financial services, is concerned about BEUC's findings. 'We have given the banks until the end of this year to show that they are implementing our recommendations,' says one of his advisors. 'If they don't, they may face a directive.'

Europe's post offices may prove swifter to act on the problem than its banks. Fourteen postal banking organisations have formed Eurogiro, a payments network with a central computer. From 17 November Eurogiro will guarantee the arrival of a payment within four days – for a standard fee equivalent to 15.40 ecus. If the threat of a directive does not spur the banks into giving their customers a better deal, perhaps Eurogiro will.

Source: *The Economist*, 7 November 1992: 96.

---

road transport have seen much development. Banks can now open branches anywhere in the EU, with their affairs regulated only by the controls imposed on the parent. The road haulage industry has been much changed by the completion of the internal market. National permits and restrictions were once a feature of this industry, but it is now possible to haul goods anywhere in the EU. Other services have not been affected much so far. Insurance and securities are likely to be liberalized somewhat in the near future, while airlines have an extension to 1997. National telephone companies have succeeded in putting off open competition indefinitely, especially for telephony.

The third freedom refers to the mobility of people. To date the EU countries have not signed or ratified an external frontiers convention, so great is their fear or uncertainty regarding immigration. This convention establishes the frontier checks which must be made at the perimeter of the EU to avoid installing internal intercountry checks. Another mobility factor not yet in force is a passport-free zone within the EU, although the inspection of EU passports within the EU is honoured more in the breach than in the practice.

The fourth freedom refers to exchange controls and capital movements. The Maastricht Treaty has effectively removed exchange controls within the EU and with countries outside the EU.

The Maastricht Treaty itself is significant in that it attempts a number of new things. First, the treaty attempts to increase the scope of the EU. As a result the EU has a very great macroeconomic impact on world markets. The nature of this influence also affects the range of areas in which the EU has taken a direct role outside the economic sphere: foreign policy, international policing activities and border controls. The Maastricht Treaty also limits the ambitions of any nascent European central government. This is the principle of subsidiarity, which states that 'in areas which do not fall within its exclusive competence the EU shall take action only where the objectives of the proposed action cannot be achieved by the member countries'.

Deregulation of airline markets

The completion of the internal market in Europe will bring with it deregulation of markets once protected by law, regulation and national edicts. For example, as of 1 January 1993, any EU airline is free to fly any international route between two EU countries. Furthermore, any airline is allowed to charge any fare it wants unless the governments of the two countries involved disapprove. By 1996 no government will be able to influence fares, and cabotage rights, the freedom to carry passengers within a single country, will increase. European airlines in a deregulated environment will face tough competition from US and Far East airlines in particular. It is expected that many of Europe's 20 major scheduled airlines will not survive deregulation.

European airlines argue that, in return for open markets in Europe, they should be allowed greater access to US destinations and the right of cabotage there. In 1992 Lufthansa was still limited to ten cities in the USA while US airlines have wide access to airports in Germany and the rest of Europe. The North Atlantic accounts for 30 per cent of Lufthansa's traffic, but like other European airlines it loses money on the route.

Many of the larger European airlines are believed to be overstaffed and inefficient, and to operate with very high costs. The large carriers in Europe, however, have a major competitive advantage in that they control Europe's

---

EXHIBIT 4.2 Europe's small airlines: like ducks in hunting season

To give the small fry a boost, the European Commission wants big carriers to give up some valuable slots. But many governments and carriers fiercely oppose the idea, and it may not pass. Entrenched airlines also have resorted to hard-nosed tactics to keep start-ups in their place. Ask Ireland's Ryanair, which began flying to Britain in 1986. After initial success with low fares, Ryanair found state owned Aer Lingus beefing up frequencies and slashing prices. To stave off a Ryanair bankruptcy, the Irish government allocated different routes to the two carriers. Having lost nearly $40 million, a slimmed down Ryanair is hoping to break even this year. What happened to Aer Lingus's bargain prices? 'When we withdrew from these routes, things returned to normal' says Ryanair CEO P. J. McGoldrick

Source: *Business Week*, 9 December 1991: 20.

---

computerized reservation system. With ready access to such systems, airlines can adjust fares quickly to match market conditions. This is an advantage for the large insider. Outsiders do not have ready access to such reservation systems and small airlines are also excluded. One of the biggest difficulties for small airlines and newcomers is the way incumbents control slots at busy airports like Heathrow (Exhibit 4.2).

Deregulation of telecommunications

Since 1988 the EU has issued six directives ordering member governments to liberalize various parts of their communications industries. These directives were aimed at reducing the monopoly position of Europe's state-owned telecommunications companies. The nature and extent of the monopoly indicated clearly to the European Commission that competition was much needed (Exhibit 4.3). The most important of these directives was the 1990 telecommunications services directive, which ordered member countries to abolish all anti-competitive restrictions in telephone services. But a temporary exemption on voice telephony, telephone calls between people, left most of the revenues of the telecommunications monopolies intact and free from competition.

Deregulation of European pharmaceutical markets

European companies dominate the world market for pharmaceutical drugs. Regulation changes by the European Commission, which will introduce a tougher trading environment, are changing that. In the EU there has not been a common policy on drug pricing, but the EU introduced a pricing transparency directive at the beginning of 1991 which ensures that prices are set according to open and objective criteria which do not favour national producers.

179

EXHIBIT 4.3 Robbery by telephone in Europe

Something peculiar happens when a telephone crosses a dotted line on a map of the EC. On average, a three minute peak rate call between two EC countries costs two and a half to three times as much as the most expensive long distance national call. This ratio rises to between five and six for off-peak calls, giving people at home the worst deal of all. The direction of a call can have a bizarre effect on its cost. A call from Madrid to Copenhagen, for instance, costs twice the price of a call from Copenhagen to Madrid; presumably the Spanish line takes the scenic route.

All this might be marginally more bearable if national calls were not so costly in most EC countries. On average, a peak-rate, long distance call made within the Community is more than 60 per cent dearer than one made from New York to Washington, DC. Fiat, Europe's second-biggest car maker, reckons it could cut its $100 million-a-year phone bill by at least $43m if it were based in America instead of Italy.

Source: *The Economist*, 26 September 1992: 19.

Before its introduction the price of each medicine was fixed in negotiations between the drug companies and national governments on a country-by-country basis. The result was substantially different prices in different countries.

Portugal, the lowest-paying EU country, pays only 68 per cent of the EU average for its drugs, followed by France and Spain, which pay 72 per cent of the average. At the other extreme, Ireland and the Netherlands pay the highest prices, at more than 130 per cent of the average (Lynn, 1991: 64). As a result of the new directive, the drugs companies are likely to witness their prices reduced by cross-border trading as it will be difficult to prevent pharmaceuticals moving from low-price to high-price countries. In response, some companies are experimenting with promoting capsules in one country, pills in another and injections in a third as a way of establishing national differences and reducing the appeal of imports (Lynn, 1991: 64).

Legal environment for marketing

There are two types of legal system which concern us: common law, which applies in the UK and all its present and former colonies; and civil law, which applies in all other countries. From a marketing point of view, the differences are not substantial. When a company is entering a contract with a foreign partner, however, the legal system applicable must be specified. Very often the civil law system of a third country, such as the Netherlands, is specified as the system to be used in the case of arbitration.

There is a fear among business people in the USA that its legal system damages the country's ability to compete in international markets. A poll of senior managers drawn from the *Business Week* 1000 found that 62 per cent believe that the USA civil justice system significantly hampers the ability of US companies to compete with Japanese and European rivals (*Business Week*, 13 April 1992: 37). It is believed that in countries such as the UK and Japan costs are held down by making it more difficult to sue and more difficult to win. In the USA each side usually pays its own legal costs regardless of the result – a system that favours litigation. In other countries, losers pay the winners' costs, which discourages frivolous suits.

The hallmarks of the US legal system – jury trials, contingency fees and punitive damages – encourage a litigious mentality among citizens and companies. Furthermore, a large proportion of legal costs in the USA and in Europe are attributable to the issue of discovery, the arrangement whereby parties may review an opponent's evidence before trial. In Japan this arrangement does not exist.

The Japanese legal system discourages litigation. The oriental culture produces an aversion for direct confrontation, which encourages the resolution of disputes privately. Barriers to litigation in Japan may clearly be observed in the legal education system. It is very difficult to get into law school in Japan and become a lawyer. In Japan and other Far East countries, when disputes arise between companies the lawyers are often the last to be told. Sales people and front-line managers are the principal problem solvers. Involving sales people helps to avoid damaging long-term business relationships.

Technological environment

The technology environment affects marketing in a number of ways, by speeding up business transactions and making them more efficient, and by providing the basis for standards.

Effect of technology change on marketing

Advances in electronic technology have revolutionized the way business is done. The impact of computers in particular has reshaped the traditional economic concepts of scale, scope and structure (Sheth, 1992: 58). Concepts such as flexible manufacturing, just-in-time and electronic data transfer have made partially if not entirely redundant the advantages associated with scale economics, hierarchical organization structures and a narrow business scope.

Improved communications technologies in some instances have reduced the importance of time and distance in doing business. Traditional marketing theories based on location – for example, retail store location, inventory management and market logistics – may be obsolete when customers and suppliers can do business at any time from anywhere (Sheth, 1992: 58).

Impact of EU standards

There is a movement towards uniform health, safety and environmental standards in the EU. At present the European Commission is focusing on between 1,500 and 2,000 health, safety, environmental and quality standards which it is seeking to standardize throughout the twelve-member community. These standards are being developed by the European Committee for Standardization (CEN), which is composed of European industry representatives, and the International Standards Organization, which has established the rules for the popular ISO 9000 quality systems. Consumer groups are not well represented on either body, so it is conceivable that products could be produced to some high technical standard that nobody wants to buy. To date the European Commission has agreed about 200 standards. Companies selling in Europe or to Europe have to meet these standards. The argument behind the harmonization of standards is that consistency breeds reliability, which is seen as a significant benefit in the Commission of the EU (Exhibit 4.4).

There is a fear that standards may reduce the ability of a company to compete, but there are benefits. Whereas formerly companies had to make different versions of products for different European countries, they are now able to produce one product for the entire European market. Common standards are favoured by strong competitors, particularly the US and Japanese motor car manufacturers interested in the large European market. Weaker companies,

---

EXHIBIT 4.4 ISO 9000 – the way to do business in the EU

The ISO 9000 guideposts from the International Standards Organization in Geneva have been described both as a management tool and a trade barrier. Either way, says Winfried Werner, head of quality at ITT Corp's Semiconductor Div. in Freiburg, Germany, 'ISO will be a must for any company in Europe.'

It may be for US companies too: Du Pont, Eastman Kodak, and other US pioneers took up ISO in the late 1980s to make sure they weren't locked out of European markets – then found it helped improve quality. The ISO 9000 premise is simple: Consistency breeds reliability. This isn't a magic bullet. 'At best, ISO minimizes the probability that you'll ship a defective product,' says Trevor Davis, a quality consultant for Coopers & Lybrand in London. But that's enough for the EC.

The EC chose ISO 9000 in 1989 to harmonize the varying technical norms of its member states. By last year, ISO compliance became part of hundreds of product safety laws all over Europe, regulating everything from medical devices to telecommunications gear. Such products account for only 15 per cent of EC trade. But German electronics giant Siemens requires ISO compliance in 50 per cent of supply contracts, and is nudging other suppliers to conform. That eliminates the need to test parts, which saves time and money.

Source: *Business Week*, 19 October 1992: 51–2.

however, may face substantial readjustments in the form of unforeseen design changes, expensive retooling, extra staff and new quality control and mainte-nance systems.

In such circumstances, companies frequently organize themselves into indus-try groupings to promote a particular standard. They also establish training programmes to help members respond to standards that have been agreed.

Physical environment

Regulations that limit the ecological damage from timber cutting, property and housing development and intensive farming have the effect of reducing jobs in those immediate businesses. But they have a positive effect on incomes of people in other industries, such as tourism and fishing. Curtailing pollution can help manufacturers to increase productivity, which can also create new jobs. Clean air and water and strong ecosystems can improve public health.

Every year throughout the EU, companies and households discard 50 million tonnes of packaging. The European Commission estimates that only about 20 per cent of this is recycled. In the 1990s, the proportion recycled should increase rapidly if proposals of the Commission are implemented. In a draft directive issued in July 1993, the Commission sought to balance the demands of environmental groups with those of industry.

One of the most contentious issues is whether individual countries in the EU should be allowed to retain even stricter recycling laws should they wish to do so. The original objective of the Commission's directive was to establish rules for the entire EU which would prevent national governments from enact-ing governmental laws that served as a barrier to trade. The most prominent exponent of this form of green protectionism, according to most big com-panies, is Germany (Exhibit 4.5).

In December 1993 the environment ministers of the EU agreed that its members should recover between 50 and 65 per cent of packaging used to transport and sell products. The agreement, which is a trade measure, was car-ried in the face of opposition from Denmark, Germany and the Netherlands, countries unwilling to accept lower ceilings for recycling than their own tough domestic targets. As a result of this directive, any country that wants to impose stricter requirements must persuade the European Commission that it has suf-ficient recycling capacity and is not surreptitiously restricting trade.

Though interest in the physical environment is growing, business is some-times reluctant to comply with requests to take greater care. The cost of envi-ronmental protection, especially for smaller firms, is often cited as the reason for this reluctance. Tax breaks and other incentives are now being considered by governments as ways of inducing change, and sometimes a flexible approach to the implementation of new environmental regulations achieves the objective.

EXHIBIT 4.5 Abolishing litter in Europe

Many exporters to Germany claim that the controversial Topfer law – named after Klaus Topfer, Germany's environment minister – puts them at a distinct disadvantage. This law started to take effect last December and requires waste collection to increase in stages until 80 per cent of packaging waste is collected by 1995. Of the waste that is collected, 90 per cent of the glass and metal will have to be recycled, and 80 per cent of the plastic and paper. Manufacturers and distributors have to take back their own packaging, or join Duales System Deutschland (DSD), an organisation set up by German industry. Members of DSD pay for the right to put a green dot on their packaging, and consumers know that any dotted pack can be left with retailers in DSD bins.

The law, and zeal of German retailers to reduce the volume of packaging to escape its most onerous provisions, is already proving a barrier to many non-German companies which have to navigate their way through the DSD's bureaucracy or repackage their goods especially for the German market. Exporters of Scotch whisky, for example, have had to take the cardboard boxes off their bottles.

The commission's own proposal is more flexible than the Topfer law. Within 10 years of the directive coming into force, 90 per cent of packaging waste (by weight) would have to be 'recovered', which means recycled, burnt for energy or composted. Moreover, 60 per cent of all packaging would have to be recycled. Governments would be required to set up their own systems for meeting these targets. Packaging would have to carry EC symbols to show whether it is recoverable, reusable or recycled. The commission unofficially estimates that it will cost seven billion ecus ($10 billion) a year to meet its target.

Source: *The Economist*, 22 August 1992. 53–4.

Impact of the green backlash

In many countries now there are rumours of a 'green backlash' as business and consumers add up the costs of protecting the environment. Some countries and some states in the USA now believe that strict environmental codes tend to drive industries away, with subsequent job losses and slower economic growth. The situation is exacerbated in times of recession. Small businesses are the loudest critics of air quality controls: dry cleaners, furniture manufacturers, car painters, and restaurants and hotels. Recycling is also getting a bad name in some countries. Although sorting waste, in the office and in the home, into paper, glass, plastic and aluminium has become habitual in many places, there is evidence that this does not protect the environment. Recycling programmes have produced a large supply of paper, glass and plastic waste, but there are few plants that can convert this rubbish into something useful. Aluminium is the only recyclable material that pays its way: it is cheaper to produce new cans from old than to make them from original raw materials.

Environmental friendliness in marketing

In regard to natural resources, there is now in most developed country markets a significantly large segment of consumers who refuse to buy products if their production is believed to damage the environment or its inhabitants: for example, cosmetics tested on animals, products packaged in styrofoam, or furniture made from wood extracted from the rain forests. Some companies have managed in their marketing communications to capitalize on their care for the environment. Anita Roddick of the Body Shop has persuaded inhabitants in the Amazon area to grow various types of edible nut. By also providing nut presses to extract oil and generate better profits than those available from extracting wood, she succeeds in retarding deforestation. However, altruistic endeavours such as this only persist if they have a positive impact on the bottom line.

Concern for the physical environment has given many companies an opportunity to respond with environmentally friendly products. In early 1991 Rubbermaid Inc. in the USA launched a litter-free lunch box which it called the 'Sidekick', featuring three plastic containers for a sandwich, a drink and one other item. The product was aimed at parents concerned for the environment. As a result Rubbermaid Inc. expected its share of the $35 million lunch box market to double to 12 per cent. In producing the 'Sidekick', Rubbermaid has exploited its market knowledge and rapid product development cycles which have given the company a strong reputation for innovation. Approximately 30 per cent of Rubbermaid's total sales are derived from products introduced in the previous five years.

Environmental life cycle analysis

Many companies in defending their record on the effects of their products on the physical environment have resorted to a 'life cycle analysis' of the effects. This means examining the environmental effects of their products and services at every stage from raw material and manufacture through distribution to consumption and disposal. Companies use life cycle analysis for three reasons:

- to discover ways of reducing pollution by their products and processes;

- to support claims made in green advertising; and

- to ward off undesirable regulatory constraints.

In a study of various kinds of orange juice in California, it was discovered that frozen concentrate, the cheapest product, had the smallest environmental side-effects. In Denmark after the introduction of a requirement for refillable containers for drinks, Tetra-Pak showed in a study that its non-refillable paper cartons could be packed closer together than glass bottles, thus reducing the number of polluting trucks needed to carry them. Cartons also need less

185

energy to refrigerate, pollute water less and require less space in landfills when finally discarded. Confronted with such evidence, the Danish government first lifted its ban on non-refillable containers and in 1993 removed the tax on milk cartons (*The Economist*, 9 October 1993: 79).

In 1992 the environment ministry in the Netherlands addressed a contentious question: which are more environmentally friendly, china coffee cups and saucers, polystyrene (styrofoam) mugs, or paper mugs? The report examined the life cycle of the cup from cradle to grave: from the extraction and processing of raw materials through production and use to final disposal. It accounted for the consumption of raw materials, the energy used in processing, transportation and cleaning, the output of hazardous substances into the air and water, and the volume of rubbish created. It ignored some other environmental effects that are more locally varied, such as noise, smell and harm to the landscape. The report concluded that the energy costs were fundamental in the analysis and paper cups do more harm than polystyrene except for their effect on water (Exhibit 4.6).

EXHIBIT 4.6 All washed up: energy or pollution

China cups and saucers start with one big handicap: they need to be washed. 'To wash a porcelain cup and saucer once, in an average dishwasher,' avers the report, 'has a greater impact on the water than the entire life cycle of a disposable cup.' The suffracants in detergents, which clean off the grease, see to that. In their impact on air, energy consumption and volume of rubbish, china cups may do less harm in the end than their disposable rivals. But each time a china cup and saucer are put through a dishwasher, they use energy, cause nasty gases to be released into the air and create a bit more solid rubbish.

Whether it is greener to drink coffee from a china cup and saucer or a plastic or paper one depends on two things: how many times the china cup and saucer are used, and how frequently they are washed. Have only one cuppa between washes, and the cup and saucer need to be used 1,800 times before they have less impact on the air during their lifetime than a polystyrene mug. That still gives china the edge: Dutch caterers reckon to use a china cup and saucer 3,000 times. But ask for a refill, and the china crockery needs to be used only 114 times before it beats polystyrene on energy use, and only 86 times before it does less damage to the air. Paper cups do more harm than polystyrene on every count except their impact on water.

The answer, says the report, is to pay more attention to the amount of energy used by dishwashers and the pollution caused by detergents. Most office workers have another answer: allow a fine patina of old coffee to develop around the inside of the mug. It may not be hygienic, but it is good for the planet.

Source: *The Economist*, 1 August 1992: 54.

Introduction to the micro marketing environment

The micro marketing environment refers to that part of the environment over which the company has some control. The remainder of the text deals with various ways the company attempts to manage its affairs within the context of a given marketing environment.

Company response to environmental change

Companies respond to environmental change by attempting to predict changes in it and by developing coping mechanisms

Predictability of environment

The degree to which the environment is unstable and unpredictable is of considerable concern to the manager. Factors which contribute to unpredictability are the rate of change in the environment, the degree to which relationships with the environment are routinized, and the degree to which the company has direct contact with the environment.

A rapidly changing environment is less predictable than a slowly changing one. Indications of a rapidly changing environment are the frequency of new product introductions, the level at which competitors enter and exit the market, and the length of the typical life cycle.

Predictability decreases as the firm has to deal with more issues in coping with the environment. For example, multitiered distribution systems give rise to greater levels of unpredictability. Companies in rapidly changing markets attempt to increase the level of predictability by developing vertical marketing systems. The activities of the large brand companies in acquiring their distributors in various markets is evidence of this approach. Firms also reduce uncertainty by routinizing relationships with the environment. This may be done by developing long-term contractual relationships. Companies also reduce uncertainty by developing adaptive organizational structures which are simple and flexible, and designed to cope easily with change.

Coping with market uncertainty

In general, companies facing an uncertain environment respond at the micro level if they believe their fortunes will be affected, or ignore change if they believe the environmental changes will not affect them or if they cannot do anything about it. In such instances, a structured response, whereby the firm

187

reduces its vulnerability to uncontrollable events by becoming more flexible and adaptable, is sometimes followed. One such approach is to broaden the product and market scope of the firm (Allaire and Firsirotu, 1989: 12). Small independent firms tend to respond to uncertainty and turbulent environments by improving existing products and services and developing new ones. A portfolio of product-markets reduces overall uncertainty and introduces stability for the firm. Also employed are new manufacturing strategies to lower product costs and strategies to compete on price. These are strategies which are believed to be predominantly within the control of the firm.

The perceived environment facing managers may be judged in terms of the rate of change occurring in key economic and market variables. Rapidly changing environments are associated with unstable public policy regimes, unpredictable changes in economic variables, and unexpected changes in customer requirements or competitor positions. The key factor is unpredictability, which calls for flexibility and devolved discretion in management. In environments which change only slowly, the firm operates to standard procedures where much of the discretion remains with senior managers.

Assignment questions

1 How can the environment of the supplier affect the marketing operations of the company? What can the company do to gain greater control over the environment?

2 Why do many manufacturers use intermediaries to distribute their products instead of doing it themselves?

3 Why is it important to assess the marketing environment?

4 Explain how changes in the demographic environment affect the fortunes of the company.

5 Describe the consequences for marketing of a period or prosperity and recession.

6 What is culture? What are the implications for the company of increased interest in health, changing roles for women and increased desire for convenience?

7 What are the components of the political and legal environment? How are these environments interrelated?

8 How does technology affect the firm's marketing efforts? Give examples of how technology can facilitate marketing.

Annotated bibliography

Abernathy, William J., Kim B. Clark and Alan M. Kantrow (1983) *Industrial Renaissance*, New York: Basic Books.

Duncan, R. (1972) 'Characteristics of organisational environments and perceived environmental uncertainty', *Administrative Science Quarterly*, **17**, 2, 313–27.

Pfeffer, Jeffrey, and G.R. Salancik (1978) *The External Control of Organisations: A resource dependence perspective*, New York: Harper and Row.

Porter, Michael E. (1980) *Competitive Strategy*, New York: The Free Press.

References

Abernathy, William J., Kim B. Clark and Alan M. Kantrow (1983) *Industrial Renaissance*, New York: Basic Books.

Allaire, Yvan, and Mihaela E. Firsirotu (1989) 'Coping with strategic uncertainty', *Sloan Management Review*, **30**, 3, 7–16.

Camillus, John C., and Deepah K. Datta (1991) 'Managing strategic issues in a turbulent environment', *Long Range Planning*, **24**, 2, 67–74.

Downey, H.K. and W. Slocum (1975) 'Uncertainty: measures, research and sources of variation', *Administrative Science Quarterly*, **20**, 4, 562–77.

Duncan, R. (1972) 'Characteristics of organisational environments and perceived environmental uncertainty', *Administrative Science Quarterly*, **17**, 2, 313–27.

European Management Forum (1984) *Report on International Industrial Competitiveness*, Geneva: European Management Forum.

Gifford, W.E., H.R. Bobbitt and J.W. Slocum (1979) 'Message characteristics and perceptions of uncertainty by organisational decision makers', *Academy of Management Journal*, **22**, 3, 458–81.

Johanson, Jan, and Lars-Gunnar Mattsson (1985) 'Marketing investments and market investment in industrial networks', *International Journal of Research in Marketing*, **2**, 3, 185–95.

Jurkovich, R. (1974) 'A core typology of organisational environments', *Administrative Science Quarterly*, **19**, 3, 380–94.

Lawrence, P.R., and J.W. Lorsch (1967) 'Differentiation and integration in complex organisations', *Administrative Science Quarterly*, **12**, 1, 1–47.

Lewis, William W., Andreas Siemen, Michael Balay, and Koki Sakate (1992) 'Service sector productivity and international competitiveness', *The McKinsey Quarterly*, **4**, 69–91.

Lynn, Mathew (1991) 'Drug companies in a fix', *International Management*, October, 62–5.

Metcalfe, J.L. (1974) 'Systems models, economic models and the casual texture of organisational environments: an approach to macro-organisation theory', *Human Relations*, **27**, 7, 639–63.

Möller, K.E. Kristian, and Mai Anttila (1987) 'Marketing capability in small manufacturing firms: a key success factor?', paper in *Contemporary Research in Marketing*, the 16th Annual Conference of the European Marketing Academy, York University, Toronto.

Pfeffer, Jeffrey, and G.R. Salancik (1978) *The External Control of Organisations: A resource dependence perspective*, New York: Harper and Row.

Porter, Michael E. (1980) *Competitive Strategy*, New York: The Free Press.
Sheth, Jagdish N. (1992) 'Emerging marketing strategies in a changing macroeconomic environment: a commentary', *International Marketing Review*, **9**, 1, 57–63.
Weitz, B., and E. Anderson (1981) 'Organizing the marketing function', in R.M. Ennis and K.J. Roering (eds), *Review of Marketing*, New York: American Marketing Association.

Case studies

Case 1: Aston Martin Lagonda Ltd

The owner of an Aston Martin is quintessentially a patriotic Briton, personified by James Bond, and HRH the Prince of Wales, who has two Astons. Rumours abound that the Princess of Wales once sat on the bonnet of one and scratched its paint work, much to HRH's fury. What is it that makes this car so precious, that a little lost paint work is enough to infuriate such a regal owner? As a past chairman of the company once said, 'Aston Martin ... is analogous to Britain.' Only 11 500 cars have been manufactured since the company was founded in 1914. Each car is hand-wrought and assembled. The signature of the man who made the engine is attached to the finished car on a brass plate.

As the car has a price-tag of £132 000, customers do not appear to be price sensitive, which considerably cushions the effects of recession. However, like many of the last bastions of all things British, the winds of change also arrived for Aston Martin Lagonda Ltd. For many years, owners like David Brown underwrote the firm's losses for love of the car. By 1987, 'Bankers were even tapping David Brown on the shoulder.' Admittedly, Aston made modest profits for two consecutive years, for the first time in its history. This was due in part to an increase in the real price of the cars, and a new company policy of demanding £25 000 deposit up-front.

In 1991 Ford took a 75 per cent stake in the British marque. Michael Haysey, Aston Martin's marketing director for the past five years, recalls, 'There were a lot of letters from Aston owners saying they wanted to buy their last true Aston and that this was going to be the end of it.' However, Ford has been careful not to publicize its Aston connection, and it has not promoted the fact that it is from the same stable as the Ford Escort. Undoubtedly, the company is mindful of the potential damage to the image of Aston's Virage and Vantage models. Victor Gauntlett, the chairman at the time, noted with

191

relief that there was 'no "Can we have a discreet Ford badge?"', claiming 'it would be better to close Aston than to ruin it' by such an action.

Car manufacturers everywhere faced the world-wide recession. Aston Martin Lagonda, previously aloof, did not go untainted by hard times. Many of its Arab consumers, still recovering after the Gulf War, defaulted on their deposits. In addition, the company's failure to read the American market properly, by having a convertible available for export, meant that the company lost out considerably in the US market, which had no interest in any other kind of Aston Martin.

Ford's influence was felt, with some subtle changes. Previously, good industrial relations did not exist at Aston Martin. There were no training programmes or skill recognition for its 400-strong workforce. Ford introduced day-release apprenticeships. Aston Martin was planning to expand its product range, by launching a new cheaper car. At £75 000, it is still in the very expensive category.

The company, despite its new ties with Ford, has shown little interest in marketing. Walter Hayes, Aston Martin's new chairman, typifies much of the company culture by saying, 'It's my opinion that if you have a product which is superior to anybody else's, you ought to survive – but there is no guarantee you will.' Inevitably with Ford's stake, a marketing orientation is bound eventually to permeate the company, alien as it is to the concept. Hayes shies away from the word. 'Lots of people have strange feelings about marketing. I'm just trying to say: we've been through a terrible recession, everybody's pessimistic about luxury cars, but don't worry about us, because we know what we are and what we're going to do.'

In 1992 the company was spending £350 000 annually on marketing; predominantly on attendance at the major car shows. There has been a realization, particularly with the launch of its new model into a very competitive segment of the market, that they should 'start to do the job more professionally'. This gradual dawning of the need for marketing may be what secures Aston Martin Lagonda's future in this highly competitive market.

Evaluate the importance of marketing to the Aston Martin Lagonda company.

Sources: 'A very distinguished marque', *Management Today*, March 1992: 56–60; 'The super-car stoops to conquer', 5 March 1992: 24–5.

This case was prepared by Nora Costello, Department of Marketing, University College Dublin, as a basis for class discussion rather than to illustrate either effective or ineffective handling of an administrative situation.

Case 2: Clashmore Containers

Clashmore Containers is the Engineering Division of the Clashmore Co-operative Society in County Wexford, one of the largest in the country. The division was formed some twenty years ago to service the stainless steel tanks and containers used in handling milk and milk products. In 1970 it began to develop and fabricate stainless steel containers for use in the many branches of the Co-op and then on request to custom-build them for other users of this type of equipment. By 1975 it was exporting stainless steel containers to the UK. Five years later, the company had developed so rapidly that a full field sales force was established in the UK. The industry consists of approximately ten major producers and a number of smaller ones. Clashmore Containers has grown to be one of the top ten mainly due to its highly competitive pricing policy. According to the sales manager, the competitors have become extremely vigorous of late, especially in product innovation. But Clashmore engineers so far have been able to place a close substitute on the market soon after a competitive innovation.

The Clashmore sales staff are completely separated from the manufacturing division, with sales offices in such centres as Manchester, Birmingham, London, Glasgow, Belfast and Dublin. The sales people are extremely active and effective in terms of sales contacts, customer relations, dispersion of product information and obtaining sales. Whenever a need arises for a new type of container, or a modification to an existing model, the sales staff contact the design engineers at the manufacturing plant in Wexford. The design engineers supply preliminary design and cost estimates to the sales staff so that specific details on capacity, size, cost and so on may be shown to a potential customer. The design engineering department is manned by a staff of very competent engineers, well versed in the various technical areas needed to design stainless steel containers. This department is accountable to the manager of the manufacturing department. Recently, this manager has received numerous complaints from the engineering department about the methods employed by the sales staff in trying to secure customers.

The problem came to a head recently when the sales staff returned with a rather large order for a radically new type of container. The engineering department had previously supplied preliminary designs and cost estimates to the sales staff, but the latter announced that what they had sold had little relation to the preliminary designs. Indeed, it was completely different from the original sketches. The complaints of the engineering department can be summarized as follows:

> The sales staff come in here and ask us for a preliminary design for a new container and we break our backs to provide them with such information on very short notice. Then they have the gall to

come back and tell us that they have sold a completely different container, for which we have done no work. It seems to me that they will sell anything the market wants, instead of what we design for them.

Another point of irritation to the engineers is the habit of sales staff in bargaining on the prices of the containers with each customer. The engineers' comment on this practice was: 'Hasn't anyone around here ever heard of a standard price?'

Evaluate the engineers' perception of the problem. What should be done?

This case was prepared by Professor Anthony C. Cunningham, Department of Marketing, University College Dublin, as a basis for class discussion, rather than to illustrate either effective or ineffective handling of an administrative situation.

Case 3: Mars ice-cream

'The problem for Mars is to avoid becoming a victim of its own success, as rivals increasingly segment the market. The company needs to redefine its target market and establish its position with consumers quickly to achieve satisfactory returns from its heavy investments in ice-cream,' suggests Clive Richardson, an industry analyst with stockbrokers Henderson Crosthwaite.

British ice-cream market, 1988

The British market, where Mars originally launched its pan-European ice-cream brand, typified market trends across Europe in 1988. Traditionally, the European market was characterized by stability, relying heavily on bulk sales of basic flavours such as vanilla. The Anglo-Dutch conglomerate Unilever, which held a commanding market share of almost 40 per cent in most European countries, dominated the market through various subsidiaries such as Walls in the UK and HB in Ireland. Unilever pursued an undifferentiated marketing approach, with the result that its ice-cream was perceived as plain and ordinary, consumed mostly by children. However, with the launch of Walls' Gino Ginelli and Vienetta, record levels of ice-cream growth were recorded in the 'premium' and 'multipacks' sectors of the take-home market in 1988. This trend, which is identified in Table 1, was the first indication of increasing consumer preference for value-added products.

It was against this background that privately owned Mars, the world's largest producer of confectionery after Nestlé of Switzerland, introduced a luxury ice-cream version of their highly successful chocolate confectionery brand. The new ice-cream, which was aimed at the latent adult market, was priced at 60p (£1.99 for four) and distributed solely through supermarkets

194

TABLE 1   UK ice-cream sector, 1987/8

	1987 (£m)	1988 (£m)	Diff. (%)
Impulse			
Wrapped	141.4	150.6	7
Scooping	84.9	87.3	3
Take home			
Multipack	86.5	108.7	26
Desserts	33.7	35.4	5
Premium	26.0	35.6	37
Block	131.5	131.0	

Source: *The Grocer*, 18 November 1989.

with little above-the-line advertising. Mars' Lockshey Ryan explained, 'Adults eat only a third of the ice-cream consumed by their children, so there is vast growth potential.'

Mars targeted the affluent adult market aged 20–45. These adults had never considered ice-cream as a luxury to be indulged. In its first year, the Mars ice-cream recorded sales of £25 million in Britain alone and was described by one financial correspondent as the outstanding new product of the year. As consumer awareness and sales grew, the marketing emphasis switched from the take-home trade to the 'impulse' purchasing sector, and from the supermarket to the corner shop. Distribution contracts where arranged with local country suppliers such as Lyons Maid in Britain, which were actually selling competing products. Philip Robinson, Walls' marketing manager, explained that 'Lyons has shown in tests that where it sells Mars ice-cream it attracts a new ice-cream buyer'. Mars' success proved that impulse ices could be sold for well above 50p, previously considered unthinkable.

European ice-cream market, 1992

Unlike five years ago, ice-cream is now considered to be among the most profitable and fastest-growing business in Europe. The catalyst was Mars' launch in 1989 of premium priced ice-cream. Almost overnight it created a thriving luxury sector. Its success has prompted consumer manufacturers such as Unilever, Scholler, Cadbury's, Nestlé and Grand Met (Haagen Dazs) to launch a stream of rival products (Table 2.).

Segmentation strategies

Simon Esberger, marketing director of Haagen Dazs, explains that his company's products are targeted at the 'young aspiring' adult segment of the premium

TABLE 2   New product launches, post-1989

	Nestlé		Grand Met	Baskin
Unilever	Lyons	Mars	Haagen Dazs	Robbins
Magnum	Klondike	Mars	Motts	Parlours
Sky	Calippo	Bounty	Gervais	
Dream		Snickers		
Cadbury		Galaxy		
Fruit & Nut		Milky Way		
Chunky		Opal Fruit		
Feast				

Source: Various

markets. 'We are not selling ice-cream, we are selling pleasure.' In effect, Haagen Dazs has successfully penetrated the target market that Mars identified, using consumer lifestyles and personality as a basis for segmentation.

Unilever responded to the threat that Mars ice-cream posed with the launch of several new products, each of which segmented the premium adult market even further: 'Dream' is aimed at women aged 20–45, 'Chunky' towards young men (20–30), 'Feast' at older teenagers, and Cadbury's 'Fruit & Nut' at married middle-age people. Both Unilever and St Ivel have introduced diet brands, 'Too Good To Be True' and 'Shape' respectively.

The launch of Walls' 'Magnum', priced at nearly £1, and the Baskin Robbins ice-cream parlours have helped create a new 'super-premium' category. When Allied-Lyons financially supported Baskin Robbins, the American chain of ice-cream parlours, it created the ultimate ice-cream, complete with a unique chain of high-class retail outlets. The final stage of the revolution was the introduction of Haagen Dazs' great US rival Klondike in several European markets. The industry's success has even prompted changes in consumers' eating habits, with the weather making less of an impact and ice-cream increasingly regarded as a dessert in its own right.

Mars ice-cream

The company's share of its three biggest ice-cream markets, the USA, the UK and Germany, is relatively low and in decline (Table 3). Mars' commitment to

TABLE 3   World ice-cream sales, 1992 (£m)

Region	Unilever	Nestlé	Scholler	Haagen Dazs	Brever	Mars
Europe	1,550	200	400	50	–	150
North America	200	150	–	200	300	100
Rest of world	150	150	–	100	–	–
Total	1,900	500	400	350	300	250

Source: *Financial Times*, 19 March 1993.

the fledgling ice-cream market was emphasized recently by the completion of the £40 million factory near Strasbourg, eastern France. But to be economic, the 50,000-tonne capacity plant needs large production volumes, which means big sales. So far its market penetration has been uneven. The bulk of its sales are believed still to be in the UK, where it had about 10 per cent of the £770 million market in 1992.

Within the adult ice-cream sector, the manufacturers have divided the market into basic ice-cream, premium and super-premium, using various segmentation techniques such as age, gender, income, personality, lifestyle and benefit expectations. Mars is now in danger of being 'stuck in the middle' with an undifferentiated strategy targeted at all adults as a 'special treat', priced at 60p. 'Mars' entry had been dramatic, their timing was impeccable,' says Henry Clark, owner of Clark Foods, a UK ice-cream manufacturer. He also suggests that the spate of new product launches has overtaken Mars and consumers are now very confused about Mars' 'premium' positioning. Clive Richardson of Henderson Crosthwaite suggests that 'Mars is rather behind in the competitive game now', while according to Simon Esberger of Haagen Dazs, 'The premium market can support only two brands.'

On what basis would you segment the ice-cream market and which segment would you suggest Mars target its brands towards should the company re-evaluate its segmentation strategy?

Sources: *Daily Telegraph*, 20 April 1990; *Financial Times*, 7 August 1990; *Financial Times*, 13 June 1992; *Financial Times*, 19 March 1993; *Financial Weekly*, 4 May 1990; *The Grocer*, 18 November 1990; *Irish Times*, 19 March 1993; *Marketing Week*, 22 May 1992; *Marketing Week*, 26 February 1993; *Sunday Times*, 12 August 1990.

This case was prepared by Derek Creevey, Department of Marketing, University College Dublin, as a basis for class discussion rather than to illustrate either effective or ineffective handling of an administrative situation.

Case 4: Cap Gemini Sogeti

Cap Gemini Sogeti is Europe's leading computer services supplier. Since managing director Serge Kampf quit Groupe Bull to found Cap Gemini, the French-based company with the entrepreneurial spirit has been a success. The company had a turnover of FFr 10 billion (ECU1.5 billion) in 1991, and was no. 4 in the industry world-wide.

However, although Cap Gemini is the market leader in France, Sweden and the Netherlands, it has less than 1 per cent of the largest IT market in the world, the USA, and has no market share in Asia. Its domestic market, France, is responsible for 40 per cent of its profits. And for the first time in 24 years, Cap's profits fell in 1991. In addition, operating margins are on a downward slide.

This decline reflects the tough recessionary times that all firms are facing. Industry commentators have suggested that the computer services market is changing, and that a shake-out is likely to occur in the industry. Competition is also becoming stiff, with the global American companies moving in on Cap's home market. 'Those against whom we've got to fight are no longer the local companies,' says Serge Kampf, 'but EDS, IBM, Arthur Andersen or AT & T.' In particular, EDS, the world leader in 'outsourcing', a practice whereby the IT service supplier runs the whole computer operation for the client, has trebled its European turnover in the last three years.

Clearly, the IT service market is moving away from a demand for the one-off customized software projects that were once the lifeblood of Cap Gemini. 'Many companies no longer see any reason to pay for custom programming when increasingly sophisticated standard software can do the trick,' says Morgan David, the Copenhagen-based service industry analyst with International Data Corporation. Companies are now demanding higher-value-added services, such as systems integration, where the supplier is responsible for the overall design, installation and maintenance of clients' orders. While growth in custom programming is falling, industry analysts predict that annual growth for systems integration and outsourcing could be greater than 20 per cent.

'Cap Gemini is facing an enormous challenge to the way it does business,' says Roger Fullton, a software and services analyst with London-based IT con-sultants Input. 'As IT purchasing habits change, the business on which they've built their success is rapidly moving out from underneath them.' In addition, American companies have targeted Europe. 'The opportunities to grow are better in Europe than anywhere else,' says Jurge Berg, managing director of EDS' European operations, 'the pressure in Europe is on Cap.'

Mindful of the need to enter growing markets and service sectors, Cap Gemini has followed an aggressive acquisition strategy. To help finance this programme, Cap teamed up with Daimler-Benz, who paid FFr1.2 billion for a 34 per cent shareholding in Sogeti, Cap Gemini's holding company. Cap Gemini's acquisitions include the French systems integrator Sesa, a 70 per cent share of Hoskyns, a UK leader in outsourcing, SCS, a German systems integrator, and Programmer, the no. 1 integration house in Sweden. In addi-tion, Cap has a joint venture agreement with Debi systemhaus, Daimler-Benz's IT services company.

Cap also established a consultancy division, Gemini Consulting, through the acquisition of French consultants Gamma International, and two US-based firms, United Research and Mac Group. Gemini Consulting is now one of the largest independent management consultancies world-wide, with over 1200 employees. This allows Cap to offer customers a more integrated range of ser-vices, comparable to those being offered by many of its competitors.

Many of these moves have met with success. The Cap Debi joint venture dominates the German market, and yields the company an additional FFr6 billion in turnover. Hoskyns, the UK arm of the company, is beaten only by Sema in the domestic market.

Following these successes, Cap Gemini's managers have set the target of being a global leader. However, before this goal is reached the company faces a number of problems: declining margins, overpayment for many of its acquisitions, and flat internal growth that was below the market level in 1991. In addition, the decentralized management structure of the company has resulted in poor communication and co-operation between operating units, meaning in effect that they operate independently. 'People's vision of the group tends to stop at national borders,' says Jacques Arnould, the former head of French operations. A big question mark also hangs over the issue of control. Daimler-Benz has the option of becoming a majority shareholder in 1995, unless the operation is bought back by Cap Gemini shareholders in late 1994.

Antoine Boivin-Champeaux, an analyst with Paris-based brokers BZW Puget Mahe, says that this push for global dominance is 'an extremely dangerous strategy', and he believes 'their only real advantage is being big'. Serge Kampf, on the other hand, sees the company's transformation as being akin to crossing a treacherous river, admitting that the river has proved to be somewhat deeper and the current stronger than expected. Although Kampf may feel that half the river is behind him, the company has yet to reach the shore safely.

What should Cap Gemini Soget do: (a) to adapt to the changing technological environment; (b) to become a global player?

Sources: 'Cap Gemini takes aim at the world', *Business Week*, 26 August 1991: 50; 'Cap Gemini's twin challenge', *International Management*, November 1992: 28–31.

This case was prepared by Nora Costello, Department of Marketing, University College Dublin, as a basis for class discussion rather than to illustrate either effective or ineffective handling of an administrative situation.

PART B

Select the value for markets, customers and competitors

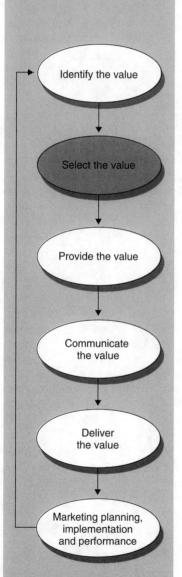

- select market values
- define customer benefits
- recognise competitive responses

Chapters

5   Analysis of markets

6   Understanding consumer markets

7   Understanding organizational markets

8   Understanding and analyzing competitors

9   Informing marketing decisions

Analysis of markets

5

Multidimensional aspects of markets
Competition in markets
Innovation and evolution of markets
Marketing management in different markets

Introduction

This chapter introduces and explains:

- different management perspectives in the company: financial, investment and market;

- the myriad kinds of market which exist;

- influences on market demand;

- the meaning of competition in markets;

- the role and importance of innovation;

- how diffusion of innovation works;

- how markets evolve; and

- management conditions existing in different kinds of market.

The focus of this chapter is on the concept of a market, emphasizing that buyers and sellers meet in some way to exchange things of value. The circumstances under which they meet determine, to a large extent, the value of the exchange. The role of competitive innovation, especially in respect of products and services, is examined and forms the basis of an understanding of how markets emerge, grow, mature and eventually decline. By way of introduction to subsequent chapters, the general marketing management conditions which exist in selected markets are described.

After studying this chapter, you should be able to do the following:

1. Define the term 'market', 'competition', and 'innovation'.

2. Apply the concept of market to products, services, people and ideas.

3. Identify the general influences on demand for a product or service.

4. Describe the nature and structure of competition in markets, distinguishing among undifferentiated, differentiated and monopoly markets.

5. Determine the impact of market structure on marketing management.

6. List the advantages of innovation in markets.

7. Describe how diffusion of innovation occurs at industry level and at company level.

8. Recognize the importance of the evolutionary stages in markets.

9. Evaluate the general approaches companies use to manage different kinds of market.

Multidimensional aspects of markets

Each firm must decide where in the market it should compete. This means selecting a market of even a part or segment of the market to serve. Two mutually supporting influences affect the company's choice. Markets arise from the interaction of customer needs and demands and from the capability of organizations to provide products and services to satisfy these needs and demands, which are primarily technology driven. The fundamental demand factor is the size of the pool of prospective buyers, i.e. the market potential. Needs and demands are dynamic, since they may be altered over time by factors such as demographic and economic trends and the evolution of other markets.

Markets may be viewed from several perspectives. There are markets for products and services, ideas and people, commodities, finance and a host of other tangible and intangible things. Originally the word 'market' referred to the place where people exchanged goods and services for money or other goods and services. Nowadays it may not be necessary to meet to transact business. Markets can exist without there being a physical location in which to transact an exchange.

A market is the circumstance under which buyers and sellers transact business. Both buyers and sellers are involved. This view of a market is different from that found in many marketing textbooks, where the sellers are viewed as the industry and the buyers viewed as the market. Kotler's (1994: 11) concept of a market as 'all the potential customers sharing a particular need or want who might be willing and able to engage in exchange to satisfy that need or want' is, therefore, too narrow. Buyers and sellers converge in the market, where the convergence implies a meeting of minds regarding the exchange of values. The value from the buyer's point of view is usually a benefit of some kind, whereas the benefit from the company's point of view is profit.

Managerial framework of the company

The company seeks to make profit in its transactions. Several groups within the company have a direct interest in company profitability. A company may be conceived as being represented by three perspectives: an investment perspective, a financial perspective and a market perspective (Figure 5.1). Profit is central to all three perspectives. The market perspective is concerned with demand and supply as they affect the market for the value under consideration. The company engages in a series of marketing activites, leading to a set of receipts and costs. A trade-off between these gives rise to profit. In the financial perspective of the business, profit contributes to the company's dividends and retained earnings, which indirectly contributes to the funds available for investment. The investment perspective considers the allocation of resources among various uses, such as physical plant and equipment, research and development, and investment in markets. Market investment and research and development investment influence the demand side of the market equation, while investment in physical facilities and research and development contribute to the supply side of the equation, the second major element in the market perspective of the company.

The three perspectives are intimately linked: market-based activities drive profit, which in turn drives the company's financial performance, which then supports investment. Investment expenditures directly influence the market. The three perspectives of the company represent an interlocking management system related to various markets.

Markets for products and services

In dealing with products and markets, it is necessary to distinguish between different levels of aggregation. First, there is the product class, which includes all things that are close substitutes for the same needs despite differences in size, colour, shape and technical configuration. Examples include all video players, personal audio equipment, washing machines and cars. Product type is the next level of aggregation and is a subset of product class wherein items differ in size, price, shape and, perhaps, form. Examples include fresh, frozen, dried and canned fruit; digital and mechanical time-pieces; leather or PVC covered diaries. At the lowest level of the product hierarchy is the brand.

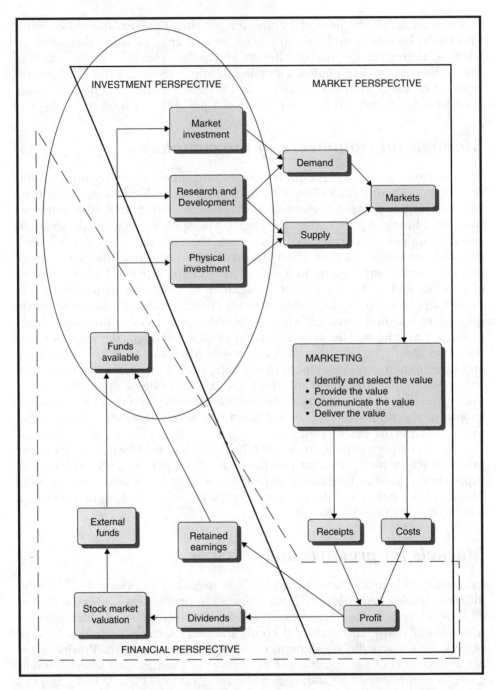

Figure 5.1 Managerial framework of the company: investment, market and financial perspectives of the firm

The principal consideration in dealing with product hierarchies suggests that the more homogeneous the level, the better the company can relate its market investment to income streams over time. The level of aggregation selected should also provide important insights into the interrelationships among the various levels in the hierarchy, especially in regard to costs.

There are also hierarchies in markets. Market hierarchies depend on the extent of segmentation in the market. As was seen earlier, segments are usually defined on the basis of similarity of buyer choice criteria as well as consumer evaluation of the various brands or products on offer. They are typically referred to as product segments. Using segments in this way, it is possible to link the product to definable groups whose preferences about product class and product type attributes are known. Obtaining such knowledge allows the firm to identify opportunities for new products. Such knowledge also provides guidelines for other elements of the marketing mix, such as promotion and pricing.

Markets for ideas and people

There are markets also for ideas and people. Though not normally seen as such, politicians, entertainers, writers and university teachers are in the market for ideas and some of them for people also. Ideas and people in a sense represent value to others. The electorate gives its vote in return for a promise to manage the country or public office in a certain way. Similarly, entertainers, writers and other people exchange ideas or the participation in some activity in return for payment.

The market for entertainment and leisure activities is very large in most countries and growing rapidly. Understanding how some of these markets function can be difficult. The sports business, for example, is very complex and includes large expenditures by the public (Exhibit 5.1). It is also very dependent on television for its revenues (Figure 5.2).

Defining a market

Many definitions may be found as to what constitutes a market. A market has been defined as 'an aggregate of people who, as individuals or as organizations, have needs for products in a product class and who have the ability, willingness, and authority to purchase such products' (Dibb *et al.*, 1991: 66). At a general level, a market is all actual and potential buyers of a product or service. At a more specific level, a consumer market is defined as all individuals and households who are actual and potential buyers of products and services for personal, family or household consumption. An industrial market contains all organizations which buy products and services as components, raw materials or equipment to be used in the provision of other products and services.

207

EXHIBIT 5.1 The sports business

It is a complex market. The suppliers are of many sorts: self-employed *players; team owners; promoters of events*. This third group includes global sporting bodies such as FIFA or the International Olympic Committee (IOC), regional and national ones, commercial promoters, team owners themselves and – in tennis and golf – groupings of players (or, in Japan's sumo wrestling, ex-players). All are jostling fiercely for their share of the loot. The ultimate source of that loot is, as ever, Joe Public, but wearing many hats: paying *spectator*; subsidy-providing *taxpayer; buyer* of sports goods; or of anything else that can be sold to Joe in his most lucrative persona – the *television watcher*.

Between suppliers and the final customer lie a host of middlemen. Most significant are the broadcasters, buying television rights for huge sums, which they in turn pull in from advertisers, programme sponsors and, increasingly, pay-TV subscribers. Next are the sponsors – of players, teams or events – who pay through the nose to have their product used (skis) or worn (shoes) or drunk by the stars, or merely named (anything from cigarettes to insurance) on advertising signs, shirts, helmets, sails, car-bodies, whatever is visible on the course and so on-screen. A bit more comes from buyers of merchandising rights – the right to sell Chicago Bull's shirts or mugs with FIFA's World Cup logo.

Greasing the ways of money almost everywhere are the agents, working with all the other categories, sometimes for several at once; on commission or – in some rights deals, for example – as principals. Do not think all the participants are equal. Some could vanish little mourned; without the mass audiences of television, today's sports market would collapse.

Source: 'Survey of the sports business', *The Economist*, 25 July 1992: 25.

Market demand refers to the demand in the market for a product class, which is the total volume that would be bought by a defined customer group in a defined time period under defined environmental conditions and marketing effort.

Influences on demand

The price the company can charge for its products or services and the price a customer is willing to pay depend on three important influences. The first of these influences is referred to as the generic demand for the product, or the demand for a general product class and related products. The second is the brand demand or those factors which influence the demand for the company's specific product or brand. The third influence is public policy, or restraints on pricing imposed by the government or other public agency (Figure 5.3).

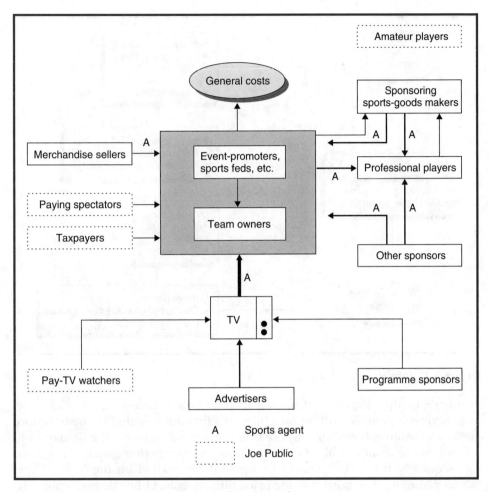

Figure 5.2 How the money rolls in the business of sport

(Source: 'Survey of the sports business', *The Economist*, 25 July 1992: 5. Copyright, *The Economist*, London 1994.)

Generic influences on demand

Generic influences on market demand are determined primarily by demographic and economic factors. An example will illustrate. Suppose a furniture factory manufactures under the label 'Superline'. The demand for furniture in general, irrespective of who makes it, is referred to as the generic demand for furniture and is influenced by demographic trends and economic factors.

Demography affects the generic demand for furniture in a number of ways. A rapidly expanding population expands the demand for furniture. But it is important to note that the increased demand for furniture will differ, depending on whether the new entrants to the population result from a high

209

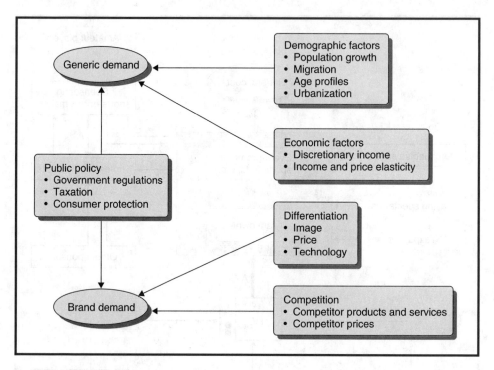

Figure 5.3   Influences on demand

birth-rate or the migration of middle-aged and older people. In the first case, the increased demand will be for children's furniture, including beds, school desks and more robust items, whereas in the second instance, the demand will be for more comfortable items perhaps in the higher price categories. Consequently, it may be possible to segment the market on the basis of age, which presents an opportunity for price differentials. Other demographic factors which influence the demand for furniture include the number of women in the population, where people live (centre city, suburbs, town, countryside) and how people live (family units, singles, apartments or houses). Some of these demographic factors will have a greater influence on the demand for the company's products than others.

Regarding economic factors, the general trend in discretionary income is an important determinant of demand. Discretionary incomes have a larger effect on the demand for some products than for others. As food purchases cannot easily be postponed, the amount of food purchased does not change as much as, say, the number of new motor cars purchased in response to a reduction in discretionary income. Of significance to pricing policy is the strength of consumer response to a change in income. With an increase in discretionary income, consumers buy proportionately more of some products than others. Luxury items are usually in this category.

210

Underlying this discussion is the concept of the elasticity of demand in response to income changes. Product categories may be income elastic or income inelastic. Products and services for which there is a large change in demand in response to a small change in income levels are referred to as income elastic. Products or services for which the demand only responds very slightly for a small change in income are known as income inelastic. Motor cars are classified as income-elastic products, whereas basic foodstuffs are classified as income-inelastic products.

Related to this concept is the concept of price elasticity. Interest here centres on the response to price changes. Products and services for which there is a substantial change in the demand as a result of a price change are referred to as price elastic. In contrast, price-inelastic products and services are those the demand for which does not change greatly as a result of a change in price. When department stores hold sales, they usually reduce the price of those items of merchandise which they believe to be price elastic, so that stocks can be cleared to make way for new styles and new products.

Influence of branding on demand

Selecting a pricing strategy for a specific brand is part of the strategy of positioning a brand. It is necessary to know the image of the brand in the customer's mind. The company must then determine how to price its product, to position it as a high-quality product or as an economy product. Deciding on the brand price is important because the company is trying to position its product in such a way as to gain adequate sales without attracting undue competitive reaction. A drop in price, for example, is one of the clearest signals that can be communicated to a competitor. Price can be changed more quickly than any of the other variables in the marketing mix. Thus it is important to determine how competitors will react and how the market will react.

Competitive reaction will depend on how substitutable competitors' products are for those of the company. An important consideration here is the amount of new technology the company and its competitors are building into competing products. If there is nothing to distinguish the company's product, product substitution will, of course, be much easier. Successful branding insulates the company from competition.

Influences of public policy on demand

The third major influence on the demand for, and hence the price of, the company's products is public policy, or broadly speaking the influence of the government and other regulatory agencies. Public policy is used to ensure the preservation of competition in an industry, to protect the consumer, to conserve resources and protect the environment, and to raise government revenues through various forms of tax which usually operate directly through the price mechanism. In the first instance, public policy may affect the price that the company charges through regulations in regard to quantity discounts (e.g. the same quantity discounts to all buyers); functional discounts (e.g. a promotion discount given to a large supermarket chain must also be given to the small independent grocery shop); and geographic price differentials (e.g. to reflect differential transport costs). Regulations which apply to these anti-competitive devices and other price-fixing arrangements are frequently changed and updated, and hence should be monitored carefully.

Consumer protection from deceptive pricing is a second area where public policy impinges on the pricing of the firm. Regulations under this heading usually involve sale prices and also influence the way a firm advertises its products.

Public policies towards the conservation of resources and the preservation of the environment are beginning to have an impact on pricing agencies. It is likely that resource conservation will play a larger role in public policies in the future. Anti-pollution devices on motor cars have raised car prices, roof insulation regulations have raised house prices, and restrictions on the disposal of farm slurry have presumably raised the price of pork and bacon. Conservation of resources also enters pricing decisions: for example, if soft-drink manufacturers and beer bottlers are required to use returnable bottles.

The environment has in the past been a free good, so that it did not enter pricing decisions, but now the environment is rapidly entering production costs as firms are required to add devices to their production systems that will reduce the pollution of air and water.

Last, and perhaps most obvious, almost every price decision is affected by government policies on taxation. All taxes add to the price level directly or indirectly. Two major forms of taxation affect prices: value added taxes, and excise duties and tariffs. Because these taxes can be high, they tend to have a very significant effect on the final price charged to the consumer, and hence on the manner in which the consumer responds to changes in price due to changes in taxation. Two products with high taxes are alcoholic beverages and cigarettes, both of which are now so heavily taxed that their price is very high. It is thought that recent increases in taxation have adversely affected the generic demand for both of these product categories, which may serve governments' public health maintenance objectives.

In the medium term, the fear of standardized, regulated, EU-wide prices appears ill-founded. There is little pressure to harmonize prices, especially for consumer products, since most consumer products are made on a country basis and few cross-border retailing companies exist. There is, as yet, very little parallel importing occurring in the EU. Furthermore, the differences which exist in products from country to country in Europe are still very substantial. Identical products also appear to be positioned very differently in different countries. It is important to note, however, that this situation may change rapidly as the large food manufacturers and retailers attempt to implement European marketing strategies.

Competition in markets

A powerful supplier is able to reduce profits in an industry by raising prices or reducing the quality of products and services supplied to that industry. The power is highest in monopolies, but weak when there are many suppliers or substitutes. In the long term, supplier cartels may be weakened by market forces. In contrast, unless an industry has unique capability, the bargaining power of customers may severely restrict its room for manoeuvre. This is especially true when buying power is concentrated in a few hands.

Within the value chain, the profitability of any link is limited by the possibility of it being by-passed by either suppliers or customers. Many large companies have integrated vertically to control suppliers and to obtain a larger share of the value added. But in a rapidly changing environment, vertically integrated businesses may easily become high-cost, inflexible manufacturers which lose out to smaller, more flexible competitors.

The competitive continuum

At some point it will become essential for the company to identify the competitive characteristics of the market in which it operates. A successful continuum exists in which markets may be very competitive at one extreme, or there may be no competition at the opposite extreme (Table 5.1). Markets perform in different ways depending on their structure.

In purely competitive markets, there are a very large number of competing suppliers of undifferentiated products with no entry barriers, whose information concerning the market is freely available and in abundant supply.

TABLE 5.1 Characteristics of the competitive continuum

	Highly ◄─────── Competitive continuum ──────► competitive	No competition		
	Pure competition	Monopolistic competition	Oligopoly	Monopoly
No. of suppliers	Inifinite	Many	Few	One
Product/service differentiation	None	Some	Significant	Total
Market information	Perfect	Imperfect	Imperfect	Perfect
Market entry	No barriers	Few barriers	Some barriers	High barriers
Market types	Commodity and undifferentiated markets	Differentiated markets	Oligopoly and monopoly markets	

Examples of purely competitive markets include unorganized farming and commodity trading. Commodity markets such as the market for grain or cattle or steel are highly competitive. Similarly, undifferentiated product-markets are highly competitive as may be found in the case of simple kitchen furniture, machine components or petrol.

In monopolistic or differentiated markets, there are many suppliers of slightly different products. Entry barriers are few and information flows are imperfect. Examples of such markets include machine tool manufacturing and unbranded clothing. Differentiated markets are characterized by a degree or element of uniqueness in the product or service, which separates it from the rest. Differentiation is central to marketing as components attempt to feature the uniqueness of their products and service in an effort to serve the differentiated needs of customers. For example, petrol companies attempt to differentiate their products by adding cleansing agents and using heavy advertising.

In some product-markets there is little or no competition. Such markets are referred to as monopoloy or oligopoly markets depending on whether there is only one supplier or a few suppliers. In monopoly markets there is only one supplier of a totally differentiated product. There are very high entry barriers, but information is freely available. The markets for the products and services of utilities are good examples of monopoly markets. Even here, there is often a degree of competition. An electric utility may be a near monopolist in the market for artificial light, but in the market for power for heating and cooking it will have to compete with gas and oil. Many countries have begun to privatize utilities with the objective of ensuring that they compete for customers in the market. In recent years, telecommunications monopolies have attracted a lot of criticism which no doubt is a factor encouraging governments to privatize them (Exhibit 5.2).

As an example, there are monopoly and near-monopoly markets in the personal computer business. Intel Corporation and Microsoft Corporation

---

EXHIBIT 5.2   High prices and poor service from monopolies

High prices and poor service from PTT [post and telecommunications systems, government owned] can complicate the logistics of conducting business across a unified Europe. Just ask John C. Sale, network strategy director for Rank Xerox Ltd. The company is hoping to save money by consolidating five European data centres into one in southwest England. But doing so would require much additional data traffic between Britain and the Continent. The cost would be $25 million over the next several years. That would nearly wipe out the potential savings. 'At this point, telecom is a barrier to our quest of operating in a single market,' Sale laments.

Source: *Business Week*, 1 June 1992: 41.

profit handsomely from near monopolies in basic personal computer technology, while personal computer manufacturers have seen net margins fall from 8.1 per cent in 1987 to 3.9 per cent in 1993. According to Nobou Mii, president of IBM's Power Personal Systems Division, 'the truth is that we've become little more than assemblers' (*Business Week*, 13 December 1993: 53). Until recently, the Ordre de Médécin had a virtual monopoly of general practitioner medical services in France. This monopoly was broken by the launch of a service under the name SOS, which provides medical services in the home and during the night that were not previously available.

In oligopolistic markets, there are few suppliers of products which are significantly different from each other. There are some entry barriers and information flows are imperfect. Examples of such markets are detergents, fuels and oil.

Competitive environment of industry

Sometimes the company has an opportunity of evaluating the potential and risk associated with a number of different industries in which it might compete. The manager is interested in determining which industries are characterized by growth, profitability and other opportunities for the firm. The manager is also interested in avoiding unattractive industries, such as those characterized by cyclical or seasonal demand, or those very exposed to international competition, or industries which experience shortages of skilled labour or other scarce resources. The firm also needs to determine whether industry conditions are sufficiently favourable to allow the achievement of the company's objectives.

According to Levitt (1960: 47) there is no such thing as a growth industry, there are only companies organized and operated to create growth opportunities. Industries that assume that growth in their markets is automatic manifest a 'self deceiving cycle of bountiful expansion and undetected decay', according to Levitt, and there are four conditions which usually guarantee this cycle:

- the belief that growth is assured by an expanding and more affluent population;

- the belief that there is no competitive substitute for the industry's major product;

- too much faith in the advantages of mass production and in associated rapidly declining unit costs; and

- preoccupation with a product that lends itself to carefully controlled scientific experimentation, improvement and manufacturing cost reduction.

Level of competition in markets

From a marketing perspective, competition arises at three levels (Figure 5.4). At the broadest level, the company faces generic competition for its product and services. In such circumstances, the customer considers money spent on one item as an opportunity forgone for expenditure on every other item. All buying opportunities are seen as substitutes for each other. In most cases, companies attempt to influence generic competition in a general way only.

For most companies, competition is addressed at the product form and brand levels. Once the buyer has decided to make a purchase in a product category, such as beverages, product form competition arises. Most beverages in the product category are considered to be in competition with each other at the product form level. Coffee may be considered to be in competition with tea, beer, soft drinks and mineral water. It may not be seen to be in competition with whisky, brandy and other liquors. Companies are very interested in knowing how their products and services compete in the product category, and are quick to point out market share and sales performance in the context of the product category.

Competition is most fierce, however, at brand level. Heavy advertising budgets are often used to support brand competition. This takes place among rival companies which devote their marketing efforts to capturing market shares from others. The nature and intensity of competition depends on the stage of evolution in the market. A new brand in the pioneering stage has virtual free rein, whereas a brand among many in the maturity stage experiences stiff competition.

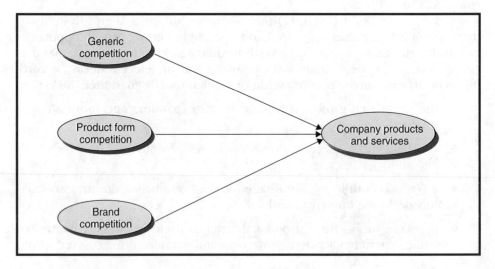

Figure 5.4　Levels of competition

Marketing in a recession

The pattern of a typical customer's purchasing changes dramatically in a recession. In periods of rapidly rising incomes and economic growth, conspicuous consumption is a common practice. In a recession, customers seek value or the right combination of product quality, fair price and good service. Value means high quality and real performance at reasonable prices and communicated through informative advertising. In a sense, the value-seeking customer of the 1990s is repudiating the excesses of the 1980s, and seeks more traditional benefits and a simpler lifestyle.

A slowdown in the growth of real incomes combined with a recognition by consumers that many private-label or unbranded products have achieved near parity with well-known or national brands has led to more difficult times for

---

EXHIBIT 5.3   Card wars – my card value is bigger than your value

Keith Kendrick, marketing chief of MasterCard International, saw the 1980s whimper to an end in focus groups he staged around the country in 1989 and 1990. In one session for Gold MasterCard holders, an ad showing a yuppie buying herself a diamond was soundly rejected. The same ad had been applauded 18 months before. The card's motto from 1985 to 1989 was 'Master the possibilities', a theme laden with the promise of self indulgence. Ads for the 1990s, by contrast, are utilitarian, prominently detailing such practical Master-Card features as cash-machine access. As MasterCard's shift shows, the long running plastic war is increasingly being fought on the battleground of value.

One issuer that's feeling the value squeeze is American Express Co. In the 1980s, the company used the tag-line 'Membership has its privileges' to triple its cards outstanding, and push charge volume worldwide to $111 billion. Charge volume is flat so far this year, however. Rivals sneer that AmEx, that 1980s avatar of conspicuous consumption, is about as poorly positioned as plastic can be in the value conscious 1990s. 'They represent something antithetical to what's going on today,' says Discover's Hodges, citing AmEx' prestige pitch and the fees of $55 and up. And rival Visa International has been pushing the idea that Visa is accepted in more places than American Express.

Some consumers are listening. Travelling in Europe a few years ago, James O. Richards, a Denver-based life insurance consultant, discovered that some places took Visa but not his American Express Gold Card. So Richards cancelled his Gold Card – with no regrets. 'I've got two Visas, and there's no annual fee,' says Richards. 'Why would I pay $75 or $100 for a card?' Yet Visa and MasterCard often match AmEx's efforts in such areas as extended warranties on items charged on the cards. Says Visa USA marketing chief Bradford Morgan: 'The only thing that worries me is if AmEx's image plummets so much that we won't be able to play off them.' AmEx is betting that adding more value will help it avoid that plunge.

Source: *Business Week*, 11 November 1991: 58.

---

mass-marketing companies particularly. The battle among credit and charge card companies illustrates the impact of this kind of development in the financial services market (Exhibit 5.3).

In a recession, the successful company provides greater value: an improved product with added features and enhanced services at a better price. Marketing in a recession places less emphasis on moulding image and establishing positions, and more on delivering value to the customer. Because it means giving more or less, marketing in a recession favours lean companies which possess cost advantages. Successful marketing in a recession does not mean discounting. By providing value it becomes possible for some companies to build brands on this concept, and if the brand is perceived to possess value, premium prices may be possible. Marketing in a recession is made easier for companies that:

- offer performance products, e.g. avoid low-quality, shoddy products and fads;

- exceed customer expectations, e.g. provide better packaging, extras included in the price and surprises to win loyalty;

- provide enhanced guarantees with no quibbles when complaints arise;

- avoid unrealistic pricing, i.e. basic quality cannot justify premium prices;

- provide consumer information in advertising, not just persuasion; and

- establish and strengthen relationships with customers, e.g. easy access to the company's products and services and a free telephone service for loyal customers.

Innovation and evolution of markets

Competition in markets based on innovation has led to products which perform old functions better and products which make new functions possible (Roman and Puett, 1983: 256). There are numerous product examples: teflon, velcro fasteners, synthetic wash-and-wear fabrics, and accelerated freeze drying. Procedural innovations can also be very significant in marketing. As operations change, especially in service businesses, the way of doing business may also have to change. Procedural innovations related to the way customers are served can result in a more effective use of resources and increased customer benefits.

Seldom is there a single dominant product technology underpinning a product-market. In most instances, companies have the choice of pursuing quite different product technologies. In examining some of the managerial issues associated with choosing among alternative product technologies, Abell

218

(1980) argued that it was first necessary for the company to define its business, which he concluded had three primary dimensions of concern for marketing managers: customer groups, customer functions and alternative technologies (Figure 5.5). Companies make decisions that define their product-market activities along each of these three dimensions. In the first case, the company serves multiple customer groups; in the second case, multiple customer functions are served; and in the last case, a business with products based on several alternative technologies is depicted. Clearly the company must make decisions regarding all three factors as it develops its marketing strategy. Markets are based on providing solutions to customer functions, for different customer groups using varying technologies.

Diffusion of innovation

An innovation is the adoption of a new idea, product or process which is likely to be useful. The presence of a number of factors increases the likelihood that an innovation will be adopted. The innovating company must seek to satisfy an existing or latent demand or need, and the solution provided must be compatible with the norms and rules of society. Other matters which must be considered include complexity, ease of trial, observability and ease of mass communication (Rogers and Shoemaker, 1971: 351–76). According to these writers, the greater the perceived complexity of the innovation, the slower the

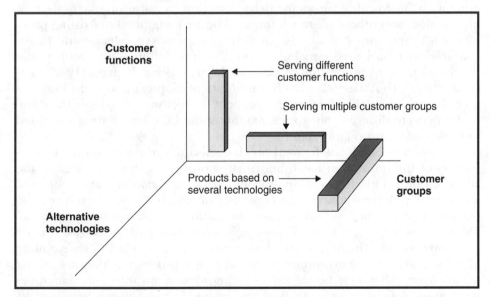

Figure 5.5   A market definition of a business in three dimensions
   (Source: Abell, 1980)

rate of adoption. Providing the innovation in small quantities or on a pilot basis may reduce risk and encourage product trial and adoption. If the customer can observe the benefits of the innovation, it is more likely to be adopted, and innovations which can be easily and frequently communicated through the media are likely to be adopted much more rapidly than innovations which require sales and merchandising support.

With an increase in the speed of invention and consequent obsolescence, life cycles have been shortened dramatically in recent years. This is particularly so in the electronics, pharmaceuticals and aviation industries. As a result, entire industries can easily become obsolete or reduced to a fraction of their former size. This technology-based, market-driven pressure is now so strong that many companies and even countries can easily be left behind in the race to compete in global markets.

It is no comfort for the company to state that it is a commodity producer, and hence can ignore the pressure for innovation. The demand for commodities is controlled by those in the more advanced sectors who need them as raw materials. Many commodity producers have sadly discovered that innovation in other industries has left them without a market for their obsolete materials.

Diffusion at the macro level

It is generally accepted that the diffusion of most products into a market follows an S-shaped pattern. At the initial stages, few people are aware of the innovation, many who are aware delay adoption because of risk or lack of information, and others are much too loyal or are committed to existing products. With time, industry sales begin to increase slowly, accelerate and finally converge on a market potential which is difficult to define. It is possible to use the diffusion of an innovation to classify adopters. Using Rogers' (1962) categories, Bagozzi (1991: 102) classifies innovation adopters into five categories according to when they first try the product. In this way, he relates the diffusion process to different categories of adopters and the lapsed time associated with their adoption (Figure 5.6).

Diffusion research has focused on characteristics of the customer, characteristics of the innovation itself, information-processing characteristics of the adopter, and the effect of interaction between adopters and potential adopters. This interaction refers to the word-of-mouth effect, which is used so extensively as a vehicle for information and influence in the diffusion process. The diffusion process is generally envisaged as consisting of five stages.

Innovators are the first to adopt an innovation. They tend to have a number of characteristics in common. Besides being venturesome, they are willing to take risks. They may be outward looking, communicative and sometimes thought of as socially aggressive, and are involved in many networks of people. They form only a small proportion of the total population in the market. This group is thought to represent about 2.5 per cent of the population at

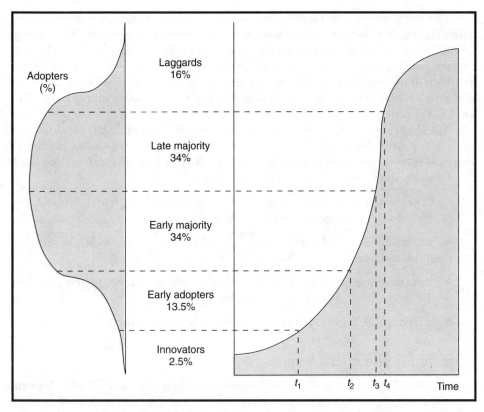

Figure 5.6 Contribution of adopters to sales over time

(Source: Bagozzi, 1991: 102. Reprinted by permission of Simon and Schuster, Copyright © 1986 by Macmillan Publishing Company Inc.)

large, although this proportion varies by product, country and extent of marketing effort.

The next group to adopt an innovation are referred to as early adopters. This group enjoys the prestige and respect that early purchasing of an innovation brings. Early adopters tend to be opinion leaders, who influence others to purchase. They might be referred to as discretionary adopters of a new product. This group represents a larger proportion of society, about 13.5 per cent of the population.

The mass market for a product is divided into two groups. The early majority are generally thought of as having status within their social class and are gregarious, communicative and attentive to sources of information. They represent a large proportion of the total population. The late majority, also a large part of the total population, tend to be less cosmopolitan and less responsive to change. People in this group tend to be less well off and older, and usually belong to one of the lower socioeconomic groupings.

The last group to purchase a new product, not surprisingly, are called laggards. This group, which may be a relatively substantial proportion of the population, tend to be price conscious and suspicious of novelty and change, receive low incomes and are conservative in most of their behaviour. Most products have reached the maturity stage of the life cycle before being purchased by laggards. Thus when the laggards have entered the market, the market has become saturated.

At industry level, there are a number of conditions which are conducive to innovation and which allow the above process to start. Innovation presumes the existence in the market of key resources. The primary resources required for the diffusion of innovations at the macro level include:

- developments in product and process technology, which enable the product to be commercialized, refined and improved;

- the availability and cost of input materials and systems which determine the cost and market attractiveness of the finished product;

- the presence or absence of an industry infrastructure, which may hasten or delay the market penetration; and

- a favourable regulatory environment to legitimize the new industry.

Diffusion at the micro level

At the micro level, potential buyers are viewed as passing through an adoption process for the product or service that results in a trial and eventually culminates in a purchase. Potential buyers are believed to follow one or a combination of two paths towards the adoption of a new product or service. The more traditional viewpoint is that the potential buyer must first be introduced to an innovation in order to become aware of its existence. In this way, the individual learns about an innovation from others, such as through a salesperson, a member of the family, a friend, a colleague or mass advertising. If the initial reception is positive, the individual's interest is aroused. Further information may be sought to evaluate the innovation. A favourable reception may lead to trial of the innovation, and confirmation of expectations may lead to adoption.

One of the most popular forms of the adoption process, popularized by Rogers (1962: 81–6) involves six stages (Figure 5.7). Potential buyers become aware of a product or brand when they learn of its existence but do not have any further information about it. In some cases, the buyer takes an interest in the product and is motivated to seek information about it. It then becomes necessary to evaluate the product or brand with a view to trying it. At the trial stage, the buyer purchases the product to test it. Adoption is said to have occurred when the customer uses the product on a regular basis. During the confirmation stage, the buyer seeks reinforcement of the adoption decision, but may reverse it if for any reason expectations are not fulfilled.

222

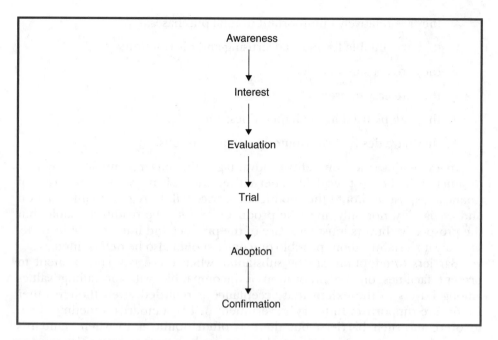

Figure 5.7   Product adoption process in consumer markets

Alternatively, the process may begin with the individual who recognizes a problem. When potential customers first recognize a need, they may search and evaluate existing products and services in seeking a solution. Sometimes they may persuade a company to provide a solution. In this situation, consultations with sales people may take place, and advice from others may also be sought. The final result is much the same as before: an innovation is evaluated, found acceptable or wanting, and as a result adopted or rejected. The initial point of departure and the process are different, but in different circumstances both descriptions may fit the selected adoption process of innovations at the micro level.

In consumer markets, high discretionary income among opinion leaders leads to faster adoption. Adoption is also rapid if the product has clear advantages over existing products and its use presents little financial, physical or social risk in adoption. Products which are easily adopted are those which are modifications of existing ideas and not a major innovation into a complete new product category. The probability of adoption of an innovation is influenced by a number of characteristics of the innovation itself (Tornatzky and Klein, 1982; Rogers, 1983). Products are considered to be relatively easy to adopt by consumers if:

- they are compatible with existing lifestyles;
- they have a perceived competitive advantage and low perceived risk;

- they are relatively unimportant in total purchases;
- they are suitable for mass advertising and distribution;
- they are consumed quickly;
- they are easy to use;
- they can be tried in small quantities; and
- they have desirable attributes which are obvious.

In evaluating the competitive advantage, the buyer compares the new product with the best available alternative, and risk is assessed in terms of financial exposure should the product or service fail. In regard to information and availability, not only must the product or service be readily available, but the prospective buyers must be aware of the product and informed of its benefits. Any uncertainty about possible outcomes should also be determined.

Barriers to adoption can be substantial when there is a commitment to present facilities or the innovation is incompatible with prevailing values among buyers to the extent that acceptance is retarded, even though other factors are supportive. Industry, government or EU standards sometimes help to overcome such barriers, but there is often doubt as to when standards encourage the adoption of new technology and when they act as a barrier to its adoption (Exhibit 5.4). Few companies will be willing to gamble on new technology or products which threaten to cannibalize existing product sales unless they are confident that they can dominate the sales of the new products. This is the reason why large powerful companies in an industry attempt to set their own standards for in-house manufacture of finished goods or components and as a basis of licensing to others.

Evolution of markets

Markets are like natural biological systems. They start, grow, mature and decline. An understanding of how markets evolve is important for the company because it is necessary to decompose the dynamics of the market into those associated with the discovery of new needs and new technologies. As a result a company must deal with the technology of need satisfaction and how it can best respond to the opportunities presented.

Role of technology in market evolution

Companies need to anticipate the evolutionary path of a market as it is affected by new needs, competitors, technology, channels and other developments. The evolution of product-markets reflects the outcome of numerous market, technological and competitive forces, each force acting within others to facilitate or inhibit the rate of sales growth or decline in a product class.

EXHIBIT 5.4 Bandwagons and barriers

Who has not been frustrated by learning that a certain piece of music is only available on compact disc, or that a blade does not fit their fancy new razor, or that a whizzy new computer game will not work on their recently purchased machine? The compatibility, or incompatibility, of products with one another often has an enormous impact on their value to consumers. So it is hardly surprising that, as new technology has increased the number of products available, firms have used technical standards as a competitive weapon. The computer and consumer-electronics industries, for example, have been repeatedly driven by standards over the past two decades.

One of the most intriguing issues is determining when standards encourage the adoption of new technology and when they act as a barrier to its adoption. Confusingly they can do both. The markets for video-cassette recorders and personal computers are two famous examples where sales, and innovation, exploded after a single, dominant standard prevailed and started a bandwagon rolling among hundreds of firms. But once entrenched, standards can also be a barrier to anything but incremental improvements compatible with the existing standard. Persuading millions of customers to abandon their video recorders or personal computers, together with all their videos and software, even for something fantastically better, is now beyond the power of any one firm.

Television broadcasting is a prime example. Incremental improvements to existing television sets are reaching a dead end. But any great, incompatible leap forward in broadcasting technology, such as high-definition television (HDTV), will succeed only if tens of millions of consumers buy new television sets. Hundreds of television stations will also have to invest in new equipment, as will thousands of programme makers and scores of equipment manufacturers.

Worse, a 'chicken and egg' dilemma faces nearly all these market participants. Consumers will not want HDTV sets until there is something to watch on them and the price is affordable. But broadcasts will have little incentive to switch to HDTV until well after consumers have begun a stampede to the new system. Programme makers, meanwhile, will have no incentive to produce HDTV programmes until broadcasters demand them. And manufacturers will not be able to sell HDTV sets in sufficient volumes to make them affordable until large numbers of consumers have taken the plunge.

Source: *The Economist*, 17 February 1993: 71.

Successful companies begin by recognizing that potential customers have a need of some kind. They also recognize that products and services exist as one solution among many to meet identified needs. A need is satisfied by some technology. A person's need for instant taste gratification in hot weather may be satisfied by traditional ice-cream. The same person's need for sweet-tasting chewy confectionery might be satisfied by a traditional chocolate-covered toffee bar. Until recently, the satisfaction of these two needs was available through the purchase of two distinct products. Now a new confectionery technology makes it possible to satisfy both these needs simultaneously, in the form of a chocolate confectionery item combined with ice-cream. A number of such products and brands compete in the market to satisfy this newly identified consumer need.

The technology available to provide products which satisfy consumer needs at different points in time evolves with innovation and invention. The choice of technology is, therefore, an important consideration for the company as it competes to serve customers' needs. There is a relationship between the evolution of technology and the product life cycle which is important for the company. Technologies have life cycles similar in shape to product life cycles, but they tend to last longer while encompassing a number of product life cycles (Kotler, 1994: 354–5). In this view, the technology life cycle emerges, grows, matures then declines (Figure 5.8). Within a given technology life cycle, a succession of product forms appear to satisfy the specific needs identified at any particular time.

New products are essential for the survival and growth of the company:

> No matter how skilled the marketing manager might be in developing new
> markets for old products, and how much manufacturing costs can be cut
> through process innovation, the time will come when existing products have
> served their purpose. Without new products to replace old ones a firm will
> ultimately wither and die. (Johne, 1988: 168)

It is essential that the company plans for and anticipates the need for new products, which enables the company partly to control the future. 'The reason why every manager should have a flow diagram of the product life cycle on his or her desk or office wall is to remind him or her that sooner or later, for better or worse, the status quo will change' (Baker, 1988: 135).

Companies must decide what technology to invest in and when to move to a new technology. Choosing which technology will succeed in becoming dominant is difficult:

> They can bet heavily on one new technology or lightly on several. If the latter,
> they are not likely to become the leader. The pioneering firm that bets heavily
> on the winning technology is likely to capture leadership. Thus, firms must
> carefully choose the strategic business areas in which they will operate.
> (Kotler, 1994: 355)

A number of additional factors influence the likelihood of success.

It is necessary to determine from the outset whether there is a market for the innovation. The problem is exacerbated the more sophisticated the technology:

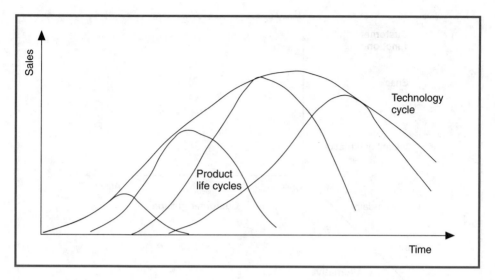

Figure 5.8 Technology and product life cycle
(Source: Adapted from Kotler, 1994)

> The higher the technology the more difficult it is to get the technical product champion of a product to address the question of the market for it. Its newness is used to discredit any comparisons with previous products and even to imply that its outstanding technical merits will result in it being bought at any cost. (Blackwell and Eilon, 1991: 6)

Pioneers and marketing innovations

In many situations, new markets emerge when somebody recognizes a latent demand among a significant group of potential customers for a product or service which does not yet exist. For example, until recently in the impulse ice-cream market, instant gratification needs have been satisfied by non-dairy products, i.e. non-dairy ice-cream and non-dairy chocolate. More recently, some ice-cream companies have recognized a latent need for more natural, richer chocolate-covered bars which would serve adults as well as children and provide benefits associated with snacks in addition to the more traditional instant gratification function (Figure 5.9).

Now the range of needs to be satisfied is much wider than before. A particular ice-cream manufacturer facing these possibilities must design a single product to cater for the entire market, or produce a range of products to satisfy the existing and new needs identified. Based on the material in Chapter 3, the manufacturer has three options:

- provide a non-dairy-based product to provide instant gratification to children;

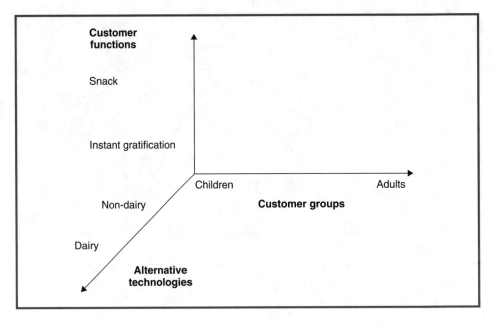

Figure 5.9 Evolution of the impulse ice-cream market: hypothetical example

- launch a number of products to meet the requirements of all segments identified; or
- provide a single product to satisfy the entire market.

In the situation described, it is unlikely that a single product would serve mass-market needs. The large branded companies such as Mars, Nestlé and Unilever have recently attempted to address latent needs for ice-cream by introducing a range of sophisticated chocolate-covered ice-cream bars aimed at the adult market.

Imitators and market expansion

If the innovation is successful, other companies will attempt to copy it. In the above example, Mars was the innovator in the ice-cream market but was soon imitated by others. It soon becomes apparent whether a new significant market exists. Subsequent market growth is likely to be influenced by the number of additional companies that enter the market, the speed of their arrival and the amount of resources they devote to market development. The extent and form of this investment depend on competitors' expectations about market potential and growth aspirations. Generally, the greater the investment and the more intense the competition, the faster sales growth is likely to be.

The innovating company must recognize that markets have characteristic selling prices and sales volumes. The innovation must be comparable to that

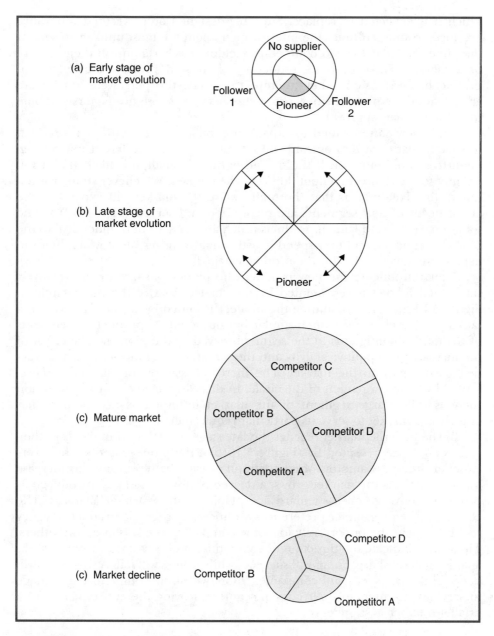

(a) Early stage of market evolution

No supplier

Follower 1

Pioneer

Follower 2

(b) Late stage of market evolution

Pioneer

(c) Mature market

Competitor C

Competitor B

Competitor D

Competitor A

(c) Market decline

Competitor B

Competitor D

Competitor A

Figure 5.10 Evolution of markets

which it is expected to replace. Superbly designed and executed innovative products costing ten times the inferior incumbent are most unlikely to sell. At the same time, entrenched competitors seldom easily relinquish their control of a market. Through price reductions, improved product attributes and product-line extensions, they attempt to reduce the perceived competitive advantage of the pioneer's new product or service. These two factors combine to influence market growth.

While new entrants tend to expand the total market for the new product, it is likely that each new entrant will attempt to serve a different market segment from the innovator. If the second entrant is small, it is likely that it will attempt to avoid direct competition with the pioneer. Whichever strategy is followed, the likelihood is that the total size of the market will expand as the latent needs of new segments are recognized and served (Figure 5.10). The followers design and launch products which are similar but not identical to the pioneer's product, and they spend heavily on advertising, all of which helps to expand the total market for the product category.

After introducing the new product, the pioneer's share of the relatively small total market is represented by the shaded area of the inner circle in Figure 5.10(a). After some time the pioneer is joined by, in this case, two imitators who develop and launch similar but not identical products in segments of the market contiguous to the segment served by the pioneer. The effect of the increased competitive activity and the spread of the innovation is to attract new customers into the market. The increased size of the market is represented by the enlargement of the circle. In this early stage of market evolution there is still a large segment of the market unserved as no company has entered the market to serve its particular requirements.

By the time the market reaches the late stage of evolution in this hypothetical example, represented by (Figure 5.10(b)), the pioneer and six followers experience a great amount of competition as each battles to hold or increase market share. As the market grows, a degree of homogeneity is introduced as providers converge on a standard acceptable to all or a large majority. The convergence of consumer preferences around an acceptable product category standard opens the opportunity for some companies to take share from others. The arrows indicate the direction of competitive moves as each company seeks a larger market share. Some will succeed, while others will fail. A shake-out will occur of the less successful companies, those with little competitive advantage in serving customers in their chosen segment, leaving the entire market to a smaller number of suppliers.

Market maturity and decline

In mature markets, tastes, preferences and product category standards have stabilized and the market is shared by a small number of successful companies. In the present case (Figure 5.10(c)), four competitors serve the entire market.

Note that the pioneer may or may not be among them. The turbulent state of the market during shake-out can sometimes cause even pioneers to exit.

Markets eventually decline due to the introduction of a new technology or the discovery of a new need not well served by existing products. As the old need disappears or a new technology with a stronger competitive advantage begins to replace the old, new market opportunities arise, thereby starting the cycle again. Other possible market evolution combinations exist. The hypothetical example discussed here illustrates the different competitive elements which exist at each stage as markets emerge, grow, mature and decline.

Marketing effort and sales potential

From the individual company's point of view, demand for its products and services is seen as a variable which is also influenced by its own marketing efforts. In some sense, the company judges that there is a sales potential which is only reached under certain competitive conditions and with the expenditure of a great amount of marketing funds (Figure 5.11). The company recognizes that sales are greater for a higher than a lower level of marketing expenditure. It is also expected, however, that as additional funds are devoted to the marketing

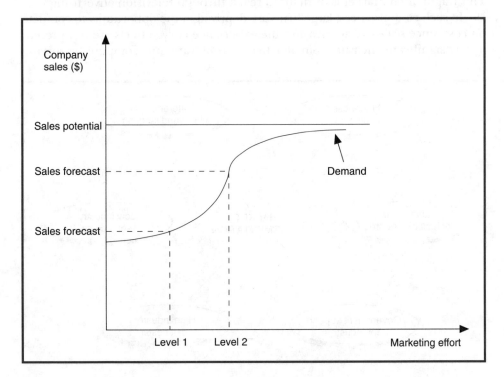

Figure 5.11 Market demand related to marketing effort

effort, the marginal increase in sales begins to decline after some point. Sales potential becomes a target which is never reached due to competition in the market and innovation.

Consolidating fragmented markets

Fragmented markets tend to be small and diffuse, and to require a great deal of customization in terms of products and the other elements of the marketing programme. Fragmentation arises from differences in tastes, languages, culture, and technical and operating standards (Figure 5.12). The interplay of these factors is a serious obstacle to market consolidation and is most obvious in European markets at present.

Large, uniform markets are hard to find. The changes in the complexion of western society have been profound. Large and rapid increases have taken place in the number of people living alone, the number of single parent families and the number of women in paid employment. As the market changes, the demand for products and brands also changes. Such changes increase the demand for convenience, variety and sophistication in products purchased. This fragmented market is difficult to reach through television advertising.

In such circumstances, large firms are deprived of the opportunity to compete on cost, since scale economies and the experience curve effects are not present in any significant measure. Smaller firms proliferate and compete by serving

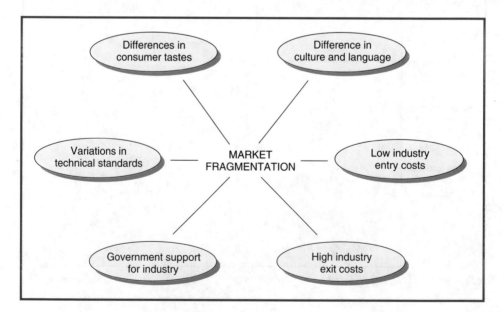

Figure 5.12 Causes of market fragmentation

speciality niches. Fragmented markets also suffer from regulated transport markets, which give rise to diseconomies of scale, giving advantage to local manufacturers. Industry entry costs tend to be low and exit costs high. To exacerbate matters, the situation is frequently made worse by the determination of national governments to protect industries which are considered strategic.

There are a number of ways in which companies may attempt to consolidate such markets (Figure 5.13). With more open markets it may be possible for firms to introduce standardized, low-cost products capable of serving most market needs, thereby replacing many specialized products: an example is Philips Matchline Series. Large companies sometimes attempt to consolidate a market by systematically raising marketing expenditures, especially advertising, to a level where firms that are not financially strong may be forced to leave. Another approach to consolidation is to acquire competitors and rationalize production capacity. The Swedish firm Esab has systematically acquired competitors to dominate the European welding industry. Consolidation may also result from a spate of heavy investment in capital equipment, which raises the minimum scale necessary to be an efficient competitor.

In many western European markets and in North American markets, a socioeconomic convergence is taking place, albeit slowly. Population growth is slowing down or is static, personal consumption is rising, and similar ownership patterns of consumer durables like cars, TVs and personal audio equipment are appearing. In many of these markets, similar penetration rates of foreign cars are in evidence. Greater numbers of women are in the paid workforce and

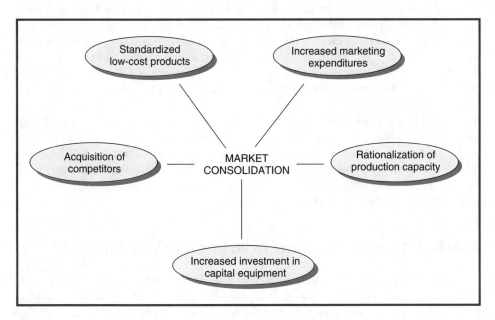

Figure 5.13 Forces for consolidation

the fashion industry is serving similar expensive and youth tastes in many of these markets.

Paralleling these developments is the increase in telecommunications traffic, air, sea and land traffic, and trade among countries. The impact of internationally available television channels and advertising is also widespread. These developments lead to increased convergence in communications among markets.

Marketing management in different markets

This section introduces the various types of markets that the company faces. A more detailed examination of consumer and organizational markets is contained in subsequent chapters.

Marketing management in consumer markets

In considering consumer markets, the company is concerned with the needs and wants of individual and households. This market is very large and in a sense is the focus of attention of all providers of value, even if they only serve the market indirectly by providing raw materials, components or supplies which are subsequently incorporated into products sold in the consumer market.

The company needs to understand how consumer markets function, how buyers behave under different circumstances, and the role of influence and persuasion in this market. It is also important to determine the size of the consumer market for the company's products and services and to know how fast the market is growing or declining. The company must be in a position to decide where the market should be segmented. This presumes a considerable understanding of consumer needs and wants under varying market conditions. The market for books is a good example, where many underlying factors may help to explain the differences in book sales in different markets (Exhibit 5.5). It is easy to assume that, because the per capita consumption of books is high in Germany or Sweden, it might be raised in India through aggressive selling. Reasoning thus would indicate a poor understanding of consumer behaviour in different markets.

Marketing management in organizational markets

Organizational markets consist of sellers and buyers who are manufacturers, distributors and retailers, and public sector agencies. Product and service transactions among these groups may be for their own use or for resale. All the organizations buy office equipment and supplies for their own use, whereas

---

EXHIBIT 5.5   The market for books

Although the United States is much the largest book market in the world, with sales of $21 billion in 1990, it ranks only third in purchases per head, according to a market research firm, Euromonitor. Western Germans lead the list, spending an avarage of $120 a year followed by the Swedes (who actually read more books), with spending of $97. Four out of five Swedes read at least one book in 1990; the average for the whole of western Europe is two out of three. Publishers fearing that the industrial-country market has become saturated might start to consider poorer places. The people of India, where English is widely used, spent just $2 a year on books in 1990; they seem a promising market for English-language publishers.

TABLE 1 Book buying, 1990

	$ per head – estimates	Market size – $ billion
Western Germany	120	7.5
Sweden	97	0.8
United States	85	21.0
Spain	67	2.6
Britain	63	3.5
France	63	3.5
Canada	60	1.6
Australia	60	1.0
Italy	51	2.0
Japan	51	5.9
South Korea	40	1.7
Soviet Union	10	3.0
Brazil	5	0.8
India	2	1.5

Source: *The Economist*, 9 May 1992: 139

manufacturers buy materials and components for further manufacture, and retailers and distributors buy for resale without further processing.

Institutions and public sector markets

Institutional markets consist of hospitals, educational institutions, prisons and other bodies that are obliged by law or regulation to provide goods and services to people in their care. Budgetary constraints and a captive client group typify the buying circumstances of these institutions. Profit is not a concern and cost minimization may not be an overriding issue, since established standards of care may dictate a quality level above that associated with minimum costs.

Public sector markets include all government, national and EU agencies, and local government bodies that buy goods and services for or on behalf of their customers, the constituents they serve. As may easily be appreciated, taken together, these represent a very large market and provide opportunities for many companies. Many individual public sector agencies wield enormous buying power, given the size of their product and service requirements. For example, the budget for health maintenance and education in most countries is a significant proportion of GDP.

Sometimes the role of marketing in serving institutions and public sector agencies is not so apparent. Procurement policies in such agencies emphasize price, since all of their decisions are in the public domain and can be reviewed in a public forum. A price emphasis encourages cost competition among potential suppliers. In addition, tight product specifications, another feature of these markets, reduce the scope for product differentiation and advertising.

Reseller markets

Distributors and retailers who buy products for resale without further processing other than packaging and display are referred to as resellers. Manufacturers co-operate with resellers to ensure their products are available at the locations where final customers can access them.

Commonalities and differences in organizational and consumer markets

It is possible to distinguish organizational markets from consumer markets in three respects. They differ in regard to market structure, buying decisions and how companies reach their customers. In regard to structure, a small number of users in organizational markets usually account for a very high proportion of total sales in that market. In addition, many industrial products sold, such as equipment and machinery, have a high unit value and are not purchased frequently. The purchasing decision for capital products can usually be postponed, something which can be difficult for consumer products.

The early literature on industrial marketing emphasized that buyers in that market were more rational than could be found in consumer markets. A degree of rationality enters into all purchases, but it is necessary to recognize that buying motivations in organizational markets are also influenced by psychological and political factors in addition to more rational economic factors, often accepted as the only basis for industrial purchases.

Buying decisions in organizational markets are also influenced by the derived demand for the products and services that their products serve as inputs. Demand in organizational markets depends on the demand for other industrial or consumer products. In this sense, the demand for the output of industrial markets is derived from the demand arising in other markets.

In most circumstances, the principal difference between the two markets stems from the influence on the buying decision itself. Several people influence the buying decision and these people may have different motives. The number of influences on the buying process and their relative importance varies from company to company and from purchase situation to purchase situation.

In organizational markets, there is usually greater emphasis on direct selling to the final user. Products have to be demonstrated, technical issues exploited and special before- and after-sales services provided. If distributors are involved in the process, they are usually customers and may be regarded as final users by the manufacturer. In this case, the manufacturer must consider providing customer satisfaction to distributors and final users.

In terms of purchasing behaviour, Cooper and Jackson (1988) identify seven differences between industrial products and consumer products:

1. There are fewer buyers for products which are more technical.

2. Larger quantities are produced.

3. Demand is derived and inelastic

4. Products serve many purposes and are usually bought for inventory, mostly raw materials and semi-finished goods.

5. Greater emphasis is placed on pre- and after-sales technical service.

6. Product packaging emphasizes protection, not promotion.

7. Competition is on the basis of specification and delivery reliability.

Reaching the customer in organizational markets is usually done in ways which are different from those found in consumer markets. For many industrial products, it may not be possible to differentiate them to any significant extent because of the need to comply with international standards and regulations. It should be noted, however, that the market sets the effective standard, and companies usually compete on standards which are more stringent than those set by regulatory authorities. In such circumstamces, product differentiation exists. More important, other elements of the marketing mix may be more easily differentiable to give competitive advantage, such as delivery, price and service.

The degree of differentiation which exists in consumer or industrial markets is an important determinant of the price premium that the company can charge. In this respect, consumer and industrial markets are similar. Homogeneous products such as staples and commodities exist in both markets, giving rise to little product differentiation and hence little price premium (Figure 5.14). At the other extreme, high differentiation exists in consumer markets of products such as clothes, cars and hotels, and in industrial markets

237

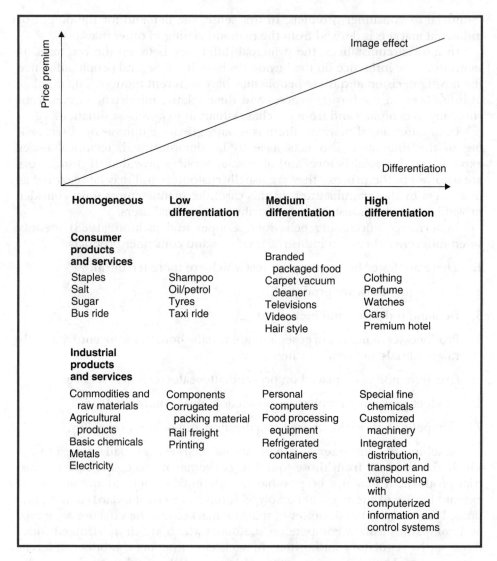

Figure 5.14 Effect of differentiation on product and service image and price premium

for products such as fine chemicals, customized equipment and integrated computer information systems. High differentiation in both cases allows the providers of these products and services to charge a price premium. Often there are as many things which are similar between industrial and consumer markets as there are elements which are different.

Developing-country markets

The efforts of developing countries to achieve growth and improved economic conditions for their people are often hampered by an inadequate industrial base. These countries are important markets for industrial products, especially as they attempt to develop their own capacity in the production of industrial and consumer products. Developing countries frequently view marketing with suspicion for two major reasons. In regard to industrial products, there is the fear that they will be placed in a position of dependence on second-rate or uncompetitive technologies and so will never be able to compete with developed countries. The second reason refers to the likelihood that the demand for imported consumer products would be so enormous that the ability to pay would not exist. Most people want to improve their living standards, and access to the mass media, particularly television, has had a powerful demonstrative effect in developing countries.

Marketing's role in these circumstances is to convince such countries that technology transfer through the importation of industrial goods can be the means of compressing the time and resources required to reach a manufacturing capability in most industries that is comparable to or better than that available in developed countries.

Wealth effect in new markets

One easy mistake for companies to make when examining different country markets, especially developing-country markets, is to compare average incomes. Comparing average incomes hides a lot of economic power elsewhere in the country. A visit to the Far East illustrates the point. Side by side are poverty and wealth. In many of the large cities, the population is growing rapidly and so are sales of consumer and industrial products. Markets in the Far East have been growing very rapidly in recent years. But how can sales grow so rapidly when average incomes there are so low? This is the question of interest to marketing companies.

The pattern of demand for any consumer good looks very much the same. Few households with incomes below a certain level buy certain consumer durables, such as colour television or cars. But large numbers of households suddenly enter the market for these products when their incomes surpass that level (Figure 5.15). Because incomes are unequally distributed, between regions and between households, a relatively small increase in average per capita income can lead to a much larger increase in the number of households in specific locations like Shanghai, Beijing, Kuala Lumpur, Bombay, Manila or Bangkok with incomes above the threshold for buying the product in question.

239

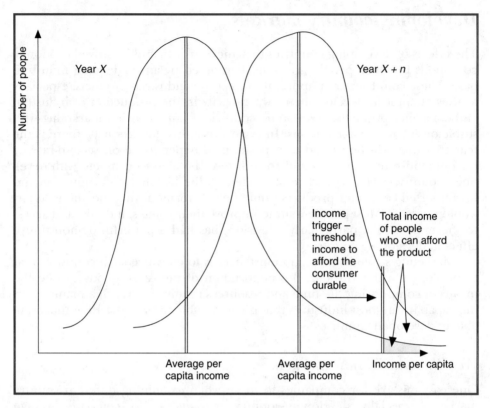

Figure 5.15 Impact of wealth effect on sales of consumer durables

The wealth effect operates as follows: the number of people and the total income of the people who can afford a particular consumer durable in year X + n is much higher than the number of people and the total income of the same group in Year X (Figure 5.15). The threshold income which allows people to buy a durable good such as a refrigerator or a car is assumed to remain the same in the two periods, but since the total income of the relevant segment increases dramatically between the two periods, the purchase impact is very significant. Very large numbers of people enter the market quite suddenly with relatively small increases in average incomes. The income of the people above the key threshold increases much faster, however, giving rise to a significant wealth effect. As average incomes rise, this wealth effect can be an important driver of consumer goods expenditures throughout the world, but particularly in developing countries.

An example illustrates the point. Based on an analysis by G.T. Management (Asia) of car sales in Malaysia, a 40 per cent increase in incomes between 1987 and 1991 was accompanied by a 290 per cent increase in car sales, mostly in Kuala Lumpur, the capital (*The Economist*, 30 October 1993:

240

EXHIBIT 5.6   Chinese consumers – next in line

The greatest consumer boom in history may be about to take place in China over the next five to ten years. This is why western companies are starting to flood into the country. Evidence of what might happen comes from theories about how wealth is generated. Consumer demand in poor countries follows a predictable pattern as incomes rise. Demand for a good does not rise smoothly but in leaps. Households with annual incomes below, say, $1,000 do not buy colour televisions; over that level, almost all of them do.

So an increase in a country's average income per head leads to a much larger increase in sales of particular consumer goods. The total amount of national income in the hands of people whose incomes allow them to buy that good expands enormously with even a modest rise in average incomes.

A recent study by McKinsey, a management consultancy, reckons that average purchasing power in China is almost 30 per cent higher than published figures indicate. This gives China 60m people with an annual income above the magic threshold of $1,000 – the threshold for spending on non-necessities like colour televisions and washing machines. The figure could well rise to 200m by 2000.

This may seem surprising in a country where the official figure for annual GNP per head is below $400. But there is a lot of unreported income in China. And high saving rates – 38 per cent of GNP – provide room for spending sprees.

The high incomes are found in China's southern and eastern coastal regions. McKinsey says five urban markets now make it over the $1,000 threshold: Schenzen and Guangzhou in the south, Shanghai in the east and Beijing and Tianjin in the north. Hong Kong's Trade Development Council adds another three: two in Guangdong province, next to Hong Kong; and Dalian in the north. McKinsey guesses the number of cities on the $1,000-list will have expanded to 16 by 2000. Others think it could be more than 50.

It is convenient that China's middle class markets are so compact, but J. Walter Thompson China, an advertising firm, cautions that they have to be approached differently. Beijing's consumers, more under the government's thumb, do not indulge themselves with the elegant clothes favoured by the Shanghainese; nor do they go for the flash that appeals to the Cantonese, who are influenced by Hong Kong television. Retailing is beginning to open up for foreigners. Yaohan, a Japanese retailer, has just opened a big shop in Beijing, and is doing well. But true visionaries reckon the thing to watch will be the rise early next century of scores of millions of Chinese above the $4,000 threshold. That is when people begin buying cars.

Source: *The Economist*, 23 January 1993: 70–1.

16). The expectation is that in similar markets throughout the Far East a similar explosion in sales will occur (Exhibit 5.6).

Assignment questions

1 Define that you mean by (a) a market, (b) competition and (c) innovation.

2 Describe the general influences on product and service demand.

3 How does market structure influence the marketing of products and services?

4 How does innovation diffusion occur, and why is an understanding of the process important for marketing management?

5 What is your understanding of the wealth effect in new emerging markets?

Annotated bibliography

Abell, Derek F. (1980) *Defining the Business: The starting point of strategic planning*, Englewood Cliffs, NJ: Prentice Hall.

Kotler, Philip (1994) *Marketing Management* (8th edn), Englewood Cliffs, NJ: Prentice Hall.

References

Abell, Derek F. (1980) *Defining the Business: The starting point of strategic planning*, Englewood Cliffs, NJ: Prentice Hall.

Bagozzi, Richard P. (1991) *Principles of Marketing Management*, New York: Macmillan.

Baker, Michael (1988) 'Innovation: key to success', in Michael Thomas and Norman E. Waite (eds), *The Marketing Digest*, Oxford: Heinemann Professional Publishing.

Blackwell, Basil, and Samuel Eilon (1991) *The Global Challenge of Innovation*, Oxford: Butterworth-Heinemann.

Cooper, R. W., and P. D. Jackson (1988) 'Unique aspects of marketing industrial services', *Industrial Marketing Magagement*, **17**, 2, 111–18.

Dibb, Sally, Lyndon Simkin, William M. Pride and O. C. Ferrell (1991) *Marketing*, Boston, Mass: Houghton Mifflin.

Johne, F. A. (1988) 'Innovation in the marketing of high technology products', in Michael Thomas and Norman E. Waite (eds.) *The Marketing Digest*, Oxford: Heinemann Professional Publishing.

Kotler, Philip (1994) *Marketing Management* (8th edn), Englewood Cliffs, NJ: Prentice Hall.

Levitt, Theodore (1960) 'Marketing myopia', *Harvard Business Review*, **38**, 4, 24–47.

Rogers, Everett M. (1962) *Diffusion of Innovation*, New York: The Free Press.

Rogers, Everett M. (1983) *Diffusion of Innovation* (3rd edn), New York: The Free Press.

Rogers, Everett M., and F. Floyd Shoemaker (1971) *Communication of Innovation: A cross cultural approach* (2nd edn), New York: The Free Press.

Roman, Daniel D., and Joseph F. Puett, Jr (1983) *International Business and Technological Innovation*, New York: North-Holland.

Tornatzky, Louis G., and Katharine J. Klein (1982) 'Innovation characteristics and innovation adoption–implementation: a meta analysis of findings', *IEEE Transaction on Engineering Management*, EM-29, **1**, 28–45.

Understanding consumer markets

6

Characteristics of consumer markets
Influence in consumer markets
Understanding consumer buyer behaviour
Consumer buying process

Introduction

This chapter introduces and explains:

- the classification of consumer products and services;

- product categories and brands;

- influences on the consumer: consumers as economic people, social influences on consumers, personal influences on consumers and marketing influences on consumers;

- how to understand consumer behaviour: the stimulus process response model and involvement in consumer purchasing; and

- the consumer buying process.

Understanding how consumer markets function means being able to classify consumer products and services in a way that will allow the company to understand how consumer markets are influenced. One of the oldest models of consumer behaviour, the consumer as 'economic man', is described and analyzed. It is noted that consumer buying behaviour is a rich collage of influences from society at large, from within the consumer and directly from companies active in the marketplace. Factors such as social characteristics and norms in society, social stratification, income levels, reference groups and the family all contribute as determinants of consumer behaviour. Similarly, personal influences such as values, beliefs, attitudes, perceptions, personality, self-concept and life-style are inner driving forces in the formation of consumer behaviour which must be understood. Lastly, it is necessary to note that marketing companies are important actors in the influence process. By understanding consumer needs and responding to them, marketing can influence consumer behaviour.

Consumer behaviour can be understood in the context of the stimulus process response model, which depicts consumers as experiencing a need stimulated externally or recognized from within, then processing the information concerning alternative solutions to that need and responding in some way to the stimulus. Various types of need are analyzed on the basis of the consumer's involvement in their purchase. Low-involvement and high-involvement purchase situations are examined, and impulse purchasing, unplanned purchasing and the hedonistic role of brands are described.

Finally, the consumer buying process is examined. Company responses to consumer needs are described in the context of the purchase situation, the consumer decision-making unit, service levels and customer satisfaction.

Having studied this chapter, you should be able to do the following:

1. Classify products and services into categories suitable for different marketing mixes.

2. Evaluate the myriad social, personal and marketing influences in consumer markets.

3. Determine the relative importance of each for different consumer groups.

4. Select the most appropriate set of influences for particular marketing situations.

5. Apply the tenets of the stimulus process response model of consumer behaviour to a consumer purchasing situation.

6. Determine the degree of involvement in consumer purchasing behaviour.

7. Trace the impact of consumer involvement to consumer behaviour and identify the implication for the marketing mix.

8. Specify the company's appropriate marketing response to the consumer buying process.

Characteristics of consumer markets

The consumer market consists of all individuals and households who acquire products, services or ideas for personal, family or household consumption. In analyzing consumer buying behaviour, the company is concerned with all the actions of individuals directly involved in acquiring and using products and services, including the decision processes which precede and determine this action. The company is also interested in actions after the purchase, since these influence subsequent consumer buying behaviour.

The study of consumer markets is difficult due to the complexity of the market. This complexity may be attributed to the consumer's need to choose among numerous brands, products and retail outlets. It is also necessary for the consumer to consider the timing and frequency, risks and costs associated with each purchase. In coping with this complex situation, the company recognizes that different people have different values, attitudes and personalities, all of which influence their buying decisions. The different occasions on which consumers make purchasing decisions influence the type of retail outlet used, the communication package which is likely to influence them, and the consideration they give to substitutes in the market.

There are some characteristics of consumer markets which condition the company's overall marketing approach. In general terms, consumer markets are end-user markets. Consumers buy products for consumption in the immediate or longer term. Buyers in industrial markets buy because the products they produce are demanded by others. For many consumer products, demand is fairly stable over time. The demand for food and other household items does not vary greatly from week to week or month to month. But in the longer term, the demand for individual products does change, sometimes dramatically. The purchase of other consumer items, particularly consumer durables such as furniture, can be postponed, of course, which makes their sales less stable and more difficult to predict.

Consumer markets tend to be geographically very dispersed and the quantities purchased tend to be relatively small. Both these factors affect the way distribution is organized in consumer markets. In some markets with very dispersed populations, it may be difficult to reach all consumers cost effectively. In large urban areas where the population is concentrated, distribution may be easier to organize and may be more cost effective. Large shopping centres, large department stores and other outlets tend to be located in centres of population with good accessibility.

Classification of consumer products and services

Consumers buy a wide range of products and services, so it is difficult to classify them in any meaningful way. People buy food, clothing, furniture, newspapers, confectionery, haircuts, cars, washing machines, vacuum cleaners, detergents, video recorders and stereo equipment, to name but a few. Several methods of classifying consumer products have been proposed. One method popular since the 1920s, which has the virtue of concentrating on the time and effort involved, divides consumer products into those which must be convenient to buy, those which the consumer expects to shop around for, and speciality products for which some searching is expected (Holton, 1958; Bucklin, 1963). The way consumer products may be classified and the marketing implications of such a classification are shown below (Table 6.1).

TABLE 6.1   Classification of consumer products and marketing characteristics

Characteristics and marketing considerations	Type of product		
	Convenience	*Shopping*	*Speciality*
Characteristics			
1. Time and effort devoted by consumer to shopping	Very little	Considerable	Cannot generalize. May go to nearby store and exert maximum effort, or may have to go to distant store and spend much time.
2. Time spent planning the purchase	Very little	Considerable	Considerable
3. How soon want is satisfied after it arises	Immediately	Relatively long time	Relatively long time
4. Are price and quality compared?	No	Yes	No
5. Price	Low	High	High
6. Frequency of purchase	Usually frequent	Infrequent	Infrequent
7. Importance	Unimportant	Often very important	Cannot generalize
Marketing considerations			
1. Length of channel	Long	Short	Short to very short
2. Importance of retailer	Any single store is relatively unimportant	Important	Very important
3. Number of outlets	As many as possible	Few	Few; often only one in market
4. Stock turnover	High	Lower	Lower
5. Gross margin	Low	High	High
6. Responsibility for advertising	Manufacturer	Retailer	Joint responsibility
7. Importance of point-of-purchase display	Very important	Less important	Less important
8. Advertising used	Manufacturer	Retailer	Manufacturer and retailer
9. Brand or store name important	Brand name	Store name	Manufacturer and retailer
10. Importance of packaging	Very important	Less important	Less important

Convenience products

With convenience products, consumers know exactly what product they wish to buy and acquiring it takes a minimum of time and effort. Convenience products do not cost a lot of money relative to the consumer's total budget, so the advantages of shopping around to compare prices and quality are not great enough to offset the extra time and effort involved. Groceries, cigarettes, confectionery, newspapers and toiletries are convenience products for most consumers.

Since convenience products are purchased frequently, they must be available in kiosks, local shops or district shopping centres. They must also be available in wide distribution, since consumers do not expect to devote much effort to their acquisition.

Shopping products

Shopping products are those which are purchased only after the consumer has been able to compare alternatives with respect to suitability, quality, price and style. Before buying shopping products, consumers visit various outlets or sections of a department store. Furniture, ladies' fashion shoes, men's suits and cars are shopping items. On a particular shopping trip, shopping products usually absorb a greater proportion of the budget than do convenience products. Purchasing frequency is lower, and considerable learning or relearning about alternatives on offer is necessary before a purchase is made.

Since people are prepared to shop around, fewer outlets are required. Because comparison is a fundamental aspect of buying shopping products, outlets carrying similar types of shopping product tend to cluster. A major advantage of department stores in regard to shopping goods is that they can provide this clustered shopping environment under one roof with a range of choice available to the shopping customer.

Speciality products

Speciality products and services have unique features and may also have strong brand identification, which make them very attractive to particular groups of people who devote considerable time to acquire them. Stave Puzzles are unique in this regard because it is so difficult to solve them. However, the company has a loyal following (Exhibit 6.1). Buyers of speciality products and services know exactly what they want; they may also have a very strong brand preference. Being so highly motivated, these consumers visit the outlets which they know stock the speciality products and brands even if inconveniently located. Exclusive menswear, prestige cars and cameras, and high-performance stereo equipment are speciality products for segments of the consumer population. In the case of speciality products, consumers generally insist on a particular product or brand and do not accept a substitute.

Very few outlets are required to serve the speciality product market, since consumers are prepared to travel. To maintain the exclusive image of the products and services involved, the manufacturer is usually obliged to award exclusive sales territories to the retail outlets carrying speciality products.

Price–effort trade-off

In this way of examining consumer products, buyers are judged to trade off effort and price in some way. It is possible, therefore, to classify the three categories in terms of price and shopping effort. Convenience products tend to be relatively low priced and require only limited shopping effort, whereas special-

---

EXHIBIT 6.1   Piece offering

Tom Peters, an American management guru, has spent years telling companies to care for their customers and, in his words, 'get innovative or get dead'. One of his favourite firms does that by selling a product invented over 200 years ago and by doing its best to infuriate those who buy it.

Stave Puzzles, of Norwich, Vermont, has prospered by taking the humble jigsaw-puzzle upmarket. Its puzzles are cut by hand from hardwood (rather than stamped by machine on card) and cost from $95 to $3,000. Many are hand-painted. Stave sells around 1,000 jigsaws each year, says Steve Richardson, the firm's founder. Despite recession, it has doubled sales revenues – which he will not disclose – over the past three years.

Only masochists need buy. Stave's puzzles have pieces faked to look like corners but which really fit in the middle, edge pieces that do not interlock, and split corner pieces that do not look like corners. Some are three-dimensional. Most fit together in a number of ways – 64 different ways in one puzzle – only one of which is correct. Meanly, none comes with a picture on the box. Generously, a bottle of aspirin comes with the trickier puzzles.

Stave's real secret, however, is its relationship with its customers. Jigsaws can be made with pieces in any shape that a customer chooses – such as the silhouette of a pet dog. If buyers solve a cryptic puzzle within each jigsaw, they win a discount off future purchases. New puzzles are tested by sending prototypes to loyal customers – who also receive free puzzles on their birthdays.

'We play with our customers,' says Mr Richardson, who reckons that selling direct is the only way for a niche business to get to know those who buy its wares. To that end, he recently sent two lobsters to a customer who was first to solve Stave's new lobster-shaped puzzle.

Has such playfulness ever backfired? 'Only once,' says Mr Richardson. Three years ago 30 customers each paid $89 for an 'April Fool' jigsaw. While most of Stave's puzzles look impossible, this one actually was. 'I had to give them all a refund,' Mr Richardson laments.

Source: *The Economist*, 14 November 1992: 72.

---

ity products are relatively high priced and require extensive shopping effort. Shopping products fall into an intermediate position (Figure 6.1).

Services

The above classification scheme ignores services. However, it is necessary to include services in any classification scheme, since they are such an important element of marketing. Services have always been a part of marketing, but their importance has not received explicit recognition in marketing management. As people move up the hierarchy of needs, their demand for services increases with the result that more services are in demand now than previously.

In recent years there has been a significant shift in the pattern of consumer expenditure in favour of services. As a general rule, people now spend a greater proportion of their income on services, and the amount spent on consumer durable and non-durable goods has declined correspondingly. As countries become better off, this trend becomes more pronounced. In the Netherlands and Ireland, for example, consumption expenditure has shifted in the past decade away from goods towards services such as health and personal care, insurance, housing, electricity and other utilities (Leeflang and van Raaij, 1993: 353; Lambkin and Bradley, 1995).

Product categories and brands

In discussing consumer involvement, it is important to distinguish between the brand, e.g. the Sony Walkman, and the generic product category, e.g. a

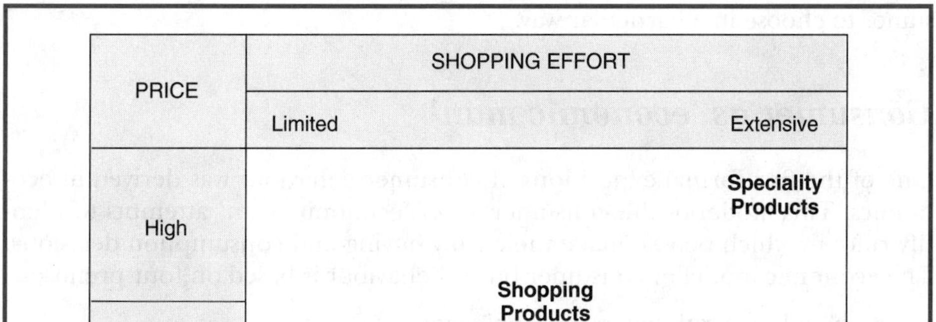

PRICE	SHOPPING EFFORT	
	Limited	Extensive
High		Speciality Products
	Shopping Products	
Low	Convenience Products	

Figure 6.1 Consumer products compared: price and effort

personal stereo system, in which the brand lies. In marketing the terms 'brand' and 'product' cannot be used synonymously. Brands carry with them a set of consistent meanings and beliefs which exist in addition to, and even in spite of, the product's physical attributes. The consumer uses these beliefs to discriminate between the competitive offerings. As brands are essentially a set of meanings, it is important to know which meanings are attributable to the brand alone, and the product category to which it belongs, and which therefore are shared to a certain extent by all the brands in that particular product category (McWilliam, 1992).

This distinction is made difficult when certain brand names dominate a product category in terms of brand share or product awareness, and are used synonymously with the product category name (e.g. Hoover for vacuum cleaner, BIC for ballpoint pens). However, the distinction is significant when discussing involvement, as brands are believed to be more involving than the product category from which they come.

Influence in consumer markets

Consumers are influenced by four sets of factors: economic, social, personal and marketing factors. Some of these are general background influences which affect the consumer's educational and cultural programming and operate as social influences. The influence of various reference groups is also believed to be substantial, especially for some classes of product. Other influences operate at the personal level on the consumer. The last set of influences refers to the direct attempt by marketing organizations to influence the consumer to choose in a particular way.

Consumer as 'economic man'

One of the first formal expositions of consumer behaviour was derived in economics. This model of the consumer as an 'economic man' attempts to identify rules by which people make their daily buying and consumption decisions. The economic model of consumer buyer behaviour is based on four premises:

- people are rational in their behaviour;
- they attempt to maximize personal satisfaction through exchange;
- they possess complete information on available alternatives; and
- no external factor influences the exchange.

Assumptions of the economic model

The first premise implies that the consumer applies a set of rules or guidelines to buying behaviour which are not changed when circumstances change. Consumer preferences, or the rank order in which the consumer chooses from among a selection of items, remains consistent if only a subset of these choices is available. The consumer may also have other guides to buying which are expected to be applied consistently. The second premise merely reflects the motivation of consumers to buy the products and services that best meet their needs and wants. People usually have limited budgets and so choose among products and services on offer to maximize their personal utility or satisfaction.

The third premise indicates that people choose from among products and services known to them. They are presumed to choose on the basis of the information available, which they believe to be accurate even though it may not be. The last premise assumes that the consumer is able to choose freely among the alternatives available. It is assumed that no outside force exists which compels the consumer to make a particular choice.

Based on the above reasoning, it is possible to develop a model of the demand for a product or service (Figure 6.2). The model is based on a series of independent variables or influences, which taken together in some fashion determine the level of the dependent variable. The dependent variable is usually a measure of the demand for the product or service in question and is often measured as sales.

Determinants of demand

The model depicted in Figure 6.2 shows demand to be influenced or determined by three types of independent variable: income, prices and tastes. Demand is expected to be positively related to changes in the level of income, the prices of substitutes and more developed tastes for the product or service. It is negatively related to changes in its own price and the price of complementary products. In the economics model, the predicted effect for a change in any one independent variable is made on the assumption that no change is made to the others, i.e. their levels are held constant. This is the often-cited *ceteris paribus* criterion, which states, for example, that as a consumer's income rises, the model predicts that more of the product will be consumed, *ceteris paribus*. The increase occurs as a result of the relaxed budget constraint, but prices and tastes are assumed to remain constant. Similarly, as the price of product X or the price of a complement rises, less of product X will be consumed. As the price of a substitute increases, more of product X will be consumed.

Tastes are particularly interesting, since much of marketing is concerned with influencing them or changing people's perceptions of them. Tastes have been identified as important determinants of consumer behaviour and often change over time. If there is a significant shift in tastes – for example,

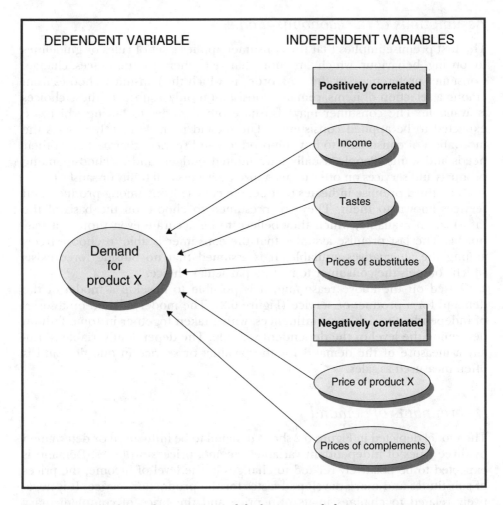

Figure 6.2   Neo-classical economic model of consumer behaviour

increased interest in CD music – then more CDs will be demanded and less of some other product, given the budgetary constraint. The particular product sacrificed will depend on the new preference ordering established as a result of the change in price.

Note that the above model contains variables which are relatively easy to identify and measure. Latent consumer decision variables do not feature. Nevertheless, the economic model helps to provide answers to questions on why people buy, what they buy, and how they make decisions. It also provides assistance in demand forecasting. But it is limited in that it does not consider many very real cultural, social and psychological factors thought to influence demand. It is also limited in that some of the independent variables used, such as income, are outside the scope of influence of managers. Tastes are considered fixed in some economic models and are thought to change only very slowly in others. Taste is known, however, to change dramatically and rapidly. All the elements of the marketing mix are believed to influence demand, but they are virtually ignored by the economic model. This is one of the reasons why economic arguments made by groups such as the Scotch Whisky Association should not hold much sway with politicians at Westminster (Exhibit 6.2).

Consumer income allocation

The way in which consumers and households allocate their income is an important consideration for the marketing company. The amount consumers and householders spend, how they allocate their expenditure over major

---

EXHIBIT 6.2   Whisky on the rocks

Fifty lucky members of Parliament have just received a seasonal gift of a bottle of whisky from the Scotch Whisky Association. This, of course, is not a bribe. The tax lobbying season is reaching its feverish climax in the run-up to Norman Lamont's budget on 16 March, and the side of each bottle is marked, in red pen, with the levels of duty in France, Spain, Italy and (highest, naturally) Britain.

The lobby plays on Britain's sentimental attachment to highland Scotland. 'The Gaelic term for Scotch (uisge beatha) means, literally, the water of life. Scotch Whisky is the water of life for many remote islands and glens where whole communities can depend on the distillery.' Thus the association's report on the economic significance of whisky. But the lobby also recognises the chancellor's practical attachment to revenue. A pub measure of whisky is taxed 23p (33 cents), compared with 12p for a glass of wine, it says. Because of this high duty, it claims, sales are falling: in 1992, tax revenue from spirits was down 2.3 per cent in real terms compared to 1991.

The association is not always so careful to allow for inflation in its calculations. In real terms, duty has come down by more than a fifth since 1980. True, wine duty is down slightly more over the period, but beer duty is sharply up. Despite this advantage, whisky sales have tumbled. This suggests that Mr Lamont and his predecessors are not to blame for whisky's problems. The British consumer is. Young Britons prefer white spirits: gin, vodka, and white rum, often in sweet cocktails with plastic umbrellas in them. Older Britons prefer wine, convinced that it is tastier, or healthier, or both.

Unfortunately for whisky, changes in taste are not susceptible to parliamentary lobbying. The industry should learn the real lesson on the bottles it is handing out to the MPs. Whisky's future lies not in privileged treatment from the chancellor, but in seeking out bigger markets in Italy, Spain, France and the rest, where Scotch remains a cachet now faded on this side of the English Channel.

Source: *The Economist*, 6 March 1993: 34.

---

product categories and within product categories, and how they make choices at the generic product level and brand level are important issues in marketing. A general income allocation scheme is shown in Figure 6.3. The household income allocation shown at level 2 to level 4 determines the overall short-run

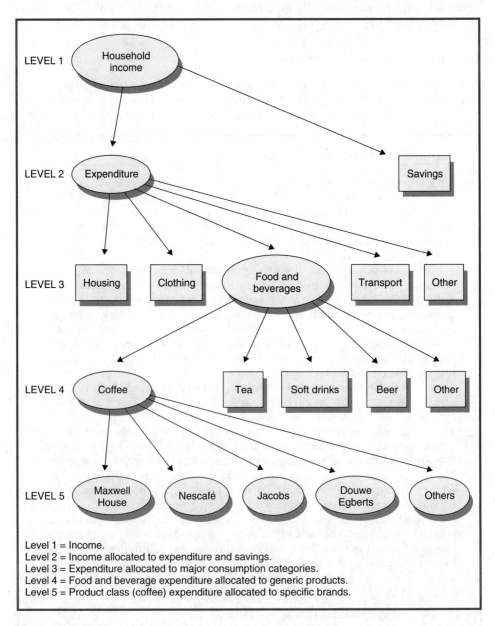

Level 1 = Income.
Level 2 = Income allocated to expenditure and savings.
Level 3 = Expenditure allocated to major consumption categories.
Level 4 = Food and beverage expenditure allocated to generic products.
Level 5 = Product class (coffee) expenditure allocated to specific brands.

Figure 6.3   Consumer income allocation process: from the general to the specific

market potential. Most companies are interested, however, in the allocation at level 5. In the example, the household is presumed interested in the purchase of coffee and must choose from among a number of well-known brands, including myriad alternatives designated as 'others'. The consumer decision process, central to consumer behaviour, occurs at this level. The various theories of consumer behaviour provide alternative ways of understanding how consumers solve such decision problems.

Social influence in consumer markets

At birth, each individual enters a process of learning to live with others. The influence from this process is subtle and emanates through social exchange rather than through formal education. Part of the learning process affects the products purchased and consumed by society. Observation and imitation are the principal ways by which products and services acquire meaning in a social context. Social influences may be classified as norms, reference groups, social class and family life cycle.

Social characteristics and social norms

It is considered important to know the social characteristics of customers and how they are influenced. By understanding the process of influence, the company may begin to understand how best to intervene in the influence process to reach the target market. Social characteristics involving group norms and role behaviour, reference groups, social class and the family are thought to be important considerations in this respect. Regarding the first, it is noted that different groups have different role norms. For example, some groups discuss their latest summer holiday abroad, while others discuss how they entertained themselves the previous night. Both have different group norms and role behaviour. Products, the purchase of which is susceptible to such influence, include sports equipment, cars, furniture and clothes.

Role behaviour in society depands on social norms, which regulate relations among individuals and so provide a guide to social behaviour. As norms reflect the values of the group, they are enforced: compliance is rewarded, while non-compliance is punished. The norms of a society clearly influence the type of products and services that members of that society purchase. To many health-conscious Americans, Kentucky Fried Chicken stands for cholesterol, sodium and fat. The company responded to this consumer shift by offering both fried chicken and non-fried items such as broiled chicken and chicken salad sandwiches. According to Kyle Craig, president of Kentucky Fried Chicken (US), the company planned a gradual replacement of the original name with the initials KFC. 'The key is to reduce the dependence on the word "fried",' said Craig (*Business Week*, 18 February 1991: 45).

257

EXHIBIT 6.3   East European consumers take national shape

Bulgarians may not have much to cheer about, but at least they have twice as many freezers as Poles. On the other hand, Poles on average have twice as many video-recorders as Czechs and Slovaks. European Russians stand twice as much chance of having a domestic telephone than Hungarians. But none of the newly independent east European countries can boast more home satellite dishes than Hungary.

These findings appear in a report published by Mintel, the UK's leading market research analyst. Mintel questioned about 1,000 people in each of Bulgaria, Czechoslovakia, Hungary, Poland and European Russia, from a wide range of occupations and locations. The survey suggested that Czech, Slovak and Hungarian households were the most likely to be equipped with the more basic consumer durables, such as a washing machine and television, while European Russian and Bulgarian homes came bottom of that particular ladder.

Car ownership is at its highest in Czechoslovakia and Hungary, with 207 and 204 cars per thousand inhabitants respectively; in Russia the figure is closer to 84. By contrast, car ownership is about 600 per thousand people in the USA and just over 400 in the UK. The survey also revealed widely different attitudes on leisure activities. Czechoslovaks were found to be keenest on sport, who topped the list for those spending time in cafés and bars. Listening to Western radio was found to be most popular in Czechoslovakia and European Russia.

Mintel also tried to gauge feelings of optimism versus pessimism, and of being risk-inclined or cautious. Czechs and Slovaks evinced the least inclination to take risks – perhaps, hazards the study, because 'they certainly have the best equipped households in the survey' – while the Polish sample indicated the highest number backing risk-inclined statements such as: 'There's not enough excitement in my life' and 'I would gladly live in another country'. Mr Peter Ayton, Mintel's senior European analyst, said that the study offered a 'guide to the relative prosperity of the region'.

Source: *Financial Times*, 23 July 1992: 2.

Social stratification and income levels

There are few, if any, completely egalitarian societies in the world, where people perform the same jobs, receive the same level of payment, live in the same kind of accommodation, receive the same education, and function under the same system of beliefs and values. In most societies there is substantial heterogeneity in each of these factors. People living and working in what were formerly egalitarian societies, in theory at least, display very different consumption behaviour in regard to consumer goods (Exhibit 6.3). People work at different jobs, receive different levels of pay and live in attractive or less attractive housing.

By grouping people according to different mixes of these variables, social classes are identified. It is believed that social class influences many aspects of consumer buying behaviour. Consumers in different social classes tend to patronize different shops, buy different products and prefer different brands. These social class differences in product purchasing give rise to psychological differences among consumers in different social classes. As a result, consumption patterns become symbols of class membership. Class membership is believed to be a stronger influence on buying behaviour than the level of income. However, the value of social class as a predictor of consumer buying behaviour does not always apply.

Occupational and income factors are the variables most commonly used to classify people socially. Other objective measures of social class include education attainment level, home address, inventory and quality of possessions. The propensity to purchase different products is thought to vary by social class. Similarly, different social classes resort to very different sources of information when making important household purchases. It is believed that people categorized as belonging to the 'lower class' are more likely than the middle classes to use in-store sources of information when purchasing expensive household items. Word of mouth among friends, and newspaper and magazines are more effective for people categorized as middle class. This means that the latter group decide what to purchase before entering the shop, by which time it will be too late to attempt to influence them, whereas newspaper advertising aimed at the former group may not be effective. In-store promotion may be more valuable for this group.

Influence of reference groups and the family

A seemingly powerful social influence is the reference group: real or imagined people with whom individuals compare themselves, or to whom they ascribe a set of standards for the purpose of modelling their own behaviour. The degree of reference group influence tends to vary by product and service type, but 'keeping up with the Joneses' is a generic form of this influence.

Reference groups consist of people with whom the individual compares his or her own behaviour. A considerable amount of stereotyping and image are usually involved: for example, 'yuppies' and small fast cars. Reference group influence is thought to vary by product and by brand, and to be stronger for some products and brands than others.

Perhaps the strongest social influence on individual buying behaviour is the family. In examining this influence from the point of view of buying behaviour, it is necessary to decide who influences the buying decision, who makes it, who purchases and who uses the item. It is possible to classify families into different stages of a life cycle, which reflect their different needs depending on the stage reached. The family cycle has been classified in several ways, each with its own appeal and popularity (Cox, 1975; Murphy and Staples, 1979).

There are a number of family characteristics at each stage of the life cycle which are thought to influence consumer buying behaviour: ages of members of the household, income levels, the number of children and the status of people (Table 6.2).

Product-markets affected by the variation in demand due to the stage of the life cycle include food, clothing, education, housing, transport and medical care. People of the same income, age and occupation may have diverse product and service needs because they are at different stages of the life cycle. Young, single, educated adults living away from home appear to spend a high proportion of their income on well-appointed apartments, small fast cars, fashionable clothing, entertainment and holidays. Middle-aged couples with

TABLE 6.2   Stages of the family life cycle and consumption characteristics

Stages of family life cycle	*Consumption characteristics*
Younger	
Single, away from home	Fashion items, especially clothes, cars, basic furniture, travel, entertainment
Married, both in paid employment, no children	Major consumer durables, more expensive furniture, small house, apartment dwelling, entertainment, travel
Married, one in paid employment, children under six	Little discretionary income, heavy mortgage, toys and medical bills, more food and basic necessities, purchase lower-priced items, consumer durables postponed
Married, both in paid employment, children over six	Consumer durables, medical and dental services, education and instruction for children, family holidays
Older	
Married, both in paid employment with dependent children	Non-essential purchases, expensive consumer durables, new cars, remortgage home, luxury items purchased, distant holiday destinations
Married, no children at home	Recreation, travel, self-improvement, home improvement, medical services. Leisure-time activities. Investments for future income protection. If retired, income and living standards fall dramatically.
Single and surviving spouse	Purchasing power remains high even if retired because of savings and investments. Income still high if working. May sell home to move to smaller dwelling.
Other older people	Purchases similar to young families with children. Unlikely to own home. Less discretionary income.

Source: Cox (1975). With permission from the American Marketing Association.

teenage children or young adults in the household spend a high proportion of their income on education, food and clothing. Older married couples with no children living at home tend to seek foreign holidays, more comfort in travel and living, and products and services aimed at self-esteem. The family life cycle helps companies to develop products, services and other elements of the marketing mix to match the consumption pattern at each stage of the cycle.

The family is considered as a major source of influence in the buying process. Husbands, wives and children all display varying degrees of influence in household purchases (Figure 6.4). Traditionally, it was believed that the

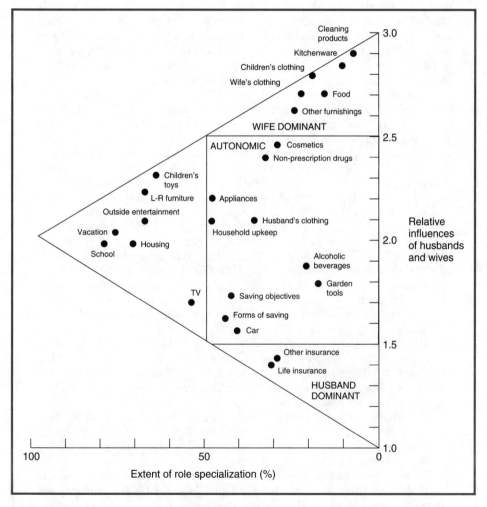

Figure 6.4   Marital roles in 25 decisions

(Source: Davis and Rigaux, 1974: 54. Reprinted by permission of the University of Chicago Press)

husband dominated decisions to buy things like insurance, the family car, garden equipment and tools, while the wife dominated decisions to buy food, children's clothing, cleaning products, cosmetics and beverages. Joint decisions applied for items such as housing, holidays, household appliances and the husband's clothing. Children are thought to be major influences in the

---

EXHIBIT 6.4   Tastes yucky, sells like hotcakes

It was green. It was vile. Her face turned red, her eyes bulged, and her mouth made a God-this-is-awful grimace. Finally, she spat it out. Then, Patricia Mariani, 4, retrieved the offending gum, ran it under the cold water, stuck it back in her mouth, and cheerfully chomped away as her sister Shannon watched. 'Its more sour than a lemon,' says Shannon, 13, a seventh grader at St Peter School in Point Pleasant Beach, NJ. 'I don't really like it. But it's probably my favourite gum. Whenever I see it, I buy it.'

The Mariani sisters are crazy about Cry Baby, a super-sour gumball that's the hottest candy to hit the confectionery market in years. The secret? Cry Baby is awful. 'Don't quote me, but it tastes like battery acid,' says a worker at Philadelphia Chewing Gum Corp., which makes the stuff.

Sour gum is blowing out of stores: One manufacturer estimates the gum will post $70 million in retail sales this year. Although the sour sensation gradually becomes sweet and eventually settles into tastelessness or a mild, tangy flavour, the first minute of chewing or sucking requires Homeric acts of courage. 'How brave are you?' dares a package of Mega Warheads, a super-sour hard candy distributed by Foreign Candy Co., which is based in Hull, Iowa. A Warhead package intones: 'CAUTION: First 50 seconds are EXTREMELY INTENSE. Hang in there!' That type of scare tactic is very effective, says Teresa Tarantino, editor of *Candy Marketer* magazine. 'Kids are challenging each other. "If you can get through this, you can get through anything."' She estimates that 50 to 60 companies make super-sour confections.

There might be another explanation for the masochistic madness. 'With sour candies, you can play tricks on your friends,' says Ron Sherman, a merchandise manager for Mr Bulky Treats & Gifts, a 148-store chain based in Troy, Mich., where Tear Jerkers are best-selling items at $5.99 per pound. 'You say, "Hey, do you want a piece of candy?" and then watch their faces get all twisted.' Sherman expects to sell $7 million to $12 million worth of sour gum and candy this year.

But what's hot today could be totally uncool tomorrow. Chris Burnett, 12, a sixth grader at Lake Bluff (Ill.) Junior High School, started chewing Tear Jerkers a couple of months ago, but he has already given them up. 'It's like hot dogs. You stop after a while,' he says.

To keep the momentum going, Sherman is test-marketing items such as Spicy Meatball Gum, a meatball-shaped gum loaded with red chili pepper. That should pass muster with the gross-meisters.

Source: *Business Week*, 18 May 1992: 30.

---

purchase of breakfast cereals and entertainment facilities, such as video players and computer games. Every year companies pander to children's tastes by introducing new fads, most of which last a season or two, then disappear (Exhibit 6.4). Nowadays, however, much of the above needs to be reviewed. Shared and joint decisions are now more common for a greater range of products and services than was the case in more traditional societies. With increased informality, the source and importance of the influence varies.

Personal influence in consumer markets

Within each person there are inner pressures and motivations which are also important determinants of consumer buyer behaviour. An individual buyer's behaviour is believed to be influenced by personality, values, beliefs and attitudes.

Values, beliefs and attitudes, and perceptions

People with different values have different preferences for product characteristics and types. Values are developed in a social context, affected by roles in society, which refer to how good or bad to the individual is the performance of an activity or the attainment of certain objectives.

Beliefs and attitudes are personal influences which affect consumer buying behaviour. Beliefs are opinions or facts which an individual holds to be true. They may be based on direct use of the product or brand, or what has been gleaned about it from advertising and word of mouth. Attitudes, on the other hand, are feelings of like or dislike towards a product or service. A potential buyer may like the low price of the Lada motor car, but dislike its poor finish. Beliefs are thought to help form attitudes. Buyers must believe that the Lada is cheap before they can like or dislike the finish. The combination of beliefs and attitudes towards the characteristics of a product or service determines the extent to which buyers like the product or service as a whole.

In attempting to understand consumer behaviour through a study of attitudes, there is an underlying assumption that attitudes affect behaviour. Attitudes are described as an overall tendency to respond in a consistently favourable or unfavourable way towards the product or service. That attitudes affect behaviour is central to the thinking of most social psychologists and marketing people, and the relationship between the two is still an active area of research. In many research studies, however, attitudes have not been found to be good predictors of behaviour. It may therefore be premature to draw conclusions on the premise that, if the company can change consumers' attitudes towards its products, it can also change their behaviour regarding these products. Many advertising agencies argue that promotional activity can change attitudes, but companies usually want to know about changes in consumers' behaviour. If there is no relationship between attitude change and behavioural change, the value of such research studies is questionable.

Personality, self-concept and lifestyle

Understanding personality traits of customers can help companies determine the importance of various product benefits. Personality factors are thought to be the reason why individuals buy products which support an idealized self-

---

EXHIBIT 6.5   Totally switched-on

The British consumer is a puzzling creature. Income ought to be a guide to expenditure, especially on expensive household goods such as televisions and microwaves. But take six European countries with higher income per head than Britain, and compare possession of consumer durables. Britain, which might be expected to rank a poverty-stricken bottom, comes top.

Tumble-dryers, microwaves, home computers, and video recorders (VCRs) give British households the biggest lead. The popularity of tumble-dryers comes as little surprise in such a sodden climate. The rest is harder to explain. Analysts suggest that sales of microwaves were given an early boost by innovative British food stores such as Marks and Spencer, which led the market in microwavable meals. A highly developed rental market helped to get the British addicted to the manifold joys of the video recorder even when they were far too expensive for most people to buy. The miracles of home computing were first realised by home-grown firms such as Acorn and Sinclair.

A broader and braver explanation is that British consumers are by nature more receptive to new technology than their continental counterparts. Between 1983 and 1990, for example, ownership of video recorders trebled. But many adults still depend on their children to work the video, the computer, even the microwave. This makes the idea of the technologically voracious British consumer seem less plausible. More likely, the British are simply more extravagant and buy hi-tech gizmos as trophies of household status. Their home is, after all, their castle.

Table 1 The gizmo league: household ownership (including rentals), 1990, %

	TV	VCR	CD player	Home computer	Microwave	Washing machine	Tumble- dryer	Dish- washer	Total score*
Britain	98	58	20	22	48	78	32	11	367
Germany+	97	42	24	16	36	88	17	34	354
Holland	98	48	43	20	19	91	23	12	354
Switzerland	93	41	39	14	15	78	27	32	339
France	94	35	23	14	25	88	12	33	324
Denmark	98	39	20	14	14	76	22	26	309
Italy	98	25	9	12	6	96	10	18	274

Source: Euromonitor: *European Marketing Data and Statistics 1992.*
*Addition of percentages. +Western Germany.

Source: *The Economist*, 12 September 1992: 39.

---

image, where the product has some symbolic value in portraying the kind of person they would like to be (Exhibit 6.5). Purchasing decisions for such people, for some products at least, may be seen as an attempt to seek consistency between their self-image and the product image.

Using gerontographics, an approach similar to psychographic and lifestyle descriptions of market segments, but acknowledging individual differences and the biological, social and experiential aspects of the ageing process, Moschis and Mathur (1993) recently reported a study of the consumer buying behaviour of the elderly in the USA. Older consumers were classified as 'healthy indulgers', 'healthy hermits', 'ailing outgoers' and 'frail recluses'. These authors developed a series of recommendations regarding the appropriate levels of the marketing mix for each of these segments (Table 6.3). A study of these data clearly indicates that the elderly behave very differently from the rest of the population and follow a very different lifestyle. This has a significant impact on the kind of products and services they seek, and also on their expectations for the other elements of the marketing mix.

Psychological influences on consumer markets

There are three aspects to psychological influences on consumer buying behaviour: perception, motivation and learning. Perception is the process

TABLE 6.3 Marketing strategies for older consumers

Market segment	Implication for marketing mix			
	Product/service	Price	Place	Promotion
Healthy indulgers (13%)	To get most out of life	Willing to pay for lifestyle; have more money than others	Like to shop: seek independence	In-store promotion; direct mail
Healthy hermits (38%)	Fulfil inner goals, not concerned with appearances	Self-actualising value, not socially driven	Direct marketing	Direct mail; print media
Ailing outgoers (34%)	Support social activity	Will pay to maintain active lifestyle	Shop selectively; welcome home delivery	Sales promotion; select mass media
Frail recluses (15%)	Home health care products to make daily living easier	Value means easier living not product durability	Direct marketing; in-home buying and direct delivery	Mass media assistance service

Source: Moschis and Mathur (1993: 49). With permission of the American Marketing Association.

by which people receive, interpret and recall information from the world about them. Perceptions are powerful influencing factors in consumer buying behaviour as they are shaped by the physical characteristics of the stimuli, the relation of the stimuli to their surroundings and the condition within the individual. The scope for advertising and product package design in this context is obvious. Shape, colour, sound, feel and, depending on the product, taste are perceived by consumers in some way, and buying behaviour is influenced by these physical perceptions. Buyers perceive a given stimulus in the context of their own frame of reference. Factors within individuals which influence this frame of reference refer mainly to the personal influences already discussed.

As a consequence of these influences, producers or services do not exist of themselves. From a marketing point of view, they are products or services only if consumers perceive that they satisfy their needs. A further consequence of these influences is that a given product is perceived differently by different consumers.

Consumer perceptions are also thought to influence behaviour, especially consumer preferences. Perceptions refer to an individual's judgements concerning the similarities and differences among a set of objects such as products or brands. Preferences refer to a ranking of these objects, regarding the extent to which they meet consumer requirements as indicated by their distance from some ideal preference point. A perceptual approach to understanding consumer behaviour is not concerned with the underlying decision process itself or with the nature of preferences and perceptions. Attention is focused on outcomes, i.e. behaviour, not the process of formulation.

In some sense, brands, products or other marketing stimuli may be represented as a set of points in multidimensional space. The axes of this space measure the perceived attributes that characterize the product or brand (Figure 6.5). The distances among the various brands are a measure of the perceived similarities of the brands for the individual consumer concerned. Brands A and C are perceived by this consumer as being relatively similar, while brand B is perceived as different. If the dimensions can be identified then the basis for this difference can also be identified. With this procedure the individual consumer's ideal or preference point can also be identified. The distance between the ideal point, X, and the various brands may be interpreted as a measure of preference. Brands or products perceived as being closer to the ideal point are preferred. In Figure 6.5, brand B is preferred to either brand A or brand C.

Motivation refers to a different range of influences on the consumer. A motive is a stimulated need which an individual seeks to satisfy, such as hunger or thirst. A need must be aroused before it can serve as a motive. It is possible to have latent needs which do not influence behaviour until they become stimulated. The source of this stimulation may be from within the individual (e.g. hunger) or external (e.g. a food advertisement). Maslow's (1970) hierarchical classification scheme of needs, as discussed in Chapter 1, is directly relevant to

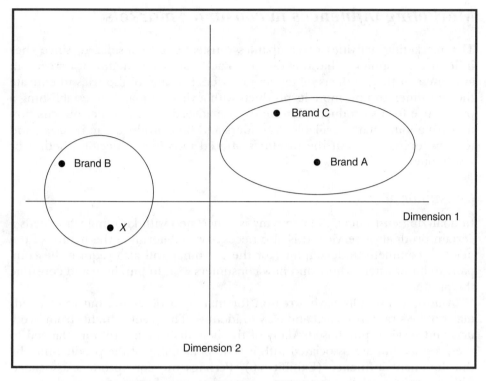

Figure 6.5 Measuring brand preferences by perception

consumer behaviour and to the possible responses that a marketing organization might make. Satisfaction of basic needs permits higher-level needs to emerge. Needs which dominate at any time are dependent on the extent of satisfaction achieved for the more basic needs. In countries suffering chronic food shortages and hunger, the other higher-level needs may be sacrificed. In more affluent societies, the needs for affiliation, prestige and self-fulfilment tend to dominate consumer buying behaviour.

The third psychological influence, learning, refers to changes in behaviour arising from experience, repeated association or insight. Consumers learn when they are positively or negatively rewarded by experience. A positive reward from using a product increases the chances of a repeat purchase. A negative award has the opposite effect.

Long understood by advocates of rote learning, the rewards do not have to be present at the time. Learning can occur through rehearsal or seeing the same thing repeatedly. Repeated advertising of some detergents reflects the use of this principle. By using the power of reasoning and insight, consumers can rely on a related past experience and incomplete new information to draw inferences about a new product or service just launched in the market.

Marketing influences in consumer markets

The marketing activities of companies must also be considered, since they influence consumer behaviour directly. Each company attempts to create an awareness of the products or services it offers for sale. It also tries to educate the consumer and promote its products with a view ultimately to establishing a preference for its products. Consumers use advertising and other information to learn about what is available, to understand how products can be used, and to form opinions about the products offered in order to decide whether or not to buy.

Consumer needs

In analyzing customers, the company is concerned with knowing who needs a certain product or service. It is also necessary to determine the nature of the need. A complete understanding of the customer will also require the company to know when, where and how consumers wish to purchase and consume the product.

Customers usually have a reason for making a purchase, but their needs may not be straightforward and easy to identify. They seek benefits from products and services purchased. Many of the benefits sought are not attached to the product, but are associated with it. The personality of the product may be the dominant influence (Exhibit 6.6). Perhaps the core product associated with a credit card is convenience, but other benefits might include a low annual charge, easy replacement if lost, easy limit extension and prestige. It may be necessary to enquire of customers what benefits they seek in a product. However, it may also be necessary to use probing techniques when consumers

---

EXHIBIT 6.6   Competitive changes in quality

Uh oh, Detroit, watch out. Once again, something extraordinary is happening in Japan. Just as US carmakers are getting their quality up to par, the Japanese are re-defining and expanding the term. The new concept is called *miryoku-teki hinshitsu* – making cars that are more than reliable, that fascinate, bewitch and delight. In plain English, it translates into 'things gone right'. In either language, it signals a campaign by the Japanese to engineer unprecedented measures of look, sound, and 'feel' into everything from family sedans to luxury models, at the same time that they continue to improve reliability. 'We've entered the second phase of quality,' proclaims Richard D. Recchia, executive vice-president at Mitsubishi Motor Sales of America Inc. 'Now, it's the personality of the product that dictates quality.' It is by this measure that Japan plans to hold its lead in quality.

Source: *Business Week*, 4 February 1991: 39.

---

cannot articulate their requirements. Latent needs and wants are difficult to discover. This is especially true of new products.

The information collected from a customer analysis enables the company to form a customer profile, which can help the company to understand who its customers are and what they desire in products and services.

Marketing channels and marketing communications

Access to the appropriate marketing channel and perhaps to a number of channels is an increasingly important dimension of marketing. As consumers seek to purchase products and services in many different locations and at different times of the day, new forms of distribution have appeared to serve these customers. For some products, it is essential that they are available in all important mass distribution outlets. For others, distribution may be selective and focus on the needs of a market niche.

Similarly, marketing communications affect the demand for consumer products in many different ways. Advertising is used to promote certain features of the company's products or services, to ensure that consumers are favourably disposed to them, establish a preference for them and eventually buy them.

Understanding consumer buying behaviour

Approaches to understanding consumer buying behaviour therefore draw heavily on the other social sciences. Four groups of factors underlie buying behaviour in consumer markets: external factors; individual factors; buying processes; and a product, service or something of value which stimulates the consumer into a buying routine (referred to as a stimulus object) (Figure 6.6).

The external factors which influence consumer buying behaviour are culture, social class, inter-household communications and other influence processes. The internal factors refer to the individual's own cognitive world, which determines the individual's reaction to stimuli. The individual's cognitive world is influenced by needs, past experience, personality, learning and attitudes, as discussed above.

The company also has a strong role to play in designing and providing appropriate stimulation to the purchase decisions. The process is dynamic: there is an interaction between the buyer and the environment. The consumer actively participates in the process by searching for information on alternatives available, by providing evaluations of products and services, and by expressions of risk. In this process the company also plays an active role by manipulating the variables under its control. The company modifies the marketing mix to accommodate the demands expressed by consumers. The more successful it

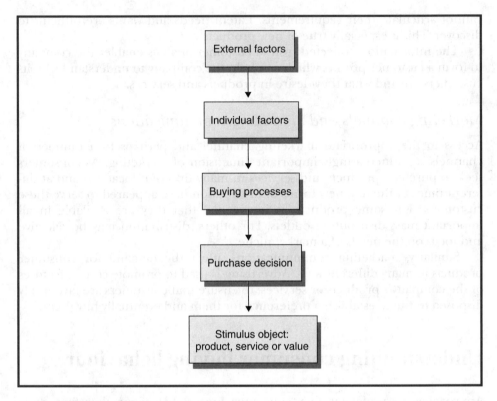

Figure 6.6   Influences on consumer buying behaviour

is in matching its marketing mix with expressed and latent demands in the market, the greater is the possibility that consumers will patronize the company's products now and in the future.

Stimulus process and consumer response

From the previous discussion it is evident that consumer behaviour is determined by a host of variables studied in different disciplines. Consumer behaviour may be described as a relationship between a stimulus of some kind, such as a new product, the way information about the innovation is processed by the consumer, and the response the consumer makes having evaluated the alternatives (Figure 6.7). The stimulus is captured by the range of elements in the marketing mix which the company can manipulate to achieve its corporate objectives. These stimuli derive from the product or service itself, or from the marketing programme developed by the company to support its products and services. A number of symbolic stimuli derive from the use of media such as television. Stimuli also include many of the conditioning variables discussed above. Chief among these are the cultural and social influences on consumer behaviour and the role of reference groups.

Process refers to the sequence of stages used in the internal processing of these influences by the consumer. This sequence highlights the cause-and-effect relationships involved in making decisions. The processes include the perceptual, physiological and inner feelings and dispositions of consumers towards the product or service being evaluated.

The third component refers to the consumer's response in terms of changes in behaviour, awareness and attention, brand comprehension, attitudes, intentions and actual purchase. This response may indicate a change in the consumer's psychological reaction to the product or service. As a result of some change in a stimulus, the consumer may be better disposed to the product, have formed a better attitude towards it, or believe it can solve a particular consumption-related problem. Alternatively, the response may be in the form of an actual change in purchasing activity. The consumer may switch from one brand to another or from one product category to another. Consumer responses may also take the form of a change in consumption practices, whereby the pattern of consumer behaviour is changed. Supermarkets frequently offer incentives to get people to shop during slack periods of the week, which involves a change in shopping practice.

Generally speaking, a great deal of interest is focused on responses which involve buying or the disposition to buy. Manufacturers spend considerable sums of money in developing and promoting their products, creating brands

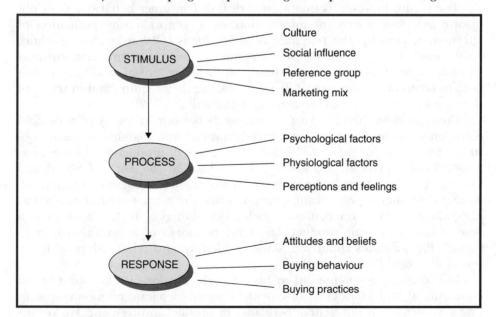

Figure 6.7 Stimulus process response model of consumer behaviour

and otherwise designing marketing efforts to influence consumer behaviour in a particular way. At the same time, consumers may be more or less disposed to these efforts. Through the influence of external stimuli and internal processing mechanisms, a convergence may occur between consumer needs and wants, and the products and services provided. On other occasions, no such convergence occurs.

It is known, however, that the same degree of interest may not be displayed for all products and services. For some products and services, consumers like to be heavily involved. Some purchases are planned, while others are unplanned and may even arise as a result of impulse. These are among the various outcomes or responses which arise in the stimulus process response model of consumer behaviour.

Involvement in consumer behaviour

Researchers of consumer behaviour have historically developed a number of complex theories in an attempt to explain and predict the behaviour of the consumer (Howard and Sheth, 1969; Engel *et al.*, 1993). These theories propose that consumers actively search for and use information to make informed choices. This implies that the consumer is an intelligent, rational, thinking and problem-solving being, who stores and evaluates sensory inputs and stimuli in making reasoned decisions.

The reality, however, is that a great deal of consumer behaviour does not involve extensive search for information, or a comprehensive evaluation of alternatives, even for the purchase of major items (Olshavsky and Granbois, 1979; Hoyer, 1984). A considerable amount of research affirms that, for most consumers, most fast-moving consumer products are 'trivial' and uninvolving both in terms of the amount of decision making they require, and in terms of their personal relevance to the consumer (McWilliam, 1992).

Consequently, theorists view consumer behaviour in terms of a twofold dichotomy: low-involvement consumer behaviour and high-involvement consumer behaviour (Engel *et al.*, 1993). The concept of product involvement has a long history in academic writing, dating back to the work of Sherif and Cantril (1947). Many involvement theories are heuristic in nature. Nonetheless, there is significant agreement that the degree of involvement has a significant impact on consumer behaviour. Inherent in the concept is a recognition that certain product classes may be more or less central to an individual's life, attitudes about self, sense of identity, and relationships with the rest of the world (Traylor, 1981).

In a qualitative component to his research, Traylor (1981) found brand commitment and product involvement to be two separate phenomena, with brand commitment not generally related to product involvement. His results showed that a consumer may be highly involved in a product without having committed himself or herself to a particular brand, or may be strongly committed to a particular brand for what is considered an uninvolving product class.

The survey research component of Traylor's (1981) research further discovered that consumer non-durables rated more as low-involvement purchase decisions, while consumer durables rated as more highly involving decisions. In addition, the relationship between product involvement and brand commitment varied across the product categories examined.

Determinants of consumer involvement

Consumer involvement is frequently measured by the degree of importance the product has to the buyer. However, a recent study (Laurent and Kapferer, 1985) has concluded that, since there really are so many different kinds of consumer involvement, efforts should be made to measure an involvement profile, rather than a single involvement level. Laurent and Kapferer's (1985) review of the literature indicated that a number of factors influenced the degree to which consumers become involved in a particular purchase:

- perceived importance of the product;
- perceived risk associated with its use;
- symbolic value of the product; and
- hedonic value of the product.

There are two aspects associated with perceived risk: the perceived importance of negative consequences in the case of poor choice; and the symbolic value attributed by the consumer to the product, its purchase or its consumption. This differentiates products and services in terms of psychosocial risk. The hedonic value of the product refers to its emotional appeal, its ability to provide pleasure and affect. Laurent and Kapferer's aim in their research was to create a valid and reliable measure for each of these facets of involvement.

Low-involvement behaviour

In an address to the Association for Consumer Research in the USA, Professor Harold Kassarjian reiterated his belief that most consumer behaviour is low involvement (Wilkie, 1990). Low-involvement purchasing assumes that the major goal in repetitive and relatively unimportant decisions is not to make an 'optimal choice', but rather to make a satisfactory choice while minimizing cognitive effort. According to Hoyer (1984), this emphasis on effort arises when there is agreement that:

- buying decisions are unimportant;

273

- buying decisions are routine; and

- there is pressure of time.

In this view of consumer buying behaviour, decisions are not important enough to individuals and do not involve a degree of risk large enough to warrant significant decision-making effort. Buying decisions are typically routine as consumers have made such decisions numerous times in the past. Regarding time pressure, most consumers do not wish to devote much time or effort on any one buying decision because a shopping trip involves numerous decisions.

Research by Beatty and Smith (1987) supports this view of limited decision making for low-involvement products, suggesting that different types of involvement seem to have a differential influence on the external search activity of a consumer. In this study, four dimensions of search were used to indicate the external search effort involved:

- media search;

- retailer search;

- interpersonal search; and

- search of neutral sources.

Media search was measured as the number of commercials that the consumer recalled having heard, read or seen on radio, in the press or on television. Retailer search was measured as the total number of hours spent inside retail stores, the total number of telephone enquiry calls made, the total number of visits to retail outlets and the total number of brands or models examined. Interpersonal search was measured by the number of friends, relatives and neighbours consulted during the search. Lastly, neutral sources were determined as the number of independent consumer or similar reports consulted while searching. Beatty and Smith's (1987) research indicates that when individuals care more about the product, they shop more, examine more alternatives, note more advertisements, and talk to more friends.

On the surface, however, marketing practitioners would appear to be at odds with this concept of low involvement, where consumers are at best buying in a routinized manner, but certainly not out of any long-term or deeper-rooted, exclusive loyalty to the brand. Many companies attach considerable value to apparently trivial brands, by declaring their brands as assets to be valued along with their other tangible assets in the balance sheet. These brand owners see branding activity as an activity designed to create high-involvement situations. The reason for branding is differentiation leading to positive discrimination, which buyers, through the competitive positioning activities of the brand owner, perceive, value and act upon (McWilliam, 1992).

If the concept of low involvement does prevail, particularly among fast-moving consumer goods (fmcg), there would seem to be no economic justification for either manufacturers or retailers in expensive branding activities.

High-involvement behaviour

High involvement conditions are believed to exist for the following types of product or brand:

- lifestyle products;
- special interest products;
- hedonic products; and
- differentiated brands.

Products which are 'lifestyle products', or used as ways of self-expression or self-concept enhancement, are considered to be high-involvement products, as are special interest products, purchased as a hobby, or related to the consumer's role or occupation (Bloch and Richins, 1983). Products and brands which provide 'pleasure' or hedonism (Laurent and Kapferer, 1985; Zaichkowsky, 1985) are also considered to be high-involvement purchases. Where there exists a high degree of brand differentiation based on the product's attributes, there is usually a high degree of involvement in the purchase due to the element of risk involved (Robertson, 1976).

Hedonic role of brands

Of particular interest when considering involvement in the purchase of brands is their hedonic role in consumer behaviour. Also important is the extent to which consumers engage in planned, unplanned and impulse purchasing.

Involvement researchers have shown that, when the motivation for purchase is a hedonic one, high-involvement conditions obtain (Zaichkowsky, 1985). Hirschman and Holbrook (1982: 92) defined hedonic consumption as designating 'those facets of consumer behaviour that relate to the multisensory, fantasy and emotive aspects of one's experience with products'. Tastes, smells, sounds, looks and tactile preferences are largely idiosyncratic and often used by people to define themselves (e.g. 'I'm a sweet-toothed person.').

Therefore, brand and product choices may be seen as highly involving, since they reaffirm these idiosyncrasies. In addition, some of these sensory sensations can be used to evoke memories or even dreams or desires. Certain brands of food such as chocolate, (e.g. the 'secret self-indulgence' of Cadbury's Flake) or perfume, evoking romantic scenes as well as actual remembered occasions, are good examples of hedonic purchases (McWilliam, 1992).

It is, of course, difficult to know whether it is the physical product which is the source of the hedonism or the brand name, as to date no research has addressed the issue of whether hedonism is experienced differently with different brands that are physically indistinguishable. Conceptually, Park *et al.* (1986) support this notion of certain purchases being 'experiential purchases' because of a certain brand image attached to the physical product.

275

Impulse purchasing

Impulse purchasing is related in much of the literature to hedonic impulses and hedonic consumption. Bellenger *et al.* (1978) claim that it is impossible to isolate and label certain products as impulse products, since individual purchasers' motivations, product information levels, environmental variables, monetary and time constraints combine to produce an impenetrable combination of variables that vary from one individual to another. In their study of grocery purchases in the United States, where they defined impulse purchases as those where the decision to buy was made in the store, it was found that almost two-fifths of purchases were impulse. In addition, impulse purchasing was found to be more important in some merchandise lines than others. It would seem that impulse purchasing is here defined so broadly that, if a person did not have a particular brand in mind before entering the store and follow through with its purchase, it would be taken as an impulse purchase. A much narrower view defines impulse buying more specifically as the kind of buying which 'often occurs when a consumer experiences a sudden, often powerful and persistent urge to buy something immediately. The impulse to buy is hedonically complex and may stimulate emotional conflict. Also, impulse buying is prone to occur with diminished regard for its consequences' (Rook, 1987: 191).

Data for the Rook study were obtained by asking respondents a set of open-ended questions about their impulse buying. The four most important behavioural features regarding impulse buying were, in order of importance:

- the presence of hedonic elements or intense feelings of pleasure and pain about the purchase;

- the unexpected, spontaneous urge to buy immediately;

- the compulsion to possess or buy something immediately; and

- the conflict between control and indulgence.

Rook found, among a high proportion of consumers, a significant disregard for consequences of a purchase: that is, the consumer's impulse or urge toward immediate action discouraged consideration of the consequence of that behaviour. For some the urge proved irresistible, despite an awareness of potentially negative consequences. An overwhelming majority, 80 per cent, of those surveyed by Rook felt that they had incurred negative consequences as a result of their impulse purchases. These negative consequences included financial problems, disappointment with the purchase, guilt feelings, disapproval by others, and spoiled non-financial plans – a diet, for example. It is evident from this research that impulse buying represents a distinctive type of consumer behaviour.

Unplanned purchasing

Unplanned purchasing is distinguished from impulse buying because it includes items for which the purchasing decision was made in the store and not prior to entering the store. Thus, all impulse buying is unplanned, but all unplanned purchases are not necessarily impulse (Iyer, 1989). Reasons cited by respondents in this study for their unplanned purchases demonstrated that purchases were partially planned or the consumer saw the item in the store. Recognition of a need is probably triggered by in-store cues, price, quality and sales promotion.

Related, perhaps, to the role of time in unplanned purchasing is the fact that some researchers have found that decision time is an effective measure of involvement. In a study by Kendall and Fenwick (1979), over 200 supermarket shoppers were timed as they chose specific items. The decision times for all consumers and products ranged from almost instantaneous, one second, to 5.5 minutes. Almost all purchases were, however, at the low end of the time range.

A classic set of studies undertaken by the Point-of-Purchase Advertising Institute (POPAI) and the E.I. Du Pont company has also examined the dynamics of consumer decisions within supermarkets. In a recent study, the buying practices of over 4,000 consumers throughout the United States were surveyed. The researchers found that most purchases that consumers make are not planned in advance; in-store decision making is the norm, rather than the exception (Wilkie, 1990). The following are the categories, in order of importance, that these researchers used to classify consumer purchase decisions:

- unplanned purchases;
- specifically planned purchases;
- purchases planned in a general way; and
- substitute purchases.

Unplanned purchases are items reflecting 'impulse' decisions, where the consumer did not report a plan to buy the item at the time of entering the supermarket. Instead, the entire decision-making process, from problem recognition to actual purchase, occurred while in the store. More than half of the purchase decisions studied fell into this category.

The next most important category referred to purchases which were specifically planned. Consumers had plans to buy a particular item before entering the store. In the third category, consumers had the general intention of buying something in the product class, but did not have a specific brand in mind when entering the store. Lastly, a very small proportion of consumers changed their minds while in the store, and substituted a related product or brand.

Over two-thirds of consumer purchase decisions were found to be made in the store. There were, however, distinct product differences in terms of the way they fitted into the above categories. While these findings do not apply uniformly across all product categories, they seem to indicate that, for certain products especially, consumer demand is not fixed, but is likely to be quite responsive to various forms of promotional effort. A high level of unplanned purchasing has important repercussions for brand building and marketing communication through advertising. It suggests that retailers through their various merchandising and sales promotion programmes both communicate with and deliver value to consumers.

Consumer buying process

The individual buying process starts when the consumer recognizes that a need exists: that is, the consumer senses a difference between actual and desired states. The consumer then proceeds through an additional three stages before arriving at a decision or outcome of the buying process (Figure 6.8). At this stage, it is necessary for the company to understand the circumstances which start the buying process. This means attempting to understand

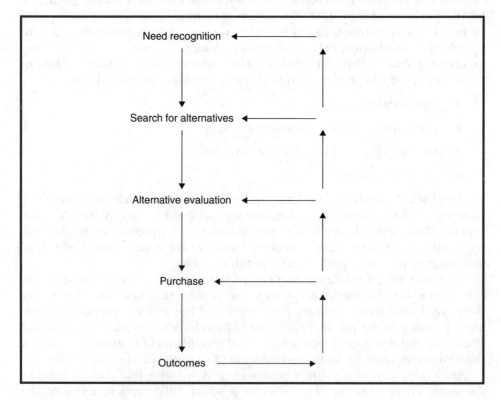

Figure 6.8 The buying decision process

which needs arise, what stimulates them and how they lead to a particular product purchase.

During the next stage, the consumer may wish to seek alternatives which could satisfy the need. The consumer may search for information about the alternatives available. A suitable product readily available may, however, satisfy the consumer who is not curious about alternatives. If the consumer decides to search for information, the company will have an interest in the information sources used. Information sources include personal sources (e.g. family, friends, colleagues); commercial sources (e.g. advertising, sales people, displays, packaging); and experiential sources (e.g. handling and using the product). The company must design its marketing programme in such a way that the consumer is aware of its products and services as alternatives.

The following stage involves an evaluation of the alternatives available or short-listed by the consumer. The company needs to know how the consumer processes the information available to arrive at a brand choice. In this regard, consumers differ in their approach to evaluation, but a number of aspects are common. Products or services are viewed by individuals as bundles of attributes. Cars are seen as transport, safety, prestige, speed and carrying capacity. Some attributes are more important than others, so consumers allocate importance weights to each attribute identified. Some buyers will view safety as more important than speed. The company can divide the market into segments according to the attributes which are important to different groups.

Consumers tend to develop a set of beliefs about where each product or brand is in regard to each attribute. This set of beliefs about a particular brand is referred to as the brand image. For a particular consumer, the brand image of a BMW may be that it is expensive, reliable and fast, while the brand image of a Lada may be that it is cheap, plain and slow.

A company will often find itself in a position where it must attempt to change consumer evaluations. It can do so in one or a combination of five different ways (Figure 6.9). The company may attempt to upgrade or modify the product in some way. This may mean changing product attributes or adding new product features. Sometimes it may be possible to promote neglected attributes, especially if the company discovers that segments of the market are susceptible to the neglected features. Through advertising and other forms of persuasion, the company may successfully alter consumers' beliefs about its own product or about competitor products. Lastly, it may be possible to change the evaluative scheme, or importance weights, used by consumers as they select among alternatives. At the end of the evaluation stage, the consumer will have ranked the alternatives available according to preference.

The purchase decision usually involves the consumer in buying the most preferred product. Two factors can intervene even at this late stage. Sometimes the attitudes of other people can influence the decision. A partner or colleague may feel that the Lada is the better choice, even though the consumer in question has already tentatively chosen the BMW. Unanticipated

279

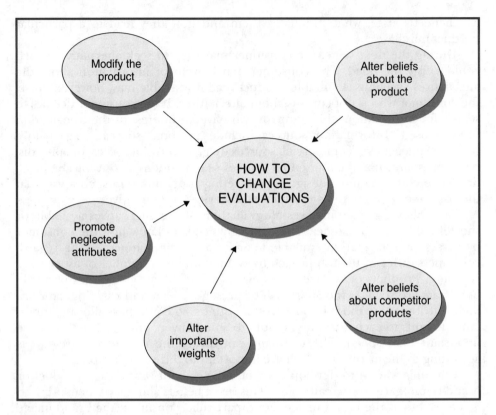

Figure 6.9   Changing consumer evaluation

events can also influence the purchase, thereby making an alternative more attractive: for example, a competitor may reduce the price of its products.

The consumer buying process continues past the purchase decision. Consumers evaluate the product purchased during use and afterwards. To the extent that consumers are satisfied, there is a greater chance that they will reward the company with repeated patronage. They may also offer unsolicited recommendations to potential consumers among their friends and neighbours. In this context, it is necessary to recognize, however, that many buyers experience anxiety after making a purchase. This is true for all but routine purchases. This anxiety is referred to as cognitive dissonance and occurs because, before purchasing, each alternative considered by the buyer was judged to have its good and bad points. After purchasing, the negative aspects of the alternative selected and the positive aspects of the products rejected create cognitive dissonance. The company is therefore concerned with post-purchase behaviour among buyers.

Responding to customer demands

Consumer purchase situation

It is possible to divide consumer purchase situations into those involving a simple routine, those involving a limited amount of problem solving and those involving an extensive amount of problem solving (Figure 6.10). Routine products are generally low priced, frequently purchased and openly displayed at point of purchase. Products which involve limited problem solving refer to the consumer's first evaluation of an unfamiliar brand, where there is a certain amount of risk involved in its purchase. Extensive problem solving arises when the consumer devotes considerable time and effort in searching for and evaluating alternatives. In such cases, the commitment stakes are high. Products in this category usually cost a lot of money and the buyer faces the prospect of having to use them for a long time. Examples are a home and a car.

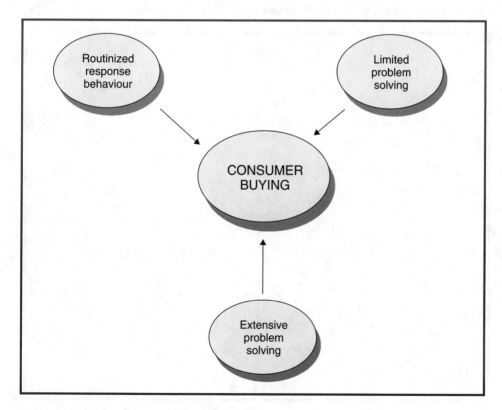

Figure 6.10   Consumer purchase situations

Decision-making unit

A decision-making unit is an individual or group involved in the decision-making process in households or families, who share common purchasing objectives and who share the risks and rewards which may arise from the decision. In each decision-making unit a number of buying roles may be identified which may be taken by one individual or shared by many in the group (Figure 6.11).

The initiator is the person who first suggests the purchase of a particular item. The influencer is the person who carries implicit or explicit influence in the final decision. The decider is the person who decides any part of the purchase decision: whether to buy, what to buy, how to buy, when to buy or where to buy. The purchaser is the person who makes the actual purchase. The user is the person who consumes the product or service.

Consumer markets are also typified by many buyers. Retail outlets must deal with large numbers of customers each day, buying anything from single items like a newspaper to the weekly grocery supplies. Coping with such diversity requires ingenuity on the part of the retailer in terms of staff training and allocation, the allocation of shelf space to products in demand, and keeping the outlet open at times suitable to customers.

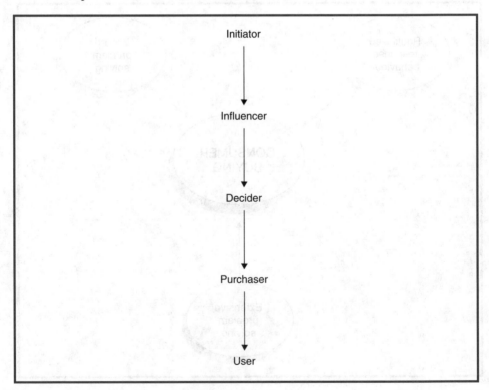

Figure 6.11 Buying roles in consumer markets

Customer service and satisfaction

Many companies have realized that profits can be made by satisfying customers. In many instances, this has meant a complete reorganization of the company from research and development and manufacturing to marketing and distribution, aimed at giving customers what they want, when they want it and how they want it. Behind the approach is a customer-focused philosophy aimed at delivering the services that customers seek, recognizing that by doing so the company too will benefit. This is also a recognition that market share and profit are derived by keeping close to remote customers.

The Japanese were among the first to recognize the need to provide customer service. The Toyota Motor Company attempted to build customer loyalty in the US market by opening a design centre there to produce cars for American tastes. The Ford Motor Company responded by adapting to customer needs. When Ford customers complained that their shoes were being scuffed because of lack of space in the rear of the car, the company sloped the floor underneath

---

EXHIBIT 6.7   How British Airways butters up the passenger

It was our first transatlantic trip with our infant daughter, and my wife and I arrived at London Heathrow Airport laden with luggage and baby gear. To our dismay, a computer failure had left check-in lines 40-deep. We were just about to settle in for an ordeal when a British Airways staffer pulled us aside. 'You don't want to wait in those queues with a baby,' he said. Grabbing our cart, he ushered us to a special desk and stood by until we checked in.

That's an impressive change for a carrier that in the early 80s was on many people's list of worst airlines. 'The attitude was, "This would be a great place to work if its wasn't for these bloody customers",' says John J. Bray, chief executive of Forum Europe Ltd, a consulting firm BA hired in 1984.

The shift started in 1983, when Colin Marshall took over as chief executive. The former CEO of Avis Inc. adopted a novel approach for BA. He asked customers what they wanted. Surveys showed that a friendly staff was twice as important as operational factors such as food service and speed of check-in for generating goodwill. Marshall and his team tirelessly preached the gospel of focusing on the customer and launched an extensive training programme.

BA also dropped some of its old, military-style hierarchy in favour of more decentralised decision-making. Marketing people helped decide which planes to buy and how to equip them. Money was poured into reservation systems, uniforms, and plane interiors. Marshall has also focused on BA's most important group of customers: business travellers. Since upgrading business class in 1987 – with wider seats, foot-rests, and expanded menus and wine lists – revenues have doubled for long hauls and risen 13 per cent in Europe.

Source: *Business Week*, 12 March 1990: 56.

the front seats and widened the space between the seat adjustment rails, which were made from plastic instead of metal. Customers have responded by making Ford one of the better motor company performers. Ford's chairman, Donald E. Peterson, remarked in the early 1980s that 'If we aren't customer driven, our cars won't be either' (*Business Week*, 12 March 1990: 52).

To be successful, a customer focus must start with a forceful commitment from senior executives (Exhibit 6.7). At the same time, it must be acknowledged that employees who deal directly with customers are in the key position to ensure that a marketing plan works. Innovative companies ensure high motivation among such employees, by empowering them to solve customer problems on the spot: for example, supermarket checkout staff being allowed to approve cheques and handle merchandise returns without consulting managers.

The performance of the company's product or service from the consumer's point of view is evaluated and a level of satisfaction determined. The greater the level of customer satisfaction, the more consumers are expected to

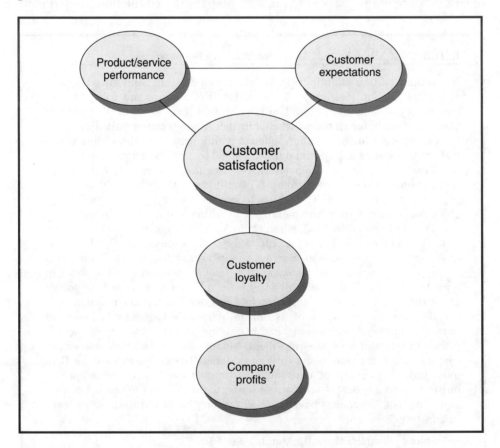

Figure 6.12   Expectations–performance ratio determines company profits

reward the company with their long-term loyalty, which should result in healthy profits over the life cycle of the product or service (Figure 6.12).

Assignment questions

1   Discuss the factors which motivate consumers to buy. Why is it important to understand these factors?

2   Discuss the influence on consumer behaviour of reference groups.

3   Describe the role of the family in consumer buying behaviour. Which family members would be involved in the purchase of: a personal computer; garden tools; a car; breakfast cereals?

4   Should the company be concerned with social class?

5   Why are attitudes of consumers important to the company?

6   What is the self-concept and what does it mean for the company? What type of purchases are likely to be heavily influenced by the ideal self-concept?

7   What can the company do to ensure that consumers perceive its products and services as intended?

8   Is the company's marketing task over once the sale is complete? Explain.

Annotated bibliography

Engel, James F., Roger D. Blackwell and Paul W. Miniard (1993) *Consumer Behaviour* (7th edn), Fort Worth, Tex.: The Dryden Press.
Wilkie, William L. (1990) *Consumer Behaviour* (2nd edn), New York: John Wiley.

References

Beatty, Sharon E., and Scott M. Smith (1987) 'External search effort: an investigation across several product categories', *Journal of Consumer Research*, **14**, 1 83–95.
Bellenger, Danny N., Dan H. Robertson and Elizabeth C. Hirschman (1978) 'Impulse buying varies by product', *Journal of Advertising*, **18**, 6, 15–28.
Bloch, Peter H., and Marsha Richins (1983): 'A theoretical model for the study of product importance perceptions', *Journal of Marketing*, **47**, 3, 69–81.
Bucklin, L.P. (1963) 'Retail strategy and the classification of consumer goods', *Journal of Marketing*, **27**, 1, 50–5.

Cox III, Eli P. (1975) 'Family purchase decision making and the process of adjustment', *Journal of Marketing Research*, **12**, May, 189–95.

Davis, Harry L., and Benny P. Rigaux (1974) 'Perceptions of marital roles in decision processes', *Journal of Consumer Research*, **1**, June, 51–62.

Engel, James F., Roger D. Blackwell and Paul W. Miniard (1993) *Consumer Behaviour* (7th edn), Fort Worth, Tex.: The Dryden Press.

Hirschman, Elizabeth C., and Morris B. Holbrook (1982) 'Hedonic consumption; emerging concepts, methods and propositions', *Journal of Marketing*, **46**, 3, 92–101.

Holton, R.H. (1958) 'The distinction between convenience goods, shopping goods and speciality goods', *Journal of Marketing*, **23**, 2, 53–6.

Howard, John A., and Jagdish N. Sheth (1969) *The Theory of Buyer Behavior*, New York: John Wiley.

Hoyer, W.D. (1984) 'An examination of consumer decision making for a common repeat purchase product', *Journal of Consumer Research*, **11**, 3, 822–9.

Iyer, Easwar S. (1989) 'Unplanned purchasing: knowledge of shopping environment and time pressure', *Journal of Retailing*, **65**, 1, 40–57.

Kendall, K.W., and Ian Fenwick (1979) 'What do you learn standing in a supermarket aisle?', *Advances in Consumer Research*, **6**, 153–60, quoted in Wilkie (1990).

Lambkin, Mary, and Frank Bradley (1995) 'The changing consumer in Ireland: recent changes in environmental variables and their consequences for future consumption and marketing', *International Journal of Research in Marketing* (forthcoming).

Laurent, Giles, and Jean-Noel Kapferer (1985) 'Measuring consumer involvement profiles', *Journal of Marketing Research*, **22**, February, 41–53.

Leeflang, P.S.H., and W.F. van Raaij (1993) 'The changing consumer in the Netherlands: recent changes in environmental variables and their consequences for future consumption and marketing', *International Journal of Research in Marketing*, **10**, 4, 345–63.

McWilliam, Gil (1992) 'Consumers' involvement in brands and product categories', in M.J. Baker (ed.), *Perspectives on Marketing Management*, Chichester: John Wiley.

Maslow, Abraham H. (1970) *Motivation and Personality* (2nd edn), New York: Harper and Row.

Moschis, George P., and Anil Mathur (1993) 'How they're acting their age', *Marketing Management* (American Marketing Association), **2**, 2, 41–50

Murphy, Patrick E., and William A. Staples (1979) 'A modernised family life cycle', *Journal of Consumer Research*, **6**, 1, 12–22.

Olshavsky, Richard W., and Donald H. Granbois (1979) 'Consumer decision making – fact or fiction?', *Journal of Consumer Research*, **6**, 2, 93–100.

Park, W.C., B.J. Jaworski and D. MacInnis (1986) 'Strategic brand concept image management', *Journal of Marketing*, **50**, 4, 135–45.

Robertson, Thomas S. (1976) 'Low commitment consumer behaviour', *Journal of Advertising Research*, **16**, 2, 19–24.

Rook, Dennis W. (1987) 'The buying impulse', *Journal of Consumer Research*, **14**, 2, 189–99.

Sherif, M., and M. Cantril (1947) *The Psychology of Ego Involvement*, New York: John Wiley.

Traylor, Mark B. (1981) 'Product involvement and brand commitment', *Journal of Advertising Research*, **21**, 6, 51–6.

Wilkie, William L. (1990) *Consumer Behaviour* (2nd edn), New York: John Wiley.

Zaichkowsky, Judith Lynn (1985) 'Measuring the involvement construct', *Journal of Consumer Research*, **12**, 3, 341–52.

Understanding organizational markets

7

Characteristics of organizational markets
Identifying buyers in organizational markets
Organizational buying behaviour

Introduction

This chapter discusses and explains:

- the nature of organizational buying;

- how industrial products may be classified;

- how organizations can develop and maintain standards by implementing quality systems;

- how organizational markets can be divided into manufacturers as customers, intermediate customers and the public sector as customer, and how each of these organizational markets may be segmented for a different mix;

- the different situations facing the organizational buyer: the need to solve a problem; a special purchasing need; ways of overcoming commercial and technical complexity;

- influences on organizational buying behaviour;

- the role of the buying centre;

- stages in industrial buying;

- the significance of supplier loyalty and ways of developing it among organizational buyers;

- an approach to designing an integrated framework of organizational buying.

Organizations usually buy products and services in response to a derived demand. Organizational markets seek a wide range of products and services, some as raw materials, others as components, others to repackage for resale and others as consumables in the manufacture of new products and services.

Standards have become a feature of organizational markets. The introduction of international standards and quality assurance systems such as the ISO 9000 series facilitates trade in industrial products, reduces costs overall and provides guaranteed quality.

Three major customer groups are recognized in organizational markets: manufacturers, intermediaries and the public sector. Each has its own needs and purposes. The buying behaviour in each type of market is different and within each market there are important segments.

Two major sets of influences on organizational buyers may be identified: those emanating from outside the buying organization and those which arise within the organization itself. A second key feature of the influence process is the stage in the buying process at which the influence occurs. Organizations go through a number of stages, moving from awareness to adoption and further to routine reordering, depending on the nature of the product and the buying situation.

Having studied this chapter, you should be able to do the following:

1. Classify organizational products and services into different categories suitable for a different marketing approach.

2. Define the circumstances in which organizational buying occurs.

3. Evaluate the contribution of standards and quality assurance systems to the growth and development of organizational markets.

4. Identify the various types of buyer in organizational markets and determine their distinct needs, wants and motivations.

5. Segment industrial markets for different marketing mixes.

6. Specify ways of identifying different organizational buying situations.

7. Recognize the myriad sources of influences on organizational buyer behaviour.

8. Evaluate the roles of members of the buying centre.

9. Specify approaches to developing loyalty among customers.

10. Develop an integrated framework to understand the organizational buying process.

Characteristics of organizational markets

Nature of organizational buying

An industrial or organizational market consists of all individuals and organizations that acquire products and services which are used in the production of products and services demanded by others. The demand for most products and services arises because of a derived demand for the finished products and services that the company produces.

The market behaviour which affects the demand for industrial products and services is generally quite different from that experienced in consumer markets. The differences arise mainly in regard to the behaviour of industrial buyers, the type of products and services purchased, and the purpose for which they are purchased.

Buying is performed by all organizations: manufacturing firms, service firms and non-profit organizations in the public and private sectors. Organizational buying is a complex process which may be divided into a number of stages taking place over time. People with different functional responsibilities are usually involved in the industrial buying process. Their influence varies at the different stages, depending on the product or service being purchased. In broad terms, organizational buying is influenced by factors in the environment, by the nature and structure of the organization itself and by the way the buying centre in the company operates (Figure 7.1).

Defining organizational buying

Organizational buying has been defined as 'the decision making process by which formal organizations establish the need for purchased products and

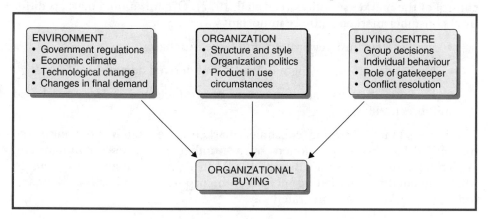

Figure 7.1 Influences in organizational buying

services and identify, evaluate and choose among alternative brands and supplies' (Webster and Wind, 1972: 2). This decision-making process includes information acquisition and search activity, in addition to developing criteria to be used in choosing among various alternatives open to the organization. In deciding on these issues, the buying organization must take account of a large number of variables in addition to the ability of the product to perform. Likewise the selling company must understand the entire process of organizational buying behaviour.

Comparisons with consumer markets

Industrial marketing is far more complex than consumer marketing because it involves a more intricate network of buying influences. The technical nature of many of the products purchased adds to the complexity of industrial marketing. Generally, the size of the purchase in money terms is greater and the buying relationship is more long term.

In the marketing of industrial products, technology is a more pervasive element, which frequently produces a technologically driven production orientation rather than a marketing orientation. This production orientation is due to the greater amount of interaction and interdependence between marketing and other functional areas, especially manufacturing, R & D and engineering. Customers in industrial markets buy for commercial reasons, whereas in consumer markets customers buy for personal gratification, for the family or household, or for individuals in the household.

In industrial markets, the purchase may be postponed for long periods even if this leads to inefficiencies. In the short term, however, industrial product buyers can decide when to buy specific items of equipment. Industrial markets are, therefore, subject to policy decisions on investment, which may be affected by many other considerations, including political factors outside the control of the market suppliers (Chisnall, 1977). Organizational markets differ from consumer markets in three important ways:

- market structure: fewer users and large purchases;

- buying decisions: buying motivation and derived demand; and

- reaching the customer: the nature of products and services purchased and direct selling.

The wisdom of treating consumer marketing separately from industrial marketing has been questioned by a number of writers (Zaltman and Wallendorf, 1979; Fern and Brown, 1984). In light of the above arguments, what is needed is a marketing mix which incorporates products, services and industrial markets in an integrated way.

Classifying industrial products

There are various ways of classifying industrial products and services. Industrial marketing is concerned with the basic industries which produce or process primary products, such as chemicals, plastics, oil, iron, steel, other metals, artificial fibres, wool and other raw materials derived from agriculture and the extractive industries. Concern also rests with industries that supply semi-manufactured components, materials and durable products, including engineering, shipbuilding, commercial vehicle assembly, electronics, heavy electrical assembly and allied industrial activities. Service industries such as finance and consultancy are sometimes treated as industrial markets.

Industrial products are frequently classified according to their application, whereas consumer products are classified according to the manner in which they are purchased. For example, industrial products have been classified as heavy equipment, light equipment, consumable supplies, component parts, raw materials, processed materials and industrial services (Haas, 1986). Jackson and Cooper (1988), however, criticize most classification schemes due to their inadequate handling of industrial services. They propose a classification which includes both goods and services, and which divides them into three major groupings (Figure 7.2).

In this classification, capital products have a long life span and involve a major capital outlay: land, buildings and major items of equipment.

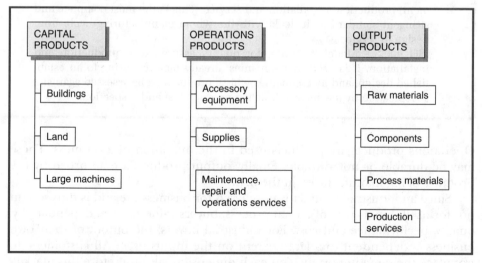

Figure 7.2 Classification of industrial products

(Source: Based on Jackson and Cooper, 1988: 116. Reprinted and adapted by permission of the publisher from Jackson, Ralph W., and Philip D. Cooper (1988) 'Unique aspects of marketing industrial services', *Industrial Marketing Management*, 17, 2, 111–18. Copyright 1988 by Elsevier Science Inc.)

EXHIBIT 7.1   ISO: a quality assurance system

In 1987 the quality standard ISO 9000 was formally adopted throughout Europe as the basis for quality systems. Concurrently, the American Standards Institute (ANSI) co-operated in adopting the series for use in the United States. Most leading companies in the field of quality assurance and industrial expertise in general have allowed their own standards to be superseded by the ISO 9000 series.

The ISO 9000 standard is a quality assurance sytem award. It originated with the International Organization for Standardization (ISO), the specialized international agency for standardization. The series was developed from the original British standard BS5750, resulting in a comprehensive series of documents applicable to organizations which design and manufacture, those which simply manufacture and those which provide services. The series sets down the minimum requirements for quality management by detailing what is necessary for the management and control of quality assurance within a company. To apply for registration, companies are required to have a documented quality system that complies with the requirements of the relevant standard.

There are six standards in the ISO 9000 series which are of particular interest to companies seeking registration:

- ISO 9000: Quality management and quality assurance standards guidelines for selection and use. This standard is for internal management use and helps also to decide which of the standards are more appropriate.
- ISO 9001 – Model 1: Model for quality assurance in design and development, production, installation and service. This is the most complete and stringent standard as it deals with the whole manufacturing cycle from design to service.
- ISO 9002 – Model 2: Model for quality assurance in production and installation. It is used by companies already manufacturing to an established design, and by companies whose product can be assessed against a specification by means of a 'finished product' test and inspection.

Operations products are products used in the operation of a business. These may be durable or non-durable. Finally, output products are absorbed by the products being manufactured in the firm.

Since an industrial product is purchased for business use and is thus sought not for itself, but as part of a total process, buyers value service, dependability, quality, performance and cost. For industrial buyers, the output of their own business is dependent to a large extent on the inputs used. All customers do not place the same importance on each dimension, and therefore this marketing orientation, which industrial firms have typically been accused of lacking, is crucial in determining the product offering required by each customer.

- ISO 9003 – Model 3: Model for quality assurance in final inspection and test. Both ISO 9002 and ISO 9003 are less stringent than ISO 9001.
- ISO 9004: Guidelines for quality management and quality system elements.
- ISO 9004 – Part 2: This standard provides guidelines for quality management in service industries.

Benefits of using ISO 9000 standards

Although the application of management to quality inevitably involves a cost in implementation, which may be particularly difficult for the smaller company, there is demonstrable evidence that there is a subsequent pay-off in profit. There are five major supplier benefits which may be identified:

- independent verification of the quality claims of a company;
- exposure to potential customers through inclusion in internationally recognized registers of companies using ISO 9000;
- evidence of effective quality control procedures now demanded by other government and financial agencies for grant aid purposes;
- recognition by multinational customers and public sector purchasing organizations; and
- cost savings through reducing the needs for multiple assessments and factory inspections.

There are clear customer benefits associated with the use of standards. Four major benefits may be identified:

- a guarantee that quality needs are being met;
- reduced inspection costs and elimination of the need for own supplier assessments;
- increased confidence in the supplier; and
- supplier selection made easier by registration.

Maintaining standards with quality systems

With the increased commercial 'quality pressures' facing many firms today, there has emerged an increased interest in quality assurance in general, and especially in quality management systems. In recent years, quality standards have become the focus of interest in the EU. The aim of quality systems such as the ISO 9000 series is to institutionalize quality as a primary activity within the firm, to emphasize high-quality design and equally high productivity, and to accelerate new product and process developments to make the companies even more competitive (Exhibit 7.1). Adopting an official quality system has been described as a preliminary and fundamental step towards a total quality strategy in the organization (Kalinosky, 1990).

Role of standards

Standards in any industry are important to customers because parts, components and sub-assemblies must fit together. Standards derive from a set of specifications and practices, or they may be embodied in a simple product such as the Sony Walkman. In the absence of standards, it is very difficult for a new industry to develop. The objective of standards is to converge shapes, sizes, taste and other configurations in such a way that the key features and components in an industry can reach a mass market. Even then not all aspects of products are standardized, which leaves open the possibility of slight differentiation and continued innovation. Eventually agreed standards are undermined by new technologies, thereby creating a new competitive environment in search of a new standard.

When the standard agreed relates to a single component or part of a product, and contains most of the value added in the product, it can be difficult for new industry entrants to differentiate themselves, and competition quickly deteriorates into rabid price battles.

In recent years, there has been an increased interest in standards especially in Europe and North America, for a number of reasons:

- harmonization of standards increases trade;

- linkage between national and international standards; and

- recognition of the value of horizontal standards.

The increased importance of trade in the European Union and the North American Free Trade Association, and between them and their major trading partners, requires a harmonization of standards for industry to benefit fully from the removal of internal trade barriers or the reduction of external barriers. Individual countries also recognize that there are competitive advantages to be gained by ensuring that national standards form the basis of an international standard. As a result, stronger countries like Germany, France and the UK in Europe, and the USA in North America, control or strongly influence the International Organization for Standardization committees established to develop new international standards. Such influence allows these countries considerable scope in shaping the ultimate standard. For example, fear has been expressed on many occasions that very rigid environmental standards may be set by countries not to protect the environment, but to protect their industries. The German paper industry is believed to have received an unfair trade advantage by the introduction of very rigid recycling regulations (Exhibit 7.2). The third reason for increased interest in standards is the trend towards developing horizontal standards which address such areas as environmental control and quality assurance across different industries and services. The ISO 9000 is the first horizontal standard to be implemented.

EXHIBIT 7.2   Rag and bone moans

Germany's Topfer law appears to be strangling Britain's paper-recycling industry. The companies paid by German industry to dispose of waste paper have such a glut of the stuff that many are paying German paper makers to take it off their hands. This, in turn, has allowed German paper makers to reduce their costs by as much as 15 per cent. British firms have lowered their prices in an effort to hold on to market share, but are losing money as a result. British paper mills are closing.

Britain's recycling industry has also been hurt by imports of German waste paper. Even after hefty transport costs, this is cheap enough to replace the British variety, but not so cheap as to lower the costs of British paper makers to the level of those of their German rivals.

The capacity of the British recycling industry has fallen by 10 per cent over the past six months. Britain recycled 34 per cent of all the paper that it consumed in 1991. But next year it is likely to recycle no more than 30 per cent of its paper. 'The Germans are using their packaging law as a means of dominating Europe's recycling industry,' claims Peter Williams, chief executive of a firm called David S. Smith, which, with 6,500 staff, is Britian's largest recycler of paper, both collecting waste and using it to make recycled paper.

German recyclers of plastic packaging are stealing a similar advantage. British Polythene Industries, which uses waste polyethylene film to make new film, has complained to the commission that it cannot compete against German firms selling new film in Britain. At one time German companies paid waste collectors DM30 ($21) for a tonne of used film; they are now paid DM500 a tonne by waste collectors, who are desperate to get rid of their stocks. British makers of polyethylene film cannot benefit from this bonanza, because transport costs make it uneconomic to ship much waste film from Germany to Britain.

Source: *The Economist*, 22 August 1992: 54.

Proprietary and open standards

Standards may be proprietary or open. Proprietary standards can be used to tie up customers and prevent competitors from entering the market. The current debate about the digital compact disc and the recent debate about video standards – Betamax and VHS – are good examples of proprietary standards on which the industry converged, so that the market for products based on agreed standards could grow.

Customers benefit from open standards to which all potential competitors have access. Open standards allow network economies to exist: for example, compatibility with an extensive range of accessory equipment, as was the case in video recording technology when the VHS system became the standard. Indeed, the standard adopted often does not reflect the best technology available, but because the industry and customers are confident that related products can be used in association, the inferior standard tends to be adopted. Thus VHS was adopted although many in the industry believed that Betamax was a better system at the time. Open standards in an industry also allow new, innovative firms to enter.

Industries set open standards on the basis of agreement among several firms in the industry, or by adopting the standard established by a single firm which becomes the industry leader. In personal audio, Sony set the standard. In microprocessing, Intel set the standard. In applications software for personal computers, Microsoft's MS-DOS Operating System software and more recently its 'Windows' are standards. Standards set by individual firms tend to be more successful and more quickly adopted than those set by industry-wide agreement, since there is frequently a lack of trust and no real incentive at industry level to standardize. The way in which the car industry evolved in the early days is a good example of the difficulty of setting standards by agreement. Modern cars follow standards established by one or two dominant global car manufacturers, especially Japanese companies.

Competitive standards

High quality, service and exclusivity are features of competitive standards which even small companies in more traditional industries can adopt. Eurobags, the manufacturer of designer shopping bags used by well-known department stores, has set the competitive standard for its industry by vertically integrating its production and using specialized modern equipment (Exhibit 7.3). This relatively small Italian company makes everything in-house, from the bags themselves to the plastic and cord handles, and the knotted silk handles provided on some premium bags.

In the car market, the Japanese set the standard that all European manufacturers in particular aim to match. In Europe, Renault has attempted to meet the challenge by cutting costs, improving quality and designing more rapidly. But as all cars are now of a high quality standard, Renault is placing more emphasis on design and style to win competitive advantage. Renault is also attempting to develop new models faster. At present new models take up to five years to develop, compared to three years for Japanese manufacturers.

In setting and applying competitive standards in an industry, suppliers as well as their products are evaluated. If the number of suppliers is large, industrial purchasers screen them to identify a few which are further evaluated. The hypothetical example of a dental drill supplier analysis for two competitors shows what might result (Table 7.1). Note that the buyer's importance weights do not change with suppliers, but their evaluations do. By weighting the suppliers' scores with the importance weights, an overall view of the two suppliers is obtained.

EXHIBIT 7.3 From bags to riches

Buy anything in a top store in Madrid, Paris or any other other big European city and your purchase will be placed in a bag bearing two names. One will proclaim tastefully the origin of the goods in the bag – Chanel or Missoni perhaps – the other, more discreetly, the origin of the bag. The chances are the second name will be that of Eurobags. Based in the Northern Italian provice of Traviso, Eurobags makes shopping bags for the top end of the market. Its client list includes Benetton, Chanel, Lacoste and Missoni. Customers of about 20,000 outlets in 18 countries take their purchases home inside a Eurobag.

The company was set up 25 years ago by Renzo Taffarello and now employs about 180 people and had a turnover last year of more than L40 billion (Ecu 26 million). About 60 per cent of sales are in the home market, with the rest of Europe providing 35 per cent. The company has a warehouse in each of the main Community countries, Taffarello says. 'That way we can guarantee deliveries in two to three days.' Production from the company's three factories is vertically integrated. 'It probably costs a bit more to do it all ourselves,' Taffarello says, 'but outside suppliers simply don't exist.'

One of the secrets of Eurobag's success lies in the 12 modern machines it bought from Japan two years ago. Their cost, more than L1.5 billion each, is a formidable barrier to the entry of new suppliers. But Taffarello has added another safeguard: he has secured a promise from the Japanese that the machines will not be sold to anyone else in Europe.

The Japanese machines, which are speedier and more flexible than rival bag-making equipment, have also given Eurobags capacity well above its immediate needs. This helps with seasonal demand cycles, which are characterised by an autumn peak and a spring low, Taffarello says. The company has also been able to reduce its delivery time by two thirds, with no more than a month needed to deliver a new line – and most of this time is taken in preparing the design and locating raw materials.

Source: *International Management*, March 1992: 38–9.

Role of quality systems

Quality systems standardize procedures and eliminate variances in production, thus helping companies conform to requirements. If strategy can be defined in terms of the dimensions of quality, it is clear that conformation has changed from just an operational view of meeting a set of specifications to a strategic consideration. This reflects an evolving effort towards continual improvement in comformation to design, by attempting to eliminate variances from design specifications and manufacturing processes.

From a manufacturing point of view, the quality–strategy link consists of product and process specifications, delivery schedules and cost goals. Management must derive correct process specifications, best delivery schedules

TABLE 7.1   Dental drill equipment supplier analysis: hypothetical example

Criteria	Importance weights	Supplier score										
		0	1	2	3	4	5	6	7	8	9	10
Technical capability	9								B		A	
Financial strength	4							A		B		
Product reliability	8				B						A	
Delivery reliability	7						A	B				
Compatibility	8				B						A	
After-sales service	8						A	B				
Price	5						A				B	

Weighted total score for supplier A = 9 × 9 + 4 x 5+ .... + 5 × 3 = 312
Weighted total score for supplier B = 9 × 5 + 4 x 8+ .... + 5 × 9 = 221

and cost goals from a reconciliation of customer needs and the firm's capabilities. Conflicts concerning specifications, schedules and costs must be resolved to the greatest extent possible prior to their delivery to manufacturing, and systems must be put in place to handle changes and unresolved conflicts. A quality system can provide a company with a means of achieving this (Tillery and Rutledge, 1991: 73).

Companies that promote the fact that they have achieved 'registered firm status' claim that having the standard is a major selling advantage, and that certification is essential in order to be taken seriously by large purchasing companies. One writer advises that the attainment of the ISO 9000 standard should be at least a significant element in a company's public relations programme, and the most important part as far as industrial firms are concerned. For suppliers it should be both a public relations programme and a strategic plan (Rothery, 1991: 125).

The ISO 9000 standard is becoming compulsory for many manufacturers which are the sub-suppliers of major international corporations. Industries which already have their own stringent standards of control (e.g. pharmaceutical, food and health care companies) are also adopting ISO 9000 as a demonstrable quality management standard.

Managing supplier quality

The majority of the parts and components that manufacturers do not produce themselves are sourced from outside suppliers. Knowledge of effective approaches for controlling supplier quality is an essential element in the achievement of product and service. It is essential to the quality effort of the organization to bring the vendors in as active participants. Through a closer interaction with this group, the company can eliminate a great number of potential quality problems (Tillery and Rutledge, 1991: 75). According to Garvin (1987), without acceptable components and materials it is difficult for a manufacturer to produce high-quality products. Careful selection and monitoring of vendors is necessary to ensure reliable and defect-free production.

Some international companies such as Boeing and AT&T will not consider suppliers which are not registered to ISO 9000 standards. The standard is an effective management tool for companies to establish whether their suppliers are using a quality system. These factors contribute to the standard being called an 'epidemic'. Companies are beginning to feel that, to place themselves in a competitive position in the marketplace, they will need ISO 9000 accreditation. Several experts contend that future European and world-wide industrial trends will be for ISO 9000-registered companies to trade with each other.

EU directive on product liability

Recent efforts have been made to set standards for industrial products in the EU with the introduction of the Council of Ministers directive on product liability. All member states are required to bring their statutes and regulations into compliance with this directive. Prior to the new directive, injured parties had to prove all elements of their claim under tort law: that is, negligence, causation and damage. Consumers had to bear the risk of legal actions, including the costs of expert witnesses. In addition, legislation was quite fragmented across member states. This new directive favours user protection, placing greater obligations on industrial producers.

The following is a brief outline of the directive and its implications for producers. First, once a defect has been found to exist, it is presumed to have existed at the time it left the producer's hands. The onus of proof now lies with the producer and not the customer. Second, defects in product design, manufacturing and product warnings may each be the basis of liability under the directive. Producers may be found liable if they have not warned people adequately of a product's dangerous properties. This could require advertising to consumers by producers who have not done so previously. The content of producer and wholesaler advertising to the trade may be affected. The content of personal selling and point-of-purchase displays may also be affected.

Third, the injured person bears only the burden of proof that the finished product is defective. Thereafter it is up to each person along the channel, i.e. retailer, wholesaler, component manufacturer and raw material manufacturer, to prove that they are not liable. If any middlemen in the distribution channel cannot clearly identify the supplier that made the product, then the middleman takes on the legal role of producer and is treated as such. Importers of products into the EU are also considered producers but not importers of products from another EU member country. In this way, liability for defects remains within the EU jurisdiction. Producers and constructive producers cannot exclude or limit their liability for defects caused in the contract with the customer. Lastly, the plaintiff customer has three years in which to file for recovery. Rights are extinguished, however, when the product is ten years old or more.

This directive is also relevant to non-EU countries, especially those with strong trade, investment and political ties with the EU. Product liability enforcement and regulation, therefore, represent a major force within the company's macro environment, and must be monitored and addressed.

Identifying buyers in organizational markets

Buyers in organizational markets are typically manufacturers, intermediaries or customers in the public sector. To identify them it may be necessary to segment the market.

Manufacturers as customers

Manufacturers as customers buy raw materials, components, and semi-finished and finished items to be used in the manufacture of final goods. Manufacturers tend to be concentrated in particular areas of a country, and hence may more easily be served than consumer markets where the population is dispersed. Furthermore, buying power for certain products tends to be concentrated in a few hands, since a few manufacturers frequently account for most of the production of specific industrial products.

Intermediate customers

Intermediate customers are organizations which buy and sell to make a profit. They are sometimes referred to as resellers. Normally they make very few changes to the products handled. Wholesalers and retailers are the largest intermediaries in this market, but other specialized distributors also exist which may also provide additional services.

Intermediate customers are also concerned with the derived demand further down the channel of distribution for the products they carry. They are particularly concerned about product obsolescence, packaging and inventory requirements, since all three variables are important considerations in their financial well-being.

Public sector markets

The public sector market is in reality a myriad of markets. It consists of institutional markets like schools, hospitals, prisons and other similar public bodies. It also consists of direct sales to government departments such as the health services and education departments. In most countries with an active public sector, the annual budgets of many of these institutions can be a multiple of the expenditure of organizations in the private sector.

Public sector tendering procedures

Many different purchasing terms are used in public sector purchasing, but it is possible to establish two broad categories of these. The first category contains terms which refer to the extent of the publicity given to a particular public sector tender or contract, while the second category contains terms based on the discretion available to the awarding authority within the public service itself.

Where it is judged that many suitably qualified suppliers exist, the publicity given to a particular tender notice is widespread. The opposite is the case where the number of potentially suitable suppliers is limited. Three tendering procedures, each implying a different level of publicity, may be identified:

- open tendering;
- selective tendering; and
- private contracting.

Open tendering procedures arise when an invitation to tender is given the widest publicity. In this situation, an unlimited number of suppliers have the opportunity of submitting bids. Selective tendering procedures occur when the invitation to tender is restricted to a predetermined list of suppliers. In this case, the invitation to tender normally takes the form of invitations sent to these suppliers. Private contracting procedures refer to the situation where the awarding authority contacts suppliers individually, usually a single supplier.

Public sector buying procedures may be further classified according to the extent of the discretion available to the awarding authority. Again it is possible to identify three procedures:

- automatic tendering;
- discretionary tendering; and
- negotiated tendering.

Automatic tendering refers to an arrangement whereby the contract is awarded on the basis of a predetermined criterion such as the lowest bid, or some other criterion either in isolation or in conjunction with price. Discretionary tendering procedures arise when a bid which is most advantageous to the buying department is accepted. The award of the contract in this instance is based on several criteria, some of which are predetermined, but which in general leave the awarding authority a certain freedom of choice. Negotiated tendering describes the situation whereby the awarding authority negotiates freely with the supplier as to the conditions of the contract. This is similar to industrial buying in most private sector situations.

Normally the public sector buying departments follow some combination of open and automatic tendering procedures. Selective tendering has recently become more important because of the lack of a large number of suitable suppliers.

Information sources used

With respect to information sources, the sales representative, technical reports and promotional materials are most commonly used. Because of the technical nature of many of the items bought by the public sector, representation usually means multiple visits to many different sections within the buying centre. To overcome the problem of contacting the official with real purchasing decision-making power, many firms selling to this sector also use a direct mailing service and advertise in the trade press.

Segmenting organizational markets

Industrial product markets are highly heterogeneous, complex and often hard to reach because of the multitude of products and uses as well as a great diversity among customers. Formulating a coherent marketing strategy can be extremely difficult in such an environment (Kluyver and Whitelark, 1986). The need for market segmentation becomes very important in these circumstances.

Failure to segment an industrial market properly can result in missed opportunities, surprise competition and even business failures (Hlavacek and Reddy, 1986). Segmentation is particularly important for the firm in international markets because the benefits that accrue from standardizing elements of the marketing strategy are realized only when similarities among situations are identified. Universal needs and similarities in buying processes are far more evident in industrial markets than in consumer markets (Day *et al.*, 1988).

Various segmentation approaches suitable for industrial markets have been proposed. A staged approach to the segmentation of industrial markets, such as the two-step approach proposed by Wind and Cardozo (1974) or the nested approach (Shapiro and Bonoma, 1984), is recommended for a more comprehensive analysis. In these approaches, macro variables such as type of industry, size of customer and product usage are relevant. Then these segments are subdivided on the basis of micro variables such as the characteristics of the decision-making unit. Such approaches capture all the variables which help to make a particular segment unique.

Sometimes managers of industrial products companies can be very receptive to the concepts of market segmentation and positioning. Doyle and Saunders (1985: 24) report how a basic chemical company used market segmentation techniques to reposition itself to compete in an attractive speciality chemical market that was radically new to it. The company in question decided to process its commodity rosins further into polymerized rosin and stabilized rosin esters, the key element in the manufacture of adhesives, to open up a whole new market segment for the company (1985: 26). These authors claim that the managers of the company were very receptive to the concepts of market segmentation and positioning due to the difficult market conditions experienced by the company when it decided to shift to the more sophisticated chemicals. This 'triggered a high felt need for a marketing oriented approach to the strategic problem facing the business' (1985: 31).

Organizational buying situations

Organizations buy a wide variety of products and services which differ in respect to the type of product, the size of the order and other characteristics such as essentiality. As a consequence, several taxonomies have appeared in the literature which address this matter. Two approaches are discussed here: the first is based on the extent of the management problems which may be associated with the buying situation, and the second refers to the functions served by the products or services once purchased.

Problem solving in industrial buying

A four-way classification based on routine order products, procedural problem products, performance problem products and political problem products has been developed by Lehmann and O'Shaughnessy (1974), which has been very popular in application. Routine order products are products which are frequently ordered and used. With such products there is no problem in learning how to use them; nor is there any question about whether the product will perform in an acceptable way.

In the case of procedural problem products, the buyer is confident that the product will be satisfactory. Problems are likely to arise with such products, however, when other staff in the buying organization have to be trained in their use. In this case the total offering is the key to patronage. The choice of supplier is greatly influenced by the extent to which a prospective supplier can persuade the buyer of the superiority of the service offered in reducing the time likely to be spent in learning how to use the product.

For performance problem products, there is some doubt regarding their ability to perform satisfactorily. The problem is one of the technical ability of the product in application. In such circumstances, the buyer tends to favour the supplier who offers appropriate technical services, provides a free trial period and is sufficiently flexible to adjust to the needs of the buying organization.

Political problem products are those which require a large capital investment for which there are attractive competing opportunities. Rivalry for the allocation of scarce funds also occurs when the product is used by several departments in the buying company.

Functional approach in industrial buying

The functional approach is adopted by Robinson *et al.* (1967) when they suggest that purchasing should be thought of as falling into three classes: a straight rebuy, a modified rebuy and a new task. During the purchasing process, behaviour is believed to depend on the level of previous experience obtained by the company, how much information is needed to make the decision, and the extent to which alternative product offerings are considered. These three aspects – newness of the buying problem, information requirements and a consideration of alternatives – are fundamental to the functional approach (Table 7.2).

The new task buying situation is one which has not arisen before in the company, and consequently there is little previous experience to draw upon. In such cases, the buyer requires a great deal of information; customers must search for alternative ways of solving the problem and must evaluate alternative suppliers. New task decisions occur infrequently, but they may develop into routine purchases and so are important to manage carefully.

Products in the modified rebuy category are purchased regularly. The buying alternatives are known, but they may be changed somewhat due to some particular circumstances such as an emergency in the buying company or something introduced by the seller. New buying influences within the firm may also cause the buyer to reconsider alternatives in the market. In the straight rebuy situation, there is usually a list of acceptable suppliers of products required on a continual or routine basis. For most industrial buying organizations, products bought on a routine basis represent a very high proportion if not a dominant part of total purchases.

The relative novelty of the purchase affects the type of negotiations and the people involved. The greater the novelty of the purchase, the lower the level of experience among buyers, the more information required to make the decision, and the greater the number of alternatives likely to be given consideration. The more repetitive the purchase, the more established and sophisticated is the buying likely to be.

This grid industrial buying framework, referred to as the buy-grid model, has been popular in empirical research studies largely because of its simplicity and intuitive appeal (Anderson *et al.*, 1987). These authors obtained the

TABLE 7.2 Types of industrial buying situation

Buying situation	Newness of problem	Information requirements	Consideration of new alternatives
New task	High	Maximum	Important
Modified rebuy	Medium	Moderate	Limited
Straight rebuy	Low	Minimal	None

Source: Adapted from Robinson *et al.* (1967).

perceptions of sales managers regarding the purchase situation in developing empirical support for aspects of the buy-grid framework. They concluded that newness and information needs are related to buyer behaviour, whereas the availability of alternatives was less associated.

Complexity in industrial buying

There is a danger that, because a firm is science or engineering based, it remains product instead of customer oriented. The complexity of the market

---

EXHIBIT 7.4 Nothing is in the bag

Airbags, already a boost to the otherwise moribund auto parts business, will be standard in most new cars by 1994. In terms of market share, the business is currently split evenly between Cleveland's TRW Inc. (1990 sales, $8.2 billion) and Chicago-based Morton International ($6.1 billion). But Morton has all the profits. Last year it earned $15 million on $163 million in airbag sales. TRW lost money, and may lose more money this year, too.

TRW should have had a big head start. Half its business is supplying automakers items like steering systems and seat belts. And it is spending $1.50 for every $1 Morton spends on airbag capital outlay. Morton, a speciality chemical firm, has little automative parts expertise. What has TRW done wrong? What did Morton do right?

TRW makes all four parts of an airbag: sensors, to detect a crash; diagnostics, which signal when to inflate the bag; the inflator, which burns sodium azide to produce nitrogen, inflating the bag; and the module that houses the contraption. By contrast, Morton makes only inflators and modules.

The difference is important because most car companies, it turns out, don't buy entire airbag systems. General Motors makes its own sensors and diagnostics, which account for about two-thirds of the cost of a $300 (wholesale) airbag. Ford makes its own diagnostics. Chrysler buys the whole system but not always from the same source.

TRW Chief Executive Joseph Gorman defends making the entire system on the grounds that, sooner or later, specialisation and economies of scale will induce carmakers to buy complete systems. 'In two or three years? I don't know,' he says. 'It will happen ultimately because we'll convince [carmakers] that's the way to go.'

Morton has concentrated its efforts on developing the best inflators, the key to airbag technology. It's helped greatly by its knowledge of solid propellants, which in turn comes from Thiokol Corp., the aerospace unit split off from Morton in 1989 after the *Challenger* disaster. 'Morton has a lot more expertise in pyrotechnics than TRW,' notes one man at Ford Motor, TRW's major customer.

Source: *Forbes*, 4 March 1991: 97.

---

for a product, and the difficulties of marketing it, should not be confused with the complexity or high technical content of the product itself.

To be useful from a marketing viewpoint, the classification of industrial products should be on the basis of the ways the products are bought and serviced rather than on technical specifications. Determining the market complexity of the product forces the firm to adopt a marketing rather than a purely technical orientation when attempting to understand industrial buyer behaviour.

Companies serving industrial markets must understand the product and market complexity they are likely to meet. Technology-oriented companies often overstate market responsiveness to their new product and underestimate the ability of existing competitors to retaliate (Doyle and Saunders, 1985). The competition between TRW and Morton International in the airbags for cars market demonstrates how the former company focused more on the technology, while the latter considered the market requirements and the specific needs of its customers (Exhibit 7.4).

Marketing complexity may be measured as the extent of interaction which must exist between the seller and buyer to bring about a successful exchange. In many cases the interaction can be extensive. Hill (1973) identifies six areas where interaction can be high (Figure 7.3). Frequently, both parties know the usual uses for the product, but the selling firm may have to identify appropriate uses or there may be a mutual examination by the buying and selling firms.

The interaction level and the associated marketing complexity rise with each of these levels of analysis. Purchases may be small orders and frequent,

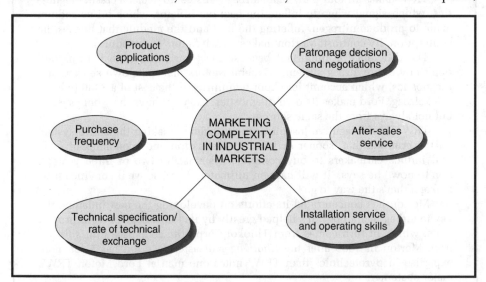

Figure 7.3   Determining marketing complexity in industrial markets
(Source: Adapted from Hill, 1973: 34)

annual or periodic, or very infrequent and large. There may be little or no standard items in the purchase, some estimating may be performed by sales staff, or the manufacturer's technical advisory team may be involved. At the same time, the rate of technological change may be fairly static, change only occasionally or be very dynamic.

The patronage decision may involve the buyer only, the buyer and one or two colleagues, or several parties including technical support staff. The negotiating time may consist of one or two calls only, several calls or protracted negotiations over a long period. The installation service may be simple, require reasonable care or require extreme care and special operating conditions. Allied to this is the level of operating ability required in the buying organization. It may be unskilled labour, semi-skilled or trained operators, or skilled technicians only. After-sales service may not be required, may be required only occasionally, or may be required frequently.

The more extensive the interaction required for each of the above, the greater the marketing complexity involved. Understanding the technical dimensions of the product is essential, but so too is understanding the buying process, the communication needs of buyers, and the negotiating positions to adopt at the various stages of the buying process.

Product complexity and commercial uncertainty

It has been suggested by Fisher (1969) that the buying responsibility in organizational markets is largely determined by product complexity and commercial uncertainty. Product complexity refers to the relationship between product technology and the extent of the customer's technical knowledge just discussed. Commercial uncertainty refers to business risk and its impact on future

COMMERCIAL UNCERTAINTY	PRODUCT COMPLEXITY	
	Low	High
High	Board Senior managers	All organization levels
Low	Purchasing manager	Design engineers manufacturing manager

Figure 7.4 Patterns of industrial buying influence
(Source: Adapted from Fisher, 1969)

company profits. It refers to the level of the investment, the order size, the length of commitment, any adjustments required elsewhere in the company, the effect on profitability, and the ease with which the effect can be forecasted.

Where product complexity and commercial risk are low, the professional buyer and his or her department carry out all the buying functions. At the other extreme, many people may be involved at different levels in the organization. When product complexity is high and commercial uncertainty is low, the technical staff tend to dominate the buying decision. When the commercial risk is high and the product complexity is low, the buying decision becomes the responsibility of specialist buyers supported by the finance department (Figure 7.4).

Organizational buying behaviour

In understanding organizational buying behaviour, it is necessary to understand the role of the buying centre, the industrial buying process and determinants of source loyalty in industrial markets.

Role of buying centre

Each organization may be conceived as having a buying centre, sometimes referred to as a decision-making unit. The buying centre has several distinct functions, which are carried out by different groups of people and must be understood by the potential supplier (Figure 7.5). Roles for members of the buying centre have been classified as: users, influencers, buyers, deciders and gatekeepers (Webster and Wind, 1972). The importance of different organizational roles varies according to the phase of the buying process. The make-up of a buying centre in terms of members and the roles fulfilled changes depending on organizational factors, the organization size and the buying situation (Wind, 1978).

Roles can be conceived fairly easily for the purchasing of products such as production materials. It is more difficult to specify roles for services. Determining who within the company is the user of transportation for inbound materials or outbound products, who is the gatekeeper or who has the decider role is a difficult task. It is quite likely that several individuals occupy the same role within the buying centre: for example, there may be several users and one individual may occupy two or more roles, such as buyer and gatekeeper.

Users can influence the buying decision in a positive way by suggesting the need for purchased materials and by defining standards of product quality, or in a negative way by refusing to work with the materials of certain suppliers for any of several reasons.

Influencers are members of the company who directly or indirectly influence buying or usage decisions. They exert their influence by defining criteria which constrain the choices that can be considered in the purchase decision, or by providing information with which to evaluate alternative buying actions. Technical personnel are significant influencers, especially in the purchase of equipment for the development of new products or processes.

Buyers have formal authority for selecting the supplier and managing the terms of the purchase. Depending upon the nature of the formal organization and its size, buyers may have such titles as purchasing manager, purchasing agent or buyer, or this responsibility and authority may reside with people other than those designated specifically as buyers – the production manager, for instance.

Deciders are those members of the buying organization who have either formal or informal power to determine the final selection of suppliers. The buyer may be the decider, but it is also possible that the buying decision is made by somebody else and that the buyer is expected to ensure proper implementation of the decision.

In practice, it is not always easy to determine when the decision is actually made and who makes it. An engineer may develop a specification which can only be met by one supplier. Thus, although purchasing agents may be the only people with formal authority to sign a buying contract, they may not be the actual deciders.

Gatekeepers are group members who control the flow of information. For instance, the buyer may have formal responsibility and authority for managing

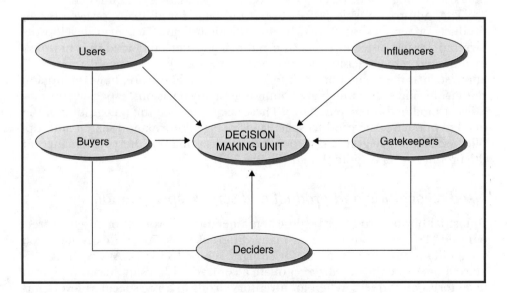

Figure 7.5 Roles in the decision-making unit

309

the relationships of a firm with vendors and potential vendors. In such a situation, the buyer is the gatekeeper with formal authority for allowing sales people to call upon the engineering department, or may be responsible for maintaining a library of catalogues.

The behaviour of individuals in formal organizations is, therefore, a complex interaction of personal, group and organizational behaviour directed at attaining goods. These behaviours frequently coalesce, but may conflict. Individuals strive to reach individual goals, but members of organizations also strive to accomplish the objectives of their groups and organizations. In well-functioning decision-making units, individuals accept the objectives of the organization as their own, while also deciding that the decision-making unit represents the best opportunity to pursue private objectives and satisfy their own requirements.

Industrial buying process

The industrial purchasing process is one of the foundations on which the marketing strategy in industrial firms is based. The other is an understanding of competitive behaviour. The buying process for industrial products is often conceptualized as a sequential process involving a number of stages. Many classifications have been proposed. One of the most widely quoted classifications is the buy-stages model (Robinson *et al.*, 1967): awareness of the problem; deciding the appropriate product to solve the problem; searching for qualified suppliers; accepting offers; placing the order; and evaluating the outcome.

The industrial buying process is not the same for all firms, or even for all products or services purchased by an individual firm. Each firm develops its own purchasing procedures. Furthermore, some steps included in a new task or modified rebuy decision are not usually necessary in a straight rebuy situation, such as the evaluation of different suppliers. There are, however, organizational buying stages which are common to many decisions, especially for new tasks or modified rebuy purchases. These stages include the recognition of the need to purchase, the product specification stage, information search and supplier evaluation, negotiating a purchase and evaluating the performance of the product or service purchased (Figure 7.6).

Need recognition and product and service specification

Industrial buying processes begin when a need for a product or service is recognized. This step can occur in many different ways. At one extreme, need recognition is routine, such as for straight rebuy decisions. Anticipating this kind of need, a company may negotiate a contract with a supplier to replenish inventories on request. When an inventory drops to a pre-specified level, purchase orders are completed and sent to a supplier. At the other extreme, a

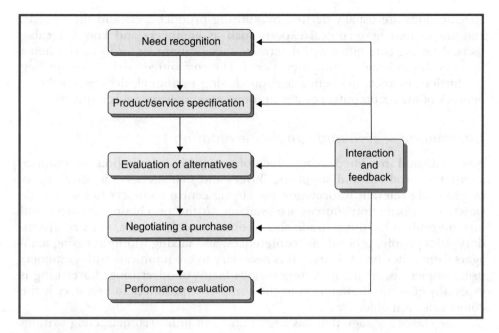

Figure 7.6 Organizational buying process

need for a product can arise because of events which happen in specific situations. For instance, the company may decide to install a computer system to process sales orders, which is a one-off purchase. The approach in both situations is different.

Having recognized a product need, members of the buying centre must determine product performance specifications. Specifications include benefits important to the user of the products as well as non-product criteria important to the buying organization. Furthermore, each member of the buying centre often has private specifications which must be met, and some of these may conflict.

Specifications range from general statements of performance requirements to detailed listings of product attributes, price and support services. For example, specifications for a dental drill unit might include:

- accuracy of measurement within specified tolerances;
- ability to accommodate drill bits produced by numerous manufacturers;
- stability of application under different conditions;
- ability to be used by dentists of different heights;
- price limit per unit; and
- rapid and dependable repair service.

311

Specifications are usually derived by studying product users and their needs, and are written by technical experts such as engineers and knowledgeable users. A buying committee may determine specifications, as for instance when a firm decides to install a computer system. The committee, perhaps comprising production, finance, marketing and purchasing personnel, decides whether a network of microcomputers or a mainframe computer system is required.

Information search and supplier evaluation

New task and modified rebuy decisions require information to evaluate alternative products and suppliers. Buyers and managers act as gatekeepers by gathering relevant information for buying centre members to use. A wide variety of information sources are available to the purchasing manager and include trade advertising, trade shows, direct mail literature, visits from vendors' sales people, professional conferences, and talking with purchasing managers from other firms. Usually it is necessary to communicate with customers using numerous media, including various forms of advertising. Advertising is especially effective if awareness of the company's products and services is the communication objective.

The classic message that has been quoted in industrial marketing writings to demonstrate the importance of developing an appropriate image and credibility before contacting buyers directly is the business magazine publishers McGraw-Hill's 'man-in-chair' advertisement (Haas, 1986). This advertisement appeared in several business advertisements over the years and featured a man sitting in a chair who says to the reader:

> 'I don't know who you are.
> I don't know your company.
> I don't know your company's product.
> I don't know what your company stands for.
> I don't know your company's customers.
> I don't know your company's record.
> I don't know your company's reputation.
> Now – what was it you wanted to sell me?'

The purpose of the advertisement was to persuade companies that selling should start before the salesperson calls on prospective customers, hence the need to advertise in business magazines.

Other forms of communication are also effective. Architects are important influencers in the construction industry as they are in a position to specify product types and even brands of products to use in particular situations. In a study of information sources used by architects, it was discovered that word-of-mouth influence from colleagues was the most important in terms of influence, whereas trade literature was the most important in terms of usage (Table

TABLE 7.3 Information sources used by architects in evaluating building materials suppliers and their influence

Source type	Use	Influence
Personal sources		
Architects in own company	4.4	3.6
Architects in other companies	2.7	2.8
Informal social contacts	2.2	1.3
Manufacturer sources		
Trade literature	4.9	3.0
Technical representatives	3.9	3.0
Direct mail	3.8	2.0
Sales representatives	3.1	1.6
Trade exhibitions	2.8	2.0
Neutral sources		
Specialist	3.6	3.4
Standards	2.8	2.9
Contractors	2.7	2.3
Product tried	2.1	1.9

Sources were rated on a scale 1–5 with the higher number reflecting very extensive usage and influence.

Source: Bradley and Hackett (1978).

7.3). It is noteworthy how important selected manufacturer sources are in terms of both usage and influence. Informal social contacts, trade exhibitions, contractors and experience did not count for much with the architects surveyed.

Supplier choice criteria

Early writings on this subject assumed that the only criterion used in the purchase of industrial products was price. It was also recognized that the initial price was only one component of the total cost. Usually with industrial products there are recurring costs which must also be considered. Since the objective of the firm is to maximize profit, the argument went, in a buying context this meant minimizing cost. It was also argued that organizational buying was more rational than consumer buying.

Later it was recognized that it is difficult to apply rationality to industrial buying as products and services become more and more complex and heterogeneous. Furthermore, it is necessary to consider the reliability of the products and services purchased, which depends on supplier credibility. As a consequence, it was necessary to extend the simple price model to include myriad attributes of the products and services purchased, such as price, quality, delivery and financial arrangements. In this respect, Microsoft has demonstrated

---

EXHIBIT 7.5   A harder sell for software

The daunting task of learning how to use a new software package (along with compatibility problems) means that most PC users tend to stay loyal to the brand they bought first: once a Lotus 1-2-3 user, always a Lotus 1-2-3 user. This generates a stream of revenue for Lotus, as users will happily pay to upgrade their software each time a new version of the spreadsheet program is released.

To win new buyers and keep them loyal, the industry has unleashed every marketing weapon it can lay its hands on. Microsoft, the giant of the industry, is selling its new Access database software for $99.99 until the end of January – down from a list price of $695. Access is aimed directly at Borland, whose Paradox database software (retail price $795) is a best-seller.

To lock PC buyers into using a range of their products (and to lock out competitors), big software firms are selling 'suites' of programs at huge discounts: Lotus's Smart-Suite combines spreadsheet, word-processing, graphics and electronic-mail software, and sells for as little as one-fifth of the $1,500 retail price for the same software sold individually: Office, Microsoft's rival package, offers PC users a similar deal. And to lure users of rival software, many firms are offering 'competitive upgrades'. WordPerfect is now offering its WordPerfect for Windows software to users of rival word-processing packages for just $129 – a 74 per cent discount.

Personal computer makers have been able to take a price war in their stride because the cost of computing power is falling by the day. The price of the Intel 386 microprocessor used in many of today's $1,000 PCs has fallen by over 40 per cent in the past year alone.

Most software firms, by contrast, will find it much harder to weather a price war, because their costs are rising. Two main factors lie behind this dilemma. The first is that software is becoming more complex – and hence costly – to write. The second factor is Microsoft. After a decade dominating the personal-computer industry with its MS-DOS operating-system software, Microsoft's latest operating system, Windows, is rapidly turning into the new industry standard. Windows is now far outselling DOS (on which it is based) and is already installed on 18 million PCs.

Unsurprisingly, Microsoft was first into the market with applications software for Windows – a head start which has allowed it to corner about half the market for Windows-based applications in America. Its competitors have taken longer than expected to launch their own Windows-based applications software. Borland, for example, has yet to release a Windows version of its successul Paradox and dBase software.

Source: *The Economist*, 7 November 1992: 79.

the power of price in holding on to existing customers and attracting the customers of competitors, while at the same time presenting buyers with all the benefits of these non-price factors (Exhibit 7.5). The fact that Microsoft has set the industry standard in its Windows has been most influential.

Buyers differ from each other in two respects which influence supplier choice. The individual characteristics of buyers dictate the importance they attach to each attribute featured in the product or service purchased. Buyers attach different importance weights to each attribute. In the private residential house market, builders have rated economic variables as being more important in supplier selection than behavioural variables, although these were also important (Banville and Dorndoff, 1973). According to Lehmann and O'Shaughnessy (1974), price was most important for political problem products, but ranks only eighth in importance for performance problem products.

The amount and type of risk involved in buying also varies by buyer. Depending on their circumstances, some buyers face greater risks than others in buying essentially the same industrial product or service. Supplier choice is therefore related to three variables: the characteristics of the supplier, the characteristics of the buyer, and the level and type of risk involved (Cardozo and Cagley, 1971).

Decision criteria for organizational buying

The numerous stages involved in industrial buying mean that a cascading hierarchical dependency exists among the choice criteria. It is likely that numerous different sets of buying criteria are involved (Möller and Laaksonen, 1984). First, buyers use one set of criteria for selecting potential suppliers to submit bids. Because the intention is to restrict or screen suppliers, cut-off levels of criteria based on supplier reputation, technical specifications and delivery capacity dominate. In evaluating bids, the same set of criteria may be used, but now a rank order of preference among the suppliers is established. The relative importance of the criteria may change as those left meet the criteria imposed.

At the stage involving negotiations with one or two potential suppliers, a third set of criteria may be used. This contains only the most important attributes which still have some variation across the bidders after the first two stages. At this stage in the negotiations, the buyer's aim is often to get the best possible price without jeopardizing quality and delivery.

Numerous stages in the industrial buying process are more in evidence for high-value and complex buying situations where competitive offers are available. In simpler, routinized buying situations, the above stages are not normally used. The stages phenomenon is complicated further by the presence of the buying centre influence on the criteria. The interaction of buying stages and buying centre members should also be assessed. In an attempt to generalize, Möller and Laaksonen (1984) develop a set of major criteria which might be used in industrial purchasing situations. These criteria, which should be

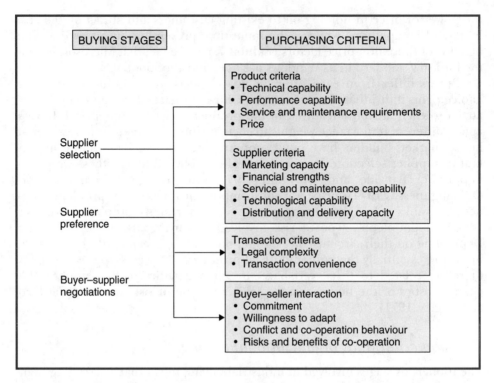

Figure 7.7 Buying stages and purchasing criteria in industrial markets
(Source: Adapted from Möller and Laaksonen. 1984)

applied in a differential manner at each of the three buying stages identified, consist of factors relating to the product itself, the supplier, the transaction and the buyer–seller interaction (Figure 7.7). These authors warn, however, that no single list of criteria, despite the degree of generality, should be applied.

Supplier loyalty in organizational markets

Having selected a supplier, it becomes necessary to decide whether to remain with that supplier. The supplier is usually interested in building repeat purchases and loyalty among customers. Knowledge of the factors which contribute to and strengthen loyalty enable the supplier company to stress them in its marketing strategy. In one study, four sets of factors were found to explain 80 per cent of the variation in source loyalty (Wind, 1970). These factors were traditional economic variables like price, quality and delivery; the buyer's previous experience with sources of supply; the organizational structure of the buying firm, including its policies and how it copes with the various influences on its decisions; and factors which simplify the buyer's work (Figure 7.8).

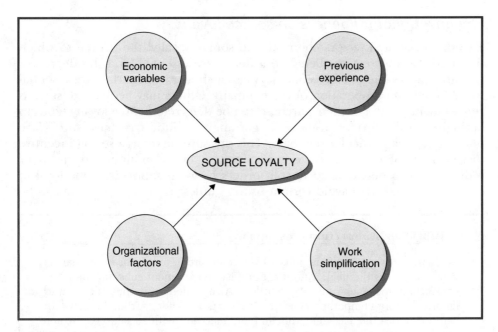

Figure 7.8 Determinants of source loyalty in industrial markets
(Source: Adapted from Wind, 1970. With permission from the American Marketing Association)

Factors determining source loyalty

Conflict over the relative importance of the economic variables often occurs. The buyer may be under simultaneous pressure from one part of the organization to reduce the cost of purchase and from another to improve quality. While these do not necessarily conflict, as the discussion on quality elsewhere shows, buyers resolve the issue by selecting sources which are optimum in respect of one variable and acceptable in terms of another. The process has been described as a 'weir effect', whereby preliminary hurdles are established to filter potential suppliers which are unable to meet specification criteria (Cunningham and White, 1974). Hence, lowest price may in one case be a determinant of supplier choice, whereas in another case an acceptable price may be a necessary qualification to be included in the short list. In the latter case, a quality or service variable may be the critical determinant.

Past experience tends to reinforce a buyer's previous decision and is likely to lead to a repeat purchase if no better supplier is identified. The effect of past experience is demonstrated in Cunningham and White (1974), who reported that 63 per cent of orders went to companies supplying machines which the buyer had previously bought. With high repeat purchases like that, it is no wonder that many industrial marketing companies consider existing customers as the best prospects for further business.

317

Organizational influences on source loyalty

Two organizational factors contribute to source loyalty: the degree to which the products and services being considered are essential, and the degree of risk involved. Some products and services such as raw materials are essential for the continuing operation of the company. Others may be needed, such as replacement plant, but their purchase can be deferred. Source loyalty tends to be higher in the former instance. Regarding risk, industrial buyers may face uncertainty in a particular purchase. This pressure serves as a strong incentive to remain loyal to sources previously used. A buyer motivated to avoid or reduce risk can be expected to split orders between suppliers, to be loyal to reliable sources, or to avoid certain sources unless no risk is perceived to be

---

EXHIBIT 7.6   Airbus cruises comfortably

Every time Airbus Industrie wins a US aircraft order, talk focuses on finance: How sweet was the deal? And did European government subsidies help the consortium make an unbeatable offer? Airbus denies it, but the chatter ignores a more compelling story: In less than a decade, Airbus Industrie of North America Inc. has gone from an inept marketer with 20 salespeople, one plane to sell, and poor customer service, to a powerhouse combination of technologically sophisticated aircraft and top-notch service, as well as the famous, too-good-to-be-true financing. The result? Airbus is now a deadly serious competitor in North America.

Airbus' hot new deal with United Airlines Inc. is proof. United in early July agreed to lease 50 narrowbody A320s from Airbus and took options for 50 more. UAL cut the $3 billion deal because it liked the planes – their range, speed, comfort, technology, and fuel efficiency. But it got a lot more than new jet technology. Airbus will train United pilots and mechanics. The clincher: Airbus will allow United to walk away from its lease on just 11 months' notice, insiders say, which reduces the airline's financial liabilities.

The marketing magic of how Airbus invaded north America is based on a four part theme:

Fired-up fleet: responding to customer need, Airbus in 1985 began adding longer-range, more powerful, and fuel-efficient planes to its product line

Inside-track: Chairman Alan Boyd expanded sales staff with industry insiders, including James Bryan, an aircraft leasing vet, and John Leahy, a former Piper Aircraft salesman

King Customer: In 1988, Airbus opened a mechanics' and pilots' training centre in Miami and, in 1991, a new parts warehouse at Washington's Dulles Airport. Both are crucial to a new emphasis on quick, reliable service

Easy terms: Airbus' innovative financing drew new orders. In 1990, Northwest got a $500 million low-interest loan in exchange for an order. Lease opt out with short notice.

Source: *Business Week*, 27 July 1992: 25.

---

involved. The marketing strategy used by Airbus Industrie to enter the US market was based on four elements which addressed these buyer concerns directly and efficiently (Exhibit 7.6).

Buyers in industrial markets frequently attempt to reduce the frequency and extent of search for alternative suppliers. They attempt to simplify their work by developing purchase routines, especially for standard products and services. In such circumstances, acceptable levels of performance on products and services are sought rather than the optimum level, since complete information on alternatives would be prohibitively expensive.

Longer-term commitment

Because demand in industrial markets is derived, it is the life cycle of customer relationships which should receive emphasis. The strategic changes of the buying firms during the life cycle of their products must be the focus of attention in an organizational buying model. The buyclass variable suggests that the level of management involvement should decrease as products progress from a new task purchase class to a straight rebuy, but during both the design and product maturity stages, purchasing involvement tends to be high (Fox and Rink, 1978).

Integrated framework of organization buying

While there are many differences between consumer markets and organizational markets as discussed above, there are also many important similarities. In both cases, it is possible to classify buyers on various criteria such as the familiarity of the company with the product or service being purchased, the nature and extent of the information sources used, and the stages in the buying decision. Each of these elements has already been discussed. The idea of a buyclass – routine, reorder, modified rebuy or new task purchase – developed by Robinson *et al.* (1967); the variation in information sources used at various

TABLE 7.4 Relationship among buyclass, information sources and stages in industrial decision

Buyclass	Information sources used	Stages in buying decision
First purchase	Impersonal	Awareness
	Advertising	Interest
	Personal	Evaluation
	Other companies Sales people	Trial
	Other users	Adoption
Routine reorder Modified rebuy	Limited information requirements	

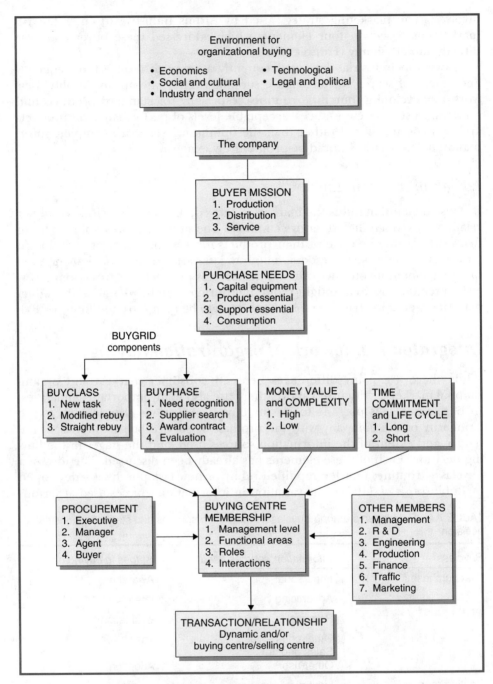

Figure 7.9 Influence and composition of buying centre in organizational markets
(Source: Based on Bradley, 1991: 413)

points in organizational buying, as documented by Ozanne and Churchill (1968); and Rogers' (1962: 306) innovation adoption stages: all these can be integrated into a single framework.

By combining these three factors, a relationship can be established which shows that a whole range of information sources are used by organizational buyers faced with a new task or first purchase situation as they move through the stages from awareness to adoption (Table 7.4). For routine reorder and modified rebuy purchases, the buyer has limited information requirements and all the important buying decision stages have been experienced.

The discussion in this chapter may be summarized by examining the important aspects of influence in organizational buying and the role of the buying centre. The interaction between the various influences and the buying centre are traced in Figure 7.9. The environment for organizational buying sets the broad parameters within which the company operates. The nature of the buying organization dictates purchase needs. The buying centre is exposed to five major influences: the buyclass, the buyphase, financial considerations, the time dimension and the purchase needs within the company. Within the buying centre there are certain additional influences, and others within the organization contribute to the buying decision. The outcome of the process is the completion of a transaction or the strengthening of a buyer–seller relationship.

Assignment questions

1 How does the demand for industrial products differ from the demand for consumer products?

2 What are the major differences between consumer and industrial buying behaviour?

3 Describe government buying procedures. Why is market orientation less important when selling to governments?

4 How does the buyclass of a purchase affect the industrial buying process?

5 What is the buying centre in a company? Describe its functions and the implications for the selling organization.

6 Describe the various stages which industrial buyers pass through during the buying process.

Annotated bibliography

Ames, B. Charles and James D. Hlavacek (1984) *Managerial Marketing for Industrial Firms,* New York: Random House, chapters 2 and 3.

Bonoma, Thomas V., and Benson P. Shapiro (1983) *Segmenting the Industrial Market*, Lexington, Mass.: Lexington Books.

Bradley, Frank (1991) *International Marketing Strategy*, London: Prentice Hall, chapter 16.

Hutt, Michael D., and Thomas W. Speh (1985) *Business Marketing Management*, Chicago: The Dryden Press, chapters 3 and 4.

References

Anderson, E., W. Chu and B. Weitz (1987) 'Industrial purchasing: an empirical explanation of the buyclass framework', *Journal of Marketing*, **51**, 3, 71–86.

Banville, G.R., and R.J. Dorndoff (1973) 'Industrial source selection behaviour – an industrial study', *Industrial Marketing Management*, **2**, 3, 251–9.

Bradley, Frank (1991) *International Marketing Strategy*, London: Prentice Hall.

Bradley, Frank and Joseph P. Hackett (1978) 'Perceived risk and search behaviour: role of architect in industrial buying', *Journal of Irish Business and Administrative Research*, **2**, 2, 10–19.

Cardozo, R.N., and J.W. Cagley (1971) 'An experimental study of industrial buyer behaviour', *Journal of Marketing Research*, **8**, 3, 329–34.

Chisnall, P.M. (1977) *Effective Industrial Marketing*, Harlow: Longman.

Cunningham, M.T., and J.G. White (1974) 'The behaviour of industrial buyers in their search for suppliers', *Journal of Management Studies*, **11**, 2, 115–28.

Day, Ellen, Richard J. Fox and Sandra M. Huszagh (1988) 'Segmenting the global market for industrial goods', *International Marketing Review*, **5**, 3, 14–27.

Doyle, Peter, and John Saunders (1985) 'Market segmentation and positioning in specialised industrial markets', *Journal of Marketing*, **49**, 2, 24–32.

Fern, Edward F., and James R. Brown (1984) 'The industrial/consumer marketing dichotomy: a case of insufficient justification', *Journal of Marketing*, **48**, 2, 68–77.

Fisher, Lawrence (1969) *Industrial Marketing*, London Business Books.

Fox, Harold W., and David R. Rink (1978) 'Purchasing role across the life cycle', *Industrial Marketing Management*, **7**, 3, 186–92.

Garvin, David (1987) 'Competing on the eight dimensions of quality', *Harvard Business Review*, **65**, 6, 101–9.

Haas, Robert W. (1986) *Industrial Marketing Management*, Boston, Mass.: Kent Publishing Co.

Hill, R.W. (1973) *Marketing Technological Products to Industry*, Oxford: Pergamon Press.

Hlavacek, James D., and N. Moham Reddy (1986) 'Identifying and qualifying industrial market segments', *European Journal of Marketing*, **20**, 2, 8–21.

Jackson, Ralph W., and Philip D. Cooper (1988) 'Unique aspects of marketing industrial services', *Industrial Marketing Management*, **17**, 2, 111–18.

Kalinosky, Ian (1990) 'The total quality system, going beyond ISO 9000', *Quality Progress*, **23**, 6, 50–4.

Kluyver, Cornelis A. de, and David B. Whitelark (1986) 'Benefit segmentation for industrial products', *Industrial Marketing Management*, **15**, 4, 273–86.

Lehmann, D.M., and J. O'Shaughnessy (1974) 'Differences in attribute performance for different industrial products', *Journal of Marketing*, **38**, 2, 36–42.

Möller, Kristian K.E., and Martii Laaksonen (1984) 'Situational dimensions and decision criteria in industrial buying: theoretical and empirical analysis', in *Proceedings of the*

International Research Seminar on Industrial Marketing, Stockholm School of Economics, 29–31 August.

Ozanne, Urban B., and Gilbert A. Churchill (1968) 'Adoption research: information sources in the industrial purchasing decision', *Proceedings,* Fall Conference, American Marketing Association.

Robinson, P.J., C.W. Farris, and Y. Wind (1967) *Industrial Buying and Creative Marketing,* Boston, Mass.: Allyn and Bacon.

Rogers, Everett M. (1962) *Diffusion of Innovations,* New York: The Free Press.

Rothery, Brian (1991) *ISO 9000,* Aldershot: Gower.

Shapiro, B.P., and T.V. Bonoma (1984) 'How to segment industrial markets', *Harvard Business Review,* **62**, 3, 104–10.

Tillery, Kenneth R., and Arthur L. Rutledge (1991) 'Quality-strategy and quality-management connections', *International Journal of Quality and Reliability Management,* **8**, 1, 71–7.

Webster, F.E., Jr, and Y. Wind (1972) *Organization Buying Behaviour,* Englewood Cliffs, NJ: Prentice Hall.

Wind, Yoram (1970) 'Industrial source loyalty', *Journal of Marketing Research,* **7**, 450–7.

Wind, Yoram (1978) 'Organizational buyer center: a research agenda', in G. Zaltman and T.V. Bonoma (eds.), *Organizational Buying Behaviour,* American Marketing Association, pp. 67–76.

Wind, Y., and R. Cardozo (1974) 'Industrial market segmentation', *Industrial Marketing Management,* **3**, March, 153–66.

Zaltman, Gerald, and Melanie Wallendorf (1979) *Consumer Behaviour: Basic findings and management implications,* New York: John Wiley.

Understanding and analyzing competitors

8

Meaning of competition in marketing
Nature of competition among firms
Developing a competitive strategy

Introduction

This chapter introduces and explains:

- the value of strategic thinking in developing competitive advantage;

- levels and scope of market competitors;

- how to assess competitors;

- the relationship between market pioneering and competitive advantage;

- the impact of technology on competition;

- the need to define quality in marketing terms;

- the link between competitive success and speed to market; and

- the hierarchy of competitive responses.

Managing marketing in the organization implies a recognition that competition takes place at the level of the industry, among strategic groups of companies at the level of the company, and at the product category and brand levels. Companies develop key success factors to compete at one or more of these levels. They seek competitive advantage in their ability to provide low-cost, high-quality differentiated products and services desired by customers.

Three major competitive elements help companies to compete. Companies which innovate and pioneer new products and services are more profitable and gain a larger share of the market. The second element is the way in which the company copes with the issue of quality. Successful companies have discovered that it is possible to compete on quality without adversely affecting cost. Related to both innovation and quality is the issue of time.

Speed to market is a competitive phenomenon of the 1990s. Speed is part of the competitive armoury of companies attempting to capture and hold on to customers. It applies in industrial, consumer and service markets. Time is the underlying resource to be economized. This means that flexibility and speed to market have joined the range of key success factors considered by companies.

Lastly, it is necessary to examine how companies respond to competition. Companies compete in a hierarchical manner. One of the more popular frameworks based on cost, differentiation and focus strategies is used to integrate the options available.

Having studied this chapter, you should be able to do the following:

1. List the elements of the strategic thinking process.

2. Recognize competition at industry, strategic group, company and product category levels.

3. Determine key success factors and sources of competitive advantage.

4. Assess the company's marketing effectiveness.

5. Specify the roles of innovation, quality and time in the company's competitive strategy.

6. Outline and evaluate strategic responses to market competition.

Meaning of competition in marketing

Strategic thinking for competitive advantage

Thinking strategically to perform a competitive analysis involves six separate activities (Figure 8.1). In carrying out a competitive analysis, most companies start by attempting to define their business, and by identifying factors such as products, markets, segments, technologies and competitors. By starting in this way, the scope of the company's activities is described. The choice of business definition depends very much on the personality, leadership qualities and vision of senior managers. In circumstances where the company is changing its competitive focus, the business definition itself may be the most important element of the business strategy.

In recent years, successful banks have redefined their business from the provision of loans and savings opportunities, to a definition which recognizes their competitive advantage: their branches and customers. Banks now appreciate that they are in the retail business and that the banks are financial shops.

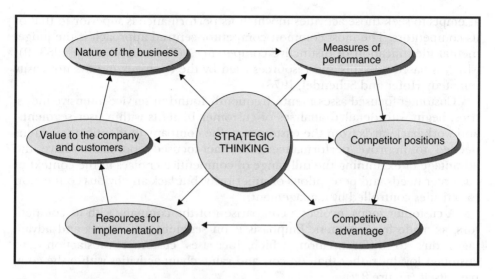

Figure 8.1 Strategic thinking in competitive analysis

Identifying competitive advantage

One approach to identify competitive advantage is to examine factors which affect profitability – market share, investment levels and margins obtained – and to compare them with industry averages or with peer companies in the industry. By following this procedure, the company identifies a short list of factors which determine success for the business. The approach, often referred to as the top-down approach, reflects judgement and industry experience.

A more intensive and analytical examination of a particular industry segment in which the company competes is an alternative way of proceeding. In this case, the company compares the way competitors do business and attempts to separate the successful from the less successful. At the same time, the company also focuses on the needs of the customer. Sony Consumer Products Company, UK, competes by giving undivided attention to three aspects of its business: the product, the brand image and customer service (Pearson, 1991). For companies like Sony, competitive analysis starts with the customer. A customer analysis is essential, otherwise the company could be completely off-target in its efforts. This approach is often referred to as the bottom-up approach.

Competitor-centred approaches, frequently used in stable, mature industries, are based on direct management comparisons with a few target competitors. These are businesses which watch costs closely, quickly match the marketing initiatives of competitors and seek a sustainable competitive edge in technology. A competitor-centred approach, used on its own, leads to a preoccupation with costs and controllable activities (Day and Wensley, 1988: 1–2).

A competitor focus means directly comparing the company with its rivals, based on relative skills and resources and their impact on costs. The company attempts to seek those activities in which its performance is superior to that of its competitors. The most common competitor-centred approach is the judge-mental identification of distinctive competences (Day and Wensley, 1988: 9), which is based on skills and resources used by the company in ways not easily imitated (Hofer and Schendel, 1978).

Customer-focused assessments, frequently found in service-intensive indus-tries, begin with detailed analyses of customer benefits within user segments, and work backwards from the customer to the company to identify the actions needed to improve performance. Customer-focused approaches have the advantage of examining the full range of competitive choices in the context of customer needs and perceptions of superiority, but lack an obvious connection to activities controlled by management.

A customer focus involves a comparison of the company with its competi-tors, as made by customers. Emphasis is on segment differences and advan-tages due to differentiation, which increases customer satisfaction and customer loyalty, rather than on cost and value chain activities within the com-pany itself (Figure 8.2).

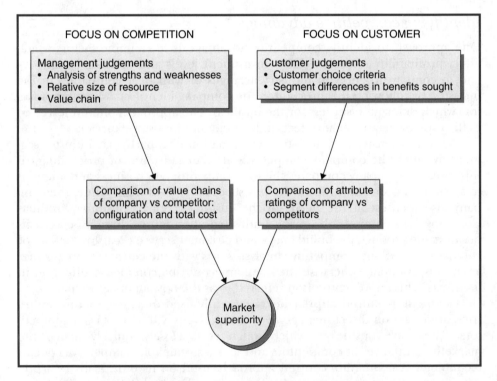

Figure 8.2 Framework for assessing competitive advantage

(Source: Adapted from Day and Wensley, 1988: 8. With permission of American Marketing Association)

In this approach, it may be possible to apply benchmarking to the company's activities. This involves rating the company's more important business practices against the best in the world, not just the best in the same industry, and then replicating those practices. In this regard, the most important benchmark may be customer satisfaction.

The next step involves a comparison between the company and its competitors. To perform this step effectively means carrying out a SWOT analysis. Relative to its competitors, the company needs to know its strengths and weaknesses; and for the market, it needs to know the opportunities and threats which exist. The analysis of strengths and weaknesses and opportunities and threats is now a conventional approach to a situation analysis. Greater value is obtained from a SWOT analysis which is limited to those factors which make a difference between success and failure. The likely areas to be included in such an analysis are political developments, manufacturing processes, technology change, products and distribution.

In this context, it is necessary to determine the various positions that competitors hold in the market. For each competitor, it is necessary to understand what customer segments it focuses on and what distinctive product or service benefits it offers. An understanding of competitors' segment focus and strengths shows what areas of the market will be most difficult to penetrate and also what areas of the market are not being serviced adequately. How competitors typically respond to changes in the market is something most companies attempt to glean from observation and other sources. Some competitors match innovations very quickly through innovations of their own, or imitate the success of others. Other competitors may be classified as price leaders or price followers. These patterns of competitive behaviour are important for the company to understand.

To visitors to Britain, Marks and Spencer is a department store with reasonable prices. The company prices to provide value for money, but the emphasis is on quality, convenience and speed of shopping. To provide the high level of service, Marks and Spencer maintains very close links with its suppliers, many of which are highly committed in terms of the level of sales dedicated to the store. 'Suppliers are given instructions from the shape of tomatoes to the food Australian sheep should eat in order to improve the wool's consistency. Quality control is draconian; the hold on prices firm. Suppliers who do meet the standards are treated loyally and paid promptly' (*The Economist*, 26 June 1993: 43).

Using competitive advantage

Once competitive advantage has been identified, the company must decide how to use it and how to respond to the competitive advantages of others. Business strategy is the management of competitive advantage with a focus on the elements required for competitive success. The strategy identified is described in terms of product development, advertising and manufacturing. It may involve product specifications that address needs not served by competitors, marketing priorities that focus on market segments from which competitors are absent, a change to a different manufacturing process that provides unique cost or quality advantages, or a pricing policy that exploits a competitor price umbrella. This approach to preparing a competitive business strategy focuses on innovation not imitation.

The company must now decide if the endeavour is worth it. The total investment in the strategy should be carefully analyzed as an integral part of the strategic thinking in the company. Some companies postpone the full financial analysis until the entire process is complete, being satisfied with approximate measures to separate the practical from the impractical at the early stages in the process.

Nature of competition among firms

Company-specific competences determine the basis of competition and so determine the success or failure of a company. For example, retailers compete on distribution skills, consumer products depend on successful advertising, consumer electronics and cars depend on engineering design. These critical capabilities change over time, however, requiring the firm to adapt. Failure occurs if the firm does not recognize the shift in critical capability, or if it cannot obtain competence in the new critical capability introduced as an innovation.

Level and scope of market competition

Loss of monopoly, new competitive products and changes in consumer tasks can produce a powerful competitive mix for companies protected by patents, trade barriers or sheer lack of competition. In December 1992 the lucrative US patent for the artificial sweetener aspartame expired, thereby jeopardizing the $700 million US market monopolized by Monsanto's Nutrasweet Company (*Business Week*, 14 December 1992: 30). Competition arising from the removal of a monopoly in consumer products markets can be equally fierce, as one Hungarian company experienced when western companies entered that market (Exhibit 8.1).

Competition at industry level

The material in this section is presented in the form of a case history of how competition in the computer industry has evolved. The section is based on a survey in *The Economist* (27 February 1993). In the past decade, personal com-

---

EXHIBIT 8.1   Toothpaste giants apply the squeeze

In the fierce competition for eastern Europe's turbulent consumer markets, it is the innocents who suffer. One of them is Tihamer Gedeon, beleaguered managing director of Caola, the Hungarian state-owned cosmetics and household chemicals manufacturer. Competition from western multinationals since imports were liberalized at the start of 1991 has broken Caola's near monopoly, reducing the company's market share to 40 per cent. Turnover has fallen in step, the 1992 forecast of Ft 4.3bn (£28.6m) representing a halving in real terms since 1990.

In toothpaste, for instance, three multinationals are battling for market share – and incidentally squeezing out Caola. Procter & Gamble has taken the lead with 30 per cent, with Colgate-Palmolive following strongly on 15 per cent and rising. Now Unilever too has entered the market with the successful launch of its Signal brand. Caught in the middle, Caola has found its share of sales falling from 70 per cent to just over 30 per cent in two years. The company now claims to have stabilised its position and ironically, it is economic depression that has given the company its temporary reprieve.

When cash-strapped Hungarian consumers compare the western price tags with cheap local products on the shelves, enough of them economise to keep Caola in business – just. But Caola faces a new threat as recovery approaches. 'We have to prepare for the time when people don't just want cheap products but have the money to buy better,' says Gedeon. Gedeon insists he relishes the competition. Caola languished in 'stagnant water' while it remained a monopoly, he explains.

Source: *Financial Times*, 3 July 1992: 10.

---

puters and the microprocessor chips on which they are based have radically changed the nature of competition in the computer industry. Until the early 1980s, nearly all computers were large number-crunching machines used by large companies to make the performance of routine administration tasks more efficient. Mainframes and minicomputers were the two computer categories available. IBM dominated the industry. Other competitors included companies such as Digital Equipment Corporation (DEC), WANG and NEC.

The products of these companies, usually referred to as systems because of their complexity, were produced in relatively small numbers for a loyal customer base which made entry to the industry difficult. The complexity of mainframes and minicomputers encouraged these firms to integrate vertically, so that all parts and software were produced within the firm. Marketing, distribution, sales and service were also provided directly by these companies. The resulting structure of the computer industry in the 1960s and 1970s looked like that shown in Figure 8.3(a).

The products and services of the various layers were purchased by customers as a single package from one supplier. The basic circuitry refers to the

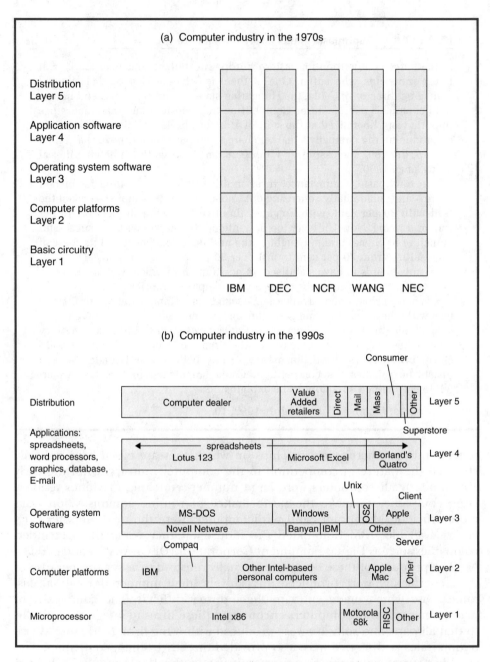

Figure 8.3 Evolution of competition in the computer industry, 1970s–1990s

(Source: Adapted from 'Survey of the computer industry', *The Economist*, 27 February 1993: 7 and 10. Copyright, *The Economist*, London 1994)

myriad wires and transistors. Computer platforms are the assembled machines, which depended on operating system software, the programming which made the machines function in response to commands emanating from application software: for example, payroll programmes and word-processing mathematical functions, both of which were based on proprietary formulae. The computer companies also carried out most of their own distribution.

With the introduction of the personal computer, almost every defining feature of the old industry has been reversed in the new computer industry of the 1980s and 1990s. The industry has moved to selling millions of inexpensive personal computers to individuals, institutions and companies of all sizes. The key success factors in personal computers are that they require little maintenance and the software to run them can be purchased in packaged form off the shelf without customization. Unlike with the large systems, purchase decisions are now made by users with little technical knowledge.

Attempting to obtain a clear view of the competitive structure of the computer industry in the 1990s is difficult as technology and competition continue to change it. The most striking aspect of the industry today is a series of horizontal layers, each containing many companies, rather than the vertically integrated structure of the 1970s. An attempt to show the difference is made in Figure 8.3(b). The originator of this diagram is Andy Grove of Intel.

Each horizontal layer represents a distinct market. Barriers to entry for new companies vary from layer to layer. But under the new regime an entrant does not have to compete across all layers, as was the case in the industry of the 1970s. As a result, competition in each layer is much more aggressive than before and profits are lower.

A number of aspects of the new competition are apparent. Because Intel and Microsoft have managed to establish de facto industry standards with their products, barriers to entry to layer 1, the microprocessor level, and layer 3, the stand-alone operating system software level, are relatively high; hence Intel's and Microsoft's dominance of these levels of competition.

Computer platforms in layer 2, which includes the assembly of personal computers, is the area of greatest competition, since Intel's dominance of microprocessors in the level below has established an industry standard allowing any technically competent firm to enter the market in layer 2. Competition in this layer has resulted in the personal computer price wars of recent years.

In layer 3, operating system software, the market is divided between the basic software needed to operate the central server of a network and the software to run client machines in the same network or stand-alone PCs. The top part of the layer is much bigger than the bottom part, which acts as servers. In the early 1990s, the bottom part was the more profitable and was growing rapidly.

Distribution occurs in layer 4, probably the layer where competition is most fierce. This is the arena in which companies such as Microsoft, Lotus, WordPerfect and Borland compete for market share. Within this layer, there are a number of distinct markets for major applications: word processing, spreadsheets, database management and graphics. Writing these complicated computer programs, which is time consuming and expensive, constitutes a formidable barrier to entry at this level. Branding and access to distribution outlets for such general-purpose software packages also serve as barriers to entry. But this does not prevent numerous small specialist firms from competing in niche applications outside the major applications listed.

The end result of this evolution is a computer industry characterized by few discernible differences between products, except price, low barriers to entry and small profit margins. The large amount of intellectual property in

---

EXHIBIT 8.2　Wrong altitude

After their worst-ever slump, airlines are starting to fill their jets with more passengers. Last year passengers started to return; world-wide air travel grew by almost seven per cent. Unfortunately for airlines, most of that growth was stimulated by fare cuts and price wars that left carriers with billions of dollars of losses. Air travel will continue to grow at about six per cent per year until 2000. The worrying bit is that airline yields are going in the opposite direction.

Airlines calculate yields as the total revenue they receive per mile, per passenger. Since the early 1970s, yields have collapsed from more than 20 cents per passenger-mile to around 13 cents last year. Boeing thinks yields may pick up this year, but will then continue a longterm decline averaging almost one per cent a year. Yields have fallen for a variety of reasons. The introduction of more-efficient wide-body jets, like the Boeing 747 and Airbus models, has resulted in cost savings that have been passed on to passengers. Deregulation of the domestic airline market in America, more competition being allowed in other countries, and airline privatisations have also boosted competition.

As such trends are set to continue, future profits will have to come from even more cost savings. Boeing reckons some of those savings will be found through further airline consolidation and the development of so-called 'mega-carriers' in alliances like that between British Airways and US Air and one being discussed between Swissair, KLM and SAS. Costs will also be driven lower with more sophisticated computer-reservations systems.

Boeing also says that international business travel is dropping as a percentage of world travel: from 16 per cent in 1985 to an estimated 14 per cent in 2010. This has already led some airlines to change their pricing strategy to try to boost yields from budget-conscious businessmen and better-off leisure travellers. Britain's Virgin Atlantic offers a 'mid-class', which consists of a business-class seat but an economy meal, for the equivalent of a full economy fare. America's Continental has launched a first-class service for a business fare. Some airline chiefs fear that apart from a few high-rollers, first-class passengers paying sky-high prices are a vanishing breed.

Source: *The Economist*, 6 March 1993: 72.

computers and their associated products, and their complexity, would indicate that competition could be contained. But rapidly changing technology and competition continue to erode margins.

Strategic groups analysis

Various recessions and the Gulf War of 1990 have had an adverse effect on the profits of the airline industry. Many airlines have attempted to cut costs, and consolidations have been quite common. The large carriers have also sought refuge in newer, more efficient aircraft. At the same time, smaller airlines are scrambling to remain competitive. The result is that the airline industry consists of a number of distinct strategic competitive groups, each attempting to serve different types of customer in different ways (Exhibit 8.2).

In the civil aeronautics sector of this industry, the repair and maintenance of engines and aircraft is a growing business. Using a strategic groups analysis, O'Reilly (1990) has positioned most of the major airframe maintenance companies relative to each other. In the airframe maintenance business, the two dominant competitive factors are price and range of aircraft, from single and multiple manufacturers, capable of being maintained (Figure 8.4). Quality is also most important, but as all competitors meet the required quality standards, it does not serve to discriminate competitors one from the other. Using strategic groups analysis and recognizing the trend to wide-bodied aircraft, O'Reilly suggests that the strategic direction for TAP and Air Lingus is to shift to the medium-price, wide-body group. These two companies had been specializing in the narrow-bodied Boeing 737. The recommendation would mean developing facilities and capability to serve wide-bodied aircraft from a number of aircraft suppliers.

Competition at company level

Competition at company level takes various forms. A number of examples drawn from services and manufacturing will illustrate how it occurs at this level. Competition in service businesses is very difficult to determine accurately. Banks, for example, serve distinct local markets, each of which is different in some respect. Branches are becoming less standardized as banks customize outlets to meet specific needs. Additional new services are also provided by automated teller machines (ATMs) outside banks. Many banks now locate their ATMs away from the branch. In this way, the customers of the two are separated: a branch could be closed down, but the bank could still retain the ATM customers.

The concepts 'competitive advantage' and 'distinctive competences' are frequently used interchangeably in the marketing literature. Both refer to the company's relative superiority in skills and resources. Superior skills refer to the firm's ability to perform specific functions more effectively than others,

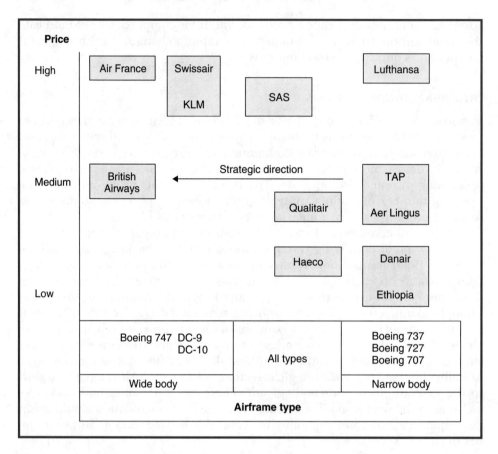

Figure 8.4   Strategic groups in airframe maintenance business
(Source: O'Reilly, 1990: 127)

such as greater precision in the manufacture of optical lenses, or its ability to identify and react quickly to a change in the market. Superior resources refer to tangible factors which give the firm a competitive advantage, such as a brand name, a distribution network, an automated manufacturing facility or a good location.

By cleverly using skills and resources for competitive advantage, the company can establish a market position which is based on cost or value (Porter, 1980; Mattsson and Johanson, 1985; Day and Wensley, 1988). A market position based on cost means performing business functions at a lower cost than competitors while maintaining competitive parity in the products manufactured. A market position based on added value means producing products and services valued highly by customers and perceived to be superior.

Since the beginning of the 1990s, Harley-Davidson Inc., the US manufacturer of heavy-duty motor cycles, has based its international strategy on aggressive marketing of a classic American image. In the early 1980s, poor quality and Japanese imports resulted in Harley-Davidson's share of the US market for large-engine bikes (i.e. more than 850cc) falling from more than 40 per cent in the mid-1970s to 23 per cent by 1983 (*Business Week*, 24 May 1993: 65). The Harley-Davidson marketing strategy of the mid-1990s is based on packaging a lifestyle, associated with magazines, clothing and enthusiasts' rallies. The company also helps to establish Harley Owners' Groups in the USA and abroad. In recent years, Honda Motorcycles was forced to change its approach to competing. Having dropped its high-quality, low-price formula in favour of more expensive technology which customers did not want, the company reverted to updating its more affordable machines (Exhibit 8.3).

Product category competition

Asking one brand in a company to compete against another brand in the same company is similar to competition between two different companies. The brand management system evolved out of the notion that brands within a company should compete with each other. Such competition creates strong incentives to excel among brand managers, but it also introduces conflict and even inefficiencies as brand managers compete for corporate resources such as advertising budgets, plant capacity and delivery services.

In growth markets, such competition may be healthy. In slow-growing markets and in recessions, too many brands may be following too few customers. Such relative brand proliferation and fragmented markets combined with increased power among retailers has forced many consumer packaged goods companies to consider competing on the basis of product categories.

Under a system of category management, advertising, sales, manufacturing and research and development report to the product category manager. Marketing strategies are developed based on integrating brand management into category management, rather than developing competing brand strategies which must also compete for resources (Exhibit 8.4). A co-ordinated approach to marketing is required. As an example of how brands sometimes compete, note that claims on appeals are often fought over by brand managers. In detergents, 'clean' or 'whiter' are words which competing brands would like to use. In cereals, 'crunchy' or 'wholesome' are competitive claims among brands. Arbitrating such disputes between brand managers can be a waste of resources, whereas promoting the category might be more profitable.

By focusing on categories instead of on brands, consumer products companies direct their attention to what competitor companies are doing. Devoting time to what rivals are doing is central to successful competition. Category management allows the company to rationalize its product line so that, instead of overlapping, each brand can have a unique and distinct market position. Under category management, the marketing manager has some control over other functions such as research and development, finance and

---

EXHIBIT 8.3 That 'vroom!' you hear is Honda Motorcycles

After 10 years on Easy Street in the US, Honda's motorcycle division wiped out when it abandoned the high-quality, low-price formula that helped it dominate the market in the 1970s. And it took the new tack just when a rising yen was slamming Japanese manufacturers in the US. Now, Honda is trying to reverse its slide by changing direction again. It has rolled out seven new models since September 1989, five of them aimed at enticing first-time riders. This fall, it will reintroduce the CB-750, the beefy, four-cylinder bike that helped make Honda No. 1 among American motorcycle riders when it was first introduced 20 years ago. In the past five years, American Honda Motor Co. has seen its market share plummet from 58 per cent to 28 per cent.

What happened to the leader of the pack? Part of the problem is demographics. But many of Honda's wounds are self-inflicted. The company had successfully carved up the motorcycle market into a multitude of niches, ranging from dirt bikes to road racers. But in 1988, Honda's US marketing officials thought they could get consumers to pay a premium for the latest in motorcycling technology. They were wrong. What's more, they tried to reposition their bikes for the upscale market just as the yen was rising sharply against the dollar. That drove customers into the arms of competitors such as Kawasaki Motor Corp. and Suzuki Motor Co., which were holding the line on price increases.

Honda made other mistakes, too. Honda's obsession with technological superiority has been its Achilles' heel. Rather than determining what the public wants, Honda has tended to add new technology and hope that demand

---

manufacturing. Such a system allows for better-planned, faster new product launches. Product-line extensions are very easy to introduce and become a very effective weapon in the armoury of the marketing manager.

Assessing competitors

Successful firms attempt to monitor their closest competitors very carefully to avoid being outmanoeuvred by technological developments. New technologies have the ability to blur the distinction between competitors, suppliers and customers. Changing technology may allow a firm that was once a customer to become a competitor. For these reasons, it is necessary to be alert to the actions of other firms in the industry.

Key success factors

Companies that develop uniquely competitive products or services can select defensible and profitable positions in the market, exploit them and then rein-will follow. Take the 1988 version of the popular Gold Wing touring motorcycle. Honda engineers developed more than 60 prototypes, redesigning everything from luggage compartments to full systems. American and Japanese engineers even tried out 20 separate engine designs and added fuel injection before they finally unveiled the line. Cost: $10,000, up from $8,500 for the 1987 model. That put the new Gold Wings beyond the reach of many.

To crawl back from the abyss Honda will try to get more Americans to use motorcycles as a viable alternative to cars, as many commuters do in Europe and the Far East. That's why the company has updated the affordable CB-750. For the first time in years, economic and political trends may be on Honda's side. Increased traffic congestion, rising fuel costs, and pollution concerns are all working to Honda's advantage. No wonder the company is looking ahead. What's in the rear-view mirror isn't pretty.

TABLE 1   Motorcycle market shares in US (%)

	1985	1987	1989
Honda	58.5	50.8	28.9
Yamaha	15.5	19.8	27.7
Kawasaki	10.2	10.2	15.6
Suzuki	9.9	11.6	14.2
Harley	4.0	6.3	13.9

Source: *Business Week*, 3 September 1990: 28–9.

vest the profits so that growth and market share are obtained. For the innovative firm, first-mover advantages apply; but as markets mature, the company attempts to capitalize on initial strong positions to build new skills and resources which keep it at the forefront of technology and market developments (Jacobson and Aaker, 1985).

Current profits tend to be the reward for past achivements. Because profitability is influenced by actions taken during many previous investment periods, it is unlikely to be an accurate measure of current competitive advantage. As a consequence, competitive advantage is a function of past profits not the other way around. It would seem, therefore, that investment in markets and marketing determines profitability, which in turn allows the company to obtain market share.

Investment in markets and marketing allows the firm to convert skills and resources into superior market positions, and performance means identifying the key success factors for the company. The key success factors of any business are the skills and resources which exert the highest degree of leverage on market positions and future performance; skills and resources that contribute most to lowering costs to or creating superior value for customers. For the

---

EXHIBIT 8.4   Before and after P & G's marketing shift

Last October, Procter & Gamble Co. (P & G) reorganised along category lines. Even reticent P & G calls this the biggest management change in more than 30 years. The reorganisation doesn't abolish brand managers, but it makes them accountable to a new corps of mini-general managers with responsibility for an entire product line – all laundry detergents, for example. The effect on advertising, budgeting, packaging and manufacturing illustrates the impact of the change. P & G advertises Tide as the best detergent for tough dirt. But brand managers for Cheer started making the same claim in ads that were pulled after the Tide group protested. Now a category manager decides how to position Tide and Cheer to avoid such conflicts.

Brand managers for Puritan and Crisco oils competed for a share of P & G's ad budget. But a category manager might decide that Puritan could benefit from stepped-up ad spending to publicise its new formula, while Crisco can coast on its strong market position for a while. Brand managers of various detergents often demanded new packages at the same time. Designers complained that the projects were hurried, and nobody got a first-rate job. Now the category manager decides which brand needs a new package first. Under the old system, a minor detergent such as Dreft had the same claim on P & G's plant as Tide – even if Tide was in the midst of a big promotion and needed more supplies. Now a manufacturing staffer reports to the category manager, helping to coordinate production.

Source: *Business Week*, 25 July 1988: 48–9.

Almarai Dairy Products Company in Saudi Arabia, the key success factors are a mixture of production, marketing and innovation skills (Table 8.1).

Sources of competitive advantage

Sources of competitive advantage are reputation, brands, tangible assets, knowledge, customer service and people. To be worthwhile, the competitive advantage must be sustainable. It must, therefore, be tangible, measurable and capable of providing competitive protection for some time. An illusory competitive advantage is one that is easily matched by competitors.

The protected position built up through early market entry, achieved in the face of inactivity by competitors, allows the pioneering firm to achieve customer loyalty, brand identification and time to build distribution, while benefiting from manufacturing scale economies which may exist. Product leadership, being the first to introduce a new product or innovative product features, can also provide an extended period of market protection.

Companies which demonstrate superior performance relative to their competitors succeed by a combination of operating effectiveness and competitive positioning. Competition based on operation efficiency is a cost-based

TABLE 8.1   Key success factors for Almarai Dairy Products Company, Saudi Arabia

Market	Skill and resource factors that create value or lower cost	Important aspects of value to the customer
Liquid milk	Production quality Packaging	Freshness and taste
Laban[1]	Marketing resources Brand building Market dominance	Texture, freshness, taste, premium goodness
Special cheeses	Innovation Respect needs/wants of customers in traditional markets	Premium goodness, consistent with traditional cultural values of Saudi society

[1]Laban is a special yoghurt-like drink which is very popular in the Middle East.

battle between competitors, whereas competition based on competitive positioning is strategic, whereby the choice of market segments to be served, the nature of the product, the channels of distribution and the manufacturing process underwrite success. Competitive advantage derives from the customer and from production factors. The ultimate competitive advantage arises when the company can efficiently mass produce everything in batches of one.

The company's competitive advantage depends on how well it chooses from a number of approaches:

- concentrating on selected market segments;

- offering differentiated products;

- using alternative distribution channels; and

- using different manufacturing processes to allow higher quality at lower prices.

In most cases, the company chooses to compete on cost and on product and service differentiation. Usually it picks a point on a continuuum between lowest delivered cost and high differentiation. On entering European markets, the Sara Lee company adopted the 'value position' and appeared to be able to compete on both dimensions (Exhibit 8.5).

Assessing market effectiveness

Marketing effectiveness is not necessarily revealed by current marketing performance. Good results and growing sales may be due to the company being in the right place at the right time, rather than having effective marketing management. This is frequently the situation during the entrepreneurial phase of a company's growth and development. The innovator frequently has

---

EXHIBIT 8.5   Sara Lee's designs on Europe's knickers

Until the late 1980s, Sara Lee's name was synonymous with wholesome (real cholesterol-laden) American food. Then Mr Bryan, company president, decided it was time for a change. So Sara Lee diversified, spending billions to gobble up companies making shoe polish, deodorant, and, especially, clothing: underwear, T-shirts, socks, sweatshirts. To some this sounded a confused recipe. In fact, all of Sara Lee's new products had two big things in common. First, they were staples, which people buy in good times and bad. Second, their markets were highly fragmented, with own-label goods accounting for most sales.

To Mr Bryan, Sara Lee's competitive advantage was clear: its experience in the food business. By extending names such as Hanes, Playtex and Champion across a variety of products, and by pouring money into advertising Sara Lee brought big-brand marketing to sectors that had never seen it before. Well-known names were then combined with low prices as the company used its know-how to squeeze manufacturing costs. Most important, Sara Lee used its established food-distribution channels for its non-food products. With its L'Eggs stockings, the firm pioneered selling hosiery in supermarkets, while hawking its upmarket Donna Karan tights in department stores.

It has worked wonders. In the year to June Sara Lee's net profits rose 15 per cent, to $620m, on sales of $13.2 billion. Sara Lee is the world's biggest maker of women's hosiery. Hanes dominates American women's underwear and is challenging its arch-rival, Fruit of the Loom, in men's. Heinz's boss, Tony O'Reilly, calls Sara Lee 'a hosiery queen masquerading as a food company'. Mr Bryan does not demur.

Wearing that disguise will not, however, get Sara Lee nearly as far in Europe. Now Sara Lee is planning to centralise its manufacturing in a place with cheap labour – Spain, Portugal or northern Africa. This is classic Sara Lee: cut costs, then offer a high-quality branded goods at a low price. That is, occupy the 'value position'.

Source: *The Economist* 14 November 1992: 80.

---

considerable discretion in the market. At this stage, the driving force is entrepreneurship rather than marketing. With acceptance of the product or service, and with the rise in competition which normally accompanies the acceptance of a new product or service, performance becomes more marketing dependent.

In a competitive environment, especially where consumers have learned how to respond to various offerings, the situation changes. Improvements in marketing in the company might improve results from good to excellent. Another company might have poor results in spite of excellent marketing planning. It depends on how well the company matches its own resources against those of the competition to attract and hold the loyalty of customers (Figure 8.5). Managing the area of overlap is the key to strategic success.

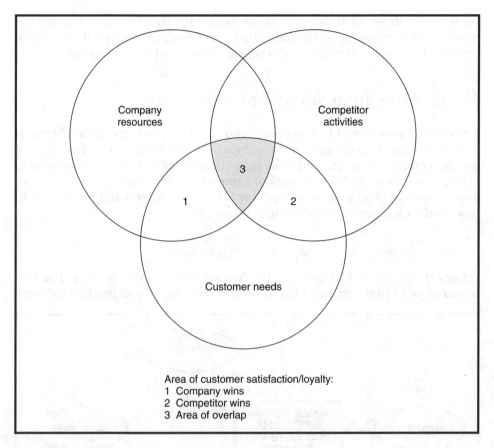

Figure 8.5   Ability of company and competitors to serve customers

Marketing effectiveness may be measured by changes in market share and profits, customer satisfaction and repeat purchasing, where customer satisfaction is measured by observing actual product performance relative to the perceived performance of competitor products (Day and Wensley, 1988: 15). The marketing effectiveness of the company in serving its customers in the face of existing and potential competition is reflected in the degree to which it exhibits five major attributes of a marketing orientation:

- a customer philosophy;

- a strategic marketing orientation;

- adequate marketing information;

- a strategic orientation; and

- a high level of operational efficiency.

343

Each of the above attributes may be measured for the company. The performance of the company on the individual attributes may then be used to indicate which elements of effective marketing action need most attention.

Competitive innovation and pioneering

Investment in successful new products and services, from investment funds or from excess funds generated in the company, tends to have the effect of raising the company's profits, which in turn contributes to the company gaining market share and additional market experience. The extra experience can lower costs and produce excess funds for further innovation and investment in new product and service development (Figure 8.6).

Market pioneers and competitive advantage

A market pioneer or first mover is the first entrant in a new market. The first mover enjoys a unit cost and a market control advantage and product differen-

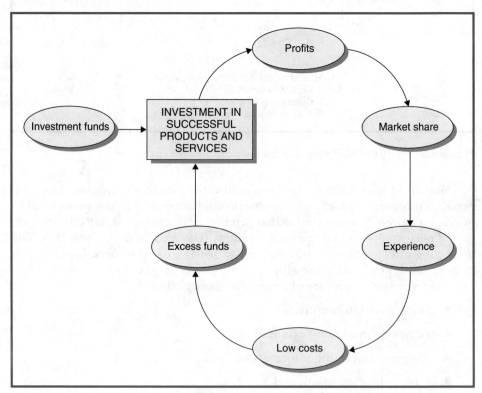

Figure 8.6   Competitive cycle in marketing

tiation advantages because it can build a large-scale operation before competitors enter the market. As output increases, overhead costs are spread over a greater volume, and unit costs decline and stay low for a relatively long period. The advantage of product differentiation stems from noting that buyers in a new product category have not yet developed brand loyalties, so that the first mover or pioneer that offers a product of acceptable quality supported by strong promotion can expect to gain market share with relative ease, and to be able to defend that share against later competition (Carpenter and Nakamoto, 1989). Very often, pioneering and competitive advantage derives from the introduction of a range of new types of product (Exhibit 8.6).

To be successful, market pioneers must invest in manufacturing to produce a broad product range to serve numerous segments through blanket

---

EXHIBIT 8.6   The high-voltage rivalry in batteries

The environmental movement is demanding a safe alternative to cadmium, a toxic heavy metal that can leach into groundwater when nickel–cadmium batteries are dumped in landfills. Consumers, meanwhile, can't get enough of portable devices, such as pocket phones, laptop computers, handheld TVs and electronic organisers – all of which need smaller, lighter, and longer-lasting batteries. Today's batteries account for up to 12 per cent of the size and 30 per cent of the weight of a notebook computer – making them one of the biggest hindrances to the continued growth of portable electronics.

Japanese companies have introduced two new rechargeable designs: nickel metal hydride and lithium ion. Close on their heels is a promising prototype called lithium polymer, which is being developed by Silicon Valley startup Valence Technology Inc. Nickel metal hydride began the '90s as the odds-on favourite to replace nicad. Besides being low in or free of cadmium, it offers about 50 per cent more energy output by weight (Table 1).

Nickel cadmium is a proven technology but cadmium is toxic. Nickel metal hydride is less toxic than nicad because metal hydride replaces cadmium. Sony sells lithium ion batteries which are small and light but expensive. Lithium polymer batteries look like sheets of foil; mass production is set for 1994.

TABLE 1   Comparison of nickel cadmium batteries with new products

	Nickel cadmium	Nickel metal hydride	Lithium ion	Lithium polymer
Energy output* (watt-hours/kilogramme)	33–50	56–60	78–115	205
Average operating voltage	1.2	1.2	3.6	2.5–3.6
Cost per watt-hour	$0.67–0.81	$1.03–1.47	$1.34–1.62	$0.08–1.50
Number of charges	1,000–2,000	1,000	500–1,200	300

Source: *Business Week*, 15 February 1993: 46–7.

coverage of the relevant distribution channels, heavily supported by promotion. Using the PIMS database, Lambkin (1992: 17) concludes that, unless a business invests sufficient resources to implement a full-scale attack on the market, then it faces a severe risk of losing share to later entrants, and perhaps also risks its long-term survival.

Sources of market pioneer advantage

There are three major sources of market pioneer advantage (Robinson and Fornell, 1985). These refer to relative consumer information advantages, relative marketing mix advantages and, through increased market share, advantages in relative direct costs (Figure 8.7).

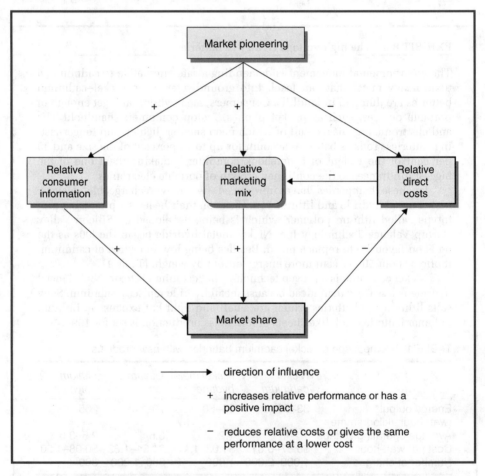

Figure 8.7   Three sources of market pioneer advantage and direction of influence
(Source: Robinson and Fornell, 1985: 306. With permission from the American Marketing Association)

346

With relative direct costs held constant, market pioneering may lead to long-lived marketing mix advantages. These represent product differentiation advantages arising from the supply side of the market. To incorporate competition, these marketing mix advantages are measured relative to competition. A stronger relative marketing mix tends to lead to a higher market share.

Market pioneering may lead to direct cost savings, in purchasing, manufacturing and physical distribution expenditure, relative to competition. These direct cost savings can be based on absolute cost or scale economy advantages. If some portion of the relative cost savings is used to provide a more attractive marketing mix, pioneers can achieve a higher market share. Market pioneering may yield relative consumer information advantages by way of product experience or familiarity, which, in turn, may provide market pioneers with higher market shares. These represent a product differentiation advantage arising from the demand side of the market.

In a US study of 371 mature consumer products businesses, pioneers had an average market share of 29 per cent, early followers 17 per cent and late entrants 12 per cent (Robinson and Fornell, 1985). Order of entry alone accounted for 18 per cent of the variation in market share. It is now generally accepted that market share is, in general, closely related to order of market entry: 'the first takes the lion's share, the second has to settle for second best, the rest fight over the scraps. We can prove this in our markets. On average, the pioneer achieves twice the share of the second man in' (Fitzgerald, 1991).

Developing a competitive strategy

The recent competitive revolution in the computer industry is a good example of rapid competitive technological change which damages some companies and offers opportunities to others.

Maintaining a strategic focus

In the latter part of the 1980s, the economics of the computer industry have been transformed by three developments: rapidly falling prices, increased computational power and, as a consequence, the rise of personal computing in all its forms. IBM, the giant of the industry, failed to cope adequately with these developments. The company's reputation and dominant position resulted from its focus on large mainframe computers introduced in the 1960s, its core business for nearly three decades. Like most of its competitors, IBM worked to proprietary standards: that is, the company did not work with the standards of other manufacturers. With little price competition and a commitment to a particular system, there was little incentive to switch from IBM hardware and customized software. Many customers, especially large firms throughout the world, voted for IBM. For almost twenty years, IBM dominated an industry which was stable, growing and very profitable.

Competing on cost and versatility

The introduction of personal computers, built with the same standardized microprocessor chips, compatible with machines produced by competitors and running standardized off-the-shelf software, produced a low-cost, high-powered option with little differentiation, which destroyed IBM's oligopoly base. As a result the price of personal computers has fallen, demand has increased very rapidly and new technology continues to be developed.

In 1981 IBM entered the personal computer market and legitimized it for the many large corporate users of computers which had hesitated to buy the stand-alone machines (*The Economist*, 19 December 1992: 57). While IBM generated very large sales for itself, it also opened the door for others to enter. IBM made it especially easy for new entrants by assembling its own personal computers using off-the-shelf components, which meant that it was easy to build machines to the same standard as IBM.

For IBM, the growth of the personal computer market was incidental to its mainframe business, where most of its profits were earned. But as chips became more powerful, so did personal computers. The growth in the PC market represented a flank attack on the mainframe market. A new segment appeared based on workstations, which were in effect a network of very powerful, but cheaper personal computers. Workstations became attractive alternatives to the mainframe computers. The cheaper alternative had in fact become the core market with the improvement in chip technology and the decline in costs. IBM had managed to promote the decline of mainframe computers, once its core business.

Factors that typically accompany high market share are above average product quality, early entry into the market and broad product lines (Buzzell and Wiersema, 1981). The PIMS evidence on how quality works to improve profitability and growth is depicted in Figure 8.8. Effective quality management involves reducing the cost of production by getting the design specifications right first time, and simultaneously producing a product perceived by customers as a quality product. The diagram illustrates the views of the PIMS researchers and of many modern management writers that effective quality management can lead to a position of both high quality and cost competitiveness.

Competing on quality

During the 1970s Motorola Inc., the US personal communications company, found itself excluded from the lucrative consumer electronics market in the USA as a result of competition, particularly from the Japanese. A major turn-

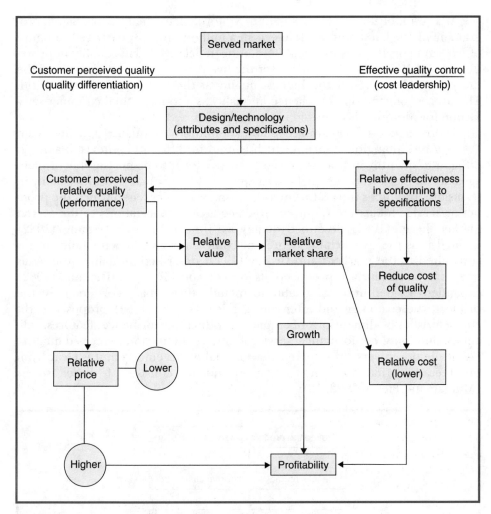

Figure 8.8 How quality drives profitability and growth
(Source: Luchs, 1986: 16. With kind permission from Elsevier Science Ltd, The Boulevard, Langford Lane, Kidlington OX5 1GB, UK)

ing point occurred in 1979 for Motorola, when it decided to compete with the Japanese in the rapidly growing personal pager market (Glynn, 1992). At the same time, the Japanese were erecting seemingly impossible technological market barriers: a monthly product failure rate of 0.5 per cent. Japanese pagers were discovered to be more than twice as reliable as the then highest-quality Motorola pager. The shock of this revelation galvanized Motorola into the first steps of a programme devoted to total customer satisfaction. In 1981 a quality programme was established in the company to increase quality tenfold by 1986.

As a result of this quality evaluation, Motorola launched the Six Sigma programme in 1987: a target of 34 defects in a million units. By early 1992 a figure of 5.5 sigma or 40 parts in a million had been achieved. This quality improvement saved Motorola $2.2 billion over the five years. The company believes the programme has given it the highest quality at the lowest costs in the world. The process of achieving excellence in quality as a route to total customer satisfaction for Motorola is captured in six steps (Figure 8.9).

There is no universally acceptable definition of quality. Quality is an abstract and intangible concept which is used in different contexts, making it difficult to quantify in strategic terms. In order for it to be measurable or manageable, an organization's quality strategy should be concerned with quality in terms of a product's fitness for intended use, or the degree to which the product or service meets the requirements, needs and expectations of the served market. Juran (1962) described quality as 'fitness for use'; Deming (1982) defined it as the 'predictable degree of conformity and dependability at low cost suited to the market'; and Crosby (1979) described a quality product as one that consistently reproduced its design specifications. Deming (1982) expanded his definition of quality to include three main cornerstones: the product, the customer and after-sales service. Garvin (1984) proposed eight characteristics or dimensions of a quality product: performance, features, reliability, durability, conformance, serviceability, aesthetics and perceived quality.

While no universally accepted view of quality has emerged, it is clear from the literature that the management of quality consists of three aspects (Morgan and Piercy, 1992: 12):

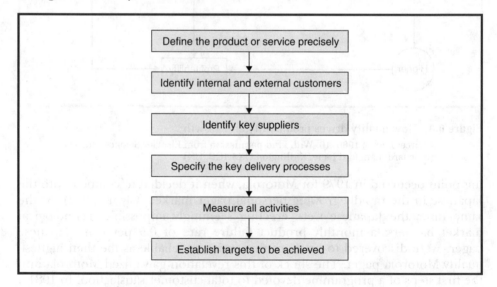

Figure 8.9 The six steps in Motorola's Six Sigma quality programme
(Source: Adapted from Glynn, 1992)

- customer focus – the provision of quality in terms of customer needs and specifications;

- process – the understanding, design and control of the process by which goods and service are produced and delivered to customers; and

- people involvement – all employees of the organisation have a role to play in quality programmes. Staff of supplier and distributor organizations may be included.

These three dimensions reconcile the often competing views of quality held by marketing and manufacturing departments. Marketing managers see the customer as the final arbiter of quality. They view quality as the degree to which a specific product satisfies the wants of a specific customer. On the other hand, manufacturing managers typically view quality as the product's conformance to specified requirements. Both views are correct, but are myopic in scope. For example, a product may conform exactly to process requirements and meet industry standards yet fail in the marketplace. Similarly, a product may be well accepted by customers, but because it fails to conform to manufacturing and design specifications, it incurs substantial reworking costs and proves unprofitable for the company in question. Effective quality management takes a broader view of the concept of quality and encompasses the three facets outlined above (Garvin, 1984).

As a competitive weapon, quality has recently come to the top of the class or near it. The Japanese use of quality as a competitive tool has led them to develop the concept aggressively from *atarimae hinshitsu*, or quality that is taken for granted, to *miryokuteki hinshitsu*, or quality that fascinates (*Business Week*, 22 October 1990). A relatively new approach to dealing with quality, defined as the absence of variation as perceived by the customer, is referred to as quality function deployment. Reducing variations that cause defects usually reduces costs too, ensuring that customers get what they pay for, a very competitive idea.

Competing on technology

Travellers between Paris and London are now able to travel by superfast train at 200 m.p.h. under the English Channel, in less than three hours from city centre to city centre – as fast as flying, but at about 75 per cent of the cost of air travel. Trains in Europe are becoming competitive again. Soon it will be possible to travel by superfast train between Seville and Berlin. In early 1993 a contract was signed to supply *trains à grand vitesse* (TGVs), which will link Amsterdam, Brussels, Cologne and Paris on new track by 1996. Behind the development of train technology and the strong competitive thrust is the objective of discplacing planes and cars on routes shorter than 500 kilometres. The French are the leaders in exporting fast-train technology. They supplied the fast trains for the Madrid–Seville line and won the contract for the Paris–Amsterdam line over the German Inter City Express (ICE). The TGV's advantage is speed: it is due to travel at 360 k.p.h. on the Paris–Brussels route. While there are many market opportunities for high-speed trains opening up in Europe and the Far East, the major competitors are closely watching developments in the USA.

Eventually a maglev line will whisk tourists from Orlando airport in Florida to Disney World, while the Swedish-built tilt train will operate in the northeast. Developers in Texas are studying the relative advantages of TGVs and tilt trains to link the state's five major cities. The advantages and disadvantages of each suggest that the tilt train is cheapest, which may suit some circumstances, while in the longer term the more sophisticated trains are likely to prevail (Table 8.2).

Tilt trains increase passenger comfort on curves by leaning into them. ABB (Asea Brown Boveri), the Swedish–Swiss industrial conglomerate, has produced an expensive tilt train operating on sensors that trigger hydraulic lifts

TABLE 8.2 The great train race: leading technologies for high-speed rail travel

	French TGV	German transrapid maglev	Swedish tilt train	US Gruman Corp. consortium maglev
Description	Runs on standard rail using electricity from overhead wires	Floats above guideway propelled by magnetic forces	Takes curves well, axles swivel on turns, while carriages tilt to offset centrifugal forces	Superconducting magnet expected to give a smoother ride than German maglev
Cost	$10–20 million per mile	$20–60 million per mile	$2–10 million per mile	$29–60 million per mile
Advantages	Fastest train on steel wheels – up to 200 m.p.h; in commercial service for 12 years	Top speed up to 300 m.p.h.	Cheapest because it works entirely on existing tracks; increases passenger comfort by leaning into turns	Lighter, possibly cheaper than German system; one of four designs developed by US consortiums
Disadvantages	Attains high speed only on new, dedicated track; noisier and slower than maglev	Expensive; requires extremely smooth guideways and computer control to keep magnets on cars from clamping on to guideways	Top speed of 150 m.p.h. on good track	Requires several more years of design and testing

Source: *Business Week*, 19 April 1993: 54–6.

352

when a carriage enters a curve at high speed. A similar but much cheaper technology is available in Spain, developed for the Talgo express train in the 1950s. This technology, owned by Patentes Talgo of Madrid, is based on a pendulum system, whereby the passenger compartments are connected to the outer frame of the train by springs. When the train enters a curve the compartments naturally lean towards the inside of the curve. It will be an interesting question to note which of the above technologies dominate, the more expensive dynamic systems or the less expensive passive systems.

Time as a competitive marketing strategy

Time-based competition or speed to market has recently been suggested as a way of increasing the flexibility to offer customers more choice and faster delivery of goods and services. By improving on speed to market, successful companies can provide the most value for the lowest cost in the least amount of time. To be competitive in such an environment, companies strive to provide speedy, low-cost, high-quality goods and services.

High-technology products arriving in the market six months late but within budget have been reported as earning 33 per cent less profits over five years, while products arriving on time and 50 per cent over budget reduce profits by only 4 per cent (McKinsey and Company, quoted in *Fortune*, 13 February 1989). Shrinking product life cycles are forcing companies to develop and launch new products more quickly to keep abreast of market demands.

The market benefits to the firm of faster new product development and commercialization are numerous. Faster new product development allows the company to:

- charge higher prices;

- adopt a shorter time horizon for forecasting sales and profits;

- increase its market share;

- provide excitement at retail level and increase consumer satisfaction; and

- obtain a greater number of product development experiences.

Being quicker to the market allows the innovator to obtain a price advantage and greater pricing discretion. It is possible to charge a price premium and to hold it, even after competitors enter the market (Figure 8.10). As competitors introduce new products in response, prices may decline. By then, however, the pioneering company will have moved down the manufacturing learning curve ahead of the competition (Figure 8.10). The pioneering firm benefits from the initial price premium and from a significant cost advantage. This tends to last over the life of the venture. There is, therefore, a continuing price and cost advantage to being first into the market.

353

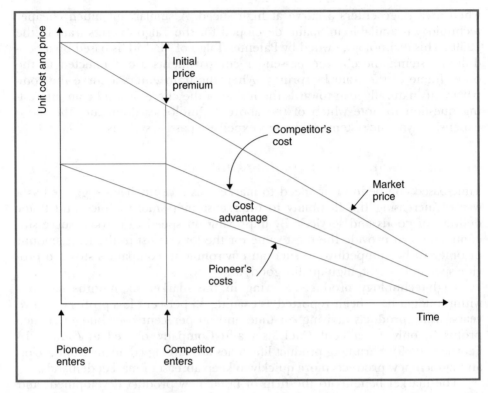

Figure 8.10 Impact of speed to market on costs and prices
(Adapted from Smith, Preston G., and Donald G. Reinersten (1991), *Developing Products in Half the Time*, New York, Van Nostrand Reinhold, p. 5)

A counter-argument is often made, whereby slow product developers justify their performance by arguing that speeding up the process can reduce quality, increase costs and perhaps limit the extent of technological benefits in the new product. Generally speaking, the opposite is true. If the right principles of new product development are applied, speedy new product development and launch can reduce costs and improve quality at the same time.

Consumers want products faster than ever. The fashionable will buy products only if the latest designs are available before rivals have them, and they will pay more for the privilege of speed. For the increasing number of faddish, fashionable, innovative customers, many companies have developed fast-response manufacturing, marketing and distribution. Benetton, for example, maintains an undyed inventory of clothes waiting to be coloured according to the latest trends. This is not a matter of cutting out unnecessary manufacturing tasks. In developing speed to market, it is necessary to examine the entire manufacturing and marketing system and to restructure it systematically.

By dramatically cutting its mortgage approval cycle from one month to a maximum of ten days, Citicorp Mortgage in the USA uses time as a competitive weapon. By targeting the home buyer and the broker, both of whom value a short approval cycle, Citicorp Mortgage provides a service that has helped it secure a 10 per cent national market share in the USA and significantly improve its financial performance (Stonich, 1990).

It has long been known that customers may be divided into segments based on their sensitivities to time and choice. The airline market is a good example, where the business traveller tends to be less sensitive to price but more sensitive to schedules than the holiday traveller.

A company's responsiveness to the needs of its customers, influences the price it receives for its goods and services and hence its profitability. The faster a company responds better to its customers than its competitors, the higher its prices, the faster its growth and the greater its profitability. The willingness of customers to pay higher prices for faster response may be measured by the time elasticity of price (Stalk and Hout, 1990: 88). Many customers will pay a high price to obtain the product or service they want very close to the time they make the purchase decision. The longer customers wait to receive the desired product or service, the more likely they are to shop around for better prices and the lower will the company's profits be. If the company's value delivery system can be altered to exploit the time elasticity of price, profits can be increased.

Strategic response to competition

In attempting to understand competitors, it was necessary to examine the nature of competition among companies, how they engage in innovation and pioneering activities, and what roles they accord to quality, technology and time in establishing a competitive position. Now it is necessary to examine how companies respond to the competitive environment. Porter's (1980) framework, reflecting cost, differentiation and focus strategies, is used as the framework for the analysis.

Generic competitive responses

Companies react in different ways to changes in competitive circumstances or to new competition. Usually they respond on a number of dimensions. When British Telecom became a private company and had to compete for customers, it began to focus on the customer. After much debate and trial and error, the company devised a three-pronged approach based on the organization and culture of the company (Figure 8.11). British Telecom attempts to provide a world-class service, develop its existing portfolio of products and services, and expand internationally.

In Porter's (1980) framework, competition is limited by the threat of substitute products and services, and the threat of new entrants. These external

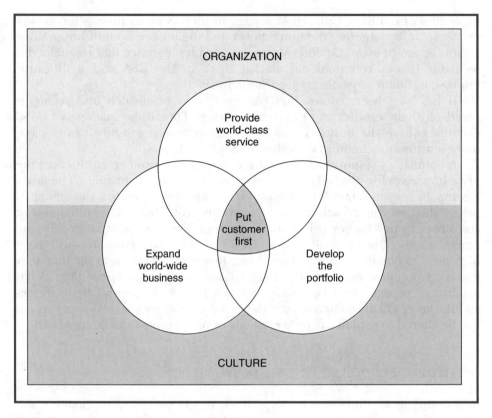

Figure 8.11   Competitive strategy at British Telecom

threats pose the greatest difficulty to incumbents attempting to respond. It is rare that dominant incumbent firms can survive the onslaught of a continuous threat from substitute products and services. For this reason, many companies succumb to new competition from manufacturers using alternative materials and technologies, and to imports from low-cost countries. According to Porter (1980), however, there are three ways in which a company can succeed (Figure 8.12). A company may be:

- a low-cost producer of products and services;

- a high-cost, differentiated producer; or

- a focused producer of unique products and services in a small, sheltered market niche.

This approach identifies opportunities for numerous companies in the same industry, since more than one means of differentiation and several market niches are usually available. Porter warns against being a follower in any of these options, or being stuck in the middle. To be successful, each competitive

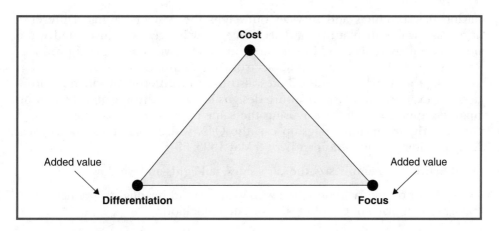

Figure 8.12 Three generic competitive strategies
(Source: Porter, 1980. Reprinted by permission of The Free Press, a Division of Simon and Schuster)

strategy requires the company to follow a specific course of action which is difficult to change in the short term.

Cost leadership, differentiation, focus and followers

As was seen earlier, the cumulative experience accruing from a high market share is a major way of achieving low costs. Low costs mean that funds can be released to support marketing or investment expenditure in order to monitor or increase market dominance. Allocating release finance to new products provides an opportunity to learn about new materials and technologies, and about new ways of managing and organizing.

Cost leadership arises for a number of reasons. By investing in larger-scale modern equipment, some manufacturing firms are able to reduce costs. The globalization of business also helps: companies marketing global brands may obtain scale economies unavailable to companies that permit regional autonomy. Global manufacturing decisions allow firms to concentrate production in larger factories in low-labour-cost countries. Low cost also derives from labour effectiveness as a result of the flexibility, co-operation and commitment of workers. To achieve cost leadership, a company must focus on controlling costs. Cost leadership must not be confused with low prices. Low costs allow companies to lower prices if they choose to penetrate markets, but they can also be used to produce profit, which in turn is used for investment purposes and contributes to maintaining market dominance.

The company which bases its competitive strategy on differentiation attempts to offer products and services which are unique or superior to those of competitors. Differentiation is a strategy favoured during the emergence of a product life cycle, when innovation attracts customers whose present value of having new products and services outweighs the cost of waiting. Differentiation also works in mature markets, since growth may be rejuvenated when new technology replaces old technology in well-known standardized products. An example is the introduction of electronics in 35mm cameras.

Design and styling are attributes also used to differentiate mature products: for example, modern furniture designs based on chrome and steel, or an upgrade appearance for a car using the same approach. Nissan has softened the austerity of Infiniti's flagship car, the Q45, with visual clues that suggest luxury inside and out (*Business Week*, 3 May 1993: 53):

- chrome to emphasize the car's sides, tail-lights and windows;

- front of the car redesigned with wrap-around headlights, fog lights and a grille in place of the old Q45's ornate medallion;

- heavier use of wood and softer leather in the interior;

- console facility for holding cups and hiding a cellular telephone; and

- key-chain remote control, with door-lock, boot-release functions and the ability to operate windows.

Branding can be used to differentiate products which otherwise might be perceived as indistinguishable. Packaging and brand image are particularly important in prestige and designer product markets. Notice the number of brand names prominently displayed on the outside of garments which were once hidden inside. Even services can be differentiated. Many successful airlines gain their reputation and share of the market by differentiating inflight and passenger-handling facilities. Quality combined with service is a powerful differentiating factor used by some supermarkets and department stores.

Competitive strategies based on differentiation require an innovative and creative approach to marketing. Differentiation also requires speed and flexibility, since imitators are many and easily flock to a success. This is the situation Quaker Oats discovered when it introduced Gatorade. The giants in the soft-drinks market responded very quickly to protect their markets (Exhibit 8.7).

Focused firms are entrepreneurial in that they constantly monitor emerging markets to judge whether new segments exist. Small companies are ideally suited to concentrate on providing customized products and services for well-defined customer groups. These companies usually lack the resources to compete on cost or market dominance. Success stems from staying very close to the customers and developing the design, manufacturing and marketing skills necessary to serve the needs of the niche. Such companies frequently extend the scope of their activities by offering related products and services also required by the customer group.

Small companies sometimes focus on niches in which they are uniquely able to survive. They attempt to avoid confrontation with major low-cost competitors by occupying niches in a separated market segment which is secluded

358

EXHIBIT 8.7   The thirst of champions

Both Coca-Cola and PepsiCo want to grab a bigger share of the sports-drink business, the fastest-growing segment of the soft-drink market. This is currently dominated by Gatorade, which is owned by Quaker Oats, a food company better known for oatmeal than soft drinks. Miffed at being left out, and convinced that sports-drink sales are set to grow even faster, Coke and Pepsi are determined to barge their way into Gatorade's market, one way or another.

Coke with PowerAde and Pepsi with All Sport are counting on their vast distribution networks to grab the market from Gatorade. Pepsi has around 1m 'sales points' and daily contact with 250,000 retailers who can be encouraged to promote All Sport. Coke's distribution clout is even greater: it has 1.5m sales points (of which 1m are vending machines). Quaker, in contrast, has only 200,000 sales points, relies on wholesalers, rather than direct contact with retailers, and has few vending machines of its own.

Quaker is hoping that Gatorade's carefully cultivated image will keep customers loyal. Basketball star Michael Jordan, a national idol, fronts Gatorade's advertising campaign and Gatorade is the official drink of America's sports establishment, from the National Football League to the Professional Golf Association. But this could change quickly once Coke and Pepsi open their wallets.

Quaker is also resorting to the time-honoured ploy of citing scientific studies to prove that the body absorbs Gatorade faster than water or any other soft drink. Coke counters that PowerAde contains more energy-packed carbohydrates than Gatorade. But Coke and Pepsi, veterans of a thousand such marketing battles, calculate that it will be taste, not scientific studies, which will impress most consumers. But Gatorade's continuing success has been partly due to the introduction of new flavours with broader appeal, which echoes the strategy of Coke and Pepsi.

Quaker's record against challengers to Gatorade is impressive. Though Gatorade already has 27 rivals in the American market, none has won more than a tiny share of sales. And Quaker has defeated attacks by Coke and Pepsi before. In 1985 Coke's food subsidiary launched a sports drink called 'Max', only to withdraw it two years later. Pepsi test-marketed Mountain Dew Sport in 1990 with success. Despite Coke's and Pepsi's muscle, it would be unwise to write off Quaker's chances.

Source: *The Economist*, 6 June 1992: 95.

---

and profitable. At the same time, the small firm cannot afford to ignore changes in customer needs. Large low-cost leaders are sensitive to opportunities in small segments and are likely to invade isolated niches. Survival for small companies means offering a wider range of products and services to customers in the niche, and being competitive in numerous niches. According to Saunders (1991: 22), success for the small firm in niche markets can also derive from:

- product standardization – limits on versions and services;

- specific focus – specialize rather than generalize;

- product quality and good value for money; and

- effective use of 'cost drivers', a narrow product line, restricted R & D expenditure, fewer new products, and reduced promotion and sales service.

Success does not depend on concentrating exclusively on one competitive position. Many successful companies are cost leaders and differentiators. The buying power, skills and expertise of companies like Motorola or Carrefour make them low-cost companies, but they trade on quality, service and brand names. Differentiation can be combined with focus to produce a successful competitive mix: Ferrari and Jaguar in cars; Bang and Olufsen in stereo musical equipment.

Market followers or imitators are companies that do not have sufficient resources, market positioning, technical skills or organizational commitment to challenge the market leaders in industries where product and service differentiation and branding are difficult to achieve. Market followers are usually to be found in price-sensitive markets, where the market rewards existing suppliers with its patronage because the products and services offered are acceptable. Common success strategies for market followers according to Saunders (1991: 21) are:

- careful market segmentation – compete only in areas where the company's special strengths are highly valued;

- efficient use of limited R & D budgets – concentrate on truly innovative products;

- emphasis on profitability rather than sales growth or market share; and

- willingness to challenge conventional wisdom – strong-willed, committed, enterpreneurial leaders.

Strategic choice for competitive success

Competitive success in marketing is a dynamic concept. The circumstances facing the company determine the approach most likely to succeed. Some companies succeed by keeping costs down and investing the profits earned in new products and services to stay ahead. Others win by differentiating their products and services to meet the needs of the market in a unique way. Smaller companies can sometimes succeed by focusing on special niches with a customized approach. Even imitators can be successful: many of the most successful marketing companies are market followers who innovate on neglected key success factors. It is necessary, however, to understand the market, its customers and competitors before choosing a particular approach. There is no unique solution to the problem of choosing a competitive strategy.

Assignment questions

1   Describe the forces which influence competition at industry level.

2   How may a company determine the strengths and weaknesses of a competitor? Why is it important to have such knowledge?

3   What approaches may be used by a company in examining the competitive positions of competitors?

4   What are the different strategies the company can adopt regarding quality?

5   How can a company compete on technology? What are the traps to be avoided?

6   What is the relationship between market pioneering and speed to market as a way of competing?

7   What risks does the firm face if it pursues a cost leadership strategy?

8   Describe the advantages and disadvantages of a differentiation strategy.

9   Is there an appropriate generic competitive strategy for small companies?

Annotated bibliography

Day, George S., and Robin Wensley (1988) 'Assessing competitive advantage: a framework for diagnosing competitive superiority', *Journal of Marketing*, 52, **2**, 1–20.
Porter, Michael E. (1980) *Competitive Strategy*, New York: The Free Press.
Stalk, George, Jr, and Thomas M. Hout (1990) *Competing Against Time*, New York: The Free Press.

References

Buzzell, Robert D., and Frederick D. Wiersema (1981) 'Successful share building strategies', *Harvard Business Review*, **59**, 1, 135–44.
Carpenter, Gregory S., and Kent Nakamoto (1989) 'Consumer preference formation and pioneering advantage', *Journal of Marketing Research*, **26**, 3, 285–98.
Crosby, Phillip B. (1979) *Quality is Free*, New York: McGraw-Hill.
Day, George S., and Robin Wensley (1988) 'Assessing competitive advantage: a framework for diagnosing competitive superiority', *Journal of Marketing*, **52**, 2, 1–20.
Deming, W. Edwards (1982) *Quality Productivity and Competitive Position*, Cambridge, Mass.: MIT.
Fitzgerald, N.W.F. (1991) 'Sustaining competitive advantage', paper presented at the National Marketing Conference, Dublin, 8 November.

Garvin, David (1984) 'What does product quality really mean?', *Sloan Management Review*, **26**, 1, 25–43.

Glynn, William (1992) 'George Fisher, Chairman and Chief Executive Officer, Motorola, speaks on quality to UCD', synopsis of a lecture, 'Total customer satisfaction – the ultimate competitive advantage', delivered by Dr George Fisher at University College Dublin, 7 October.

Hofer, Charles W., and D. Schendel (1978) *Strategy Formulation: Analytical concepts*, West Publishing Co., Minneapolis.

Jacobson, Robert, and David A. Aaker (1985) 'Is market share all that it's cracked up to be?' *Journal of Marketing*, **49**, 4, 11–22.

Juran, Joseph (1962) *Quality Control Handbook* (2nd edn), London: McGraw-Hill.

Lambkin, Mary (1992) 'Pioneering new markets: a comparison of market share winners and losers', *International Journal of Research in Marketing*, **9**, 1, 5–22.

Luchs, Robert (1986) 'Successful businesses compete on quality – not costs', *Long Range Planning*, **19**, 1, 12–17.

Mattsson, Lars Gunnar, and Jan Johanson (1985) 'Marketing investments and market investments in industrial networks', *International Journal of Research in Marketing*, **2**, 3, 185–95.

Morgan, Neil, and Nigel Piercy (1992) 'Market-led quality', *Industrial Marketing Management*, **21**, 2, 111–18.

O'Reilly, William Kevin (1990) 'Airmotive Ireland', unpublished UBA dissertation, Graduate School of Business, University College Dublin.

Pearson, David (1991) 'Global advantage – the Sony story', paper presented at the National Marketing Conference, Dublin, 8 November.

Porter, Michael E. (1980) *Competitive Strategy*, New York: The Free Press.

Robinson, Wiliam T., and Claes Fornell (1985) 'Sources of market pioneering advantage in consumer goods industries', *Journal of Marketing Research*, **22**, August, 305–17.

Saunders, John (1991) 'Marketing and competitive success', in Michael J. Baker (ed.), *The Marketing Handbook* (2nd edn), Oxford: Butterworth-Heinemann.

Smith, Preston G., and Donald G. Reinertsen (1991) *Developing Products in Half the Time*, New York: Van Nostrand Reinhold.

Stalk, George, Jr, and Thomas M. Hout (1990) *Competing Against Time*, New York: The Free Press.

Stonich, Paul J. (1990) 'Time: the next strategic frontier', *Planning Review*, **18**, 6, 4–7 and 46–8.

Informing marketing decisions

9

Need for marketing information
Meaning of marketing research
Sources of marketing research data
Data measurement and scaling
Reporting marketing research results

Introduction

This chapter introduces and explains:

- the scope of the information requirement in marketing management;

- the need to convert data into knowledge;

- the nature of the information required with special reference to customer information;

- the nature and purpose of marketing research;

- marketing decisions and problems;

- how to design a marketing research project;

- the value of desk research and the role of field research;

- the use of questionnaires in marketing research;

- selected methods of data measurement and scaling techniques; and

- the importance of an appropriate presentation strategy for the research results.

Informing marketing decisions is an essential ingredient of marketing management. This chapter introduces the reader to the nature and significance of data, information and knowledge, and the distinctions among them, in the context of managing the marketing process in the organization. The emphasis is on understanding the research process in marketing, so that the reader can evaluate the need for marketing research and specify the most appropriate approach to carrying out a research study and evaluating research results. The marketing manager must be able to recognize the need for marketing research, specify the various kinds of research problem encountered and be able to design a research study which would provide the required information. Various approaches to collecting and measuring marketing research data and presenting the results are discussed.

Having studied this chapter, you should be able to define the phrases listed above in your own words, and you should be able to:

1. Describe the difference among descriptive, strategic and operational information requirements.

2. Specify the precise information required to estimate market potential, to understand customer product and service requirements, and to understand marketing practices in a particular field.

3. Outline approaches to sales and demand forecasting.

4. Design a research framework or paradigm to assist in data collection and analysis.

5. Formulate marketing research problems.

6. Evaluate the various sources of data.

7. Recognize the distinction among exploratory, descriptive and causality research, and know when to use each.

8. Evaluate questionnaire designs and decide the appropriateness of each design for personal, telephone or mail surveys.

9. Evaluate different approaches to measuring or scaling data in marketing research and recognize the appropriateness of each.

10. Design an effective presentation strategy for research results, recognizing the need for oral and written presentations.

Need for marketing information

Marketing decision makers are usually faced with a time constraint and must make decisions rather quickly, so the timelines and accuracy of information are important. As marketing activities become increasingly complex and broader in scope, the nature of the marketing information required also changes. Marketing information must be comprehensive and sophisticated, and have a wide angle of focus. At the same time, it is necessary to note that the decision maker is faced with a data explosion, which forces the company to screen data for effective and efficient generation of useful information.

Scope of the information requirement

In general terms, marketing information is required to help the firm to discover the sales potential for a particular product or service. Observing the trends in the music business and the need to research the market for music albums and discs, Paul Keogh, managing director of Polygram Ireland, reported that:

> We are not a very market-oriented business. We use promotional tools applied to a very production-oriented environment. The A & R [artist and repertoire] man is king. He equates to the chemist in the pharmaceutical business. The A & R man often gives the view that 'there is no need to research this new band – we were there, we saw the crowd reaction'. But marketing techniques are creeping in as investments get larger, sales become harder to get and return on investment not as guaranteed anymore.

A sharper focus on the value of information even in a business as traditional as music is required. Various approaches are being adopted to suit the particular needs of this business (Exhibit 9.1).

Information is also needed on ways of achieving success with the product or service. In specific terms, marketing information provides answers to the following issues:

- identity and description of the market segments offering greatest sales potential;
- attributes of the product most in demand and any adaptation needed;
- expected sales revenues at different prices;
- alternative marketing options for the product; and
- costs of achieving marketing objectives.

Descriptive, strategic and operational information

The nature of the information needed may be separated into descriptive information about the market itself, strategic marketing information, and information concerning operational issues (Figure 9.1.). Regarding descriptive information on the market itself, the company may be interested in knowing

---

EXHIBIT 9.1   Promised Land of music

Suppose that ways of affecting the reproduction of music will continue to become more widespread, perhaps evolving out of video games or the Rapman's children. In addition to new hardware, this calls for recordings of music that are in the right format to be tinkered with by the listener. The record companies will thus have something new to sell when home-taping erodes their old markets.

Some of the big record companies are pondering that new dawn. As its audiences get older and technology gives it more power, the business is starting to realise it needs new ways to sell. Some corners of the record business are beginning to be less dependent on the old philosophy of throwing albums at fickle teenagers and just hoping for the best. Consider compilations. The practice of making tapes of favourite album tracks at home on a cassette recorder, for use in a Walkman or at a party, has created a large new market for pre-packaged compilation albums. These now account for 16 per cent of album sales in Britain. American record companies have barely discovered them. They acknowledge that they should have done, and hope that marketing them on television and by direct mail will (belatedly) work wonders in America as it has done in Britain.

Putting together a successful compilation album involves something that the record business has never liked confessing to: pre-production research. This means playing music to test audiences and using their responses to design the product. Increasingly sophisticated ways of doing this for compilation albums are being developed. And the technique has often been used to pick out which album tracks to release as singles. But the idea that such a thing might have a wider application is regarded as anathema by most A & R men. They are in the business of cultivating artistic talent: you cannot tell a musician what to play any more than you can test market Proust and then tell him to put in less stuff about his mother.

Source: 'The music business', *The Economist*, 21 December 1991: 17.

---

which markets hold the greatest promise, and within these markets which segments are likely to be more lucrative than others. It is also necessary to determine risk levels in the market. The company must also decide where to start in the market, which means deciding the timing of market entry and the sequence of subsequent markets to enter.

The strategic marketing decisions the company faces, for which information is required, are the competitive position to adopt and the most appropriate entry mode. It is also necessary to have information on the timing of market entry, so that optimum benefit can be obtained especially in new product markets.

Operational decisions for which information is required refer to issues arising in implementing the marketing programme. The company is concerned

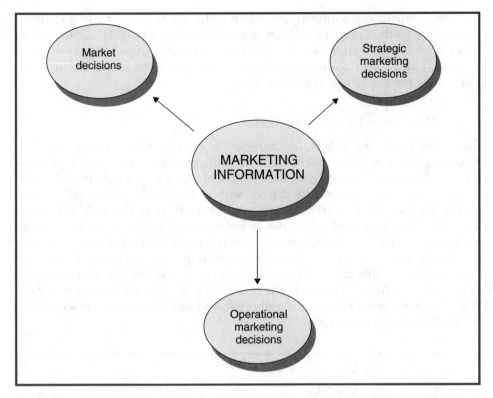

Figure 9.1 Marketing information required for marketing decisions

about the relative emphasis to place on the elements of the marketing mix. It is also necessary to have operational marketing information when the product has been in the market for some time and it becomes necessary to fine tune or calibrate levels of the elements of the marketing mix.

There are a number of circumstances when the need for marketing information is greater. Rapid changes in the environment generally increase the need for marketing information. New government initiatives to regulate industry or to protect the environment have the same effect. Artificial barriers in the availability of resources similarly affect the need for information. For example, during wars involving Middle East countries, the supply of oil and its price tend to be affected adversely. Companies need to know how the impact will affect them and the alternatives available before they can plan their production and marketing programmes.

A second set of circumstances involves the cost of new ventures and the rate of technological change. For example, rapidly falling prices for microchips reduce costs, but because such chips can become obsolete relatively quickly, the company is doubly affected. In this case, the firm must attempt to predict technology changes and microchip prices.

367

The company seeks information when a change in the marketing environment presents the company with an opportunity to improve its circumstances or its performance. Alternatively, when the company's market performance associated with a previous decision does not meet required standards, information will be needed to rectify the situation.

Converting data into knowledge

Good decisions are based on knowledge of the issues being decided. Knowledge derives from information, and information, as seen above, is based on data. Data refers to raw, unsorted, unstructured sets of numbers and observations. These data are obtained from within the company, through market observations and from market research, and contribute to the body of theoretical and conceptual marketing knowledge (Figure 9.2). Data, especially those available from published sources, are abundant and relatively cheap. They are considered to be 'noisy', unorganized and frequently irrelevant. There are many concerns with databases available to the marketing company. For the present, it is sufficient to refer to the matter of accuracy and relevance of data. Published data generally are not well organized, are sometimes irrelevant and are available only occasionally.

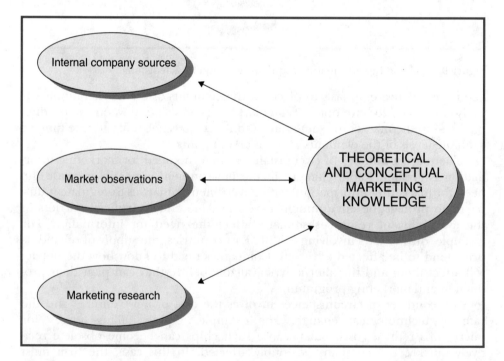

Figure 9.2 Elements of a marketing information system

Information is much more useful to the decision maker than raw data. By imposing a structure and a purpose in the search through data, the company develops useful information to help make decisions. Information is focused on a marketing problem, and its relevance and value are easy to judge. This is a matter of seeking quality in the marketing information developed. Frequently, managers do not have access to the appropriate methods for handling information. Here is a situation where modelling marketing phenomena based on data and information could be instrumental in improving the process by which decision makers deal with existing information (Leeflang, 1995). Leeflang also argues that marketing models provide a structure which helps in deciding what information should be produced and which areas of marketing research are likely to be the most fruitful.

Information made available to the company is in some way internalized and absorbed by managers into individual decision systems. Information which has been processed in this way is knowledge, and it refers to how the manager reacts to the information provided. To convert information into knowledge it is necessary to have an analytic framework as an information processor.

Marketing information system

In 'The elephant's child', Rudyard Kipling identifies the kind of questions which are very useful in obtaining marketing information. He refers to these questions as his 'six honest serving men':

> I keep six honest serving-men
> (They taught me all I knew);
> Their names are *What* and *Why* and *When*
> And *How* and *Where* and *Who*
> I send them over land and sea,
> I send them east and west;
> But after they have worked for me
> I give them all a rest

The company which succeeds in obtaining answers to the questions what, why, when, how, where and who, in regard to customers and competitors for its products and services, will have gone a long way to understanding how to respond to market opportunities in a competitive fashion.

- Why? Need for information.
- What? Context of information sought.
- How? Collecting and analyzing data.
- Where? Sources of information.
- When? Timing and quality of information.
- Who? Recipient of information.

369

A marketing information system which provides answers to the above questions when applied to a specific marketing research question contains three components (Figure 9.3). Environmental issues refer at the general level to the macro marketing environment and to specific matters dealing with customers. The marketing information system itself refers to internal sources of information, marketing intelligence and marketing research. Lastly, the information flows to the company to assist in decision making.

The benefits of a functioning marketing information system are obvious to the user. A well-designed practical marketing information system controls the distortion and loss of information in data and provides faster, more complete and less expensive information extraction to serve management decisions. A good system allows the company simultaneously to monitor a variety of activities in the marketplace.

Information on market potential

Access through distribution channels to potential customers is an important set of factors to be quantified (Figure 9.4). It is important to recognize any government or trade barriers which may exist. Blocked channels, a feature in certain markets, may make it impossible to reach customers, thereby forcing the company to seek an alternative channel. If the company intends selling

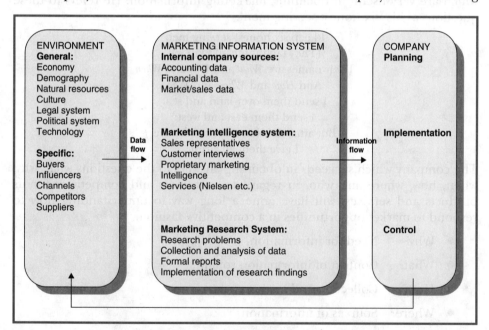

Figure 9.3   A marketing information system
(Source: Bradley and Ward, 1983)

abroad, it will have to consider non-tariff barriers to trade, licence and registration fees, and hidden internal taxes. Tariffs and quotas are still a feature of
some country markets and there may also be currency restrictions which prevent the company repatriating its revenues.

Regulations, which include health and safety regulations and those regulations designed to protect the environment, must also be considered. There
may be country restrictions on the company's products if it attempts to export
certain kinds of product, such as alcoholic beverages in some markets, food
ingredients and others. Regulations on currency and tax invariably apply in
national and international markets. In recent years, the growth of regulations
on packaging, advertising and ingredients, in food and beverages especially,
has given companies great cause for concern. These are regulations which
change periodically and keeping abreast of them requires considerable attention on the part of the company.

Under the second set of factors, market size and sales growth, concern
rests in establishing levels and trends in consumption, geographic patterns
and the impact of segmentation. For industrial products, it is also necessary to
measure the extent of derived demand for the product or service as trends in
final markets dictate demand in industrial markets. Under this heading the
company will also need to quantify other, broader factors which affect
demand. Among the more important of these factors are social and cultural
trends, economic development and the physical environment.

The third set of factors to be examined is the price structure in the market.
The company needs determine the prices to end-users and, if it is a consumer
product or service, the price points involved. Other factors influencing prices
and costs should also be evaluated, such as ex-factory prices, trade mark-ups,
transport costs and tariffs if the company is considering exporting.

Fourth, it is necessary to examine the competitive structure of the market.
In evaluating competition, domestic production, its volume and growth
trends, must be examined. Frequently, there is a correlation between production and consumption after making allowances for foreign trade and inventory. It is especially important under this heading to examine market
structures. This means identifying major competitors, estimating their market
shares, and knowing where their plants are located and their capacity. If possible, information on future plans, especially regarding capacity additions and
technology changes, is most helpful. The company must also attempt to measure the strength of competitors, which means obtaining information on their
size and other special advantages, such as the provisions of valuable patents
and trademarks. There may be other factors that determine success levels
among competitors and that should be identified, such as the marketing
knowledge and skills of the competitors' staff. During this analysis the company has an opportunity of identifying gaps in product lines.

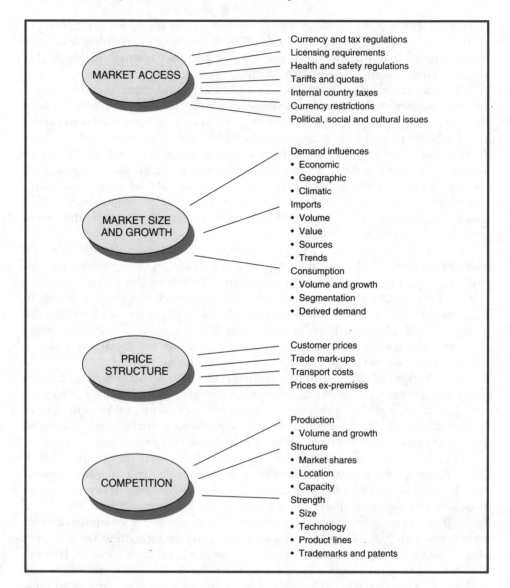

Figure 9.4   Factors influencing market potential

Information on products and services

In determining product information requirements, three sets of factors dominate the consideration: the core product itself; its transport and storage; and associated information and promotion (Figure 9.5). The other elements of the marketing mix are discussed under the heading of marketing practices below.

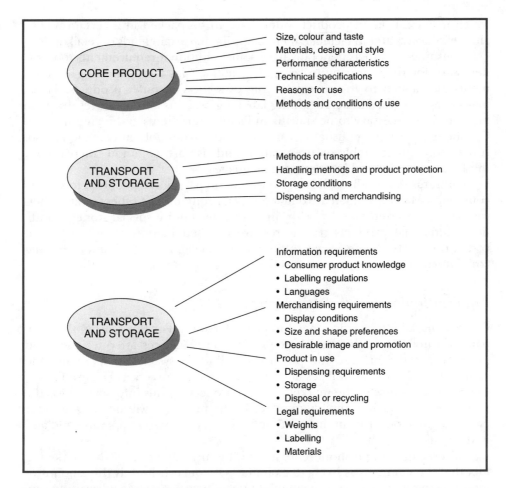

Figure 9.5 Factors influencing product requirements

Regarding the product itself, issues such as colour, taste, size, design, styling and materials used must be considered. Other product factors include the performance characteristics of the product, its technical specifications, and advertising and promotion as a persuasive justification for product use, including methods and conditions of use.

Packaging has two aspects: the physical aspect, which serves the protective function; and the promotion and information functions, which can be very effective, especially for consumer products sold into mass distribution. Consumer packaging offers the company great opportunities for product and brand promotion. The design, use of colour, shape and size of the package all have an influence on consumer choice. To design packaging with protection as an objective, concern rests with knowing the transport methods, handling methods and equipment used, the storage conditions and any marketing requirements which may exist. Food products often have to be packed in a certain way to allow easy access and to facilitate merchandising in certain kinds of retail outlet.

Consumer products generally have some additional requirements too. It is necessary for the company to recognize that special merchandising requirements may attach to the successful sale of some consumer products. There may be legal requirements regarding labelling, weights and measures. In some markets, it is necessary to be specific in listing ingredients and materials used. Consumer packaging usually carries other types of information also. Instructions on assembly or preparation and use are common. Increasingly, these must be prepared in numerous languages.

For industrial products, it is also necessary to pay special attention to storage conditions. Materials which are dangerous, can contaminate others or are otherwise at risk, or are themselves risky in some way, require special storage conditions. Industrial products usually require detailed identification marks and codes. It may also be necessary to design the packaging in such a way that the contents can easily be removed and the packaging returned for further use.

Information on marketing practices

Current marketing practices need to be understood. For this reason, the company will need to understand how products and services are advertised and promoted in the market, the physical distribution system in operation, the channels used, pricing policies and customer service practices (Figure 9.6). If the company is new to the market, it will be collecting this information for the first time, whereas if it already operates in the market it will need to monitor changes which occur from time to time in the way the system operates and also in the costs involved.

Advertising and promotion are among the first elements of the marketing mix that the company is likely to examine. Of concern here is the amount of money being used to advertise competing products. Very large advertising support for a competitor's product is in itself a barrier to market entry which is difficult for the underresourced company to overcome. At the same time, it may be necessary to match or surpass competitors to hold or increase market share, or to gain a foothold in the market if the company is considering a new entry.

During the review, the company will also examine the advertising media and techniques used, and the level of expenditure on each. Of greater importance is information concerning competitor products that may be obtained from a study of the content of the advertising. The sales messages and the positioning intended may be obtained from a close study of advertising content.

Sometimes companies allocate part of their advertising and promotional budget to distributors and retailers in their efforts to push their products down the channel of distribution. It is a question of balancing how much to spend on consumer or ultimate user advertising and how much to spend on intermediaries. In recent years, the power of retailers in many traditional

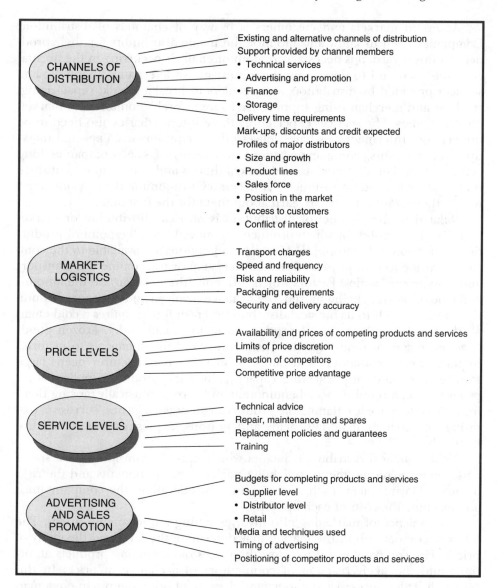

Figure 9.6   Researching marketing practices

branded products markets has forced manufacturers to spend a greater proportion of their advertising budget on retailer-controlled promotions. It may
also be necessary to determine the timing sequence and geographic spread of
the budget for advertising and promotion. A greater relative expenditure in
one area of the country or at a particular time may indicate a competitor
strength there or the onset of some new marketing activity.

375

Access to markets and customers is by way of channels of distribution. Companies need to know and monitor the major distributors for their products. In this regard, it is necessary to monitor changes occurring in the normal channels used and to determine the advantages of alternative channels. The services provided by distributors and retailers in breaking bulk, repackaging, stocking and merchandizing support are factors closely monitored by marketing companies. The services expected by these intermediaries also need to be understood. Intermediaries have delivery time requirements, expected mark-ups and discounts, credit expectations and terms of sale. Companies long active in a market will understand these conditions and expectations, but since they change from time to time it is necessary to monitor them. Companies new to the market will have to learn about them for the first time.

Related to the channel of distribution is physical distribution or market logistics: the methods by which products are moved from the point of production to the point of consumption. Two broad options are available to the company: provide its own physical distribution system or use commercial transport and storage companies. Factors which influence the decision are the amount and type of product being moved, the distance involved and any special conditions which attach to its physical distribution. Fresh food requires a cold chain all the way from the point of production to the retail outlet. Frozen goods have more special requirements. The delivery of bulk chemicals to factories requires special containers and tanks. A furniture manufacturer needs large storage space and large carrying capacity, since the product is bulky. Other products which require special equipment and care in physically moving them from place to place are flammable products, compressed gasses, corrosive, oxidizing and irritant materials, acids and poisons, explosives and radioactive materials.

Other physical distribution factors which must be considered are speed and frequency requirements, reliability, packaging requirements and the risks involved. Having taken each of these into consideration, the company must also examine the costs of each option.

The practice of marketing also involves setting and changing prices. The levels of competition in the market may determine the level and flexibility of prices. The company needs to know the prices of competing products at any time, and the likely reaction of competitors to a change in price. In this regard, it is also necessary to understand the role of premium pricing in a market and the practice of discounting. Sometimes companies new to the market develop relatively low prices as a market entry strategy. In consumer markets, many products are sold at price points. The company has some flexibility below the price point, but cannot stray above it because the market expects the product to be available at that price point.

Many companies compete by providing an excellent customer service. In some markets, a certain level of customer service is expected. Customer service varies depending on the technical advice given, the policy on replacing defective products, guarantees, repair and maintenance. These service features apply in both industrial and consumer markets. Training may also be a feature of consumer service in industrial markets.

Information on customers

Having accurate and reliable information on customers is an essential ingredient in marketing management. Many marketing companies, however, claim that they know who their customers are and that a methodical approach to collecting information on customers is necessary. The problem is that companies may know who their customers are, but the important thing is to know who they are likely to be in the future. In claiming that they know who their customers are, companies are stating that they know which companies or individuals are most likely to buy their products and services in the following three to six months. This is usually a relatively easy matter, since under normal circumstances signed contracts or agreements will account for most short-term revenues in some markets at least. With the aid of modern technology, especially powerful personal computers and appropriate software, companies can develop a customer information file which is easily accessible and designed to aid decision making. A customer information file for a commercial bank would draw upon computer-based data systems (Figure 9.7). For organizations like banks, on-line customer information is a common feature. Periodic marketing efforts directed at customers are also quite common.

It is essential, however, that the company look beyond the short term and attempt to identify customers for the longer term. Buyers and other decision makers move from organization to organization, and buyers for the company's products this year may be different next year. Decision makers who are important today may not be important in the future.

Sales forecasting

Companies attempt to estimate the value of a market to them by forecasting sales. Company demand is related in some way to market demand. By forecasting the size and configuration of market demand, it is possible subsequently to obtain an estimate of future company sales (Figure 9.8). There is a wide range of sales forecasting techniques available. Some are valuable, while others are quite complicated and the added value in complying with their rigid assumptions may not warrant their use by many companies, especially smaller companies or companies operating in a very turbulent environment. To help choose a particular approach, the company is concerned with the accuracy of the forecasts, the time period to which they apply and the data requirements. Previous experience with a particular approach may be the overriding consideration in choosing the forecasting method.

Five approaches which find favour among companies are: extrapolation of

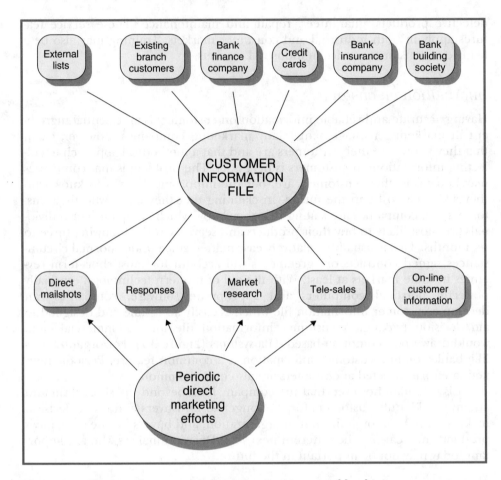

Figure 9.7   Sources of customer information in commercial banking

past sales, sales correlations, sales force opinions, buyer interviews and test marketing. Simple extrapolation techniques present as a sales forecast for one time period the sales actually achieved in the previous time period. The use of correlation techniques depends on the assumption that the historical relationship between two variables, one of which is independent of the product-market under examination, will continue into the future. A valuable source of information about the market is the company's sales force. Companies frequently use the opinions of the sales force to build a market forecast.

Sometimes customers are able to provide valuable opinions on their own future buying intentions. Surveys of buyer intentions are quite common, especially in consumer durables and investment goods. Such surveys are often used in the motor industry when manufacturers attempt to gauge existing customers' likelihood of changing to a new model. A sophisticated variant of this

378

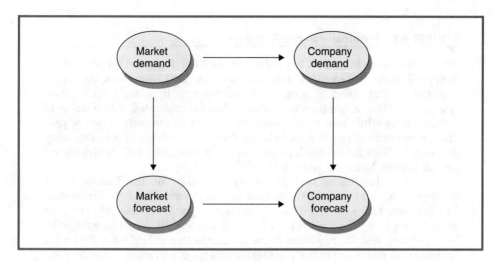

Figure 9.8 Forecasting market and company demand

approach applies to services in an attempt to model people's likely reaction to new films before they have been produced (Exhibit 9.2).

For new products, the company may have to carry out a test market to derive a forecast for the entire market. Test marketing is in effect a mini market launch of a new product into an environment which simulates the ultimate market for which it is designed. Test marketing is used where the commercial and market risk associated with the demand of the new product is high. Where a large investment is at stake, a test market is advised.

Quality and cost of information

The quality of the information available to the company may be evaluated on the basis of:

- relevance;
- accuracy;
- timeliness;
- compatibility; and
- cost.

Secondary sources of data usually provide information which is of limited value, since it is collected and prepared for a wide audience with wide needs. Such data may be irrelevant to the task. There may also be a statutory reason for collecting it in the first place, making it unlikely that the results would have specific and precise commercial value. Before engaging in a detailed search

379

EXHIBIT 9.2 Terminator 9: you'll love it

Film makers have long tried to predict whether the dog-eared script on their desk will make a box-office hit. As early as 1937 America's Audience Research Institute tried to gauge audience reaction by using brief, written synopses of films. Since then the industry has experimented with a string of techniques, ranging from sneak previews of films in the early stages of production to crude attempts at correlating the characteristics of a forthcoming film (e.g. violent, funny, erotic) with cinema attendance at films already on general release. None has worked well.

   Jehoshua Eliashberg and Mohanbir Sawhney, of the University of Pennsylvania, reckon they have at least part of the answer to the film industry's problem. Films are an odd sort of consumer good, because they are 'purchases' with little or no prior knowledge of whether they will be enjoyable. Dr Eliashberg and Dr Sawhney hope to change that. They have devised a mathematical model to predict whether cinema-goers will enjoy a specific film.

   The model relies on established personality-testing techniques to assess would-be film goers. First, it measures each against a sensation-seeking scale: do they seek adventures or new experiences, are they easily bored, and so on. Second, it assesses their emotional state (pleased or displeased, aroused or relaxed). Third, it measures the cinema-goer's tendency to undergo mood changes. The model then predicts likely enjoyment levels for each individual by correlating all three factors with the film's excitement and pleasure content, as assessed scene-by-scene by a trio of independent judges.

   The Pennsylvania pair admit that their model needs refining. But even in its existing state it might be used to test scripts or to determine the right target audience for a given film. Used on a scene-by-scene basis, it might also suggest script changes before too much money had been spent – although such 'market-driven editing' is unlikely to be a match for the average film director's ego.

   Other enormous egos might have to watch out, too. If all a film-goer needs to help him decide what to see are his own test score, the judges' assessments and some deft number crunching, he hardly needs critics to tell him what to do. Palmtop computers may soon substitute for the palmy streets of Cannes.

   Source: *The Economist*, 4 July 1992: 83.

---

of such sources, the company should determine the potential usefulness of the data.

   Accuracy is an issue which arises in connection with sampling and methods of collection. Incorrect sampling procedures tend to generate the wrong type of data. Defective administration of the data collection task can also reduce accuracy. It is also necessary to judge the objectivity of the supplier of the data. Timeliness, referring to the currency of the data used, may be a key consideration.

Generally, the company is interested in making comparisons of one period with another, a product with that of a competititor, or one market with another. The issue of compatibility arises frequently, especially when dealing with secondary sources of data. Statistics collected in different years may not be comparable because different categories are involved or definitions have changed. Each of these factors gives rise to compatibility problems. Furthermore, the data required are frequently not available.

Information is not costless. The company faces the cost of data collection, analysis, storage and interpretation. Frequently, there is a significant cost of organizing the data so that it can be used. The cost of updating the data, adding names and pieces of data and discarding old data, must also be borne by the company.

Market intelligence

A distinction is made between a market research system and a marketing intelligence system. The former is a set of static, independent, information-collecting activities carried out periodically, while the latter is a continuous dynamic system for collecting and managing marketing information gleaned from a wide variety of sources.

Marketing intelligence is based on personal activities and the collection and analysis of printed or recorded material on markets and competitors. Personal contacts and information sources are very popular with many companies, but documentary and computer-based sources have proliferated with the revolution in communications and information technology.

A practical marketing intelligence system helps to filter, condense and evaluate great quantities of data to yield marketing information in more manageable form. Marketing intelligence helps to corroborate the information developed in formal marketing research studies, and may be used to improve the implementation and control of marketing plans.

Meaning of marketing research

For many marketing decisions, the information needs dictate that the company carry out a specific investigation of the market. This involves understanding the nature and purpose of marketing research and establishing a framework to carry out the research.

Nature and purpose of marketing research

Marketing research is a search for knowledge and understanding, an enquiry into the nature of, the reasons for and the consequences of any particular set of circumstances. It begins with a question or a problem, the nature of which varies. For this to be answerable by research, real-world observation should be able to provide the required information. Marketing research has two objectives:

- to know and understand market-based phenomena; and

- to be able to do something more efficiently.

Satisfying the first objective is a scientific matter as it contributes to the development of a body of principles which permit the understanding and prediction of a whole range of human interactions in marketing. Satisfying the second objective reflects a more immediate and practical emphasis. A wide variety of practical concerns in the company may present topics for marketing research:

- information to decide whether there is a need for some new distribution facility, product or service (e.g. need for a new cold storage facility in the docks area);

- information about probable consequences of various courses of action to allow the company to decide among alternatives (e.g. impact of an advertising campaign); or

- information to predict some future course of events in order to plan appropriate action (e.g. likely launch by a competitor of an imitative product).

Marketing research refers to the efforts of defining the problem to be examined, assessing existing knowledge, extending it to concepts, testing hypotheses through the analysis of meaningful data, and evaluating the original concepts critically with a view to making significant contributions to understanding and application (Zaltman *et al.*, 1973). The results of the research help to provide explanations, make predictions, support marketing control and contribute through various forms of dissemination to a new body of marketing knowledge (Figure 9.9).

This framework should not be mistaken for a model of the actual research process itself, which differs from the above paradigm in two respects: first, the research process almost never follows the neat sequential pattern suggested; and second, there are many interrelationships and additional decisions, such as the kind of data needed, the most efficient means of collection, how to develop and test the data collection instrument, planning the research, and deciding and providing the budget.

Marketing decisions and problems

Formulating the problem is the first step in the marketing research process. Only if marketing researchers know the problem that the company wants to solve can they be sure that they will design a project that will provide the

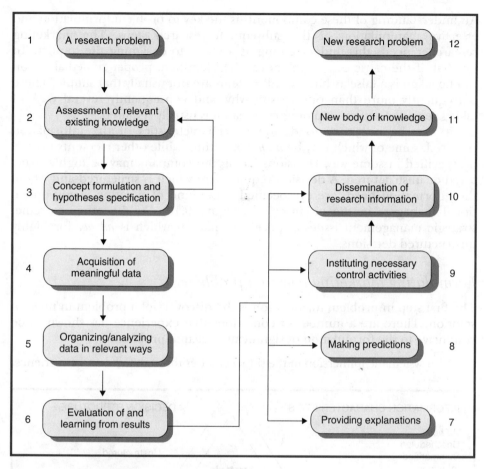

Figure 9.9 A paradigm of the marketing research process
(Source: Based on Zaltman *et al.*, 1973)

pertinent information. Indeed, much initial marketing research is done to help management to recognize the existence of problems. Typically, a general management problem is identified which must be subdivided into one or more research problems. To do this the researcher must know:

- who the decision makers are, the environment in which they operate, and the resources available for research;

- the measurable objectives or goals that the decisions makers hope to obtain; and

- the possible courses of action which may be used to solve the problem and the consequences of the alternative courses of action.

An understanding of these components is the key to problem formulation and effective manipulation of the subsequent research steps. The marketing researcher needs this understanding as a guide to designing the inquiry. To say that, if the cause of a problem can be identified, proper remedial action can be taken is a false assumption. Problems are not usually that simple. There is frequently more than one reason why, and consequently several ways of taking remedial action. Exploratory research is usually required.

It may be necessary to decide the characteristics of the information required, some of which may be *ad hoc* in nature, while other elements may be prespecified in some way. Decisions facing the company may be highly structured or unstructured. A decision requirement which is structured and where the information needs are prespecified is the kind of situation facing operational managers in the organization (Figure 9.10). At the other extreme, strategic management issues require information which is *ad hoc* for highly unstructured decisions.

Formulating marketing research problems

The first step in problem formulation is the discovery of a problem in need of solution. There are a number of conditions that experience has shown to be conducive to the formulation of significant research problems:

- a systematic immersion in the subject matter through first-hand experience;

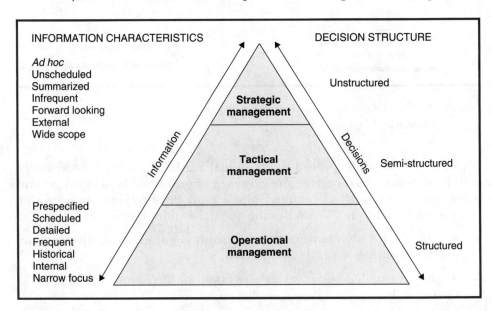

Figure 9.10   Characteristics of information and decisions
(Source: Adapted from O'Brien, 1990. By permission of Richard D. Irwin)

- a study of existing literature; and

- a survey of experts.

In order to experience a systematic immersion in the subject matter or topic of interest, it may be necessary to carry out an exploratory study to increase the investigator's familiarity with the phenomenon to be examined in a subsequent, more highly structured study. Theory is often either too general or too specific to provide clear guidance for empirical research. It is generally necessary to obtain experience that will be helpful in formulating relevant hypotheses for a more definitive investigation.

Literature search and survey of experts

One of the simplest ways of economizing effort in research is to review or build upon the work already done by others. The focus of the review should be on hypotheses that may serve as leads to future investigation. Hypotheses may have been implicitly stated by previous researchers. The task then is to gather the various hypotheses that have been put forward, to evaluate their usefulness as a basis for future research, and to consider whether they suggest new hypotheses. This is not an easy task:

> It is an utterly superficial view that the truth is to be found by studying the facts. It is superficial because no inquiry can ever get underway until and unless some difficulty is felt in a practical or theoretical situation. It is the difficulty, or problem, which guides our search for some order among the facts, in terms of which the difficulty is to be removed. (Cohen and Nagel, 1934: 199).

However, in purely exploratory research, hypotheses will not have been formulated at all. The task then is to review the available material with sensitivity to the hypotheses that may be derived from it.

In many cases, a literature survey will be time consuming. In some cases, no research of significance will have been done on the topic of interest. Without a thorough search of journals and other reports which are likely to carry material on the topic, the marketing researcher cannot comment on the relevance of existing literature. Professional organizations, research groups and voluntary organizations are sources of unpublished research which may be of interest. Furthermore, it may be a mistake to confine the literature survey to studies that are immediately relevant to the researcher's area of interest. Perhaps it would be more fruitful to apply concepts or theories developed in completely different research contexts to the topic of interest.

A survey of experts on the topic of interest can provide very useful results. Only a small proportion of existing knowledge and experience is in written form. Many people are specialists in their own area of endeavour, and acquire in the routine of their work a reservoir of experience that could be of value in helping the researcher.

The aim of a survey of experts is to gain insight into relationships between variables rather than to get an accurate picture of current practices. The researcher seeks provocative ideas and useful insights, not a statistical description of the business or market. A survey of experts, besides being a good source of hypotheses, can provide information on the practical possibilities of doing different types of research: which factors can be controlled, which cannot, and what co-operation will be forthcoming.

The primary value of surveying experts is that it may lead to asking more significant questions in the final study than would otherwise have been possible. In developing hypotheses to be tested, the researcher attempts to abstract the important elements of the problem situation and represent them so that they are simple enough to be understood and manipulated, yet realistic enough to portray the essentials of the situation.

Designing a market research project

Having identified the research problem to be analyzed, it is necessary to design a procedure whereby data can be collected to reject or support it. Research design means planning this procedure so that data will be collected which are relevant to the problem under investigation. Research design is the complete sequence of steps taken ahead of time to ensure that the appropriate data will be obtained in a way which permits an objective analysis leading to valid inferences with respect to the stated problem.

There are at least three reasons why research should be designed: to predetermine the level of inaccuracy in the results which will be tolerated, to collect relevant data and to determine ways of improving the methods of research inquiry. Research design is an insurance against failure: it is economical in the long run because it is less likely to result in fruitless inquiry. Architects design houses in such a way that when built they generally do not fall. Similarly, marketing researchers design research in such a way that the value of the findings does not collapse due to poor research methodology. Second, it is more fruitful to collect relevant data at the outset. The time consumed in trying to find out what the data mean after collection based on weak methodology is much greater than the time required to design an inquiry which yields data the meaning of which is known when being collected. The delay involved may be worthwhile. Failure to plan the research may produce more inaccuracy and greater longer-term cost than would a well-designed research project which does not meet the completion deadline.

Third, the researcher has other obligations besides finding answers to immediate problems. The title 'researchers' carries with it the obligation to seek improved ways of inquiring. Marketing researchers are rarely content with the methods of inquiry used.

There are three general purposes which a research study might serve.

Corresponding with each purpose is a specific study design. First, an exploratory study is used to gain familiarity with a phenomenon in order to formulate more precise research problems and to develop a set of testable research hypotheses. Second, a descriptive study is used to portray accurately the characteristics of a particular set of individuals or situation. Third, a study design to test hypotheses of a causal relationship between variables may be required.

Exploratory, descriptive and causality marketing research studies

An exploratory marketing research study should be considered as an initial step in a continuous research process. Here the major design emphasis is to gain ideas and insights rather than definite conclusions. Three approaches to exploratory research may be identified: a review of the literature, a survey of experts and immersion in the subject matter. These have already been discussed at some length.

The purpose of an exploratory study is to transfer an initially vaguely defined problem into one with more precise meaning. Frequent changes in the research procedure are necessary in order to provide for the collection of data relevant to the emerging hypotheses. Consequently, the design of such studies is characterized by flexibility and versatility. The researcher seeks information to enable specific research questions and hypotheses about the problem to be stated.

It is important to remember that exploratory studies merely lead to insights or hypotheses, they do not test or demonstrate them. An exploratory study must always be regarded as a first step. More carefully controlled studies are needed to test whether the hypotheses that emerge have general applicability. A classic example of the need for exploratory research arises in the following: 'We're not getting the sales results we thought we would. What's wrong?' The marketing researcher might guess at a number of factors:

- the product might be inferior in quality and style;
- the wrong channels of distribution might be used;
- there might be too few sales people; or
- the advertising appeals might be irrelevant.

Since the number of possible difficulties is almost infinite, it is impractical to test them all. Exploratory research is required to find the most likely explanations for subsequent detailed research.

In the case of descriptive research, the researcher usually starts with an initial specific hypothesis, but not always. It is appropriate to make three comments concerning descriptive research which distinguish it from purely exploratory studies:

- concern lies with research questions which presuppose much prior information about the problem to be investigated;

387

- the researcher must be able to define clearly what is to measured, and adequate methods for measuring it must be identified; and

- the researcher must be able to specify who is to be included in the definition of a 'given population'.

In regard to the last point, should it be manufacturing or service firms, or middle or upper management? There is no room for flexibility in a descriptive study. There is a need for a clear formulation of what and who is to be measured, and the techniques for valid and reliable measurement must be specified. Because the aim is to obtain complete and accurate information, the research design must make much greater provision for protection against bias than is required in exploratory studies.

Descriptive studies are not limited to any one form of data collection. It is possible to employ a number of techniques:

- interviews;

- questionnaires;

- systematic direct observation; and

- company or industry records.

Whichever technique is used, the procedure must be carefully planned.

Information collected in descriptive studies may be used to draw inferences concerning the relationship between the variables involved. The information collected may also be used to make aggregate predictions and even predictions concerning the frequency distribution of sales by the income level of consumers. However, no causality is implied. The basic principle involved in descriptive studies is to find correlates of the behaviour desired at the time the predictive statement is made.

The design implications for causality studies require an experiment of some kind. Procedures which reduce bias and increase reliability, but also permit inferences about causality, are required. Experiments as such are not always required. Causality studies are much more complex. First, it is necessary to understand what is meant by causality. In research, interest centres on finding a multiplicity of determining conditions which taken together make the occurrence of a single event probable. Marketing researchers seek to find the necessary and sufficient conditions for an event to occur. Rarely does the researcher expect one single factor or condition that is both necessary and sufficient to bring about an event.

In marketing research, it is not just the necessary and sufficient conditions for an event that are sought, but also the myriad contributory conditions which exist to explain the existence or occurrence of an event. Indeed, much of the emphasis is placed on examining contributory conditions and how they operate.

Finally, in marketing research, when the researcher states that two variables are related, it is essential to ask how they are related. There should be a clear statement of the nature of the mechanism whereby one variable affects another.

Sources of marketing research data

Sources of data for decision makers may be found within the company itself or outside. A search of company records is a useful way to start a research project. The next stage might be to engage in desk research of published material. Only when these two sources are exhausted would the researcher engage in field research.

Search of company records

Internal sources of data include sales records, delivery records, prices and quotations, advertising budgets and media used, sales call reports and previous research studies or marketing evaluation reports.

Internal company data are the most accessible and least expensive potential source of information. Such data are also available at short notice. Only when internal sources have been exhausted should outside sources be used. Internal company data are not available for new products or new markets, but comparisons may be made with existing product-markets which can help the decision maker. As the information required becomes more product-market specific, the value of internal data declines.

Desk research

To be efficient in desk research, the company begins by finding out what published data are available. Secondary sources of data are collected by agencies without a specific commercial purpose. These include government census data, family expenditure surveys, trade association data, international production and trade statistics, and surveys and market audits published periodically by market research companies. Desk research of secondary sources of data is useful when examining a subject for the first time, as the company may not be very familiar with the market or conditions in the industry. As a consequence, the research generally works from the general to the specific (Figure 9.11).

Starting at a more general level, it is possible to sift the information available at each stage by first examining what is available in general guides. Then the research moves from the general to specific guides, and from there to specific information sources. The problems which arise in desk research are

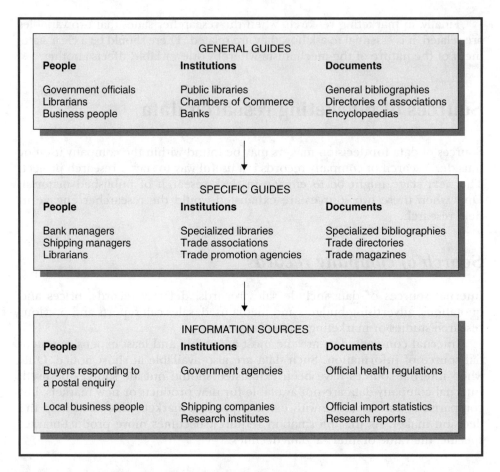

Figure 9.11   The route to information in desk research

(Source: Adapted from *Introduction to Export Market Research*, Geneva: International Trade Centre (UNCTAD/GATT), 1978)

principally those of developing search and retrieval skills. It is necessary to have these skills otherwise useful information may be by-passed in the process. Search and retrieval skills refer to the ability of the researcher systematically to apply a routine in order to identify and locate the required information irrespective of where it appears. Desk research is concerned with obtaining answers to questions like: 'how many people buy the product?' and 'how much do they buy?' The benefits of systematically searching through information sources are threefold:

- the topic can be assessed in light of previous research work;

- the various perspectives can clarify the field research approach to be adopted in the field work; and

- statistical and market findings may reinforce an argument.

It is very difficult to know at what point the desk research routine should stop and field research should begin. It may be possible to obtain all the information necessary through desk research. Usually, however, statistics and other information available may be too vague. Inexperienced researchers usually want to rush into field research often with ill-prepared questions, and thereby miss the opportunity of obtaining the information needed much more efficiently. At some stage, the value of desk research will be exhausted and it will be necessary to carry out field research.

Sources of desk research data

Censuses and registrations are the more common sources of secondary data. Censuses are useful for sales forecasting, market potential studies, and facility location studies. Registrations provide data on issues which are examined routinely under some legal requirement: new cars, marriages, births, deaths, income tax returns, social security payments, export licences and food manufacturing licences are good examples. It is particularly easy to obtain data on issues where a subsidy or tax is involved.

A frequently used source of desk research data is reports prepared on a commercial basis to provide details on market trends, consumer expenditures, advertising trends and similar commercially useful matters. Many organizations supply such information, which is valuable to a wide audience: for example, EIU Reports, Mintel Reports and the Nielsen Reporter. Other useful sources of marketing information may also be consulted:

- Books. Data for topics of current interest may be out of date, but books frequently contain data found nowhere else. Rapid production of books has enabled publishers to compete successfully with periodicals.

- Magazines, journals, periodicals. Indexed articles in magazines, journals and periodicals provide useful research material on most subjects of interest.

- Newspapers. Newspapers frequently contain valuable data of all types, statistical, political and financial. Many papers carry periodical in-depth analyses of industry sectors, countries or institutions.

- Government documents. Governments publish statistical information and many useful reports of a very high calibre.

- Directories. Business or trade directories carry a wide variety of information on products, sources of supply, names and addresses of individual companies and product listings.

- Miscellaneous sources. These include annuals, atlases, special reports and anniversary productions.

Evaluating secondary data

In attempting to evaluate secondary data, the researcher must answer the following questions:

- how pertinent are the data?
- who collected the data and why were they collected?
- what method was used to collect the data?
- is there evidence of careful work?

Answers to the above questions are necessary if the researcher is properly to evaluate secondary sources. In relation to the first point, it is necessary to review the limitations of secondary data listed below. In relation to the second point, it should be noted that if the collection and publication of the data are a function of the agency with specific designation to do so then the data are likely to be accurate. In some cases, data sources are suspect because of the motivation of the collectors. In regard to the third point, note that where weaknesses are mentioned it is likely that further camouflaging may exist. Other questions to ask include:

- were the subsamples large enough and were they chosen from the universe of interest?
- are the data carefully analyzed and are the results clearly presented?
- are the tables in the study consistent with each other?
- are the conclusions supported by the data?

Desk research is frequently complicated by the lack of uniformity in the compilation of the statistics, and sometimes the statistics are merely crude estimates. The marketing researcher is often faced with the problems of interpreting data collected from secondary sources. In choosing sources of secondary data, the researcher must pay close attention to whether the source:

- covers the topic comprehensively and precisely;
- provides the desired information in a readily understood manner;
- approaches the topic in an appropriate manner;
- covers the appropriate period of time; and
- is readily accessible.

In regard to the last point, when it is difficult to locate a source for cost or other reasons, it may be worth considering a more convenient, but possibly inferior, source.

Field research

Desk research relies on information that others have recorded for some other purpose. When the researcher has studied what others have done, it may be necessary to search for additional information in primary sources, including information gathered by means of a specifically designed questionnaire, interviews or observation study. Information obtained by asking questions is called original or primary information. Frequently, it is referred to as field research.

Field research is research actually carried out within the market. It is concerned with specific questions like 'what kind of product is required?' 'in what sizes?', 'in what colours?', 'in what flavours?' and 'at what power levels?' External sources of data may be primary sources, such as data collected for the company by market research agencies. These studies are usually highly focused and designed with a specific research purpose. They take the form of surveys, consumer panels, in-store experiments and competitive intelligence.

As the cost of field research can be high, it is generally carried out in markets offering the greatest potential as indicated in the desk research. Before carrying out the field research, the company must decide which markets should be examined and precisely what information is required. The cost of the research must be related to the value of the information likely to be obtained.

Other kinds of primary data include original reports, letters and notes, diaries and personal observation. This type of data is frequently referred to as 'raw' because they have not been subjected to interpretation and analysis by others. No one else has added any biases to the data.

Means of collecting primary data

A variety of techniques are used for gathering information by means of surveying a sample of a universe of interest in a field study. The more commonly used field research techniques are personal interviews, telephone interviews, postal surveys and observation studies (Figure 9.12).

Several different methods are used to obtain information from people. They involve asking them questions or presenting them with situations, securing their reactions, and then determining how they will behave in a practical situation based on their responses to the survey. Primary data may be obtained by means of:

- mail questionnaire;
- interview questionnaire;
- telephone interview; and
- observation.

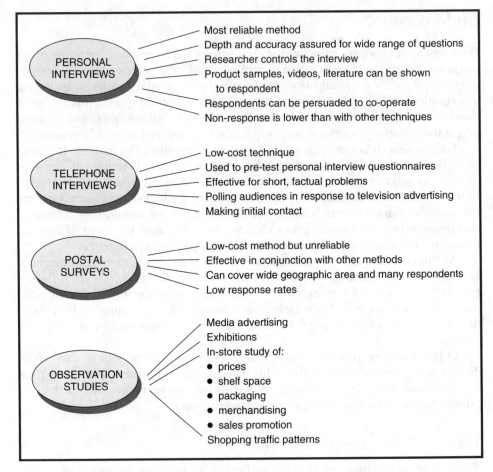

Figure 9.12 Techniques of field research

One of the simplest approaches to collecting primary data is to mail a questionnaire to selected potential respondents for completion in their own time. There are several advantages in using a mail questionnaire.

- low cost for each response;

- ease of securing responses from and efficient coverage of a wide geographic area;

- respondents can be assured of anonymity;

- easier to secure information from 'hard-to-see' people; and

- interviewer bias is avoided.

There are also a number of disadvantages in using a mail questionnaire:

- biased results are possible, since people who are well disposed or not well disposed to the central issues raised are more likely to respond than people who are relatively indifferent to the issues;

- the questionnaire must be relatively brief to obtain any response at all;

- it is frequently difficult to ascertain whether the respondent or some-one else in the organization completed the questionnaire;

- respondents to mail questionnaires are usually reluctant to expand on their answers because of the effort involved;

- respondents may be unable to classify items in a similar manner, so there may be inconsistency of responses across respondents on attitudes;

- bias from a low response rate, lack of knowledge or deliberate attempt to mislead; and

- it is difficult to select a representative sample.

For these reasons, the researcher is never quite certain that the information collected is really representative of the sample of interest. In an interview it is possible to conduct a more lengthy discussion than is usually possible by mail. It may also be easier to gain the confidence of the respondent in an interview to obtain information on sensitive issues.

The interview questionnaire has a number of advantages:

- relatively complicated issues can be treated successfully, and prompt cards can be used to assist the interview process;

- sensitive issues can be successfully examined; and

- additional information can easily be obtained at relatively low cost.

The interview questionnaire also has a number of disadvantages, even though it is still the most extensively used method of collecting primary data:

- relatively high unit cost – only a limited number can be completed each day;

- interviewer bias may exist, perhaps caused by a lack of empathy between interviewer and respondent; and

- interview questionnaires tend to be time consuming.

The third way of collecting primary information is by using the telephone. The advantages of using a telephone interview include the following:

- telephone interviews are relatively inexpensive;

- many respondents are easily accessible by telephone; and

- simple information can be obtained quickly and easily.

There are also a number of major disadvantages in using the telephone interview:

- the questioning process must be short and uncomplicated;
- questions requiring discussion or careful thought should not usually be included;
- sometimes it is not possible to reach the desired respondent by telephone;
- a steady flow of conversation must be maintained, making it difficult to pause or reflect;
- it is difficult to judge respondents' attitudes and reactions; and
- confidential information is rarely given on the telephone.

The telephone interview is used extensively in industrial marketing research, where many of the above restrictions do not apply.

Irrespective of the types of questionnaire used, whether mail, interview or telephone, there are advantages and disadvantages with each. The advantages are as follows:

- a questionnaire is highly adaptable to a specific situation;
- a questionnaire can result in the speedy collection of data;
- supplementary data may be available at little extra cost;
- data are collected under conditions similar to those where the results are to be applied, i.e. the natural environment.
- questionnaire data are relatively inexpensive to collect.

The disadvantages are as follows:

- questionnaire surveys are expensive when the cost of eliminating uncontrolled variables is considered;
- misunderstanding on the part of the respondent;
- uncooperative respondents may bias the results;
- respondents may deliberately attempt to bias the results;
- respondents may have no knowledge of the topic; and
- the respondent's memory may be faulty.

For these reasons, it is necessary to supplement questionnaire survey data by other methods. A great deal of information can be collected simply by observing marketing-related phenomena. Researchers can observe how shoppers select a cut of meat, or whether they confer with friends before selecting a jacket. It is also possible to collect other types of information through observation, such as watching traffic patterns, counting shoppers, noting people's restaurant habits, observing materials moving into and out of factories, and studying displays in shop windows.

Observation studies such as these are useful in that the information collected is more likely to be accurate than is the case with some personal interviews. Observational research may be used in an attempt to avoid biases which arise due to memory lapses, halo or indirect effects and other influences. Data which seem 'too trivial' to the respondent may usefully be collected through observation: for example, whether drivers secure seat belts before or after starting the engine, or whether a customer selects a product from a shelf or a dumper display in a supermarket.

Observational research also has a number of disadvantages. By observing behaviour, the researcher is able to see what happens, but is not given any indication of why it happens. Second, with observational research it is not usually possible to employ rigorous experimental or sampling control, although there have been many successful pricing and promotion experiments organized in supermarkets.

Types of survey information available

Irrespective of the method of collecting primary data, respondents may be asked to supply information on a wide range of topics. Data gathered by means of a survey include factual information, opinions and a combination of the two. Respondents supplying factual information, such as the amount of meat purchased, the number of hours worked, the amount of money spent on advertising, or wages, usually do so from memory or records. Opinion data may be the direct recording of the respondent's opinion or his or her opinions as interpreted by the interviewer. In neither of these cases is any attempt made to control or influence the conditions under which the questions are asked.

Structure and disguise in marketing research

Whichever type of survey is used to collect primary data, it is important to ask the right questions. It is often said that nothing is easier to prepare than a poor questionnaire, and nothing is more difficult than a good one. There are, however, a few rules which, if carefully followed, greatly enhance the chance of success. Almost every detail of the questionnaire is important.

One of the most important issues is to decide how structured the questionnaire should be to obtain the desired results, and whether the study should be disguised. Questionnaires may, therefore, be of four basic types:

- structured, disguised;
- structured, non-disguised;

- disguised, non-structured; and

- non-disguised, non-structured.

In a structured and disguised questionnaire, the respondent does not know the objective of the questioning process and is expected to answer a prescribed list of questions in a forced choice situation. The results are easy to tabulate and analyze, but this type of questionnaire is difficult to design.

In a structured and non-disguised questionnaire, the objectives of the questions are clear to the respondent. The respondent is expected to answer a prescribed list of questions. In this case the interviewer is not as likely to bias the results as in the previous situation. Most marketing research surveys fall into this category. Again the results are easy to tabulate and analyze, but the questionnaire is difficult to design.

In a non-structured and disguised questionnaire, the respondent does not know the objective of the questioning and the interviewer adapts the questions as the interview progresses. Projective techniques using standardized probes and stimuli fall into this type of questioning. Interpretation of the results tends to be subjective and requires highly trained personnel. This type of question-naire is frequently used to obtain information on subconscious and socially unacceptable attitudes.

In a non-structured and non-disguised questionnaire, the objectives are clear to the respondent and the interviewer uses a general list of questions to probe the respondent with during the interview. Bias is easily introduced, but this type of questioning can be very useful at the exploratory stage of the research project. In-depth interviews fall into this category, and these tend to be expensive to administer and difficult to analyze since comparisons are difficult.

The function of a questionnaire is to translate research objectives into specific questions and to motivate the respondent to co-operate. Hence, there is a need for a pre-test of any data collection instrument to determine how accurately the questions reflect what the interviewer wants from respondents. Furthermore, the questionnaire must be standardized so that inter-respondent comparisons of observations on the measurement variable can be obtained. Furthermore, a standardized questionnaire introduces an element of speed and accuracy into recording and analyzing the data. Some questionnaires must be designed for particular circumstances, hence the layout, format and structure are important as they facilitate completion. Structured questionnaires like that used by IBERIA, the Spanish national airline, are easy to administer, complete and analyze. Notice the detail obtained and the pre-coding which facilitates analysis (Exhibit 9.3).

Data measurement and scaling

Having specified the kind of information required and the format of its collection, it is necessary to decide how the data should be scaled or measured. This is a matter of deciding on the measurement units. Methods of data measurement have universal application, but some are more popular in marketing than others. This section introduces a small number of such scales, and the reader is referred to the many excellent marketing research books for further study.

Methods of data measurement

There are numerous methods used to measure and collect data for marketing research studies. Some are relatively simple, while others are very sophisticated and beyond the scope of this book. Two of the more popular approaches, Likert scales and semantic differentials, are introduced, and two less well-known but more analytical techniques, multidimensional scaling and conjoint analysis, are introduced.

Likert scale and semantic differential

Both of these approaches to scaling or measuring data are very popular in marketing research. Likert scales are based on the precept that individuals can accurately rate a statement in terms of their agreement or disagreement with it. This is done by asking respondents to indicate their reaction to a statement on the following or similar continuum:

Strongly agree	Agree	Uncertain	Disagree	Strongly disagree
1	2	3	4	5

Associated with each of the responses is a scale of 1–5. It is arbitrary whether 5 is chosen to represent the most favourable or the least favourable response. What does matter is that, when the decision has been taken regarding the scoring of responses, it is rigorously maintained. It is normal practice that, if the researcher decides a score of 5 should represent the most favourable response, then positive item statements would have a 5 for strongly agree responses and a 1 for strongly disagree responses. Unfavourable item statements should be scored in reverse order. For each individual, the scores on all items are totalled. The scores obtained for individuals on the selected evaluative items are totalled to get a final overall attitude score.

The semantic differential enables the researcher to examine both the direction and the intensity of respondents' factual knowledge or beliefs. This is done by asking respondents to indicate their position on a set of bipolar

EXHIBIT 9.3   Iberia in-flight customer questionnaire

The following is a simple questionnaire prepared by IBERIA, the Spanish national airline, to obtain information from its customers. Of particular interest to IBERIA was the awareness customers had of its Municolor holidays. The questionnaire was available in four languages: Spanish, English, German and French. The following is the English version. The letter of introduction requesting completion of the questionnaire has been adapted slightly from the original.

Dear Passenger:
We need your co-operation which will enable us to offer you a better service. We have prepared this questionnaire which we ask you to complete during this flight. There is no need to include your name and address. We are grateful for the time taken to complete the questionnaire and for your valuable assistance. Many thanks on behalf of IBERIA.

Carlos Argullo
Commercial Director

Date _____   Flight No. _____

From _____   To _____

01   Your permanent residence:

    Country _____   City/Town _____

02   What is your reason for travel?

    01 ❑   Business
    02 ❑   Holidays/Tourism
    03 ❑   Visiting friends or relations
    04 ❑   Educational
    05 ❑   Working abroad, travelling to or from your home country
    06 ❑   Others

03   How long have you been away or how long do you intend to be away?

    01 ❑   Part of a day   04 ❑   15–30 days
    02 ❑   1–6 days   05 ❑   31–60 days
    03 ❑   7–14 days   06 ❑   More than 60 days

04   Where did you acquire your ticket?

    Country _____   City/Town _____

05   How many flights have you made during the last 12 months?

    01 ❑   One flight   03 ❑   3–6 flights
    02 ❑   2 flights   04 ❑   More than 7 flights

06   What is your final destination for this journey?

Country _____   City/Town _____

07   Why did you choose IBERIA for this journey?

01   ❏   The convenient schedule
02   ❏   Previous experience of Iberia
03   ❏   On the recommendation of your travel agent
04   ❏   On the recommendation of friends or relatives
05   ❏   As part of an organized tour or inclusive holiday
06   ❏   Because of the country of origin of the airline
07   ❏   Because of your impression of the airline
08   ❏   Other reasons

08   What type of fare did you pay?

01   ❏   Normal (first or tourist class)
02   ❏   Included in the total price of an organized tour or inclusive holiday
03   ❏   Other (Please state type) _____

09   Do you know about or have you made use of the special discounts and/or
     special low fares available on Iberia services?

	Known	Used	Unknown
Iberiabono, US $99	01 ❏	06 ❏	11 ❏
Spouse Fares (Europe)	02 ❏	07 ❏	12 ❏
Common Interest Group Discount	03 ❏	08 ❏	13 ❏
Excursion	04 ❏	09 ❏	14 ❏
Others (Please state type)	05 ❏	10 ❏	15 ❏

10   Have you heard about IBERIA's Mundicolor Holidays?
     Have you taken a Mundicolor Holiday?

01   ❏   No, I have not heard of Mundicolor
02   ❏   Yes, I have heard of Mundicolor
03   ❏   I have taken a Mundicolor holiday

11   By which means have you been made aware of our special fares, inclu-
     sive holidays, etc?

01   ❏   By friends or relations
02   ❏   By your travel agent
03   ❏   Through advertisements
04   ❏   By requesting information from IBERIA offices
05   ❏   I am not aware of IBERIA's special fares
06   ❏   I am not aware of IBERIA's inclusive holidays

---

12 Have you seen IBERIA's advertisements? If so, where?

    01 ❏ Cinema
    02 ❏ Newspaper
    03 ❏ Radio
    04 ❏ Posters
    05 ❏ Magazines
    06 ❏ TV
    07 ❏ I have not seen them
    08 ❏ Others (Please state) _____

13 Please can you give your age, sex and occupation?

	Age			Sex
01 ❏	12–22		05 ❏	Male
02 ❏	23–35		06 ❏	Female
03 ❏	36–50			
04 ❏	Over 50			

---

adjectives. Thus a company's corporate image might be obtained by asking a group of respondents to rate it on the following scale:

	Extremely	Very	Fairly	Neither	Fairly	Very	Extremely	
Powerful	–	–	–	–	–	–	–	Weak
Reliable	–	–	–	–	–	–	–	Unreliable
Modern	–	–	–	–	–	–	–	Old-fashioned
Friendly	–	–	–	–	–	–	–	Unfriendly

Sometimes the scale intervals are made more explicit through the use of headings on the scales, as in the above example, but these are not necessary and may be omitted.

A major advantage of the semantic differential is that it is relatively easy to compare the responses of many different respondents. If we assume equal intervals, the researcher can assign scores to responses and calculate the average score given by a group on any dimension. It is also possible, in addition to presenting the profiles, to test differences in means and other measures. It is essential to ensure that the items being tested are relevant to the final analysis, and the adjectival statements developed by the researcher must also be appropriate. The semantic differential has achieved a wide reputation in the following areas of marketing analysis:

- comparing corporate images both among existing suppliers and against an 'ideal';

- comparing brands and services;

Occupation

07 ❏ Company director, senior management, professional, owner
08 ❏ Executive, technician, middle management, sales executive,
representative, self employed
09 ❏ Other forms of employment
10 ❏ Housewife
11 ❏ Student
12 ❏ Retired
13 ❏ Emigrant
14 ❏ Others (Please specify) _____

- determining attitudes to several factors; and
- analyzing the effectiveness of marketing programmes.

It is an extremely versatile technique, but one with which care must be taken, especially in specifying the bipolar scales to be used.

Multidimensional scaling and conjoint analysis

Multidimensional scaling can be applied to metric, interval-scaled data, non-metric data or data which are only rank ordered or nominal scaled. Again, concern rests with the relationship among elements or among pairs of elements. These elements can be characteristics of stimuli, people or both. In multidimensional scaling, no attempt is made to describe the underlying decision process of the sample respondents, or why perceptions and preferences are what they are. The researcher concentrates on the outcomes, the end result, and not the process of formulation. The multidimensional scaling concept can be illustrated geometrically through a set of points in multidimensional space. The axes of this space represent the perceived attributes which characterize the stimuli: the flavour of brand A beer, etc. In a market with four beers, an individual might locate them as shown in Figure 9.13. It is assumed that only two dimensions are relevant: flavour and strength.

Figure 9.13 is a perceptual map of how an individual consumer might perceive four existing beer brands. The position of this respondent's ideal beer is also indicated. It is assumed that the distance between the various brands on the map is a measure of perceived similarity of the brands. Brands A and C are

403

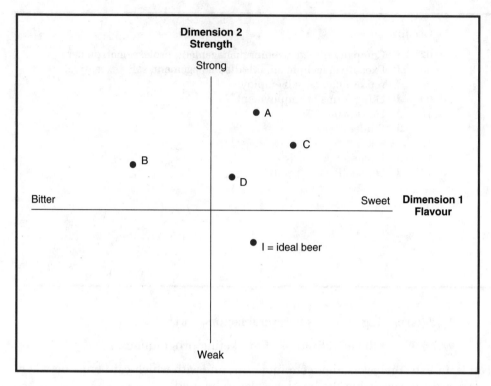

Figure 9.13 Perceptual map of four brands of beer using multidimensional scaling

perceived to be relatively similar to each other by the hypothetical respondent, while Brand B is perceived to be very different. All beers are perceived to be stronger than the ideal beer for this consumer. By naming the dimensions involved, it is possible to establish a basis for the differences in perception. The task of naming the dimensions may be easy for experts in the beer indus-try, since they can judge from the relative positions of the competing brands the basis underlying consumers' evaluation.

Conjoint measurement represents a relatively new theoretical framework for simultaneously measuring the individual as well as the joint effects of a set of independent variables. These are collapsed on to a single variable which is not numerical, i.e. a utility function of some kind. Conjoint measurement, which is similar in spirit to multidimensional scaling, allows the researcher to develop interval-scaled effects from rank-order responses. Marketing questions which might be examined by conjoint measurement are typified by the follow-ing example (Green and Tull 1978):

- what combination of product benefits should be implemented in the form of a new product by the manufacturer of self-polishing floor waxes?

404

- having settled on a product formulation that affects certain consumer benefits, what type of package should be designed to connote these benefits psychologically to the consumer?

Conjoint measurement algorithms enable the researcher to translate ordinally collected data on a combination of items into a utility function.

Reporting marketing research results

For a marketing research report to be accepted by management, it must represent a valid attempt to meet the objectives specified. The objectives of the study should be presented and the research design described. The marketing research report writer should also describe the analysis performed on the data and should, if requested, suggest a course of action. To ensure that the report is used, the marketing researcher should:

- consider the reader's background, experience and role in decision making;

- keep the report short and concise;

- follow a natural writing style, use ordinary language and avoid jargon;

- address the research objective but avoid extraneous material;

- ensure the accuracy of all statistical information presented;

- illustrate the report with charts, diagrams and tables; and

- accord more space to important items.

Presentation strategy

No matter what the quality of the research on a project, much of the acceptance of the results depends on the way they are communicated to various audiences. Thus if the researcher wants action as a result of the work, a great deal of effort must be made to convince others of the value of the research. In any event, the researcher will have to consider the type of presentation to make, and to whom and how and where and what conditions must be present to allow maximum effectiveness. The researcher may make a written presentation, an oral presentation or a combination of both written and oral presentation.

All too often the researcher spends weeks or even months gathering and analyzing information, a day or so in writing up the report, but only five minutes in making the presentation. The researcher should set the presentation stage properly by securing the time necessary for an appropriate presentation. There is a right time and climate for explaining the purpose of a report, what is accomplished, what is not accomplished. The end of the project is as important as the beginning. The writer should plan the strategy of the presentation with the following considerations in mind:

- who should be there when the report is presented?
- what needs to be said or explained?
- what visual and other aids should be utilized?
- what advance work is needed and with whom before the study is presented?

Identity of reader and audience

It is important to know for whom the researcher is writing. With respect to internal reports, this is usually a fairly simple task. The writer knows, for example, that the director of sales or marketing or the head of human resources will read, analyze and act on the report, or that the report is for all departments. Special care must be taken when the report is being written for a decision maker whose orientation may be finance, accounting or human resources, or anyone who is not used to marketing jargon. When a report has both internal and external readership, however, the problem becomes more complex.

The written report

A reader of a report needs to be told enough about the study that it can be placed in its general scientific context and the accuracy of its methods judged. Readers should be able to form an opinion of how seriously to accept the findings. The report should include sufficient detail that the reader could repeat the study with other subject material. Thus a report should cover the following points:

- statement of the problem with which the study is concerned;
- research procedures – study design, nature of sample, data collection procedures and methods of statistical analysis;
- results – description and presentation; and
- discussion of the implications drawn from the results.

Oral presentations

An oral presentation may be used to introduce or summarize a detailed written report, or it may be structured to interpret the findings of a general report for a special audience. Regardless of the objectives, the oral presentation should be considered a prime opportunity to convey important research findings and to stimulate interest in specific research activities. Inadequate preparation does an injustice to the total research endeavour, and reflects negatively on the researcher. A well-prepared oral presentation has three benefits:

- it brings the research findings to the immediate attention of the people who matter;

- it ensures that the written report is not automatically placed on the shelf; and

- it helps busy executives or managers to realize quickly the significance and worth of the research findings.

Assignment questions

1 List the kinds of question that marketing research attempts to answer.

2 Describe the elements of a marketing information system.

3 How would you assess the quality and value of marketing information?

4 What is the difference between marketing research and marketing intelligence?

5 When should the company engage in marketing research?

6 Describe what is meant by secondary and primary sources of data.

7 How can primary data be obtained?

8 Outline a simple approach to scaling and measuring marketing research data.

Annotated bibliography

Crimp, Margaret (1981) *The Marketing Research Process*, Englewood Cliffs, NJ: Prentice Hall.

Fitzroy, Peter T. (1976) *Analytical Methods for Marketing Management*, London: McGraw-Hill, chapter 2.

Green, Paul E., and Donald S. Tull (1978) *Research for Marketing Decisions* (4th edn), Englewood Cliffs, NJ: Prentice Hall, chapters 6, 9, 13, 14, 15 and 16.

Webb, John R. (1992) *Understanding and Designing Marketing Research*, London: Academic Press.

Weiers, Ronald M. (1988) *Marketing Research* (2nd edn), Englewood Cliffs, NJ: Prentice Hall.

References

Bradley, M. Frank, and J. J. Ward (1983) *Export Marketing Research*, Geneva: International Trade Centre (UNCTAD/GATT).

Cohen, Morris R., and Ernest Nagel (1934) *An Introduction to Logic and Scientific Method*, London: George Routledge and Sons.

Green, Paul E., and Donald S. Tull (1978) *Research for Marketing Decisions* (4th edn), Englewood Cliffs, NJ: Prentice Hall.

Leeflang, Peter S.H. (1995) 'Modelling markets', in Michael J. Baker (ed.), *Marketing: Theory and practice* (3rd edn), Basingstoke: Macmillan.

O'Brien, James A. (1990) *Management Information Systems: A managerial end user perspective*, Homewood, Ill.: Richard D. Irwin.

Zaltman, Gerald, Christian R.A. Pinson, and Reinhard Angelmar (1973) *Metatheory and Consumer Research*, New York: Holt, Rinehart and Winston.

Case studies

Case 5: Skilball

Take an English entrepreneur with a good idea for a lottery game. Take an Irishman with years of experience in the lottery business. Take a few cash-rich investors on board. Add them all together and you have the bones of a company with a projected turnover of £3 billion in five years. The Englishman, Anthony Fenwick, laboured for fourteen years to put the game together. It was essentially an electronic spot-the-ball competition where entrants were given a card with six football pictures on it. They had to mark where they thought the ball was within a grid of thirty-six smaller squares. It was the hope of the games backers that it would replace the football pools as Britain's biggest lottery earner. The Irishman was Frank Flannery, who took a three-year leave of absence from the Rehabilitation Institute in Ireland, where he ran a successful lottery game, to take up the position as managing director of the company.

Golden Grid, the company that launched Skilball in April 1990, forecast that it would recoup £340 million in revenue in its first year and rise to £800 million in three years. Skilball claimed that it would become British Telecom's second largest customer, representing one-sixth of British Telecom's new business. Charities were to 'get an £800 million windfall' and the Golden Grid Company spoke of becoming 'Britain's biggest lottery and the largest donor to charity in the world'.

Golden Grid did not lack financial backers. Spurred on by the hope of quick riches, the company, prior to launching the game, had secured £12 million from several, mainly Irish investors. Independent Newspapers paid out £3.2 million for a 20 per cent stake. Two large Irish investment companies, Allied Combined Trust and Irish Life Assurance Company, took 10 per cent and 5.6 per cent stakes in the company respectively. There were also some smaller Irish investors. In the end the company was oversubscribed by £3.5 million. Another £8 million was raised from Control Data Corporation, an

American computer group which installed the main computer for the game. It secured a ten-year contract to maintain and operate Skilball's complicated state-of-the-art technology. The company had years of experience of similar on-line lottery games in the USA.

Initially it was decided to concentrate the service in the Greater London area, central Scotland and the north-west. The launch was accompanied by an advertising campaign in which celebrities from the world of sport such as Jimmy Greaves and Ian St John played leading roles. A £1.5 million ten-week TV campaign backed by a £250,000 radio and a £60,000 press and poster campaign launched the lottery in the London region alone. Philip Robinson, Golden Grid's sales and marketing director, claimed that 'Golden Grid will do for scratch cards what Cadbury's did for confectionery.'

Almost immediately the investors' hopes were dashed. The game simply did not attract a large enough audience. Instead of millions, only thousands were playing. Worse still, the company had spent almost all of its initial £20 million cash injection. After only five weeks in operation the company was forced to return to its shareholders, who were asked to subscribe to a £2 million rights issue. One shareholder explained, 'We were left in little doubt that the whole venture would have been abandoned in a matter of weeks without the extra cash. I think all the investors had looked at this as a high risk enterprise but we were still very disappointed.' Ultimately, few of the Irish investors took up their full rights. Independent Newspapers only partly subscribed. It invested a further £290,000; a full rights subscription would have cost it £420,000. Irish Life decided to cut its losses and did not put up any more money. Control Data, which had already invested £8 million, agreed to lend Golden Grid a further £2 million. Coupled with the rights money received, this made a total new cash injection of £4 million.

The UK's lottery and gambling laws restricted a single prize to £12,500, where there is no skill involved. The allure of other national lotteries worldwide lies in a rolling jackpot which makes millionaires out of street cleaners, and builds magic into the brand. Skilball (as the name suggests) demanded a degree of dexterity, so the law permitted Golden Grid to give out as much money on a single prize as it wanted to. What was once a major selling point of the game now left Golden Grid in an expensive dilemma. If it abandoned the game without paying the promised jackpot, it would lose credibility with retailers and players for any future ventures. Instead, it had to wait for a jackpot winner. The newspaper that carried the names of the winners also told the public that Skilball was coming off the market. At that stage, total turnover had come to around £1 million, a far cry from the £340 million predicted by the company. Total losses for the five-month period were conservatively put at about £11 million.

Skilball had the allure of a big prize game, but it lacked distribution. There were some problems with the number of computer terminals. The game was launched with only 600 terminals in operation. It had been hoped to increase this to 8,000 by the end of the first year. By the time play was suspended the company had only 6,000 terminals in operation. Many British retailers, including the larger chains, felt it was not worth giving up valuable shop space to the Skilball computer for a mere 5 per cent commission. The disappointing number of terminals installed was a major blow to Golden Grid. In addition, it was rumoured that Skilball had met with some technical difficulties at the same time as the rights issue. Control Data, however, strongly refuted this claim.

Many commentators on the Skilball disaster suggested that the problems were not with technology but with people. The British public simply did not take to the game. The retailers realized this early on. One Chelsea newsagent reported that his takings slumped from £550 in the first week to £150 in the second. A similar trend was noted almost everywhere.

The small number of players turned out to be good news for some. One player, Nigel Needham from London, played the game for seven weeks and won a prize almost every time. On week seven he hit the jackpot, receiving a payout of £340,000. That particular week, three of the six winners reportedly came from one tiny suburb in London, Thames Ditton.

Regular players were, however, in the minority. Most people were just not interested. 'We thought when we launched it that the game would be simple and straightforward enough,' said one company executive. 'But we found unexpectedly that some people had problems with it.' It had been hoped that the advertising campaign would iron out these difficulties. However, executives now admit that it missed its intended audience. People still did not understand the game after the campaign. Another contributing factor to Skilball's failure was seen to be management's decision to introduce the on-line Skilball game before they introduced a scratch card instant game. The general trend in America and Ireland was to introduce a simple scratch card game first.

All in all, the Skilball fiasco left a hole in the pockets of investors, but failed to dampen their enthusiasm. Sadder but hopefully wiser, the Golden Grid Company is reportedly set to try again.

Carry out a complete SWOT analysis of Golden Grid plc. Should Golden Grid try again? Justify your answer.

Sources: *Marketing*, 25 October 1990: 2–3; *British Telecom World*, June 1990: 32, 33, 42; *Business and Finance*, 15 November 1990: 3–5, 14.

This case was prepared by Dympna M. Hughes, Department of Marketing, University College Dublin, as a basis for class discussion rather than to illustrate either the effective or ineffective handling of an administrative situation.

Case 6: British Airways

When Mike Batt, the North American Director for British Airways, was asked if BA was expecting to lose market share (40 per cent in 1991) on its North Atlantic routes, he replied: 'Lord King and Sir Colin Marshall [chairman and managing director of BA respectively] expect us to hold market share. But I think they understand we may lose some of our market. What we are really talking about here is holding as much as we can. Damage limitation.is the name of the game.'

North Atlantic route

Since the early 1980s, British Airways, ranked seventh in the world in 1992 (Table 1), has pursued the dream of becoming a truly 'global' airline. To achieve this, BA has invested heavily in North America since the late 1980s. In December 1992, BA completed a deal to invest $300 million in return for a 24.6 per cent share of USAir. This BA/USAir alliance was set to challenge American Airlines as the world's biggest airline. The alliance had the potential to link BA's European and Asian routes with USAir's domestic network in the USA. The lynch pin was BA's ability to maintain its dominant hold of the North Atlantic route.

In 1991, Pan Am and TWA agreed to sell landing rights, which they had held at Heathrow for decades, to the two strongest US carriers: American Airlines and United Airlines. At a stroke, the nature of the North Atlantic route changed. Instead of being played between two weak competitors and one very strong one, it was now being played between three of the strongest players in the world.

TABLE 1   World's top airlines, 1992

	No. of passengers (million)	Fleet size (no. of aircraft)
American	86.0	672
United	66.7	536
Delta	83.1	551
Aeroflot	62.6	437
Northwest	43.0	359
Continental	38.8	319
British Airways	25.4	229
USAir	54.7	445
Air France	32.7	220
Japan Airlines	24.0	103
Lufthansa	27.9	219
TWA	22.4	172

Source: *The Economist*, 12 June 1993.

American and United were the largest and second largest airlines in the world respectively. In order to develop as global airlines, both companies have had to develop a strong business over the Atlantic. Some industry analysts suggest that it may be worth losing money on the Atlantic to build the global brand. Both airlines deny this. 'I don't believe it is wise just to buy market share, even if you could afford to do it,' says United's vice-president David Coltman. The stakes were high. According to Mike Batt, it boiled down to a marketing battle: a war fought at 50,000 feet, over canapés and bottles of fine wine, with smiling staff and comfy headrests as the main weapons.

World airline industry

Despite years of air travel growth, airlines as a whole rarely produce healthy profits. According to the OECD, throughout the boom years of 1980s the combined operating profits of the world's airlines amounted to just 2.7 per cent of revenues, while in the first three years of the 1990s the combined losses of the world's airlines wiped out the entire previous decade of profits (Table 2).

Most industry experts argue that this was due to more than just recession. 'Essentially airlines have reduced prices beyond their break-even point,' one industry executive suggested. As the industry was deregulated, direct competition increased dramatically. In the early 1990s, the industry entered into a deep-rooted recession, causing a downturn in passenger numbers, particularly in the numbers of lucrative first-class and business travellers. With the industry suffering from overcapacity and the airlines struggling to fill seats, the competitors turned to price cutting. As a result of these trends, about a quarter of the entire capacity of the American airline industry (considered the most efficient in the world) was in bankruptcy protection (Chapter XI) by 1993.

Marketing strategies

'Our strength is the level of our service,' explains Mike Batt. By offering a superior-quality service, BA has appealed mainly to the high-yield business-class and first-class passengers. 'Quality service has been part of our culture for a long time now,' says Batt. 'It is something that is built into the way we operate, rather than something we are just trying to introduce on to the North Atlantic routes. And it is something that is very difficult to develop suddenly. Anyone will tell you that the standards just aren't the same in the US.'

TABLE 2   World airlines financial results ($bn)

	1986	1987	1988	1989	1990	1991	1992
Net profit/loss	−0.1	1.3	2.0	0.3	−3.0	−4.2	−5.0

Source: *The Economist*, 12 June 1993.

The US airlines have their own strategic strengths. One of their most successful ploys was the price-oriented, frequent-flyer programme, a sophisticated marketing device used for locking customers into an airline by rewarding regular flight with free travel. BA was forced to launch its 'Latitudes' scheme in 1992 as a direct response to this powerful tool. Most industry analysts agreed that European airlines have seldom competed on price; rather they have a highly developed culture of competing on quality. In the USA, where price wars between airlines have been long and vicious, airlines concentrated on keeping costs lean, and were worried less about quality. BA was betting heavy on its quality edge.

BA's competitors suggest that there may be a flaw in the emphasis BA places on quality. 'The truth is most passengers don't care about how cute the hostesses are, or the vintage of the wine,' says one executive. 'All they care about is how much it costs them.' In the USA, unlike Europe, the airlines compete largely on price. Both United Airlines and American had positioned themselves as price leaders. 'Some of the US airlines are just going into major corporate customers and saying, "Look, tell us what price we have to take to win this business, and we'll take it",' says one industry insider.

The North Atlantic is not the exclusive arena of BA, United and American. Delta, Virgin and Aeroflot had also taken advantage of the deregulation (Table 3). Virgin Atlantic had been a particular thorn in BA's side. By operating a 'no-frills' service on the North Atlantic route, Virgin had forced BA to respond with a reduction of over 5 per cent in its prices since 1991.

The challenge for BA

The Atlantic is BA's most valuable route network, accounting for £1.6 billion of the total turnover of £4 billion last year, and making profits of £158 million, out of a total of £167 million. More importantly, the dream of a truly global airline may depend on BA's ability to compete successfully in the North Atlantic route. David Coltman, vice-president for United Airlines in Europe, suggests that 'BA have established a market share out of all proportion to what they would normally expect, because of the historical weakness of the competition on the Atlantic routes.'

TABLE 3   Major North Atlantic competitors, 1991

Airline	Flights per week	Seats per week
British Airways	278	83000
American Airlines	168	35000
United Airlines	122	30000
Virgin Atlantic	84	30000

Source: *Management Today*, 1 November 1991.

Identify the marketing strategies of BA United Airlines, American Airlines and Virgin Atlantic. Should BA continue with its strategy?

Sources: *The Economist*, 12 June 1993; *Management Today*, 1 November 1991: 48–52.

This case was prepared by Derek Creevey, Department of Marketing, University College, Dublin, as a basis for class discussion rather than to illustrate either effective or ineffective handling of an administrative situation.

Case 7: Nintendo

'An excavator was working overtime in the Nevada desert in 1984. It was burying millions of unsold computer game cartridges, casualties of one of the most spectacular consumer fads of modern times.'

It was an obscure Japanese company, Nintendo, which had been making playing-cards for more than a hundred years, that was responsible for raising this deceased entertainment industry from the grave with the introduction of Nintendo Entertaining System in 1986. By 1993 Nintendo had added a staggering 10 per cent on to the much lamented US–Japan trade deficit. At around £1 billion a year, Nintendo's earnings were bigger than Microsoft's or IBM's, while in 1992 Nintendo earned twice as much as the electronics giant Sony, on a sixth of its sales and a tenth of the staff. Although Nintendo's performance on the stock market had been spectacular, however, it was eclipsed by Sega. Since the middle of 1989 Nintendo's shares had risen by more than 65 per cent, at a time when the Nikkei Dow had fallen by 40 per cent. But Sega's shares stood at more than 650 per cent higher.

Mario the Plumber vs Sonic the Hedgehog

The original game consoles were based upon 8-bit processing technology. The capabilities of these machines allowed the game hero to run forwards and backwards and jump around. The cult status of one such hero, Nintendo's 'Super Mario', the adventurous Brooklyn plumber, boosted Nintendo to the no. 1 spot with 90 per cent of the American and Japanese markets. According to Peter Skinner, marketing manager at Sega's software manufacture Hamleys, 'Somehow Sega's Sonic the Hedgehog has not caught on, but in many ways he is a more endearing character.' Skinner attributes the popularity of the Nintendo system to its established position on the market: the Nintendo system was introduced two years before Sega's. For some, price might also play a part. In early 1991 Nintendo's hand-held 'Game Boy' retailed at £79.99, compared to Sega's 'Game Gear' costing £109.99.

Though the original Nintendo system dominated the world after 1986, Sega Enterprises of Japan beat Nintendo in the race to introduce the first

16-bit television game machine. The Sega Megadrive, launched in America in 1989 and Europe in 1990, could provide more exciting graphics, better animation and a more impressive range of stunts. When Nintendo finally launched its 16-bit Super-Nintendo console some sixteen months later, sales were slower than expected. In fact, during 1991 for every one system Nintendo sold, Sega sold two.

The Sega Megadrive, priced at £20 cheaper, was well established on the market before Super-Nintendo. The Sega Megadrive also had the advantage, unlike Nintendo, of being able to play games designed for the original Sega (8-bit) machine. Sega games software (priced at £30–40), with over five times as many games available as Nintendo (priced at £45) had more 'street cred'. Hence, by 1991 the trials and tribulations of a bionic hedgehog had overtaken Super Mario Brothers in popularity.

World-wide, Nintendo was still the dominant player, primarily because of its first-mover advantage in Japan and the USA. However, with the Japanese and the US markets fast approaching saturation – penetration levels in households with children are 40 and 30 per cent respectively – Europe with its larger profit margins was the principal 'battleground'. The European market was considered to be three or four years behind the US and Japanese markets. Nintendo and Sega had been locked in price competition in the USA since October 1992, when the rivals cut the price of their video games systems to $99. Nintendo had been charging $199.99 and Sega $149.95.

Press button 'B' for more than two players

In 1992 both Atari and Commodore (Amiga AI200) introduced 32-bit 'home entertainment systems'. As well as offering faster and more powerful graphics (using a 32-bit processor), these machines are also capable of running other software such as educational packages. However, these systems are priced at £400, considerably more than the Nintendo or Sega games consoles, which cost about £150.

On 16 February 1993 Fujitsu, the world's second largest computer company after IBM, introduced CD technology with the launch of the 'multimedia video games machine' called 'Marty'. With 100 times the memory capacity of conventional game cartridges, the new CD-ROM (compact disc read-only memory) provided better-quality graphics and faster action. Meanwhile, other companies such as Philips and Tandy of the USA also launched their own CD-based multi-media machines.

Game plans

In the area of technology, Nintendo had lost its position as market leader. Sega was perceived as more technologically advanced. First on to the market with its 16-bit console, it was expected to introduce 'Mega CD' for the 1993

TABLE 1   Chronological order of product launches

Year	Technology	Market
1986	Nintendo Entertainment System (8-bit)	USA and Japan
1987	Nintendo Entertainment System (8-bit)	Europe
1988	Sega Entertainment System (8-bit)	Global
1989	Sega Megadrive (16-bit)	USA and Japan
1990	Sega Megadrive (16-bit)	Europe
1991	Super Nintendo (16-bit)	Global
1992	Atari and Commodore (32-bit)	Global
1993	Fujitsu, Philips and Tandy CD-ROM	Global
1993	Sega CD	Global
1994	Sega Satellite TV	Europe
1994	Nintendo CD	N/A

Source: Derived from various articles and reports.

Christmas season (Table 1), while Nintendo had scheduled the introduction of its CD-based system for 1995. This new technology, which allows users to interact with characters in Hollywood films, came about because of an alliance with Sony and Warner Brothers. 'Up to this point, video games have had animated characters. Sega CD allows players to control real actors. Its like being in movie theatre and controlling the actors on screen,' says Mr Doug Glen, Sega's group marketing director.

According to Mike Haynes, marketing director of Nintendo, 'We don't want a technology race. Future games are bound to be CD based, but it's vital to wait until it's commercially sound. Sega CD does not offer sufficient new features to justify the mooted £270 price tag.' Haynes defines his objectives for 1993 as maximization of Nintendo's cartridge-led business by serving the existing hardware with new game titles.

Philip Ley, marketing director of Sega Europe, explained that his advertising and positioning strategy was based on 'credibility' as opposed to Nintendo's 'product benefit' strategy. Ley explains, 'Our positioning is designed to make the brand part of the consumer's lifestyle – we are going for a depth of brand, like a Coke or a Levi's.' At Nintendo, on the other hand, Haynes says, 'We believe 100 per cent in product benefits.' He points out that, although Nintendo outspends Sega by almost two to one in advertising, it is very much profit benefit oriented and is less overtly 'creative' than Sega's advertising initiatives.

417

Level ten: for advanced players

It was expected that by early 1994 Europe would have its first 'interactive games television channel' with the introduction of the Sega Satellite channel. Philip Ley, Sega's European marketing director, explains: 'In this industry, a month can represent a year. You are continually under pressure to produce something new and it's up to marketing to keep the edge.'

> 1. **How do you think Nintendo's more passive technology strategy will affect its market share?**
>
> 2. **Since 1991 Nintendo has lost market share to Sega. What changes would you make to Nintendo's European marketing strategy, specifically its positioning, product, pricing and promotional activities?**

Sources: *The Independent*, 7 June 1993; *Marketing Week*, 19 February 1993; *Financial Times*, 17 October 1992, 20 December 1992, 17 February 1993; *The Times*, 8 January 1992, 9 January 1993; *Daily Telegraph*, 5 June 1992; *The Independent on Sunday*, 20 June 1993.

This case was prepared by Derek Creevey, Department of Marketing, University College Dublin, as a basis for class discussion rather than to illustrate either effective or ineffective handling of an administrative situation.

Case 8: Babycham

Babycham, the pear-based sparkling perry, was the first drink developed specifically for women and was introduced by Showerings in the 1950s. In 1992 Showerings, Vine Products and Whiteways became the Gaymer Group after a £140 million buyout. By 1993, after a two-year brand rethink, Babycham was finally growing up. The Gaymer Group's marketing director, Elaine Robinson, set up Project Sparkle to mastermind the Babycham relaunch. The relevant company executives were involved in the project together with the advertising agency, packaging designers and a number of specialist market research houses. Their intention was to produce a mass-market drink with a positioning relevant to women in the 1990s. In discussing their market research techniques, Elaine Robinson admitted that 'Every idea, every research finding, had to be tested against young and old consumers, loyal and lapsed drinkers.'

Babycham had been a brand with sales of close to £50 million a year. However, sales of the product had been in steady decline since the 1970s and it had been losing contact with the core under-35 age group. In the mid to late 1980s it was claimed that six million people drank Babycham regularly. By 1993, that figure was down to four million – and those who did drink it, did so less frequently.

The team's research identified a number of factors to be considered in the formulation of their marketing strategy:

- Almost three-quarters of all women (73 per cent) had consumed Babycham at some stage and most had fond memories of it. By 1993, four out of five people in this 73 per cent were 'lapsed' Babycham drinkers.
- Babycham labelling and advertisements had evolved over time, but the product and the positioning had stayed much the same, despite the fact that women's attitudes and roles had changed. Many saw Babycham as girlish and naïve.
- The 'deer' logo reinforced the young, naïve, girlie image.
- Consumers did not take a dislike to Babycham, but rather drifted away as they discovered other drinks.
- There was a widespread view that the product was too sweet. However, in blind tasting, it outperformed everything that was tested against it.
- A single product – 'classic' or 'original' Babycham – would not be enough to span the target market.
- Loyal Babycham drinkers welcomed the concept of product change.
- All the consumer groups believed that the Babycham 10cl bottle, unchanged since the 1950s, was too small. In an age when it was common to find women drinking beer, cider or lager, Babycham drinkers were often embarrassed to find themselves sitting with empty glasses while waiting for the rest of the company to finish their drinks.
- Consumers associated three things with the Babycham packaging: the small bottle (which they disliked), the deer (about which they had mixed feelings) and the blue colour.
- A myth, stemming from the small bottle size, was that Babycham was weak in alcohol. In fact, it was comparable with many beers.
- Ms Robinson had been pondering these research findings, trying to establish the way she wanted to reposition the 'new' Babycham. In her opinion, 'It is a relaunch in the fullest sense – not just a tarting up of the packaging.'

Considering the accumulated market research findings, how would you advise Elaine Robinson and her team in their efforts to relaunch the Babycham brand?

Source: 'Why that cute Babycham deer just had to die', *Marketing*, 24 June 1993.

This case was prepared by Jacqui McWilliams, Department of Marketing, University College Dublin, as a basis for class discussion rather than to illustrate either the effective or ineffective handling of an administrative situation.

Case 9: Philips

The faltering $28 billion Dutch electronics company, Philips, needed revital-
izing – quickly. It had suffered heavy losses in recent years, and consequently
cut its workforce by 20 per cent. After a loss of $2.36 billion in 1990, Philips
had profits of $668 million on sales of $31.7 billion in 1991, primarily due to
the cost-cutting operations.

The potential light at the end of the tunnel was Philips' innovations in
consumer electronics. Philips had pinned its hopes on such leading-edge technologies as the digital compact cassette (DCC), and the compact disc interactive
(CD-I). Philips' digital compact cassette was pitched against Sony's MiniDisc
(MD), in a high-risk strategy to find the replacement for the 'analogue' audio
cassette, and decide the future format for global audio systems (Table 1). This on-
going battle between the two electronic giants was a far cry from the co-operation
between Philips and Sony when they launched the compact disc (CD), and
tolled the deathknell for the vinyl LP. Both formats represented substantial
investments by the companies. Sony spent $100 million in MiniDisc develop-
ment and plant retooling, while Philips spent $55 million on its technology.

The two firms decided to go separate routes, each seeking the spoils of
producing the industry standard, where vast sales of speakers, receivers and
other audio components would fall to the victor. There were also potential
hardware sales of 180 million cassette players annually, as well as royalties
for each DCC or MD unit sold, in perpetuity. Both Sony and Philips benefited
from royalties from the sales of CDs. The clash was reminiscent of the battle
between Matsushita Electrical Industrial Co. and Sony, to establish VHS as *the*
video standard. The Sony Betamax VCR was subsequently vanquished in the
early 1980s.

David Pearson, managing director of Sony UK, claimed that its MiniDisc
was more than just an improvement on the CD; that it was a 'revolutionary
format'. The MD looked like a square floppy disc and had a number of features specific to it. It had digital recording and playback facilities, and offered
a maximum recording time of 74 uninterrupted minutes. The new minidisc
players did not skip when jarred as is the case with mobile CDs in Discmans
and car stereos. Sony also claimed that it had sound quality 'approaching that
of CD'. However, to ensure record industry backing, the sound quality distinction had to be made, or demand for the older system could disappear.

Sony targeted its new format at the mobile young 'Nintendo' generation.
From its experience with the Walkman, launched in defiance of expert opinion when cassette sales were falling, Sony believed that the ability to listen to
music on the move was a vital ingredient when it came to format
acceptability. Therefore, Sony only launched the new MiniDisc in portable
form, and had no immediate plans to introduce static decks for home use.
This strategy also ensured that the CD player remained at home. Therefore,

sales were stimulated without killing the demand for CDs and CD players. 'MiniDisc is a move that will rejuvenate the Walkman market,' explained Steve Dowdle, Sony's marketing director. The CD failed to make significant inroads in the 'mobile' target market because of its bulk and expense. It is ironic that Sony pushed the MiniDisc as a portable CD player, in effect, as a replacement for its own Walkman, which was still a big earner for the company.

There appeared to be just one stumbling block to Sony's youth-target approach – the price. The basic MiniDisc player, which cannot record, comes with a price tag in the region of £400. In addition, MiniDisc albums cost the same price as equivalent CDs. This pricing strategy was a deliberate ploy so as not to cannibalize the established CD market, but could have been a turn-off for the 'Nintendo' generation, who purchased 40 per cent of all music sold.

Sony had no immediate plans to advertise the MiniDisc, claiming that awareness was already quite high. Their most pressing priority was to

TABLE 1   Battle for your ear: how the two formats compare as of November 1992

Philips' DCC	MiniDisc
Philips' DCC 900 player (£500) on the market now. Portable, midi and in-car versions due 'in the spring'	Playback only MZ-2P (£400), record and playback MZ-1 (£500), MDX-U1 in-car player (£850) on sale end Dec.
Digital recording and playback with CD sound	Digital recording and playback with 'near CD quality' sound
Maximum recording time 2 × 45 minutes on C90 tape	Maximum recording time – uninterrupted 74 minutes
Text mode displays album, artist and track title	Text mode displays album, artist and track title
Tape decks can play existing audio cassettes	Players work only with MiniDisc
Tape format means players can be jogged without affecting sound	Memory buffer gives a ten-second back-up if laser is knocked off-track
Direct track access – but winding can take up to 30 seconds	Direct track access within 3 seconds
Other DCC players due shortly from Panasonic, Technics and Marantz	Sharp and Sanyo have recently 'shown' products at trade shows
Philips owns Polygram	Sony bought CBS
Artists exclusive to DCC include U2, Dire Straits, Van Morrison, Luciano Pavarotti	Artists exclusive to MiniDisc include Michael Jackson, Bruce Springsteen, Michael Bolton
TV and press advertising running now; Dire Straits lined up for world promotional tour	No ads this year – but an 'intense' PR campaign

Source: *Marketing*, 26 November 1992: 22–3.

'educate' in-store sales people. 'What we're going to do is make sure the guy on the shop floor knows the benefits of MiniDisc, and can convey that to the consumer.' Press advertisements were scheduled to follow in 1993.

Philips' DCC had similar advantages to the MiniDisc, in that it offered CD-quality sound, and also had digital recording and playback. As it was in tape format, the tape could be jogged without affecting sound. The maximum recording time was 2 × 45 minutes on a C90 tape. Although there was direct track access, winding of the tape could take up to 30 seconds. However, a major advantage was that old-style 'analogue' cassettes could be played on the new format players. Philips' group marketing director, Ray Harris, believed that this 'backward compatibility' was vital, and that anything else was tantamount to 'throwing out the baby with the bath water'. 'Sony says that CD took off even though you couldn't play your old records on it,' said Harris. 'But I remember in the early days there was a hell of a lot of resistance from consumers worried about their vinyl collections becoming obsolete.'

Philips' positioning was clear. The DCC was a replacement for traditional cassette recorders, but was also able to play old cassettes. This function was particularly important in the light of Philips' research, which showed that the average western household owned 50 to 60 audio cassette tapes, as well as three cassette players or recorders (including in-car systems). Philips had also set clear pricing policies: the company aimed to bring hardware prices down to mass-market levels as soon as possible, to the point of engaging in 'normative pricing'. 'In the end, whatever the technology, it had to be affordable to the consumer – otherwise we're all kidding ourselves,' asserted Harris.

It was too early to tell what direction pricing and positioning strategies would take. Certainly, these could be determining factors for future technology. Robert Heiblum, president of Denon America Inc., which made players for both companies, claimed that 'the war will be won over marketing'. Gary Thorne, president of a retail chain in Minneapolis, added, 'Whichever brings more brands and more product variations to market, the better the chances of success.' Both companies realized the crucial importance of the availability of pre-recorded albums in either format, to ensure product acceptability. It was here that Sony appeared not to fare so well. Polygram Inc., 80 per cent owned by Philips and five other major music companies, had pledged to launch 500 titles for DCC in 1992 alone. On the other hand, besides Sony Music Entertainment, the MiniDisc had received backing from just one other music company, Thorn EMI plc.

There was a considerable danger that consumers, bewildered and bombarded with the proliferation of new products, formats and technology, continually being offered by the electronic companies, would not have the confidence to purchase what may become obsolete in a few years' time. Retailers were carrying both, to let the consumer decide. Neither Sony nor Philips was taking any chances, as both had licensed the other's technology. This battle was just one that could secure Philips' future. The old adage, 'there's nothing like the sight of a noose to focus the mind', seemed particularly pertinent.

Who is likely to win the technological and marketing battle of the new audio format, and why? What are the key marketing arguments in favour of each format?

Sources: *Business Week*, 27 May 1991: 36–7; 5 August 1991: 14–19, 15 June 1992: 40; *International Management*, September 1992: 26; *Marketing*, 19 November 1992: 3; 26 November 1992: 22–3.

This case was prepared by Nora Costello, Department of Marketing, University College Dublin, as a basis for class discussion rather than to illustrate either effective or ineffective handling of an administrative situation.

PART C

Provide the value for customers

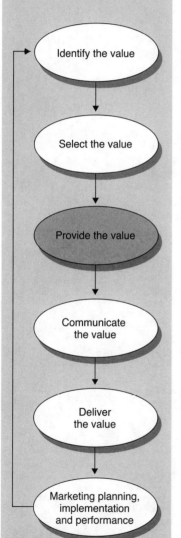

- design products and services
- process and procurement decisions
- manufacture and source
- manage branding
- price

Chapters

Product and service marketing decisions

10

Meaning of products to consumers
Nature of product marketing
Product design and quality
Managing products through the life cycle
Managing the product portfolio
Product and service company fit
Managing services in marketing

Introduction

This chapter introduces and explains:

- the product concept in marketing;
- ways of classifying products;
- core products and benefits;
- the role of product design;
- packaging the product;
- product warranties and guarantees;
- costs in the product life cycle;
- the ideal product life cycle;
- product class, product form and brand life cycles;
- innovation and product life cycles;
- market entry barriers and the product life cycle;
- the company as a multiproduct organization;

- product mix decisions; and

- positioning products and services.

An understanding of the role of products is fundamental to an understanding of marketing. Of central importance is the hierarchy of dimensions associated with the product concept. At the most fundamental level, there is the core product with the associated benefits. Near the top of the hierarchy is the augmented product and all the additional services, extras and differentiating factors that go with it. The idea of the potential product leads to a discussion of product life cycles and new products. A detailed examination of the managerial implications of the product life cycle and all of its stages shows how the company can develop and adapt its products to meet consumer needs and competitive challenges at each stage. The need to manage the company's portfolio of products in the context of an overall growth strategy for the company is examined. Ideas on product development and innovation are introduced, and product and service positioning is discussed.

Having studied this chapter, you should be able to define the phrases listed above in your own words, and you should be able to do the following:

1. Describe the four dimensions of the product.

2. State how you would evaluate product benefits.

3. Classify products in managerially useful ways.

4. Specify the functions of packaging, warranties and guarantees.

5. Outline the influences on the product or service for each stage of its life cycle.

6. Recognize the role of innovation in renewing life cycles.

7. Evaluate various approaches to managing a portfolio of services.

8. Understand the meaning of positioning and the reasons for repositioning.

9. Outline approaches to managing services.

Meaning of products to consumers

The product is central to marketing, and product management decisions are fundamental to the performance of the company. It is necessary, therefore, to understand the role of the product in the activities of the firm, the value of products to buyers, and the competitive responses made by other firms in the industry. Companies must first understand the nature and significance of products in marketing, and place special emphasis on the meaning of the product and its various dimensions and associated benefits. It may also be necessary to classify products and services with a view to integrating the products to services continuum. The company must also consider the various dimensions of the product, showing a progression from the core product, to the augmented product, to the potential product. Managing the company's product portfolio, including the product-market fit and dimensions of the product mix, are fundamental marketing management tasks.

Product and services concepts in marketing

A product has been defined as 'the need satisfying offering of a firm' (McCarthy and Perreault, 1990: 218), or anything than can be offered to someone to satisfy a need or want, or 'everything, both favourable and unfavourable, that one receives in an exchange' (Dibb *et al.*, 1991: 208). More formally, 'a product is anything that can be offered to a market for attention, acquisition, use or consumption, that might satisfy a want or need' (Kotler, 1994: 432). A product has also been defined as a set of tangible and intangible attributes, including packaging, colour, price, quality, brand, and the services and reputation of the seller. A product may be a tangible good, service, place, person or idea (Stanton *et al.*, 1991: 168–9). A product is, therefore, anything that satisfies the customer, and increasingly it is something which has embodied in it a high level of service. The consumption of products and services is the way in which users attempt to satisfy needs.

Dimensions of the product

There are four major aspects or dimensions associated with a product. First, the physical or core product consists of the physical appearance and quality as perceived by the customer and/or user. This refers to the product's functional utility. Second, the product is also presented to the customer in some way which involves packaging and promotion. Product packaging refers to the way the product is protected and promoted as it moves through the channels of distribution to the customer. It also includes any instructions provided, technical advice and warranties. In addition, the packaging of a product may be more broadly defined to include the brand name, delivery and installation arrangements, and after-sales service.

The third aspect of the product is the way a firm communicates the benefits associated with using the product to its customers. Product communications refer to the way the benefits of the product are explained and promoted to customers. Product communications also refer to the emphasis which may be placed on the psychological attributes of the product. Fourth, concern rests with the image of the product in the market. The manufacturer is concerned about the image that market intermediaries and final users have of the product. Producers tend to be judged against a set of criteria including customer needs. In some sense, there should be agreement between the manufacturer's image and the user's image of the product. Customer needs tend to vary from time to time, and circumstances may determine the exact form that the product should take. Eastman Kodak Co. responded to the element of convenience, not available with regular cameras, when it launched its disposable camera (Exhibit 10.1).

Product benefits and satisfaction

It is acknowledged that, underlying these aspects of the product, customers seek to buy benefits and satisfaction. In buying food, the customer seeks sustenance and taste; in buying a car, the customer seeks safety, style and transport;

EXHIBIT 10.1   The hottest thing since the flashbulb

The guests at Diane and L.J. Palazesi's wedding in Boston earlier this year found a surprise on each table: a disposable camera. Afraid the professional photographer would miss those spontaneous moments that define a wedding, the bride and groom bought a dozen of the $11 cameras and invited guests to take candid snaps. Several hours and hundreds of flashes later, guests simply dumped the cameras in a bag to be shipped off to the developer. 'We got a lot of really fun pictures,' says Diane. 'It was a great idea.'

Fun. Cheap. Easy to use. That potent combination has turned the disposable camera – basically a roll of film with a cheap plastic case and lens – into the hottest thing in photography. Sales in the US zoomed 50 per cent last year, with no sign of levelling off. Projected sales for 1992 are 22 million units in the US, or about $200 million at retail.

To make sure the enthusiasm doesn't wane, Eastman Kodak Co., with about 65 per cent of the US market for disposables, and Fuji Photo Film USA Inc., with about 25 per cent, are rolling out niche products for everything from underwater photography, to close-ups of baby. When Fuji pioneered disposable cameras in Japan in 1986, few in the film business expected them to click. After all, most people already had cameras. And disposables were slow to catch on in the US, where they were introduced by Kodak in late 1987.

But as the public grew more familiar with the product, the disposable started to sell itself by filling needs that regular cameras can't. One giant need: being there when your fancy Minolta or Canon isn't. Peter M. Palermo, general manager of Kodak's consumer imaging division, figures about half of purchases are made by people who left their regular cameras at home. Buying a new camera would be extravagant; an $8 to $12 disposable is cheap by comparison, even with the added cost of processing. 'Don't think of it as a camera, think of it as convenient film,' says John J. Ruf, a partner at New England Consulting Group in Westport, Conn.

Source: *Business Week*, 7 September, 1992: 60.

---

in buying furniture, the customer buys comfort and durability; in buying the services of a medical specialist, the customer relates to an accumulated reputation and an ability to solve medical problems. Because products and services are perceived by customers as bundles of benefits, the emphasis in marketing should be on these benefits. Customers buy benefits to satisfy their needs and wants. The product is, therefore, fundamental to the company's existence and its marketing strategy. While the four elements which constitute the product concept are more obvious in consumer product markets, they also have a central role to play in industrial product and service markets. The concept of a product has deliberately been defined to include consumer products, industrial products and services.

Several managerial and product policy implications arise from examining products in this way. It is necessary to have information on all four areas before a policy can be formed. Any contemplated innovation or design change to a product or the product mix should only follow a comprehensive examination of its impact on the other aspects of the product. Desirable innovation in one area may have undesirable side-effects elsewhere. A less expensive packaging material may reduce the product's ability to withstand contamination or damage from other products in storage or transit. Less expensive packaging may also interfere with the customer's perceived image of product quality.

Products, services and benefits

The products that people buy are mostly physical goods like furniture, beer, cars, newspapers and textbooks. Things like medical care, education, shoe repair, the theatre and hotel accommodation are services which are produced by somebody and are also classified as products. In the same sense, some people are products: sports stars, singers and national and international politicians. In one sense or another, we purchase what they package and sell, whether it is athletic prowess, rock music or a particular political policy or idea. Similarly, places can be products. A place like Atlanta can be promoted as a holiday centre, as the place to see the 1996 Olympic Games, or as a base for industrial investment. An organization can also be marketed and must, therefore, be considered as a product. Many people feel positive towards the Red Cross, the Red Crescent, the Worldwide Fund for Nature and Amnesty International, and support them financially. Products consist, therefore, of a wide range of physical things, services, people and organizations which can be packaged in some way and marketed to a significant group of customers.

Frequently in the literature, the concepts of products, goods and services are confused, which leads to considerable misunderstandings. Much of the difficulty arises from the mistaken view that products are tangible physical goods only. Using tangibility as the dominant distinguishing feature between products and services, Shostack (1977) has shown that a continuum represents the situation better than a dichotomous relationship. For Shostack, salt is at the

431

tangible end of the continuum, whereas teaching is at the intangible end, and products and services like cosmetics, fast food and advertising agencies are somewhere in the centre of this continuum (Figure 10.1). This led Shostack (1977) to place different products on a tangible–intangible spectrum, ranging from goods and services on one side to intangible services on the other side, which emphasizes the different demands on marketing. Tangibility in the product is, therefore, a factor which helps in understanding some of the problems of marketing. The key point to note is that the emphasis changes on moving along the continuum, but not the fundamental principle of the relevance of marketing in all its dimensions.

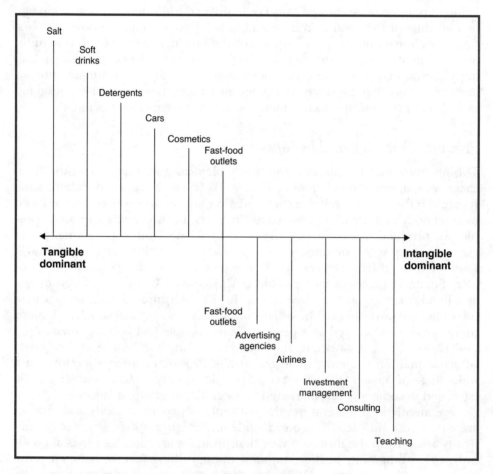

Figure 10.1 Product tangibility: goods, services and ideas
(Source: Shostack, 1977: 77. With permission of the American Marketing Association)

Approaches to classifying products

Products may be classified in different ways to assist companies in developing cohesive marketing strategies. Classifying products by degree of durability, tangibility and type of user are the three most common approaches found in practice.

Durability of products

Using the durability criterion, products may be classified as durable, non-durable or services. Durable products are tangible, survive many uses and are relatively expensive; they usually require more personal selling; and consumers take longer to decide to purchase durable products, have greater concerns regarding their suitability and so require greater after-sales service than other types of product. Durable products command higher margins and require manufacturer guarantees. Examples of durable products are washing machines, pneumatic drills, cameras, cars, photocopiers and computers.

Non-durable products are also tangible, but are normally consumed in one or a few uses. They are purchased frequently, cost relatively little and are consumed relatively fast. Generally, non-durable products must be widely distributed and heavily advertised to remind customers of their existence. They tend to carry a small margin and require awareness and reinforcement advertising to prevent consumers shifting to alternatives. Examples of non-durable products are washing-up liquid, dairy products, bread, petrol, engine oil and building materials.

Products as services refer to activities, benefits or satisfaction offered for sale. Services are intangible products which are inseparable from the provider and perishable. Services require high levels of quality control, supplier credibility and flexibility. A major challenge to marketing is to make the benefits of purchasing the service somehow real to consumers. People who provide the service are usually fundamental to its success, since consumers often judge the service by the providers. That is why front-line people are so important in service marketing. Examples of services are shoe repair, hairdressing, theatre, restaurants, public transport, three-phase electricity for industrial use, freight services, telecommunications, financial services and marketing research services.

Goods and services as products

From the previous discussion, it should be clear that any product purchased may be a good, a service or a mixture of the two. A product is a solution to a problem or the satisfaction of a need. A good is a physical thing which is tangible and can be touched, seen and owned, whereas a service is an intangible deed performed by one person for another. It may be difficult to know exactly what is provided when a service is purchased, but this should be a relatively easy matter to determine in the case of a good. In most cases, however, products purchased are a combination of goods and services, having tangible and intangible elements.

Four major characteristics distinguish the marketing of products which are predominantly services from those which are predominantly goods. Services are:

- intangible;
- perishable;
- less standardized; and
- simultaneously involve producers and buyers in the exchange.

Services are characterized as intangible: they cannot be seen, held, touched, smelt or felt before purchase. As a result, the company providing the service emphasizes the benefits to be derived from the service, rather than the service itself. This may be done by visualizing the benefits in promotional material and by documentary evidence outlining favourable facts to support claims made.

Services are perishable and cannot be stored. Empty seats on a plane, unused telephone time and idle waiters in a restaurant all represent lost business. As a result, services are usually sold first and then produced and consumed at the same time. The combination of service perishability and a fluctuating demand presents difficulties in planning, pricing and promoting the service. Differential pricing may be used to shift some of the demand from peak to off-peak periods, and clever reservation systems are increasingly being used to manage fluctuating demand for hotels, airlines and other services.

The third characteristic of services marketing refers to the variability or lack of standardization which exists. Standardization is not always possible, since services depend on who provides them and the circumstances in which they are provided. For example, an airline does not give the same quality of service on each trip. Many factors intervene which affect the quality of the service provided. Companies invest in staff selection and training to ensure that customer satisfaction levels are acceptable.

The fourth characteristic which distinguishes services from goods refers to inseparability, or the simultaneous participation by buyer and seller in the production and sale of the service. The interaction of buyer and seller in the production and consumption of many services is very high. For example, doctors produce and dispense almost all of their services at the same time, and they require the presence of the patient for the services to be performed. Inseparability usually means that direct sale is the only possible distribution channel and is, therefore, a limit to the extent of the market for such services.

Users of products

The third major way of classifying products is to refer to the user. Consumer products are those purchased by the ultimate consumer or on behalf of the final consumer, whereas industrial products are those used in the production of other products. In many cases, the distinction is clear and serves its purpose: J & B Rare Whisky and Christian Dior accessories are clearly consumer products, whereas sheet stcel and three-phase electricity are clearly industrial products.

Some products may serve both the consumer and industrial markets. Cars may be sold to consumers as final products or to industrial firms as part of a fleet. Each warrants a separate marketing approach. If the car were viewed as a consumer product, greater emphasis would be placed on trade-in allowances, personal financial packages and after-sales service. If it were viewed as an industrial product, discounts, leasing arrangements and replacement policies would be more important. By focusing on the user, the company is in a better position to develop suitable marketing strategies.

Nature of product marketing

Associated with every product or service is a core benefit. In addition, however, there are other benefits that the buyer expects. The product can be augmented in various ways. Furthermore, products can be differentiated to suit the needs of particular groups of customers. Related matters include product design, packaging and guarantees or warranties.

Core products and benefits

An alternative way of looking at products is to examine the various dimensions of marketing associated with the product (Figure 10.2). Fundamental to every product is a core benefit which is the basic service or benefit that the customer seeks. This involves the physical appearance of the product, its quality and its ability to satisfy user needs, including functional utility. Another way of treating the core product is to recognize that people have basic needs to be satisfied or problems to be solved. The core product is used by customers to solve problems and satisfy these needs. In the case of rock music, it may be entertainment, camaraderie, or social protest. In the case of a restaurant, it may be a wholesome tasty meal. In the case of a car, it may be transport to work, weekly shopping trips or enjoyment.

Concept of a generic product

Having identified the core benefit, the task facing the company is to convert the core benefit into a generic or basic version of the product which will eventually be sold. Thus, a car consists of a box-like body, made of steel, plastic and

435

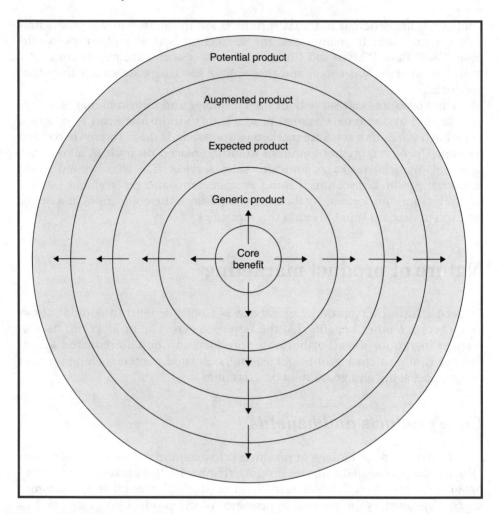

Figure 10.2 Dimensions of the product

glass, which has an engine and four wheels. Associated with the concept of generic product are benefits to be obtained from its use; product features are not stressed. Generic product concepts evolve with time. The generic product concept 'computer' has evolved from being a large machine with complicated software, which dominated a specially equipped room, to a small desk-top unit or even a hand-held unit completely under the control of the user. Generic products are also easy to recognize. The names by which they are known immediately convey a sense of recognition for most people: a racehorse, a bicycle, a cup, a hair cut, a rock concert, a parliamentary speech.

Water is a generic product which some companies are trying to change by bottling 'mineral water' and 'spring water'. Many companies have successfully branded spring water which may be no different from tap water. There is considerable uncertainty surrounding the benefits people seek when they buy bottled water: are they buying natural mineral water or spring water? According to some people, the demand for bottled water is sustained by imagined tastes and fear of ordinary tap water (Exhibit 10.2).

The third dimension refers to the expected product, or the set of attributes that customers normally expect when they purchase a product. Car buyers, for example, expect that the vehicle they purchase will travel at certain speeds, carry a certain number of passengers and their baggage safely, cost so much to run and maintain, and not corrode or rust.

EXHIBIT 10.2　Bottled water – eauverdose?

A decade ago selling bottled water to the British seemed as sensible as selling snow to Eskimos. Yet in the 10 years from 1982, demand surged by over 1,000 per cent. Last year, the British drank 520 million litres of bottled water, eight per cent up on the previous year. In restaurants, fashionable clients have switched from wine to water; even McDonald's is selling water to accompany its burgers.

There are two main types of bottle water: natural mineral water (the premium product) and spring water. Starting up as a bottler of natural mineral water is a tortuous process, requiring several years of tests and approval by a host of authorities. The water must be bottled at source without being tampered with. Rules on spring water are much looser – which can encourage cowboy bottlers. Spring water can be subjected to a host of treatments after extraction from the ground. Yet bottle labels for spring water often brim with pictures of fountains and mountains. In fact, though regulations on mineral water are more demanding, spring water can be sold for as much. Research shows that consumers – more fool they – are more attracted by the word 'spring' than 'mineral'.

The British consumer still has a long way to go to catch up with most other Europeans. The French, Belgians and Italians down ten times as much. The traditional reason for drinking bottled water is the poorer quality of tap water. But tap water is subject to more rigorous treatments than bottled water. A survey by the Consumers' Association suggested that still bottled water contains much higher numbers of bacteria than tap water, and that most natural mineral waters are low in mineral content.

So what advantage is left to bottled water, save crafty marketing and (in some cases) bubbles? Taste, say the connoisseurs. Drinkers often complain they detect a chemical tang in tap water. But even people in the industry suspect that demand for bottled water is sustained by imagined tastes and unmerited fears about contamination. 'As far as I'm concerned,' concedes one bottler of natural mineral water, 'there's nothing wrong with tap water.'

Source: *The Economist*, 14 August 1993: 35.

Differentiated products

By adding additional services and benefits, the company turns the expected product into an augmented product, which is the fourth product dimension to be considered. It is these additional benefits and services which help to distinguish the company's product from those of competitors. The Japanese car manufacturer, Toyota, augments its products by providing, in the Corolla, power steering, a four-speaker stereo radio cassette player with quick-release anti-theft mechanism, remote control mirrors and headlamp levellers as standard features. Image is also an important feature of car marketing, and country of origin may be a differentiating factor and a key determinant in making a purchase (Exhibit 10.3).

In competitive markets, companies seek as many opportunities as possible for augmenting their products. Added benefits through product augmentations become the fundamental basis for branding, which is discussed in Chapter 12. With more competition, however, augmented product benefits soon become expected product benefits.

At the same time, in certain economic conditions two major segments

---

EXHIBIT 10.3   Advantage, Mitsubishi!

The Plymouth Laser and the Mitsubishi Eclipse are identical sports coupés built by Diamondstar Motors, a 50–50 partnership between Chrysler and Mitsubishi. (The same vehicle is sold as an Eagle Talon by Jeep/ Eagle dealers.) Whatever the nameplate, the zippy car sells for $11,000 for a basic model, around $17,500 for a souped-up version. Last year Chrysler's 3,000 dealers sold 40,000 Lasers while Mitsubishi's 500 dealers sold 50,000 Eclipses. That astounding difference – 100 cars per Mitsubishi dealer, 13 per Chrysler dealer – says a lot about the image problem facing American cars these days. Jeep dealers did only slightly better than Chrysler dealers, selling 28,000 Talons, or about 18 per dealer.

A recent survey by *Popular Mechanics* found many US car buyers say they'd rather buy American than Japanese if the cars were similar. Here's a case where the Japanese and American are more than similar; they're identical. Yet the Japanese nameplate outsells the American. Why? Part of the problem is image. 'People perceive the Japanese car to be better quality. It's a lot easier to sell an Eclipse than a Laser,' says Ira Rosenberg, who should know. He owns adjoining Plymouth and Mitsubishi dealerships in Crystal Lake, Ill.

In his television commercials, Chrysler Chairman Lee Iacocca blames his competitive problems on Japan's overblown image for quality. 'Our cars are very bit as good as the Japanese,' he insists – and with substantial evidence to back his claim. But to the extent the problem is image, not quality, Chrysler has some work to do.

Source: *Forbes*, 18 March 1991: 100 and 104.

---

appear: one that competes on the basis of augmented products, and the other which competes on the basis of the expected product. In a recession, witness the growth of economy supermarkets paralleling the growth of premium price and service food outlets. Similarly, car manufacturers produce augmented products for the premium or luxury end of the market, while also producing economy models for the expected product market. These product markets may exist side by side within the same country or region.

The fifth dimension of the product refers to all possible future innovations in the product. The potential product refers to the evolutionary process through which the product may go. As companies search for new ways of satisfying customer needs, potential new products are identified which help to distinguish the company's products. The car of the future might include a range of benefits which amount to a sophisticated mobile office, as telephone, facsimile and on-board interactive computers are added. The recent introduction of digital CD musical equipment, which allows the owners effectively to write their own music from the myriad compositions available, is another example of a potential product (Exhibit 10.4).

Role of product design

Design is a broad-based discipline concerned with control, order and communications which are not purely visual. Design is also concerned with technology, language, symbols, values and beliefs (Lowe and Hunter, 1991: 1151). Based on this view of design, product perceptions, preferences and attribute trade-offs are central to the design process in marketing. It is important that all three are considered simultaneously. There is little point in establishing trade-offs among product attributes if those attributes are not important to the customer. Similarly, understanding product and service perceptions while ignoring preferences is also myopic.

Product design means searching for a set of key features or appeals that are special or even unique to the product or customer group. By agreeing on the basic benefits, the company is in a better position to serve customer needs. Product design is considered as 'the designation of the key benefits the product is to provide, the psychological positioning of these benefits versus competitive products, and the fulfilment of the product promises by physical features' (Urban and Hauser, 1980: 155). These key benefits form the foundation on which all elements of the marketing strategy are built. It is possible to apply these design principles to all kinds of products, including ordinary everyday kitchen utensils.

Alessi SpA, the family-owned kitchen utensils company located in the Italian Alpine village of Crusinallo, north of Milan, has turned metal bashing into a designer business (*Forbes*, 24 December 1990: 46). This company has gained an international reputation as one of the finest design teams in the

---

EXHIBIT 10.4   Redefining the recorded music business

Today's record companies will have to learn how to do something more sophisticated than making and distributing physical objects. They will increasingly need to market and sell information in the form of music, which is not quite the same thing. Today's passive audiences will be able to take more of the music business into their own hands, and there are increasing signs that they want to do so. They will be able to make recordings at home (from digital radio and other things) which are indistinguishable from what they can buy in shops today; or they will have customised recordings made for them in the descendants of today's record shops. They are already straining to do more with the music than just play back someone else's performance exactly as it was recorded in a studio.

The record companies will thus become more like the music publishers of old, making their money from facilitating and licensing the recording the performance of music. The phenomenon that will eventually force this role on them is digitalisation. Digitalisation implies three main things. First, that music can be faithfully recorded on a durable medium. That part has already happened, and saved the music business without changing it much. Second, that such recordings can be compressed and distributed in new ways. That is just beginning in America. Third, it implies that computers can speak the language of music.

This third consequence is already starting to transform the composition and production of popular music; some of today's hit records are made by one person with a bedroom-full of computer equipment. It will ultimately affect the way music is consumed as well. It is a fair bet that more popular music will come packaged as part of videogames, to take the simplest example.

Source: 'The music business', a supplement in *The Economist*, 21 December 1991: 4.

---

world. The company confirms the view that many modern consumers define themselves through images conferred by the brands they buy, rather than by other variables such as age, culture and social circumstances used in segmentation studies. Alessi managed to extend brand preference to kitchen utensils for people who wish to flaunt their refined tastes. The secret of Alessi's success is that it is not just producing function that counts, but also what the product adds to the customer's self-image. According to Alberto Alessi, 'companies in Italy came the furthest and fastest in understanding that design is a business and not just a part of product marketing' (*Forbes*, 24 December 1990: 46).

Miniaturization is a product feature which the Japanese have dominated for years. Now this concept is being applied to personal computers with great effect. Computer companies have recently battled with each other to introduce a notebook computer. Sub-notebooks, which are about one-third smaller than the average notebook model and weigh about two kilograms, have also

TABLE 10.1   Ways of designing a PC

Features	Hewlett-Packard Omnibook 300	IBM Thinkpad 500
Weight	1.3 kilograms	1.7 kilograms
Chip	386SXL	486SLC2
Hard disk	20 to 40 megabytes	85 to 170 megabytes
Screen	23-CM reflective	18.8-CM backlit
Keyboard	27.3 × 10.8 cm	22.9 × 9.5 cm
Battery life	3–9 hours	4–6 hours
	(AA batteries)	(rechargeable batteries)
Price	$1,950–$2,395	$1,999–$2,499

Source: *Business Week*, 26 July 1993: 52.

entered the market. There is a trade-off in reducing size, however. In these tiny computers, the size of the keyboard, the quality of the screen and the efficiency of the microprocessing chip are not as good as those found in larger models. The ways of designing a notebook PC give Hewlett-Packard and IBM advantages in different areas (Table 10.1). In addition to the more obvious differences, the sub-notebook from IBM has an easy-to-read backlit screen, its keyboard is 10 per cent smaller than a full-size keyboard and the screen is small (*Business Week*, 26 July 1993: 52). Hewlett-Packard Company's Omnibook 300 has a larger screen, but it is not lit, which makes it difficult to read in poor lighting conditions. It has a full-size keyboard, however, and can function for up to nine hours on four AA batteries.

The design features which have allowed computer manufacturers to squeeze more product features into less space include better technology, better power management features to extend the battery life, and energy-saving devices.

Product design and quality

The issue of quality as a competitive element in the company's strategy was examined in Chapter 8. Quality is what the customer thinks it is, and design contributes to it. It is necessary, however, to be precise in the meaning of quality and design, and how they should be implemented. In this regard, it is necessary to translate technical proficiency into product and service attributes desired by the customer. Quality must relate and contribute to customer satisfaction. At the same time, the company must also benefit from providing quality products and services. This means decomposing customer demand into its elements and relating those elements to the functions performed by the product objectively and compared to the competition. This evaluation allows the company to judge how well the customer is satisfied.

Many Japanese companies realized that, while they could manufacture reliable products, they were weaker in getting product designs right the first time.

Furthermore, many companies also realized that they did not take customer needs and preferences into account, and hence relied very little on market research. New products that fall short of customer requirements have to be redesigned. Quality function management, originated by Yoji Akao of the University of Tanagawa and his colleague, Shigeen Miguno, demonstrated how design considerations could be deployed to every element of competition in such a way that the need to redesign faulty products was eliminated (*Business Week*, 2 December 1991: 27).

An example of a hypothetical pencil company Writesharp illustrates the procedure referred to above (*Business Week*, 2 December 1991: 28–9). Assume that Writesharp has two major competitors, X and Y. The company recognizes that the attributes desired in a pencil by customers are 'easy to hold'; 'does not smear'; 'the point lasts'; and 'the pencil does not roll in the user's hand' (Figure 10.3). Company research has shown that customers attach different weights to each of these attributes. Writesharp's research has also shown certain correlations between these customer demands and physical characteristics that a pencil might possess: pencil length; time between sharpening; lead dust; and hexagonality. For example, there is a strong correlation between lead dust, measured as particles for each line of text written, and smearing. There is a possible correlation between pencil length and rolling.

In terms of satisfaction levels, Writesharp is perceived to be better than competitors on 'easy to hold', so the company's target is to maintain that standard. Competitor Y and Writesharp deliver the same high level of satisfaction in regard to smearing, so there is no scope for improvement here. Competitor X provides greater satisfaction levels in regard to 'point last', so Writesharp expects to improve this attribute. Writesharp has no competitive advantage on 'rolling', so it will attempt to improve satisfaction levels relative to competitors.

At present, Writesharp's price is 15 cents, its market share is 16 per cent and the profit on each pencil is two cents. With the improvements it expects price to be 16 cents, share to be 20 per cent and profit to double.

The company expects to achieve this level of performance by improving the quality of its product. The company has prepared a set of benchmarks to use in its evaluation. Writesharp's aim is to improve significantly on its own performance on each functional characteristic, to exceed its two competitors on three of them and to match competitor X on hexagonality.

If Writesharp's analysis is correct, if it meets the benchmarks set and if customer satisfaction materializes as expected, company performance in terms of price, share and profit should improve as a result of the improved quality.

Quality and design can be built into all kinds of products and services. The above example illustrates the need to be precise in the meaning of quality, and to translate elements of quality and design as perceived important by customers into physical reality.

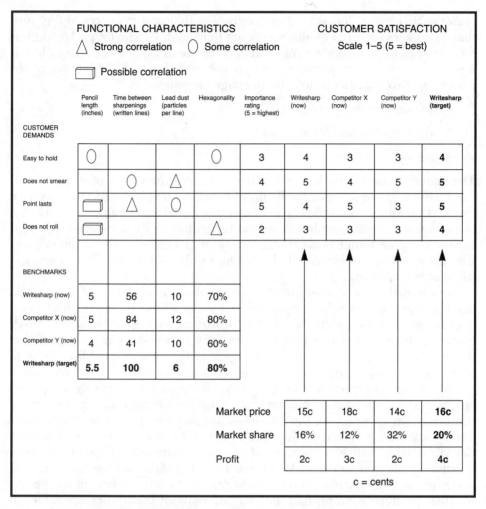

Figure 10.3 A sharper pencil through quality function deployment
(Source: *Business Week*, 2 December 1991: 28–9)

Role of packaging

Pre-packaging brought with it considerable advantages to manufacturers. They could make direct contact with customers through the medium of the package, creating images and appeals to stimulate purchase. In the early days of pre-packaging, many products were of different or dubious quality, so pre-packaging allowed the manufacturer to provide assurance to customers that the contents were unlikely to have been adulterated or interfered with in any way.

Having chosen an image for the product, the manufacturer attempted to preserve that image for as long as possible, so that customers could feel sure that a consistent level of quality was being delivered. Gradually, packaging was seen not just in its protective role and as a vehicle to carry information, but as a way to promote the product through the creation of a unique image. In packaging, three factors contribute to image formation:

- the outline design of the package;
- the use of strong colour; and
- the overall shape.

The materials used in packaging frequently restrict the variety of shapes which can be used. There are many well-known examples where designs in glass have fostered a strong brand image, e.g. Coca-Cola, Bovril and Orangina. Packaging colour plays a crucial role in immediate recognition. Often, before the design registers, the customer is aware of the colour associated with the brand, e.g. the yellow of Colman's mustard, the red and white of Campbell soups and the white of Siúcra sugar.

In the early ears of mass merchandizing, the overall design of many packaged products relied on a typographic statement of the company's name and general information about the product. Complex package designs were used, however, on many of the packaged versions of well-known brands. These designs remained substantially unchanged as the brands established themselves in the market. In some cases, the packaging is still the same, e.g. Lyle's golden syrup. The pressure for shopping efficiency and convenience associated with the modern supermarket has resulted in a dramatic simplification of the image. In this regime, the emphasis has switched to simple, clean, clear and eye-catching packaging. This shift is part of the brand debasement process described later, which a number of manufacturers have wittingly or even unwittingly allowed to occur. With brand proliferation and overemphasis on shelf appeal, some manufacturers are beginning to reintroduce an old design for their products to imply that the contents embody the wholesome values of earlier days. For these brands at least, it may be possible to add value through an emphasis on visual nostalgia.

Importance of packaging in marketing

For many products, industrial and consumer, the buyer's first contact is with the package. Packaging is an important part of the product and intimately bound up with its marketing. Only recently have companies seen packaging in a positive light. Formerly, packaging was seen as a production activity, as a cost to be minimized, serving purely functional and protective needs. Now, however, the marketing significance of packaging is fully recognized, especially in consumer product markets. The growth of self-service and automatic vending machines, scarce shelf space in supermarkets, increased safety concerns, the trend towards snacking and individual product portions, and the use of the microwave oven have all challenged companies in their approach to packaging. Furthermore, with the increased number of new products available, it is necessary to be ever vigilant regarding the strong promotional values which may be obtained from good packaging.

The pressure on the packaging industry has resulted in new types of package and container, new types of can opener and protective caps for medicine bottles and dangerous liquids. For many consumer products, the package must serve as a promotional vehicle and be suitable for transportation, storage in the cupboard or freezer, and even cooking in the microwave. Soup and vegetable companies are beginning to shift away from traditional cans to new containers capable of use in microwave ovens.

Packaging for protection

Packaging protects the product in transit and prevents the contents from interference. A major benefit of packaging is the printed information addressed to the consumer, such as directions on use, production composition, recipes and other data required to satisfy legal requirements. Packaged products are also easier to handle and more convenient. On arrival at a port, baled timber is easier to handle by fork-lift equipment than loose boards. Ease of product use through the addition of special features like dispensers, reusable containers and a non-drip lip can give a competitive advantage.

While packaging is important from a marketing point of view, the growing concern about waste disposal has led to greater use of recyclable and biodegradable materials for packaging. The need for environmentally friendly packaging is becoming very clear. While there have been many admonitions from governments, industry and consumer groups concerning the need to protect the environment, however, there is still a degree of ambivalence concerning the matter which can make it difficult for companies to make the most appropriate response. It would seem that convenience is a consumer benefit which overrides concern for the environment in the USA, whereas the reverse is true in Europe (Exhibit 10.5).

Packaging for promotion

There are distinct promotional advantages which stem from effective design, shape and colour. These latter two factors appear to have influenced the success of Ty Nant spring water in the US market (Exhibit 10.6). Packaging helps to identify products especially at point of purchase. The advertising copy on the package lasts only as long as the product remains in the package. For some products, the package is the only way to differentiate the product contained. In photocopying paper, for example, one brand is considered as good as another, so the package may be used to differentiate one supplier from another.

EXHIBIT 10.5   Pressure on packaging

Making matters worse has been the double standard of American consumers, who, unlike their European counterparts, seem unwilling to accept changes in packaging to protect the environment.

In Europe, Procter & Gamble Co. began packaging its Vizir and Lenor brands of detergents in concentrated form, thus requiring less packaging than ready to use detergents, forcing consumers to mix the concentrate with water in a reusable bottle. European consumers readily accepted the innovation in the interests of environmental protection. When P & G tried to do the same thing with its best-selling Downy fabric softener in the US, sales plummeted. Deborah D. Anderson, head of Procter & Gamble Co.'s three year old environmental task force on trash, believes 'American consumers want convenience ... and, contrary to popular belief, won't favour one product over another simply because it generates less waste.' Other firms have learned that marketing lesson at great expense.

In response to environmentalist pressures, H.J. Heinz Co. sought to abandon its plastic squeeze bottles for ketchup and return to traditional glass bottles. But the plastic squeeze bottles had captured one-third of the US ketchup market and their share was increasing every day. Company market researchers quickly found that consumers were unwilling to return to glass bottles, because 'you can't squeeze glass'.

PepsiCo Inc., the second largest US soft-drink maker, tried bottling its soft drinks in three-litre plastic bottles to reduce the use of plastic. But consumers found the big container too bulky to pour conveniently and often too big for their refrigerators.

Source: *Food Processing*, February 1990: 33–4.

Packaging and labelling for different markets

When packaging and labelling products for foreign customers, manufacturers must ensure that they comply with legislation in the target market, and they must present the product in a way that recognizes cultural and linguistic differences. Labelling legislation in the EU is very complex, making such decisions difficult. In food marketing, for example, EU harmonization means that a company which meets all the requirements on ingredients, names, quantities and use-by dates in one EU country should be able to enter another without difficulty. The EU labelling directive 79/112 states, however, that food producers must display information about their products in a language easily understood by local-market customers.

Complete harmonization is unlikely for another reason. Even when the basic design and lettering on a package are the same in different markets, manufacturers may decide to use a different message or slogan. Although Unilever launched its new Sun Progress dishwasher powder in a standard pack-

---

EXHIBIT 10.6   Ty Nant big blue

Not since Tom Jones's first stateside tour have so many Americans been clam-
ouring to get their hands on a Welsh artefact. Ty Nant, a brand of spring water
from Lampeter, in Wales, is all the rage. In Georgetown, chintzy shops display dozens of bottles in their windows. In New York, nightclubs charge $5
and more for 11 fluid ounces, pacifying customers by allowing them to keep
the empties.

The spring is about as far from the fleshpots of New York and
Washington as you can get, spiritually as well as physically. Ty Nant (Welsh
for 'the house by the stream') is a 350-year-old farm in rural mid-Wales.
Geoffrey and Gwenllian Lockwood bought the place in 1977, and spent
almost a decade renovating it. For water they relied on a natural spring on
their land. In 1986 they had the idea of bottling the spring water and selling
it locally. The couple tried fitfully to break into the American market, only to
be frustrated by the country's fearsome bureaucracy. In late 1991, they sold
Ty Nant to a joint venture owned by Biscaldi, an Italian beer distributor, and
Alfonso Guerrero, a Mexican-born American entrepreneur.

Ty Nant sold 1.8 million bottles in the United States in 1992, and,
according to Mr Guerrero, is well on its way to selling 8.5 million this year.
The water's success has little to do with its taste (rather bland) or its healthi-
ness (it is very low in sodium, but so are most other designer waters), and
everything to do with the cobalt-blue bottle. 'It's incredible, the power of this
package,' says Mr Guerrero from his Welsh headquarters.

Source: *The Economist*, 10 July 1993: 48.

---

aging design, research in France, Germany, Italy and the UK revealed widely
different consumer priorities (*Financial Times*, 13 October 1993: 23). The
result was that, when Sun Progress was launched in Germany in 1990, the message on the packaging stressed the product's environmental attributes. When
it was later launched in the UK, the emphasis was on value for money and the
fact that it would not cause damage to fine china.

Warranties and guarantees and satisfaction

A statement indicating the liability of the manufacturer for product defects is a
warranty and an implied guarantee of replacement or repair. Warranties are
important in the context of increasing product liability claims. Court rulings
nowadays tend to hold the manufacturer liable for product defects. The provision of full warranties represents a significant marketing advantage for the
company willing to offer it. Japanese motor manufacturers' six-year anti-
corrosion warranty on cars has been very effective. The general purpose of a
warranty is to provide buyers with an assurance that they will be compensated

in the event of the product failing to perform satisfactorily. In recent years, there has been a shift from *caveat emptor* to *caveat vendor*, 'let the seller beware!'

With product parity and many brands virtually turning into commodities, and with continuous recessions, often the only way for a company to distinguish itself is to offer guarantees of satisfaction. Satisfaction is very personal, is based on judgement and is difficult to measure objectively. In regard to quality, the company's products may reach the market with zero defects, but satisfaction is based 'more on the customer's somewhat fuzzy expectations than on his outright needs' (*Forbes*, 24 December 1990: 106). In addressing problems regarding customer satisfaction, successful companies concentrate on those problems that have the greatest impact on brand loyalty. It is also necessary to be specific when questioning customers regarding satisfaction. The following is the approach adopted by Xerox (*Forbes*, 24 December 1990: 107):

- ask administrators how they like the billing process;
- ask machine operators how well the machines work; and
- ask purchasing agents about their relationship with the local sales office.

Satisfaction is different for different people in the buying organization and must be measured at each level if the company is to use it in its marketing planning.

Managing products through the life cycle

The product life cycle provides the firm with an understanding of the sales behaviour of products in the market. The primary use of the product life cycle is to focus the firm's attention on a specific product or brand in the market. Fundamental to understanding the product cycle concept is the belief that market and competitive characteristics change from one stage to the next, and that these changes have significant implications for marketing strategy. Each stage, therefore, presents a different challenge to the firm. By identifying the location of a product in the cycle, an appropriate marketing plan can be developed. The different stages also recognize that profits and cash flow increase and decrease at different rates throughout the life cycle.

Planning in the life cycle

The concept of the life cycle and its value as an analytical tool were discussed in Chapter 3. Here a number of additional aspects are examined: in particular, the value of the life cycle as a planning tool in the company.

Costs in the life cycle

Before a product is launched, the company incurs considerable costs, many of which continue after the product is available in the market. Three sets of costs have been identified and analyzed in a life cycle framework. These help to illustrate how costs impact on product planning (Scheuble, 1964). For a considerable period before launch, the company must spend money on marketing research, market testing and promotion to ensure that when the new product is launched it will be accepted by the market (Figure 10.4). In addition, there is a heavy expenditure on product research, engineering and development work. Prototypes and sample products based on primitive designs may have to be produced which are subsequently modified and finalized, thereby contributing to manufacturing cost. These costs continue for some time after the product is launched.

After launch, sales increase slowly at first, and if expectations are realized, they soon begin to take off and increase rapidly, quickly reaching a revenue-rich period of maturity. From this, they decline in a controlled fashion under management control. During the initial stages, advertising costs tend to be very high relative to sales. Other marketing costs are also significant during these stages. The result is that direct marketing and other organization costs continue to rise for a considerable period.

According to this framework, investment recovery begins after the product is launched, but the product is in the maturity stage before break-even is reached. There is considerable debate regarding the precise point at which the investment recovery line reaches the point of break-even. However, the broad thrust of the framework has been accepted: products reach profitability later in the life cycle and the greatest level of profits is to be made in the mature and decline stages, depending on how the product is managed throughout the life cycle.

Sales in the life cycle

In the early stages of the life cycle, the company is interested in ensuring rapid sales growth so that it can reach a high plateau where it knows that profits can be made. On reaching this plateau, the company is faced with a different set of problems.

The 80:20 rule, frequently mentioned in management texts, states that 80 per cent of a company's profits are derived from 20 per cent of its sales. This also indicates that 80 per cent of its products produce only 20 per cent of the profits, and suggests that many companies do not have an active product replacement policy. They are prepared to add new products to the portfolio, but reluctant to delete older products. Customer objections to product deletion may sometimes ensure that the company retains a particular product in its portfolio (Avlonitis, 1983). Carrying a weak product can be very expensive in

449

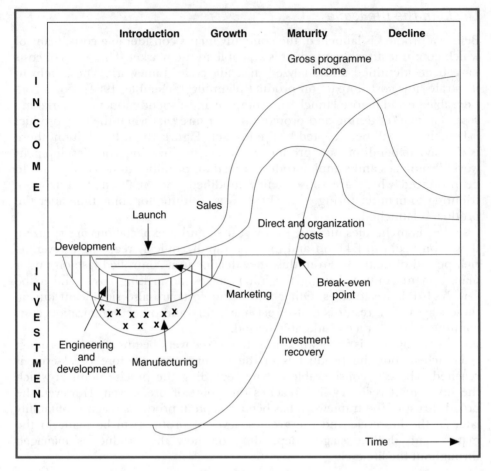

Figure 10.4 Product life cycle: planning emphasis

(Source: Adapted from Scheuble, 1964. Reprinted by permission of Harvard Business School Press from Scheuble, P.A. (1964), 'ROI for new product planning', *Harvard Business Review*, **42**, 6, 110–20. Copyright © 1964 by the President and Fellows of Harvard College)

terms of overheads, missed profits, management time and the general opportunity cost of not developing the better products in the portfolio.

The manufacturer should decide when it is appropriate to withdraw marketing support for a product and either let it go into decline or consciously withdraw it from the market. Critics of the life cycle concept argue that the cycle itself is 'a dependent variable which is determined by marketing actions; it is not an independent variable to which companies should adapt their marketing programmes' (Dhalla and Yuspeh, 1976: 125). For some companies, therefore, the product life cycle can be a dangerous self-fulfilling concept, though it need not be. Some companies with a product in the maturity stage of the life cycle, believing in the inevitability of its prediction, tend to withdraw marketing support too soon in favour of newer products, with the result that the mature product goes into a terminal decline. Management then believe that their actions were anyway justified, whereas the product might have stayed in the mature stage for much longer. The decline stage results from the company's marketing strategy rather than from some inevitability. Poor marketing support for products in the late phase of the maturity stage and in the decline stage is frequently the major determinant of premature decline.

Ideal product life cycle

In the ideal product life cycle, the product development period is short, and therefore the product development costs are low (Figure 10.5). The introduction and growth periods are also short. Sales reach a high plateau relatively quickly, which results in maximization of revenues. The maturity period lasts much longer, giving the company an opportunity to earn profits over an extended period. The decline stage tends to be prolonged, indicating that profits fall gradually rather than suddenly. A firm launching a new product should attempt to forecast the shape of the product life cycle by referring to those factors which influence the length of each stage. Development time is shorter and less costly for routine products than for high-technology products, for example. Thus new perfumes, new snacks and so on do not involve much

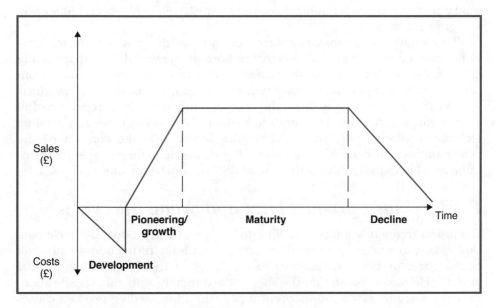

Figure 10.5   The ideal product life cycle
(Source: Adapted from Goldman and Muller, 1982: cited in Kotler, 1991: 353).

development time, whereas high-technology industrial products may require much research and development, engineering time and cost.

The product life cycle shown in Figure 10.5 is an ideal life cycle whereas that shown in Figure 10.4 is a generalized life cycle. Life cycles vary greatly from product to product (Rink and Swan, 1979). The shape of the life cycle may depend on whether products are classified as low-learning or high-learning products (Wasson, 1978). For low-learning products, sales lifts off quickly because little learning is required by the customer and the benefits of purchase are readily understood. The result is a rapidly rising life cycle during the pioneering stage. Because considerable education of the customer is required, high-learning products tend to have an extended pioneering stage and sales are slower to materialize. The result is a rather flat life cycle during the pioneering and growth stages.

The length of the pioneering and growth stage will be short under the following conditions:

- the product does not require setting up a new infrastructure of distribution channels;

- distributors readily accept and promote the new product; and

- consumers have an interest in the product, adopt it early and give it favourable word-of-mouth promotion.

These conditions apply to many familiar consumer products. They are less valid for many high-technology products, which require longer pioneering and growth stages.

The length of the maturity stage depends on the extent to which consumer tastes and product technology are fairly stable and the company maintains leadership in the market. Companies make the most money from products which experience a long maturity period. In contrast, for products where the maturity stage is short, the company might not even recover its full investment. The decline stage tends to be long if consumer tastes and product technology change only slowly. The more brand loyal the consumers, the slower the rate of decline. The lower the exit barriers, the faster some firms will exit, which will slow down the rate of decline for the remaining firms.

Product class, product form and brand life cycles

Confusion frequently arises regarding the scope of the product life cycle concept. Many researchers attempt to apply it without distinction to product classes (beer or biscuits), product forms (lager or digestive) and individual brands (Heineken or McVities). There is a difficulty with this classification, however, since there are no theoretical principles for dividing product classes into product forms. By far the largest confusion arises in regard to the practice by manufacturers of using the same brand for different product forms, and even for products in different product classes. To avoid total confusion it may be necessary in a discussion of product management to define what is meant by the terms 'product class', 'product form' and 'brand'.

Product form and brand life cycles

The life cycle of a product form refers to the total sales of all brands, and the overall shape of growth defines the stage. More specifically, the life cycle for a product form is made up of three dynamic components: the ageing of existing brands, the entrance of new brands and the exit of other brands (Barksdale and Harris, 1982: 76). At any stage of the life cycle for a product form, there may be brands that are growing, others that are maturing and some that are declining. The life cycle for an individual brand could take place entirely within a single stage of the life cycle for the product form.

It is clear, therefore, that the life cycles for product forms and brands are very different, although of the same general shape. The life cycle of an individual brand is the sales history of that brand. Brand life cycles tend to be the shortest of all three types of life cycle. At the same time, some brands have a very long life, such as Hoover, Mars, Cadbury and Lifebuoy.

Length of product life cycle

The length of the product life cycle is different for product classes, product forms and brands. Product classes have the longest life cycles and brands generally the shortest. Some brands, however, have been in existence for more than 50 years. The nature of the product appears to have an impact on the length of the life cycle. In the music business, the commercial life of a single 45 r.p.m. record was sixteen weeks in the late 1970s (Meenaghan and Turnbull, 1981). An ethical drug studied in the 1960s was found to have a pioneering stage of four weeks, a growth stage of twelve weeks and a maturity stage of fifteen months, and was commercially dead after two years (Cox, 1967). Measurement equipment for industrial markets was found to experience a four-year pioneering stage, a three-year growth stage and a maturity stage of three years (Cunningham, 1969).

It is generally agreed that the product life cycle is an accurate model of the sales histories of product forms and individual brands, although in a general sense the concept also applies to product classes. Product classes are believed to have the longest life cycles and reflect society values. Hence, they remain for a long time in the mature stage of the life cycle. Because society changes, product class sales also change, albeit only slowly. Some well-known product classes appear now to be under threat of decline in various societies for many reasons: tobacco, alcoholic spirits, heavy beers, wines and fatty foods. Other newer product classes are clearly in the introduction or growth stages of the life cycle: CD players, cordless telephones and videography.

Life cycle for frequently purchased products

When estimating life cycle sales, the management of the company need to know whether they will be high enough to yield a satisfactory profit. For frequently purchased low-learning products like ice-cream, the product life cycle sales that can be expected resemble Figure 10.6. The number of first-time buyers initially increases and then decreases as fewer are left, assuming a fixed population. Repeat purchases occur soon, providing that the new product satisfies some fraction of people who become steady customers. The sales curve eventually falls to a plateau representing a level of steady repeat purchase volume; by this time the product is no longer in the class of new products.

For a frequently purchased new product, the seller has to estimate repeat sales as well as first-time sales. This is because the unit value of frequently purchased products is low, and repeat purchases take place soon after the introduction. A high rate of repeat purchasing means that customers are satisfied; sales are likely to stay high even after all first-time purchases take place. The seller notes the percentage of repeat purchases that take place in each repeat purchase class – those who buy once, twice, and three times and so on. Some products and brands are bought a few times and dropped. It is important to estimate whether the repeat purchase ratio is likely to rise or fall, and at what rate, with each repeat purchase class. A second peak in the life cycle representing the impact of repeat sales has been found for ethical drugs (Cox, 1967),

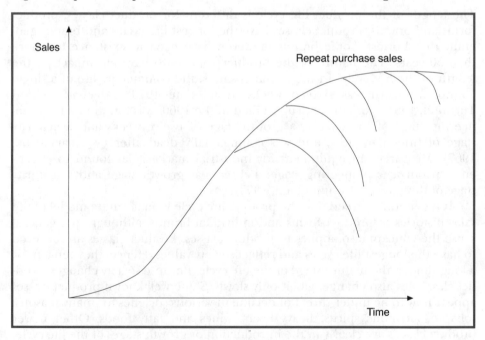

Figure 10.6 Product life cycle for frequently purchased products

454

several studies in the food industry (The Nielsen Researcher, 1968) and industrial fluid measurement devices (Cunningham, 1969).

Innovation in the product life cycle

The two concepts of product life cycle and product innovation lead to several
implications and practical consequences when the firm is deciding its product
policy. Very few products are completely immune to technical obsolescence,
changes in consumer or industry demand, replacement by substitutes or competitive reaction. Life cycle and innovation changes have no in-built reliable
time pattern, so prediction regarding the life expectation of a specific product
is very speculative.

Product innovation and product life cycles are closely related concepts.
Many products evolve from simple to more sophisticated forms with time. This
development takes place due to changes in production techniques, new developments in packaging, the availability of new ingredients or components, or
more simply as a result of changes in fashion, customer preferences or attitudes. The extent of innovation in products such as computers, telecommunications and aircraft is highly visible and their impact on our daily lives is
considerable. The innovation which has occurred in machine tools and robot-
ics is less obvious, but has an equally positive impact on our lives. Innovation
also occurs in ordinary consumer products which may be taken for granted.

Innovation in packaged consumer products

In the detergent market, there have been numerous product innovations over
an extended period which have been positive (Figure 10.7). With the introduction of synthetics based on a new technology in the late 1940s and early
1950s, laundry powder innovations were motivated by changes in demand and
the need for product differentiation. Low-sudsing powders were required
when front-loading washing machines became popular. Biodegradable synthetic powders were the industry's response to accusations of pollution.
Bioactive powders contain enzymes which are more effective for certain types
of organic stain.

The only insurance for the company against obsolescence is a consistent
policy of product innovation. According to a senior director at Unilever plc
and Unilever NV:

> detergents is a technology driven business: we can prove it. All the
> developments since the 40s that have permanently and profitably shifted
> market standing, have had at their core a better product. The competitor who
> delivers superior technology, and delivers it first, will win. This means sinking
> large capital sums into the ground in anticipation of demand, often on scant

455

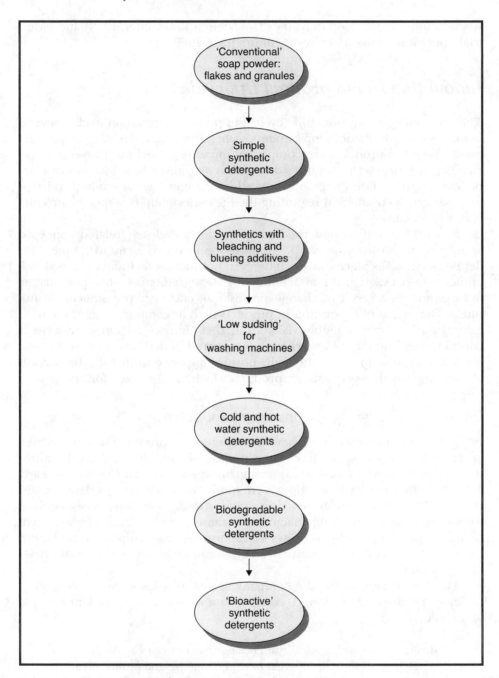

Figure 10.7   Product innovation over time: laundry powder
(Source: Adapted with permission from International Trade Centre (UNCTAD/GATT) training material).

evidence. When we get it wrong it leaves us with an expensive white elephant – or an expensive car park in one of our factories! It means entering the new markets which recent geopolitical changes have opened up while there are still economic and political risks. It means extending our brands around the world without necessarily collecting the finest points of market research evidence in Uruguay or Vietnam. (Fitzgerald, 1991).

Innovation in technical products

The pace of product innovation, especially in high technology, has increased in recent years as companies recognize that speed to market means profits. In microprocessors, for example, two developments are noteworthy. First, the pace of new competition in microprocessors development has increased significantly. Second, the time taken to develop and launch each new generation has shortened considerably. Since 1979 Intel Corp. has developed and launched the 286, the 386 and the 486 microprocessor. It took Intel about five years to develop and launch the 486 chip, but new generations are expected to take less time. In the period 1990 to 1996, Intel expects to launch three new generations of microprocessors (Figure 10.8).

Because the first company to market gains the lion's share of the market and profits, even in a commodity market such as chips, Intel's activities have attracted a great deal of attention from competitors. When Intel Corp. introduces a new generation microprocessor such as the 586, the company does not usually hold the market to itself for very long. Competitive designs tend to be launched, sometimes within weeks.

It is reported that NexGen Microsystems Inc. had a 586 chip ready for launch to match Intel's August 1992 launch. NexGen waited to examine Intel's specifications before putting the final touches to its own designs (*Business Week*, 3 August 1992: 45). Cyrix Corporation is another cloner which watches Intel Corp. very closely. In January 1992, Cyrix introduced its workalike version of Intel's 486 microprocessor with the eventual ambition of beating Intel to market. Not only has the pace of innovation increased in Intel, but the extent of overlap between one generation of technology and the next has been reduced considerably. Design work on the 686 chip began very soon after the design work began on the 586, for example. The pressure on companies to innovate is, therefore, considerable.

Market entry barriers and the product life cycle

The ideal product life cycle as described above, needless to say, may never be found in practice. It is a hypothetical presentation of expectations if ideal circumstances were present in the market. Competitive actions, changing technologies, government regulations and fickle customers all contribute to producing

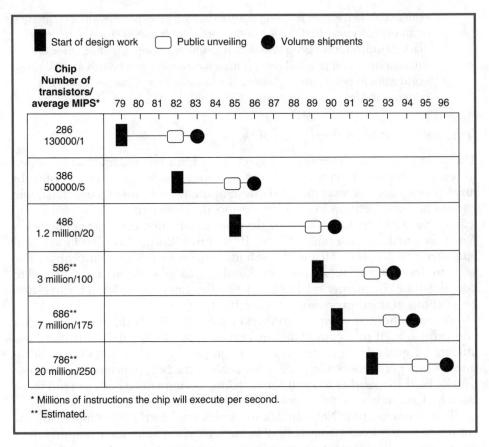

Figure 10.8 The pace of product innovations at Intel Corporation
(Source: *Business Week*, 1 June 1992: 50)

a different shape and duration for the life cycle. An unexpected market entry barrier is also likely to change the shape of the life cycle dramatically.

A barrier to entry may be interpreted as an unanticipated longer product development time, a steep development cost, a long time in the pioneering and growth stages, and an uncertain and possible rapid decline due to demand technology changes or competitive market entries (Figure 10.9). This figure is a modification of Figure 10.5, describing the ideal product life cycle.

Managing the product portfolio

For many firms, a small number of products contribute a large share of the profits. In this context, the firm must ensure that it has developed an appro-

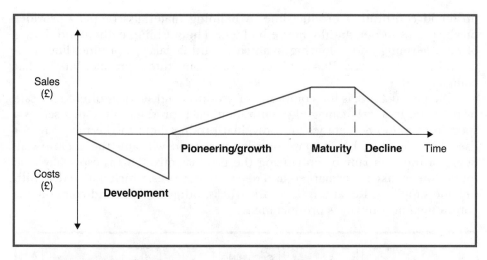

Figure 10.9   Possible effects of barriers to market entry on the product life cycle
(Source: Adapted from Goldman and Muller, 1982; cited in Kotler, 1994: 358)

priate product-market fit and that the product mix is balanced in such a way to meet customer requirements while contributing a profit for the firm. To meet these objectives, the company attempts to protect its best-selling products, delete marginal ones and relocate marketing support to newer products with growth potential. In the process, the firm is careful to take account of cost and demand interactions which may exist within its portfolio of products.

Product mix decisions

Most companies are multiproduct organizations. In managing this situation, a distinction may be made among individual product items, product lines and the product mix or product portfolio. The first refers to individual product items which are identified separately on a price list. Product items include, for example, different flavours of ice-cream on a restaurant menu, different styles of women's summer dresses, and different sizes of industrial compressors used in the construction industry to drive drilling and cutting equipment. A product item for the Renault Motor Company would be a specific version of a product which has a separate designation in the price list. The Renault Clio 1.1 litre, three-door hatchback is a product item in Renault's product mix.

Product lines refer to a group of products which satisfy a particular class of needs. They may be used together, possess common physical or technical characteristics, be sold to the same customer groups, be sold through the same channels and retail outlets, or fall within the same price category. Clearly, product lines are highly variable and their composition depends greatly on how the manager views the market. All forms of soap, detergent and washing-

459

up liquid constitute a product line. A building materials company provides product lines in demand by house builders. The washing, cutting and drying of hair, perming and colouring, manicures and facials are product lines provided by beauty salons. Renault's motor cars constitute a product line in that company.

The product mix is the composite of products and services offered for sale by the firm. In a well-managed organization, each product in the mix serves a specific purpose. Sometimes an individual product item in the mix may not itself be profitable, but it may contribute to good will and the overall well-being of the company by enhancing the product mix. This is especially true for customers like supermarkets and department stores, which like to deal with full-line suppliers. Renault motor cars, trucks, other vehicles and components constitute that company's product mix.

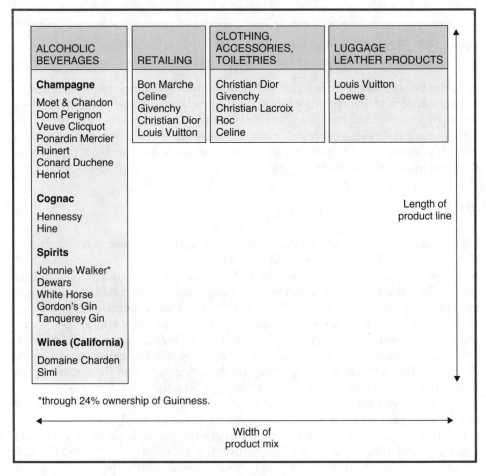

Figure 10.10 Product and service portfolio at LVMH

In managing the product mix, the company is concerned with a portfolio of products and services, and must be concerned with decisions at three different levels: the depth of the product mix, its breadth and its consistency. The depth of the product mix refers to the average number of product items offered by the organization within each product line. The LVMH Group may be seen to have four lines of alcoholic beverages, five distinct branded clothing, accessory and toiletry lines, two luggage and leather products lines and five major retail service chains (Figure 10.10). By increasing the depth of the product mix, the company may attract customers with very different needs and wants. The breadth of the product mix refers to the number of different product lines found in the firm. Breadth of product mix depends on the definition of established product-line boundaries. By increasing the breadth of the product mix, the company may capitalize on its good reputation and skill in existing markets. The consistency of the product mix refers to how closely related the product lines are in customer use, distribution channels, technology and production techniques. By increasing consistency, the company may acquire an unparalleled reputation in a particular area of endeavour.

These four dimensions of the product portfolio indicate the ways in which

---

Johnson and Johnson consumer products

Band-Aids
Johnson's baby oil
Johnson's baby powder
Johnson's baby shampoo
Reach toothbrushes

McNeill consumer products

Pediacare medicines
Tylenol products

Personal Products

Carefree sanitary pads
Serenity Super Plus Guards (incontinence)
Stayfree Maxi Pads

Jensen Pharmaceutica

Anesthesia drugs
Hismanal antihistamine

Lifescan

One Touch II
Blood glucose
Monitor

Advanced care products

Fact Plus (pregnancy tests)
Micatin (athlete's foot)
Monistat 7 (yeast infections)

Ethicon

Ligatures
Sutures

Iolab

Intraocular lenses
Microsurgical gear

Ortho-pharmaceutical

Birth control pills
Diaphragms
Retin-A acne cream
Terazol 3 vaginal cream (antifungal)

OrthoBiotech

Procrit (anemia)

Figure 10.11 Johnson and Johnson's product mix

461

the company can expand its business: broaden the product mix by adding new product lines, make each product line longer, deepen the product mix by adding new versions to selected products, and change the product-line consistency. Increasing product-line consistency helps the company acquire a stronger reputation in a reduced number of areas, whereas reducing consistency allows the firm to compete in several areas. Johnson and Johnson has a very wide product mix, ranging from anaesthetics and birth control drugs to Band-Aids, baby powder, baby oils and contact lenses (Figure 10.11). Johnson and Johnson's 166 operating companies are constantly changing to keep this mix of products up to date. The company uses ten product categories to classify its products.

Companies in pursuit of profits tend to carry shorter lines of products selected to succeed. Companies in pursuit of market growth and share tend to carry longer lines as they are less concerned when some products fail. There are other reasons why a company's product line tends to grow. Excess production capacity encourages the development of new products and, frequently, intermediaries and the company's own sales force seek new products to satisfy their customers. With a greater number of products being added to the line, many costs also rise, especially design, inventory, transportation and promotional costs. Eventually product-line growth is checked and the firm may even prune a number of less profitable items from its line.

Product and service company fit

Companies must determine the appropriateness of the match or fit between the range of products in its portfolio and its resources, size and configuration. This raises questions of balancing the portfolio of products and services provided by the company, the company's approach to new product and service development, and the conditions for success in this endeavour. The company must also be aware of the traps in new product development.

Balancing the product portfolio

In attempting to maintain a balance in its portfolio of products and services, the company must ensure that an appropriate fit exists between itself and the products and services provided. To maintain this balance, companies sometimes attempt to extend the life cycle, and they may even relaunch existing products under a new formulation or into a different niche or segment of the market.

Product–market fit

To establish the extent to which the organization's products fit customer or market requirements, it is necessary to start with an understanding of customer needs (Figure 10.12). The next step is to determine the product's actual or perceived strengths and weaknesses among customers. During the third stage, some customers will purchase and use the product and then apply the benefit of the product to their expressed needs. To the extent that the product meets their requirements, customers are satisfied or dissatisfied, which in turn influences the actual or perceived product strengths and weaknesses.

Manufacturers, through research, can only be partly accurate when it comes to designing products and matching product attributes with consumer needs. It is also necessary to observe how consumers use the product. Avon

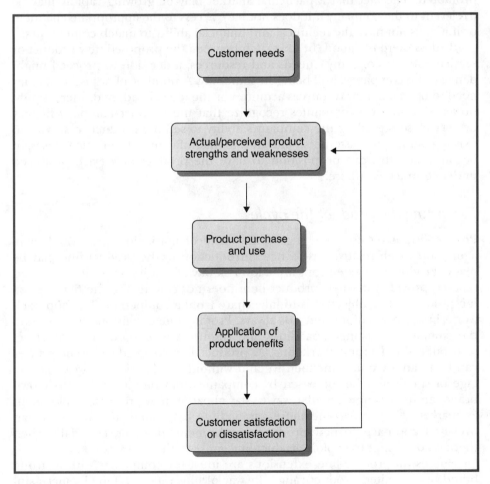

Figure 10.12 Testing for product-market fit

Products Inc. discovered that its bath oil brand Skin-So-Soft, a 30-year-old brand, was being applied by consumers directly on their skin, which worked well as an insect repellent. In 1988 Avon packaged Skin-So-Soft in spray containers and in one month sales quadrupled to $10 million.

Product–company fit

Sometimes products do not fit well with the company's existing resources and it may be necessary to acquire additional resources. In this regard, successful product innovators first examine their customer base, the existing distribution channels, the existing marketing programme, in-company skills, and the capital and working capital situation to see to what extent they fit with the new idea being promoted. The fact that a particular market may be growing rapidly may be irrelevant to the company if it does not have access to the appropriate channels, or if it does not have the technical and financial ability to match competitors.

Unless there is a good 'fit' or match between the proposed new product or service and the company's needs and resources, a decision to proceed might damage the company's well-being in some way. A number of adjustments may need to be made, new resources acquired or the idea abandoned. Increasingly, however, innovative companies recognize that the product–company fit may be very close regarding the company's ability to sell the product or service to existing and new customers, but not to manufacture it. In such cases, it becomes an attractive proposition to have the product or service produced under contract elsewhere.

Extending the product life cycle

Product-line extensions are a great favourite of marketing and brand managers, since with relative ease a new introduction to the product line may be made. Product-line extensions are a low-risk way of gaining share in a crowded market, provided the new product item does not cannibalize the firm's existing products. The objective is to take share from a competitor. The approach works in some situations, but not always. Product-line extensions capitalize on the company's existing capabilities and resources in design, manufacturing, distribution and brand marketing. A product launch in ideal circumstances can be relatively quick, inexpensive and without much risk. The great advantage of speed may be increased by companies that buy in under their own brand, an increasingly popular way to stay ahead in new product development as market changes become more rapid. Line extensions are sometimes an overused approach to new product development, however, especially when there is an attempt to exploit product-line gaps which may not exist.

Successful product-line extensions are ideal for companies with a strong brand but a limited product range. By way of illustration, L'Oréal's successful DRAKKAR scent for men was quickly extended to include DRAKKAR Noir for men preferring a heavier scent. However, such product-line extensions are unlikely to work in the dairy cabinet in supermarkets or in certain sectors of the car market. The danger of too much dependence on product-line extensions as a way of developing and launching new products is that very quickly the customer could face a proliferation of indistinguishable products, which serve only to dilute the company image and damage its costs position.

The principal way of extending the length of the company's product line is by stretching it upwards or downwards. Every firm serves only part of the total possible range of needs. It may be possible for the company to stretch its product line up or down that range. Companies in the lower end of the market may attempt to trade upwards, attracted by higher profits or better growth rates. Trading up means adding a higher-priced, prestige product to a line to attract a higher-income market. One of the major difficulties faced in attempting to stretch the product line upwards is that of credibility among customers. They may not believe that the firm is capable of producing products for the high end of the market. In addition, the company's sales people may not be adequately trained and competitors are unlikely to remain passive. Competitors may counter-attack in the lower end of the market.

Other companies initially located in the high end of the market stretch the line downwards by introducing promotional versions of their products to attract customers on price. Trading down like this means adding a lower-priced item to the firm's line of prestige products. Behind downward line stretching is the view that consumers will trade up once they see the better versions of the product. In such cases, the promotional version of the product must support the company's high market image. One of the dangers of downward line stretching is that of product-line cannibalization. The company could ultimately be worse off if customers switch away from high market items towards the promotional versions of the product.

Relaunching existing products

There are circumstances in which the company may decide it is appropriate to relaunch a product that is either not performing well in the market or in danger of decline. Before starting a relaunch process, the company should clearly understand the reasons behind the potential demise of the product, and should have the resources required to ensure that the relaunch process is successful. A successful relaunch requires that the product is not obsolete in all market segments or applications. It helps greatly if the product still enjoys a brand franchise with associated loyalty. It is important too that the relaunch should not be the first of a long series of attempts to repair the product, but should open opportunities for substantial growth and profits.

There are a number of approaches to relaunching a weak product. The company may engage in a face-lifting exercise by rapidly introducing a number of line extensions. Alternatively, it may be possible to focus on more efficient sales management techniques to produce a better-motivated sales force, which might reactivate dormant accounts among other activities. Some companies successfully relaunch products by developing aggressive advertising and promotion programmes to lift product sales. Unless there is something of substance in such campaigns, reaching new users or identifying new product attributes in demand, the effect may be only temporary. Lastly, some companies relaunch products based on a revised pricing structure, which involves a total repositioning of the product. Frequent price repositioning involves a shift from premium pricing of the product to economy pricing which can attract a different customer group.

Product diversity and deletion

The product mix strategy is determined by long-run profit and sales objectives, by growth aspirations and by the company's attitude towards risk. As a consequence, it is difficult to state what the ideal product mix should be for any company. It is easier to speculate as to what might be a suboptimal situation. A number of occurrences suggest a suboptimal product mix for a company: recurring excess production, storage or transport facilities, high profit dependency on a small number of products, an underutilized sales force and a persistent decline in sales or profits.

Unilever has been attempting to resolve discrepancies among some of its frozen food products in international markets. The Cornetto cone is being standardized to one design from the fifteen or so different cone shapes of a few years ago. The same is true for other Unilever food products. The result will be that, instead of formulating their own recipes from the start, operating companies within the Unilever Group will increasingly draw on common ingredients. Here is an attempt by a large international company to standardize its approach to various markets.

The easiest products to harmonize for different country tastes are impulse items such as ice-cream bars. The closer a particular food comes to being part of the consumer's stable diet, however, the more difficult it becomes to transfer internationally. It is not easy to be successful in this endeavour. Bird's Eye Walls, Unilever's frozen food subsidiary, has made seven unsuccessful attempts in five years to create a UK market for Carte d'Or, a premium ice-cream which sells well in continental Europe. In 1991 the company realized that its very wide portfolio needed to be harmonized to take account of the overlapping which had occurred, and also to exploit the challenges of a wider European market (Exhibit 10.7).

In coping with these problems, companies abandon poor-performing products, modify those with potential and develop new products. Companies delete products for which there is an uneconomic demand, or which require excessive management time relative to profit contribution, and also old-fashioned products which damage the company's image. Product modification

---

EXHIBIT 10.7   Unilever harmonizes product mix to compete

In the old days, when each operating company developed products only for its local market, launching them in other countries could take up to seven years. Today, priorities have been reversed. 'We are trying more strongly for international products,' says Manfred Stach, head of Union, Unilever's largest German foods subsidiary. 'Only if there really is a distinct difference in taste do you go for the local aspect.'

Two recent product introductions demonstrate the new approach. Magnum, a chocolate-coated ice-cream bar, was launched Europe-wide in 18 months. Ragu, the best-selling spaghetti sauce in the US made by Cheseborough Ponds, was successfully rolled out across Europe after Unilever acquired the American company in 1987. The only concession to local custom was to change the name to Raguletto in Germany to meet trade description rules.

Unilever is also trying to iron out discrepancies between similar existing products. The Cornetto cone is being standardised on one design, while the variety of chicken soup flavourings has been much reduced. But simultaneous international product launches can be risky, particularly since they often preclude extensive local test-marketing. The skill lies in judging where harmonisation will not be noticed by consumers – and where genuine differences in local taste will create resistance. In general the easiest products to harmonise are impulse buys, such as ice-cream bars. But the closer a particular food comes to being part of consumers' staple diet, the harder it becomes to transfer across borders.

Source: *Financial Times*, 28 October 1991: 14.

---

involves a change in the tangible or intangible product attributes, and may be achieved by product reformulation or redesign, or changing sizes and features.

Too many weak products in the firm's portfolio eventually weaken the company's ability to introduce new products, which adversely affects future prospects. Before removing a weak product from the product portfolio, however, a number of factors should be considered. First, the product under threat may help to fill out and complete the company's product line. Second, sometimes because of cost interactions, a product may help to cover fixed costs even though its own sales performance is not up to standard. Third, a weak product may sell as a complement to other products in the product mix and may be indirectly contributing to profits. Lastly, a significant group of customers may want the product, which for good will or other long-term reasons the company may wish to delay a decision to eliminate.

Market share and cash flow

It is now generally agreed that market leadership and profitability depend on market share. Greater market share at any stage in the life cycle enables the firm to achieve greater production and marketing economies. A company whose share falls radically in a particular segment soon joins the marginal suppliers in the industry and experiences the disadvantages such a role implies, including the loss of pricing initiative. Firms usually seek to establish themselves in the market early in the life cycle. Market share is easier to obtain for innovators. In more mature markets, as the sales curve flattens, gains in the market share only come at very high cost. Each extra percentage share of the mature market costs much more than a similar gain at the introduction or growth stages. Buying market share at the mature stage of the life cycle may not be justifiable in profit terms.

Successful product innovation depends on how well the firm manages its cash flows. As was seen in the section dealing with the product life cycle, products which are growing rapidly require relatively large amounts of cash. Products which are growing slowly in mature markets tend to generate cash. Combining these two observations, two conclusions follow. First, the investment required to maintain market share is a function of the growth rate in that market. If the growth rate is high, a high level of investment in plant, equipment and inventory is required, if sales of the product are to grow as fast as or faster than the market, i.e. to retain or improve share position. Second, in a given market or product category, the profitability of competing products is a function of their market share. Products with large market shares, which dominate the segment, tend to have high margins and thus generate a substantial amount of cash.

A powerful message regarding the dynamic management of the company's portfolio of products emerges from these two principles. Products which have a high market share but are experiencing slow growth should be managed to generate cash. The low growth rate means that the reinvestment needed in the products themselves is less than the earnings being generated. Deliberate control is required to ensure that the earnings from such mature products are not all reinvested in themselves, but are applied to new products in the pioneering and growth stages of the life cycle.

Products with high growth rates are unlikely to be able to produce their own investment funds. In high-growth markets, there is a high demand for funds to maintain or extend market share. In such circumstances, companies transfer cash from mature businesses to products with rapidly growing sales, to enable them to grow faster than the market, achieve a dominant position and forgo current profits for market position and longer-term profits.

This approach to analyzing product-markets has been popularized by the Boston Consulting Group through its well known growth–share matrix. Products are classified according to their relative share position and the growth rates of the market they serve. The principles behind this approach were discussed in Chapter 3. Relative market share is used instead of absolute market share, as it indicates the competitive strength of a firm in a given market segment (Figure 10.13).

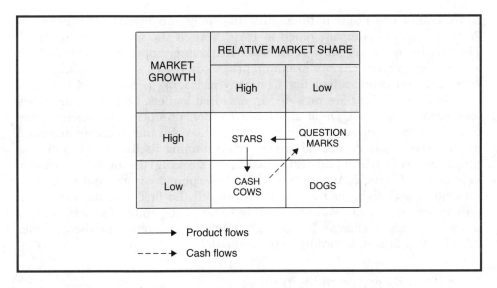

Figure 10.13   Product-market growth–share matrix

Based on the conclusions drawn, the recommended cash flow is also shown. A successful firm applies the surplus cash generated by the cash cows to the needy products classified as question marks, to ensure that the latter in time become stars and eventually cash cows themselves. In this way, the product portfolio is managed as a whole to provide a balance between cash generation now and future cash generation, by aiming for dominant share positions in growth markets.

Positioning products and services

Positioning is the process by which the company defines a market role for a product relative to others. The ability of a company to compete effectively in the market is determined by its success in positioning its products and services appropriately relative to the needs of selected market segments and relative to competing products and services. The process of market positioning is based on an integration or synthesis of customer analysis and competitor analysis.

The first step in deciding the appropriate positioning in the minds of customers for new products is to identify the benefits that customers seek when buying in the product category. It also means deciding the appropriate segments to serve. Once the benefits and segments are known, it is necessary to determine the importance of each benefit for each market segment. Positioning then involves matching an appropriate mix of differentiated benefits with a specific segment whose needs are not satisfied by competing products and services. In this way, positioning may avoid a full-scale direct attack on competitors.

Earlier companies were admonished to 'forget the steak, sell the sizzle'.

Some companies position themselves by doing the reverse. Clarins SA, a French cosmetics company based in Paris, 'forgets the sizzle, sells the steak'. This company works with a no-frills marketing approach, advertises in women's magazines, charges premium prices and places a solid emphasis in its advertising on product benefits. Company packaging is plain, and extensive technical descriptions are provided in enclosed leaflets. Compared to its better-known rivals like L'Oréal and Estee Lauder, producers of Lancôme and Clinique respectively, Clarins could not spend lavish sums to create luxurious images. Hence the double advantage of positioning itself as a 'no nonsense substance over style brand with advertising stressing the product's natural ingredients' (*Forbes*, 5 August 1991: 87). The company is also quite adept at innovation and niche marketing. It introduced the first 'climate controlled' skin treatment called 'Multi-Active Day Cream', the molecular structure of which responds to changes in humidity, releasing different ingredients under different conditions, according to the company.

Product and service repositioning

Product positioning depends on the image created by promotion, pricing and distribution, in addition to the intrinsic product benefits. By consciously positioning a product or service, the company accurately addresses the needs of customers and thereby avoids confusion in cluttered markets, in which precisely positioned competitive products are more likely to enjoy success. Market positions are not, however, set in stone; they are established relative to competing products and customer needs, both of which may change, necessitating a change in the company's positioning strategy.

Changing the position of a product, or repositioning it, may be an alternative to modifying it physically. Companies regularly reposition their products by changing elements of the marketing mix, such as pricing, promotion, distribution or packaging. Some companies reposition to take market share from competitors, while others do it to avoid direct competition. Using price to stimulate customers to 'trade up' or 'trade down' is a form of positioning based on price. The images created by television advertising may also be used to reposition products. In this regard, tea is usually accepted as an ordinary beverage, very much a commodity to be enjoyed by millions of people. While this is so, it is not uniquely so, as has been demonstrated by Republic of Tea, a successful niche marketing company (Exhibit 10.8).

Managing services in marketing

Traditional service companies have often confused their operations with manufacturing. Approaching quality in a service company with a manufacturing

---

EXHIBIT 10.8   Tea mind with the Republic of Tea

Convinced that most Americans have never tasted a good cup of tea, the forty-something Mel and Patricia Ziegler, along with their partner Bill Rosenzweig, 33, are out to convert the coffee-drinking public. To do it they've launched Republic of Tea. It markets 21 types of natural tea through department stores and gourmet shops across the country. Packaged in cylindrical tins decorated with whimsical water colours, the full-leaf and herbal teas carry such names as Mango, Ceylon, Tea of Inquiry, and Sky Between the Branches.

The leaves aren't exactly cheap: Republic's teas, sold loose or bagged in round 'pillows', cost from $6 to $16 for a 60-cup canister, depending on variety. That's three to five times as expensive as Lipton's. But Neiman Marcus, Macy's, Bloomingdale's and Nature Co. have all signed on. 'The packaging is gorgeous,' gushes Jennifer A. Panchenko, who signed Republic of Tea for Dayton Hudson Department Store Co. 'The whole line is very '90s.'

Republic believes that Americans want to slow down the frantic pace of their lives. So just as the partners created an image of action and adventure with Banana Republic (the Indiana Jones look), they want customers to associate their products with what Mel Zeigler calls 'tea mind'. That's why the motto is 'Sip by Sip, not Gulp by Gulp'. Mel Ziegler, who is not Republic's chairman but its minister of leaves, says: 'Tea is as much a metaphor for life as it is a product.' The Company is based – no surprise here – in Marin County, California, across the Golden Gate Bridge from San Francisco.

While Republic's partners frequently equate sipping good tea with drinking fine wine, neighbouring Napa Valley isn't exactly in a panic. Although alcohol consumption is down, not even Ziegler expects a big switch from wine to tea.

It's the $3.5 billion coffee market the Republic is really after. 'If we got two or three [market share percentage] points from coffee, we would become the dominant speciality tea company,' Ziegler says. The company hopes to cash in on consumers' efforts to cut back on caffeine: Tea contains far less than coffee. So far, the company says, it is on the track to sell $500,000 worth of tea by next June and to build up to $2.1 million by 1994.

Source: *Business Week*, 7 December 1992: 60.

---

mentality does not appear to work. In such companies, service is defined in terms of meeting company standards that measure such things as the average time waiting in queues or the number of complaints received. These approaches fail to measure the quality of service provided to customers now lost to the company because the service provided was poor. These measures do not relate customer service directly to the bottom line. It would be better to measure customer loyalty, on an appropriate basis, through repeat purchasing of the service provided. Successful service companies monitor the quality and value of their services in order to increase customer retention rates. Loyal customers are also cheaper to deal with and hence costs are also reduced.

It is difficult to improve quality in services due to the fleeting nature of its product. Since it is the 'front office' worker who talks to the customer, this has implications for training and support. Successful service companies cope with the issue by hiring, training and developing the right employees. Quality in service also requires technology support, such as better telephone systems for customer service representatives and lap-top computers for sales staff. Some service companies believe there is a role for marketing in their business, while others do not.

Julian Rivers, marketing director of the Dillons Bookstore Group in London, is quoted as saying, 'Book shopping should be marketed as a leisure activity; it needs marketing for excitement and discovery' (*Marketing*, 25 April 1991: 23). According to Rivers, books are 'undermarketed in the UK by both booksellers and publishers'. In Foyles, the other large bookstore, owner Christine Foyle is reputed as saying about marketing, 'We are already sufficiently high profile for it not to be necessary.' Foyle's approach seems to be 'We don't want to push customers into buying what we want to sell them' (*Marketing*, 25 April 1991: 23). Both approaches emphasize that book buying is a leisure activity and that, in the UK at least, there is scope for both approaches.

In the 1990s in the USA and Europe, airline service quality has become an oxymoron. While airlines provide safe transportation, many of them treat their customers as objects to be jostled, inconvenienced, treated rudely, held in numerous queuing systems and otherwise badly treated (Exhibit 10.9). As airline companies jostle for share of deregulated markets or endeavour to survive, their focus appears to be on making returns in a complex capital-intensive business and emphasizes a production orientation. Some airlines

---

EXHIBIT 10.9   Straighten up and fly right

Minneapolis business consultant Bruce K. Symonds travels a lot. He has twiddled his thumbs through countless delays, missed many connections, lost a few bags. He expects the worst from air travel. But even this jaded passenger blew his top on a recent United Airlines flight to Toronto. After the packed plane pulled onto the tarmac in a blowing thunderstorm, it inched along for an hour behind a string of other jets. Then an engine failed and took 45 minutes to restart. By takeoff time, Symonds had been sweating in his seat for two and a half hours.

Symonds didn't blame United for the weather or the engine. What irked him was the airline's attitude. Despite the long delay, the crew offered nary drink nor an apology. And when Symonds asked why the passengers couldn't have waited out the storm in the terminal, a flight attendant said that United prefers that its planes 'leave the gate on time' even if it means a wait on the runway.

Source: *Business Week*, 2 December 1991: 62.

---

excel at providing a quality service in such an environment and have gained a well-deserved reputation for it, such as British Airways and Singapore Airlines. But heavy expenditure on advertising the service component of air travel, developing frequent-flier programmes to lock in customers, responding to new low-fare entrants by cutting fares, and then raising them again when upstarts have been pushed out of the market, is not the answer.

The current trend towards developing hub-and-spoke systems so that an increasing number of passengers are funnelled like packages into larger flight routes to recover huge fixed costs is a further demonstration of a lack of customer orientation. By developing sophisticated computer reservation systems, which exclude competitors and manipulate fares to match expected demand, airlines need discount only a few seats, hence the highly mobile separating curtain between tourist and business class on most airlines. These approaches to service marketing alienate customers.

Assignment questions

1 What is meant by a product and a service?

2 Describe the distinguishing features of services and outline their implications for marketing.

3 Describe the concept of the product life cycle and discuss its implications for marketing management.

4 How does design and packaging facilitate the marketing of consumer products?

5 If an item in the product mix is not contributing to the firm's profits, should it be eliminated?

6 When is it appropriate to introduce line extensions?

7 When is it profitable to relaunch a product?

8 How should the company's product portfolio be managed to maximize cash flow?

Annotated bibliography

Dibb, Sally, Lyndon Simkin, William M. Pride and O.C. Ferrell (1991) *Marketing*, European Edition, Boston, Mass.: Houghton Mifflin, chapter 7.

Kotler, Philp (1994) *Marketing Management* (8th edn), Englewood Cliffs, NJ: Prentice Hall, chapter 14.

McCarthy, E. Jerome, and William D. Perreault, Jr (1990) *Basic Marketing* (10th edn), Homewood, Ill.: Richard D. Irwin, chapters 9 and 10.

Stanton, William J., Michael J. Etzel and Bruce J. Walker (1991) *Fundamentals of Marketing* (9th edn), New York: McGraw-Hill, chapters 7 and 8.

References

Avlonitis, George J. (1983) 'Ethics and product elimination', *Management Decision*, **21**, 2, 37–45.

Barksdale, Hiram C., and Clyde E. Harris, Jr (1982) 'Portfolio analysis and the product life cycle', *Long Range Planning*, **15**, 6, 74–83.

Cox, William E. Jr (1967) 'Product life cycles as marketing models,' *Journal of Business*, **40**, 4, 375–84.

Cunningham, Malcolm J. (1969) 'The application of product life cycle to corporate strategy: some research findings', *British Journal of Marketing*, 3, Spring, 32–44.

Dhalla, Nariman K., and Sonia Yuspeh (1976) 'Forget the product life cycle concept', *Harvard Business Review*, **54**, 1, 102–12.

Dibb, Sally, Lyndon Simkin, William M. Pride and O.C. Ferrell (1991) *Marketing*, European Edition, Boston, Mass.: Houghton Mifflin Company.

Fitzgerald, N.W.A. (1991) 'Competitive marketing strategies in fast moving consumer goods', paper delivered at the National Marketing Conference, Jury's Hotel, Dublin, 8 November.

Goldman, Arieh, and Eitan Muller (1982) 'Measuring shape patterns of product life cycles: implications for marketing strategy', paper presented at the Jerusalem School of Business Administration, Hebrew University of Jerusalem, August.

Kotler, Philip (1994) *Marketing Management* (8th edn), Englewood Cliffs, NJ: Prentice Hall.

Lowe, Andy, and Ross B. Hunter (1991) 'The role of design and marketing management in the culture of innovation', in *Marketing Thought Around the World*, Proceedings of the European Marketing Academy Conference, University College Dublin, Ireland.

McCarthy, E. Jerome, and William D. Perreault, Jr (1990), *Basic Marketing* (10th edn), Homewood, Ill.: Richard D. Irwin.

Meenaghan, A., and Peter W. Turnbull (1981) 'The application of product life cycle theory to popular record marketing', *European Journal of Marketing*, **15**, 5, 1–50.

The Nielsen Researcher (1968) **26**, 1, 1–19.

Rink, David R., and John E. Swan (1979) 'Product life cycle research: a literature review', *Journal of Business Research*, **78**, 3, 218–42.

Scheuble, P.A. (1964) 'ROI for new product planning', *Harvard Business Review*, **42**, 6, 110–20.

Shostack, G. Lynn (1977) 'Breaking free from product marketing', *Journal of Marketing*, **41**, 2, 73–80.

Stanton, William J., Michael J. Etzel and Bruce J. Walker (1991) *Fundamentals of Marketing* (9th edn), New York: McGraw-Hill.

Urban, Glen L., and John R. Hauser (1980) *Design and Marketing of New Products*, Englewood Cliffs, NJ: Prentice Hall.

Wasson, Chester R. (1978) *Dynamic Competitive Strategies and Product Life Cycles* (3rd edn), Austin, Tex.: Austin Press.

Developing new products and services

11

Need for new products and services
New product and service development as
marketing innovation
Process of new product and service
development

Introduction

This chapter introduces and explains:

- the meaning of new product and service innovation;

- how companies attempt to balance their product and service portfolios;

- ways of developing new products and services;

- criteria for success and failure in new product and service development;

- traps in new product development;

- how innovations are diffused throughout the market;

- the role of new products and services in competitive success, market share and profits;

- the stages of new product and service development;

- the importance of timing in launching products and services; and

- possible ways of avoiding new product and service failure.

New products and services are essential for the growth and survival of the company. At the same time, the risks associated with innovation are very high. In developing new products and services, the company must recognize that they demand considerable managerial attention to ensure that innovations succeed. This means understanding how innovations may be applied commercially, and how new products and services can improve the performance of the company. To succeed the company must be able to take an innovation through a series of stages from idea to commercialization. At the same time, it is necessary to recognize that the timing of market entry and launch can be critical for success. Lastly, it is important that the company develop an approach to avoid failure in its attempts to develop new products and services.

Having studied this chapter, you should be able to define the phrases listed above in your own words, and you should be able to do the following:

1. Recognize the importance of new product and service decisions.

2. Outline approaches to new product development.

3. Avoid the various traps in new product development, especially the competitive delusion trap, the restricted scope and competence traps, the market illusion trap and the market analysis failure trap.

4. Recognize how technology push and market pull can converge to produce beneficial innovations.

5. Specify the nature and significance of each of the stages in the process of new product development.

6. State how to cope with the timing decision of new product and service launch.

7. Develop criteria to prevent failure.

Need for new products and services

There are numerous reasons why companies develop new products and services. There may be a gap in the company's existing product line, or the market for the company's existing products may have been saturated and new sources of growth must be found. Sometimes innovative companies discover new procedures which lead to new product development possibilities. Innovation is a theme which drives most successful companies. For example, the *raison d'être* of the Johnson and Johnson Company seems to be innovation. Products introduced by that company in the past five years account for about 25 per cent of total company sales. Two other reasons may be found for developing new products: excess production capacity and the opportunity to shorten the life cycle of competitor products.

New product objectives

New products and services are important to the company for a number of reasons. They serve to stabilize sales, contribute to company growth and reduce risk through diversification. New products can also make more efficient use of distribution channels. They can also enhance the company's image as an innovator. In some cases, new products can be developed from the waste materials of existing products, which has both a cost and profit effect and an environmental benefit.

New product development activity is greater in some countries than in others. It tends to be greater in Japan and the USA than it does in Europe. New product launches in the non-alcoholic beverages category reached 700 in Japan in 1991 compared to 435 for the USA and 16 for Germany (Ohbora *et al.*, 1992: 53). These authors estimate that there was only one new biscuit product launch in Germany in 1991, while 200 were launched in Japan. Two new coffee products were launched in Germany, while in the USA it was 67 (Table 11.1). In recent years, however, there is evidence that the number of new product launches in Japan in all product categories has fallen considerably.

New product development opportunities

The value of new products to the company is unambiguous. The firm may see a gap in its existing product line and attempt to fill it by developing a new product. New products help to stabilize irregular sales patterns of existing products, they contribute to company growth and they reduce risk through diversification and the application of the portfolio concept to the company's product mix. New products can mean more efficient use of established channels of distribution. They may also use waste materials or by-products from existing products and processes, and thereby enhance the company's image. This reason is related to the excess production capacity that companies sometimes experience. Furthermore, the company may discover that the market for its existing products is saturated and that it is necessary to seek new sources of growth.

Successful innovators may discover new processes, leading to new product development. This might have the added advantage that introduction could

TABLE 11.1   Selected new grocery product launches, 1991

Product category	Germany	Japan	USA
Non-alcoholic beverages	16	700	435
Biscuits	1	200	170
Coffee	2	24	67

Source: Ohbora *et al.* (1992: 53). By permission of McKinsey and Co.

serve to shorten the life cycle of competing products. Shortening the life cycle of competitor products has become a major feature of the strategic arsenal of a number of well-known companies. In the early 1970s, the Olivetti company was rejuvenated as a result of its introduction of the then new electronic typewriters. The Canon Company succeeded in attenuating the life cycle of some large photocopying machines through its introduction of feature-laden small photocopiers. Similarly, Brother with its expanding line of portable electronic typewriters damaged sales of existing desk-top products. An inversion of the product life cycle may be used to plan company growth (Weber, 1976). As a result of Weber's analysis, it is possible to identify a series of gaps in the market attributable to various causes (Figure 11.1).

New product and service innovation

From a marketing point of view, an innovation is anything perceived as new by potential adopters. The newness may be incorporated in products, services or ideas. The perceived innovative characteristics of an innovation determine the rate and extent of adoption. A number of characteristics of the innovation itself are thought to influence the likelihood of adoption (Tornatzky and

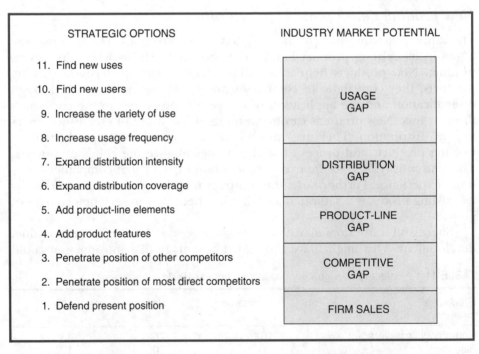

Figure 11.1   Identifying new product development opportunities

(Source: Adapted from Weber, 1976: 18. With kind permission from Elsevier Science Ltd, The Boulevard, Langford Lane, Kidlington, OX5 1GB, UK)

Klein, 1982; Rogers, 1983). The characteristics of the innovation featured by these authors are relative advantage, compatibility, complexity, trialability, observability, uncertainty and diffusion obstruction.

The perceived superiority of the innovation over that which it replaces is a measure of its relative advantage in the market. Its consistency with existing life-styles and ways of working and procedures indicates how compatible the inno-vation is. If it is not relatively easy to understand how the innovation works and how it can be implemented, it may be perceived as too complex for adoption. To what extent is it possible to experiment with the innovation before adoption is an important question. If the investment is high, adopters may wish to place the innovation on trial for some time before deciding. If the consequences of adopting the innovation are clearly observable to the adopter, by way of greater efficiency from a new piece of equipment or complimentary glances from passers-by for a new jacket, the innovation will have met the observability criterion.

Successful product innovations meet customer needs competitively, whereas failures tend to be based on an illusory innovation. While it is neces-sary to keep abreast of new technological developments in an industry, it is not always easy and can be extremely risky and expensive:

> My business is currently pioneering two radical new forms of detergent. We make a 'building block' detergent in Germany that allows consumers to use only the chemicals they need for any set of circumstances – dramatically reducing the environmental load. We're also making products for auto dosing in washing machines; you fill containers in the machine with products – it does the rest. Ownership of these expensive machines is tiny and growing only slowly: it may be a decade before we can make money out of the products we supply. Both of these products have limited consumer appeal today. But we will keep going because we believe it will be important in the future and because we will only learn by being active in the market. (Fitzgerald, 1991)

New product-market decisions

It is possible to classify new products in terms of product objectives defined in two dimensions: the newness of the product in terms of technology change; and the newness of the market entered in terms of the difference from exist-ing markets. The company may have numerous new product development decisions to make, depending on circumstances. By relating marketing deci-sions to new product development decisions, Johnson and Jones (1957) derive nine new product development objectives that the company might pursue (Figure 11.2). A number of these, particularly those involving minor changes to existing products, were discussed in Chapter 10. In this chapter, the discus-sion centres on innovation, which means introducing completely new products to existing and to new markets. The discussion may reflect the circumstances associated with improvements and adaptation of technology.

NEW MARKET	Reposition brand new use	Extend market	Diversify
NEW MARKETING MIX	Remerchandize	Improve product	Extend product lines
NO CHANGE	Serve existing product markets	Reformulate product	Innovate
Marketing decisions	NO CHANGE	IMPROVED TECHNOLOGY	NEW TECHNOLOGY
	Product decisions		

Figure 11.2 New product development objectives
(Source: Adapted from Johnson and Jones, 1957: 507)

The most innovative and daring approach is to diversify, which requires a lot of marketing analysis and resources before it can be considered as a possibility. Marketing risk rises as the new product development decision moves further away from the origin. By improving the technology only, without changing market decisions, the company is reforming the product. A new technology would mean a product innovation.

The more interesting decisions involve a change in products and markets. A combination of improved technology and a new marketing mix allows the company to introduce an improved product (Exhibit 11.1). An improved technology in a new market means deciding to extend the market, while a new marketing mix and a new technology means an extension to the company's product lines. A combination of a new technology and a new market involves a decision to diversify. The further the company moves from serving existing product-markets, the greater the risk involved. The decision to diversify involves the greatest risk.

The Mars group had many alternatives open to it when it decided to introduce the range of ice-cream versions of its well-known confectionery brands: Mars, Snickers, Milky Way and Bounty. Both the traditional confectionery and ice-cream markets were highly fragmented, and awaited consolidation through an innovative intervention such as designed and implemented by Mars. The decision taken by Mars regarding product replacement in the market was an

---

EXHIBIT 11.1   Step-by-step new product development at Nike

Last February, 186 athletes from Alaska to the Virgin Islands laced up new running shoes and hit the road. They had specific instructions: cover at least 45 miles a week, don't worry about stepping on rocks and glass, then report on how well the shoes held up to Nike Inc., in Beaverton, Ore.

These runners, all volunteers, are a key part of Nike's product-development process. They were testing its newest model, the Air 180; it marks what Nike calls the next evolution of its air-cushioning technology. But so far, runners' comments have resulted in only minor modifications to ensure that the shoe holds up past 500 miles – enough to last most amateur runners a while. Nike foresees a big market for the 180.

The saga of the Air 180 illustrates the curious blend of high and low technology that goes into top-selling athletic shoes. Nike has learned the hard way to push its technology. In 1979, the company introduced the air-cushioning system. But in the mid-1980s, it focused too much on fashion and was overtaken by Reebok International Ltd as the industry leader. In 1987, Nike fought back, carrying marketing to athletic performance with the Visible Air line shoes with a tiny window in the heel so consumers can see the air bag. That spurred sales of all Air products. And in 18 months, Nike has surpassed Reebok in both market share (25 per cent vs 23 per cent) and sales. Now, Nike's engineers, not its fashion designers, call the shots.

On Wall Street, some question claims of new technology in the marketing-oriented athletic-shoe business. 'Nike'll Air you until you're Aired out,' says Kidder, Peasbody & Co.'s Gary Jacobson. 'The question is, are they engineering a better, more technological sneaker or a more marketable sneaker?' Adds one university foot expert: 'It's a good product, but not miles better than what others are doing.'

Source: *Business Week*, 13 August 1990: 42.

---

innovation, since the constituents of the product are constituents which were not before combined in ice-cream form. The Mars products use real dairy ice-cream containing 5 per cent butterfat, and are wrapped in real milk chocolate. The average ice-cream bar on the market prior to this contained non-milk fat covered in a chocolate-flavoured coating.

Developing new products and services

Developing new products is a risky business. Business magazines and research reports regularly carry stories of very high failure rates. Levels of 80 per cent failure for new product introductions are frequently reported. Products fail for technical reasons and for marketing reasons. It is important to note that a product which is a technical success can be a marketing failure. At the same time, few companies can ignore the need to develop new products, since they are the life blood of future profits in the company.

In the 1990s, companies attempt to compete on quality in their products and services. But unless this quality is translated meaningfully for the customer, the new product is unlikely to succeed. It is important, therefore, that the company understands how success and failure arise in new product introductions.

New product success and failure

Many reasons may be adduced to explain the success and failure of new products. Successful firms are known to evaluate new product development ideas using four important criteria:

- prospects for sales and profits;
- capital or investment cost associated with the new venture;
- competitive feasibility; and
- strategic desirability.

Based on the perceptions of managers of industrial product companies, the following lists of success and failure factors appear to capture the range of experience reasonably well.

Reasons for new product success

The six most important variables which contribute to new product development success, in order of importance are:

- significant customer/user benefits;
- synergy with existing marketing skills;
- synergy with existing technical and manufacturing skills;
- high product quality;
- appropriate targeting and pricing strategies; and
- distribution channel support.

As a consequence, success factors in new product development may be identified as:

- speed;
- cost leadership;
- perceived superiority among customers; and

- use of familiar distribution channels and existing customer bases to ensure initial success.

In regard to speed to market, companies have the option of buying in the new product under their own logo.

Reasons for new product failure

Many reasons have been cited for product failure. The seven most frequently encountered reasons are:

- inadequate market research;
- high development costs;
- short life of the innovation;
- lack of marketing skills;
- high production costs;
- lack of competitive advantage; and
- corporate pride.

Inadequate market research can result in exaggerated sales projections. Sometimes development costs are higher than originally planned. The new product may be rendered obsolete by a competitor sooner than anticipated; this competitive matching shortens the life of the innovation. Many companies are skilled in innovation and new product development, but do not possess adequate marketing skills or distribution capabilities for the product. High production costs are also a well-known cause of product failure; companies are frequently unable to reduce production costs quickly enough to be competitive in the market. Another reason for product failure is that the product had no real points of superiority, thereby resulting in a lack of competitive advantage. Lastly, there are situations where, during the product development process, the new product team and others in the company realize that the product is going to fail, but for reasons of corporate pride the process is continued instead of dropping it and thereby cutting losses.

Very soon after the launch of Kodak's Photo CD product, doubts were cast on its market viability. Some thought that the product was 'over-engineered', too sophisticated and expensive for the task to which it would be devoted, particularly when many more accessible and competitively priced alternatives existed (Exhibit 11.2).

The six most important variables which contribute to new product development failure in order of importance are:

- the market is too competitive;

EXHIBIT 11.2   Smile – you're on compact disc!

Bill Smith, owner of a small Boston photo-lab, slips a gold-coloured compact disc out of its case and inserts it into a black machine. Within seconds, a colour photo of Boston Red Sox pitcher Roger Clemens pops up on the nearby TV. Clemens is in midpitch, frozen just as the ball is leaving his hand. Fingering his remote control, Smith zooms in on Clemens' arm. The colours remain luminescent, the resolution good. 'This', says Smith, 'is the future of photography.' The folks at Eastman Kodak Co. surely hope so. Kodak has a lot riding on Photo CD, which is just part of a broader push by the Rochester (NY) company to revitalise and protect its core photo business. After years of solid growth, US sales of amateur film stagnated in 1990 and 1991. Growth in international sales also slowed markedly. Some analysts blame the popularity of camcorders; others the economy.

Looming on the horizon is an even bigger threat: electronic photography. It's a hybrid system, allowing photographers to capture images on ordinary film. Then, a photo finisher could 'digitize' the image so it might later be manipulated, stored and transmitted with relative ease. 'We've changed the rules of the game,' says Stephen S. Stepnes, a general manager of the Photo CD project.

But will anybody buy it? The price of the Photo CD player – which can also play audio CDs – is just the beginning. A photographer must take a roll of film for ordinary developing, then pay an additional $20 or more to get those pictures scanned onto a Kodak CD. 'To me, it's simply a fancy way of looking at slides,' says Paul D'Andrea, president of Mystic Color Lab Inc., a mailorder photo finisher.

Next year, Kodak will spend a quarter of its ad budget on Photo CD alone. But if that doesn't give sluggish film sales a much-needed boost, Kodak may be left wondering if a fancy slide projector is really the wave of the future.

Source: *Business Week*, 10 August 1992: 26.

- insufficient market research performed prior to launch;
- the product is not new or novel to the market;
- the product offers negligible savings or other benefits to users;
- inadequate sales force allocation or training; and
- inadequate promotion and advertising strategies.

The first is an environmental factor outside the control of the firm. The marketing company is in a position substantially to reduce the likelihood of failure due to the remaining five factors, by taking appropriate actions and decisions during the new product development process.

Avoiding product failure

At each step in the process, product ideas and proposals are rejected. The attrition rate is highest in the early stages. Because sunk investment increases as the new idea moves through the process, the cost of losing new production development prospects increases. Very rigid screening devices at the early stages are recommended. A product with no real advantage over existing products faces an uphill battle against established products. An imitative product may be successful in new markets, but true innovations, products with unique features and advantages, usually prove to be more successful.

No matter how much technical effort is invested in developing a new product, it may not meet performance expectations. The problem usually arises when a substantial amount of resources have already been sunk on development and the company decides to introduce the product even though its performance characteristics are not as good as originally expected. If the gap is too large between desired and actual product characteristics, the product is likely to fail at the commercial stage.

Either the lack of marketing research or faulty research may cause a new product to fail. Good research information can also help to determine desired product characteristics, market target decisions and product positioning.

There are risks of being too early or too late in entering a market. Preoccupation with the development of a new product and neglect of the commercial stage sometimes occurs in industrial product companies with highly technical products.

Traps in new product development

It is a relatively simple matter to fall into one of the traps associated with developing new products. These traps may arise under any of five different types: competitive delusion, market scope, competence, illusory innovation, and marketing analysis and strategy (Figure 11.3).

Competitive delusion trap

Competitive delusion refers to the situation where companies believe that their approach is right and that they can take on the world without much opposition. Frequently, such companies have new product development launch plans which are much too ambitious. Because it is extremely difficult to launch into several markets simultaneously, it may be necessary to fine tune products for specific markets. It is likely that, no matter how standardized the product is expected to be, it will need some calibration for different markets within a country and across countries. For this reason, to avoid competitive delusion, companies may be advised to adopt a roll-out sequence through a

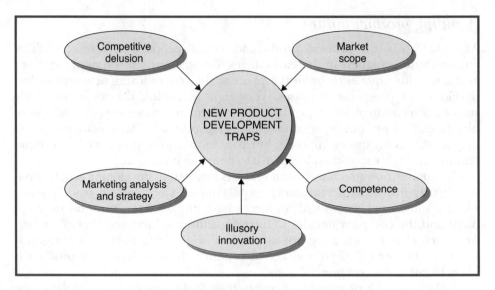

Figure 11.3   Traps in new product development

series of smaller test markets first, before going national or tackling large international markets.

Some managers would object to this advice based on the idea that new products should be introduced quickly into many markets so that sales rise quickly. The difficulty which arises is that few companies have the resources to match the requirements of the approach to launching a product. If the firm does not have the resources, quality problems may emerge and intermediaries and customers may start to have doubts about the new product and the company's entire product mix.

Competitive delusion also arises from corporate pride. On occasion a new product about to be launched is tipped in the trade press to be a loser, and market research may have already indicated as much to the company, but for reasons of corporate pride the product is launched when it should have been dropped.

Restricted scope and competence traps

The second trap is to have a much too restricted scope of the appropriate market. Companies which fall into this trap are often located in small national markets or in reasonably protected regional markets. Without being overly ambitious and falling into the competitive delusion trap, it may be advisable to design the new product in such a way that, without heavy modification costs, it can subsequently be introduced into wider markets. In many cases, companies need to plan for international markets from the outset to allow for the market-

486

ing barriers which arise, such as language, culture and technical standards. Companies attempting to maintain control over market scope tend to carry out product and market tests in a number of national and international markets early in the process, to obtain a wider vision of the overall potential for their new product.

The third new product development trap refers to the company's competence in the area and its cost structure. In many markets, there are strong competitors who are difficult to dislodge. It may be foolhardy to attack international market leaders, particularly if the company does not have a distinct competence in a number of areas. Success may depend on a competence which includes cost leadership, quality or access to distribution outlets. The company may also face the situation where development costs are substantially higher than expected. After launch, the company may experience production costs which do not fall quickly enough.

Market illusion and market analysis failure

The most highly publicized trap in new product development is that the innovation is a market illusion. Here it is necessary to recall that an innovation is what is perceived by the customer to be an innovation. Unfortunately, companies often develop products which have no real points of superiority. The source of this problem can sometimes be traced to a company philosophy based on technology push. The danger is that technically excellent products may be produced, but may be perceived as not having any exceptional value. An allied danger is that the product may be matched or rendered obsolete by the competition sooner than expected. There are many examples of products which have fallen into this trap, including Kodak's disc cameras, RCA's video disc player, IBM's PC Jr and Philip's motivational feedback loudspeakers.

The most fundamental trap in new product development refers to marketing analysis and strategy. Weak marketing in the company is often the reason why some companies fall into the traps listed above. Many reasons may be identified. In some cases, the market research is inadequate and sales projections are over-optimistic. In other cases, a marketing strategy of aggressive entry-level pricing may achieve initially high sales, but at the cost of low profits. In general, such companies do not have adequate marketing know-how or distribution capabilities for the product, or fail to implement them properly. Sometimes companies and even entire industries misjudge trends among consumers, or misinterpret them to end up producing highly sophisticated and technical solutions when customers seek simple solutions to their problems. This was the situation facing the more expensive end of the Japanese camera business in 1992 (Exhibit 11.3).

EXHIBIT 11.3   Throwaway high-tech cameras

Now that microchip technology has made it possible for even the most ham-fisted holiday maker to take photos like the best professional, consumers suddenly seem bored by the whole idea. This is proving a disaster for Japan's camera makers.

Out of the 26 million cameras sold in America last year, fewer than one million were fancy, auto-focusing models. Japanese makers managed to export only 3.3 million of their top-of-the-range single-lens reflex cameras in 1991 – down from a peak of 6.4 million in 1981. Today many consumers prefer simpler, handier and even throw-away models with few high-margin accessories. Once lauded and feared as the most ruthless of Japanese exporters, the country's camera makers swept competitors aside by dazzling consumers with clever new technologies. Now it seems to be their turn to be swept aside.

The quickest to exploit, and encourage, these trends has been Fuji Photo Film. With a 70 per cent share of the Japanese market for film and second worldwide only to Eastman Kodak, Fuji has attacked the camera market with gusto, catching traditional camera makers off guard with a range of startlingly successful disposable cameras.

At the other end of the market, the aficionados who once spent lavishly on the latest wizardry from Nikon, Minolta or Canon now tote the new generation of palm-sized video cameras offered by electronic giants such as Sony, Matsushita and Hitachi. Worse, those still buying cameras could not care less about grain size, depth-of-field, l/f numbers and other photo-babble. All most consumers want is convenience, at rock-bottom prices. The high-tech skills carefully acquired over decades by Japanese camera makers are having to be redeployed to be worth anything.

Source: *The Economist*, 29 February 1992: 76.

New product and service development as marketing innovation

Shrinking product life cycles are forcing companies to develop and launch new products more quickly to keep abreast of market demand. Improved design technologies help speed up the development process. Greater flexibility in the use of components or ingredients contributes to the process by permitting many variations on a theme to be used, such as cereals, nuts and fruit as ingredients in confectionery. Sometimes new product and service development can come from attempts to reinvent the wheel (Exhibit 11.4). As a consequence, it is necessary to understand how innovation occurs and how it is diffused. It is also important to recognize that new products and services

EXHIBIT 11.4   Reinventing the wheel

For a century or more bicycles have been much the same shape. Yet the business of making bicycles is now dominated not by cost-cutting mass-producers so much as trend-setting innovators. The cause is partly new technology; but also the transformation of bicycling from a transport industry to a hobby. The space-age creations whizzing around the Barcelona velodrome at this month's Olympics are one example. British sports fans were abuzz at the record-breaking, gold-medal exploits of Chris Boardman and his 'aerodynamic bike'. Meanwhile, in the Olympic village competitors switched in droves to a drag-reducing wheel that can save them a precious ten minutes in a 100-mile time trial.

The wheel, originally created for the American Olympic team using a supercomputer, is the fruit of collaboration between Du Pont, a chemicals giant, and Specialized Bicycle Components, based in Morgan Hill, California. The firm regularly joins up with others not best known for their cycling connections. Unlike most of the inventors pedalling their wares this week in Spain, Specialized has a record of turning technological leads into commercial success.

Specialized's mix of innovation and smart marketing was the key to this success. Products tested by its professional racing team are typically on sale within a year. It consults, and bombards with product information, the independent dealers who are its main sales outlets. The two-thirds of bikes that are sold through chain stores are mostly cheaper than the $300 minimum price of a Specialized cycle.

A risk is that cycling's current innovative phase will be as short lived as the equivalent period a century ago, when designers added pedals and decided that two equally sized wheels were better than one giant wheel and one tiny one. If a new 'standard' emerges for the bicycle, one that can be cheaply mass-produced and sold off-the-shelf in chainstores, Specialized may find its market vanishing in the face of competition from producers better suited to bulk manufacturer and distribution. Cheap and cheerful mountain bikes are selling increasingly well in shops across America.

Mr Sinyard reckons there is plenty of innovation to come, and has a research team working on the 'bike of the future'. Besides, there will always be Olympians desperate to shave a few seconds off their time.

Source: *The Economist*, 1 August 1992: 57–8.

frequently appear as a result of a convergence of product and market technologies. Companies must also recognize that the benefits of innovation must be perceived as such by potential users.

Innovation and diffusion processes in marketing

The marketing strategy adopted by the innovation supplier can have a significant influence on the diffusion rate (Frambach, 1993). In some situations a group of suppliers together promote the innovation to ensure it is accepted in the market, while in other situations a unique marketing approach by an individual firm is followed (Easingwood and Beard, 1989). By considering customer requirements early in the product development process, the ultimate fit between technical aspects and customer needs will be improved (Håkansson, 1982).

The needs of the adopter influence the adopter's behaviour. Four sets of characteristics are thought to influence this behaviour (Figure 11.4). Perhaps the most important are the characteristics of the innovation itself. Also impor-

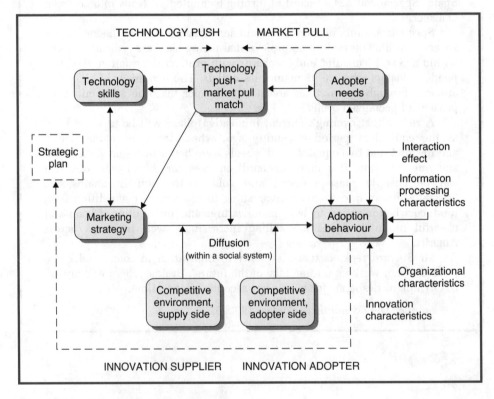

Figure 11.4 Innovation push and market pull
(Adapted from Frambach, 1993: 35)

tant are the characteristics of the adopting organization, the information-processing features of the organization and the interaction effects caused by the innovation within the adopting organization.

Convergence of technology push and market pull

On the supply side, the innovation supplier prepares a marketing strategy to push the new technology or innovation. This is influenced by the technical capacity of the innovator and the nature of the diffusion process in the particular product-market in question. As a result of these two pressures, a convergence occurs between the technology push of the innovation supplier and the market pull of the innovation adopter (Figure 11.4). Innovation push and market pull are considered to be part of the same network of relationships involving suppliers and customers.

A marketing innovation, however, is any new market or technology change which represents an innovative intervention in the market. It is anything perceived as new by potential adopters: a new product, a new service or a new idea.

Benefits and consequences of an innovation

The characteristics of the innovation determine the level of adoption in the market. For an innovation to be adopted, there must be an advantage associated with its use which is higher or better than that of competitors. The superiority of the innovation determines its relative advantage over competitors (Figure 11.5). The innovation company also checks for consistency between the innovation and the lifestyles of the target market. To be successful an innovation must be compatible. There is little point in attempting to introduce an innovation which conflicts with the culture, religion or mores of society, or behaviour which is incompatible with the lifestyles in the target market.

It is also necessary that the innovation can be understood by potential users and is easy to implement. This refers to the issue of complexity. In industrial markets, many products are highly complex, sometimes much too complex for the intended task. Such mismatching gives rise to difficulties in understanding and applying the innovation. Before adopting something new, consumers or users often like to try the innovation without committing to it, particularly if it involves a large cost or a significant change in work practices in the buying organization. It is important, therefore, to allow potential customers to try the innovation to determine if it works for them.

Experimentation with the innovation before final commitment allows trial-ability, which is a desirable feature of any innovation. To accomplish trial-ability, companies often make the product available as samples. Food products are frequently available by way of a sales promotion in supermarkets to allow potential customers to try them. In industrial markets, potential customers

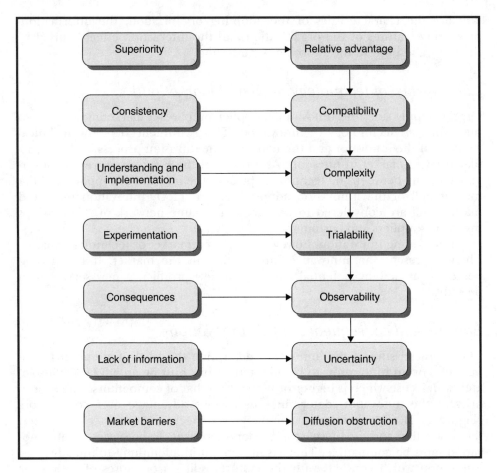

Figure 11.5   Adoption of market innovation

may be allowed to use a piece of equipment for some time before deciding whether to purchase it.

Potential users of the product will also wish to determine the consequence of adopting the innovation. It is important, therefore, that the innovation results in an observable improvement for the buyer. Observability may refer to a visible improvement in a person's attire as a consequence of purchasing a new jacket, or the saving of 2 per cent in production costs as a consequence of installing a new computer-controlled metal-cutting machine.

Lack of information about the innovation and its application can result in uncertainty, and artificial market barriers can obstruct the diffusion of the innovation. Diffusion of innovation in marketing is concerned with the process by which the application and use of the innovation spreads through-out the target market. The adoption of innovation is seen as a process which diffuses throughout society. Not everybody adopts the innovation at the same time. There are leaders and laggards in the process. Observing this type of behaviour and based on research work, Rogers (1983) provided the information on the timing of adoption of a new product or idea which was discussed in Chapter 5. He represented this as a normal distribution curve irrespective of the length of time involved.

Competitive success depends on speed to market

The key element in marketing competition today is speed to market. This is especially true in high-technology products, but also true in any product likely to experience obsolescence, seasonality, fashion or changing consumer tastes. The market benefits to the company of faster new product development and commercialization are numerous, as discussed in detail in Chapter 8.

Maintaining product quality with speed

If the right principles of new product development are applied, speedy new product development and launch can reduce costs and improve quality at the same time. Product-line and resource planning are critical elements in rapid new product development. Forecasting the resources which will be required in the medium term, conducting market research and developing cost-estimating methods are among the elements of planning which will speed up new product development. They are also likely to lead to lower costs, improved quality and greater improvements in the new product development process.

The improved market position, increases in company experience and brand enhancement associated with rapid new product development suggest that it is much better to identify and correct deficiencies than to allow competitors to achieve and enhance market positions which will be very difficult to regain. In such circumstances, the innovator possesses many advantages over its rivals.

Process of new product and service development

A fundamental aspect of new product development in successful companies is that innovation is not an event, it is a process. For successful companies, innovation is part of their routine. Because there is a great deal of uncertainty and risk involved, successful companies use a structured approach to integrate the crucial parts of the process.

The process of bringing new products to the market can be very risky and can involve large financial and time investments at many stages. This is especially true in the case of fast-moving consumer products. In calculating the

---

EXHIBIT 11.5   Developing and launching a new brand: Bailey's Original Irish Cream Liqueur

In the early 1970s Gilbeys of Ireland Limited faced a rapidly changing environment which would affect the market for alcoholic beverages in a number of fundamental ways. By developing a whole new product category, the company responded to the opportunities arising in world markets at the time. Hence was created Bailey's Original Irish Cream Liqueur, marketed by R & A Bailey and Co. Limited, a subsidiary of Gilbeys of Ireland. A summary of the approach to new product development and launch in the company demonstrates many of the critical steps in the process:

Idea generation

● 'Think Tank' of senior managers of Gilbeys meet to scan the environment for opportunities.
● Wish to design a product which would use 'Irishness' concept and reflect natural healthy countryside.

Screening

● Examination of traditional areas of the spirit market is made:
  – vermouth-type products – already developed;
  – green vodka – 'green' concepts already covered;
  – whiskey and cream – unique Irish combination.

---

cost, it is necessary to include the cost of the time spent in research and development, capital investment in plant and equipment, warehousing and distribution costs, packaging and advertising development costs, and launch and promotional support costs. For well-known brand companies, there is the additional risk of damaging the company's overall reputation if failure should occur. Customers remember product failures for years. The greatest risk of all, however, is not to innovate, which will guarantee the ultimate demise of the company.

Stages in the new product development process

The new product development process may be divided into six stages:

● new idea/concept generation and screening;

● development and testing of the new idea/concept;

● business and marketing analysis;

● product development and testing;

Market research

- Traditional market segments (whisky, gin, vodka) maturing rapidly.
- Swing to lighter-alcohol products.
- Swing to more exciting new products.
- Growing importance of women in the market.
- Liqueur segment not dominated by any one major brand.

Product development

- Product concept relatively simple.
- Chemistry difficult – whiskey and cream don't mix.
- Focus group studies in London and New York have inconclusive results.
- Experts – 'too sweet'.
- Pilot plant established in Dublin in 1974.
- Packaging developed:
  - Irish but not stagy;
  - 'Bailey's' name easy to say and identify in most languages;
  - legally protectable.

Commercialization

- Irish national launch in 1974.
- 19,000 cases sold in 1975.
- Test marketed in Holland and UK in 1975.

- test marketing; and

- commercialization.

Many very successful companies are known to have developed a step-by-step approach to new product development. When the R & A Bailey and Company Limited launched its Bailey's Original Irish Cream Liqueur brand in the early 1970s, the company followed a staged approach similar to that outlined above (Exhibit 11.5).

In the early stages of new product development, the manager gathers sufficient data to decide whether an opportunity is worthwhile. A particularly appropriate source of information on new product development opportunities is published research on changing consumer lifestyles. In recent years, for instance, there has been a move to snacking and more informal eating, greater emphasis on products for older people as the population ages, and a change in the type of furniture purchased as people move into smaller houses and apartments, and as single-person households are established. Detail is not required at this stage. Comprehensive market research can be carried out later.

In these preliminary stages, qualitative research is used to eliminate concepts that are unlikely to succeed for various reasons. The qualitative research gives guidance on how the concept may be refined during later stages. It may be sufficient to discuss the project in outline form with distributors, retailers or journalists from the trade press, who can provide a great deal of qualitative information. This approach may be essential in poorly researched markets or certain industrial product markets.

The crucial aspect of research at this stage is to eliminate projects which have no likelihood of market acceptance. Research may prevent the company from accepting a new product idea just because corporate strategy requires new products to be launched on some prescribed basis. At this stage, it is also necessary to determine the extent to which the perceived opportunity can remain viable in the face of competitive retaliation. It is unlikely that competitors will remain passive in the face of a challenging new product.

Idea generation and screening

Generating new ideas and concepts means having a continuous systematic procedure for searching for new product opportunities. In this regard, it is generally believed that customers are the best source of new ideas, followed by competitors and the sales force. New product development consultants and scientists do not appear to be as highly rated in generating new concepts and ideas for development into products. Sometimes accidents help to produce

---

EXHIBIT 11.6   A star material is born, accidentally

Last year, Onio State University announced that a screw-up by one of its undergraduates had created a superstrong, lightweight material. Now, the university is trying to convert serendipity into cash by working with auto manufacturers and electronics companies that would like to use the material, known as Co-Continuous Ceramic Composite, or C^4.

C^4 came to life in 1990, when undergraduate Michael Breslin accidentally let a ceramic container full of aluminium heat up far beyond aluminium's melting point of 660 °C. The ceramic became saturated with aluminium. It proved to be strong but not brittle, good at conducting heat, wear-resistant, and only about half the density of steel. Plus, its ingredients are cheap: Silica for the ceramic is only about $1.50 a kilogram, while aluminium runs about $2.20 a kilogram.

An Ohio State team that includes Breslin, now a graduate student, is working with General Motors, Ford, General Electric, Cummins Engine, and others to design and test components made from C^4. Breslin says the composite can be modified for particular jobs – for example, to provide extra wear resistance in a brake rotor. Ohio State materials scientist Glenn Daehn says C^4 could start appearing in cars by 1997.

Source: *Business Week*, 24 January 1994: 39.

---

new products, as may be seen in the way one new, very strong material was discovered in 1990 (Exhibit 11.6). In these cases, scientists stumble on new discoveries which subsequently have very high commercial value.

In the process of new product development, the company first analyzes the current market situation and the capabilities in the company, and simultaneously carries out a market opportunity analysis and search (Figure 11.6). The first step in the process is to generate new ideas and concepts. This involves a continuous, systematic search for new product opportunities, in which senior management in the company define a new product development strategy.

The company must then refine the new concepts or ideas and screen them, using criteria such as product features, market opportunities, the competitive situation, company capability and the availability of finance. Ideas which have been screened through research and corporate fit criteria and have survived must pass through several further stages of refinement. Some companies at this stage propose a conceptual checklist for the project. The detailed criteria applied here are:

- identity of market segment;

- product description;

- technical features;

- customer benefits;

- competitive advantage; and

- manufacturing process.

In applying the above criteria, the company may use a numerical weighting evaluative system to relate the market potential of the new product idea to the company's ability to develop and launch it (Table 11.2). Scores are

TABLE 11.2   Product idea rating scheme: an example

Product success requirements	Relative weight	Company competence	Score
Company personality	0.20	6	1.2
Marketing	0.20	9	1.8
R & D	0.20	7	1.4
Personnel	0.15	6	0.9
Finance	0.10	9	0.9
Production	0.05	8	0.4
Location and facilities	0.05	2	0.1
Purchasing and supplies	0.05	3	0.3
Total	1.00		7.0

Note: Rating scale: poor = 0.0–4.0; fair = 4.1–7.5; good = 7.6–10.0

Source: Adapted from Richman (1962). Copyright 1962 by the Foundation for the School of Business at Indiana University. Used with permission.

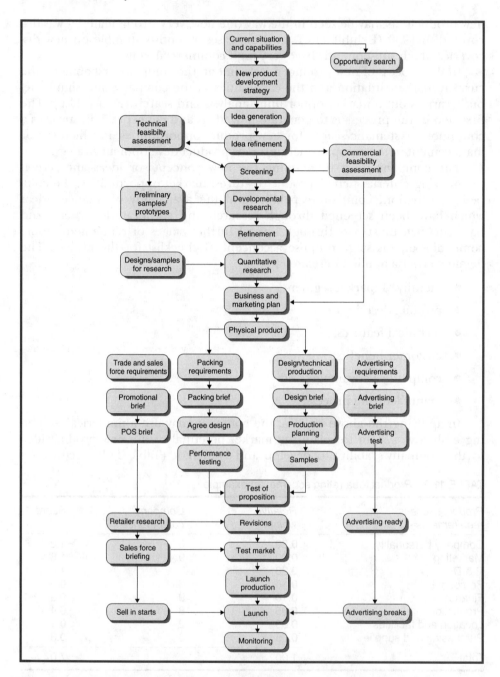

Figure 11.6 The process of new product development

(Source: Adapted from 'Marketing Guide 7: New Product Development', supplement in *Marketing* (UK), 11 May, 25–8).

allocated to new product development ideas depending on how well they meet the criteria in the company's various markets. Two benefits of this evaluative process may be identified. First, a ranking of projects is established which ensures that the most likely success receives immediate attention and, if for any reason it falls out of consideration at a later stage, that others have been identified for development. Second, the approach provides a clear objective basis for evaluating possible new products.

In carrying out more detailed research, the company may reserve the services of a specialist market research house, or it may have the resources internally to do the research itself. Various types of research may be performed at this stage, mainly based on focus groups. Whatever the nature of the research, it is necessary to separate responses into those which are substantive and those which are superficial.

Concept development and testing

During the second stage, the company carries out two types of feasibility study: a commercial feasibility study to judge if the new idea proposed is commercially sound; and a techical feasibility study to determine if the appropriate technical requirements and standards can be met. It is also usually necessary to produce designs and samples for quantitative research during this stage. This development and testing of the new idea moves the process from the stage of considering a product idea to dealing with a product concept and deciding an appropriate product image.

The commercial feasibility assessment is a form of business analysis which attempts to identify product success requirements and company competences. Financial projections, market analyses, sales projections, and estimates of profit margins and likely costs are made at this point. During this stage, the company attempts to identify the product features and market opportunities which might be developed. At this stage, too, the company assesses competitive factors, company capability and the financial requirements associated with proceeding further.

The company faces the possibility of making two types of mistake. It may decide not to proceed with a new product development idea, which is then taken up and made successful by a competitor. Alternatively, it may decide to proceed with an idea which turns out to be a failure. Two types of product failure are recognized:

- an absolute product failure which loses money, but in which variable costs are covered and a contribution is made to fixed costs; and

- a relative product failure which yields a profit less than the company's expected rate of return.

To reduce the probability of failure, many companies use a new product development checklist. By way of illustration of the procedures involved, nineteen factors are used to evaluate four hypothetical markets A, B, C and D in Table 11.3. Note that the evaluation recognizes long-term market prospects and the ability of the sales force to carry the new product as most important; potential customer age profile and other age group characteristics, and company image, are not important factors in evaluating this new product and its potential performance in the four markets.

Based on the factors selected and the evaluative scores obtained, usually done on the basis of management judgement, market A most closely meets the requirements, having obtained a score of 54. Market D is very unattractive. Indeed, the low scores obtained for all markets would lead the company to question the wisdom of entering any of them. Some companies, using frameworks like this, would decide an appropriate cut-off score before carrying out the evaluation.

Development research involves extending the concept or idea further and testing it. It means taking the product idea through the product concept stage and identifying an appropriate product image for it. It may be necessary, therefore, to create prototypes, carry out product functional tests and consumer tests. During this stage, the product concept is described to a sample of potential customers. They are told about the features of the product and may be shown a product mock-up or drawing of what it would look like. There are a number of advantages associated with concept testing (McGuire, 1973: 34):

TABLE 11.3   An illustration of market screening: assessing a new product in four hypothetical markets

Factor	Maximum score	Market A	B	C	D
Sterling sales trend	6	6	3	0	0
Volume trend	8	4	4	−4	−4
Long-term prospects	12	0	12	0	0
Current market size	6	0	0	−3	6
Buying by class	2	1	2	0	1
Age group characteristics	4	0	2	0	0
Age profile	2	1	2	1	1
Economic factors	10	5	10	0	5
Seasonality	6	−3	3	3	0
Penetration of branding	6	6	3	0	0
Companies in the market	10	10	5	5	5
Marketing/sales ratio	6	3	3	3	0
Product differentiation	10	5	5	0	0
Company image	4	0	−2	4	2
Brand images	8	0	0	8	0
Technology	10	5	−5	5	0
Buying resources	6	0	0	3	3
Sales force	12	6	6	0	0
Distribution	10	5	−5	10	0
Total	138	54	48	35	19

- it can be done quickly and before the product prototypes need to be developed;

- it can often be done early enough to make any project modifications indicated at little cost;

- it is relatively inexpensive as compared with later-stage research possibilities;

- it involves less danger of premature disclosure of the concept to competitors than does test marketing;

- it can help planners make sound choices from among alternative concepts being considered;

- it can help define and prove the existence of a suitable target market; and

- it can assist planners in developing the right produce and appeals for that market.

The test is, therefore, only an approximate measure of customer reactions. Concept testing is a service provided by specialist research companies, but it may be performed within the company if resources are available and care is taken. McGuire (1973: 65) also provides a set of guidelines for carrying out a concept test which focus on the critical steps involved:

- clarify the functions that the new product would perform, possible situations in which it could be used, and how it would be used;

- portray the product's characteristics in terms that will be understood readily by the respondent;

- provide a comparison of the product's likely physical and performance characteristics with those of any existing competitive products that perform a similar function;

- cite the product's principal advantages and disadvantages; and

- indicate an expected price or price range.

Business and marketing analysis

The third stage of the process involves a business and marketing analysis to produce a marketing plan. It is necessary at this stage to specify product success requirements and to identify company competences. Financial and sales projections are part of the process, and estimates of profit margins and development costs are also provided. At this stage, the company also describes the target market in considerable detail. It determines the appropriate positioning for the new products, its likely sales, market shares to be achieved and profit objectives. Appropriate price levels are decided, the distribution channel is

501

selected and the marketing budget for the first year is determined. The company also outlines the long-term sales and profits goals and marketing programme for the new product. Commercial feasibility therefore has an important role to play at this stage too.

In preparing a business and marketing plan, it is necessary to describe the market to be served and how the product should be positioned. It is also necessary to prepare a set of market share and profit objectives for the new venture. Underlying this analysis is the requirement of specifying an appropriate price, the level of distribution likely to be achieved in the first year and a marketing budget for that year. It is also necessary to specify long-term sales and profit objectives, and to outline the nature of the marketing programme for the longer term.

Product development and testing

During the fourth stage, the product is developed and tested. Numerous functional tests are carried out, and selected consumer tests are also administered. This is a very busy time in the company. Two sets of activities take place simultaneously. One set of activities involves deciding the appropriate packaging requirements for the product, its design and tests of performance, while the other set of activities involves product design, technical and production factors involved in production planning and the development of a sample product. At this stage, too, the proposition may again be tested, leading to some revision, particularly if retailers or other channel members have an opportunity to express their opinions.

Market testing

During the fifth stage, the company market tests the new product, having briefed the sales force. The product and proposed mix of marketing activities are introduced into authentic buyer settings to test product acceptance and market size. Revisions may still be necessary, hence the need for a flexible approach (Exhibit 11.7).

It will also be necessary to carry out quantitative research through consumer surveys or interviews with buyers in industrial markets, depending on the nature of the new product. At this stage, the company attempts to measure the extent to which potential customers are interested in the product, how they assess it compared to competing products, the features they like and dislike, the extent to which they are likely to purchase, and the price they would expect to pay. Other aspects of the marketing mix will also be researched as the product moves through the development process, including packaging, advertising copy and merchandising.

EXHIBIT 11.7   Office furniture as you like it!

Winston Churchill preferred to work standing at his desk. Now, another Brit, designer Geoff Hollington, has made it easy for everyone else to follow in Churchill's footsteps. A height-adjustable desk is the centrepiece of his Relay line of office furniture, made by Herman Miller Inc., in Zeeland, Mich.

Relay's flexibility was such a radical departure that Herman Miller used an unusual technique to test the concept. Hollington's first Relay design had been killed because its components could not be fastened together easily by office workers. So in 1989, the company gave eight employees prototypes of a new Relay system, then videotaped them using it. They quickly warmed to its malleability, shifting pieces more frequently than Hollington anticipated. Some altered the desk height as often as every few minutes. They also pulled wheeled tables and stands into tight wagon-like clusters, to create a larger work space.

The designer also used the tapes to fine-tune the components. For example, he added shelves to the credenza at heights that are handy to the adjustable desk. And it was obvious that office employees rarely used the line's small, rolling 'tool caddy', so it got the axe.

Source: *Business Week*, 8 June 1992: 68.

Commercialization of a new product

Market testing presumably gives management enough information to decide whether to launch the new product. If the company goes ahead with commecialization, it will face its largest costs to date. The company will have to contract for manufacture, or build or rent a full-scale manufacturing facility. The size of the plant will be a critical decision variable. The company can build a plant smaller than called for by the sales forecast, to be on the safe side, but it will then run the risk of missed opportunities in the market if the product takes off. In such circumstances, the company is in danger of handing over the potential of a well-cultivated market to flexible competitors who are capable of moving fast to imitate the company's new product. Another very large cost is the marketing cost associated with commercialization, which can be very high depending on the size of the market and the marketing tasks to be performed.

The final stage is to commercialize the product by launching it in the market. At the launch stage, the entire sales promotion activity, working with the trade and sales force and, particularly, retailers, converges with the advertising support process. The timing of market entry, the geographic market segments to be served, the target customer groups in each segment and the introductory marketing strategy are determined at this stage.

The new product development process described above is quite typical of the situation facing most companies. The details vary by company and circumstance.

EXHIBIT 11.8   New product development process in Tipperary Cereals Ltd

Tipperary Cereals Limited operates up-to-date plant and equipment to extrude cereals of different kinds from raw materials, such as wheat, rice and maize. The plant of 29 000 square feet, which was taken over by the company in 1985, is located on the Industrial Estate in Thurles, Ireland. Until about 1980 cereal processing was very traditional. It was based on technology introduced about the turn of the century, was capital intensive and operated on the batch system. For this reason, cereals could only be produced on a large scale because of economies, thus favouring the large multinationals. New entrants to the industry were not attracted by these conditions.

About 1980 a heat extrusion technology based on modern processing techniques (high temperature, high pressure, short cooking time) was introduced and applied to the snack food and cereal-processing sectors of the food industry. As a consequence, the bulk of breakfast cereals are now produced using the modern technology. The impact of the new technology is enormous: the traditional method of producing crisp rice took six hours, whereas Tipperary Cereals can produce an improved crisp rice in six minutes! The heat extrusion process, while capital intensive, is energy efficient and uses less labour than the traditional method. Plants may be operated at a lower scale of production. Being a recent innovation, however, very little background data have been published, nor is there any relevant database available in the public domain.

Tipperary Cereals has developed its own database and expertise over the previous five years and has become very skilful in the application of the technology to cereal production. The large companies prefer to work with small

---

Developing a new cereal food ingredient for the confectionery industry brand leader on a co-packing basis was a problem faced by Tipperary Cereals Limited in the early 1990s. The product development sequence resembles that discussed above in considerable detail (Exhibit 11.8). In industrial markets, new product development is usually carried out in close co-operation with existing and potential customers. The development sequence for the introduction and launch of a co-packing agreement, whereby this small cereal manufacturer prepared ingredients to be used in branded confectionery items for a large consumer products company, demonstrates the resource and time commitment, and the level of interaction involved (Figure 11.7).

Timing of new product launch

The product may be launched immediately into the national or international markets, or it may be moved into the market in stages, one national market

specialist firms like Tipperary Cereals, which have extensive knowledge and proprietary databases, rather than incur the cost of developing their own and investing in the specialist equipment necessary to apply the technology. Tipperary Cereals is a specialist, highly skilled producer of cereal ingredients and a niche player in this new market.

The development by Tipperary Cereals of a cereal for co-packing or of specialized cereal ingredients is a very detailed process involving the company and the customer throughout a process which, in extreme circumstances, can take more than three years to complete. Normally, however, it takes from eight to twelve weeks for the company and its customers to define the product concept and to evaluate costs. At this stage, most of the activity takes place within Tipperary Cereals, where the concept and prototypes are developed.

During the second stage, which can take from ten to twenty weeks, the prototype is reviewed and accepted. Market research findings and costings are evaluated in stage three. Storage tests are also carried out. At the end of this stage, the product is accepted or rejected. This stage can last from ten to twenty weeks. In some special cases, storage tests have lasted a full year. The next stage involves confirming packaging, finalizing quality assurances for process, and packaging and delivering the product to the customer's premises. The product is tested on the market during the next stage, which means monitoring consumer reaction, assessing transit stability factors, agreeing quality assurance acceptability standards and market research. This stage can last for between twelve and twenty-six weeks. Finally, a new cycle begins with subsequent product development phases for new product versions.

area at a time. Indeed, a geographic roll-out may be appropriate in larger national markets like Germany, the UK or the USA. This roll-out approach may be favoured when the supply of the product is limited or market tests were not conducted in every market. Sometimes companies launch a new product or service internationally at the same time because a competitive market and cost lead can be obtained. Very large companies may also have the resources to go for an international or global launch. To obtain adequate market coverage, it is often advisable to use familiar distribution channels and customer bases to ensure initial success.

Within the roll-out markets, the company must target its distribution and promotion to the best prospects. Prime prospects for a new consumer product would ideally be heavy users and opinion leaders prepared to give the new product positive word-of-mouth support and capable of being reached at low cost. The company must develop an action plan for introducing the new product into the roll-out markets. It must allocate the marketing budget among the marketing mix elements and sequence the various activities.

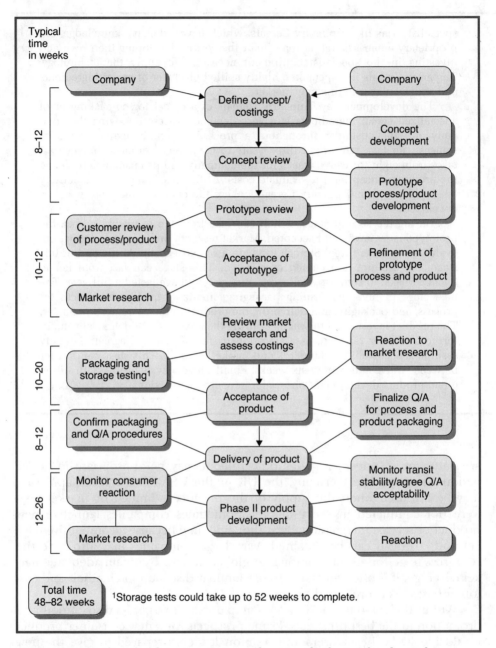

Figure 11.7 Outline development sequence for co-pack of specialized cereal ingredients products

Timing the market entry

In commercializing a new product, market-entry timing can be critical. Suppose a company has almost completed the development work on its new product and hears about a competitor nearing the end of its development work. The company faces three choices:

- to be the first to enter the market;

- to enter at the same time as a competitor; or

- to wait until after a competitor has been in the market for some time, and to enter with the benefit of knowing what is acceptable and what is not.

The first firm entering a market usually enjoys 'first-mover advantages', consisting of locking up some key distributors and customers, and gaining reputational leadership and the other benefits discussed in earlier chapters. On the other hand, if the product is rushed to the market before it is working properly, the company can acquire a flawed image. This was a danger which faced Merck and Co. when it introduced Proscar, a prostate drug. Critics believed the company had moved to market without sufficient testing. To counteract the criticism, the drug was introduced at a price much lower than expected (Exhibit 11.9).

The firm might time its entry with the competitor. If the competitor rushes to launch, the company does the same. If the competitor takes its time, the company also takes its time, using the extra time to refine its product. The company might want the promotional costs of launching to be borne by both of them.

Lastly, the firm might delay its launch until after the competitor has entered. There are three potential advantages. The competitor will have borne the cost of educating the market. The competitor's product may reveal faults that the late entrant can avoid. And the company can learn the size of the market.

The timing decision involves additional considerations. If the new product replaces an older product, the company might delay the introduction until the old product's stock is sold. If the product is highly seasonal, it might be held back until the right season.

Roll-out market entry

The company must decide whether to launch the new product in a single locality, a region, several regions, the national market, or the international market. Few companies have the confidence, capital and capacity to launch new products into full national distribution immediately, except in small-country markets. They develop a planned market roll-out over time.

In roll-out marketing, the company has to rate the alternative markets for their attractiveness. The major rating criteria are market potential, company's,

---

EXHIBIT 11.9   Critics ganging up on Merck's new wonder drug

As recently as April, at Merck and Co.'s annual meeting, Chairman Dr P. Roy Vagelos confidently predicted that Proscar, the company's new prostate drug, would be a $1 billion-a-year blockbuster. Good thing Vagelos didn't say when. Merck may have to wait for its big payoff until it overcomes worries about Proscar's safety and effectiveness.

Even before the Food & Drug Administration approved Proscar on June 19, many urologists had their doubts. Fewer than one-third of the men who used it during clinical tests reported a significant easing of urinary discomfort from prostate enlargement. 'There is a lot of scepticism this drug is not as powerful as it was thought to be,' says Dr Peter D. Scardino, chairman of urology at Houston's Baylor College of Medicine. Still, given that 10 million older men may have enlarged prostates and the drug will sell to druggists for $511 a year, Proscar's potential seems huge.

But other drawbacks may limit the drug's acceptance. It's impossible to predict who will benefit from it, so patients must try it for six months to see if it works. And those it helps must take it daily for life. So, many men may continue to opt simply to live with mild prostate conditions. And many of those with more severe problems may still choose surgery.

The other big worries about Proscar are cancer-related. Its harshest critic may be Dr William J. Catalona, head of urologic surgery at Washington University Medical Centre in St Louis, who was one of Merck's consultants on the drug. He argues that the FDA shouldn't have approved Proscar without further testing its long-term effect on prostrate-specific antigen, or PSA, in the blood. PSA testing increasingly is used by doctors to look for early signs of prostate cancer, which kills some 34,000 US men a year. Catalona, who has seen Merck's confidential data on Proscar, argues that the drug could make PSA testing ineffective. He complained to the FDA in February that 'this most important safety issue has not been adequately addressed'.

Another concern is whether – and how – Proscar will affect non-life threatening prostate cancer that is common in older men. Some cancer specialists worry that Proscar may accelerate the growth of some tumours. 'If you

---

local reputation, cost of filling the pipeline, quality of research data in that area, influence of the area on other areas, and competitive penetration. In this way, the company ranks the prime markets and develops a geographical roll-out plan. Larger companies attempt a global roll-out for products they believe have potential for world markets. Global marketing has become a feature of consumer durable products and many companies develop products with the intention of serving the global market. In developing the Mondeo model, Ford of Europe Inc. was attempting to produce a car which would succeed where the Fiesta had failed (Exhibit 11.10).

give this drug to patients who might have cancer in their prostates, albeit unknown, what will happen to the cancer?' frets Dr Paul H. Lange, chairman of urology at the University of Washington School of Medicine in Seattle, site of some Proscar testing. 'Will it do better or worse? That's unknown.'

Merck says tests so far show that Proscar is safe. Indeed, there are some signs, says Merck research chief Dr Edward M. Scolnick, that the drug may actually block some early cancer growth. The company plans a study with the National Cancer Institute to see if that is the case. In the meantime, Merck is pricing Proscar to sell. The price to druggists it set on June 22 – $1.40 a pill, or $511 for a year's worth – is well below the $730 annual charge analysts expected. Patients will also get a free two-month dose in their first year, plus one free month per year until 1995.

Some analysts doubt discount pricing will help Proscar much. Industry follower Hemant K. Shah figures the drug won't hit $1 billion in annual sales until perhaps 1998, four years later than he once thought. Patricia P. Lea of Vector Securities International Inc. sees no more than $500 million in yearly sales by 1997. 'I do not think it is a particularly good drug,' she says. Such doubts are one good reason that Merck stock has tumbled recently.

Arguments for Proscar:

- The only approved alternative to prostrate surgery
- Eases urinary discomfort in some older men
- Sometimes modestly shrinks swollen prostates

Arguments against Proscar:

- May interfere with detection of prostate cancer
- Effective for only 31 per cent of users
- No positive effects for six months – if ever

Source: *Business Week*, 20 July 1992: 31.

Assignment questions

1 Why is it important for the firm periodically to produce new products or services? What are the various sources for new production ideas?

2 How do the characteristics of a new product influence its rate of adoption? Consider the case of the microwave oven.

3 What is an innovation? What are the implications of new product/service adoption for the company?

EXHIBIT 11.10   Ford of Europe: from Escort to Mondeo – concept of a global car

For two humiliating years, Ford of Europe Inc. has been vying for billing as Europe's worst-performing car maker. To get back in fighting trim, the most critical part of Ford's turnaround plan is a flood of new products, spread over the next three years. In that effort nothing is more important than the Mondeo, a midsize car unveiled on January 6.

In a $6 billion programme, the new car is another effort by Ford to develop a 'world car'. 'It's what Ford of Europe is hinging a complete turn-around on,' says William Fike, the company's president. Ford's European dealers are hungry for the new model. No wonder. For too long, Ford left a gap in its mid-market product line and has relied on smaller models such as the Escort, which proved a design and financial embarrassment. Ford Motor Co.'s concept seemed great at the time – building a new 'world car' that would satisfy every taste from Detroit to Düsseldorf. But the result, the Escort, proved to be one of the grandest corporate foul-ups ever. To make the Escort, Ford set out to pool design, engineering and manufacturing from both North America and Europe. But rivalries were so intense that Ford ended up producing two very distinct models. When they finally hit the road in 1981, the North American and European versions shared nothing other than one part – a water-pump seal the size of a thumbnail.

Hoping history won't repeat itself, Ford now is betting $6 billion on the Mondeo, an even more ambitious world car. The front-wheel-drive Mondeo, priced at around $18,000 in Europe, is designed to replace the aging, 10 year old Sierra line in Europe and next year the Tempo/Topaz line in the US.

Ford executives figure that the convergence of emission standards, safety regulations, and, above all, consumer tastes in the Old and New Worlds make a single car worthwhile. Unlike the 1981 Escort, the US and European versions of the Mondeo will have 75 per cent common parts, although the US version will be slightly longer and have more chrome. While initial costs are higher, they are more than offset by the savings from engineering one, rather than two, cars. Even so, Ford execs admit, the final product isn't a dramatic head-turner. Ford is counting on such features as standard airbags and side impact bars, plus good fuel efficiency, to produce a winner.

Source: *Business Week*, 18 January 1993: 17–18.

---

4   Why do many new product ideas fail?

5   Discuss the various new product development traps.

6   What does the business analysis stage of the new product development process involve?

7   Discuss the need for concept development and testing in the new product development process.

8 What is test marketing? Discuss its advantages and disadvantages.

9 Discuss the importance of timing in market entry.

Annotated bibliography

Crawford, C. Merle (1983) *New Products Management*, Homewood, Ill.: Richard D. Irwin.

Hisrich, Robert D., and Michael P. Peters (1984) *Marketing Decisions for New and Mature Products: Planning, development and control*, Columbus, Ohio: Charles E. Merrill, chapters 8–11.

Kotler, Philip (1994) *Marketing Management* (8th edn), Englewood Cliffs, NJ: Prentice Hall, chapter 13.

McCarthy, E. Jerome, and William D. Perreault, Jr (1990) *Basic Marketing* (10th edn), Homewood, Ill.: Richard D. Irwin, chapter 10.

Stanton, William J., Michael J. Etzel and Bruce J. Walker (1991) *Fundamentals of Marketing* (9th edn), New York: McGraw-Hill, chapter 7.

Urban, Glen L., and John R. Hauser (1980) *Design and Marketing of New Products*, Englewood Cliffs, NJ: Prentice Hall, chapters 1–3.

References

Easingwood, Chris, and Charles Beard (1989) 'High technology launch strategies in the UK', *Industrial Marketing Management*, **18**, 2, 125–38.

Fitzgerald, N.W.F. (1991) 'Sustaining competitive advantage', paper presented at the National Marketing Conference, Dublin, 8 November.

Frambach, Ruud (1993) 'An integrated model of organisational adoption and diffusion of innovations', *European Journal of Marketing*, **27**, 5, 22–41.

Håkansson, Håken (ed.) (1982) *International Marketing and Purchasing of Industrial Goods: An interaction approach*, Chichester: John Wiley.

Johnson, Samuel C., and Conrad Jones (1957) 'How to organize for new products', *Harvard Business Review*, **35**, 3, 49–62.

McGuire E. Patrick (1973) *Evaluating New Product Development Proposals*, New York: The Conference Board.

Ohbora, Tatsino, Andrew Parsons and Hajo Riesenbeck (1992) 'Alternative routes to global marketing', *The McKinsey Quarterly*, **3**, 52–74.

Richman, Barry M. (1962) 'A rating scale for product innovation', *Business Horizons*, **5**, Summer, 37–44.

Rogers, Everett M. (1983) *Diffusion of Innovations*, (3rd edn), New York: The Free Press.

Tornatzky, Louis G., and Katherine J. Klein (1982) 'Innovation characteristics and innovation adoption-implementation: a meta analysis of findings', *IEEE Transactions on Engineering Management*, EM-29, 1, 28–45.

Weber, John A. (1976) 'Planning corporate growth with invested product life cycles', *Long Range Planning*, **9**, 5, 12–29.

Brand management decisions

12

Nature and purpose of branding
Building equity in the brand
Brand decisions
Managing the brand in the longer term

Introduction

This chapter introduces and explains:

- the difference between products, services and brands;

- the meaning of added value and how companies brand added values;

- the different perspectives on brand equity;

- the role of luxury in branding;

- manufacturer and customer benefits of branding;

- manufacturer and private-label brand decisions;

- the nature and role of generic brands;

- the use of brand extensions;

- competition from private label and threats to branding;

- relaunching the brand;

- how brands can be mismanaged;

- how companies position their brands; and

- the wheel of branding.

Branding is concerned with identifying and developing the added values associated with products and services. A product is something with a functional purpose. A brand serves a functional purpose, but its value derives from a unique balance between functional benefits and differentiated benefits. Uniqueness is the hallmark of a brand. Brands have become the centre of attention in recent years due to the brand equity debate. There are various perspectives on brand equity: financial, marketing and customer. Ultimately, the brand must provide something extra in all three areas for it to succeed. Profits, marketing power and customer loyalty should each be greater in regard to branding. The company must decide what type of brand name to use, whether it should be a manufacturer brand or a private label. The decision regarding branding can involve the company in significant levels of investment. In the longer term, brands face the inevitability of a life cycle if the brand is not managed. Companies frequently upgrade, relaunch and reposition their brands to protect their markets.

Having studied this chapter, you should be able to define the terms listed above in your own words, and you should be able to do the following:

1. Define branding and outline its purpose.

2. Outline the main issues in the debate on brand equity.

3. Specify the benefits of branding to the manufacturer and customer.

4. Evaluate the advantages and disadvantages of using manufacturer brands and private-label brands.

5. Recognize that brands may have a life cycle.

6. Evaluate different approaches to managing the brand in the longer term.

7. Specify the way that brand extensions are used.

8. Understand the meaning of brand positioning and know how companies position and reposition their brands.

Nature and purpose of branding

Successful brands attempt to balance functional benefits, which prompt the customer to use any brand in the product category, and discriminatory benefits, which prompt the customer to choose one brand rather than another. Because they are more tangible, functional benefits sometimes receive greater attention than the discriminating benefits. Successful firms do not focus exclusively on the functional benefits, over which they exercise greater control, at the expense of the added values, which may be psychological factors over which they have only limited control.

Successful brands depend on large marketing budgets because the level of commitment required is high. Branding also requires special management skills and a long-term perspective. Life cycle considerations may still apply as branding does not confer complete immunity from competitive threats and innovation.

Products, services or brands

The creation of successful brands means starting with a tangible product or service which, after the manufacturer or owner has incorporated design and quality, developed appropriate packaging and decided a suitable brand name, becomes the basic brand (Figure 12.1). The next stage is to augment the basic brand by providing a range of basic ancillary services not associated with the core brand. These include guarantees, credit and purchase terms, customer service, installation, and training and delivery. Associated with the augmented brand is a particular advertising emphasis which contributes to the overall brand image. By manipulating each of these attributes of the brand, and adding others yet to be discovered, the company eventually reaches the state of having produced a potential brand which will replace the existing brand sometime in the future.

Purpose of branding

As pre-packed products, especially in the fast-moving consumer products sector, come into common use and are accepted in different societies, manufacturers are presented with an opportunity to exercise some control over the way their products are accepted by a rapidly growing, dispersed mass market. As markets become impersonal, with increasing physical and time distance between the manufacturer or producer and the customer, some way has to be found to maintain the association of a name and a product with its producer. In these circumstances, the evolution of brands affords customers the opportunity of forming product perceptions in terms of packaging and design, product quality and performance, value and image. The branding of products and services is thought, therefore, to have three purposes:

- to conform to the legal patent protection the inventor may have;

- to guarantee quality and homogeneity in markets where buyers and producers cannot meet face to face; and

- to differentiate products and services in a competitive environment.

Branding has been an important aspect of marketing for centuries, but brand names are of more recent origin. They first appeared in the sixteenth century when whiskey distillers burned or branded their name on to the top of each wooden vessel in which the whiskey was shipped, thus identifying the dis-

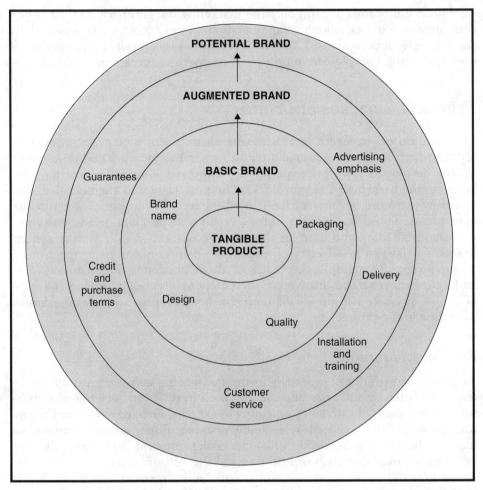

Figure 12.1 Creation of successful brands

    (Source: Adapted from Levitt, 1983. Reprinted by permission of Harvard Business School Press from Levitt, Theodore (1983), *The Marketing Imagination*, Collier Macmillan. Copyright © 1983 by the President and Fellows of Harvard College)

tiller to the consumer and preventing tavern owners from substituting cheaper products, two purposes of branding which are still important today.

    The brand concept evolved in the eighteenth century as the names of places of origin, famous people and even animals replaced producer names in an effort to strengthen the association of the brand name with the product, thus making it easier for consumers to remember the producer's product and to distinguish it from the competition. In the nineteenth century, brands began to be used to enhance the product's perceived value through such associations. The purposes and strategies of branding have evolved even further in the twentieth century.

Definition of branding

A brand is any combination of name, symbol and design which identifies a product or service and differentiates it from competitors. An economist's view of branding, which is held in some regard by marketing managers in companies selling well-known international brands, is as follows: 'various brands of a certain article which in fact are almost exactly alike may be sold as different qualities under names and labels which will induce rich and snobbish buyers to divide themselves from poorer buyers' (Robinson, 1933: 180–1). Alternatively, 'a successful brand is a name, symbol, design or some combination, which identifies the "product" of a particular organisation as having a sustainable differential advantage' (Doyle, 1991: 336).

A brand is a name, symbol, design or mark that enhances the value of the product, thus providing functional benefits plus *added* values that some consumers value sufficiently to buy.

> What turns a product into a brand is that the physical product is combined with something else, symbols, images, feelings, to produce an idea which is more than and different from the sum of the parts. The two, product and symbolism, live and grow with and on one another in a partnership and mutual exchange … as a sort of attachment or 'symbiosis' which consumers have for their brands and the advertising surrounding them. (Lannon and Cooper, 1983: 205).

Brand equity is the added value with which a given brand endows a product (Jones, 1986). The brand also legally protects from imitation any unique features that the underlying product might have, while at the same time conveying to the customer a set of quality attributes which help to build loyalty and repeat purchases of the brand.

Branding added values

A brand, as we have seen, offers added values that some customers value sufficiently to buy. Added values are believed to arise from three sources (Jones, 1986):

- from experience of using the brand;
- from the kind of people who use the brand; and
- from a belief that the brand is effective.

First, added values emanate from experience with the brand: familiarity, reliability, risk reduction, personality and character. Added values also come from the kind of people who use the brand – rich and snobbish, young and glamorous – and user associations fostered by advertising. Third, added values arise

517

from a belief that the brand is effective. Experience of using the brand allows the user to become familiar with the brand and to test it for reliability. The risk associated with the use of the brand may be reduced with continued use.

Brands are thought of as having personalities which represent these attributes. Brand personality has two dimensions: the rational characteristics associated with the brand, and the way brand values are communicated (Figure 12.2).

Branding may also work like an ingredient of its own. The branding of some proprietary drugs is thought to affect the mind's influence over body processes for some people: 'branding works like an ingredient of its own interacting with the pharmacological active ingredients to produce something more powerful than an unbranded tablet' (Lannon and Cooper, 1983: 206). Added values may also come from the appearance of the brand, which is the prime function of packaging and applies to consumer and industrial products.

These psychological aspects are just as important as the functional aspects. The image the product has gives rise to conative components of the brand which represent real benefits to the customer. Branding is a claim to uniqueness. The success of Aqua Libra table water brand is thought to derive from the scarcity factor surrounding its availability. The process technology involved in Unilever's Vienetta ice-cream protects this brand from imitators and so gives the brand its uniqueness.

Brands mean different things to different consumers. Uncovering the meaning of the brand to consumers allows the company to satisfy needs precisely and determines:

- exact benefits expected from a product;

- benefits sought but not satisfied by existing brands; and

- benefits a market segment may be educated to seek which are not considered at present.

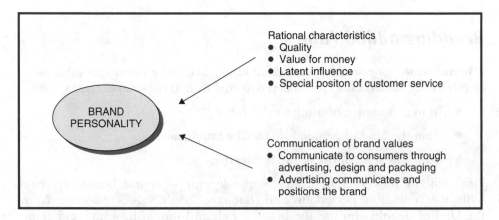

Figure 12.2 Personality of the brand

Branding functional and differentiated benefits

In branding added values, the company identifies and stresses the functional benefits of using the brand which are associated with the product class. The company also emphasizes, and sometimes concentrates on, the differentiated benefits of using the brand, which means focusing on the brand itself (Figure 12.3). The source of these benefits may be the experience that the consumer has obtained from using the brand, user associations which tend to be fostered by advertising, the effectiveness of the brand in meeting the expectations laid down for it by consumers, and its appearance, design and packaging, which can also provide great appeal to branded consumer and industrial products. Attempts have been made to brand what have traditionally been seen as commodities, initially focusing on the functional benefits. A recent attempt to brand the humble nail as user friendly is an illustration of how a basic steel product can be branded (Exhibit 12.1).

The definition of branding provided above also emphasizes that only some consumers value the brand sufficiently to buy it. Tastes differ so widely that no

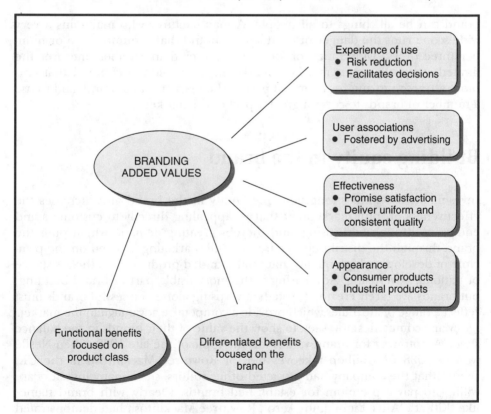

Figure 12.3 Branding means adding value

EXHIBIT 12.1   Branding the unbrandable

The humble nail is always cited in economics textbooks as the classic example of an impossible product to brand. Now, however, Scottish company Hammerhead Nails is trying to prove them wrong. The Edinburgh-based advertising agency Ash Gupta Communications will be running the company's campaign through trade and DIY magazines. The ads will highlight the company's logo – 'a derivative of tartan' – on the head of the nail. In addition, the nails are to be made 'user friendly' with the introduction of colour coded tips.

Hammerhead, formerly known as Cal-fast, has a 20 per cent share of the UK market. Now it aims to become the brand synonymous with nails, an area, claims Hammerhead, 'which is largely ignored by the multinationals'. This latest attempt to brand a product regarded as a commodity begs the question 'What next?'

Source: *Marketing*, 24 April 1989: 9.

---

brand can be all things to all people. A manufacturer who maintains a very wide scope runs the danger of producing a brand that is number two or number three over a wide range of attributes, rather than number one over the limited range that matters. Many marketing professionals contend that it is more attractive to aim for a limited part of the market with a brand, and to use a number of brands to cover a greater part of the market.

Building equity in the brand

Investment in brands strengthens the equity in the brand and increases the effectiveness of 'pull marketing': that is, appealing directly to customers and end-users through advertising, and thereby creating demand which pulls the brand through the distribution channels. Pull marketing is based on the principle of developing high-quality, national branded products with the assistance of national advertising. Advertising is the most visible part of brand building, but brands are rarely created through advertising alone. Successful brands must reflect a range of attributes which provide a competitive advantage in the market.

Many companies now seek to show the value of their brands in the balance sheet. Accounting for brand values was the topic of the late 1980s when Nestlé won its 1988 £2.5 billion takeover bid for Rowntree Mackintosh in the UK. Before that the company had attracted other suitors, since many investors are willing to pay a premium for established brands. Clearly, with brand names like 'KitKat', 'After Eight' and 'Aero', Rowntree Mackintosh had demonstrated to consumers and the market what is in a name, but had not convinced

---

EXHIBIT 12.2   Rowntree demonstrates what's in a name

Jacobs Suchard's dawn raid on Rowntree last Wednesday highlighted how little credit the London market gives companies for their strong brand names. The shares, idling at 477p on Wednesday morning, closed at 710p on Friday. With the benefit of hindsight the city admits Rowntree was under priced. But it remains true that American institutions, European markets and international conglomerates are all willing to pay a premium for established brands which British institutions will not.

Suchard's action seems almost a rerun of the General Cinema double raid on Cadbury Schweppes last year which gave the American cinema and drink bottling group around 18 p.c. at share prices up to £1 less than the current level. Rowntree is a medium-sized company with very large brands. KitKat is the second best selling sweet in the world, but such is Rowntree's lack of financial muscle it cannot exploit KitKat's full potential and has to allow Hershey to manufacture KitKat under franchise in America. Cadbury is in the same boat, it has to license Schweppes production in America, and so to a lesser extent are United Biscuits and Rank Hovis McDougall. All have risen in the light of Suchard's move, Cadbury put on 21p on Friday to 292p and United Biscuits 12 to 277p, although some reinvestment of Suchard's cash could be a factor.

As an investment branded names are excellent defensive holdings. It takes years to build up a brand name into the position where it can dominate a market and reap the premium profits accordingly. Many people will pay 3p more for a tin of Heinz baked beans than the store's brand, or 30p more for a jar of Hellmans mayonnaise. In the wrong hands a brand can be easily ruined, Smiths crisps was starved of investment when part of the ailing Huntley & Palmer, as was Golden Wonder for a time under Imperial Group's ownership.

As far as brand names are concerned the London market knows the price of all things but the value of nothing, to paraphrase Oscar Wilde.

Source: *Daily Telegraph*, 18 April 1988: 22.

---

investors in the City of London (Exhibit 12.2). Rowntree had placed no value on its range of chocolate and confectionery brands, and had indicated a shareholder interest of only £400 million.

Financial evaluation of brands

The need for brand evaluation has been recognized as a result of these developments and the more recent acquisitions such as Pillsbury in the USA by Grand Metropolitan in the UK, and of Kraft by Philip Morris in the USA. In addition, a number of well-known companies have been broken up or have experienced a leveraged buyout for their brands, such as the $6.2 billion break-up of Beatrice company and $2.5 billion leveraged buyout of RJR Nabisco in the USA. In each case the buyers and break-up venturists believed they could sell well-known brands or use them more effectively than existing owners and managers.

Brand value or brand equity is a measure of the intrinsic utility of a brand to consumers. It is the outcome of long-term investments designed to build a sustainable, differential advantage for the company relative to competitors (Doyle, 1990). The financial institutions have expressed a great deal of interest in brand equity. Of particular interest are the present and future earnings and incremental cash flows relative to unbranded goods, where the main purpose is the valuation of brands as intangible assets to be included in the company's published financial statements (Kamakura and Russell, 1993: 9). The London-based Interbrand consulting group uses a procedure based on a multiple of profit and price-earnings (P/E), which reflect brand strength, to measure the financial value of the brand (Kamakura and Russell, 1993: 9). Brand strength is also composed of subjective ratings of the brand, including market leadership, brand stability, internationalization, stability in the product category, trademark protection, and advertising and promotional support.

Perspectives on brand equity

In response to these developments, many companies now attempt formally to value their brands. One approach is to account for the history of the brand, its market share or dominance in the market, and the accumulated advertising support (Wentz, 1989). This assessment is then applied to the earnings contribution of the previous three years for individual brands using common valuation procedures. This provides an objective current-use value known as 'open market value' or 'goodwill' value. The healthier balance sheet then allows the company to acquire, expand or internationalize its endeavours. Brand equity has been defined as 'the differential effect of brand knowledge on consumer responses to the marketing of a brand' (Keller, 1993: 1).

Manufacturer's view of brand equity

Successful brands perform a number of valuable services for their owners. They project a positive identifiable image of the seller, they promise and deliver a uniform and consistent quality, and they provide a guarantee of satisfaction.

Brand equity can be measured by the incremental cash flow from associating the brand with the product. This arises if it can be shown that the brand results in higher sales with the brand than without it. Incremental cash flow also arises from premium pricing and reduced promotional expenditure. Brand equity also gives the firm certain competitive advantages. A strong brand can serve as an umbrella under which to launch new products or to license existing products. Resurrecting an old brand with high consumer awareness may be easier than creating a new brand in some instances. An example is the Singer brand, formerly used on sewing machines, which is now used on computers. Well-established brands can be resilient in times of crisis, periods of neglect by the company or shifts in consumer preferences, such as during the Tylenol product-tampering crisis of 1982. An important strategic component of brand equity is brand dominance: that is, the ability of a brand to dominate a product category, thus providing ownership of the category. Examples are McDonald's in the fast-food service, Heinz in beans, and Hoover in household vacuum cleaning machines.

Brands help to create customer loyalty and repeat purchasing behaviour as they help to differentiate the company's brand from competing products. Brand loyalty gives sellers some protection from competition and greater control in planning their market mix. Well-established brands form a barrier to market entry by competitors. They now have a greater hurdle to cross if they want to get customer attention and patronage.

Increased margins associated with the added values of the branded product make it more attractive than the generic product from the company's viewpoint. The company may also at some point wish to introduce a new product to the market. This may easily be facilitated through an extension of the brand to the new product.

A powerful brand name is said to have consumer franchise. This is apparent when a sufficient number of customers demand the brand and refuse a substitute, even if the price of the substitute is lower. Companies that develop a brand with a strong consumer franchise are somewhat insulated from competitors' promotional strategies. A successful brand also means market power in the distribution channel. A strong brand with a heavy customer franchise receives the respect of an otherwise indifferent or antagonistic retailer.

Retailer's view of brand equity

From the retailer's point of view, brand equity relates to the leverage which is possible over other products in the market. Easier acceptance and wider distribution provide the source of the equity. Well-known consumer brands pay lower slotting fees and are given more shelf facings for new products than weaker brands. Brand leverage also protects against private labels. Less leverage means that market shares are eroded and less expensive generic brands become dominant. Some retailer brands are more innovative than national brands and they are aggressively promoted by the large retail chains.

There is evidence that distributors want brand names as a means of making the product easier to manage in a number of respects:

- easier to handle;
- easier to identify suppliers;

- easier to maintain quality standards; and

- easier to increase buyer preference.

Consumer's view of brand equity

From the customer's point of view, successful branding means lower uncertainty in purchasing. There is also less need for an extensive decision-making process on the part of the customer. Brands carry with them certain assurances of product quality and reliability in use. Product identification in large, cluttered supermarkets, department stores or mass merchandising outlets is facilitated. There are also psychological benefits to the customer in using brands.

Brand equity is reflected in the improved attitude towards the product using the brand, where attitude means the association between the branded product and the evaluation of that product which is stored in an individual's memory (Fazio, 1986). Consumers also desire brand names to help them to identify differences and to shop more efficiently.

Brands provide cues in coping with many competing products in the market and the confusion associated with the plethora of advertising messages (Figure 12.4). Habit also has a significant role to play in consumer choice, especially with low-involvement products. Sometimes brand preferences are based on perceptions which are highly influenced by branding. Branding also positively influences attitudes towards industrial products and services. Lastly, branding is thought to influence consumer aspirations by concentrating on brand attributes that influence consumers who may not be in a position to buy the brand now, but who may be in the future.

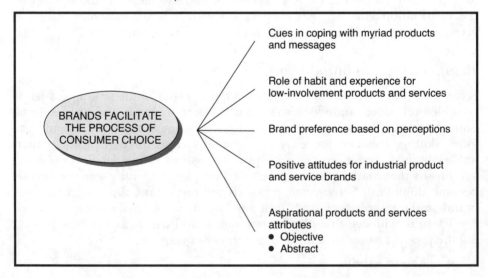

Figure 12.4 Branding functions

Brand equity and customer loyalty

Brand equity is that feature of the brands which allows the firm to differentiate it and increase customer loyalty. The attachment to the brand established over time makes brand extensions possible, thereby allowing the brand to withstand price competition. Price inelasticity is often used as a measure of brand equity. In a world of myriad brands, it is difficult, however, for individual brands to establish a strong equity base.

The durability of brands attests to the equity built into them over time. In a range of product categories, the leading brand in the US market in 1923 was the same in 1991 (Table 12.1). Of the nine brands listed, only one had slipped and that was from first place to second place in the toothpaste product category. Successful brands tend to be relatively stable over time, reflecting the investment in brand equity.

The brand's ability to maintain a long-term competitive advantage in the market is another way of considering brand equity. Indeed, higher-priced brands, often perceived to be of higher quality, are relatively less vulnerable to competitive price reductions than are lower-priced brands (Blattberg and Wisniewski, 1989). According to Watkins (1986: 36), 'The success of an existing brand may be judged primarily by its price level compared with other brands, as this is the most visible evidence of success of the branding policy.'

Brand equity also applies to services. Having and using a Big Eight accounting firm brand name, for example, is associated with premium audit fees. The Big Eight spend considerable resources to protect and enhance their reputation and brand name, an effort which is rewarded with higher fee income of about 4 per cent, the brand name itself being responsible for a large part of the fee premium (Firth, 1993: 386).

TABLE 12.1   Durability of brands in the USA

Product category	Leading brand in 1923	Rank in 1991
Cameras	Kodak	1
Canned fruit	Del Monte	1
Chewing gum	Wrigley's	1
Crackers	Nabisco	1
Razors	Gillette	1
Soft drinks	Coca-Cola	1
Soup	Campbells	1
Soap	Ivory	1
Toothpaste	Colgate	2

Source: *Business Week*, 8 July 1991: 34.

Quality and luxury in branding

There is a relationship between quality and luxury which is captured by some brands. Quality is a distinguishing factor in luxury, but not the only one. Quality is not the major reason why people buy luxury. 'If you want technique get a Rolex or a Piaget,' stated Alain-Dominique Perrin of Cartier, 'we're not selling watches to tell the time. We're selling them to people who belong to a certain social class. People buy luxury because they are looking for recognition. They want to show-off' (*International Management*, December 1987: 24–6). The marketing of luxury depends on brand image not retailing. According to Perrin, 'Tiffany's, the US jeweller or Ralph Lauren, the US fashion designer are "assured" flops overseas because their name represents a store or a product more than a style.' Not everybody would agree with Perrin, but the intangible psychological benefits associated with luxury are successfully captured in well-known brands.

Branding competitive advantage

Perceived quality is a major determinant of brand strength. Quality helps to increase market share, which results in lower unit costs through scale economies and, because differentiation and quality are possible at the same time, the company may be able to charge a higher price.

Sustainable competitive advantage is derived from superior customer service. Improved manufacturing technology allows imitators to thrive, but the corporate culture of an organization is not so easily copied, which allows it to develop and sustain its differential advantage.

As was seen in Chapter 8, pioneers have a clear competitive advantage. Being first to the market does not necessarily mean being the first to develop a new technology; it means being the first to obtain a competitive share of the consumer's mind. In this regard, Clifford and Cavanagh (1985) found that pioneering brands earned on average more than one-third higher returns on market investments than late entrants. When there is no competition, it is much easier to obtain share of mind, since the consumer does not have any substitutes. That is why true innovation rather than imitation has more lasting competitive advantage. Highly differentiated markets or markets where differentiation can be developed are very attractive to pioneers and innovating companies.

To build a luxury image it is essential that the high-quality products sold must be identifiable, hence the LV initials for Louis Vuitton, the green and red motif for Gucci and the C for Cartier. Successful luxury goods companies also trademark their name to protect it from counterfeiters and from transfer to other products. Advertising centres on the name and image of the company, not the product. Luxury products are usually restricted in supply. It is said that Rolls-Royce traditionally followed the policy of building sufficient cars to just

---

EXHIBIT 12.3   Has the flying lady lost her shine?

Donna Summer, an American rock star, confided in a recent interview that though she could afford to buy a Rolls-Royce, 'it would hurt for me to drive it into a neighbourhood where people were having a hard time.' She settled for a humble Range Rover.

The world's most famous luxury-car maker, it seems, may have run into a snag: could riding in a Roller require just too thick a skin? If so, nemesis could threaten for Rolls-Royce and its cars with the flying lady mascot on their radiator grills. Things certainly look ominous in the showrooms. On 24 February it announced that after decades of bumper profits, world-wide sales slumped from 3,333 in 1990 to just 1,723, last year – their lowest level since 1968. The collapse helped to drag Vickers, the British engineering group that owns the car maker, into a £12.4m ($22m) loss.

Vickers blames a deep recession for the slump in sales, especially in the company's two main markets – Britain and America. It is, after all, hard for a company chairman to justify splashing out £93,000 for one of the cheapest models – a Rolls-Royce Silver Spirit, rated by Britain's *Car* magazine as a 'glorious artefact' – while handing out redundancy notices. Even the British ambassador to the United Nations is now to be seen not in a Rolls but a Lincoln (made by America's Ford).

Car sales revolve around branding as much as engine performance. Rolls-Royce has kept its image highly polished. Officials privately winced when John Lennon painted his Rolls-Royce Phantom in psychedelic colours or when Bhagwan Shree Rajneesh, a mystic, ordered yet another Rolls-Royce to add to his collection, which eventually numbered more than 90. Perhaps they were right to worry. Wider Rolls-ownership may have cost the brand much of its former exclusiveness, and replaced it with a lethal whiff of vulgarity.

Compelled to rely more on the intrinsic worth of the product, in terms of value for money, the car's salesmen have an even tougher problem. A luxury Japanese car can now do everything a Rolls-Royce can – at a quarter of the price. The image of a Rolls-Royce as a state-of-the-art car is becoming harder and more expensive to sustain. It may be that Rolls-Royce will have to embrace the nostalgia business, making models that are resolutely of a different era, to keep its famous flying lady on the road.

Source: *The Economist*, 29 February 1992: 40.

---

miss satisfying demand. It is the scarcity factor which maintains the Rolls-Royce investment value. Once the scarcity factor no longer exists, there is little attraction associated with such brands, which then become debased (Exhibit 12.3).

Market entry in a luxury goods market

In such luxury goods markets, entry is usually at the top end, since an image of exclusivity and sophisticated quality is desired. But initial entry into the upper end of the market has become increasingly costly, which results in only very few new entrants. The major new entrant in the fashion market in the 1980s was Christian Lacroix of France. The opportunity is open to such luxury goods and fashion companies subsequently to move down market, having diluted the product in some way and priced it for the economy market. Giorgio Armani, one of the world's most successful fashion houses, receives most of its revenues from its less expensive Emporio Armani perfume, accessories and jeans lines. Crucial at the lower end of markets for perfume, clothing, accessories or sunglasses is the image and reputation created at the upper end of the market.

As luxury brands depend on exclusivity for their success, each of the above strategies has imbedded in it the danger of damage to the brand. By extending the brand to other goods, making the brand accessible to large numbers of people through lower prices, or internationalizing it, the exclusivity factor is weakened. The trade-off for these companies is to continue making profits without damaging the brand. This means careful and selective use of advertising and promotion. It also usually means targeted advertising, not mass media advertising. As important and perhaps more important is the need to control distribution, the element of the marketing mix which is difficult to control due to brand stretching and internationalization. A product retains exclusivity only if it is not available everywhere, and where it is available is also important. Outlets must be such as to promote the desired image.

Trends in branding

It is possible to identify three trends which together have promoted the growth of brands, especially consumer brands: diversification, accessibility and internationalization (Figure 12.5). By differentiation or stretching a brand, the company can attract new segments. If the umbrella is to provide a less expensive product line, the brand will rapidly serve numerous new segments more price sensitive than the original market. Many well-known branded goods companies, especially in luxury goods, have licensed their names and logos to manufacturers which actually make the products. Perhaps the best known examples of such brand extensions and licensing arrangement are to be found in the fashion product markets, such as luggage and watches. 'Le Must de Cartier' is the very successful brand used by Cartier to launch a less expensive line of watches and accessories.

Within this development the second trend may be identified. In shifting away from the very expensive exclusive end of the market, luxury brands are being made more accessible to large numbers of people. Many people who cannot afford a Cartier watch might be able to aspire to owning one while buying a wallet, which is expensive by normal standards but does not cost a fortune in absolute terms. If the luxury brand is made accessible through scarves, ties, second lines of watches, perfumes or wallets, people can enter the world of the exclusive brand to satisfy their need to demonstrate success, belonging or arrival. An example is Ralph Lauren's 'Polo' brand.

The third development which has promoted the growth of the brand is internationalization. The owners of many well-known branded goods internationalized their businesses through establishing chains of boutiques, using specialist distributors or working with certain department stores for exclusive merchandising space, devoted to promoting their products in a way consistent with the predetermined brand image. Louis Vuitton is one of the best-known examples of a company which followed the route of the boutique.

In recent years, these or other benefits do not seem to be so much in demand by consumers, however. In a study carried out by Grey Advertising Inc. in 1991 in the USA, 61 per cent of consumers registered brand names as an assurance of quality – a drop of six percentage points since July 1989. In the same study, 66 per cent reported that they were trading down to lower-priced brands (*Business Week*, 23 September 1991: 53). Brands are being devalued. A survey by DDB Needham Worldwide (*Business Week*, 8 July 1991: 34) found that 62 per cent of consumers in 1990 reported that they only buy well-known brand names, compared 77 per cent in 1975.

Brand decisions

Three principal approaches to branding may be identified. There are manufacturer brands (e.g. Heinz, Cadbury, Komatsu), there are private-label brands (e.g. Safeway, Carrefour, St Michael) and there are generic brands (e.g. Yellow Pack).

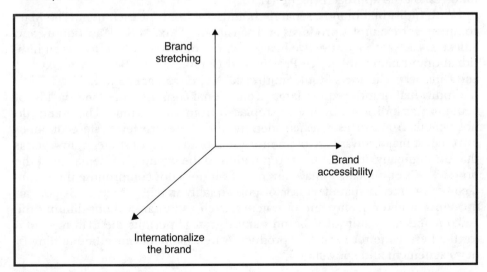

Figure 12.5 Growth of the brand

At the broadest level, it is necessary to decide whether manufacturer branding or private-label branding is the more appropriate. Within manufacturer brand decisions, it is necessary to decide among individual brands, family brands or a combination. Private-label branding raises the issue of retailer power and the shift in consumer preferences. Decisions may also have to be made regarding generic branding.

Manufacturer brand decisions

Manufacturer brands usually contain the name of the manufacturer, such as Miele electrical products. These brands appeal to a wide range of consumers who desire low risk of poor product performance, good quality, status and convenience shopping. Manufacturer brands are quite well known and trusted because quality control is strictly maintained. The brand name is identifiable and presents a distinctive image to shoppers. Manufacturers normally produce a number of product alternatives under their brand names.

Manufacturers sell their brands in many competing retailer outlets, spend large sums promoting them and frequently run co-operative advertisements with retailers so that costs are shared.

Using individual brand names

Manufacturers which brand their products face a decision of whether to use individual or family brands or a combination. There are advantages and disadvantages to each approach (Figure 12.6).

With individual brands, separate brands are used for each item. The Mars company, for example, produces and sells Mars, Twix, Milky Way, Bounty and Snickers, each with a distinctive image. Other companies which follow an individual brand name policy are Procter and Gamble (Tide, Bold, Daz, Oxydol) and Guinness (Guinness Stout, Smithwicks Ale, Harp Lager and Kaliber).

Individual brands require large promotional costs and there may be loss of continuity as individual brands are replaced from time to time. The brands do not benefit from an established identity and there are few scale economies involved. A major advantage of an individual brand names strategy, however, is that the company does not tie its reputation to the product's acceptance. If the product fails or appears to have low quality, it does not compromise the manufacturer's name. A manufacturer of good-quality watches, such as Seiko, can introduce a lower-quality line of watches, such as Pulsar, without diluting the Seiko name. The individual brand names strategy permits the firm to search for the best name for each new product. A new name permits the building of new excitement and conviction.

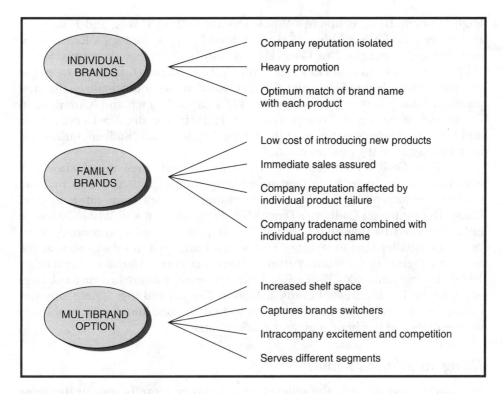

Figure 12.6 Manufacturer brand options

Using family brand names

With family brands one name is used for several products, such as Heinz Beans and Heinz Tomato Ketchup. Other companies which follow the family brand name policy are General Electric and Philips. The cost of introducing a new product will be less. There is no need for name research or for expensive advertising to create brand name recognition. Furthermore, a well-known and reputable family brand will tend to guarantee an acceptable level of sales for the new product. The major disadvantages are that a company's overall image may be adversely affected if individual products fail the acceptance test.

Thus, the Campbell Soup Company introduces new soups under its brand name with extreme simplicity and instant recognition. Philips in Europe also uses its name on all of its products, but since its products vary in quality, most people expect only average quality in a Philips product. This hurts the sales of its superior products. Here is a case where individual branding might be better, or the company might avoid putting its own name on its weaker products.

A combination of a company tradename with individual product names is a policy followed in the breakfast cereals market by the Edward D. Flahavan Milling Company Limited, producers of Flahavan's Progress Oatmeal, Flahavan's Fibre

531

High Crunchy Bran, Flahavan's Wholewheat and Bran Flakes, and Flahavan's Hot O'tees, by Kellogg's (e.g. Kellogg's Rice Crispies, Kellogg's Raisin Bran and Kellogg's Crunchy Nut Corn Flakes) and by Weetabix (Weetabix Ready Brek, Weetabix Fruit and Fibre, and Weetabix Wholebran). In these cases the company name legitimizes while the individual name individualizes the new product. Thus 'Quaker Oats' in Quaker Oats Cap'n Crunch and 'Guinness' in Guinness-Kaliber use the company's reputation in the breakfast cereal field and beer markets respectively, while 'Cap'n Crunch' and 'Kaliber' individualize and dramatize the new products.

In 1986 Cadbury-Schweppes in the UK grouped three major chocolate brands under a single $5 million advertising campaign, which also had the effect of reducing the number of advertising agencies from three to one. Under the campaign Cadbury's Dairy Milk, Fruit and Nut and Whole Nut were linked for the first time in a national TV campaign aimed a promoting lower-price and smaller bars to younger customers. Cadbury's move was seen at the time as a logical step towards cutting advertising costs (*Marketing*, September 1986). In the same way, Bird's Eye Walls gathered various frozen food lines together under umbrella brands to rationalize advertising. These are two examples of companies converting individual brands into family brands to reduce costs and to obtain a greater market impact.

Using multibrand names

In a multibrand strategy, the seller develops two or more brands in the same product category. This marketing practice was pioneered by Procter and Gamble when it introduced Cheer detergent as a competitor for its already successful Tide. Although the sales of Tide dropped slightly, the combined sales of Cheer and Tide were higher. Procter and Gamble now markets eight detergent brands.

Manufacturers adopt multibrand strategies for several reasons:

- they can gain more shelf space, thus increasing the retailer's dependence on their brands;

- few consumers are so loyal to a brand that they will not try another – capture 'brand switchers' by offering several brands;

- creating new brands develops excitement and efficiency within the manufacturer's organization – brand managers in Procter and Gamble, and Beecham's, for example, compete to outperform each other; and

- each brand is positioned to capture a different market segment – Mars' four brands of ice-cream are aimed at different segments of the market.

In deciding whether to introduce another brand as part of a multibrand strategy, the manufacturer considers such issues as:

- the uniqueness of the brand;

- its credibility among consumers; and

- the degree to which the new brand is expected to cannibalize competitor's brands rather than the manufacturer's other brands.

The company will also want to determine whether the new brand's sales will cover the cost of product development and promotion. A major pitfall in introducing new brands is that each might obtain only a small market share, and few might be profitable. Ideally, a company's brands should cannibalize competitor brands and not each other.

Private-label brands

It has been a tradition that manufacturers sold their products under their own brand name, but in the past two or three decades there has been considerable growth in private-label distributor brands, whereby channel members such as retailers are able to sell products using their own brand name or label. By doing so, these retailers do not incur the large promotional cost normally associated with manufacturers brands. Part of this cost saving is usually passed on to the consumer in the form of a lower price, while at the same time producing a higher profit margin for the retailer. Private-label brands mean that retailers have greater control over pricing. They also have greater control over the supplier, since they have become more powerful.

Retailer power and private label

For less powerful suppliers, especially new small companies, the retailer is seen as an ally in the attempt to enter the market. The cost of launching a new brand, especially in retail consumer markets, has become financially prohibitive for all except the large, well-endowed companies. In addition, in recent years there have been many new products developed which seek scarce retail shelf space. In such circumstances, the retailer has become more powerful and is in a position to arbitrate on new entries to the market. This shift in power has given retailers and other distributors the opportunity of developing their own private-label brands. Retailers with a good reputation for customer service can transfer that reputation to products they have manufactured under their own name.

Sometimes manufacturers also produce for the private-label market. They might follow this parallel policy if faced with excess capacity, and may consider it worthwhile also to produce for private label in an attempt to reduce unit operating costs. Such a policy can be successful provided the private-label products can be sold in a differentiated way in a market segment separate from the segment where the manufacturer's own brands are sold.

Private brands appeal to price-conscious consumers. When private brands offer good quality at a lower price, they are purchased. Consumers are willing to accept some risk regarding quality, but store loyalty influences consumers in believing that the products are reliable. Usually, private brands are similar in quality to manufacturer brands, although packaging is less important. Assortments are limited and the brands are unknown to shoppers who do not patronize the store. The marketing focus is to attract and retain customers who are loyal to the store and exert control over the marketing plan for these private-label brands.

Private-label markets are often served by smaller and weaker firms which do not have the resources to develop their own brands. Entry to the market by the private-label route frequently gives the aggressive small firm the opportunity to compete ultimately with the large brand companies. A poorly served private-label segment provides a strategic opportunity for the new smaller entrant. At the same time, private-label mass merchandisers may be very interested in providing an entry point to mass distribution. Japanese consumer electronics manufacturers entered the US market in the 1950s by observing that a private-label opportunity existed that had been ignored by US manufacturers. The latter were then only concerned with selling national brand merchandise to the high-margin trade.

Growth of private-label brands

The growth of private brands through the 1970s and 1980s primarily reflects and is part of the reason for the increased power of retailers, especially in food retailing. As more and more grocery sales have become concentrated in the hands of fewer retail chains, such as Aldi in Germany, Carrefour in France, and Tesco and Safeway in the UK, they have begun to market products under their own private brand names and thereby to transfer customer loyalty to the supermarket from the manufacturer.

It is generally believed that private-label branding does not adversely affect the brand leader in any category. Private labels are usually sold side by side with brand leaders. Indeed, most supermarkets can ill afford to be without the product category brand leader. If a private label competes with the no. 3 and no. 4 brand, the brand leader may welcome the arrival of strong private-label brands. The launching of O'Lacy's' private label to match the quality of branded category leaders, selling for 15 to 20 per cent less and yielding higher gross margins, is a unique attempt to create a European retail brand from scratch (Exhibit 12.4).

In the UK, the Northern Foods Company recognized a major gap in the market in producing private-label products for major retailers. This £1.2 billion company was established to carry out new product development for the retailers Marks and Spencer, Tesco and others. The company's competitive advantage is being able to respond quickly with new food products to the exact specifications of the major retailers, and these products are distributed under the retailer's private label. New product development and speed are the key competitive advantages of such companies.

In a similar way, Pauls Foods, a UK company, has linked with H & C Cereals in France to develop private-label marketing there. In France and other continental European countries, private-label marketing has not been developed to any extent, relying solely on the private labelling of commodity foods. The leaders in private-label marketing are UK companies. One of the objectives of this joint venture is the provision of marketing services to demonstrate to the retail trade in France and elsewhere the manner in which private-label marketing works, and to move the retail trade there from commodity private labels to sophisticated private-label brands.

Generic brands

A further development of private-label brands has been the growth of generic grocery products. For most products, generic brands are of lower quality than manufacturer or private brands. In packaged food products, for example, contents may vary in size, have less strength and use more filler. Pharmaceutical generics are an exception to this, being a close approximation to manufacturers' brands. Labels and packages are simplified, assortments are limited and brands are not well known. Distribution costs are much lower. Generic brands are not well advertised and receive secondary shelf space. The major marketing goal is to offer low-priced, lower-quality items to consumers interested in economy.

In socioeconomic terms, middle-class housewives are now relatively heavy buyers of own label or generics, but there is a marked swing towards the purchase of private-label brands among housewives with young families in urban areas.

Retail distribution of brands

One key factor influencing the immediate success or failure of a new brand is the manufacturer's ability to get it into distribution. For well-known brand names this is generally not a difficult task. If the brand sells well in the early stages, the public will demand it and word will get around, so that more and more retailers will want to stock it to participate in its success. Functional superiority is very important to retailers, and as it contributes to the success of the brand, it draws commitment from the retailer.

For a new brand with growing distribution, retailers running out of stock or unable to obtain deliveries may cause widespread switching away from the brand to competitors. If the desired brand is not available, consumers on entering the shop face a dilemma. They will normally buy a substitute brand if the brand they seek is not available. According to Nielsen data for the USA, this will happen in 58 per cent of cases. Retailers realize that, in the case of the

535

EXHIBIT 12.4   O'Lacy's says it!

Who is Isabelle O'Lacy? This attractive young woman smiles out of television commercials across Europe, and her face is all over supermarket shelves on products bearing her name. She is one of the marketing breakthroughs of the year, the woman every continental housewife is meant to want to be. Yet mystery surrounds her identity. She exists: she answers customers' letters and occasionally makes lightning guest visits to stores. She even owns shares in a company named after her. Yet Isabelle O'Lacy is not her real name. The reason given is that she is a private person, and wants to stay that way.

This Greta Garbo of the supermarket aisles is the brainchild of Fred Lachotzki, vice chairman of Asko Deutsche Kaufhaus. She is also the solution to a problem facing the German retailing chain. Three years ago, Lachotzki recognised that Asko was locked in an unequal struggle with its biggest suppliers, whose powerful international brands and production scale gave them muscle which few retailers could match. None of the obvious solutions looked attractive. One was for Asko to introduce more products under its own label, which theoretically offered higher margins. In practice, however, continental supermarkets have been conspicuously less successful than British retailers in making own-label products pay.

The upshot is O'Lacy's, a unique attempt to create a European retail brand from scratch. Barely 18 months since it was launched, it has spread to more than 500 food and household products in stores in Germany, the Netherlands and Sweden. Though Lachotzki will not disclose sales, he says they exceed those of many medium-sized food manufacturers. Since Asko introduced

---

missing brand, 42 per cent of customers will leave the shop with no purchase in the product category. This represents a loss of business to the retailer.

With the loss of sales, manufacturers even more than retailers will continue to pay a significant penalty for their inability to gain effective distribution for their brands. Inadequate distribution access to customers is a problem which is in the interests of both manufacturers and retailers to solve.

Managing the brand in the longer term

Managing the brand in the longer run usually means a combination of relatively heavy advertising and at some stage a modification to the product for a relaunch. A number of additional changes also support the long-term life of the brand (Figure 12.7).

To protect the brand in the long run, it is usually necessary to have continued and growing advertising expenditure. The advertising in this situation usually emphasizes those added values that have become the brand's unique property.

O'Lacy's products, its gross margins have increased by a percentage point. Furthermore, Asko has found that three quarters of its customers now recognise the O'Lacy's name. Central to O'Lacy's success is its personalised brand format. Lachotzki says the name Isabelle O'Lacy was chosen because it sounded suitably international and was found by market research to suggest quality and good value.

The O'Lacy's company defines the broad specifications, pricing and basic package design of every product. The iron rule is that products should match the quality of branded category leaders in each country, sell for 15–20 per cent less and yield higher gross margins. Manufacturing and packaging arrangements are left up to the retailers, though the O'Lacy's company regularly checks the quality of products. These are now made by more than 200 suppliers, including a German subsidiary of the Anglo-Dutch Unilever group.

O'Lacy's seeks to cope with differences in national consumer attitudes – and minimise development costs – by modelling its products and packaging closely on the brand leaders. In Germany, for instance, its coffee packages have a green label, just like Jacobs, the best-selling brand. But in the Netherlands, O'Lacy's uses a red label, like Douwe Egberts, the market leader. Lachotzki says the brand leaders do not object to such tactics. Before Asko launched O'Lacy's in Germany, he explained its strategy to its 60 biggest branded suppliers. 'I reminded them that increased competition always hurts the number three and four brands, not the market leaders,' he said.

Source: *Financial Times*, 19 December 1991: 10.

Longer-term brand protection may also involve repositioning the brand to cater for new market segments. This may also mean modifying the product in some way, which of itself is a way of extending the life of a brand. The company must be concerned with the possible cannibalization of existing brands that can result from the introduction of brand extensions and the encouragement of private labels.

Brand life cycles

If not continually managed and upgraded, brands have a life cycle and soon reach maturity. Some can maintain a relatively constant market share in the face of competition, while others lose out and decline altogether. It is believed that many brands lose market share as a result of a conscious transfer of resources from existing brands to new brands without proper consideration of the need to maintain the existing brands. For a single product category of household products in the USA, Jones (1986) has reported that for the period 1936–77 only two of the five most important brands in 1936 were still on the market in

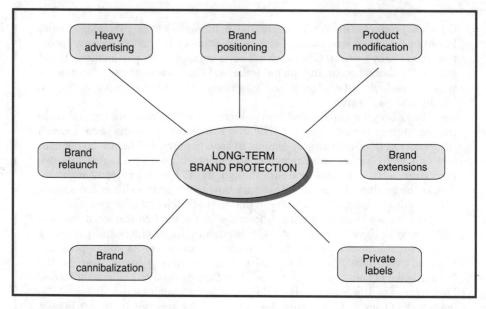

Figure 12.7   Long-term brand management

1977, and with severely reduced market shares; of the twelve most important brands introduced since 1949, four had disappeared by 1977, and brand leadership had changed hands five times due to a failure to keep up to date.

In regard to brand building, it is the pressure of competition which dictates the pace of innovation, not inevitability. Experience and research show that brands do reach maturity and maintain relatively constant permanent levels of market share in the face of competition. The decline stage of the product life cycle is under manufacturer control. Products can become obsolete; brands need not become obsolete if adapted functionally to remain competitive. The company in this position may need to launch product variations as Procter and Gamble did in the USA with Tide and Liquid Tide, and Unilever did in the UK with Persil and Persil Automatic. This poses an important question for management: how many brands lose market share by an unnecessary transfer of resources from old to new?

Influences on a new brand

The fortunes of a new brand may be influenced by a number of factors: achieving customer trial, differentiation, the brand name and pricing.

Achieving customer trial

Achieving customer trial is the first problem facing the manufacturer of a new brand. One of the most effective ways of achieving awareness and trial is through consumer promotions which encourage people to try the product. Repeat purchasing is, however, very dependent on customer satisfaction regarding the functional performance of the brand. The new brand must deliver the benefits promised. Functional benefits provide support for the other elements of the marketing mix. The brand's functional performance also helps to specify the more likely market segments to address in advertising.

In attempting to decide the appropriate market segments and in order to obtain a quick response, likely prospects for the new brand may be found among existing users of the product category. It is advisable, therefore, to promote the new brand specifically at existing competitive brands. A consumer franchise will not protect an existing brand from a well-advertised technical breakthrough. It then becomes a question of identifying the brands from which the company wishes to take business. If it is a totally new concept, such as the creation of a new product category, these latter issues do not apply.

Brand differentiation, brand name and premium pricing

In consumer product markets, it is more the practice that consumers switch from one brand to another than that they remain always loyal (Oxendfeldt and Moore, 1978). Brand differentiation is, therefore, a general phenomenon in that usage differentiation among consumers does not appear to exist. A range of competing brands will be used by the same kind of people, so multi-brand purchasing is normal behaviour. The danger in this for the new brand is that its introduction may cannibalize the company's existing brands. To overcome this possibility, companies attempt, where possible, to introduce new brands into different but contiguous segments of the segmented market.

The choice of brand name can be significant. Added values embodied in a well-known brand name may be transferred to a new product. This is the rationale for umbrella branding in product-line extensions. It is noteworthy, however, that cannibalization is greater for products in competition within a product line. It is likely that the competition, and hence the cannibalization, between Tide and Liquid Tide is greater than that between Ivory bar soap and Ivory shampoo. Umbrella branding saves promotional costs by relying on the added values of other brands carrying the umbrella name.

Premium prices are justified for functional improvements over existing brands. Premium pricing also draws attention to the innovation, and the cash generated helps to find the high cost of sampling by above- and below-the-line expenditures.

Combining the key competitive factors

The unique combination of the factors discussed above establishes a personality for the brand. Brand personality is derived from the rational characteristics associated with the brand and from the way brand values are communicated. Rational characteristics refer to factors such as quality and value for money, latent influences which may be present and the special position the firm gives to customer service. Brand values are communicated to consumers through advertising, design and packaging. Advertising communicates and positions the brand. The personality of the brand is a strong driving force behind successful brands.

Managing brand extensions

One of the most popular means of managing the brand in the longer term is to extend the brand name to other product categories. Brand extension or umbrella branding is a favourite device of companies in the possession of a strong brand which management believes will extend to other areas. It does not always work, however, as the BIC Company discovered when it attempted to extend its well-known brand name to a completely different product category, perfume. One of the possible difficulties facing BIC may have been that perfume may be perceived not as disposable and utilitarian like a ball-point pen or a plastic shaving razor, but rather as a product for which an emotional attachment is important. Brand extensions are, however, relatively easy to arrange, hence their popularity. In evaluating the wisdom of brand extension, it is necessary to examine the company's overall brand strategy and the financial implications as measured by market share changes and advertising efficiency (Smith and Park, 1992). This evaluation should take account of three sets of characteristics: those associated with the brand itself, those associated with the extension and those concerning the market for the brand extension (Figure 12.8).

Umbrella branding, taking an existing brand and applying it to a different product category, sometimes referred to as brand stretching, can be very profitable. An example is 'Les Must de Cartier' for a new line of consumer trinkets such as scarves, wallets, cigarette lighters and writing pens. Firms that are successful in developing umbrella brands exploit the recognition value and reputation of a brand name in a new product area and obtain very high margins in doing so. This strategy is an accepted way of quickly and inexpensively entering a new market. After Quaker Oats' success with Cap'n Crunch dry breakfast cereal, the company used the brand name and cartoon character to launch a line of ice-cream bars, T-shirts and other products. Honda Motor Company used its name to launch its new power lawnmower. Umbrella branding is especially popular in the food and beverage industries: ice-cream versions of the Mars Bar and Milky Way, Chicken McNuggets and McPizzas are well-known examples.

As a strategy, brand extension offers a number of advantages. A strong brand

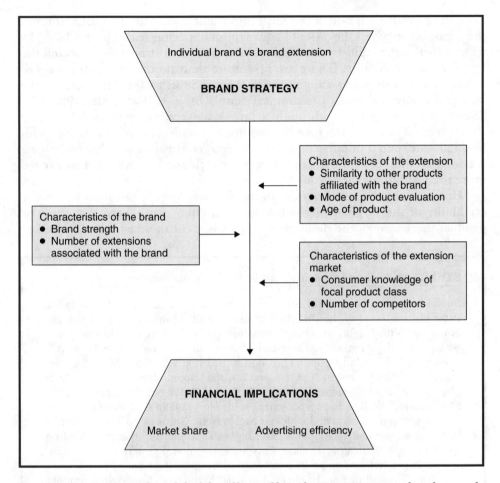

Figure 12.8 Conceptual model of the effects of brand extensions on market share and advertising efficiency

(Source: Smith and Park, 1992: 298, with slight modifications. With permission of the American Marketing Association)

name gives a new product instant recognition. Brand stretching can be profitable as it saves money. The company saves the advertising costs involved in familiarizing consumers with a new name. Thus people would ordinarily respond positively to Pierre Cardin wine or Porsche sunglasses or Mars ice-cream bars.

An established brand name makes a new product attractive by promoting a range of desirable associations and images. Not only do umbrella branded products need less advertising, but consumers are also more willing to give brand names they already know an initial trial.

Tylenol, a most successful brand, is managed by the McNeill Consumer Products Company, a division of Johnson and Johnson. At present, McNeill

Consumer Products is one of the most important and innovative companies in the group. It survived the Tylenol packaging tampering scares of the 1980s by using a forthright publicity campaign. Tylenol's recent strategy is to stretch the brand name to its limits. There are now more than twenty shapes and sizes of Tylenol in five categories, ranging from Tylenol Sinus to Tylenol Allergy and a new group formulation of Children's Tylenol (*Business Week*, 4 May 1992: 55). The brand is maintained through a large-scale commitment to advertising which keeps Tylenol to the fore in consumers' minds, and good relations with hospital staff keep it popular there too, thereby confirming its value and giving it added credibility with consumers. Sales of Tylenol are estimated to exceed more than $1 billion each year.

However, there are dangers in umbrella branding. It can undermine the credibility of the original product. Consumers may not believe that the new product shares any of the desirable characteristics of the established brand, or

---

EXHIBIT 12.5   Brand stretching can be fun but dangerous!

Stretching a brand can be lucrative, but it can also be dangerous. Listen to Mr Peter Philips, head of the British subsidary of CPC International: 'If you get brand-stretching right, you can travel further for less money. If you get it wrong, you risk weakening the core values of the original product.' Brand-stretching is especially popular in food and drink. America's Mars has just launched an ice cream in America and Europe named after its famous chocolate bar, which in America is known as the Milky Way and in Europe as the Mars bar. McDonald's is experimenting with McPizzas in its American stores, having previously launched Chicken McNuggets. Guinness, a British drinks firm, has introduced a Tanqueray Sterling Vodka to partner its market-leading American gin. Chicago's Quaker Oats recently unveiled a range of micro-waveable sandwiches under its crusty old porridge-oats name.

Brand-stretching may be cheap, but what happens to the original product if the new product flops? Does it take the brand name with it? Unilever's oil and spreads subsidiary, Van Den Berghs & Jurgens, is due to find out; the company's new low-calories salad dressings, which use the same name as its market-leading flora margarine, have been a failure. Not even a well-known name can save a product that tastes wrong.

Badly thought-out brand-stretches can be hideously inappropriate. Imagine a Pepsi single malt whiskey or Chanel galoshes. In 1979 Levi Strauss introduced a line of slacks and blazers under the name David Hunter. They were marketed as 'classically tailored clothes, from Levi'. A contradiction in terms? The men who buy classically tailored clothes thought so too, and the range sank without trace. Brands risk hurting themselves if they indulge in too many acrobatics. On the other hand, says Unilever's Mr Perry, 'they take a tremendous amount of mismanagement to destroy'.

Source: *The Economist*, 5 May 1990: 69–71.

they may simply forget what was attractive about the original brand. The brand name may be inappropriate to the new product, even if it is well made and satisfying: consider buying Texaco olive oil or Harpic dairy products! And the brand name may lose its special positioning in the consumer's mind through overuse (Exhibit 12.5).

Threats to branding

In recent years there have been a number of threats to brands. The major threats to branding arise from three sources: perceived product parity; lack of innovation and product proliferation; and the rise of own- or private-label brands (Figure 12.9).

Perceived product parity

In regard to perceived product parity, the argument is made that there is now no discernible difference between rival brands across a broad range of products. Manufacturing technology has raised the quality of many products while innovations are minor and easy to imitate. The lack of uniqueness which arises and the better technology which is available result in an abundance of new products. At the same time, advertising reinforces the belief that brands are similar.

Perceived product parity
- No discernible difference between rival brands across broad range of products
- Manufacturing technology has revised the quality of many products
- Innovations are minor and easy to imitate
- Lack of uniqueness and better technology result in abundance of new products
- Associated advertising reinforces the belief in brand similarity

Lack of innovation and increased product proliferation leads to dominance of promotion
- Undifferentiated product proliferation
- Shelf space auctions (discounts; 'hello' money)
- Advertising budgets diverted into promotions
- Less money available for advertising
- More power to retailers, giving them more price discretion
- Well-known brands sold below cost as loss leaders

Rise of own-label brands
- Strong own-label tradition in some countries in selected product categories
- Rise of own label in Europe and USA in 'immune' product categories
- Own-label quality and sales impact pose threat to established brands

---

Figure 12.9   Threats to branding

Proliferation of undifferentiated products

The second major threat refers to the proliferation of undifferentiated products, which has meant that retailers are in a position to auction access to consumers through extensive use of discounts and 'hello' money for new products seeking first-time display. In this situation, the advertising budget tends to be diverted into sales promotions and less money is available for advertising. This shift gives greater power to retailers and it also gives them greater price discretion with the result that many well-known brands are sold at below cost.

The shift in emphasis from above-the-line advertising to below-the-line promotion has given rise to doubts about the value of branding. It has been

---

EXHIBIT 12.6   A fierce brand of consumer warfare

Competition from retailers' own private-label goods and cut-price branded merchandise is causing much discomfort in the US to large household and personal products manufacturers – P&G, Colgate-Palmolive and Anglo-Dutch Unilever – at a time when they are locked among themselves in a fierce battle for market-share, both in North America and around the world. This intensifying competition prompted P&G to announce last week that it will cut 13,000 jobs, or 12 per cent of its worldwide labour force, and close about 30 factories, about 20 per cent of the total.

The restructuring raises fresh questions about consumers' brand loyalty and the size of the price premium big manufacturers such as P&G can command nowadays over cut-price rivals. Its international business, which now accounts for more than 50 per cent of revenues, is still growing strongly, with volume sales up 10 per cent in 1992–93. But profit margins internationally are lower than in the US, which P&G has been relying on to fund the global push. Yet, the US market has been weak, with P&G's sales volumes up just one per cent over the past year, due to recession. This has intensified competition and the temporary dislocation caused by a radical change in the group's marketing strategy to a system called 'value-pricing'.

Under the old system, P&G ran trade promotions to boost sales, offering big but periodic discounts to retailers and wholesalers. This was inefficient, since it encouraged the buyers to stockpile discounted goods and forced P&G to keep extra manufacturing capacity to handle big swings in demand. The new system, introduced on 70 per cent of P&G's US products over the past two years, cuts trade promotions and uses the savings to lower prices throughout the year. The change has angered some retailers, who relied on the promotions for a good part of their profits, rather than passing them onto consumers; as a result P&G's market share initially suffered.

However, the company insists that both its volume and market share have begun recovering over the past six to nine months and that its value pricing brands are performing significantly better than those on the old system.

Source: *Financial Times*, 19 July 1993: 23.

---

argued that advertising is no longer as effective as it was and that consumers are more price sensitive and responsive to sales promotions (Exhibit 12.6).

Private-label competition

Private-label brands tend to increase their share in times of recession, when customers are more price conscious. It is uncertain, however, whether the shift to private-label products is a temporary phenomenon based on recession, or the result of a more fundamental shift of attitude among cost-conscious consumers. There is also a strong private-label tradition in some countries in selected product categories. Many food products in the UK are sold very successfully under private-label brands. In recent years, private-label branding has increased in the USA and a number of European countries. These trends pose a significant threat to established manufacturer brands.

Private-label brands may be used to access an untapped market, so that the company's brand continues to serve a designated market niche. Private-label branding may also be used to determine whether a new market segment exists for which the company might develop an exclusive own brand at some future date. The challenge for branded consumer products under these circumstances is to ensure that the premium they charge reflects consumers' perceptions of the competitive superiority of their products. It is important to note that in this context the consumer perceptions depend not only on price but also on advertising.

The premium charged for branded products is expected to be associated with a degree of exclusivity. The spread of many brands in middle-range fashion items has reduced the exclusivity element, with the result that consumers can tire of brands and turn to a plainer lifestyle which may have its own benefits. The trend in Japan to 'no-brand' products may be cited to illustrate this point (Exhibit 12.7).

Relaunching the brand

To ensure that brands continue to grow in the long term, successful companies allocate increasing advertising budgets and emphasize the added values which have become the unique property of the brand. Frequently, however, it becomes necessary to relaunch the brand with a new marketing mix to support it, especially if a brand has wilted for a time on the market. Holding brand share by continually adding to the advertising budget without upgrading the brand itself is a form of financial suicide.

A brand relaunch does not always succeed. Sometimes companies leave it too late to relaunch a brand which has been poorly supported. To be successful, the first requirement is that the reason for the fall in share or the decline in fortunes of the brand must be clearly understood. A temporary decline due

---

EXHIBIT 12.7   Muji – the Japanese anti-brand brand

Try to imagine that you are a 22-year-old woman office worker living at home with your parents in Japan. You spend most of your Y160,000 ($1,200) monthly pay packet on yourself. Elegant in your Jean Paul Gaultier dress, Hermès scarf draped casually around the neck, gold Cartier watch on your wrist and Chanel handbag dangling from the shoulder, you step jauntily into the office lift. Seconds later the doors open and – horrors – in steps another lady decked out in precisely the same designer-brand uniform, then another, and yet another. Many Tokyo office buildings are now full of young Japanese women who dress exactly alike.

Jaded by the ubiquity of fancy brand names, many of Japan's conspicuous consumers are now turning to 'no-brand' goods in what looks like a forlorn attempt to display some individuality. The trend-setter has been Seibu, a department-store chain that goes after the affluent young. Inside Seibu's flagship store in Tokyo, one section sells only Mujirushi ryohin ('no brand/good quality') products. Their labels say only what materials are used and the country of origin – mostly China, Hong Kong, South Korea, Thailand or India. The products are easy to spot because of their simple design, plain colours, high quality and reasonable pricing.

Two years ago the group established a separate company, Ryohin Keikaku, to handle an expanded line of Muji goods, which today includes 1,800 items. Ryohin Keikaku now has 201 outlets in Japan and two overseas and plans to open 20–30 more outlets in East Asia over the next few years, if Muji products prove as popular abroad as they have been at home. Many fashionable young Japanese would not be caught dead in anything else.

Source: *The Economist*, 14 March 1992: 80.

---

to a temporary withdrawal of marketing support or concentrated competitive attention is one thing, but longer-term neglect is another. The brand must not be obsolete in all applications or market segments for the relaunch to work. It must have a franchise that still commands loyalty. The relaunch should not be the first of a long series of repairs, but should pave the way for durable market performance.

Where the brand is relaunched, product improvements added may be evaluated alongside the established and accepted battery of functional benefits that the brand provides. Relaunching a brand gives the company an occasional opportunity to sharpen the attention of existing and potential users. It also allows the introduction of new variants, such as new types, flavours and colours, which can add market share without cannibalizing existing sales. In most relaunches of a brand, companies make adept use of the word 'new', a concept which is found to be of value for a long time afterwards.

Ways of relaunching a brand

There are a number of ways in which a company might relaunch a brand. A facelift for existing products under the brand and a quick introduction of line extensions may bring a positive response. Aggressive, new-look advertising and promotion is sometimes used in successful relaunches. A careful revision of the pricing structure, which may involve a total repositioning of the product or service, is another way of relaunching a product.

Moving from near the top of the market in women's ready-to-wear into the lower-to-medium price range is an example of how a company in the fashion industry might relaunch its range of products. Combined with these strategies it may be necessary to focus on sales force efficiency, with special attention being paid to ways of motivating the sales force and ways of reactivating slow or dormant accounts.

Brand mismanagement

There is much evidence available indicating that established brands are survivors and keep going for a long time. It is relatively easy, however, for a company to neglect the valuable equity created over years and to precipitate the decline that leads to brand erosion and the eventual demise of the brand. Six interrelated factors are thought to contribute to brand erosion, here referred to as the vicious cycle of brand debasement (Figure 12.10).

Focus on the short term

There has been a shift in philosophy among many companies which, through financial pressure or the need to serve short-run targets, have adopted a harsh short-run perspective. The inexorable trend towards short-term financial results forces most companies to set short-term corporate strategies for the rest of the organization. Long-term brand building in such circumstances is virtually impossible. As a result, brand managers must increase short-run sales instead of investing in image advertising to develop and nurture brands. In such circumstances, many companies shift budgets away from advertising into sales promotions such as coupons, contests and lotteries.

Where companies experience great pressure to produce quarterly sales results, the impact of image-building advertising is frequently difficult to see, and its value is not so obvious compared to price discounts or coupons, which result in a quick, easily measured sales response. Such developments often lead to a brand being turned into a commodity, sold on the basis of price only.

These short-term corporate objectives play into the hands of powerful retailers. By denying their brands the support required, manufacturers have abrogated their right to control the brand to retailers, who demand even

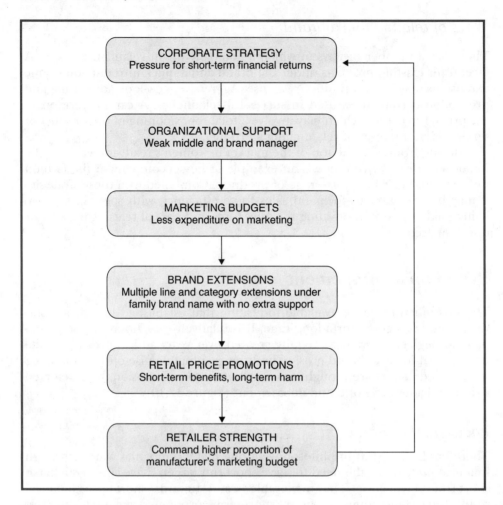

Figure 12.10 Vicious cycle of brand debasement

higher percentages of promotion budgets for in-store promotions and other locally focused activities. Brands are further weakened, thereby increasing the pressure for corporate-imposed short-term financial returns.

Lack of marketing support

Within the company, support for the brand may have been weakened. Brand management has traditionally been the responsibility of middle and junior managers, who must also show short-term results. These managers, because they are relatively junior, may not have the experience or corporate clout to protect company brands. Sometimes companies reduce advertising, believing that the brand can sustain itself without such support.

Spending less on advertising is the third factor which directly contributes to the erosion of brands. The risk in cutting advertising budgets is that the brand will go into decline. In the USA, Mars Inc. outstripped the Hershey Foods Corporation as the country's largest chocolate maker because it spent more to advertise M & M's and its other brands than Hershey did.

With less money to spend and a greater pressure to show short-term returns, product-line and category extensions under family brands multiply, but with no accompanying image-builder effort. As a result, brand values dissipate and decline.

In an effort to defend customer franchise and forestall the evil day of complete decline, companies have little choice but to turn to in-store price and sales promotions to encourage the trial of well-known brands. While this has immediate benefits in terms of the short-term financial objectives of the company, it has decidedly sinister long-term effects.

Overexposure to sales promotion

Retailer power has arisen in large part due to checkout scanning devices, which enable supermarkets to see which products sell and to allocate shelf space accordingly. To hold on to valued shelf space, suppliers must agree to trade discounts, contributions to retailer advertising budgets or fees for in-store displays. These fees have grown enormously because the increase in the number of new products has made shelf space that much more scarce. Having to pay for it leaves manufacturers with much less for brand advertising. Donnelly Marketing, an American research house, estimates that US companies now spend 70 per cent of their marketing budgets on promotions, leaving just 30 per cent for advertising. In 1980 the proportion for advertising was 43 per cent and for promotions was 57 per cent (*Business Week*, 23 September 1991: 55).

Impact of recession

The recession of the 1980s and early 1990s raised doubts in people's minds about the value of advertising and branding. Heavy advertising campaigns have made consumers weary of the clamour of advertising messages. As consumers have become less receptive, consumer loyalty to brands has eroded and many products are seen as commodities distinguished only by price.

Positioning the brand

Positioning is the process by which the company defines what it wishes a product or service to stand for in the market, relative to the needs of specific market segments and relative to competitive brands. The ability of an organization to compete effectively in any given market is determined in large measure by its ability to position its products appropriately. Product positioning requires a synthesis of consumer analysis and competitor analysis. The company also attempts to identify a range of benefits that customers use to make decisions. This helps it to identify relevant market segments. The company must evaluate the relative importance of each benefit in each segment.

Analysis of competitive offerings involves not merely a review of product features and other marketing mix strategies, but also an evaluation of competitive advertising content. The image generated by advertisements and the nature of the slogans employed may constitute a major positioning tool, especially for personal products such as cosmetics, liquor and apparel.

Effective brand positioning

Following this consumer analysis, management must consider the degree to which existing products in the category are perceived to deliver strong performance on each of the benefits of interest to customers. In choosing a position for a product, the company must match an appropriate package of benefits, clearly differentiated from competitive products on important dimensions, with a specific target segment whose needs are not fully satisfied by existing products. Positioning permits a company to develop a more effective and parsimonious approach to competition rather than competing head-on.

Product positions often reflect not only intrinsic product characteristics, but also the image created by promotional strategies, pricing decisions and the choice of distribution channels. A study of the perceptions of a group of senior executives of various Irish and Scotch whisky brands suggests that, for this group, two underlying evaluative criteria were important, modernity and smoothness (Figure 12.11). Notice how many of the brands are clustered together, with the exception of Powers, perceived as rough and old-fashioned. Selective use of alternative brand names in multibrand companies may also contribute to the achievement of the desired image. For instance, the Mercury name, owned by the Ford Motor Company, carries connotations for car buyers different from those of the Ford brand itself.

Effective positioning is essential to a product's success. If the company does not consciously position its products, consumers will be confused and competitive products which are accurately positioned may enjoy an advantage. At the same time, a product's positioning must not be too rigid. Positions are held relative to other competitive products and relative to consumer needs. Both may change, necessitating a change in positioning. Different national and local tastes make truly standardized products a rarity, especially in Europe. Even the global brand Nescafé is sold in 50 combinations of strength, taste and flavour in different European markets. The brand, of course, is constant, which is the key to brand management.

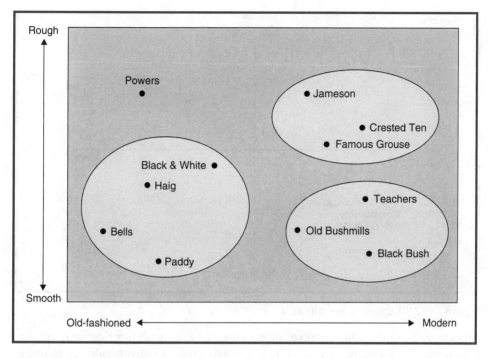

Figure 12.11 Positioning of whisky brands

Repositioning of the brand

As an alternative to physical modification of an existing product, firms some-times elect to reposition their products simply by changing some or all of the elements of the marketing mix: advertising and promotion, distribution strat-egy, pricing or packaging. The Lucozade brand was repositioned from being a drink for people who are ill to being an isotonic beverage. It was effectively repositioned from being perceived as old and for the infirm, with emphasis on sickness and convalescence, to being a soothing drink for the active consumer, emphasizing compatibility with the body, a remedy, soothing and revital-ization. The success of this repositioning strategy is that Lucozade now serves a number of segments along the diagonal line in Figure 12.12, not just one posi-tion. A revision of the entire marketing mix, including a change in product features, may also accompany a repositioning strategy. Sometimes reposition-ing may represent a deliberate attempt to attack another firm's products and erode its market share; in other instances, the objective may be to avoid head-to-head competition by moving into alternative market segments which are attractive, but which are not well served by existing products.

Repositioning along price and quality dimensions or in regard to the func-tion served is generally referred to as 'trading up' or 'trading down'. However,

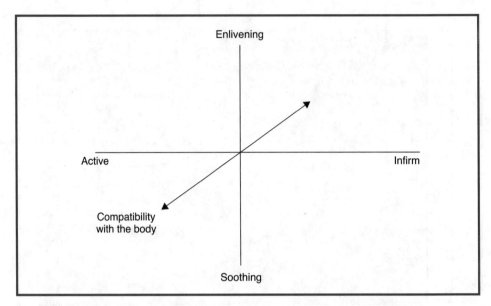

Figure 12.12   Lucozade repositioning

repositioning may also involve sideways moves in which price and quality remain little changed, but modifications are made to the product's tangible benefits or image. The aim is to enhance its appeal to different types of consumer or for alternative end-uses. Repositioning a traditional brand which has been neglected for many years and overstretched can be very expensive, but it is necessary if the brand is to survive (Exhibit 12.8).

Examples of repositioning existing products include advertising a deodorant formally promoted only to women as 'the deodorant for all the family'; reducing the price of a felt-tip pen to take advantage of a perceived market need for a lower-price model; and modifying the assortment at a supermarket chain to improve its appeal to family groups.

Different segments, different positions

Companies sometimes take a brand which has been successful in one market and reposition it to serve emerging needs in another segment. This may require considerable retargeting on new customer groups that the company or brand did not previously serve. The US whiskey company Brown-Forman's efforts to reposition its well-known whiskey brand Jack Daniels is a good example of repositioning:

> As the brand has gotten [sic] bigger we have kept looking for places to find new drinkers ... vodka has done alright with women, but women are a big untapped category for whiskey. We felt there was potential, especially with up-

---

EXHIBIT 12.8   At Gucci, la vita is no longer so dolce

When Maurizio Gucci, grandson of the founder, captured control of Gucci in 1988, things seemed to be looking up for the first time in years. The company had been battered by suits and countersuits among feuding Gucci relatives until a white knight arrived in the shape of Investcorp. Fresh from a highly profitable turnaround of Tiffany & Co., Investcorp paid an estimated $160 million for half of Gucci. Maurizio, buying out relatives' shares, wound up with the other 50 per cent and management control.

With backing from Investcorp, he then went ahead with one of the biggest – and most expensive – brand repositions ever attempted in luxury goods. In the 1980s, a rudderless Gucci had lost cachet by indiscriminately putting its name and trademark red-and-green band on more than 10,000 items. Quality went down the drain. To restore Gucci's exclusive lustre, Maurizio slashed the number of products to barely 200 and poured millions into refurbishing flagship shops in key markets.

Unfortunately, the repositioning has yet to produce a profit. The focus on big-ticket items, such as cashmere throws and 18-karat gold baubles, may be hurting sales by offering little to middle-class consumers.

Source: *Business Week*, 16 November 1992: 21.

---

scale working women who make their own brand decisions. (Gordon Hendry, media planner with the company in *Advertising Age*, 27 July 1981: 34.)

There are dangers in repositioning, however, especially when the company moves too far from the original position. A repositioning strategy should not confuse the consumer. The Parker Pen Company in Europe fell foul of this problem when it attempted for many years to straddle two markets: the mass market at low prices and the exclusive market at premium prices. Regular losses were the norm. According to Jacques Margry, Parker Group Area Manager for Europe, 'by going down market we confused the customer, since the consumer no longer knew what Parker stood for. We were all over the place, dissipating advertising' (*Business Life* (British Airways Inflight Magazine), June 1992: 27). Within a few years of a reorganization in 1986 based on a repositioning of the brand, not as high as Mont Blanc and not as basic as BIC, Parker claimed a 53 per cent share of the 'writing instrument' market in Europe, nine times the nearest rival, and achieved pre-tax profits of £13.3 million.

Wheel of branding

As in retailing, there is also a wheel of branding. In the 1950s, fast-moving consumer goods companies depended on product managers. The growth of brand management indicated a shift in the culture of society. The emergence of brands may have been a by-product of the creation of a consumer-led society, indicating that manufacturers had shifted from an attitude based on selling everything they could make after a long period of scarcity, to producing what would sell.

Rise and fall of the brand manager

In the 1960s, the marketing world was one of well-known brands like Coca-Cola, Nescafé, Bovril, Persil and Kellogg's. But the environment has changed. The pressure on margins, the increased emphasis on price due to the oil crisis of the 1970s and the recessions of the 1980s, and the thrust to internationalize the brand have changed the role of branding and the brand manager particularly. Another change which has had a profound effect on the life of the brand manager is the growth in the power of retailers.

Traditionally, brand managers were responsible for all aspects of brand development, growth and maintenance. They were responsible for integrating all management functions to ensure the success of the brand. This included research and development, production, sales, advertising, pricing and sales promotion activities. The brand manager had to be able to communicate effectively with the other functional areas of the business. In this world, the manufacturer was dominant, the retailer weak and the middlemen subservient to both. In such an environment, the brand manager was king.

As margins dwindled and costs became a major issue, particularly the rising cost of advertising, and as retailers became more powerful, the power of the brand manager was dramatically reduced.

In regard to pricing, the national account managers who provide retailers with attractive discount structures have become more important than brand managers. In addition, the greater pressure on margins has also affected the brand manager's control of promotional expenditure and new product development, functions once tightly guarded by the brand manager.

Growth of retailer power

Retailer power has been a most serious contributory factor in the decline of the brand manager. All retailers want to be treated the same in regard to price and promotions, but they each want to be treated differently in regard to the product service mix. This poses a difficulty for manufacturers, many of which find that four or five retail customers account for 50 per cent of their trade, and that six to nine will account for 75 per cent. Retailers for these manufacturers have become a very powerful bargaining group. As a consequence, in most European countries, regions of the USA and large parts of other developed countries, ten to twelve large retailers control the grocery trade and each seeks a different product and service mix from suppliers. In addition, major brands frequently represent a very small proportion of the retailer's total sales. It is not surprising, therefore, that retailers command a powerful position.

In such a competitive environment, manufacturers attempt to ensure accurate co-ordination between national accounts managers and brand managers. This is an integration of marketing and sales, and the distinction between the two is less important than formerly. In such a regime, it is possible for brand managers to have profit on their brands identified for each customer as well as knowing the overall cash contribution. Techniques such as direct product profitability (DPP) assist in such allocation. This new emphasis on financial returns is enhanced by the use of new techniques and information technology.

From brand to category management

Because of their growing power, retailers are no longer passive observers of interbrand competition at the manufacturer level. Retailers are not brand oriented but category oriented as they are concerned about entire categories: the confectionery category, the detergent category, the dairy foods category, etc. They are not really concerned about whether consumers reach for Mars or Cadbury's, Tide or Cheer, Yoplait or Danone. The retailer is also in a position to demand shelf promotion allowances and 'hello' money. Very few manufacturers can afford the advertising and promotional inefficiency of two or more of its own brands competing for the customer's attention. To the retailer, therefore, it makes sense to have a Cadbury's coupon this week, a Danone money-off promotion next week and an end-of-aisle display of Mars products the week after. Category management, not brand management, has become the important criteria for both manufacturers and retailers.

In the restricted world of financial controls, functional departments within the company, like sales and finance, are given responsibility for those aspects of brand management that they desire. This has had a negative effect on marketing-led growth and innovation. The intervention of other functional areas has meant that strategic brand management has been compromised. In the 1980s, brand management has become a tactical concern of the company with the result that the equity in many well-known brands has been undermined or debased.

Brand managers are today much more financially aware, and are leaving manufacturing companies to work with large retailers with the result that their role is poorly defined. Retailers and financial services institutions have in recent years become attractive places of work for people who traditionally would have worked in large branded manufacturing companies. Traditional ways of managing the brand have been neglected in many situations.

International and Eurobranding

At the present stage of development of the European market, it is difficult to know to what extent a company should attempt to harmonize its brand

---

EXHIBIT 12.9   Just one Cornetto!

While consumers are increasingly prepared to try new and exotic foods, these usually remain niche products. According to Allan Price, chairman of Birds Eye Wall's, Unilever's UK frozen foods subsidiary, about five varieties of staple food account for three quarters of sales in every national market, with the rest divided between 10 or more niche products. Yet there are exceptions. Lasagne has become virtually a staple food in many European – and American – households. By contrast, Birds Eye Wall's has made seven unsuccessful attempts in five years to create a UK market for Carte d'Or, a premium ice-cream which sells well on the continent. Attempts to interest British consumers in frozen herbs – Unilever's most profitable frozen product in Germany – have also flopped. So have efforts to emulate another German success, a gourmet frozen fish dish. 'We have had it on the market twice, and it's failed twice. We're going to try again because this is something we've got to make work,' says Price determinedly.

Even if products cannot always be transferred successfully across borders, the marketing concepts and experience behind them can be. An example is Du Darfst (literally, 'You May'), a range of healthy eating foods launched in Germany 18 years ago and now an umbrella brand covering 120 different products there. As concern with healthy eating has spread, the Du Darfst formula has been adapted to other countries and re-christened Effi in France and Delite in Britain. One advantage is that the brand can be supported by common trans-European advertising campaigns, cutting marketing costs.

Unilever companies are also applying each other's brands to new products. Birds Eye Wall's, for instance, has extended to frozen foods the Gino Ginelli ice-cream brand developed in Germany. So far, the tactic has produced mixed results. It has worked well with pizza, but not with pasta. The approach can involve costly pitfalls. When Unilever set out to extend Healthy Options, a British line of ready meals, to other European countries two years ago, it learned too late that many prohibit use of the word healthy in a product name.

Source: *Financial Times*, 28 October 1991: 14.

---

strategy. One side of the argument states that local differences will keep markets fragmented for many years. This is particularly true in culture-bound businesses such as food. In this case, product innovation and brand development might continue to remain as a national phenomenon with little concern for other European or international markets. Developing a harmonized product and brand strategy may not be so easy in all circumstances (Exhibit 12.9).

The other side of the argument holds that many products would benefit from a European or international perspective in their development and management. In the food industry, this would certainly apply to food ingredients, but also to ready-to-eat frozen foods. The debate will continue for some time, but to the extent that markets and consumer tastes converge, there will be increased pressure for greater harmonization in product and brand development strategies. In recent years, a number of companies in the DIY industry have indicated that the development of international and European brands is feasible (Exhibit 12.10).

EXHIBIT 12.10   Building DIY brands in Europe

The lack of home ownership on the Continent has stunted the growth of DIY retailing because there is less demand for the staple products on a consumer basis. When a local authority or private landlord owns a property, most of the decoration is left up to them so they call in contract decorators who buy materials through trade outlets. The low level of retail trade in Europe has led to low levels of branded, consumer-oriented products such as paint, which tends to be treated as a commodity product. In the UK, ICI has led the way in the paint market by creating strong brand identity for its paint under the Dulux name.

The original Dulux concept was to apply some of the lessons of consumer goods marketing to what had been a commodity or own brand market. Now the company hopes to repeat the success by making Dulux into a pan-European brand. As its growth strategy is largely dependent on the acquisition of existing European paint makers it faces the problem of how to convert the local brand to the Dulux name. In France it has bought the Valentine paint company and brand, which has about 20 per cent of the French market. It has so far branded it ICI Valentine, and is now wondering how to incorporate the Dulux name on to the packaging.

But another UK paint maker is taking a different route. Crown Berger, part of Williams Holdings, had formed a European division to exploit not just the European paint market, but other DIY products, such as the Polycell range and Rawlplugs, both strong brands owned by Williams. But Crown Berger Europe is tackling the European paint market in the exact opposite way to ICI. Instead of one pan-European brand, Crown Berger is planning to attack through regional brands. The Crown brand is a dominant second in the UK – while the Berger brand that it bought from Germany's Hoechst is market leader in Ireland and Portugal.

There is something of a paradox involved in bringing slick professionalism to a market that is based on the part-time efforts of amateurs, but the growth of the market seems to depend on it. Consumers like the confidence that well-known brands bring to DIY. In that respect the marketing challenge involved in European DIY is in branding and confidence building. It is an approach that has worked in the UK, and could work in the rest of Europe, as long as the DIY instruction books are translated into French, German, Italian, Spanish, Greek...

Source: 'Marketing in Europe: Special Report', in *Marketing*, 20 April 1989: 35–7.

Brand names in Europe

One of the difficulties of branding is that the brand name chosen for one market may not work in another. This is a special problem in Europe as new opportunities appear and companies attempt to take brands across borders. Some brand names lose their impact in different markets. The decision facing the manufacturer or brand owner is whether to change the brand name when entering a new market.

Many manufacturers decide not to change brand names that are well established in different countries, recognizing that the country loyalty factor might be lost in any such attempt. The Unilever brand names for its main detergent in various countries Omo, Persil, Presto, Via, Skip and All, have been maintained because the company feared it would lose customers to change them. Packaging was, however, standardized so that travellers from one country to another would recognize the familiar shape and colour, and hopefully remain loyal. Mars, the US-owned confectionery manufacturer, did harmonize one of its brand names across markets with great success. The 'Snickers' confectionery bar once known as 'Marathon' in the UK was harmonized successfully by alerting customers well in advance of the change, using a 'flash' notice in the packaging stating that the product was soon to be called 'Snickers'. For a period after the name change, the 'flash' changed to 'formerly known as Marathon'.

In some cases, brand names translate so badly that they must be changed lest they convey wrong meanings or cause offence. Selling 'Irish Mist Liqueur' or 'Body Mist' anti-perspirant products in Germany would be ill-advised because of the meaning of the word 'mist' in German. In other cases, although the company is very successful, the brand name used in most markets cannot be extended very much due to the meaning of the brand which is conveyed (Exhibit 12.11).

Assignment questions

1   What is a brand? How can branding help in marketing consumer products?

2   Should manufacturers of consumer products always brand their products?

3   Discuss and decide whether a family brand, or an individual brand policy, is more appropriate for a line of consumer electronic products.

4   What is meant by brand equity and how does the company increase it? How may it be measured?

5   What are the roles for quality, style and differentiation in the branding of luxury goods?

EXHIBIT 12.11   Who ya gonna call?

If you were a rat, there is one company whose strategy you might follow with interest: the dreaded Rentokil. But behind the firm's unglamorous image lurks far more than a bunch of rat-catchers. Rentokil is one of Britain's most successful service businesses. When Clive Thompson took over as chief executive in 1982, most of the firm's sales came from exterminating British pests and treating damp British homes for woodworm and rot. Today Rentokil operates in more than 40 countries and – along with chasing rats – offers a range of environmental services including the provision and care of tropical plants for offices, disposing of medical waste, and cleaning offices, shops, kitchens and other nooks and crannies.

Mr Thompson's achievement has been to transform a firm once considered a polluting rat-poisoner into one purveying greenery and cleanliness. Demand for its services is fuelled by nightmares of legionnaire's disease, sick-building syndrome, the spread of AIDS and every type of food poisoning. Any customer indifferent to such threats has yet to talk to a Rentokil salesman. Apart from hitching up to the green machine, Mr Thompson's second good insight was that the fragmented industries supplying cleaning and pest-control services were ripe for a dependable, branded service providing corporate customers with as much reassurance as cleanliness. Firms trying to guard against an embarrassing environmental disaster, however remote, rarely quibble over price.

With real, or imagined, environmental threats proliferating faster than ever, Rentokil's future looks bright – provided the company can maintain the quality of its services and thus its premium pricing. Mr Thompson confidently aims to continue increasing Rentokil's profits by 20 per cent or more a year indefinitely.

Three possible constraints face the company. First, Rentokil itself could become entangled in an environmental disaster. It has already settled out of court two British cases of alleged poisoning, without admitting any liability. Second, the company's high profitability and growth are bound to attract competitors. But replicating Rentokil's service operation will not be easy. BET, another British corporate-services conglomerate, ran into trouble after buying too many unrelated businesses too quickly and failing to establish a premium brand.

Ironically, Rentokil's very success at creating such a brand now limits the types of services it can offer. '"Rentokil" is a terrible name in any language,' admits Mr Thompson ruefully. The company considered going into the funeral and retirement-home businesses, but decided that its name would be an insurmountable obstacle. Changing the name in which it has invested so much, or nurturing a collection of brands, is too late and too risky, argues Mr Thompson.

Source: *The Economist*, 6 March 1993: 68 and 71.

6 How does the brand life cycle differ from the product life cycle? How have long-established brands avoided decline?

7 Branding is under threat from various sources. What are these and how may they be counteracted by the branded goods company?

Annotated bibliography

Jones, John Philip (1986) *What's in a Name?*, Aldershot: Gower.

Keller, Kevin Lane (1993) 'Conceptualising, measuring and managing customer-based brand equity', *Journal of Marketing*, **57**, 1, 1–22.

Watkins, Trevor (1986) *The Economics of the Brand: A marketing analysis*, London: McGraw-Hill.

References

Blattberg, R.C., and K.J. Wisniewski (1989) 'Price induced patterns of competition', *Marketing Science*, **8**, Fall, 291–309.

Clifford, Donald K., and Richard E. Cavanagh (1985) *The Winning Performance: How America's high- and midsize growth companies succeed*, New York: Bantam Books.

Doyle, Peter (1990): 'Building successful brands: the strategic options', *Journal of Consumer Marketing*, **7**, Spring, 5–20.

Doyle, Peter (1991) 'Branding', in M.J. Baker (ed.), *The Marketing Book*, Oxford: Butterworth-Heinemann.

Fazio, Russell H. (1986) 'How do attitudes guide behaviour?' in R.M. Sorentino and E.T. Higgins (eds.), *Handbook of Motivation and Cognition: Foundations of social behaviour*, New York: Guilford Press.

Firth, Michael (1993) 'Price setting and the value of a strong brand name', *International Journal of Research in Marketing*, **10**, 4, 381–6.

Jones, John Philip (1986) *What's in a Name?*, Aldershot: Gower.

Kamakura, Wagner A., and Gary J. Russell (1993) 'Measuring brand values with scanner data', *International Journal of Research in Marketing*, **10**, 1, 9–22.

Keller, Kevin Lane (1993) 'Conceptualising, measuring and managing customer-based brand equity', *Journal of Marketing*, **57**, 1, 1–22.

Lannon, J., and P. Cooper (1983) 'Humanistic advertising: a holistic cultural perspective', *International Journal of Advertising*, **2**, 3, 195–213.

Oxendfeldt, Alfred R., and William L. Moore (1978) 'Customer or competitor: which guideline for marketing?', *Management Review*, August, 43–8.

Robinson, Joan (1933) *The Economics of Imperfect Competition* (reprinted 1950), London: Macmillan.

Smith, Daniel and C. Whan Park (1992) 'The effects of brand extensions on market share and advertising efficiency', *Journal of Marketing Research*, **29**, 3, 296–313.

Watkins, Trevor (1986) *The Economics of the Brand: A marketing analysis*, London: McGraw-Hill.

Wentz, Laurel (1989) 'How experts value brands', *Advertising Age*, 16 January.

Pricing decisions and methods

13

Introduction

This chapter introduces and explains:

- the differences among prices, costs and values;
- the impact of public policy on pricing;
- the influence of costs on price;
- how companies engage in price-cost planning;
- the significance of cost, competition and market-oriented pricing;
- how to formulate a pricing strategy;
- how companies price for different markets and circumstances;
- how companies respond to price changes;
- the dangers of the price trap;
- the limits of price discretion; and
- the various tactical approaches to pricing.

Price is a measure of value, usually expressed in monetary terms, which is agreed in some fashion between a buyer and seller in an exchange. In marketing management, price is the element of the marketing mix which serves to generate revenue, hence the setting of price is a crucial decision.

There are many influences on pricing. It is necessary to understand the impact of public policy on prices. Governments and other public institutions take a great deal of interest in the price mechanism, usually in a role of protecting consumers, but also to regulate markets and with a keen eye on monopoly profits which might arise. There are also company influences on price which relate to the cost of providing products and services, and the experience gained by the company over time.

Companies adopt different approaches to pricing. Perhaps the most popular approach is to add a margin to costs and arrive at the price charged. Numerous versions of cost-oriented pricing exist. Their principal attraction is their simplicity. Companies also have regard for the competition in setting prices, but this approach too has its limitations. It is difficult to know whether the price charged will generate sufficient profits. Market-oriented pricing attempts to understand the needs of customers and to relate them to conditions in the company in the setting of prices.

Pricing has a number of strategic dimensions which the company must consider. These relate to the nature of the product and the sensitivity of the market. Companies sometimes price to penetrate markets, to skim them or to achieve early cash recovery from the market. Different pricing strategies are required in each instance. There are also tactical aspects of pricing which the company must understand. These relate to the psychological aspects of pricing, discounts and calibrating price levels in relation to the other elements of the marketing mix.

When you have studied this chapter, you should be able to define the terms used above in your own words, and you should be able to do the following:

1. Understand the role of price in marketing management.

2. Specify the relationship among demand, supply and demand price elasticity.

3. Determine the importance of internal company influences on pricing.

4. Recognize the influence of fixed costs, excess capacity experience and scale effects in setting prices.

5. Understand and apply cost-oriented approaches to pricing.

6. Determine when to use competition-oriented pricing.

7. Specify the appropriateness of market-oriented pricing methods.

8. Recognize when penetration pricing, price skimming and early cash recovery pricing are appropriate.

9. Avoid the price trap, while recognizing the limits of pricing discounts.

10. Recognize the role of price flexibility in tactical competition.

562

Meaning of price in marketing

Prices reflect values: the value sellers believe their product possesses and, if sold at that price, the value to the buyer also. Pricing is important to the economy and the company. In the economy, it is the mechanism used to allocate resources among competing uses. In the company, it is the basis for generating profits. Price reflects corporate objectives and policies, and is an important element in the marketing mix. It is the only element in the marketing mix which generates revenue directly; the others are cost elements. For that reason, price is often used by firms to offset weaknesses in the other elements in the marketing mix. Price change can be made more quickly than changes in the product, channels of distribution, advertising and personal selling. A price change is relatively unambiguous and easily understood, so it is easy to communicate it to buyers. For these reasons, price changes are frequently used for defensive and offensive strategies.

Pricing has a strategic aspect which gives it a longer-term focus, and it has a tactical focus in the short term. In forming pricing strategy, the company

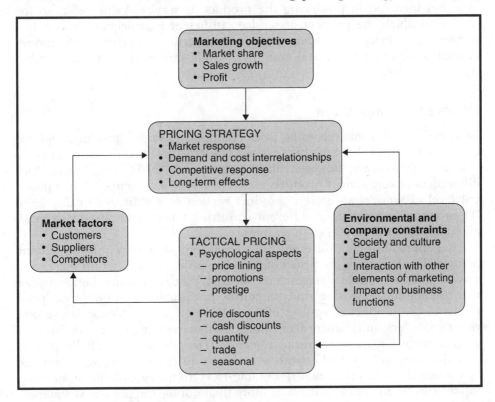

Figure 13.1   Role of pricing in marketing management

563

must first determine or adopt a set of marketing objectives relevant to pricing (Biswas *et al.*, 1993). It must also be concerned with environmental and company constraints and with market-specific factors (Figure 13.1). Pricing strategy is concerned with how the market responds, how demand and costs are interrelated, and how competitors respond, particularly in the longer term. Tactical factors are concerned with the psychological aspects of pricing and the value and effectiveness of price discounting. It is a shorter-term orientation.

Prices, costs and values

In spite of the importance of managing price, many companies do not charge the most appropriate price for their products. The most common mistakes include: pricing on the basis of costs only, so that firms fail to take sufficient account of demand intensity and customer psychology; failure to revise price often enough to capitalize on changed market conditions; and setting the price independently of the other elements of the marketing mix.

Three words often cause confusion: cost, value and price. Cost refers to all expenses incurred in producing the product or service. Value refers to the degree to which the product or service satisfies or is anticipated to satisfy a defined need. Price arises when a transaction occurs and refers to the money equivalent by which seller and customer benefits are matched to the satisfaction of both parties.

Prices and competition

Consumers expect markets to be price competitive, so that products and services which deliver the same benefits are similarly priced. Differentiated products and services are, however, likely to be priced at different levels. Price differences among similar products may reflect a lack of competition, a different level of service, a different product version or a different quality level. When comparing prices in different countries it is also important to make allowance for different taxation regimes.

In general, however, different price levels indicate different levels of competition. By comparing the prices of the same products in different markets, it may be possible to make a judgement concerning the relationship between price and competition. A pricing study of consumer durables at two different price points in the product categories of portable televisions, table-top televisions, video recorders and camcorders, indicates that very high price differences exist between European countries (*Financial Times*, 3 August 1992: 2). In general, Germany and the Netherlands were the low-price countries, while Italy and Spain were the high-price countries (Table 13.1). In the case of one of the table-top televisions, the price in Italy was more than double the price in Germany.

The intention under EU competition and market policies is that these

TABLE 13.1 Comparative dealer prices charged by a consumer electronics manufacturer for products sold in the EC, March 1992

Product	Country	Lowest price (DM)	Country	Highest price (DM)	Difference (%)
Portable TVs					
Model A	Germany	434	Spain	596	137
Model B	Netherlands	408	Italy	560	137
Table-top TVs					
Model A	Germany	922	Italy	2,000	217
Model B	Germany	1,270	Spain	1,764	139
VCRs					
Model A	Netherlands	675	Italy	885	131
Model B	Germany	1,383	Spain	1,873	135
Camcorders					
Model A	Germany	1,126	Italy	1,632	145
Model B	Germany	995	Italy	1,323	133

Note: Conversion to D-Marks at prevailing exchange rates. The survey did not include Britain.

Source: *Financial Times*, 3 August 1992: 2. With permission.

price differences will disappear. To the extent that they are caused by marketing institutional barriers such as inefficient distribution systems, the price convergence will be slow in coming. In the meantime, manufacturers and retailers can expect a considerable amount of parallel imports as consumers attempt to obtain the benefit of the lower prices by buying in the low-price country and taking the products home (Exhibit 13.1).

Supply, demand and elasticity

It is generally agreed that a host of factors influence price sensitivity and the demand for a product or service. For many years, economists have examined the integration of demand and supply and discussed the effect on price. Price sensitivity occurs for many reasons discussed in other chapters. Here concern rests with determining the relationship between the demand for a product or service and its supply. This is captured in the concept of price elasticity of demand. Price elasticity of demand is expressed as:

$$\frac{\text{Percentage change in quantity demanded}}{\text{Percentage change in price}}$$

The less elastic the demand, the more it pays the seller to raise the price, other things being equal. Suppose the buyer response to price changes was elastic.

EXHIBIT 13.1   Price flaws undermine EU's single market hopes

Of all the companies which have agitated for faster European economic integration, none has done so for longer of more loudly than Philips, the large Dutch electronics manufacturer. Indeed Philips claims to have invented the single European market, and top executives have repeatedly called for its speedy realisation. Yet, when it comes to applying the single market's central principles – total liberalisation of trade and unrestricted price competition across EU borders – Philips' business practices appear to diverge from its lofty rhetoric.

The company freely admits the trade prices it charges for the same products vary, though it will not say by how much. It also says it supplies products to dealers only for sale in their own countries and refuses to supply them for re-export to other EU countries – so-called parallel importing. 'If an authorised Philips dealer in Italy asked us to sell him products in the Netherlands, we would tell him, very politely, that we have a distributor in Italy and he should buy his products there,' said Mr Jack Reemers, a spokesman at Philips' Eindhoven headquarters. Mr Reemers said Philips had no intention of changing its approach once the single market took effect at the end of this year by unifying its prices across the EU. 'What have unified prices got to do with the single market?' he said, adding that the company planned to continue existing policies 'until the end of the world'.

In consumer electronics, wide price differentials are far from unique to Philips, according to electrical retailers. They say the prices of leading brands such as Grundig of Germany and Panasonic and Sony of Japan also vary substantially. Expert International and Euronics, two pan-European associations of small electrical retailers, say the prices of many of these companies' products

---

Under these circumstances, demand is elastic at all points on the demand curve (Figure 13.2(a)). If price is lowered from £10 to £9 for each unit, the increase in revenue more than compensates for the revenue lost due to the price decrease. Total revenue increases from £1,000 to £1,260. If, however, prices are raised to £11, the increased revenue due to the higher unit price is insufficient to compensate for the sales decline. Total revenue declines from £1,000 to £825.

The situation is quite the reverse when demand is inelastic, as may be seen from Figure 13.2(b). A decrease in price results in a decline in total revenues to £972, while an increase in price results in an increased total revenue of £1,045.

The concept of elasticity is important in pricing decisions if it can help the manager decide the most appropriate price to charge for the company's products. Recall also that it is a neat summary measure of how customers respond to price changes. If the company knows what determines price elasticity of demand, it is in a better position to estimate how consumers respond to price changes, and it is thus in a better position to decide on the price to charge. There are four circumstances in which demand is likely to be less elastic, where:

are 25–35 per cent higher in Italy and Spain than in Germany and the Netherlands. The difference can in some cases be 50 per cent or more. Mr Wim van den Toorn, Export's managing director, said exceptionally high trade prices depressed dealers' margins. He claims variation in the cost of distribution, transport and manufacturers' contributions to after-sales service give rise to differences of less than 5 per cent in prices across Europe. 'We know what the costs are. We ship goods to our dealers using the same transport companies, trucks and roads as our suppliers,' he said. He and other retailers complain price differentials are maintained by obstacles to cross-border product flows. 'Suppliers never say explicitly in their dealership agreements that you can't make parallel imports,' he said. 'But if you know the business, you can read between the lines. And what the suppliers are saying is "we can make life very difficult for you".

'If we bought Philips or Sony products in the Netherlands and sold them in Spain, the suppliers would boycott our dealers. Or maybe they would be told that certain spare parts they needed would be out of stock.' Mr Van den Toorn's fears are shared by Mr Macel Vloemans, head of Euronics which, unlike Expert, has tried to make parallel imports. It is currently trying to buy 10,000 Philishave razors in the Netherlands for dealers in Italy, where Mr Vloemans says the price is 20 per cent higher. However Mr Vloemans says such attempts have repeatedly run into outright refusal or resistance. 'If I buy products for parallel imports, suppliers won't do repairs, send spare parts or provide service manuals. They can also threaten to remove dealer discounts,' he said.

Source: *Financial Times*, 3 August 1992: 2.

- there are few or no substitutes or competitors;
- buyers do not readily notice the higher price;
- buyers are slow to change their buying habits and search for lower prices; and
- buyers believe that the higher prices are justified by quality improvements, normal inflation and similar factors.

If demand is elastic rather than inelastic, a seller might consider lowering the price, since a lower price will produce more revenue. This price policy makes sense so long as the costs of producing and selling more do not increase disproportionately.

A complete market-oriented approach to pricing appears to be appropriate when an emphasis on demand and customers is required. It is inappropriate if used unethically and if it ignores cost and profit considerations. In such circumstances, the company's reputation and financial viability are at stake.

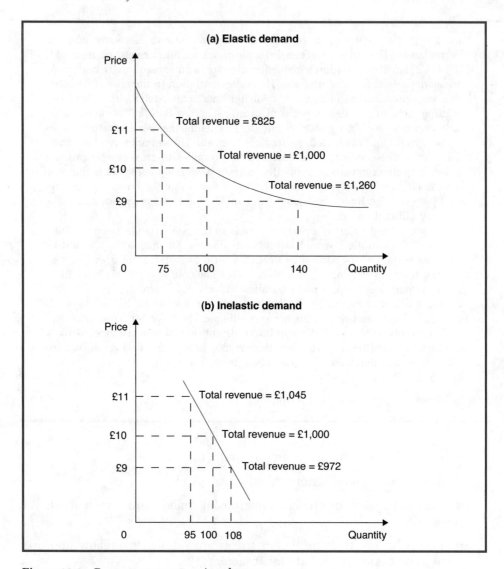

Figure 13.2 Buyer response to price changes

Major influences on the pricing decision

Two major influences affect the pricing decision process in the company: public policy and internal company factors.

Public policy influence on pricing

Public policy influence on pricing stems from public concerns for the general environment, and the public and social constraints which emanate from these concerns. Public policy influences are usually manifested in the form of laws and regulations which affect companies in their pricing decisions.

The pricing environment

Price decisions are influenced by a constellation of factors (Figure 13.3). Costs come first to mind, but there are other factors, such as company marketing objectives, the reaction of competitors, and the response of intermediaries in the channel of distribution (Oxendfeldt, 1991). Price levels and price changes induce a series of reactions among these groups of interested parties which cannot be ignored. Pricing is such a sensitive issue that in most countries aspects of pricing are controlled or regulated by governments. Lastly, it is essential to examine the response of buyers to price decisions. In recent years, US consumers have witnessed a steady increase in the real price of cars, making allowance for changes in models and inflation (Exhibit 13.2). Some markets are more price sensitive than others. Price perceptions vary by product, by market and by customer group (Monroe, 1973). Each of these factors must be considered when arriving at a price decision.

Impact of public policy

Government agencies and public policy bodies influence price in many ways. In regulated industries such as utilities, railways and airlines, public authorities

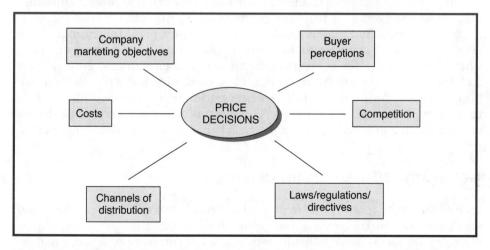

Figure 13.3 Influences on pricing

EXHIBIT 13.2   The price is high

Car firms in America are running into a new version of an old problem: their cars cost too much. Although new car sales are up about three per cent this year in America, industry analysts fret that the numbers would be better if American motorists were not suffering from 'sticker shock'. The average new car now costs $17,692; in 1983 the sticker price was $10,640 and in 1973 just $4,052. Measured another way, the typical American buyer will work 25.5 weeks to pay for a new car this year, compared to 22.5 weeks in 1983 and 17.5 weeks in 1973.

For years, America's car makers have insisted that their prices were rising slower than the rate of inflation. But the figures they quote are usually calculated on a 'comparably-equipped' basis, which allows them to juggle the figures to account for any new standard features, such as air conditioning or electric windows. And the manufacturers' numbers usually do not include the added cost of meeting new federal standards for safety, emissions and fuel-economy. So an advertised price rise of $250 might actually mean an extra $1,000.

General Motors' answer is a new 'value-pricing' strategy based around so-called special editions, which all come equipped with the popular extras, such as air conditioning, that most buyers order anyway. Thus a Special Edition Chevrolet Caprice will cost $18,995 while last year's model cost £20,042. Similarly, Ford's 'one-price' programme offers five different body styles of the Ford Escort for the same price. The snag with this strategy is that it phases out the rebates and other sales incentives that can shave $1,000 or more off the price of a new car.

Source: *The Economist*, 14 August 1993: 63.

---

may approve or reject price changes. Their stated concern is to protect consumer interests while allowing the regulated company sufficient profit to expand capacity as demand grows, and a 'reasonable' return on investment. Increasingly, however, regulation has come to be seen as protecting inefficient companies, which does nothing for consumers. In an era of open markets, governments and bodies like the European Commission recognize the need for international competition in many of the services traditionally protected for strategic reasons by individual governments. The move is a recognition that protected markets mean inefficient production, which benefits nobody in the longer term.

Company influences on pricing

One of the major reasons why firms find it difficult to price their products and services relates to the relative ease with which information on costs may be obtained, but the relative difficulty with which information on demand may be obtained.

Internal constraints on pricing policy

Three internal constraints on the firm's price policy may be identified:

- the nature of the business;
- the availability of market information; and
- corporate resources.

It is necessary to be very precise in describing the nature of the business. 'Superline Furniture manufactures a range of soft furniture for the first-time home buyer. The units are hard wearing, of modular design and suitable for the smaller home and apartment. Superline competes on quality and price and matches import competition for this range of furniture.' This is an example of the detail required. A precise definition of the business determines the products that the company produces and the nature of the markets to be served. The products manufactured identify the firm with a certain industry, while the market served specifies the firms, industries and products with which the company competes, and the dimensions of competition: price, quality and service. Such information is vital to determining the price to charge for the company's products, even though it is more difficult to obtain than cost information.

Second, many companies do not possess good information on the market, so they accept the going market price. In this case, profits depend very largely on the firm's ability to minimize costs. The third internal constraint on the company's price policy is the nature and extent of its corporate resources. It is the company's financial and marketing resources which have the greatest impact on price policy.

Influence of costs on price

The cost of manufacturing a product or producing a service may be variable or fixed. The annual depreciation on a chemical plant is considered as a fixed cost and so is labour. The costs of running the plant, materials and power, would be considered as variable. These latter vary directly with the finished chemicals produced in the plant. If fixed costs make up a large proportion of total cost, pricing to get maximum plant utilization is the dominant consideration.

Until the company covers its fixed costs it loses money. After fixed costs have been met, each incremental sale contributes a proportionally large amount to profits. If variable costs are a relatively large proportion of total costs, pricing to maximize the difference between the variable cost of each unit produced and the price, or unit contribution, is the key consideration for profits. Here the manufacturer attempts to maximize unit prices while reducing variable costs.

In the first situation, the objective of the chemical plant will be to produce sufficient revenue to cover its fixed costs and above that to achieve maximum plant utilization to make profits. In the second case, the company prices to cover the relatively high variable costs on each unit and gain sufficient contribution to make a profit having amortized the fixed costs.

Sometimes companies experience underutilization of plant and equipment, and price below full cost. Companies with high fixed costs are known to accept business at prices which cover variable cost, but which also make a contribution to overheads. Their ambition is to struggle through bad times and maintain staff and other key resources. A second situation arises when companies sometimes price below full costs is to win a large order. By taking such business, the company expects its unit costs to fall. Later the company may attempt to raise price again. Attempting to offset short-term losses with longer-term profits may be a foolhardy strategy, since there are no guarantees that the losses will be offset.

The cost of a product or service is not, therefore, a single indisputable number. Price–cost planning is needed in a number of circumstances, especially when the situation changes in the company or in the competitive environment (Figure 13.4). The calculation of relevant cost depends on the judgement and objectives of managers. Relevant costs depend on the company's marketing objectives. Six steps may be identified in evaluating the cost–price structure in a company:

- define the existing price structure;
- identify the prices of competing products for each item in the product line;
- decide which product items need attention;
- calculate the profitability of the current product/service mix;
- identify products and services for price changes; and
- define the new price structure in the company.

Value of accumulated experience

With experience in producing a product or service, the company is able to do it better and cheaper. The learning involved is captured in Oscar Wilde's claim that 'Experience is the name everyone gives to their mistakes.' The experience curve describes a pattern of declining cost, whereby the total value-added costs in an enterprise, i.e. the costs of all purchases except components, decline in real terms as cumulative experience increases. Included in these costs are manufacturing overheads, advertising, distribution, sales and general administrative costs.

The experience curve is specific and predictable. Each time cumulative production doubles, the value-added cost in real terms declines by a fixed percentage which varies from situation to situation. For example, in an industry with an 80 per cent experience curve, each time the total accumulated

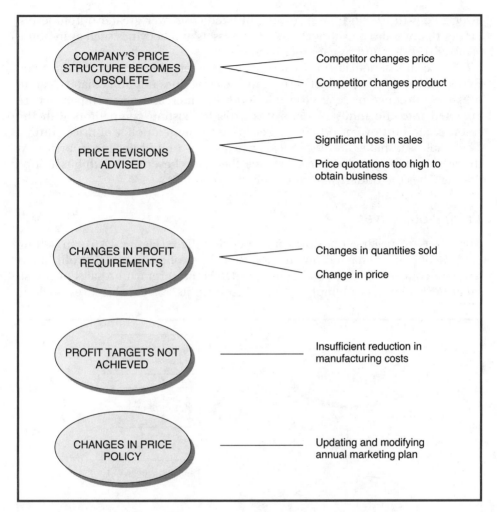

Figure 13.4　Need for price–cost planning

production doubles, the cost is reduced by 20 per cent, i.e. to 80 per cent of its previous value.

The sources of advantages which determine the slope of experience curve are numerous. With time and repetition companies learn how to make products better and more efficiently, and to incorporate technological improvements in production. It is often possible to redesign products during their life cycle, which can lead to a reduction in the number of parts, switching to better materials and miniaturization. Replacing fabricated metal with plastic is an example of the first, while an application of the second and third can reduce the number and size of components in a product.

Scale effects also reduce costs. These reflect the efficiencies which are

573

associated with size and the spreading of fixed costs over greater output levels. Larger operations can support specialized assets and activities such as in-house legal, advertising and research services.

There are beneficial implications of the experience curve for the firm. Excess demand for a product early in its life cycle does not immediately lead to pressure to reduce price as costs fall. As profits increase, new competitors are attracted into the industry, or profits provide existing competitors with the resources to improve or retain market share through a policy of price cutting. The result is a shake-out of the weaker firms and a rapid decline in prices. As the market stabilizes after the shake-out, the market eventually exhibits a slope that matches the underlying experience curve.

Pricing objectives

Three sets of pricing objectives may be identified (Figure 13.5). In setting prices, companies may be highly motivated by profit objectives. Profit objectives are concerned with obtaining a predetermined return on sales or investment, or even an attempt to maximize profits. Sales objectives include

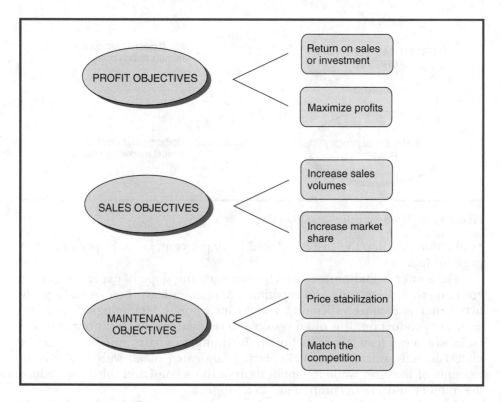

Figure 13.5 Pricing objectives

574

attempts to increase sales volumes or market share. Maintenance objectives are concerned with issues such as price stabilization in the market and with meeting competitive pricing behaviour. Pricing for market share, for example, is an objective frequently associated with Japanese companies (Exhibit 13.3).

Alternative methods of pricing

In this section the three major approaches to pricing are examined:

- cost-oriented pricing;
- competition-oriented pricing; and
- demand-oriented or market-based pricing.

Each of these approaches is discussed in a separate section below. Then the information on these three approaches is integrated in a section which deals with establishing the limits of pricing discretion in the firm.

Cost-oriented pricing

Four variations of a cost-oriented approach to pricing are described (Figure 13.6). It is emphasized that the discussion is about a variation on a theme. The

---

EXHIBIT 13.3   A curious pricing system

The Japanese company's obsession with markets rather than profits is logical in an extremely competitive environment where profitability is pushed down to market-clearing levels, and survival depends more on keeping up with the competition and anticipating the market than on the state of the bottom line at any given moment.

This obsession is reflected in everything from the organisation of production through marketing strategies to the pricing of new products. Japanese pricing reverses western practice. It is standard in the West to specify a product, than add up the costs of its components, including overheads and profit, to arrive at a selling price. Most Japanese companies start with a target market share; then they estimate what price will enable them to reach that share; then they work backwards to push down the cost of everything that goes into the product, until the target price is met. This tends not only to drive down costs (because it makes everyone involved re-think his bit of the product) but speeds up innovations as well.

Source: *The Economist*, 4 April 1992: 24.

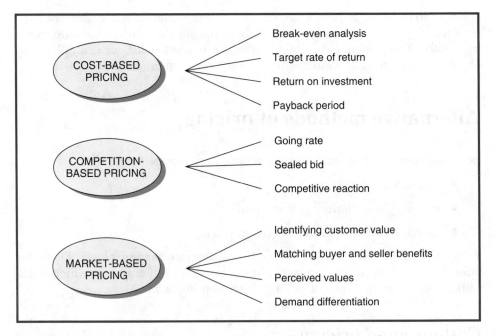

Figure 13.6 Methods of pricing

concept of a break-even price is examined first, since it is central to the other approaches listed. Companies sometimes use one, all four, or a combination of these cost approaches depending on circumstances.

Break-even analysis

The break-even formula for a product, which suggest what sales must be to cover costs, can be derived easily:

> Product total profit = Product total revenue − Product total cost

This simple formula may be expanded by examining the elements of revenue and cost in more detail:

> Profit = (Price × Quantity sold) − [Fixed costs + (Variable costs × Quantity sold)]

or in easily recognizable symbols:

> $\pi(\text{profit}) = PQ - [FC + (VC \times Q)]$

At the break-even point, total profit is zero, i.e. the company is neither losing nor gaining on the venture. Therefore, the following can be stated:

> $\pi(\text{profit}) = PQ - [FC + (VC \times Q)]$

576

which is the same as:

$$\pi = Q(P - VC) - FC$$

which is the same as:

$$-Q(P - VC) = -FC$$

Now if we divide both sides of the equation by $-(P-VC)$ we obtain

$$Q = \frac{FC}{P-VC}$$

which is the break-even quantity in units. Sales may be expressed in units or value terms. The formula, in words, is as follows:

$$\text{Sales quantity (in units) to break even} = \frac{\text{Fixed costs}}{\text{Price} - \text{Variable costs}}$$

While the above appears technical, it is necessary to appreciate that break-even analysis is not a complicated concept. It simply answers the question, 'What must company sales be, at a given price, to cover fixed costs?'

An example will illustrate the concept. Suppose ABC Photocopying Services Ltd charges $0.10 for each colour copied page. If fixed costs, equipment, space and overheads of running this small service unit are $27,000 each year and the variable costs of producing each photocopy are $0.04, ABC Photocopying Services Ltd can compute its break-even point as follows:

$$\text{Break-even quantity in units} = \frac{\$27,000}{\$0.10 - \$0.04} = 450,000 \text{ copies}$$

At this level of output, total revenues would be $45,000 (Figure 13.7). If ABC Photocopying Services Ltd were to sell each copy at $0.12, the margin would increase to $0.06, so the company would break even at a lower quantity. Specifically, the break-even point would be ($27,000/$0.08) = 337,500 copies. In this analysis, the possibility of diminishing returns in production has been ignored, which might increase costs. The effect of market saturation has also not been considered, which would require lower prices to attract marginal buyers. Nevertheless, the principles of break-even analysis are illustrated using constant costs and constant prices.

Target rate of return

A more likely financial goal than break-even is a target rate of return on investment. This rate, which the company must select as part of its pricing policy, is multiplied by the investment involved and entered into the break-even formula above as part of fixed costs. Thus, suppose the investment required to develop and test a new form of 3D photocopying was $50,000 and the desired rate of return on investment was 20 per cent. Then $10,000 ($50,000 × 0.20) must be added to the fixed costs in the formula:

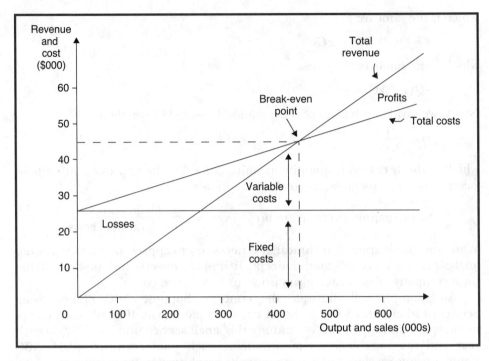

Figure 13.7   Break-even analysis for pricing

Break-even for a 20 per cent target rate of return on investment =
$$\frac{\$27,000 + \$10,000}{\$0.10 - \$0.04} = 616,667 \text{ copies}$$

In attempting to achieve a target rate of return, the company must set its price to give a specified target rate of return on total costs at a standard volume, in the present example 20 per cent rate of return on investment. The company first estimates total costs at various output levels covering the capacity range in the company and then estimates the capacity at which the company expects to operate a planning period. It is then possible to calculate the total cost of output at this level of capacity utilization. The company then sets a target rate of return, such as 20 per cent rate of return on investment:

(Total cost + Required return)/Output level = Price per unit

The approach is appropriate as there is a focus on profits. Its weakness is that it uses an estimate of sales to set prices, but we know that price influences sales!

Return on investment

Sometimes there is difficulty understanding precisely what is included under the term 'investment' in the previous formula. From the point of view of financial analysis, it is necessary to distinguish between return on assets and return on equity. A rate of return is specific to a definite time period, generally a year. The more times the company uses its investment during a year, the higher the rate of return. For example, if the company earns 10 per cent on its investment every six months, it is earning 20 per cent per year because it is turning its assets over twice a year.

Turnover, a very important concept for pricing policies, is the basis for the success of the discount stores: they lower the price–cost margins on those products for which consumer response is highest, i.e. highly price elastic. The increased volume thus obtained by the discount stores enables them to turn over their assets many times per year, which more than offsets the lower margins. To see how this works in practice, a few definitions are necessary:

$$\text{Turnover} = \frac{\text{Sales}}{\text{Total investment}}$$

$$\text{Earnings} - \text{Sales Ratio} = \frac{\text{Earnings}}{\text{Sales}}$$

Return on investment = Earnings as a ratio of sales multiplied by turnover

$$\frac{\text{Earnings}}{\text{Sales}} \times \frac{\text{Sales}}{\text{Total investment}}$$

To illustrate, suppose a local newsagent had earnings (sales less cost of sales) of £25,000 on an annual sales volume of £250,000. Thus earnings as a percentage of sales would be 10 per cent. If total investment (inventories, accounts receivable, cash and permanent investment) was £250,000, the retailer's investment turnover for the year would be 1.0 (£250,000/£250,000 = 1.0). The rate of return on investment is 10 per cent (10% × 1.0 × 100 = 10%). Now suppose the retailer recognizes that the demand for the products carried is elastic and a decision is taken to lower the margin to 8 per cent of sales. Suppose further that, as a result of the price reduction, sales double to £500,000 per year. The retailer's turnover is now 2.0 (£500,000/£250,000 = 2.0) and the annual return on investment is now 16 per cent because the investment is being used twice per year.

Payback period

Suppose a company has an idea for a new product or a new venture. It might wish to estimate how long it will take before the original investment is recoverd or paid back. The payback concept combines the estimates of demand and break-even units. The formula is:

$$\text{Payback period (in years)} = \frac{\text{Break-even (in units)}}{\text{Annual demand (in units)}}$$

An illustration will demonstrate the use of the formula. Suppose the break-even point for a new product is 100,000 units, but the annual demand (the amount the company expects to sell in a year) is only 50,000 units. The payback period is then two years. If the break-even point were lowered to 75,000 units, the payback period would be reduced to 18 months.

Break-even pricing is used by a large number of firms because it is easy to use and allows the firm to compare the profit consequences of alternative sets of prices. To make profits, the firm has to sell a quantity greater than the break-even quantity. Alternatively, a higher price allows the firm to break even at a lower quantity and thus reach profitability sooner.

Limitations of cost-based pricing

The weaknesses of cost-based approaches are that they ignore market demand, they are rigid and frequently they are not profit oriented. It is frequently difficult to discover the real costs of products and processes. It is not always easy to decide what are the appropriate costs to include and disagreement can easily occur. This riddle of cost management means that managers must be very careful when referring to cost structures as a guide to pricing.

Cost-oriented approaches to pricing may be appropriate if the average unit cost and the price elasticity of demand are constant over the relevant range of sales. In such circumstances, the industry may have discovered the optimum mark-up on cost. Cost approaches are also reasonably simple to apply, and if all competitors behave similarly, they are seen as being socially fair.

There are a number of reasons why too much emphasis on costs is not recommended. Once the company focuses attention exclusively on the cost–price relationship, it removes all possibility of introducing innovativeness into the market. Matching prices to costs also means that the company has little discretion remaining when it attempts to set the other variables in the marketing mix. For example, a cost–price emphasis which produces only mariginal profits is unlikely to encourage product improvement. A cost emphasis also tends to reduce the number of new product ventures among firms which insist on recovering product research and development costs in the early stages of a new product launch.

Too much emphasis on costs of production rather than on the market or demand side of the equation gives rise to two major managerial deficiencies. First, companies tend to evaluate profits in terms of profit per unit sold rather than in terms of profit generated on a certain turnover. Second, a cost emphasis provides little scope for market segmentation or product positioning on the basis of price perception. Galleries Lafayette and Prisunic carry similar ranges of merchandise, sell at very different price levels to different market segments and yet are both profitable firms. Of course, these firms vary on other elements of the marketing mix besides price, but the price images created by the two firms are important dimensions in their competitive armoury.

Competition-oriented pricing

While all companies should be aware of competitive marketing influences, it is known that many firms rely almost entirely on the competition to determine price. These companies set price at a level which is at, just above, or just below the prices obtaining in the market. The guiding force in setting price is the behaviour of competitors. Companies that price in this fashion are said to follow a competition-oriented pricing policy. The two major forms of competition-oriented pricing are: going-rate pricing and sealed-bid pricing.

Going-rate pricing

This approach to pricing means charging the going rate for the job or the product, or the price normally charged in the market. Going-rate pricing is popular with companies that find it difficult to measure costs, and which also find it difficult to estimate likely demand. These firms believe that, since going-rate pricing represents the collective wisdom of the industry concerning the price to charge, it should yield a fair return on investment. An additional benefit often cited is that going-rate pricing is the least disruptive of industrial harmony. On the demand side, going-rate pricing is attractive to firms wishing to follow established market leaders, presuming that well-organized firms know the price that the market will bear.

Going-rate pricing primarily characterizes pricing policies followed in markets where the product is homogeneous. While the company selling a homogeneous product in a highly competitive market has very little choice about the setting of price, however, to do so blindly over time without reference to the company's own costs and the demand for its product is short-sighted and can easily lead to poor pricing policies and even the demise of the company. The collective wisdom of the industry or the reasons behind the market leader's behaviour may not be appropriate for all companies that rely on going-rate pricing.

Sealed-bid pricing

This approach to pricing, also known as competitive bidding, dominates in those situations where companies compete for contracts to supply original equipment of a capital nature. It is also used extensively for all kinds of products in government or public body purchasing whereby companies compete on the basis of tenders.

The tender is the company's offer price and is a good example of pricing based on expectations of how competitors will price rather than on a rigid relation to the company's own costs or estimate of demand. The objective of the firm is to get the contract and this usually means attempting to set the price at a level below that of the other bidders. When companies do not have the resources to determine the pricing behaviour of competitors, they tend to rely on their cost information in setting the price. Sometimes companies tender below cost to keep plant and equipment occupied.

Going-rate pricing and tendering are inappropriate to the extent that there is no pricing discretion. If products or services are differentiated, the company misses an opportunity for greater profits by not using a more demand-oriented approach in pricing.

Competitive price reaction

Competitive activity in the market imposes a constraint on what the company can charge for its products and services. The provider of undifferentiated products which prices above the market price quickly loses sales. If the provider lowers prices, others may do so also, or risk losing sales. The extent to which the company is constrained by competitors in setting price reflects the degree of differentiation in the product or service. A highly differentiated product or service can command a price premium.

There are three sets of circumstances when a firm prices above the competition:

- to avoid selling below cost;

- to protect revenues from a large established customer base; and

- to boost cash flow and exit the market.

In regard to the first point, for some companies, selling at the market price means selling below cost, which they try to avoid. Firms in this category are under threat and face the possibility of early closure or eventual exit from the market. On the second point, large companies with an established customer base, facing an aggressive price competitor, may decide that it is less damaging in the short run to hold prices firm and give up a small proportion of the market, but avoid losing substantial unit profits from its large customer base. The danger is, of course, that the small competitor becomes a dominant force in the market. The third set of circumstances arises when a firm deliberately prices above market price even though its products and services are not highly differentiated. The firm may intend eventually to get out of the business and in the meantime follows a strategy of harvesting: that is, it yields market share, reduces selling and advertising support, but significantly increases cash flow and profits.

Where there are frequent price changes, a price leader may emerge which dominates the influence on market prices. Price leaders give direction to price patterns in the market by initiating and defending price increases or decreases. They may demonstrate leadership by not following the price moves of other firms in the market. Price leaders become the price reference point in the industry, but the price leader can exert influence only to a limited extent. The underlying structure of the market and the supply/demand balance provide the substantial influence on price.

Market-oriented pricing

Market- or demand-oriented pricing, as the name suggests, is an approach to pricing which examines the intensity of demand expressed by consumers or users of a given product. The objective is to set price at a level which reflects the intensity of demand: a high price might be charged where there is a high

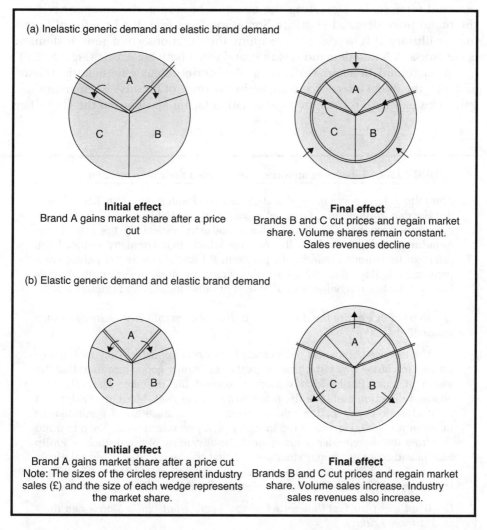

Figure 13.8 Possible market responses to a price cut at different demand elasticities

degree of interest in the product, and a low price charged when demand is weak, even though unit costs may be the same in both instances. Frequently, these approaches are referred to under the heading 'pricing according to what the market will bear'.

Brand demand elasticity

Markets respond in different ways to price changes. Companies in general attempt to reduce the price elasticity of demand for their products or services. One very effective way of doing so is to build equity into the company's products and services. By increasing the effect of branding, the company reduces the brand price demand elasticity. Sometimes, however, the benefits of branding are illusory. It is necessary to examine the situations when generic demand is inelastic and brand demand is elastic, and when both are elastic (Figure 13.8).

When brand demand is elastic and generic demand is inelastic (Figure 13.8(a)), the initial effect of a decrease in the price of brand A is a market share gain. This may have represented the situation facing Marlboro in the USA when

---

EXHIBIT 13.4   Tobacco companies have created their own monster

The following is a synopsis of a *Business Week* interview with Karl M. van der Heyden, former chief financial officer at R.J.R. Nabisco, in which he discusses the recent trends in the tobacco industry, especially the events surrounding 'Marlboro Friday', the day on which that company reduced the prices of its famous brand by 40 per cent. R.J.R. Nabisco is the parent company of R.J. Reynolds Tobacco Co., owners of premium cigarette brands Camel, Winston and Salem and of budget brands Monarch and Doral.

Q   *To what extent are the dire straits of the tobacco industry really of its own making?*

A   The tobacco companies have created their own monster. They took prices up way too fast – way faster than any other consumer-goods [product] that I'm aware of. And Philip Morris made a second big mistake: They abruptly changed direction and took the price down 40 per cent. Marlboro Friday was a cataclysmic event for the tobacco companies because all of a sudden, so much profit was taken out of the industry on a permanent basis. Keep in mind that from the shareholder point of view, the advantage of these stocks – Philip Morris and other consumer stocks – was that they were considered relatively steady. And Philip Morris taking this abrupt action shattered that whole image, not just for itself but for the other food and tobacco companies as well.

Q   *What was your first thought when you heard what Philip Morris had done on Marlboro Friday?*

---

it reduced its prices by 40 per cent, recognizing that the brand effect had diminished (Exhibit 13.4). The final effect of such a price change might show brand B and brand C reducing prices to meet the reduction in brand A's price. In such circumstances, market shares in sales volume terms remain constant, but sales revenues decline due to the lost revenue arising from the price reduction.

When both brand demand and generic demand are elastic (Figure 13.8(b)), the initial effect of a price reduction is that brand A gains market share. The final effect after the prices of brand B and brand C have been reduced is that shares are regained, but volume sales increase and industry revenues also increase. Some computer software packages are produced which appear to fit this configuration (Exhibit 13.5).

In a study of 105 brands, Broadbent (1980: 536) discovered quite a variation in price elasticity of demand. The average price elasticity of demand for all 105 brands was −1.32. It was more than −2.0 for 21 brands, between −1.50 and −1.99 for 16 brands and between −1.0 and −1.49 for 26 brands. Only 42 brands had an elasticity less than −1.0. The elasticity for 20 brands was in the range −0.50 to −0.99 and for 22 brands it was in the range 0.00 to −0.49.

A Complete shock. And basically, a feeling ... why? Why are they doing this? I still don't understand it to this day.

Q *After working so many years to stabilize RJR Nabisco's finances, what was it like to have so many gains washed away in the past few months?*

A The LBO experience, the R.J.R. Nabisco experience, was exhilarating, particularly in the early stages. This has recently been overshadowed. Tobacco is a beleaguered industry. The pressure's just on. The diversification efforts of tobacco companies in the 1980s into food, which both R.J. Reynolds and Philip Morris pursued, was a flawed strategy. There are few synergies between tobaco and food, even in the distribution and retail areas. So the only reason that these companies did this is [because they feared] the tobacco business one of these days was going away.

Q *What strategies will branded-goods companies have to use to combat the increased threats by private labels and other lower-cost products?*

A They will have to get the price-value in line, nobody will be able to sell their stuff if the gap is too large. And there will be an increased fragmentation of products offered. The national branded companies will have to be more attuned to the ethnic preferences of consumers in different parts of the country. The branded companies aren't going to allow private labels to take over; they're going to do everything to keep [their dominance] in place.

Source: *Business Week*, 30 August 1993: 45.

EXHIBIT 13.5   The shooting war in software

When Borland International Inc. announced a new version of its spreadsheet programme, Quattro Pro, for the cut-rate price of $50 in August, competitors were not impressed. At a conference a few weeks later an audience of industry executives was asked whether they thought the move was brilliant or desperate. The tally: 82 per cent said desperate.

If so, much of the software industry seems to be approaching desperation. The price war that has infected the PC hardware business for the past few years is now solidly entrenched in software as well. Programs which used to sell for $300 are now available for $100. There are lots of reasons for the price plunge. One is the declining price of PC hardware – off 32 per cent last year, according to International Data Corp. It's hard to sell a $500 word-processing programme for a $1,000 computer. Then there are suites: groups of programmes sold in bundles that list for 50 per cent off the retail price of the individual package – and retail for 45 per cent to 70 per cent off that. Finally, there are the price wars in various categories, often sparked by a competitor thirsting for market share or entering a new area. Microsoft Corp. dove into data bases by offering its $495 Access package for $99 during a three-month promotion – and sold an astounding 750,000 copies. Now, Computer Associates International Inc. has gone Microsoft one better: it's literally giving away more than a million packages to break into new markets.

It all adds up to a dismal spiral. Promotional prices tend to become permanent – or close to it. That's because they're followed by so-called competitive upgrades, discounts offered to owners of competing products. Of course, there is a bright side to discounting pricing. 'There's a fundamental elasticity of demand,' says Richard Rabins, chief executive of alphas Software Corp., a

---

Value pricing

In recent years, there has been criticism of the high prices of some branded products. In recessionary times, consumers resist price increases and price premiums. Many consumers reduce their purchases or trade down to lower-priced products, thereby avoiding branded products. A number of large branded product companies have responded to these trends by reducing the prices of their well-known brands, but they have also reduced the number and size of sales promotions. This combination of lower list prices and the elimination of or severe reduction in promotions is referred to as value pricing. By lowering prices and eliminating promotions and discounts, companies attempt to even out the swings in demand that such promotions cause. The diminution or reduction of sales promotions tends to aggravate retailers, but on balance it is welcomed by consumers and manufacturers with well-known brands who are strong enough to implement value pricing.

maker of $50 and $60 databases and graphics programs. 'You should be able to sell more software to more people if the price is lower.' And once they pare costs, if the volume materialises, software makers say profits will rebound. Software makes Aldus Corp, and Synmantec Inc., for example, both reported good results in the September quarter.

Indeed, Borland Chief Executive Philippe Kahn gloats that he sold 500,000 copies of Quattro Pro 5.0 in just 45 days, a goal he hadn't expected to reach for five months. 'We've never seen anything like this,' says Kahn. The higher volumes, he adds, reduce his cost of materials from about $13 per package to about $9.

And, he insists, the low price will lure buyers from the suites. After he explained this strategy at the Agenda conference, at least a few members of the audience were converted: A second poll cut the 'desperate' votes to 48 per cent. Not exactly a ringing endorsement, but perhaps a first small sign of hope.

TABLE 1   The incredible shrinking price tag for Quattro Pro

Release date	September 1990	March 1992	September 1993
Version	Quattro Pro 2.0	Quattro Pro 4.0	Quattro Pro 5.0
List price	$495.00	$495.00	$99.95
Store price	$99.95(a)	$99.95(b)	$49.95(c)

(a) for those who owned competing products
(b) became list price in January 1993
(c) applied to January 1994

Source: Adapted from *Business Week*, 8 November 1993: 86–8.

Identifying customer value

It is difficult, however, to price according to the value to the customer, since it is difficult to determine that value. The perceived value of the product may be different for different market segments. Different market segments may place different values on the different attributes that constitute the product or service. The level of competition in the market helps to determine the level of perceived value. The ability of the buyer to substitute one competitive offering for another helps to determine the effective upper band to perceived value.

In many situations, prices reflect values and quality in items purchased. Prices also reflect the newness of technology and the degree of finish and styling in industrial equipment and consumer durables. Price–quality relationships are an important feature of many markets. In the market for consumer electronics, quality and price are important discriminating variables (Figure 13.9). In this case, suppliers of electronics were evaluated by store buyers to determine similarities and preferences. Using multidimensional scaling, the two most important underlying evaluative criteria were price and quality. These two variables serve to discriminate simultaneously among suppliers and buyers, and a number of groups or segments are identified. ABC Durables was perceived to be a high-quality supplier with price on the high side. Two department stores, A and B, also positioned themselves in this segment. The two discount stores were clearly seen as having a low price but a medium level of quality. The three general merchandisers were seen at a slightly higher price-quality level. The brand leader and two other major competitors were judged to supply high-priced products at a relatively low level of quality. This would give considerable concern to each of these suppliers, particularly the brand leader, which may have been living on past investment in a brand now in need of renewal.

In buying a small car as an entry vehicle or as a second car for the family, buyers recognize that the relatively low prices reflect old technology and low performance levels. Some of the new small car imports available in Europe have been described as 'a great deal of metal for the money but heavy to drive and poorly made' or 'based on designs that Fiat abandoned decades ago'.

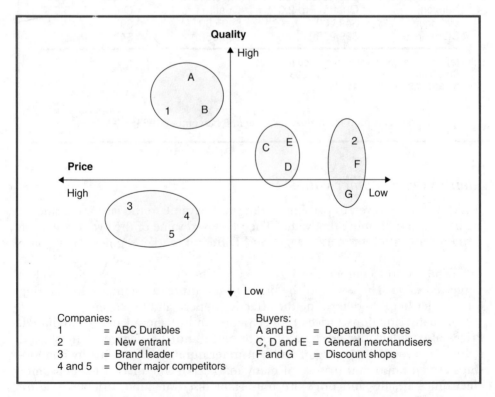

Figure 13.9 Perceptual map of suppliers and store buyers in the consumer electronics market

Some cars which may be based on older technology are nevertheless seen as providing good value for money in the price bracket in question, which is one of the reasons why the VW Polo ran into some pricing difficulties in 1991–2 in the UK (Exhibit 13.6).

Perceived value pricing

Under this approach to pricing, the company bases its pricing decision on the product's perceived value. Here the buyer's perception of value and not the seller's level of cost is taken as the key to pricing. Perceived value pricing is in line with the modern marketing concept of product positioning. The firm develops a product for a particular target market with a particular market positining in mind with respect to price, quality and service. The company thus makes an initial decision on the value of the product to the consumer and the acceptable price level. The next step for the firm is to estimate the volume it can sell at this price and cost. If the result is positive, the product is selected for development; if negative, the idea is dropped.

R & A Bailey and Company Limited followed such a pricing strategy for Bailey's Original Irish Cream Liqueur. The company decided to position the new brand in the exclusive end of the liqueur market and accordingly charged a relatively high price. Imitators, economy products and other substitutes have come and gone, but the successful high-price/quality image has stood this now universally known brand in good stead. The key to perceived value pricing is

---

EXHIBIT 13.6   Buying a second car, a time to watch the price not the clock

Selecting a new company car is one of life's more pleasant tasks. A generous budget means you can pick and choose to your heart's content. But choosing a second car, from taxed income, is altogether different: the all-important factor is the price. If you need proof, just ask Volkswagen's marketing men. The company's entry level Polo Fox enjoyed all the benefits of being a member of the VW family, with reliability, quality, design integrity, style and panache all taken for granted. Dealers should have been turning buyers away.

The fact that they weren't is partly due to the recession, but mainly down to the price tag, a hefty £6,661 – considerably more than the rivals. After discounting, of course, the prices moved far closer together, but the private buyer tended to forget that and did not consider the Polo in the first place. So, instead of having a car that cost a mint, VW cut dealer margins, lowering the price to just under £6,000. As the advertisement proclaimed: 'For once, a Volkswagen falls below your expectations.'

Indeed, at under £7,000, a 'new' car's average age is around 10 years old. And that's the problem when buying a new car on a limited budget: from a technological point of view, it's a case of 'all our yesterdays'.

Source: *Financial Times*, 25 July 1992: 4.

---

to make an accurate determination of the market's perception of the value of the total offer, i.e. the product and accompanying services.

Companies with an inflated view of the value of their offer may be over-pricing. In some cases, companies underestimate the perceived value and charge less than would be acceptable. Good use of perceived value pricing requires a detailed understanding of likely consumer responses to price changes. This applies to products, services, ideas and sports stars (Exhibit 13.7).

EXHIBIT 13.7   Lure of the lira

As Europe's finest soccer players took to the field in Sweden for the European Nations' Championship, the stands filled with cashmere-coated scouts from Italy, flexing their chequebooks. Many of the stars on display in Sweden already play for Italian clubs. Ruud Gullit, 'Marco Golo' van Basten and Frank Rijkaard of Holland turn out for AC Milan. The home-town hero, Thomas Brolin of Sweden plays his club football for Parma. England's lone goal-scorer, David Platt, will move from Bari in southern Italy to Juventus of Turin next season. No fewer than seven of Germany's first-choice team play their club football in Italy. Rumours are already swirling about the new stars who emerged in Italy – men like Dennis Bergkamp of Holland and Brian Laudrup of Denmark. Will they be the next to get an irresistible offer to play in Italy?

With their fine stadiums, large crowds and plutocratic patrons, like Gianni Agnelli of Juventus and Silvio Berlusconi of AC Milan, the rich Italian clubs can outspend all but a handful of foreign rivals. The best-paid player in Italy is thought to be Marco van Basten, the man who missed a vital shot in Stockholm. His salary is put at $2.5m a year. By contrast, the best-paid player in Britain, John Barnes of Liverpool, earns about $900,000 a year and the top Germans about $1m. Claudio Caniggia of Argentina, Careca of Brazil and other South American stars have also flocked to Italy. As a result Italy's top soccer division, Serie A, is getting ever closer to becoming a world league.

A comparison between the staffs of England's Tottenham Hotspur and Italy's Inter Milan is instructive. Three foreigners to play for Inter last season – Lothar Mattheus, Andreas Brehme and Jürgen Klinsmann – were all members of the West German team which won the World Cup in 1990. Tottenham, by contrast, has just sold its best English player, Paul Gascoigne, to Italy's Lazio for nearly $10 million. Its foreign staff includes a Norwegian goal-keeper, an Icelandic defender and a Moroccan midfielder.

But in football, as in any other team sport, buying expensive foreigners does not guarantee success. Imported players can outshine, and so eventually demoralise, home-grown players. Italian clubs failed to win any of the three big European club competitions this year. Italy's national side may also be suffering. When the best teams in Europe arrived in Stockholm, flights from Rome were chock-a-block with expensive footballers – but not with Italians. Italy failed to qualify for the European Nations' Championship.

Source: *The Economist*, 27 June 1992: 102.

Demand-differentiated pricing

Differentiation indicates the extent to which buyers perceive differences between the products and services offered for sale and the extent to which their buying decisions are influenced by such differences. It is generally believed that the greater the degree of differentiation, the wider will be the spread of acceptable prices. The differentiated product or service may be sold at two or more prices, but usually these prices do not reflect a proportional difference in the marginal costs of producing the differentiation.

Successful differentiation depends on the company's ability to associate with its products or services benefits which are measurable in terms of tangible values or which, if non-quantifiable, are nevertheless real. Non-quantifiable benefits would include a reduction in consumer perceived risk, the desire for prestige and the desire to be seen as a leader by one's peer group. Because of the diffuse nature of the benefits which arise from differentiation, it is easy to appreciate that there are many forms which may be applied to products and services and, hence, to prices.

Products and services may be differentiated on the basis of technical performance, packaging, styling, taste, advertising and other benefits, such as the use of time and geographic location. Demand-oriented approaches to pricing are appropriate when the company wants to give a customer emphasis or a demand emphasis. They are inappropriate if used unethically or if their use changes the company's reputation. They are also inappropriate where they ignore costs and profit considerations. Pricing at the level that the market would bear is rarely a good practice, since it is usually perceived as exploitation and may, therefore, be considered as disreputable. The company must also consider the longer-term consequences of its actions.

Strategic aspects of pricing

Price must be used within overall marketing strategy to support the other marketing mix variables (Tellis, 1986). Marketing strategies tend to dictate the pricing strategy to use in a particular set of circumstances. To be useful, pricing strategies must be specific and practical, and assist the company in pricing for different marketing circumstances (Figure 13.10).

Marketing strategies which might be examined by a marketing manager include market penetration, market development, market segmentation, new product development or the modification of existing products to suit new markets, such as an export market. Associated with each marketing strategy is a set of pricing strategies. Pricing strategies often found in practice include penetration pricing, price skimming, early cash recovery pricing, and product-line and promotional pricing.

591

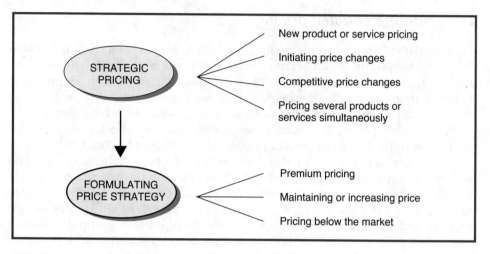

Figure 13.10 Strategic aspects of pricing

It is necessary first to determine when pricing is a strategic problem. Strategic pricing is a problem in four general situations, when:

- a company sets price for the first time;

- circumstances force the company to consider a price change;

- the competition initiates a price change; or

- the firm produces several products that are interrelated on the demand side or on the cost side.

Two generalizations regarding pricing strategy may be made. First, the strategy should be tailored to the particular circumstances of the firm and of its markets. Second, the strategy should be regarded as a means of implementing the marketing plan, which in turn should serve the ends of the company's overall objectives.

Formulating price strategy

There are five steps in formulating a pricing strategy. In the first step, a situation analysis is performed, which is a summary of the current business situation along key market and competitive dimensions. In the second step, the firm attempts to identify an appropriate set of strategic options which depends on marketing objectives. Three approaches to pricing strategy may be identified:

- pricing at or below the market, depending on the company's competitive strength, which results in low profit and cash flow immediately, but higher profit later;

- maintaining or increasing price, which means profits and cash flow now; or

- premium pricing, which means maximum profit and cash flow in the short term.

The option dictated by the market may be in conflict with legitimate management goals: for example, the market may dictate growth in share at the expense of current profitability, while management may want maximum profit now to invest in other projects. In attempting to accomplish selected goals, such as introducing new products, improving service and designing special promotions, the company must define a strategy for price, which is the third step.

During the fourth step, it is necessary to specify profit goals for the firm, which means deciding the appropriate gross margin percentage. This depends on the firm's profitability, its market share strategy and its management expectations.

Lastly, an effective assessment of competitive reaction to the company's marketing strategy requires some basic information and evaluation of the financial and technical strengths and weaknesses of the company's major competitors, together with their non-product strengths and weaknesses, marketing strategy and historical reactions to competitive moves, with a view to determining how they are likely to respond to a price initiative by the company.

Pricing for market segments

For most companies the market is a series of market segments, each requiring a distinct marketing mix, which means separate prices. Pricing for different market segments means considering the possibility of price skimming, using penetration pricing or combining these two to recover cash early. It is also necessary to determine the appropriate price level for the company, given customer and competitive circumstances (Figure 13.11).

Penetration pricing, price skimming and early cash recovery pricing

Companies sometimes face the choice in the introductory stage of the product life cycle of skimming the market by pricing high to maximize short-run unit contribution, or penetrating the market by pricing low to maximize unit volume and thereby pre-empt competition. Sometimes the decision is to combine both approaches over time in a sequenced way as the life cycle evolves.

Each of these price strategies is used by firms when introducing new products or services. The choice of strategy depends on the objectives of the firm and the circumstances in the market. Penetration pricing and price skimming

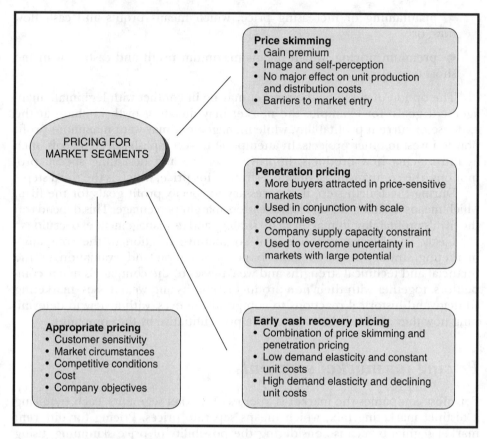

Figure 13.11 Pricing for market segments

are distinct strategies, whereas early cash recovery pricing may refer to a high or a low price depending on market circumstances.

Price skimming

There are many marketing circumstances where it is possible for a firm to take advantage of the tendency of some buyers to pay more for a product than others because the product, for one reason or another, has a high present value to them. A price skimming strategy is designed to gain a premium from these buyers. After a period, for some product categories, the premium segment becomes saturated so the company gradually reduces price to draw in the more price-sensitive segments of the market. However, there are always a few people in small groups who are willing to pay high prices for what they want. Apart from strong need of the product, they may also have substantial resources so that price is of little concern within the context of the money they spend. Image and self-perception are important determinants of the size of the price-skimming segment.

A price-skimming strategy makes good marketing sense when one of the following three sets of conditions exists:

- the segment of the market prepared to pay the premium price is such that the revenues forgone from charging a low initial price would be significant;

- the company's unit production and distribution cost function is relatively flat over the entire range of output, i.e. there are no benefits from experience so that costs fall with increases in output; or

- the premium to be charged is not so large that it will entice competitors into the market.

The implication of the second condition is that the unit costs of producing and distributing a smaller amount must not be so high that they cancel the advantage of charging the premium price. The last point refers to the issue of exclusivity, which appeals to the top end of the market.

On the cost side, a price-skimming strategy works well where there are significant entry barriers such as patents, high development costs, raw material controls, or high and sustained promotional costs. For example, Sony introduced its transistorized portable TV at a high price. Initially, Sony did not have to worry about competition due to the long lead time needed in developing a portable TV. As a result, it could afford to go for the high-price market segment first. Eventually, it moved to a lower price and started mass producing the TVs. It is important to note that, for a price-skimming strategy to work, the quality produced must be relevant to the requirements of the premium segment. A distinct advantage of this stragety is that it leaves room for a price reduction, subject to costs, if a market miscalculation has been made. It is always easier to reduce price than to raise it once a product has been established on the market.

A skimming strategy by an innovator may encourage others to enter the market at lower prices. This often occurs in fast-moving consumer products and in fashion, where innovative products are relatively easy to imitate. In such circumstances, the imitators often capture the mass market, leaving the exclusive segments to innovators.

Penetration pricing

One way of achieving a large share of the market for a new product is to set a relatively low price initially to stimulate demand. There are a number of conditions any one of which might favour such a pricing strategy. If the market appears to be highly price sensitive, setting a low price may bring additional buyers into the market. Existing market prices are undercut by so much as to make it impossible for competitors to follow. If the firm succeeds, it will experience a large increase in sales volume. Penetration pricing can unlock markets that may not even have been anticipated. For example, initially only the commercial and industrial markets for microcomputers were developed, but now that prices are falling rapidly, the much larger personal market is making its impact felt.

When a product is being produced under conditions which give rise to scale economies, a low initial price permits the firm to move to a lower position on its cost curve. The more experience the firm has in producing the product, the lower its costs.

A danger with a market penetration strategy is that it may encourage demand far in excess of the firm's capacity to supply. A strategy of penetration pricing is based on the assumption that the company will attract a very large number of new customers and that a large new market will develop. The key to this strategy is that the competition must be unable to compete with the company on price. This means that penetration prices must be significantly below existing market prices, otherwise the competition will match or better the lower price. Should this happen, the penetration price strategy would be in danger of turning into a price war based on promotional prices. To follow a price penetration strategy, therefore, the company's technology and cost structure must be such as to allow it to separate itself significantly from competitors on price.

Penetration pricing is appropriate for defect-free products for which there is a very large potential market. It is unlikely to benefit products which require explanation in the early stages of the life cycle. In such circumstances, low prices are unlikely to overcome market uncertainty. Furthermore, the company needs to have sufficient production capacity and have ready access to distribution channels to respond quickly to market demand. Successful penetration pricing depends on an element of surprise to constrain competitors' ability to respond.

Pricing for early cash recovery

Sometimes companies do not believe that the market for their product will exist for a long period, or they experience a shortage of cash, or survival is their overriding objective. In such circumstances, the future is too uncertain to justify patient market cultivation and the company tends to set a price which will bring in cash at an earlier stage rather than in the longer term.

Early cash recovery pricing is a combination of price skimming and penetration pricing, played out at different time periods (Figure 13.12). Whereas price skimming refers primarily to markets which are small, exclusive and not highly price sensitive, it is conceivable that for some products the company might wish to charge a high price now, and when capacity is fully operational to lower the price to attract the much larger mass market. It may be possible to use the two pricing strategies in tandem over a period of time. The circumstances under which this strategy works are limited. Market conditions again dictate whether the price should be high, price skimming, or low, penetration pricing. Two sets of conditions are identified:

- the presence of a low demand elasticity and constant unit production and distribution costs means that the firm can maximize immediate cash flow through a high-price strategy;

- the presence of a high demand elasticity and declining unit costs means that the company can maximize immediate cash flow through a low-price strategy.

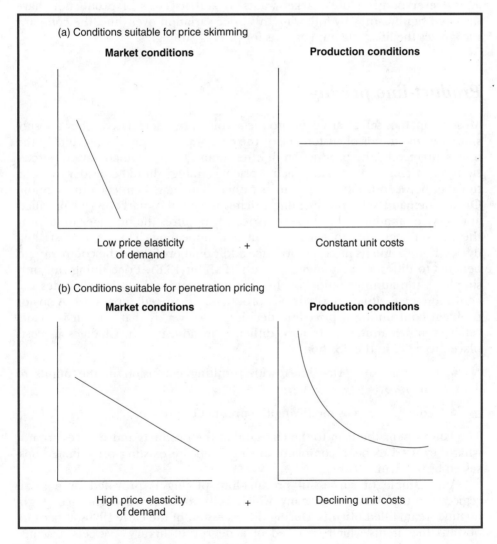

Figure 13.12 Early cash recovery pricing

Provide the value for customers

The choice of strategy depends on the company's objectives and its view of market conditions.

From the discussion above it should be clear that market conditions should dictate the appropriate price to charge. Low demand elasticity and constant unit costs favour a high price, whereas a high demand elasticity and declining unit costs favour a low price (Figure 13.12). The first set of conditions outlined above is typically found when a new product is first introduced to the market and for a short period thereafter, while the second set of conditions is found later when the product becomes well known, everybody or almost everybody in the market wants it, and its costs of production have declined significantly. By following this price variation over time, the company recognizes the life cycle implications for pricing strategies.

Product-line pricing

Most companies sell a variety of products which are interrelated. They are substitutes in the minds of customers, or the cost of producing one product in the line is affected by the production of other items, both of which have repercussions for pricing strategy. An effective pricing strategy should consider the relationship between the firm's products rather than view them each in isolation. On the demand side, product-line pricing means the marketing of products and services at a limited number of prices. It requires the manager to identify the market segments to which the firm is appealing. The firm must then decide how to line its prices to produce additional profits for the company and benefits to different customer segments (Exhibit 13.8). Price lining not only simplifies the administration of the pricing structure, but also alleviates the confusion of a situation where all products are priced separately. A major problem confronting a price-line decision, however, is that once it is made, retailers and manufacturers have difficulty in adjusting it. Changes in costs place the seller in the position of:

- changing the price lines, with resulting confusion in the minds of customers; or
- reducing costs by modifying the product or service.

The latter opens the firm to the charge that the products and services are not what they used to be, a complaint arising from the existing price image possessed by the firm.

An example of successful product-line pricing is provided by a small regional confectionery company which sells a range of high-price, high-quality, cream-filled biscuits. During the recession of the early 1990s, it became obvious that items which smacked of a degree of luxury – sweets, biscuits, cakes – were bound to lose some customers, and that others would be more

---

EXHIBIT 13.8   Product-line pricing, sending multiple signals

Price lining, the practice of offering two, three or four brands or qualities of the same product at different prices, is a well accepted device used to establish a value concept in the consumer mind. For example, witness what the retailer has done with ground meat. Another variation of this principle is premium pricing over competition. In fact one of the most positive ways of convincing the shopper that you have an inferior product is to constantly undersell your competitor.

Some years ago in a simple demonstration of this principle we ran a test in 12 supermarkets over a three week period in which we offered identical apples side by side with one lot priced two pounds for 19 cents and the other two pounds for 23 cents. I shall never forget my experience in putting up the first display one early Monday morning. A graduate student and I were stacking two pound bags of apples on the counter working out of the same shipping container on the floor. I was filling the 23 cents display and he was filling the 19 cents side. A shopper came in, looked at both displays and at the common shipping container from which we were working. She then asked, 'Well, what's the difference?' Without a pause the graduate student simply replied, 'These are two for 19 cents and these are two for 23 cents.' The shopper picked up two bags of the 23c apples and put them in her cart. Over a three week period in 12 supermarkets over 40 per cent of the apples sold were from the 23 cent side of the display.

Source: 'Principles of product pricing', speech by Max E. Brunk, Professor of Marketing, Cornell University, Ithaca, NY, to the *58th Annual Meeting of the American Meat Institute*, Palmer House, Chicago, 23 September 1963.

---

discerning about price and quality. Customers began to seek value for money more deliberately than before, thus creating a new value segment. To serve this segment, the firm broadened its product line by introducing a new brand of cream-filled biscuits which they priced above the cheapest available, but well below the more expensive products in the market, including their own established brands. The brand name already established helped to overcome doubts on quality that customers requiring a cheaper biscuit might have. The biscuits were very successful, capturing most of the new segment. At the same time, the new product did not adversely affect the demand for the existing brands, as they appealed to a different market segment.

Demand interrelationships

Two products are interrelated on the demand side when the price of one affects the demand for the other. The expression 'cross elasticity of demand' is often used to express this relationship. A positive cross elasticity of demand means that two products are substitutes. In most instances, the product items in a manufacturer's line of products are substitutes for each other, but not perfect substitutes. For example, a prospective car buyer can obtain higher quality, better styling or extra features by paying more money, and the seller is able to attract a wider range of buyer types and perhaps induce buyers to trade up to the more expensive versions when the manufacturer offers a multiple line of products.

The manufacturer's problem is how to price these versions to obtain the greatest overall revenue. If a vehicle manufacturer lowered the price of the luxury cars in the line, this would decrease the demand for the lower-priced cars, increase the demand for items such as expensive seat covering and stereo sound equipment, and probably not affect the demand for the manufacturer's range of farm tractors and trucks. Before changing the price of any single item in the line, the manufacturer should consider the various cross elasticities of demand to determine the overall impact on profitability.

Cost interrelationships

Two products are interrelated on the cost side when a change in the level of production of one affects the cost of the other. By-products and joint products are related in this sense. A reduction in the level of output of one product thus related results in higher unit costs of the second because the overhead is spread over fewer units. For this reason, the marketing manager must consider the cost interactions before changing the price of a single product in the line.

Finally, various products in a company line are exposed to different degrees of competition. Sellers may have little latitude in pricing products in their line where existing or potential competition is keen. Price discretion varies in other cases. The structure of prices for products and services in the line should reflect not only costs, but also the profit opportunities in the market.

Responding to price changes

Before responding to a price change initiated by a competitor, it may be advisable to examine the company's costs, competitor costs and the degree of price resistance in the market. It is necessary to determine:

- why the competitor has changed price;
- the permanence of the price change;
- the effect on market share; and
- competitor reaction to company price change.

The competitor may be trying to capture a greater share of the market by attempting to respond to changes in costs, or perhaps attempting to provoke an industry-wide price change in response to a change in industry demand. The firm's response depends on whether the price change is permanent, a temporary affair to move surplus stocks, or an endeavour to promote a product line. If the price change is ignored, market share may be affected in some way. There is also a possibility that other firms in the industry will respond. The last point is a matter of determining how the competition will react to each of the alternative options available to the company.

The price trap

The decision to lower price is a difficult one for the company, since it can easily fall into a classic price trap. The price trap arises when a market becomes price sensitive and competitors begin to discount. If the company decides to maintain price levels, a series of events may occur which could leave it worse off

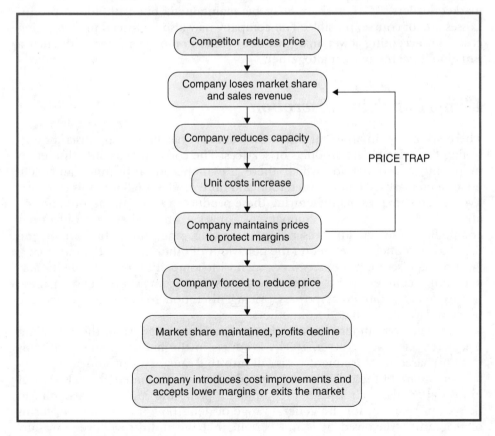

Figure 13.13   The price trap

than before (Figure 13.13). Assuming product substitutability in the market, the company's sales will begin to fall and market share will be lost. In evaluating its position, the company may be well advised to recognize the danger of too much confidence in the value of product differentiation to protect it from price competition. Product differentiation which existed may have vanished with time and improvements in competing products.

In such circumstances, the company may be forced to reduce prices to protect its market share. In some instances, companies raise prices in an attempt to recover lost overheads. Normally, however, revenue is lost. As the situation becomes more serious, the company begins to reduce excess capacity and plants may be closed. Faced with rising unit costs, declining sales volumes and low profitability, the company may finally decide to regain lost ground by following a discounting strategy, which, because it is forced upon it, is often indiscriminate. When the company decides to discount to maintain or rebuild market share, it must be confident that it possesses a cost advantage over competitors and that the products in question have quality parity with those of market leaders. Market share may be maintained, but with lower profits. Losses are, of course, possible. The company may also be forced into reducing costs and accepting lower margins. Sometimes companies faced with such a situation leave the market altogether.

Limits of pricing discretion

There are many situations in which the company has little or no discretion in setting the price for its products or services. The company has little discretion in pricing a product for which there are numerous substitutes and well-established markets. Unprocessed food and fibre products fall into this category. Typically, companies manufacturing these products are also numerous and relatively small. In contrast, a company in a market where there are only a few competitors also has little discretion in pricing, since the behaviour of one firm has an immediate effect on the behaviour of other firms in the industry.

Pricing discretion remains very much with companies that operate in markets with a competitive structure that places them somewhere between these two extremes. Companies possess pricing discretion for products which are perceived as differentiated from others.

For many consumer products, buyers are not very aware of the prevailing prices (Dickson and Sawyer, 1990). Products in the luxury classes and items not purchased on a frequent basis fall into this category. Consumers are usually very aware of the prices of staples and regularly purchased items. Buyers of industrial goods, such as capital equipment, plant and raw materials, tend to be very price aware for the general range of items bought. However, in terms of magnitudes involved, it is not certain that the industrial buyers are any more aware of prevailing prices than are final consumers.

If price awareness is low, the company will be less inhibited in raising prices. It would be dangerous to assume, however, that prices can be changed with impunity in such situations. When price awareness is low, companies intent on lowering prices sometimes attempt to increase the level of price awareness in the market so that they can oust rivals. Information on price awareness may be a useful guide to marketing activity, by indicating those products for which a policy involving a strong emphasis on price would be most, or least, appropriate. Price awareness for services as distinct from products tends to be very uneven, since it is difficult to quantify something intangible such as a service, the dimensions of which change frequently. Companies frequently display low price awareness for many services such as transportation, which has marketing implications worth noting.

In situations and markets where the level of price awareness is high, the firm must take great care to ensure that its prices are not out of line with competitive products. Should the firm wish to charge a different set of prices, it would be well advised to ensure that its products are well differentiated in the eyes of its customers.

The value of a product or service to the best prospective customer fixes the ceiling for pricing, while cost sets the floor. Between the cost floor and the appropriate value ceiling is a gap. This gap varies depending upon the type of product and customer involved. Setting the price within this gap depends upon the company's analysis of such factors as the nature and type of competition, the overall marketing programme used and various public policy considerations.

Tactical aspects of pricing

So far pricing strategy has been discussed: whether to use a high price or a low price and the subsequent repercussions. It is now necessary to establish specific prices within the context of the chosen pricing strategy. Two categories of pricing tactics are available, psychological pricing and discount pricing, both of which are related indirectly to the overall pricing strategy (Figure 13.14).

Psychological pricing

The final price for a product or service must take the psychology of the buyer into account. It is possible to identify at least three ways of doing this. While they deal primarily with retail marketing, some psychological pricing tactics are also relevant to industrial markets.

The first psychological pricing tactic identified is price lining, introduced previously. Suppose a local retailer of men's clothes carries suits selling at three price levels, £220, £330 and £470. Customers will associate low, average

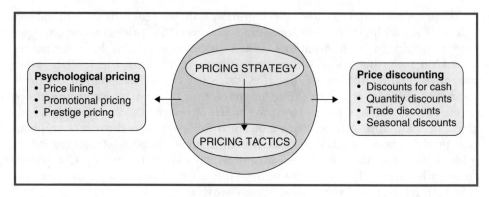

Figure 13.14   Tactical aspects of pricing

and high-quality suits with the thre points indicated by the three prices. Even if the three prices are changed moderately, men are likely to continue buying suits at their customary price point. Customers are not sensitive to small changes in price points for some products and services. The demand curve in such circumstances may be perceived as a series of steps at the various price points, indicating the need to price within a range (Figure 13.15).

Promotional pricing is a tactic designed to appeal to customers' tendency to respond to special, low or bargain prices. Grocery stores, supermarkets and department stores often price a few of their products below their normal mark-up or even below cost. These are called loss leaders and are used to

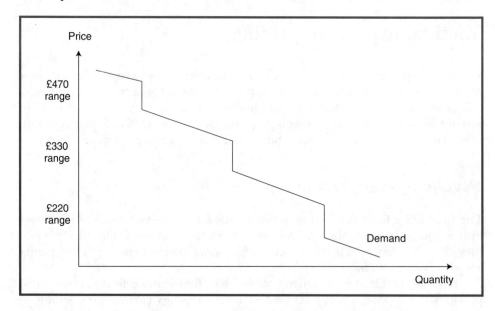

Figure 13.15   Price points in marketing and demand for men's jackets

attract customers into the store in the hope that they will buy other things at normal mark-up. A few examples will illustrate. Corner grocery stores frequently price cigarettes below cost. Department stores use the January sales to attract weary customers back to the stores after the hectic pre-Christmas shopping period. Supermarkets frequently use a staple like butter or bread as a loss leader to get people to shop there.

Prestige pricing is a psychological tactic which may also be used. Buyers of certain products often take price as a sign of product or service quality, as with exclusive cars, medical and hospital treatments and exclusive schooling. Note that it is not easy to evaluate the quality of these products and services before making a purchase. In these instances, the price has symbolic connotations that the seller must consider. However, if a company attempts prestige pricing and if the price set is too high, the buyer's credibility may be strained and distrust created.

Price discounting

In discussing pricing, phrases like 'nobody pays the list price' may frequently be heard. Two important features of that statement are, first, that there is a list price and, second, that sellers tend to discount from the list price. Discounts are allowances that are sometimes offered to dealers and customers as special incentives.

There are five major types of discount. Perhaps the best known are cash discounts, which are offered to buyers who pay their bills promptly. Such discounts have become customary in many industries and serve the purpose of improving the seller's liquidity and reducing credit collection costs and bad debts. The second type of discounting tactic is the quantity discount, which is an offer of a price reduction to buyers who buy larger volumes. A typical example would be '£10 per unit for less than 100 units; £9 per unit for 100 or more units'. The seller who gives quantity discounts reduces selling expenses, inventory and transportation costs.

Sometimes manufacturers seek the assistance of intermediaries in selling, storing, record keeping and market research. To ensure this support they use trade or functional discounts. A typical example would be when a manufacturer of refrigerators quotes a retail list price of £500 and discounts of 40 and 10 per cent. In this case the product would cost the retailer £300 (£500 less 40 per cent) and the wholesaler would pay £270 (£300 less 10 per cent).

A fourth type of discount in frequent use is the seasonal discount. This type of discount is an offer of a price reduction to buyers who buy merchandise or services out of season, or at a time other than during peak demand. Seasonal discounts allow the seller to maintain production levels during the year. Hotels and airlines offer seasonal and other related discounts in the off-peak periods. Telephone charges are lower at night and during weekends. Electricity charges may be lower at night. Such discounts attract the discretionary spender or user.

Lastly, a discount with which we are all familiar is the allowance off list price for a trade-in. Trade-in allowances are most common in the motor trade, but may also be found in some consumer durable goods categories such as electric cookers, bicycles and cameras. Trade-in allowances are also found in plant and capital equipment markets.

Pricing and marketing mix

Pricing strategy must reinforce the company's overall marketing strategy. For example, the desire for a quality image and a full service operation would preclude a discount pricing strategy. This quality image may require greater product research and development costs, higher-quality retail outlets, and more exclusive promotion. On the other hand, the buyer may be willing to travel further, pay cash and carry the product home if the price is discounted enough. Thus, whatever pricing strategy is selected, it must be related to all of the elements in the marketing mix.

Product–price interaction

The two best-known pricing strategies which were discussed above, price skimming and penetration pricing, are associated with the evolution of the product life cycle. Early in the life of a new product, there are few competitors and research and development costs are high, as are initial promotional costs. The initial adopters of the new product tend not to be sensitive to price, so price is relatively inelastic. It is for this reason that a skimming strategy may work early in the life cycle of the new product. The higher margins help to cover the extra costs of marketing at this stage. When initial demand has been met, it may be time to lower the price, thereby appealing to the segment of the market that is more price elastic, which means changing the strategy to penetration pricing. If the timing of the price reduction is accurate, it attracts new market segments and discourages competitors which have been attracted by the large margin.

The character of the product may establish a price range that is acceptable to the customer. Product positioning or repositioning can be achieved through the careful use of the price mechanism (Exhibit 13.9). These characteristics also determine the appropriate channel of distribution. Convenience products such as toilet soap, cigarettes and newspapers must be conveniently located and competitively priced. A speciality product such as a high-quality perfume or a sophisticated stereo unit may be sold through exclusive shops and priced high.

EXHIBIT 13.9   Altima's positioning secret

Critics called it underpowered and too small for a family sedan. The styling was too unconventional for conservative baby boomers. Besides, the sceptics wondered, did Nissan Motor Co. have the marketing savvy to successfully launch a midsize car, the biggest and most competitive segment of the automobile industry? Turns out the critics were wrong. Indeed, Nissan's Altima may well be the hottest car in the sluggish auto market. Its secret? The sticker price – an eye popping $13,000 for the base model. Even the better-equipped versions run $1,500 below the Honda Accord and a good $2,000 less than a comparably equipped Toyota Camry. 'Nissan's hit a home run,' says Christopher W. Cedergren, senior vice-president of Auto Pacific Group, a Santa Ana (California) market researcher, 'and the reason is price.'

Nissan ascribes the Altima's success to its decision to hold the line on size and price when competitors, with such models as the Toyota Camry and Mazda 626, were moving upmarket with bigger cars. 'We saw a big vacuum developing, and we knew that there were still a lot of people shopping for a $15,000 car instead of a $20,000 car,' says Earl J. Hesterberg, vice-president and general manager of the company's Nissan Division. The 39-year-old Hesterberg gets full credit for masterminding the launch of the Altima, Nissan insiders say. Hesterberg also won a hard-fought battle with the Japanese parent company to price the car well below its competitors. 'We were more aggressive on pricing than our finance people thought we should be,' he says, 'but we wanted to make sure we jolted the public.'

Hesterberg wants nothing less than to use the Altima to create a new image of reliability and quality for Nissan, which has watched its sales in the US slide by more than one-third since their 1985 peak. To that end, he has focused virtually all of Nissan's national advertising budget – an estimated $120 million – on the Altima and on the company's new Quest minivan.

The campaign positions the Altima as a car that is as finely crafted as luxury models but at a fraction of the price. The ads poke gentle fun at archrival Toyota Motor Co. by mimicking the techniques – such as balancing 10 wine glasses on the car hood – that Toyota uses to show off its Lexus luxury sedan, which costs three times as much. Says Larry Miller, general manager of Chrysler Corporation's Jeep Eagle Division: 'The ads are fantastic.' For Nissan, the early results look fantastic as well.

Source: *Business Week*, 18 January 1993: 29.

Channel-price interaction

The selection of a channel of distribution usually determines the channel discount structure. Some channels have 'traditional' discounts. It is important to note that trade discounts are usually given in exchange for some service related to the product.

Many aspects of marketing a product can be considered as a distribution management problem. For example, if prices or costs rise, for whatever reason, it is necessary to determine who benefits or bears the brunt of the changes. When distribution margins are calculated in percentage rather than in fixed amounts per unit, even small changes in costs have a magnified effect on final selling prices. This is referred to as the multiplier effect of cost change. The effect on the company's revenue of changes in the final price is partly absorbed in the margins at the various stages if their percentages remain unchanged. This is referred to as the absorber effect of cost changes.

It is important to recognize the existence of these two effects and to know how to use them effectively in pricing. Four ways to control for these effects are:

- when the cost of a product increases, avoid excessive increases in the final customer price by freezing the margins of intermediaries at the money amount allowed before costs increased;

- when the cost of a product decreases, gain full advantage in the final price by adjusting margins downward;

- when the final customer price decreases, resist attempts of intermediaries to maintain money margins by applying a higher percentage – freeze the percentages;

- when the final customer price increases, resist the attempt of intermediaries to profit excessively – freeze the money margin.

The extent to which companies can follow the above guidelines depends very much on the power they have in the distribution channels. Very often the most they can do is to share the advantages of the movements in the margins and prices with their intermediaries.

Communications–price interaction

The strong interactions between advertising and pricing strategies can be explained by the fact that price changes must be communicated. Advertising is most effective when the message it communicates is easily understood. Changes in price are relatively unambiguous and therefore may easily be communicated through advertising.

The importance of the interaction between personal selling and pricing strategies depends on whether the sales people control prices or whether prices are used to control the sales people. The first situation is typical of industrial marketing. In many forms of industrial selling, the price is negotiated by the salesperson either through pricing the product or by altering the offer for a trade-in. When pricing decisions are centralized in head office, the pricing strategy may be used to control the sales people. Compensation schemes may be based on margins, so that the sales force do not sell only the easy, low-margin products. Similar compensation-pricing methods can encourage sales people to spend their efforts on profitable customers and profitable order sizes.

Assignment questions

1 What factors influence the price elasticity of demand for a product? What do you think would be the effect of a price increase for bread? Hovis bread? Personal computers?

2 Discuss the relevance of competitor prices in the pricing decision.

3 Discuss the advantages and disadvantages of cost approaches to price determination.

4 What conditions are necessary for price differentiation to work? Can you think of any organizations which use this approach to pricing? How do they do it?

5 What are the differences between price skimming and prestige pricing?

6 What is penetration pricing? When is this pricing strategy most suitable?

7 Discuss three methods of psychological pricing. What method do you think would be most appropriate in pricing a service? A perfume? A newspaper? Why?

8 In which situation is a firm likely to use a flexible pricing strategy? What are the disadvantages of such a pricing strategy?

Annotated bibliography

Bagozzi, Richard P. (1991) *Principles of Marketing Management*, New York: Macmillan, chapters 12 and 13.

Dibb, Sally, Lyndon Simkin, William M. Pride and O.C. Ferrall (1991) *Marketing*, European Edition, Boston, Mass: Houghton-Mifflin Company, chapters 16 and 17.

Kotler, Philip (1984) *Marketing Management* (8th edn.), Englewood Cliffs, NJ: chapter 19.

Morgan, Rory (1989) 'Pricing as a marketing tool', in Michael J. Thomas (ed.), *Marketing Handbook* (3rd edn), Aldershot: Gower.

Winkler, John (1991) 'Pricing' in Michael Baker (ed.) *The Marketing Book* (2nd edn), Oxford: Butterworth-Heinemann.

References

Biswas, Abhijit, Elizabeth J. Wilson and Jane W. Licata (1993) 'Reference pricing studies in marketing: a synthesis of research results', *Journal of Business Research*, **27**, 3, 239–56.

Broadbent, Simon (1980) 'Price and advertising: volume and profit', *Admap*, November, 532–40.

Dickson, P., and A. Sawyer (1990) 'The price knowledge and search of supermarket shoppers', *Journal of Marketing*, **54**, 3, 42–53.

Monroe, K.B. (1973) 'Buyer's subjective perceptions of price', *Journal of Marketing Research*, **10** February, 70–80.

Oxenfeldt, A.R. (1991) 'A decision making structure for price decisions', in Ben. M. Enis and Keith K. Cox (eds.), *Marketing Classics* (7th edn), Boston: Allyn and Bacon, pp. 428–36.

Tellis, G.T. (1986) 'Beyond the many faces of price: an integration of pricing strategies', *Journal of Marketing*, **50**, 4, 146–60.

Case studies

Case 10: Johnson Group Cleaners

As the board meeting reconvened, Terry Greer, chairman of Johnson Group Cleaners, was still undecided on the whole question of acquiring a national trading name. The UK director, Richard Zerny, had initiated a full meeting of the company's board to discuss the possibility of introducing one single national brand name for their retail operation. Up to this point, the group had been operating under eleven different local trading names.

Zerny firmly believed that there were some real gains to be made by using an integrated national brand name. Standardization of the company's products, packages and promotional activities could permit substantial cost savings, as well as increasing consumer brand awareness and providing a greater consistency in dealing with customers.

Greer wasn't so sure. Although the concept of a national brand looked appealing on paper, he had grave doubts about whether it could be successfully applied to his business. He had previously stated during a board meeting: 'The real trick about the dry cleaning business is that it cannot be run successfully as a big business.' On this occasion Zerny had interrupted him, saying: 'That's a rather mysterious attitude for a man at the helm of the world's biggest dry cleaning firm.'

Greer, who didn't like to be challenged, retorted:

> There might be economies of scale to be achieved in terms of, say, packaging, but you have to consider the other side. Dry cleaning falls into the category of begrudged expenditure. People by and large don't say, 'Hooray: let's go to the dry cleaners.' What they want is not the best, but the least bad, and that means the nearest. People aren't going to walk an extra half-mile just because you have a national trading name.

As Greer left the meeting, he reflected on the principles that had enabled him to build a small family business into the world's largest dry cleaning operation with a turnover of £149.4 million. At the time of this latest board meeting, the Johnson Group ran some 750 shops in the UK, over 25 per cent of the market.

Johnson was built on the format of what Greer called a 'multiple cottage industry'. Of the Group's 750 UK outlets, the majority were acquired by direct purchase rather than through organic growth. The strategy was to acquire successful outlets and keep the current management in place because of their knowledge of the locality and their consumers. The group was built on decentralized flexibility. Apart from fiercely scrutinized number crunching, interference from Johnson's minuscule (seven-man) headquarters team was confined to those areas where centralization led to greater efficiencies, notably in the realms of purchasing, and financial and technical advice. At the same time, local boards were given complete freedom over everything from pricing to promotion strategies.

According to Greer, by operating as a 'multiple cottage industry', the company had reaped the double benefit of cut-price local advertising rates and national buying clout. But the real advantage came in the flexibility afforded in each geographic market. A good example of this successful strategy was the Group's Liverpool chain, which operated under the 'Prestige' name. Research showed that Prestige's customers spent an average 70 minutes in their local supermarket. Prestige introduced a very successful one-hour return service, so customers could accomplish two chores at once. Greer believed that this flexibility was necessary to succeed at local level.

By operating under the eleven different local trading names, Johnson was able to position each of its operations slightly differently, within each of the geographical areas. Designer beer on one's tailored suit in Exeter was removed by the local high-class Kneel's, while Bristol's domestic dry cleaning was serviced by middle of the range Bollom's.

However, since his arrival 18 months ago, Richard Zerny had challenged Terry Greer's company philosophy on more than one occasion. Zerny argued that the benefits that would accrue from operating under one national name would outweigh any disadvantages from potential loss of flexibility. In fact he believed that the only disadvantage associated with the national name strategy was that the image of several of their current operations would have to be reviewed. Zerny felt that increased brand awareness, cost advantages from marketing economies of scale, and greater consistency in dealing with customers, particularly in pricing policies, outweighed any repositioning problems.

Should Johnson Group Cleaners adopt a national trading name?

Source: 'Johnson's passion for dirty work', *Management Today*, June 1991: 59.

This case was prepared by Derek Creevey, Department of Marketing, University College Dublin, as a basis for class discussion rather than to illustrate either effective or ineffective handling of an administrative situation.

Case 11: Gillette Sensor

A Boots Chemist (UK) survey has shown that a majority of women think a man is more sexy when he is clean shaven. Unfortunately for men, shaving has always been a complicated and hazardous ritual, liable to take up to 3,350 hours of a man's life. The company that introduced a razor that made the arduous affair of shaving easier, safer and more comfortable was on to a winner, it was thought.

Such a winner took a long time, and a lot of money, to get off the ground – thirteen years and $200 million development costs, in all. In addition, the lengthy development process was fraught with technological problems, management conflicts and financial difficulties.

The origins of this winner took root in 1977. An engineer in the Gillette Company (Britain) had already worked out how to create a thinner razor blade that would make existing Gillette cartridges easier to clean. He then had the idea of setting these thinner blades on springs, so that, as a man shaved, the blades would follow the contours of the face. He made a simple prototype, and passed it to the boss of the Gillette Company's Reading research facility. The boss liked the idea, but it took some time for the innovation to come to the forefront, and be developed as 'Sensor', Gillette's new high-tech razor.

The Gillette engineers had considerable work ahead of them to develop the innovation. There were many technical difficulties in developing a razor with floating parts. Originally, they thought that the blades could sit on tiny rubber tubes filled with a compressible fluid. This idea, however, proved to be too costly and complicated for mass manufacturing. In addition, they had to mount the skin guard, which stretches the skin before the blades shear the stubble, on somewhat firmer springs than rubber tubes. The engineers in Boston had an alternative idea. They moulded plastic springs into the blade cartridge itself, but in doing so created further problems. The styrene plastic which they had used in the past to mould blade cartridges for all razors had a tendency to lose its bounce over time. The solution the engineers came up with was a resin called Noryl, which was stronger and kept its bounce.

By 1983 Gillette was able to test a Sensor Prototype with 500 men. The results were encouraging. However, the Boston engineers still faced the problem of how to mass-manufacture the complicated innovation. 'We went to bed at night without the foggiest notion of how we were going to solve this one,' recalled Donald L. Chaulk, director of Gillette's shaving technology laboratory. The independently 'floating' Sensor blades posed the greatest problem – these blades, while no thicker than a sheet of paper, had to be rigid enough to hold their shape. The solution devised was to attach each blade to a thicker steel support bar.

This presented a whole new set of manufacturing problems. Glue was too messy and expensive to attach the support bar. Gillette's engineers solved the problem by building a prototype laser that would spot-weld each blade to a support, but without creating the heat that would damage the blade edge. Although complex, this process had the advantage of being difficult for competitors to copy. 'Clearly, it's a difficult bit of manufacturing,' admitted Norman R. Proulx, president of Wilkinson Sword North America, one of Gillette's principal rivals.

At this time, Gillette executives faced a series of financial headaches in the form of potential takeover bids. The first was from Revlon Inc., which offered $4.1 billion for the company. Then Comiston Partners, a New York investment firm, attempted to gain control of the board of directors. During the proxy battle, Gillette's chairman, Colman Mockler, in an effort to win over shareholders, told them of a revolutionary, top-secret 'shaving technology' that would guarantee fat profits for many years. 'We held on to the company, in part, by promising a big winner,' said Robert Murray, a Gillette vice-president. 'Sensor was a symbol of the "new Gillette". If it failed to deliver, we would have been vulnerable all over again.'

Despite desperately needing all its cash to fight off these take-over battles, the company's board granted the project more funds in 1986 and 1987, for the development of manufacturing equipment. Many financial analysts remained sceptical. 'When you're trying to conserve cash, the last thing you do is roll out a multi-million dollar new product,' said Andrew Shore, an analyst with Shearson Lehman Hutton.

US and European management had conflicting ideas, amid the technical difficulties. The US side, recognizing the popularity of disposables, wanted both disposable and permanent versions of Sensor. The European operations felt that there was too much emphasis on disposables. They pointed out that there were greater profit margins and growth in the market for up-market 'system' products, i.e. those razors with a handle and replacement cartridges. In addition, wet shaving had been growing in popularity, albeit slowly, over the previous five years at the expense of electric shavers.

In the end, as a result of the reorganization brought about by the Revlon bid, Gillette decided in 1988 to de-emphasize disposables. As a result, European executives replaced the Boston vice-presidents in the Safety Razor Group. The head of European operations, John Symons, was brought to Boston as executive vice-president. Symons was one of the few managers who had disagreed with the commonly held opinion that the razor market was moving towards commoditization. He felt that Gillette had to 'change the playing field'. He acknowledged, however, that the shift away from disposable razors 'created a lot of difficulties within the company'. The new Safety Razor team cancelled plans for development of the disposable version. They also abandoned the plastic handle originally planned for the new system razor, in favour of a more classy stainless steel handle. They set a production deadline, and told engineers, 'For the foreseeable future, Sensor is your life.'

Gillette was faced with many difficult decisions with respect to the launch of Sensor. The company had two options. It could launch it gradually in a select number of markets, and thus gauge consumer reaction and adjust the marketing campaign accordingly. Alternatively, Gillette could aim at the high-risk strategy of launching Sensor with a highly visible advertising strategy, throughout America and Europe. If successful, the latter option would reap tremendous rewards. On the other hand, if Sensor failed, other Gillette products would suffer as well. There was a lot at stake.

Gillette chose the more risky strategy, and added to the risk by using identical television commercials (apart from language) in every market, as it simultaneously launched Sensor in America and Europe. Gillette's long-term advertising agency, BBDO, was first called in to boost the Gillette corporate image, to set the stage for Sensor. The $80 million subsequently spent was badly needed. Older men remembered Gillette and its 'look sharp, feel sharp, be sharp' advertisements of the 1950s. In contrast, younger men had no image to match the Gillette name. 'When I think "Gillette", I think "hollow, plastic and blue",' said one young stockbroker. The campaign's slogan was 'Gillette – the best a man can get.' The corporate image advertisement, featuring pulsing music and strong-yet-sensitive men in various sporting activities or cradling babies, was very popular and highly effective. So much so that, for the actual Sensor launch, BBDO used much of the existing advertisement and just substituted in new computer-animated pictures showing how the floating Sensor blades worked.

The advertising campaign was just a small part of the launch. Considerable amounts of money were spent on public relations, packaging and design. To bring consistency with the corporate branding strategy Gillette was aiming for, it was decided that the Gillette name should be as big as the actual razor inside the package.

Identify the steps involved in the development of the new Gillette Sensor. Would you have recommended a different course of action at any stage in the process? Justify these recommendations.

Sources: *Business Week*, 29 January 1990: 62–3; 28 September 1992: 102–4; *Evening Standard*, 5 February 1992: 19; *The Economist*, 15 August 1992: 57–8; *Marketing*, 27 August 1992: 22–3.

This case was prepared by Nora Costello, Department of Marketing, University College Dublin, as a basis for class discussion rather than to illustrate either effective or ineffective handling of an administrative situation.

Case 12: Channel Tunnel

Christopher Garnett, the commercial director for the Eurotunnel, was faced with a challenging task: how does one 'manage a truly binational brand and make it work in five nations'?

As it drew closer to the offical opening in May 1994, speculation and criticism concerning the £10 billion Eurotunnel project intensified. According to Brian Langford, marketing director of P & O European Ferries, 'The closer we get to it, the clearer it becomes that there is absolutely no need for a channel tunnel. It has been an enormous waste of money, just an ego-trip for the politicians either side of the water, and it has criminally destroyed acres of Kent countryside' (*Marketing*, 5 August 1993). Such criticism reveals the apprehension which was then escalating among the Eurotunnel's main competitors, the ferry companies. The Tunnel would allow people to go to Waterloo Station in London, get on a train as a passenger and arrive in Paris three hours later courtesy of British Rail or SNCF (the French rail system), the two national train companies who bought the right to half of the trips through the Tunnel. However, if passengers wanted to take a car, they would have to travel to Folkestone and put their car on the shuttle.

Since 1988, cross-Channel ferry operators had invested approximately £1 billion in making their services more attractive and competitive. Of all the routes being fought for, the Dover-Calais route was currently valued at around £600 million per annum. Some observers estimated that the Tunnel would expand the business to around £800 million. The ferry operators which were on collision course with the Tunnel (specifically 'Le Shuttle' – the shuttle service which would take cars, motorbikes, lorries or bicycles regularly through the Tunnel) on the Dover to Calais short sea crossing were P & O and Stena Sealink with conventional ferries (a 75-minute crossing) and Hoverspeed with its Hovercraft (35 minutes), in addition to a Seacat service from 21 June to 25 September (50 minutes). Due to the fact that the speed factor was becoming a key issue in cross-Channel travel, Stena Sealink was rumoured to be introducing a Catamaran-style ferry which could do the crossing in 45 minutes. With the Tunnel introduction, passenger shuttles each carrying up to 120 cars and 800 passengers were expected to run every 15 minutes at peak times. The 50 km journey would take approximately 35 minutes. The marketing director at Sally Ferries was confident that, despite the speed emphasis, she would not lose many passengers when the Tunnel opened: 'We would have already lost them to Hovercraft.'

The ferry companies were intensifying their advertising and promotional strategies in anticipation of the Tunnel's opening. When so little was known about the marketing strategy which Eurotunnel intended to adopt, the ferry companies were faced with the difficulty of deciding how to pitch their own marketing and advertising messages. These companies now realized the importance which attached to customer loyalty and they were therefore beginning to invest in target marketing and direct marketing through database development.

In 1993, a price war began between the cross-Channel operators, and it was expected that the issue of pricing would be even more important when the Tunnel opened. According to Christopher Garnett, 'A price war is inevitable: the ferry companies may well position themselves to attract different parts of the market, but they will have to persuade people to make two or three trips and not just one in order to maintain capacity. The only way they will do this is by reducing prices.' Eurotunnel had already announced that its prices would be 'broadly in line' with those charged by the ferries, but its strategy would be to charge for each car rather than for each passenger.

Garnett had £25 million to spend on a pan-European marketing campaign for the Tunnel. However, despite the substantial marketing budget, his task of strategy formulation would not be an easy one. According to Garnett, 'The perception people abroad have of the Tunnel is different to that of British people. There they think it's wonderful, visionary, inspirational and they are very proud of it. Here people are more practical, they want to know exactly what it is and what it does and how it works.' In addition, it was felt that because the British are an island race, asking them to consider continental Europe as part of their territory would involve a considerable change of psyche which would probably take a number of years to achieve. Furthermore, inconsistencies between the French and British rail systems were likely to cause further problems. In France, the express trains would run on purpose-built, high-speed lines at up to 200 m.p.h. On the British side, they would have to run with commuter trains on existing tracks and could be lucky to manage 60 m.p.h.

Because travelling by fast ferry or by a rail tunnel link would both involve breaking a journey to the continent, it was thought that the expected battle would be won on customer service, speed of check-in and minimum bureaucracy. However, surveys indicated that up to half of the UK population was allergic to the idea of spending about 45 minutes under water. Their concerns included terrorism, flooding, fire, being stuck in a broken-down train and anxiety that the roof might cave in. Concern was twice as high as worries about aeroplanes and boats. 'There is terrible confusion in consumers' minds,' admits Garnett.

In marketing its binational service, the company would have to communicate with a vast array of different constituencies, leisure travellers, business travellers, freight companies, bankers, investors and manufacturers. According to Christopher Garnett the first step would involve 'turning this company from money, muck and muddle as a construction company to a service transportation company'.

1. What recommendations would you make to Christopher Garnett regarding the formulation of a binational marketing strategy for the

Tunnel, which will cement the identity of this service product while taking the various target markets/audiences into account? What steps should the Eurotunnel management take to overcome the public's fear and misconceptions regarding the Tunnel?

2. What should the Tunnel management do to differentiate their product further from those offered by the ferry companies?

Sources: *Financial Times*, 23 March 1993; 3 April 1993; *The Independent*, 4 May 1993; *Lloyd's List*, 1 March 1993; 27 April 1993; *Marketing*, 9 July 1992; 5 August 1993; *Sunday Telegraph*, 28 March 1993; *The Times*, 8 August 1992.

This case was prepared by Jacqui McWilliams, Department of Marketing, University College Dublin, as a basis for class discussion rather than to illustrate either effective or ineffective handling of an administrative situation.

Case 13: LEGO

Toy manufacturer LEGO, with an annual turnover of DKK10 billion, had a well-established brand name. At the end of 1991, the board of directors at LEGO received the results of consumer surveys which they had commissioned. The 'image power' survey by Landor Associates at the end of 1991 represented 10,000 adults between the ages of 18 and 65 and was conducted in the United States, Japan and many parts of Europe (Belgium, France, Italy, Holland, Spain, the UK and Sweden).

Image power was defined as a measurement of a brand's strength or impact, combining the consumers' awareness of the leading (global) brands with their perception of the brands' quality. When the survey results were collated, they revealed that in the USA and Japan the LEGO brand was not placed among the top ten, but the European results were encouraging. LEGO was fifth in the rankings after four automobile brands, Mercedes-Benz, Rolls-Royce, Porsche and BMW, and ahead of brands such as Nestlé, Rolex, Jaguar and Ferrari.

In the USA, the five top brands were IBM, Disney, Coca-Cola, Duracell and Levis. In Japan they were Sony, Panasonic, Seiko, Canon and Honda. In addition, an American survey carried out in Europe, the USA and Japan shows that LEGO ranked thirteen overall, while a similar survey by a German market analysis firm shows that LEGO, with a score of 67 per cent, is the best-known brand of toy in the new German states. Matchbox ranked second with a score of 41 per cent.

The board of directors at LEGO had decided to take advantage of this strong brand power and hired a vice-president for a new business area, LEGO Licensing A/S. The purpose of this company was to generate royalties from appropriate business partners that use the LEGO brand name in marketing their own products. The board had learned that Coca-Cola, for example, earned more than DKK3 billion in royalties using a brand-milking strategy, where the brand name, in certain product areas, was sold to the highest bidder.

> **Assume that the president of LEGO has hired you to analyze the potential possibilties in this new business area. You are asked to address the following tasks:**
>
> **1. What products would you recommend in connection with any licensing agreement of the LEGO brand name?**
>
> **2. What type of products would be appropriate?**
>
> **3. What conditions should be met in choosing an appropriate partner?**
>
> **4. Which positive attributes can LEGO offer a potential business partner?**
>
> **5. What can the licensee offer LEGO?**

This case was prepared by Svend Hollensen and Marcus J. Schmidt, Copenhagen Business School, and published in scener fra dansk erhversliv. *The text was edited and adapted by Dympna Hughes, Department of Marketing, University College Dublin, as a basis for class discussion rather than to illustrate either the effective or ineffective handling of an administrative situation. Original translation by Lynn Kahle, Copehagen College of Engineering. Published with permission of Handelshojokolens Forlag [Copenhagen Business School Press].*

Case 14: Philip Morris

Phrases such as 'Black Monday' or 'White Wednesday' are normally reserved for cataclysmic events on the stock exchange, but Philip Morris's decision to slash the price of its top selling Marlboro cigarette brand by almost 20 per cent has been accorded similar status. The day on which the price cut was announced, 2 April 1993, has entered the history books as 'Marlboro Friday'.

For years Marlboro has been one of the world's top brands, commanding 22 per cent of the £31 billion ($46 billion) US cigarette market (Table 1). The price cut both created mayhem in the highly profitable US cigarette market and jolted the whole consumer products sector. Products which traded on marketing imagery suddenly encountered growing resistance. Grocery manufacturers' brands were coming under increasing pressure from supermarkets' cheaper own-label lines, while discount retailers were flourishing.

Overnight the price of Marlboro's was slashed by 40 cents per pack to stave off the brand's market-share deterioration. The company's stock sank fourteen points accordingly, and pulled down the stocks of other consumer goods companies. This represented a marked change from the 1980s when Philip Morris raised prices on Marlboro twice a year, with little consumer

TABLE 1 Top ten brands: US market shares, 1991 (volume)

Brand	%
1. Marlboro	25.8
2. Winston	7.5
3. Salem	5.4
4. Newport	4.7
5. Kool	4.6
6. Doral	4.6
7. Camel	4.0
8. Benson & Hedges	3.2
9. Merit	3.1
10. Virginia Slims	2.8

resistance. 'Those easy profits were able to mask their marketing inefficien-cies,' says Murray Hillman, president of the Strategy Workshop, a New York consulting firm. Suddenly everything depended on Marlboro's ability to 'do more with less'.

The Marlboro brand accounted for 60 per cent of Philip Morris USA sales and 75 per cent of its operating income in 1993. Largely because of 'Marlboro Friday', analysts estimated that the parent company's world-wide operating income slipped to $9.3 billion in 1993 from £11 billion in 1992. Shares were reduced from $64 to $49 and consequently $13 billion in share capital went up in smoke. Most analysts felt that the Marlboro Cowboy had committed suicide with his own rifle.

Three months after 'Black Friday', the dust showed little sign of settling. Philip Morris announced that the Marlboro price cut – previously presented as a temporary, market-testing move – was being made permanent and extended to the rest of its premium brands, including Virginia Slims and Benson & Hedges. The company also announced price changes in discount cigarettes, a market which was virtually non-existent a decade earlier, but by 1993 commanded approximately 40 per cent of total US cigarette sales. Ironically, Philip Morris, a late entrant to the discount market, was by April 1993 one of the segment leaders, with an estimated 33 per cent market share, roughly the same as arch rival R.J. Reynolds.

The company increased the price of its cheapest brands (so-called 'deep discounts') by around six cents a pack, and moved its mid-range brands, which are deeply discounted through trade promotions, down to that level. The result was a two-tier price structure rather than a three-tier one, which was perceived as being technically easier for the consumer to understand and cheaper for the company to administer. These discount price increases aimed at narrowing the gap between premium and cheap cigarettes to the point where consumer purchases are guided more by perceptions of quality than by price. Marlboro, Philip Morris reasoned, would regain ground, and its increased sales would offset the loss of profits from lower prices.

With these changes, the average retail price of a pack of discounted Philip Morris cigarettes was $1.31 – approximately 45 cents lower than a pack of Marlboro, selling for $1.70 to $1.80. Before April 1993, discount cigarettes were $1 or more cheaper than Marlboro's $2.20 pack.

Six months on, Philip Morris was able to produce figures which suggested that this strategy was working. However, this did not mean that all was well. It appeared that much of Marlboro's gain had come from other premium brands, including Philip Morris's own. Gary Black, an analyst at Stanford C. Bernstein, the US brokerage, reckoned that only about half of the increase had come from discount brands. Mr Black went on to warn that Marlboro could lose up to half of its total market share gain since April 1993, because he felt that consumers would revert to other premium cigarettes as they followed Marlboro's lead and cut their prices in turn.

Many analysts were also far from certain that the 45 cents a pack differential between premium brands and discounts, which Philip Morris imposed on the market, would stick. They suspected that smaller manufacturers of discount brands would cut prices to maintain their market share, creating a new ultra-low price, third tier. At the very least, it was thought that these smaller manufacturers would not follow Philip Morris's price increases.

> **What in your opinion led to Philip Morris's adoption of this price-cutting strategy? Evaluate the company's pricing strategy. Would you have done things differently?**

Source: *Financial Times*, 2 April 1993: 17; 13 April 1993: 14; 23 July 1993: 21; *Business Week*, 31 January 1994: 44–5; *Capital*, December 1993: 43.

This case was prepared by Dympna Hughes, Department of Marketing, University College Dublin for the purpose of class discussion rather than to illustrate either effective or ineffective handling of an administrative situation.

PART D

Communicate the value to customers

- advertising and public relations
- direct marketing
- personal selling

Chapters

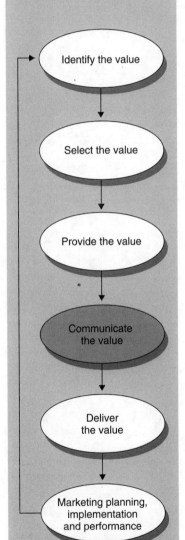

Identify the value

Select the value

Provide the value

Communicate the value

Deliver the value

Marketing planning, implementation and performance

Marketing communications: advertising and public relations

14

Role of promotion in marketing
Communications process in marketing
Nature and scope of advertising
Managing the advertising process
Evaluation of advertising effectiveness
Role of public relations
Sponsorship in marketing

Introduction

This chapter introduces and explains:

- the role of promotion as a marketing investment;

- the impact of promotion on the buyer;

- how effective communications are developed;

- the elements of promotion;

- the nature of advertising with special emphasis on products and services;

- the relationship between advertising and social issues;

- how companies develop an advertising strategy, set advertising objectives, decide the media message and schedule and establish the budget;

- the function of advertising agency support;

- the way companies determine the value of advertising;

- the role of publicity and public relations;

- how companies develop and manage relationships with the media; and

625

- the growing importance of commercial sponsorship and its use by companies to promote self-image.

Marketing communications is an important element of the marketing mix. The company must communicate with its customers to ensure that they know about the value provided by the company. It is necessary to establish communications objectives, determine the nature of the message to be communicated, select the audience to be addressed, and specify the expected response. It is management responsibility to allocate a budget across the various elements of broadcast, print and other promotion media to achieve objectives.

Advertising is a high-profile promotions medium used to reach a mass market. Companies advertise their products and services and themselves in a competitive way. They must develop an advertising strategy and establish specific objectives to be attained. This also means deciding the message, the advertising theme to use, and the timing and scheduling of media exposure. Usually companies call upon the assistance of advertising agencies in implementing advertising strategy. It is also necessary to evaluate the effectiveness of advertising, which means determining the value of advertising to the company and its customers. Other aspects of communications may complement the role of advertising. Public relations are sometimes used to capitalize on good news concerning the company, and are also effective in dampening the effects of bad news. Increasingly, companies are turning to the sponsorship of events which promote a self-image developed by the company. Companies tend to associate themselves and their products and services with the characteristics and lifestyles of people who feature in such events.

Having studied this chapter, you should be able to define the terms used above in your own words, and you should be able to do the following:

1. Specify the effects of promotion on the demand for a product or service.

2. Outline the tasks in the communications process.

3. List the advantages of broadcast and print media.

4. Determine the important factors in deciding the promotion mix.

5. Evaluate the contribution of 'push' and 'pull' communications in the marketing channel.

6. Understand the roles of comparative and generic advertising.

7. Identify the key elements in forming an advertising strategy.

8. Decide the message, its schedule and its timing, and be able to outline a brief to the advertising agency.

9. Specify ways of evaluating the effectiveness of advertising.

10. Recognize the value of public relations and know when it should be used.

11. Understand some of the reasons why companies are turning towards commercial sponsorship to promote themselves, their products and their services.

Role of promotion in marketing

Promotion is any form of communication used by an organization to inform, influence or remind people and other organizations about its products, services, ideas, image and identity, and impact on society. Communication may be by means of the organization's brands, its sales force or the mass media. Marketing communications may emphasize information, persuasion or reinforcement of various themes, such as product performance, sociability, fear, humour or comparisons with competitors. There are several categories of audience: consumers, owners, government, consumer associations, suppliers, company staff and the general public. Because each of these audiences is different in terms of objectives, knowledge and needs, communications are different.

Promotion as marketing investment

Most promotional expenditure is an investment, an outlay made today to produce future benefits, so the important consideration from the advertiser's point of view is future cash flows accruing from the promotion. Promotion is not just a current expense to produce immediate benefits, although it works by stimulating sales in the short run. Short-run sales stimulate brand or product use and the long-run accumulation of added values which arise as a consequence. The long-term effect of promotion is through the long-term use of the product or brand and not so much due to the brand itself.

Effect of promotion

Usually the greatest part of the company's promotional budget is spent on its products and services with the objective of ensuring that customers become aware and eventually buy. The effect of promotion is to change the demand curve for the company's products and services. Two effects on the demand curve may be observed (Figure 14.1). First, with promotion the demand curve shifts up and to the right, so that greater quantities are purchased at the same price. In Figure 14.1(a) sales increase from S_1 to S_2 at price P. Second, the shape of the demand curve changes (Figure 14.1(b)). For price increases from P_1 to P_2 the demand curve has become more inelastic than without promotion, and for a decline in price from P_1 to P_3 demand has become more elastic than before. A price increase with promotion results in a smaller decline in sales, from S_1 to S_3, than would have been expected had the old demand curve

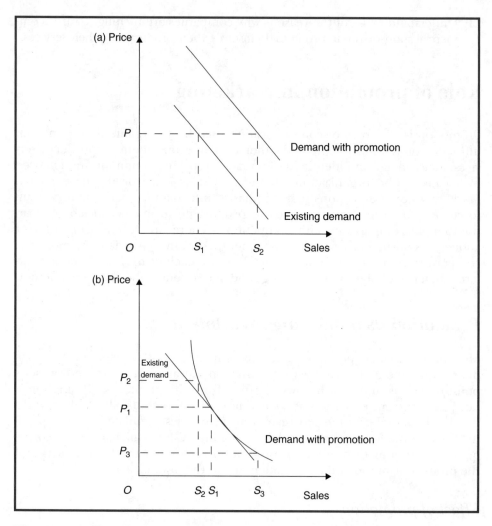

Figure 14.1 Effect of promotion on product or service demand

remained in place. A price decrease with promotion results in a greater increase in sales, from S_1 to S_3, than would have been expected had the old demand curve remained.

Objectives of promotion

It is essential to know the objective of the promotion if its effectiveness is to be evaluated. The company must identify the specific objectives to be accomplished during a particular period as a result of a set of promotional expenditures. Objectives include:

- conveying information to buyers;
- creating brand preferences; and
- producing sales.

These are complicated objectives and difficult to separate from one another. In reality, different effects may result from a particular promotional expenditure. Setting objectives for promotion requires an understanding of the influence process.

In advertising, two fundamental tendencies or 'laws' determine the behaviour of buyers: slow learning and fast forgetting (Figure 14.2). The law of slow learning states that buyers are slow to accept the benefits of new products and processes. Consumers respond on an incremental basis so that they need a lot of reminding and reinforcement of learned ideas and customer appeals. For these reasons, advertising must be substantial and frequent.

The second tendency, the law of fast forgetting, states that buyers are quick to forget. Other concerns and competitive activity may divert attention away from the company's products or services. There is a need, therefore, to constantly remind, update and emphasize the benefits of the company's offerings. Sales may decline slowly when advertising is reduced or withdrawn because they also respond to the history of the company's advertising (Vidale and Wolfe, 1957). A substantial carry-over effect implies that the company should devote relatively more resources to advertising as a strategic variable and not just a tactical response to short-term considerations.

Buyers are thought to go through a number of stages in being influenced by promotion. The company must recognize these stages and the different

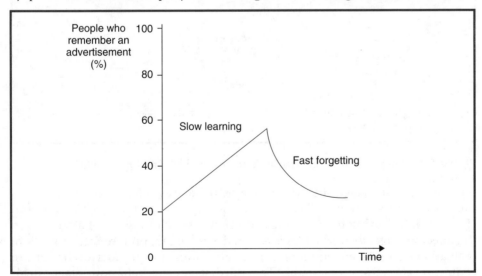

Figure 14.2 Slow learning and fast forgetting

629

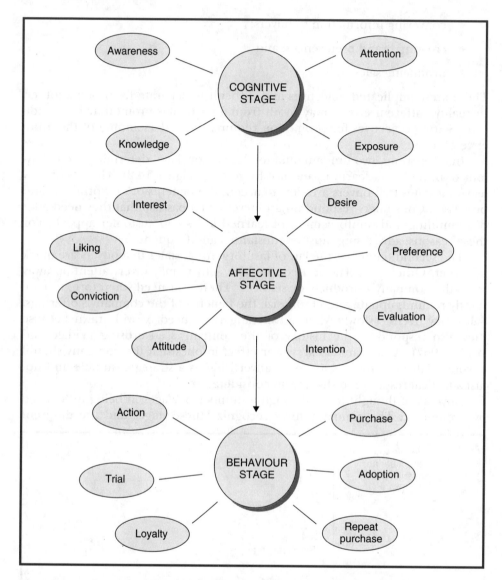

Figure 14.3 Stages in consumer decision process and advertising emphasis

objectives at each stage. In the first stage, objectives refer to cognitive issues such as awareness, attention, knowledge and exposure to the product or brand (Figure 14.3). During the next stage, objectives switch to issues of affection. In the affective stage, issues such as interest, desire, liking, preference, conviction, evaluation, attitude and intention associated with the product or brand are central to advertising objectives. The third stage, the behaviour stage, deals with action, purchase and other behavioural objectives.

The objectives of promotion change with different stages of the product life cycle. For new products or services, customers must be informed and product attributes recognized before customers can develop a favourable disposition towards them. For products at a later stage in the life cycle, consumer awareness is less important, but persuasion or the conversion of product knowledge into product liking becomes important. For mature products, the emphasis is on reminding customers and reinforcing existing positive beliefs.

Impact of promotion on the buyer

The different forms of promotion affect buyers in different ways depending on the purchase decision stage. At the pre-purchase stage, the company wishes to increase awareness, knowledge and even preference for its products and services. At the buying stage, the aim is to create satisfaction. At the post-purchase stage, the company seeks to promote loyalty among its customers. The different forms of promotion vary in their effectivenes in achieving these aims at each stage of the buying process (Figure 14.4). Advertising is more effective in creating awareness, raising the knowledge level and establishing preferences than is sales promotion or personal selling.

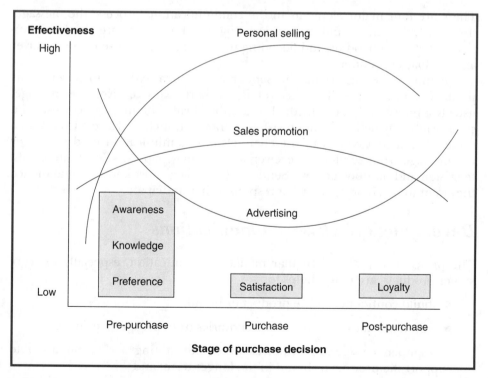

Figure 14.4   Impact of communication mix on buyer

631

Personal selling and sales promotion, because they are interactive and provide incentives to buy, are more effective in increasing satisfaction at the purchase stage. Advertising again dominates the influence in the post-purchase stage. By reinforcing the desired attributes, advertising reassures and is very effective in raising loyalty and hence increasing repeat purchases.

It is difficult to judge how much emphasis the advertisier should give to each objective at each stage. It is possible to over- or underpromote in any of the stages. At the pre-purchase stage, it is possible to create too much awareness and too high a preference for a new product. When the Gillette company launched the new 'Sensor' razor in January 1990 in the USA, it failed to judge the impact of its advertising, so retailers were left short. The company's response was to divert production to the US market that was destined for the European markets, and to postpone some of its advertising spending until the second half of 1992. Advertising money may be wasted if the product is not available. Also it may build up resentment among retailers and consumers.

Communications process in marketing

There are four major elements in the communications process: the message, the media, the sender and the receiver (Figure 14.5). There are also four principal functions: encoding and decoding the messages, response by the receiver and feedback to sender.

In the marketing arena, the sender is the firm wishing to advertise its products and services. The receiver is the party who receives the message, usually a household, an individual or another firm. The message consists of a set of symbols which the sender wishes to transmit, such as 'Have a Coke and a smile'. The media consist of the channels of communication used to convey the message from sender to receiver, such as newspapers, sales conferences, television and outdoor posters. Senders of messages must know what audience they want to reach, why, and what responses they anticipate.

Developing effective communications

The principal benefits of regular media communication, especially for consumer products, are that it helps to:

- build confidence in the product or brand;

- stimulate sales and encourage enquiries from prospective customers;

- dampen competitor advances by demonstrating a determination to support the product or brand in the longer term; and

- increase the frequency of purchasing.

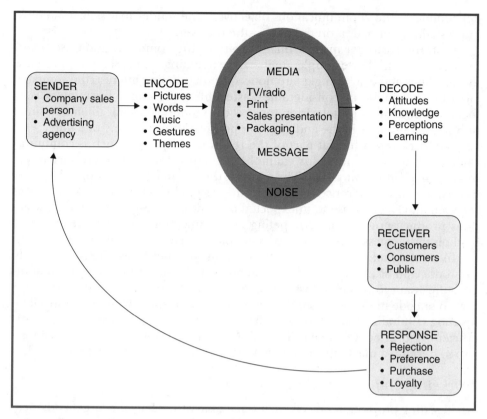

Figure 14.5 The communications process

Tasks in the communications process

Companies pay a great deal of attention to the four elements of the communications process. Even greater concern is required for the four functions. The process of converting thought into symbolic form or encoding (e.g. deciding the appropriate set of words and illustrations to be used on an outdoor billboard poster) requires great care, attention and planning. Encoding of the message must take account of the way the target audience is likely to decode it. Similarly, decoding of the message, or the process by which the receiver assigns meaning to the symbols transmitted by the sender, raises the possibility of misunderstanding or misinterpretation. The receiver uses language, symbols and illustrations to internalize the meaning of the message being transferred. The possibility of error is greater when the communication is between different language or cultural groups.

Of considerable concern to the sender of messages in marketing is the response by the receiver. Here a range of reactions may be anticipated, depending on the communications objectives. The sender may seek awareness, interest, desire or action on the part of the receiver.

First, the customer must be made aware of the communication itself, and hence its content. For example, deliberately irritating advertisements, provocative headings and catchy jingles are noticed. In developing interest, the company faces the possibility of considerable waste unless the communication is very focused. Advertising on television for new car models faces this dilemma, since only a small number in the audience are potential buyers at any one time.

Feedback refers to that part of the receiver's response which is communicated back to the sender: for example, a request for further product information or product purchase. Throughout the communications process there is a danger of interference or noise in the system, which distorts the message received and so gives rise to unexpected or undesired responses. Many distractions produce noise: other competing communications, inappropriate use of symbols in the message sent, or a preoccupied receiver of the message.

In treating marketing communications in the above way, the factors likely to produce an effective response are identified. Senders must know what audience they want to reach and what responses they desire. They must understand how to encode messages in such a way as to avoid misunderstanding, especially if strong cultural factors are present. The message must be transmitted through efficient and effective media directed at the target audience. It is necessary also to develop a mechanism by which the nature of responses is understood.

Marketing communication objectives

When setting promotion objectives, it is necessary to specify the target audience, the desired response, the message and the media (Figure 14.6). It is necessary to decide who the target audience is before sending a message. By knowing the audience, it is possible to know what to say and how to say it. Frequently, the audience for marketing communications are influencers, deciders, users or buyers. These may be individuals, households, other companies or the general public. The nature of the target audience influences the company's decisions on marketing communications. The basic issues in marketing communication may be identified by answering a number of questions based on who, what, how and when:

- who does the company wish to inform?
- what outcome does it wish to influence?
- what message best achieves these objectives?
- what media are most appropriate?
- when should the company communicate?
- how much should the budget be?
- how effective is the marketing communication?

Communications objectives may be divided into three categories:

- those dealing with the pre-purchase situation, such as the level of awareness, product or service knowledge and established preferences;

- those dealing with the purchase situation itself and the level of satisfaction involved; and

- those dealing with the post-purchase situation which relate to issues of loyalty.

The firm must also seek an effective means of communication, which means deciding among the various media involved, such as advertising, publicity, sales promotion and personal selling. The company may concentrate on one of these, but is more likely to consider a mix of a number of them.

In selecting a form of promotion, the company may wish to inform or influence potential customers, or it may wish to reinforce a particular message in its communication. Some media are more effective than others in serving each of these objectives (Table 14.1). It is generally thought that advertising is most effective in influencing a potential customer. Publicity is very effective,

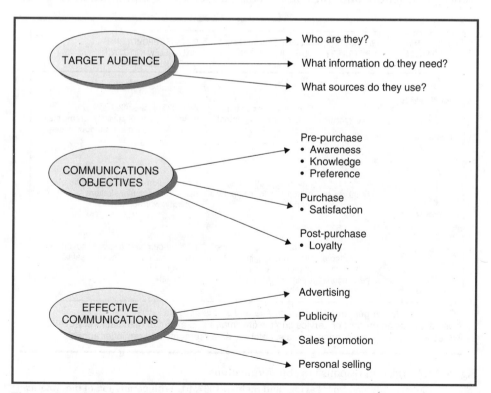

Figure 14.6   Key dimensions of marketing communications

TABLE 14.1 Effectiveness of different forms of promotion

Forms of promotion	Promotion objectives		
	Inform	*Influence*	*Reinforce*
Advertising	3	5	2
Publicity	5	2	1
Sales promotion	2	3	5
Personal selling	3	2	5

Note: 5 = very effective; 1 = not very effective.

however, in informing potential customers of the value of a product, service or idea. Sales promotion and personal selling are judged to be very effective in reinforcing the effects of the other media when the potential consumer has reached the point of purchase. At this stage, publicity is not very effective.

When the company has identified the target audience, it is necessary to decide the desired response. The hierarchy of effects model posited by Lavidge and Steiner (1961) suggests a set of intermediate and long-term promotional objectives the firm might pursue: awareness, knowledge, liking, preference, conviction and purchase. This model ties communications to the

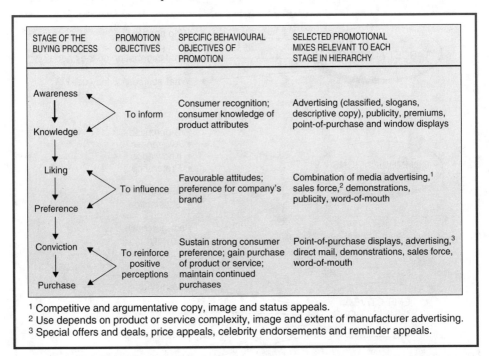

¹ Competitive and argumentative copy, image and status appeals.
² Use depends on product or service complexity, image and extent of manufacturer advertising.
³ Special offers and deals, price appeals, celebrity endorsements and reminder appeals.

Figure 14.7 Desired response to communications

(Source: Adapted from Lavidge and Steiner, 1967: 61. With permission of the American Marketing Association)

636

buying decision process. Processes and methods associated with the hierarchy of effects model are shown in Figure 14.7.

Hierarchy of effects models like this one link communications to the buyer's decision processes. For marketing communications to be effective, they must accomplish the communication objectives, such as achieving awareness, stimulating interest and providing knowledge. In this way the target audience moves from the situation of recognizing a problem to searching for possible solutions, to evaluating alternatives, to choice and purchase.

The nature of the audience, the state of 'buyer readiness' and the response that the company expects influence the allocation of the communications budget. Companies rely more heavily on advertising if the communications objective is awareness. Advertising is important throughout the process of moving the consumers from awareness to purchase (Figure 14.8). Publicity is more effective at the early stages, while sales promotion is effective throughout but more so at the point of purchase. Personal selling is most effective in supporting the purchase decision.

The message and the media

Central to marketing communications is the preparation of a message which will influence people to act in a desired way. To be effective the message must

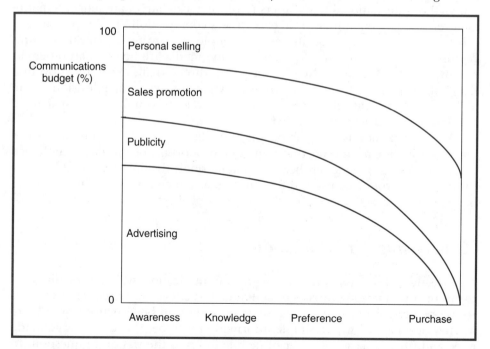

Figure 14.8 Communications mix and buyer readiness

hold the attention of the audience, should not be misunderstood and should be memorable. These decisions are more likely to produce the desired results when message content and context are considered. Message content refers to what is being communicated to target audiences. The context of the message refers to how the message content is communicated. Context deals with issues such as actors, nature of copy, use of colour and themes. In deciding on content and context, creativity may be an important consideration. A creative approach may be based on detailed information regarding the lifestyle, product benefits and competitive offers among members of the target audience. The advertising message must reflect the needs of the market and the ability of companies to serve the market. In recent years, advertising has become much more focused on segments and on variation in the market.

When the company has decided on the appropriate message, it must then decide how to deliver the message to the target audience. For this there are many different types of media, the more important of which are the print media (newspapers, magazines), the electronic media (television and radio), the postal media (direct mail, catalogues), outdoor media, publicity, sales promotion and sales people (Figure 14.9). Sales promotion includes merchandising, trade shows and exhibitions.

Companies select media to reach their target audience. A consumer products company is likely to use the mass media such as television, radio and national or international newspapers to reach a wide target audience. A manufacturer of heavy equipment is likely to use a combination of sales people and direct mail to reach a specific set of people in buying organizations who require detailed technical information. Some media are better than others in enhancing the message. Newspapers and direct mail excel in providing detailed technical information, while a major advantage of television is the ability to demonstrate the product in use. For some companies, cost may be the dominant factor in making a choice.

Most companies use a combination of media to deliver their message, since there is a higher likelihood that a greater proportion of the target audience will be reached. It is generally believed that no single medium reaches everybody in the target group. By using different media, the company can also vary the nature of the message and exploit the hierarchy of effects model to greater effect.

Advertising and the media

Advertising is an impersonal form of communication which uses different forms of print and broadcast media. Radio and television are popular vehicles to use in advertising. The spoken word on radio can be effective where there are few newspapers, where simple information is to be passed to a target audience and where a large number of people listen to the station in question. In contrast, advertising on television combines the advantages of the spoken

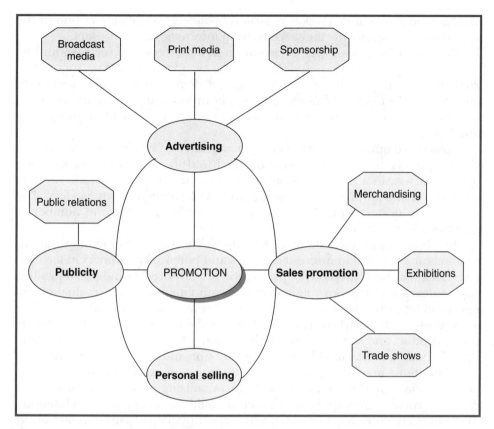

Figure 14.9 Types of communications media

word with visual form. Television is an expensive communications medium. Because of the costs involved and the large audiences reached, television is particularly appropriate when a consumer products company is trying to reach a very wide mass market. In these circumstances it can be cost effective.

The print media consist of the press: daily or weekly newspapers and magazines which appear weekly or monthly. Usually newspapers and magazines are aimed at a particular readership.

Advertising appearing in magazines reaches fewer people than it would in newspapers, but because it is concentrated on a particular type of reader, its desired impact may be greater. Examples are women's and special interest magazines. Magazines do not date as easily as newspapers, and they tend to be read by many people.

The key factor in assessing the value of a newspaper or magazine as a medium of communication is readership and not just circulation. Many publications have several readers for each copy. Another fact to be considered is the purchasing power of the readers. Selecting the best newspaper to reach senior managers in national markets is regarded by media consultants as one of the most difficult assignments they receive from international advertisers.

Personal selling is an oral presentation in a conversation format with one or more prospective buyers for the purpose of ultimately selling something. Publicity is an impersonal encouragement of demand for a good, service or idea, derived by placing commercially significant news about it in the press, on the radio, on television or in another medium which is not paid for by an identified sponsor.

Posters are quite popular in certain areas and for certain kinds of product. Usually posters are placed in areas of much traffic, such as on the side of a busy motorway, in a railway station or in a busy street. Locations where there are large numbers of people passing are good candidates for posters. The value of the poster depends on its size, the traffic flow and the number of people who actually see it.

Exhibitions and trade shows or fairs allow the company to demonstrate its products and services to interested parties and potential customers in a convenient location. Such methods of promotion are favoured by industrial product companies, since it is possible to clarify requirements, obtain evaluations of new product introductions, assess competitors and determine the conditions for success in the market. Trade fairs and exhibitions are also used in consumer product and service markets. In Germany, for example, exhibitions and trade fairs are a most valuable form of promotion and are used extensively.

Exhibitions may be organized by a trade group, an independent exhibition organizer or the company itself. In organizing its own exhibition, the company usually hires space in a hotel or building designed for exhibitions. Trade fairs are especially associated with exporting. Participation in one of the well-known trade fairs is often the first step in developing export markets.

Sales promotion refers to communication activities other than advertising, publicity, personal selling or sponsorship, which stimulate consumer purchases and dealer effectiveness: merchandising, trade shows, exhibitions and other non-recurring selling efforts. Sales promotions involve in-store demonstrations, special offers, samples, coupons, and customer and trade competitions which stimulate short-run sales and promote customer interest. Merchandising in retail outlets has become very important in recent years due to the pressure for shelf space from an increasing number of competing products. Many manufacturing companies use special teams of merchandisers to ensure effective presentation of products, and occasionally arrange special displays as part of a sales promotion endeavour.

Media advertising expenditures

Since 1990 newspapers in America, western Europe and Japan have suffered their worst slump in 50 years, and advertising revenue and circulation have

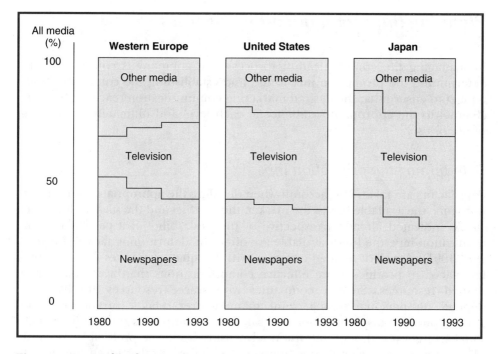

Figure 14.10   Media advertising expenditures in western Europe, United States and Japan
(Source: Adapted from *The Economist*, 31 October 1992: 72. Copyright, *The Economist*, London 1994)

both declined. The downturn is one thing, but advertisers have now shifted their attention to television with the trend to deregulation, especially in Europe (Figure 14.10). As a result, newspaper advertising has declined dramatically in recent years.

Newspaper circulations have also declined due to television. In the 1960s, about 75 per cent of Americans read a paper daily; the figure for the early 1990s is 50 per cent. Meanwhile television viewing has increased dramatically (*The Economist*, 31 October 1992: 71).

There is a general belief, however, that television can only do so much damage to newspapers. Television advertising expenditure tends to peak in developed countries at around 25–30 per cent of total advertising expenditure. It is easier to target an audience with local and regional newspapers than it is with television, which tends to be national or international in scope. Television is also likely to experience strong competition from telecommunications companies intent on sending information and advertising directly to homes. Another development which could adversely affect the growth of television advertising is the potential for households to customize what is displayed on their screens through paid cable and other forms of pre-paid programming. It is uncertain how advertising messages will receive an airing in such circumstances.

Planning the communications process

In managing the communications process, the company is concerned with determining the promotion mix to use and establishing the communications budget to ensure that the desired marketing communication reaches down the channel to the appropriate audience at each level and ultimately to the consumer or user.

Determining the promotion mix

Four factors are taken into account when deciding the appropriate communications mix: the available funds, the market, the product and the stage of life cycle.

As indicated already, irrespective of the desirability of a particular communication mix, the funds available are often the determining factor (Rossiter *et al.* 1991). A well-developed company with adequate resources is usually better placed to produce more effective communications than a company with limited resources. Smaller companies with scarce resources are likely to depend on personal selling, joint manufacturer–retailer promotions and general-purpose displays at point of sale. Such companies often rely on personal selling even though television advertising would be preferable. Because of resource considerations, the company can afford a salesperson but not an advertising budget.

The nature of the market also influences the communications decision. Personal selling may be adequate for a small local market. For an extensive market, television advertising may be necessary. The geographic scope of the market is, therefore, an important factor. Related to the scope of the market is the degree of concentration in the market. The smaller the number of potential buyers, the more effective is personal selling compared to advertising.

The type of customer also influences the decision. The communications decision depends on whether the company is attempting to reach final consumers, intermediaries or industrial users. Related to this point is audience heterogeneity. A target audience consisting of a homogeneous customer group requires a different communication mix from a market consisting of many different customer groups.

In allocating the promotion budget, consumer product manufacturers are likely to spend most of it on advertising, with a considerable amount on sales promotions, less on personal selling and a relatively small amount on public relations (Figure 14.11). The opposite tends to be the case for industrial products. Here personal selling dominates with advertising and sales promotion absorbing a smaller proportion. The proportion spent on public relations tends to remain the same. These proportions tend to fluctuate with changes in the environment and the circumstances facing individual companies. As national or international advertising becomes expensive and ineffective in

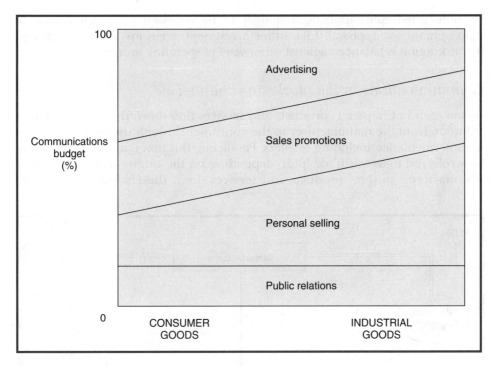

Figure 14.11 Communications mix in industrial and consumer goods markets

reaching target audiences, some firms prefer to target customers more closely by using sales promotions and even personal selling.

A company like Black and Decker, selling heavy-duty drills used only by furniture manufacturers, may be able to use personal selling effectively. When it sells drills to the DIY sector, the company may decide to use a combination of media with greater emphasis on television advertising. In such cases, personal selling would be much too expensive and even ineffective.

Communications budget

Two alternative ways of developing a promotional budget may be identified. The top-down approach is used when the company applies an upper limit on the amount to be spent for promotion. This approach and the percentage of sales approach are similar and very popular in situations where company planning is dominated by a financial view of the world, whereby financial managers allocate a certain fixed proportion of forecast sales to promotion without a detailed treatment of how the money should be spent.

The bottom-up approach is a more logical approach, involving decisions on the combination of message content, context and media required to achieve specified communications objectives. The total cost of the plan becomes a recommended communications budget to be reviewed by senior company management for approval. Like other investment decisions, the use of funds for promotion is balanced against other ways of spending money.

Communications in the marketing channel

As was seen in Chapter 1, products and services flow down the channel of distribution from the manufacturer to the consumer through the various marketing intermediaries, including retailers. Paralleling this flow is a communications flow referred to as 'push' or 'pull' depending on the origin of the force. The manufacturer 'pushes' products and services down the channel by personal

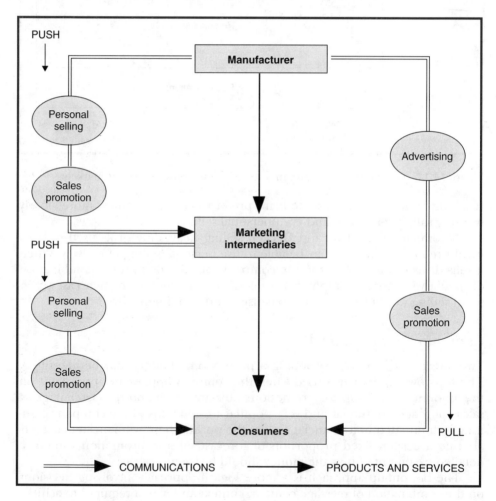

Figure 14.12   Communications in the marketing channel: push vs pull

selling and sales promotion. The target audience is the next member in the channel, in this case a marketing intermediary (Figure 14.12). The marketing intermediary in turn promotes the products and services to consumers, again, with a heavy dependence on personal selling and sales promotion. In both cases other forms of promotion may be used, but personal selling and sales promotion are thought to be more effective in pushing products and services through the channel.

Manufacturers or providers use a combination of advertising and sales promotion to pull products and services down through the channel. By promoting them to the final consumer through advertising and by providing point-of-sale incentives to purchase, products and services are pulled through the channel. Consumers, motivated by advertising or seeing a sales promotion, demand the products and services at the point of retail. Again, other forms of promotion are used in conjunction with advertising and promotion, but these two dominate.

Nature and scope of advertising

For many people, the world of advertising is one of exaggerated claims, hard sell and persuasive tactics to get people to buy products they do not want. While there may be an element of truth in some of these claims, it is generally accepted that people who work in advertising cloud themselves in a language of their own which confuses clients, consumers and the general public, and which, if it were made more available, would obviate the difficulties encountered (Exhibit 14.1).

Nature of advertising

Advertising is any form of mass communications which is paid for by somebody to transfer a message containing elements of information and persuasion regarding the potential purchase of a product, service, or idea to people whom the advertiser wishes to reach, who may or may not be receptive (Vaughn, 1980). Advertising is a one-way mass medium access to large audiences with the ability to communicate quickly, indiscriminately and at low cost for each viewer reached.

Advertising decisions

The advertiser faces two decisions: the media decision and the copy decision. The media decision involves choice among a mix of newspapers, magazines, television and radio stations, and about the timing and size or length of the

---

EXHIBIT 14.1   Advertising 'bizzwords'

An advertising agency is launching a new campaign. No. An *above-the-line outfit* is going to *roll out* a multi-million-pound *push*, that *breaks* at the end of the month in an intensive *burst* aimed at a *targeted niche market*. The clients are assured that there'll be no *scattershotting* of the *adspend* here. The agency is not just an agency, of course, but a *fully-integrated one-stop shop*, with subsidiaries in design, PR, point-of-sale, direct marketing and a range of *below-the-line* and *through-the-line* activities which offer clients the chance to *cherry-pick* whatever they require. All the services are described at exhaustive and boastful length on the agency's *video showreel*.

The agency's *creatives*, planners, *suits* and *media guys* have been working for months on the campaign. The *roughs* have been *conceptualised* (and *concepts roughed*), *cartoon animatics* made, ideas *triangulated* and *flagpoled*, research groups convened, a *production house* appointed, fists banged, heads clutched and lunch bills run up. The client has argued with the suits, the suits with the planners, the planners with the media men, and the creatives with everyone. But finally, with all the team in a state of diplomatic exhaustion, and the *final line*, the ultimate *creative execution* bearing not the slightest resemblance to those first, primitive roughs – we're ready.

The campaign, everyone at the agency agrees, is brilliant *impactful* and just right for the *ad-literate generation*. Gone are the days when you could get away with a hard sell: *golden corn ads* which *wallyised* the poor consumer with *doughnuts* –jingles – of the most irritating and mindless variety. The finished ad is high on *stun factors*, it's got great *stand-out* and early *instant recall research* shows that the consumer *take-out* is very favourable.

But what's this? Only a few months after the initial run, the rumours begin. The *roll-out* has stopped rolling, and the agency's masterpiece has only been seen in a few households in the Grampian region. The marketing director has been seen having lunch with whizz-kids from three to four other *top-shops*, and had reportedly seen *credentials presentations* from at least six others. A company spokesman denies there's any problem. There's a great relationship with the agency, he insists: all that's going on is a *statutory three-year review* of the account. A week later, the agency is fired. No, not fired. The agency's *slice* has gone elsewhere as part of an *international re-alignment* prompted by a *reprioritising* of *long-term strategic objectives*. Besides, the agency say, the *ratecard spend* has been negligible for most of the past year.

The new agency has a different story. 'We're proud to be associated with this great historic and multi-billion brand, which we'll be pushing in a rolled-out, niche-oriented campaign ...' it says.

Source: *Business Life* (British Airways Inflight Magazine), June 1992: 30.

advertisement. The media decision is essentially a matter of cost effectiveness. The major influences on the media decision maker are the estimates of the audience exposure rates and the costs of the different media vehicles.

The copy decision, the word and illustrations of the advertisement itself, refers to the content and context of the advertisement. Decisions on copy involve creativity and a focus on good ideas to attract the attention of the target audience to help promote the products, services or ideas of the advertiser. The creative decision is usually not constrained by costs so much as by the imagination of the people employed to produce the copy and decide the illustrations. A clever, well-conceived, small or short advertisement often obtains better results than a larger or longer but cluttered version which has little impact. Though more difficult to measure, this qualitative aspect of advertising is considered very important. Many advertising agencies are chosen on the basis of their creative proposals rather than their media expertise.

Once the media budget, the advertising message, the copy and the appropriate illustrations are decided, the company must choose the media alternatives to use, the number of insertions in each, their timing and their size, their duration, and colour options in each case to produce the most cost-effective impact given the advertising budget. The output of this media decision process is referred to as the media schedule.

Advertising products and services

In advertising products and services, companies are primarily concerned with competition. Consequently, how well a company's advertising compares with that of competitors to obtain a 'share of the consumer's mind' is a key consideration. Similarly, companies are interested in brand advertising, so developments in the area of generic advertising also hold considerable interest.

Comparative advertising

While the legislation in many countries permits advertising which claims that X's detergent washes whiter than Y's, advertising agents tend to be opposed to comparative advertising, which they believe is not creative, mimics and tends to be ineffective. Comparative advertising of this nature may rebound on the company, especially if the incumbent is well resourced or is the market leader and decides to respond to such claims. In such a counterattack, the market leader's product is likely to remain in the consumer's mind. However, there is pressure for more consumer information, such as comparative unit prices, from consumers and consumer groups, which makes comparison inevitable.

Most comparisons which are enshrined in legislation allow an objective comparison of intrinsic, significant and verifiable qualities of products and

647

services. The products and services being compared must be of the same nature and sold under the same conditions, so comparisons between a large supermarket and a small corner store would not be permitted. Claims made must not be untruthful, misleading or denigrating.

Generic advertising

The word 'genus' originally referred to a category of biological classifications comprising related organisms, usually consisting of several species. For corporate decisions, species become brands and generic categories are specific product lines, such as wine, beer, whiskey and dairy products. The concept of generic advertising may be clearly seen in the various advertising campaigns using this form of communication: for example, 'Drink More Milk', 'Do More Exercise' or 'Eat Healthy Foods'. The purchasing rationale behind generics is price, since they are given much less advertising support.

Generic advertising aims to influence the industry demand curve, whereas brand advertising is concerned with the demand for a particular brand. Increases in the quantities demanded as a result of generic advertising also benefit the individual brand. Furthermore, because of the generic elements in brand advertising, competitive brand advertising serves to expand the total market for the product class.

The reason for producing generics is an attempt to capture any segment of the market that has developed antibodies against, and hence immunity to, advertising. Generics are also frequently the subject of government-supported export promotion programmes for entire product lines – Scotch whisky, French wine, New Zealand kiwi fruit.

Advertising consumer products to men

Companies have recently begun to pay greater attention to a once neglected segment – the male shopper. Attempts are being made to entice them to buy products which have been traditionally purchased by women. Advertising on television may be seen which shows men cuddling small babies, shopping for good bargains in supermarkets, and buying diet yoghurts and spreadable butters. In recent years, there has also been a very large increase in the advertising of cosmetics for men. Much of this shift in emphasis reflects the number of women working outside the home, resulting in men purchasing products heretofore the prerogative of women. In preparing advertising, most companies have been careful to recognize the potential ego damage which could arise from the tradition that men only buy alcohol, cars, computers and consumer electronics. This is changing as a convergence occurs between the male and female segments of the market.

Advertising and social issues

Advertising is sometimes judged to be manipulative, meaning that it can manipulate customers into making decisions against their best interests. This argument states that some advertising appeals to subconscious motives and that there may also be indirect emotional appeals. The argument that the customer is manipulated at the subconscious level by advertising was most strongly supported in the highly publicized subliminal advertising experiments carried out by James Vicary in the late 1950s, in which he subliminally flashed the phrase 'Drink Coke' and 'Eat Popcorn' on a cinema screen every five seconds. (Engel *et al.*, 1993: 394). The tests were reputed to have increased cola sales by 57 per cent and popcorn sales by 18 per cent in a six-week period, which at face value suggested manipulation. But as the test did not employ even rudimentary controls and has not been replicated, there is considerable doubt as to the conclusions (Aaker and Myers, 1975: 539). Motivation research is unlikely, therefore, to give an advertiser control over an audience.

Attitudes towards advertising

People have different opinions regarding advertising. In a survey of UK consumers, Wendy Gordon of The Research Business, a consultancy company, used cluster analysis to identify the key factors that resulted in four clusters among housewives of equal size:

- the 'end does not justify the means' cluster;
- 'advertising is trash' cluster;
- 'advertising is rewarding' cluster; and
- the 'advertisements are better than the programmes' cluster.

For people in the first cluster, advertising manipulates the public and it is out to sell. These people are suspicious of advertising. They also believe that the only role for advertising is to inform the public about new products and services, and that the only advertising which works is that which entertains and is humorous.

People in the 'advertising is trash' cluster tend to be articulate and intelligent, often older and defensive about advertising. They are unwilling to consider how it works, and are the lightest viewers or readers. They are unappreciative of advertising, reject the concept of advertising as an art form and claim never to be influenced by it.

The 'advertising is rewarding' group critically appreciate advertising for its technical sophistication, take a lively interest in it and differentiate clearly between 'good' and 'bad' advertising. They relate the quality of the advertising message to the image of the product or service being promoted.

Lastly, the 'advertisements are better than the programmes' group prefer the advertisements, are trustful of advertising and enjoy it. This group is ideal from the point of view of the advertisers, since they neither dislike nor distrust any of the information they receive. They tend to be older, less well off and heavier viewers of television.

Offensive and fear appeals in advertising

The appeals used in advertising frequently give rise to offence. The use of sex in advertising is usually singled out for criticism, depending on the country and culture involved. In response, the advertising industry claims that, as long as advertising is not obscene and reflects society and its collective lifestyle, it is acceptable. This school of thought argues that sex portrayed in advertising, for example, is part of the contemporary world. Others argue that sex is overused and suggest that good advertising can be created without titillating.

Fear appeals have also been criticized, since their intent is to create anxiety that can supposedly be alleviated by the advertised product, service or action. Advertising using fear appeals informs consumers of the risks of not using products like deodorants and insurance, and of using products such as tobacco and alcohol (Assael, 1987: 543). Insurance companies use fear appeals in promoting health and life insurance plans, and governments use it to encourage people to stop smoking. Women appear to respond more easily to fear appeals than men, particularly in regard to anti-smoking campaigns. This suggests a segmented approach to fear appeal advertising, involving stronger fear appeals targeted at men (Quinn *et al.*, 1992: 365). These authors conclude that fear appeals are a potent form of advertising, particularly when the message strategy and content reflect market segments.

Intrusive advertising

Advertising can be intrusive, particularly when boring advertisements are used repeatedly throughout a long campaign. The number of exposures to the same advertisement is the key variable to be considered. Bursts of advertising surrounding particular events or important dates run the risk of causing irritation and make the advertising less intrusive. Humorous and entertaining advertising has demonstrated its ability to survive heavy repetition.

Advertising has an effect not only on what people buy and on their activities, but also on their attitudes and lifestyles. While there are many sources of social influence which have a causal impact on lifestyles there seems to be little argument that advertising can have a powerful effect on lifestyles and attitudes. This is demonstrated by the Lynx advertising campaign against the fur trade in the UK (Exhibit 14.2). The fur industry in the USA, through its Fur Information Council of America (FICA), has attempted to counteract these campaigns, and the effect of the recession, by defending wearing fur as a

---

EXHIBIT 14.2   Lynx advertising and ideology

It is extraordinary to think that granny would habitually hang a dead fox around her neck before venturing out of an evening, or that it was considered 'smart' for society ladies to step out looking as though they were the object of desire for a thousand amorous weasels. But the changing face of fashion and the raising of Green consciousness means that, while we still sport leather shoes, it is rare to see a fur coat in the UK – even in the coldest of winters.

The organisation most strongly associated with the decline of the fur trade in Britain is Lynx. Established in 1985 by former Greenpeace worker Mark Glover, Lynx came to prominence with the *cause célèbre* of a cinema ad that showed a catwalk model trailing blood from a fur coat. Shot by David Bailey, the campaign immortalised the line: 'It took 13 dumb animals to make this and only one to wear it.' The organisation hammered home its point that fur was an unacceptable fashion choice by commissioning posters shot by Veggies prefect Linda McCartney, with the headlines 'Rich Bitch' above a woman in a fur coat, and 'Poor Bitch' above a picture of a dead fox.

The marketing and merchandising that emerged from Lynx's Nottingham headquarters was of the then fashionable hard-nosed variety; in a matter of months, the Lynx tee-shirt became a staple garment of the socially aware wardrobe. While the RSPCA's ads relied on shock value – piles of dead dogs etc. – Lynx was branding trendy duffel bags and other consumer durables.

The targets of the Lynx campaign were the rich and vain, which gave the organisation a twin appeal for supporters of ideologically sound causes. But while the fur-buying classes bore the brunt of public disaffection, it was the trade which Lynx successfully sought to curtail. Retail figures for fur sales are not readily available but, according to the Department of Trade and Industry, the fur manufacturing business was worth some £106 million in 1985. By last year, this figure has dwindled to £15 million. The number of fur farms in the UK has also fallen – from between 50 and 60 to 27 during the past 18 months, according to Lynx. More importantly to Lynx, High Street fur retailers were hit hard, with 60 per cent going out of business.

Glover feels a measure of satisfaction at the organisation's achievements: 'It worked as a retail campaign at an almost unprecedented level. It just goes to show what the power of advertising can do.'

Source: *The Observer*, 19 July 1992: 40.

---

matter of choice. New advertising by the FICA is much stronger, with print advertisements focusing on fashion, showing women on the beach stylishly swathed in sumptuous fur, with the tag: 'The way it reveals, the way it embraces, the way it reveals. Fur more than any other fabric' (*Marketing News*, 8 November 1993: 1). The advertising battle between the two groups is likely to continue.

Advertising to children

Concerns about social issues in advertising are magnified when children are involved, since it is believed that they lack the perceptual defences of adults and are more likely to be misled or deceived. In some European countries, advertising directed at children is banned, or banned after a certain time in the evening, or there are rigid restrictions on the kind of advertising which may be used if children are likely to be part of the audience. The social need for control or regulation appears justified on the basis of research which shows that distrust of advertising increases with age among children (Ward, 1972: 38).

Growth of infomercials

A new form of direct response marketing, 'infomercials', is presented generally as a half-hour television talk show or new programme featuring a well-known celebrity, who is paid for the part and may also receive a commission on sales. It is estimated that Cher was paid about $1m for her part in the 'Aquasentials' haircare products infomercial (*Financial Times*, 5 March 1992: 18).

In the early days, 'infomercials' concentrated on selling dubious products such as miracle cures for baldness, impotence and obesity. Charges by consumer advocate groups of deceptive advertising and a decision by the infomercial sponsors themselves to police their activities have legitimized many of the infomercial activities. New terms, such as 'direct-response television' are used to distance the activity from the disreputable actions of previous years. Nevertheless the format of the informercial makes it difficult for viewers to distinguish between advertising and regular programming.

Advertisers welcome infomercials because of their low cost. A 30-minute infomercial can cost about the same as a 30-second network advertising spot because of differences in production and airtime costs (*Financial Times*, 5 November 1992: 18). The sponsors of informercials have yet to succeed in attracting well-known advertised products to their format. Cable television systems and satellite vehicles assist in the endeavour, especially in the USA. In Europe, however, progress has been slower.

Infomercials broadcast across Europe face obstacles which cause less concern in the USA: language and cultural differences, myriad legislative structures which affect product claims, and advertising and packaging which also vary from country to country. According to David Corman, president of Quantum, a company which takes programmes produced by its US parent and re-edits them for European use:

> Europeans seem to demand a higher standard of packaging, quality, value for money and services [than American audiences]. All instructions [on the products] must be translated into all languages; products must meet all regulations whether EC or local; and our programmes are dubbed into different languages, currently German, French, Dutch and Swedish. (*Financial Times*, 5 November 1992: 18)

Managing the advertising process

The advertising process consists of a number of stages. The company must decide the appropriate advertising strategy to employ, establish a set of objectives to be attained, decide the message to be communicated, select the mix of media to use, and decide the budget and advertising support necessary.

Advertising strategy

In deciding an advertising strategy, successful companies concentrate on systematically reaching the right audience with a clear convincing message. Many companies fail this test by being preoccupied with popular or fashionable advertising, whereby the audience is attracted to the theme, but not to the product or service advertised. It is necessary, therefore, to set specific communications objectives for each advertising campaign, and these should not be confused with the company's marketing objectives. Pre-testing, where feasible, to measure the probable impact of a campaign is also necessary. In such circumstances, it is necessary to have an advance plan for measuring the final results of a campaign, which should be implemented by a disinterested party.

It is generally believed that it is more effective to concentrate the promotion budget on newer or faster-growing products than to spend too much on products in decline, unless they have been upgraded in some way. Successful companies also monitor competitor advertising very closely and are prepared to respond quickly to any prolonged or unusually intensive advertising expenditure by a serious rival.

Successful companies also pay attention to the timing of their advertising campaigns. By maintaining a steady, low level of advertising throughout the year, Swissair attempts to convince the business traveller that it is always there to serve, and that its services are designed to accommodate the travel demands of the business traveller. In contrast, Kodak allocates most of its advertising budget to a few short, intensive campaigns during peak sales periods, stressing holidays and gift giving. Sometimes a combination of approaches is necessary: regular local press advertising throughout the year and a few intensive advertising bursts linked to new products, sales promotions and seasonal buying patterns.

Building and reinforcing loyalty

Generally, a single promotional event or a single advertisement has a limited effect because of recall decay among audiences. To maintain awareness, some repetition and continuity is required. Companies and advertising agencies

---

EXHIBIT 14.3   You must remember this

With loyalty to brands eroding, and new brands more difficult to establish than ever, American advertisers are casting a longing eye at the good old days. And they are hoping that consumers, jaded by today's barrage of advertising, will do the same. With so many potential customers entering, or already in, middle age, companies are trying to catch their fancy by reviving the jingles most of them imbibed with their mother's milk.

Coca-Cola is using Humphrey Bogart, Louis Armstrong and other golden oldies to sell the 'classic' version of its mainstay, Coke. Campbell's soup is once again 'mmm, mmm good'. Alka-Seltzer is re-running a series of advertisements carrying the punch line, 'I can't believe I ate the whole thing'. Rice-A-Roni is doing great business with the old slogan, 'that San Francisco treat', read over the hustle and bustle of the city's famous trams. Such tunes were so drummed into America's first television generation that most baby boomers can still hear them in their sleep. The way things are going, it is only a matter of time before a company advertises its products as 'old' rather than 'new and improved'. Corn anyone?

Source: *The Economist*, 1 February 1992: 80.

---

speak of advertising campaigns in addressing this issue. It is difficult to recognize the optimum level of promotional investment. Prolonged exposure to a particular advertisement can lead to boredom, lack of notice or even rejection. There may, therefore, be too much promotion in a given period (Aaker and Carman, 1982). With loyalty to brands eroding, companies seek alternative messages and themes to hold on to customers, even introducing a degree of nostalgia into advertisements (Exhibit 14.3).

Likewise, there may be too little promotion, resulting in a negligible impact. The management task here is to judge the minimum promotion in each period that will accomplish the promotional objectives. Applying this principle to advertising, Langhoff (1967) showed the effect of advertising repetition, an advertising campaign, on the individual by observing the impact on cognition or knowledge, while at the same time measuring affect, or the individual's feelings or disposition towards the product advertised (Figure 14.13).

The higher the cognition effect, the more likely is the product or service to be purchased and repurchased. Note that there is very little substitution between cognition and affect in contributing to the probability of a purchase. The diagram also suggests that a considerable investment in raising the level of knowledge and the positive attitude towards the product or service is necessary for any impact to occur. Only by relatively intensive investment in promotion is loyalty and product-in-use knowledge achieved, indicating that the buyer has reached the high loyalty threshold.

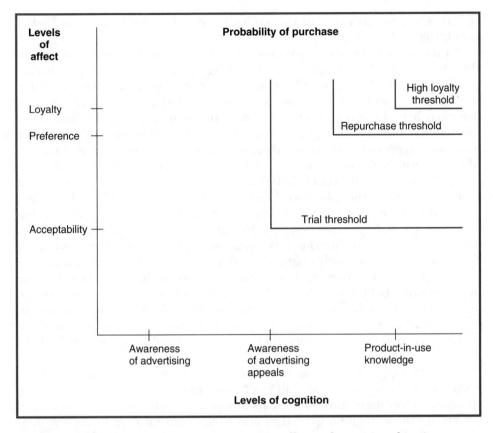

Figure 14.13 Evaluating a promotion campaign: affect and cognition objectives
(Source: Langhoff, 1967. With permission)

Advertising themes

Advertising themes can also be used to reposition a brand or launch a new version of a brand. In the mid-1980s, Maxwell House discovered that its well-known coffee brand was beginning to lose its image as it suffered from an association with cigarette smokers, nervousness and old age. Other beverages were preferred by young active people. Ordinary coffee consumption had been in decline and only decaffeinated and special coffees were increasing.

To counteract this image the company developed its premium Maxwell House Private Collection label, with whole beans and first-quality ground coffee. The company also decided to be very selective regarding the availability of the new product: it was made available in only the small proportion of supermarkets known to serve young shoppers. Advertising in magazines like *Bon Appetit* emphasized relaxation, and according to Stephen B. Morris, president of Maxwell House, it was a 'private coffee for private moods' (*Business Week*, 2 March 1987: 47).

In the car market safety and, more recently, driveability have been acceptable themes on which to base an advertising campaign. For the past twenty years or so Volvo has reflected a consistent image based on safety, reliability and durability, with the safety message becoming dominant. Until recently, there has been little reason to shift the emphasis from safety, but now other car manufacturers have begun to realize that safety sells cars and a number have been aggressively attacking Volvo's position. A statement in *Autocar and Motor* underlines the competition which Volvo now faces in its selected safety niche: 'Many cars – Mercedes, BMWs and Audis in particular – have every bit as strong a claim to the title of world's safest car' (*Campaign*, 19 June 1992: 18).

In more recent advertising, Volvo has emphasized driveability and styling in addition to safety. Advertising for the new Volvo 850 model promotes its handling and performance qualities, emphasizing the theme, 'It drives like it's alive'. Across Europe, each country has developed its own execution for the same positions of the Volvo 850 as an exciting drive. In Italy the claim is made that 'You won't believe it's a Volvo'. Driveability and safety may be the message Volvo wishes to communicate. For some products, deciding the appropriate message may be a difficult task. In periods of recession it may be very difficult to strike the right message, since there are many possible options available to the company (Lasky *et al.*, 1989).

In 1993 Burger King in the USA put its advertising account up for review. According to James Adamson, CEO of Burger King, the company was seeking an agency to promote the company's 'back to basics' philosophy. According to Adamson, 'we sell hamburgers, fries and Cokes, and we have to get the message out that we do it better than anyone else' (*Business Week*, 29 November 1992: 80). In 1993 Burger King's share fell to 6.5 per cent of the fast-food market, down from 8.5 per cent in 1986 (Figure 14.14). Throughout the period 1974–93 Burger King changed its advertising theme and emphasis quite a number of times in an endeavour to seek a winning theme.

Advertising agency support

At some stage, the company draws upon the support of advertising agencies. Good advertising usually means using outside agencies. Successful companies tend to be meticulous in their choice of agency, and very critical in evaluating creative work and media plans submitted. In most cases, advertising agencies provide a very extensive service to marketing companies. To use these services effectively, the company must understand the functions performed by advertising agencies and must be able to brief the agency to ensure that the service provided is precisely what the company wants.

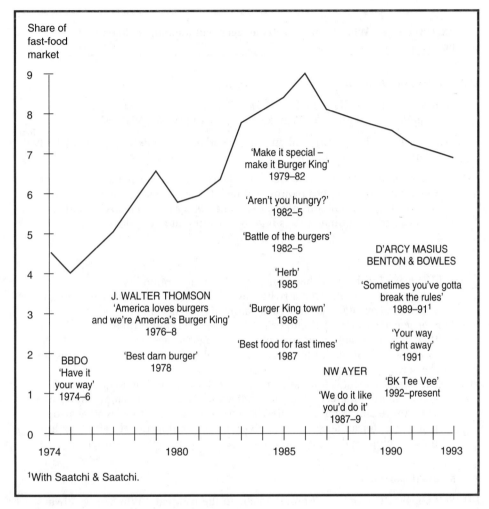

Share of
fast-food
market

'Make it special –
make it Burger King'
1979–82

'Aren't you hungry?'
1982–5

'Battle of the burgers'
1982–5

'Herb'
1985

J. WALTER THOMSON
'America loves burgers
and we're America's Burger King'
1976–8

'Burger King town'
1986

'Best food for fast times'
1987

D'ARCY MASIUS
BENTON & BOWLES

'Sometimes you've gotta
break the rules'
1989–91[1]

'Your way
right away'
1991

BBDO
'Have it
your way'
1974–6

'Best darn burger'
1978

NW AYER

'We do it like
you'd do it'
1987–9

'BK Tee Vee'
1992–present

[1]With Saatchi & Saatchi.

Figure 14.14   Burger King advertising messages, 1974–92
(Source: Adapted from *Business Week*, 29 November 1993)

Functions of advertising agencies

An advertising agency consists of marketing and market research people who decide with the client the most effective message to be communicated to the public. It also consists of copywriters and artists who create memorable and persuasive methods of communicating this message. There are media planners and buyers in advertising agencies whose jobs it is to decide the most effective means of communication for the message. Advertising agencies also have television, radio and print production specialists to ensure high standards of reproduction. John Fanning, managing director of McConnells Advertising

---

EXHIBIT 14.4   What is an advertising agency: Functions defined and analyzed

---

Creative department

Self-image: I'm really too talented for all this. I should be writing a real book or painting real pictures. Why are everybody else such Wallies?

Rest of agency view: Overpaid and underworked. How do they get away with coming in late and I don't?

Objective assessment: Like all creative activities the job is demanding and often lonely, and it does require real talent. It is not enough any more to be 'professional'. There are increasing demands for more creativity and for a greater understanding of consumer behaviour and psychology.

Account executive

Self-image: Too busy to have any. In perpetual motion trying to extract a coherent brief from clients (who never know what they want to say) and explain the result to the creative department (who never know how to say it).

Rest of agency view: An 'empty suit' – spend so much time at lunch that they forget or are incapable of presenting the agency's work with the drama and delicacy it deserves. Can't decide whether they are working for the agency or the client.

Objective assessment: Mentally and physically demanding. Requires considerably more intellectual capacity than a well-known 'empty suit' jibe would indicate. Real talent lies in letting either client or creative people take credit for an account executive's ideas – unfortunately any length of time developing this attribute leads to severe personality disorders.

Media department

Self-image: The only *real* professionals in the company. Why are we always the last to be given credit for a job well done?

Agency in Dublin, has provided a succinct summary of the nature of an advertising agency (Exhibit 14.4).

Briefing the advertising agency

In briefing an advertising agency, the company must provide answers to four questions:

- what is the product or service?
- who will buy it?

Rest of agency view: Why are media presentations so boring?

Objective assessment: By some criteria, the *most* technical area in the agency. Probably have more right to feel neglected than other departments. Clients in particular should give this area more attention – they could save more money here than by trying to cut corners on production costs.

Accounts/data processing

Self-image: The agency would collapse if we weren't as efficient and hard working as we are.

Rest of agency view: Why do they delay paying my expenses as if it was their own money?

Objective assessment: Still regarded as a 'Cinderella' department, but recessions and the cash flow and other financial problems facing some agencies have forced a much more professional approach to agency financial management.

Production

Self-image: The only *real* professionals in the company – cannot understand the appalling level of technical knowledge of account executives and creative people nowadays. When I was young, account executives actually knew the difference between a block and a bromide.

Rest of agency view: Why can't they just get on with the job instead of explaining the technical bits?

Objective assessment: Rapidly changing communications technology and the client's concern over production costs have meant a much more important role for this department.

Source: Adapted from John Fanning, 'We know what it is – but what does it do?' Advertising – Special Report, *Irish Times*, 28 March 1985: 21.

- why should they buy it?

- when should the product be promoted?

The answer to the first question describes the product in detail – size, shape, colour and varieties – and emphasizes performance factors – the product gives better value for money, or has exclusive physical features (e.g. is easy to open). The answer to the second question defines the target market for the product. It may be necessary to describe the typical consumer in qualitative and statistical terms.

The answer to the third question, 'why should they buy it?' gives reasons for purchasing the product, adding psychological appeals to the rational reasons above. Recall Elmer Wheeler's dictum, 'Emphasize the sizzle, not the sausage.' The 'why' refers to the sizzle, the 'what' to the sausage. The answer to the fourth question, 'when will the product be promoted?' refers to product availability, the launch date for the campaign and the probable duration of the campaign. The answer to this question has direct implications for the available budget.

Wilson Hartnell Advertising and Marketing Ltd, a Dublin-based marketing communications company, has developed a basic brief to assist advertisers in preparing a briefing document (Figure 14.15). The basic brief contains a capsule which attempts to summarize the whole brief; it is the essence of the communication. Note the concentration on the simple, direct, but fundamental questions: what, who why, and when.

For advertising to be effective, it should establish preference in the consumer's mind for one particular brand, to persuade them to try it and to continue using it. The Unilever Company has developed ten principles for good advertising (Figure 14.16). Advertising should be presented in such a way that it addresses the needs of consumers: the case for purchasing a product or service should be presented as the consumer sees it, not as the manufacturer sees it. Good advertising concentrates on memorable reasons for trying a product – the emphasis is placed on selected consumer benefits to avoid a scatter-gun approach which would diffuse the impact of the advertising. The company should also emphasize the product attribute with the greatest appeal to

What is the product?	'Gobble' is a new candy bar which combines the consistency of toffee with the fruit flavours of strawberry, lemon and orange, each coloured appropriately. Available in two sizes, regular and jumbo size, it is long lasting and has a strong fruity flavour. Unit prices 12p and 16p.
Who will buy the product?	Children 9–14 years – urban bias.
Why will they buy the product?	'Gobble' has an unusual new taste. It is reasonably priced, long lasting and provides a real change from the existing range of countline options.
When will they buy it?	Launch September. ? second phase January – February.
Budget	£30,000 (including production costs).
Capsule	You must experience the unique, fruity taste of 'Gobble' – a taste that lasts and lasts!

Figure 14.15   The basic brief: a typical example

(Source: *Input*, 2.2, April 1977, a newsletter produced by Wilson Hartnell Advertising and Marketing Ltd)

- Consumer / user oriented

- Concentrates on one selling idea

- Emphasizes most persuasive idea

- Presents unique / competitive feature

- Involves the consumer / user

- Is credible and sincere

- Is simple, clear and complete

- Associates the selling idea with the brand name

- Exploits the medium

- Makes the sale

Figure 14.16   Principles of effective advertising
(Source: Adapted from material produced by the Marketing Division of Unilever Company).

consumers, which implies pre-testing of advertising and research to ensure that this property exists in the advertisement.

Successful advertising contains a promise of some unique benefit, quantity or quality not available elsewhere, and it appeals to the consumer's own interest by attempting to solve some problem experienced by the consumer. Advertising must also be credible and sincere. The advertising must be perceived to be honest and should not mislead.

Most advertisers also attempt to avoid misunderstanding by saying what is intended, so advertisements should be simple, clear and complete. It is also necessary to link the brand name with the central selling idea. Some advertising fits better with one medium than another, so it is important to take full advantage of the physical characteristics and the mood to which the particular medium predisposes consumers. Finally, for advertising to be good, it should establish among consumers a wish to buy so strong that simple merchandising techniques will be sufficient to serve as a gentle reminder.

Evaluation of advertising effectiveness

Value of advertising

Advertising is valuable from the perspective of the advertiser and the audience. Companies expect advertising to have strong positive communications effects and advertisements should also be able to sell. Advertising therefore has identifiable value to the company, but it is also of value to consumers.

Value of advertising to the company

In examining the value of an advertisement to the company, it is necessary to distinguish between reach and frequency. Reach is defined as the net number of people exposed one or more times to the company's advertising campaign. Frequency is the number of exposures received by the average person who is reached at least once by the campaign. The reason for distinguishing between reach and frequency is that advertisers place different emphasis on each at different times. If, for example, the objective is to convey information about a special offer then awareness is sufficient and it is necessary for the message to be received only once to motivate an appropriate response. In this case, reach is more important than frequency.

If, however, the company is attempting to build brand acceptance and believes that this is a function of the number of times the brand is mentioned, the advertiser is likely to seek frequency rather than reach among a particular group of consumers. The average number of times each consumer is reached is more important than the number of people reached.

Value of advertising to consumers

The value of advertising to the consumer and the degree to which it is perceived to be truthful varies from one product to the next, depending on the kind of information the consumer needs when choosing a product (Davis *et al.*, 1991). These researchers have divided products into four broad categories, each of which they claim is advertised in a different way: search goods, short-term experience goods, long-term experience goods, and goods where experience is of little value (Table 14.2). For search goods, consumers do not depend on the manufacturer to supply evaluative information, since they can easily find out for themselves if the goods are worth buying. Advertising of such products is likely to be honest because lies or exaggerations will be obvious. Advertising of such products will tend to be low.

Consumers are usually not able to learn all they need to know about short-term experience goods before buying them, but they will know very soon after the first purchase. An example would be non-alcoholic beer or instant coffee. Again the advertiser must be accurate in advertising these products, but heavy advertising of such products signals to consumers that the products will be a permanent feature in the market and that shopping for a better alternative is unlikely to be worthwhile. Many of the fast-moving food brands fall into this category. The fact that Coca-Cola is willing to spend a very large sum of money to hire Elton John and much more to broadcast him around the world tells consumers that the company will continue to make Diet Coke available for a long

TABLE 14.2   Advertising expenditures for different kinds of product

Product categories	Advertising–sales ratios (% sales)
Search goods	
Curtains	1.17
Jeans	0.19
Jewellery	0.38
Category average	1.79
Short-term experience goods	
Facial tissues	3.14
Instant coffee	7.09
Lager	1.26
Category average	3.56
Long-term experience goods	
Analgesics	12.39
Cat food	4.90
Hair conditioner	20.29
Category average	5.04
Goods where experience is of little value	
CD players	0.26
Dishwashers	5.41
Motor cars	1.58
Category average	0.41

Source: Adapted from Davis *et al.* (1991: 12). By permission of Oxford University Press.

time to come. Whether Elton John actually likes the drink or whether the advertisement is trendy and manipulative is probably irrelevant to most consumers.

In contrast, consumers cannot discover the quality or usefulness of long-term experience goods, such as skin-care creams and motor oil, without buying them repeatedly over a long period of time. In the case of such products, the consumer benefits greatly from truthful advertising. At the same time, advertisers could get away with misrepresentation or exaggerated claims for a long time before buyers discovered the ruse. But eventually, misleading advertising is discovered. It is not enough to claim that such products are better than rival products; it is important that consumers are convinced that the advertiser will keep them in the market for a long time by advertising more than rivals. For these products, the amount spent on advertising may be just as important as the direct advertising message. This suggests that advertising will be heaviest for products such as shampoo, pain relief pills or pet food which the consumer can only evaluate over the long run.

Products for which experience is of little value are mostly bought just once or very infrequently. Examples are refrigerators and washing machines.

Consumers seek truthful advertising, but because low-quality producers could misrepresent their goods and be undetected for a long time, such goods are lightly advertised.

Regulation of advertising

Advertising in Europe is controlled by domestic laws, national voluntary rules imposed by advertising standards authorities, and more recently by EU directives that are legally binding within all member states of the EU. These latter deal with health and safety issues and with the difficult-to-define 'cultural integrity of European broadcast media'. But there are many differences in these regulations. In some countries, Germany is an example, advertising is condoned on state television only if it appears in long-block broadcasts within clearly specified time periods. In other countries, such as Luxembourg, a defined proportion of advertising material must be produced locally. Certain categories of business are prevented from advertising at all on television: for example, retailers in France.

Several self-regulatory bodies representing the advertising industry, advertisers, agencies and media owners already exist in EU countries. In general, the rules of these bodies reflect the recommendations of the International Code of Advertising Practice produced by the International Chamber of Commerce.

Regulation of advertising to children and the responsibility for public authorities to protect a nation's health are not solely the prerogative of EU countries. Many other countries operate similar restrictions, and when the media deviate from accepted norms a great deal of public concern is caused. This occurred when the Camel Tobacco Company launched its Joe Camel advertising campaign in the USA a few years ago (Exhibit 14.5).

EU advertising directive

EU directives on advertising are aimed to prevent misleading advertising, but allow governments of member countries to introduce their own legislation to achieve the desired objective. At present, EU directives affect some television advertisements, the use of firm- or brand-specific comparisons and misleading advertising. The most important directive to date is that affecting cross-border television broadcasting. This directive, which came into effect in 1992, guarantees freedom of transmission in broadcasting across national borders and lays down minimum rules on the nature of the advertising. Each country is responsible for applying the directive, which sets limits on the airtime devoted to commercials, bans television advertising of tobacco and prescription drugs, and provides guidelines for alcohol advertising, advertising to children and sponsorship of television programmes.

EXHIBIT 14.5   I'd toddle a mile for a Camel

From 1987 to 1990, R.J. Reynolds Tobacco Co. saw its share of Camel filter cigarettes jump from 2.7 per cent to 3.1 per cent – some leap for an ageing brand when US cigarette sales are sinking. The No. 2 tobacco manufacturer resuscitated the brand largely through a four-year-old campaign featuring a cartoon character of its camel mascot. Now, it's looking as if the extra market share may have come at a steep price.

Anti smoking crusaders and health officials have repeatedly criticised the cartoon dromedary as an effort to target underage smokers. After long denying these charges, Reynolds now also must fend off dramatic new evidence published in the December 11 issue of the *Journal of the American Medical Association*. The journal reports that old Joe Camel, as the character is called, entices kids to light up. The studies cited in JAMA no doubt will bring other tobacco companies into the debate, not to mention alcohol marketers who also have come under fire for ads that may appeal to kids.

According to the studies published in JAMA, teenagers are far better able than adults to identify the camel logo (Table 1). One study even found that kids as young as three identify the cartoon with cigarettes. More chilling: one study concluded that Camel's share of the market of underage children who smoke is nearly 33 per cent – up from less than a pecentage point before the Old Joe campaign got rolling. 'We're hoping this information leads to a complete ban of cigarette advertising,' says Dr Joseph R. DiFranza, a University of Massachusetts Medical School researcher who worked on one of the studies.

Reynolds contests the studios' results. It cites a US Office of Smoking & Health study issued this year that says eight per cent of kids aged 12 to 18 who smoke choose Camels. The average Camel smoker, Reynolds says, is 35. 'Just because children can identify our logo doesn't mean they will use the product,' a Reynolds spokeswoman says.

TABLE 1   Old Joe has caught fire with teens

	Students (%)	Adults (%)
Have seen Old Joe	97.7	72.2
Know the product	97.5	67.0
Think Ads look cool	58.0	39.9
Like Joe as a friend	35.0	14.4
Smokers who identify Camel as favourite brand	33.0	8.7

The above are the results of a survey of 1,055 students ages 12 to 19 years, and 345 adults, ages 21 to 87 years, on Camel's Old Joe advertisements.

Source: *Business Week*, 23 December 1991: 28.

Role of public relations

Public relations is part of the company's communications mix. Companies use publicity and public relations for very specific purposes which, if used effectively, complement the other elements of the communications mix.

Publicity and public relations

Publicity refers to free promotion of the company's products and services in the media. It is usually the result of a newsworthy aspect of the company's activities being captured by the media. Media coverage of items such as the development or introduction of a new product by a company falls into the realm of publicity. It takes the form of press releases, press conferences and press exclusives. Companies frequently orchestrate their own publicity in situations where the event or circumstance has broad appeal. Publicity may help to promote a positive image of the company among relatively detached third parties. Like public relations, publicity may be managed in the company itself or by a specialist company.

Public relations, which is closely related to publicity, is also part of the company's communications mix, and is used to inform selected groups about the company and its products with a view to building a basis of understanding and trust for product-specific communications activities. Public relations, described as being good at getting credit for something, refers to activities aimed at creating, maintaining or enhancing the company's reputation among groups, such as the government, financial institutions and employees, whose goodwill and understanding promote its future prosperity. Large, well-established companies whose prosperity is tied to the development of the economy at large pay special attention to public relations. Public relations may be managed within the company or on an agency basis by a specialist company.

Nature and scope of public relations

Public relations is any non-personal communication in the form of news about the company or its products which is carried by the mass media. Public relations helps the company to build a reputation for its products and an image for itself. Well-planned public relations activities can benefit the company by obtaining media exposure for products or the company itself which would cost much more if advertising were used.

Public relations has been defined as 'the deliberate planned and sustained effort to establish and maintain mutual understanding between an organisation and its public' (Institute of Public Relations, 1986). It is concerned with the behaviour of the company, its products, services and people, which gives rise to public knowledge about the organization. Public relations is not 'free advertising' or 'propaganda', but rather a communications vehicle which must be planned and implemented as part of a marketing communications strategy. Public relations helps to develop a personality for the organization.

Public relations activities at company level are usually aimed at corporate image building among the general public, stakeholders, government officials, consumer and advocacy groups, and suppliers (Nakra, 1991). Public relations aimed at selling a product is usually targeted at customer segments, influencers and the general public.

Public relations is generally restricted in the types of objective which can be achieved. Because it uses news stories in the media, there is little opportunity to present persuasive reasons for buying a product or service. It is impossible to make a direct appeal to customers to buy the product. Public relations in these circumstances plays an educational role rather than a persuasive role in the marketing communications process.

Developing relationships with media

Many companies develop a fear of the media, sometimes with good reason. The role of the media is to communicate newsworthy items to their customers. Companies often have newsworthy items to report which are positive and show the company in a good light as a good corporate citizen. At other times, the company may be less fortunate in regard to what has become newsworthy. In both cases, the relationship with the media must be managed. Sometimes these relationships are very well managed and provide a lesson to others (Exhibit 14.6).

EXHIBIT 14.6   Public relations

The United States swimming team gave a massed press conference the other day and did it awfully well. So they should: they have been given official written instructions on how to be interviewed. This is summarised thus: 'One; take control of your interview. Have two or three points you want to get across to the media and hammer away at those points. Repetition may be necessary. Two; look and act like a champion. Comb your hair, wear your sweats, smile, sit up, speak up, establish eye contact, avoid um, uh, and you know. Three; be positive even when things didn't go your way. Relax and enjoy your interview. Four; finally, remember that it is your interview. You control what you say and the direction the interview is taking.'

If Kenny Dalglish would like a copy of that, he has only to give me a call.

Source: *The Times* (London), 25 July 1992: 36.

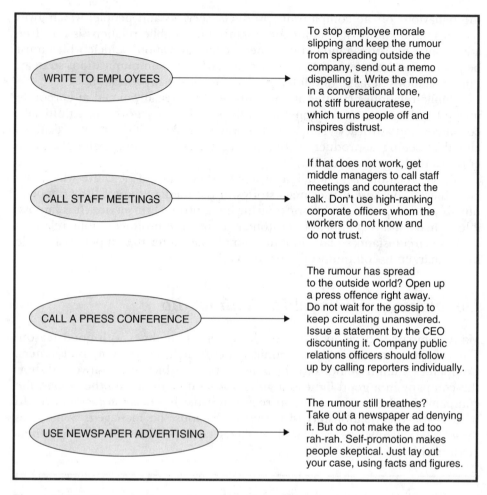

To stop employee morale slipping and keep the rumour from spreading outside the company, send out a memo dispelling it. Write the memo in a conversational tone, not stiff bureaucratese, which turns people off and inspires distrust.

WRITE TO EMPLOYEES

If that does not work, get middle managers to call staff meetings and counteract the talk. Don't use high-ranking corporate officers whom the workers do not know and do not trust.

CALL STAFF MEETINGS

The rumour has spread to the outside world? Open up a press offence right away. Do not wait for the gossip to keep circulating unanswered. Issue a statement by the CEO discounting it. Company public relations officers should follow up by calling reporters individually.

CALL A PRESS CONFERENCE

The rumour still breathes? Take out a newspaper ad denying it. But do not make the ad too rah-rah. Self-promotion makes people skeptical. Just lay out your case, using facts and figures.

USE NEWSPAPER ADVERTISING

Figure 14.17 Four ways to quash an untrue rumour
(Source: *Business Week*, 24 December 1990: 80)

Managing community relations

In the past, public relations companies focused on refurbishing a company or product image after a catastrophe occurred. The newer approach aims at stopping gossip about an event that has not occurred, and may never occur. Taking on a rumour is hazardous, since denying a rumour has the perverse effect of also spreading it. Furthermore, some rumours do actually come true, in which case silence is advised. But, where possible, companies are advised to refute ill-founded rumours quickly on the basis that facts, fully disclosed, will drive out the distortions of rumour. Professor Irv Schenkler of New York University advocates a series of steps to stop a false rumour: memos to employees, meetings, press conferences and advertising (Figure 14.17).

Rumours take root because in some way they are plausible. They should be addressed immediately and comprehensively (Exhibit 14.7). Deciding whether to use advertising, sales promotion or public relations is usually difficult for the company. Public relations works best to provide long-term solutions to

---

EXHIBIT 14.7 Boxed in at Jack in the Box

The tragedy began with a $2.69 'Kid's Meal'. On January 11, Michael Nole, 2, happily tore into the dinnertime cheeseburger bought for him at the Jack in the Box restaurant on South 56th Street in Tacoma, Wash. The next night, the boy, stricken with severe stomach cramps and bloody diarrhoea, was admitted to Children's Hospital & Medical Centre in Seattle. Ten days later, Michael died of kidney and heart failure.

Crisis on such a scale is never easy going, but Jack in the Box's response was hardly smooth. True, the company's 12-person crisis team, working from a plan devised in the mid-1980s, quickly scrapped nearly 20,000 pounds of hamburger patties prepared at meat plants where the bacteria were suspected of originating. It also changed meat suppliers, installing a toll-free number to field consumer complaints, and instructed employees to turn up the cooking heat to kill the deadly germ.

But it took nearly a week for the company to admit publicly its responsibility for the poisonings. Even then, the admission seemed half-hearted. At a Seattle news conference, Jack in the Box President Robert J. Nugent attempted to deflect blame – first criticizing state health authorities for not telling his company about new cooking regulations, then pointing a finger at Vons Cos., which supplied the meat. That performance didn't win many public-relations points. Instead, nervous customers defected to other burger joints in droves.

What could Jack in the Box have done? Closing every store for a week or more for a thorough inspection – a strategy recalling Johnson & Johnson's nationwide withdrawal of Tylenol capsules in 1982 – would have effectively dramatized the company's concern, says Richard Zien, who represented the chain in the mid-1980s and is now president of ad agency Mendelsohn/Zien Advertising Inc. Furthermore, Zien says, Foodmaker should have extended immediately the apologetic ads it ran in Seattle to other important cities. 'Their biggest market is in LA,' says Zien. 'Do you think we don't read newspapers in LA?' More than anything else, Foodmaker should have moved faster. Its offer to cover victims' hospital costs came two weeks after news of the first poisoning. And the ad campaign, featuring Chairman Jack W. Goodall Jr, simply didn't keep pace with rumour and gossip. Jack in the Box will eventually regain lost customers, but that could take time. Three years ago, Perrier Group was slow to acknowledge problems with benzene in its water. US sales have returned only slowly.

Source: *Business Week*, 15 February 1993: 36.

---

rather general problems. Public relations is unlikely, therefore, to provide an effective solution to a sales decline problem or being bypassed in the advertising stakes by a competitor. A combination of advertising and sales promotion would be preferable in such circumstances.

Sponsorship in marketing

A casual observer of the marketing communications scene might be forgiven for believing that sponsored cultural, social, sporting and educational events

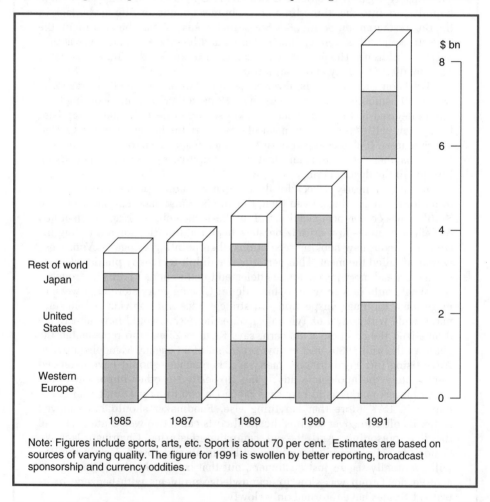

Note: Figures include sports, arts, etc. Sport is about 70 per cent. Estimates are based on sources of varying quality. The figure for 1991 is swollen by better reporting, broadcast sponsorship and currency oddities.

Figure 14.18 Total sponsorship by region

(Source: 'A survey of the sports business', supplement to *The Economist*, 25 July 1992: 8. Copyright, *The Economist*, London 1994)

are now the way companies have of advertising themselves, their products and their services. In recent years, there has been much growth in marketing expenditures by sponsors of such events (Figure 14.18). A sponsor has been defined by the *Oxford English Dictionary* as 'an advertiser who pays for a broad-

---

EXHIBIT 14.8   The Maecenas touch

They are true amateurs, training for the world's most famous (if often famously tedious) event for such people – 16 healthy young men and two girls who will cox them in the annual Oxford and Cambridge boat race on the Thames. And over their crests is blazoned the name of a brand of gin. True, they are unlabelled during the race itself, but surely the fuddy-duddy British must be appalled. No longer. If it moves, they know, it's sponsored – and if it is not sponsored, it probably should not be there. That is sport today, except that the thing sponsored may be immobile, indeed intangible: a player, a horse, a yacht, a team, a league, a stadium, an event, a series of events or even a non-event, like some sports broadcasts.

Nor does today's sponsor just pay its money and get its brand-name on a cap or a racket or a few boards placed round the ground for the cameras. The cameras are crucial, but the well-run sponsorship gets closer than that. For the sponsored, it may bring not just money but equipment and technical help: Seiko will pour money into timing the Barcelona Olympics, Kodak into aiding photographers there. For the sponsor, it means chances for spectators to sample products, skyboxes at the baseball stadium, hospitality tents near the 18th green, opportunities for the company's clients (or its own dealers) to meet, be photographed with, or maybe play a few holes with the great man.

But much sponsorship is image-promoting, always hard to quantify. The trade is working on that, though. And one thing is sure: well-chosen sponsorship buys more screen-time per dollar than commercials. What sort of time, though? Not only must the image be right; it should not, ideally, be struggling with a host of rival images before the same camera lens.

Clutter like this is common in advertising. Yet wise sponsors – and event-promoters – eschew clutter. The 1980 winter Olympics had 381 sponsors, each paying peanuts and getting peanuts back. Peter Ueberroth, the man who made Olympics pay, cut the figure at the 1984 Los Angeles summer games to fewer than 40. Then the IOC took a centralising grip. Barcelona has 12 IOC-picked global sponsors (paying $175 million in all, plus many services in kind), nine big players/service-providers from Spain and 14 mostly local, smaller ones.

In the search for the right image, one thing matters even more than the sports: the success. There is an obvious risk in sponsoring teams or players: only a few can do well. Fine, if your pick is Mr Mansell, or Michael Jordan, basketballing genius of the Chicago Bulls. For sponsors that can afford it, a well chosen – or specially created – event, well managed, is a safer, if usually far costlier bet.

Source: 'Sports business survey', *The Economist*, 25 July 1992: 7–8.

cast programme into which advertisements of his are introduced'. Commercial sponsorship has been defined as 'an investment, in cash or in kind, in an activity, in return for access to the exploitable commercial potential associated with that activity' (Meenaghan, 1991: 36). The sponsor obtains the audience exposure potential which the activity sponsored has, and the image associated with the activity in terms of how it is perceived. As with advertising, the company invests money in sponsorship for an expected return on the investment.

Sponsorships reflect self-image

Successful sponsorship means that the activity sponsored must reflect the company's vision of itself and its products and services. Some activities are acceptable and some are not. In recent years, sports sponsorship has become very significant in total communications expenditures. The emphasis on sport has been acknowledged by commentators and academic writers (Abratt and Grobler, 1989; Marshall and Cook, 1992). A company may decide to sponsor sports but not the arts, individuals but not teams, rock music but not classical. These are general policy criteria which are company specific. In recent years, there has been a rush to sponsor sporting activities, which possibly indicates a shift in lifestyles which attract certain kinds of commercial sponsorship (Exhibit 14.8).

Assignment questions

1 How would you describe the impact of promotion on a buyer?

2 What are the more important considerations in setting communications objectives?

3 Describe the components of the communications process and the potential difficulties the manager may encounter in attempting to influence it.

4 What is pre-testing in relation to advertising?

5 Discuss the factors affecting the firm's choice of advertising medium.

6 Discuss the use of advertising in stimulating the demand for a product.

7 What are the advantages of 'push' and 'pull' communications in the marketing channel?

8 Why have social issues in advertising become so important in recent years?

9 How is advertising used to build the brand and brand loyalty?

Annotated bibliography

Aaker, David A., and John G. Myers (1975) *Advertising Management*, Englewood Cliffs, NJ: Prentice Hall.

Cateora, Philip R. (1993) *International Marketing* (8th edn), Homewood, Ill.: Richard D. Irwin.

Howard, Wilfred (ed.) (1990) *The Practice of Public Relations*, Oxford: Heinemann Professional Publishing, chapters 3 and 5.

Greener, Tony (1990) *The Secrets of Successful Public Relations*, Oxford: Butterworth-Heinemann, chapters 1, 2 and 7.

Jefkins, Frank (1988) *Public Relations Techniques*, Oxford: Butterworth-Heinemann.

Kotler, Philip (1994) *Marketing Management* (8th edn), Englewood Cliffs, NJ: chapters 21 and 22.

References

Aaker, David A., and John G. Myers (1975) *Advertising Management*, Englewood Cliffs, NJ: Prentice Hall.

Aaker, R.L., and J.M. Carman (1982) 'Are you over advertising?', *Journal of Advertising Research*, **22** 4, 57–70.

Abratt, R., and P.S. Grobler (1989) 'The evaluation of sports sponsorship', *International Journal of Advertising*, **8**, 4, 311–26.

Assael, Henry (1987) *Consumer Behaviour and Marketing Action* (3rd edn), Boston, Mass.: Kent Publishing Co.

Davis, Evan, John Kay and Jonathan Star (1991) 'Is advertising rational?' *Business Strategy Review*, **2**, 3, 1–23.

Engel, James F., David T. Kollat and Paul W. Miniard (1993) *Consumer Behaviour* (7th edn), Fort Worth, Tex.: The Dryden Press.

Institute of Public Relations (1986) 'Definition of public relations', London: Institute of Public Relations.

Langhoff, Peter (1967) 'Options in campaign evaluations', *Journal of Advertising Research*, **7** 4, 41–7.

Lasky, Henry A., Ellen Day and Melvin R. Crask(1989) 'Typology of main messages strategies for television commercials', *Journal of Advertising*, **18**, 1, 36–41.

Lavidge, Robert J., and Gary A. Steiner (1961) 'A model for predictive measurements of advertising effectiveness', *Journal of Marketing*, **25**, 6, 59–62.

Marshall, D.W., and G. Cook (1992) 'The corporate (sports) sponsor', *International Journal of Advertising*, **11**, 4, 307–24.

Meenaghan, Tony (1991) 'The role of sponsorship in the marketing communications mix', *International Journal of Advertising*, **10**, 1, 35–47.

Nakra, Prema (1991) 'The changing role of public relations in marketing communications', *Public Relations Quarterly*, **36**, 1, 42–5.

Quinn, Valerie, Tony Meenaghan and Teresa Brannick (1992) 'Fear appeals: segmentation is the way to go', *International Journal of Advertising*, **11**, 1, 355–66.

673

Rossiter, John R., Larry Percy and Robert J. Donovan (1991) 'A better advertising planning grid', *Journal of Advertising Research*, **31**, 5, 11–21.

Vaughn, Richard (1980) 'How advertising works: a planning model', *Journal of Advertising Research*, **20**, 5, 27–33.

Vidale, M. and H. Wolfe (1957) 'An operational research study of sales response to advertising', *Operations Research*, **5**, 3, 370–81.

Ward, Scott (1972) 'Children reactions to commercials', *Journal of Advertising Research*, **12**, 2, 37–47.

Direct marketing

15

Introduction

This chapter introduces and explains:

- the nature and significance of direct marketing as a means of communication in marketing management;

- operational aspects of direct marketing;

- the benefits of direct marketing;

- how an interactive marketing system works;

- the role of direct marketing in prospecting for new customers;

- the relationship between direct marketing and retailing;

- ways of increasing customer loyalty;

- the application of databases in direct marketing;

- growing privacy and environmental concerns; and

- how to integrate direct response advertising with image advertising.

One of the key elements of marketing management is the communication of value to customers. In the previous chapter, mass communications were examined. This chapter examines how direct marketing, which targets individuals, may be used to communicate the value to actual and potential customers. The key element of direct marketing is the development and maintenance of a detailed customer database specifying historical buying behaviour, which may be statistically manipulated to produce market segments that can then be directly served with a customized marketing package.

The growth of direct marketing may be attributed to the rising cost and possible ineffectiveness of mass communications and the possibility of an accurate focus on individual customers in direct marketing. Direct marketing requires a sophisticated up-to-date database capable of being exploited by modern computer, mail and telecommunications technologies. Allied to these developments are developments in direct response advertising, which can be used to support direct marketing activities. Direct marketing has become an important aspect of marketing communications and has been used successfully in many different circumstances.

Having studied this chapter, you should be able to define in your own words the phrases listed above, and you should be able to do the following:

1. Define direct marketing in operational terms as part of an interactive marketing system.

2. Specify the ways in which direct marketing can be used to build personal customer relationships.

3. List the communications benefits of direct marketing.

4. State the relationship between direct marketing and advertising.

5. Demonstrate how it can be used to acquire new customers and establish loyalty among existing customers.

6. Recognize the role of computer and telecommunication technologies in the development and maintenance of essential databases.

7. Specify ways of integrating direct marketing and direct response advertising with image advertising.

Growth of direct marketing

A major influence on the growth of direct marketing has been the increasing cost of television advertising. Increased fragmentation in the market and the need to identify more specific lifestyles and interests have also resulted in mass media becoming less effective for all aspects of the communication task. The value of direct marketing is relatively easy to assess, given that a small local area can be targeted before a large-scale campaign is decided. Besides the selective nature and cost effectiveness of direct marketing, it is also personal in that it can reach people in their homes or businesses with a message that is of personal interest to them.

Compiling an accurate database is essential for direct marketing. Without such a database, accurately targeted audience listings cannot be produced. Modern software technology enables companies to store detailed information on the lifestyles of large numbers of consumers classified in various ways. Data protection and the right of individuals to privacy have, however, become important marketing management issues in recent years.

High-technology customer relationship

Direct marketing requires a maintained database of information to record names of customers, actual and potential, and a means of maintaining direct communication with the customer. It is a form of marketing in which the providers of products and services bypass all intermediary channels of distribution in reaching the buyer. It is different from direct mail, direct response advertising and sales promotion. Direct marketing is aimed at building long-term relationships with customers (Cross, 1992: 33). In doing so, it exploits high-technology communications.

Catalogue companies were the first to recognize the power of building direct relationships with customers. In more recent times, a number of financial houses have followed their example. Other service organizations are now

---

EXHIBIT 15.1   What's in a relationship?

The problem with the old mass-marketing philosophies is that they create or maintain distant relationships. Prospects and customers are the passive recipients of one-way communications from manufacturers. Strategies are based on numbers games – frequency of ad impressions rather than measurable results. The customer's needs for recognition and affiliation with the manufacturer are ignored and sometimes abused.

The new marketing recognises that the highest levels of human needs – those concerned with involvement and individualisation – can be addressed as part of the seller–buyer relationship. People may respond to an American Express Gold advertisement that appeals to their desire for uniqueness and distinction. But once they've signed up, they want ongoing recognition of that uniqueness.

A database makes it possible to recognise customers as individuals, to get them involved as active participants in the relationship, engaged in a direct dialogue with you. Your interactions in this relationship are driven not by a numbers game, but by information about each prospect or customer as an individual.

Source: *Direct Marketing*, October 1992: 35.

---

using the approach, including airlines, car-hire companies, hotels and holiday resorts. Retailers and manufacturers are also beginning to experiment with direct marketing. Customer databases based on direct marketing help to establish close relationships between the company and the customer (Exhibit 15.1).

Nature of direct marketing

Direct marketing consists of three components: direct response advertising, which leads to the sale; the development of an effective customer database; and the direct building of customer relationships to increase sales and profits. Direct marketing is an approach to marketing which is driven by a database which implies that the company knows who its customers are, and that it communicates with them in appropriate ways through enhanced and refined means of communication. It is a highly targeted approach to marketing, which also implies that the company knows who are not among its customers. Customer information management is critical and two-way communication with customers may lead to high loyalty.

There are three requirements for effective direct marketing: a sophisticated computerized database; an effective delivery medium; and an efficient delivery system (Figure 15.1). The database is the engine which drives direct marketing. It enables the company to differentiate between customers and non-customers and to communicate with them in different ways. Mass communications can be a very blunt instrument. Direct marketing hones mass communication into a refined and precise tool.

In addition to an effective database, it is also essential to have an efficient medium and an efficient delivery system. The delivery medium requires access to sophisticated printing services which can personalize mailings and target customers at competitive prices. An efficient delivery system usually means having an effective postal system which is competitively priced.

The value of direct marketing in the 1990s is due in no small way to the revolution in contemporary technologies, most notably data processing and telecommunications, both of which are becoming more widely available through becoming cheaper.

Interactive marketing system

Direct marketing, for the Direct Marketing Association in the USA, has been defined as an interactive system of marketing that uses one or more advertising media to effect a measurable response and or transaction at any location (Stone, 1982). A number of faults have been found with this definition (Bauer and Miglautsch, 1992). First, all advertising and sales promotions can be

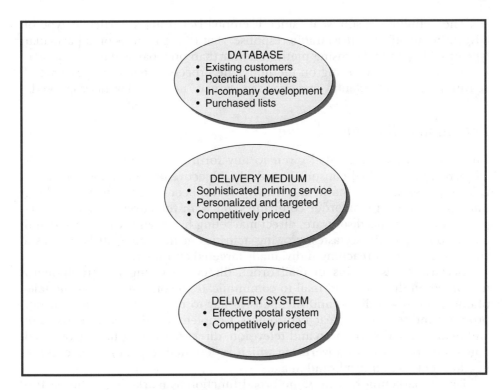

Figure 15.1 Requirements for effective direct marketing

viewed as an interactive system of marketing, since consumers can react in terms of brand recognition, recall, purchase intent and purchase. Indeed, personal selling is perhaps more interactive than direct marketing, since the salesperson interacts with the prospect or customer in a person-to-person context.

The second limitation with this approach to defining direct marketing is that most consumer reactions to advertising can be measured in terms of recognition, recall and purchase intent as well as actual purchase. Direct marketing does, however, measure individual-level responses. Third, to say that the response can occur at any location simply means that the consumer is not required to travel to a fixed retail location. This does not help to distinguish between direct marketing and direct selling and telemarketing.

The above definition was extended to 'require the existence and maintenance of a database' (Hoke, 1988: 30). This definition is an operational definition as it extends the focus from direct response advertising to include the collection and maintenance of individual consumer responses in a computer database. Such a database contains classification details on consumers, but also contains transaction information. The database may contain demographic and psychographic profiles as well. The distinguishing feature of this aspect is that data at the individual consumer level are obtained.

The definition is still weak, since it emphasizes using a particular type of advertising to effect a measurable response: that is, the focus is on a particular type of selling and advertising method rather than on a particular type of marketing. By narrowly focusing on methods, the process of marketing as a set of activities designed to identify and satisfy consumers' needs and wants is ignored.

Definition of direct marketing

Direct marketing is the label given to any form of communication directly addressed to individual consumers with the objective of generating a measurable response to some marketing activity. It has been in existence for a long time. It began with mail-order companies, but with the advent of cheap computers and customized software, direct marketing has been revolutionized and has become one of the fastest-growing activities in marketing. It is seen as a cost-effective way of reaching individually targeted customers.

Because of its origins in mail order, direct marketing has traditionally depended on the press and mail to communicate to consumers. Now the telephone is a quick, reliable and inexpensive way to request information, order products and services, or reach customers. Coupled with the recent expansion and democratization of radio and television, direct marketing has encouraged a new style of broadcast advertising which is designed to generate a response in addition to building a brand image.

Direct marketing has the same broad function as marketing – the performance of the entire range of activities required to provide customers with products, services and ideas desired – but in addition requires a maintained database of information to record the names of actual and potential customers and a means of maintaining direct communication with customers (British Direct Marketing Association, 1989). Direct marketing attempts to communicate the value to customers using sophisticated targeting methods.

Direct marketing in operational terms

Recognizing the weakness of the various definitions of direct marketing, Bauer and Miglautsch (1992: 10) propose the following operational definition: 'Direct marketing is a relational marketing process of prospecting, conversion and maintenance that involves information feedback and control at the individual level by using direct response advertising with tracking codes.' This definition, which emphasizes the operational content of direct marketing, consists of four properties:

- relational marketing;
- the process of prospecting, conversion and maintenance;

- information feedback and control at the individual level; and

- direct response advertising with tracking codes.

The first property refers to some minimum of regular repeat contact with customers by direct response advertising, mailings or telephone calls to customers and repeat orders from customers. Prospecting, or name acquisition, is an on-going activity of finding new customers to build the customer file. The second major on-going activity is conversion, which focuses on changing the status of a respondent to a higher disposition towards purchase and loyalty. The third on-going activity refers to the need to maintain customer interest and purchase.

Information feedback at the individual level refers to the detailed customer information and transaction data that constitute the company file on customers. When transaction data are analyzed and used in marketing decisions, they become information feedback. Companies can develop customer segmentation models to select particular customers for various types of special contact.

Lastly, direct marketing involves direct response advertising with tracking codes (Bauer and Miglautsch, 1992). Connecting direct response advertising to tracking codes is the basis for developing a customer file of transaction information for future marketing decisions. The tracking code should be unique for each direct response advertisement in order to identify the source of the response. For press advertising, the tracking code is usually an alphanumeric code printed on the mail-in coupon that identifies the specific advertisement in a specific media vehicle issue. For direct mail and telephone orders, similar procedures are followed. Some kind of tracking code is necessary to monitor, measure and analyze responses to a particular direct response advertisement and a set of direct response advertisements for customer lifetime value analyses.

Benefits of direct marketing

Direct marketing is an approach to marketing that involves the company knowing who its customers are, understanding that not everybody is a customer, communicating in relevant ways with customers and prospects, enhancing and refining the relevance of the communications and doing all of the above through a database. Successful direct marketing can be accomplished with any and all combinations of media and distribution channels. Direct marketing is not, therefore, a medium, or a channel, or a methodology; it is a comprehensive approach to marketing and to identifying, reaching and serving the needs of customers.

The principal benefits of any direct marketing technique are the accuracy with which customers can be reached, due to the targeting involved in using computer databases; the measurable effect of direct marketing, allowing the

681

company to determine its impact in the short term; the quality of the message, due to the ability to provide sophisticated copy appropriately printed; and the low cost of the delivered message, especially compared with advertising (Figure 15.2).

Direct marketing communications and advertising

The attractions of direct marketing for many companies are that short-term sales effects are easy to quantify, whereas the short-term effects of mass communications such as advertising are less easy to measure. Advertising, as was seen in the previous chapter, addresses longer-term brand values and is essentially a social phenomenon because it is public. Direct marketing by its nature, however, is essentially a private form of communication which ignores the social aspect of consumption.

Direct marketing is like advertising in a number of respects. Properly used it can reinforce the brand values created and maintained by advertising. Like advertising it is also an above-the-line expenditure, since it represents actual outlays as opposed to sacrificing profit. In both of these respects direct marketing is different from sales promotion, which is a 'below-the-line' expenditure which may erode brand values if used excessively.

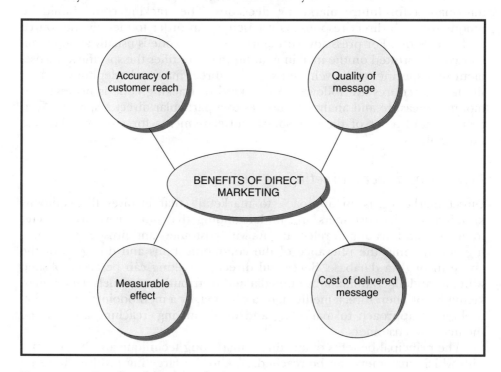

Figure 15.2 Benefits of direct marketing

Building personal relationships

Direct marketing is not just concerned with the first order or sale. The aim of most direct marketing activities is to create and encourage a personal relationship between the company and its customers which lasts a long time. Such relationships encourage people to become increasingly receptive to information about new products and services. Skilfully prepared and well-designed mail shots are an ideal way to build company–customer relationships.

The banks and other financial institutions have discovered the value of direct marketing, and increasingly the manufacturers of expensive consumer products such as cars are also using it. Dell Computer Corporation provides an

---

EXHIBIT 15.2   Dell: mail order was supposed to fail

When executives at Dell Computer Corp. decided to march on Europe in 1987, they knew they had to win over a sceptical public. European customers had never bought big-ticket items through the mail – the only way Dell planned to distribute them. 'In every country, they told us mail order would not work,' says Andrew R. Harris, senior vice-president for international operations at the Austin (Tex.) company. The Texans, deep discounters, also found that European buyers have a long established prejudice: High price equals good quality, low price means shoddy.

Yet Dell has stunned rivals and nay-sayers by going from no European sales to some $240 million for the year ending 3 February. European sales, 95 per cent to business customers, have become a key part of Dell's revenue picture. They will constitute nearly 30 per cent of the estimated $870 million Dell rings up this year, almost double the 1988 share. Even Dell is surprised by its growth spurt, particularly among corporate buyers. 'Having bought one or two times, they find they need better service – or may not need the extra features of an IBM or Compaq machine,' says Elizabeth Montgomery, a computer market researcher at Britain's Inteco. 'They just need something reliable and Dell fits the bill.'

To get doubting European buyers to give its PCs a try, Dell waged an intense 'education programme' – really a series of ads in computer magazines and direct mailings throughout Britain and the Continent. The campaign, printed in several different languages, stressed Dell's reputation for quality, service and price. The tagline in most ads: 'It's Best to Be Direct.'

For Dell, the pickings have been best on the Continent, where PC prices, set by European companies such as Groupe Bull's Zenith Data Systems and Olivetti, were double those in the USA. As Dell has swept into Germany, France, Sweden, Italy, the Netherlands, and Finland, rivals have had to slash their prices. 'Dell is sort of a beacon,' Harris says. That may be overstating it a touch. But considering that most people dismissed Dell when it arrived, he can be excused for beaming.

Source: *Business Week*, 20 January 1992: 56.

---

excellent example of the value of direct marketing based on price competition as a way of entering a new market for a relatively expensive durable product (Exhibit 15.2). Companies like Dell can very quickly achieve a share of the market through price competition where incumbents are vulnerable. However, a 'cherry picking' exercise is very difficult to sustain for durable products like computers, where after-sales service and advice are required. As Dell discovered, it is difficult to use direct marketing to expand sales beyond a limited range. Nevertheless, direct marketing is becoming a central feature of the communications mix of many organizations.

Computers are now so accessible and easy to use that company sales people can easily monitor and keep track of their customers and prospects with greater precision than ever before. Simple personal computers with the appropriate software can help companies to communicate the right message to the right people at exactly the right time.

Role of direct marketing in prospecting

Direct marketing is designed to encourage loyalty and increased sales. At the same time, it is not sufficient to work with existing customers; it is also necessary to attract new customers not yet in the market and the customers of competitors. Prospecting, seeking new customers to add to the existing database of customers, is fundamental to direct marketing, since it helps to provide a source of future sales and revenues.

Prospecting, or customer and lead acquisition, has been referred to as 'front-end' marketing, since the people involved in the company are different from those at the 'back end'. The responsibility of the front-end marketing team is to acquire new, first-time customers, acquire new leads or enquiries, and convert leads into first-time customers, to maximize the number of new names on the customer list while minimizing the cost of building the list (Schmid, 1992: 39). Few direct marketing companies expect to make money in the prospecting side of the business. The central objective is to locate the highest-quality names at the lowest possible cost (Figure 15.3).

Direct marketing can also be used in circumstances where it is difficult to identify possible customers. In the USA, the Upjohn Company successfully used an integrated direct marketing approach in prospecting for new customers for its new prescription hair-loss treatment drug, Rogaine, even though doctors have to prescribe the drug, which is sold in pharmacies (Hoke, 1992). Upjohn realized that there was no list of people with hair-loss problems, so it had to develop its own list and an effective way of reaching afflicted people. A direct marketing campaign was the solution.

Direct marketing and retailing

There is a great deal of evidence available which suggests that many fast-moving consumer goods companies are placing their direct marketing activities

684

FRONT-END MARKETING	
Objectives	**Measuring performance**
• Acquire new, first-time customers • Acquire new leads • Acquire new enquiries • Convert leads and enquiries into customers • Minimize cost of building customer file	• Cost per customer • Cost per lead • Cost per name • Cost of conversion

BACK-END MARKETING	
Objectives	**Measuring performance**
• Convert first-time buyers into repeat buyers • Maximize number of mailings to customer list • Maximize profits	• Growth of repeat purchaser file • Number of customer mailings per year • Return on investment • Return on sales • Value of a customer over three years

Figure 15.3   Front-end, back-end concept of direct marketing
(Source: Schmid, 1992: 39. Reprinted by permission of John Wiley and Sons Inc.)

into the promotions budget. These companies see increased promotion budgets as a way of creating action at retail level, as customers become accustomed to using other forms of marketing activity such as sales promotion, event marketing and direct marketing. In such cases, these forms of marketing communication are included with sales promotion, and direct marketing loses its identity as a valuable means of marketing communication. In Chapter 19 sales promotion is shown to have a legitimate tactical role in marketing as a means of producing immediate short-run sales. Direct marketing, in contrast, is aimed at building long-term customer relationships.

Packaged goods companies have always been interested in direct marketing, but merely as a sales promotion tool. This is frequently in conflict with the general view that direct marketing is a strategic way of developing long-term marketing relationships. Through sales promotions, fast-moving packaged goods companies have accumulated many names and addresses. This does not reflect a direct marketing approach, and direct marketing in such circumstances is being strategically driven by the sales promotion side of the business rather than by the need to build longer-term relationships and loyalty.

Direct marketing process

In general, the process of direct marketing involves a manufacturer, a direct marketing company, a channel and a consumer (Figure 15.4). Many direct

685

marketing companies do not manufacture the products they sell, but of course they may. The direct marketing firm sends an advertising message, usually in the form of a direct response advertisement, to the consumer. This message is usually transmitted through the mass media, press, radio and television. It is possible, however, for the message to be sent person-to-person directly or by telephone. Direct marketing may, therefore, use any channel of communication to transmit the direct response advertising message.

The consumers who decide to respond usually transmit their responses by mail or by telephone to the advertiser. If an order is placed, a tracking code becomes part of the transaction to identify the specific sales message and source of the consumer's name and other details. When the direct marketing company has received the order, the merchandise is sent directly to the customer through the fulfilment channel, usually the mail system.

Increasing customer loyalty

Customers can be very loyal to a product, brand or company, or they may express no loyalty at all. The degree to which they are loyal depends on a number of factors, but loyalty itself is most important for the direct marketing company as repeat purchases and lifetime sales are the life blood of companies engaged in direct marketing. Direct marketing may be used to increase customer loyalty in a number of ways (Figure 15.5).

At the first stage, awareness is the important feature. At this point, customer loyalty does not exist, since the customer is unaware of the company or its products. Awareness results from obtaining a greater 'share of mind' than competitors. Appropriate images may be created through advertising. At the awareness stage, advertising is perhaps the most powerful communications medium. Advertising also helps to identify the values in the product or service being offered. By appealing to higher-level needs, advertising can produce interest in the product or service, desire for it and action. By identifying the

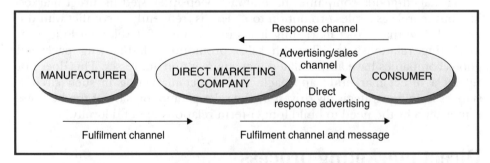

Figure 15.4 Direct marketing process: message, response and fulfilment channels
(Source: Adapted from Bauer *et al.*, 1992: 15. Reprinted by permission of John Wiley and Sons Inc.)

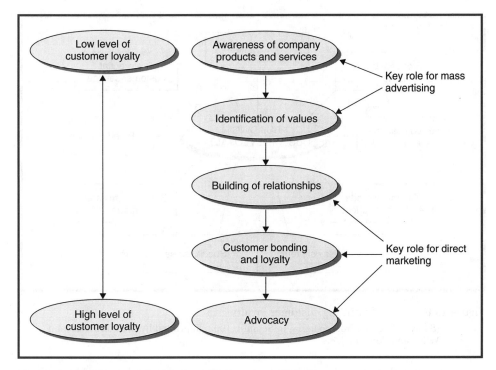

Figure 15.5   Direct marketing increases customer loyalty

value and communicating it in this way, advertising obtains strong product identification. The key role for mass advertising is evident in these two early stages in the development of customer loyalty.

During the next stage, a relationship between the company and the customer is established. There is a direct exchange of benefits. The company provides customized products, services and information. In return, customers provide more information about themselves and their needs. Greater loyalty is established and sales increase. At this stage, the first important role for direct marketing arises. The opportunity now exists for two-way mail or telephone communication based on a database.

In the next stage, the company attempts to establish a strong link between the customer and the company by integrating the company's products and services with the customer's lifestyle. During this period the relationship between company and customer is highly interactive. The relationship becomes a private one, leading to a customized, exclusive treatment. Regular two-way communication becomes essential to this exclusivity. There are numerous ways of building customer loyalty through direct marketing (Figure 15.6). Many of these are very familiar. Frequent buyer benefits, gifts and preferred services are perhaps the more popular. Direct marketing activities allow them to be packaged in a customized way that can be tailored to the needs of the individual

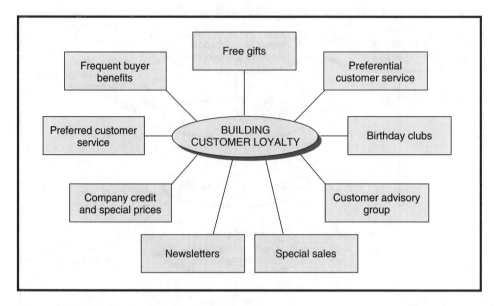

Figure 15.6   Ways of building customer loyalty
(Source: Adapted from material in Schmid, 1992. Reprinted by permission of John Wiley and Sons Inc.)

customer with the objective of building and strengthening loyalty. Mass advertising is less important at this stage and may detract from the relationship.

The expected result of customizing the marketing programme in this way is the establishment of trust and close relationships between the company and its customers. These valued relationships receive commercially significant expression in word-of-mouth promotion and advocacy for the company's products and services. When customers reach the stage of being advocates for the company's products and services, the ideal partnership has been established (Exhibit 15.3).

Evolution and use of marketing databases

Database marketing was recognized as a separate marketing entity when companies found that they could statistically analyze their customer data to produce sophisticated segmentation models, which allowed them to offer a given product or service only to those people who demonstrated a high probability of purchase. As a result, database marketing was recognized as an effective way of soliciting sales and of qualifying sales prospects.

Information technology in marketing

Modern information technology may be used to assemble and manipulate data on demographic trends and competitors. In this way, the company may be

---

EXHIBIT 15.3   An ideal partnership

The US is where some of the best examples of direct marketing stem from. Huggies nappies, a Kimberley Clark brand, had been coming under increasing pressure from Procter and Gamble's Pampers, the market leader. It determined to fight a rearguard action.

Targeting existing and expectant mothers, it built up a database using pre and post-natal clinic lists, targeted surveys and on-pack data capture. Kimberley-Clark's agency, The Rapp Collins Partnership, then created a series of nine magazines, offering practical and relevant advice, entitled *The Beginning Years*. It incorporated all the best known sales techniques: a 'member-get-member' or in this case 'mother-get-mother' device; money-off coupons and a staggered three-monthly distribution schedule so that parents would always get the relevant issue. The results, according to Rapp Collins' UK marketing director, Jonathan Clark, show that the company was justified in choosing this route. 'Brand share of Huggies has increased significantly since the incorporation of a direct marketing programme,' he says, 'while loyalty tracking studies indicate there is less brand-switching and, therefore, greater incremental sales for the brand.'

Two years on, the programme is still running, and has been refined in the process. 'It's such a natural,' says Clark. 'It provides all the help and reassurance that parents need.'

Source: *Marketing*, 17 September 1992: 24–5.

---

able to identify new market niches, develop new products and avoid inventory pressures. As part of this process, many companies now provide a call-free telephone service for customer enquiries and complaints. From the information collected in this way, it is possible to develop ideas for product and service improvements and for new products. Many companies also use computer technology to short-list potential customers before contacting them by telephone. The combination of the two technologies, computers and telecommunications, can help reduce the size of the sales force and reduce costs.

An increasing number of companies supply their sales people with portable computers so that they can receive messages faster and enter orders directly, both of which mean quicker deliveries, better cash flow and less paperwork. By creating exclusive computer communications with customers for order entries in this way, and by the exchange of product and service data, the company develops loyal customers and makes it difficult for competitors to attract the company's customers away from it.

Computer and information technology in the form of video discs and other software may be used to train staff, especially sales staff. New products and services can be explained to sales people in this way. Indeed, the use of video material in promotions is growing rapidly. Many customers, especially for industrial products and services, appreciate being able to see the product and service in use as they consider it for adoption. A promotional video can help in this regard.

Information technologies make whole new operations possible. The application of information technologies and especially the machine-read universal product codes has allowed express delivery companies to extend their services to traditional freight businesses requiring security and constant information on products as they move through the market logistics system.

Identifying decision makers

Modern information technology, especially database marketing, is a dynamic tool which requires constant updating and maintenance. A database list which is not maintained ceases to be a useful marketing tool. It is essential to keep the list current and to add new names to it on a regular basis. To have currency, a database must be updated with information on new prospects who are emerging as possible customers. At the same time, the names of people no longer interested in the product should be dropped from the database. Some companies send newsletters or information sheets on a quarterly or six-monthly basis to customers, asking for feedback on which products were of greatest interest. In mailing product literature, companies usually include a 'bounce back' card giving prospects an opportunity to request additional information or a sales call. In addition, respondents are given the opportunity of having their names removed from the list.

The most successful database marketing companies use their lists for telemarketing surveys to monitor market trends and identify emerging customer needs. The time gained and the speed to market allows such companies to outpace rivals who may be only beginning to recognize the gap in the market. Telemarketing also allows the company to keep the customer list up to date.

The telephone is just one of a number of ways companies have of maintaining a current database. Many companies frequently advertise in the media, use public relations efforts, and attend trade shows and exhibitions to maintain contact with existing customers and to reach new ones. Usually it is necessary to develop a communications strategy balanced between the need to reach short-term and longer-term prospects (Figure 15.7). A typical approach might be to adopt a narrow-angle vertical focus through various media to reach short-term prospects. This vertical or narrow-focused effort concentrates scarce resources where short-term results are likely to be greatest. A wide-angle horizontal approach using the same media is necessary to identify new emerging segments with sales potential. By following this procedure, the company ensures that its database is maintained with a balanced mix of short-term and long-term prospects for each segment served.

Databases also offer the possibility of better customer service. Accurate database marketing allows the firm to fulfil orders more rapidly, track orders, and provide information and technical assistance and to develop relationships.

690

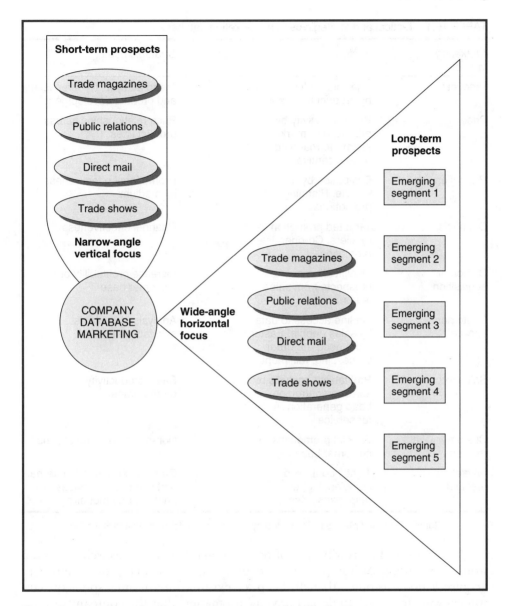

Figure 15.7 Balanced communications mix to identify prospects

Relationship management implies continuing contact with customers between sales cycles. Direct marketing databases can also support strategic marketing decisions as well as tactical decisions. Roberts (1992) has analysed a range of marketing variables which can be supported both tactically and strategically by the use of database marketing (Table 15.1).

TABLE 15.1   Tactical and strategic uses of marketing databases

Marketing variable	Tactical uses	Strategic uses
Product	Analysis (Sales, margins by product line, region)	Trend analysis for forecasting and product development
Price	Price sensitivity by product and market segment. Planning price incentives	Price relationships across product lines
Promotion	Evaluation by medium vehicle. Planning promotions	Promotional effectiveness by medium
Channels	Targeted promotion to retailers. Co-operative promotions	Channel effectiveness
Customer acquisition	Qualification of prospects from sales leads	Increase profitability of customer base
Customer service	On-line access to data by sales people. Faster, more accurate order processing, fulfilment	Analysis of contacts, satisfaction levels
Sales force	Profitability analysis by salesperson/region. Lead generation. Access for service	Sales productivity programmes
Customer relations	Special promotions to customer base	Non-sales communications
Marketing research	Tightly controlled samples, higher responses rates	Combine survey with internal and external databases for analysis and modelling

Source: Roberts (1992: 54). Reprinted by permission of John Wiley and Sons Inc.

In regard to the growing use of database marketing, it is as well to heed a word of warning. Although it is true that it can cost many times more to acquire a new customer than to keep an existing one, money spent on customers who are about to depart anyway, no matter what the company does, is wasted. It becomes important, therefore, to maintain the database, to keep it fresh and to ensure that it is relevant.

It is also necessary to determine where most of the company's effort is being devoted: on generating additional sales and revenue, on keeping existing customers, or on reducing expenses by avoiding contacting people who simply will not buy. As Richardson (1993) suggests, non-marketing to customers deserves perhaps as much attention and resource dedication as the concept of database marketing itself (Exhibit 15.4). According to Richardson, 'the cheapest and most beneficial way to double your sales response rate is to get the same number of responses while cutting the size of your mailing in half' (Richardson, 1993: 6).

Applications of databases in direct marketing

According to Roberts (1992: 52), database marketing is 'the application of statistical analysis and modelling techniques to computerised, individual level data sets, used (a) to support the development of cost effective marketing programmes that communicate directly with targeted customers and prospects, and (b) to track and evaluate the results of specific promotional efforts'. This excludes many marketing research activities in addition to many other marketing management and support activities. Database marketing involves a planned

---

EXHIBIT 15.4   Sometimes database 'non-marketing' is the way to go

'Not' marketing to people who won't buy could save the company more money than additional sales revenue might generate. Thus we have data-base 'non-marketing'. Do you know what junk mail is? Junk mail is doing all the right things for all the wrong people. The creative was good; the message was well-conceived; the pricing was right; the timing was well-correlated to the season; and the product was well-made. Unfortunately, 97 per cent of the people you sent the mailing to had no need, interest, or desire for the product.

Right now you may be saying to yourself, 'Everybody knows that you shouldn't market to people who won't buy. We already spend lots of money refining our lists and building models to find people who will buy.' Notice where the emphasis is: finding people who *will* buy. Have you ever built a model to identify the people who won't buy? Are you still sending promotional material to people who have not purchased anything from you in the last 12 months, or the last 24 months, or ever? Have you deleted their names from your data base? If not, why not?

Customer retention is a hot topic today. It closely relates to the concept of 'the lifetime value of a customer'. In many companies, a lot of time and money is spent trying to identify customers who are likely to close their accounts. Having identified these potential attriters, the company usually begins a proactive campaign aimed at getting them to stay. In many cases, this produces desirable results. However, if the proactive retention programme succeeded in keeping 25 per cent of the customers from leaving, it failed at preventing the other 75 per cent from leaving. The company spent 75 per cent of its budget trying to save customers who probably were going to cease being customers no matter what the company tried to do for them.

Source: Richardson (1993).

---

communication with targeted customers and prospects over an extended period to promote repeat purchases of related products and services.

The application of a database in direct marketing implies a statistical modelling of customer behaviour through in-depth quantitative analysis. Contacting everybody on a mailing list is not database marketing; rather it is necessary to manipulate the database statistically first. It is also necessary to note that the data are collected and maintained at the individual level: that is, at the level of the individual customer, household or business organization. The analysis is performed and the marketing activity is designed at the level of the individual unit.

The database also allows the company to monitor and evaluate the effectiveness of each contact with customers or prospects, which enables better management decisions regarding product design, pricing, segmentation and media choice. A carefully planned programme of marketing communications can also be used to cross-sell, upgrade and otherwise promote the sale of substitute and complementary products and services.

Media revolution and direct marketing

The media revolution which is taking place is beginning to transform conventional media into direct response media. Telecommunications is the agent of change. The press, television or outdoor advertising is likely to produce a measurable response in terms of the extent of dialogue that arises, and in regard to the continued development of the database itself. The telephone is a powerful means of acquiring new customers.

Role of direct mail

Direct mail is a mass medium which includes any form of promotional or informational material sent by mail to a target audience. It includes direct response advertisements, sales advertisements and discount coupons. Direct response advertisements sent in the mail are a very specific form of direct mail advertising.

Direct mail is still the most favoured medium for customer communications. The primary use of direct mail is to maintain and reinforce brand loyalties. Because of environmental and privacy issues, direct mail is likely to become more accurate, attractive and customer value driven. Otherwise public policy constraints will force it into a minor position.

Focused communications medium

Direct mail is a specific communications medium employed by companies to reach target markets. Mail is sent directly to a person whom the company wishes to influence. The receiver has the option of examining the material on receipt or deferring it for more leisurely study. Products and services advertised may be ordered through the mail or by telephone. Direct mail is characterized by three factors (Stone, 1982):

- it makes a definite sales offer;

- it contains all the information necessary to make a decision; and

- it contains a response device such as a mail coupon or telephone number.

For direct mail to be successful, it is necessary to have accurate mailing lists readily available, and the postal and telephone system must be cost effective and able to access the company's target market. Financial institutions have been very extensive users of direct mail, since they can easily use their databases to reach customers.

Direct mail is the most commonly used mass medium for direct response advertising. In preparing direct mail for promotional purposes, the company recognizes that some forms of promotional material are likely to be better in obtaining qualified leads than others. In addition to the mail, direct marketing companies use other forms of advertising, such as magazine inserts, press advertising and the broadcast media.

Concerns for privacy and environment

The average US household receives 4.3 pieces of mail each mailing date (Rosenfield, 1991: 2). In reality, good direct mail prospects receive much more than the average. The result of this barrage of mail is diminishing response rates, a concern about the environment, and a concern for privacy. While concern for the environment and privacy is less in the USA, the impact of the deluge of direct mail in many European countries, most notably Germany, has given rise to considerable debate.

Concern for the environment and concern for privacy place direct marketing companies on a collision course, since as they attempt to address one of these problems they exacerbate the other (Figure 15.8). By moving along the horizontal axis, direct marketing companies display a greater concern for the environment. But targeting customers, actual and potential, means collecting and using information about them. Increasing data collection and usage demonstrate less concern for the privacy issue. A trade-off is required. A high concern for privacy means junk mail and less concern for the environment, while a high concern for the environment means a low concern for privacy. The danger from the viewpoint of direct marketing companies is that the public authorities will regulate direct mail in a way which will damage customer communications.

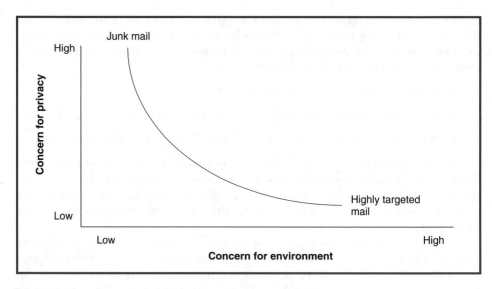

Figure 15.8   Direct mail privacy–environment trade-off

Role of telecommunications

The widespread availability of telephones in most western European countries and in North America has ensured that this means of communication can be used as a powerful medium for transmitting advertising messages and transacting an exchange. The efficiency and economy of the telephone system can be instrumental in reducing the transaction costs of doing business. The diffusion of telephones in a market indicates the number of customers who can directly call in orders by telephone in response to a direct mail offer (Akhter, 1988). A typical mail offer provides information about a product or service and at the same time encourages a positive response by the mail or telephone.

As income increases, in-home shopping becomes more attractive to consumers because of the reduced time committed to shopping (Lumpkin and Hawes, 1985). Other factors are also important. The increased participation of women in the workforce influences the growth of direct mail. Using income, availability of telephones and participation of women in the workforce as explanatory variables, Akhter (1992: 27) found that income and telephone possession are significantly related to per capita direct mail volume in the twelve EU countries. According to Akhter, a possible explanation for the lack of statistical significance of women in the workforce can be sought in the strategies of companies engaged in direct marketing: it is likely that they are targeting households regardless of the occupational status of women (Akhter, 1992: 28).

Direct selling and telemarketing

Neither direct selling nor telemarketing should be confused with direct marketing. This section, which is based on an evaluation of Bauer and Miglautsch (1992: 15–17), attempts to explain the differences among direct marketing, direct selling and telemarketing, three terms in common usage and often confused.

Direct selling is often confused with direct marketing because of the word 'direct'. Avon Cosmetics and Encyclopaedia Britannica are examples of direct selling companies. Direct selling, once very popular in the West, is now being used quite frequently in eastern Europe (Exhibit 15.5). In such companies, the selling is often carried out indirectly through agents or commission sales people who have little status or contact with the 'direct selling' company. Indeed, the producers of the cosmetics and encyclopedias rarely know who their end customers are, and they are usually not in a position to monitor the responses of consumers. Instead, they sell their products through commission agents or to sales intermediaries who are independent contractors (Bauer and Miglautsch, 1992: 15–17). These sales people are the ones who sell 'direct' to consumers (Figure 15.9). Usually the sales message and response are transmitted directly between people and no permanent record is kept by the firm

---

EXHIBIT 15.5   Direct selling to make up for lost time in Poland

Until 1990, eastern Europe was *terra incognita* for Jonas af Jochnick. As chairman of Oriflame, the Brussels-based cosmetics firm, af Jochnick concentrated on direct selling throughout western Europe, Mexico and Chile. But once the communist regimes collapsed in eastern Europe, he jumped at the opportunity to start selling in a region which had been starved of consumer goods.

His first venture was in Poland. Instead of exporting his wares to the country, af Jochnick took a gamble. He bought Karmeila, a Polish cosmetics factory, and has never looked back. In just three years, Oriflame has blossomed in Poland. It now has more than 50,000 sales assistants who spend their time criss-crossing the country, encouraging Poles to buy a wide range of cosmetics without leaving their homes. 'It has been a remarkable development,' said af Jochnick. Last year, Oriflame's turnover in Poland and other countries in eastern Europe rose to £6.4m compared with the previous year's turnover of £2.7m. Its total turnover was £83.6m.

The eastern Europe consumer can be put off by the barrage of television and newspaper advertising at a time when most countries are facing high unemployment. Af Jochnick has tried to overcome this problem in three ways. He makes sure the consumer can afford his products – through careful market research. In addition, his staff, mostly women, are hired locally, which means that customers are not intimidated by the thought of a foreigner stealing his or her job.

Source: *Financial Times*, 7 October 1992: 15.

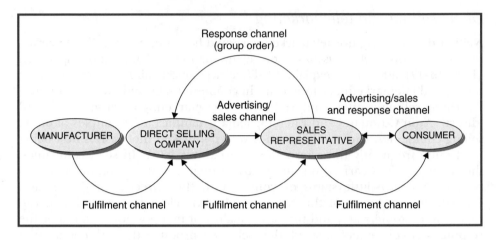

Figure 15.9 Direct selling process
(Source: Bauer and Miglautsch, 1992. Reprinted by permission of John Wiley and Sons Inc.)

about the transaction. As may be seen in the diagram, the communication is interactive between the salesperson and the consumer. Only if a complete history of transactions is maintained on each customer and prospect is direct marketing involved.

Most of the activity in telemarketing of consumer products is merely person-to-person telephone selling (Figure 15.10). In telemarketing, rarely is the sales transaction permanently recorded and used as input for future telemarketing decisions and activities. As no customer files are developed and maintained, no on-going relationship develops between the company and customer. Telemarketing is not direct marketing, therefore, but simply 'cold call' telephone selling in the old tradition of door-to-door selling.

Business-to-business telemarketing may, however, be a part of direct marketing, since companies which use a telephone to contact prospects and customers may be using direct marketing (Bauer and Miglautsch, 1992: 15–17) if they:

- use a tracking code for relating the sales message to the sales transaction information;

- permanently record the transaction information; and

- use it for future marketing activities, such as database maintenance.

The key point to note is that direct marketing involves collecting and maintaining a complete history of customer transactions, to be used in designing future marketing activities to be applied in reaching and serving these customers. This database of historical transactions and consumer behaviour should be capable of statistical manipulation on a computer to segment the market better with a view to accurately targeting customers and prospects.

698

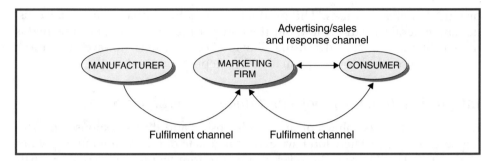

Figure 15.10 Telemarketing process
(Source: Bauer and Miglautsch, 1992. Reprinted by permission of John Wiley and Sons Inc.)

Direct response advertising

The Direct Marketing Association in the USA defines direct response advertising as 'any paid advertising where the intention is to solicit a direct response by including a response device'. A direct response advertisement must contain a definite offer, information necessary to make the decision and specific directions for response, usually including a toll-free telephone number or a free-post response coupon (Stone, 1982). Direct response advertising is one of the promotional techniques used in direct marketing.

Direct response and image advertising

Direct response advertising is quite different from image advertising. It is interactive in that an offer is made and a response device is provided. There is a greater opportunity to segment the advertising messages, since direct response advertising is usually sent to individual consumers. By monitoring response rates, the company may more objectively measure the success of its communications, since respondents and non-respondents can be identified.

Direct response advertising, with its emphasis on the solicitation of quantifiable responses, such as sales, enquiries and leads, is very much part of the sales school (Woodside and Motes, 1980) rather than the hierarchy of advertising effects school (Lavidge and Steiner, 1961). The sales school argues that advertising effectiveness should be measured on its ability to generate sales, whereas the hierarchy of advertising effects school argues that the objective of advertising is to move consumers from awareness to preference to purchase.

Direct response advertising is not normally used to create product or service differentiation through images. Rather the copy in direct response advertising is usually replete with details, examples and clever anecdotes (Mitchell, 1986). Advertising copy tends to provide greater detail regarding potential product benefits and uses. The production costs for direct response advertising are generally relatively low, but the cost per thousand audience reached is higher than with image advertising. The level of wastage is, however, lower as a targeted approach through the mail or by telephone is used.

Integrating direct response and image advertising

For decades the disciplines of image advertising and direct response advertising have been segregated and have existed in a state of mutual toleration (Peltier *et al.*, 1992: 41). There is, however, a pressure to integrate the two, due partly to a recognition of a weakness of each, especially when used alone. The relative efficiency of image advertising is threatened by increasing production and placement costs, while the effectiveness of direct response advertising is in jeopardy due to rising costs, media saturation, tune-out factors and consumer perceived abuses (Peltier *et al.*, 1992; Russell and Lane, 1990: 336). Hence, the integration of the two approaches holds promise for some scholars and managers.

Image advertising and direct response advertising are not mutually exclusive strategies for success, since direct marketing efforts are closely linked to behavioural responses, while image-oriented messages are closely linked to mental processes. As such, incorporating both image and direct response components into a communications mix may jointly maximize their unique strengths, while minimizing their weaknesses (Peltier *et al.*, 1992: 41).

According to Peltier *et al.* (1992), image and direct response advertising may be operationalized as a bipolar scale. These authors have developed an approach to determine the extent to which a particular advertisement may be designed as 'image majority', 'response majority' or 'balanced' (Exhibit 15.6). There are many circumstances where each strategy can and should be used independently. There are other circumstances where a blend of image and direct response advertising may be successful. This integrated form of advertising would fall somewhere between the two extremes on the bipolar scale, and could jointly maximize the unique benefits of the two forms (Table 15.2).

Image-majority advertisements are designed to create or enhance imagery, but some response is desired. Frequently an offer is associated with the advertisement. Since the primary objective of image-majority advertisements is to build brand image, the offer should contribute to the image-building process. An example is an offer of a videotape describing the product in greater detail, included in the advertisement together with a toll-free number. Similarly, devices such as prizes, gifts and properly designed and co-ordinated brochures can influence the brand image. Generally, the company also seeks some form of commitment or participation by consumers. The individual who responds with a relatively small initial commitment, such as a telephone call for a free videotape, is more likely to respond to a subsequently larger request, such as to buy a resort-based holiday. Image-majority advertisements may, therefore, influence a respondent's 'readiness to buy'.

EXHIBIT 15.6   Integrating image and direct response advertising

---

Advertisers typically have embraced an either/or strategy for their communications. Pure image advertising and pure direct response advertising are valuable communication strategies, each in its own right. Many scenarios exist where each strategy can and should be used independently. Many other scenarios exist, however, where a blending of image and direct response advertising communication strategies may reap significant rewards. This 'integrated' form of advertising, which would fall in-between direct and image advertising, could jointly maximize their unique benefits.

The decision to integrate image and direct response techniques suggests the development of an instrument which can evaluate the position that a given message maintains on the image/direct response continuum. Positions located along the continuum incorporate varying degrees of each strategy's axioms or principles.

The key dimensions that may be used to distinguish image and direct response advertising are summarized in Table 15.2 in the text. The dimensions are quantifiable and assist in assessing the image–direct response profile. Each dimension is evaluated on a five-point scale. Once each dimension has been evaluated, a 'mean' score can be calculated for the ad. Using this scale, the image/direct response continuum (and individual advertisements) can be segregated into the following general categories: image-majority ads (mean score = 1.0–2.0), balanced ads (2.01–3.99), and response-majority ads (mean score = 4.0–5.0).

The primary advantage of this instrument is that it provides greater objectivity in evaluating where any given advertisement lies on the image–direct response continuum. In practice, however, a certain degree of subjectivity will exist due to the fact that individual evaluators may have differing opinions as to how certain ads rate across the various dimensions.

As both traditional and direct marketers realize that they can better meet a variety of objectives by utilizing a mix of pure image, image-majority, response-majority, and pure response messages within a single campaign, the instrument may prove useful from a strategic standpoint in determining how to manipulate messages in order to achieve that exact mix.

Source: Adapted from Peltier *et al.* (1992).

Response-majority advertisements are designed to obtain an immediate measurable consumer response, and so are most closely classified as direct response advertising. Response-majority advertising messages, however, aspire to build at least a limited long-term brand image as well (Peltier *et al.*, 1992: 46). The impact of the promotional copy used in the advertisements on qualifying sales leads can vary significantly depending on its focus and emphasis (Table 15.3).

In balanced advertisements there is a considerable mix of image effects

TABLE 15.2   Image–direct response continuum: an instrument for evaluating image/direct response profile

Image	1	2	3	4	5	Direct response
No response device	–	–	–	–	–	Strong response device[1]
Awareness/attitudes	–	–	–	–	–	Response
Uses imagery	–	–	–	–	–	Does not use imagery
Uses emotions	–	–	–	–	–	Uses reason
Uses little information	–	–	–	–	–	Much information
Attitude towards brand	–	–	–	–	–	Attitude towards product
High message frequency	–	–	–	–	–	Low message frequency
High production values	–	–	–	–	–	Low production values

[1] A '5' rating on this dimension implies that the response device is directed towards making a sale. Lower scores would be appropriate for different types of response (e.g. set up appointment, call for information, etc.). How these other responses are scored will probably differ across evaluators.

Source: Peltier *et al.* (1992). Reprinted by permission of John Wiley and Sons Inc.

and direct response effects. These advertisements retain characteristics of pure image and pure direct response communication strategies. Considerable emphasis is placed on image enhancement through the use of creative techniques consistent with image building. Second, there is an emphasis on sales

TABLE 15.3   Impact of promotional copy on lead qualification

Greater likelihood of obtaining qualified leads	Greater likelihood of obtaining less qualified leads
Send for our free booklet, we'll have our salesperson deliver it.	Your return of the enclosed postcard will register you in our million dollar sweepstakes.
Agree to a demonstration and we'll give you a valuable booklet that will help you to evaluate your needs.	Use our postage freecard to send for our free booklet. No salesperson will call.
Call our 800 number with your questions. Our telephone consultants will tell you how our product can respond precisely to your needs.	Agree to a demonstration and we'll send you a $19.95 pocket calculator absolutely free.
Send $500 along with the answers to the enclosed questionnaire and we will prepare a customized sales analysis for your firm.	You have definitely won two of the following prizes. Call our 800 number to make arrangements to pick up your gifts and enjoy a tour of our beautiful ocean-view resort.

We'll tell you how you can increase your profits overnight.

Source: Jolson (1988: 193). Reprinted by permission of the publisher from Jolson, Marvin A. (1988) 'Qualifying sales leads: the tight and loose approaches', *Industrial Marketing Management*, **17**, 3, 188–96. Copyright 1988 by Elsevier Science Inc.

generation, usually obtained through the generous use of detailed copy with phrases such as 'act now', 'limited offer', 'special promotion' and 'free offer'.

Assignment questions

1 What is meant by direct marketing and what are its benefits?

2 What is the role of interaction in direct marketing and how is it achieved?

3 Is direct marketing a communications technique or an approach to marketing?

4 What is the function of the database in direct marketing?

5 How has the growth of direct marketing been influenced by the media revolution?

6 How can image advertising and direct response advertising be integrated?

Annotated bibliography

Although aspects of direct marketing have been practised for a number of years, this communications approach has yet to be fully integrated into the marketing management literature. At least two publications are devoted exclusively to publishing material on direct marketing: the *Journal of Direct Marketing* and the trade magazine *Direct Marketing*. Both of these publications carry extensive coverage of the topic.

References

Akhter, Syed H. (1988) 'Direct marketing infrastructure: an indicator of direct marketing potential in foreign markets', *Journal of Direct Marketing*, **2**, Winter, 13–27.

Akhter, Syed H. (1992) 'The influence of socioeconomic and technological factors on direct mail volume in western european economies', *Journal of Direct Marketing*, **6**, 1, 23–8.

Bauer, Connie L., and John Miglautsch (1992) 'A conceptual definition of direct marketing', *Journal of Direct Marketing*, **6**, 2, 7–17.

British Direct Marketing Association (1989) *The BDMA Direct Marketing Code of Practice*, London: British Direct Marketing Association.

Cross, Richard H. (1992) 'The five degrees of customer bonding', *Direct Marketing*, **55**, 6, 33–5 and 58.

Hoke, Henry R. Jr (1988) 'Direct marketing – what is it?', *Direct Marketing*, **51**, 4, 32.

Hoke, Henry R. Jr (1992) 'UpJohn's database fuels sales growth', *Direct Marketing*, **54**, 12, 28–31.

Jolson, Marvin A. (1988) 'Qualifying sales leads: the tight and loose approaches', *Industrial Marketing Management*, **17**, 3, 188–96.

Lavidge R., and G.A. Steiner (1961) 'A model for predictive measurement of advertising effectiveness', *Journal of Marketing,* **25**, 6, 59–62.

Lumpkin, James R., and Jon M. Hawes (1985) 'Retailing without stores: an examination of catalogue shoppers', *Journal of Business Research,* **13**, 139–51.

Mitchell, Andrew A. (1986) 'The effect of verbal and visual components of advertisements on brand attitudes and attitude toward the ad', *Journal of Consumer Research,* **13**, 1, 12–24.

Peltier, James W., Barbara Mueller and Richard G. Rosen (1992) 'Direct response versus image advertising', *Journal of Direct Marketing,* **6**, 1, 40–8.

Richardson, Randall K. (1993) 'Sometimes database "non-marketing" is the way to go', *Marketing News,* 24 May, 6.

Roberts, Mary Lou (1992) 'Expanding the role of the direct marketing database', *Journal of Direct Marketing,* **6**, 2, 51–60.

Rosenfield, James (1991) 'Direct marketing myth and reality', *Business and Finance,* 2–3.

Russell, J. Thomas, and Ronald Lane (eds.) (1990) *Kleppner's Advertising Procedure* (11th edn), Englewood Cliffs, NJ: Prentice Hall.

Schmid, Jack (1992) 'Growth and profit strategies in a maturing industry', *Direct Marketing* **55**, 8, 39–41.

Stone, Bob (1982) 'Direct marketing', *Advertising Age,* 5 July 17–27.

Woodside, Arch. G., and William H. Motes (1980) 'Image versus direct response advertising', *Journal of Advertising Research,* **20**, 4, 31–7.

Personal selling

16

Nature of personal selling
Roles and tasks of the sales force
Recruitment, remuneration and renewal

Introduction

This chapter introduces and explains:

- sales force objectives and tasks;

- the evolution of consultative selling;

- the relationship between product type and personal selling;

- the process of selling;

- how sales people negotiate a sale;

- the importance of recruiting and remunerating a sales force;

- ways of renewing selling abilities in a company;

- the various ways that companies organize their sales force with an emphasis on effectiveness;

- the need to give autonomy to the sales force; and

- the impact of cultural and legal constraints on selling in an international setting.

Selling is a dynamic two-way communication which provides information in a flexible way that can be adapted to the specific needs of customers. Selling is part of the communications mix, but it is much more focused than mass communications like advertising. It is customized, as occurs in direct marketing, but is performed by an individual or a team in personal contact with customers.

Marketing management is concerned with the management of the selling process, which means understanding and agreeing the roles and tasks of the sales force, such as prospecting, communicating, negotiating, collecting information and servicing accounts. The company must acknowledge that in recent years the selling tasks have evolved. Selling is now considered more of a consultative activity between the company and its customers, emphasizing relationships and loyalty, and is not just about short-term sales gains. Hence, it is important that the company pay meticulous attention to the recruitment, remuneration and renewal of its sales force. Because selling is an expensive function, it is also necessary to seek high productivity levels, which derive from sales support by way of back-office staff, personal computers and access to relevant databases.

In organizational terms, marketing management attempts to integrate the sales force with the other marketing activities in the company by according them a degree of marketing autonomy in recognition of their flexibility and understanding of local customer bases. An effective sales force is one which serves two masters well – the company and the customer – where both of these meet, in the marketplace.

Having studied this chapter, you should be able to define the terms used above in your own words and you should be able to do the following:

1. Define what is meant by selling and negotiating.

2. Specify the objectives and tasks of the sales force.

3. Recognize the role of personal selling as an element of the company's communications mix.

4. Understand the process of selling and recognize the role of prospecting, sales conferences, sales literature and the personal sales call.

5. Specify the steps in the negotiations process, state how to cope with objections, and recognize the importance of language at different stages in the process.

6. Evaluate the different approaches to recruiting and remunerating the sales force.

7. Evaluate how companies attempt to improve sales force productivity.

8. Specify ways of organizing the sales force, recognizing the need for marketing autonomy.

Nature of personal selling

Personal selling means informing and pursuing customers through interpersonal communications directly associated with a particular transaction. Personal selling tends to be the most expensive element in the company's communication mix, because in most instances sales people represent an overhead for the company. Because the salesperson is trained to be flexible, knowledgeable and adaptable concerning the company's products, personal selling can be a very effective and powerful means of communication. By understanding the sales and communication objectives of the company, the salesperson can adapt the communication message as the need arises. The salesperson is in a position to customize the message to suit the needs of individual customers. Such a dynamic link optimizes the effectiveness of marketing communications, whereby a message can be adapted or tailored instantaneously to the reaction of each individual buyer. Personal selling is most effective where close relationships between supplier and customer need to be established. The more complex and technical the buying–selling relationship, the more effective is personal selling likely to be rather than other means of communication.

General role of personal selling

Personal selling plays a unique role in the marketing mix by establishing a set of relevant intercommunicative relationships between sellers and buyers of economic goods and services (Robinson and Stidsen, 1967: 260). Although supported by advertising, sales promotions and technical support, personal selling is the dominant, demand-stimulating force in the communication mix. This is often referred to as 'push strategy.' 'Pull strategy' relates to a more passive role for personal selling, engaging in channel assistance and market intelligence, and strengthening buyer–seller relationships (Hutt and Speh, 1985: 422, 430; Kotler, 1994: 625, 630).

Successful personal selling depends on the company recognizing the unique requirements of each customer in each relevant market segment. The sales force is then used to meet the needs of these segments. Personal selling is, therefore, a most labour-intensive and expensive means of marketing communications.

Personal selling and negotiations defined

Selling is defined by Kotler (1994) as the part of promotion involving an oral presentation in a conversation with one or more prospective buyers for the purpose of making a sale. Selling is a dynamic two-way communication which provides information in a flexible way that can be adapted to the needs of specific customers. Because it is focused and feedback is possible, selling can be less wasteful than advertising, but is complemented by it.

Negotiation may be defined as any sequence of written or verbal communication processes whereby parties to both common and conflicting commercial interests and of differing backgrounds consider the form of any joint action they might take in pursuit of their individual objectives, which will define or redefine the terms of their interdependence or relationship.

Roles and tasks of the sales force

The sales force has been described as 'a valuable source of up-to-date information about a whole range of marketing developments occurring at the individual customer location where they acquire business' (Moss, 1979: 94). As a result, sales people educate their customers in the latest technical developments and report back opportunities in the marketplace to their companies. For example, new product developments, faults in the company's products disclosed in customer complaints, and analysis of customers and competitors in the market are among the concerns of a salesperson and assist the company in future planning.

Sales force objectives and tasks

The objectives of the sales force are selling, servicing, prospecting, communicating, information gathering and allocating goods in the marketplace. Arising out of these objectives, a number of selling tasks may be identified (Figure 16.1). It is difficult to establish priorities among this list of tasks. Those tasks which are treated with a certain degree of glamour are the 'front-end' tasks of prospecting and negotiating and selling. The other more 'back-end'

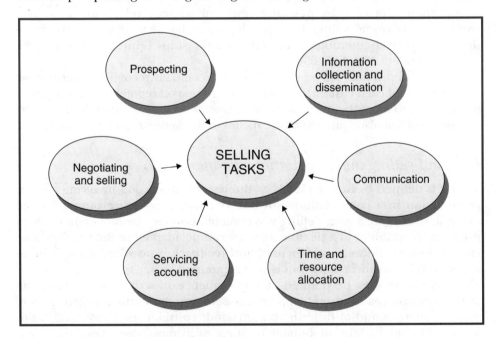

Figure 16.1   Important tasks in selling

tasks, such as collecting and disseminating information, communications, time and resource allocation and servicing accounts are no less important even if they are less glamorous. They are essential to the success of selling. Companies sometimes provide a sales support staff to carry out some of these tasks.

Personal selling as marketing communication

Personal selling has been described as the most effective tool of the promotions mix (Reeder *et al.*, 1987). The many strategies employed by sales people have been discussed at length in these and other writings on the subject. The art of selling has not really changed over the years, but selling and buying styles change from person to person along the dimensions of the salesperson's concern for the sale to concern for the customer (Blake and Mouton, 1970: 4). A positive correlation of both these variables is the most consistent with effective marketing. Hutt and Speh (1985) outline emerging industrial selling styles as consultative, negotiation, systems selling and team selling. In regard to industrial products, Shapiro and Posner (1976) have developed a systematic procedure for 'making the major sale':

- develop a profile of a company's needs and key personnel;

- justify the purchase to the buyer;

- co-ordinate the company's resources to present a more attractive sales package;

- make the sales 'pitch'; and

- close the sale and maintain the account.

When Motorola wanted to enter the highly specialized market for transformers that allow fluorescent systems to function, it developed a sales pitch focused clearly on the value of its new product to customers (Exhibit 16.1).

Changing focus in personal selling

A number of decades ago, selling meant that the company knew its customers, understood their needs and knew how its products and services could meet those needs. Sales people were sought out by shoppers and other buyers for their knowledgeable approach to business. Customer service was central to this approach. With mass marketing and the pressure for short-term results, however, competition has intensified and markets have become more complex. This change inaugurated a period of high-pressure sales techniques, reflecting great concern for the sale but little for the customer. The rise of scientific management, emphasizing narrowly focused expertise and functional specialization, is also thought to have contributed to a lack of customer orientation.

709

EXHIBIT 16.1   Motorola wants to light up another market

Motorola Inc. spent much of the 1980s fighting off assaults by Japanese rivals in its cellular phone, semiconductor, and pager businesses. Motorola not only survived – it triumphed by passionately embracing a single concept: quality. Despite its success, Motorola hasn't used what it learned about quality to invade new markets. Until now. The Schaumburg (Ill.) company was set on 3 October to announce the formation of Motorola Lighting Inc. The new subsidiary will produce electronic ballasts, the transformers that run fluorescent-lighting systems. By coupling a high-quality product and intensive customer service, Motorola bets it can grab world-wide market shares from old Japanese foes Toshiba and Matsushita, as well as the Netherlands' Philips. The first step: Conquer the $700 million (1.5 billion units) US market. MLI President Levy Katzir is confident: 'We're going to build a big business.'

Here's how Motorola is plugging its electronic fixtures for fluorescent lights vs the standard electro-magnetic variety:

Motorola's Sales Pitch:

Motorola	Standard
Needs 120 watts to power	Needs 180 watts to power
No irritating flicker	Flicker causes eyestrain
Weight: 2 pounds	Weight: 8 pounds

Source: *Business Week*, 14 October 1991: 14.

Customers rebelled, but for many years there was little response from manufacturers. They were still very production oriented, caring little for developments in the market. In this era, to be a salesperson was almost equivalent to being an outcast in society. Terms like 'ignorant' sales assistants and 'shady' car dealers abounded, often with good reason, especially in the USA (Exhibit 16.2). Fortunately, selling is becoming much more professional and such methods are unlikely to be tolerated, though from time to time investigative reports on 'hard' selling raise the spectre of disreputable methods of selling.

Evolution of consultative selling

In an era when there has been a shift from product-driven to market-driven selling, reflecting competitive product and price parities, companies must still distinguish themselves and their products from the competition. One of the solutions to this dilemma is to offer value-added service by discovering exactly what customers need and satisfying that need. Sales people have a key role to play in these circumstances: they deliver the service.

EXHIBIT 16.2   High-pressure sales tactics used in US motor industry

1. Selling the Payments: Focusing discussions on the monthly payments to divert the shopper's attention from the total price of the car.

2. The Slam Dunk: negotiating a price that earns a high profit on a sale to an unsophisticated and unsuspecting buyer.

3. The Heavy Turnover System: The highest in high-pressure tactics. Shopper is shown into a small windowless 'sweatroom' where a succession of salespeople wear down his or her resistance.

4. Low-Balling: A comparison shopper is quoted an absurdly low price. After finding only higher prices elsewhere, the buyer returns to find sales manager won't approve the quoted price. Salesperson then negotiates a higher price.

5. The Hull–Dobbs Technique: Named after two salesmen reputed to shine at this tactic. Basic goal: Make the shopper feel trapped until a sale is closed by holding on to a big deposit, or obtaining and refusing to return the keys to the customer's present car.

6. Stealing the Trade-In: Offering an extremely low price on the new car, but buying the customer's old car for a ridiculously low price. The trade-in then yields a big profit.

7. The Puppy Dog: Let customer take car home thinking the deal is closed except for minor details. Customer, already attached to car, returns next day to find the 'details' may include a jump in interest costs.

Source: *Business Week*, 6 April 1992: 73.

Increasingly, the ability of the company to match performance with customer expectations depends on the ability of the sales force to orchestrate the company's response to customer needs. In such circumstances, sales people must demonstrate trustworthiness and an ability to solve problems, even if the solution does not include the company's products or services.

Characteristics of consultative selling

The most important characteristics that customers seek in sales people are business and product knowledge, communications skills, a customer orientation and concern for the longevity of the account (Figure 16.2). All four characteristics rely on the salesperson's consultative ability to understand the customer's business, and to be a problem solver and an efficient provider of services aimed at satisfying customer needs.

The consultative ability requires sales people to be willing to share their knowledge and understanding of the business and product environment, so that customers can better serve their customers. Usually it is necessary to share state-of-the-art information without pressing for a sale. The purpose is to keep the customer informed of business developments. The service thus provided becomes the key to future sales.

Consultative sales people need to be able to combine the older selling skills with the newer consultative skills. Sales people must continue to prospect, enquire, support and close deals. Their skills are being refined to ask the right questions, which depends on knowing the customer's business, knowing how to control the sales process and being able to establish and maintain a relationship. Successful sales people are able to strike an acceptable balance between achieving short-run sales targets and cultivating and maintaining long-term relationships with customers. The ultimate goal of sales people is to master the basic skills of selling within a consultative framework.

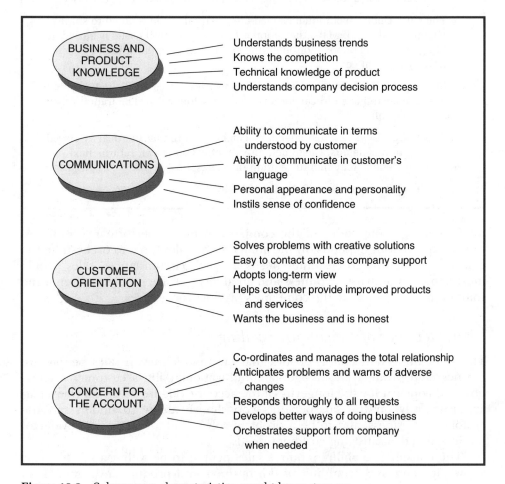

Figure 16.2   Salesperson characteristics sought by customers

Developing a team approach

Successful consultative selling means being part of a team with the resources to satisfy customer enquiries and needs. Customers expect consistent, dependable performance from products and services, and the salesperson is seen as the provider. The salesperson orchestrates the company's resources, people and information, to address the customer's needs. Rather than being a simple dyadic relationship of salesperson–customer, it becomes an integrated marketing programme where concern centres on the longevity of the account and the underlying relationship.

Companies attempting to shift from product-driven selling to market-driven selling based on customer consultation are faced with a dilemma: how

---

EXHIBIT 16.3   A science to selling boxes in Jefferson Smurfit

When General Electric Co. expanded a no-frost refrigerator line produced at its plant in Decatur, Ala., in 1990, Jefferson Smurfit Corp. went the extra mile. Smurfit, a major packaging supplier, had a new plant scheduled to come on-line in 1991 to feed the Decatur facility, but GE needed more shipping boxes, pronto. So, Smurfit assigned a co-ordinator to juggle production from three plants – and sometimes even divert product intended for other customers to keep Decatur humming. 'You don't do that for anybody,' explains Ron L. Yates, Smurfit's vice-president for sales and marketing. 'But we have a relationship with GE that promises long-term volume.'

That kind of hustling helped win St Louis-based Smurfit, the nation's second-largest maker of corrugated packaging, the GE appliance unit's 'Distinguished Suppliers Award'. No wonder partnership selling has become a rallying cry at $4.5 billion Smurfit and scores of other business-to-business sellers. Customers such as GE are increasingly channelling hefty orders to fewer vendors. In return, suppliers must improve quality by sharing proprietary information, delivering products on a sometimes quirky schedule, and joining problem-solving teams.

That kind of selling can also shelter a supplier from the bruising struggle of competing only on price. 'Today, it's not just getting the price but getting the best value – and there are a lot of pieces to value,' explains Joseph F. Bradley, vice-president for procurement at Emerson Electric Co., a big Smurfit customer that has cut its supplier count by 65 per cent. 'You want to earn profits jointly by reducing costs, but you can only work that intensely with a few suppliers who understand the changed role of sales.'

There's no turning back. 'Industrial salespeople are going to have to face the fact that we're not going back to the old ways,' cautions Yates, who expects partnership sales to account for 20 per cent of Smurfit revenues by 1997. 'If you don't follow your customers into partnering, then you'll be locked out – and your competitor will be the one doing the selling.'

Source: *Business Week*, 3 August 1992: 43–4.

to manage the trade-off between short-run sales revenues and long-term customer relationships. In allowing the sales force to negotiate price, credit terms and other conditions to improve customer satisfaction, there is a danger of jeopardizing the predictability of revenues and production schedules. Achieving the appropriate balance between traditional selling and consultative selling requires a change in behaviour in the company (Exhibit 16.3). In an environment where the pressure is on sales people to close sales deals and get business to produce short-term revenues, it is difficult to conceive of the kind of partnership with customers that is implied in consultative selling.

Product type and personal selling

Advances in advertising and promotional techniques have reduced the importance of personal selling in some markets. Impersonal selling, involving little buyer–seller interaction, may not be suitable for high-value-added industrial goods which require a high degree of problem solving, demonstration and instruction. The influence of product type should be examined to ascertain the role of personal selling in marketing communications.

Personal selling is concerned not just with the transfer of products and services in exchange for money, but also with persuading customers to buy or to increase the size of the order. The importance of personal selling increases directly, therefore, with the size of a particular order. For example, very expensive machines are not usually sold through advertising or mail order, likewise toothpaste or cigarettes are not usually sold directly to consumers by a sales person. However, there was a time when the second was done, and with developments in communications and direct marketing, the first may also occur at some point in the near future.

Matching the sales force with the product and channel

In some cases, companies misjudge the appropriateness of chosen ways of selling their products and services. Even when products are expected to succeed, failure is likely if the appropriate distribution channel combined with technical sales support is not available. A study by Robert G. Cooper of McMaster University in Canada shows that new product managers double their chances of success when they successfully match a new product with the right sales force and distribution system (*Business Week*, 16 August 1993: 37). Bicycle maker Huffy Corporation did not heed such advice when it introduced its Cross Sport, a combination mountain and racer bike (Exhibit 16.4).

For most industrial goods and services, such as office equipment, building materials, management consulting and computer systems, it requires the expertise and knowledge of well-trained sales people to link the firm's offering to customer needs. In this context it is important for the company to create

---

EXHIBIT 16.4   Matching the sales force and distribution channels

Huffy Corp., the successful $700 million bike maker, did careful research before it launched a new bicycle it dubbed the Cross Sport, a combination of the sturdy mountain bike popular with teenagers and the thin-framed, nimbler racing bike. Huffy conducted two separate series of market focus groups in the shopping malls across the country, where randomly selected children and adults viewed the bikes and ranked them. The bikes met with shoppers' approval. So far, so good. In the summer of 1991, Cross Sports were shipped out to mass retailers, such as the Kmart and Toys 'Я' Us chains, where Huffy already did most of its business. That was the mistake.

As Richard L. Molen, Huffy president and chief executive, explains the company's slip-up, the researchers missed one key piece of information. These special, hybrid bikes, aimed at adults and, at $159, priced 15 per cent higher than other Huffy bikes, needed individual sales attention by the sort of knowledgeable sales people who work only in bike speciality shops. Instead, Huffy's Cross Sports were supposed to be sold by the harried general sales-people at mass retailers such as Kmart. Result: 'It was a $5 million mistake,' says Molen. By 1992, the company had slashed Cross Sport production 75 per cent, and recorded an earnings drop of 30 per cent.

Source: *Business Week*, 16 August 1993: 37.

---

awareness and a rapport with the target audience, and to solicit sales for existing products, while continually monitoring customer reactions and market opportunities and developments.

Personal selling for technical products

Personal selling is dominant in industrial markets because the number of potential customers is relatively small compared with consumer markets, and purchases are usually considerably larger. In industrial markets, companies use personal selling as the traditional means of communication between themselves and buyers. The task of the industrial sales force differs from that of the consumer sales force in two important ways:

- they make fewer sales calls each day; and
- they spend much more time with each customer in liaising and problem solving.

For consumer products, a 'pull strategy' based on advertising and other non-personal techniques is used. In consumer mass marketing, where the selling process relies heavily on demand stimulation by brand and heavy merchandising, the pure selling function has dwindled to a pale shadow of what it was before the advent of self-service. In consumer markets, self-selection, self-service, catalogues and automatic vending have become widely accepted.

Personal selling is most effective in any market where the product or service is technical in nature and requires a considerable amount of knowledge on the part of the salesperson. In situations where demonstration of the product is important, the role of personal selling becomes essential. Such circumstances arise when a new technical product is being introduced to the market.

Process of selling

Selling involves many stages: prospecting for new qualified customers; understanding the customer decision-making process and developing the sales approach, including sales literature; contacting the customer and making a personal sales call; presenting the product or service to the customer; negotiating the sale; and managing and supporting the account (Figure 16.3).

Prospecting is an important endeavour in the overall selling process, and can be rewarding in terms of ultimate selling success. Successful prospecting for new customers or clients requires the company to reduce the difficulty of 'cold calling' a potential customer by first reaching them with a public relations effort. In this way, it is easier to obtain an appointment to discuss the possible sale.

During the presentation it is important to emphasize needs and problems facing the potential buyer. The company's products and services must be presented as solutions to problems. The company normally presents a number of possible options at different price levels, not a take-it-or-leave-it package.

Effective sales prospecting systems

Prospecting is the search for sales leads to identify potential customers. Prospecting is not only in the salesperson's domain; it is a team responsibility requiring techniques designed to give each salesperson constant support. Jolson and Wotrulea (1992: 59) note that 'nothing can happen until the selling firm finds a "prospect" for its products. Without a prospect there can be no meaningful sales presentation ... and surely no sale.' Efficient prospecting means:

- minimizing sales time spent with people who are not potential customers;

- saving travel time/expenses through better planning of sales calls;

- providing optimum background information on prospects to help make smoother calls and easier sales; and

- creating a meticulous customer or prospect databank for efficient use.

Modern prospecting increasingly uses computers to segment the market as follows:

- types of product used by prospect;

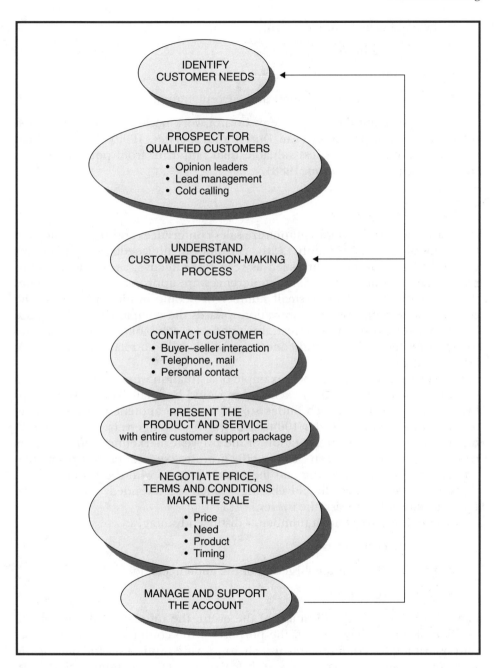

Figure 16.3   Sequential process of effective selling

- type of business and location;

- purchasing history;

- competition in the area; and

- prospect's current suppliers and current equipment.

Many marketing database systems do not work because they produce too many unqualified prospects (Van Doren and Stickney, 1990). Even qualified sales leads are sometimes less valuable than enquiries from potential buyers who are less qualified (Jolson, 1988).

Sales conferences

Companies are beginning to emphasize sales conferences and presentations in their overall communications with customers, intermediaries and other groups. Sales conferences are seen as very cost effective, since client groups may be targeted accurately. Sales conferences are appropriate for companies that can identify a relatively small number of people inside and outside the company whose attitude and motivation towards the company's well-being are likely to have the greatest effect. Included are companies with large sales forces or dealer networks, and companies which sell to a relatively small number of customers.

Car manufacturing is a good example of a situation where, relatively speaking, the number of dealers in each region would be small. There are perhaps five or six key people in each outlet, so that the total audience for a sales conference could be of the order 100 to 200, which would be very manageable. A new product launch or presentation of the five-year marketing plan to dealers in such an environment can be very effective. Real success derives from combining the information-giving and motivation process with the normal above-the-line activity, especially advertising, which is intended to encourage potential customers to visit the dealer.

Sales conferences have a number of distinct advantages:

- they are cost effective;

- they permit accurate targeting of the audience; and

- they are very flexible.

Flexibility surrounds the duration of the event, the number of delegates, the location of the conference and the purpose of the conference. The principal purpose of a sales conference is usually to provide motivation for staff or the sales force, training programmes and dealer or retailer communications. In recent years, financial institutions have become significant users of sales conferences, followed by retail organizations and industrial groups.

Sales literature and direct mail

Sales literature is any printed material containing information about a product or service for sale. It includes leaflets, catalogues and price lists. Most items of sales literature describe the products or services offered, emphasize their advantages and selling points, and indicate how and where they may be obtained. Increasingly, sales literature is produced in the form of multilingual leaflets aimed at a number of markets.

The great advantage of sales literature is that it can be read when convenient to the customer. Sales literature is often used to support other forms of communication, especially personal visits, exhibitions and trade shows. Well-designed sales literature presented during a sales visit can have a very favourable effect on a prospective buyer. Many prospective customers judge a company and its products by the quality and appearance of its sales literature.

As was seen in Chapter 15, direct mail means sending materials, including sales literature, through the mail to customers or prospective customers. It is a useful low-cost way of communicating with selected customers when a personal visit is not an option or is too expensive. Direct mail also serves as an effective back-up or follow-up to personal selling at trade shows or exhibitions.

The first decision in direct mail is to identify the kinds of people to be contacted. This implies having an accurate list of names and addresses. Directories and direct mail agencies may be used to obtain such a list. Most successful companies prepare their own lists as they get to know the important decision makers in buying organizations or households. Lists built within the company from experience are generally better than any to be purchased from outside agents. It is generally believed that direct mail should be customized and sent to a named person with an interest in the product or service offered.

It is then necessary to decide what is to be sent to the people on the lists and what kind of sales literature should be used. The company must, therefore, also design effective sales literature, which means stating something about the product or service offered and deciding on the best approach to promotion.

Personal sales call

The personal sales call is no longer a cost-effective means of satisfying a customer's need for information. Without the cushion of large margins, companies can no longer afford to invest as much time in the selling cycle as previously. This is especially true for complex products and services that require the provision of large quantities of specific customized information, demonstrating how a particular product or service provides a cost-effective solution which is competitively superior to that of their rivals. To achieve this objective through personal sales calls would be very expensive.

It is necessary, therefore, that companies use other ways of identifying sales leads, collecting information on potential customers, providing tailor-made presentations and maintaining regular contact with the potential customer during the selling cycle, while avoiding the high cost of the personal sales call. Part of the solution may be a combination of the computer and the telephone (Van Gaasbeck, 1993). The telephone can be used in prospecting for new customers if the company can identify its target customer group. By asking the right questions at an early stage in the selling cycle, the company can customize a personal sales visit to cater for the potential customer's most immediate needs. Alternatively, a sales seminar achieves the same object but is much more effective, since instead of dealing with one person at a time the company makes its presentation to a large interested group. Trade shows and exhibitions are very attractive in terms of prospecting scale effects.

At the next stage, the company can qualify the sales leads generated by telephone before sending sales literature or making a sales call. It is essential to avoid wasting the time of valuable sales people. Before making the personal sales call, it may be possible to send the potential customer a demonstration video or computer disc with a brochure and other descriptive material outlining the benefits associated with the product or service. The sales calls which arise from the follow-up telephone call are more likely to be made to interested customers who are likely to buy.

Negotiating the sale

Three aspects of negotiating the sale are important. First, it is necessary to recognize the various steps in the process. Second, the salesperson must be able to cope with objections which potential buyers may raise. Lastly, it is necessary to pay particular attention to the type and style of language used throughout the negotiations process. This is especially true when the buyer or seller or both are not working in their native language, as can so easily occur in open markets.

Steps in the negotiations process

There are five key steps in the negotiations process (Figure 16.4). Having identified the customer's need or problem to be solved, the salesperson makes a written or oral presentation to ensure that negotiations begin. When the negotiation range is established, and the parties recognize that a transaction could result, it becomes necessary to demonstrate a willingness to move from entrenched positions. When both parties trust each other and want to develop a relationship, a willingness to move from an entrenched position is likely to be reciprocated. In the process, verbal and non-verbal signs are used to demonstrate a willingness to progress.

In the next stage, an attempt is made to develop an acceptable proposal for solving the customer's problem. Assuming that the company's products or

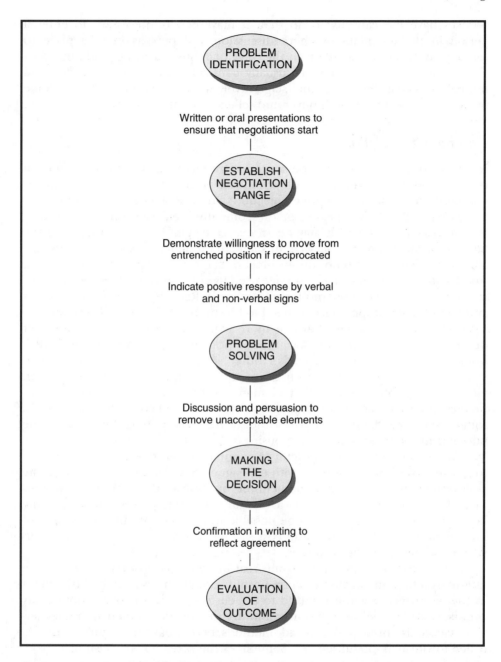

Figure 16.4   Key steps in the negotiations process

services have the capacity to do that, it may then be necessary to enter a period in the negotiations where discussion and persuasion take place to remove unacceptable elements in the offer or request. Having made the decision to purchase, the terms are usually confirmed in writing to reflect the mutual understanding. The final stage involves an evaluation of the outcome from the perspective of both buyer and seller.

Coping with objections

In negotiating a sale, the salesperson must frequently deal with objections on the part of the customer. These objections may take many forms: a need objection, a product objection, a price objection, a timing objection or an objection to dealing with the salesperson or the company itself. Customers often deny that any need exists, which may be an excuse or genuine unawareness of the benefits of the product or service. In such circumstances, a salesperson usually attempts a demonstration of the product or service to emphasize the benefits. An objection to the product or service itself usually indicates that the customer requires more information and technical details. Recent product improvements and technical developments may need to be emphasized by the salesperson.

Almost every sale, especially of more expensive items such as consumer durables or industrial products, can face a price objection. A major reason for price objections is the existence of other suppliers which are prepared to reduce price to obtain the business. In such circumstances, the salesperson attempts to emphasize the other elements of the deal: easy payment terms, finance, product quality, delivery, after-sales service and company reliability. In some cases it may be necessary to withdraw from the potential deal, since the salesperson should seek profitable business.

The timing objection is difficult to counteract. Customers sometimes want to 'think it over' or to discuss it with colleagues. Such attempts at delaying the consummation of a deal may be genuine or tactical. By responding with an incentive such as a premium or a discount, the salesperson may overcome both types of delay. It may also be possible to demonstrate the advantages of immediate purchase through the cost savings which the new product or service would mean for the customer.

Lastly, customers may have some real or imagined grievance against the salesperson or company itself. Open hostility usually arises from bad treatment in the past which was not resolved to the customer's satisfaction: poor-quality products, broken delivery promises and, frequently, inadequate after-sales service. Good listening abilities and methods of establishing future trust are called for in such circumstances. Sometimes the problem is a clash of personalities, in which case it may be worth considering substituting someone else for the task.

When the salesperson has responded to objections, it is usually time to attempt to close the sale. Many salespeople are reluctant to attempt closure for many reasons, fear of rejection by the buyer being one of the more commonly cited. Customers, however, expect to be asked for their order, so it is important for the salesperson to attempt a close. Many successful sales people attempt to close a deal many times during the negotiations process, recognizing that it is difficult to judge the most appropriate timing. In such circumstances, the advice is often given that the salesperson should 'close early and often' in the sales process. Trial closes are part of this process and when they are effective the customer accepts the proposition and the deal can be closed.

There are many forms of closing a sale. The two most commonly used forms, which to an extent include all the others, are the summary close and the concessionary close. The summary close, very popular in western society and based on Cartesian thinking, is perhaps the most common. The benefits of the purchase as accepted by the customer are summarized during the selling process and combined with an action plan requiring customer commitment.

The concessionary close is popular in price-sensitive markets and where customers have raised a timing objection. It is also common in eastern societies, reflecting oriental thinking based on a complete understanding of the offer before any commitment by the customer can be made. Extra product may be offered if the sale is completed within a certain time period, or free delivery may be offered or some other allowance given. The purpose is to make a dramatic concession that will overcome the customer's remaining resistance. Examples of special concessions in retailing include advertising allowances, point-of-purchase displays and longer credit terms. All are concessions used to close a deal. As they can be expensive, they are offered only at the very end of the selling process to obtain agreement from the customer.

Language of negotiations

In many instances, the seller must cope with objections. Objections should be seen as positive because they allow the seller to adapt the product or service to the potential customer's needs. Listening to objections and, when reasonable, agreeing with them defuses unnecessary debate and increases the prospect of mutual benefit. The language used in negotiating a sale can be a powerful ally or detractor. Certain words suggest negative outcomes and are frequently avoided: 'failure', 'recession' and 'problem'. Other words are more likely to be seen in a positive light: 'benefits', 'solutions' and 'total satisfaction'. Positive language helps the parties to reach a close.

At some stage in the negotiations process, it will be necessary to ask for the business. If the selling process has been well prepared, the seller tends to confront indecision head-on by attempting to determine the nature of the obstacle to progress.

Customer satisfaction must be actual practice in the organization, not just a slogan. The acid test of customer satisfaction is whether the company checks its own behaviour or that of its customer when something goes wrong. The company should seek to meet its customers' latent needs, those needs which customers do not consciously realize they value.

Recruitment, remuneration and renewal

Sales management is one of the areas which gives rise to great difficulty in marketing management. Three aspects of sales management which concern the company are: how to recruit good sales people; how to remunerate them; and how to train and retrain them. Changing competitive circumstances require the firm constantly to renew its selling capability.

Recruiting and remunerating an effective sales force

The firm should have a clear written statement of the characteristics required to succeed in different selling jobs in the company. It is important to examine character profiles and place an emphasis on psychology rather than on job descriptions. There is an old adage in sales management that it is possible to teach sales recruits to look good and have an acceptable appearance, and to teach them to negotiate, but potential recruits must want to sell! Because of the cost of hiring and holding people, companies are increasingly using meticulous recruitment methods in their attempts to hire the right kind of people for the selling task.

Sales force remuneration

With increasing product-market complexity and competition, many companies face intense pressure for short-term sales results. In such an environment, the emphasis in the selling process on understanding customers and knowing how company products meet their needs has almost disappeared. In some businesses, selling is still focused on high-pressure techniques rather than on customer service. Insurance, home improvement and timesharing resort apartments have featured in the press in this regard. To redress this situation, companies are beginning to reassert the need to treat their customers as essential resources. This means changing the way things are sold, the way people are trained and paid, and the way the company is organized. Even in the car industry the older disreputable methods are no longer seen as appropriate (Exhibit 16.5). Selling is now being viewed again as part of marketing, relating directly to product development, advertising, pricing, distribution and especially communications.

There is no one remuneration or reward system suitable in all circumstances. All systems have their strong and their weak points. The company is

---

EXHIBIT 16.5   Car dealers with souls?

Car shoppers have long dreaded the hard-sell tactics practised in many auto showrooms. But with few alternatives open to consumers, dealers felt little pressure to change. Now, though, the success of customer-friendly brands, such as Toyota's Lexus on the high end and Saturn at the entry level, is fuelling a reform movement in car retailing. Car makers from Hyundai Motor America to Ford Motor Co. are constructing ways to simplify pricing and reward salespeople for actually satisfying customers.

One simple improvement is to end haggling, which can leave customers angry and bewildered. Among Saturn dealers, negotiating is largely out, thanks to a policy of sticking with suggested retail prices that still leave a $1,200 profit per car for dealers. In Saturn showrooms, options are packaged together into a few simple choices.

Some dealers aren't waiting for Detroit. J.D Power & Associates reckons there are more than 30 dealers trying some variation on the fixed price, no-haggle sales approach. One is Earl D. Stewart, a Pontiac dealer in West Palm Beach, Fla., who last December decided he had enough of the old ways. Says Stewart: 'We've operated on the edge of credibility a long time.' Stewart ditched his commissioned sales staff, hired salaried order-takers, and slapped low, non-negotiable prices on every car on the lot. Stewart also has his trade-ins auctioned off; if they fetch more than he offered, the customer gets a check for the difference. So far, the response is good: Sales tripled from 30 cars a month to about 90 in January and February. Stewart expects to sell about 110 cars in March, even though he has cut advertising spending by 85 per cent.

It's a more daunting task to re-educate established dealerships steeped in traditional sales techniques. This spring Chrysler Corp. is kicking off a $25 million programme to educate 100,000 employees at the 5,000 dealers nation-wide selling its brands. Much of Chrysler's programme sounds like good old common sense. It will include tips from Chrysler's research showing that customers particularly resent gouging tactics such as sudden jumps in finance charges and mandatory service contracts. And it will teach new skills – such as selling to women as if they are sentient adults. All too often now, 'the salesman will say, "Honey, get your husband, and we'll talk turkey",' says Theodore Cunningham, executive vice-president for sales and marketing.

Source: *Business Week*, 6 April 1992: 72–3.

---

unlikely to succeed unless it is prepared to accommodate changes in the environment. Second, remuneration and motivation are linked intimately, so they must be considered carefully. The principal options available are: salary only; a combination of salary and commission; and salary, commission and bonus (Figure 16.5). There are advantages and disadvantages associated with each approach. Remuneration based on commission only is appropriate when sales people have only weak links to the company, when they are hired for the short term only, or when the company is quite uncertain about the nature and size of the market for the product being sold. Arrangements involving a combination of salary and commission may collapse, since it is difficult to establish an appropriate relationship between the two. Whichever approach is used, it is important that the company ensures that sales force remuneration relates directly to the firm's marketing objectives.

Companies have reacted in various ways to the new views of selling. Commission-based compensation plans have been dropped or reviewed, the selling job is seen not as exclusively that of the sales force but as that of every-

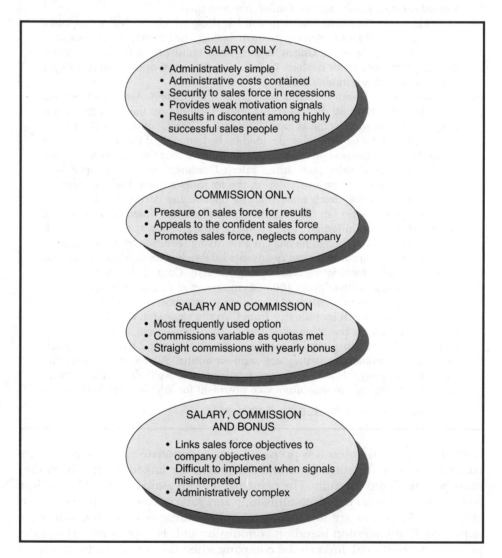

Figure 16.5   Alternative ways of remunerating the sales force

body in the organization, and companies have begun to realize that they exist to serve customers, profitably.

Renewing selling abilities

There is a lot of advice available on the 'best way' to update and train a sales-force. The approach taken depends very much on the circumstances in the company. A company departing on a totally new endeavour, such as launching a range of new products in a new market, will require a different type of sales force from a company operating in a competitive, growing or maturing market. In the latter case, a few suggestions may be made with some degree of confidence. It would seem generally true that a company should use the experience of its established and knowledgeable sales people first before calling in outsiders.

A review of recent training literature and applications shows that, in updating sales people, a number of topics are more frequently the focus of training programmes than others:

- product knowledge and applications;
- time management;
- individual sales and negotiations techniques; and
- prospecting techniques.

Most effective training programmes may be successfully delivered through:

- short group meetings or seminars;
- occasional long seminars;
- video cassettes; and
- printed matter for questions.

In all circumstances it is important to emphasize flexibility and adaptability in the design of training programmes and in the sales people trained. Successful companies have developed policies involving investment in continuous training programmes aimed at keeping their sales force current and competitive.

Company commitment to the customer

In any company, success means focusing the entire organization on customers. Focusing on customers for many companies means changing the way chief executives view their role, the way sales people are hired and trained, and the way sales people are motivated and paid (Figure 16.6). It is necessary to inspire top-down in most organizations. This means that managers must

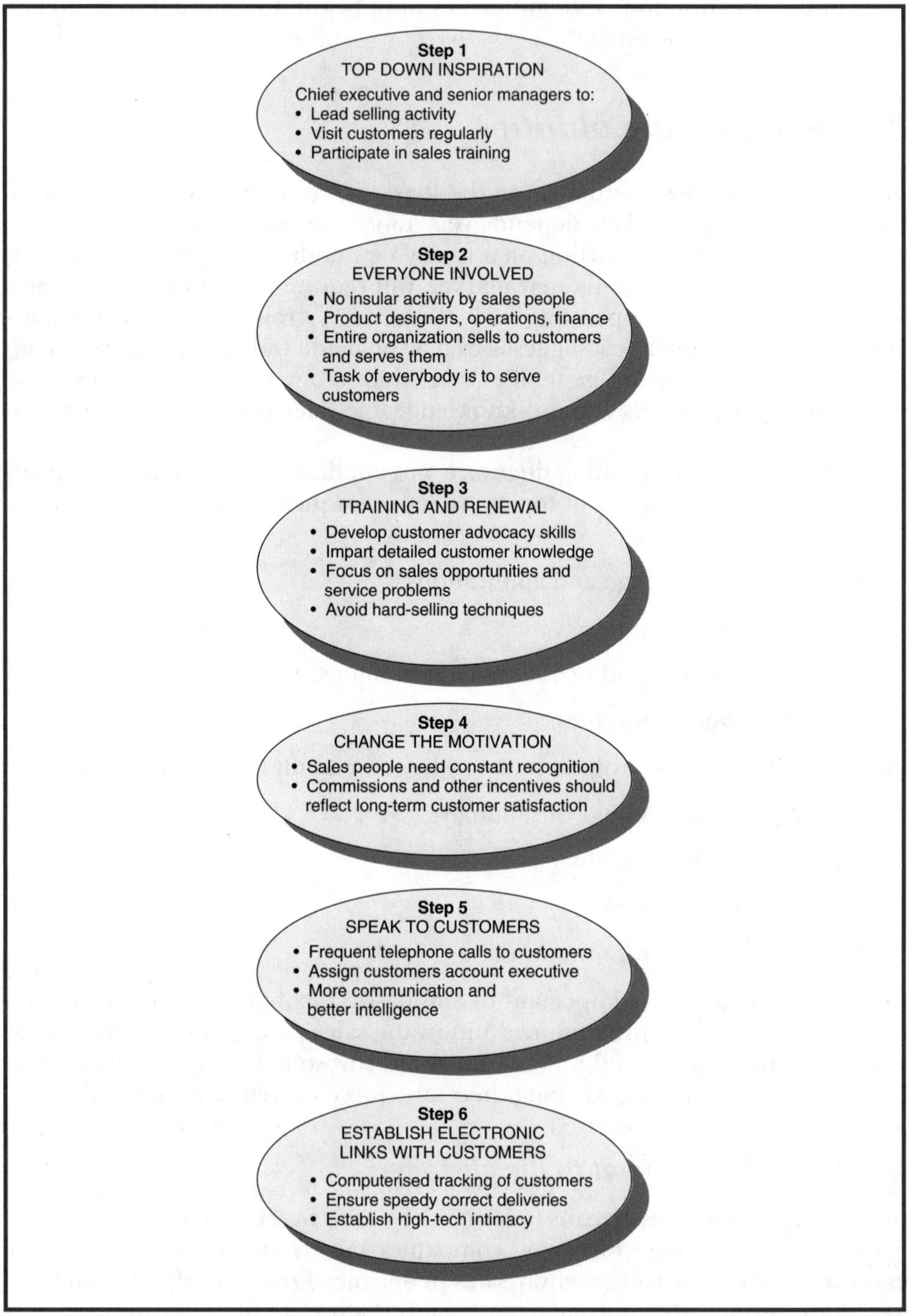

Step 1
TOP DOWN INSPIRATION
Chief executive and senior managers to:
• Lead selling activity
• Visit customers regularly
• Participate in sales training

Step 2
EVERYONE INVOLVED
• No insular activity by sales people
• Product designers, operations, finance
• Entire organization sells to customers
  and serves them
• Task of everybody is to serve
  customers

Step 3
TRAINING AND RENEWAL
• Develop customer advocacy skills
• Impart detailed customer knowledge
• Focus on sales opportunities and
  service problems
• Avoid hard-selling techniques

Step 4
CHANGE THE MOTIVATION
• Sales people need constant recognition
• Commissions and other incentives should
  reflect long-term customer satisfaction

Step 5
SPEAK TO CUSTOMERS
• Frequent telephone calls to customers
• Assign customers account executive
• More communication and
  better intelligence

Step 6
ESTABLISH ELECTRONIC
LINKS WITH CUSTOMERS
• Computerised tracking of customers
• Ensure speedy correct deliveries
• Establish high-tech intimacy

Figure 16.6   Keys to better selling

frequently visit customers and be involved with the sales team in actual selling and in training sessions. It is also important that everybody in the company from product designers to section managers and finance people is involved in selling. No longer is it acceptable for the salesperson to act in splendid isolation. It is everybody's task to serve customers.

Sales people to be effective must become advocates for the customer's needs. High-pressure selling techniques do not have a place in customer-oriented companies interested in delivering value. Training in new skills designed to allow the salesperson to obtain detailed knowledge of his or her customers' business is required. This approach supports the salesperson in identifying new sales and service opportunities. It is also essential that companies change their motivation system. Sales people thrive on constant recognition, which is not necessarily derived from commissions. The successful marketing company attempts to build into the remuneration package measures of long-term customer satisfaction.

Most companies usually find that it is necessary to maintain regular communications with customers by making frequent telephone calls and, if feasible, appointing an account executive responsible for the customer's business with the company. Customer loyalty is built on attention, communication and company commitment. Regular customer contact has the added advantage that it provides an opportunity for collecting accurate marketing intelligence.

Lastly, it may be necessary, if not just advisable, to establish computerized marketing and distribution technology to monitor customer relationships and ensure that the right products arrive at the right customer premises. Such systems also make ordering much easier and provide what has become known as 'high-tech' intimacy with the customer.

Improving sales force productivity

In the 1990s, low cost and high quality are essential ingredients for success in marketing. The next arena for competition seems to be sales and customer service. The consulting firm Bain and Co. in Boston, Massachusetts, has produced research showing that raising the company's customer-retention rate by two percentage points has the same effect on profits as cutting costs by 10 per cent (*Business Week*, 3 August 1992: 39).

It is possible to identify sales force conditions which are likely to translate into sales and share improvement. Successful companies tend to give the sales force more marketing autonomy. Sales force management may be improved in a number of ways (Figure 16.7).

The costs associated with personal selling are very high. Expenses include recruitment, remuneration, transport, entertainment, sales management, secretarial support and training. Selling across international borders increases these costs even further. A geographical organization of the sales force may

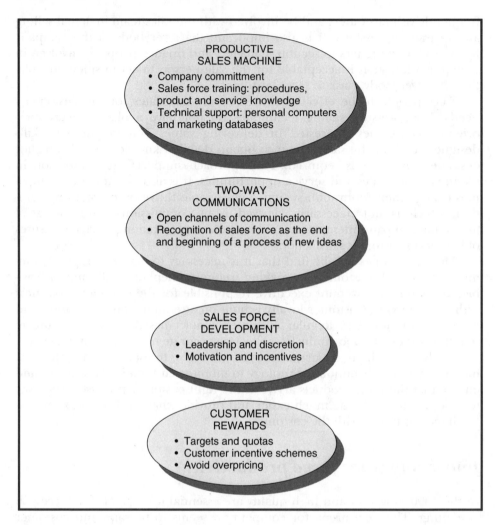

Figure 16.7   Improving sales force productivity

reduce travel costs, but the salesperson must be able to perform all of the selling tasks in each sales territory. This can prove rather difficult if the products have diverse applications. A critical mass of demand is required to offset such costs.

Use of computers in selling

According to many commentators, the sales force is the single largest marketing cost in large companies. Productivity is therefore a big issue in managing the sales force. Computers and sales force automation tools are being used to support sales. Computer technology is now being used to transform the selling

---

EXHIBIT 16.6   Anatomy of the sales process: before and after the lap-top

Before the lap-top	After the lap-top
Step 1 Sales person contacts sales administration for a rundown on the best leads.	A powerful lap-top computer dials into the corporate network to give the sales rep access to most vital information. It can prepare memos, send faxes and communicate via electronic mail. It can show customized marketing presentations, too.
Step 2 Salesperson requests sales literature and other fresh material from marketing	A single call back to head quarters network can tap into all relevant department data bases. The lap-top can validate configurations of complex products, too.
Step 3 After the order, it's time to check with the pricing, credit and manufacturing departments. There may be dozens of calls before the order is closed.	
Step 4 A final check with manufacturing and shipping confirms delivery date.	

Source: *Business Week*, 25 October 1993: 68–9.

---

function from an art based on exaggeration to a thoroughly scientific business.

Before this investment in sales technology, company sales people would typically spend days getting quotations and proposals typed and mailed to customers. Telephone calling and paper chases lasting days were normal. Now that lap-top computers handle much of the process, price quotations can be available in a matter of hours not weeks. Orders tend to have fewer errors and take much less time to process. The computer can be used to garner the collective intelligence of the company in support of the sales force (Exhibit 16.6).

The sales process, for many industrial products particularly, involves many sections of the company that often operate independently of each other and have separate information systems. In such a company, the value of personal computer support is unambiguous. In many circumstances, the modern salesperson complements the traditional skills of selling with sophisticated technology to support the selling process (Exhibit 16.7).

The installation of a computer-based management information system may not always be the solution, and is expensive, difficult and fraught with danger. Firms which have tried it have found that obtaining relevant, usable data is a time-consuming, research-intensive process. Companies typically source the following as potential databases:

- routine buyer information;

- sales call reports;

- trade and industry associations;

- market research and advertising responses; and

- specialized off-the-shelf databanks.

Defining prospecting criteria which are of most value to the sales force is extremely difficult. Getting the sales force and marketing people to use a computer-based management information system is not a teaching but a learning process. Firms which successfully implement a management information system usually start in a simple but practical way. Common problems found with many systems include:

- superficiality – names and addresses, but nothing on buying habits;

- cumbrousness – it has plenty of data but no information, i.e. it is not 'user-friendly'; and

- inaccessibility: 'how do I get screen time if they don't give me a portable?'

Organization of the sales force

Many textbooks on marketing and sales management devote considerable space to describing traditional or classical approaches to organizing the sales force. Detailed organization charts are provided to illustrate the appropriate

---

EXHIBIT 16.7   Complementing the sales call with the computer

An architect imports a computer file containing a library of a plumbing fixture manufacturer's products into her CAD system. She uses the information to help her specify fixtures for the kitchen in a new home design. In the past she would have called in a sales representative to get the specifications she needed. The computerised catalogue also contains stock numbers, making the order process easier when the fixtures are finally needed for installation. Although the order may still be placed with a person, the computer file packages information that used to be the expertise of a sales representative.

Source: Van Gaasbeck (1993: 22).

---

configuration for different types of company. It is also necessary to consider sales effectiveness in designing the sales organization and building into it the mechanisms for renewal, so that the company's marketing objectives are continuously attained. In the modern company, this may mean allocating a degree of marketing autonomy to the sales force, while at the same time providing the company with sufficient back-up support.

Classical organization of the salesforce

The sales force may be structured according to territory, product or customer, or a combination of these (Figure 16.8). The most common form of industrial sales organization is geographical. Here, each salesperson sells all of the firm's products in a defined area. By reducing travel distance and time between customers, this method usually minimizes costs. Likewise, sales people know clearly the customers and prospects that fall within their area of responsibility. However, each salesperson must be able to perform all of the selling tasks for all customers in that territory.

A product-oriented sales organization is one in which each salesperson specializes in relatively narrow components of the total product line, and hence becomes more adept at communicating with members of buying centres. By learning the specific requirements of a particular industry, the salesperson is more prepared to identify and respond to buying influences.

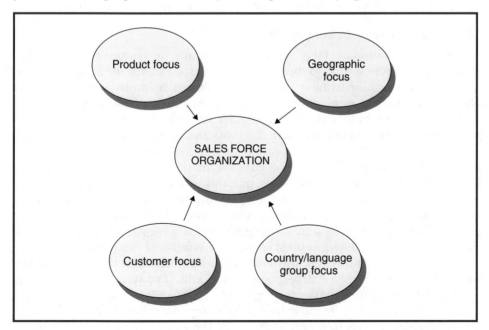

Figure 16.8 Ways of organizing the sales force

733

Effective sales force organisation

The sales force conditions likely to translate into significant sales and share gains are:

- better organization of the sales force;
- absolutely meticulous training and recruitment;
- systematic improvement of prospecting techniques; and
- effective remuneration packages.

Concentration in these four areas seems the most efficient route to high-productivity sales management among companies. Sales people are central to marketing negotiations. Much of selling is the ability to negotiate exchange terms favourable to the company. The salesperson as negotiator must be able to understand the customer's needs and wants, and be able to judge how best to serve these in the context of the resources available to the company.

Sales people should, therefore, be given a focal position in the implementation of strategy in the company. People negotiate relationships with counterparts in buying organizations. They must also take account of the buyer's customers. In developing a negotiations stance, sales people seek information about the needs and preferences of customers on a continuous basis and especially before any change in strategy. It is important to assess any changes which may occur in power relationships between the company and its customers.

Sales force with marketing autonomy

There is a trend in many large successful companies to convert some regional or local sales forces into autonomous marketing staff under the strict guidance of the marketing department. Giving the sales force more autonomy is an attractive option for some companies. It means shifting from a system based on calling on distributors, retailers and other customers to spending more time meeting advertising agency creative directors and media buyers to create local advertising campaigns. Research shows that a converted sales force can obtain good deals locally which make for effective marketing. A dynamic and well-trained sales force can frequently move quickly to create tie-ins with local retailers to celebrate some local event which may involve sponsorship. In this regard it is worth noting that captive audiences are especially receptive to locally targeted efforts: a few years ago Campbell's Soups gave canned soup a boost through well-positioned signs on ski lifts at Ski Windham Resort in New York.

Sales force remuneration and motivation are intimately linked. All remuneration systems have their strong and weak points. The system chosen should promote the company's marketing objectives. Regular updating and retraining of the sales force is a feature in strong companies. Successful companies attempt to design a simple organization for the sales force to ensure regular communication between sales and other departments in the company.

Cultural and legal issues in selling

Language problems often exist in selling, especially when diverse markets such as occur in the EU are involved. Sales people who cannot converse with a high degree of fluency in the language of the country, and often in the dialect of a region, will not create a favourable impression on the buyer. As a result, foreign nationals are often employed in this capacity most of the time, otherwise training costs would be too great and training would also run the risk of being ineffective.

Likewise, door-to-door selling may be threatening to various cultures: socialist countries regard this form of selling as predatory (Carson, 1967: 401). It is unlikely that such influences will have been completely eliminated in the former USSR and Eastern Bloc countries.

Variations of selling techniques have to be taken into consideration to accommodate local customs. For example, Avon Cosmetics may have to alter its approaching styles across countries. Also, Tupperware altered its 'party' approach in Nigeria and selected 'mammies' to sponsor such events in the open (Carson, 1967: 402).

There are also various legal restrictions which hamper the operation of personal selling in many countries, such as visas prohibiting long-term assignments in Eastern Bloc countries. There may also be legislation against certain forms of personal selling, especially door-to-door selling of consumer goods, as in Denmark (Carson, 1967: 401). Government agencies and legislators are responsible for protecting consumers and businesses against each other. The regulations of such agencies must be adhered to by both buyers and sellers as they develop products and services and overall marketing strategies.

Regulatory authorities attempt to overcome any misrepresentation in selling, but high-pressure sales techniques such as the 'Bait and Switch' method (whereby a salesperson pushes a more sophisticated, expensive model or pretends the original (cheaper) one is not available) are more difficult to monitor by such agencies. As a result of 'fear selling', often on a door-to-door basis, many countries have introduced a 'cooling off' law to allow the prospective purchaser to reconsider the situation.

Assignment questions

1 Describe how selling fits into marketing and explain why it is referred to as the dynamic element of the marketing communications mix.

2 What are the major tasks and objectives of the company salesforce?

3 Industrial selling has been described as 'consultative'. What does this mean and what are the implications for the salesperson?

4 When is a team approach to selling appropriate?

5 Personal selling is more important is some product-markets than in others. Discuss.

6 What are the requirements for personal selling in regard to technical products?

7 Describe the personal selling process.

8 What are the key dimensions in negotiating a sale?

9 Recruiting and compensating the salesforce are among the more difficult marketing management tasks. Discuss.

10 How may the organization improve the productivity of its salesforce?

11 Describe the various approaches to salesforce organization and suggest ways of designing an effective salesforce.

12 Describe the more important cultural and legal issues which affect the selling function in your country.

Annotated bibliography

Claubaugh, Maurice, Jr, and Jessie L. Forbes (1992) *Professional Selling: A relationship approach*, St Paul, Minn.: West Publishing Co.

Kotler, P. (1994) *Marketing Management: Analysis, planning and control* (8th edn), Englewood Cliffs, NJ: Prentice Hall, chapter 25.

McCarthy, E. Jerome, and William D. Perreault, Jr (1993) *Basic Marketing* (11th edn), Homewood, Ill.: Richard D. Irwin, chapter 16.

References

Blake, Robert R., and J.S. Mouton (1970) *The Grid for Sales Excellence*, New York: McGraw-Hill.

Carson, D. (1967) *International Marketing: A comparative systems approach*, New York: John Wiley.

Hutt, M.D., and T.W. Speh (1985) *Industrial Marketing Management: A strategic view of business markets* (2nd edn), Chicago: CBS College Publishing (Dryden).

Jolson, Marvin A. (1988) 'Qualifying sales leads: the tight and loose approaches', *Industrial Marketing Management*, **17**, 3, 189–96.

Jolson, Marvin A., and Thomas R. Wotrulea (1992) 'Selling and sales management in action: prospecting: a new look at an old challenge', *Journal of Personal Selling and Sales Management*, **12**, 4, 59–66.

Kotler, P. (1994) *Marketing Management: Analysis, planning and control* (8th edn), Englewood Cliffs, NJ: Prentice Hall.

Moss, C. (1979) 'Industrial salesmen as a source of marketing intelligence', *European Journal of Marketing*, **13**, 3, 94–102.

Reeder, R.R., E.G. Brierty and B.H. Reeder (1987) *Industrial Marketing: Analysis, planning and control*, Englewood Cliffs, NJ: Prentice Hall.

Robinson, P.J. and B. Stidsen (1967) *Personal Selling in a Modern Perspective*, Boston, Mass.: Allyn and Bacon.

Shapiro, B.P., and R.S. Posner (1976) 'Making the major sale', *Harvard Business Review*, **54**, 2, 68–78.

Van Doren, Davis C., and Thomas A. Stickney (1990) 'How to develop a database for sales leads', *Industrial Marketing Management*, **19**, 3, 201–8.

Van Gaasbeck, Richard (1993) 'Marketers can't afford to invest more in personal sales calls', *Marketing News*, 13 September, **27**, 19, 22.

Case studies

Case 15: Oral Hygiene (HK) Ltd

Oral Hygiene (HK) Ltd was an international affiliate of Oral Hygiene International, with its head offices in the USA. The company marketed mouth wash, toothpaste, dental floss and numerous other oral hygiene products. They were widely accepted by local consumers. New product introductions were given high priority by top management as continuous launches of new products were seen as the life blood for further growth.

Lily Lau, a group product manager, was assigned to study the feasibility of launching a toothbrush available in soft and medium bristles on to the Hong Kong market. The product had already proven to be highly successful in the United States and throughout Europe. Senior management in the local company were very eager to ensure a successful launch, as the toothbrush represented an entirely new product line. A successful launch could make tremendous inroads for the company into the toothbrush market, which would enable the company to claim brand representation in all segments of the oral hygiene market.

The toothbrush market was fully developed at 100 per cent penetration. Volume growth was therefore likely to relate to population growth (approximately 2–3 per cent per year). Brand share could only be achieved at the expense of the competition. The brands on the market with their respective brand share were as shown in Table 1.

The three largest brands were all priced under $3.30, with Dental East appealing to the older age group and Pink D purchased more frequently among the lower-income groups. Golden Unicorn, in particular, was associated with soft bristles that did not hurt gums. Consumers in general were found to prefer soft to medium bristles to hard ones.

Lily also completed a comprehensive study on possible brand names and 'Dura' was selected. A full launch plan was prepared and a three-year marketing plan, incorporating the HQ prime objective of gaining a 10 per cent brand

TABLE 1   Toothbrush brands and market share

Brand	Market share (%)
Golden Unicorn	21.6
Dental East	18.2
Pink D	17.1
Whitie	9.9
Tootsie	8.2
Tiger	6.6
Moca	6.2
Fresh-Dent	2.9
Chisdom	2.9
Others	6.4

share and a 15 per cent marketing contribution by year 3, was summarized as shown in Table 2. The price in year 1 was to be $4.30 per unit.

Senior management appeared to be quite pleased with Lily's presentation. Tom Smith, the managing director, felt certain that the regional vice-president would fully support the proposed marketing plan. Two weeks later, Rick Reynolds, the Asia-Pacific regional vice-president arrived on his quarterly business trip and Lily presented her Dura launch plan again. Rick looked bothered as he began reviewing the projected three-year plan. 'The sales and market share figures look fine to me, Lily, but do you think it's likely that we will be able to achieve them?'

TABLE 2   Dura Toothbrushes (soft and medium bristles) year projected marketing plan

	Year 1[1]	Year 2	Year 3[2]
Unit sales	550,000	890,000	1,190,000
$ sales	2,365,000	3,827,000	5,712,000
	(100.0%)	(100.0%)	(100.0%)
$ gross profit	1,064,250	1,722,150	2,684,640
Margin (45.0%)	(45.0%)	(45.0%)	(47.0%)[3]
$ advertising	800,000	1,000,000	1,400,000[4]
	(33.8%)	(26.1%)	(24.5%)
$ promotion	600,000	400,000	400,000
(including dental profession)	(25.4%)	(10.5%)	(7.0%)
$ marketing	−335,750	−322,150	884,640
Contribution	(14.2%)	(8.4%)	(15.5%)
Unit market size	11,200,000	11,420,000	11,640,000
Projected market share	4.91%	7.79%	10.22%

[1]March–December only.
[2]Built-in price increase of 11.63 per cent to $4.80 per unit.
[3]Gross profit would be improved through cost reduction by sourcing from Korea when manufacturing came on stream in year 2.
[4]Cantonese-dubbed US commercials would be replaced by new local commercials. $150,000 was set aside for production costs.

740

'Yes,' replied Lily, 'our toothbrush has the unique selling point that it has been well portrayed in our US commercial launch. This could be effectively dubbed into Cantonese. I think there should be no problem in gaining customer awareness and from that sales. Responses to our dubbed commercial testing were very positive and given the market situation – no toothbrush is as yet being advertised on TV – I think we have a competitive advantage there. After all, our target market is very much influenced by the American way of life and the American ideal.'

'I am not against TV advertising, Lily,' replied Rick, 'but we want to project Dura as a premium "professional" product like Fresh-Dent. We have to price it on a par with Fresh-Dent to achieve that image. Part of the budget will have to be used to promote the product among the dental profession who, we hope, will recommend the product in turn to their patients. This strategy has already proven most successful in Europe.'

At this point Tom interrupted the conversation and agreed the point that Dura should be positioned in the same price bracket as Fresh-Dent. Less should be spent on a TV advertising campaign, and the product should be promoted more extensively among dentists. Lily tried to explain that local dentists were still unconvinced by the idea of preventative dentistry and argued that 'below-the-line' promotional money should be made available from funds to cover the cost of sending free samples and posters to the 800 larger and more established practices in Hong Kong.

As Lily pointed out to her colleagues, 'Hong Kong is a different market altogether. Fresh-Dent is priced at $6.60, which is 100 per cent more than other market leaders. My suggestion of pricing our product at $4.30 is already 30 per cent higher than almost all other toothbrushes, and although a premium price may help the development of a "professional" image, at a 100 per cent premium we will definitely price ourselves out of the market altogether. Look at what Fresh-Dent has achieved over the past 10 years or so – a 2.9 per cent stagnant market share gained via dental health promotion through dentists. Don't forget that our prime objective is to gain a 10 per cent share of the market by year 3 with a hefty 15 per cent marketing contribution. How can we possibly do that without the aid of heavy TV advertising? It is the most likely way to generate demand in a short period of time. Frankly, I would not be able to take responsibility for this brand confidently unless you approve of my launch as is.'

There was silence as Lily looked questioningly at Tom for his reaction. 'Well, Lily,' said Rick, 'I am not pushing you into a decision right away. I know you understand the importance of this launch. Take your time and think over my suggestions. When you are ready, discuss it with Tom and fax me your decision. But mind you, my dear, if you stick to your original recommendations, you had better make sure that all the objectives are attained. Otherwise, I need not tell you what might happen.'

1. Was Lily being rash in insisting that projected sales and market shares of Dura were likely to be attained? What factors are likely to hinder these objectives?

2. What do you think of Rick Reynolds's proposed pricing strategy, i.e. pricing in relation to Fresh-Dent in order to project a 'professional' image for Dura?

3. Should Lily reconsider switching part of the advertising money into promotional funds for targeting the dental profession?

4. How would you like Tom Smith, the managing director, to be your boss?

5. What actions would you recommend Lily to take, given the way the meeting ended?

This case was prepared by Loretta Ho, Department of Business Studies, Hong Kong Polytechnic, and adapted by Dympna Hughes, Department of Marketing, University College Dublin, for the purpose of class discussion rather than to illustrate either effective or ineffective handling of an administrative situation.

Case 16: Adidas

For many years, Adidas and Puma running shoes had dominated Europe's athletic and shoe apparel market, and had also had a strong presence in the USA. US companies Nike and Reebok, with their 50 per cent share of the US market, were also making their way into Europe. Although Adidas still reigned as no. 1 in Europe, it was facing a serious challenge from the American contenders for this position, with Puma relegated to fourth place in many shoe categories. Meanwhile, as Adidas sales in Europe were slowing down, Nike and Reebok sales were accelerating. In 1991, Nike's sales were up 100 per cent from the previous year.

The European market was vital to the future growth and earnings of Nike and Reebok, as US sales had begun to stagnate. As a result, both companies had been shipping their surplus stocks to Europe and dropping their prices. Europe was regarded as an obvious move as it was widely recognized that many Europeans had a fascination with all things American.

In the fight for market share, brand differentiation had become key. Reebok and Nike had achieved this through their own unique positioning. Reebok stressed performance first, and style second. Each shoe was developed with a sport in mind and designed to appeal to all age groups. Its advertising aimed to reflect ordinary people and events at the 'heart of sport'. Nike, on the other hand, sold its shoes on the basis of individualism, and one-on-one sportsmanship. Its advertisements tried to give an understanding of the emotional aspect of playing sport, and it used high-profile celebrity endorsements, such as that of basketball's star, Michael Jordan.

Another crucial element for all companies in this competitive market was product innovation. Nike was acknowledged as having the leading edge in R & D, but the others were far from dormant. In 1992, Reebok unveiled its 'Pump' system, and Puma revealed the 'Disc' system that did away with shoelaces, both of which generated considerable interest. The onslaught from Nike and Reebok, with their heavy advertising spending, had come at a particularly bad time for Adidas and Puma. Both companies had suffered losses in recent years, due to unfocused marketing, high costs and excessive product ranges. The problems were particularly acute for Adidas, which with up to 1,200 variations and styles of shoes, and poorly co-ordinated marketing, had angered and alienated many distributors.

In addition, Adidas faced financial problems. There were doubts as to whether or not the new owner, French entrepreneur Bernard Tapie, had the money to invest to effect a turnaround. He claimed that 'brand awareness is huge – its a question of revitalizing Adidas' heritage as *the* sports shoe company, and shrugging off its "has-been" feel'.

Others were not so convinced. 'The markets are at a cross-roads,' said brand manager Grant Allen of Reebok UK. 'The growth curve has just come off its initial steep rise. There is still growth, but it has slowed. In the 1980s, it was fuelled by the rise of health and fitness, high levels of disposable income, and consumers' preoccupation with brand values. The challenge now is to translate that surge into durability for the brands in an environment with radically changed values and changing demographics.'

What should Adidas do to meet this 'challenge'?

Source: 'Where Nike and Reebok have plenty of running room', *Business Week*, 11 March 1991: 44–5; *Financial Times*, 6 July 1992; *Marketing Week*, 11 November 1992.

This case was prepared by Nora Costello, Department of Marketing, University College Dublin, as a basis for class discussion rather than to illustrate either effective or ineffective handling of an administrative situation.

Case 17: IBM

On 3 September 1992, the IBM Personal Computer (PC) operation was reborn as IBM-PC Co. However, apart from the addition of an existing IBM marketing section and a new company name, little else had changed. The same products, problems and management remained. On 9 September 1992, the first series of IBM's new PC models, the new PS/1s, was introduced. This two-year-old line now came in three versions:

- *Entry-level computers:* Three versions – essential, for small businesses; Expert, for advanced buyers; Consultant, for home offices.

- *High-end PCs:* Overhauling PS/2 line with more powerful desktop, server and notebook models.

- *For the price war:* New ValuePoint, positioned between PS/1 and PS/2, aimed at Compaq's Prolinea.

On 20 October 1992, IBM's ValuePoint line was finally introduced. Prices for the PCs started at a Compaq-matching $795 and carried plenty of service and support in addition to a powerful brand name. The company also revamped its big business PS/2s line. The ValuePoint series used 386 and 486 micro-processors that were faster than most others. Unlike Compaq's Prolinea range, which was distributed through mass merchants, the ValuePoint was positioned primarily for the corporate buyer. The computers were to be sold by PS/2 dealers as well as through an 800 number, direct response IBM unit in Atlanta.

However, some dealers were sceptical about IBM's marketing strategy. According to Bill Fairfield, president of InaCom Corp., an Omaha-based dealer chain, 'There's going to be a great deal of confusion about how all these lines fit together. They face a significant job in teaching the dealers.'

The competition

The three leading companies in the PC sector are IBM, Compaq and Apple. Compaq ranked second behind IBM in IBM-compatible PCs. In June 1992, Compaq computers heard the repeated hints by IBM officials of IBM's inten-tion to expand and upgrade its PC segment by introducing a low-priced line. Compaq had a four-month headstart in introducing its new Prolinea PCs with-out having to compete against comparable IBM machines. The company had spent the previous eight months transforming itself by cutting costs by more than 30 per cent and basically rethinking its entire business. Its Prolinea range was priced at the competitive price of $795.

Apple Computers were not IBM-compatible. Apple's gross margins, at 40 per cent, seemed impressive, but were considered to be unsustainably high, and the company had been striving to expand beyond its extremely profitable niche. Indicative of some anxiety about Apple's prospects as an independent company was CEO John Scully's unsuccessful attempt to merge Apple with IBM in the spring of 1992.

A savage price war began in the industry in early 1992. The market value fell by 20 per cent in the second quarter of 1992 compared with the first three months of the year. In the same week IBM announced its intention to match its competitors, price cut for price cut. Apple cut its PC prices by up to 50 per cent, and Compaq, having already cut its PC prices to launch its Prolinea range, laid off 100 staff and shut its service operation in Scotland. Steve Walker, the

IBM marketing programmes manager, predicted 'immense shake-out – companies are operating on such thin margins they can't generate any money to keep themselves in business'. Other industry observers forecast that the emphasis will shift from that of pricing to other elements of the marketing mix.

Assuming that Steve Walker's 'industry shake-out' predictions are accurate, what strategy should IBM adopt in order to ensure its place in the future computer industry?

Sources: *Business Week*, 21 September 1992; *Fortune*, 14 June 1993; *Marketing*, 15 October 1992.

This case was prepared by Jacqui McWilliams, Department of Marketing, University College Dublin, as a basis for class discussion rather than to illustrate either effective or ineffective handling of an administrative situation.

Case 18: Buitoni

In late 1992, Duncan MacCallum, UK marketing manager for Nestlé's Buitoni brand, wanted to adopt a completely radical approach to building his brand. In the UK, the Buitoni brand could be found across a variety of foods – ranging from dry pasta to ready-made lasagne. The brand existed in a market dominated by own-label (which accounted for 58 per cent of £100 million dry-pasta sales). Buitoni marketing, together with McCann communications, were plotting new 'revolutionary' ideas. MacCallum was adamant that the strategy chosen would ensure that consumers would pay Buitoni's 10 per cent price premium.

A number of factors spurred MacCallum's determination to search for an innovative marketing approach. First, the growth of retailer power had obstructed the manufacturers' path of communications to the consumer. According to Peter Brabeck, Nestlé's group executive vice-president, 'It is clear it has become more difficult to get directly to the consumer.' It was no longer enough to expect retailers to sell a product – a great deal of effort had to be exercised to create demand. Advances in information technology worked in the retailers' favour, making it riskier and more expensive for manufacturers to launch their products. Through retailers' scanning systems, product success or failure could be detected quicker than ever. Furthermore, competition had intensified in this market, which had become stagnant by nature. Manufacturers were no longer contending with the old form of 'own label'. As Brabeck observed, 'We have a branded competitor in retailers [with own-label products] who are doing the job very well.'

In addition, the Nestlé management felt that the 'mass consumers' who used to react to mass advertising no longer existed. Brabeck was of the opinion that 'In the past, consumers wanted what their neighbours had. The modern consumer wants what the neighbour does not have. We have to approach him in an individual way.' Paul Baxter, marketing director of Gateway's (UK supermarket chain) commented, 'It's about time manufacturers started recognizing there is a consumer out there. It's something retailers have been doing for years.'

The management team also thought that mass advertising was becoming less and less cost effective. The proliferation of satellite and new terrestrial channels was making it increasingly difficult to reach the targeted customer. According to Brabeck, 'We will always need advertising to have public appeal, but that alone will not be enough.' The Nestlé management had a £2.5 million promotional budget for the UK at their disposal. The company was beginning to realize the importance of technology and alternative distribution channel use, and it was eager to develop its 'new' strategy before its competitors changed their strategic direction. It was keeping a very close eye on competitors such as Unilever, Philip Morris and BSN. MacCallum summed up the company's intentions: 'We're not sitting here blasé in an ivory tower thinking that mere [advertising] presence will sell a product. We're trying a different approach.'

> **Should Duncan MacCallum and his team endeavour to formulate and implement a 'radically' different approach to building the Buitoni brand? If so, why? What suggestions would you make to them?**

Source: 'Nestlé adopts the personal touch', *Marketing*, 19 November 1992.

This case was prepared by Jacqui McWilliams, Department of Marketing, University College Dublin, as a basis for class discussion rather than to illustrate either the effective or ineffective handling of an administrative situation.

PART E

Deliver the value to customers

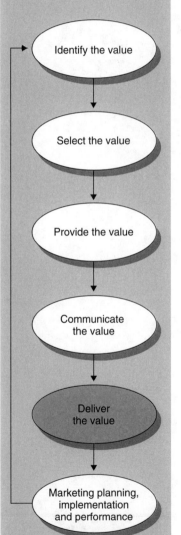

Identify the value

Select the value

Provide the value

Communicate the value

Deliver the value

Marketing planning, implementation and performance

- Distribution channels
- Market logistics
- Sales promotion

Managing distribution channels

17

Nature and function of marketing channels
Developing a distribution policy
Formulating a distribution strategy
Managing channels of distribution
Power, conflict and co-operation in the
channel

Introduction

This chapter introduces and explains:

- the nature of marketing channels;

- functions of marketing channels;

- the distribution channel as a vertical market;

- effective management of distribution channels;

- strategic goals for distribution;

- marketing channel decisions;

- intensity of market coverage;

- selecting and motivating intermediaries;

- evaluating distributors;

- sources of channel power; and

- managing channel conflict.

Distribution in marketing management is about delivering value to the customer. More precisely, marketing channels involve the organizational arrangements the company makes to deliver its products and services to the customer or user. Marketing channels perform the function of accumulating product and services into assortments required by customers, and ensuring that this assortment is delivered to the location desired at the time required and in the quantities demanded. Wholesalers and retailers play a key role in this process. Retailers have become the dominant organizations in the distribution network.

In developing a distribution strategy, the company decides the appropriate way to reach its customers. This may be through intense distribution or selection or exclusive distribution, depending on objectives and the nature of the product, the service and the market. In managing the marketing channel, the company must select, motivate and evaluate distributors. Because marketing channels comprise a set of interdependent organizations, conflict can arise among channel partners. Power is used to manage this conflict so that the channel system develops and grows. From time to time channel members on one or more levels dominate this power relationship. At present, in the fast-moving consumer goods industries, large retailers, especially supermarkets, dominate and lead the marketing channel.

Having studied this chapter, you should be able to define in your own words the phrases listed above, and you should be able to do the following:

1. Discuss the concept of a distribution channel in marketing management.

2. Specify the form and meaning of traditional distribution channels, multiple channels and direct distribution.

3. Identify the benefits of distribution and evaluate the role of intermediaries.

4. Specify the objectives of different channel members.

5. Recognize the interdependence existing among channel members.

6. Outline tactical and strategic decisions to be made in channel management.

7. Evaluate the important factors in selecting a channel and channel partner.

8. Specify the intensity of market coverage required.

9. Decide how to motivate and evaluate intermediaries.

10. Understand how conflict arises in channel management and recognize the role of power in managing conflict.

Nature and function of marketing channels

Defining a business using the traditional product-market concept ignores the levels of business at which the company may operate. Companies frequently change the level in response to market opportunities. Donnelly Mirrors, a specialist company in the auto industry, integrated forward to enter the French market for prismatic mirrors for cars and trucks. Rank Xerox and IBM have established retail shops to reach small business customers. There is, however, a trade-off between the increased control and return gained from vertical integration compared to the increased risk and loss of flexibility associated with the investment at different levels of business.

The marketing channel as an area of study is perhaps the only major concept in marketing not borrowed from another discipline (Mallen, 1967). On the other hand, it is an area which has been relatively neglected by marketing scholars, particularly in terms of the analytical concepts and tools required for the objective description, measurement and comparison of channel components and channel systems.

Distribution channel as a vertical marketing system

Two very different forms of marketing channel exist. Conventional marketing channels consist of a set of independent firms – manufacturer, wholesaler and retailer – and the user. Each is considered a separate entity. The manufacturer and the intermediaries seek to maximize their own profits, even if this means lower profits for other firms in the distribution channel. As independent companies, each recognizes the others as independent entities outside its control.

A vertical marketing system consists of the manufacturer, wholesalers, retailers and users all acting in unison to maximize profits or benefits for the system as a whole. In a vertical marketing system, one channel member may own all the others or may use a franchising arrangement to control the system, or it may be able to exert power and influence in the system to attain system objectives. The vertical marketing system may be dominated by a firm at any level within the system. A successful vertical marketing system controls channel behaviour and eliminates the conflict which results from individual intermediaries following individual objectives.

In most cases, there is no such thing as the best channel or set of channels for the company's products over a planning period. A channel is a set of intermediary companies, people or agents who manage the movement of products and services from the manufacturer to the final user. All firms which take title to the product, or assist in transferring the title as it moves from manufacturer to consumer, form part of the distribution channel. Channels may be short or long. Typical channels used in the marketing of consumer and industrial products are shown in Figure 17.1. Variations of these forms may be found in practice.

The value of marketing intermediaries may be judged by their superior efficiency in making products widely available and accessible to target markets. Marketing intermediaries, at all positions in the marketing channel, on account of their experience, their specialization, their contacts and their scale,

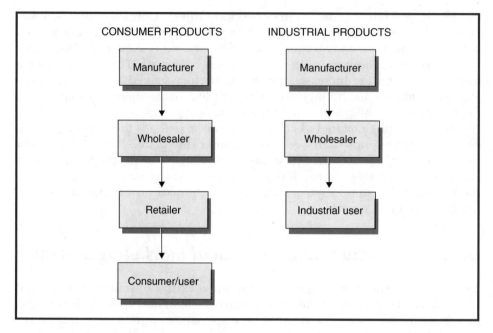

Figure 17.1 Typical channels in the marketing of consumer and industrial products

offer the manufacturing company more than it can usually achieve on its own. The entire channel helps to provide customer value.

Concept of a distribution channel

A marketing channel is a set of interdependent agencies that, by the exchange of products and services, provides time, place and possession utilities to make that product or service available for final consumption. These three utility factors are required in addition to the form utility provided by the manufacturer. A product is complete when all four dimensions have been included.

In any channel configuration, there are combinations of manufacturers, agents, distributors, wholesalers, retailers and end-users. Also included is the host of support agencies which facilitate the passage of title and the physical movement of products. These include transport companies, banks, other lending agencies and advertising agencies.

The channels chosen for a company's products intimately affect every other marketing decision, and involve the firm in relatively long-term commitments of resources and long-term, sometimes contractual, relationships with other firms. It has been suggested that the concept of channels of distribution is one of the most fundamental, original and enduring concepts in the marketing literature (Stern, 1969: 1).

In this context it is necessary to distinguish clearly between the concept of 'channels' and the concept of 'physical distribution'. Channels are defined as the vertical marketing system of forces, conditions and institutions associated with the sequential passage of a product or service through two or more markets, or sets of contractual relationships through which the exchange of goods or services is consummated (Bucklin and Stasch, 1970). Marketing channels have also been viewed as 'sets of interdependent organisations involved in the process of making a product or service available for use or consumption' (Stern and El Ansary, 1988: 3). The relationship among the various organizations providing distribution services has given rise to the concept of distribution channels as political economies (Stern and Reve, 1980). Physical distribution, on the other hand, is viewed as the functional areas of marketing associated with inventory and transportation, or the temporal and spatial inputs to the logistic system within the channel (Heskett, 1966).

Marketing channel decisions are linked to other marketing mix decisions. Pricing and advertising depend to a large extent on whether the firm has access to large full-scale intermediaries like department stores or medium-size economy stores found in most cities. Pricing, product management, sales force training and distributor support are intimately linked. Likewise, a channel decision is a relatively long-term decision as commitments are usually made for at least a year, and usually a longer period is implied.

Traditional marketing channels

The traditional marketing channel is from manufacturer to wholesaler to retailer to user. It is the method used by hundreds of small manufacturers of firms producing limited lines of products and by small retailers. Small firms with limited financial resources use wholesalers as immediate sources of funds and as a marketing arm to reach a myriad of retailers which stock their products.

Likewise, small retailers rely on wholesalers as buying agents to ensure a balanced inventory of products produced in various regions of the world. For industrial products, industrial distributors are normally used in a channel consisting of manufacturer, wholesaler and industrial user. These wholesalers assist in the marketing of small accessory equipment and operating supplies, such as building supplies, office supplies and small hand tools.

Multiple channels

In designing a channel system it is necessary to recognize that many firms are multichannel business units: that is, they offer identical products to consumers in the same market through a variety of different outlets. Beer sales through public houses and supermarkets and increasingly through private clubs are a good example of the use of multiple channels. Likewise, Michelin tyres are sold directly to Citroën, where they serve as a fabricated part of new Citroën cars. They are also found in car accessory shops and some garages. Each channel enables the manufacturer to serve a different market.

Complex industrial products favour direct distribution through the company's own sales force. Standard components, on the other hand, can be distributed efficiently through third-party distributors. Sometimes companies organize the distribution of industrial products through specializing by customer, which means taking account of product applications. Organization distribution based on selection applications is a way for the smaller company to use its limited resources effectively, and for the larger company to protect against such niche strategies by offering applications expertise across a range of product users (Corey *et al.*, 1989: 113).

An alternative way to organize distribution, in industrial markets particularly, is to have size-of-account company sales teams serving large customers directly, while independent distributors are used to reach the smaller users.

Direct distribution

The simplest, most direct marketing channel is not necessarily the best, as evidenced by the relatively small percentage of total sales that move through this channel. As was seen above, direct distribution can be very effective in industrial markets. However, only a very small proportion of all consumer products are candidates for direct distribution. Encyclopaedia Britannica, Tupperware, Avon and numerous mail-order houses are examples of firms which use the direct marketing channel.

Direct marketing channels are much more important in the industrial products market: capital equipment, fabricated parts and raw materials are distributed through direct contacts between producer and user.

Functions of marketing channels

The management of marketing channels and distribution focuses on the delivery of products and services to the final user. It is by distribution through a marketing channel that products are made available for consumption. Marketing channels are the paths that products follow from producer to user. Distribution is the marketing function which ensures that the flow actually takes place.

Identifying benefits of distribution

Channels of distribution provide three major benefits: those associated with time, location and conveyancing. A time benefit means having the product available when the user wants it. Fashion fairs take place months before the relevant season. Ladies' fashion shoes for the summer season are produced during the previous winter. Long lead times are required to produce the necessary quantities and to transport the finished product to the retail outlet.

In regard to the second benefit, location, note that since few customers are willing to devote the time and energy to seek out the manufacturer, retailers provide a supply of products in locations convenient to the user. Retail shops, vending machines and mail-order catalogues provide the means of conveniently supplying products to the user.

Marketing channels also provide a means for title to the product to be transferred from the manufacturer to the buyer. The purchaser obtains physical possession of the product, and the title of ownership of the product at the retail outlet. The importance of the distribution channel in transferring title to products is much more apparent for industrial products, in situations where a financial institution may be involved in facilitating the sale, and where products are exported or imported.

Usually, the manufacturer provides none of these benefits. The manufacturer normally provides only those benefits associated with the product itself. Delivery of products means creating time, location and possession benefits. Users cannot obtain a finished product unless it is transported to where it is required, stored until such time as it is required, and eventually exchanged for money or bartered. These three benefits are inseparable from the product itself; there can be no complete product without incorporating all three into the product or service.

Functions of wholesalers

Wholesaling involves the activities of people or firms which sell to retailers, other wholesalers or industrial users, but which do not sell in significant amounts to ultimate consumers. The major function of a wholesaler or distributor is to break bulk and send small orders to the retailer, thereby realizing substantial savings on physical distribution costs. Functions performed by wholesalers today have emerged as a result of:

- large-scale mass production in distant factories;
- product volumes manufactured on a speculative basis;
- the need for product adaptation to suit intermediaries and final users; and
- increases in the quantities and varieties of products available.

The sorting process of wholesalers is the key to their economic viability. Hundreds of pairs of Levi jeans are produced in a single cutting, but they are ultimately sold one pair at a time in myriad retail stores. The distribution channel brings about a convergence in the quantities and characteristics of products manufactured with the quantities and characteristics consumed.

Wholesaling has been under increasing pressure from manufacturers which have expanded the scale of their factories, broadened their product lines and integrated forward into distribution. A more serious threat at the other end of the channel comes from the chain stores, especially supermarkets.

These outlets, in their endeavours to obtain large volumes of supplies at low cost, have in recent years bypassed many of the wholesalers and gone directly to manufacturers. This has caused serious friction in the channel of distribution.

Function of retailers

Retailing consists of all the activities involved in the sale of products and services to the ultimate consumer. The buying motive for a retail sale is usually satisfaction stemming from the final consumption of the item purchased. Retailing includes sales through shops, the mail, door-to-door selling and automatic vending machines. It also includes all outlets that seek to serve ultimate consumers: hotels, hospitals, schools, banks and other financial institutions.

Retailing has been and continues to be affected by the emergence of new institutions as well as the evolution of existing ones. This is especially evident in regard to department stores, chain stores or supermarkets, discount houses and various forms of non-store retailing (Figure 17.2). A new form of retailing which has become popular is the specialized retailer of consumer durables sometimes referred to as a 'category killer'. These retailers tend to locate on the periphery of large cities (Exhibit 17.1).

Each form of retailing has its own peculiar strengths and weaknesses. Frequently, the same products are found in different types of retail outlet, thus showing how the manufacturer can reach different market segments. The different types of retail outlet attempt to maintain an assortment of products and services to cater for specific market segments. Thus it is possible to think of price-conscious shoppers who might frequent discount stores more often than they would department stores. The images created for these retail outlets provide customers with certain cues when they go shopping.

It is important for manufacturers to avoid using inappropriate outlets. For example, it is unlikely that manufacturers of exclusive ladies' evening gowns would retail them through a discount house or a mail-order company. They are more likely to use a speciality boutique. Similarly, the processor of a special pâté might consider the food counter in a well-known department store like Harrods in London or Galleries Lafayette in Paris and at the same time use the delicatessen counter in some of the supermarket chains. It is important to match the services provided by the retailer with product and customer needs.

Improving the performance of retailers

Retailer performance is usually improved by the prospect of more profit, less capital investment, fewer user complaints, lower training costs, and more repeat business. Small retailers may need assistance in accounting, financing and inventory control. Support may also mean giving immediate personal attention to retailer grievances. Sales managers should know retailers personally and ensure that incentives and other rewards reach them.

STORES AND SHOPPING CENTRES

Department stores
Retail wide variety of products, organized on a departmental basis; large sales; sell mainly to women; located in high street and shopping centres; offer many 'free' services e.g. packaging, delivery (Harrods of London, Galleries Lafayette of Paris, Corte Ingles of Madrid).

Speciality stores
Retail broad selection of restricted class of merchandise; small or medium-sized establishments or boutiques; soft goods (clothing, linens etc.); durables (kitchen utensils, appliances etc.).

Chain stores/supermarkets
Central ownership and management; buying power combined with managerial efficiencies; low margins and high turnover; offer complete stock of dry groceries, fresh meat, perishable produce, dairy products; convenience goods, non-food merchandise; self-service (Sainsbury, Tesco in the UK, Rallye, Casino in France, Aldi in Germany). Other forms of chain store/supermarket include voluntary and symbol groups (associations of retailers usually established on the initiative of a wholesaler); associated retailers remain independent, e.g. Spar, VG.

Discount houses
Broad merchandise assortment (soft and hard goods); price is main sales appeal; relatively low operating cost ratios; relatively inexpensive buildings, equipment and fixtures; self-service; limited customer services; rapid merchandise turnover; large leased premises.

Planned shopping centres
Integrated developments under single ownership, co-ordinated and complete shopping facilities; adequate parking; rental space is leased; joint advertising and public relations among stores in the centre.

NON-STORE RETAILING

Automatic vending machines
Stable products of low unit value; convenience products; operating costs high because of expensive machines, stocking time and maintenance costs; high prices and margins.

Mail-order houses
Receive orders and make deliveries by mail, parcel post or freight deliveries; catalogue stores; strong guarantees/liberal return policies, postage/delivery costs keep prices close to those of conventional retailers.

Door-to-door selling
Direct sales to ultimate consumer in houses; demonstration/return after trial service; cash transactions; low overhead costs; heavy travel costs; high turnover of sales people.

Figure 17.2 Characteristics of selected forms of retailing

In all cases, sales managers should be prepared to negotiate ambitious but realistic sales goals with retail outlets. One way of doing this is to monitor each retailer's performance monthly and by product through a computerized information system. If targets are not met, sales managers often visit retailers to express concern. Positive problem solving not criticism is usually sufficient. Performance of the marketing channel and the role of retailers in the channel

---

EXHIBIT 17.1   Category killers

What exactly is a 'category killer', and why are they getting so much press coverage in Europe? This dramatic label seems to have surfaced in the EU only within the last year, popular among marketing practitioners wanting to describe the fantastic success of highly focused retailers. Though the definition varies slightly across the Atlantic, the general profile of the killers is nearly the same: out of town; large; highly focused on particular categories; relying on the motto 'everyday low prices'; carrying a wide merchandise selection, often at lower margins; selling higher volumes than competitors; and leaning toward minimal to self-service staffing. Perhaps you have seen one of these retailers in your neighbourhood.

These sector masters appear in the brown goods electronics, clothing, do-it-yourself home improvement, furniture, office supplies, sporting goods, toys, and white goods electronics sectors. None seem to survive in a highly specialised grocery or food product area, suggesting that short shelf lives and the demand by consumers for convenience have staved them off.

The efficiencies for the retailer come in the form of global sourcing and supply chains while stocking internationally recognised brand names. Success stories of European origin include IKEA (pan-European furniture), Castorama (French do-it-yourself), Bauhaus (German do-it-yourself), PC World (UK hardware/software), Darty (French electronics), Office World (Swiss office products/stationery), and Olympic Sportsworld (UK sporting goods).

The Americans with an interest in Europe include Toys 'Я' Us, Lenscrafters, CostCo/Price Club (first store opening in the UK shortly), PIP Photocopying, Sports Authority (K Mart owned), T.J. Maxx, Staples (a joint venture with UK's Kingfisher), Blockbuster Video and Home Depot. Obviously, all these killers share an interest in one thing: providing better value, selection, and price to consumers no matter which side of the Atlantic they are on.

Source: Allyson L. Stewart, 'Category killers get major attention in EC', *Marketing News*, 8 November 1993: 9.

---

may be evaluated in terms of four criteria: the ability of the system to provide goods and services in the quantities desired; at the time needed; at the locations desired; and displayed in combination with complementary and substitute items to meet market demand and provide assortment breadth (Figure 17.3).

Developing a distribution policy

The type of distribution policy employed depends on the product itself and on other marketing policies. The nature of the product determines to a large

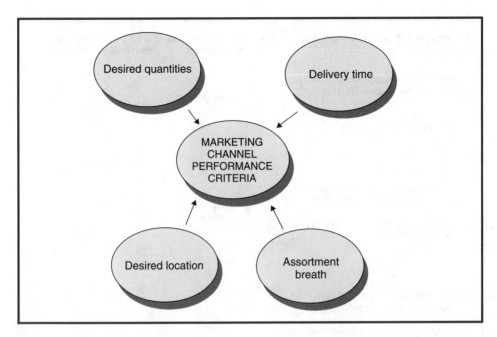

Figure 17.3   Performance measures in the marketing channel

extent whether users rely on providers or distributors as primary sources of technical information and supply availability. If the product is technically complex, users desire a direct relationship with the source of product technology (Corey *et al.*, 1989: 45). For industrial products, the source is usually the original equipment manfucturer, but it could be other channel members if they have accumulated the necessary technical skills. In such circumstances, gaining sales volume in the short run is not an appropriate goal for many firms, and uncontrolled distribution is likely to bring with it some serious long-term problems. It may be more appropriate to build up good demand relationships between the manufacturer and the customer.

In developing a distribution policy for consumer products, it is necessary to examine the relationship between product type and likely form of distribution, while taking into account the patronage motives of consumers. Here it is necessary to distinguish among convenience products, which are purchased frequently, immediately and with the minimum of effort in comparison and buying (e.g. cigarettes, newspapers, confectionery); shopping products, which involve much comparison regarding suitability, quality, price and style in the process of selection and purchase (e.g. furniture, used cars, dress apparel and major appliances); and speciality products, which have unique characteristics or brand identification for which buyers are habitually willing to make a special buying effort (e.g. stereo components, photographic equipment). Detailed knowledge of buyer behaviour is essential, therefore, in forming distribution policy (Figure 17.4).

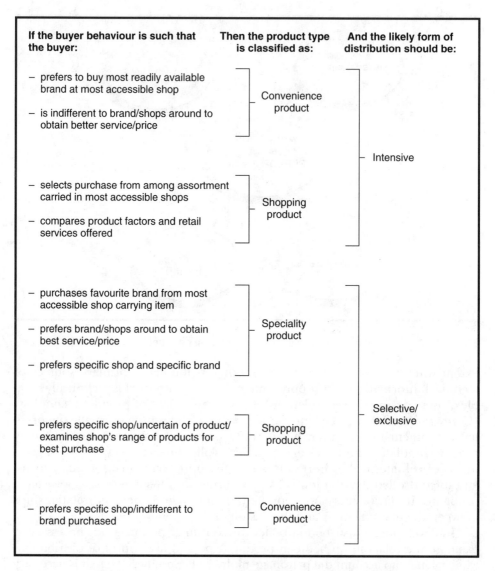

Figure 17.4 Relationship between buyer behaviour, product type and form of distribution

Effective management of distribution channels

Marketing is concerned in the broadest terms with the process of consumption and the behaviour of buyers and sellers in that process. Distribution, on the other hand, is concerned with achieving availability for that consumption. Competition in marketing channels is not defined by horizontal relationships

760

involving wholesalers or retailers only. Competition is a system phenomenon involving the entire distribution system, comprising the entire network of interrelated institutions and agencies. The way that individual manufacturers and distributors co-ordinate their activities determines the viability of one channel configuration over another, comprising different institutions and agencies handling similar or substitutable products.

Objectives of channel members

In developing the ideal channel system design, it is necessary to achieve a subtle blending of the needs and objectives of all parties in the system – producer, consumer and intermediaries (Proudman, 1976: 15). The way that this process might be balanced is illustrated in Figure 17.5. The ultimate criterion for eval-

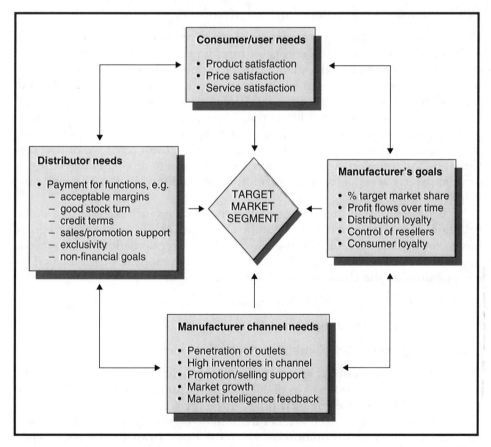

Figure 17.5 Balancing channel member needs

(Source: Proudman, 1976: 15. Reprinted by permission of the Chartered Institute of Marketing)

761

uating the pay-off of alternative channel systems for the manufacturer or inter-mediary is profit flows over time, related to the resource commitments involved in each alternative and the associated risks. Resources include man-agement skills and the financial assets of the firm.

The manufacturer identifies a set of goals related to market share, profit, reseller relationships and customer loyalty, which are translated into channel needs regarding penetration of outlets, inventories, promotion, sales growth and market information. The distributor in turn must be paid for the func-tions performed, and other non-financial goals are usually involved. Lastly, the distribution channel must be capable of serving consumer needs satisfaction. These criteria are established for each target marketing in the company's port-folio of markets.

Interdependence among channel members

Most important to the implementation of effective channel management is an understanding that channels consist of interdependent institutions and agen-cies. Tasks performed by the manufacturer support wholesaler activities. This type of dependency is essential in order to divide labour effectively and achieve the objectives of the channel. It also creates conflict in the channel. Conflicts, some of which are beneficial, often arise in a distribution channel over how much inventory should be carried by various members, or who has the right to represent a particular product within a given territory, or why dis-tributors and retailers are sometimes bypassed when direct selling is used. Conflict which arises as a result of mutual dependence in the channel con-tributes to innovation.

It is necessary that the roles of each channel member be defined for a dis-tribution system to be effective. Within a channel this requires some agree-ment concerning the domain of each member: the population to be served, the segment and territory to be covered, and the functions to be performed by each member in the channel. To achieve this three steps are necessary:

- identify the relevant market segment;
- establish market targets; and
- specify precise relationships between channel members.

To specify relationships we make use of the concept of a channel flow in making products and services available for consumption. Stern and El Ansary (1988) have identified eight such flows: three are forward flows only, two are reverse flows only and three are bi-directional (Figure 17.6). Physical posses-sion, ownership and promotion are forward flows from producers to con-sumers. Negotiation, financing and risking flows move in both directions, ordering and payments are backward flows. A ninth flow could be added which is a backward flow, that of market intelligence.

762

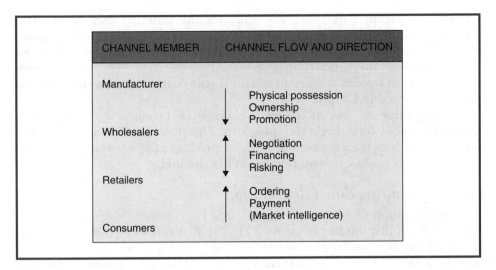

Figure 17.6 Marketing flows in distribution channels
(Source: Adapted from Stern and El-Ansary 1988: 13–14).

Any time that inventories are held by a channel member involves a financing operation. When a wholesaler takes title and assumes physical possession of a product, the wholesaler is financing the manufacturer, since there are inventory-carrying costs. Thus when manufacturers are freed from holding inventory, they may reinvest the funds in further production. Other examples of backward financing are found when store buyers commit themselves to purchasing a large volume of fashion products prior to production. The commitment may be factored and the cash used by the manufacturer.

Forward financing flows are also common. Manufacturers of cars and durable goods often arrange with banks and lending institutions to make finance available to final consumers and to wholesalers and retailers as well.

Level of service in distribution channel

The service level of a marketing channel may be thought of as purchase size, delivery time, retail outlet location and range of products available. It is difficult to measure quantitatively the performance of a channel in terms of the service provided, but a qualitative assessment of some of the changes which have recently occurred is possible. In recent years, consumers have been buying larger quantities, requiring less service from the channel in this respect. The increase in transaction size permits retailers to buy in larger quantities, which reduces the need for wholesaling services. In turn, these developments permit lower distribution costs, since marketing channel service outputs are reduced, and thus lower prices to consumer are possible.

At the same time, however, consumers or industrial buyers continue to be unwilling to accept longer delivery times for the products they desire. The unwillingness of buyers to postpone purchases or accept longer delivery times is rewarded not by lower prices, but by rapid or immediate acquisition and consumption of the product in question. Possession of the product when desired is of paramount importance. This is part of the phenomenon 'time to market' discussed in Chapter 8.

Rising affluence has increased the range of products that consumers would like to buy on a single shopping trip. This poses additional distribution problems, such as the provision of broader product ranges within a shop and increases in specualtive inventories within the channel.

Factors favouring direct distribution

The configuration of four sets of factors to a large extent determines the viability of direct distribution (Figure 17.7). The first relates to the capability of the company. It is necessary that the company have sufficient resources available to support a direct marketing approach. This will usually involve the establishment and maintenance of a sales force. The company will also need to have sufficient time available to develop direct distribution before potential competition becomes a threat.

The second set of factors relates to product and service characteristics. When the manufacturer's staff are required in selling and servicing, because of the complexity of the product, direct distribution is favoured. Computer

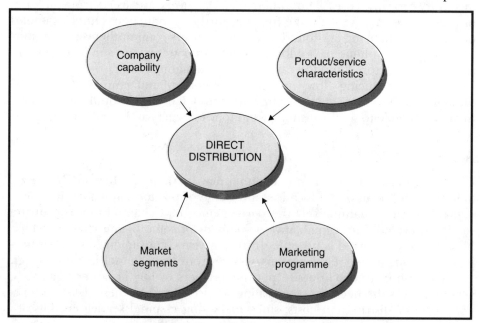

Figure 17.7   Factors favouring direct distribution

sales and service fall into this category. A wide product line also favours direct distribution, since the sales force carries a broad range of products (e.g., Avon and Tupperware). Direct distribution is also favoured in many industrial markets where product application assistance is required. Process control panels usually fall into this category, for example. Direct distribution is also favoured where product technology is changing rapidly.

Market segments with relatively few customers tend to favour direct distribution, especially if purchases are large in terms of quantity or price. It is also favoured when customers are geographically concentrated and when there is sufficient margin to support personal selling or direct marketing efforts. Direct distribution is also attractive when the purchase decision involves a major long-term commitment by the buyer.

The nature of the marketing programme or marketing mix also determines to some extent whether direct distribution is likely to be successful. It is more likely to be successful when personal selling is an important feature of the marketing mix, and when normal intermediary functions such as storage, local credit and repackaging can be performed by the manufacturer or are not required.

Tactical and strategic distribution management

Sometimes the company discovers that the distribution channel is not performing as well as it should. There are a number of tactical moves the company can make to optimize the existing channel configuration. Strategic change can only be implemented in the longer term, however. Short-term changes which can be relatively easily introduced include:

- more frequent and timely delivery of products to key outlets;
- setting strict sales quotas for each product line for various retailers;
- better profit opportunities for retailers;
- more advertising and promotion support;
- improved incentive systems for sales people; and
- manufacturer–retailer agreed plans to eliminate weaknesses in the system.

In the mid-term, it may be necessary to develop new channels, especially when traditional channels are saturated or blocked. In some situations, particularly in opening up new markets, manufacturers may have to design a distribution system to provide a retail structure on which future development can occur (Exhibit 17.2). It may also be necessary to develop new retailers and to change the manufacturer's perception of what are 'appropriate' ways to reach customers. Distributing L'eggs Hosiery in an egg-shaped container, which assisted supermarkets to sell a non-traditional product, and selling bubble packs of batteries in variety shops and supermarkets in addition to electrical goods outlets, are illustrations of mid-term changes that can be introduced.

EXHIBIT 17.2   Distribution in the People's Republic of China

Without doubt the biggest constraint in marketing consumer goods in China is distribution. There are myriad problems: unreliable and inexperienced wholesalers; credit risks; and transportation bottlenecks. For packaged food manufacturers, the biggest problem lies at the retail level. Specifically, the distribution system for packaged food remains unsophisticated and incredibly fragmented.

While it is generally true that a firm could have products distributed on a huge scale almost instantly by selling to all comers, that firm would have no control over how its products were sold. Many would end up in an open-street environment where turnover is generally low and products quickly deteriorate.

Manufacturers hoping to distribute in a controlled fashion are presented with the following options:

- Products can be sold in the limited number of 'A' stores, such as department stores.

- The other choices are 'B' and 'C' stores, such as traditional small retailers.

The latter are frequented often by many people, but not all of these consumers can afford packaged food.

Although few firms have long years of experience in the market, one lesson is already clear: the successful firms have their own sales forces and merchandisers. While wholesalers can be quite efficient at getting goods from point A to point B, they are not concerned with getting the products on the shelf, ensuring they are priced properly and preventing damaged goods from being put on sale. In 1990, about 60 per cent of sales in Guangdong were ex-warehouse, with customers picking up the product themselves. Now, only about 20 per cent of sales is done that way. The rest of the retailers expect the goods to be delivered to them.

Source: 'China supplement', *Business Asia*, 17 January 1994: 7.

In the longer term, new and multiple channels may be developed. A trend towards direct marketing in some industries is in evidence, but such direct contact with customers is unlikely to be feasible in some situations: for example, in food distribution where there is a requirement for a cold chain, when it is difficult to locate customers and when cultural barriers exist. Another development is franchising, which is a low-cost way of distribution in many industrial and service sectors particularly. This may be viable for well-organized companies possessing strong brand names, proven marketing skills and products that are difficult to imitate.

Strategic goals for the distribution channel

The company has five strategic goals for the distribution channel serving customers (Cateora, 1993: 459–61). While Cateora has recently added a sixth C – the capital required – concern here rests with cost, control, coverage, character and continuity, referred to as the five Cs (Figure 17.8).

In regard to cost, companies must consider the capital or investment cost of developing a marketing channel and also the cost of maintaining it. The maintenance costs include the direct expenditure of a sales force or the margins and commission of distributors.

Using its own sales force gives the company maximum control, although it imposes additional cost burdens. As channels grow longer, the ability of the manufacturer to control price, sales volumes, promotional methods and type of outlet used is diminished. Many firms do not attempt to control the final destiny of their products and are satisfied merely to use the services of a distributor, which in turn passes them to others for further distribution. Such a firm can hardly be expected to know where its product is going, what volume of sales can be expected and so on.

The third major goal for the marketing channel is target market coverage. This means gaining the optimum volume of sales obtainable in each segment, securing a reasonable market share and attaining satisfactory market penetration. Coverage also includes the concept of full representation of all the company's product lines. Sometimes distributors are willing to take the high-margin products in the manufacturer's line and will neglect or refuse to handle other products which the manufacturer might wish to emphasize. Indeed, broadened product lines may make it possible to have a dedicated sales force in the market that could not be supported by single products or a limited range of products.

The fourth goal is to ensure that the marketing channel fits the character of both the company and the markets in which it is doing business. Sometimes fitting or matching the two characters is impossible. In such circumstances, some firms leave a market rather than compromise on company standards. In other instances, company standards are adhered to and local channel characteristics are ignored, resulting in serious distribution problems. Such conflicts are common especially in longer channels and in intermediate markets.

Lastly, if a channel is to perform consistently, it must have continuity. This reason by itself encourages many companies to set up their own sales force and distribution organization. Channels of distribution often pose longevity problems. Many distributors have little loyalty to their suppliers. They handle brands in good times when the line is making money, but will quickly reject such products within a season or year if they fail to perform during that period. Less well-known brands are particularly vulnerable to this type of threat in the larger retail outlets. Supplier allegiance is easily tempted by

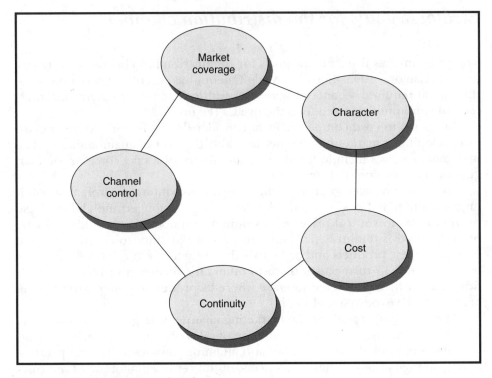

Figure 17.8   The five Cs in distribution
(Source: Based on Cateora, 1993: 459–61. By permission of Richard D. Irwin)

larger margins, better promotional allowances and other types of inducement. These are the issues which give rise to the greatest difficulty between manufacturers and retailers.

In building and managing the overall marketing channel strategy, the five Cs must be matched, balanced and harmonized with one another to build a service-oriented and cost-effective distribution organization. The company's entire distribution strategy should be one of balancing the desirable goals of minimizing distribution cost and maximizing the advantages of the other four Cs.

Formulating a distribution strategy

Marketing channel decisions

Selecting a marketing channel means deciding who the company is going to work with in the distribution system. The decision to work together may be mutual. In making the choice, some factors are important to intermediaries while a separate set are important to the manufacturer (Table 17.1).

TABLE 17.1 Manufacturer and intermediary selection criteria

Factors important to intermediaries in establishing relationships with manufacturers	Factors important to manufacturer in selecting intermediaries
1. Manufacturer's product/brand image and trade reputation of manufacturer.	1. Contacts and relationships with customers in target markets.
2. Support/assistance provided.	2. Capabilities, reputation and past performance for sales and service.
3. Compatibility of product with existing line.	3. Match of functions provided with manufacturer's needs.
4. Potential profit contribution of product to intermediary.	4. Potential contribution of manufacturer's product or service to intermediary's needs (profit, contribution, gaps in line, existing products, etc.).
5. Anticipated reaction of channel members to addition of manufacturer to channel system.	5. Probability of effective long-term working relationship.
6. Estimated start-up costs in adding new product.	6. Financial status and management ability.

Factors affecting choice of channel

A major determinant of channel structure is whether the product is intended for the consumer or industrial market. Industrial buyers usually prefer to deal directly with the manufacturer, but most consumers make their purchases from retail stores. Products which are sold to both industrial users and consumer are likely to be sold through multiple channels.

Product characteristics also play a role in determining marketing channel structure. Perishable products such as fruit and vegetables, and fashion garments with short life cycles, typically move through relatively short channels direct to the retailer or ultimate user. Bakeries distribute their bread and cake products direct from the bakery to the retail shelves, and in some markets within a short distance of its premises, through van sales direct to the consumer. Daily doorstep milk deliveries are still a feature in some towns and cities. Complex products, such as custom-made installations or mainframe computer equipment, are also typically sold direct from the manufacturer to the buyer. In contrast, the more standardized a product and the less perishable, the more indirect the channel is likely to be. Such items are usually distributed by wholesalers.

Another generalization concerning marketing channels is: the lower the unit value of the product, the longer the channel. Installations and more expensive industrial and consumer products use shorter, more direct channels.

The characteristics of the manufacturer can also determine the structure of the marketing channel. Companies with adequate financial, marketing and managerial resources may be less inclined to use intermediaries. Financially strong manufacturers can develop their own sales force, warehouse their products and grant credit to retailers or consumers. Weaker firms must rely on wholesalers and other intermediaries for these functions, and production-oriented firms may be forced to use the marketing expertise of an intermediary.

A company with a broad product line is better able to market its products directly to retailers or industrial users, since its sales force can offer a variety of products to their customers and thus spread marketing costs over a number of products and make direct marketing more feasible.

Environmental factors which tend to affect channel choice are usually legal and regulatory matters. For example, channel choice may be affected if there are laws concerning exclusivity and compensation of intermediaries and agents. Environmental protection regulations constrain manufacturers in the amount and type of material used. These issues are discussed in more detail in Chapter 18.

Choosing a marketing channel

Every company faces a series of alternatives relating to making its product or service available and accessible to consumers. Assume an established manufacturer of basic chemicals which is facing declining profits and is considering marketing a product that can be used to kill lice on caged birds such as budgerigars. Assume further that the product is a significant departure from the company's present consumer marketing, and that present channels of distribution are far from ideal in reaching the caged-bird market effectively. The company might use a four-step approach as follows:

- itemize alternative outlets used to purchase the product;
- determine how much of the product is sold through each outlet;
- specify the primary channels to reach the outlets; and
- measure the relevant factors at each of the previous steps.

The first step in determining the type of intermediary to use in reaching this market would be to itemize alternative ways in which caged-bird owners could purchase the lice powder. The buyer represents the starting point in channel design. The caged-bird owner may obtain the product from at least five sources:

- conventional retail outlets (e.g. hardware stores, pharmacies);
- specialized pet supply shops and equipment retailers;
- mass retailer outlets (e.g., supermarkets, department stores and discount houses);

- caged-bird clubs; and

- direct marketing companies.

In the second step, management attempts to assess the relative volumes of lice powder that move through each of these types of outlet, their relative rates of growth and their relative profitability as channels. The company also attempts to learn from caged-bird owners the value they play on price, convenience, packaging and the effectiveness of the lice powder, in order to assess further the relative standing of the various outlets in facilitating delivery of these features.

The next step in the analysis of alternatives is to specify the primary channel patterns that the company might follow in reaching these outlets or markets. Five radically different paths that the firm might take to market the new product are:

- present distributors of industrial chemicals;

- new distributors already selling to the caged-bird trade;

- buying a small company already in this market to gain access to its distributors;

- selling the chemical in bulk to companies already in the market; and

- packaging and selling the chemical through direct mail to caged-bird owners.

Each of these alternatives has advantages which should be analyzed in qualitative and quantitative terms.

Intensity of market coverage

Judging from behaviour in the market, it would seem that Unilever defines adequate distribution for Lux soap as almost every supermarket, discount store, pharmacy and variety store. Some products require intensive distribution, others may be distributed through selective outlets, while others may require exclusive distribution.

Intensive, selective and exclusive distribution

Manufacturers of convenience products, such as toothpaste, which attempt to provide a saturation coverage of their potential markets are the prime users of intensive distribution. Soft drinks, cigarettes, sweets, newspapers and magazines are made available in convenient locations to enable the buyer to obtain the desired article with a minimum of effort. Mass coverage and low unit prices make the use of widespread distribution almost mandatory. Goodyear changed its approach to selling tyres when it realized that it was being so exclusive in its selection of outlets that insufficient buyers had an opportunity to purchase. By making the tyres available in much more extensive distribution, company fortunes improved (Exhibit 17.3).

Not all products benefit from intensive distribution. A policy of selective distribution means selecting a small number of retailers to handle the firm's product line. Motor manufacturers follow a policy of selective distribution. Very few car dealers handle Ford, Nissan, Fiat, Renault, Citroën, Volvo and Toyota cars at the same time. Usually a number of dealers are appointed for a given area. A large city might be served by five or six dealers. By limiting the number of retailers, the firm may reduce its total marketing costs while establishing better working relationships within the channel. Co-operative advertising can be used for mutual benefit. Marginal retailers are avoided. Where service is important, dealer training and assistance are usually provided by the manufacturer. Price cutting is less likely, since fewer dealers are involved.

Manufacturers sometimes grant exclusive rights to a distributor or dealer to sell in a geographic region – an extreme form of selective distribution. Imported durable consumer goods, expensive car marques and industrial equipment are frequently handled on an exclusive basis. Some market coverage may be sacrificed through a policy of exclusive distribution, but it is often offset through the development and maintenance of an image of quality and prestige for the products, and the reduced marketing costs associated with a small number of accounts. Both manufacturer and retailer co-operate closely in decisions concerning advertising and promotion, stocks to be carried by the retailer and prices. There are a number of advantages and disadvantages associated with selective or exclusive distribution, and by implication intensive distribution (Table 17.2). Active participation from the retailer, implied in selective and exclusive distribution, is particularly desirable when:

- the product requires demonstration (e.g. cars, video recorders, microwave ovens);

- after-sales service is required;

- the price is relatively high, since the dealer has to make a greater effort to sell it; and

- the company wants to sell a range of products.

The manufacturer usually gives selective and exclusive dealers sales promotion and advertising support;

- support in finding customers;

- advice on how to reduce retail costs; and

- supplier credit and interest-free loans for new endeavours.

EXHIBIT 17.3 Goodyear is gunning its marketing engine

Stanley C. Gault wants to know what Goodyear Tyre and Rubber Co. has done for the customer lately. Gault's goal: to recapture the market share lost by the flagship Goodyear brand. On March 3, Goodyear took its biggest step yet to regain lost ground, jolting its dealers by announcing that it would sell seven Goodyear-brand tyre lines through Sears, Roebuck & Co.

Drastic measures were probably in order. Goodyear has seen the share of the US replacement car-tyre market held by its name brand fall from roughly 15 per cent to 12 per cent since 1987. A big reason for the drop is that Goodyear simply wasn't putting its tyres where shoppers would buy them. Increasingly, consumers are buying their tyres at multibrand discount outlets as well as warehouse clubs (Table 1). Alone among US tyre makers, Goodyear has sold its brand almost exclusively through its own stores and independent dealers loyal to Goodyear. Those stores have a pricey image, says Gault, and potential customers who do come in encounter a selection that hasn't changed much lately.

TABLE 1 How the tyre business is turning: share of US car-tyre sales

Type of outlet	1982 (%)	1992[1] (%)
Traditional multibrand	44	44
Discount multibrand	7	15
Mass merchandisers	20	14
Company-owned	10	9
Service stations	11	8
Warehouse clubs	–	6
Other	8	4
Total	100	100

[1] Estimate.
Data: Goodyear Tyre and Rubber Co.

Hooking up with Sears puts more Goodyear-brand tyres where customers roll by. Sears sells 9.5 million tyres a year, more than any other retailer. Goodyear hopes to sell up to 2.5 million tyres a year at Sears, which could erase half of the market-share loss. Of course, that assumes that Goodyear won't lose any sales by its long-time dealers, some of whom are feeling slighted. That points up the two-pronged hazard of the move to Sears: Dealers are restive while the company's brand-name tyres still aren't available in the fast growing discount outlets. Gault insists that the whole Goodyear family will prosper from the new marketing approach. Some dealers disagree. Yet whether they'll start selling rival brands remains to be seen.

Source: *Business Week*, 16 March 1992: 32.

TABLE 17.2   Evaluating selective and exclusive distribution

Advantages	Disadvantages
1. Shorter distance and lapsed time between manufacturer and outlet: improves manufacturer control of outlet; can respond more quickly to turnover fluctuations at retail level.	1. Easy to lose potential customers to competing brands: difficult to find the product quickly in shops.
2. Guarantees more retailer effort: selective/exclusive rights; increase manufacturer control.	2. Provokes additional competition: retailers not on your books may deal in competing brands.
3. Larger margins for retailers.	3. Smaller market share: choosing among retailers in area may mean less overall sales.
4. Lower distribution costs for manufacturer.	4. Reduces advertising effectiveness: advertising must include dealer costs to avoid customer loss through selection of wrong shops.

Distribution intensity required

In selecting distribution for its products, the company faces a trade-off between market coverage and market control. Exclusive distribution gives greater control, whereas increased market coverage may be obtained by intensive distribution (Figure 17.9). This is a matter of considering the appropriate breadth for the channel. The issue of channel breadth focuses attention on the distinction among convenience products, shopping products and speciality products (Holton, 1958; Bucklin, 1963) already discussed in Chapter 6. Companies selling fast-moving consumer products, especially well-known brands, insist on access to consumers through the distribution channel. Many consumer product companies own their distributors to control and guarantee distribution (Exhibit 17.4).

Many manufacturers attempt to sell their products through as many retailers as possible. The motivation derives from the belief that retail shelf space is directly related to share of market, and thus the objective is to distribute products as widely and as intensively as possible. The more intensive the distribution, however, the less likely is the manufacturer to be able to support the retailer or other intermediaries.

In selective distribution, more than one intermediary exists. Selective distribution is frequently followed by clothing manufacturers. By limiting the number of intermediaries, the manufacturer is in a position to provide some reseller support. Using fewer outlets reduces the shopping convenience compared with intensive distribution.

Only one reseller is used in a system based on exclusive distribution. Exclusivity is granted by the manufacturer in the expectation that it will

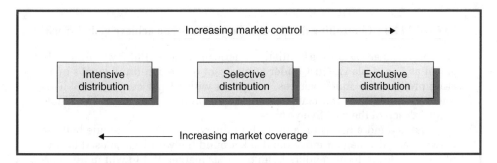

Figure 17.9   Market coverage or market control

encourage the reseller to provide strong selling support. It is assumed that consumers will be willing to seek the exclusive outlet in the area which carries the brand concerned.

Managing channels of distribution

Once the firm has decided on a distribution policy and channel design, it must manage the channel. It does this in three ways: selecting channel partners, motivating them and evaluating them.

Selecting and motivating intermediaries

Taking the problem of channel partner selection first, the manufacturer must decide on the intermediary characteristics that provide the best indication of their competence. It is important to know how long a prospective distributor has been in business, its growth record, solvency, co-operativeness and reputation. In the case of a department store or supermarket, location, future growth potential and type of clientele are important characteristics for examination.

So far it has been assumed that it is easy to find a suitable distributor. There are many manufacturers, however, who find it difficult for small food manufacturers to obtain shelf space in supermarkets and other grocery outlets.

It is also essential to motivate intermediaries to perform well. Motivation is a complex issue, since there are grounds for both co-operation and conflict between manufacturers and distributors. The manufacturer should attempt to understand the needs of the particular distributor or retailer. Channel partners are frequently criticized by manufacturers because they do not stress a given brand, or because their salesperson's knowledge of the product is not adequate, or because they neglect certain customers. Shortcomings from the manufacturer's perspective must also be examined from the intermediary's viewpoint. Four points are relevant (Figure 17.10).

775

EXHIBIT 17.4   Controlling distribution helps Coca-Cola achieve global reach

Few products are as quintessentially American as Coke. But few are as truly global as Coca-Cola Co. Just under 80 per cent of the soft-drink giant's operating profits come from overseas, compared with 51 per cent in 1985. This international blitz is the main reason Coke's profits have surged by double digits in each of the past five years.

Taking a more hands-on approach to the company's world-wide bottling network has also helped move the drink around the world. Coke used to simply leave sales to local vendors in an overseas market. But to win more international consumers over to Coke and away from such local fare as tea, coffee, wine and bottled water, the company figured the soft drink would have to be more available and affordable. So Coke not only expanded and modernised its distribution system but also began to demand more of a say in its bottlers' operations.

Coke will occasionally own 100 per cent of a bottler. In the former East Germany for instance Coke snapped up five bottling plants from the state just after the Berlin Wall fell in 1989, ensuring its place in the newly expanded German market. The quick action paid off. Last year, the company sold 80 million cases of soft drinks in the former GDR, up from none in 1988. Now that Coke has a stronger say in its bottling system, it can more easily apply its marketing savvy around the world.

Source: *Business Week*, 13 July 1992: 39.

It is important, therefore, that manufacturers recognize that the first step in motivating others is to see the situation from their viewpoint, which may mean forging a long-term partnership with distributors. Manufacturers must have a clear idea of what they expect from their distributors and what the distributors can expect from manufacturers in terms of:

- market coverage;
- product availability;
- market development;
- technical advice; and
- service and marketing information.

By cultivating a sense of partnership in the distribution channel, it may be possible to convince intermediaries, retailers in particular, that they make profits through being part of a marketing system linking manufacturer, distributor and buyer, and that it is not always necessary to seek profits primarily on the buying side through an adversarial relation with the supplier.

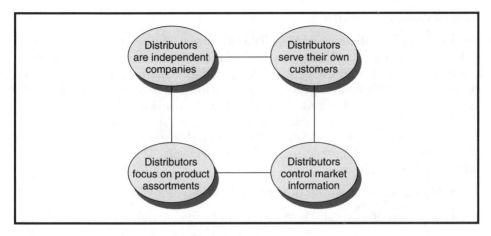

Figure 17.10   Influences on intermediary motivation

Evaluating distributors

It may be possible to manage the marketing channel by occasionally evaluating distributor performance against certain standards. Much argument can be avoided if standards of performance and sanctions for not complying with these standards are agreed between the manufacturer and channel member at the outset. The areas requiring explicit agreement are:

- sales intensity and coverage;
- average inventory levels;
- customer delivery time;
- treatment of damaged or lost products;
- co-operation on promotional and training programmes; and
- distributor services to be provided to the customer.

Manufacturers frequently use sales quotas to define performance expectations. Car and appliance manufacturers use quotas. In some cases, these quotas are treated only as guidelines; in others, they represent serious standards. One of the better ways of motivating distributors is to set quotas and to compare each distributor's sales performance for a period against its performance in the preceding period. The average percentage of improvement or decline for a group of distributors can be used as a norm. In this way, under-achievement can be identified and the underlying reasons sought with a view to a possible solution.

The distribution audit

From time to time the company is faced with the necessity of auditing its distribution arrangements. Changes in the marketing environment, new competition or changes within the company itself can give rise to the need for such a review. A distribution audit provides the basis for a change of distribution strategy in response to changed circumstances. It provides management with details of inefficiencies and early warnings of possible obsolescence of channels. Methods of auditing the marketing channel might include a comparison of net sales to costs incurred in serving it effectively. The analysis would also include an examination of:

- the different channels used by each product line;
- the costs of maintaining each channel and cost trends;
- the sales trends and sales volumes of each channel;
- the types and numbers of end-users served by each channel;
- the number of intermediaries involved in each channel;
- the degree of control over channels and the balance of bargaining power;
- contractual obligations, contract expiry dates, exclusivity rights; and
- the channels used by main competitors.

The distribution audit must be detailed and periodic to be effective. It requires considerable commitment of management time and resources.

Power, conflict and co-operation in the channel

Marketing channel performances may be evaluated by referring to economic performance and financial considerations (El-Ansary and Stern, 1972) or to relational activities linking common interests (Arndt, 1979; Noordewier *et al.*, 1990) and the use of power which creates penalties for non-compliance (Dwyer and Oh, 1987, 1988). In their pursuit of channel dominance, retailers are quick to exert their power over manufacturers when they can (Exhibit 17.5).

Sources of channel power

The ability of channel leaders to exercise control in their distribution channel stems from their access to a set of economic, social and psychological resources that gives them the opportunity to exercise power. This power may be used in a process of exchange, whereby the channel leader secures com-

---

EXHIBIT 17.5   Clout! More and more, retail giants rule the marketplace

The folks at Totes Inc. thought up a pretty nifty product. They took a heavy pair of socks, stuck rubbery treads on them to provide traction on slippery floors, and called the result slipper socks. High fashion, no. Big business, yes: A year after introducing them in 1988 Totes was selling 14 million pairs a year. Kmart Corp. and Wal-Mart Stores Inc. alone accounted for as many as 1.5 million pairs. But not for long. Within two years, both giant discounters had found suppliers that made knockoff slipper socks for less. They dropped Totes – and lowered the price of their knockoffs 25 per cent or more, to under $3 a pair.

For this $200 million Cincinnati based marketer, such reversals are the price of doing business with huge mass merchants. These days, Totes executives figure their new products have a year, at most, before these retailers crowd them out with lower-priced knockoffs. Says President Ronald Best: 'You're constantly faced with a decision: Can I afford to deal with these guys?' The brutal truth: 'You can't afford not to.'

In category after category, giant 'power retailers' are using sophisticated inventory management, finely tuned selections, and, above all, competitive pricing to crowd out weaker players. The key to its clout, says Wal-Mart's Chief Executive David Glass: 'We're probably in a better position to determine specifically what the customer wants to buy than is the manufacturer.' More and more, they're telling even the mightiest of manufacturers what goods to make, in what colours and sizes, and how to ship them and when. But that's only the beginning. Some vendors complain, usually off the record, of an unceasing barrage of demands from retailers, who want everything from discounts for new store openings to payments of fines for shipping errors to huge numbers of free samples. Says Best, 'You really have to have your act together to deal with these guys.' And there's the rub. The growing clout of big retailers tends to favour big suppliers at the expense of the little guys. It's usually only the largest manufacturers that have the capacity to produce, on time, the huge quantities required by Wal-Mart and its ilk. And only a supplier with multiple product line, a Unilever or a P & G, can offer big retailers an efficient way to buy many different products.

Source: *Business Week*, 21 December 1992: 40–2.

---

pliance from channel members in return for rewards given to co-operating channel members or penalities imposed on non-cooperative members.

Power may accrue to the leader as a result of the environment facing firms (Figure 17.11). The environment consists of the demand conditions in the market, the technology in use, the nature and extent of competition, any legal constraints which may exist, and the ability of the channel leader to capitalize on these forces and to mitigate their effect on other channel members.

However, the power of channel leaders may also reflect their own characteristics, in terms of experience, history and management. In this context it

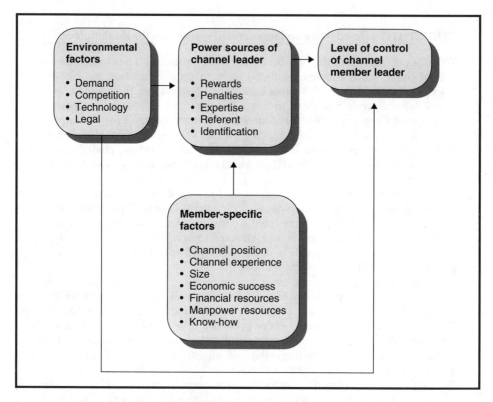

Figure 17.11   Power and control in marketing channels
(Source: Adapted from Stern and El-Ansary, 1988: 412)

should be noted that channel objectives of members change through the product life cycle. During the introductory stage, little or no control is desired because the market is begining to open. In contrast, at the maturity stage, deeper penetration is desired, so the need to ensure delivery and to develop and maintain loyalty is greater, and there is a greater need for more control. Channel members seek a channel leader to impose this discipline and harness the efforts of the entire channel.

Managing channel conflict

In attempting to manage conflict that arises in the channel, companies usually discover that one of the important sources of conflict is confusion about channel roles. Once the source has been identified, it is then necessary to develop a strategy for dealing with it. Sometimes power can be used to manage conflict and turn it to good effect. The question of conflict in the channel has been examined by Rosson and Ford (1980), who found that there was strong empirical support for the hypothesis that low levels of conflict are associated with high performance in the channel.

Conflict in channel roles

The individual firm improves its market performance by recognizing its vertical interdependence with other organizations in achieving its marketing objectives. Successful exchange in a marketing channel requires the specification of a role relationship for each channel member. The ensuing interdependence can give rise to conflict and the subsequent use of power to resolve the conflict. It is necessary to recognize that there is an interrelation among role specification, conflict and the use of power in attempting to specify appropriate roles to ensure conformity and thereby resolve conflict (Figure 17.12).

The overall objective of the effective use of power is to improve the performance of the channel. Role specification means defining appropriate behaviour for firms occupying each position in the distribution system. The firm selects a channel position which reflects its goals, expectations and values.

Role prescriptions are determined by the norms that channel members set for each other, or are dictated by the channel leader. They indicate what each member desires from all channel members, including themselves relative to their respective degree of participation in the channel. Role consensus enables channel members to anticipate the behaviour of others and to operate collectively in a unified manner.

Functional interdependence requires a certain minimum level of co-operation to accomplish the channel tasks assigned or specified, but companies seek to be autonomous and independent. They manifest a mixture of co-operative and autonomous motives, which can lead to conflict. Channel conflict arises

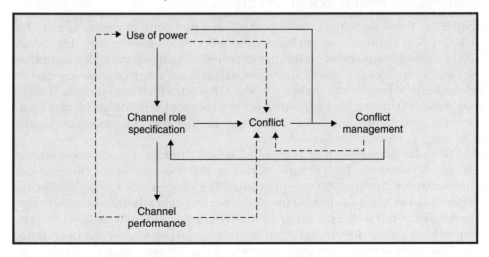

Figure 17.12 Conflict and power related to channel performance

when one channel member perceives another to be impeding the achievement of its goals and restricting its role performance. For example, large retailers, especially large supermarkets, frequently have objectives which are incompatible with those of small manufacturers.

Domain conflict may also exist, whereby manufacturers compete with some of their own wholesalers, a situation which frequently occurs when manufacturers decide to use multiple channels (Cespedes and Corey, 1990). Price competition for an identical product sold through different channels may give rise to this form of channel conflict. An example would be an article of women's clothing sold through the ladies' section in a department store, sold in a traditional drapery store in the suburbs, or sold in a boutique. Such price competition can be damaging to the carefully cultivated image the manufacturer has created.

There is, therefore, often considerable friction in the distribution channel, much of which occurs because intermediaries:

- are exclusively tied to competitors;

- will not expand their range of products;

- do not accept the terms of sale they are offered;

- are not suitable but there is no alternative available;

- have large turnover and hence exert power regarding price and discounts; and

- wish to promote their own brands and not those of the manufacturer.

Strategies to manage channel conflict

There are three principal ways to manage channel conflict and to ensure that it is directed to improving performance rather than allowing it to degenerate into a destructive element within the channel: bargaining strategies, boundary strategies and interpretation strategies. Bargaining involves agreeing certain commitments between the parties in the channel, which may include making concessions. Underlying bargaining is the process of rewarding channel members for compliance, the possibility of threatening others for non-compliance and using compromise where effective.

Boundary strategies may be applied by the sales force and people in purchasing departments. Both groups operate on the boundary of the company and interact with other companies and groups. The process may involve diplomatic representation between channel members. Success depends on how well channel members consult with each other to resolve conflict before it matures. Success depends on a clear understanding of organizational procedures and operations.

The third response involves agreeing on the interpretation of roles and functions within the channel. In attempting to agree appropriate roles for each other, channel members frequently become members of each other's trade associations and chambers of commerce and industry.

In all situations, a degree of channel leadership is required where the primary objective is to manage the entire channel. Generally, power is used to co-ordinate, specify and implement channel synergy. The most successful retailer–supplier relationships involve compromise and a delicate balancing of

---

EXHIBIT 17.6   Category killers consolidate manufacturers

In some businesses, the emergence of category-killer merchants is forcing a consolidation among manufacturers that mirrors the concentration among retailers. Take the toy industry, where Toys 'Я' Us Inc. controls some 20 per cent of the retail market. The manufacturing side today is dominated by just six companies, while a decade ago, no one toy-maker controlled more than five per cent of the market. The crucial difference today is that the best retailers are harnessing powerful information systems to stock what customers want, when they want it. And they expect suppliers to act quickly on that knowledge.

Increasingly, manufacturers are seeking input from retailers at the earliest stages of product development. To better serve their retail customers, other consumer-goods giants are revamping not just their product lines but their very organisational structures. Consider Bordon Inc. 'We've had 28 different people dealing with Wal-Mart.' The fragmentation meant that Borden had little muscle in the marketplace. Borden will meld its eight sales organisations, six distribution operations, and five information systems into one to deal with big customers.

The most successful retailer–supplier relationships involve compromise and a delicate balancing of interests. Many point to the Gitano Group Inc. as a supplier that lost its balance. The trendy apparel maker watched its revenues soar from $30 million in 1980 to $780 million in 1991. A good share of the growth came from Wal-Mart, which last year accounted for 26 per cent of the company's sales. In fact, Gitano sells too much to Wal-Mart. As a result, other retailers have started to shy away from Gitano as an over exposed and under priced brand. The relationship with Wal-Mart, says one former high-ranking executive is 'what killed the brand'. Working with the chain, he says, was like 'dancing with a gorilla, and suddenly you're married to it'.

Adding to the manufacturer worries is Wal-Mart's edict a year ago that it would no longer deal with the most independent brokers and manufacturer's representatives. Wal-Mart says that it needs direct communication with its vendors. Indeed, cherishing smaller retailers may become a key strategy for a supplier aiming to keep some clout for itself. But what if the growing clout of powerful retailers stifles too many small companies and forces too many large ones to dodge risks? The close ties between retailers and their surviving suppliers could ultimately end up raising consumer prices and reducing innovation.

Source: *Business Week*, 21 December 1992: 43–4.

interests. Increasingly, however, channel integration and consolidation are being driven by powerful retailers (Exhibit 17.6).

Using channel power to manage conflict

A constructive use of power can also ensure that conflict is a positive force in the system. Power is the ability of one channel member to get another to do what the latter would not otherwise have done. There are five sources of power in the channel (Figure 17.13). Rewards are beliefs by one firm that a second firm has the ability to mediate rewards for it: for example, provide wider margins and promotional allowances. Coercion refers to the belief that some form of sanction will ensue if the firm fails to conform. Sanctions might include margin reduction, slowing down of shipments, reduced territory rights and other such restrictions. Expertise refers to the company's perception that another possesses special knowledge: for example, manufacturers providing managerial training for marketing intermediaries. Referent power refers to the identification of one firm with another and reflects the attraction of being thus associated. The power arising from legitimacy stems from values internalized by one firm, giving it the feeling that the other has a right to exert influence and that the first has an obligation to accept it.

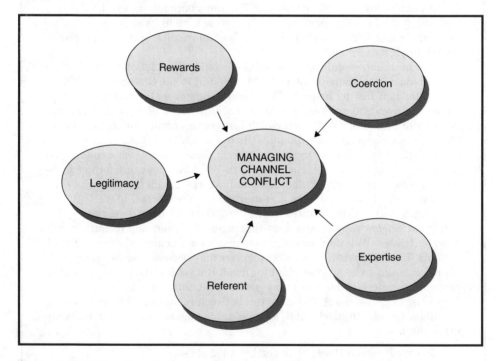

Figure 17.13   Use of power to manage channel conflict

The ability of one company to exert power indicates that a dependent relationship exists in the channel. One company in some way depends on the more powerful company. Dependence and power are issues much discussed in the channel literature. Dependence is the potency of external groups in the company's environment (Pfeffer and Salancik, 1978: 52). In contrast, power is the ability of one company to influence the decisions or behaviour of another (El-Ansary and Stern, 1972).

Dependence of buyers on sellers and the power of the former over the latter may be viewed from the perspective of the buyer and seller. From the buyer's perspective, dependence represents the seller's ability to contribute needed resources to the success of the buyer's operations (e.g. merchandising equipment and training programmes), and is the basis of the seller's power. From the seller's perspective, the basis for buyer dependence represents the seller's ability to create distinct buyer advantages unattainable from alternative suppliers.

In markets for industrial products, the supplier of an original brand may escalate the distributor's switching costs by calling directly on user-customers to encourage their shifting to another distributor as a source of supply (Corey *et al.*, 1989: 143). Seller activities contributing to buyer efficiency also help to motivate buyers to remain loyal and committed to the relationship. The reverse may also be true: that the seller depends on the buyer for an outlet for the product and an efficient way of reaching the final user. In some situations, dependence is mutual. In retail markets today, especially with the concentration in food retailing, manufacturers are very dependent on a handful of large buyers in any national country market.

The use of power is something separate. Power may be used as a defensive weapon to regulate the relationship between buyer and seller by influencing responses. Power also may be used to create barriers that prevent competing products from reaching distributors or reduce the access of such products to distributor customers. Suppliers sometimes demand that distributors discontinue dealing with certain sellers, or require that their products receive special attention. The response of distributors may reflect the level of dependence: when dependence is low, distributors may not tolerate the burden and may turn to alternatives (Bucklin, 1973). When dependence is high, distributors may comply but take some action in an attempt to lessen future dependence.

Many authors have attempted to explain sources of power and the emergence of leaders within channels of distribution. One author argues that channel leaders emerge when the environment is threatening (Etgar, 1977). These threats arise from:

- product/service demand characteristics;
- the technology used and the risk of obsolescence;
- the level of channel competition for space; and
- the need for control.

Controlling the marketing channel

The ability of the company to control its intermediaries is a key part of the company's distribution strategy. Control is an issue particularly where the channel used is independent rather than integrated. Channel control is characterized by the degree of congruence between distributor goals and those of the supplier. It also refers to the amount, and relevance, of market information feedback from the channel, and whether the distributor conforms to certain standards determined by the supplier.

Smaller firms have particular problems in this area and often find that they must trade off control against the cost of that control. Channel control is affected by whom the company sees as the immediate customer, the intermediary or the final customer and user, and whether the company takes a passive or an active interest in the market for the product or service in question.

If there is too much control, one party may perceive a loss of autonomy, which introduces conflict. The use of economic variables can introduce a feeling of conflict between a supplier and a retailer, whereas non-economic incentives such as providing expert advice or reliable market-related information can increase independence and create the opportunity for control while reducing the feeling of conflict (Brown *et al.*, 1983: 77).

Developing countervailing channel power

While the power of a company to influence the actions of its intermediaries is primarily a function of its power sources and the dependence of the intermediary on the company, a third factor must be considered: the intermediary's countervailing power. According to Etgar (1977), countervailing power is believed to arise from:

- customer loyalty;
- the intermediary's volume;
- acquisitions of other intermediaries;
- the advertising sales ratio; and
- the strength of an intermediary's assocations.

If strong countervailing powers exist in a channel, then a distributor will find that monetary rewards and threats will be more effective than the use of non-monetary reward systems (Etgar, 1976, 1977). In practical terms, this means that the acceptance of controls will be easier where an exchange relationship exists: that is, where the intermediary accepts controls in return for a high level of service.

Evaluating distribution channels: an illustration

Performance in marketing channels means the provision of an acceptable level of service. Acceptance of the concept of service as a marketing tool has not been universal. Indeed, many companies fail not because their products are not wanted, but because they fail to deliver them in the quantities and at the time expected. Some companies use service to capitalize on their market position. Air freight and courier delivery companies were quick to exploit the service concept. Service for these firms is a major marketing platform. Here a high-cost transport mode is seen to offer important cost trade-offs because of the impact it can have on the customer's own service if affirmative answers to the following three questions are forthcoming:

- does it matter how long it takes the company to deliver an order?
- must it always be the right company?
- will substitutions be acceptable?

Only a monopoly could answer these questions in the negative. Having first determined the importance of the distribution service offering in a particular market, the company must then determine the costs and benefits of the various service alternatives available. Given that a service offered implies customer costs absorbed, will the customer response be worthwhile? In this way, it is possible for the company to segment its market based on service levels.

Short-term improvements

In the short term, there are a number of things the company can do to improve the distribution of its products and services.

- more frequent and timely delivery of goods to key outlets;
- setting stricter sales quotas per product line for various channels, and reviewing results more closely and more frequently;
- creating better profit opportunities for distributors – easier terms, more advertising and promotion support, etc.;
- more powerful incentive systems for sales people;
- problem-solving sessions where manufacturers and distributors forge joint plans to eliminate weaknesses in the system; and
- being serious about sanctions against poor performers in the distribution system.

Long-term improvements

In the longer term, it will be necessary to examine alternatives involving an investment in existing channels or the development of new channels. It may be necessary to change the company's perception of what are appropriate channels to reach customers. Companies sometimes attempt to develop new channels when traditional channels are saturated or blocked. While it is possible to develop new channels, it is necessary to recognize that the issue may be not the ownership of the channel, but market access and control.

Long-term strength in distribution is likely to come from channel multiplicity and flexibility. Franchising, for example, is a low-cost distribution device in many industrial sectors. It may be viable for well-organized firms possessing strong brand names, products which are difficult to imitate and proven marketing skills.

Direct contact with customers and users has been increasing at a rapid rate. In this regard, improvements in telecommunications are creating an electronic marketplace which may revolutionize distribution in virtually every industry. Electronic channel systems drastically reduce paperwork and increase the speed at which orders can be placed, recorded and fulfilled. The added speed and ease of use often make customers rely on the systems to such a degree that they become virtual captives, as the costs of switching from exceptionally efficient suppliers are usually substantial. The first firms in an industry to develop viable electronic distribution are frequently able to lure customers away from less advanced rivals.

Importance of periodic evaluation

Measuring the performance of the distribution channel is a task the company should address from time to time. By assessing performance, the company provides the basis for imminent decisions that need to be taken regarding distribution strategies which should be revised. Such an analysis of distribution provides the company with details of inefficiencies and an early warning of the possible obsolescence of certain channels. It is dangerous, for example, to ignore a disturbing cost trend in a distribution channel.

Companies attempt to avoid such traps by periodically evaluating the efficiencies of individual channels. In carrying out such an analysis, companies compare net sales to costs, where costs include administrative costs, transport costs, storage and other relevant costs, such as financial carrying charges. A popular measurement approach is to compare the sales growth provided by a channel to its cost growth over the same period. It is when the costs of maintaing a channel accelerate faster than its sales growth that corrective action should be taken. In measuring the performance of individual channels, the analysis should address the following issues:

- different channels used for each product line;

- costs of maintaining each channel and cost trends;
- sales trends and sales volume of each channel;
- types and numbers of end-users served by each channel;
- the number of distributors involved in each channel;
- the degree of control over channels and the balance of bargaining power;
- contractual obligations, contract expiry dates and exclusivity rights;
- channels used by main competitors.

Assignment questions

1 How do the characteristics of the following products affect the length and type of the distribution channel for each: (a) ball-point pens; (b) bread; (c) a haircut; (d) insurance; and (e) a dishwasher?

2 When would the use of multiple channels be appropriate? What are the problems associated with such a strategy?

3 Why are industrial products usually distributed directly to the customer?

4 Discuss the appropriateness of an intensive distribution policy for the following products: (a) stereo equipment; (b) milk; (c) office equipment; (d) a Rolls-Royce motor car; and (e) Christian Dior perfume.

5 What are the functions of the channel leader? Under what circumstances would (a) a manufacturer and (b) a retailer be a suitable channel leader?

6 How does conflict arise between manufacturers and retailers?

Annotated bibliography

Cateora, Philip R. (1993) *International Marketing* (8th edn), Homewood, Ill.: Richard D. Irwin, chapter 14.

Corey, E. Raymond, Frank V. Cespedes and V. Kasturi Rangan (1989) *Going to Market*, Boston, Mass.: Harvard Business School Press, chapters 1–8.

Hutt, Michael D., and Thomas W. Speh (1985) *Business Marketing Management* (3rd edn), Chicago, The Dryden Press, chapter 13.

Stern, Louis W., and Adel I. El-Ansary (1988) *Marketing Channels* (3rd edn), Englewood Cliffs, NJ: Prentice Hall.

References

Arndt, J. (1979) 'Toward a concept of domesticated markets', *Journal of Marketing*, **43**, 4, 69–75.

Brown, James R., and Robert F. Lusch and Darrel D. Muehling (1983) 'Conflict and power dependence relations in retailer–supplier channels', *Journal of Retailing*, **59**, 4, 53–81.

Bucklin, L.P. (1963) 'Retail strategy and the classification of consumer goods', *Journal of Marketing* **27**, 1, 50–5.

Bucklin, L.P. (1973) 'A theory of channel control', *Journal of Marketing*, **37**, 1, 39–47.

Bucklin, L.P., and Stanley F. Stasch (1970) 'Problems in the study of vertical marketing systems', in Louis P. Bucklin (ed.), *Vertical Marketing Systems*, Glenview, Ill.: Scott Foresman.

Cateora, Philip R. (1993) *International Marketing* (8th edn), Homewood, Ill.: Richard D. Irwin.

Cespedes, Frank V., and E. Raymond Corey (1990) 'Managing multiple channels', *Business Horizons*, **33**, 4, 66–77.

Corey, E. Raymond, Frank V. Cespedes and V. Kasturi Rangan (1989) *Going to Market*, Boston, Mass.: Harvard Busines School Press.

Dwyer, F.R., and S. Oh (1987) 'Output sector munificence effects on the international political economy of marketing channels', *Journal of Marketing Research*, **24**, 4, 347–58.

Dwyer, F.R., and S. Oh (1988) 'A transaction cost perspective on vertical contractual structure and interchannel competitive strategies', *Journal of Marketing*, **52**, 2, 21–34.

El-Ansary, A.I., and L.W. Stern (1972) 'Power measurement in the distribution channel', *Journal of Marketing Research*, **9**, February, 47–52.

Etgar, Michael (1976) 'Channel domination and countervailing power in distributive channels', *Journal of Marketing Research*, **8**, August, 254–62.

Etgar, Michael (1977) 'Channel environment and channel leadership', *Journal of Marketing Research*, **14** February, 69–76.

Heskett, J.L. (1966) 'A missing link in physical distribution design', *Journal of Marketing*, **30**, 4, 37–41.

Holton, R.H. (1958) 'The distinction between convenience goods, shopping goods and speciality goods', *Journal of Marketing*, **23**, July, 53–6.

Mallen, B.E. (1967) *The Marketing Channel: A conceptual viewpoint*, New York: John Wiley.

Noordewier, T.G., G. John and J.R. Nevin (1990) 'Performance outcomes of purchasing arrangements in industrial buyer–vendor relationships', *Journal of Marketing*, **54**, 4, 80–93.

Pfeffer, J., and G.R. Salancik (1978) *The External Control of Organizations*, New York: Harper and Row.

Proudman, A.J. (1976) 'Distribution channels: analytical aspects of the marketing system', *The Quarterly Review of Marketing*, **2**, 2, 8–16.

Rosson, Ph. J., and I.D. Ford (1980) 'Stake conflict and performance in export marketing channels', *Management International Review*, **20**, 4, 31–7.

Stern, L.W. (ed.) (1969) *Distribution Channels: Behavioural dimensions*, Boston, Mass: Houghton Mifflin.

Stern, Louis W., and Adel I. El-Ansary (1988) *Marketing Channels* (3rd edn), Englewood Cliffs, NJ: Prentice Hall.

Stern, Louis W., and T. Reve (1980) 'Distribution channels as political economies: a framework for comparative analysis', *Journal of Marketing*, **44**, 3, 52–64.

Managing market logistics

18

Marketing strategy and market logistics
Market logistics system
Market logistics decisions
European dimensions of market logistics

Introduction

This chapter introduces and explains:

- the concept of physical distribution;

- ways of measuring performance in physical distribution;

- product and customer requirements of the physical distribution system;

- how the transportation, storage and materials-handling systems work;

- the total cost concept and its application;

- the key elements in a logistics service;

- how companies provide a customer service;

- how service levels are measured;

- the significance of market logistics for time-sensitive deliveries; and

- market logistics in application.

Managing market logistics concerns the physical delivery of value to customers. It deals with all the move–store activities in the channel of distribution as products move from the point of manufacture to the point of consumption or use. Often referred to as physical distribution, market logistics emphasizes service to customers: the terms are interchangeable. The market logistics system comprises the transportation system, the storage system and the materials-handling system.

The total cost concept applied to market logistics activities attempts to minimize the total distribution system cost, subject to delivering a desired level of customer service, while making a profit for the company. There are cost and revenue factors to be considered. Various elements of customer service are also discussed and the role of time in delivering value is examined. The chapter ends with a brief discussion of recent developments in European retailing and branding, and shows how a number of companies use market logistics as an effective element of marketing strategy.

Having studied this chapter, you should be able to define the phrases listed above in your own words, and you should be able to do the following:

1. Define what is meant by market logistics.

2. Explain how companies use market logistics to compete on product innovation, service and cost.

3. Specify the tasks involved in managing market logistics.

4. Identify product and customer service requirements in designing or modifying a market logistics system.

5. Outline ways of measuring service performance levels.

6. Evaluate the level of service, suitability and cost of various transportation modes.

7. Integrate decisions on inventory into the overall physical distribution decision.

8. Apply total cost analysis to the market logistics decision.

9. Recognize market logistics trade-offs.

10. Specify key elements in customer service, recognizing the impact of cost and quality.

11. Decide the importance of time in the physical distribution function.

12. Demonstrate the impact that market logistics decisions can have on the company's overall marketing strategy.

Marketing strategy and market logistics

Marketing strategies influence many aspects of market logistics. Different marketing strategies have different implications for the market logistics goals that a company might pursue (Shapiro, 1984). They also influence inventory and transport policies and can impact on the logistics network maintained by the company (Table 18.1). Competitive strategies may be developed in regard to product innovation, customer service levels and cost leadership.

The company's competitive strategy has defined implications for market logistics. The market logistics goal for the innovating company is availability, rapid delivery for the consumer service company and minimum cost for the cost leader. In a similar way, the kind of competitive strategy adopted influences inventory, transport and logistics network decisions (Table 18.1).

Concept of physical distribution

Both marketing and manufacturing people consider logistics activities as part of their responsibilities. The responsibility of marketing for physical distribution includes field warehousing, customer service and to some extent inventory

TABLE 18.1   Obtaining competitive leverage through market logistics

Market logistics implications	Competitive strategy		
	Product innovation	Customer service	Cost leadership
Goals	Availability Flexibility to volume shifts Flexibility to product changes Cope with small orders Cope with erratic order frequencies	Rapid delivery Consistent delivery Availability Flexibility to customer changes	Minimum cost with acceptable level of service
Inventory	Tension between immediate widespread availability and obsolescence	Establish market presence with rapid consistent delivery	Minimal inventory which ensures acceptable service
Transport	Premium rapid transport Use common carrier Less than truck load shipments	Mix of short-haul and long-haul services Emergency service available Own transport to provide short-haul service	Low-cost transport High utilization Volume discounts for large direct shipments Own transport for better control and lower cost
Logistics network	Non-existent – direct delivery to customer Use public/leased warehousing if necessary	Multiechelon system likely	Centralized Consolidated Rationalized Automated

Source: Adapted with modifications from Shapiro (1984: 125). Reprinted by permission of Harvard Business School Press from Shapiro, Roy D. (1984) 'Get Leverage from Logistics', *Harvard Business Review*, **62**, 3, 119–26. Copyright © 1984 by the President and Fellows of Harvard College.

management. On the other hand, manufacturing people manage such logistic activities as traffic, finished goods inventories at the factory, purchasing and overall production scheduling. There is a potential overlap between marketing and manufacturing with respect to responsibility for market logistics activities.

Market logistics plays a very important role in delivering industrial and consumer products at the high service levels and low costs increasingly demanded throughout the supply chain. As companies expand in size and scope, the need for further investment in logistics technology increases accordingly. 'In logistics, there are no economies of scale; large companies are no faster than small businesses. They need technology to offset the complexity of their large operations,' says Joachim Miebach of Miebach Logistics, one of Europe's largest logistics consultancies (*Financial Times*, 27 January 1992: 4).

Market logistics task

The market logistics task is to co-ordinate and optimize the activities of suppliers, users, channel intermediaries and customers, so that the entire supply chain is managed in such a way that value added at each stage flows from suppliers to ultimate consumers. Market logistics or physical distribution involves planning, implementing and controlling the physical flows of materials and final goods from points of origin to points of use to meet customer requirements at a profit (Kotler, 1994: 585). 'The goal of logistics strategy is to organize companies to compete across the span of their markets without having to over charge some customers or under serve others. It means building distinct approaches to different groups of customers' (Fuller *et al.*, 1993: 91).

Physical distribution is a process involving a large number of interdependent activities concerned with the efficient movement of products from the point of production to the consumer or user. There are five tasks associated with physical distribution:

- determining the places where stocks have to be held and designing a storage system;
- introducing a materials-handling system;
- introducing and maintaining a stock control system;
- devising procedures for processing orders; and
- selecting a transportation system.

Market logistics defined

Market logistics, often referred to as physical distribution, is the term employed to describe the broad range of activities involved in the efficient movement of finished products from suppliers to users and consumers. In some cases, it involves the movement of raw materials from their source to the place of product manufacture. These activities include transportation, warehousing, materials handling, protective packaging, inventory management, plant and warehouse locations, order processing and customer delivery services.

In attempting to define the meaning of market logistics or, more precisely, physical distribution, it is useful to note that it adds time and place utility to the form utility provided in the factory. Pope (1974: 154) attempts a more exact definition: 'distribution is a part of the science of business logistics, whereby the right amount of product is made available at the place where demand for it exists at the time it exists'. According to Pope, distribution is the vital link between manufacturing and marketing.

Market logistics is also part of broader-based business logistics, which is:

> the planning, organising and controlling of all move–store activities that facilitate product flow from the point of raw material acquisition to the point of final consumption, and of the attendant information flows, for the purpose of providing a sufficient level of customer service consistent with the costs incurred for overcoming the resistance of time and space in providing the service. (Ballou, 1985: 8).

An earlier definition of logistics refers to 'the management of all activities which facilitate movement and co-ordination of supply and demand in the creation of time and place utility in goods' (Heskett *et al.*, 1964: 21).

Physical distribution management has been defined as 'the generic term widely used for the management of the flow of goods and services from the point of origin to the point of consumption' (Stern and El-Ansary, 1988: 144). Alternatively, Bowersox (1978: 60) has defined physical distribution as the co-ordination of the 'relationship between company facilities and middlemen which will result in completion of the time and place aspects of marketing with the result that both goods and their titles are moved to the market'.

Marketing, manufacturing and logistics

Because of its service characteristics, market logistics must interface and interact with the demands of marketing and manufacturing (Figure 18.1). Marketing means identifying customer values to be provided, communicated and delivered by the company. The market logistics–marketing interface involves providing a certain level of customer service, decisions regarding packaging and decisions regarding the most appropriate retail outlet. The interface also has implications for information flows both within the company and into the company.

Market logistics also interacts with manufacturing. Manufacturing is concerned with company operations and materials handling, manufacturing schedules and quality control. It is also concerned with equipment maintenance.

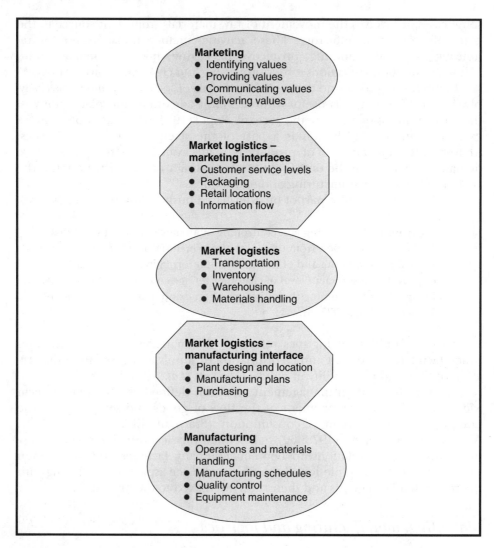

Figure 18.1 Market logistics interfaces

The interface with market logistics concerns plant design and location, manufacturing plans and purchasing decisions.

The interface between manufacturing and marketing activities becomes a management problem. The management of marketing or manufacturing in isolation can lead to overall sub-optimal behaviour for the firm. To manage interface activities effectively, some form of co-operation among the functions involved needs to be established. However, it should be noted that some of the most difficult administrative problems arise from interfunctional conflict when attempting to manage interface activities.

Measuring performance in physical distribution

Suppose that a company has developed its distribution system and wishes to examine whether or not it meets objectives set. As in many aspects of management, the company might try to measure the output of the system.

Measuring customer service levels

A basic output of a physical distribution system, as noted already, is the level of customer service. Customer service represents one of the key competitive benefits that a company can offer potential customers in order to attract their business. The principal way in which services are reflected is in the delivery of the product or service down the channel, so that consumption can take place where, when and in the form required. Performance is reflected very much in the physical distribution of the product or service and whether this activity is done well or badly. From the customer's view, service means several things:

- the speed of filling and delivering normal orders;

- the supplier's willingness to meet customer emergency needs;

- the care with which goods are delivered, so that they arrive in good condition;

- the supplier's readiness to take back defective goods and resupply quickly;

- the availability of installation and repair services and parts from the supplier;

- the supplier's willingness to carry inventory for customers; and

- service charges, i.e. whether services are 'free' or separately priced.

The company's task is to determine the relative importance of these various customer services to its target customers, and it is also necessary to know what competitors are offering. The company must decide on a competitively viable mix of customer services. Of all the services listed above, the first one, delivery time, is typically the most important to customers. Customers want goods and services delivered at the promised time. Late delivery of needed parts or services can leave expensive equipment, labour and even whole factories idle.

Influences on customer service requirements

Several factors influence the optimal level of customer service. Customers use objective criteria based on an evaluation of their perceived needs and also evaluate competitive offers of service. Four major factors are believed to dominate customer requirements:

797

- competitor's normal delivery time;
- whether expensive operations are dependent upon delivery;
- the cost of supplying higher levels of service;
- the loyalty enjoyed by the company – the higher the loyalty, the less the company must offer in the way of a delivery-time advantage.

In regard to the first point, note that the company risks losing or failing to attract customers if it offers a lower standard; and to offer a higher standard would be costly and might even lead competitors to increase their service levels, thus raising everyone's costs. Also note in regard to the third point that a company is not going to improve the delivery time at a high cost unless this will substantially improve sales. Once the company decides on a delivery-time standard, it can then design the physical distribution system to meet that standard with a high degree of reliability.

Market logistics system

The logistics element within a firm varies considerably with the type of business and how management perceives the scope of logistics and associated decision problems. A representative list of market logistics elements for a firm with substantial logistics costs illustrates these points (Figure 18.2).

Product and customer requirements

In designing a market logistics system, it is necessary to consider the product itself and customer requirements. The design of a market logistics system starts in the market and works backwards to the point of production. Concepts and implications arising out of physical distribution considerations should, therefore, emphasize market factors rather than manufacturing issues only.

Product characteristics

In discussing the product in relation to the market logistics system, due regard must be paid to a number of characteristics, such as value–weight ratios, perishability, volume, fragility and environmental danger. These attributes of the product affect decisions regarding the cost of transportation, the way goods are packed and stored, and how they are handled.

The higher the value of the product, the easier it is to absorb distribution costs and the more likely that a high-service-level logistics system design can be supported. It is necessary, however, to take account of weight as most logistics

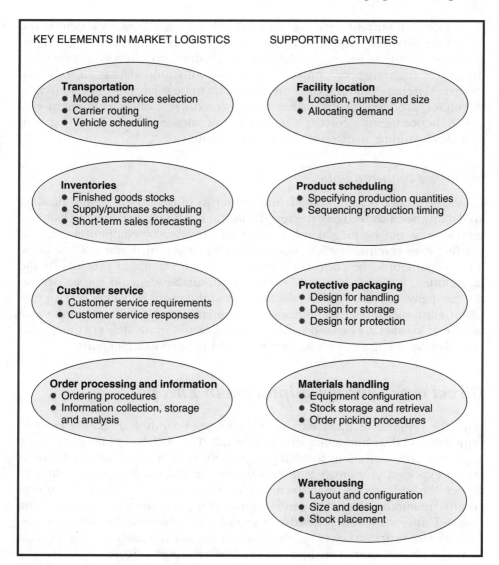

KEY ELEMENTS IN MARKET LOGISTICS

SUPPORTING ACTIVITIES

Transportation
- Mode and service selection
- Carrier routing
- Vehicle scheduling

Facility location
- Location, number and size
- Allocating demand

Inventories
- Finished goods stocks
- Supply/purchase scheduling
- Short-term sales forecasting

Product scheduling
- Specifying production quantities
- Sequencing production timing

Customer service
- Customer service requirements
- Customer service responses

Protective packaging
- Design for handling
- Design for storage
- Design for protection

Order processing and information
- Ordering procedures
- Information collection, storage and analysis

Materials handling
- Equipment configuration
- Stock storage and retrieval
- Order picking procedures

Warehousing
- Layout and configuration
- Size and design
- Stock placement

Figure 18.2 Elements of market logistics and supporting activities
(Source: Adapted from Ballou, 1985: 10–11)

costs correlate with weight, not with value. Low value to weight products, such as grain, timber and ore, incur relatively high logistics costs compared to high value to weight products such as specialized components, medical analysis equipment and certain luxury goods like expensive watches and perfumes. Storage costs for low value to weight products tend to be low because the capital invested in inventories is low. As the value to weight ratio increases, transportation costs decline but storage costs rise, creating a cost trade-off.

Another important determinant of the design of a logistics system is the weight to volume or bulk ratio. When the weight to volume ratio is high, transportation costs tend to be low relative to sales values, since the weight-carrying capacity of the transport equipment is usually fully utilized (e.g. steel, books, ingots). Materials-handling costs are also likely to be relatively low. Low weight to volume products do not utilize transportation or storage equipment efficiently, hence logistics costs as a proportion of sales tend to be high (e.g. self-assembly furniture, mattresses, foam-filled cushions).

Customer requirements

Customer service is frequently defined in terms of delivery time and product availability, such as next-day delivery from stock. The importance of customer service must not be judged relative to that provided by competitors only. If product sales revenue is a function of the service provided and not just costs, the company must be concerned with how much service to provide. At the same time, customers generally exhibit an insatiable demand for service, so the company must in addition take account of the profit impact of service provision. Customer service elements which companies use to compete in the area of market logistics are order-processing time, assembly time, delivery time, accuracy of order filling and consistency in each of the previous elements.

Direct cross-border shipments in Europe

With the removal of trade barriers in Europe and other areas, the costs of transport and distribution are expected to fall. The abolition of border checks, expensive administration, form-filling procedures and circulation restrictions are all expected to improve significantly the distribution of goods in the EU. Under the old regime, manufacturers exported goods from one European country to another. Under the new regime, it may be possible to dispatch the goods. Under such a regime, direct cross-border shipping becomes increasingly attractive for many firms that have historically consolidated shipments to replenish inventories in local national warehouses (Figure 18.3(a)). The alignment of warehousing operations with natural service areas irrespective of national border is an expected result of this improved situation (Figure 18.3(b)).

Companies in Europe are now better positioned to secure benefits from a reconfiguration of market logistics. To obtain the benefits, companies must ensure that regional or country marketing and sales work effectively with logistics when the change from a geographically based structure to a market-based structure is implemented.

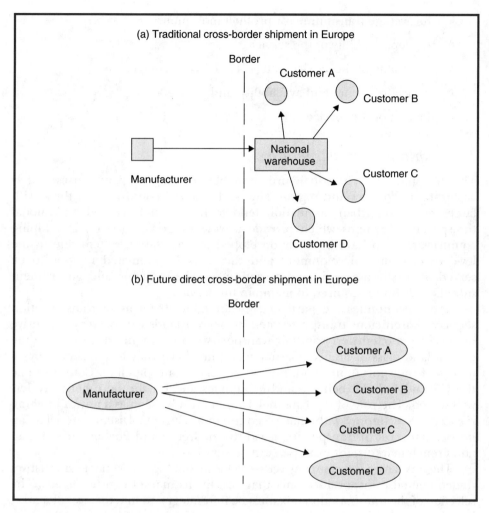

Figure 18.3 Alternative cross-border shipping methods
(Source: O'Laughlin *et al.*, 1993: 63)

The transportation system

The requirements for transportation services vary greatly from one company to another and from one customer to another. Transportation provides space and time utility in the movement of products and services to customers. It links production to markets and refers to the entire system for physically distributing products and services. A transportation system is characterized by five elements (Ballou, 1985: 35):

- the average transit time for product movement;
- the dependability of the service;
- the quality of the service in terms of loss or damage;
- service frequency and availability; and
- the cost of the service.

Transportation infrastructure

The transportation infrastructure available to the company varies widely according to country and region. Highly developed countries and those with large centres of urban population tend to have well-developed multimodal transportation systems which provide a wide range of services. Developing countries tend to have a poorly developed transportation system due to the level of economic development and the sparsely populated regions to be served. In such cases, rail transportation may be available and government subsidies are often required to maintain the services.

Island economies are particularly vulnerable in terms of transportation services. An efficient transport system to serve islands can be very expensive because an efficient ferry and air transport system is required. In Europe the central land mass of France, Germany and northern Italy is well served by all modes of transportation: road, rail, air, waterway and pipeline. Countries like the UK and Ireland, being island economies and on the periphery, are less well served. The role of the Channel Tunnel must be seen as a way of integrating the UK economy with that of continental Europe. Distance too has an impact. The cost of transporting goods from Greece and Portugal to German and French markets, for example, can be very high.

The task facing the company is to select from among the available alternatives the combined transportation mix that best fits its market logistics needs. The selection of the transportation mix must be fully integrated into the overall market logistics configuration in order to design a cost-effective service-balanced system.

Underlying the transportation decision is a complex system of national government regulations and EU directives which affect rate structures and restrictions. Regulations on driving times, rate charges and prices, access to cities and environmental protection all affect the modal choice available.

European rail traffic

All over Europe, superfast trains are beginning to dominate the passenger travel market. Within a few years it is expected that superfast trains will be able to travel between Seville and Berlin and between Rome and London. By 1996 Paris, Brussels, Amsterdam and Cologne will be linked by *trains à grand vitesse* (TGV). In France the objective is to compete with cars and planes on journeys shorter than 500 km. France is the leader in exporting fast-train technology. French companies supplied the trains for the Madrid–Seville line completed for Expo 1992 and they won the contract for the Paris–Amsterdam line over the German Inter City Express (ICE). The TGV's competitive advantage is speed: it is due to travel at 225 m.p.h. on the Paris–Brussels route, for example.

In Europe in the twenty-first century, the major traffic flows are expected to be from north to south, linking the industrial centres of France, Germany and Italy which together account for over 80 per cent of national passenger rail traffic in the member countries of the Community of European Railways (CER) (*Financial Times*, 9 May 1989: 37).

The conventional wisdom among railway authorities is that rail can best compete with road and air transport over distances of between 200 km and 1,000 km. In this regard, the TGV from Paris to Lyons has attracted 40 per cent of its traffic from the airlines and 25 per cent from the motorways (*Financial Times*, 9 May 1989: 38). Outside these limits, potential customers are likely to choose either the car or air transport. That makes Europe well suited to the development of rail services because of the large number of relatively affluent and highly mobile urban populations concentrated in a relatively small area.

The transport directorate of the European Commission reports strong support for a Europe-wide high-speed rail network, which it sees as both a unifying force within the EU and an environmentally preferable alternative to motorway construction. The CER suggests (Figure 18.4) that the main north–south traffic flows will be:

- a French Atlantic corridor serving Lille, Paris, Bordeaux, Madrid and Lisbon;

- a French corridor from Lille to Lyons and Marseilles; and

- an X-shaped double corridor starting in Amsterdam and Copenhagen/Hamburg in the north, converging in the Rhine/Main region of Germany and continuing to Milan, Rome and Naples in one direction and Munich and Vienna in the other.

In addition, there will be five east–west corridors linking:

- Lille, Brussels, Cologne and Hamburg;

- Paris, Lorraine, Saar/Alsace, Frankfurt, Stuttgart and Munich;

- Lyons, Geneva, Berne, Zurich, Stuttgart and Munich;

- Lyons, Turin, Milan, Venice and Trieste; and

- Madrid, Barcelona, Marseilles, Nice and northern Italy.

Taking this perspective, the UK, Ireland and Scandinavia are seen as peripheral markets within Europe, isolated by geography. The real importance of the Channel Tunnel is that it should allow the UK to participate in this revitalization

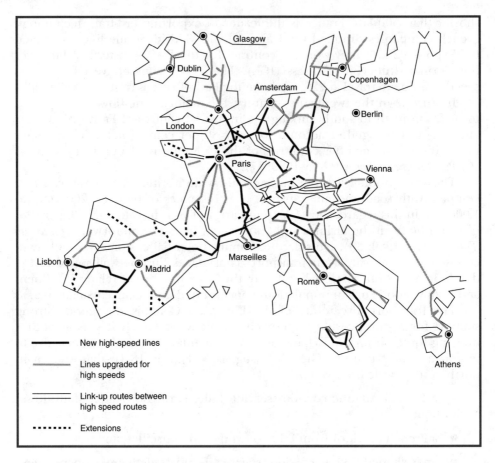

Figure 18.4   Future of EU transport links

(Source: *Financial Times*, 9 May 1989: 37. With permission)

of the European rail network, which is expected to take place in the next twenty years or so.

The improvement in European rail systems is likely to result in greater efficiency in the transportation of goods and people. The impact on journey times between major cities demonstrates the strong competitive element in the rail companies' strategy. Significant reductions in times are expected during the period to 1995 and after. Between 1980 and 1995 train journey times between London and Brussels are expected to fall from seven hours to two hours (Table 18.2). From London to Frankfurt the time is expected to fall to seven hours by 1995, and the Paris–Barcelona time may also decline to seven hours. The Alps are expected to continue resisting much improvement in journeys to Milan, but the opening of new tunnels is expected to have a significant impact on times to that city.

TABLE 18.2   Train journey times between selected EU cities, 1980–2000

Destination	From Brussels				From London				From Paris			
	1980	*1987*	*1995*	*GA¹*	*1980*	*1987*	*1995*	*GA*	*1980*	*1987*	*1995*	*GA*
Brussels	–	–	–	–	8	4.5	2.5	–	3	2		
London	7	6	2	–	–	–	–	–	6	5	3	–
Paris	1.75	1.75	1.75	1.75	6	5	3	–	–	–	–	–
Amsterdam		3		2		11		4		5.5	3.5	2.5
Hamburg	6	5		2						10	6.5	
Frankfurt	6	5	2.5	2	13	10	7	5			5	3
Munich	9	6	5.5	5					10	9	–	5
Basle	6			4	–	14	9	6			4.5	3
Milan	12	8	7	6.5					9	8	–	5.5
Lyons	8	6		3	11	8	–	4	4.5	–	2.5	2
Barcelona	16	14	8	6					12	10	7	4.5
Cologne					10	7.5	3	–	–	5.5	3	–

¹GA = '*Grand Avenir*'

Source: *Financial Times*, 9 May 1989: 38. With permission.

The storage system

The management of inventories, especially of perishables, fashion items or other time-dependent products and services, is one of the riskiest areas of marketing management. Deciding on a particular inventory assortment and subsequent market allocation in anticipation of future sales is a central aspect of marketing management, especially in fast-moving consumer goods businesses. Overstocking of unwanted items increases costs and reduces profitability through additional warehousing costs, obsolescence, insurance and deterioration in the product stored. The costs of maintaining inventory comprise three main elements:

- the costs of storage space;
- interest on the capital employed to finance stocks; and
- risk due to spoilage, loss and obsolescence.

Balancing shortages and excesses

Inventory management attempts to achieve a balance between shortages in the retail outlets and excess stock. Issues such as the replenishment cycle and economic order quantities must be managed. The storage system involves the maintenance of an appropriate level of inventories and the provision of supporting warehouse facilities and the necessary materials-handling equipment.

The ideal inventory arrangement would consist of manufacturing to a customer's specifications, which would not require any stocks of raw materials or finished goods in anticipation of future sales. While such an inventory-free arrangement is unlikely to be practicable in many circumstances, it is well to note that money tied up in stocks has an opportunity cost. Financial management in a company suggests that inventories should be kept very low to improve cash flow, but marketing demands an adequate supply of finished goods inventories to protect against stock-outs and lost sales. Gillette faced this problem as it reduced its warehousing facilities in Europe (Exhibit 18.1). Generally, most companies carry an average inventory which exceeds their basic requirements. The development of a sound policy regarding the level of stock to hold is one of the most difficult storage decisions facing the company. The focal point of such policy formulation is the establishment of the appropriate level of average inventory to hold.

EXHIBIT 18.1   Gillette reduces warehousing in Europe

Warehousing and customer service are often perceived as the last bastions of control that sales and marketing organizations have to ensure good customer service, while production and procurement are buffered from sales and marketing by the distribution function. In the fmcg [fast-moving consumer goods] industry, the separation of distribution from sales can be exceptionally difficult because of the inherently promotion-intensive nature of the consumer goods market. In this environment, local management often insists on retaining control of the design, building and delivery of vital promotional programmes.

Gillette faced this hurdle as it endeavoured to reduce warehousing facilities in Europe. Gillette's products, including blades for the Sensor, TracII, and Contour shaving systems, are totally pan-European in branding, formulation, packaging, and the use of pictograms for user instructions. Gillette is leveraging this approach to achieve greater centralization, moving from 13 country-based warehouses to five regional distribution centres.

As part of its warehouse restructuring effort, Gillette faced the question of how to configure and ship promotional/special packs locally while removing local warehouses. Gillette's organization has historically given control of promotional designs to local sales/marketing teams because of their close ties to customers. Local marketing groups have felt that local or store-specific packs and displays are better controlled and more quickly shipped from a local warehouse. In addition, it is costly to move special packs and displays over long distances. As a result, the issue of how and where to build and ship promotional packs impeded Gillette's warehouse reduction effort. Gillette overcame this hurdle by implementing strategically located stockless depots at a national level from which special packs can be configured and distributed to local markets.

Source: O'Laughlin *et al.* (1993: 153 and 158).

Flexible manufacturing systems

Flexible manufacturing systems allow companies to postpone the completion of tasks until the precise product configuration required is certain. The storage system must complement this by being able to respond to customer needs. Combining the two developments, the implication for the manufacturer is to produce what it is currently selling. This avoids having to estimate precise product configurations a long time in advance of their being purchased by customers. Producing for order rather than for the forecasts substantially cuts down inventory costs and risks (Kotler, 1994: 591).

Materials-handling system

Materials handling in the market logistics system tends to be concentrated around storage or warehousing facilities. There are four major materials-handling functions which must be performed (Bowersox, 1978: 197):

- receiving;
- transfer;
- selection; and
- shipping.

These four elements of materials handling apply to materials management before manufacture, transfer within the plant, and physical distribution of finished goods. The type of product being handled influences the system used. A basic difference exists in the handling of bulk materials, such as cement, chemicals or water, and finished goods, such as cosmetics in individual packages within cartons.

Modern materials-handling systems may be classified as mechanized or automated. A combination of labour and handling equipment is used in mechanized systems to facilitate receiving, processing, transfer and shipping of some goods. Automated systems attempt to minimize the labour involved by substituting sophisticated robotic equipment to perform the same and additional tasks, often more efficiently and at less expense.

As was seen in previous sections, conventional manufacturing systems produce batches of product based on sales forecasts. These products are placed in inventory to await receipts of orders. With flexible manufacturing and just-in-time delivery, part of the traditional warehousing function can be eliminated. Daily production and postponed finishing to a point adjacent to shipping reduces materials handling and storage. Less materials-handling equipment is required and fewer materials-handling people are needed. Product quality may be increased by eliminating the opportunity for wastage, deterioration and damage.

807

Market logistics decisions

There are four functional aspects of market logistics in the firm and one organizational dimension. Market logistics functional decisions must be made in the areas of transportation and warehousing, materials handling, stock control and ordering procedures. Decisions must also be made with respect to the organizational responsibility for market logistics (Figure 18.5).

Total cost concept

In evaluating the company's market logistics functions, it is necessary to adopt a total system cost approach. In simple terms that means analyzing the distribution impact on each cost within the company and then selecting for more detailed scrutiny those costs strongly affected by market logistics policies and practices. In the next stage, it is necessary to gather data for measuring the profit impact that alternative logistics decisions would have on each of the activities. Lastly, it is necessary to identify appropriate logistics policies which will help to maximize profits.

While stated in very simple terms, this three-step approach involves quite a lot of work and the outcome is not always clear. The creative part associated

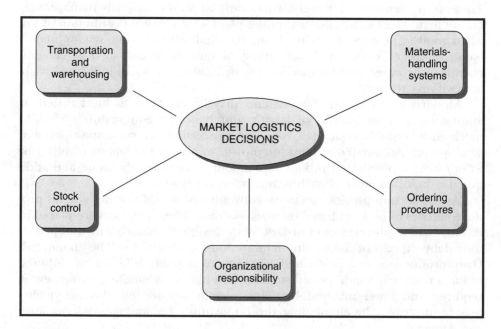

Figure 18.5 Market logistics decisions

with the first step requires considerable skill and knowledge of distribution systems. The operational detail in the second step is time consuming and expensive. Here it is easy to discuss these matters generally, but it is necessary to examine the detail of packaging, transport handling and storage in each particular case. The last step requires the attention of senior management as it has company-wide implications.

Market logistics trade-offs

The importance of systematic cost analysis and control in itself should not be overemphasized, since physical distribution is part of a wider operation which adds value as well as cost to the marketing of products. Distribution-related costs are not the responsibility of any one department. They result from the complex set of interrelationships involving all of the functions of business (Le Kashman and Stolle, 1965: 36). The management of market logistics in many companies provides a clear demonstration of the sub-optimality and faulty claims of advantage associated with functional specialization and scale economies.

In physical distribution, the manufacturer or product provider normally locates, selects and pays for the services of agencies involved in physical distribution. As a general rule, whoever owns the product, i.e. has the title, pays for the services of the facilitating agencies employed (McCallery, 1992: 43). This is quite different from the practice associated with the use of other facilitating agencies, which are normally paid by the channel member requiring the services.

From the perspective of the distribution channel as a whole, the objective is to minimize the cost of handling for the total channel. This usually means minimizing the number of levels in the process. A second principle is to reduce the volume of the product held anywhere in the channel compatible with supplying expected demand at each stage in the distribution process. A third principle, often referred to as the principle of postponement, refers to the guideline of delaying as much as possible the breaking of bulk loads into heterogeneous assortments. These principles raise the need to consider trade-offs among the attributes and characteristics of the logistics system to achieve the objectives specified.

An alternative way of examining these trade-offs is to observe what happens to total logistics costs with the introduction of some change, such as a new courier service or a new shipping route. Market logistics costs are composed of a number of interrelated components of varying sizes (Figure 18.6). In the situation depicted, market logistics costs after introducing the new service are lower than before. As a result of increasing the number of local distribution centres, inventory-carrying costs and local distribution costs have risen, but the overall market logistics costs have been reduced. Introducing the new service has produced a positive trade-off in the form of lower total logistics costs. The reduction in total logistics costs stems from the improvement in transport costs, stock-out costs, and communications and order-processing costs.

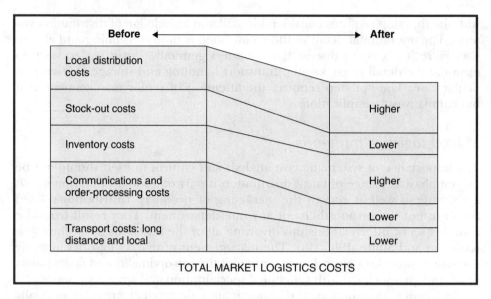

Figure 18.6   Trade-offs in market logistics costs associated with introducing a new service: hypothetical example

The identification of such cost trade-offs is the key to integrated market logistics management, which also means a positive impact on company profits through cost savings and increased sales resulting from improved customer service.

Total cost analysis

Total cost analysis is a decision methodology which allows the company to design an appropriate market logistics system. Storage facilities are used in physical distribution as long as their costs, including local delivery, are equal to or less than the total cost of direct shipments to customers. The total transportation cost declines as storage facilities are added to the logistics network (Figure 18.7). The reduction in transportation costs arises from consolidated volume shipments to storage facilities, combined with short-haul small local shipments from warehouse locations to customers. The optimum number of storage facilities to produce the lowest total transportation cost is identified this way.

In the present case, the low point on the total transportation cost curve is at five storage facilities. If storage facilities are added beyond the optimum number, total transportation costs increase. The principal reason for the cost increase is that the quantity of consolidated volume shipments to each warehouse decreases, which results in a higher unit transport cost, and the frequency of in-bound small shipments to the storage facilities increases. As more and more storage facilities are added to the network, the benefits of consolidation are reduced and transportation costs rise at an increasing rate.

810

With an increased number of storage facilities in the system, total inventory increases, so that total costs related to inventory commitment increase with each facility added. The lowest total cost, taking account of storage and transport, occurs at four storage facilities (Figure 18.7). The identification of the least total cost combination of storage facilities and transportation arrangements illustrates the potential for trade-offs among elements of cost in the system. Note that the lowest total cost point for the logistics system is not at the point of least cost for either transportation or storage. This is the central feature of total cost analysis in a market logistics system.

Market logistics service

The third-party provision of market logistics services is quite a common feature of business. The most common form of market logistics services provided by third parties is general haulage, usually supplied by small local companies providing a low degree of service customization (Figure 18.8). Express delivery services are also widely available. These are usually provided by larger companies, but the level of customization is still low. In groupage, whereby numerous customers share the same container or truck or rail wagon, the level of service customization is relatively low. Groupage is usually provided by medium-size

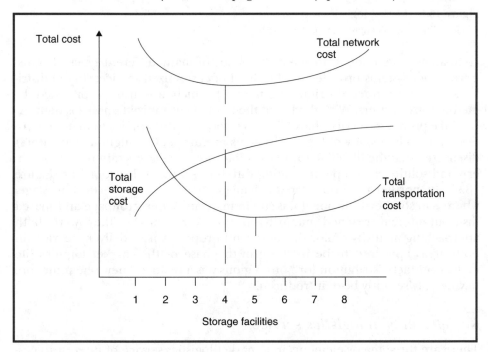

Figure 18.7 Total costs in market logistics

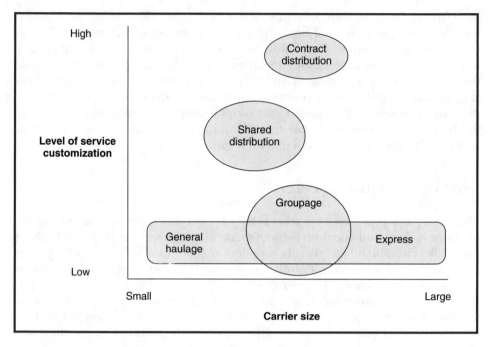

Figure 18.8   Market logistics services
(Source: O'Laughlin *et al.*, 1993: 75)

companies large enough to serve the needs of many different types of transport. Other systems provide a higher level of customized service: shared distribution and contract distribution, both of which are usually provided by medium-size carriers. With the latter, the level of customized service is high.

Like products, services have life cycles too, and this applies to market logistics services. In a study of logistics systems in Europe, O'Laughlin *et al.* (1993) discovered that the life cycle for market logistics systems was different in northern and southern Europe, indicating different stages of development (Figure 18.9). In northern Europe general haulage had reached the decline stage, whereas in southern Europe it was still in maturity. While groupage and shared distribution had reached maturity in northern Europe, they were both approaching maturity rapidly in southern Europe. Express delivery services in both areas appeared to be in the growth phase of the market logistics life cycle. Contract distribution for both regions was a relatively new phenomenon, having only recently been introduced.

Key elements in logistics service

There are three major elements in a market logistics service of interest to customers: order cycle length, its consistency and customer requirements. The

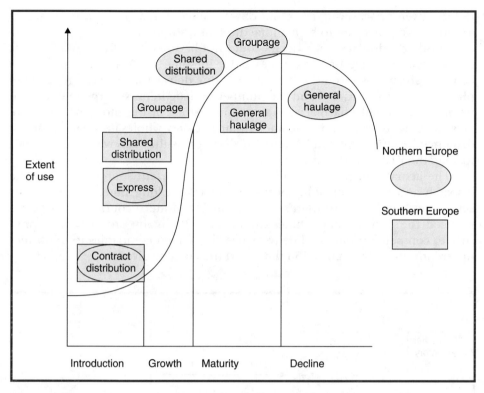

Figure 18.9   Logistics service life cycles
(Source: O'Laughlin *et al.*, 1993: 76)

order cycle length refers to the lapsed time between placing an order and receiving the product or service. Customers develop a set of expectations regarding lead times, and anything which delays the length of the cycle reduces customer service levels.

When a customer places an order, three factors influence the length of time it takes for delivery: order transmission time (the time it takes for the order to reach the seller), order preparation time (or the time taken to prepare, assemble and dispatch the order) and the actual transportation time (Figure 18.10). Transportation time is assumed to be longer than order transmission time and order preparation time. This need not necessarily be so. Individual circumstances can determine the precise relationships involved.

In most situations, order transmission time can be relatively instantaneous, especially if sales people use hand-held computers. In many cases, however, retailers, wholesalers and other intermediaries dispatch orders in batches to manufacturers, thus introducing a delay into the system. The time taken to prepare an order can be considerable, depending on the nature of the product. Some furniture manufacturers, for example, only make to order, to reduce inventory-carrying costs and obsolescence. It may take up to six weeks for an item of furniture to be manufactured and shipped.

In other industries, such delays could not be tolerated. Retail pharmacists expect delivery twice or three times a day in some cities. In most parts of a country, pharmacists would receive at least one delivery a day. Storage space in pharmacies is so restricted and the number of drug items so large that it is not feasible for a retail pharmacist to maintain a stock of the thousands of products demanded from time to time. In such cases, wholesale pharmacists or drug manufacturers prepare orders for dispatch as they receive them in order to keep their customers satisfied.

The actual transportation time is also an important source of delay. The dispatch and receipt of bulky products can take a long time, whereas many small items can be transported relatively quickly. Modern courier services have reduced the transportation times dramatically for many products. The pressure to compete on time and delivery has also forced companies to think very differently about transportation times and the costs involved.

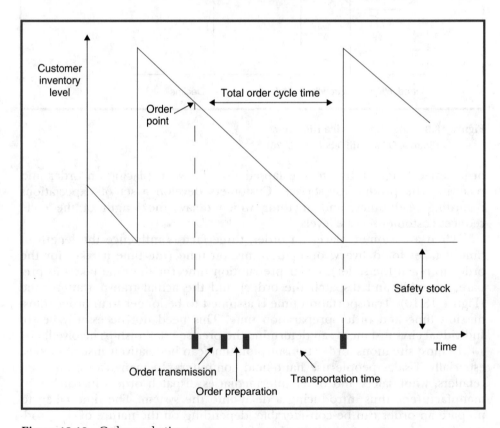

Figure 18.10 Order cycle time

The second major feature of a market logistics service is the consistency of lead times. Consistency in order cycle length or lead time may be an important element in customer service and subsequent purchase decisions. The consistency of lead times may be derived by observing a pattern of order cycles. A popular measure of order cycle consistency is the coefficient of lead time variation, derived as a ratio:

$$\frac{\text{Standard deviation of order cycle lengths}}{\text{Average length of cycle}}$$

The third element refers to customer requirements. While it is difficult to determine what is meant by customer requirements, it is nevertheless important to ensure that the correct product quantities are delivered and received in good condition. Being able to deliver from inventory is a frequently used measure of customer service, hence the need to maintain safety stocks. Only with experience of a particular business and an assessment of customer needs can the appropriate level of safety stock be determined.

Given that service offered implies customers' costs absorbed, the company will wish to determine how the customer will respond and if the response is worthwhile. Logistics services may be used to segment a market by the response of customers to the level of service offered. On examination it may transpire that too high a level of service is being offered. In such circumstances, a small reduction in the level of service may not noticeably affect sales, but may have a marked effect on logistics system costs.

Providing customer service

Customer service has become a central feature of the logistics system in companies. There are many dimensions of market logistics which affect the level of customer service (Figure 18.11). Delivery speed, and attention and care for the products carried, are perhaps the better-known aspects of market logistics. Customer service also means the provision of an emergency service when required, an installation and repair service, and an inventory service. Market logistics companies must also consider the issue of returns and resupply which arises in some industries. Lastly, there is the issue of service charge policy. Decisions in each of these areas affect the level of service provided, the costs involved and, hence, the profit outcome. It is important that the company pay considerable attention to detail in selecting the appropriate portfolio of logistics services.

Low-cost, high-quality service

In some companies, too much emphasis in total distribution planning has been placed on approaches and techniques that will produce the lowest

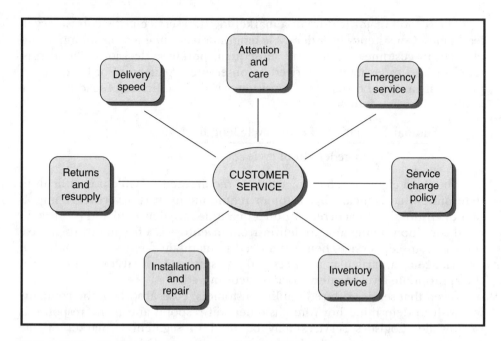

Figure 18.11   Dimensions of market logistics services

possible physical distribution system cost. Cost minimization does not necessarily mean profit maximization. Conversely, a policy of service maximization is unlikely to lead to an optimal profit situation either. There is a trade-off between the level of service offered and the other system costs that will result in an optimal profit situation. The logistics manager should seek a situation where the logistics contribution is maximized. Distribution is an element in the marketing mix, an aid to selling, and is therefore an activity that can contribute to company profitability if managed properly.

The linkages in the market logistics system demonstrate the trade-offs which may arise when considering elements of cost and service (Figure 18.12). In quadrant 1 a total systems cost curve is shown which has been derived from a total cost analysis in which costs are expressed as a function of the level of service offered. Quadrant 2 postulates the familiar S-shaped response curve, with areas of diminishing returns at low and high levels of service. Quadrant 3 incorporates several sets of cost data and suggests that sales revenue, net of direct manufacturing costs, is an increasing function of sales, i.e. economies of scale are reflected in the cost of manufacture. Quadrant 4 merely serves to project total costs on to the net revenue axis and this provides an estimate of the market logistics contribution to the fixed costs of the operation and profits.

It is apparent from the solid lines in Figure 18.12 that contribution is not being maximized where system costs are at minimum. The reason for this is the sensitivity of the market to the distribution service offered, which is repre-

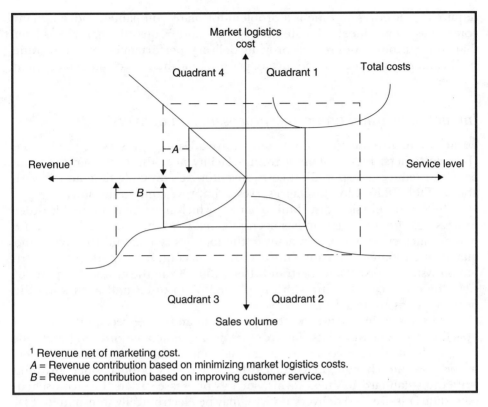

Figure 18.12 Market logistics revenue and cost linkages
(Source: Pope, 1974. With permission)

sented by the shape of the response function in quadrant 2. The lowest system cost does not permit a sufficiently high level of service to be offered to take advantage of the increasing returns to service.

The objective of logistics system management is to develop that logistics system which minimizes total costs while providing a level of service consonant with customer satisfaction. For this to happen, it is necessary to have a correct identification of the form of the cost–service–revenue relationships in the system.

Time-sensitive delivery

Physical distribution includes several factors that affect the company's costs, and its ability to provide a just-in-time service and serve customers. These include location, order processing, inventory planning, transportation and materials handling (O'Neal and Bertrand, 1991: 146). Each distribution activity must be examined to determine its influence on the customer service elements

817

required. Delivering on time is a problem for many companies. Indeed, many companies do not meet the date they agree – and frequently that date is later than the customer desires. Improving delivery performance might provide such companies with a competitive edge, or allow them to challenge efficient competitors.

Impact of location and order processing on delivery

Location can give the company a competitive advantage in serving just-in-time (JIT) customers. By dispatching from a facility near the customer, the company can reduce transportation costs, inventory, credit cycle time and its variability (Table 18.3). Closeness also serves to improve communications.

The second physical distribution activity which must be examined is order processing. Order processing has been referred to as the 'nerve centre' of the system, since customer orders activate the logistics system and the speed and quality of customer–company information flows continuously affect the distribution system (O'Neal and Bertrand, 1991: 150). From the customer's point of view, the order cycle begins with the placing of an order and ends when the ordered goods are received.

The elapsed time between order placement and order receipt depends on how the customer transmits the order. Slow unpredictable ordering methods such as the mail have come under threat from newer methods such as electronic data interchange (EDI). EDI is becoming very popular since anything written on standard business forms, such as purchase orders, invoices, schedules, status reports and delivery notices, may be electronically transmitted. EDI offers the company and customers several benefits, including less paperwork, more accuracy in transmitted information, a shorter order cycle and improved operations planning (O'Neal and Bertrand, 1991: 153). When customers use EDI, order transmission time drops virtually to zero and human errors associated with document preparation may also be eliminated.

TABLE 18.3   Influence of physical distribution on customer service

Elements of customer service	Physical distribution activities				
	Facility location	Order processing	Materials handling	Inventory	Transportation
Product quality		x	x		x
Frequent deliveries	x		x	x	x
Small lot sizes	x		x		x
Exact quantity		x	x	x	x
Precise deliveries		x	x		x
Minimum cycle time	x	x	x	x	x
Lowest total cost	x	x	x	x	x

Source: O'Neal and Bertrand (1991: 146).

Impact of materials handling and inventory on delivery

Materials handling plays an important role in inventory reduction, since it may represent a significant part of the cost of manufacturing. Effective materials-handling practice also has a time component which can contribute to improved service and productivity. According to O'Neal and Bertrand (1991: 167), there are five benefits of time-related materials-handling practice:

- it eliminates handling wherever possible by renewing buffer stocks and keeping active inventories to a minimum;

- it minimizes the distance that inventory moves within supplier and customer plants;

- it minimizes goods in process and handling costs by reducing lot size and handling the materials only once;

- it ensures uniform product flow – having continuous small lots with precise pick-up times and delivery circumvents congestion and delay;

- it minimizes losses from waste, breakage and theft, since only minimal product quantities are processed.

The concept of just in time is often seen as a way of reducing inventories, even though it applies to all aspects of the value delivery system. In fact, the just-in-time concept has its own costs, which have until recently been ignored or not quantified properly. The costs to the environment of the extra traffic congestion and pollution are important considerations and have a strong impact on market logistics (Exhibit 18.2). The question which arises in this respect is: how can an efficient inventory system be compatible with attaining quality output for the company and society? By synchronizing production with the customer's systems, the supplier can significantly reduce the production cycle to allow greater production flexibility, thereby eliminating the need for buffer or safety stocks. Buffer stocks signal waste in the company due to poor organization and operational problems.

Impact of transportation on delivery

Transportation is the final link in moving the product to the customer's premises. A very high proportion of the total elapsed time in an order cycle is absorbed by transportation. In some situations, companies use dedicated carriers to provide next-day or second-next-day delivery within substantial distances. Within Europe the growth of express carriers in shipping goods is partly explained by the need for rapid transportation to serve customers' time requirements. The demand for speed to market has been a windfall to express carrier companies (Exhibit 18.3).

EXHIBIT 18.2   'Just in time' is becoming just a pain

Toshio Yamamoto sells snacks and drinks from his 'papa-mama' shop in a Tokyo suburb. More than 30 wholesalers trundle over at his beck and call, no matter how small the order. He likes to keep deliveries to just one day's worth of rice balls, dried squid, and red-bean rolls. 'My customers demand freshness,' Yamamoto explains. 'And besides, I don't have any place to put it.'

Yamamoto is using a technique that has helped make Japan's manufacturers world-class. The 'just-in-time' (JIT) system means frequent delivery of parts to an assembly line in small lots. Suppliers and assemblers synchronise their production cycles. And when all runs smoothly, efficiency rises and defects drop. But Japan is finding that too much of a good thing means trouble, particularly in retailing. Wholesalers now scurry with half-empty trucks to drop as little as $15 worth of products at one outlet. The result: clogged traffic, noxious fumes, a shortage of truck drivers, and rising prices. 'Just-in-time has gone too far,' gripes Takashi Kashara, general manager of logistics for wholesaler Meiji-ya Co. 'It's crazy.'

Just in time is also hurting the environment as truck exhaust strangles roadside residents. Then there's the problem of getting enough drivers. Ten years of growth nearly doubled the volume of freight delivered by truck to more than 270 billion tons last year. Ideally, these volumes require 1.3 million drivers, but Japan has only 1 million. To attract new drivers, including women, transport companies have installed power steering to their trucks and added ladies' rooms to warehouses. But women drivers remain scarce.

To unblock the arteries, a number of manufacturers are setting up warehousing systems outside towns and cities to receive the bulk of deliveries. But the retail industry remains the real bottleneck, and some leaders in the industry are scurrying after solutions. By careful scheduling, 7-Eleven Stores has managed to slash the number of trucks visiting each store per day from 70 to 12. 'The key isn't frequent delivery, it's optimum delivery,' says Moriya Unozawa, director of distribution.

Source: *Business Week*, 17 June 1991: 24.

European dimensions of market logistics

The opening up of European Union markets and the accession of neighbouring countries has created market logistics opportunities and challenges for companies serving these markets. The diverse geographic profiles, the demographic configuration and the diversity of purchasing power throughout the EU raises special issues. In a comprehensive study of European logistics systems, O'Laughlin *et al.* (1993) outline a number of scenarios for the development of logistics in a European context. This section draws on that report to outline some of these developments for European retailing, for fast-moving consumer goods businesses, and for the role of branding in a market logistics setting.

EXHIBIT 18.3   Speed to market a windfall to express couriers

When Toyota Motor Corp. decided to build its transplant in Burneston England it wanted to find the speediest way to get the plant to meet tough just-in-time delivery schedules. Today, containers chock-full of parts are at the loading dock every morning by eight.

To get such service, Toyota turned to an outsider: DHL International, the Brussels-based courier company. With goods flowing faster across Europe's borders since the European Community opened its single market 1 January, DHL and other major air-express companies are getting more and more calls to do freight forwarding, inventory control, billing, invoicing and other back-office functions that used to be the preserve of truckers, warehouses, or manufacturers themselves. Once content with documents and parcels, DHL, United Parcel Service, Federal Express and others find themselves hauling time-sensitive goods that range from Cray super computers to Volvo bumpers. The more intense battle of the couriers has begun. 'With border barriers down, customers are increasingly saying, "I want that product tomorrow",' says Patrick Lupo, DHL International's chairman.

To get out front, DHL announced on 4 February that it will spend $1.25 billion in the next four years buying land, warehouses and goods-tracking computers to beef up logistics capabilities, mostly in Europe. With global competition forcing manufacturers to focus on core business, the trend toward going outside for distribution should last, says Martin White, a logistics consultant with Coopers & Lybrand. That's not news to DHL. It made a third of its $2.8 billion in 1992 revenues from logistics services, up from just 10 per cent five years ago. Revenues are set to jump 40 per cent this year, twice the industry rate, says Lupo.

Source: *Business Week*, 22 February 1993: 17.

Market logistics in retailing

The opportunities afforded retailing in Europe illustrate very well the interaction between marketing strategies and logistics decisions. Retailers with different formats among their individual outlets tend to have decentralized market logistics operations, while retailers that maintain a common format often centralize their logistics arrangements. At the same time, companies selling standardized products tend to follow a marketing strategy based on standardization. As a result, product similarity, demand patterns and replenishment cycles tend to be associated with a common retail format. A retail firm with a centralized logistics organization is better positioned to exploit the synergistic effects associated with common products, demand patterns and replenishment cycles occurring in an area populated with stores of a common format (O'Laughlin *et al.*, 1993: 136). The operational synergies are a primary driver of centralized logistics.

Deliver the value to customers

Marketing strategies and market logistics

Four different types of market logistics strategy, based on the relationship between the form of logistics organization and the marketing strategy adopted, have been identified for major retailers in Europe (Figure 18.13).

The co-operative strategy involves groups of independent firms, such as Spar, Eurogroup and Co-op, that have pooled operations to concentrate purchasing power and store management know-how across national borders. The European Retail Association (ERA), including Argyll in the UK, Casino in France and

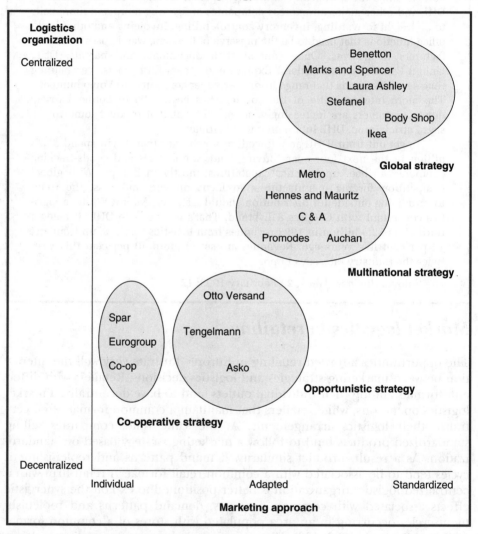

Figure 18.13 . Internationalization strategies of retailers
(Source: O'Laughlin *et al.*, 1993: 135)

Ahold in Germany, was the first to join forces in 1989. These groups are able to negotiate better prices from suppliers and also reduce logistics costs.

The acquisition of retailers in other markets to internationalize the business very quickly is a strategy followed by some retailers. Acquiring other retailers but allowing the distinct business formats to remain is an opportunistic strategy. In such cases, market logistics is also likely to continue decentralized. Tengelmann, the large German retailer, uses this strategy throughout the world. It has acquired A & P in the US, Löwa in Austria, Groep in the Netherlands, KD in France and now controls Gateway in the UK.

With a multinational strategy, the aim is to develop the company's same marketing strategy in another country with some adaptation to account for local preferences. The market logistics organization is likely to be more centralized, while reflecting local circumstances. Companies which have pursued a multinational strategy with some success in Europe are Metro, Hennes Mauritz, C & A, Promodes and Auchan.

A global strategy involves exporting an identical concept to many foreign countries. It often works in niche segments of the market, where consumer preferences are similar across markets. The focus is on a universal standardized approach to marketing strategy and logistics, with little attention to local preferences. Companies which follow such a strategy include Benetton, Marks and Spencer, Stefanel, Laura Ashley, Ikea and the Body Shop. When successful, such strategies produce scale economies in procurement, distribution, store layout and branding.

Market logistics in fast-moving consumer goods industries

While the European fast-moving consumer goods industry includes thousands of manufacturers, the industry is dominated by a few companies selling well-known brand name products. Delivery patterns in this industry sector are changing rapidly. Retailer-owned regional warehouses throughout the EU have reduced the number of direct store deliveries. In this regime there is little room for wholesalers, which are becoming virtually extinct. For retailers and manufacturers alike, inventory control mechanisms have become very sophisticated and information technology has contributed significantly to logistics management. With such developments, integrated market logistics management is possible. By centralizing decisions regarding logistics, companies are able to leverage scale economies in production and distribution.

Market logistics network configuration

Network reconfiguration occurs at the country level and at European level. Companies focus on country-level rationalization in order to reduce operating costs. This usually means reducing warehouses to one or two in each country market served. But it may not be possible to go much further. Congestion, transport and other social costs may limit the efforts of companies to centralize completely.

A complete centralization of the market logistics function to serve a large market area like Europe would probably have an adverse effect on service levels. In such cases there would be pressure for additional facilities rather than fewer. Furthermore, changes in a company's physical distribution network to take advantage of scale economies and open markets require the company to develop new skills and practices. A centralized physical distribution facility in Europe implies a knowledge of freight forwarding and an ability to introduce flexible lead times for a wide range of markets. There is, therefore, a trade-off between the level of service and the cost of its provision.

Centralizing the market logistic function results in a greater number of national and international product flows to serve customers in Europe. The increase in cross-border product movements by a major consumer products company, experienced as a result of changing its physical distribution network, illustrates the point (Figure 18.14). The extra product flow gives rise to additional costs and indicates the need for additional management skills and resources. In such circumstances, attempts to centralize the market logistics function to the detriment of total systems costs and service are undesirable.

Branding and logistics

Standardization or customization of the product, its formulation, the brand and its packaging throughout the EU can have a significant impact on market logistics decisions. A fully centralized production and distribution system may derive scale economies as benefits. Such benefits might accrue for a standardized branded product like the Gillette Sensor razor (Table 18.4). A logistics response based on a product design to allow customization at the latest stages of production, such as may be found in bundled manufacturing, produces benefits such as the rationalization of the range of components, thereby simplifying in-bound shipping and improving quality. Hobnobs, the United Biscuit brand in central Europe, is an example.

Sometimes it is necessary to defer the final configuration of the product until it reaches the market. The logistics of deferred finishing provide the same benefits as bundled manufacturing. There are many situations where the company must pack and label its products at a local warehouse. Deferred packing allows production scale economies, less inventory and a higher level of customer service. Fuji film is an example of a brand with pan-European acceptance, while Aquafresh and Odol toothpaste are examples of regionally accepted brands. In some cases, there is little opportunity for a market logistics reconfiguration and the benefits to the company would be marginal. Odol mouthwash would be an example of such a product.

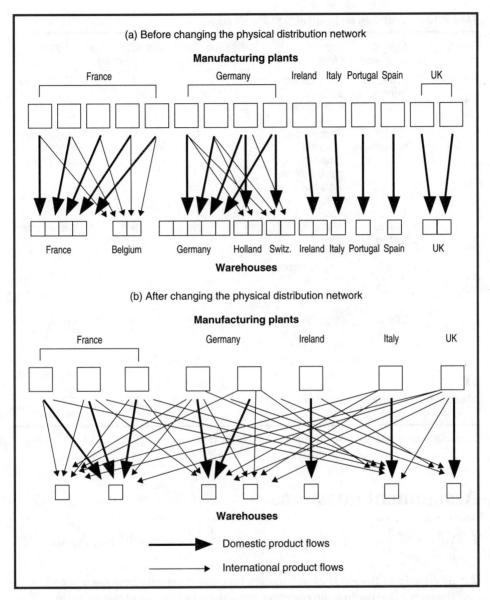

Figure 18.14 Effects of changes in fast-moving consumer goods distribution networks
(Source: Adapted from O'Laughlin *et al.*, 1993: 158)

TABLE 18.4   Branding and market logistics strategies

Product standardization	Logistics organization	Potential benefits	Pan-European branding	Standardized product	Standardized packaging	Products and brands
Standardized	Centralized operations	Production and distribution scale economies	Yes	Yes	Yes	Gillette Sensor razor
	Bundled manufacturing	Rationalization of range of components In-bound shipping and quality improved	Yes	No	Yes	United Biscuits Hobnobs in central Europe
Partial	Deferred finishing	Rationalization of range of components In-bound shipping and quality improved	Yes	No	No	Nescafé coffee
	Deferred packing	Production scale economies, less inventory, high levels of customer service	Yes	Yes	No	Fuji film
			No	Yes	No	Aquafresh Odol toothpaste
Differentiated	Decentralized operations	Limited	No	No	No	Odol mouthwash

Source: Adapted from O'Laughlin *et al.* (1993: 154).

Assignment questions

1   What is the total cost concept in market logistics management? Why is it so important?

2   By organizing the physical distribution function separately from the other elements of marketing, the company introduces another set of management interfaces. What are these and why are they of concern?

3   What are the key elements and activities of market logistics as applied to (a) a computer components manufacturer; (b) a dairy products co-operative, (c) a clothing manufacturer; and (d) a pharmaceutical company?

4   State how each physical distribution decision affects the manufacturer or producer of (a) beer; (b) expensive jewellery; (c) natural gas; and (d) farm machinery.

5 What is the disproportionate risk in holding of inventory by retailers? Why is there a tendency to push inventory back up the distribution channel?

6 How are marketing strategies in fast-moving consumer goods business affected by market logistics considerations?

Annotated bibliography

Ballou, Ronald H. (1985) *Business Logistics Management* (2nd edn), Englewood Cliffs, NJ: Prentice Hall.

Coyle, John J., Edward J. Bardi and C. John Langley Jr (1992) *The Management of Business Logistics* (5th edn), St. Paul, Minn.: West Publishing Co.

Fuller, Joseph B., James O'Connor and Richard Rawlinson (1993) 'Tailored logistics: the next advantage', *Harvard Business Review*, **71**, 3, 87–98.

Le Kashman, Raymond, and John F. Stolle (1965) 'The total cost approach to distribution', *Business Horizons*, **8**, Winter, 33–46.

Pope, A.L. (1964) 'The concept and cost elements of physical distribution', *International Journal of Physical Distribution*, **4**, 3, 149–65.

References

Ballou, Ronald H. (1985) *Business Logistics Management* (2nd edn), Englewood Cliffs, NJ: Prentice Hall.

Bowersox, Donald J. (1978) *Logistical Management* (2nd edn), New York: Macmillan.

Fuller, Joseph B., James O'Connor and Richard Rawlinson (1993) 'Tailored logistics: the next advantage', *Harvard Business Review*, **71**, 3, 87–98.

Heskitt, J.L., Robert M. Ivie and Nicholas A. Glaskowsky, Jr (1964) *Business Logistics: Management of physical supply and distribution*, New York: The Ronald Press.

Kotler, Philip (1994) *Marketing Management*, Englewood Cliffs, NJ: Prentice Hall.

Le Kashman, Raymond, and John F. Stolle (1965) 'The total cost approach to distribution', *Business Horizons*, **8**, Winter, 33–46.

McCallery, Russell W. (1992) *Marketing Channel Development and Management*, Westport, Conn.: Quorura.

O'Laughlin, Kevin A., James Cooper and Eric Cabocel (1993) *Reconfiguring European Logistics Systems*, Oak Brook, Ill.: Council of Logistics Management.

O'Neal, Charles, and Kate Bertrand (1991) *Developing a Winning JIT Marketing Strategy*, Englewood Cliffs, NJ: Prentice Hall.

Pope, A.L. (1974) 'The concept and cost elements of physical distribution', *International Journal of Physical Distribution*, **4**, 3, 149–65.

Shapiro, Roy D. (1984) 'Get leverage from logistics', *Harvard Business Review*, **62**, 3, 119–26.

Stern, Louis W., and Adel I. El-Ansary (1988) *Marketing Channels* (3rd edn), Englewood Cliffs, NJ: Prentice Hall.

Sales promotion

19

Sales promotion in marketing management
Methods of sales promotion
Power of retailers in the channel
Managing sales promotion

Introduction

This chapter introduces and explains:

- the need for sales promotion and the reasons behind its recent growth;

- sales promotion tasks in trade and consumer promotions;

- how to gain and maintain access to customers;

- manufacturer attitudes toward sales promotion;

- the need to advertise sales promotions;

- the dilemma of sales promotion; and

- how to determine the effectiveness of sales promotions.

As population growth slows down during economic recessions, manufacturers feel the pressure to move product, sometimes at almost any cost. Sales promotion is most effective in moving product in the short term. Demand from retailers combined with competition from private-label and other manufacturers are two powerful additional pressures on manufacturers to increase or maintain sales promotions budgets. The decline in brand loyalty among the more fickle consumers and the fragmentation of media also contribute to the growth of sales promotion. Furthermore, there has been increased pressure from company owners and stakeholders for short-term financial returns, which motivates company managers to favour the short term and hence sales promotions. Many different methods of sales promotion may be found in practice. They can be divided into sales promotions directed at the trade and those directed at consumers. The precise form chosen depends on the nature of the promotion task to be achieved.

Sales promotion policies are largely dictated by powerful retailers, whose marketing objectives may be very different from those of the manufacturer or brand owner. The conflicts which occur give rise to market distortions and a short-term, myopic view of the markets. Manufacturers face the dilemma of choosing between short-term sales, which are essential for survival, and longer-term brand development, which gives the company independence and longer-term wealth. In attempting to cope with this dilemma effectively, the company must integrate sales promotion decisions into overall marketing strategy decisions.

Having studied this chapter, you should be able to define the terms listed above in your own words, and you should be able to do the following:

1. Define the meaning of sales promotion.

2. Recognize that sales promotion complements the other communications elements with the benefit of an immediate response.

3. Judge the value of promotions as a silent sales force.

4. Determine the appropriate use of sales promotion at different stages of the life cycle.

5. Identify particular product-market situations where sales promotion may be required.

6. List, explain and evaluate the various methods used in trade and consumer sales promotion.

7. Recognize the appopriateness of each method to achieve selected marketing objectives.

8. Determine how sales promotion can distort the market and debase the value of brands.

9. Recognize the need to integrate sales promotion into marketing strategy.

10. Specify the circumstances where sales promotion can be effective in achieving the company's marketing objectives.

Sales promotion in marketing management

In recent years, sales promotion has become a very important marketing management topic. To understand how to use it and when to use it, the company must first examine the need for sales promotion under different circumstances. It is also necessary to understand the sales promotion tasks to be carried out in the company from time to time. The growth of sales promotion may be attributed to the increased emphasis by companies on short-term returns. Sales promotion is eminently suited for supporting short-term marketing objectives. Other factors encouraging the use of sales promotion include the ability to tailor promotions to almost any marketing situation at different stages of the product life cycle and for different product-market situations. Many companies have also sales-promoted services successfully.

Need for sales promotion

Three sets of factors give rise to the increased pressure on manufacturers to consider sales promotions as an important or even as a key element in the communications mix: environmental factors, market factors and organizational factors. The first refers principally to population and economic factors. As population growth slows and as economic recessions occur, manufacturers feel the pressure to maintain sales, sometimes at almost any cost. Sales promotion is most effective in influencing sales in the short term.

The market itself is the second source of pressure. Demand from retailers and competition from private-label and other manufacturers are two powerful pressures on manufacturers which increase or maintain sales promotions budgets. Two other factors related to these are the decline in brand loyalty among the more fickle consumers and the fragmentation of media, especially in larger markets in Europe and the USA, where no single network is capable of serving all the market in a cost-effective manner.

The third pressure, perhaps the greatest, comes from within the firm itself. The pressure for short-term financial returns or unit volume sales combines with compensating systems based on short-term targets to send a powerful signal to managers and companies in favour of sales promotions.

Benefits of immediate response

As population growth slows in a market area, the large annual increases in consumption once expected by consumer product companies are no longer a feature. Furthermore, real product innovation has been absent for a number of years in consumer markets especially. Product modifications have been minor, and imitation rather than innovation has been the basis of much product development. In these circumstances, it is difficult to differentiate brands in ways which are meaningful to the consumer. The short-term solution to such a slow-down in product sales has been price-cutting promotions to attract customers and temporary boost sales.

The effect of these developments is that as soon as one promotion ends another begins, which gives more power to retailers, especially supermarkets, as they control the promotions and access to the shelves. In some markets, retailers can command fees, discounts and other promotional support from manufacturers amounting to between 30 and 40 per cent of the total advertising and promotion budget.

Defining sales promotion

Sales promotion is frequently treated as a residual promotion tool: in other words, a promotion activity which cannot be classified as advertising, publicity or personal selling must be sales promotion. The American Marketing Association defines sales promotion in such terms: 'those marketing activities other than personal selling, advertising and publicity that stimulate consumer purchasing and dealer effectiveness, such as displays, shows and exhibitions, demonstrations and various non recurrent selling efforts'. The Council of Sales Promotion Agencies in the USA considers sales promotion to consist of couponing, refunds and rebates, sweepstakes and contests, allowances, educational programmes, promotional public relations, meetings, premiums and incentives, promotional packaging, point of purchase and display, and trade shows (Bowman, 1985).

Sales promotion has been defined as 'the direct inducement or incentive to the sales force, the distributor, or the consumer, with the primary objective of creating an immediate sale' (Schultz and Robinson, 1988: 8). Dibb *et al.* (1994: 473) have defined it as 'an activity or material that acts as a direct inducement, offering added value or incentive to the product, to re-sellers, salespersons, or consumers'. Alternatively, it may be described as 'a more direct form of persuasion based frequently on external incentives rather than inherent product benefits which is designed to stimulate immediate purchase and to "move sales forward" more rapidly than would otherwise occur' (Rossiter and Percy, 1987: 4). Kotler (1994: 664) states that 'sales promotion consists of a diverse collection of incentive tools, mostly short term, designed to stimulate quicker and/or greater purchase of particular products/services by consumers or the trade'.

Sales promotion tasks

The tasks associated with sales promotion depend on the general marketing and communications objectives that the company establishes. In a general way, sales promotion tasks are designed around attempts by the company to complement its marketing communications at the point of sale. Sales promotion is used effectively when other elements of the marketing mix achieve their objectives of getting the potential customer or user to the point where the product or service might be purchased. The need for the promotion is to encourage consumers or users to select the company's product, service or brand from among the myriad of others available in cluttered retail outlets. Sales promotion in effect becomes a silent sales force, encouraging people to select one offer over the others.

Identifying general sales promotion objectives

There are two types of sales promotion. Sales promotion may be aimed at the trade or at consumers. Four sets of objectives for trade promotions and seven objectives for consumer promotions have been identified (Schultz and Robinson, 1988: 51–75). Trade promotion objectives in general complement objectives established for consumer sales promotion. The tasks of trade promotions are to provide in-store sales support, a change in the location of inventories, improvement in distribution and motivation to channel partners (Figure 19.1). Consumer promotions have many objectives depending on the circumstances, including trial of new products and services, and greater use of existing ones.

Complementary marketing communication

Sales promotion attempts to promote the movement of products through channels of distribution by stimulating sales people and providing additional incentives to channel intermediaries and consumers. Sales promotions increase in number and in strength as product markets become crowded, and decrease with product and service differentiation and scarcity in the markets.

Promotion has both strengths and weaknesses in the communication mix. It can help to create a positive attitude towards the product or service being sold, by adding value to its sale. It represents an inducement to purchase, an additional direct incentive aimed at stimulating immediate purchases rather than sales at some future date. Sales promotions are very flexible and may be

TRADE PROMOTIONS	CONSUMER PROMOTIONS
• In-store sales support • Change trade inventories • Improve product distribution • Motivate channel partners	• Obtain product trial • Encourage loyalty • Promote more frequent purchases • Encourage consumers to trade up • Introduce new or improved products, new packaging, or new product sizes • Neutralize competitive sales promotion or advertising • Capitalize on special circumstances

Figure 19.1   Objectives for sales promotion
(Source: Adapted from Schultz and Robinson, 1988)

used at any stage of a new product or service introduction, enhancing a sales message delivered by advertising and personal selling. They may also stiffen the resolve of sales people and intermediaries in promoting the company's products and services.

At the same time, there are limitations and risks with sales promotions (Quelch *et al.*, 1987). As they are temporary communications devices, they have limited value for the long-term sustained promotional campaigns which would be required, for instance, in building a brand franchise. Sales promotion must be used in conjunction with other promotional tools, since it supplements or complements but does not replace other forms of marketing communication (Abraham and Lodish, 1990). Because sales promotions are non-recurring, the talent and investment that are devoted to developing them are lost. Perhaps the most serious limitation of sales promotion is that, if it is used too frequently to promote a branded product or service, damage to the brand image may occur, which suggests either a weakness or an oversupply of the product or service being promoted.

Sales promotion complements other marketing mix elements at various points in the marketing channel. Trade promotion is used by the manufacturer to encourage distributors to behave in a certain way with respect to the manufacturer's products and services (Figure 19.2). The manufacturer also designs sales promotions which are implemented directly at consumer level. Sales force promotions are also a feature of manufacturer sales promotion activity. It may be necessary for the manufacturer to promote a new marketing mix to its own sales force. Alternatively, changes in the existing marketing mix may need to be promoted: for example, a new product version, a new package, or new price terms.

As may be seen, distributors and retailers are both recipients of sales promotion activities and senders of such activities in the form of retail promotions. The task for the manufacturer is to ensure that all types of promotion are co-ordinated and that no element conflicts with any other. This is very difficult to achieve, since retailers typically have very different objectives from manufacturers.

The silent sales force

Sales promotion is normally aimed at the same consumer promotion targets as advertising and personal selling. Since this promotion target usually needs to be reached more than once before a sale is made, the overlap may be beneficial rather than wasteful, as the buyer's interest in purchasing may be increased. At times, buyers may be difficult to reach through advertisments or sales people, but may be contacted by means of a trade show, an exhibition or some other sales promotion device. This is especially true of international promotion, where trade shows serve a useful purpose in identifying and contacting potential customers. The various promotion tools, including advertising, public relations and personal selling, can accomplish more together than if used separately.

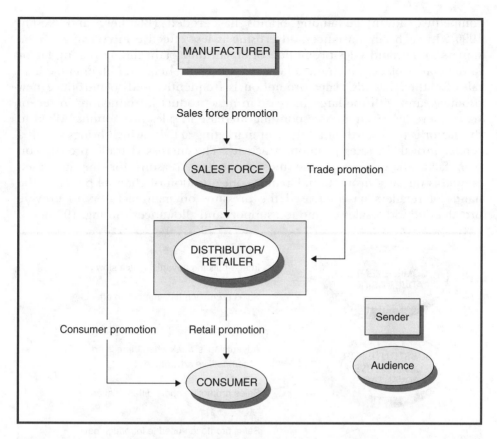

Figure 19.2   Sales promotion in the marketing channel

In promoting a packaged product sold through supermarkets, extensive advertising support is usually provided. However, since no salesperson is present to close the sale, a sales promotion device such as packaging often serves as a silent salesperson to fill the void. Likewise, advertising is often used to merchandise a good promotion to the proper markets, such as when contests, coupons or premiums receive advertising support. One use of company sales meetings as a promotion device is to provide adequate information and details on new products, policies and promotion programmes to sales people, so that they can explain and merchandise the offering to their customers.

Growth in sales promotion

Growth in the use of sales promotion may be attributed to a number of causes (Figure 19.3). Sales promotions complement advertising, particularly the type of advertising which is aimed at image building or establishing a brand franchise, since the results are immediate. Sales promotion is also popular where competitive advantage among brands has eroded (Blattberg and Neslin, 1990). In such circumstances, advertising is less effective in convincing consumers to buy, and sales promotion offers an important differentiating factor in the marketplace, which manufacturers recognize helps to obtain immediate sales for their brands. Sales promotion is frequently used to introduce new products, and with the large increase in new product introductions in recent years, there has been a corresponding increase in sales promotions. Allied to this factor is the growth of all types of marketing activity, which brings with it a similar growth in sales promotion activity. The increased trade pressure on manufacturers is perhaps the most important reasons for the increased emphasis on sales promotion. Greater concentration of channel power in the hands of retailers has increased the pressure on manufacturers to provide broader and wider sales promotion support and allowances (Strang, 1976).

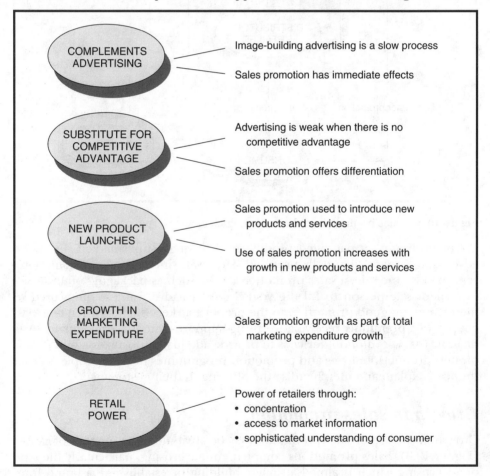

Figure 19.3 Growth in sales promotion

Short-term marketing objectives

In recent years, managers have been unwilling or unable to resist the pressure from their sales and marketing people and from retailers who implicitly conspire to continue a marketing communications system heavily dependent on sales promotion.

This conspiracy arises for a number of reasons. When company annual profit goals are unlikely to be achieved, it is a relatively easy matter to cut advertising expenditure, which has a longer-term effect, than sales promotion budgets, which have a more immediate and visible effect in sales volumes. A second reason for the increase in sales promotion is that sales volumes, not values, are still used by many companies as the basis on which to evaluate and reward retailers and compensate sales people. Evaluation methods based on volume may not reflect a profitability criterion, especially when heavy sales promotions are involved. At the same time, brand managers may face a conflicting situation. They are often held accountable for a combination of profit and volume or share gains. This inconsistency in compensation systems and the use of different criteria for brand managers and sales managers can lead to conflict.

Another reason for the relative growth of sales promotions may be the relative ease with which their effectiveness may be judged compared to advertising. By using intuitive or qualitative measures, advertising agencies and brand managers have damaged their case. The use of qualitative measures such as recall tests, advertising monitoring and tracking studies, and relating these quantitatively to sales results, could make a stronger argument for advertising by deriving advertising and promotion elasticities (Jones, 1990).

Life cycle effects

Marketing practitioners consider the stage in the product life cycle as an important influence on how marketing budgets are allocated between advertising and promotion. The advertising to promotion ratio changes over the life cycle (Strang *et al.* 1975: 39). Frequently, when product categories reach the mature or declining stages of the life cycle, brand differentiation also declines and brands proliferate in the market. Using the PIMS database, Quelch *et al.* (1984) conclude that the lower the differentiation, the higher the ratio of promotion expenditure to sales.

Market maturity leads to less differentiation and therefore an increase in price and promotion responsiveness. Furthermore, consumers have learned, as a result of manufacturer's intiatives, to respond to promotions. It may also be true that the effect of advertising may decline as markets mature. With increases in advertising, its marginal productivity declines compared to trade and consumer sales promotion.

As the relative importance of sales promotion in the communication mix grows, manufacturers and some retailers have begun to question its value. As a greater proportion of the marketing communications budget is devoted to sales promotion, the incremental benefits gained may not be worth the cost. According to Donnelley Marketing, an American market research company, media advertising in 1989 in the US packaged goods industry accounted for 43 per cent of marketing communications budgets, while trade promotions accounted for 34 per cent and consumer promotions 23 per cent. By 1992 the proportion spent on media advertising had fallen to 27 per cent, trade promotions had increased to 45 per cent and consumer promotions had increased to 28 per cent (Figure 19.4).

Product-market considerations

A number of characteristics of the product and the competitive environment influence the allocation of the marketing communication budget between advertising and promotion (Strang *et al.*, 1975). According to these authors, lower levels of promotion relative to advertising are associated with brands that:

- have profit contributions above the company average;
- have a high degree of brand loyalty;
- have a strong competitive differentiation;
- have a high degree of risk associated with the purchase;
- are in the growth or maturity stages of the life cycle; and
- have a large market share.

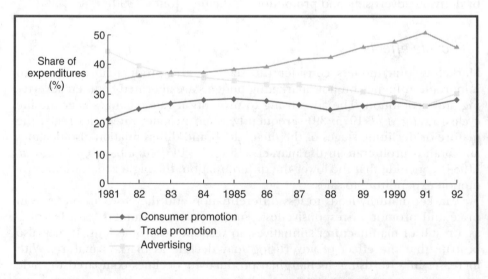

Figure 19.4 Promotional expenditures by packaged goods firms in the USA, 1981–92
(Source: Adapted from Mohr and Low, 1993: 35. With permission of the American Marketing Association.)

These authors conclude that higher levels of promotion relative to advertising are associated with brands that:

- have a profit contribution rate below the company average;
- have little brand loyalty;
- have little competitive differentiation;
- are directed towards children;
- are purchased with little planning;
- are in the introductory or decling stages of the life cycle;
- have a pronounced seasonal sales pattern;
- have a small share of the market;
- compete with promotion-oriented companies; and
- compete in markets where private labels are important.

Sometimes companies spend large amounts of money to achieve a marketing objective. The battle of market share between Ford and Honda in the US car market is a good example. Ford used very substantial rebates to convince consumers that their car was better than Honda (Exhibit 19.1). Ford must consider the longer-term value of such promotions, and whether attempts to encourage loyalty and competitive differentiation in other ways would have been more worthwhile.

Sales promotion of services

The difference between products and services as far as sales promotions are concerned is that the forms of promotion activity are different given the characteristics of target audiences and the appropriateness of the devices available.

There has been a major increase in sales promotion activity in many service markets in recent years. Services cannot be stored, however, which has particular implications for the use of sales promotional practices aimed at spreading the load of service use more evenly. Off-peak attractive pricing schemes, such as the 'happy hour' in bars or cheaper entrance charges to cinemas for early and late shows, are examples of ways of price-promoting services.

In practice, most sales promotion schemes apply to services, although they are often disguised and go under other names. A solicitor may waive the fee for certain minor services – a price cut as a reward for loyalty. A management consultant may offer an amount of time free of charge, which is a form of sampling. All of these are types of sales promotion. While there may be ethical constraints on the use of certain sales promotion practices in the professions and other service sectors, since their use may be regarded as too aggressive by professional associations, they are nevertheless becoming a feature of such markets.

EXHIBIT 19.1   Top of the car lots

'Every day on the fax they sent over something saying "sell Taurus, sell Taurus",' says Scott Runyan, general manager of Crown Ford, in Roswell, Georgia. And that is what Mr Runyan and other Ford dealers did until the car nudged out the Honda Accord as the best selling car in America. The Accord had topped the sales charts every year since 1989, much to the annoyance of Detroit. But last year, in a fearsome battle, Ford clinched victory when it sold 409,751 Taurus cars. American buyers bought 393,477 Honda Accords, some of which are made in America and some imported from Japan.

Ford had to open the corporate coffers to ensure its win. Industry analysts estimate that Ford spent $50m on rebates and other incentives to lure customers into its showrooms. Buyers could sign a two-year lease on a fully equipped Taurus for just $248 a month with a $1,500 down payment. With a sticker price of $18,600, the same car normally carries a monthly lease payment of $320. Honda countered with leases carrying monthly rates as low as $199.

Ford is convinced it was worth it. 'It makes a statement about Ford. It means we're making products the American public likes,' says Ross Roberts, general manager of the Ford division that makes the car. Anyone who watches American television will soon hear the same message in a series of TV commercials that will boast about Taurus's victory over the Accord. Ford has used similar ads before to gloat about its sales leadership in the market for pick-up trucks, which many Americans drive like cars. Ford's F-series pick-up is actually the nation's best-selling vehicle.

Source: *The Economist*, 16 January 1993: 67.

Methods of sales promotion

Companies use many different types of sales promotion technique in an effort to attract customers. A very extensive range of alternatives, each with its own strengths and weaknesses, is available to the company considering promoting its products or services (Figure 19.5). The fact that so many different techniques exist may indicate that many of them serve only very specific purposes, and that there is no convenient subset of techniques available for general application.

Trade and consumer promotions

Sales promotions to the trade and to consumers are the most common versions in use. Trade promotion attempts to move product through the channel, provide price incentives, merchandise, assist in co-operative advertising and

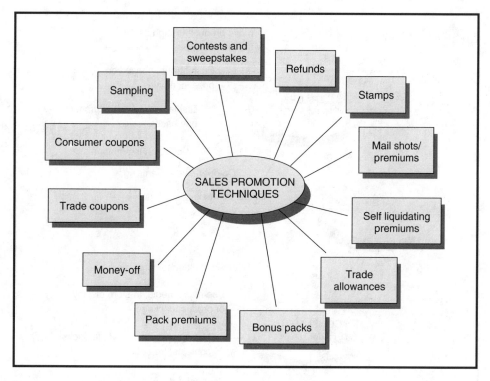

Figure 19.5   Sales promotion techniques

implement dealer contests (Figure 19.6). Consumer promotion uses various forms of direct incentives to encourage the consumer to buy the manufacturer's product rather than some other. Very often the mass media are used to advertise the sales promotion itself.

Sales promotion to the trade

Sales promotion involving the trade attempts to accomplish one or both of the following objectives: to increase sales of the product to channel members, so they in turn promote increased sales to the ultimate consumer or carry a larger inventory of the product; and to increase the distribution of the product to new geographic markets, new types of distributor, or new retail categories. Trade promotions are designed to produce short-term sales increases, shelf space, merchandising improvements and other point-of-sale benefits for the manufacturer.

When intermediaries are helped to increase their sales and profits, the manufacturer also benefits through increased sales and profits, greater intermediary loyalty, and more co-operation in promoting the manufacturer's

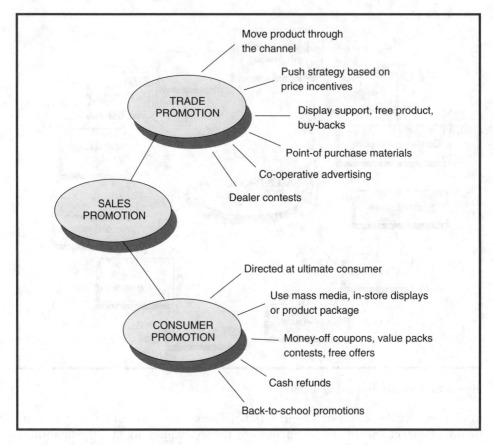

Figure 19.6 Sales promotion to the trade and consumer

products and brands. A large variety of sales promotion devices are available for a manufacturer to use in helping intermediaries. Which one is employed depends somewhat on the nature of the product, the distributor and dealer preferences, competition, the time of year and the limitations of the company budget. Continuous contact between the company salesperson and intermediaries is necessary to secure the active support required for good sales results.

Point-of-purchase and merchandising support

Many tools are used for promoting to intermediaries. Point-of-purchase material consists of the promotion material placed in retail stores. A wide variety of point-of-purchase material is furnished to retailers by manufacturers, such as posters, banners, streamers, price cards, racks, signs, displays and cartons. This material can be distributed to retailers through wholesalers, company sales people or display crews. The large sums of money spent on it are justified by the increase in self-service merchandising and the increasing amount of unplanned purchases made in supermarkets.

Trade promotion may consist of payments to the trade for services rendered. This payment usually takes the form of a discount for featuring, displaying or advertising the brand for a specified time period. Consumer prices are not lowered; the discount covers services rendered to the manufacturer. Alternatively, a trade promotion may consist of a buying allowance, which is a discount to the trade in order to promote purchases and reduce retail prices, thereby stimulating retail sales. It is recognized that low-margin sales are generally ineffective in producing incremental profits. Trade promotions succeed only if some consumer incentive accompanies them: a lower price, a store display, a premium or a refund. The consumer must recognize the value of the incentive and favour it over competing offers for the duration of the promotion.

In general terms, sales promotion aimed at retailers attempts to provide visible merchandising support for product sales at retail level. The retailer is seen as an integral part of the sales promotion programme. Manufacturers frequently obtain retailer support for a price promotion by providing a pre-priced combination package of the product. Alternatively, the manufacturer may reduce the price of the product, display this information on the product and encourage the retailer to pass the benefits on to customers. The most common form of support under this heading is sales promotion and point-of-sale materials developed and provided by the manfucturer.

Trade deals and price promotion

By far the most significant trade promotions are those involving trade deals. Trade deals are designed to secure distribution of a product and encourage retailers to give it promotional support that it would not receive under normal conditions. These incentives are given in exchange for superior store locations for products, special displays or special promotional support. There are four basic types of trade deal:

- buying allowances;
- advertising and display allowances;
- buy-back allowances; and
- free goods.

Since trade deals offer retailers an opportunity for increased profits, they are particularly effective in securing retail merchandising support. However, they can be quite expensive for the manufacturer, and co-operation may not be as great as desired.

A trade deal involving a price reduction of some kind, such as an allowance against invoices or a stocking allowance, is frequently used when the manufacturer is planning a major advertising or consumer sales promotion campaign. The objective is to ensure that there will be sufficient stocks of the product available at retail level. Sometimes manufacturers wish to reduce inventories at retail level. This occurs when new or improved products are planned. Under such circumstances, the manufacturer wishes to remove all old products from the channel system. Merchandising allowances may be used to reduce inventories.

Sales promotion may be used to introduce the product to new distributors and even to new markets. By offering a sales promotion, a reduced price or free product, for example, the manufacturer may attract new retailers to carry it. Sales promotion is not, however, a substitute for a well-conceived distribution programme in the company.

'Hello' or 'push' money is a special monetary incentive to retailers, especially supermarkets, to push a particular line or brand of goods. It is given by the manufacturer as a special reward for selling the manufacturer's product. Hello money is best used when retail sales people are a vital link in selling to the customer.

Motivating the sales force

As a sales motivation tool, sales promotion has a lot to offer. Sales contests, expensive prizes for staff, and gifts for retail store managers associated with product purchases are all highly motivating mechanisms for promoting product sales. The objective is to ensure that the people selling to the trade and to final consumers are enthusiastic about their task. It needs to be remembered, however, that sales promotion is not a substitute for a well-trained and product-knowledgeable sales force. Sales promotion is what it says: the promotion of sales to complement other marketing activities.

Trade shows and exhibitions

Trade shows and exhibitions are another form of sales promotion used with the trade. Many manufacturers of consumer and industrial goods exhibit their products at trade shows. Trade show visitors are able to see demonstrations of new products or innovations in existing products.

Consumers sales promotion

Some sales promotion devices attempt to persuade consumers directly to purchase a product, go to a certain retail store, or take advantage of a premium, contest, coupon or temporary price reduction. There are two basic types of consumer sales promotion devices: those that reach them in retail stores, such as new packaging, in-store demonstrations, premiums and price-off promotions; and those that reach them at home, such as samples, money refund offers, contests and sweepstakes.

As with trade promotion, consumer sales promotion is designed to assist in the promotion of consumer-level sales, especially in the immediate and short term. Sales promotion does not build brand loyalty or consumer franchise, and it cannot reverse a sales decline; nor can it be used to persuade people to accept a product or service they do not want. Sales promotion cannot compensate for inadequate levels of advertising or the wrong form of advertising, and it cannot overcome other product or pricing problems. Sales promotion at consumer level is designed to support the other elements of the marketing mix. Its uniqueness is that it is customized to produce an immediate consumer response.

Objectives of consumer sales promotion

At the consumer level, sales promotion serves to attain seven major objectives (Schultz and Robinson, 1988). As a short-term incentive, sales promotions may be used to obtain consumer trial of new products. Sampling is one of the best ways of obtaining trial for a new product, especially foods and beverages where taste is involved. Sales promotion may be used to obtain an initial trial, but the product in service must deliver the benefits otherwise repeat sales will be low or disappear altogether.

Campaigns frequently use premiums and savings plans to establish loyalty by providing something of value to be accumulated with product or service purchases. In this way, repeat purchase and repeat usage may be derived at a relatively low sales promotion cost.

Sales promotion may be used to encourage more frequent purchases. If new uses are identified for an established product, consumers can be encouraged to buy it more frequently or in greater quantities at each purchase occasion. Recipes showing how a food can be used in alternative ways extend the life cycle and are an attractive sales promotion technique. On occasion, companies producing complementary products or services attempt to develop a 'tie-in' sales promotion to increase the purchase and use of both products and services: for example, a sales promotion related to a brand of gin and a brand of tonic; or 'Paddy' and 'Red', a promotion aimed at increasing the consumption of Paddy Whiskey in conjunction with red lemonade as a mixer.

Sometimes companies use sales promotions to encourage consumers to trade up to larger pack sizes or more profitable products. Usually this objective is achieved through a price promotion or a combination deal involving the present product and the product being promoted. The image of the product being traded up is central to the success of this type of sales promotion. A good image usually means a successful trade-up through sales promotion.

In introducing new products, improved products, new packaging or new sizes, companies frequently use sales promotions to acquaint consumers of the changes. A combination of heavy advertising and focused sales promotion tends to be the choice of companies in such circumstances. The consumer knows the product's benefits, so the sales promotion is used to obtain additional sales immediately.

Sales promotions are often used to offset competitive advertising and sales promotion activities. Indeed, an astute use of sales promotion can build upon competitor advertising. When a competitor launches a heavy media advertising campaign for a product, consumer interest in the product category is raised. By the clever use of point-of-sales promotion, the company can capture some of the newly created interest in the product category, thereby turning the competitor's advertising to the company's advantage.

Lastly, sales promotion may be used in conjunction with special circumstances. A special event in a locality or region may be a suitable occasion for a focused sales promotion which is highly targeted on local consumers. Another example of special circumstances is the use of sales promotion to stem a normal seasonal decline in sales. In the period immediately after Christmas and other busy holidays, television and radio companies frequently offer heavily discounted advertising time to keep the schedules occupied. Many products and services experience a seasonal sales pattern which is susceptible to some degree to change through the use of sales promotion.

Permanent or temporary sales gain

Consumer sales promotions generally need to be accompanied by some form of mass communication. As a consequence, the product must be available in a wide range of outlets, so that the offer can be availed of. A consumer promotion builds market share temporarily. Some of the new customers will soon fall away again, so the objective is to achieve an ultimate share greater than before the promotion was introduced.

Companies, of course, expect there to be a permanent gain as a result of the promotion. But sales promotions are not always successful. Some promotions succeed only in attracting one-time new users, or provide the product at a lower price to some regular customers who are subsequently lost when they refuse to pay the normal price for the product at the end of the promotion. In this way, a poorly designed and executed sales promotion can cost money in the short term and cause longer-term market share loss.

In the hypothetical example in Figure 19.7, consumer promotions are shown to work sometimes, but there are circumstances when they do not. The company is shown to obtain a temporary increase in market share during the period of the sales promotion, but as soon as the promotion is over the original market configuration reappears. In the permanent loss situation, during the period of the promotion consumers substitute the sales-promoted or 'deal' product for regular purchases, stock up on it and afterwards increase regular purchases, but to a level lower than existed before the promotion.

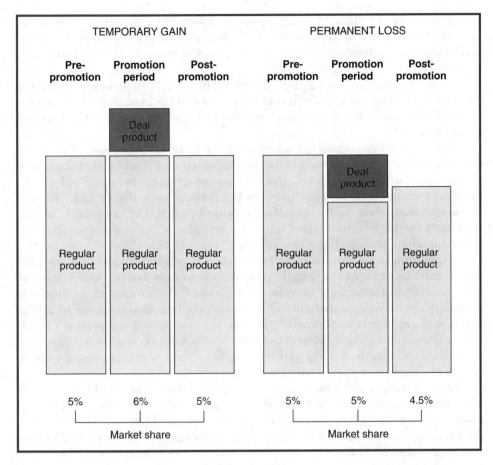

Figure 19.7 How consumer promotions sometimes work: hypothetical example

Supermarkets can jeopardize manufacturers' sales promotion plays by forward buying special wholesale deals, which allows them to stock up far more product than they expect to sell during the promotion. After the promotion period, these supermarkets obtain a wider margin by selling the surplus product at the regular price. Some supermarkets have also been suspected of diverting some of the low-priced products by selling to a retailer outside the promotion area through an intermediary which does the diverting (*Business Week*, 17 February 1992: 80).

In-store sales promotion techniques

Packaging may be viewed as an in-store sales promotion device. When consumers know little about competing products or regard them as being about equal in quality, the sales advantage may come from the package as a stimulant at the point of purchase. Packaging has two functions to perform: product protection and the communication and promotion of product benefits to the consumers. A handsomely designed package is not enough. It must project an attractive image to target markets. Competitive marketing environments accelerate the rate of packaging changes. The effects of ecology, pollution controls, consumerism and high material costs can be expected to exert continued upward pressure on the packaging budgets of many consumer product manufacturers.

In-store demonstrations are a very popular form of sales promotion. Such demonstrations are performed by people supplied and paid by manufacturers to demonstrate their products. In-store demonstrations are used effectively where consumers can be convinced to buy having seen the product in use. Demonstrations are a high-cost sales promotion device that can usually be justified only for high-volume sales. They are popular with food manufacturers, especially when introducing a new product.

A premium is an item of merchandise that is offered free or at a low cost as a reward to buyers of a specific product. Premiums are not often used in new product introductions because they confuse the consumer by drawing attention away from the benefits of the new product. The purpose of a premium is to get buyers of competing products to switch to the company's product and become regular customers. A premium should be readily recognizable to consumers. Products such as toys, watches, glasses, inexpensive jewellery and clocks have been successfully used as premiums.

Trading stamps are a bonus given for buying from a particular retail outlet. Trading stamps have been used with great success by grocery retailers, petrol stations and other convenience goods outlets. They are used to build sales volume for low-margin products in a highly competitive market. Trading stamps programmes are difficult to discontinue once started because many fickle consumers change their purchasing loyalties in the absence of an incentive like stamps.

Price-off promotions are sales promotion devices that offer consumers a specified amount of money off the regular retail price of a product, and state the amount of the reduction on the package. Price promotion sends an unambiguous message that immediate purchase delivers consumer value (Farris and Quelch, 1987). Consumer deals are increasingly common in the marketing of low-priced, frequently bought, non-durable products. Price dealing is more effective on newer brands than on established ones. The frequency of money-off promotions must be carefully watched as too high a frequency can cheapen the image of the brand.

In-home sales promotion techniques

Sampling is a sales promotion technique which may be used in attempting to reach new users, or to provide an inducement to purchase a new product.

Sampling is effective for food and similar products which benefit from tastings and similar forms of product testing not available in advertising. It is known that sampling can convert some triers of a product to be users. It is an expensive technique, however, as it may involve special packaging and other support. Sampling is not justified for well-established or mature products, slow turnover products, products with a narrow profit margin and products that are perishable, heavy, bulky or fragile. It is unparalleled, however, in its efficiency in introducing a new improved product: it can build a higher level of sales volume faster than most other types of sales promotion.

A coupon is a certificate that, when presented for redemption at a retail store, entitles the bearer to a specified saving on the purchase of a particular product or brand. Most coupons are distributed by manufacturers through the mail, in printed publications and on product packages. Coupons can be very versatile sales promotion devices and are used for many purposes. They are frequently used to get consumers to try a new or improved product, to encourage the repeat purchase of a new product after its initial trial, or to increase the use of an established product. The largest users of coupons have been grocery manufacturers, but health product and beauty aid manufacturers also use coupons in volume. With sophisticated computer programming, couponing can be used in very precise ways to attract competitors' customers to the company's products (Exhibit 19.2).

Money refund offers are promotion devices which return a sum of money through the mail to consumers who supply proof of purchase of a particular product to the manufacturer. Money refund offers are used primarily to encourage trial of a product. They are a low-cost sales promotion device because of the low redemption rates. They are least effective in marketing high-volume products where competitors promote their products heavily, but most effective in product categories where limited amounts of sales promotion activities take place.

Contests and sweepstakes create a high level of consumer interest and are strong supporters of other sales promotion devices. Companies that run contests and sweepstakes must be careful, however, to avoid having them classified as lotteries, which in some countries may be illegal. Most companies find it to their advantage to let a professional organization handle the planning, development and operation of contests or sweepstakes. Keeping the goodwill of the losers is a most delicate and important task, since they will far outnumber the winners and the company will want them to continue to purchase the product.

Sales promotion for new product-markets

Consumer coupons are used by companies to obtain trial and to convert one-time buyers into users. One margarine company used a promotion based on selective product characteristics of their well-established margarine brand to attract customers to try its new cheddar-style alternative to cheese (Exhibit 19.3). Consumer coupons may also be used to encourage consumers to trade

---

EXHIBIT 19.2   Buy theirs, get ours free

Americans of all ages redeem millions of coupons in supermarkets; in Europe the practice, long shunned, is catching on fast. The trouble is the imprecision of coupons: too many go either to consumers with no interest in the product (shampoo coupons to bald men, cat-food offers to goldfish owners) or to those who would have bought the brand anyway, at full price.

Catalina Marketing, a small California company, has invented an ingenious way to make coupons far more precise. It sells a computer system which eavesdrops on the flow of data from the cash-register scanners that read bar codes on packages. When someone buys a product that sets off a 'trigger' programmed into the Catalina computer, a printer near the till spits out a coupon, which is then given to the happy shopper with the change. Catalina's product has proved a big hit and has already been installed in nearly 5,000 American supermarkets.

The system lets companies take aim at their competitors' customers with brutal precision. To encourage consumers to switch from another cookie brand to, say, Nabisco's Chips Ahoy, Catalina's system spits out a discount coupon for Chips Ahoy each time the scanner reads the bar code for a rival brand. Nabisco wants Chips Ahoy munchers to try its other products, Catalina spits out a coupon for those. 'The name of the game is to market directly to the right consumer,' says Catalina President George W. Off. According to data trackers A.C. Nielsen Co., an average of 9.4 per cent of Catalina's checkout coupons are redeemed at stores, compared with 2.5 per cent of free-standing coupons – the kind in the Sunday papers.

In August the company made its first foray into Europe by helping to set up a British licensee, Catalina Electronic Marketing, which has already persuaded Asda, Britain's fourth-biggest grocery chain, to try its product. And yet Catalina may have a tougher time in Britain, where a few big chains dominate the market. John Eustace, Catalina's managing director in Britain, worries that this country's supermarkets may not be keen to help manufacturers' brands compete with their own popular private-label products. Perhaps. More likely, British retailers will take a lesson from American supermarket chains, which quickly discovered how to use the Catalina system to boost their own sales, such as offering their cash-back discounts or free food to free-spending shoppers, at the expense of local competitors.

Despite its success, Catalina's system may have a flaw. It depends for success on what Mr Gottesman calls the 'cloud of unknowing'. If consumers know which purchases trigger a coupon, they might be tempted to buy one product at full price simply to get a discount on another: Pepsi would be encouraging people to buy Coke at full price to get Pepsi at a discount, in effect subsidising its competitor. Staying one step ahead of smart shoppers may become as important as beating a rival.

Source: *The Economist*, 5 September 1992: 66; *Business Week*, 5 April 1993: 50.

up to a larger size or to increase product usage. Because they are used in a profile way by many companies, and because misredemption is also a problem, they have become an expensive way of delivery money-off value to consumers.

Trade coupons are offered by retailers, usually in conjunction with the manufacturer. From the manufacturer's viewpoint, trade coupons help to build distribution and reduce inventories. They also help to obtain premium in-store displays away from the usual shelf position. Because the retailer offers the trade coupon, the brand image is not adversely affected in a direct way. Trade coupons can be expensive if the retailer is able to demand allowances to cover expenses.

Trade allowances are highly controversial. Sometimes spoken of as bribes to the trade and referred to as 'hello' money, they have become almost essential for the company attempting to obtain access to distribution and to build up trade inventories. There is little or no consumer involvement, so trade allowances are unlikely to benefit manufacturers. Trade allowances can be abused as their use reflects the power of retailers to dictate the terms and conditions under which new products are admitted to scarce shelf space.

Similar to money-offs and trade allowances, refunds can create in-store excitement at a reasonable cost. Refunds are effective in building brand loyalty especially when multiple purchases are required. They are not considered very useful for trials, and retailers prefer store coupons. Originally, refunds were in the form of cash, but it is more usual nowadays to offer a coupon valid for the repurchase of the promoted brand.

Sales promotion for mature product-markets

Money-off techniques are used to build up consumer-level inventories, which remove customers temporarily from the market and thereby weakens competitors. Because money-off schemes attract price-conscious buyers, there is the danger that once the regular price is restored, the customer will revert to private or generic labels. Money-off techniques produce a temporary increase in sales, but nothing lasting. Repeated use of money-off schemes can debase the brand to such an extent that it will eventually be purchased only when available as a money-off brand. The size of the money-off is also important, as unknown brands may require a considerable discount before any effect is evident. Furthermore, the money-off must reach the consumer for it to have any benefit. If retailers keep most of the money-off, the consumer may not respond at all.

A pack premium is a sales promotion technique whereby the manufacturer offers a useful product in association with the brand being promoted. Pack premiums may help to increase product usage if the premium is directly related to the way the product is used: coffee cups with coffee, a simple razor with shaving cream, or a novelty spoon with breakfast cereals aimed at children. Pack premiums are often perceived by consumers as representing greater value for money spent than is obtainable with money-offs or coupons. Pack premiums can extend the brand advertising and image to the point of sale.

851

EXHIBIT 19.3   Flora sales promotion: cheese friend or foe – 50p off!

The following sales promotion was used by a subsidiary of Unilever to promote its cheddar-style product. The data in the figures given are estimates based on diagrams in the promotional material. The material was in the form of a brochure-like insert affixed to the lid of the Flora margarine tub.

Cheese is traditionally seen as a healthy and nutritious food since it contains more protein than meat, fish or eggs. It is also a very good source of calcium, vitamins and minerals. However, what is not so widely known is that the average pound of traditional cheddar cheese is made from a whole gallon of full-fat milk. So gram for gram, its saturated fat content is similar to that found in pork sausages, beef burgers and cakes. How do we solve the dilemma of a food which is high in saturated fat and at the same time a valuable source of nutrients?

Well it's simple! By following Flora's healthy tips for 'Keeping Cheese in Check' you can still enjoy cheesy goodness and be kind to your heart at the same time:

Try nibbling on some fresh fruit and vegetables
Keep an eye out for hidden cheeses
Cut down on the amount of cheese used
Try a different variety of cheese
Better still, try Flora's cheddar style alternative cheese

Flora's cheddar style alternative is made and matured in the traditional way but most of the milk fat has been replaced with sunflower oil which is high in polyunsaturates and low in saturates ... So whether you are concerned about your own or your family's fat intake, or you just enjoy the quality and taste that you have come to expect from Flora, why not try this delicious option.

50p off your next purchase of Flora's delicious alternative to cheese cheddar style and buy four packs of Flora's delicious alternative to cheese cheddar style and get the attractive cheeseboard – Free!

Accompanying the above text the two figures opposite appeared without comment.

Source: Sales promotion literature for Flora's alternative to cheese, cheddar style, available in supermarkets in 1992. (Note that the diagrams are approximations based on small originals in the sales promotion literature.)

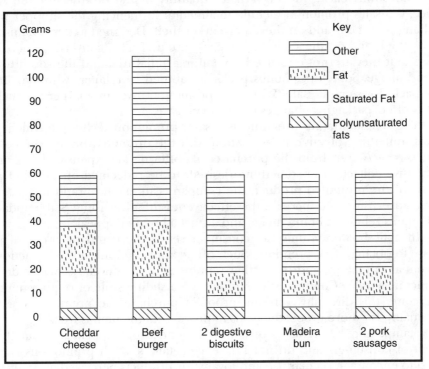

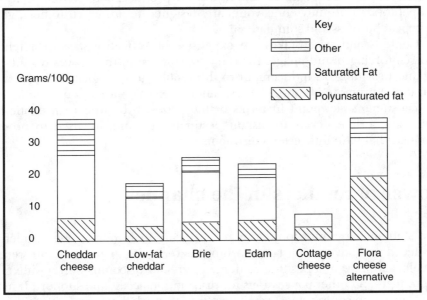

The bonus pack, offering greater quantity of the product for the same price, is a sales promotion technique aimed at influencing the shopper while walking past the brand on the supermarket shelf. Designed as a mechanism to move the brand off the shelf, bonus packs are useful for converting triers into users, but they are not effective in obtaining initial trial and they do little for brand image. Sometimes bonus packs are abused by retailers who may break the packs for separate sale. When the promotion involves a larger jar, such as with coffee, packaging changes can be expensive.

The self-liquidating premium is a sales promotion technique which provides something of value in assocation with the promoted brand, the cost of which is recovered from the purchaser. By offering an expensive book or an expensive collection of something desired, to be redeemed on proof of purchase of the promoted product, the company can extend brand image, reinforce advertising and increase the effectiveness of advertising. Self-liquidating premiums reinforce brand image and attract a broader appeal.

In mail-shot premiums the consumer sends the company proof of purchase to obtain a free premium. Such offers appeal to only a small fraction of potential purchases, and offers that require multiple purchase proofs do not attract new users. Companies sometimes use a sliding scale of requirements to overcome this difficulty: for one proof of purchase the premium is a self-liquidator, for more proofs the deals improve until the item is free.

Stamps and other forms of continuity endeavour appeal to a small segment of consumers and do not influence retailers. Such promotions can be used to encourage regular use and loyalty for products perceived at parity with competitors. Continuity endeavours are designed to attract customers, generate repeat business and stimulate sales.

Contests and sweepstakes are expensive but effective ways of extending and reinforcing brand image, focusing consumers on the company's advertising and providing an inducement to the retailer to give special display attention to the promoted brand. Contests and sweepstakes are often valuable from the consumer's viewpoint in terms of the prizes to be won (e.g. exotic holidays, cars, airline tickets to distant destinations), and are used to promote products that have little else to distinguish them.

Power of retailers in the channel

The shift in bargaining power in recent years in favour of the retailer has produced an adversarial relationship between manufacturer and retailer. Retailers are now in a position to demand greater discounts over a wide range of products and other concessions for distribution access and support. If manufacturers fail to comply, most retailers refuse to stock their product.

Access to customers

The threat of loss of access to customers through distribution outlets is very effective, especially for retailers which are able to play off one competitor against another, or which feature private-label products. Sales promotion budgets are frequently decided on the basis of this fear; they have become the cost of doing business through retailers. It has been essential to run sales promotions in order to keep retailers satisfied. The adversarial relationship thus developed favours only one partner in the deal, which ultimately has a destabilizing effect on the manufacturer–retailer relationship.

Channel power, or the importance of the manufacturer to the retailer and the importance of the retailer to the manufacturer, is a dominant influence on the marketing cost ratio between advertising and promotion (Quelch *et al.*, 1984). The promotion to sales ratio tends to be lower when the manufacturer is considered important by the retailer, when the manufacturer is not dependent on a single distribution channel and when the retailer has higher margins.

In recent years, channel power has shifted to retailers. A number of reasons may be found for this power shift in the channel. One of the reasons is that retailers, due to the scarcity of display space and increased retail advertising budgets, are unable to cope with the number of promotions offered by manufacturers. Manufacturers must, therefore, bid for space and attention.

Gaining access to new customer bases through third-party promotion deals has become very popular among brand companies in recent years. By cross-promoting their products and services, two or more companies can access the established customer base of partner companies in the promotion. For such promotions to be successful, there have to be benefits for at least three parties: the two sponsoring companies and the customer (Exhibit 19.4).

Concentration of buying power

At the same time, there has been a concentration of buying power in fewer hands at the retail level, which has also resulted in channel power shifting to the retail sector. In more recent times, these buyers, especially the supermarkets, have improved their information systems through the use of scanner data to such an extent that daily product sales tracking is possible, whereby the best circumstances for the sale of a company's product can be determined.

As the balance of channel power has shifted to the retailer, the ability of manufacturers to determine the communication mix as between advertising and promotion has been reduced. Because manufacturers' promotional payments contribute directly to retailer profits, it is not surprising, in the circumstances described, that retailers have such a dominant influence in increasing the promotion to advertising ratio. The ability of retailers to delist products, reduce shelf space, price contrary to manufacturers' wishes and reduce in-store merchandising support means that the retailer has the upper hand in a relationship which in the past two decades has become increasingly adversarial.

855

EXHIBIT 19.4   Do free flights really build brands?

BA and Sainsbury, Boots and British Rail, Thomas Cook and Sony, Bird's Eye Menumaster and National Express. It seems you can't buy anything these days without the retailers or manufacturers trying to pack you off on a holiday. In the third week of their 'Buy and Fly' promotion, BA and Sainsbury are all smiles. 'We're delighted. There's a discernible increase in our trade,' says Sainsbury director of marketing Anthony Rees. 'Exceeded all expectations,' says Robert Ayling, director of marketing and operations at BA.

The big promotion sticks to all the fundamentals of third party deals and collection schemes: make it easy on the customer, give them tangible added value, stick with a brand that's your equal, ensure that the staff are onside. Except one. Keep a link between the promotion and the brand. Pedigree Chum and Guide Dogs for the Blind, Fuji Film and Air Miles. Partner promotions with a clear thematic link, goes the theory, are the ones that make a firm contribution to long-term brand values. International air travel and food shopping? Fundamentally linked? Hardly?

First, a look at the positives. The promotion works, says Sainsbury, because the two brands share a common status. 'It's the World's Favourite Airline and Britain's favourite supermarket,' says Rees. Sainsbury, which foots the 'substantial' bill for advertising the promotion, gets increased sales. BA isn't giving flights away. It is offering a discount on seats which might otherwise have flown empty or gone through the bucket shops. In return it gets access to Sainsbury customers: people who haven't tried BA and established BA fliers taking an extra trip. The only negative element, says BA, is the danger of dilution. Giving a 30 per cent discount to a customer who would have bought at the full price anyway is galling. But the airline is confident that it has minimised dilution by timing and promotion in the low season and targeting it at economy customers: 'it's in a class of seat where we need to encourage trial'.

So far, so good, but what's food got to do with economy air travel? Rees says: 'people have been travelling for some years and that has inspired an awful lot of changes in the food market. Many popular dishes are from other countries. International cuisine is really very important there.' Interesting stuff. But surely a little tenuous. Nick Godliman, of the Travel Portfolio, the unit BA set up in February this year to co-ordinate third party promotions, says the lack of a strong link doesn't matter. It's the commonalty of audience, not of brand, that's important. 'There isn't a better match.'

Godliman is confident that this one is a success. 'For a proper third party promotion to work there has to be something in it for us, something in it for the other brand and something for the customer. If that's all there you ought to be able to find a way of making it happen. We mustn't forget that at the end of the day that's what makes the promotion work.' Right. But what would really make them sing is a fundamental commonalty of brand values. And you have to look hard to find that.

Source: Adapted from Clare Sambrook, 'Do free flights really build brands?', *Marketing*, 15 October 1992: 11.

Manufacturer attitudes towards sales promotion

In recent years there has been evidence that some of the very large consumer product companies have begun to resist the pressure for trade and consumer promotions. These companies attempt to introduce price stability and value by an everyday low-pricing policy.

Sales promotion distortion

There is a general belief that the plethora of sales promotions has distorted the traditional business of retailers. Much of the support system, once under the control of manufacturers, has shifted to or been duplicated at retail level, thereby introducing inefficiency in the system. Supermarkets now require storage space for the promoted products, transportation to move them around and office staff to administer the entire operation. Arising from this shift of operations to the retail level, there is a view that only a small proportion of the benefit, 20 to 25 per cent according to some estimates, ever reaches the consumer in the form of lower prices. The remainder goes to the retailers or is lost in inefficiencies (Exhibit 19.5).

EXHIBIT 19.5   The trade promotion two-step

Here is an example of how one supermarket could benefit from a promotion. The process occurs in five steps:

Step 1   For one week only, Super Colossal Products offers a special promotional price on Kleenup detergent to UK stores: ECU20 a case, or 20 per cent off list price.

Step 2   Buy-Now Supermarkets of Happytown, England, orders 10,000 cases. Super Colossal expects Buy-Now to use the 20 per cent savings to promote Kleenup by passing the savings on to shoppers.

Step 3   Super Colossal allocates funds to Buy-Now to promote Kleenup. Buy-Now uses some funds for advertising and keeps the rest. It sells only 5,000 cases at a discounted price to shoppers.

Step 4   Buy-Now later sells 3,000 cases to shoppers in its stores at the normal, higher price.

Step 5   Buy-Now sells the remaining 2,000 cases at a slight mark-up to XYZ Markets, Belfast, Northern Ireland, where Super Colossal has not offered the special price available in England.

Source: Adapted with modifications from *Business Week*, 17 February 1992: 80.

Avoiding brand debasement

There are costs at manufacturer level, too, as it is necessary to produce in peaks and troughs to meet the increased demand and subsequent decline. Trade promotions have been singled out as costly affairs for the manufacturers concerned (Buzzell *et al.*, 1990). A more fundamental cost is the debasing of brands created by continuous sales promotions, which encourage many shoppers to purchase products only when 'on sale'. Powerful manufacturers have begun to strike back by reducing discounts offered to retailers for some but not all products in the portfolio, thereby leaving the total purchase cost to retailers at about the same as before.

By following this pricing and sales promotion approach, these companies expect that the lower prices will eliminate the manufacturing and distribution inefficiencies caused by sales promotions, allow a decrease in regular retail prices to consumers, and eventually restore brand loyalty among consumers. Such a strategy can work only if the manufacturer has a portfolio of well-known brands in demand which the retailer is reluctant to boycott. The fear from the manufacturer's viewpoint is that competitors will continue to offer retailers attractive concessions in order to control greater shelf space. If the more powerful manufacturers withstand this pressure, the weaker competitors could then face increased competition from discounts if they continue to offer deals to the supermarkets.

There has been considerable debate concerning the effects of sales promotion on brand equity. The general view is that sales promotion has a negative effect. While advertising is believed to increase market share, brands that are heavily sales promoted tend to lose market share (Strang *et al.*, 1975). Product sampling tends to be an exception, since it can help to build awareness, especially for a new product. In the case of packaged goods, retail promotions benefit brand leaders over weaker brands (Blattberg and Neslin, 1990). The consumer perceives a strong brand to be a quality product, so it can claim a higher price. A sales-promoted brand, however, is perceived as being of lower quality, otherwise it would not need to be promoted (Dodson *et al.*, 1978).

Managing sales promotion

In the consumer products market, the sales promotion tools more frequently used to promote consumer goods and services are: point-of-purchase displays, money-off promotions and coupons, and in-store demonstrations. For example, in the clothing business, suppliers frequently send samples of colours and materials for a range of clothing articles to store buyers. In the food business, it is usual to send samples of the product offered to ensure that the buyer is favourably disposed.

'Value-added' promotions, such as giving a jar of cranberry sauce with every turkey sold during a particular sales period near Christmas, tend to be more effective than 'value-subtracted' promotions, such as giving £0.50 off the price of the turkey.

Advertising sales promotions

Because there are so many sales promotions competing for the buyer's attention at any time, retailers and some manufacturers have become cynical about their value unless the promotion itself is advertised. This is particularly true in the case of less well-known brands. The brand itself and its packaging can advertise the sales promotion in the case of well-known brands. The brand becomes the advertising medium. Clearly, therefore, it is necessary to consider sales promotion, a below-the-line activity, as part of image formation generated through advertising.

The advertising must, of course, be very focused. The intention in advertising a promotion is to encourage consumers to do something immediately, such as cut out a coupon from the newspaper, call into a store before a certain day, or make a telephone call. Advertising normally associated with image building produces a longer-term effect.

Dilemma of sales promotion

Extended use of sales promotion poses a dilemma for the company. While sales promotion may be effective in obtaining short-term sales and other desired behavioural change, the possible long-term damage to brands raises the issue of the need to integrate sales promotion into marketing strategy and not to treat sales promotion budgets as residuals to be used when all else is presumed to have failed. It may also be necessary to review the increasingly short-term approach that companies and brand managers have adopted. In developing a set of criteria to determine the value of sales promotion, the company should pay attention to both short- and long-term marketing objectives.

Integrating sales promotion in marketing strategy

Many companies recognize that sales promotion is an essential part of doing business in the modern world. They also recognize that there is a difference between actual practice in the use of sales promotion and the way it might optionally be used. This ineffective use of sales promotion may often stem from management attitudes that treat promotion as distinct from marketing strategy, rather than as an integral part of it.

Companies often see marketing strategy as something to be applied in the longer term, whereas sales promotion means providing flexible funds to meet short-term volume and profit objectives. The two are rarely seen as part of the same process to achieve company objectives. More effective use of sales promotion would come, therefore, from an improved integration in sales promotion planning and implementation between brand management and sales as well as between brand management and the other functional areas.

A failure to treat sales promotion as an integral part of marketing strategy may give rise to unrelated selling and advertising plans in the company, and the dilution of decision-making authority over the sales promotion budget. This lack of integration may prevent the establishment of cohesive advertising and promotion strategies, and may produce an inappropriate balance in the allocation of marketing efforts. 'Advertising and promotion are complementary parts of brand strategy; yet, in practice, their theme development, budgeting and implementation may be separate' (Strang *et al.*, 1975: 9).

In practice, short-term sales needs prevent the identification and enforcement of sales promotion performance criteria, which results in additional management difficulties at brand owner level. For sales promotion to be effective, it is essential that companies establish appropriate, measurable sales objectives related to the product items sold to different market segments. It is ineffective to use sales promotion objectives related to price reduction, retail advertising display and volume sales which are not focused on particular groups of customers who are of interest to the brand owner.

Sales promotion treated as a residual

Part of the difficulty stems from the practice of treating sales promotional budgets as a residual expense, not as funding for strategically planned and implemented programmes (Ruch, 1987: 12). Budgets for sales promotion programmes are more influenced by short-term volume and profit considerations than by objectives for using the funds to achieve tactical or strategic business objectives for the brand. Very frequently, sales promotion budgets are established and money is spent on programmes without setting objectives or testing the performance of sales promotion programmes.

Brand manager perspective

One of the better ways of improving sales promotion productivity is to improve the integration between brand management and sales (Ruch, 1987: 14). It is essential, therefore, to obtain sales force opinions on the design of sales promotions, and it is necessary to involve them at every stage of the planning and implementation of the promotion. With the concentration of retail power, it may be necessary in developing sales promotion to focus more on the retailer than on the product, which means taking the sales force into confidence regarding the promotion. Otherwise it may fail. Successful specialized sales promotions depend on being closer to the retailer and the sales force.

In some companies, brand managers are promoted very quickly to positions of greater importance. This results in inexperience and a short-term orientation among brand managers. The rapid turnover of brand managers means that little accumulated experience remains at the level of brand management in the company. A quick career path through brand management means that brand managers rarely have time to understand sales force and retail trade issues sufficiently in order to manage sales promotions effectively.

Increasing managers' time horizons to a three- to five-year planning period is not easy. At the same time, enduring brand strength requires a long-term focus. One way to ease into a longer-term focus is to reduce trade spending gradually over the course of several years, rather than take a drastic reduction in any current period (Mohr and Low, 1993: 37–8). Managers, the sales force and retailers are unlikely to complain about such reductions if their compensation systems are adjusted accordingly. Mohr and Low suggest that sales quotas should be gradually reduced in proportion to trade spending. Furthermore, as retailers move to just-in-time delivery, they may be less inclined to buy excess inventory, since that involves storage.

Appropriate evaluative criteria

Companies can further avoid the problem by designing evaluation systems for the sales force which include incremental profits from volume gains where evaluation criteria are uniform for brand and sales managers. Mohr and Low (1993: 33) make two further suggestions to ease the problem with sales promotions. First, they note, manufacturers and retailers get more value out of trade promotion by using techniques such as direct product profitability, compensating retailers for long-term growth, co-operative advertising and joint promotions.

In regard to the second point, if retailers adopted an everyday low-price policy, the haggling over trade promotion deals would end. Replacing trade promotions, which often produce wide swings in sales and prices, with relatively stable, low prices would ease the time and cost pressures of implementing price promotions and reduce any mistrust that exists between manufacturers and retailers and between business and consumers. Before engaging in a programme of sales promotion, the company should deliberately determine the key success factors required for the particular situation facing it (Hardy, 1986). It is unlikely, however, that retailers with strong private-label brands would be so accommodating in situations where the real competition is between private-label brands and brands ranked third or fourth. Accommodation is easier to find for dominant brands where mutual interest exists.

Effectiveness of sales promotions

Sales promotion is designed to support the sales force and its merchandising efforts, to gain acceptance and the active support of intermediaries, especially retailers, and to increase the sales of the product to the consumers.

In a detailed review of the literature on the importance of promotion in marketing communications, Ruch (1987) noted that most of the research findings are derived from studies of a few brands in a limited number of geographic areas. According to Ruch, five findings which have a degree of general application are:

- every study involving multiple brands and product categories shows important brand and category differences in promotion responses;

- brand-loyal buyers use promotion to 'stock up' and to adjust the frequency of purchase to the size of the inventory built up from promotional purchases;

- brand-loyal buyers do not provide much long-term incremental volume to the company;

- incremental volume from promotions comes from infrequent users of the brand rather than from loyal users or non-users; and

- the effectiveness of a promotion depends on both retailer response and consumer response.

The first conclusion is of very little help to managers other than to warn them that it is important to study the circumstances in their own product-market. As Ruch (1987) suggests, however, the methodologies used in the literature reviewed could be adapted for individual company studies. Retailer responses may be positive (e.g. merchandising support) or negative (e.g. forward buying or transhipment to non-deal areas). Consumer responses may consist of awareness that the promotion exists. Consumer response may also reflect a profitability trade-off between future sales to loyal buyers and immediate promotion-induced brand switching by infrequent buyers.

Characteristics of effective promotions

Sales promotions are most effective when:

- a new brand is being introduced;

- a major product improvement in an established brand is being communicated to the market;

- the brand being promoted is already enjoying competitive success;

- the company is trying to increase store distribution, and sales promotion is used to help sell to intermediaries; and

- a branded product is being advertised, and sales promotion is used to amplify the results of the advertising.

Characteristics of ineffective promotions

Sales promotions are usually ineffective under the following circumstances:

- established brands with no product improvements;

- established brands in decline;

- brands where sales promotions are established as a way of doing business; and

- product classes where intensive competition exists on consumer sales promotions.

EXHIBIT 19.6   Hoover sacks three executives after fiasco over offer

Hoover has fired three top executives after admitting that its ill-fated and controversial free flights offer will lose at least £20 million. The company's US owners meanwhile sent a task force into Hoover's South Wales headquarters with orders to clear up the wreckage from the sales promotion that succeeded beyond its wildest dreams. Under the offer anyone buying a Hoover product costing more than £100 was eligible for two free return air tickets to the US or Europe. Customers purchasing the cheapest qualifying product, a £119 vacuum cleaner, could receive two tickets to New York, costing Hoover more than £500.

Hoover refused to say how many customers had entered the promotion or what the total bill would be. According to some estimates, however, up to 100,000 people may have applied for free tickets – suggesting that the cost will be much higher than £20 million. The promotion was at the centre of controversy almost from the minute it was launched last August, with customers flooding into shops selling Hoover products but then finding it difficult in some cases to obtain their free flights. The British Labour Party called on the Department of Trade and Industry to investigate while trading standards officers in Mid-Glamorgan, where Hoover's head offices are based, received more than 300 complaints.

Although the offer ceased at the end of January, customers may apply to travel on flights any time up to next April. The executives dismissed are the managing director of Hoover Limited and President of Hoover Europe, and the two directors most closely involved with the promotion, Hoover vice-president of marketing, and the director of marketing services.

Source: *Irish Times*, 31 March 1993: 14.

Deliver the value to customers

When the Hoover Company in the UK introduced a sales promotion whereby, for a consumer expenditure of a little over £100, the purchaser was eligible for two free return air tickets to the USA or destinations within Europe, the promotion was ineffective from the company's point of view, but very attractive from the purchaser's perspective. Clearly the implications of the sales promotion offer were not properly assessed in this case (Exhibit 19.6).

Assignment questions

1   Define what is meant by a trade sales promotion and a consumer sales promotion.

2   How does sales promotion fit into the marketing mix?

3   Can sales promotion be used at different stages of the product life cycle?

4   When is sales promotion appropriate and what are the sales promotion techniques which should be used?

5   Does sales promotion damage or support the brand?

6   How can an effective sales promotion campaign be designed?

Annotated bibliography

Blattberg, Robert C., and Scott A. Neslin (1990) *Sales Promotion: Concepts, methods and strategies* Englewood Cliffs, NJ: Prentice Hall.
Rossiter, John, and Larry Percy (1987) *Advertising and Promotion Management*, New York: McGraw-Hill, chapters 12–14.
Stanley, Richard E. (1977) *Promotion, Publicity, Personal Selling Sales Promotion*, Englewood Cliffs, NJ: Prentice Hall, chapter 15.

References

Abraham, M.M., and L.M. Lodish (1990) 'Getting the most out of advertising and promotion', *Harvard Business Review*, **68**, 3, 50–60.
Blattberg, Robert C., and Scott A. Neslin (1985) 'Sales promotion: the long and short of it', *Marketing Letters*, **1**, 1, 81–97.
Blattberg, Robert C., and Scott A. Neslin (1990) *Sales Promotion: Concepts, methods and strategies*, Englewood Cliffs, NJ: Prentice Hall.
Bowman, Russell D. (1985) *Profit on the Dotted Line: Coupons and rebates*, Chicago: Commerce Communications Inc.

Buzzell, R.D., J.A. Quelch and W.J. Salmon (1990) 'The costly bargain of trade promotion', *Harvard Business Review*, **68**, 2, 141–9.

Dibb, Sally, Lyndon Simkin, William M. Pride, and O.C. Ferrell (1994) *Marketing* (2nd European edn), Boston, Mass.: Houghton Mifflin.

Dodson, Joe A., Alice Tybout and Brian Steinthal (1978) 'Impact of deals and deal retraction on brand switching', *Journal of Marketing Research*, **15**, February, 81.

Farris, P.W., and J.A. Quelch (1987) 'In defence of price promotion', *Sloan Management Review*, **29**, 1, 63–9.

Hardy, F.G. (1986) 'Key success factors for manufacturers' sales promotions in package goods', *Journal of Marketing*, **50**, 3, 13–23.

Jones, John P. (1990) 'The double jeopardy of sales promotions', *Harvard Business Review*, **68**, 5, 145–52.

Kotler, Philip (1994) *Marketing Management* (8th edn), Englewood Cliffs, NJ: Prentice Hall.

Mohr, Jackki J., and George S. Low (1993) 'Escaping the catch-22 of trade promotion spending', *Marketing Management*, **2**, 2, 31–9.

Quelch, John A., Cheri T. Marshall and Dae R. Chang (1984) 'Structural determinants of ratios of promotion and advertising to sales', in Katherine E. Jocz (ed.) *Research on Sales Promotion: Collected papers*, Marketing Science Institute Report No. 84–104, Cambridge, Mass.

Quelch, John A., S.A. Neslin and L.B. Olsen (1987) 'Opportunities and risks of durable goods promotion', *Sloan Management Review*, **28**, 2, 27–38.

Rossiter, John, and Larry Percy (1987) *Advertising and Promotion Management*, New York: McGraw-Hill.

Ruch, Dudley (1987) *Effective Sales Promotion Lessons for Today: A review of twenty years of Marketing Science Institute sponsored research*, Marketing Science Institute Report, No. 87–108, Cambridge Mass.

Schultz, Don E., and William A. Robinson (1988) *Sales Promotion Management*, Lincolnwood, Ill.: NTC Business Books.

Strang, Roger A. (1976) 'Sale promotion – fast growth, faulty management', *Harvard Business Review*, **54**, 4, 115–25.

Strang, Roger, A., Robert M. Prentice and Alden G. Clayton (1975) *The Relationship Between Advertising and Promotion in Brand Strategy*, Marketing Science Institute Report No. 75–119, Cambridge, Mass.

Case studies

Case 19: Chupa Chups

P.T. Barnum's calculation that a sucker is born every minute appears rather conservative these days, especially when one considers about 60,000 suckers at any given moment are sucking a Chupa Chup, the world's hottest selling lollipop. Mr Enriqué Bernat, the chairman of Chupa Chups, may be a sucker, but he certainly is no fool. Chupa Chups – which translated from Spanish means Suck Suckers – sold 785 million lollipops in all shapes, sizes and flavours in 1992. From their sales in almost one hundred countries, Chupa Chups have collected 14.2 billion pesetas ($120 million) in revenue.

But even with marketing experience from Iceland to Japan, Russia has proven to be the Spanish lollipop makers' biggest challenge. As early as 1988, Chupa Chups was considering establishing a local presence in Russia. Since the 1970s the Spanish company had been selling its products to the Soviet market on a barter basis. In return, the company received honey and other foodstuffs, as well as space on board Soviet ships to transport its products to its customers scattered across the five continents.

In 1989, the company began negotiations on the formation of a joint venture with the First Confectionery Kombinat of Leningrad, its target partner, and Lengoragroprom, the local regulatory body for the food industry. A joint venture contract was signed in October 1990, and the joint venture was officially registered eleven months later under the name Leningrad Chupa Chups. Under this agreement the Spanish partner retained a 75 per cent share of the holdings. Start-up preparations took a year. Chupa Chups had to lease production equipment to the joint venture to replace the Kombinat's antiquated equipment, which was on average 25–30 years old. During this time, things were far from being all sugar and spice. Initially, according to Juan Llabaria, the joint venture's general manager, it was difficult to get state-owned plants to produce in small quantities and deliver on time.

867

In August 1991, the Chupa Chups Company began efforts to overhaul a former bread factory in St Petersburg, about the same time as attempts to overthrow Soviet leader Mikhail Gorbachev picked up momentum. Within a matter of months, Chupa Chups Soviet market dissolved into fifteen markets, many with new currencies, laws and regulations. 'All the rules of the game changed on us,' says Miguel Otero, managing director of international ventures. 'We didn't know how much money we were making, who our associates were, how to sell or even where we were going to find sugar.' Nor was there any guarantee that the company's contracts would be honoured. As communism's icons fell one after another, even the name of the venture had to be changed – from Leningrad Chupa Chups to Neva Chupa Chups.

One important factor did, however, remain constant. Russian consumers still appeared to be prepared to buy Chupa Chups. No matter how high inflation was or how unstable the currency became, Chupa Chups sold briskly at black market prices on Moscow streets. To the Russians, Chupa chups represented a brightly wrapped taste of western civilization at an affordable price.

While Chupa Chups had no local competitors, small quantities of imported lollipops could be found on the market. Juan Llabaria, the joint venture's general manager, was not concerned because the imports were distributed inconsistently and were generally priced much higher than Chupa Chups' locally produced sweets. Lower energy, labour and other production costs in Russia allowed Chupa Chups to sell its product at about half the price in the West ($0.06–0.07 rather than $0.10–0.15). The lollipops were initially available in kiosks and big supermarkets in Moscow, but local confusion about the ice-cream flavoured Chupa Chups led to their withdrawal. Russians found it odd that 'ice-cream' would be sitting on a shelf without melting, and the rumour mill started spreading stories about strange synthetics.

From the outset, distributing the lollipops throughout Russia proved to be a formidable task. Dutch-born marketing director, Wim Van Brakel, summarized the problem thus: 'If you sell cars and you have one dealer in St Petersburg and one in Moscow, you can probably sell a lot of cars. With lollipops two shops wouldn't get you anywhere.' Distributors had a tendency to overstock, buying a larger amount of the product than they could sell. The Spanish parent company's principal objective was to convince them to buy smaller quantities of product more frequently. Because sales were for roubles and inflation was high, the company preferred advance payment for goods, 100 per cent for new wholesalers and 50 per cent for a distributor with which the company had an established relationship.

Notwithstanding day-to-day difficulties, Chupa Chups had big plans for the market. The company intended to double its production to one million units per day, hiring 18 additional line workers to bring the total to 59. It also hoped to increase market penetration by building up its distribution channels. However, before this plan could be realized, the St Petersburg joint venture was faced with considerable supply and distribution challenges. The reward of overcoming these hurdles would be access to a large and uncrowded market.

> **Identify the supply and demand challenges facing Chupa Chups and write a short report advising the marketing department what it can do to meet these challenges successfully.**

Sources: *European Business*, no. 01421, 28–31 January 1993; *Wall Street Journal Europe*, 5–6 March 1993; *Business Eastern Europe*, 4 October 1993: 5.

This case was prepared by Dympna Hughes, Department of Marketing, University College Dublin, for the purpose of class discussion rather than to illustrate either the effective or ineffective handling of an administrative situation.

Case 20: Cooley Distillery

Dr John Teeling, chairman of Cooley Distillery Group, was approached by several international beverage companies with a proposal that they distribute Cooley's uniquely blended Irish whiskies. Teeling was faced with the choice of whether the company should attempt to develop an independent brand or merely manufacture a product controlled and distributed by an industry giant.

For over twelve months Cooley's has been canvassed by Irish Distillers and its parent Pernod-Ricard, and by Grand Metropolitan and Allied Lyons, to enter into a distribution agreement. Dr Teeling, the charismatic university lecturer turned entrepreneur, had mixed feelings about such an agreement. Undoubtedly entering into an agreement with one of the industry's global players would give the company access to vital distribution channels. However, this would virtually demote Cooley's role to acting as an industry sub-supplier, operating on lower margins and dependent on the whims of its larger partner.

Cooley's roots go back to the early 1980s when Dr Teeling dreamed of marketing a high-quality blended Irish whiskey, aimed at the top end of the market. Teeling felt that, by using a unique combination of temperature, light and humidity, the taste of this new whiskey could be made to reflect the growing consumer preference for a lighter and sweeter-tasting alcoholic beverage. To this end the company was producing at the rate of 20,000 cases of whiskey per week in 1993.

Although the company's two whiskey products, 'Tyrconnell' and 'Lockes', had been available for sale since 1992, Cooley had been unable to secure a suitable distributor. The world whiskey market was dominated by a small number of very powerful international companies with exclusive distribution networks and well-established global brands. United Distillers controlled 30 distillers and sold 20.2 million cases in 1990, which accounted for nearly 40 per cent of the world whiskey market. Hiram Walker/Allied Lyons controlled nearly 16 per cent of the market. International Distillers and Vintners, through its prestigious J & B Rare brand, controlled more than 8 per cent of the world market.

The Cooley Distillery Group was funded almost entirely under special tax savings instruments devised by the Irish government to encourage investment in Irish indigenous industry. Unfortunately, Cooley's was unable to source further equity from this scheme, while it had already made extensive use of debt. In 1990 the company exported about 5,000 cases of branded gin and vodka to Europe, the Middle East and South America. It was producing and selling about 25,000 cases of spirits (gins, vodkas, rums and grain spirits) as well as a selection of sherries to the Irish licensed trade in 1993. The company achieved this by using small local distributors.

Dr Teeling was 'confident that a highly profitable market exists for a new independent Irish whiskey company'. At the time it was believed that, if Cooley successfully developed a distribution network itself, the long-term gains in return on investment, company growth and brand value could be highly lucrative. The major drawback was that it would be a very slow process, and with limited capital available it would be a high-risk route. However, if Teeling entered into a partnership agreement with a larger international organization, the company would have access to exclusive distribution networks, thereby guaranteeing a level of sales and a source of revenue. In return, the international company would control supply to the market and influence the positioning and promotional strategies, so that there would be a minimal amount of direct competition with its own whiskey brands. Of course, the larger partner would also require a substantial share of the margins.

Should the Cooley Distillery Group enter into an agreement with a larger international beverage company?

Source: *Irish Times*, 19 February 1993.

This case was prepared by Derek Creevey, Department of Marketing, University College Dublin, as a basis for class discussion rather than to illustrate either effective or ineffective handling of an administrative situation.

Case 21: CityJet

Conventional wisdom in the airline business holds that the successful airlines of the future must be either huge global carriers with interlocking networks, air-miles programmes and other economies of scale, or small and nifty regional operators such as America's Southwest Airlines. Virgin Atlantic Airways was an affront to such dogma. Richard Branson, the owner of Virgin, believed that his company could be both small and global. His company was founded on two philosophies: that in airlines big is ugly; and that small airlines must compete on something other than price. Otherwise, he said, 'sooner or later the big companies can squash you'.

These philosophies were tested as the bigger airlines improved their service to match those offered by Virgin's long-haul flights. Virgin, however, successfully staved off the competition 'through aggressive marketing, friendly service and extensive inflight entertainment', which included masseuses, tailors and even gambling on some routes.

Virgin was also expanding into the short-haul market within Europe. Here Branson's trump card was to franchise Virgin's name to other small airlines. Under such an agreement, the franchisees could easily get landing slots under new EC regulations. This was in fact the first time that such an exercise in franchising had been used in the airline business.

In theory, franchising could deliver extra revenues without investment or direct risk. However, much depended on the brand name, which was already well established. In order to offset any risks if the franchisee did not keep up required standards, 'Virgin tries to protect itself by training the franchisee's staff, installing the operating systems and reserving the right to withdraw the brand name at 24 hours' notice if it is unhappy with how it is being used.'

There were certain disadvantages to being small, however. It was possible for travellers on big carriers to clock up more air miles because of their huge networks. When they came to spend their air miles, larger airlines provided a wider choice of destination. In practice, Virgin's London–Dublin route (CityJet), now the second busiest after London–Paris, was the only branded service currently in operation. Although CityJet was a wholly owned Irish airline, travellers on the route were left in little doubt as to who set the standards. The check-in desk at Dublin Airport had a Virgin Airways sign overhead, the check-in staff wore Virgin uniforms and the planes were in Virgin's red and white livery.

CityJet's service got off to a 'turbulent' start in February 1994. Its strategy, in order to win the custom of the 700,000 business travellers who yearly fly the route, was to differentiate itself by using London City Airport in London's Docklands. From here it claimed to be less than 20 minutes from the City, whereas Heathrow is an hour away by underground from central London. Most commuter traffic associated with such airlines as Aer Lingus and British Midland uses Heathrow, one of the world's busiest airports. Unfortunately for the fledgling airline, the new service coincided with major engineering works on one of the road tunnels under the river Thames in central London. The resultant traffic jams more than doubled the travel times from London City Airport to the City. On its third day in operation, the new service had yet another stroke of bad luck, when a plane was forced to return to Dublin shortly after take-off because a crack had developed in its windscreen.

More than 2.4 million people flew between Dublin and London in 1993, and volume on the route was expected to grow by 5 per cent in 1994. But business service statistics available suggested that volume growth alone was not going to be enough to allow the newcomer to take the share of the market it seeks. The market shares of the Dublin to London route claimed by the four airlines that flew on it in 1993 amounted to 110 per cent. CityJet also expected to achieve some 5 per cent of market share in 1994. Such figures suggest that there would have to be a major shake-out on the route.

Aer Lingus was still the largest carrier on the route, claiming 50 per cent market share. However, what would happen to the Dublin to London route following its restructuring was still unclear. According to estimates, the debt and other financial problems of Aer Lingus meant that the national carrier might not be able to establish such a stand-alone operation before 1996, when it was hoped that Aer Lingus would have returned to profit.

It was thought unlikely that CityJet would attract traffic from Ryanair. Ryanair offered the cheapest standard fares on the route and had the added attraction of flying into the relatively uncongested airports of Luton and Stansted, both of which are situated north of London. Ryanair claimed to have 30 per cent of the traffic between Dublin and London, and its unrestricted business fare of £199 was significantly less than the £236 and £237 fares offered by the other four airlines (Table 1). 'We offer a no-frills, value for money service and are not in the business of competing in terms of the number of sausages we offer,' explained Ryanair's marketing manager, Ms Valerie O'Leary.

CityJet did not rate very highly its chances of taking customers away from British Airways Express. British Airways Express, which flies into Gatwick Airport south of London, claimed to have 3 per cent of the market. Mr Brad Burgess, the managing director of CityFlyer, the company which operated British Airways Express, said that 'the target market for the Dublin to Gatwick route is business and leisure travel to southern England and as a feeder for international flights from Gatwick'. He refuted any claim that British Airways Express was concentrating on business passengers travelling to London.

In the meantime, Virgin was still embroiled in a 'dirty tricks' row with

TABLE 1   Weekday business services to London

Airline	Route	Business fare	Flight time	Journey to City	First flight from Dublin	Last flight from London
Aer Lingus	Dublin/Heathrow	£237	70 mins	45 mins	7.00 a.m.	20.45 p.m. 22.10 (Fri.)
Ryanair	Dublin/Stanstead	£199	60 mins	41 mins	7.25 a.m.	20.20 p.m.
	Dublin/Luton	£199	60 mins	46 mins	8.00 a.m.	19.45 p.m.
British Midland	Dublin/Heathrow	£237	60 mins	45 mins	6.50 a.m.	20.45 p.m.
BA Express	Dublin/Gatwick	£236	90 mins	30 mins	6.30 a.m.	21.30 p.m.
CityJet	Dublin/London	£237	70 mins	16 mins	7.15 a.m.	19.35 p.m. 21.25 (Fri.)

British Airways, this time in America. In 1993, the company filed an anti-trust suit in New York against British Airways and was seeking some $325 million in damages. Could such a distraction be the cause of Virgin missing the proverbial boat when it comes to market share on the Dublin to London route?

1.   **Evaluate Virgin's service against that of its competitors in terms of choice and quality of service.**

2.   **What conditions will be necessary for Virgin to obtain an adequate share of the business?**

3.   **Is Virgin likely to succeed on the route? Explain your answer.**

Sources: *The Economist*, 22 January 1994: 61–2; *Irish Times*, Friday 14 January 1994: 12.

This case was prepared by Dympna Hughes, Department of Marketing, University College Dublin, as a basis for class discussion rather than to illustrate either effective or ineffective handling of an administrative situation.

Case 22: Donegal Foods

Sean McCarthy, managing director of a small snack food company in Donegal in north-west Ireland, believed that the time was right to expand sales of its successful range of adult snack 'Snippets' into the UK market. The company manufactured and distributed a range of snack foods, crisps, peanuts and extruded adult snacks, with varying degrees of success. Its range of flavoured crisps for children had wide distribution throughout Ireland. While the peanut brand had been successful until the early 1980s, a flood of well-branded and promoted imported lines badly affected its market share. Donegal Foods was now manufacturing a number of private-label peanuts and Sean McCarthy was considering whether to discontinue the branded lines of peanuts.

In 1984 McCarthy identified a growing segment in the adult snack food market. After eighteen months of research, sourcing the right plant and equipment and positioning the product range, Donegal Foods launched Snippets in September 1986, initially in cheese flavours and later in bacon and scampi varieties. The range soon enjoyed a high share position in the adult snack market.

McCarthy had two important appointments within a ten-day period. He had to meet his bank manager in Donegal to discuss a number of issues, in particular an update on Donegal Foods' payback arrangements on the new plant and equipment. He had to allay concerns regarding a slow-down in sales of the original core business, peanuts. But, more importantly, he had to discuss with his bank manager the issue of raising finance to launch Snippets into the UK market. The second meeting was in Manchester. An Bord Trachtala (Irish Exporting Board) had arranged a meeting for him with a potential food distributor/agent which handles a number of major food lines in the area.

Donegal Foods had already analyzed the UK snack market with some care, and its secondary sources indicated that, although the children's segment of the market was very competitive, no adult extruded snack brand yet dominated the market. McCarthy believed that Snippets had potential in both the retail and off-licence trade.

In order to prepare for both of these meetings, McCarthy had to be clear in his own mind about a suitable market-entry strategy. Choosing the right distributor was only part of the problem. A number of other issues also needed to be addressed. How much would it cost to launch a brand nationally into a very competitive market sector? And would it be possible to use the same brand strategy and packaging in the UK market as in Ireland? Also, since snack foods had a limited shelf life, what distribution problems would arise in attempting to get the product from Donegal on to a shelf in Cornwall in a fresh condition?

> **Draw up a list of issues which you think Sean McCarthy should discuss with the distributor in Manchester, and outline what you feel the optimal arrangement would be. How should Sean promote sales of the Snippets product on the British market? Explain your suggestions.**

This case was devised by Brenda Cullen, Department of Marketing, University College Dublin, for the purpose of class discussion rather than to illustrate either the effective or ineffective handling of an administrative situation. Donegal Foods is a disguised company.

PART F

Planning, implementation and performance in marketing management

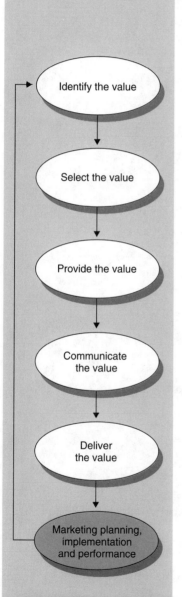

- Marketing planning
- Implementing marketing decisions
- Measuring performance

Chapters

Marketing planning   **2**

Introduction

This chapter introduces and explains:

- the need for an integrated approach to marketing and the role of marketing planning in that process;

- the effect of market conditions on planning;

- how portfolio analysis can be applied in a company;

- the steps in the marketing planning process;

- how companies review markets and perform a situation analysis;

- the necessity for reviewing marketing objectives; and

- the background to preparing a marketing plan.

Marketing planning is a detailed analytical and applied set of activities by which the company determines the best way to implement marketing strategies. Marketing strategies are integrated in a comprehensive framework within the marketing plan. Marketing planning is a process by which the company understands the marketing environment, and the needs and wants of customers, while recognizing that competing firms also serve the market. It also means recognizing the company's strengths and weaknesses in serving customers. Companies attempt to develop strategies to build on their strengths while coping with their weaknesses. Analyzing the market and the company's competitive position allows the company to place its products and services in a portfolio that has significant strategic planning implications. A case study of a hypothetical company, Alpha Foods Limited, applies the portfolio framework in the development of a new product to illustrate the planning approach adopted. The portfolio analysis is the starting point and indicates the precise ways in which the company can develop its product portfolio by improving existing products and adding new ones.

The marketing planning process consists of a number of stages, including assessing existing product-markets, preparing a detailed financial statement, reviewing the market situation, obtaining and analyzing the relevant data, developing appropriate marketing objectives, sequencing and timing marketing activities to implement marketing strategy, and preparing and controlling a detailed operational marketing plan.

When you have studied this chapter, you should be able to define the terms listed above in your own words, and you should be able to do the following:

1. Distinguish between strategic and tactical planning.

2. Define marketing planning.

3. Determine the value of marketing planning to the company, especially in turbulent times.

4. Recognize the different approaches to planning and state how the company can organize for planning.

5. Establish product positions in a portfolio using the procedure used by Alpha Foods Limited.

6. Specify the steps in the marketing planning process.

7. Outline a precise approach to developing a marketing plan for a company.

8. Determine how the company's marketing objectives might change and how the company can cope with such change within a marketing plan.

9. Prepare in outline form an operational marketing plan.

Strategic marketing decisions

Marketing strategy is a process which consists of analyzing market opportunities, specifying objectives, developing plans and monitoring performance (Boyd and Larréché, 1978). The concept of strategic marketing emphasizes the need to define appropriate targets before determining the composition of the marketing mix (Oxendfeldt, 1962). An alternative but related view of marketing strategy involves a statement of intent regarding the company's market objectives and choices of product-markets (Catry and Chevalier, 1974).

Strategic market planning involves the management of any business unit in the dual tasks of anticipating and responding to changes which affect the market for their products (Abell, 1978). It is concerned with the composition and allocation of the marketing mix over all product-markets of interest to the firm. It is, therefore, company specific and stresses the individual elements of the marketing mix, such as the product, its price, its promotion and its distribution. The overall objective of strategic marketing planning is to identify that portfolio of product-market activities which provides the best return on the company's investment.

Strategic marketing planning

Successful companies usually know where they are going and plan to get there. Planning the marketing effort means carefully designing and implementing a strategic and operational framework within which the company can operate. Marketing planning is a logical sequence of activities leading to the setting of marketing objectives and the formulation of plans for achieving them (McDonald, 1989: 13). A marketing plan consists of objectives and a carefully thought-out marketing programme.

Integrated approach to marketing

There are many barriers to the introduction of marketing planning in the company. Many companies have been successful without formal strategic or operational planning. Others, especially smaller firms, claim that they have no time for planning, since they are too busy running their companies. Still others claim that market conditions change too rapidly for planning to be of any value; they are victims of a turbulent competitive environment, buffeted by the winds of change without direction or control.

The alternative to planning marketing activities is to engage in periodic fire fighting and crisis management, which is a reactionary approach to customers and competitors. Marketing planning, however, is concerned with knowing how to operate in the market and deciding the appropriate course of action before events catch up with the company. The philosophy behind marketing planning is that an integrated approach is likely to be more successful than disparate endeavours taken in response to unanticipated changes among customers and competitors. In marketing planning, the manager is attempting to answer six questions:

- where are we now?
- how did we get here?

- where are we going?
- what must be done?
- who should do it?
- when should it be done?

Answers to these questions are likely to improve the company's marketing performance. Marketing planning encourages a systematic approach to strategic thinking and a better co-ordination of marketing efforts. It also allows the company to anticipate developments in the market.

Marketing plans are normally developed for a new company, a new venture or a new product and updated periodically, but at least yearly. Roll-over planning on a continuous basis is becoming increasingly popular among firms with good information-processing facilities and skills. Constant monitoring of the market allows quick tactical changes to be made if a sudden change is noted. Many different managers in the company contribute to the plan: manufacturing, advertising and sales people add components or sections to the plan and also update them on a periodic basis.

There are two types of marketing plan: a strategic marketing plan and an operational marketing plan. The strategic marketing plan specifies a course of action for the company for up to five years. It is a long-term view of the company in the context of its customers and competitors, actual and potential. The operational marketing plan covers the details of how the strategic plan is to be implemented in the first twelve months. All marketing plans should indicate who in the company is responsible for each marketing activity, and how these activities are to be accomplished. It is also necessary to provide time schedules and budgets.

Stages in marketing planning

There are five management stages in marketing planning, which correspond to the need for analysis, forecasting and making assumptions, resolving strategic issues, developing market strategies and organizing for marketing (Day, 1984). The analysis stage involves a detailed examination of the marketing environment, customers and competitors, and an internal analysis of the company itself (Figure 20.1). A number of chapters at the beginning of this book were devoted to these issues. In regard to forecasting and assumptions, the company must attempt to forecast or assume likely changes in the environment among its customers and competitors, and determine how its own resource base is likely to develop during the planning period.

During the third stage, the company attempts to resolve strategic issues that arise, which means carrying out a SWOT analysis for the company. The identification of the strengths and weaknesses derives from a simultaneous analysis of customers, competitors and the company itself, and allows the com-

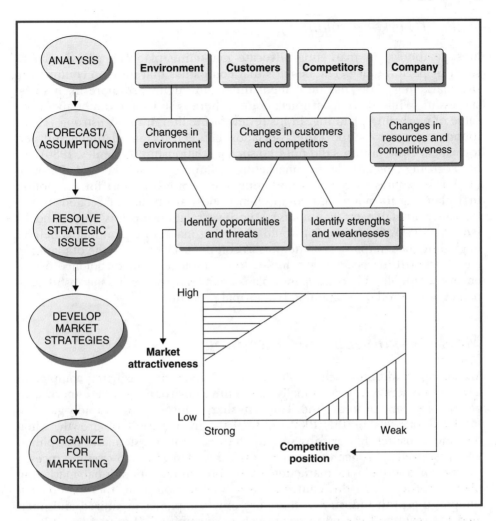

Figure 20.1 Stages in marketing planning

(Source: Adapted with modifications from Day, George S. (1984) Strategic Market Planning, St Paul, Minn., West Publishing Co. Copyright © 1984, West Publishing Co. All rights reserved)

pany to assess its competitive position, which may be strong or weak or somewhere in between. The identification of opportunities and threats derives from a simultaneous analysis of the environment, customers and competitors, and allows the company to determine the attractiveness of its various markets. Now it becomes possible for the company to develop a set of appropriate market strategies. The last stage is to organize the marketing endeavour to implement the strategies decided.

Value of marketing planning

Most textbooks on marketing advocate marketing planning as essential to superior performance. The belief is that companies that develop comprehensive marketing plans and implement them thoroughly are more likely to be successful. While these assertions abound, there is still some doubt about the value of marketing planning. In his review of the literature, Armstrong (1982) found evidence to support the association between formal planning and performance. Other authors did not find such a relationship (Greenley, 1986).

Focusing specifically on marketing planning, Lysonski and Pecotich (1992), in a study of New Zealand companies, found support for the notion that planning formality and comprehensiveness are positively related to performance in stable environments. A positive relationship was also found by Hooley (1984). On balance it would seem that marketing planning is helpful in guiding the company as it attempts to compete. The time frame of planning has shortened in recent years due to the complexity and turbulence of the environment. Flexible contingency plans are a feature in most successful companies, where roll-over planning is a normal procedure.

Market conditions and planning

Marketing conditions in the 1990s are best characterized as being complex in a rapidly changing, internationally competitive environment where markets in general are static or in decline. This is in sharp contrast to the rapidly growing insulated markets of the 1960s and 1970s. In a period of growth, when demand consistently outstrips supply, the need for a systematic, disciplined and organized approach to the market is less evident. In such circumstances, a short-term approach to marketing based on annual operational marketing plans is sufficient. In this context, it is as well to note that 'there is no such thing as a growth industry ... there are only companies organized and operated to create and capitalize on growth opportunities' (Levitt, 1960: 47). In the turbulent conditions of the 1990s, circumstances dictate a more rational and strategic approach to markets and marketing.

The industry dynamics model popularized by Porter (1980) and others, including the McKinsey Company, helps to place company planning in context. Four pressures from the external environment influence the system in which the company operates: government regulation, economic trends, international developments and social values (Figure 20.2). The industry environment is characterized by influences from suppliers and customers, by the threat of substitutes, and by the structure of the industry in which the company operates. Changes in any one of these variables determines, to some extent, the pattern of company development. These issues were discussed in Chapter 4.

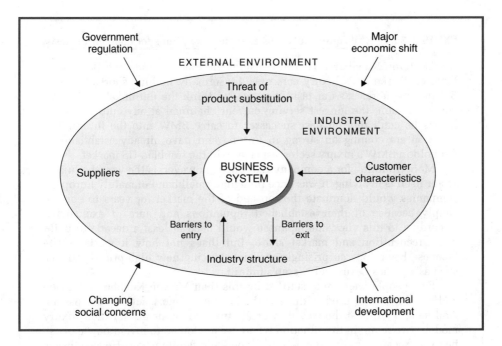

Figure 20.2 Industry dynamics model
(Source: Adapted from McKinsey and Co., 1983: 34)

Marketing planning for turbulent times

Market changes may be so far reaching that the competence of the company to continue to compete effectively is questioned. Observing these circumstances led Abell (1980) to develop the concept of strategic windows, or the need to focus on the limited periods during which the fit or match between the key requirements of a market and the particular competences of the firm are at an optimum. If such a strategic posture is not adopted:

> by failing to grasp the nettle of strategic orientation in plans that identify and develop their distinctive competences, companies have become, or will increasingly become casualties during the 1990s ... By developing short term tactical marketing plans first and then extrapolating them, managers merely succeed in extrapolating their own shortcomings. (McDonald, 1989: 16).

Sometimes strategic marketing planning calls for lower costs in the company and even a relocation of production facilities, which may damage the brand (Exhibit 20.1).

It is necessary at the outset to understand the difference between strategic marketing and operational or tactical marketing. McDonald (1989: 16–17) argues that companies with an effective marketing strategy and inefficient

---

EXHIBIT 20.1 BMW pulls out stops as it studies options for controlling costs

Eberhard von Kuenheim used to consider the idea of producing Bayerische Motoren Werke AG's luxury cars outside Germany nothing short of heresy. But not anymore. 'It's our task', he says, 'to think the unthinkable.' But Mr von Kuenheim, the longest serving current chairman at any auto producer, knows he can't rely on past successes to carry BMW into the future. The Japanese are coming on strong in Europe and have already established a foothold in BMW's luxury sector, especially in the troubled US market.

More troubling for a company like BMW, however, is the way the luxury sector itself is evolving. It was once thought a small band of mainly European companies would dominate the top end of the market for years to come – simply because of their established reputations and aura of exclusivity. According to this view, the Japanese would need at least a decade to build name recognition and market share. But that's not how it worked. The Japanese have done surprisingly well introducing new high-priced models, such as Toyota's Lexus and Nissan's Infiniti.

Few people were more startled by this than Mr von Kuenheim. Urbane and aristocratic, he used to dismiss the Japanese almost without discussion. And he still sniffs at the way they create trendy new names for their luxury models: 'we're not in the situation where we are forced to invent new names', he says, 'because we can stay with our good, old family name'. He also insists BMW only has one 'true competitor' – Mercedes-Benz AG, the car-making division of Daimler-Benz AG.

But even if nothing comes of it, the fact that BMW is looking overseas marks an important departure. Mr von Kuenheim is deeply aware that his cars are closely identified with their 'Made in Germany' label, and he often talks in hushed tones about the need to protect the trademark. But he says the increasing globalization of the auto market is making this less relevant. 'Our car must come from BMW, wherever the factory is situated,' he says. 'And that means that it comes under the same rules for quality and reliability' as a BMW built in Germany.

Source: *Wall Street Journal*, 19 February 1992, 1 and 5.

---

marketing operations merely survive (Figure 20.3). Companies which fall on the left side of the matrix, i.e. have ineffective marketing strategies, are destined to die. The short view does not protect the firm from the vicissitudes of the marketing environment. In this context, only firms with a strategic orientation are likely to remain in existence.

Different approaches to marketing

Companies in the same industry in two different countries often approach the market in quite different ways. The use of planning, new manufacturing

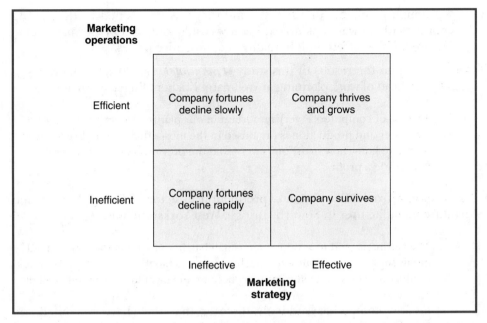

Figure 20.3 Marketing strategy and marketing operations
(Source: Adapted from McDonald, 1989: 17).

technologies and computer information systems can be very different in different countries. In this regard, the manufacturers of kitchen cabinets in the former West Germany and in the UK are very different. The National Institute of Economic and Social Research in the UK reported in a study published in 1987 (*Financial Times*, 20 November 1987), that the manufacturers there were competitively weak and vulnerable because of:

- acute skills shortages exacerbated by superficial training programmes;
- restricted use of computers for production scheduling; and
- inadequate and outdated equipment, resulting in frequent breakdowns.

According to this study, the results of such weaknesses for the competitive position of UK companies were:

- output per employee in German plants was twice that in UK, in some processes;
- productivity in the German furniture industry as a whole was 66 per cent higher than in the UK;
- German manufacturers exported about 33 per cent of their output, while UK companies exported only 4 per cent;

- though profitable in 1987, UK industry was threatened by developing countries which were able to exploit low-cost labour, and by German manufacturers which offered high quality at competitive prices.

Commenting on the results of this study (*Financial Times*, 20 November 1987), Hans Grabs, head of work planning at Wellmann Kuchen, Enger, Germany, stated:

> The use of computers is very important in our plants. Orders go into the computer and production is organised in the most efficient way. Every day at 9 a.m. we know how many units were sold the previous day and whether we have made a profit.

The response from Mike Runack, production director at Ram HI, a kitchen furniture manufacturer in Sowerby Bridge, West Yorkshire, was:

> The Germans tend to produce very small batches of kitchens and they need highly sophisticated computer machinery to enable them to do that. We mass produce and do not need computers because the machines are running all day.

Frequently, companies suddenly discover that they have remained too complacent for too long and realize that their traditional market has disappeared or become a fraction of the size it once was, or, more likely, that brand values are no longer what they were. The short-term response of some companies is to cut costs and seek a financial solution, which may give temporary respite. In the longer term, however, financial rectitude without value-providing products and services may be limiting. Developing an appropriate product and service marketing strategy which will take a company beyond a maturing market franchise is the key to success and not easily found (Exhibit 20.2).

Organizing for marketing planning

Marketing planning involves people at all levels in the company. In particular, it seeks a commitment of people at senior levels. At the very senior level, i.e. at board and chief executive levels, commitment is likely to be very high in regard to selecting planning issues, developing and evaluating corporate strategies, and approving strategies and operational plans (Table 20.1). Commitment at senior and middle manager levels is likely to be high when diagnosing the development of business unit or product-market strategies and their evaluation, and very high in the implementation of chosen strategies, strategic and operational.

Techniques used in marketing planning

There are many options available to the company in regard to selecting a technique for marketing planning (Figure 20.4). A review of the literature

---

EXHIBIT 20.2   Campbell is bubbling, but for how long?

When David W. Johnson arrived at Campbell Soup Co. 18 months ago, he found a financially ailing, inefficient company that was, well, in deep soup. Johnson wielded a very big knife. He shuttered or sold 20 plants world-wide, got rid of roughly 15.5 per cent of Campbell's 51,700-odd work force, and yanked unprofitable products lines off store shelves. The crash diet, though painful, is paying off: Campbell's profits have become the second fastest-growing in the food industry behind Kellogg Co.

So the ever-frugal Johnson can rest easy, right? Only at his own peril. True, his cost-cutting blitz has delivered a stunning profit rebound: Campbell's net profits hit $316.8 million for the nine months ended on April 28, up 31 per cent over the year-ago period. But there's concern that Johnson's penny-pinching ways may hurt Campbell over the long haul. It's one thing to take a machete to Campbell's bloated overhead. It's quite another to fashion a workable product and marketing strategy that will carry Campbell beyond its maturing soup franchise.

What's especially disconcerting is that Campbell's profit gains have been accompanied by anaemic sales numbers – 1.9 per cent gain, to $4.86 billion, in this fiscal year's first nine months. More worrisome, Johnson is squeezing more cash out of existing lines through price hikes, one reason for the company's soft sales. Take canned soup: Last year, a three per cent over-all price increase resulted in a four per cent drop in unit sales, according to Information Resources Inc., a market-tracking service.

Price hikes have also hurt sales of Campbell's Pepperidge Farm premium-prices Goldfish crackers and its Franco-American pasta line. 'They're sowing the seeds of future problems by milking their brands instead of investing in them and investing in new brands,' says Al Ries, chairman of Trout and Ries marketing consultants in Greenwich, Conn. Indeed, Campbell's advertising budget – which trade publications place at $200 million or so a year – hasn't budged much from last year.

Source: *Business Week*, 17 June 1991: 67–8.

---

indicates that financial modelling is the technique most in use by marketing planners. Many of these financial models are quite simply representations of the world of marketing, while others have been adopted to accommodate many of the more important marketing dimensions.

The more popular techniques used in marketing which have direct applicability are life cycle analysis, portfolio methods and segmentation techniques. These have already been discussed in Chapter 3. Other techniques are useful additions. Scenario forecasting, industry modelling and learning have only tenuous relevance to marketing planning, particularly in regard to applications.

TABLE 20.1   Role of the manager in the marketing planning process

Steps in marketing planning	Management commitment	
	Board and chief executive	Senior and middle managers
Background		
Organizing the process	Low	Low
Selecting planning issues	High	Medium
Business position diagnosis	Medium	High
Identification of strategic alternatives		
Corporate strategies	High	Low
Business strategies	Medium	High
Evaluation and selection of strategies	High	High
Implementation of marketing planning decisions		
Approving strategies	High	High
Approving annual plans	High	High
Formulating implementation plans	Low	High

Source: Adapted from McKinsey and Co. (1983: 16).

Portfolio analysis and marketing planning

This section examines the key issues the company must consider when analyzing its portfolio of products and services. A hypothetical company, Alpha Foods Limited, is used to demonstrate how market portfolio analysis is applied so that the company can derive the foundations for an effective marketing plan.

Critical factors in portfolio analysis

In the analysis depicted in Figure 20.1 above, markets were classified on their attractiveness and the company was judged on its competitive position. This analysis helps to identify a number of development alternatives or investment opportunities for the company (Figure 20.5). Opportunities in highly attractive markets in which the company has a strong competitive position should be developed. The decision in these circumstances would be to invest for growth. Opportunities which arise in unattractive markets in which the company is weak should usually be ignored. The interesting opportunities are those that fall in the middle. Some of these are questionable, while others may prove worthwhile. These are investments which the company might wish to develop opportunistically. If the company does not possess the skills or knowledge to develop such markets, it might be possible to acquire them. The other

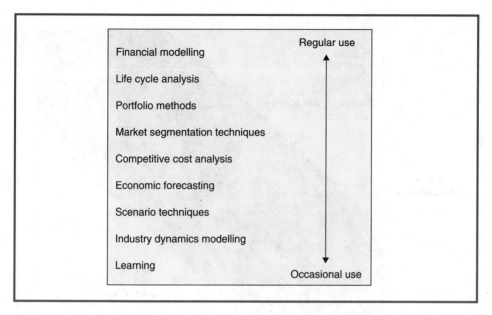

Figure 20.4 Techniques used in marketing planning
   (Source: Adapted from McKinsey and Co., 1983: 18)

situation arises where the market is not very attractive, but the company is very strong there. There may be no good reason to abandon such markets just because they do not fit the attractiveness and competitive position criteria.

In general, the company manages a portfolio of products which are spread around the portfolio. Using the Boston Consulting Group growth–share matrix, these products may be classified as question marks, stars, cash cows or dogs. The reasoning behind this classification was discussed in Chapter 3. Here it is used to demonstrate that the company would normally wish to have a balanced portfolio of products (Figure 20.6). Note that the cash cows are important in terms of sales. These are the products which produce surplus cash to ensure that the questionable successes become star products and avoid becoming dogs to be removed. Many companies support a balanced portfolio like that illustrated.

Seeking balance in the product portfolio is crucial in terms of the allocation of scarce marketing resources. It is important that the company has a range of products at different stages of development. A range of question marks, some stars and a few well-established cash cows is a very attractive portfolio. Viable product portfolios have already been discussed in Chapter 3. The portfolio in Figure 20.7(a) is very attractive, but it would be difficult to maintain since there is only one cash cow available to support the life cycle development of many others. This would be especially true in high-technology companies.

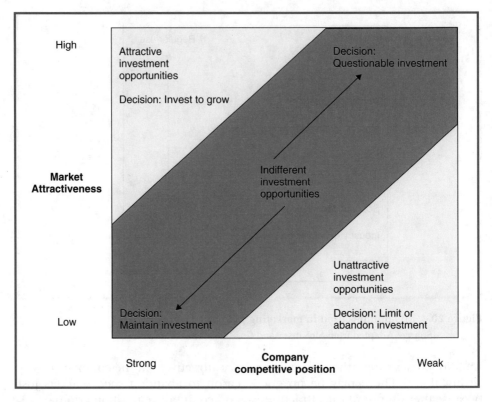

Figure 20.5   Portfolio analysis of market and marketing investment opportunities

Most companies could not support the portfolio shown in Figure 20.7(b), since question marks are cash users and the company has no cash cows. Unless it has a surfeit of cash from elsewhere, this company is a candidate for takeover or quick demise. Lastly, the company illustrated in Figure 20.7(c) is in trouble. Most of its sales are from dogs in markets with low growth and in which the company is not competitive. This company is likely to liquidate its other assets.

Portfolio analysis in Alpha Foods Limited

The value of portfolio analysis to the company is that it depicts the position of the company's products relative to one another and, in a general sense, relative to conditions in the market. For it to be of practical value, it is necessary to view portfolio analysis as having two aspects, a static view and a more dynamic view. Usually the company would start with a static view and then shift to a dynamic view. A static analysis involves using the criteria discussed above to

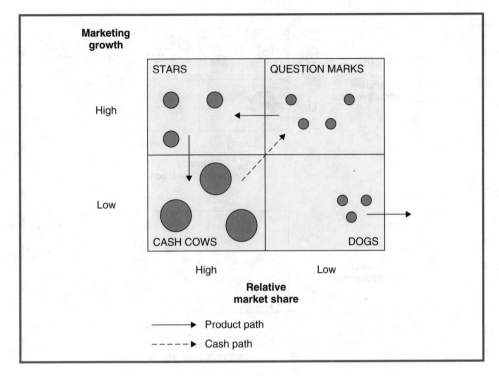

Figure 20.6 The BCG product portfolio matrix

assess the attractiveness of the market and the company's competitive position in the market relative to competitors. Proceeding in this fashion, it is possible to assign the company's products in a preliminary portfolio classification. A case illustration will help to demonstrate the value of portfolio analysis in assisting the company in understanding its present market position.

Markets for Alpha Foods Limited

Assume that an imaginary company, Alpha Foods Limited, is interessted in using a portfolio analysis to judge the likely position of a proposed new oven-ready bread-crumbed chicken kiev product, sold under refrigerated conditions. To do so the company would first attempt to assess the attractiveness of a particular market for the proposed investment along the lines of the analysis indicated above. The results of this analysis might look something like that shown in Table 20.2.

The first step in the process of measuring the attractiveness of the market might be to measure present market size. Market research might indicate three possible sizes: $10 million, $7.5 million and $5 million. The most likely outcome is expected to be $7.5 million. The next step would be, again

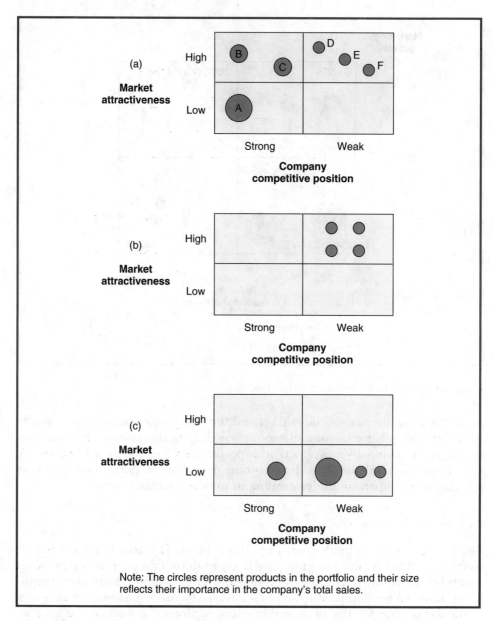

Figure 20.7 Viability of product portfolios

TABLE 20.2   Measuring market attractiveness for Alpha Foods Ltd

Market attractiveness factors	Importance weights	Preference ranks			Measures
		100	50	0	
		Possible market outcomes			
Market size ($ million)	0.20	10	7.5	5	10
Sales volume growth (%)	0.25	>15	10	<5	25
Profitability (%)	0.30	>20	15	<10	15
Opportunity to segment	0.05	High	Some	Limited	5
Long-term trends	0.20	Above average	Average	Below average	20
Total					75

through research, to establish the volume sales growth in the market. Three estimates are provided: more than 15 per cent, 10 per cent and less than 5 per cent. The most likely outcome expected is a greater than 15 per cent volume growth. The company would then estimate profitability and three possible outcomes, like those shown in the table, might be provided by company analysts, with less than 10 per cent being the most likely. It is further assumed that opportunities to segment the market are expected to be high, and long-term trends are expected to be above average for the industry.

At this point the firm will explicitly or implicitly allocate importance weights to each of these factors in assessing market attractiveness. Assume that the firm gives the greatest weight (0.30) to profitability, and believes that segmentation possibilities are of least importance (0.05). Multiplying these weights by the preference ranking for the most likely outcome, and aggregating over all factors, produces a market attractiveness score.

The market attractiveness score is computed as follows: market size = 10 (0.20 × 50); sales volume growth = 25 (0.25 × 100); profitability = 15 (0.30 × 50); segmentation opportunities = 5 (0.05 × 100) and long-term trends = 20 (0.20 × 100). The total market attractiveness score of 75 is a summation of the individual scores obtained. The importance weights are internal company judgements of the importance of each of the attractiveness factors evaluated. There is nothing sacrosanct about the list used here. A different or more extensive list might be used.

Alpha Foods' competitive position

A similar procedure is followed in deriving the firm's competitive position (Table 20.3). In this case a great deal more judgement and internal company information is required. The importance weights are determined by management, and the position of Alpha Foods Limited on the evaluative factors is assessed with reference to internal company data and competitive market information.

By following this procedure, the company discovers that it scores the same as the industry average on new technology and innovation capability, that its product quality is no better or worse than the industry average, and that it is above average on cost of distribution. It is below average on a number of important factors, such as manufacturing efficiency, share of market and net effective distribution (Table 20.3). As in the previous case, the importance weights are multiplied by the preference ranks for the expected positions of Alpha Foods Limited to derive a company competition position equal to 35.

The result of this analysis is presented in Figure 20.8. Note that the proposed new product venture is classified as a questionable investment. Alpha Foods Limited now faces a number of interesting issues. It may be possible to improve utilization of the firm's current capacity, or perhaps the company should consider reducing capacity. Alternatively, the company may be able to raise profits by adding volume through better distribution and share increases in the market. The company might also consider introducing a number of new related products to form a new product line instead of just one new product, thereby providing greater consumer choice. The analysis performed so far is too limited to allow the company to decide what to do.

Dynamic analysis of Alpha Foods' portfolio

Alpha Foods Limited uses a dynamic analysis of its portfolio to reposition its products in the market growth–share matrix. The company can maintain or change the portfolio classification of each of its products by following a three-step process. First, it must access capacity to maintain or change the existing classification. Second, it must prepare a benchmark strategy, which includes a statement of assumptions, likely competitive reactions and risk as indicated in Figure 20.1 above. Third, the company will need to develop a set of alternative

TABLE 20.3   Measuring Alpha Foods' competitive position

Competitive position factors	Importance Weights	Preference ranks			Measures
		100	50	0	
		Above average	Average	Below average	
New technology	0.20		✓		10
Manufacturing efficiency	0.15			✓	0
Product quality	0.20		✓		10
Market share	0.10			✓	0
Cost of distribution	0.15	✓			15
Net effective distribution	0.20			✓	0
Total					35

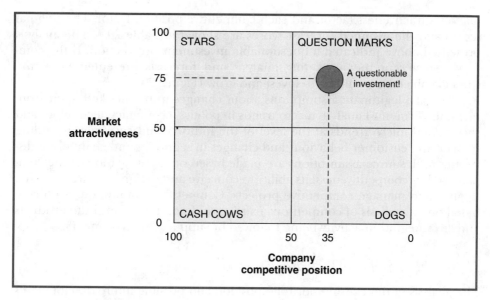

Figure 20.8   Portfolio analysis for Alpha Foods Ltd

strategies, such as the possibility of introducing a range of new products. It may also be necessary to develop a contingency plan for high-risk situations.

Marketing analysis is usually based on qualitative judgements supported by research and analysis. There are a series of questions that managers must answer before it is possible to develop a detailed marketing plan. The company will be concerned to know how:

- the environment will change;
- financial performance will be affected;
- costs will change;
- product technology will change;
- process technology will change;
- the character of competition will change;
- competitors are likely to redefine their activities;
- competitors are likely to change their investment and functional strategies;
- customer behaviour is likely to change; and
- market segmentation may be influenced.

In the next step of the analysis, it is necessary to assume that the manager of Alpha Foods Limited has developed a set of three-year forecasts for each market attractiveness factor and each competitive position factor. The original scores and the assumed forecast scores are shown in Table 20.4. The analysis presented above indicated a questionable investment proposition. If the company can accept the marketing analysis and forecasts presented here, the strategic objective would be to invest and grow (Figure 20.9).

To make legitimate assumptions about changes in the marketing environment, the firm must analyze macro trends in politics, economics, technology and society, and micro trends at the level of the industry and customer, including market size, customer behaviour and changes in segments and channels of distribution. Resource assumptions are made based on an evaluation of the company and its competitiveness: its ability to conceive and design, produce, market, finance and manage competitive projects. Competitive assumptions are made based on an analysis of competitors, existing and potential, substitute products and any integration activity being followed by suppliers and customers.

Using the benchmark strategy

The analysis of the existing portfolio position and possible future developments presented in Figure 20.8 provides Alpha Foods Limited with a benchmark or starting strategy. The company now has a benchmark strategy for each product reflecting the existing situation and a focus on the key strategic issues and needs of the company, with an accompanying risk assessment based on the key assumptions. Most companies support a starting strategy with possible additional new product options and, where the risk is great, with a contingency

TABLE 20.4   Market attractiveness and competitive position forecasts

Sources of change	Actual score Year t	Forecast score Year t + 3
Market attractiveness		
Market size	10	15
Sales volume growth	25	25
Profitability	15	25
Opportunity to segment	5	5
Long-term trends	20	20
Total	75	90
Company business position		
New technology	10	15
Manufacturing efficiency	0	10
Product quality	10	20
Share of market	0	10
Cost of distribution	15	20
Net effective distribution	0	5
Total	35	80

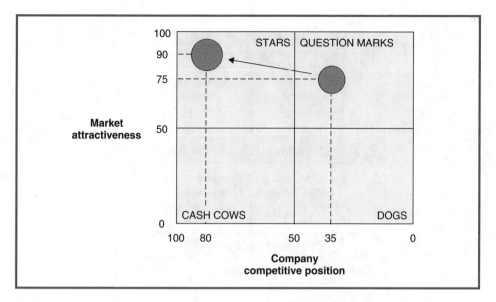

Figure 20.9   Benchmark strategy portfolio analysis for Alpha Foods Ltd

plan. By preparing a marketing plan in this way, the company is in a better position to obtain an accurate assessment of the long-term needs in the market.

In summary, the benefits of the portfolio concept in strategic marketing planning for the company are that it:

- provides a uniform measurement system to evaluate all product lines;

- assists in identifying key issues and needs, for individual products and for the company;

- classifies product lines in terms of invest to grow, invest to maintain, or limit investment categories;

- evaluates the portfolio of current products and businesses in terms of these classifications;

- identifies the need for new products and businesses; and

- focuses marketing planning and operations on key issues, and suggests how resources might be allocated.

Developing the market plan

In developing a market plan, it is necessary to understand the marketing planning process and how to carry out a market review and situation analysis. As

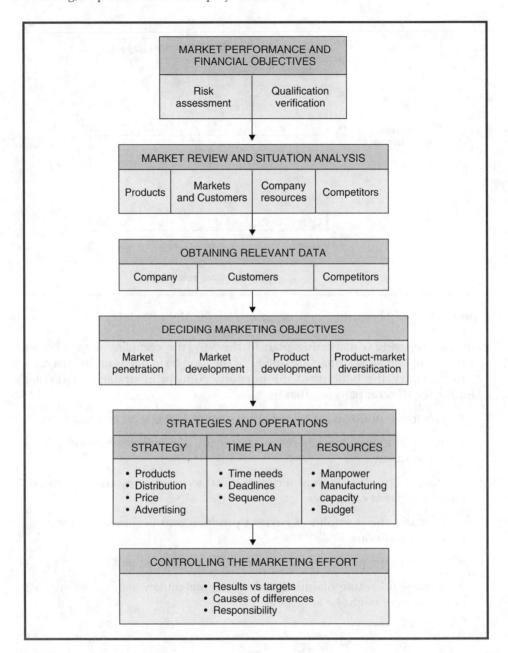

Figure 20.10   The marketing planning process

planning should be a regular activity in the company, it is also necessary to review marketing objectives from time to time to accommodate changes in the environment, among competitors and among customers. The company must also be able to prepare a detailed marketing plan with operational content.

Marketing planning process

There are six steps in the preparation of a marketing plan (Figure 20.10). First, it is necessary to have an assessment of the company's marketing performance to date and a statement of its financial objectives. Second, it is necessary to carry out a situation analysis or a review of the existing market conditions. Third, the company will have to obtain and evaluate relevant industry and market data. During the fourth stage the company specifies its marketing objectives. In the fifth stage, activities, budgets and schedules are identified and determined. Lastly, it is necessary to implement and control the marketing effort.

Marketing performance and financial objectives

There are two generic approaches to improving the company's marketing performance. One is to increase sales volume in some way. The second is to

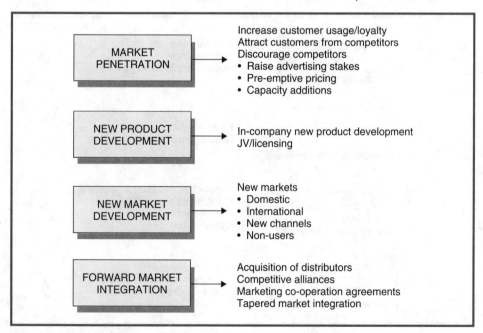

Figure 20.11   Improving marketing performance by increasing sales volume: principal options

improve profitability in the firm. The principal options in increasing sales volume are to increase the firm's penetration of its markets, develop new products, develop new markets and integrate forward into the distribution channel (Figure 20.11). Each of these strategies may be employed by companies, depending on the circumstances and the resources available. Small innovation companies tend to concentrate on penetrating existing markets and engage in new product development strategies. Larger companies have the resources to develop new markets and even to acquire distributors. Increasingly, large companies are attempting to guarantee access to their customers by acquiring their distributors, especially in international markets.

In attempting to improve profitability, the company faces four principal options (Figure 20.12). It can increase profit yield in various ways and it can attempt to reduce costs. Some companies successfully raise profits by adopting a selective and focused approach. They attempt to rationalize segments, distribution channels and the product line. Companies also attempt to increase profits by integrating backwards through the acquisition of suppliers.

The starting point for any marketing plan is usually a corporate financial requirement by which the firm must meet a financial objective, such as 20 per cent ROI or a similar objective. It then becomes the function of the marketing area to attempt to meet that requirement through its marketing and sales activities. In situations where the financial requirement is greater than the

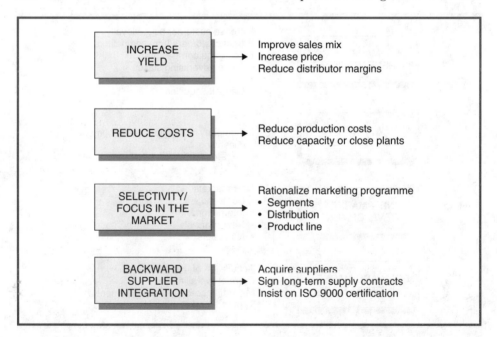

Figure 20.12 Improving marketing performance by improved profitability: principal options

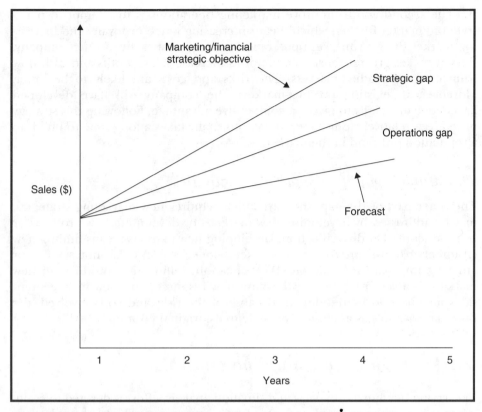

Figure 20.13   Strategic and operations gap analysis
(Source: McDonald, 1989: 128)

current long-run sales forecast, there is a gap which must somehow be filled (Figure 20.13). This gap can be divided into components which relate to improvements in existing operations and those which relate to a strategic shift in the company towards new products or new markets or both (McDonald, 1989: 128).

The operations gap: improving marketing operations

The marketing operations gap may be filled through improved marketing productivity, i.e. improving the marketing efficiency of existing operations, which means emphasizing a better product mix, additional and better sales calls, reducing costs, increasing prices, reducing discounts and generally using company assets more intensively. Improving productivity is usually directly associated with costs and revenues. Unless the approach can discriminate in favour of likely successes and not damage sales of particular products, this approach may be limited.

901

The second way to improve marketing operations is to attempt to penetrate the market further, which means increasing usage or loyalty and increasing market share. A market penetration strategy is attractive to the company, since it makes greater sense to attempt to increase sales, profits and cash flow from existing product-markets. The risks and costs are likely to be lower. Moreover, in existing product-markets, the company will have developed knowledge and skills to give it a competitive advantage. Following this strategy may take a relatively long time, since it normally takes a long time to build up a reputation or brand in the market.

The strategic gap: new marketing activities

The other part of the gap, the part which requires new marketing strategies, may be addressed by developing new markets, by developing new products or by product-market diversification. Developing new markets means finding new customer groups, entering new market segments previously not served, or entering international markets. Diversification, selling new products to new markets, is a very risky strategy because new resources and new management skills may have to be developed. Because of the risks and costs involved, the firm may wish to stay as close as possible to its original position.

Market review and situation analysis

In carrying out a market review and situation analysis, effort is devoted to evaluating the performance of the company's existing products and markets. Account is also taken of the firm's financial, manufacturing, technological and manpower resources. The situation analysis also deals with an examination of external factors, such as changes in the environment, changes in the market, the likelihood of new markets and changes in technology. The analysis provides management with a very detailed and precise answer to the questions. what business is the company in and how does it rate in that business? A situation analysis may present the firm with an operational business definition regarding its various product-markets.

Marketing planning in Alpha Foods Limited

In the case of Alpha Foods Limited, the company might observe changes in eating habits which would favour the introduction of the new oven-ready fresh chicken kiev product. Perhaps research has shown that taste and quality have become more important; a greater emphasis on health is noticed, discouraging the consumption of cholesterol and fatty foods; and convenience and ethnic values are recognized. Alongside these trends, Alpha Foods has observed a trend to more informal eating and snacking.

A market environmental analysis to support the above view would show a trend towards smaller households, informality in home meals, individual choice among members of the household, greater use of microwave ovens, and fewer items served at each meal. The role of women in society would also be a determining factor. Convenience would be an element in the demand for oven-ready foods by women in the labour force.

The implication for Alpha Foods in developing the new product is a greater interest in a product which would be relatively quick to prepare, modular in design and available as a single-serve food.

On the competitive front, Alpha Foods must attempt to provide a product which meets quality and taste standards higher than those currently available in the market. The company may have to incorporate more nutrition in each serving, depending on the segment to be served. At the same time, Alpha Foods must recognize that there is an increasing amount of food consumed in restaurants and canteens, and as packed lunches. The phenomenal growth in snacking, particularly among younger people, must also be considered.

As a result of this analysis, Alpha Foods might introduce the oven-ready chicken kiev as a main meal alternative for the busy household. The product would be sold in a portion-controlled way, and would be of high quality and added value in the form of convenience. The positioning would be a convenient, high-quality, good-tasting, portion-controlled oven-ready chicken kiev product.

Marketing planning questions

In analyzing the present market situation, it is necessary to ask the right questions so that the answers can be useful in marketing planning. As noted already, simple questions such as Rudyard Kipling's six honest serving-men: who, what, how, when, where and why ('The Elephant's Child') serve the purpose quite well. Kipling's serving-men help to decide which customer segments should be served, depending on the fit or match with the company's resources.

The question 'who buys?' indicates the precise market. The question 'what do the customers buy?' specifies the benefits associated with the product or service. The question 'how do customers decide?' helps identify approaches to pricing, selling and advertising. The question 'when do they buy?' assists with distribution decisions and pricing decisions. The question 'where do customers buy?' focuses attention on the issue of distribution channels and the kinds of outlet which are appropriate. The question 'why do they buy?' captures the impact of the entire marketing mix. The 'why' focuses on all the reasons and conditions associated with buying; it covers functional and psychological reasons. Salesman Elmer Wheeler's famous dictum 'sell the sizzle, not the sausage' should be modified to allow the 'why' question to focus on 'the sizzle *and* the sausage'!

The 'what', 'how' and 'why' questions together help to define the business. A business may be defined in one of two ways: in terms of the served market or in terms of the products and services of which it is comprised (Abell and Hammond, 1979). Served market is a definition based on the demand side, whereas emphasis on products and services reflects a concern with the supply side. Taking both together reflects the three dimensions of concern to the marketing manager (Figure 20.14). The scope of a business may be defined by choices along each of these dimensions.

The customer segment dimension refers to the question 'who buys or who is being served?' Several alternative classifications based on geography, usage, industry, demography, buying behaviour and other segmentation methods may be appropriate. Customers segments are groups of people or organizations with similar needs, all sharing characteristics which are strategically relevant to the company.

The customer function dimension refers to the question 'what need is being satisfied?' Sometimes products are multifunctional and serve clusters of related needs, while in other situations the company serves multiple customer functions with separate products or services. The company provides a mix of benefits sought by customers to solve problems. These benefits include the product itself, supporting services and other enhancements. The pattern of benefits sought is dictated by the application contemplated by customers.

The technology dimension refers to the question 'how are customers being satisfied?' The technologies refer to the alternative ways a particular

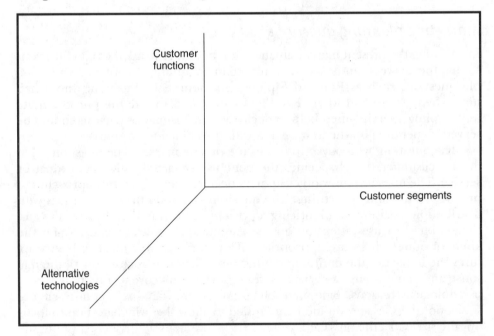

Figure 20.14   A marketing definition of business
 (Source: Abell, 1980)

function can be performed. Frequently, the company has a choice of several different technologies to satisfy the same desire.

Refining the product-market dimension in the way suggested by Abell helps Alpha Foods in two important ways. By recognizing the interaction of product technology with manufacturing, the need to co-ordinate marketing and product design issues is highlighted, and market segments are identified for which the firm might differentiate its products and services. The approach also highlights potential problems. A broad definition of the business along the customer segment dimension may achieve manufacturing cost advantages, but it fragments the sales, distribution and service activities. A broad definition along the customer function dimension, by serving a broad number of related functions, runs the risk of uneconomic dispersion of technological and manufacturing resources (Day, 1981). At the same time, too narrow a business definition may endanger Alpha Foods. A relatively broad definition may be necessary to allow change to occur, and thereby ensure the continued survival of the company.

Obtaining relevant data

The first stage in preparing the marketing plan involves obtaining as much information about the market as is relevant. This means obtaining facts and data on customers, competitors and other environmental issues. It is rarely possible to obtain all the data desired, since that would be too expensive and take too much time. Completeness is less important than relevance, which may be decisive for subsequent stages.

However, the manager should apply a qualitative assessment to the data obtained. Data should not be taken at face value. To avoid the risks of basing the plan on incorrect data or unverified opinions, there should be a conscious effort to ensure reliability through detailed verification. Generally, the company will need to obtain data on many factors (Figure 20.15).

In preparing the marketing plan, it is also necessary to evaluate the information collected. This means placing the information in context and assessing the relative importance of each element of information. The firm must make a realistic assessment of the market for the product. It is also necessary to examine pricing problems, distribution matters, advertising and sales promotion at different levels of expenditure. Subsequent steps in the planning process depend on an objective evaluation of the information available. It is important to examine the weaknesses as well as the opportunities.

Because planning deals with likely future outcomes, it is important for success that in analyzing problems and opportunities, and assigning priorities to them, realistic assumptions about future developments are made. Assumptions and forecasts must take account of trends in the total market, changes in market shares, price levels, competitive offers, changes in consumer attitudes, and

MARKET:	Size of total market and trends
	Shares held by competing brands/manufacturers
	Seasonal and regional variations
CUSTOMERS/USERS:	Customer identity (nature, type, demographics)
	Purchase timing, location and frequency
	Product in use and why purchased
	Perceived quality and benefits
	Brand and advertising recall
COMPETITORS:	Identity and products/services
	Areas of strength (quality, design, price, distribution, etc.)
	New product launches
	Innovation
PRODUCT:	Benefits and quality related to competition
	Cost, price and price structures
	Packaging and design
	Alternatives and substitutes
	Product developments and innovations
CHANNELS OF DISTRIBUTION:	Types of intermediary and their relative importance
	Turnover and stock levels in different types of outlet
	Frequency of stock-outs
	Power of distributors and retailers
	Transport and storage facilities and cost

Figure 20.15   Fact finding for market planning: a checklist

distribution patterns. Frequently, existing trends will continue for some time and forecasting becomes a relatively straightforward matter. Developments which are not readily discernible from existing trends can, however, cause problems.

Reviewing marketing objectives

Having performed a situation analysis, carried out a market review and evaluated the information available, it is necessary to decide the marketing objectives which should be pursued. Objectives relate to the desired future position of the company. Objectives, to be effective, should be specific and precise, and should relate to both the short term and the long term. It appears that in 1988 the Clorox Company in the USA may not have given adequate consideration to the marketing objectives set for its detergents in light of the subsequent awesome attack by Procter & Gamble in what it considered its core market (Exhibit 20.3).

> **EXHIBIT 20.3 A bright idea that Clorox wishes it never had**
>
> Back in 1988, Clorox Co. decided to take on consumer-products colossus Procter & Gamble Co. in the detergent market. Clorox invested upwards of $225 million over the past three years to develop and distribute its detergent products. But it couldn't come close to matching the marketing might of P & G and Unilever. Consider that Clorox spent $2 million last year on all its detergent advertising, compared with $62 million that P & G shelled out for its Tide brands alone. Few were surprised, then, when Clorox CEO Charles R. 'Chick' Weaver finally hoisted the white flag in late May and announced a retreat from the business.
>
> But having picked this fight, Clorox may not find it so easy to back out. Soon after it launched Clorox Detergent, the detergent–bleach combination it's now yanking, P & G unveiled its own combo, Tide with Bleach. While the product had been in the works for years, P & G picked up the pace to counter Clorox. By early 1989, P & G had Tide with Bleach in place nation-wide, backed by a promotional and advertising blitz. Thanks to P & G's overwhelming marketing muscle, Tide with Bleach quickly captured 17 per cent of the market becoming the No. 2 brand behind regular Tide.
>
> Problem is, that product didn't just trounce the Clorox detergent brand: it's also stealing sales from some of Clorox' core bleach offerings. And Clorox' surrender in the detergent market leaves the company without a big new growth vehicle. Worse, Clorox' adventure in detergent may have created a Frankenstein. 'By opening up the whole bleach–detergent business, they raised some doubts in consumers' minds about whether they really need a separate bottle of bleach,' says William Newbury, an analyst with College Retirement Equities Fund, an institutional shareholder. One immediate victim appears to be Clorox II, the company's fabric-safe, non chlorine bleach. Clorox concedes that sales are five per cent to 10 per cent behind last year.
>
> That smarts: Clorox II is a high-margin item that contributes an estimated 10 per cent of the company's profits. To shore up the business, Clorox is preparing new TV ads, and it's offering retailers incentives to improve bleach displays. So far, demand for its flagship Clorox Bleach hasn't been hit by the combo brands. But that market has been flat and is under attack from generic products.
>
> Source: *Business Week*, 24 June 1991: 43–4.

Intentions and objectives

Very few firms have a clear idea of their desired future position. Fewer still have these carefully thought out and committed to paper. Many firms also confuse intentions with objectives. A statement declaring that the company plans to achieve a 10 per cent share of the market or plans to export to Germany are not objectives and cannot aid the planning process. Such statements are mere wishes or aspirations. For objectives to be valuable, they should be written, clear, specific and measurable, so that the firm can subsequently determine if they have been achieved.

Objectives should relate to the nature of the firm, i.e. they should be achievable by the firm. There is no point in attempting the impossible. Objectives should also be relevant to the tasks to be accomplished. An objective specifying that the firm should increase its customer base without stating anything about its size or value could be futile. To be useful for planning and guiding the company's strategy, objectives should cover products, markets, sales and profit goals. The statement of objectives is only concerned with the final result; it is not concerned with how these results are to be achieved. Selecting and deciding on the ways and means is a concern for strategy.

Determining marketing objectives means that clear and concise decisions must be formulated as to what the marketing effort should accomplish. The emphasis is on purpose rather than on ways and means. it is not possible to agree on a marketing activity before the aim of the activity is defined. The key factors in deciding marketing objectives in 1985 for Pharmacia AB, the Swedish pharmaceutical company, according to Carl Erike Sjoberg, the executive vice-president, were:

- keep the customer in focus by developing innovative solutions to customer problems;

- co-perate with reliable partners;

- maintain a strong financial position, which is necessary for all research-intensive firms;

- develop and operate a unique business planning system;

- use new products for new markets (e.g. Healon for the ophthalmologist market); and

- subsequently add complementary products.

Long- and short-term objectives

It is useful in practice to distinguish between long-term and short-term objectives. A long-term objective is a broad aim which need not be quantified and related to a time period. Thus, 'market dominance' and 'increasing sales and profits' are long-term objectives. In contrast, short-term objectives need to be both quantified and made specific as to time. To 'increase sales by 15 per cent in 1996' is a short-term objective.

An excellent starting point in setting marketing objectives is to simplify the company's competitive situation into two sets of considerations: concern for the product and concern for the market. The simple matrix in Figure 20.16 provides a useful framework to examine what the company sells and to whom.

In this framework, four courses of action or four sets of marketing objectives for the company may be identified:

- sell existing products to existing markets;
- sell existing products to new markets;
- develop new products for existing markets; and
- develop new products for new markets.

In the longer term, the only way to stay in business is to sell something to someone. This is the essence of a product-market strategy, which means selecting a way of achieving company objectives through the range of products and services that the firm offers to its chosen market segments. A product-marketing strategy, because it deals with the longer term, represents a commitment to the future direction of the firm. The first set of objectives above refers to a strategy of penetrating existing markets, while the second refers to developing them. The third refers to developing new products, while the fourth is a combination referring to objectives of diversifying into new products and new markets at the same time.

General and specific objectives

There must furthermore be a clear distinction between general marketing objectives and specific objectives for the marketing mix, i.e. advertising, product

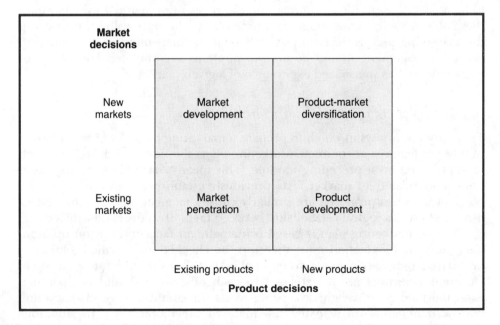

Figure 20.16 Deciding marketing objectives

design and packaging, distribution and sales. This distinction is critical for a number of reasons. First, each marketing mix element has a definite place and function within the total marketing mix; it can accomplish certain things that the other marketing mix elements cannot accomplish. Second, without specific objectives and measurable tasks for each element of the marketing mix, it will not be possible to tell whether a change in sales is attributable to advertising, or to product improvements, or to a better selling effort, or to price changes.

To ensure that results achieved can be measured and attributed to the element of the marketing mix which caused them, these specific objectives must be stated in short-term language, i.e. specific as to time and degree. Thus a proper advertising objective would be 'to increase consumer awareness of the product from 25 per cent to 40 per cent in 1996' rather than 'to communicate the idea that the product tastes better than its competitors'. Little will be gained by setting aims so high that achieving them is virtually impossible within the time period covered by the plan and with the means available.

Preparing the marketing plan

The fifth stage involves preparing the marketing plan, developing a marketing strategy and specifying tactics. The marketing plan should be written and should analyze the basic market data; provide precise statements or objectives to be achieved; describe all the measures and activities planned to help attain these objectives and state budget and time plans. The responsibility for writing the marketing plan is likely to rest with senior management in the company. Senior management should be able to apply its accumulated knowledge of marketing and its specialized experience of a given market.

Marketing facts, objectives and activities

There are many ways in which to prepare a marketing plan. All of them have a number of features in common. Marketing plans should be modular, with each module based on a preceding module. This means that objectives are based upon and related to market facts previously established and analyzed. The plans or activities proposed are similarly chosen to meet the objectives established. There is a logical relationship between facts, objectives and activity.

A good marketing plan is based principally on facts and not on opinion. Each item of information must therefore be checked and verified. Opinions may have a part to play in a marketing plan, but they should be stated as such. Different objectives must be related to each other and should not conflict; each must be given weight according to its importance. A good marketing plan also depends on activities adequate to meet objectives. In situations where this is not the case, it will be necessary to scale down the objectives to achievable levels or to use a different strategy, which has implications for resources.

Planning is concerned with selecting marketing activities, timing and resource allocation. In selecting marketing activities, the firm is concerned with identifying those activities which are most likely to allow the attainment of the objectives. This means deciding 'the appropriate marketing mix or marketing programme. Sometimes companies focus on one element of the marketing mix when developing a marketing strategy. Usually, however, it is a combination which works. For L'Eggs, a focus on pricing and branding appears to have been a strong competitive combination (Exhibit 20.4). In deciding the marketing mix, individual products, pricing, advertising and distribution strategies within an overall marketing operations framework are agreed.

In preparing the marketing plan, it is also important to establish a time schedule which can be incorporated into the operational plan. It is also necessary to decide the resources needed, which means dealing with manpower, manufacturing materials and financial support. At this stage it is also necessary to specify roles for people in different parts of the company, and the company's expectations of outside agencies and intermediaries such as banks, advertising agencies, distributors and transport companies. Lastly, the company is concerned with determining how the objectives will be attained. The basic principle to be applied in deciding the appropriate marketing activity is that the objective should govern the means: no activity should be justified unless it is clearly related to the accomplishment of an objective.

At the same time it is necessary to prepare a budget in sufficient detail that all expenditures necessary to implement the plan are identified and can be provided. There are several methods to determine a marketing budget. A number of rules apply in preparing the budget. All expenditure items should be referred to specific objectives. The associated marketing activity should be specified in detail, so that everybody knows how it was derived and as much cost detail as possible is provided. A spending plan should also be provided to show where the money is to be spent and the interrelationships involved in the overall plan.

Controlling the marketing effort

Because the environment changes and unforeseen circumstances outside the company's control occur, even well-prepared plans encounter difficulty. It is necessary, therefore, to establish a mechanism which allows the manager to compare actual marketing performances with planned performance throughout the planning period.

Sales should be only one yardstick for determining a plan's effectiveness. In addition to regular sales reporting, there should be specific controls for each individual activity proposed in the plan. Thus, the regular measurement of distribution effectiveness and distribution intensity should be included, together with procedures for measuring the effectiveness of advertising. In

---

EXHIBIT 20.4 This marketing effort has L'Eggs

Mention Sara Lee Corp. and visions of cheesecake and chocolate brownies immediately spring to mind. Just look at the non-food brands in the Chicago conglomerate's shopping bag: Hanes men's underwear, L'Eggs nylons, Bali bras, Pach leather goods, to name a few. With lessons learned from peddling pound cakes and pork sausages, Sara Lee has transformed itself into a consumer-products powerhouse with increasingly global ambitions.

Sara Lee Chairman John H. Bryan has global aspirations for Sara Lee. He has already quietly built up a $3.2 billion business in Europe through acquisitions. Sara Lee now ranks No. 4 among U.S.-based consumer-products companies with operations there, trailing Philip Morris, Coca-Cola, and Procter & Gamble. And it's growing fast. On November 18, Sara Lee acquired Playtex Apparel Inc. – the US brassiere maker with a strong position in Europe – in a deal valued at $590 million. Says Brian, who's also eyeing markets in Asia and Mexico: 'Our mission is to be a premier global, branded consumer packaged-goods company.'

To get there, Bryan will rely on the same marketing recipe that Sara Lee has used to such great effect back at home. Here's how it works: The company zeroes in on a fragmented consumer market, typically dominated by sleepy private-label manufacturers. Bryan buys an existing player or two for quick economies of scale. Next he works to improve brand image – but prices its offerings competitively.

In 1988, Bryan saw an opportunity to expand dramatically and pounced. That year, Sara Lee acquired a 50 per cent stake in rival Pannill Knitting Co., and a year later it snapped up the rest. Bryan then quickly converted most of Pannill's products to the powerful Hanes label, the underwear brand the company acquired in 1979. The move significantly broadened the reach of Hanes' product line – and its clout with retailers. Bryan had assembled a full line of casual wear with a broad retail network.

Competitive pricing is key to Bryan's strategy, so manufacturing must be razor-sharp. Much of the credit for those lower costs goes to Bryan's efficient marketing tactics. Once he has latched onto a winning brand, he extends the name to numerous related products. The idea is to make sure that as many items as possible share the glow cast by a strong brand name. For example, since buying Dim, France's leading hosiery maker, in 1990, Sara Lee has sewn the label on men's underwear and T-shirts.

Cross-promotions are the key. For instance, a package of L'Eggs hosiery may contain a $1-off coupon for an Hanes sweatshirt. Sara Lee is already Europe's No. 2 coffee company with such brands as Douwe Egberts and Van Nelle.

Source: *Business Week*, 23 December 1991: 72–3.

practice, the marketing plan should specify the controls which are to be used. Control of the marketing plan serves a dual purpose: to enable corrections to be made in costs, advertising spending and distribution efforts, throughout the planning period; and to supply new information for the preparation of the subsequent marketing plan.

Discussion questions

1 Discuss the considerations involved in deciding marketing objectives.

2 Discuss the need for market opportunity analysis. What are the main considerations to take into account in such an analysis?

3 Distinguish between strategic and tactical planning.

4 Evaluate the role of portfolio models in marketing planning.

5 How useful is marketing segmentation as an aid to planning?

6 What are the principal decisions to be made during the planning of a marketing programme?

7 Describe the factors used to position a business in the market attractiveness/competitive position framework.

8 What precise steps must the company take in developing a marketing plan?

Annotated bibliography

Abell, Derek F. (1980) *Defining the Business: The starting point of strategic planning*, Englewood Cliffs, NJ: Prentice Hall.

Day, George S. (1984) *Strategic Market Planning*, St Paul, Minn.: West Publishing Co.

McDonald, Malcolm (1989) *Marketing Plans* (2nd edn), Oxford: Heinemann Professional Publishing.

Ward, Keith (1989) *Financial Aspects of Marketing*, Oxford: Heinemann Professional Publishing, chapters 2, 3, 8 and 9.

References

Abell, Derek F. (1978) 'Strategic windows', *Journal of Marketing*, **42**, 3, 21–6.

Abell, Derek F. (1980) *Defining the Business: The starting point of strategic planning*, Englewood Cliffs, NJ: Prentice Hall.

Abell, Derek F., and John S. Hammond (1979) *Strategic Market Planning*, Englewood Cliffs, NJ: Prentice Hall.

Armstrong, J.S. (1982) 'The value of formal planning for strategic decisions: review of empirical research', *Strategic Management Journal*, **3**, 4, 197–211.

Boyd, Harper W., Jr, and Jean-Claude Larréché (1978) 'The foundations of marketing strategy', in Gerald Zaltman and Thomas V. Bonoma (eds.), *Review of Marketing 1978*, Chicago: American Marketing Association.

Catry, Bernard, and Michel Chevalier (1974) 'Market share strategy and the product life cycle', *Journal of Marketing*, **38**, 4, 29–34.

Day, George S. (1981) 'Analytical approaches to strategic market planning', in Ben M. Enis and Kenneth J. Roering (eds.), *Review of Marketing 1981*, Chicago: American Marketing Association.

Day, George S. (1984) *Strategic Market Planning*, St Paul, Minn.: West Publishing Co.

Greenley, G.E. (1986) 'Does strategic planning improve company performance?', *Long Range Planning*, **19**, 2, 101–9.

Hooley, G.J. (1984) 'The implementation of strategic marketing techniques in British industry', *International Journal of Research in Marketing*, **1**, 2, 153–62.

Levitt, Theodore (1960) 'Marketing myopia', *Harvard Business Review*, **38**, 4, 24–47.

Lysonski, S., and A. Pecotich (1992) 'Strategic marketing planning, environmental uncertainty and performance', *International Journal of Research in Marketing*, **9**, 3, 247–55.

McDonald, Malcolm (1989) *Marketing Plans* (2nd edn), Oxford: Heinemann Professional Publishing.

McKinsey and Co. (1983) 'From long range planning to strategic management', paper presented at the Ninth International Planning Conference, Paris, 2–4 March.

Oxendfeldt, Alfred R. (1962) 'The formulation of a market strategy', in Eugene J. Kelley and William Lazer (eds.), *Managerial Marketing: Perspectives and viewpoints*, Homewood, Ill.: Richard D. Irwin.

Porter, Michael E. (1980) *Competitive Strategy* New York: The Free Press.

Marketing implementation, performance and control

21

Process of marketing implementation
Marketing performance evaluation
Strategic marketing control

Introduction

This chapter introduces and explains:

- the meaning of marketing implementation;

- how companies organize for marketing;

- how companies evaluate performance in their marketing activities;

- how companies control marketing operations; and

- the need to review performance standards.

Marketing implementation considers the issue of putting marketing strategy into practice. It is a marketing management task which requires the skills of co-ordination, communication and thoroughness in application. Companies organize themselves for marketing in different ways. Sometimes organizing along functional lines is best suited to the company's needs, particularly if the company is small or produces few products or services. Organizing by product and brand focuses attention on the marketing strategy implementation needs of the company's products and services. Companies also organize with a focus on customers. While a strong customer focus is less common, a lot of attention is being given to this format, and informal networks have been found essential for success.

Measuring marketing performance means deciding appropriate measurement criteria. Criteria used include marketing and financial measures. Marketing measures deal with causes and include factors such as customer satisfaction, loyalty, new product introductions, market share and sales growth. Financial measures deal with effects and include profit, cash flow and return on investment. Both sets of measures are necessary and must be integrated.

Strategic control of marketing operations is essential. This usually means applying a series of performance measures, including marketing and financial measures, to ensure that the marketing strategy being implemented remains on course and that company objectives are met. Some of the performance standards used need to be revised from time to time.

When you have studied this chapter, you should be able to define the terms used above in your own words, and you should be able to do the following:

1. Decide how companies develop an organizational commitment to marketing.

2. Determine the importance of human resources in the implementation of marketing strategy.

3. Identify the marketing skills necessary for marketing implementation.

4. Evaluate the strengths and weaknesses of a number of organizational structures in common use.

5. Recognize the importance of informal organizational networks in the company.

6. Choose appropriate performance criteria to evaluate marketing performance.

7. Demonstrate the relation between cost control and marketing effectiveness.

8. Decide appropriate ways of controlling marketing operations.

9. Review performance standards and propose improvements.

Process of marketing implementation

Once the strategic marketing plan has been developed, it requires an organizational structure for its implementation. Daft and MacIntosh (1984) conceptualized the strategic plan as emanating from a strategic planning group and being implemented top-down through formal control systems. Four management control systems help to ensure the strategic marketing plan is implemented: budget, performance appraisal, policies and procedures, and statistical reports (Figure 21.1).

The budget is concerned with producing an annual plan with monthly measurement of actual outcomes against budget. Performance appraisal deals with a more detailed marketing audit and review of company performance for the entire year. The information collected is used in preparing the second- and third-year annual plans. Policies and procedures refer to standing guidelines and company practices. Usually these are not considered in the planning

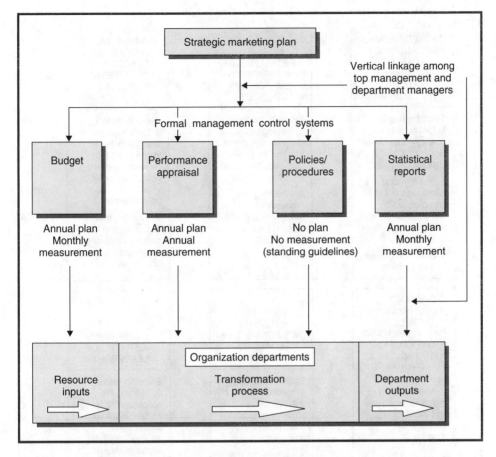

Figure 21.1   Management process for strategy implementation
(Source: Daft and McIntosh, 1984: 53. With permission of *Journal of Management*)

effort or measured in any way. They are part of the corporate culture of the company and reflect 'the way things are done'. Lastly, statistical reports are prepared to provide monthly measurement against the annual plan.

Each of these components affects the different sections in the company which operationalize marketing strategy through acquiring resources and transforming them in a predetermined way to produce outputs from the process.

Meaning of marketing implementation

Implementing market strategy is as important as formulating it. Marketing strategy implication means managing strategic change in the company's approach to its markets. There are numerous tasks associated with this

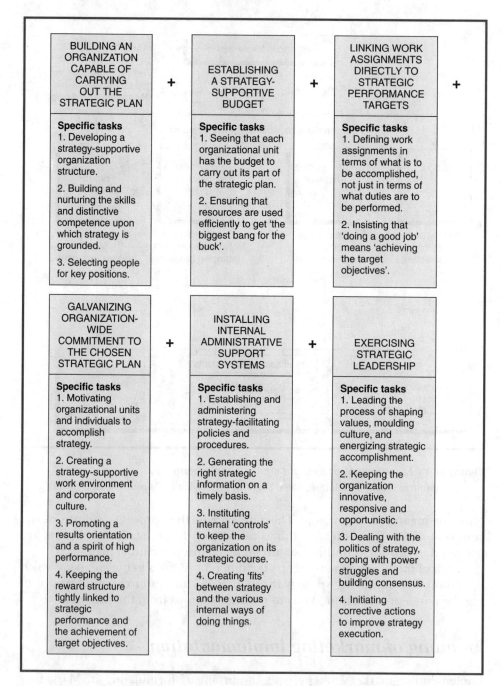

Figure 21.2   Administrative components of strategy formulation

(Source: Thompson and Strickland, 1993: 219. By permission of Richard D. Irwin)

process. For Thompson and Strickland (1993) implementation means integrating six important management tasks: building an organization capable of implementing the strategic plan, providing an adequate budget, linking tasks to performance targets, ensuring organizational commitment to the plan, establishing a support system and giving the endeavour the necessary leadership (Figure 21.2).

Organizational commitment

The traditional view is that the company's ability to implement its strategy depends on the relationship in the company between strategy and structure. A

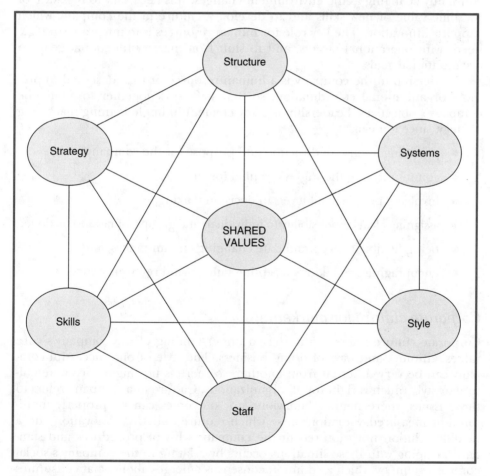

Figure 21.3 Integrating the administrative fit: the McKinsey 7S framework
(Source: Peters and Waterman, 1982: 10. Reprinted by permission of HarperCollins Publishers Inc.)

modern view of the process admits that many more organizational variables are involved. Indeed, there are many frameworks proposed, each of which purports to integrate the various influences. One very popular framework is the McKinsey 7S framework (Figure 21.3). The top three elements, strategy, structure and systems, are the hardware elements, while the remaining four are the software elements. A number of these are discussed below.

Human resources in marketing management

A rapidly changing marketing environment requires flexibility regarding staffing in the company. The knowledge base required within a company is constantly changing as the environment changes. It is necessary to be aware of the time value of new skills and to develop a culture in the company which supports innovation. The key role for human resources is to integrate strategic needs with operational targets, and to shift from narrow functional goals to organizational goals.

Leadership in the company is a human resource process designed to promote organizational co-ordination, so that staff work together to attain the company's objectives. Leadership is a key element in implementing marketing strategy, since it means:

- providing a sense of direction and purpose for the company;
- communicating the values essential for success;
- involving people at all levels in decision making;
- assigning clear responsibility to individuals and groups for tasks to be done;
- being flexible to accommodate changing circumstances; and
- encouraging risk taking, accepting failures and rewarding success.

Corporate culture for marketing

Corporate culture refers to the shared understanding of the company's core values, attitudes and ways of doing business. The style of one successful company can be very different from another, so there is no single corporate culture or style which is right for all organizations. Culture in a company refers to those issues where neither behaviour nor outcomes can be properly monitored or measured. Situations arise which require initiative, innovation and a flexible solution not captured in the company's list of procedures and standards. Coping with these situations occurs by relating to the company's social control system, by which a common consensus emerges about what constitutes appropriate attitudes and behaviour. Corporate culture in an organization is a social control system.

Culture in a company can be a driving force for progress, or for retardation if not properly managed. A strong culture can achieve success, or it may prevent an innovation. Managing culture requires constant communication from senior managers so that consistent expectations about important issues are developed. For example, smaller organizations need an entrepreneurial culture to emerge into a period of growth. A more strategic type of culture may be required for the company which has reached the growth stage and can envisage a maturity stage of the business in the near future. Promoting a particular style or culture in the company may be critical for successful implementation of marketing strategy.

Developing marketing skills

The marketing function in the company is an effective way of integrating and co-ordinating company efforts. Marketing people must be able to work with people from many other functional areas. This requires good communication skills and an ability to think strategically, so that short-term issues do not cloud the longer-term thrust of the company. Other marketing skills which must be developed are the ability to respond to customer needs, ensuring quality in company products and services, and the ability to work in multidisciplinary teams to promote creativity and encourage initiative in the company.

Training and staff renewal programmes are an essential ingredient of skill development for marketing implementation. Knowledge, innovation and change help to drive the company towards customer satisfaction, sales, profits and market share. A wide range of skills and learning experiences in the company help to realize personal and corporate goals.

Organizing for marketing

The organizational framework of a company provides a structure for the implementation of marketing strategy. It is with an organizational structure that company staff obtain authority and responsibility to guide and promote desired relationships among people. The company must respond to environmental change and to internal demands, including marketing strategy. There is a constant need to monitor and change the organizational configuration of the company. Hierarchical organizational structures, more popular in static times, have become less popular in recent years. Horizontal organizations have arisen to respond flexibly to changing environmental circumstances. There is, therefore, no such thing as an ideal organization and no unique way of matching marketing strategy with organizational structure.

Functional organization

A company organized along functional lines is particularly popular among smaller companies. Here each functional area has a manager ensuring that designated tasks are carried out (Figure 21.4). Such an organizational structure works well for single-product companies or where there is only a small portfolio of products and services and few markets. It is also suitable when specialization by function is considered appropriate, and authority for major decisions is centralized with the marketing manager or director.

Product and brand manager organization

As the company grows, the product portfolio is likely to become more complex and difficult to manage by a purely functional organization. The kinds of problem which arise include the allocation of advertising budgets, sales force, manufacturing time and physical distribution. It may be necessary to introduce a product or brand manager structure (Figure 21.5).

The advantage of the product or brand manager organization is that it allows for increased specialization in marketing. This type of organization is frequently extended to give individual managers responsibility for brands. These brand managers report to managers responsible for particular product categories, who in turn report to a group product manager. This organizational structure gives each product manager responsibility for sales and profits, and thereby concentrates management attention on the key needs of the product-market in question.

In a product or brand manager format, responsibility for promotion shifts to the product manager. It is not usual, however, for product managers to have much say over the sales force, pricing or distribution. In recent years, product managers have become more powerful in that discretion once available to brand managers is being eroded. Many companies now accord considerable authority to product managers to ensure that brand managers do not compete with one another for promotional budgets, manufacturing time, the right to use certain advertising themes and other important marketing factors.

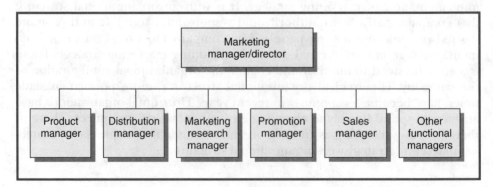

Figure 21.4   Functional marketing organization

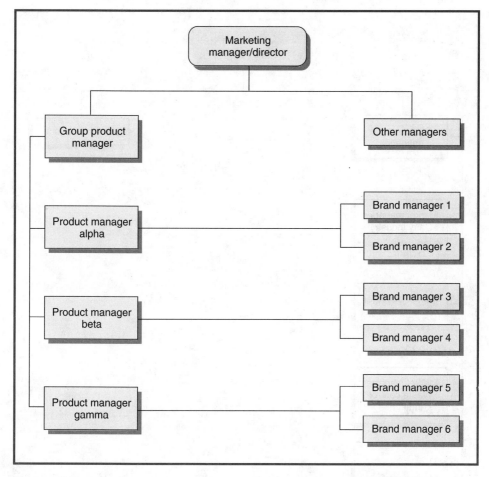

Figure 21.5   Product/brand manager organization

Market-focused organization

An organizational focus on customers or the market requires the company to develop a market-oriented structure (Figure 21.6). A market-oriented structure reflects differentiation in the market, as occurs, for example, in international markets. A market structure may be appropriate when there are different customer groups, each with different needs and each buying sufficiently large quantities of the company's products to warrant a separate organizational response. Companies organized along market lines can develop separate marketing mixes for each market. This structure may take several forms, such as consumer and industrial markets, domestic and export markets, or arrangement by industry, as would occur if the company were selling to various industries.

923

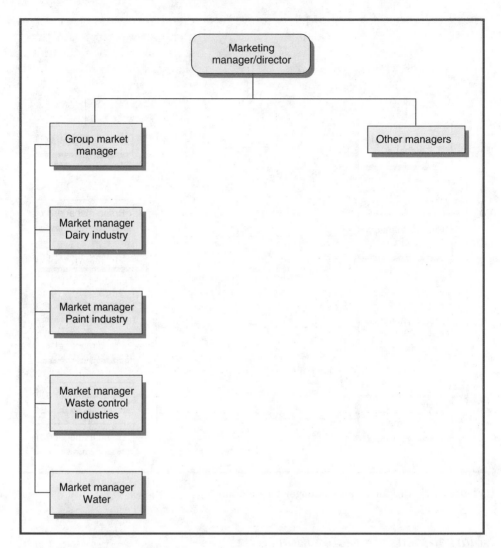

Figure 21.6 Market organisation structure

The example shown in the figure might reflect the organizational structure of a company selling sophisticated liquid particle filters.

Most organizational structures show the managing director or chief executive at the top of the organizational chart, and brand managers or detail people at the bottom, serving customers in the market. Increasingly, companies attempt to focus their organizations on customers, which means designing a flatter organization with fewer levels of command in which the customer appears as part of the organizational chart. Some companies have even placed the customer on top (Figure 21.7). This organizational structure shows senior management serving world-wide networks, which in turn ensures the provision of products and services with a focus on different customer groups. Each layer in the organization is seen as the customer group for the one below it. A focus on internal markets such as this ensures that the ultimate customer, who is placed on top, is appropriately served.

Other formal organizational structures may also be found in companies. Very large companies with many different businesses operating in many markets might adopt a divisional structure whereby one of the forms outlined above is repeated for each major division.

Informal marketing organization

In addition to formal organization structures, individual companies develop and encourage informal networks which promote good working relationships. These networks of contacts with the company develop over time and arise from attempts by companies to implement marketing strategies. Informal contacts may arise between the product manager and the transport people or the sales people. Some companies establish committees to help smooth formal relationships. Indeed, companies increasingly support informal groups drawn from many parts of an organization with special interest in developing new product-markets. Product innovations very often result from informal networks and groups within companies rather than from the formal structure.

In the 1970s and early 1980s in Europe, and in the middle 1980s in the

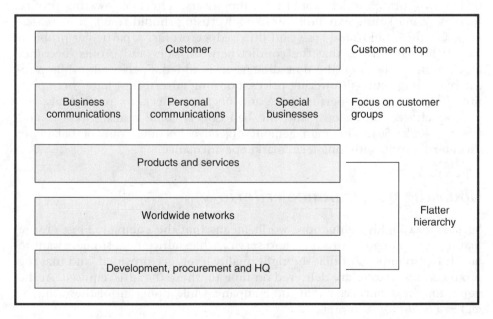

Figure 21.7 Organizational structure at British Telecom, 1993

925

USA, a trend towards more flexible organizational forms best depicted as networks began to appear (Håkanson, 1982; Miles and Snow, 1986). These new forms emphasized partnerships between companies, based on teams drawn from a number of co-operating companies, jointly to develop converging technologies aimed at some product-markets. In such arrangements, the traditional hierarchical reporting and control systems have less value. The fundamental principles of these networks are flexibility, specialization and relationship management, to respond quickly to accelerating change in technology, competition and customer preferences (Webster, 1992: 4–5).

Marketing performance evaluation

According to financial analysts and economics correspondents, the objective of the company is to maximize shareholder value. In practice, such a goal rarely dominates the strategic thinking of managers. Managers display additional objectives usually involving a combination of sales, measured as turnover, and profits, measured as return on investment. Sales are important because they are a source of profit growth in the company and reflect management rewards such as bonuses and promotion. Profits are important because they are used to satisfy shareholders and are required in raising new capital.

These two objectives are in potential conflict, since sales can be increased by lowering prices, which would have the adverse effect of lowering profits. Increasing marketing expenditures like advertising should result in increased sales, but this would raise costs and thus reduce profits. A particular problem facing the company is that the conflict between sales and profits 'becomes much more acute when the time dimension is added. Specifically, while positive marketing actions (lowering prices, boosting advertising) have these positive effects on market performance and negative effects on profitability, the positive effects come slowly and the bad effects come quickly' (Doyle and Hooley, 1992: 60). The management objective becomes one of balancing short-term profits with long-term market performance.

Choosing performance criteria

Success in a highly competitive world means that the company must ensure that it is providing the products and services that sufficient customers want to buy. It is also important that the right quality levels are provided, and that the products and services are delivered on time to where they are required. At the same time, it is necessary that the company, while doing all of these things, makes a profit for its owners.

The company must, therefore, develop a set of performance criteria which allows it to measure its marketing activities and its financial position as a result of those endeavours. Profit measures, cash flow and return on investment measures are all financial criteria which show the effects of marketing activities. Financial evaluations do not identify the key success factors in the business, however, nor do they focus on what the company is doing well or badly. Marketing performance criteria, on the other hand, deal with causes not effects. It is much more useful from a management point of view to discover the contribution of product innovation, customer satisfaction, product and service quality or on-time delivery to the company's success.

There is still a strong tradition of using financial criteria. A fixation with financial criteria leads companies to ignore the less tangible non-financial measures, although these are the real drivers of corporate success over the middle to long term (Peters, 1987). However, there is a weakness in the non-financial performance measures. To date there has been little success in developing explicit links from marketing to financial criteria. Furthermore, companies and managers are still judged on financial criteria. Until a clear link is established, it is likely that marketing criteria will continue to be treated with a degree of scepticism. 'When you can measure what you are speaking about and express it in numbers, you know something about it. When you cannot express it in numbers, your knowledge is of a meagre and unsatisfactory kind' (Lord Kelvin, physicist, in Singleton-Green, 1993: 53). Whichever set of measures is chosen, it is as well to recall the old adage 'you get what you measure'. In choosing performance criteria, the company recognizes that the system must:

- be customer/user driven;
- support manufacturing strategy in the company;
- be capable of change;
- be simple and easy to understand;
- include financial and marketing criteria; and
- provide positive reinforcement in the company.

Marketing evaluation and control

The company begins by setting some marketing activities in motion. This may result from the development of a new marketing plan, or from adjusting or updating a marketing plan which had been in operation during the previous time period (Figure 21.8). The next step in the process is to establish a set of performance standards by which the marketing activity can be evaluated. These performance standards may already exist in the company, having evolved over many years of application. It may be necessary, however, to modify the standards in use when environmental circumstances change or when marketing objectives change. The standard should be appropriate to determine whether objectives have been achieved. Some of the material in this section is drawn from Bradley (1991).

During the next stage, the company audits its marketing activity in order to evaluate marketing performance. This is a detailed assessment of marketing implementation and an evaluation of performance against budget. One very popular measure of marketing performance is the extent to which actual sales are more or less than budgeted sales for a given period. Marketing control takes the form of a cost analysis and marketing performance analysis in relation to sales in the company. The cost analysis addresses the issue of improving efficiency without jeopardizing present or future sales volume or profit targets, while marketing performance focuses on the cause and effect relationship between marketing inputs and outputs to decide how much money should be spent in the various marketing activities (Thomas, 1986). If targets are not met, the company may need to take corrective action of some form. It may be sufficient to modify the plan or expectations, so that the appropriate performance signal can be used to influence marketing activities. In this fashion, the marketing plan is evaluated and controlled.

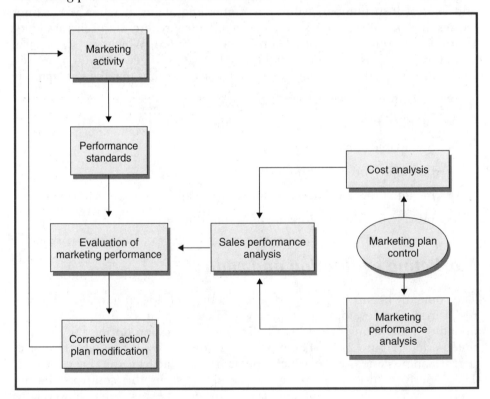

Figure 21.8   Marketing plan evaluation and control

Measuring marketing performance

The objective of the company is to create a multidimensional management process capable of identifying and responding to diversity, dynamism and complexity in the marketing environment. Only effective firms survive in this environment. Effectiveness derives from the management of demands of the various interest groups upon which the firm depends for resources and support (Pfeffer and Salancik, 1978: 2–3). The company is linked to its environment by federations, associations, customer–supplier relationships, competitive relationships and the cultural and legal framework which defines and controls the nature and boundaries of these relationships.

The behaviour of the company depends upon the company itself, its structure, its leadership, its procedures and its goals. It also depends on the environment and the particular contingencies and constraints deriving from that environment. The company must manage these relationships.

Managers bring four implementation skills to the marketing task: interacting, allocating, monitoring and organizing (Bonoma, 1984: 75). Bonoma suggests that the marketing task by its nature is one of influencing others inside and outside the firm. There are internal and external conditions over which the manager has no direct control, but which must be influenced. The manager must also allocate time and resources among the various tasks involved in implementing marketing strategy. Monitoring is a task which must be done; some firms cope very poorly with it, spending too much time collecting data and not enough time developing managerially useful information. Finally, good implementation means having the ability to develop informal networks and relationships both within the firm and outside it to address problems as they arise. According to Bonoma (1984: 75), customized informal organization facilitates good implementation.

In assessing marketing performance, companies are concerned with measuring the efficiency of the use of marketing inputs, the influence of mediating factors, and the nature and level of marketing outputs (Bonoma and Clarke, 1988). Many of these, which Bonoma and Clarke derived from an extensive literature search, are already familiar. These authors identify eleven input measures, twenty-five mediating factors, divided into market characteristics, product characteristics, customer characteristics and task characteristics, and twelve output measures (Figure 21.9). Very few companies measure all the variables outlined. Many companies use a subset of these variables and monitor their behaviour over time. Measures of marketing performance that can be used, provided the company has developed a useful computerized information system, include:

- new product introductions each year;
- product modification introduced each year;
- customer orders processed on day received (order response time);

929

- on-time delivery;

- order cancellations or charges;

- customer satisfaction score;

- customer complaints;

- product defects;

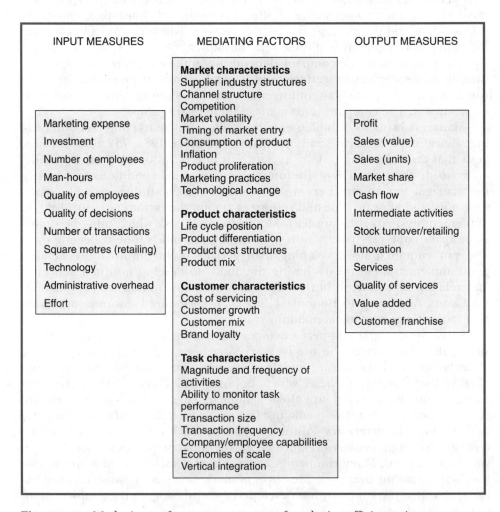

Figure 21.9   Marketing performance: measures of marketing efficiency, inputs, mediating factors and outputs

(Source: Adapted from Bonoma and Clarke, 1988: 35–7. Reprinted by permission of Harvard Business School Press from Bonoma, Thomas V., and Bruce H. Clarke (1988) *Marketing Performance Assessment*, Boston, Mass.: Harvard Business School Press. Copyright © 1988 by the President and Fellows of Harvard College.)

- health and safety standards met; and
- customer loyalty index.

Sales performance analysis

Analysis of sales performance is usually performed on the basis of the relation-ship of the company's actual sales in a given period to planned or budgeted sales. The company first establishes an overall sales budget for a year and then divides it into components corresponding to sales territories, salesperson and product group. By some criterion accepted by the company, sales quotas are established in this way and actual performance is measured against quota. An example illustrates the principal of sales performance analysis. Assume the

TABLE 21.1   Sales performance analysis in Beta Pharmaceuticals Ltd

Region, sales representative and product	Actual sales (ECU 000s)	Sales quota (ECU 000s)	Performance (%)
Regional sales performance			
North	8,386	8,228	102
South	6,468	6,380	101
East	4,928	5,280	93
West	5,509	5,632	98
Total	25,291	25,520	99
Sales performance in East Region			
Sales representative:			
Peter Bowbrick	1,373	1,320	104
Jerome Tuillier	968	1,408	69
Wolfgang Sultz	1,478	1,390	106
Jenny Simonsen	1,109	1,162	95
Retail sales performance	*East Region Jerome Tuillier*		
Pharmacy A	114	246	46
Pharmacy B	123	195	63
Pharmacy C	106	177	60
Pharmacy D	114	229	50
Pharmacy E	264	364	73
Other pharmacies	247	197	125
Product sales performance	*Jerome Tuillier*		
Bcardio H	141	123	115
Dermatex B	282	757	37
Hepatex C	264	264	100
Acnecidin Stystemic	193	176	110
Acnecidin Topical	88	88	100

hypothetical company Beta Pharmaceuticals Ltd sells five separate products to pharmacies in four regions. The company uses sales representatives in each region and there are four in the East Region (Table 21.1). In the example, actual sales of Beta Pharmaceuticals Ltd products amounted to ECU 25,291,000 in the year reviewed. The total sales quota for that year was ECU 25,520,000.

The analysis shows that overall the company achieved 99 per cent of the sales quota established, and sales performance in the North Region and South Region was above quota, while the other two regions were below quota. Sales representatives Peter Bowbrick and Wolfgang Sultz exceeded their quotas, while Jenny Simonsen and Jerome Tuillier did not meet quota; the latter was quite significantly below quota.

In an effort to determine the problem with Jerome Tuillier's area, Beta Pharmaceuticals Ltd carried out a sales analysis by pharmacy and by product. In the five major pharmacies, this sales representative was very much below target. Only in the myriad small shops did he exceed quota. It would also seem, from the product sales analysis, that Tuillier's problem lies with Dermatex B.

By proceeding in this way, Beta Pharmaceuticals Ltd can determine precisely where it is not meeting quota, and may decide to provide additional marketing support in the areas showing concern. Alternatively, it may be necessary to adjust sales quotas downward for some products in some markets. In the hypothetical example above, another possible explanation may be that Jerome Tuillier lacks selling experience, which might indicate a need for training and other support.

Financial performance criteria

While non-financial criteria such as market share or sales growth may be used in determining the value of a market investment, many firms employ a version of return on investment as the means of measuring the long-run profit performance of their operations. It is generally essential that both approaches are used in an integrated way, although, as has been already noted, full integration of the two approaches still eludes management thinking.

Where return on investment is used, a number of comparisons are possible: comparisons with similar companies in the market, or with the company's operations in different markets, or with targets established before entering the market. Unless historical measures such as the above indicate the relative returns to be expected from future investments, there is no point in using any of the above measures. The most important comparison that can be made is between actual results and ex-ante budgeted figures, since a post-investment audit can help a firm to learn from its mistakes as well as its successes (Shapiro, 1985).

The appropriate measures to use in evaluating and controlling operations depend on the nature of the business. For marketing-oriented companies, market share, sales growth or the costs associated with generating a unit of sales revenue may be the most relevant measures. These measures would seem appropriate for industrial products companies, consumer products companies and services companies.

The important point is to use those measures which experience has shown are the key indicators of performance in the business. An important objective in deciding on the approach to performance valuation is to ensure that managers and other staff are motivated to attain corporate objectives. A well-designed marketing strategy which does not capture the imagination and support of managers at all levels is likely to fail. It is thus necessary, in selecting the performance criteria, to anticipate managerial reaction. Ultimately, all performance measures are subjective, since the choice of which measure to stress in particular circumstances is a matter of judgement for the individual firm (Shapiro, 1985: 231).

Benchmarking the performance

In the competitive marketing environment of the 1990s, companies that do not evaluate their performance against the competition and predetermined standards are likely to fail. Both provide an external benchmark to evaluate performance. It is necessary to establish benchmarks so that the company can

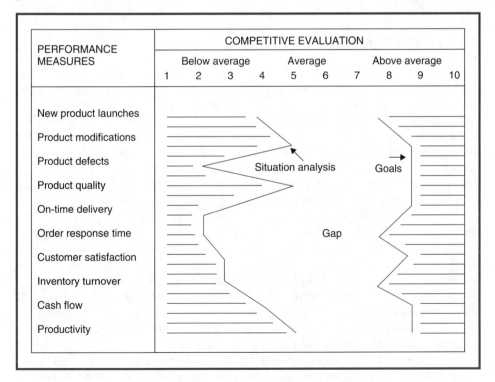

Figure 21.10   Performance gap analysis

determine whether a performance gap exists. A performance analysis begins with a situation analysis of a set of results-oriented performance measures, and goals are established by senior managers in the company in consultation with middle- and lower-ranking managers (Figure 21.10). The goals established reflect external benchmarks indicating competitors' performance. Goals may be changed for a variety of operational or strategic reasons. A comparison is made between the actual situation and goals, and the difference represents the performance gap.

Competitive benchmarking information may be obtained from a variety of sources: customers, suppliers, machinery manufacturers, technical journals and the trade press. Financial benchmarks such as inventory turnover and operating profit may be found in business publications and from marketing intelligence.

Strategic marketing control

To apply strategic marketing control systems, it is necessary first to understand the meaning of marketing control: how cost control and marketing effectiveness are related.

Meaning of marketing control

The need to pursue marketing opportunities selectively raises the issue of finding an agreed strategic framework for marketing control. Unfortunately, there has been very little interaction of concepts and theories in marketing strategy and planning with those of finance and managerial accounting, the traditional disciplines which deal with management control. While the importance of market share objectives, market size and growth rates, and good forecasts have been recognized, procedures for marketing control have not yet been successfully related to these key factors (Hulbert and Toy, 1984: 452). Good control systems are necessary for implementation of marketing strategies.

A framework for control provides a system for attempting to ensure that 'things don't go wrong during the implementation of strategies ... to ensure ... the achievement of organizational and business objectives, with profits being extracted for separate attention' (Greenley, 1989: 369). Control and implementation are serious and complex management issues in the company.

Periodically, the company decides to undertake a critical review of its overall marketing effectiveness in its various markets. Because marketing suffers from rapid obsolescence of objectives, policies, strategies and operational programmes, the company should regularly reassess its overall approach to the market (Kotler, 1994). Strategic control for Kotler means auditing the company's marketing activities to evaluate its marketing effectiveness. According to Kotler (1994: 756), the marketing effectiveness of a company is reflected in the degree to which it exhibits five major attributes of a marketing orientation: customer philosophy; integrated marketing organization; adequate marketing information; strategic orientation; and operational efficiency.

Success usually means developing a marketing strategy involving a combination of initiatives by the company under each of the above headings. These initiatives may involve new or redesigned products, different distribution channels, expanded or improved production facilities with an emphasis on cost competitiveness, pricing with an emphasis on the ability to retaliate to influence the behaviour of competitors, and even perhaps the acquisition or establishment of associated companies in the market. All such initiatives require increased marketing expenditure.

Some of the above initiatives may be managed within the company's long-term strategy, while others would fit into annual marketing plans. Some marketing expenditures and price changes are tactical matters, the concern solely of product or brand managers or the sales force. It is the combination of these initiatives that comprises the cost of the strategy.

The manner in which companies cost marketing strategies varies according to the size and nature of the expansion, the size, corporate culture and structure of the company, and the type of management involved. Sometimes the chief executives of very large companies take all decisions and develop and monitor marketing strategies. In other cases, even small subsidiaries are required to prepare detailed cost analyses of marketing strategies. Increasingly, larger firms take a greater interest in how they organize to implement strategies.

Cost control and marketing effectiveness

In developing a marketing strategy, it is necessary to identify the costs which arise under a number of headings. The major headings under which costs arise are management time, new staff required, training programmes and any development work. Most new market strategies require a reorganization in the way the company functions. The costs of such reorganization must also be included.

New marketing strategies frequently involve the acquisition of know-how, development costs and capital investment. The costs of each of these must also be included. Furthermore, it is necessary to include production, distribution and marketing costs, any income forgone through reduced prices and a contribution to overheads.

In costing the marketing strategy, the firm distinguishes among expenditures which are budget items, annual investment decisions or components of the three- to five-year marketing plan. Good management requires a cost control effort on the part of the company. A key measure of cost control is to relate net income received to sales revenues:

$$\text{Cost control effort} = \frac{\text{Net income}}{\text{Sales revenue}}$$

At the same time, the firm can measure its marketing effectiveness by relating sales revenues to the assets used in the enterprise:

$$\text{Marketing effectiveness} = \frac{\text{Sales revenues}}{\text{Assets}}$$

By combining cost control efforts with marketing effectiveness, it is possible to measure the company's return on investment. Return on investment is marketing effectiveness weighted by cost control effort:

$$\text{Return on investment} = (\text{Cost control}) \times (\text{Marketing effectiveness})$$

$$\frac{\text{Net incomes}}{\text{Total assets}} = \frac{\text{Net incomes}}{\text{Sales}} \times \frac{\text{Sales}}{\text{Total assets}}$$

The first ratio to the right of the equals sign, net income divided by sales, measures cost control in the company, i.e. the amount of gross profit the company obtains in the market. The second ratio, sales divided by total assets, measures marketing effectiveness in the company, i.e. the level of sales that the company obtains from the total resources at its disposal. This formula owes its origins to the DuPont Company, which developed it to measure new wealth created, i.e. net income, compared to all the resources that the company could employ in the creation of that wealth, i.e. total assets.

By plotting the company's cost control performance against its marketing effectiveness, it is possible to derive the company's return on investment. Numerous combinations of cost control effort and marketing effectiveness produce a given return on investment. By plotting the ratios over a number of years, the company determines whether its emphasis on marketing or cost control has been more fruitful.

To illustrate the principles involved, the short historical performances of two hypothetical firms, Alpha Foods Ltd and Beta Pharmaceuticals Ltd, are used (Figure 21.11). The details of the process involved are available in Mobley and McKeown (1987a, 1987b). As can be seen, Alpha Foods, which launched the new chicken kiev product during year 1, experienced a decline in cost control between year 1 and year 2, while marketing effectiveness did not change sufficiently to compensate for this loss. Understanding the costs of entering a market, and particularly the costs of new product preparation, is a common problem. The result is that return on investment declined to 20 per cent. For such a business, it is generally believed that a return of 20–25 per cent would be much too low, and that the company should attempt to raise its return to at least 40 per cent to satisfy profit and development requirements fully. Acknowledging this problem and the need for greater profits, Alpha Foods plans a balanced growth of its operations to obtain a return on investment in year 3 of 40 per cent. It plans to reach its target by improvements on the cost side and by improved marketing effectiveness.

The return on investment in year 2 for Alpha Foods and Beta Pharmaceuticals was the same, 20 per cent. Beta Pharmaceuticals, however,

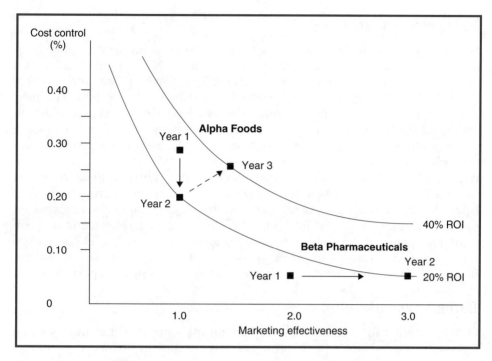

Figure 21.11   Cost control and marketing effectiveness for balanced growth
(Source: Molby and McKeown, 1987a, 1987b. With the permission of the American
Marketing Association)

achieved its 20 per cent ROI through a much more effective marketing effort;
it made 3 ECUs of sales for every 1 ECU of assets. The performance of Alpha
Foods was 1 ECU of sales for each 1 ECU of assets, but its productive efficiency
was 20 per cent compared to 5 per cent for Beta Pharmaceuticals.

Marketing operations evaluated on the basis of return on investment can,
however, produce undesired results. In such an evaluative system, longer-term
performance may be ignored by managers. In order to boost returns, essential
equipment may not be replaced even when such investment is required for
longer-term growth. This is so because new investments increase the asset base,
the denominator in the equation above, and also because return on investment measured on a historical cost basis will be greater than investment measured on a replacement cost basis.

Controlling marketing operations

Marketing operations may be controlled in a variety of ways. The most popular
ways are to use sales quotas, financial controls and cash flow management
techniques. It is necessary to maintain a long-term view as well as a short-term
view in deciding the appropriate method.

937

Using sales quotas

Sometimes companies monitor sales from one year to the next to judge performance, good or poor depending on the trend. Other companies adopt a more formal sales control approach, where sales might be classified by country or region of a foreign market, by customer, and by product group. The next step would be to determine appropriate criteria to decide the sales level which should fall into each category. The company might develop an index to measure the importance of each of the categories used. An analysis of previous sales might be used to establish quotas which, over time, are adjusted to accommodate changes in the market. Usually, effective sales control systems require a variable standard, as implied here. If economic activity in a particular market is very high and developing rapidly, sales in that market might also be expected to grow. Similarly, a decline in the market should also be reflected in a downward adjustment of the quota. The assumption behind such a sales control system is that factors causing an expansion or contraction in the market beyond the influence of the company should not be used in evaluating sales performance.

Using financial controls

Having decided to expand, the company must ensure that the strategy to be followed is costed properly. It must also decide how to finance the strategy, from internal resources or from selected external sources. Finally, good financial management dictates that the expansion strategy should not jeopardize the survival and growth of the company.

The costs of entering and expanding in slow-growth markets are particularly high. Expansion for the company, even in industries which are not capital intensive, requires large cash outlays, the postponement of income, and skilful marketing and financial management. For success it is thus necessary to co-ordinate marketing strategies and financial planning. Where the company does not properly relate its marketing strategy to its financial resources, this lack of co-ordination can lead to collapse.

The costing and financial control of marketing strategies are difficult tasks for most companies and can be very complicated. Marketing strategies can be difficult to quantify; they refer to the longer term and consist of numerous steps with varying impacts. It is difficult in costing strategies to separate costs into fixed costs, variable costs and cash flow projections. To overcome these difficulties, successful companies attempt to ensure that control rests with financial, marketing and general management people, since such a team effort is likely to produce a better understanding of the cost implications of marketing strategy.

Cash flow management

The significance of cash flow may be gleaned by observing the difference between profits and cash flow. A brief review of these concepts illustrates the point. There are two reasons why cash flow is very unlike profit. First, there is a lapse of time between obtaining raw materials and employing labour to produce the product for sale, and the actual sale of the product. Second, there is the influence of credit. Cash is not necessarily paid out for the materials and labour at the time they are used. Similarly, cash may not be received at the time the sale is made.

In contrast, profit is the difference between two sums: the prices customers pay; and the total of prices the firm agrees to pay for all the inputs used in preparing the product or service for sale. Profit is the difference between agreed prices.

Cash flow is money lodged to a bank account, less cash withdrawals from that account in any given period. Most deposits arise when customer receipts are received for products and services previously sold. Disbursements generally arise when the firm pays for the goods and services previously purchased. Cash flow is the difference between money lodged in the bank and the money withdrawn from the bank. The size of the cash flow and its direction, positive or negative, depends every bit as much upon when the money is lodged or withdrawn as upon how much is deposited or withdrawn. Profit is therefore very different from cash flow. It is possible to have a very profitable business, but still fail due to poor cash flow performance.

The significance arises most dramatically as the company expands. A major benefit of examining the company's cash flow requirements related to new marketing strategy is that the amount of financing required to carry out the anticipated expansion programme is determined. Associated with most expansions are larger purchases of raw materials and other inputs, more sophisticated machinery, access to sources of finance and additional sales people. An instinctive urge to expand has led many companies into the growth trap. Herein lies the dilemma for many companies. The company operationalizes marketing strategies, not just for increased sales; many companies also require the cash flow generated to support new product development, to support the acquisition of new technologies, and to invest in marketing channels.

In general, a faster growth in sales should produce an attractive increase in profits. There may, however, be an adverse impact on cash flow. The company may experience impressive growth in many of its markets with an equally impressive growth in earnings and at the same time face a severe financial constraint. Sales growth in most businesses consumes cash. As was seen above, cash is needed to purchase items such as raw materials, services and merchandise when preparing the product or service for sale. Growth in sales requires that greater quantities of these items be bought in anticipation of future sales. Cash is also needed to support the business at its now larger size, while awaiting payment from customers for larger sales. Consequently, during periods of rapid growth the cash flow is characteristically negative. It is perfectly normal to find that a business is growing profitably while bank balances are negative.

The company that introduces its products to a new market usually finds that, initially, sales growth is slow, the company incurs losses and cash flow is negative. While customers may be innovative, there are few of them and the company needs a lot of money to develop the market. At this stage, the company is attempting to move potential customers from awareness to adoption. Initial success brings with it rapid sales growth, which requires considerable amounts of cash to service it. The company may have to lower prices slightly and incur extra costs to improve the product in an effort to penetrate distribution channels. Such developments exacerbate the pressure on cash flows in the company.

Current earnings and profits

The managers of marketing operations evaluated on the basis of current earnings are likely to emphasize short-run profits and neglect long-run profits. This is particularly true if managers are frequently moved from brand to brand, or product to product, which would allow them to avoid the longer-term consequences of their actions. These actions could involve reducing advertising and general marketing expenditures, reducing research and development work under their control, and not spending sufficient sums on staff training and development.

As was seen in Chapter 19, too great an emphasis on sales promotion may be symptomatic of longer-term marketing myopia. Because circumstances can be different in different markets and outside the control of management, performance measures based on sales, profits or return on investment can be misleading at best, and inaccurate at worst. For this reason, companies frequently compare actual results with budgeted estimates. Variances in costs and revenues can then be examined to determine whether these are affected by outside events or caused mainly by management intervention.

Reviewing performance standards

Designing an effective implementation and control system is not an easy task. A range of possible controls were discussed in preceding sections. A comprehensive treatment of the subject would mean an evaluation of the effectiveness of the company on the following criteria (Newman and Logan, 1976: 512):

- profitability (percentage of sales and return on investment);
- market position;
- productivity (costs and sales improvements);
- leadership in technological research;
- development of key people (technical and managerial); and
- attitudes (employees and public).

The above list places considerable emphasis on strength for future company growth and current profitability. As may be judged, therefore, real control of marketing strategy implementation in the firm is more comprehensive than a simple examination of how well the company performed in the past.

Unless corrective action is taken, when performance standards are not met or when new opportunities appear, the process of implementation and control in the company is an empty exercise. As soon as a deviation from standard is detected, the causes of the variation should be investigated. A number of causes may be identified: obstacles arising in operating conditions; poor communications leading to misunderstanding; inadequate training; lack of required basic skills; or inadequate incentives (Newman and Logan, 1976: 509). Corrective action sometimes leads to a change in the targets. An evaluation of the operating conditions, leadership training and motivation may reveal unrealistic standards in relation to the company and its markets. In such circumstances, it would be important to revise the standards. In circumstances where the performance evaluation indicates results better than expected, new higher standards might be established if improved circumstances are likely to continue.

Assignment questions

1 What is meant by marketing implementation?

2 How important is marketing organization in marketing implementation?

3 Can you explain why the brand manager organizational structure may be under threat?

4 What is meant by a market-focused organization?

5 What are the relevant criteria which may be used in marketing performance assessment?

6 Describe the relationship between financial performance and marketing performance. Do they measure the same things?

7 Describe an approach to strategic marketing control involving financial and marketing factors.

8 Why is cash flow management so important in marketing management?

9 When is it necessary to review marketing performance standards?

Annotated bibliography

Bonoma, Thomas K., and Bruce H. Clarke (1988) *Marketing Performance Assessment*, Boston, Mass.: Harvard Business School Press.

Bradley, Frank (1991) *International Marketing Strategy*, Hemel Hempstead: Prentice Hall, chapter 20.
Sevin, C.H. (1965) *Marketing Productivity Analysis*, New York: McGraw-Hill.

References

Bonoma, Thomas V. (1984) 'Making your marketing strategy work', *Harvard Business Review*, **62**, 2, 67–76.
Bonoma, Thomas V., and Bruce H. Clarke (1988) *Marketing Performance Assessment*, Boston, Mass.: Harvard Business School Press.
Bradley, Frank (1991) *International Marketing Strategy*, Hemel Hempstead: Prentice Hall.
Daft, Richard L., and Norman B. McIntosh (1984) 'The nature and use of formal control systems for management control and strategy implementation', *Journal of Management*, **10**, 1, 43–66.
Doyle, Peter, and Graham J. Hooley (1992) 'Strategic orientation and corporate performance', *International Journal of Research in Marketing*, **9**, 1, 59–73.
Greenley, Gordon E. (1989) *Strategic Management*, New York: Prentice Hall.
Håkanson, Haken (1982) *International Marketing and Purchasing of Industrial Goods*, Chichester: John Wiley.
Hulbert, James M., and Norman E. Toy (1984) 'A strategic framework for marketing control', in Barton A. Weitz and Robin Wensley (eds.), *Strategic Marketing*, Boston, Mass.: Kent Publishing Co.
Kotler, Philip (1994) *Marketing Management* (8th edn), Englewood Cliffs, NJ: Prentice Hall.
Miles, Raymond E., and Charles C. Snow (1986) 'Organisations: new concepts for new forms', *California Management Review*, **28**, 3, 62–73.
Mobley, Lou, and Kate McKeown (1987a) 'ROI revisited', *Intrapreneurial Excellence* (American Management Association), April, 1 and 4.
Mobley, Lou, and Kate McKeown (1987b) 'Balanced growth plans – an ROI breakthrough', *Growth Strategies* (American Management Association), June, 3.
Newman, William, and James P. Logan (1976) *Strategy, Policy and Central Management* (7th edn), Cincinnati: South Western Publishing Co.
Peters, Tom (1987) *Thriving on Chaos*, London: Macmillan.
Peters, Thomas J., and Robert H. Waterman, Jr (1982) *In Search of Excellence*, New York: Harper and Row.
Pfeffer, Jeffrey, and Gerald R. Salancik (1978) *The External Control of Organizations*, New York: Harper and Row.
Shapiro, Alan C. (1985) 'Evaluation and control of foreign operations', in Heidi Vernon Wortzel and Lawrence H. Wortzel (eds.), *Strategic Management of Multinational Corporations: The essentials*, New York: John Wiley.
Singleton-Green, Brian (1993) 'If it matters – measure it', *Accountancy*, May, 52–3.
Thomas, Michael J. (1986) 'Marketing productivity analysis: a research report', *Marketing Intelligence and Planning*, **4**, 2, 3–71.
Thompson Arthur A., Jr, and A.J. Strickland III (1993) *Strategic Management: Concepts and cases* (7th edn), Homewood, Ill.: Richard D. Irwin.
Webster, Frederick E., Jr (1992) 'The changing role of marketing in the corporation', *Journal of Marketing*, **56**, 4, 1–17.

Case studies

Case 23: The Kid's Daily News

In September 1989, a Chinese newspaper printed in colour was launched in Hong Kong for children aged from six to fourteen. The newspaper was called *The Kid's Daily News*. Before this there were already many weekly, biweekly and monthly picture books, magazines and newspapers with children as their target readers. Some of them had been in the market for over ten years. In addition, there were many books, audio and video tapes in the same market. However, *The Kid's Daily News* was the first and only daily newspaper especially for children.

The objective of this newspaper was 'to let children have their own newspaper'. It was owned by a successful industrialist, Mr Chan, the managing director of a listed company. The idea of running this newspaper was reported to have originated from a request by his seven-year-old daughter, who asked for the international page to read when he was reading his newspaper one day. Believing that there was similar need for other children in Hong Kong, he decided to run a newspaper solely for children. The newspaper was launched within a few months.

Population estimates indicated that there were about 730,000 children in the six to fourteen age group in 1989. Their total annual consumption was estimated to be HK$430 million. If the newspaper was successful, the profits could be very considerable. However, people in the publishing business were generally pessimistic about this idea, because running a newspaper involved a large investment and high risks. Usually it takes a long time to establish a sizeable number of 'stable' readers, and the market was regarded by most as almost completely saturated. There were also other forms of mass media competing in essentially the same market. Consequently, it was very difficult for a new entrant to survive in such an environment. In Japan and Taiwan, children's newspapers had proven successful to a certain degree, but only as limited circulation publications.

943

A large initial investment was made to start *The Kid's Daily News*. A team of 60 experienced and professional journalists, child educators and business executives were employed to run the newspaper. Their monthly salary bill was estimated to be HK$1 million. The total of other fixed costs was estimated at HK$160,000 per month. HK$5 million was used in the initial launch and advertising promotion. This covered 600,000 free samples for schoolchildren, free admission to Ocean Park, a special carnival there for children under fourteen years old who bought the newspaper on the first day, a large donation to a charity organization, television and printed advertising, and lots of publicity activities. The heavy advertising and innovative idea attracted widespread attention in the Chinese-speaking community.

The newspaper covered local and international news, scientific and geographic features, interesting events, stories, cartoons, games and puzzles. It was written in a simple style for children and was printed in colour, with many pictures. Since it was found to be difficult to identify the preferences and tastes of the readers, the style of the newspaper kept changing after the launch. The basic format which evolved was that the first two pages contained news stories and the remaining fourteen were typically made up of the kinds of entertainment mentioned above. It was sold at the same price as that then prevailing for other Chinese newspapers: HK$2.00 per copy. Later it was increased to HK$2.50.

When the newspaper was first launched, it enjoyed great success. Over 70,000 copies were sold on the first day. In the following days of the week the sales stayed at around 50,000–60,000 copies. However, the sales started to decline after one month. In November 1989, sales of 50,000–60,000 were only achieved on Sundays. Sales on weekdays dropped to 30,000 copies.

Research indicated that most of the readership had to go to school early in the morning. With many other attractions and heavy school workloads, they did not develop a firm habit of reading the newspapers everyday. Many of them had limited pocket money and relied almost entirely on their parents buying *The Kid's Daily News* for them on Sundays. Their most popular column was the cartoons. Several new competitors soon appeared with similar ideas and the same target group. One of them was delivered free alongside a popular weekly women's magazine with a circulation of over 100,000. Another was a weekly cartoon book, with primary students as its target readers.

The Kid's Daily News tried to encourage children to develop a regular reading habit by encouraging them to subscribe through their regular schools. It was found to be very difficult to get the co-operation of school administrators. The total subscription through this channel was only a few thousand. They also developed a direct delivery service. It was found too costly and was soon abandoned. Most parents bought the newspaper for their children with the intention that they would improve their reading skills, develop a reading habit and learn more from it. However, many of the children soon lost interest in reading the articles, preferring just to read cartoons. This was not what

TABLE 1   *The Kid's Daily News* estimated daily income and expenses

Daily sales (copies)	Total expenses (HK$)	Total income (HK$)	Net profit/loss (HK$)
100,000	116,000	123,000	7,000
80,000	100,000	101,000	1,000
60,000	84,000	79,000	−5,000
40,000	68,000	57,000	−11,000
20,000	52,000	35,000	−17,000

Source: *Capital 11*, 1989: 49.

most of the readers' parents wanted, so they lost interest in buying the newspaper. It was also discovered that the circulation of *The Kid's Daily News* was affected by the common practice among school children of circulating it among their classmates.

The ex-factory price to wholesalers was some HK$1.10 per copy. Against this the basic (variable) production cost of the newspaper was fluctuating around the HK$0.80 per copy. The fixed and semi-fixed costs (rent etc. and wages) came to approximately HK$3,600 per day. It suffered a heavy loss with a daily circulation of only 30,000–40,000. Another major source of income apart from the direct sales revenue was advertisements. However, very few products were found to be suitable for advertising in a children's newspaper. Advertising agencies were also hesitant about recommending a newspaper with an 'unstable' readership to their clients. On average the newspaper only got half a page of colour advertisements and one page of black and white advertisements per day. The daily income from advertisements was about HK$13,000 on average. The loss to the company was estimated to be about HK$12,000–14,000 per day. By the end of March 1990, the company had already lost HK$21 million.

In view of the losses, the company tried to boost its sales by increasing the proportion of cartoons, and to reduce its overhead costs: for example, by employing some artists from China at lower wages. At the end of 1990, the format was changed to a weekly newspaper, but this proved insufficient to stem the losses and the paper eventually closed in May 1991.

Assess the viability of a children's newspaper, such as *The Kid's Daily News*, in Hong Kong in 1989. How would you evaluate the product development process of *The Kid's Daily News*?

This case was prepared by Jenny Ling, Department of Business Studies, Hong Kong Polytechnic, Hong Kong, and adapted by Dympna Hughes, Department of Marketing, University College Dublin, for the purpose of class discussion rather than to illustrate either effective or ineffective handling of an administrative situation.

Case 24: Sironimo

Part A

Cusenier is a well-known French company which has been producing and selling alcoholic and non-alcoholic drinks since 1857. Among its range of products was the famous syrup sold under the brand name Cusenier until 1968 and then under the brand name Freezor until 1977. Cordial is a popular drink in France, made from a mixture of fruit extracts and sugar which is added to water, and its sweet taste is specifically targeted at children. Cusenier, however, was becoming increasingly concerned about the growing threat of its main competitor, Teisseire, which was gaining market share. Cusenier tried to counterattack in the 1980s with a Pam-Pam brand, but this was a failure.

The company then launched a range of products which had two innovative features: a one-litre bottle, which was made in a plastic called PET. Teisseire used aluminium for its 75 centilitre bottles. The launching of this new product (which could in fact be interpreted as a relaunch) was only partially successful, in that the sales only increased slightly before falling again after 1988 (Figure 1). The company began looking for new ideas to regain the market share that had been lost over the years.

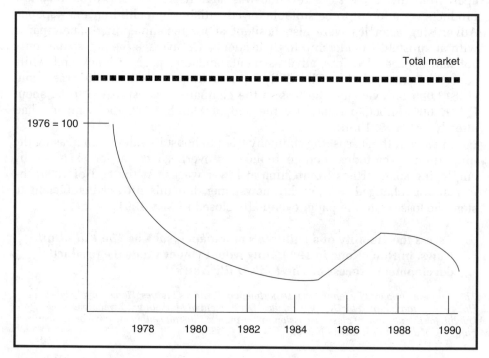

Figure 1 Total market sales trends, 1976–90

In 1991, Cusenier developed a new product concept called 'Sironimo'. This product consisted of new 0.75 litre bottles in the shape of skittles, which meant that the bottle was not only a container, but once emptied would become a game for children. The range consisted of eight flavours: orange, lemon, apple, strawberry, mint, pomegranate (which is the most popular syrup flavour in France), raspberry and blackcurrant. Each flavour in turn was associated with an animal: orange with a lion, strawberry with a monkey, blackcurrant with a koala bear, etc. The word 'Sironimo' is a play on words, a contraction of the two words 'sirop-animaux' (syrup and animals). The idea was to try to make mothers buy the entire range of products (so as to have the complete set to play skittles). This, it was hoped, would indirectly and subconsciously build up brand loyalty. The target market was children between four and eleven years old.

The company launched the product in 1991 and devoted a huge budget to a television advertising campaign in order to build produce awareness. The strategy considered the childen as the natural initiators of product selection as opposed to their mothers. The price was 13–15 francs per bottle, which was between 15 and 30 per cent more expensive than equivalent products offered by Sironimo's competitors. The company was also aware of research in the USA which measured the influence of children on purchases made by their mothers (Table 1). Managers wondered if these findings would apply in France, Germany or the UK.

1. Is the Sironimo product and concept strong enough to allow such a price difference with competitors? How can this be measured?

2. What message would you develop for the advertising campaign?

3. Evaluate the company's strategy of targeting its advertising campaign at children as opposed to their parents.

4. Try to forecast sales using the data in Table 1.

TABLE 1   Frequency of children's attempts to influence purchases and the percentage of mothers 'usually' yielding

Products	Frequency of requests[1]				Mothers acceptance (%)			
	5–7 years	8–10 years	10–12 years	Total	5–7 years	8–10 years	10–12 years	Total
Breakfast cereal	1.26	1.59	1.97	1.59	88	91	83	87
Soft drinks	2.00	2.03	2.00	2.01	38	47	54	46
Candy	1.60	2.09	2.17	1.93	40	28	57	42
Game, toy	1.24	1.63	2.17	1.65	57	59	46	54
Toothpaste	2.29	2.31	2.60	2.39	36	44	40	39

[1] On a scale 1 = often; 4 = never.

Source: S. Ward and D.R. Wackman, 'Children's purchase influence attempts and parental yielding', *Journal of Marketing Research*, **9**, 316–19.

Part B

In 1992, the company began to think of developing its brand internationally. Why should its product not be successful abroad, if it appeals to young French children? The first task was to select a number of countries which could be potential markets. The first country suggested was Germany because of its proximity to France and the fact that it is France's closest trading partner. However, it soon became apparent that this task was not going to be as easy as was initially hoped. This was due to the fact that there was no syrup market in existence in Germany as yet.

1.   Should the managers launch their syrup in Germany and try to build awareness for such a new product concept?

2.   In the case of Germany, what should be the main aspects of an advertising and promotion campaign? What tools, which media and what budget would you recommend?

Part C

The second potential target export market on which the company focused attention was the UK. Research found that a syrup market *per se* was not in existence there, even though a similar product called 'squash' was being sold throughout the country. The differences beteeen squash and Sironimo were as follows: squash had more sugar, less fruit and more preservatives, and was less expensive (approximately 40 per cent less). The squash product only existed in one flavour – orange.

The company then wondered, given these differences, if it should launch Sironimo in England. The first question was whether to adapt the product or leave it as it was. Furthermore, the company considered whether it should change the name of the product and whether the concept of a dual-purpose container should be retained in this market.

The company was also concerned about the price and quality differential between its product and the average squash brand. The available alternatives included launching exactly the same product, assuming there was a demand for a high-quality product with more fruit content, less sugar and fewer additives than were contained in the squash product. On the other hand, they could adapt the product to local tastes, developing a modified product which would have a taste and appeal somewhere between Sironimo and the traditional squash drink.

1.   You have been commissioned to draw up a marketing plan for the launch of the Sironimo product in England. What are your recommendations with respect to: the product, the brand, the positioning strategy, the target market, the price and the communication strategy?

2. **Should the orange-flavoured syrup be priced in line with the other flavours and should the same marketing mix as the other flavours be applied? Justify your answer.**

This case was prepared by Benoît Heilbrunn, Department of Marketing, University College Dublin, and adapted by Dympna Hughes, Department of Marketing, University College Dublin, as a basis for class discussion rather than to illustrate either effective or ineffective handling of an administrative situation.

Case 25: Beauty Products (HK) Ltd

Beauty Products (HK) Ltd was a well-known toiletries company with a number of market leaders among its product mix. One of its most profitable lines was a moderately priced range of skin-care products that consisted of Soft & Supple Lotion, Cream and Oil, which together controlled most of the market. S & S Lotion was the major contributor to profits. However, top management was very concerned that the growth of the skin-care line had not been keeping pace with market category growth. Chris Chow, director of the product group, was given the task of identifying the main contributors to this problem and of making recommendations as to how to arrest the line's declining market position. Chris was highly experienced in this area. He had worked for the company for six years and was responsible for approximately 50 per cent of the company's product range.

To provide him with an objective assessment of the problem, Chris appointed HUG Research Consultants, who carried out research of the market. Cluster

TABLE 1 Segments of the skin-care market

	Market segment			
	A	*B*	*C*	*D*
% of user market	32	38	18	12
Demographics	Females 24+, lower and middle-band incomes	Young adults, all income groups	Females 18–30, upper income	Females and males, middle and upper income brackets
Characteristics	All-purpose	Cheap; for face and hand use	Face only	Hands and Body
Main brand representation	S & S Lotion; S & S Cream; Oil of the Orient	S & S Lotion; S & S Cream; S & S Oil	Bella; Oil of the Orient	Youth; Kool

TABLE 2   Skin-care market, 1983–7

	1983	1984	1985	1986	1987
Market size	250	287	309	462	490
Index vs 1 year ago	(104)	(115)	(108)	(150)	(106)
S & S Lotion % unit share	36	36	35	34	33
S & S Oil % unit share	17	17	13	10	9
S & S Cream % unit share	6	6	6	5	5

analysis revealed that the market could be divided into four major segments summarized in Table 1.

The research also confirmed that the volume share of the three brands had been declining gradually over the previous three years (Table 2).

The skin-care market was growing. Penetration stood at 82 per cent in 1987, an increase of 18 per cent in one year. The proliferation of smaller brands may have been one of the factors supporting the market's expansion. The exceptionally dry weather experienced at the end of 1986 brought marginal users into the regular users category, bringing the total market expansion up 50 per cent.

Chris had a hunch that there was a degree of cannibalization among the brands themselves, but the research in the HUG report could not illustrate this. The combined growth of the product line did, however, fall short of the category expansion. Chris found it surprising that each of his three products was present in only the two largest segments of the market. This, he felt, signalled consumer confusion over the three brand identities, which in turn would explain his theory of 'self-cannibalization'.

To test his hypothesis, Chris led three focus group studies with the help of his research associates. The studies revealed that, among the three groups, the products were seen as having exactly the same attributes. It was thus concluded that a significant amount of competition must exist between the different product groupings.

Chris decided that an examination of the current brand positioning might shed some light on the problem. Calling his product managers together, he asked each of them to write out the exact positioning of their respective brands. The three product managers came up with the following product positionings.

S & S Lotion

Brand positioning: to persuade females 20 to 36 years old that S & S Lotion is a pure and mild moisturizer that softens skin because of its unique formula.

Advertising: to convince younger women that S & S Lotion is the purest, gentlest and most moisturizing lotion available, and can give them naturally soft and supple skin.

TV commercials:	S & S Lotion gives you skin that is just as soft and smooth as your child's.

S & S Cream

Brand positioning:	to stimulate usage among adult females 22+, selling on uniquely milder attributes of the product, which provides deep-down moisturizing and nourishment for the skin when used as a night cream.
Advertising:	to convince prospective clients that S & S Cream is a pure night cream which will provide the deep-down nourishment necessary to keep skin delicate and youthful.
TV commercials:	S & S Cream is a pure night cream for deep-down moisturizing which will keep skin looking fresh and young.

S & S Oil

Brand positioning:	to convince young female consumers that S & S Oil is a superior moisturizer that keeps skin softer and more supple after a bath.
Advertising:	to convince prospective customers that S & S Oil is a superior moisturizing product for the entire body with recommended usage after a bath.
Commercials (printed matter):	S & S Oil softens and moisturizes the skin like no other product can.

The lotion and cream positioning had remained unchanged since 1985. The two commercials had been in use for the previous two years. Share of voice was very high with the lotion product but was low with cream. The share of voice held by S & S Oil was unclear as its advertising campaign was in a very early stage. The oil was not advertised until May 1988.

In analyzing the positioning of the brands, it was very clear to Chris that the lotion was bought primarily for facial application and not, as had been thought, as an all-over moisturiser. S & S Cream was used only as a night facial cream. It thus transpired that the only difference in the usage patterns of those who purchased these products was the time of application. Oil was the only product to be clearly positioned – an after-bath moisturiser for overall body usage. Further analysis of HUG Consultancy's findings indicated that 40 per cent of consumers used more than one brand of skin-care products. This trend was most noticeable among users who quoted S & S among their list of skin-care products purchases. And so Chris was left pondering what course of action he should recommend to his superiors.

1.   Was Chris Chow correct in concluding that self-cannibalization exists in the skin-care line?

2.   Looking at the product positioning of S & S Lotion and Cream, as described by the product managers, do you agree with Chris's analysis that the lotion and the cream were in fact targeting different purposes and time applications, and therefore should not necessarily be competing against each other?

3.   Do you think that low share of voice might be the main contributing factor to the customer's inability to perceive difference between the lotion and the cream?

4.   Oil was clearly positioned as an after-bath moisturizer. How could it appear only in segment A, for face and hand usage only?

5.   If you were Chris, what course of action would you recommend to top management?

This case was prepared by Loretta Ho, Department of Business Studies, Hong Kong Polytechnic, Hong Kong, and adapted by Dympna Hughes, Department of Marketing, University College Dublin, for the purpose of class discussion rather than to illustrate either the effective or ineffective handling of an administrative situation.

Case 26: Grundfos

The Grundfos company was founded in 1945 by Poul Due Jensen under the name 'Bjerringbro Pressestoberi og Masinfabrik'. Initially, Poul Due Jensen was a plumber and smith, serving the needs of the residents of his locality. His construction of the first pump for the new waterworks in Bjerringboro, Denmark, proved to be a seminal event in the company's history, when the neighbouring farms started to show interest in the electric motor-driven pump, as a replacement for the existing hand pumps.

Exporting the pumps began in 1948–9 to Norway and Sweden, where the pumps were used for water supply works in small towns and on large farms. In 1959 the company took a significant step when it started production of the circulation pump for central-heating systems, which at that time were becoming a part of housing in Europe. From the outset, the pumps proved successful. However, Grundfos was not the only circulation-pump manufacturer; there was a large plant in Germany and two in France. Grundfos had two relative advantages over these competitors: lower material usage and a more simplified manufacturing process. Consequently, the company was the world's largest producer of circulation pumps for heating systems.

Poul Due Jensen died in 1977 and his son, Niels Due Jensen, took over the management of the firm. Niels continued the expansion initiated by his father and the company is still owned by the Due Jensen family today.

Products and applications

Instead of marketing single products, Grundfos chooses to cater to a number of customer needs. There are four applications or business areas:

- Building services: anything that Grundfos could offer a non-governmental building, e.g. water supply, heating, air conditioning.

- Industry/light applications: pumps used in connection with production processes in industry.

- Water supply/municipal: pumps used in connection with water supply and the public sector.

- Environmental: new applications in the environmental sector.

Of the four applications, building services (the main product is the circulation pump) contributed 50–60 per cent of total turnover, Grundfos' production of approximately five million circulation pumps per year translated into a market share for circulation pumps of approximately 50 per cent, more than triple that of any competitor (Figure 1). This was definitely a cash cow, which contributed to the development costs in connection with the new 'environmental' business area.

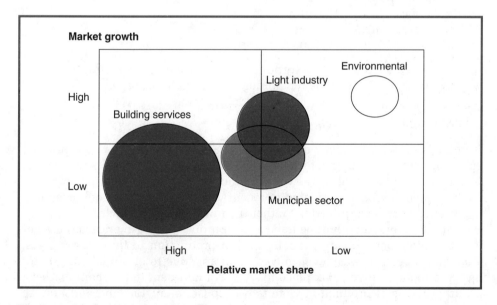

Figure 1 Market growth in Grundfos

TABLE 1   Statistical profile of Grundfos

DKK million	1991/2	1990/1	1989/0	1988/9	1987/8
Turnover	4,537	3,995	3,380	3,182	2,665
Net profit before tax	476	435	352	309	188
Consolidated assets	1,906	1,611	1,334	1,247	1,052
Number of employees	7,514	7,179	6,616	5,906	5,794

The water supply area was the application on which Grundfos was founded at the end of the 1940s, while the environmental area was new and looked as if it could offer exciting business prospects. In 1989, the company launched a product concept for the location and pumping out of polluted ground water.

Financial development

Grundfos has had very positive financial growth (Table 1). The annual report included all the companies connected to the overall firm. Turnover outside Denmark accounted for 95 per cent of the total, and the company's turnover was divided geographically as follows:

	%
Western Europe	60
North America	15
Far East	20
Other countries	5
	100

Approximately 90 per cent of turnover outside Denmark was through company-owned subsidiaries. The remainder was through local agents.

Grundfos' international organization

Grundfos' relative advantage in the value chain lay primarily within product technology and within the international sales organization of subsidiaries. Grundfos recognized that it was very product oriented, although the company had become more market oriented in recent years. The company achieved this by focusing more on applications rather than individual products.

Grundfos worked with three trade areas: Europe, North America and the Far East. Grundfos had already partially moved production to these three areas, although production was never moved to an area due to cheap labour. Rather these production moves took place to show commitment to the main markets. In Europe, parts of production were moved to Germany, England and France. In the beginning of the expansion of the international sales and service organization, it was very important for Grundfos to be seen as a local manufacturer, since some of the countries did not have a tradition of buying foreign products. When there was the financial basis for it (sufficiently high turnover in a market), Grundfos established its own subsidiary. Typically, an agent was hired as president for the new subsidiary. These takeovers were 'friendly', with one or two exceptions. Today, Grundfos has subsidiaries in twenty countries. The basic company philosophy is 'we can and will do it ourselves'.

Organizational issues: subsidiaries and headquarters

The company headquarters in Bjerringbro is divided into three functional areas: production; finance and accounting; and sales and marketing. A director is responsible for each functional area.

The subsidiaries, in principle, were categorized in the same manner, such that the individual function in the subsidiary (with the exception of sales and marketing) referred to the same functional area in Bjerringbro. For example, the financial director of the Italian subsidiary agreed on the internal accounting procedures with the financial director in Bjerringbro. Concerning the overall financial results for the Italian subsidiary, the president referred directly to Niels Due Jensen.

Reference lines with respect to sales and marketing were somewhat more complex, in that there was a regional director as a link between the subsidiary and headquarters. Grundfos' marketing organization was divided into six regions (Northern Europe, Central Europe, Southern Europe, America, South East Asia and Overseas) with a regional director for each. Their task was to develop, co-ordinate and manage the collective marketing effort in the region. The sales and marketing director in, for example, the Italian subsidiary, referred to the regional director for Southern Europe, who in return referred to the director of sales and marketing at headquarters.

1.   Discuss Grundfos' product-market strategy in relation to the internationalization process.

2.   Describe the advantages and disadvantages of the development of the current international marketing organization.

3.   On the basis of Grundfos' internationalization thus far, sketch and evaluate potential future development opportunities with respect to the international marketing organization.

This case was prepared by Svend Hollensen and Marcus J. Schmidt, Copenhagen Business School, and published in Scener fra dansk erhvervsliv. *The text was edited and adapted by Dympna Hughes, Department of Marketing, University College Dublin, as a basis for class discussion rather than to illustrate either effective or ineffective handling of an administrative situation. Original translation by Lynn Kahle, Copenhagen College of Engineering. Published with the permission of Handelshojkolens Forlag [Copenhagen Business School Press].*

General index

Index

Index of firms and brands

Name index